A History of Scottish Women's Writing

A History of
Scottish Women's Writing

Edited by
Douglas Gifford and Dorothy McMillan

Edinburgh University Press

Edinburgh University Press,
22 George Square, Edinburgh

Typeset in Goudy by Bibliocraft, Dundee,
and printed and bound in Great Britain at the University Press, Cambridge

A CIP record for this book is available from the British Library

ISBN 0 7486 0742 0 (hardback)
ISBN 0 7486 0916 4 (paperback)

The Publisher acknowledges subsidy from

THE SCOTTISH ARTS COUNCIL

towards the publication of this volume.

Contents

Contents

Introduction:
A History of Scottish Women's Writing

Douglas Gifford and Dorothy McMillan

Histories of Scottish literature have tended in recent years to include more women, notably more in the case of the most recent four-volume history which had more space to be generous with.[1] It seems, however, that gradualism in writing the history of Scottish women's writing will not be enough to secure for women a more than vestigial presence in whatever larger stories are being told about either the national or the female canons, at least not till the next millennium. There are valid objections to separatist stories, some of which are put by contributors to this volume, but even if the only justification that can be offered for separatism is that it carves out more space to talk about women's writing, then that seems good enough to be going on with. Nor do the stories that are told about women's writing in this volume ignore its intimate relations with work by men. And reconsideration of the contribution of women to the total achievement of writing in Scotland seems particularly appropriate now, when so many suggestions are being made that individual writers, periods and topics have not been adequately assessed. From early Gaelic women poets and Mary, Queen of Scots to the eighteenth-century travellers and Joanna Baillie, from the role of women in balladry to the long and impressive tradition of Scottish women novelists who seem at last to be coming into their own, Scottish literature presents a terrain which has not hitherto been mapped in a relief which shows where its women came from, and the real contribution they make to Scottish culture and culture generally.

The relative absence of women from the official histories of Scottish writing is one thing. Perhaps more alarming and more in need of protest is the regular exclusion of Scottish women from general histories and anthologies of women's writing. Mrs Oliphant, Susan Ferrier and now some twentieth-century writers are recognised but it is taking far too long for many others to find their places. Recent feminist activity in Romantic studies has forced interest again in a number of late eighteenth- and early nineteenth-century Scottish women poets, notably Joanna Baillie, but a huge number of women writers from Scotland still remain as ladies in waiting. For example, the influence of the Norton Anthologies on what gets taught in institutions of higher education is simply undeniable. The British publication of *The Norton Anthology of Literature by Women* was delayed by copyright problems but eventually appeared in 1996: nothing from Scottish literature, not even one short story from Mrs Oliphant, finds a place.[2] On one hand, then, Scottish women's writing arguably suffers from the double bind of being Scottish and being by women. On the other hand, however, as will emerge at many points in this volume, the whole notion of *Scottish* women's writing is itself open to a continuing questioning which constantly produces redefinition, a process reflected in the construction and edition of this History which at times turned the dream of recording women's achievement into nightmare in its conjunction of need and difficulty. In the absence of a canon (perhaps more of a help than a hindrance in contemporary reassessment), selection of writers, topics and periods had to be by joint decision in the light of general peer agreement – and this of course threw up continual debate as to what constitutes a 'Scottish' writer or work. Should Jane Porter's fiction – outstandingly, her profoundly influential *The Scottish Chiefs* of 1810, which helped inspire the epic 'Scotch fiction' of Scott, Hogg, and their many nineteenth-century followers – be ignored because she was English? Most of her childhood was in Edinburgh, where her mother was a friend of Walter Scott, but two-thirds of her life was spent in London. Trevor Royle includes her in *The Macmillan Companion to Scottish Literature* (1983; revised as *The Mainstream Companion to Scottish Literature*, 1993), presumably on the grounds of her significance for Scottish letters – and she is discussed in this volume. A similar question arises regarding Rebecca West, who was of Irish-Scottish ancestry. Her novel of 1922 which explores two generations of the suffragette movement, *The Judge*, is substantially located in Edinburgh and its culture, and her monumental account of the history and ideology of the Balkans, *Black Lamb and Grey Falcon* (1942), was republished as a Scottish Classic in 1993 in the Canongate Classics series. This volume refers to her in passing, however, choosing to see her work overall as properly belonging elsewhere. In contrast, however, is the case of Margaret Elphinstone, the contemporary novelist. She is English, but her novels, set in the Borders and in the Northern islands, and her teaching and writing in Scottish literature at Strathclyde University, together with her assessment of her own place, in terms of choice of residence and creative tradition, as being fundamentally Scottish, place her firmly within our history.

Questions such as these have been some of the main concerns of both editors and contributors over the period of the history's evolution. And they are such central areas of concern that this introduction may be permitted to illustrate some of the considerations involved, using the life and work of two women writers as examples. The first, Catharine Trotter Cockburn, is a relatively well-known woman of letters of the first half of the eighteenth century. She gained entrance to *The Dictionary of National Biography* (DNB), and although she has not since been widely written about, some of her drama at least is available.[3] Catharine Cockburn was both a precocious and a prolific writer. She wrote verses when she was only fourteen, and her first play, *Agnes de Castro*, was performed at the Theatre Royal in 1695 before she was twenty, beginning a bizarre writing career. She knew both Congreve and Farquhar, who valued her opinion; her tragedy, *Fatal Friendship*, was successfully produced at Lincoln's Inn Fields in 1698; and she was one of nine women writers who contributed poems on the death of Dryden. As well as writing two further plays, she turned her hand to philosophy and, in spite of an intervening conversion to Roman Catholicism, wrote a defence of Locke's *Essay* (the writing of which seems to have driven her back to the Church of England). Locke was grateful, acknowledging her support and sending her a present of books. In 1708 she married Patrick Cockburn, a Scottish divine, educated at the University of Edinburgh and in Holland. Cockburn had curacies in Suffolk and London before being forced to give up his livings because of his scruples about taking the oath of abjuration. Later he took the oath and in 1726 was appointed minister of St Paul's episcopal chapel in Aberdeen. He was, however, obliged to move from Aberdeen to Morpeth in Northumberland in 1737 where he had been preferred to Long Horsley vicarage. While Catharine Cockburn was raising her family she wrote little besides letters to family and friends. In 1726 and 1727 she turned again to philosophy, once more defending Locke; in 1737 she wrote an essay on moral obligation which she was unable to publish until 1743; 1747 saw the publication of a treatise with a preface by Warburton which accepts and defends the ethical theory of Samuel Clarke: 'It is not,' tartly remarks the *DNB*, 'much to the credit of her philosophical acuteness that she does not perceive it to be inconsistent with the theories of her old teacher'.[4] It remains uncertain, however, that she is most usefully characterised as a *Scottish* woman writer. If she is, it is on account of two claims. First, although she was born in London in 1679, daughter of a naval commander, David Trotter, who died while she was still a baby, her mother, Sarah Ballenden was connected with an old Scottish family.[5] Her second claim depends, of course, on her marriage and residence in Aberdeen.

In terms of the first claim, there is no evidence that either Catharine or her mother made much of this connection during her early life, although her good connection may have had something to do with the pension of £20 a year that Mrs Trotter received from Queen Anne. Catharine Cockburn's plays and her defence of Locke seem to have little to tell us about Scottish pressures; a commitment to philosophical thought cannot yet be claimed as a specially northern tendency. She sits comfortably among the group of English writers of the Restoration period, and she as much as Anne Killigrew seems to have qualified for Dryden's equivocal praise, 'What next she had design'd, Heaven only knows'.[6] In terms of her marriage and residence in Aberdeen, however, her letters from Aberdeen do indicate a clear sense of local difference: writing to her niece, Mrs Arbuthnot, in 1735, she whimsically speculates on the young women of Aberdeen reading Homer and imagining 'the princess *Nausicaa* going with her cloaths to wash, as it were to the *Dan Burn*'. And when Catharine Cockburn's friend and advocate, George Burnet, himself a Scot from Kethnay near Aberdeen, praised Cockburn's work to Sophia Charlotta, Electress of Hanover, Sophia wrote that she was 'charmed with the agreeable picture, which he had drawn of the new Scots Sappho, who seemed to deserve all the great things, which he had said of her'.[7] Sophia was responding not to her actual experience of Cockburn's work but rather to Burnet's eulogy and it is not clear if Burnet described Cockburn as Scottish or if Sophia herself felt Scottish connections – she was the granddaughter of Elizabeth of Bohemia, the 'Queen of Hearts', and daughter of James I – and perhaps, proud of her own difference, associated Catharine Cockburn with herself.

In one sense it would be pleasing to begin a consideration of eighteenth-century Scottish women's writing with Catharine Cockburn especially since there was little that she did not dare: she was certainly an early woman of letters. Yet from another perspective it is perhaps proper to exclude her as insufficiently Scottish in the concerns of her writing and as already appropriated by the English tradition which groups her with London Restoration writers. Further, there remains a nagging sense that Sophia's appellation, rather than being wholly complimentary, is a potentially diminishing one. After all the formula 'the Scottish whatever' deflates even when it seems to compliment, carrying with it the implication that this is the best that that benighted nation is likely to achieve.

There are always risks as well as benefits in the appropriation of specific figures with equivocal claims to belong and one of them is to open oneself to the accusation of manipulation in order to bolster the numbers and achievement of Scottish women. And perhaps the decisive point which puts Catharine Cockburn into this Introduction and keeps her out of the main text is her firm inclusion in the new edition of *The Oxford Companion to English Literature*. In this she comes after the 'Scots poet and song-writer', Alicia Cockburn: Catharine Cockburn's origins are not even mentioned.[8]

The second writer who exemplifies editorial concern regarding inclusion is an almost wholly forgotten late Victorian woman. Mrs J. L. Story (Janet Leith Maughan), completed and published her *Early Reminiscences* in 1911 when she was eighty-three years old. And she had much to remember, even from the early part of her life. In 1863 she had married Robert Herbert Story, then minister of Rosneath but subsequently Professor of Church History at the University of Glasgow, where he became Principal in 1898. She features in *The Dictionary of National Biography* merely as an appendix to the entry for her husband but before her marriage to the great man to be she was herself already the author of three novels, the most famous, then and now, her first, *Charley Nugent; Or, Passages in the Life of a Sub* (1860).[9] She enjoyed some fame even before her marriage and had met with Thackeray.

Charley Nugent is not without interest, particularly in terms of gender. For this young woman chooses a male narrator, who becomes a soldier. The story, as the title suggests, is episodic and contains much that is sentimental and moralistic. It opens, however, in an appealingly modern manner with immediate dialogue, and the narrative voice has some interesting shifts from past into present tense. Altogether its narrative techniques suggest a writer aware of the possibilities of her craft. Janet Story's young narrator is probably not in the end a very convincing male voice but her attempts to give him a gendered perception display an awareness of areas of thought and feeling accessible to women only through genuine acts of imaginative appropriation, together with some supportive irony (Charley Nugent makes the comically bewildered admission that he 'never can conceive what ladies find to write about when staying in a country house'). More tellingly, however, her use of a male narrator allows horrific descriptions of military punishments and more effective protest against them than could be made by the voice of an inexperienced young woman: 'His back was soon all raw and bleeding, and heavy drops of crimson blood fell on the ground every time that the cat was raised.'[10] Nugent reflects, 'It may be a necessary punishment; wiser heads than mine deny the possibility of entirely abolishing it; but oh! it is a humiliating and a degrading spectacle'.

In spite of her successful early life, Janet Story is apologetic in her introduction to her reminiscences:

> For many years past, my children and a few intimate friends have urged me strongly to place on record some of the old family histories and curious anecdotes with which I had frequently entertained them.[11]

Mrs Story was an old lady and may have lost some of her earlier confidence, yet that need to justify writing, or more especially going into print, will resonate throughout the early part of this volume, as will the frequent justification that publication has been urged by family and friends.

At the same time, however, once Mrs Story has committed herself to the task of memory she is unable, even in her recollecting old age, to repress the joy that her own youthful creativity gives her. Of her first novel she remarks: 'Of all my novels *Charley Nugent* was the best, I put my first fruits, the *cream* of my life into it'. (ER, p. 318) And this exuberance and joy of creation will prove a common feature of the writing experience of the women who appear in this volume.

Mrs Story begins by situating herself as Scottish while registering the pluralism of origin which is for her inseparable from that situating act:

> I am thoroughly cosmopolitan as regards my birth and parentage, for my father was an Englishman, my mother a Scotswoman, I was born in India, and the greater part of my life has been passed in Scotland; so I have always considered myself Scotch, though I have been told that the nationality of the father determined that of the children. (*ER*, p. 2)

That kind of relationship between nationalism and cosmopolitanism also signals some of the problems involved in defining the parameters of this volume. How then shall we recognise a Scottish woman writer? How can we produce a history when we are unsure about the raw material which might constitute it?

With Catharine Cockburn and Mrs Story we encounter paradigmatic problems, yet neither is quite in our history. Although they are invoked here in its Introduction, we have relegated them to the paratext or the margins of the history; in the case of Catharine Cockburn to some extent because of previous English appropriation; in the case of Janet Story, because in spite of the interesting problems she raises, her work simply does not survive close critical scrutiny. The editors may perhaps be accused of 'smuggling in' these writers while pretending to keep them out. But in the end we would hope that our honest confusion over boundaries is more of a strength than a weakness.

That is to say that the attempt to construct a history of Scottish women's writing will, we believe, inevitably produce results that will throw up inconsistencies – someone will always be able to claim that it is nonsense to include or nonsense to exclude. But then Nonsense as a genre has traditionally offered an oblique commentary on what is taken to be common sense and has as a result provoked emotional and intellectual enquiry. And so we hope in this way to acknowledge, even in part to promote, the construction of counter-canons in the very act of adumbrating the canon itself.

Doubtless this preamble seems an attempt to excuse insufficiently draconian editorial principles. We admit that this accusation must be faced because it is, at least in part, the experience of encountering the unexpected presences and absences in our originally commissioned material that has made us more fully aware of the problematic nature of the subject matter. We originally believed that we had adequately mapped out the field but have discovered that much more may be discussed under our initial heading than we had imagined and much less yields itself to generalisation than we had sanguinely supposed.

Some kind of drive towards unifying generalisation may seem, however, to be built in to the whole project, given that we have kept the title, *A History of Scottish Women's Writing*. In qualifying the possibility of such generalisation, are we perhaps betraying our effort in advance of its promulgation? If we look for a moment at the wider history of the reclamation of women's writing the issue may become clearer. In the absence of a clearly visible female literary tradition the first immediate resource is to look for a hidden continuity and to seek a consistent, though subterranean, story in writing by women. Very roughly this resource is characterisable by Gilbert and Gubar's *The Madwoman in the Attic* which finds in nineteenth-century female writing a secret story of resentment and protest.[12] It is not to denigrate this and other early exploratory work in the reclamation of women's writing to suggest that the stories that are told by Gilbert and Gubar and their successors began as thrillers, exciting new stories, and have ended up as romances, as comforting fictions which minimise difference and dissension among women. That is to say that the earlier methodologies and assumptions involved in the construction of a woman's tradition, indeed the whole notion of such a separate yet internally homogeneous tradition, are now under persistent scrutiny by feminist and other critics. Betsy Erkkila in her *The Wicked Sisters: Women Poets, Literary History and Discord* teases out the paradox at the heart of her own and other attempts to discuss women's writing:

> Against the tendency of earlier feminist critics to celebrate women writers and the female literary tradition, and to heroize strong literary foremothers and communities of women, this book considers the historical struggles and conflicts among women poets, as well as the problems of difference and otherness among and within women poets themselves . . . Whereas earlier feminists tended to treat women's literary history as something that was there to be recuperated and reclaimed by literary critics, the model that this study proposes is historically contingent: it treats the woman writer, women's writing, and women's literary history as cultural constructs, formulated by particular persons, in particular contexts, to serve particular political, social and aesthetic ends. And thus this study proposes a model of women's literary history that engages the central paradox of feminism; it does its work even as it recognizes the instability and potential impossibility of its subject.[13]

There are a number of relevant points here. The first is that a smooth story of sisterhood and continuity, subterranean or otherwise, may involve papering over the cracks, the ideological or aesthetic fissures between women writers. And it is also to recognise that women writers may often not have looked to 'mothers' or 'sisters' but rather to 'fathers' and 'brothers' as their literary forebears and present supports. The consequences of such relationships may not always be happy but we will be telling a deceptive story if we try to ignore them. Scott's relationships with his contemporary women writers can be read, for example, as supportive or patronising; MacDiarmid's as more obviously dismissive. On the other hand it seems clear that despite her concern with female experience Liz Lochhead's early literary relationships were primarily and fruitfully with male writers.

Perhaps most importantly we are aware that the aim of this volume to construct a version of the history of Scottish women's writing is not wholly revolutionary and certainly far from innocent. It is very much a function of its place and time. It is not the first attempt to celebrate Scottish women as a group[14] and we recognise that Scottish women writers were probably less ignored in biographical volumes and anthologies before 1900 than after. Many of the pre-twentieth-century women discussed are in *The Dictionary of National Biography* as well as in more specifically Scottish biographical dictionaries. Joseph Irving's popular one-volume *Book of Eminent Scotsmen* despite its apparently excluding name actually includes over seventy women of whom about fifty are writers of some kind.[15] Indeed the contributors to this volume have from time to time had the chastening experience of realising that if they speak of unjust neglect the accusing finger is pointing not at their literary forebears but at themselves. At least in terms of availability of texts things have, however, a little improved in the last fifteen or so years. Canongate Classics in particular have been generous in their allocation of space to women writers. And Catherine Kerrigan's anthology of Scottish women's poetry has notably claimed more space for writers who could not be included in less nationally oriented collections.[16] Kerrigan's volume did not please everyone, but it is a notable act of reclamation and celebration and it would have been a poor thing if it had provoked no dissent.

As editors, we are fully aware, then, of the paradox of necessity and impossibility of which Erkkila speaks. We are fortunate, however, that such paradoxes have become the playful bases of much postmodern theory. This volume is thus constrained and liberated by being a late twentieth-century history of Scottish women's writing. It accordingly commits itself to contemporary notions of plurality, fluidity, unlocatability, and indeterminacy, while recognising the penalties of such commitment. What we have tried to do is recognise the place that contemporary theory and contemporary politics have in generating ways of constructing a literary canon and ways of reading that canon without committing ourselves to one or other theoretical school or political position. By this we mean that we want this History to refuse the fixity of theory, including even that postmodern theory that pretends to refuse fixity.

We have four terms in our title that are in various ways open to question: 'History', 'Scottish,' 'Women' and 'Writing'. This need not, however, lead to silence or confusion; rather the process of questioning itself becomes a process of elucidation. The problem of writing women's literary history has been much addressed in practice and in theory over the last twenty-five years. Three recent attempts are particularly relevant for our purposes: one is Erkkila's discussion of American women poets, although the scope of this volume is considerably smaller than our own; another is Elaine Showalter's *Sister's Choice* which comes after her treatment of English writers in *A Literature of Their Own* and attempts to address the question of an American tradition;[17] the third is Margaret Ezell's *Writing Women's Literary History* which focuses both on pre-1700 writing and also critiques earlier attempts, from the eighteenth century on, at constructing traditions of women's writing.[18] Erkkila and Ezell are both suspicious about the good faith of some earlier attempts to construct female traditions whether or not within nations or periods. They suspect that the desire to find coherence and consistency invites the fudging of difference and division among women. Yet in spite of a large amount of common ground, Erkkila rejects French feminist theory while Ezell embraces it: and, confusingly perhaps, their reasons for opposite, even hostile, theoretical positions are similar. Both want to retain the notion of difference but while Erkkila argues that the essentialism of French feminism elides difference between women, Ezell claims that, more importantly, it insists on difference between feminine and masculine writing. Ezell feels that French feminism is the only theoretical position which secures notions of difference while Erkkila worries that it always finds the same difference. Whatever their theoretical starting point, however, they are both worried, as are many of the contributors to this volume, that the feminist effort to shape a tradition of women's writing needs to claim difference to validate its activity but persistently runs the risk of being trapped by the very difference that it claims.

Yet what these two critics have in common is probably more important than this theoretical distinction which may be read more as a debate about terminology than as evidence of a fundamental division in approach. Significantly, both Erkkila and Ezell insist on history. They, like the contributors to this volume, are interested in women writing within history and responding not in a generalised way to women's lot but to the specific circumstances of their historical moment. They are also conscious that their predecessors in feminist criticism and, of course, they themselves, are writing within history and that their work is provisional, although it need not therefore be tentative or effacing.

Ezell shows how the model of women's frustrated or defeated literary aspirations that is presented by Virginia Woolf, the story of Judith Shakepeare, is an appealing fiction which subsequent feminists have rather carelessly treated as fact. She argues:

> [Woolf] is a great novelist, an inspired analyst of the process of literary creation – but she is
> not a great historian, and it is unfair to demand that she act in such a role. She was bound

by the limitations of the historiography of her day. We, on the other hand have taken a text
designed to be provocative and to stimulate further research into women's lives in the past
and canonized it as history.[19]

Ezell claims that Virginia Woolf overstates the extent to which the ambitions of girls were
frustrated, their freedoms restricted by oppressive male institutions; and that she is also
hampered in her approach to past writing by her assumption that the commercial success
of print is what women writers should be aiming for. Commercial success is unlikely to
be necessary for writers from the upper classes; and consequently Woolf undervalues the
productions of aristocratic women who, however interesting, are nevertheless seen by
her as amateurs and even scribblers. Even Germaine Greer, whose *Kissing the Rod: An
Anthology of Seventeenth-Century Women's Verse* (1988) includes 400 pages of selections
from forty-five writers, still tends, somewhat against her own evidence, to see these early
women writers as 'isolated and vulnerable' and as private figures. Greer does, however,
recognise that for men and women during the Renaissance and Restoration literary
reputation did not depend on print. And Ezell argues most convincingly that the care with
which manuscripts were prepared, the existence of some of them in multiple copies and
preservative bindings, argues a readership and a willingness on the part of the women to
achieve public eminence and a readiness on the part of male and female readers to give
it to them.

We hope to have negotiated with some success some of the problems that Margaret
Ezell discusses. The early chapters of the history recognise the place of women in literary
history who are not middle class, who may have been peasants or who certainly were
ladies. Evidence of early work by women is unfortunately sparse in Scotland outside the
Gaelic tradition but Sarah M. Dunnigan certainly manages to show a group of women who
were not suppressed or intimidated by their male contemporaries and who were certainly
willing to be made public, even if they were not seeking publication in print. These early
chapters also recognise the place in literary history, even if it is a different kind of place,
of women who may not have 'written' at all. At the same time it is impossible to deny that
some aristocratic women did think that to be publicly known as a writer was a violation
of privacy and rank – Lady Louisa Stuart for example was outraged by the invasion of her
seclusion that publicity involved. And a number of our contributors clearly show that
professional writing, or at least writing for publication, usually had a financial motive as
well as a desire for public recognition and fame, identifying the middle classes as the area
in which these motives are most strongly observed. In valorising kinds of writing that have
not usually been canonised, care must be taken not to go too far in the other direction
by undervaluing the activities of those writers of the later eighteenth and nineteenth
centuries who wrote to pay the rent, or educate their children – or who did indeed write
with a view to public recognition and fame.

Elaine Showalter's *A Literature of Their Own* (1977) was the first extended study of this
drive by women writers towards professionalism and towards the assumption of a place
in the market. Studying women's novels from Brontë to Eliot, it takes its title from John
Stuart Mill's perception that 'If women lived in a different country from men and had
never read any of their writings, they would have a literature of their own' and is largely
driven by the intention of demonstrating that even though they live in the same 'country'
as men, women have nevertheless consciously or serendipitously developed that literature
of their own.[20] Given the motivations of the study it is unsurprising that Showalter did not
also take on board the problem that the women she speaks of did not all live in the same

country as each other. Showalter includes a biographical appendix which lists 213 women, 'the most prominent literary women born in England after 1800'.[21] Setting aside a number of women born in Australia or New Zealand or India or South Africa or France, usually because of the mainly colonial pursuits of their fathers, thirteen were born in Ireland, one in Wales and ten in Scotland. The last group comprises Catherine Sinclair, Jane Cross-Simpson, Margaret Oliphant, Eliza Brightwen, Isa Craig, Lucy Walford, Mary Elizabeth Hawker, Mrs Desmond Humphreys ('Rita'), Helen Bannerman, and Naomi Mitchison. As well as these differences in birthplace there are, of course, women who spent much of their lives in varieties of border crossings, like Caroline Norton, Sheridan's granddaughter of Irish ancestry, whose first disastrous marriage was to the English barrister, George Norton, but who in later life married William Stirling-Maxwell and lived finally in Pollok House just outside Glasgow; or Doris Lessing herself, born in Persia of an English father and a mother who variously described herself as Scottish or Welsh, and who was raised in Rhodesia before settling in London. Showalter's project is to establish a story about female experience and the linguistic struggles of women writers to render that experience. But so determined is she to do so that she elides those particularities of place and class that in many ways distinguish, for example, Mary Brunton and Virginia Woolf even more significantly than the years that separate them. Showalter quotes Brunton as an example of the female writer who feared the removal of anonymity; Virginia Woolf is discussed chiefly in terms of her desire for aesthetic androgyny. Both postures in their different ways avoid specific placement of the female. Showalter takes Woolf to task, however, for her comparison of women writers and American writers: she quotes Woolf's claim that women should try to transcend their femaleness just as Americans would do better to forget their Americanness:

> It is easy enough to see that Mr Anderson, for example, would be a much more perfect artist if he could forget that he is an American; he would write better prose if he could use all words impartially, new or old, English or American; classical or slang.[22]

Showalter responds:

> I suspect that few readers will agree that the great flaw in American literature is its national consciousness, its insistence on exploring what is local and special in American culture, or its use of the language which that culture has generated. The sort of perfect artist who can forget where he comes from is a figure more pathetic than heroic.[23]

But what Showalter misses is that it is her security of class and of belonging to the linguistic centre that makes Woolf see Anderson as struggling from the cultural and linguistic backwoods. Showalter might have come closer to the importance of place to the writers she deals with had she attended to Mary Brunton's remarks in a letter to Joanna Baillie: 'I hope you will be so national as to let me say, that a pretty little English knoll is not half so exhilarating as the top of a Scotch hill'. Brunton also notes that returning to the Scottish Highlands after having been so long 'among the stupid plodding Lowlanders' she is 'struck with many little *Celticisms*, which would have escaped me a dozen of years ago'.[24] The tussle with nation, or at least with place, distinguishes Brunton from Woolf more than their gender links them.

Elaine Showalter does, however, turn to her own nation and to the place of women's writing within it in *Sister's Choice*. In the opening remarks of that book Showalter speaks with some apology about her earlier work on British writing: 'If there were cultural nuances I had missed, local idioms I got wrong, historical details I scrambled, critics kindly refrained from pointing them out. Overtly, at least, nationality did not seem to be an issue in the 1970s'.[25] It is probably true that in the 1970s women were still so pleased to find out that they might have a literature that they were not too worried about its provenance; but we will not, we hope, be considered churlish when, twenty-five years later, we point out that there were indeed cultural nuances which were missed.

Showalter still believes – wrongly, we think – that 'English women's writing, until the past few decades, was racially homogenous and regionally compact, with little ethnic, religious, or even class diversity'.[26] But in *Sister's Choice* Showalter is generally much more conscious both of the pressure for a totalising figure for women's writing in a national tradition and of the need to resist it even while providing it. The title is taken from the name of the quilt pattern worked by Celie and Sophia in Alice Walker's *The Color Purple*. 'For Walker,' Showalter says, 'the pieced quilt is an emblem of a universalist, interracial, and intertextual tradition'.[27] It remains as an emblem of women's unity, but its representation of unity in diversity signals a desire for a joining of cultures and traditions that does not remove individual distinction. Showalter concludes her book with a chapter entitled 'Common Threads' which in turn takes its name from a documentary about the Aids quilt project. This enormous commemorative quilt had by 1988 been exhibited in twenty-five major American cities; now it has become so huge that it can no longer be shown whole. The quilt tradition has grown out of the communal culture of women but has, as it were, been developed to include sophisticated patterns within its overall design. It offers, therefore, a powerful figure for women's literary culture and cultures:

> To recognize that the tradition of American women's writing is exploding, multicultural, contradictory, and dispersed is yet not to abandon the critical effort to piece it together, not into a monument, but into a literary quilt that offers a new map of a changing America, an America whose literature and culture must be replotted and remapped.[28]

The figure of the quilt does its work very well insofar as it insists on diversity, change and renewal; the only negative aspect of the quilt as emblem is perhaps that it can no longer be seen whole.

Scottish women's culture does not provide a figure like the quilt. But the absence of a unifying figure does not mean that there is no desire for both the sense of common purpose and the need for particularity and distinction.

Establishing a Scottish tradition is certainly as problematic as establishing an American one. The Scottish patch may seem comparatively small, but it is very old, with old traditions – even if, as Anne Frater points out in her chapter on older Gaelic poetry, Gaelic women were not so much allowed to be bards in their communities as singers of the praises of male bards. And mention of Gaelic poets reminds that we must recognise that many of our writers have had very different ideas of what constitutes their national identity, while many will not have engaged consciously with any notion at all of nationality. Even if we can demonstrate what we feel to be specifically Scottish concerns and modes, these are necessarily derived *ex post facto* and should not be allowed to obscure those areas that do not seem to fit. We reiterate that we do not want falsely to impose a uniform story, and we do not want to trim or snip off the bits that spoil a conveniently envisaged shape. If the Scottish tradition that emerges from this volume appears inconsistent, fitful, contradictory, even exotic, then something important will have been achieved.

We can, however, claim with some confidence that what has in the past been perceived as the 'Scottish Tradition in Literature' has been both male generated and male fixated, particularly on Burns, Scott, Stevenson and MacDiarmid, in ways that are not true of English writing. Even where women writers have been admitted to the canon of the academies, in the work of Susan Ferrier or Margaret Oliphant or Marion Angus, these writers have always been seen as 'minor', seen not merely as unequal to their male Scottish counterparts but as junior literary sisters of English women writers such as Jane Austen, George Eliot, and the Brontës. Indeed Margaret Oliphant herself who wrote close on one hundred novels establishes in her autobiography her own secondary position and the peculiarly female circumstances that conditioned it:

> I have been tempted to begin writing by George Eliot's life – with that curious kind of self-compassion which one cannot get clear of. I wonder if I am a little envious of her? I always avoid considering formally what my own mind is worth. I have never had any theory on the subject. I have written because it gave me pleasure, because it came natural to me, because it was like talking or breathing, besides the big fact that it was necessary for me to work for my children . . . How I have been handicapped in life! Should I have done better if I had been kept, like her, in a mental greenhouse and taken care of?[29]

But that odd note of resentment that longs to put George Eliot down even while recognising her pre-eminence is paradoxically a version of what the English women's tradition has had to contend with. It is in some ways as much a cross as a blessing that England has its 'Famous Five', as feminist literary historians sometimes wearily call them. Jane, Charlotte, Emily, George and Virginia continue to shut out the light from many perfectly healthy plants, amongst them until recently even Anne Brontë and Elizabeth Barrett.

In the end the editors have come to feel that the absence of a recognised 'history' and the absence of a canon of writings is the great strength of the whole enterprise. This astonishing lack of constraint has become more of a cause for celebration than regret. We are aware that what this volume does is to present a series of possibilities, to envisage a kind of fluid paradigm. It does not present a canon; it offers instead some possible maps of the country and a series of possible routes through it.

We recognise, however, that every act of recollection involves a concomitant act of forgetting – or perhaps, more radically, excluding. Memory involves shape and love but memory is also prejudice. We have tried to allow for shape and love and individual choice within the areas we have defined. And this seems proper: to require contributors always to write about specific women might well have imposed a story in advance of the potential constituents of that story. But storytellers are excluders as well as celebrators and may well pass by a writer who recalcitrantly refuses to fit the particular tale that is being told. We do not claim that this volume is never guilty of prejudice or bias. By committing ourselves to a history of Scottish women's writing we are aware of the dangers of seeming to make definitive choices where these are in fact provisional. It would have been fascinating and worthwhile to write this history serially by simply allowing people to write about what they themselves found interesting, in this manner allowing the account to construct itself. This would after all have reflected changing positions in determining canon, and changing personal tastes in establishing what is deemed valuable and lasting. But this would, we believe, have allowed prejudice to come in too strongly and definition to disappear too completely. This history depends inevitably on the choices of late twentieth-century critics who are armed with every sense of the relativity of their prejudices except the sense of how to overcome them. The editors accept this failing, without which their perceptions would be inhuman, and accept the implication that almost immediately this history will itself join the history of histories.

At the same time, of course, we do not want to seem to be presenting what is here in a lukewarm manner. We admit our omissions but are committed to our inclusions. All the work that is discussed in this volume is of aesthetic or cultural significance, and usually both. That said, the contributions to this volume unsurprisingly come to a number of different conclusions about the conditions under which women have written over the centuries. Here again the story turns out to be a complex one which sometimes provokes anger but just as often becomes celebration. And Scottishness, like gender, turns out to be more a matter of the imagination than of logic. There is thus no essential Scottishness discernible as a thread throughout the writing discussed in this volume but Scottishness, even when scarcely perceived by the writers as an issue, indeed sometimes especially when it is not, is everywhere to be imagined, even as is the nation itself. It is kept alive by our contributors in their acts of criticism.

We also recognise the recurrent imaginative bonds of sisterhood, of women being good to women – Nan Shepherd's encouragement of Jessie Kesson; Helena Shire's determined publication of Olive Fraser. There are examples too of productive women's coteries, groups of writers within a period, from the eighteenth-century ladies to such groupings as that of Carswell, Muir and Shepherd as well as mutually supportive groups of contemporary women writers; one of the most moving examples of sisterhood is, of course, that lifelong relationship of love and art which sustained the separate and joint work of the Findlater sisters.

It will be clear that in respecting the variousness of these acts of imagination and sisterhood we have assumed a radically non-intrusive version of editorial practice as far as critical and theoretical approaches are concerned. Although we designed the broad shape of the volume to a very large extent we have respected the choices of writers and texts made by our contributors. We have been equally non-intrusive in our refusal to insist on a uniform format for individual contributions. We came to believe as chapters came in that their formats were generally well led by their material, and that to insist, for example, that footnotes be kept to a specific minimum or maximum would force writers to distort their material. We also recognised that some contributors properly saw their material as demanding a thematic approach while others saw chronological or generic groupings as more likely to enable them to tell the story that they wished to tell. Consequently, to take both ends of the spectrum, Dunnigan's chapter on early writing is heavily footnoted as befits the scholarship that informs it, while Chapman's witty essay on contemporary popular novels is only lightly referenced in a way that equally fits its differently angled enquiry. And in terms of overall organisation, McMillan's chapters on twentieth-century poetry allow chronology to dominate while McDonald's reading of twentieth-century drama privileges a thematic treatment.

All of these chapters deal with groups of writers and are likely, therefore, to be different in construction from chapters on individual writers which by their nature prescribe the treatment of an oeuvre. The decisions about which writers deserve individual treatment are likely to be among the most contentious. They are also generally the most conservative decisions and consequently most liable to be called in question by the very volume that makes them. Yet given the relatively small body of critical writing about the work of most of the writers in this volume, it seems likely that the prevailing eminence of our individually treated writers will survive for some time into the future. It is hard too to imagine the reputations of writers of nineteenth-century Scottish fiction such as Susan Ferrier, Mary Brunton, Margaret Oliphant, and the Findlater sisters being displaced by new names. But, as we have already suggested, their eminence is not as established or secure as that of their English counterparts, and consequently there is more scope for non-aggressive revaluation than there is south of the border. In this respect Scottish and Irish writing come together in the sense that both groups offer the possibility of consistent and exciting revaluation and reintroduction. It is tempting to suggest as a consequence of its very restlessness an eventual refusal on the part of these cultures to join in that activity of competition that has previously characterised the formation of canons.

We are aware, however, that a history, especially in so far as it is retrospective, allows certain texts to be read as cultural documents alongside others that we might, in spite of current levelling theoretical approaches, want to privilege as having special aesthetic primacy. It is probably a necessary condition of a history of writing that some of the past writing that it discusses is not of as high a quality as some of the contemporary writing that it leaves out. This is particularly true of Scottish women's writing – there is a case for claiming that this volume should be followed as soon as possible by a book focusing specifically on writing from the second half of the twentieth century for only then will it be possible to do justice to the many fine writers missed out of this volume or disposed of in a sentence or a phrase. As editors we are conscious of having exploited editorial rights in taking on a disproportionate number of chapters and a disproportionate amount of space; but we make no apology for so doing, given our obligation to complement the chapters which emerged, and our realisation of the sheer size of achievement in certain areas. Even then – as in Gifford's chapter on contemporary fiction, 'Tradition and Continuity' – we are very much aware of the omissions. And more specifically, we are aware of areas which it simply did not prove possible to examine in proper focus – for example, although the non-fiction prose of earlier writers is dealt with in some detail, and although the non-fiction of individual twentieth-century writers such as Willa Muir and Naomi Mitchison is dealt with in their separate chapters, it did not prove possible to look at twentieth-century achievement in this genre in a separate chapter. It remains for future researchers to consider together works such as Helen Cruickshank's *Octobiography*, Christian Miller's *A Childhood in Scotland*, Elizabeth Macpherson's *Letters From a Scottish Village*, Janet Tessier du Croix's *Divided Loyalties*, Evelyn Cowan's *Spring Remembered*, and impressive contemporary works like *Finding Peggy* by Meg Henderson. These, and extensive prose work by others like Agnes Muir Mackenzie, Marian McNeill, and the modern writers of urban memoirs like Janetta Bowie, Molly Weir, and Isobel Neill, deserve fuller consideration alongside the non-fiction by novelists like the Findlaters, Carswell, Muir, Shepherd, Mitchison, and Spark.

The structure of the volume is perhaps idiosyncratic, but we hope that our generally chronological development of the history will help the reader see periods and movements in a way which is helpful in placing individual works and writers. Chapters with more wide-ranging cultural coverage were more difficult to place – Hagemann on women and nation, or Burness on women's awareness between 1780–1920; in cases like these we have tried as far as possible to place chapters where their general discussion merges with our sequential layout.

In the end we hope that the forty-three chapters make their own statements in ways which combine to say what women connected with a part of Europe, for long recognised from within and without, as different from other parts, including England, thought and felt. Overall, we do feel that this volume succeeds in being celebratory in the sense that it opens up possibilities of reading: it aims to reveal and release texts, not to fix and preserve them. And above all it hopes to introduce the work of both known and forgotten writers to an audience within and far beyond Scotland.

Notes

1.   A *History of Scottish Literature*, general editor Cairns Craig, 4 vols (Aberdeen University Press, Aberdeen, 1987–8).
2.   *The Norton Anthology of Literature by Women: The Traditions in English*, compiled by Sandra M. Gilbert and Susan Gubar, 2nd edn (W. W. Norton, New York London, 1996).
3.   Fidelis Morgan (ed.), *The Female Wits: Women Playwrights of the Restoration* (Virago Press, London, 1981).
4.   The information about Catharine Trotter Cockburn's life is taken from the *DNB* and from the biographical account by Thomas Birch which precedes *The Works of Mrs Catharine Cockburn, Theological, Moral, Dramatic and Poetical*, 2 vols (printed for J. & P. Knapton, London, 1751).
5.   *DNB*; Birch says that Trotter too was of Scots descent.
6.   John Dryden, 'To the Pious Memory of the Accomplisht Young Lady Mrs Anne Killigrew', VII, 1. 146.
7.   Cockburn, *Works*, I, iii.
8.   Margaret Drabble (ed.), *The Oxford Companion to English Literature*, 5th edn (Oxford University Press, Oxford, 1985).
9.   *Charley Nugent; Or, Passages in the Life of a Sub* (London, 1860). Mrs Story wrote six novels altogether, three before and three after her marriage. It was not, however, until she published a book for children, *Kitty Fisher, the Orange Girl* (Marr, Glasgow, 1881), that her name appeared on the title page. She wrote two volumes of reminiscences – in 1911 and *Late* in 1913. Both volumes of reminiscences bear her name.
10. *Charley Nugent*, p. 23; p. 31.
11. J. L. Story, *Early Reminiscences* [ER] (Maclehose & Sons, Glasgow, 1911), p. 1.
12. Sandra M. Gilbert and Susan Gubar, *The Madwoman in the Attic: The Woman Writer and the Nineteenth Century Literary Imagination* (Yale University Press, New Haven, Connecticut, 1979).
13. Betsy Erkkila, *The Wicked Sisters: Women Poets, Literary History, and Discord* (Oxford University Press, Oxford, 1992), p. 4.
14. These include Harry Graham, *A Group of Scottish Women* (Methuen, London, 1908); Eunice G. Murray, *Scottish Women in Bygone Days* (Gowans & Gray, Glasgow, 1930; and the more recent but sadly out of print in Britain, Rosalind Marshall, *Virgins and Viragos* (Academy Chicago, Chicago, 1983).
15. *The Book of Scotsmen Eminent for achievements in Arms and Arts, Church and State, Law. Legislation, and Literature, Commerce, Science, Travel and Philanthropy*, compiled and arranged by Joseph Irving (Alexander Gardner, Paisley, 1881).
16. Catherine Kerrigan (ed.), *An Anthology of Scottish Women Poets* (Edinburgh University Press, Edinburgh, 1991).
17. Elaine Showalter, *A Literature of Their Own: British Women Novelists from Brontë to Lessing* (Princeton University Press, Princeton, 1977). References are to the revised edition (Virago Press, London, 1982); *Sister's Choice: Tradition and Change in American Women's Writing* (Clarendon Press, Oxford, 1991).
18. Margaret J. Ezell, *Writing Women's Literary History* (Johns Hopkins University Press, Baltimore and London, 1993).
19. Ezell, *Women's Literary History*, pp. 49–50.
20. Showalter, *A Literature of Their Own*, pp. 3–4.
21. *A Literature of Their Own*, pp. 320–50.
22. *A Literature of Their Own*, p. 290.
23. *A Literature if Their Own*, p. 290.

24. Mary Brunton, *Emmeline, with Some Other Pieces*, ed. Caroline Franklin (Routledge/Thoemmes Press, London, 1992), lxii.
25. Showalter, *Sister's Choice*, p. 2.
26. *Sister's Choice*, pp. 2–3.
27. *Sister's Choice*, p. 20.
28. *Sister's Choice*, p. 175.
29. Margaret Oliphant, *Autobiography and Letters*, ed. Mrs Harry Coghill, with an introduction by Q. D. Leavis (Leicester University Press, Leicester, 1974), pp. 4–5.

1

The Gaelic Tradition up to 1750

Anne C. Frater

The vast majority of the Gaelic poems composed by women which have survived from before 1750 date from the sixteenth and early seventeenth centuries. There are almost 200 songs from this period composed by women, with over thirty named authors, illustrating the lasting appeal of these old songs and, thus, the skill of those who made them. The clan system all that period was in decline, and with it the stranglehold of the literate bardic class on certain types of poetry, while the political turmoil of the age provided both opportunity and occasion for women to step into the breach left by the professional bards. Many of the vernacular poets who come to notice at this time were themselves from the higher strata of Gaelic society, and familiar with the forms and structures of bardic verse, which they combined with the vernacular language to create a new form of poetry, based on stress rather than on the syllabic counts of Classical Common Gaelic. The majority of these 'new' poets, especially the women, were unlettered, although highly literate, or perhaps more accurately, articulate. Their libraries were in their heads, and their often *ex tempore* compositions display a thorough knowledge of Clan history and Gaelic legend, while their memories of other songs were used as a framework on which to build their own. This same memory is the means by which the songs were passed down from generation to generation so that, although the 'literature' of Gaelic-speaking women in Scotland is virtually non-existent up to 1750, and beyond, their literary productions are plentiful.

The earliest datable songs which have been attributed to female authors, however, were composed by members of the literate aristocracy. Aithbhreac nighean Coirceadail's lament for her husband,[1] the warden of Castle Sween in Knapdale, is composed in the *rannaigheacht mhor* syllabic metre, using Classical Gaelic, and drawing on the examples of bardic elegy for her imagery in praise of her husband. Iseabail Ní Mheic Cailéin was influenced by the fashion for courtly love poetry, which probably reached Scotland from France via Ireland, in the subject matter for two of her poems.[2] The third poem which has been ascribed to Iseabail,[3] probably Isabella Stewart, wife of Colin, first Earl of Argyll,[4] is at the opposite end of the poetic spectrum, in content if not in style, and is certainly not the type of verse which one might expect from a woman of her status.

The earliest vernacular poem by a woman which has survived is *Cumba Mhic an Tòisich* (The lament for Mackintosh), dating from the first quarter of the sixteenth century.

Despite the title by which it is commonly known, the subject of the song seems not to have been a chief of Mackintosh, as he is named as Eòghan, and there were no chiefs of Mackintosh by that name. The traditional story behind the song is that it was composed by a woman whose husband was killed on their wedding-day:

> Bha mi 'm bhréidich, am ghruagaich,
> Am bhréidich, am ghruagaich,
> Am bhréidich, am ghruagaich
> 'S am bhantraich 's an aon uair ud.[5]

> (I was a kerched woman, a maiden,
> A kerched woman, a maiden,
> A kerched woman, a maiden
> And a widow all in that one hour.)[5]

One must conclude with this song that, while the story behind it is historically based, somewhere in the oral transmission the name of the clan to which Eòghan belonged has been lost, and that of Mackintosh mistakenly inserted. Conversely, the story connected with the lament for Gregor MacGregor of Glenstrae, known as Griogal Cridhe (Beloved Gregor) is one for which there is solid historical evidence. Gregor of Glenstrae was beheaded at Taymouth Castle in 1570, having been captured and tried as an outlaw by his father-in-law, Duncan Campbell of Glenlyon. Gregor had eloped wth Glenlyon's daughter, thwarting the match with the Baron of Dull which her father had planned for her, and adding to the anger already felt by Glenlyon over Gregor's refusal to take the Campbell name in return for his protection. The composer of the lament was forced to watch her husband's execution at the hands of her father, and her rejection of her own clan for their actions, as well as her love for Gregor, is bitterly expressed in her song:

> Mallachd aig maithibh is aig càirdean
>   Rinn mo chràdh air an-dòigh,
> Thàinig gun fhios air mo ghràdh-sa
>   Is a thug fo smachd e le foill . . .

> Is truagh nach robh m' athair an galair,
>   Agus Cailean Liath am plàigh,
> Ged bhiodh nighean an Ruadhanaich
>   Suathadh bas is làmh . . .

> Is mór a b' annsa bhith aig Griogair
>   Fo bhrata ruibeach ròin,
> Na aig baran crìon na Dalach
>   A' giùlan sìoda is sròil.[6]

> (A curse on gentles and friends
> Who have rent me thus with pain,
> Who caught my darling unawares
> And made him captive by guile . . . [7]

> I wish my father were in a sickness
> And Grey Colin in a plague
> Though Ruthven's daughter would be
> Rubbing her palms and hands . . . [8]
>
> Far better to be with Gregor
> Under tattered sealskin cloak
> Than tied to the wrinkled Baron of Dull
> Wearing satin and silk . . . [9])

In a way, this song, addressed by Gregor's wife to their child, combines two of the types of song which it was permissible for a woman to compose, the keen and the lullaby; however, although the song is addressed to a child, the focus is on the child's father, Gregor, and more particularly on the wife's grief at his loss. There is none of the praise of the warrior found in bardic elegy, physical description is limited to *Griogair bàn nam basan geala* (Fair Gregor of the white palms) and his martial prowess, although alluded to, is not detailed. This poem is not a detached bardic production, based on rules and forms, it is an outpouring of emotion in which the wife's anguish acts as a testament to the character of the dead man.

Elegy and lament form a large part of the songs composed by women, while songs of straightforward praise are relatively rare. This is probably because panegyric poetry was the domain of the bards, a strictly male order, and it was frowned upon for women to attempt to follow their example; instead they were restricted to work-songs, cradle-songs and laments. It may be in order to refute allegations of straying into Bardic territory that several songs by women contain words to the effect that 'If I was a poet I would make a song', while the quality of the poems themselves dispels any doubts about the composer's ability to versify; even Màiri nighean Alasdair Ruaidh, the best-known bardess of the seventeenth century, defended herself from the charge of having composed a panegyric with the words 'chan e òran a th' ann ach crònan' (it is not a song, but a croon).[10] The discouragement of women from composing may also have had some basis in the belief, common in Ireland and therefore not improbable in Gaelic Scotland, that a female poet in a poetic family would be the last of the line with the gift of verse: by composing poetry which strayed outside the acceptable bounds for a bardess she may have been considered to have been destroying the inheritance which should have been passed on to her sons.[11]

Few female poets actually did compose panegyric poetry which was not in the form of a lament or a lullaby. The main exceptions were Màiri nighean Alasdair Ruaidh, Diorbhail Nic a' Bhriuthainn, Mairearad nighean Lachlainn and Sìleas na Ceapaich, all of whom belonged to the upper strata of Gaelic society. Màiri nighean Alasdair Ruaidh composed poems of praise to Sir Norman MacLeod of Berneray, the brother of her chief, Iain Breac, which points to her having been a member of Sir Norman's household, rather than that of Dunvegan. It would hardly have been politic to devote so much attention to Norman and his sons if the chief, Iain Breac, was her patron. If she composed a lament on the death of Iain Breac, it has not survived; certainly her lament for Sir Norman is filled with imagery and emotion:

> Mo chràdhgal bochd
> Mar a thà mi nochd
> Is mi gun tàmh gun fhois gun sunnd . . .

> Is a bhith smuainteachadh ort
> A chràidh mo am chorp
> Is a chnàmh na roisg bho m' shùil.
>
> (Sad and heart-sore my weeping,
> for I find myself tonight
> without rest, without peace, without cheer . . .
>
> It is hard thinking of thee
> that hath tortured my body
> and wasted the lashes from mine eyes.)[12]

It is said by some that these songs were the reason for Màiri's exile, as the Chief was so angered by her obvious preference for his brother and his family.

Only one song by Diorbhail Nic a' Bhriuthainn, *Alasdair a laoigh mo chéille*, survives with a specific ascription to her. In this, she sings the praises of Alasdair Mac Colla, the MacDonald warrior who was behind so much of the success of Montrose's army during the war against the Covenanters. The song seems to have been composed on Alasdair's journey through the islands, recruiting men to fight alongside him with Montrose, and contains the idea of *tearc eugmhais* found in the Celtic legends, where a woman falls in love with a warrior, without ever meeting him, through accounts of his exploits.[13] The text of the poem describes Alasdair in detail, recounting his prowess as a warrior and his personal appearance, but, although Diorbhail uses terms of endearment for Alasdair and states what she would do if she met him, there is no evidence that she actually did so:

> Mo chruit, mo chlàrsach is m' fhidheall,
> Mo theud-ciùil 's gach àit am bithinn;
> Nuair a bha mi òg 's mi 'm nighinn
> 'S e thogadh m' inntinn thu thighinn;
> Gheibheadh tu mo phòg gun bhruidhinn . . . [14]
>
> (My lute, my harp, my fiddle,
> My musical strings in each place I would be;
> When I was a young girl
> It would raise my spirits if you would come;
> You would have my kiss without asking . . .)

The panegyric verse of Sìleas na Ceapaich is composed from a clan perspective, praising the Clan Donald for their support for, and actions during, the Earl of Mar's rebellion in 1715. Her poetry is unashamedly partisan and political, following the Rising from the raising of the Royal Standard to the defeat at Sheriffmuir which marked the end of the campaign. However, Sìleas is not blind to the political machinations which were to blame for the failure of the rising, and she is not afraid to name those whom she considers to have betrayed their principles in order to safeguard their own prosperity. In her song to King James's Army, she addresses those who surrendered in order to protect their estates from forfeiture with the words:

> Rinn sibh cleas a' choin sholair
> Thug a cholba 'n a chraos leis:

'Nuair a chunnaic e fhaileas
Thug e starradh g' a fhaotainn;
'Nuair a chaill e na bh' aige
Dh' fhàg sin acrach re shaogh'l e . . .

(You have done what the foraging dog did,
Who carried his limb of meat in his mouth:
When he saw its reflection
He made to catch it:
When he lost all he had
It left him hungry for the rest of his life.)[15]

Mairearad nighean Lachlainn's panegyric verse was also politically motivated, although her concern was not so much with national issues as with the erosion of the power of the Macleans of Duart, and its replacement with Campbell rule. Mairearad may actually have been a MacDonald by birth, but, having a Maclean mother, and living in Maclean territory, her main focus is inevitably the downfall of the family of Duart through the machinations of the Campbells. Her pride in her own clan, and her contempt for the usurpers and their often underhand methods, is evident in her poetry, and is summed up in her song to Sir John Maclean:

Na Leathanaich bu phrìseil iad,
Bu mhoralach nan inntinn iad;
'N diugh crom-cheannach 's ann chìtear iad,
'S e teann lagh a thug strìochdadh asd';
Is mairg a bha cho dìleas riutha
Riamh do rìgh no 'phrionnsa.

Gum b' fheàrr bhith cealgach, innleachdach,
Mar bha 'ur naimhdean mìorunach;
'S e dh'fhàgadh làidir, lìonmhor sibh.
'S e 'dheanadh gnothach cinnteach dhuibh,
A bhith cho faicleach crìonta
Is gun b' fhiach leibh a bhith tionndadh.[16]

(The Macleans were greatly valued,
Their minds were dignified;
Now they are seen with bowed heads,
It was a hard law which caused them to submit;
Never were any as faithful as them
To King or to prince.

It would be better to be deceitful and cunning
As your malicious enemies were;
That would leave you strong and numerous.
It would make things certain for you
If you were so wary and cautious
That treachery was worth your while.)

But most of the panegyric praise employed by female poets, even by Sìleas na Ceapaich, Màiri nighean Alasdair Ruaidh and Mairearad nighean Lachlainn, occurs in laments. Sìleas composed laments to her husband, her daughter, Anna, MacDonald of Sleat, and to the harper, Lachlann Dall; but her finest work in this form is addressed to Alasdair Dubh of Glengarry. *Alasdair a Gleanna Garadh* contains the longest list of kennings in Gaelic verse, comparing Alasdair to noble trees and animals in order to illustrate his power, martial prowess, generosity and appearance:

> Bu tu 'n lasair dhearg 'gan losgadh,
> Bu tu sgoltadh iad gu 'n sàiltibh,
> Bu tu curaidh cur a' chatha,
> Bu tu 'n laoch gun athadh làimhe;
> Bu tu 'm bradan anns an fhìor-uisg,
> Fìreun air an eunlaith's àirde,
> Bu tu 'n leómhann thar gach beathach,
> Bu tu damh leathann na cràice.

> Bu tu 'n loch nach fhaoidhte thaomadh,
> Bu tu tobar faoilidh na slàinte,
> Bu tu Beinn Nibheis thar gach aonach,
> Bu tu chreag nach fhaoidte theàrnadh;
> Bu tu clach uachdair a' chaisteil,
> Bu tu leac leathan na sràide,
> Bu tu leug lòghmhor nam buadhan,
> Bu tu clach uasal an fhàinne.

> Bu tu 'n t-iubhar thar gach coillidh,
> Bu tu 'n darach daingean làidir,
> Bu tu 'n cuileann 's bu tu 'n draigheann,
> Bu tu 'n t-abhall molach blàthmhor;
> Cha robh do dhàimh ris a' chritheann,
> Na do dhligheadh ris an fheàrna;
> Cha robh bheag ionnad de 'n leamhan;
> Bu tu leannan nam ban àlainn.

> (You were a red torch to burn them,
> You would cleave them to the heels,
> You were a hero for waging battle,
> You were a champion whose arm never flinched.
> You were the salmon in fresh water,
> The eagle in the highest flock,
> You were the lion above all beasts,
> You were the stout antlered stag.

> You were an undrainable loch,
> You were the liberal fount of health;
> You were Ben Nevis above every moor,
> You were an unscalable crag.
> You were the top-stone of the castle,

> You were the broad flag of the street,
> You were a priceless gem,
> You were the jewel in the ring.
>
> You were the yew above every forest,
> You were the strong steadfast oak,
> You were the holly and the blackthorn,
> You were the apple-tree, rough-barked and many-flowered.
> You had no kinship with the aspen,
> Owed no bond to the alder;
> There was none of the lime-tree in you;
> You were the darling of beautiful women.)[17]

Mairearad nighean Lachlainn's finest production, and her best known, is also a lament, *Gaoir nam Ban Muileach*. Composed in 1716, after the death of Sir John Maclean, it is a lament for her people and her homeland as much as for her chief. Mairearad lived through the Campbell invasion of Mull, seeing the hereditary lands of the Macleans being wrested from them with the charter rather than the sword; and any hopes of the situation changing died with the failure of the Jacobite Rising of 1715, which the Macleans had wholeheartedly joined, and the death of Sir John shortly afterwards. The political situation is referred to early on in the poem, with Mairearad lamenting the misfortune suffered by Sir John in his life, as well as his death far from home:

> Chuireadh aon mhac Shir Ailein
> As a chòirichean fearainn,
> Le fìor fòirneart's le aindeoin;
> Ach 's e lom sgrìob an t-earraich so 'chràidh mi.[18]
>
> (Sir Alan's only son
> Was forced out of his rightful territory
> Violently and unwillingly;
> But this springtime's calamity is what has caused my anguish.)

The bardic use of the convention of pathetic fallacy, where nature joins in mourning a worthy leader, is employed in order to illustrate Sir John's nobility, and this is followed by a vivid image of the perilous state of the clan without their chief:

> Cò an neach dha bheil sùilean
> Do nach soilleir, am mùthadh
> 'Tha air teachd air ar dùthaich
> Bho 'n là chaill sinn an t-aon fhear
> Fo làimh Dhé ghabh dhinn cùram;
> Fhrois gach abhall a h-ùbhlan,
> Dh' fhalbh gach blàth agus ùr-ròs,
> 'S tha ar coill' air a rùsgadh de 'h-àilleachd.
>
> Oirnne thàinig an dìobhail!
> Tha Sir Iain a dhìth oirnn,
> 'S Clann-Ghilleoin air an dìobradh,

Iad gun iteach, gun linnidh,
Iad am measg an luchd mìoruin
Is a fulang gach mì-mhodh,
Ged nach ann ri feall-innleachd a bha iad.[19]

(Where is the man who has eyes
To whom the smothering which has come
Over our country is not clear
Since the day we lost the one man
Under God's hand who took care of us;
Every apple tree has dropped its apples,
Every blossom and fresh rose has gone,
And our wood is stripped of its beauty.

A calamity has befallen us!
We are without Sir Iain,
And the Clan Maclean forsaken,
Without plumage, without a brood,
But like plucked geese
Amongst their enemies,
Suffering insults,
Although they were not accustomed to deceit.)

Mairearad nighean Lachlan was not the only woman to deal with clan concerns, especially when these related also to national politics. Several clans suffered as a result of the political choices made by their leaders, and also through the manipulation of the law by their rivals. Perhaps the most famously persecuted of the clans were the MacGregors, whose lands were gradually taken over by the Campbells, although their downfall had begun much earlier when they followed their feudal superior, MacDougall of Lorn, against Robert the Bruce.[20] Through this, they lost their rights to the territories on which they lived, making them an easy prey for their new Campbell overlords. Apart from *Griogal Cridhe*, there are several MacGregor poems, but only one of these, *Clann Ghriogair air Fògradh* (The Fugitive Clan Gregor) can with reasonable certainty be ascribed to a woman. The traditional story is that it was sung by a woman, who was sheltering fugitives in her home, to the pursuers of the MacGregors, in order to throw them off the trail.[21] The beginning of the song would certainly give the impression that she had not seen any of her clansmen for some time:

Is mi suidhe an so am ònar
    Air còmhnard an rathaid,

Dh' fheuch am faic mi fear-fuadain,
    Tighinn o Chruachan a' cheathaich,

Bheir dhomh sgeul air Clann Ghriogair
    No fios cia 'n do ghabh iad.[22]

(I sit here alone
    On the level part of the road,

> Trying to see the fugitives
>   Coming from Cruachan of the mist,
>
> Who will give me news of Clan Gregor
>   Or information as to where they have gone.)

The tact of the poetess only extends to her concealment of the whereabouts of the fugitives, and does not prevent her from praising the quality and habits of her clansmen; nor does prudence prevent her from gloating over the infamous murder of the King's forester in Glenartney, for which the MacGregors were blamed:[23]

> Is ann a rinn sibh an t-sidheann anmoch
>   Anns a' ghleann am bi an ceathach.
>
> Dh' fhàg sibh an t-Eòin bòidheach
>   Air a' mhòintich na laighe,
>
> Na starsnaich air fèithe
>   An dèidh a reubadh le claidheamh.[24]
>
> (You were late hunting
>   In the misty glen.
>
> You left the bonny John
>   Lying on the moor,
>
> As a stepping-stone over a bog
>   After being ripped by the sword.)

The majority of the clan-related songs, however, are connected to the major political upheavals in Scotland in the seventeenth and eighteenth centuries. Montrose's campaign against the Covenanters gave rise to songs of praise, such as *Alasdair a laoigh mo chéille*, and songs of victory, but also to laments for the fallen. What is interesting with this particular campaign is that there are Gaelic women's songs from both sides of the conflict, especially in connection with the battle of Inverlochy, a victory for Montrose. The songs, however, reflect the perception in the Highland areas at the time, that Alasdair mac Colla, not Montrose, was the leader of the Royalist forces; certainly both he and his followers were in a large measure the driving force in the campaign, as they saw it, against the Campbells. Inverlochy was not viewed as a battle between Royalists and Covenanters, but as one between the MacDonalds and the Campbells, or at least between the northern and island clans against their most powerful foe. Blood, not politics, spurred the armies on, and the ties of blood are the moving force behind what is possibly the most tragic lament connected to Inverlochy, *Turus mo Chreich thug mi 'Chola* (My journey to Coll was my ruin). Fionnghal Campbell was married to Maclean of Coll, and the mother of Hector Roy, both of whom fought alongside Montrose at Inverlochy; but she was also the sister of Campbell of Auchinbreck, the leader of the Covenant forces, who was killed in the battle. Fionnghal reportedly went mad with grief after her brother's death, but this seems not to have been a case of of divided loyalties, rather a result of her loyalty lying with one clan although she was both the mother and the wife of leading members of another. She makes it clear in her lament that her marriage was not a happy one, and she curses her own son for the part he played in the conflict which led to her brother's death:

Eachainn Ruaidh de 'n fhine dhona,
'S coma leam ged thèid thu dholaidh,
'S ged a bhiodh do shliochd gun toradh.[25]

(Hector Roy of the wicked clan,
Little I care if you should be injured,
Even if your offspring were without fruit.)

The lament closes with Fionnghal making it clear just which side she is on, while her bitterness towards the Macleans, the MacDonalds, and the Irish who fought with Alasdair mac Colla is all too evident:

Nan robh mis' an Inbhir-Lòchaidh,
'S claidheamh da-fhaobhair am dhòrnaibh,
'S neart agam gu m' mhiann is eòlas,
Dheanainn fuil ann, dheanainn stròiceadh,
Air na Leathanaich 's Clann Dòmhnaill;
Bhiodh na h-Eireannaich gun deò annt',
Is na Duibhnich bheirinn beò as.[26]

(If I were in Inverlochy
With a double-edged sword in my hands,
And strength as I would wish, and skill,
There would be blood there, and tearing asunder
Of the Macleans and Clan Donald;
The Irish would be lifeless,
And the Campbells I would take out alive.)

The Campbell women were loyal to their clan and their menfolk, but this did not extend to an unquestioning acceptance of the actions of their chief at Inverlochy. Argyll did not take part in the battle, preferring instead to watch from the safety of his ship in which, once it was clear that the day belonged to the Royalists, he fled from the scene. For this he was blamed, not only by the men of his clan captured after the battle, but also by women such as the widow of Campbell of Glenfaochan, who had lost everything because of him:

Mharbh iad m' athair is m' fhear-pòsda,
'S mo thriùir mhacanan òga,
'S mo cheathrar bhràithrean ga 'n stròiceadh,
'S mo naoidhnear cho-dhaltan bòidheach.[27]

(They killed my father and my husband,
And my three young sons,
And my four brothers ripped apart,
And my nine handsome foster-brothers.)

There is no praise of her chief, only disdain for the cowardly action of the man in whose cause eighteen of her menfolk had died:

Thug Mac Cailein Mòr an linn' air,
'S leig e 'n sgrìob ud air a chinneadh.

(Mac Cailean Mor took to the sea.
And allowed that calamity to befall his clan.)[28]

There is only one song connected to Claverhouse's rising, in 1689, which ended at
Killiecrankie, attributed to a woman: the lament for Angus Og, brother of Alasdair of
Glengarry, composed by his wife. The lament is mainly in the panegyric mould, and the
speaker refers to Gaelic legend in the heroic reference which she employs in order to
illustrate her grief:

> Tha mo chridhe na bhlaidhean,
> 'S tearc mo leithid ri fhaotainn,
> Mar mac Fhinn, a's e aosda,
> Ann an deidh Cloinne Baoisge,
> Cho truagh 's a bha Deardir,
> An deidh a gràidh thoirt do Naoise.[29]

> (My heart is in pieces,
> My like is not to be found,
> I am like the son of Finn in his old age
> After the children of Baoisge,
> As pitiful as Deirdre
> When she gave her love to Naoise.)

The next major upheaval in Scotland came with the Earl of Mar's Rising in 1715. The
poems of Sìleas na Ceapaich on this subject give a very partisan MacDonald perspective
on events, but although her description of the actions of some clans may be deemed unfair,
in many ways her judgement is accurate, especially regarding the political leanings of
several clan leaders and the petty jealousies which endangered, and eventually destroyed,
the Rising. The other bardesses who composed songs connected with the Rising are more
concerned with individual participants. In *Chunnaic mise mo leannan*, a girl describes
watching her sweetheart leave for battle, and wishes good fortune on Clan Donald;[30] while
Chì mi, chì mi, chì mi thall ud is a song for Allan of Clanranald, who died at Sheriffmuir.[31]
Forfeiture of their estates followed for the Jacobite leaders after the failure of the '15,
and this made them wary of committing themselves once again to the Jacobite cause
in 1745. Their clansfolk were not so, seeing reason only for rejoicing in the news that
Prince Charles Edward Stuart had arrived in Scotland to reclaim his father's throne. The
MacDonald bardess, Nighean Aonghais Oig, opens her song of welcome with a confident
assertion that the rule of the House of Hanover (often referred to in Jacobite poetry as
pigs) will soon be at an end:

> An ulaidh phrìseil bha uainne
> 'S ann a fhuair sinn an dràsd' i,
> Gu 'm b' i sud an leug bhuadhach
> 'G a ceangal suas leis na gràsan;
> Ged leig Dia greis air adhart
> Do 'n mhuic bhith cladhach ad àite,
> Nis o thionndaidh a' chuibhle
> Thèid gach traoitear fo 'r sàiltean.[32]

(The precious treasure which was away from us
  Has now returned to us,
That was the victorious jewel
  Bound up with grace;
Although for a short while God allowed
  The pig to be digging in your place,
Now that the wheel (of fortune) has turned
  Every traitor will be under our heels.)

A similar sentiment is expressed by a woman of the Stewart family, whose song of welcome to Prince Charles contains the declaration:

An t-òg tionnsgalach gasda,
Prionnsa Teàrlach nam baiteal,
Thèid meàrlach rìgh Shasunn a ghèilleadh.[33]

(The adventurous handsome youth,
Prince Charles of the battles,
The thieving king of England will yield [to him].)

The most outstanding song connected with the Rising of 1745, however, is the lament composed by Christina Ferguson for her husband, William Chisholm, who died at Culloden. *Mo rùn geal òg* (My young white love) is full of love for, and pride in her husband; while her own pitiful state is alluded to, it is by no means the focus of the lament:

Och! a Theàrlaich òig Stiùbhairt,
  'S e do chùis rinn mo lèireadh,
Thug thu bhuam gach nì bh' agam,
  Ann an cogadh na d' aobhar:
Cha chrodh a's cha chaoirich,
  Tha mi caoidh, ach mo chèile,
Ge do dh'fhàgte mi 'm aonar,
  Gun sian 's an t-saoghal ach lèine.
                                        Mo rùn geal òg.[34]

(Oh! Young Charles Stuart,
Your cause has wounded me,
All that I had you have taken from me
In a battle on your behalf:
It is not sheep or cattle
That I lament, but my husband,
Although I have been left alone
With nothing in the world but a shirt.
My young white love.)

The poet concentrates on the merit of her husband, praising everything about him, even his drinking prowess, and she only refers to herself in terms of her husband, or his absence. Some of her claims may be conventionally extravagant, but the sense of the great love of Christina and William, and her devastation at the news of his death, is strong and poignant:

> Bha mi greis ann am barail
>   Gu 'm bu mhaireann mo chèile,
> 'S gun tigeadh tu dhachaigh
>   Le aighear 's le h-eibhneas,
> Ach tha 'n t-àm air dhol tharais,
>   'S chan fhaic mi fear t' eugais,
> Gus an tèid mi fo 'n talamh
>   Cha dealaich do spèis rium.
>   Mo rùn geal òg.

> (For a while I thought
>   That my husband was still alive,
> And that you would come home
>   With joy and gladness,
> But the time has passed
>   And I will not see one like you,
> Until I am put in the ground
>   I will not stop loving you.
> My young white love.)

I have, of course, been able to discuss only a small selection of almost 200 songs composed by women in Gaelic in the period up to 1750, but I have, I hope, conveyed their impressive stylistic range and variety of subject matter.[35]

Notes

1. W. J. Watson (ed.), *Scottish Verse from the Book of the Dean of Lismore*, (Oliver & Boyd, Edinburgh, 1978), p. 60.
2. T. Rathile (Thomas Francis O'Rahilly), *Dánta Grádha* (Cork University Press, Cork, 1926; 1976), p. 74. See also Watson, *Scottish Verse*, p. 307.
3. E. C. Quiggin (ed.), *Poems from the Book of the Dean of Lismore* (Cambridge University Press, Cambridge, 1937), p. 78.
4. Watson, *Scottish Verse*, p. 307.
5. *A Collection of Ancient and Modern Gaelic Poems and Songs* (J. Gillies, Perth, 1786), p. 204.
6. Catherine Kerrigan (ed.), *An Anthology of Scottish Women Poets* (Edinburgh University Press, Edinburgh, 1991), p. 56.
7. D. S. Thomson, *An Introduction to Gaelic Poetry* (Gollancz, London, 1974), p. 108.
8. Somhairle Mac Gill-eain (Sorley MacLean), *Ris a' Bhruthaich* (Acair, Stornoway, 1985), p. 71.
9. Derick Thomson, *An Introduction to Gaelic Poetry* (Victor Gollancz, London, 1973), p. 108.
10. J. Mackenzie, *Sàr-obair nam Bàrd Gaelach* (N. Macleod, Edinburgh, 1904), p. 24.
11. E. O. hAnluain (ed.), *Leath na Spéire* (An Clochomhar Tta, Dublin, 1992), pp. 15–16.
12. J. C. Watson, *Gaelic Songs of Mary MacLeod* (Oliver & Boyd, for the Scottish Gaelic Texts Society, Edinburgh, 1965), pp. 96–7.
13. D. Stevenson, *Alasdair Mac Colla and the Highland Problem in the Seventeenth Century* (Donald, Edinburgh, 1980), p. 99.
14. *Guth na Bliadhna* (*The Voice of the Year*), vol. X (1913), p. 352.
15. C. O. Baoill, *Bàrdachd Shìlis na Ceapaich* (Edinburgh, 1972), pp. 46–7.
16. A. Maclean Sinclair, *Na Bàird Leathanach*, vol. 1 (Haszard & Moore, Charlottetown, P. E. I., 1898), p. 187.

17.   C. O. Baoill, *Bàrdachd Shìlis na Ceapaich*, pp. 72–3.
18.   Sinclair, *Na Bàird Leathanach*, vol. 1, p. 192.
19.   Sinclair, *Na Bàird Leathanach*, vol. 1, p. 192.
20.   A. G. M. MacGregor, *History of the Clan Gregor*, vol. 1 (W. Brown, Turnbull & Spears, Edinburgh, 1898), pp. 27–8.
21.   T. Pattison, *The Gaelic Bards and Original Poems* (A. Sinclair, Glasgow, 1890), p. 123.
22.   Kerrigan, *An Anthology*, p. 38.
23.   MacGregor, *History*, p. 204.
24.   Kerrigan, *An Anthology*, p. 38.
25.   *Transactions of the Gaelic Society of Inverness*, vol. XXVI, p. 238.
26.   *Transactions etc*, vol. XXVI, p. 238.
27.   A. Maclean Sinclair, *Mactalla nan Tùr* (Mac-Talla Publishing Co. Ltd, Sydney, C. B., 1901), p. 92.
28.   Sinclair, *Mactalla nan Tùr*, p. 92.
29.   A. & D. Stewart, *Cochruinneacha taoghta de shaothair nam Bàrd Gaelach* (Clodh-bhuailt le T. Stiuart, Edinburgh, 1804), p. 96.
30.   J. L. Campbell & F. Collinson, *Hebridean Folksongs*, vol. III (Clarendon Press, Oxford, 1981), p. 156.
31.   *Transactions of the Gaelic Society of Inverness*, vol. XXVII, p. 397.
32.   J. L. Campbell, *Highland Songs of the Forty-five* rev. edn (Scottish Academic Press for the Scottish Gaelic Texts Society, Edinburgh, 1984), p. 22.
33.   T. Sinton, *The Poetry of Badenoch* (Northern Counties Publishing Co., Inverness, 1906), p. 206.
34.   Mackenzie, *Sàr-obair nam Bàrd Gaelach*, p. 409.
35.   For further material not already referred to in the notes see: W. J. Watson, *Bàrdachd Ghàidhlig* (Stirling, 1959); *Scottish Gaelic Studies*, vol. XI, p. 3, p. 171; *The Clan MacLeod Magazine* (1954), p. 134; *Transactions of the Gaelic Society of Inverness*, vol. XLV, p. 98; vol. XLII, p. 30; vol. XLI, p. 11.

2

Scottish Women Writers c.1560–c.1650

Sarah M. Dunnigan

Early writing by Scottish women has been insufficiently explored. R. J. Lyall claims that the later sixteenth and early seventeenth centuries are seldom examined in Scottish literary studies.[1] Recognition of the achievement of women's writing from a 'Scottish Renaissance' earlier than MacDiarmid's occurs within an already neglected period. This chapter adopts a chronological approach and asks certain questions. Why does the 'early Scottish women writer' emerge, seemingly *ex nihilo*, in the mid-sixteenth century? No counterpart of the French female *trobairitz*, for example, seems to exist in fourteenth- or fifteenth-century Scotland. The orality of much medieval culture and the probable loss of fragile manuscript material may explain this curious silence. How does the seventy years gulf between Mary Stuart and Anna Hume affect their responses to the inheritance of 'male-authored' secular love poetics? Is the sensual, baroque aesthetic of Mary's Catholic penitent an absolute counterpart to the Protestant dreamer of Elizabeth Melville's allegory? The interest of these works, even in this brief evocation, should demonstrate that women of the Scottish Renaissance attained the 'authoritie' which Knox sought to deny them, at least in intellect and imagination.

Christian Lindsay (fl.1580s)

Christian Lindsay may be considered doubly unique: she alone of the writers considered in this chapter seems to have engaged in writing as a communal rather than solitary practice, and to have received some critical acknowledgement. Helena Shire first commented on the existence of a 'lady poetaster' in the literary and intellectual courtly elite of James VI's self-proclaimed Castalian band.[2] (Even if we consider the possibility that her name may have been playfully invented for the poetic role-play practised by this coterie, it still importantly signifies the incursion of a female voice.) Her identity is revealed in James's wry piece of poetic advice to Alexander Montgomerie. Lindsay's alleged words sanction the king's criticism of his 'maister' poet's hubris:

> Nor yett woulde ye not call to memorie
> What grounde ye gave to Christian Lindsay by it
> For now she sayes which makes us all full sorie
> Your craft to lie . . .

Montgomerie's sonnet, 'My best belovit brother of the band', bestows on her a different kind of honour, desiring that Lindsay's art will enshrine the memory of the literary quartet composed of Robert Hudson, Montgomerie, 'old Scot and Robert Semple'. Only here, in the final couplet, is the poem's rumbustious rhetoric subdued: 'Quhen we are dead that all our dayis bot daffis/Let Christian Lyndesay wryt our epitaphis'.[3]

That the surviving work of this admired Castalian poet should be confined to one extant sonnet, 'Oft haive I hard, bot ofter fund it treu',[4] is sadly ironic. Knowledge of Lindsay's life is similarly slender. One early editor of James's poetry cites a possible reference to 'Christian Lindsay, spouse to John of Dunrod, sheriff of Lanark'; while Shire proposes (without identifying her source) a birthdate 'by 1558, of the Crawford family, a cousin of the courtier Bp. of Ross'.[5] On the evidence of Lindsay's own words, we may suppose her a highly educated gentlewoman of James VI's court who gained entry by approval rather than through trespass into a male literary elite.

Inscribed 'christian lyndesay to robert hudsone', Lindsay's poem is addressed to one of James's pre-eminent poet-musicians:

> *Montgomrie* that such hope did once conceave
> Of thy guid will, nou finds all is forgotten
> Though not bot kyndnes he did at the craiv
> He finds thy freindschip as it rypis is rotten
> The smeikie smeithis cairs not his passit travell
> Bot leivis him lingring deing of the gravell.

Although the sonnet cannot be precisely dated, it was probably written in the late 1580s or early 1590s. The antagonism described evokes the period of Montgomerie's expulsion from the king's favour and the consequent fragility of the Castalian ethos. Composed in the interlacing rhyme scheme of the archetypal late sixteenth-century Scottish sonnet, the poem's moral, contemplative theme reflects the mode's emancipation in Scotland from a purely amatory subject. As a typical Castalian poem, concerned with the circle's political and social vagaries, it forms a moving coda to Montgomerie's series of sonnets which complain of royal and social exclusion. Lindsay's poem appears as an act both of pity and homage. Her poetic voice assumes the rhetoric of authority (conferred by both James's and Montgomerie's allusions) by which she acts as intercessor on behalf of one condemned 'in exyle'.

The verbal reminiscence of 'smeikie smeithis' to Montgomerie's conceit of Castalian poetic creation in 'My best belovit brother' provides evidence of the coterie's mutual poetic knowledge. This intertextuality allows Lindsay to present Hudson with an image which also signifies affectionate praise. Irony is distilled from her expansion of Montgomerie's metaphor: 'travell' aligns poetic exertion with physical graft and Montgomerie's effort to forge 'freindschip'. The poem's colloquial tenor suggests Lindsay's tonal imitation of Montgomerie's sequence. Yet the gently cadenced intimacy, 'Bot (Robene) faith . . . ', is a prelude to successive barbs. Allusion to the 'Courteour' *per se*, and the detached voice of moral commentator (in line 1, censure is delicately displaced by a wry caesural pause) postpone direct accusation until line 6. The complement of 'ye did not me beguyll' is qualified surreptitiously: 'If thou *had* wit . . . '. Such verbal guile seems to enact the vice of courtly duplicity of which Hudson is implicitly accused in the first quatrain. While Lindsay, or her rhetorical persona, speaks on behalf of Montgomerie, this other 'ventriloquism' sustains imitation of the expedient courtier: 'why then Adieu' impersonates the indifference which culminates in the couplet's striking image of suffering and its neglect. The present participle, 'deing', 'stills' the poet's death into a kind of eternity. Lindsay has become the epitaphic writer of Montgomerie's poetic jest.

The sonnet yields richly to analysis (displaying the aural, especially alliterative, mannerism of Castalian poetry, and thus revealing a poet sensitive to the tools of her craft). Lindsay's significance is greater than her extant work. As a woman, Lindsay is subsumed into what was conceived as a 'brotherhood', or in James's words, a 'sacred brethren'. The group's poetic rhetoric, especially its posture of convivial *bonhomie*, is consciously 'masculinist': writing is engendered by 'pen and drinke'. What Lindsay's sonnet implies is the 'invisibility', or irrelevance, of her gender to the extent that she adopts this rhetoric of intimacy. Her mordant exposure of Hudson's cruelty scarcely conforms to Castiglione's prescription for the Renaissance woman to possess 'a certain sweetnesse in language that may delite, wherby she may gentlie entertein all kinde of men'.[6] Montgomerie's honorific task for Lindsay might nevertheless be felt as a subtle act of exclusion: while the male quartet indulge in foolery ('all our dayis bot daffis'), a poetic sister can ensure their immortality. Perhaps more acutely, one regrets that Christian Lindsay, a writer to her peers rather than a woman writer, has not bequeathed work other than 'occasional'.

Mary Stuart (1542–87)

In contrast, Mary Stuart, Queen of Scots, has left not only an enduring myth but the most considerable poetic *corpus* of these writers. Her extant written work consists of a 66-line elegy; two poems to Queen Elizabeth; sixteen sonnets (excluding that addressed to Elizabeth); a sextain which belongs to the 'sequence' of eleven secular sonnets; the 'Méditation' of 100 lines; two poems, each of two quatrains, one addressed to Ronsard, the other to the Bishop of Ross; one quatrain preserved in Anne of Lorraine's Mass Book; a Book of Hours with quatrains and fragmentary lines; an essay in prose; voluminous letters, as well as the alleged couplets inscribed on glass at Buxton Wells and at Fotheringay, and the 'Tetrasticha ou Quatrains a Son fils', recorded in Drummond's library. Only the controversial secular love sonnets and the 'Méditation', were published within her lifetime.

Until Robin Bell's edition of 1992, *Bittersweet within my Heart* (Pavilion, reprinted 1995), Mary's poetry was virtually inaccessible.[7] Julian Sharman published *Poems of Mary Queen of Scots* (Basil Montagu Pickering) in 1873 with a dismissive critical introduction. P. Stewart-Mackenzie Arbuthnot provided in *Queen Mary's Book* (London, 1907) original texts and translations, extensive bibliographical details, and deep commitment to her subject. Prior to the latter excellent anthology, Mary's poetry appeared selectively in essentially historiographical works: for example, Samuel Jebb's *De Vita et Rebus Gestis Mariae Scotorum Reginae* (London, 1725), and in 1854 in Walter Goodall's *An Examination of the Letters said to be written by Mary Queen of Scots to James, Earl of Bothwell* (Edinburgh, 1854). With a few minor exceptions, Mary's work has been entirely excluded from the Scottish canon, and criticism consequently is scarce.[8]

Yet despite the complexity of the surviving textual sources, Mary's writings offer a distinct evolution. As if an extended Platonic sequence, the secular love of her early poetic life gives way to the renunciation of her final religious contemplations. Indeed, Mary's intellectual and spiritual biography might be construed from her own words, and not from the hagiography or denunciations of others during her lifetime to the present.

Yet it is important that her work should be granted a measure of autonomy from her life. In her last sonnet, 'Que suis ie hélas', Mary's penitent divests herself of the power of prayer: instead, 'vous, amis, qui m'avez tenue chère'; *you, my friends who have loved me so true* (l. 9) will speak. The hesitant, often faintly inscribed fragments of the Book of Hours illustrate her struggle to find poetic articulation. Her poetry, in seeking its own vindication ('pour dire et publier'; *To proclaim and tell*)[9] should not be diminished by attempts to correlate author and text. For this reason, in the present context I separate the 'Casket Sonnets', the eleven sonnets and the sextain 'avowit to be writtin by the Quene of Scottis', allegedly professing her love for James Hepburn, Lord Bothwell, from their historical controversies. The text in which they were first published, *Ane Detectioun of the Duinges of Marie Quene of Scottis . . . Translated out of the Latine quhilke was written by G. B.* (1571), attests their discovery in 'ane small gilt cofer nat fully ane foote long, beyng garnisht in sondry places with the Romaine letter F under ane kyngis crowne, quhairin were certaine letters and writynges well knawin . . . '. Their authenticity is seemingly inextricable from the enigma of Mary's innocence and integrity in Darnley's murder. Yet, contrary to the scepticism of Ronsard and sustained by contemporary biographers, to propose Mary's authorship need not convict her (as the *Detectioun* would have it) of 'mad loue, infamous adulterie, and vile passione'. Why should we not credit Mary with sufficient artfulness to create a rhetorical, as opposed to a purely personal, lyric voice?

One may propose this reservation and yet believe that writing served as Mary's consolation (the long 'Méditation', was conceived as a response to another work of religious affirmation), and became an act reserved for the privacy of manuscript and personal book. Both her religious and secular pieces define the nature of inwardness, seeking to cultivate in the loving heart and the religious soul sufficient purity. The reader may often feel that she is trespassing as a privileged but guilty eavesdropper. Yet, to borrow the metaphor of French feminism's reading strategy as 'hearing' the silent or the forbidden (*inter-dit*), we should listen to Mary's poetic 'voices' but also read them as literary artefacts.

Mary's earliest extant poem, 'En mon triste et doux chant', both realises yet contradicts Ronsard's portrait of the 'jeune espousée en plainte doloureuse'. The elegy first appeared in the *Vies des Dames de France illustres* by Pierre de Bourdeilles, Seigneur de Brantôme (c.1540–1614) and published posthumously at Leyden by Jean Sambix in 1665.[10] This self-consciously proclaimed homage of love to Francis II, Mary's first husband, is defined as a song or *chanson* that almost ingenuously announces its own conclusion ('Mets chanson ici fin', l. 61). The term may simply allude to the mutuality of poetry and music (a medieval concept which Ronsard would shortly endorse in the 'Abbrége de l'Art Poétique François' of 1565), or imply that it was intended to be sung. Mary's musical gifts were attested by Sir James Melville's *Memoirs*, and she may have composed the two galliards which bear her name. It is certainly conceivable that she either composed or performed a setting for this elegy.[11]

Though tonally 'triste et doux'; *sad and quiet* (l. 1), the elegy emphasises the mourning self, the bereaved female lover, rather than the object of lamentation. Veiled resentment towards the sacrificed promise of 'meilleurs ans' may even be sensed:

> Qui en mon doux printemps
> Et fleur de ma jeunesse
> Toutes les peines sens
> D'un extrême tristesse,
> Et en rien n'ai plaisir
> Qu'en regret et désir. (ll. 13–18)

(In my springtime's gladness
And flower of my young heart,
I feel the deepest sadness
Of the most grievous hurt.
Nothing now my heart can fire
But regret and desire.)

This honest anger at death, as if a thoughtless absence, is succeeded by joyfully invoked 'presences'. The mourner first conceives herself as a conventional lover, imbued with a Petrarchan 'visage/De violettes' (ll. 28–9), and reflecting in pastoral solitude. Lines 37 8, 'Si en quelque séjour,/Soit en bois ou en pré; *And thus I always stay/Whether in wood or meadow*, present an imperfect *locus amoenus* where time is not transcended but conspicuously annotated. Yet transcendence is achieved through visions of the beloved, as if to invert the medieval convention of the *donna angelicata*, that combine assured factuality (the simple, repetitive 'je vois' authenticates the visionary) with imaginative delicacy:

Si parfois vers ces lieux
Viens à dresser ma vue,
Le doux trait de ses yeux
Je vois en une nue;
Soudain je vois en l'eau
Comme dans un tombeau. (ll. 43–8)

(Sometimes in such a place
His image comes to me.
The sweet smile on his face
Up in a cloud I see.
Then sudden in the mere
I see his funeral bier.)

The beauty of this epiphany does not conceal its conceptual grace. The beloved's manifestations suggest both his unearthliness – the painterly image of the cloud implying his distant divinity – and his literal belonging to the earth as the imagistic solidity of 'tombeau' finds immediate contrast with the evanescent 'l'eau'. Narcissus-like, the lover perceives in her own watery reflection the image of the beloved: literally, her self becomes one with his. This unity attains an intimacy – 'Toujours est près de moi'; *He is near me always* (l. 54) – of sensual immediacy: 'Je le sens qu'il me touche'; *I can feel his touch* (l. 52). Mary's poem is a celebratory hymn, without religious sanction, to the continuity of love beyond death and not an elegy for its impossibility. In the last stanza, 'refrain' implies the endless invocation of her self-renewing love; here too is found the earliest expression of 'amour vrai', that testament of secular and devotional ardour which attains to a philosophy in Mary's writing.

Mets chanson ici fin
A si triste complainte
Dont sera le refrain:

Amour vrai et non feint
Pour la séparation
N'aura diminution. (ll. 61–6)

(I shall cease my song now,
My sad lament shall end
Whose burden aye shall show

True love can not pretend
And, though we are apart,
Grows no less in my heart.)

The love, or rather loves, enshrined in the twelve 'casket' poems, the first sonnet sequence written in Scotland as John Durkan noted,[12] differ from the elegy's in one profound respect: they require perpetual justification. To present the desiring 'I' of a Renaissance love discourse as feminine was itself to rise against an entrenched poetic ideology. Petrarchistic and Platonic love sequences, in the sixteenth century written largely by male poets, branded Renaissance literary love as the preserve of men. The text which declares how and why *she* loves is thus a genuinely revolutionary inversion of woman's usual discursive position as the object of poetic discourse.[13] The invocation to a watchful Christ in the first sonnet implies that the lover is subject to divine judgement; but scrutiny is also worldly. Her love is spectacle for 'un méchant rapporteur'/*ane wicked reporter* (st. 11, l. 10); but as she is judged, so she judges also. Mary's sequence claims a certain uniqueness for eschewing the conventional 'I/thou' paradigm of poetic love in favour of a more dramatic triad. There is the lover who writes, her beloved but also her rival, the latter's wife. Love's contingencies are skilfully exposed. The lover's (imagined) knowledge is partial, her self-vindications part of the amatory persuasion, her judgements often imagined: 'Quand vous l'aimiez' (st. 5), for example, re-enacts her rival's sexual frigidity, and her 'imperfection' of complacency.

Truthful love can be validated only by the faithfulness of the written word to the inner feeling. By 'paroles fardées'; *paintit wordis* (st. 6, 1.9), the other incriminates herself, and the lover himself by granting them faith. This concern with the consonance of word and feeling may be perceived in other contemporary Scottish and French amatory poetry. This effort to purge poetic love of its feigning hyperbole (a rhetorical manoeuvre itself) is often critically construed as 'anti-Petrarchism'. Yet in Mary's allusions to rhetorical feigning, the fictionality of love has a wider compass than the purely verbal. Unlike the rival's Epicurean desire, love as conceived by the 'je' is a moral and spiritual absolute. 'Amour vrai' enables the lover to perfect herself. The other's condemned 'imperfection' is offered in stark opposition to the speaker's desire to render herself fit 'pour lui':

Pour lui j'attends toute bonne fortune.
Pour lui je veux garder santé et vie.
Pour lui tout vertu de suivre j'ai envie.
Et sans changer me trouvera toute une.

(st. 8, ll. 11–14)

(For him I attend all good fortune,
For him I will conserve health and life,
For him I desyre to ensew courage,
And he shall euer find me unchangeable.)

This is ardent self-abnegation. Yet sacrifice of 'nom et conscience' (st. 1, l. 11), 'bien, heur . . . contentement' (st. 8, l. 8), is made in pursuit of an earthly love that is, in essence, of unearthly significance. Worldly renunciation is small loss when the lover is 'seul bien . . . seul espérance' (st. 7, l. 3) incarnate. Aspects of amatory neoplatonism may be sensed, not merely in the virtuous beloved, but in the lover's spiritual lack which requires fulfilment or completion by another. This reflects a facet of Neoplatonic love doctrine which posits that the lover must render her/himself worthy of an exchange of love. In Marsilio Ficino's commentary on Plato's *Symposium* (one of the most deeply influential of the Renaissance love treatises which were held in Mary's Holyrood library), love brings cause both to mourn and rejoice: aspiration to the beloved's state of goodness is partly destruction and loss of one's original self. In her sonnets, Mary strives to retain her 'self', her physical and spiritual identity; in the elegy, she becomes one with the beloved, her image perceived by implication in his reflection. To prove herself worthy, she will enrol as a devoted pupil of 'la science . . . /pour toujours vous complaire'; *the knowledge . . . /that I may ever please you'* (st. 10, ll. 10–11). Love (in particular, conjugal love) will be refashioned into a relationship founded on moral and spiritual equality. Subjugation, conveyed by 'Et votre volonté de la mienne suivre'; *And to follow your wyll wyth myne* (st. 10, l. 8), is the means to an end, that of a lover known 'truly' ('Et ferai tant qu'en vrai connaîtra'; *And sall do so mikle that he shall know*, st. 8, l. 7), and a love secured by the absolute of 'foi'. Yet this ideal love remains a postulate. Unlike the elegy's celebratory imagined realm, the conceived ideal of Mary's sequence is internally contradicted, riven by ironies that create its peculiar emotional power.

The beloved is not a Platonic ideal. Of this the lover is fiercely conscious. Giving faith to 'her', the false as opposed to true lover, he is vehemently censured by a series of rhetorically intense accusations:

> Vous ignorez l'amour que je vous porte.
> Vous soupçonnez qu'autre amour me transporte.
> Vous estimez mes paroles du vent.
> Vous dépeignez de cire mon las coeur.
> Vous me pensez femme sans jugement.
>
>   (st. 7, ll. 9–13)

> (you do nat knaw the loue I beare to you.
> you suspect that other love transporteth me.
> you thinke my wordes be but wind.
> you paint my wery hart, as it were of waxe,
> you imagine me a woman without iugement.)

Several orthodoxies are inverted (principally woman's irrationality as evoked by the implied allusion to theological, philosophical and literary thought) as the lover desires not to be effaced into female archetype. Fundamentally, 'l'amour d'un tel amant' (st. 6, l. 3) is flawed by a sacrilege which renders exquisitely sensitive (or defamiliarises) the act of reading as a woman. In a later sonnet, she confesses,

> Pour lui aussi j'ai jeté mainte larme.
> Premier, quand il se fit de ce corps possesseur
> Duquel alors il n'avait pas le coeur.
>
>   (st. 9, ll. 1–3)

> (For him also I powred out many teares,
> First when he made himselfe possessor of thys body,
> Of the quhilk then he had nat the hart.)

Psychologically and rhetorically, the lover's physical violation is inordinately greater than any sensual transcendence (in Montgomerie often playful) of Petrarchan chasteness. She depicts herself as an impersonalised body. 'Ce corps' implies that in the beloved's (and her own?) vision she is mere matter. Petrarchan lachrymosity sheds its usual import of melancholy to communicate the physical grief of rape. The beloved's own violation in the second quatrain still sustains the imagery of tears but is deepened by that of blood. These associative images intensify the original violation verbally and emotionally. The abstract neoplatonic idiom is violently displaced, and the conceit of a love attaining unto death (compare st. 10, ll. 13–14) diminished by her contemplated suicide:

> Puis me donna une autre dure alarme
> Quand il versa de son sang mainte dragme
> Dont de grief il me vint laisser douleur
> Qu'il me pensa ôter la vie et frayeur
> De perdre las le seul rampart qui m'arme.
>
> > (st. 9, ll. 4–8)

> (Efter he did geue me one uther hard charge,
> Quhen he bled of his blude great quantitie,
> Through the great sorrow of the quhilk came to me that dolour
> That almost caryit away my life, and the feire
> To lese the onely strength that armit me.)

Is her life's lost sustaining force ('le seul rampart') the beloved, or her now violated spiritual and physical dignity? Such contradictions render Mary's sonnets deeply unorthodox. Ironically, this sonnet is a prelude to subsequent avowals of faith; the ultimate line itself solicits a mutual unity, 'l'alliance', between violator and possessed. Mary's sequence invites psychological analyses; certainly its emotional extremities cannot be reduced to an instance of Catullan 'odi et amo' or Petrarchan oxymoron. Nor can Renaissance philosophies of love be invoked to resolve what may at best be perceived as the difficult truths of desire. My own feeling is that the poems were never conceived as a sequence which possesses a definitive temporal and logical unity. When the lover suddenly embraces 'de vous seul' in line 14 of the last sonnet, the vigilant Christ invoked in the opening text's first line may be solicited again. Lines 1–13 refer to the earthly beloved by the pronouns 'le' and 'lui', suggesting his absence. Indeed, in each of the sonnets the lover speaks or soliloquises in rhetorical isolation; 'ou je languis ici' evokes both a physical and emotional solitude. Imaginative consolation, and the presence of her God are the lover's solace.

Mary's sacred poetry, composed in the last decade of her life, can be sensed as an extension rather than contradiction of the earlier period. Both the 'Méditation' and the sonnet, 'L'ire de Dieu par le sang n'apaise', were published by John Leslie, Bishop of Ross, (1527–96) in the first book of his *Libri duo: Quorum uno, Piae afflicti animi consolationes remedia: altero, Animi tranquilli munimentum et conservatio Continentur* (Paris, 1574), which he dedicated to Mary (the poem also appears later in *Lettres et Traitez chréstiens, par David Home en Dunbar*, Bergerac, 1613). Mary's lyric addressed to Leslie, 'Puisque Dieu a, par sa bonté immense', was printed in the 1593 French edition of the *Consolations*. The *Libri duo* were composed during the period of Leslie's imprisonment in London, 1571–4. Educated in Scotland and France, he accompanied Mary to England in 1568 after appointment to his bishopric in 1566. There, he acted as Mary's chief representative at Elizabeth's court. Mary's preserved letters to Leslie convey tenderness and trust. The latter's sensitivity to her suffering can be felt in his pro-Marian treatises. In his *Negotiations*, Leslie declares 'I . . . therewith sent a Testimony of (Mary's) diligent perusing of the first treaty of the Godly meditations, out of which she had drawn summary collections, and at the same in French meetre'. Mary, in a letter from Sheffield in 1572, and published in the 1574 edition, writes of the solace afforded 'in carcere conscriptum' by Leslie's prose treatise. Mary's 'Méditation' is intertextual through its verbal resonances with Leslie's text. Yet the latter's overarching consolation – eternal life by contemplation of divine glory – is expressed with greater tentativeness. This is poignantly felt in the two quatrains addressed to Leslie and published in the 1595 edition of *Piae afflicti*. Joy for Leslie's own deliverance from prison is tempered in the second quatrain by the desire that God may also pity 'ma longue souffrance', l. 8.

These poems, combined with the other three devotional sonnets found in manuscript[14] and the fragments inscribed in the Book of Hours, seem in their cumulative power responses to the implied challenge of the earliest, the 'Méditation': how can the desecrated spiritual soul attain the salvation which is assured but arduously earned? Mary's secular lover, seeking to prove her 'mérite', has deep affinities with the Catholic penitent for whom grace (tellingly conceived as a 'nearness' to Christ rather than reunion: 'Méd'., l. 101; 'O Signeur Dieu', l. 13) is won by inward purity, those of 'de bon coeur' ('Méd'., l. 45), rather than by the Calvinist elect. On this point, one feels that Mary is sustaining a theological dialogue with Knox:

> Mais qui pourra, O Père très humain,
> Avoir cet heur, si tu n'y mets la main
> D'abondonner son péché et offense
> En ayant fait condigne pénitence?
> (Méd., ll. 49–52)

> (But which of us, O kindest Father, still
> Can claim this fortune, save it be thy will
> That he abandon sin and all offence
> By having made a worthy penitence?)

Inner sanctity is exalted as the only true possession of 'Amour et foi' ('Méd'., l. 68) since

> L'ire de Dieu par le sang ne s'apaise
> De boeufs, ni boucs, épandus sur l'autel
> Ni par encens ou sacrifice
> Le souverain ne reçoit aucune aise

> (The wrath of God is not appeased by blood
> Of goats nor oxen on the altar laid;
> No incense nor any sacrifice made
> Brings satisfaction to the Lord our God.)

The true altar at which to worship Christ is not burdened by excess rituals but held within: 'mon lieu de franchise' is, literally, her inner *sanctum*.

The 'Méditation' appears to possess two rhetorical voices: one which espouses a general 'medievalistic' moral piety (in conventions of the *vanitas*, *de casibus principibus*, the mutability of fortune and beauty), the other an individual narrative, exemplary 'de maux, de tourments, et d'ennuis'; *of sorrows, torments and of strife* (l. 92). Prayer thus replaces homily.

> Par quoi, Seigneur et Père Souverain,
> Regarde-moi de ton visage serein,
> Dont regardas la femme pécheresse
> Qui à tes pieds pleuvait ses maux sans cesse;
> Dont regardas Pierre pareillement
> Qui jà t'avait nié par jurement.
> Et comme à eux donne-moi cette grâce . . .
>
> (ll. 57–64)

> (Therefore, O almighty Father and Lord,
> Look upon me with thy benign regard
> As you looked on that woman full of sin
> Who at thy feet poured out her ceaseless pain;
> As you looked upon Peter just the same,
> He who had already forsworn thy name.
> And, as to them, grant me thy grace I pray . . .)

Mary's allusion to the archetypal penitent, Mary Magdalene, is common in religious poetry, but here has particular pathos through its resonant feminine sexuality. In pursuit of grace, Mary's penitent depicts a Christ who is alternately tender and irreconcilable. 'O Signeur Dieu resceuez ma priere' communicates its spiritual intensity by an insistent rhetoric. The 'priere' presents a type of heroic martyr – 'Je defendray à la derni carriere'; *I shall defend thee while I still draw air* (l. 4) – who demands unconditionally that Christ purge her of earthly frailties. The passionate fierceness and abnegation twinned below recall the Donne of the Holy Sonnets:

> Tu veulx Signeur estre maitre du cueur
> Viens donc Signeur et fays ta demeure
> Pour en chasser lamour et la rancueur . . .
>
> (ll. 9–11)

> (You wish, Lord, to be master of my heart.
> Come then O Lord and make me your redoubt
> That earthly love and hate be driven out . . .)

The true faith, as Mary herself defined Catholicism, binds the rhetorical and spiritual fabric of all her devotional writings except the last, 'Que suis ie helas'. The first quatrain is a striking expression of spiritual dereliction. The inward 'foi' conceived earlier as a palpable possession is realised by an image of bodily dissolution. Bereft of humanity (without her 'cueur' now beyond suffering), and conceived as as a passive object acted upon, a quasi-platonic shadow, Mary's last poetic self here evokes the later philosophical, 'baroque' pathos of Drummond, not least the closure of all life.

> Je ne suis fors qu'un corps priue de cueur
> vn ombre vayn vn obiect de malheur
> Qui n'a plus rien que de mourir enuie
> (ll. 2–4)

> (I am but a body whose heart's torn away,
> A vain shadow, an object of misery
> Who has nothing left but death-in-life.)

In the final couplet, allusion to 'la ioye infinie', l. 14, intimates the divine consolation. But Mary's sacred poetry claims most power when illuminating, as above in full anguish, the human frailty for which her 'Mère, l'Eglise' ('Méd'., l. 79) cannot wholly compensate.

Mary's writing is more than the sum of these secular and devotional pieces. Their shared resonances – fidelity to inner and systematic faith, the sanctity of the lover or penitent's imagined ideals – draw out the spiritual cohesion of Mary's early and late works. Yet fuller study of Mary's extant *corpus* should also examine the structural dynamics of her sonnets, the most exigent of poetic forms; her wordplay that delights in semantic incongruities; the prose piece on the nature of adversity. In 'Adamas loquitur', a gracefully wrought plea for clemency to Elizabeth which depicts the precious stone as an emblem of Mary's worthy heart, one perceives a playful, pictorial mannerism. The quatrains in her Book of Hours literally display the process of her creativity. These poetic fragments cannot be precisely dated (though '1579' is inscribed on one leaf), and can only be fully comprehended in their original iconographic context.[15] On f. 81v, for example, Mary's lines are closely compressed, flowing into each other in an erratic hand, seeming incomplete as they meet the book's margins. Inscribed in a fragile, inconsistent hand across and around exquisitely illuminated borders, these miniature poems impress as tightly conceived, epiphanic moments of thought and feeling.

> les heures ie guide et le iour
> par l'ordre exacte de ma carriere
> quittant mon triste seiour
> pour isy croistre ma lumiere

> (I guide the hours and guide the day
> Because my course is true and right
> And thus I quit my own sad stay
> That here I may increase my light.)

The sun's ceaseless motion provides an apt figure for the measurable constancy of the 'I'. Richly, the single conceit promises light's inevitable replenishment (strength or hope to mitigate 'tristesse') yet perhaps poignantly implying that she herself, the 'I' which is the sun or this world's own centre, obscures sustaining light. This peculiar visionary quality is embodied by the recurrent verbal emblem of 'un bel ange': an image of divine beauty or a 'guardian angel' known intimately. Several of these aphoristic poems meditate upon the nature of time: as philosophical necessity and as hopeful transience. One feels that Mary's Book itself embodies the two temporal perspectives of the human and eternal that remain her poetic constant. The body of the text (scriptural quotation and prayer) enshrines the immutable divine word; but Mary's imperfect, often incomplete, words physically mirror her sense of human pathos, as if to prefigure the marginality to which modern Scottish literary histories have unjustly consigned them.

Mary's work may be perceived as embodying the Franco-Scottish poetic alliance of Renaissance literature. The inventory of her library contains French poetry of the Pléiade and pre-Pléiade periods, and in 1583 she writes but fails to send a brief poetic 'epistle' to Ronsard. Instead she gave the illustrious French poet (who died a few years later) a casket of 2000 ecus inscribed 'A Ronsard, l'Apollon de la Source des Muses'. The two quatrains depict Mary as a commemorative poet, praising Ronsard yet asking that he be immured from 'de malheurs'. In general, the Platonising aspect of her secular love poetry may be traced to the amatory Platonism of, for example, Pontus de Tyard and Joachim du Bellay. This philosophical impulse in Mary's poetry is later deepened by the intellectually complex love sequences of Fowler and Drummond.

Mary Beaton (c.1543–c.1597); Elizabeth Douglas (fl. 1587); Mary Oxlie (early 1600s)

The artistic culture of Mary's reign in the mid-1560s is at last being reappraised as a period of poetic and musical sophistication.[16] Did Mary's aesthetic sensibility inspire women at her Scottish court to take 'la main au papier', recalling Brantôme's account of her Latin oration at the French court on women's rights 'de sçavoir les lettres et artz liberaux'? Regrettably, there is no evidence. Male poetry remained the dominant 'anxiety of influence' for several professedly aspirant women writers. One sonnet addressed to William Fowler proves the exception. Signed 'M.L.B', it has been ascribed to Lady Mary Beaton, one of the four 'Maries' castigated by Knox. The daughter of Robert Beaton of Creich, her mother was a French lady-in-waiting at the Scottish court. In 1548, she went to France with the royal entourage where she received her education, and later married Alexander Ogilvy of Boyne. She was certainly known to Fowler: his incomplete 'lamentatioun of the desolat olympia furth of the tent cantt of Ariosto' is dedicated to 'the right honorable Ladye Marye Betoun Ladye Boine'. Her 'Sonet', found among Fowler's manuscripts (NLS MS 2065, f. 6r) and composed in the Castalian interlaced rhyme scheme, urges that Fowler will only attain true poetic laurels if he 'lay . . . adowne' his lute, the instrument of love song:

> For thow maist on a stronger piller staye
> The giftis wherwith the heavens have thee instorde
> If thou the learned *Thuskan* wolde assaye
> And in thy tyme his *Triumphes* doe record (ll. 5–8)

Petrarch's *Trionfi* emerges as the only text dedicated to 'Iehouas high eternall prayes'. Interestingly, it appears of deep significance for three of these writers. Anna Hume's translation, discussed below, provides one powerful rationale. William Fowler's vernacular translation of 1587, 'The Triumphs of the Most Famous Poet Mr. Frances Petrarke Translated out of italian into inglish by Mr. Wm Fouler P. of Hauicke' (EUL Dr. De. 1. 10) was certainly welcomed by his poetic coterie. The persuasive rhetoric of Beaton's sonnet, 'if thou . . . *wolde* assaye' (my italics), implies that her poem inspired 'frend fouler' to undertake the Scots Petrarchan rendering: proof of the influence of the creative female Muse![17]

The two dedicatory poems appended to Fowler's MS translation among 'verces writen by sundrie hands', and written 'in praise of M^r. W^m. Foular her freind' by 'E.D.', may be identified as Elizabeth Douglas, the 'Contess of Erroll', to whom Fowler dedicates a sonnet. The youngest daughter of William Douglas, Earl of Morton (d. 1606), she married Francis Hay, ninth Earl of Errol (d. 1631) who gained his earldom in 1585 despite incurring royal condemnation by being a converted Catholic. Elizabeth Douglas was his third wife, and she bore him three sons and eight daughters. Her sonnets should not be conceived as mere acts of homage. The neglect of early women writers is due partly to underevaluation of the genres in which they found expression. Though the dedicatory poem of praise is not an exclusively female genre, its evident popularity with the early woman writer may arise from its decorous displacement of attention from the poet to her object of praise. Both Douglas's sonnets omit allusion to the poetic 'I'. The first, 'The glorious greiks dois praise thair *Homers* quill', displays exuberant rhetorical hyperbole in its vision of a renaissance of Scottish literary arts which surpass other European vernaculars. This may be a conscious allusion to James VI's prescriptive outline for a Scottish renaissance in 'Ane Schort Treatise, conteining some reulis and cautelis to be obseruit and eschewit in Scottis Poesie' (1584). Interestingly, the sonnet which James himself contributed to Fowler's 'Triumphes' invokes classical and European poets in a similar praise *topos* to Douglas. The latter's final line, 'They all do yeild Sen foular doith arrywe', is announced jubilantly, anticipated by the careful rhetorical balancing of the previous lines:

> The Spanzoll laughs (sawe Lucan) all to scorne
> And France for *Ronsard* stands and settis him owt
> The better sort for *Bartas* blawis the horne
> And Ingland thinks thair *Surrye* first but dout
> To praise their owen these countreis gois about
> Italian lykes *Petrarchas* noble grace
> Who well deserwis first place amangs that rout
> Bot *Foular* thow dois now thame all deface . . . (ll. 5–12)

The generous concession to Petrarch in line 11 is a wry piece of poetic hubris. Douglas's second sonnet commemorates Fowler's incarnation of a second Laura in the person of Lady Jean Fleming to whom Fowler dedicates his work. Douglas skilfully adapts her eulogy to both poet and patron: 'How may thye fame o *Foular* than be small/Who sings Dame Lauras praise but feinzeit all'. The final couplet, 'O Ladye liwe! thy foular the extolls/ Whose golden pen thy name in fame Inrolls', deploys the common renaissance *topos* of poetic immortality, used especially as a persuasive strategy on the female beloveds of secular love lyrics. Not only does Douglas glorify Fowler's propitious renaissance role but exemplifies her own literary erudition under the modest guise of praise. The catalogue of classical and European poets in the first sonnet, and the Homeric allusion in the first quatrain of its companion piece discreetly yet impressively signify aesthetic and linguistic learning.

This ebullience contrasts with the poetic *apologia* for female creativity 'To William Drummond of Hawthornden' signed by 'Mary Oxlie of Morpet', appended to the 1656 edition of Drummond's *Poems*. Her identity is complex. Edward Phillips, in the section of his *Theatrum Poetarum* (London, 1675) entitled 'Women Among the Moderns Eminent for Poetry', declares her a 'Scotch Poetess' but confusingly names her 'Mary Morpeth'. David Masson's biography of Drummond perhaps sheds light on this confusion of surname and nationality. He proposes that Phillips obtained this and other dedicatory poems from Drummond's brother-in-law, Sir John Scot of Scotstarvet. If the original ascription, 'Mary Oxlie of Morpet', is assumed the most reliable, it might be proposed that this Northumbrian poet perhaps moved to Scotland, and there participated in a literary milieu created by Drummond (with whom Anna Hume, discussed below, seems to have corresponded).[18]

> Then do not sparkes with your bright Suns compare,
> Perfection in a Woman's worke is rare;
> From an untroubled mind should Verses flow;
> My discontents makes mine too muddy show;
> And hoarse encumbrances of houshold care
> Where these remaine, the muses ne're repaire.

The 'Judith Shakespeare' of Virginia Woolf's imagination is here embodied: the distaff defeats the pen. Candour and pathos are fully present: the woman writer creates less, and less well, because of domestic duty ('hoarse' appositely conveying the effort to articulate) and psychological anxieties. Nevertheless, in the poem's substance such humility is contradicted. Despite her reluctance to impinge on male discourse, Oxlie beautifully recreates, or imitates, Drummond's sensuous, melancholic idiom:

> But when thy Muse, dissolv'd in show'rs,
> Wailes that peerles Prince of ours,
> Cropt by too untimely Fate,
> Her mourning doth exasperate
> Senselesse things to see thee moane,
> Stones do weep, and Trees do groane,
> Birds in aire, Fishes in flood,
> Beasts in field forsake their food,
> The Nymphs forgoing all their Bow'rs
> Teare their Chaplets deckt with Flow'rs . . . (ll. 39–48)

Here, Oxlie alludes to Drummond's *Tears on the Death of Moeliades* (1613); earlier, she alludes to the Auristella of *Poems* (1616). Lines 33–8 imaginatively propose that 'the Tree-turn'd *Daphne*' will crown the poet with the laurel 'garland', an image that has been conceived as a reply to the commendatory sonnet of William Alexander.[19] Oxlie provides further evidence that the literary coterie and its mainly manuscript culture provided an apt medium in which women could write (perhaps prolifically as implied by Phillips's allusion to 'many other things in Poetry' by Oxlie) without conforming to the perceived 'unfeminine' audacity of writing for publication.[20] Drummond's extant letter to Anna Hume, for example, attests that Hume had sufficient confidence to give the famous poet samples of her work. Her 'delicate verses' met with a more favourable response than Southey's to Charlotte Brontë two hundred years later:

> Alas my Muses are of no such Value to deserve the Blason of so pregnant and rare a Wit. Perhaps ye raised them to show the Highnes of your Spirit, which ever transcendeth mean Measures; or to make known how excellently ye can praise any Thing that you please. But howsoever (Praise being the Reward of Virtue, and proceeding from so sound a Judgement,

and one so praise-worthy) I will think hereafter my Muses worthy of Praise, because ye held them such.[21]

Drummond may have served as a literary mentor to Oxlie, and to other women whose writing never gained the small distinction granted to the former by the printed dedicatory verse.

Mary Maitland (fl.1586)

In reconstructing women's role in the production of early Scottish literature, a measure of creative licence must be allowed. In proposing that Mary Maitland, previously recognised as the transcriber of the Maitland Quarto of 1587, may also be the author of one, or more, of its anonymous pieces, I plead guilty of such licence.[22] Here first is the provocative allusion to Mary Maitland, poet:

> If sapho saige for saphic songe so sueit
> did pleid for prais & place amangs the nyne
> if trustie talk with raillis so trew do meit
> amids the gods dois duell that dame devyne.
>
> And now of lait that lustie ladie rair
> Olimpia o lampe of latine land
> so doeth thy workes unto this day declair
> for lyflie art Who list thy Vers to scand.
>
> A thrid o Maistres Marie maik I pray
> & put in vre your Worthie vertewis all
> for famous is your fleing fame I say
> hyd not so haut a hairt in slugish thrall. (ll. 1–12)

The anonymous writer then declares, 'a plesant poet perfyte sall ye be' (1.14).[23] The resonance of the Sapphic allusion is discussed later but the 'Olimpia' of line 6 may be suggestively identified as Olympia Morata (1526–55), Protestant convert, prolific Italian humanist and *poeta docta*. A figure who inspired the admiration of later women writers, she wrote in Greek of her creative freedom: 'I, a woman, have dropped the symbols of my sex,/Yarn, shuttle, basket, thread,/I love but the flowered Parnassus . . .'.[24] Yet the third stanza of the Quarto lyric implies that Mary Maitland is a poet *manqué*; her 'slugish thrall' may allude to her task of the manuscript's transcription. In reference to her father, the writer Sir Richard Maitland of Lethington (1496–1586), the Quarto's 1918 editor, W. E. Craigie, comments that 'the daughter writing from the dictation of the venerable old bard would form an admirable subject for painting'.[25] The more demanding nature of the task when perceived as a creative effort is gained from the following stanza which may be by this early Miltonic daughter:

> Ye heauinlie goddis & goddessis
> ye most celestiall
> Vnto my muse your helpis doe bend
> & for your aydis I call

> & thow diana ladye bricht
> with nymphes of chastetie
> Graunt me your favours I requeist
> to end this worthelie.[26]

The appeal to the 'heauinlie' deities is an orthodox classical device often deployed by Castalian poets. That to Diana may allude to another of the Quarto's poems in which a visionary narrator claims, '*Marie* thocht in this wod did appeir/*maitland* and gold scho gave me aboundantlie . . . ', ll. 41–2 (my italics).[27] This punningly conceived 'Mary Maitland' bears a 'trie' which signifies 'trew Virginitie' (l. 45), the prelude to a vision of various goddesses which includes 'diana' (l. 61), aptly the mythological figure of chastity. In the lyric which may be Maitland's own, Diana may be invoked as the guardian of women, or of the aspiring woman writer in particular. The goddess may be here refer to a new female poetic lineage incontrast to Apollo, the poetic icon of the Castalian 'brethren'. As Tilde A. Sankovitch comments, 'For male authors, that power of self-expression [was] grounded in their legitimate descent from the divine father, Apollo . . . For women poets that fabled paternity is meaningless . . .'.[28]

The Maitland Quarto is characterised by its moral intensity, derived from poetic commentaries of contemporary social and political relevance by Mary's father. This reforming tone also informs the manuscript's lyrics of secular love. 'As phoebus in his spheris bricht'[29] is its most intense manifestation, an anonymous poem of considerable wit and beauty proclaiming the love, characteristically expressed as 'freindschip', of one woman for another:

> Wald michtie loue grant me the hap
> With yow to haue your brutus pairt
> and metamorphosing our schap
> My sex intill his vaill convert
> No brutus then sould caus us smart
> as we doe now vnhappie wemen
> Then sould we bayth with Ioyfull hairt
> honour and bliss ye band of hymen. (ll. 41–8)

The poem's complexity cannot here be fully illustrated (for example, its possible debt to two elegies by Ronsard and de Tyard) but its importance lies in its delicate, often witty, recastings of the rhetoric of the orthodox heterosexual Renaissance lyric;[30] its ironic use of the Platonic 'luif of vertew'; and the genuine uniqueness of its female homoeroticism in late sixteenth-century Scottish and English poetry. While a feminine persona does not entail female authorship, the allusion to Maitland's 'sapphic song' in this extraordinary expression of lesbian love, and possible affinities between both provokes conjecture. It is not yet established whether Sappho's love lyrics (published in a French edition of Anacreon in 1554 and 1556) were interpreted at the time as declarations of same-sex love; 'saphic songe', the expression of the Quarto lyric addressed to Maitland, at any rate may have evoked the intense female desire of Ovid's epistle, Sappho to Phaon (a male beloved). That a female transcriber may use the convention of anonymity in a MS collection for the covert inclusion of her own poetry is attested by other studies. Elaine Hobby has written that 'much forgotten women's writing' lies within poetic miscellanies and song collections.[31] The Bannatyne Manuscript of 1568, for example, presents many anonymous lyrics for which we should consider at least the possibility of female authorship. Mary Maitland is thus a crucial if enigmatic poetic presence.

Elizabeth Melville (fl.1603)

'Tak the pen in your hands and seik a blessing': as a prolific writer, Elizabeth Melville obeyed her own imperative.[32] Her extant work consists of *Ane Godlie Dreme* first published in 1603 by Robert Charteris in Edinburgh, a long and dense allegorical vision reprinted throughout the seventeenth century, one sonnet and one lyric in MS, and personal correspondence. She was virtually canonised by Alexander Hume in the preface to his *Spiritual Songs and Sonnets* of 1599, as 'a Ladie chosen of God to bee one of his saincts'; the acts of writing and prayer are one – poetry is her piety incarnate. The tenor of Melville's life can be sensed with less rhetorical intensity in the 1666 autobiography of John Livingstone, the nonconformist minister. In the first decades of the seventeenth century, Melville visited the Lanarkshire home of his father, the Reverend William Livingstone. As one of the 'sundry gracious Christians' who impressed him in childhood, Melville subsequently sustained a deep spiritual relationship with him, as her letters testify. She writes in consolation to Livingstone, possibly during his excommunication in Ireland (1632–4) as an itinerant preacher seeking 'reformation of religion'.[33] This empathy and tenacity of faith also invest her earlier sonnet (in English) to John Welsh (c. 1570–1622), the dissenting minister imprisoned for alleged treason against the monarchy, with powerful spiritual conviction.[34]

Through her faith Melville acquired a public reputation. Livingstone records that at a religious meeting in 1630 at Shotts, her 'priuat devotion' became an extraordinary spectacle of devotional ecstasy:

> William Ridge of Adderny coming into the room, and hearing her have great motion upon her, although she spake not out, he desired her to speak out, saying, that there was none in the room but him and her woman . . . She did soe, and the door being opened, the room filled full. She continued in prayer, with wonderfull assistance, for large three hours time.[35]

Her principal work was written, as stated on the titlepage, 'at the requeist of friends': when publishing was conceived as a Christian act, she could eschew Oxlie's humility. Religion (specifically Calvinism) permitted Melville a voice by which to preach and write, the kind of spiritual autonomy articulated by Margaret Fell in 1667: 'And whereas it is said, I permit not a woman to speak, as saith the Law: but where Women are led by the Spirit of God, they are not under the Law . . . '.[36] The titlepage admission authenticates the sense of Melville's vision as divine revelation. The pronouncement that, 'This is ane Dreme, and yit I thocht it best/To wryte the same, and keip it still in mynde;/Becaus I knew' (ll. 329–30) may deliberately recall the Angel's words to John in Revelation, 'Write what you see in a book'.

Melville's poem gains its structural and intellectual framework from the dream vision, a convention with a long classical and medieval heritage. Her debt extends to verbal reminiscence of the dreamer's doubt regarding verity: 'I *thocht* thair did appeir', (l. 90).[37] The narrative may be simply summarised as follows. After mourning fallen humankind, the narrator sleeps and is visited by an angelic vision who is revealed as Christ. The figure leads the dreamer through a variety of physical trials; the dreamer is tempted to end the journey at a 'Castell fair' but is shown, and ultimately rescued from, the horror of Purgatory beneath. On wakening, the dreamer expounds the allegorical significances of the journey which culminate in the final stanza's hymn to divine creation and mercy. The vision may be conceived as a female spiritual 'autobiography' which has English precursors in *The Book of Margery Kempe* and in Juliana of Norwich's *Showings of Divine Love*. Though the text neither identifies nor intimates the gender of the narrator, the preface presents it as the confession of 'M. M. Gentelwoman in Culross'.[38] The deictic change in stanza six from 'I' to 'we' signifies that Melville's spiritual dreamer, her 'self', is representative of the religious soul. The 'mark of gender' is not an issue, for all are equal before Christ. Doctrinally, the poem's religion is not universal but deeply Calvinistic. Unlike Mary Stuart's penitent, fearing her unworthiness before God, Melville's narrator belongs to the spiritual elite, or elect, of God's 'chosin Sancts' (l. 426), from the outset. While imploring Christ to 'cum and saif thy awin Elect', (l. 41), the dreamer's spiritual malaise is paradoxical since the doctrine of election does not admit doubt of one's salvation. Rather, Christ's self-revelation assures the dreamer, who has chided Him for his tardiness, of the transience of 'this fals and iron age' (l. 10). Melville's poem cannot express the religious anguish or sense of worldly loss which imbue Mary's sacred writings. For some, its power may be purely poetic.

The dreamer's relationship to the figure of Christ, one of intimate tutelage, is symbolised by the image of His extended arm or hand. To endure the physically arduous pilgrimage, she must 'grip' Christ 'fast' (l. 160), 'as he did gif command' (l. 224), a repeated imperative (l. 293), which culminates in the visionary allusion to Psalm 18:35:

> Into the feild may wee nocht baldlie byde,
> Quhen hee sall help us, with his michtie hand,
> Quha sits abone, and reules baith sea and land (ll. 443–5)

Christ's appearance in stanza twelve recalls the visitation of the *donna angelicata* or female beloved in such Scottish visionary texts as *The Kingis Quair* and Drummond's last song in *Poems* (1616). Indeed, its language evokes a secularised vision as Melville strives to realise the intensity of devotional love. The sleeping (l. 34, alluding to Ps. 44:23) and concealed (l. 39) Christ is revealed as

> Ane Angell bricht, with visage schyning cleir,
> With luifing luiks, and with ane smyling cheir:
> He askit mee, 'Quhy art thou thus sad? (ll. 92–4)

The eighteenth stanza endorses this covert metaphor of the Christian soul as the Bride, and Christ as the Bridegroom: 'I am thy spous that brings thee store of grace;/I am thy luif quhom thow wald faine embrace' (ll. 130–1). This simple declaration is Melville's deepest realisation of the Canticles metaphor, lacking the mystical quality of Drummond's religious sonnets. Yet as a whole, Melville's poem celebrates the consummation of this spiritual relationship. The dreamer's impatience signifies yearning, her 'heavie hearts desyre' (l. 118), for its true realisation in death: 'I long for Heaven, my heritage is thair,/ I long to live with my Redeimer deir', (ll. 111–12). Yearning, deferral and fulfilment constitute the poem's separate thematic movements which intertwine in stanzas xxx and xxxi. The dreamer's falsely imagined sanctity receives Christ's rebuke for such spiritual hubris:

> I was sa neir, I thocht my voyage endit;
> I ran befoir and socht not his convoy
> Nor speirit the way, becaus I thocht I kend it;
> On staitlie steps maist stoutlie I ascendit,
> Without his help, I thocht to enter thair;
> Hee followit fast, and was richt sair offendit,
> And haistelie did draw mee down the stair. (ll. 233–9)

Melville's conceit of the Christian pilgrimage is derived from biblical metaphors, such as the 'path of life' from Ps. 16:11. She powerfully aligns the state of melancholy (not identified as religious until st. iv) with the associated notion of literal and emotional exile. The dispossessed 'strangers and exiles' of Hebrews 11:13 appear, almost *verbatim*, in the exhortation: 'Lyke pilgrims puir, and strangers in exyle,/Throw fair and foull, your journey ye mon tak' (ll. 355–6). While the reader swiftly realises that Melville uses the Bible as a verbal and conceptual tool, it is important to perceive how and why her text becomes such a seamless allusive weave. Direct scriptural quotation (from Matthew 26:41, the 'waik . . . flesh, strang spreit' of ll. 153–4; 164) is combined with broader metaphors entrenched within the Christian imagination (in 1.53, the state of childlikeness from Matthew 18:3, Mark 10: 14–15). Noting such citations is not mere pedantry. Melville's recreation of profound Biblical moments reveals not simply her 'godliness' (as Hume would phrase it) but a writerly sensitivity to the the innate poetic inflexions of Scripture. Melville chooses an image or conceit from which she distils its metaphorical potential, recalling it in the final 'exposition' which subsumes the literal into the symbolic. One such conceit, the Christian life conceived as natural fruition, may serve as illustration.

> I loath to live, I wishe desolvit to be:
> My spreit dois lang, and thristeth after thee,
> As thristie ground requyres ane shoure of raine;
> My heart is dry, as fruitles barren tree
> I feill my selfe, how can I heir remaine! (ll. 84–8)

The simile, its likely biblical *loci* of Ps. 32:4, Ps. 1:3, and Ps. 42:2, is delicately anticipated by the preceding image of dissolution in 1.84, and recalled by ll. 431–2: 'Quhen clouds ar past the weather will grow cleir,/Ye saw in teares, bot ye sall reap in joy'. The latter line (again allied to several scriptural sources) is a miniature inversion of the previous simile: decay becomes fruition as the revelation brings the dreamer's faith to flower.

While such metaphorical 'interlacing' suggests that Melville is not content merely to quote Scripture, a simile such as the last may seem flawed by its transparency, and a certain triteness perceived in the analogy, 'Quhen clouds ar past . . . .'. Some contemporary readers may also feel estranged by the 'dogmatism' of Melville's tone. Her dreamer proclaims, rather than seeks to persuade, the miraculous simplicity of her new knowledge of Christ and salvation: 'Rin out your race, ye mon not faint nor tyre,/Nor sit, nor stand, nor turne back againe' (ll. 393–4). The dreamer awakes suddenly, as do all medieval dreamers, to discover that salvation is an absolute truth: 'I knaw, I sall it finde at last' (l. 326).

In Melville's allegory and her early seventeenth-century faith, intellectual doubt has no place. The limpid simplicity of the last quotation is the ideal medium for proclamation. For myself, the *Dreme* impinges most when verbal delicacy is struck. The image of the angelic wings serves first to convey hubris (l. 71), the myth of Icarus (st. li1), and when nearest to biblical precedents, the idea of divine shelter (l. 303): 'Under his wings I thocht mee for to hyde'. Spiritual refuge is united with a certain capriciousness.

'Away vaine world bewitcher of my heart' is a lyric of worldly renunciation and of love for 'Chryst allone' (l. 28). Found in the chief source for Montgomerie's poetry, the Margaret Ker MS (EUL De. 3. 70, ff. 81r–v, inscribed 'To the Toon of Sall I let hir go'), the lyric has been attributed both to Melville and, recently by R. J. Lyall, to Alexander Montgomerie. Melville's claim to authorship is sanctioned by publication as an appendix to the 1603 and 1606 editions of *Ane Godlie Dreme*, considerably anglicised, and is the text reproduced here. As suggested by the music's title, the lyric (which appears in the MS after Montgomerie's poems which conclude with *finis*; only text and music for 'Come my children dere' follow) is most probably a religious reworking (or *contrafactum*) of a secular love song. Melville had ample precedent for this in the *Gude and Godlie Ballatis* of 1567 by which 'profane' songs became ('changeit into') 'godly'. The poem has close affinities with Melville's *Dreme*. The intimate framework of the devotional 'I' and 'Sweete Christ' (l. 20) re-enacts the *Dreme's* struggle between the individual and worldliness. The *Dreme* proclaims the latter's 'subtle slights' (l. 9) as the trinity of the 'Devill, the World' (l. 357) and the Flesh. Spiritual succour is again Symbolised by the 'helping hand' (l. 21). If by Melville, the text reveals her command of a new stanzaic structure and metrical variation within the stanzaic unit itself. Its cadenced voice is aptly musical: 'A thousand tymes away, ah stay no more' (l. 19). The effect of litany is derived from the last stanza's echoic phrases which announce that temptation is shunned:

> Let the world be gone, I'll loue Christ alone,
> Let the world be gone, I care not
> Christ is my loue allone, I feare not. (ll. 28–30).

In each of these texts, Melville manages to entwine religous didacticism with emotion. From her letters, Melville emerges as both preacher and poet. Written to Livingstone and her wayward son at court, they are a vivid testament to her faith (the death of her husband in 1631 is stoically announced) and her rhetorical skill. The extract below from a letter of 1631 to Livingstone demonstrates a rhetorically refined prose style (note the structural balance and amplification), intensified by aural effects and imbued with the scriptural idiom which is Melville's creative staple:

> curage deir brother all is in loue all works together for the best. ye must be hewin and hamerd doun and drest, and prepaired before ye be a LEWING STON fitt for his building . . . up your harte then and prepair for the battell. put on the wholl armour of god tho[t] ye be waik ye haue a strong captaine . . . your treasur and treasurer who keips all in stoir. the stock an the anwell is in his awin hand and he drops doun drop and drop as ye haue neid.[39]

Anna Hume (*fl*.1644)

As Melville renders 'Goddes worde' (Knox's phrase) into Scots, so forty-one years later Anna Hume distils Petrarch into English in *The Triumphs of Love: Chastity: Death: Translated out of Petrarch By M[ris] Anna Hume*, published by Evan Tyler in Edinburgh in 1644. Hume's neglect (comparatively greater than Melville's) is compounded because her extant work is a translation and her medium of expression English, albeit an elegant variant in finely chiselled couplets. Anglicisation has evoked critical prejudice in contemporary criticism of early seventeenth-century Scottish poetry: Anna Hume's work may be considered one of its many oversights. What follows is a brief critical defence of Hume's poem which seeks to establish the significance of the medieval Petrarch 'rewritten' by a mid-seventeenth-century woman. For Hume, the myth of Laura, the beloved, needs reappraisal. The creative and the critical impulses are thus mutual.

Recent studies emphasise the literary and cultural independence of the translation from the 'source text'. Hume's *Triumphs* – of love, chastity and death, thus the first three of Petrarch's six – should also be understood as a statement of her own creative independence, and emancipation from her status as another Miltonic daughter. It is alleged that she translated the Latin poems of her father, Sir David Hume of Godscroft (c. 1560–c. 1630), and evidence survives that she superintended the publication of his *History of the House and Race of Douglas and Angus*. Hume acted as an apologist for this work:

> It is not the least happinesse I enjoy by my returne to my Countrey, that I have found this Piece amongst my Fathers scattered Papers; it is here in his own method, wᵗout addition or change, I cannot say, wᵗout defect.⁴⁰

As a writer, Hume appears to favour self-denial rather than self-glorification. She praises Drummond and the Princess Elizabeth of Bohemia to whom her *Triumphs* are dedicated. Yet Hume's choice of the latter as her literary patron is interesting for the light it sheds on her intellectual preoccupations. The daughter of Queen Elizabeth of Bohemia, herself the prodigiously gifted child of James VI and Anne, Princess Elizabeth was renowned for her artistic and intellectual court *salons*. As Hume declares, 'True glory of [her] sex' indeed (first dedicatory poem, sig. A2, 1.9). The apparent lack of documentary evidence is frustrating: did Hume herself participate in this enlightened feminine *milieu* at Elizabeth's court (the letter above records a foreign journey)? Evidence of the wider literary endeavours which Drummond's letter presupposes appears in the second dedicatory poem: 'Nor is it gratitude, because y'have been/Pleas'd to approve some others you have seen' ('Another to her Highnesse', sig. A3, ll. 7–8). Surely this is proof of Hume's acquaintance with Elizabeth.

Though the subject of a number of earlier translations,⁴¹ Hume judiciously chose the *Trionfi* to emulate 'great Petrarch's name' (sig. A2, 1.14). The *Rime* had flourished as the quintessence of secular (and masculine) love in England in the 1590s while Scottish Petrarchan-influenced amatory poetry preceded and extended this English period. Hume may have feared the accusation of impropriety that a woman writer's translation might incur apart from its relative literary obsolescence in the 1640s. Revealingly, Hume emphasises the independence of her new translation, claiming that she never saw 'the *Trionfi* in any other language but *Italian*'. Though this may be an expedient rhetorical device, Hume's writing owes little or no verbal debt to Lord Morley's or Mary Sidney's versions, for example. Whether she possessed first-hand knowledge of these, or more importantly of William Fowler's MS translation, cannot be established. Yet it is illuminating to compare Hume's translation with the latter's to illustrate two profoundly differing aesthetic responses to the same text.

In the third triumph of love, Hume's narrator disclaims all 'bold hyperboles' in conveying Laura's beauty.

> No bold Hyperboles I need to feare
> My humble stile cannot enough come neare
> The truth; my words are like a little stream
> Compar'd with th' Ocean, so large a theame
> Is that high prayse . . . (ll. 139–43)

While rendering the *exusatio* of Petrarch's text, this aptly describes Hume's overall literary strategy which favours brevity and *pointe*, neatly accommodated by her epigrammatic iambic couplet and far removed from Fowler's alexandrines which have been critically censured for their *longeurs*. While Hume's debt to Fowler has been claimed by R. D. S. Jack,[42] her later text seems to constitute an almost conscious stylistic refutation of the earlier translation. Many examples may be offered where Hume's compression contrasts with Fowler's expansion. The opening preface to the third of the first triumphs, where the curious lover invites an explanation of the processional triumph of love, finds nine lines in Hume (the catalogue of Love's *exempla* is shortened) compared to Fowler's sixteen. At times this concision displays the delicate parallelisms and chiasma of Popean couplets such as I.ii.20: 'When Love did Friendship, Friendship Love control'. Sensitivity to colloquial rhythms appears when Hume accommodates the syntactical qualifications and grammatical elisions of voice to her rigorous metre. On his adversary, Love, the narrator declares:

> . . . nor can I be
> Reveng'd, as I expected once; for he,
> Who tortures me and others, is abused
> By her; she'le not be caught, and long hath used
> (Rebellious as he is!) to shun his warres,
> And is a Sunne amidst the lesser starres . . . (I, iii, 127–32)

On occasions, Hume's stylistic grace becomes inappropriately terse. Atalanta's fate is conveyed by delicate, amusing apposition – 'But three gold apples and a lovely face,/ Slackt her quick paces, till she lost the race' (I.i. 156–7) – but the full poignancy of Narcissus' self-adoration is sacrificed to a hurried crispness: '*Narcissus* too, the foolish fair/ Who for his owne love did himselfe destroy:/He had so much, he nothing could enjoy' (I, i, 136–8).

Fowler's embellished style may arise from a desire to wrest from the *Trionfi* its full emotional and intellectual significances. This striving towards a medieval resonance produces effects of both rhetorical bathos and deeply lyrical beauty. Hume's translation does not wholly avoid the former and often rails to achieve the latter. In general, Hume's attentiveness to textual detail rather than emotive power grants her greater verbal precision than Fowler. She renders 'un aureo crine' as 'one onely hair of gold' (III, i, 96) in contrast to Fowler's 'hair as fyne as gould', retaining Petrarch's emblematic significance. Hume's final couplet expresses the Petrarchan consolation, 'Ella, gia mossa, disse: Al creder mio/Tu stara' in terra senza me gran tempo', as 'She going thus replide; I do believe,/That without me on earth you long must live' (III, ii, 165–6). The imperative 'must' embodies a sense of both inevitability, and painful necessity without choice, for the bereaved lover. This sensitive ambiguity is more redolent of Drummond's *Poems*, 'The Second Part', song ii, than the assurance of Fowler's 'thow sall but me drywe furth thy dayes and long in earth sall liwe'.

Issues of semantic delicacy are debated in the commentaries that Hume attaches to each 'chapter'. In these 'Annotations' (not placed around the body of the main text as the traditional medieval or renaissance commentary), Hume exhibits erudition as well as 'personality'. While Hume's commentaries owe much to the medieval technique of moral and philosophical 'expositioun' (as Gavin Douglas's narrator justified his Virgilian text), the expositor often resigns her impersonal learned stance to communicate freely. Likely quibbles are pre-empted: of the phrase 'Side-wayes cast' in line 161, she notes,

> The place seemeth imperfect, but is not, for hee compareth himselfe in his last contemplation of the miserie of Lovers after his experience, (which hee had not much heeded before) to a man, who neglecteth a piece of rare work or picture, by haste or other thoughts; and when hee is past, considers it more seriously, either standing still, or going on w^t his eye fixed on it. (I, iv, pp. 57–8)

Hume's dependence on the cited 'Italian Commentary' is not absolute: on one textual point, she declares that it 'makes a long and needlesse discourse' (III, ii, p. 96). She does not allude to her 'Italian Commentar' or 'Commentary' when defining mythic or historical figures but when clarifying points of semantic ambiguity. Jack suggests that Fowler, and therefore Hume, use Bernardino Daniello da Lucca's edition of 1549, *Sonetti, Canzoni e Triomphe de M. Francesco Petrarca*. Yet equally Hume may have used another notable commentary such as Alessandro Vellutello's *Il Petrarcha con l'Espositione* (Venice, 1545). For example, her allusion to the 'Religious vertues' (p. 67 in reference to 1. 64) as 'Faith and Hope' corresponds to Vellutello's comment, f. 172v, 'altramente dette theologiche, cio e fede e speranza'; indeed she may have been working from both Italian texts (her single reference to 'the Italian Commentary in the life of Petrarch' may suggest a debt to Daniello's inclusion of the 'vita e costumi del poeta', ff. i–iij).

As if the *Trionfi*'s philosophical and emotional burden requires lightening, the exegesis is often sprightly:

> *Lethe flood, 103. line.*] Forgetfulnesse, an excellent cure for love, and the tooth-ake.
> *Diamonds, etc. 104. line.*] Diamonds is thought maketh the wearers constant: *Topaises* make chaste, for which two causes they were worn by ladies of old, but I hope they are not needfull now. (II, p. 68)

For the most part, Hume does not write with tongue in cheek. While the *Trionfi* impressed late medieval commentators as a complex moral and religious allegory of the soul, Hume is alert to how it permits Laura, Petrach's *inamorata*, to be articulate as opposed to her role in the *Rime*. Her avowed 'aime' is to deepen her disclosure:

> If any aske me, What is then my end?
> 'Tis to approve my selfe a reall friend
> To chaste *Lauretta*, whom since I have tane
> From the dark Cloyster, where she did remain
> Unmarkt, because unknown
> ('Another to her Highnesse', sig. A3, ll. 17–21)

This strikingly prefigures Christina Rossetti's late Victorian illumination of the still, silent feminine icons of Dante and Petrarch in her 'Monna Innominata. A Sonnet of Sonnets'.

Mary Stuart's sonnets voice feminine desire within the codified, symbolic system of poetic love. In contrast, Hume's work re-presents, literally reincarnates, Laura. Hume empathises with her female subject, presuming to 'speak' on her behalf: '*Petrarch*, whom she thought would be more hurt by her death then her selfe, in regard of his extreme affection' (III, i, p. 84). Hume's Laura is allowed to express her love. Her *Triumphs* are a conscious contribution to the *querelle des femmes* debate which was resurgent in the European Renaissance, and charted with particular vehemence in Scottish texts from the fifteenth to the seventeenth centuries. Hume defends maligned women of literary mythology: both Juno, 'troublesomly jealous, if shee can be called jealous, that had so much wrong' (II, p. 67), and Dido, to whom 'the wrong done . . . by *Virgil*' is at least amended by Petrarch, 'for which I thanke him' (II, p. 70). Hume's work conforms to that definition of translation given by another scholar, poet and feminist, Marie de Gournay, in 1623: 'to engender a work anew . . . because [the ancient writers] have to be decomposed by profound and penetrating reflection'.[43]

This chapter has considered almost 100 years of early Scottish women's writing. An impressive diversity emerges. But the work considered does not give the whole picture. Early literature in Gaelic by women can provide illuminating cultural comparison with these 'lowland' texts. At the close of the sixteenth century, Esther Inglis (1571–1624), a Frenchwoman resident in Edinburgh from early childhood, was a prolific calligrapher and illustrator of literary and religious manuscripts. Several of her works are dedicated to the Scottish poet, Sir David Murray of Gorthy (1567–1629). Her *Psalms of David*, dedicated to Queen Elizabeth 'De Lislebourg en Ecosse', contains dedicatory poems both to Elizabeth and Inglis herself, including one by the Scottish poet, John Johnston (1570–1624), who contributed to the *Delitiae poetarum scotorum* (1637).[44] As an artist, she extends our vision of the variety of aesthetic creativity engaged in by women.

Helen Livingston's (d.1627) posthumously published renunciation of her Catholic faith, *The Confession and Conversion of my Lady C. of L* (John Wreittoun, Edinburgh, 1629) suggests again that the definition of early women's writing in Scotland must encompass more than the purely 'literary'. Helen (or Eleanor) Livingston (*née* Hay), with her husband, Alexander Livingston, Earl of Linlithgow, educated James VI's daughter, Elizabeth, until 1603. Once revealed as a devout Catholic, her life became an endless struggle to evade the tyranny of the Scottish Presbytery who issued orders for her excommunication from 1596 until her death in 1627. She appears briefly in the autobiography of John Livingstone (Melville's religious 'brother'), in which her daughter solicits him to attend 'her Mother, the Countess of Linlithgow who was a-dying, and had been all her days a Papist, but some while before had deserted that religion'.[45] Presented as a personal renunciation of faith, 'most joyfullie, and constantlie uttered, and declared before many honorable men and women . . . sealed and subscryved by the right religious, most noble, and truely wise Lady', the text was most likely a forced confession (whereby the words are not her own) yet ironically possesses authenticating expressions of 'I belieue', 'I thinke', 'I perceaue'. Livingstone's text is a moving record of persecution.[46]

The beautiful complaint entitled 'Lady Laudian's Lament', both an elegy on mortality ('Lyk floures we fade and die', 1.8) and moral exhortation ('In prime tyme of our youthe we suld/The seede of vertue sowe', ll. 25–6), may be by Lady Ann Ker in the early seventeenth century.[47] While attribution remains uncertain, the text itself is neglected, not least the sudden, closing stance of humility studded with irony:

> I have bewrayed my want of will
> In dooinge yor desyre
> The waikenes of a womans witt

> Be not in natures ffault
> Ffor lack of education ffit
> Makes nature oft to hault. (ll. 69–74)

The issue of education and the extent of women's literacy in early modern Scotland is pertinent. For Margaret Cavendish, writing in England in 1655, male 'power and authority' was consolidated by women's lack of access to university education and cultural travel: 'We are become like worms that only live in the dull earth of ignorance, winding ourselves sometimes out by the help of some refreshing rain of good educations, which seldom is given us; for we are kept like birds in cages to hop up and down in our houses, not suffered to fly abroad . . .'.[48] The writers discussed here were socially privileged, belonging to the educated aristocratic and upper classes or, as in Mary Stuart's case, intellectually nurtured by a royal humanist education. Further insight might be gleaned from knowledge of authors and reading materials available to these literary women. Anneli Meurman-Solin at Helsinki University has already begun a socio-linguistic study based on a database of sixteenth- and seventeenth-century Scottish women's letters.[49]

In seeking to establish the cultural milieu of the educated Scottish gentlewoman, the manuscript of Lady Margaret Wemyss may serve as an apt epilogue. This collection of Scottish and French lute music, and of lyrics identifiably Scottish and English, was transcribed by 'me margarat Wymes with my hand' between the ages of twelve and eighteen.[50] Margaret Wemyss was born at Falkland on 24 September 1630, daughter of David, second Earl of Wemyss (1610–79) and Anna Balfour (d.1649). Her name appears twice on the manuscript's flyleaf. A sizeable number of blank folios in her 'Booke' suggest that it remained incomplete, a notion attested on knowledge of its transcriber's tragic death at eighteen. An important document providing evidence that late sixteenth-century Scottish lyric and music was sustained in aristocratic circles, Wemyss's manuscript exemplifies the archetypal Renaissance female education which placed the lute among skills of 'learning French, singing . . . the virginalls, and dancing'.[51] Yet it also conveys a love of poetry, of 'som fine verces and Lines' (f. 11r), that buoyantly transcends what Renaissance educational treatises condemned as 'ballades, songs, sonettes, and ditties of daliance' that corrupt 'a weake and delicate young gentlewoman'.[52] Is it naive to conceive Margaret Wemyss as an aspiring poet, her promise sacrificed to a poignantly early death? Perhaps. Yet imagining a young woman on the margins of a small cultivated social gathering, hearing and copying Scottish poetry that is sung or declaimed, one is persuaded even more of the need to seek critical redress to Anna Hume's inquiry, 'What is then my end?'[53]

Notes

1. R. J. Lyall, '"A New Maid Channoun?" Redefining the Canonical in Medieval and Renaissance Scottish Literature', *Studies in Scottish Literature* XXVI (1991), 1–19.
2. Helena Shire, *Song, Dance and Poetry of the Court of Scotland under King James VI* (Cambridge University Press, Cambridge, 1969), pp. 88, 95, 97. *New Poems by James I of England from a hitherto unpublished manuscript (Add. 24195) in the British Museum*, ed. Allan F. Westcott (Columbia University Press, 1911).
3. 'To Robert Hudsone', *The Poems of Alexander Montgomerie* ed. James Cranstoun, 2 vols (William Blackwood, Edinburgh and London, 1887), I, p. 101.
4. Poem xxx in the Margaret Ker MS (EUL De.3.70), the most substantial source of Montgomerie's poetry, on f. 68v. Published in Cranstoun, pp. 103–4, but assumed to be a persona of Montgomerie (p. 340).

5.   Westcott, p. 104; Helena Shire, *Alexander Montgomerie: A Selection of his Poems and Songs* (The Saltire Classics) (Oliver & Boyd, Edinburgh, 1960), p. 52.

6.   Count Baldassare Castiglione, *The Book of the Courtier*, translated by Sir Thomas Hoby and edited by Virginia Cox (Everyman, London, 1994), p. 215.

7.   The original French texts of Mary's work presented here are transcribed where possible from the original MSS with orthography modernised as little as possible. In the case of the secular love sequence (where no MS exists in Mary's handwriting), the texts used are those of the secular love sequence (where no MS exists in Mary's handwriting), the texts used are those of the earliest published edition of the *Detectioun of the duinges of Marie Quene of Scottis*. For ease of reference, I give the modern verse translations of Bell's edition with the exception again of the sonnet sequence which is taken from the Anglo-Scots translation that accompanied the original French poems in the same edition of the *Detectioun*. Though their language and grammar may seem at times idiosyncratic and inelegant, these texts merit inclusion as a reception or intepretation of these complex sonnets within Mary's own lifetime.

8.   Brief extracts of Mary's poetry appear in several nineteenth-century French anthologies. The exceptions to the Scottish omission of Mary's writing are James G. Watson, *The Poets and Poetry of Scotland 1219–1876* (London, 1876–7), pp. 57–9, and *An Anthology of Scottish Women Poets* ed. Catherine Kerrigan (Edinburgh University Press, Edinburgh, 1991), p. 153 (which did not present Mary's original texts).

   Critical appraisal thus far is confined to a brief résumé in Betty Travitsky's invaluable anthology, *The Paradise of Women: Writings by English Women of the Renaissance* (Greenwood Press, London, 1981), pp. 187–92; Sarah M. Dunnigan, '"The Consolation of Poetry": a study of the poetry of Mary Stuart c.1560–87' (undergrad. diss., Glasgow University, 1993), and 'Rewriting the Renaissance language of love and desire: the "bodily burdein" in the poetry of Mary, Queen of Scots', in *Gramma* 4 (1996), pp. 181–95.

9.   'il fault plus que la renommee/pour dire et publier', f. 81v of the Book of Hours (see n. 39); Bell, p. 90: Never again in all my fame must I/Proclaim and tell.

10.   The 'Discours troisième sur la Reyne d'Escosse, jadis reyne de Nostre France' is reproduced in *Recueil des Dames*, ed. Roger Gaucheron (Librairie Payot, Paris, 1926), pp. 42–89. Brantôme accompanied Mary on her return to Scotland in 1561: an account of their relationship is found in Anne-Marie Cocula-Vaillières, *Brantôme: Amour et gloire au temps des Valois* (Albin Michel, Paris, 1986), pp. 95–101, 260–2.

11.   See John Purser, *Scotland's Music: A History of Scottish Music from the Earliest Times to the Present Day* (Mainstream, Edinburgh, 1992), p. 103.

12.   John Durkan, 'The Library of Mary Queen of Scots', *Innes Review*, XXXVIII (1988), pp. 71–101 (p. 79). It is interesting to note that the first sonnet sequence in English literature can also be claimed by a woman, Anne Lok, who wrote *A Meditation of a Penitent Sinner* (1560).

13.   On the implications of this see, for example, Ann Rosalind Jones, 'Assimilation with a Difference: Renaissance Women Poets and Literary influence', *Yale French Studies* 62 (1981), 'Feminist Readings: French Texts/American Contexts', pp. 135–53.

14.   'O Signeur Dieu resceuez ma priere', 'Donnes Signeur dones moy pasciance' and 'Que suis ie helas', are found on ff. 22r, 22v and 24r of MS Add.c.92 of the Bodleian Library, Oxford. With the exception of the last, they give evidence of many corrections and emendments.

15.   The original Book of Hours is preserved in the library at St Petersburg but those folios (81v, 129v, 130r, 158v and 159r) inscribed with her poetry are reproduced in NLS Adv. MS 81.5.8. The quatrains are published by Mackenzie-Arbuthnot, pp. 113–15, and by Labanoff, v. vii, pp. 346–52. See also C. Piazzi Smyth, 'Notes respecting an illuminated manuscript on vellum, which formerly belonged to Mary Queen of Scots', *Proceedings of the Society of Antiquaries of Scotland*, vol. III, part iii (1859–60), pp. 394–403.

16.   See Michael Lynch, 'Queen Mary's Triumph: the Baptismal Celebrations in Stirling in December 1566', *Scottish Historical Review* 69 (1990), pp. 1–21; see also Purser, pp. 81–124, and D. James Ross, *Musick Fyne: Robert Carver and the Art of Music in Sixteenth Century Scotland* (Mercat Press, Edinburgh, 1993), pp. 115–48.

17.   Beaton's sonnet is published in *The Works of William Fowler*, 3 vols (Blackwood, Edinburgh and London, 1914, 1940), I, p. 393. Her authorship was

first proposed in Fowler's *Works*, III, ed. Henry W. Meikle, James Craigie, and John Purves, p. 30.

18.   The lyric is found on sigs A8r–v of *Poems by that most famous wit William Drummond of Hawthornden* (London, 1656), and published in Travitsky, pp. 139–41, and in *Kissing the Rod: an Anthology of Seventeenth Century Women's Verse* ed. Germaine Greer *et al.* (Virago Press Ltd, London, 1988), pp. 79–82. The entry in *A Biographical Dictionary of Women Writers 1580–1720*, ed. Maureen Bell, George Parfitt and Simon Shepherd (Harvester Wheatsheaf, Brighton, 1990), p. 148, reverts to the original 'Mary Oxlie', claiming that 'the Oxleys were an important family in Morpeth'. See David Masson, *Drummond of Hawthornden: the Story of his Life and Writings* (Macmillan, London, 1873), p. 474.

19.   Greer, p. 81. Though signed 'Parthenius', the sonnet is by William Alexander (identified in L. E. Kastner (ed.), *The Poetical Works of William Drummond of Hawthornden*, 2 vols (Blackwood, Edinburgh and London, 1913), I, p. 157. The relevant lines of the sonnet are 9–14, printed in Kastner, I, ci–cii, first published in *Drummond's Poems* (1616).

20.   See Ann Rosalind Jones, 'Nets and Bridles: early modern conduct books and sixteenth century women's lyrics', *The Ideology of Conduct: Essays on Literature and the History of Sexuality*, ed. Nancy Armstrong and Leonard Tennenhouse (Methuen, London, 1987), pp. 39–72.

21.   NLS MS 2061 (letter no. 30), published (n.d. but identified as being addressed to Hume) in *The Works of William Drummond of Hawthornden* (James Watson, Edinburgh, 1711), p. 139.

22.   'Marie Maitland 1586' is inscribed twice on the manuscript. All references are made to the *Maitland Quarto Manuscript*, ed. W. A. Craigie (Blackwood, Edinburgh and London, 1920).

23.   *Quarto*, p. 257, 'To your self'.

24.   Translation from Margaret L. King, *Women of the Renaissance* (University of Chicago Press, Chicago, 1991), pp. 180–1. Bathsua Makin, for example, in *An Essay To Revive the Antient Education of Gentlewomen* (1673), praises her achievements (see the edition by Paula L. Barbour (The Augustan Reprint Society, Publication Number 202, University of California, 1980), pp. 9–10.

25.   The *Maitland Folio Manuscript*, 2 vols (Blackwood, Edinburgh and London, 1919–27), II, p. 16.

26.   *Quarto*, p. 258.

27.   'Intill ane morning mirthfullest of may', *Quarto*, pp. 223–5.

28.   *French Women Writers and the Book: Myths of Access and Desire* (Syracuse University Press, 1988), p. 55.

29.   *Quarto*, pp. 160–2.

30.   The poem has recently received critical attention. See Janet Mueller, 'Lesbian Erotics: the Utopian Trope of Donne's "Sappho to Philaenis"', *Homosexuality in Renaissance and Enlightenment England: Literary Representations in Historical Context*, ed. Claude J. Summers (Haworth Press, 1992), pp. 103–24 (she is dismissive of the poem's 'reticent locutions, hyperbolic compliments, and thwarted yearnings . . . ', p. 111); Jane Farnsworth, 'Voicing Female desire in "Poem XLIX", *Studies in English Literature 1500–1900*, vol. 36, no. 1 (1996), 57–72; Sarah Dunnigan, 'Reclaiming the language of love and desire in the Scottish Renaissance: Mary, Queen of Scots and the late sixteenth century female-voiced love lyric', paper presented to the Eighth International Conference on Medieval and Renaissance Scottish Language and Literature, St Hilda's College, Oxford, 17–21 August 1996.

31.   See, for example, Elizabeth Heale, 'Women and the Courtly Love lyric: the Devonshire MS (BL Additional 17492), *MLR* 90, part 2 (1995), 296–313; Elaine Hobby, *Virtue of Necessity: English Women's Writing 1646–1688* (Virago Press Ltd, London, 1988), pp. 206–7.

32.   Elizabeth Melville, letter to John Livingstone, 10 December 1631: EUL La. III. 347.

33.   'The Life of Mr. John Livingstone, Minister of the Gospell, written by himself during his banishment in Holland, for the cause of Christ', and his 'Memorable Characters and Remarkable Passages of Divine Providence exemplified in the lives of some of the most eminent ministers and professors in the Church of Scotland collected by Mr. John Livingstone, late Minister of Ancrum', *Select Biographies edited for the Wodrow Society, chiefly from MSS in the Library of the Faculty of Advocates*, ed. W. K. Tweedie, 2 vols (Edinburgh, 1855), I, pp.

127–97; 293–348. On pp. 351–70 of this volume, her letters (presently held in EUL Laing collection) are transcribed. A brief biography of Melville can be found in Greer, pp. 32–3; Bell *et al*, p. 135; *Dictionary of British Women Writers*, ed. Janet Todd (Routledge, London, 1989) pp. 461–2. Further details can be gleaned from David Laing's introduction to both editions and in *DNB*, vol. XI, pp. 419–20.

34.   'A Sonnet sent to Blackness To Mr John Welsh by yᵉ Lady Culross', NLS Wodrow MS 29, no. 4, f. 11r; published in Laing, p. 281 and xxxii; Greer, pp. 33–4; Kerrigan, p. 156. A biography of John Welsh (c. 1570–1622) can be found in 'The History of Mr. John Welsh Minister of the Gospel at Ayr, ascribed to James Kirkton, *Select Biographies*, I, pp. 1–61.

35.   'Memorable Characters', ed. Tweedie, I, pp. 347.

36.   *Woman's Speaking Justified*, Introduction by David J. Latt (The Augustan Reprint Society, number 194, University of California, 1979), p. 13.

37.   The text here of *Ane Godlie Dreme* is based on the first 1603 edition. It is reproduced in David Laing, *Early Popular Poetry of Scotland and the Northern Border*, 2 vols (London, first published 1822), pp. 279–301; *Early Metrical Tales including the History of Sir Eger, Sir Gryme and Sir Greysteill* (Edinburgh, first published 1826), pp. 149–69; *Poems of Alexander Hume*, ed. Alexander Lawson (Blackwood, Edinburgh and London, 1902), pp. 184–98. Extracts are published in Greer, pp. 32–8; Travitsky pp. 25–8; Kerrigan pp. 154–6.

38.   'M.M' has been understood to represent 'Mistress Melville'. She therefore publishes under her maiden name (she married John Colville and was known by the title Lady Colville of Culross). This provides persuasive but not conclusive evidence for her authorship of the *Dreme*.

39.   Orthography and punctuation from original in EUL La. III. 347; published (with punctuation) by Tweedie, pp. 361–2.

40.   Letter to 'the Right Hon. Archibald, Lord of Angus, eldest sonne to William, Marquess of Douglas, one of the Lords of his Majesties Privie Councell in the Kingdome of Scotland', dated December 11, 1643, from Edinburgh, found in NLS copy of David Hume's *A General History of Scotland* (London 1657). A brief biography is given in *DNB*, vol. 28, pp. 213–4, Bell *et al*. p. 112; Greer, p. 100. The text given here is that of the 1644 edition (it was not republished). Short extracts are printed in Greer, pp. 101–5.

41.   Earlier European translations are cited by D. D. Carnicelli, *Lord Morleys Tryumphes of Fraunces Petrarcke: The First English Translation of the Trionfi* (Harvard University Press, 1971), pp. 28–37. Interestingly, Mary Sidney (1561–1621) translated (but did not publish) the 'Triumph of Death'. D. G. Rees, 'Petrarch's Trionfo della Morte in English', *Italian Studies* VII (1952), pp. 82–96, condemns Hume's translation in comparison to others: 'Mrs. Anna Hume . . . offers a spectacle of joyless confidence, perhaps not altogether out of keeping with an age which produced the severity of Puritanism' (p. 90).

42.   R. D. S. Jack, *The Italian Influence on Scottish Literature* (Edinburgh University Press, Edinburgh, 1972), pp. 79–80. Apart from Irvine (*Lives*, p. 296; *History*, p. 464), Professor Jack is the only Scottish critic to acknowledge Hume's work.

43.   Cited in Theo Hermans, 'Images of Translation, Metaphor and Imagery in the Renaissance Discourse on Translation', *The Manipulation of Literature: Studies in Literary Translation*, ed. Theo Hermans (Croom Helm, London, 1985), pp. 103–35 (p. 124).

44.   See *DNB*, vol. 30, pp. 346–7; David Laing, 'Notes relating to Mrs Esther (Langlois or) Inglis, the Celebrated Calligraphist, with an enumeration of Manuscript Volumes written by her between the years 1586 and 1624', Proceedings of the Society of Antiquaries of Scotland (1866–70), *Publication of the Bibliographical Society of America* pp. 284–309; A. H. Scott-Elliot and Elspeth Yeo, 'Calligraphic manuscripts of Esther Inglis (1571–1624): A Catalogue', 84 (1990), pp. 11–86; Bell, p. 118; Travitsky, pp. 24–5; Duncan Macmillan, *A History of Scottish Art* (Mainstream, Edinburgh, 1990), p. 65. A letter by Inglis, dated 1620 at Edinburgh, to James VI is preserved (NLS Adv. 33.1.6, f. 35r).

45.   *Select Biographies*, vol. 1, p. 137.

46.   There is a facsimile of the *Confession and Conversion* introduced by George P. Johnston (Edinburgh, 1924). Livingston is discussed in Bell, pp. 282–3.

47.   Identified by William Dauney, *Ancient Scottish Melodies* (Maitland Club, Edinburgh, 1838), p. 264, as the wife of Mark Ker (d. 1609), and endorsed by Shire, p. 257. R. J.

Lyall, p. 7, doubts the attribution. Lady Lothian' may also refer to another Anne Ker, the daughter of Sir Robert, Earl of Lothian; only after marriage to William Ker of Ancrum and his attainment of the earldom in 1631 did she properly accede to the title, Lady or Countess of Lothian (*The Scots Peerage*, vol. 5, pp. 459–60). An early seventeenth-century Scottish music manuscript (NLS MS 5448) inscribed 'L.A.K.', possibly Lady Ann Ker, may render her authorship more persuasive. Musical text and sources for the lament are given in *Musica Britannica* XV: *Music of Scotland 1500–1700*, ed. Kenneth Elliott and Helena Mennie Shire (Stainer and Bell, 1975), pp. 188, 220. The verbal text given is incomplete: its full stanzas are found in EUL MS 436.

48.   Cavendish's *Philosophical and Physical Opinions*, cited by Hobby, p. 190.

49.   Anneli Meurman-Solin, 'Gender-Based Differences in Renaissance Scots', paper presented to the Eighth International Conference on Medieval and Renaissance Scottish Language and Literature, St Hilda's College, Oxford, 17–21 August 1996.

50.   A full history, description and musicological analysis of the MS can be found in Matthew Spring, 'The Lady Margaret Wemyss Manuscript', *The Lute* 27 (1987), 5–79. Spring identifies the English lyrics, four by Robert Ayton, and one by Montgomerie, but not a sonnet from William Fowler's 'The Tarantula of Love'. Purser, p. 159, notes other music manuscripts written by young women in the seventeenth century. I am indebted to Robert MacKillop for knowledge of the Wemyss MS.

51.   *The Memoirs of Anne, Lady Halkett and Ann, Lady Fanshawe*, edited with an introduction by John Loftis (Oxford, Clarendon Press, 1979), p. 110.

52.   Thomas Salter, *A Mirrhor mete for all Mothers, Matrones, and Maidens, intituled the Mirrhor of Modestie* (1579), cited in Louis B. Wright, 'The Reading of Renaissance Englishwomen', *SP* 28 (1931), 139–57 (p. 141); the second phrase from Giovanni Michele Bruto's *The necessaire, fit, and convenient Education of a yong gentlewoman* (1598), cited by Carroll Camden, *The Elizabethan Woman: A Panorama of English Womanhood 1540–1640* (Cleacer-Hume Press Limited, London, 1952), p. 547.

53.   The social, political and cultural contexts of the early woman writer are illuminated (though not from a specifically Scottish perspective) by the following: Margaret L. King, *Women of the Renaissance* (University of Chicago Press, Chicago, 1991); Sherrin Marshall (ed.), *Women in Reformation and Counter-Reformation Europe: Public and Private Worlds* (Indiana University Press, Indiana, 1989); Linda Woodbridge, *Women and the English Renaissance: Literature and the Nature of Womankind* (Harvester, Hemel Hempstead, 1984).

Although the writers discussed here are more fully understood when restored to, rather than artificially estranged from, their contemporary Scottish literary context, further fruitful comparison may be drawn with English (and European) women writers of the period. Betty Travitsky's *The Paradise of Women: Writings by Englishwomen of the Renaissance* (Greenwood Press, 1981) remains the most comprehensive and catholic of anthologies. Although its perspective is anglocentric, it contains the fullest representation of early Scottish women writers to date. Helpful criticism of writers who prove interesting analogues to their Scottish contemporaries can be found in the essays of *Women Writers of the Renaissance and Reformation*, ed. Katharina M. Wilson (University of Georgia Press, 1987); Tilde Sankovitch, 'Inventing Authority of Origin: the Difficult Enterprise', in Mary-Beth Rose (ed.), *Women in the Middle Ages and the Renaissance: Literary and Historical Perspectives* (Syracuse University Press, 1986); Elaine V. Beilin, *Redeeming Eve: Women Writers of the English Renaissance* (Princeton University Press, 1987); Louise Schleiner, *Tudor and Stuart Women Writers* (Indiana University Press, 1994). See also Ann Rosalind Jones, 'Surprising Fame: Renaissance Gender Ideologies and Women's Lyric', in Nancy K. Miller (ed.), *The Poetics of Gender* (Columbia University Press, 1986) pp. 74–95, and *The Currency of Eros* (Indiana University Press, 1990).

3

Old Singing Women and the
Canons of Scottish Balladry and Song

Mary Ellen Brown

When, sometime in 1825 or 1826, a Scottish ballad and song collector and editor wrote a heading in his collecting notebook titled 'old singing women', he was doing two things: first of all he was reminding himself of possessors of songs whom he had met or become aware of; many of them were women, so many in fact that he could provide a list. But the phrase also implicitly carries a wider assumption, that is, that women were somehow connected with this form of vernacular literature, perhaps not to the exclusion of men, but certainly in profusion. This chapter takes William Motherwell's words as text and will seek to explore both the general and specific relationships of women to balladry and song, most particularly those examples which have circulated orally, bear certain stylistic marks of that mode of transmission, and which exist, invariably, in multiple versions.[1]

Antiquarian collections of ballads and songs began to appear in Scotland with considerable regularity towards the end of the eighteenth century and continued to be an extremely popular publication item well into the first half of the nineteenth. It may well be, as David Daiches suggests, that such antiquarian endeavours began as discrete, acceptable, and positive forms of nationalism.[2] Most editions of ballads included texts, often prefaced with laudatory remarks about the nature of this presumably Scottish form of literature. Seldom was there any music, seldom were critical questions raised, except in passing. One issue often alluded to was the question of authorship and the related one of origins. Where did this material come from? Who created it? When? Why? The texts were thought to be old. Some enthusiasts were sure that they had been created by minstrels, perhaps first as romances later 'broken' down into the narrative songs called ballads or alternately, first as ballads, then developed into romances: 'Hind Horn'/'King Horn' (Child 17) being the prime exemplar of this approach. And the texts were thought to contain some ineffable essence of Scottishness, a quality that merited particular attention during a period of seemingly headlong Anglicisation, as in the words of Peter Buchan:

> The ancient Ballads of Caledonia are venerated by those lovers of their country who delight in the native imagery of their homes, and in hearing the martial and warlike deeds of their forefathers said or sung in the enchanting voice of their fair country-women.[3]

Such statements and ideas introduced the often heavily edited or reconstructed texts, which typically appeared on the printed page as though they were poems, that is, without musical notation.

The first published collections were based on manuscript materials and provided almost no hint of provenance or authorship, thus opening the way for scholarly speculation. Suggesting that minstrels were responsible for the earliest ballads gave them a certain antique literary prestige, certainly a better pedigree than the simple sobriquet used later – anonymous. How could literature be anonymous? Someone must have written the materials. As late as 1849 there was an elaborate attempt to provide an author for the very best of the texts, those frequently styled romantic ballads: Robert Chambers, building on earlier suggestions by David Laing and others, hypothesised that one Elizabeth Halket, later Lady Wardlaw (born 15 April 1677, died 1727), was the author not only of 'Hardyknute' – attributed to her earlier in Percy's *Reliques of Ancient English Poetry* and in Ramsay's *Evergreen* – but also of 'Sir Patrick Spens' (Child 58), 'Gil Morrice' (Child 83), 'Edward, Edward' (Child 13), 'Jew's Daughter' (Child 155), 'Young Waters' (Child 94), 'Edom o' Gordon' (Child 178), 'Bonny Earl of Murray' (Child 181), and other exemplars of note, either wholly or partially her work. Chambers's argument was that the frequently anthologised romantic ballads probably were not older than the eighteenth century, were stylistically similar to one another, and must have been written by the author of 'Hardyknute'.

First published anonymously in 1719, 'Hardyknute' describes a warrior by that name, called on by the king to help rebuff the Norse invasions. After successfully helping the king, he returns home to discover that his wife, daughter and one son are missing; he is filled with fear for their safety, which humanises his military prowess. The text deals with the invasion of Haco, King of Norway, during Alexander III's reign. David Laing had earlier noted the similarities between 'Hardyknute' and 'Sir Patrick Spens', the latter often said to refer to the voyage taking that same Alexander's daughter to Norway to marry King Eric in 1281. Chambers's theory too used the comparison with 'Sir Patrick Spens' as its cornerstone. Others were quick to respond, even naming the hypothesis the 'Lady Wardlaw Heresy'; Norval Clyne replied somewhat condescendingly:

> If Mr Robert Chambers has, in his recent publication on the Romantic Scottish Ballads, propounded the correct doctrine as to the authorship of the pieces he particularly refers to, . . . A number of Scottish Ballads, hitherto supposed to be the production of various unknown rhymers living at different periods and in different parts of the country, will have to be assigned to one Scottish lady who amused herself with verse-making, 'and cutting paper with her scissors', in the early part of last century. Let such a claim be established, and she deserves a bust in marble.[4]

Clyne's demolition of Chambers's theory makes fascinating reading. Referring to Chambers's attribution of some twenty-five of the 'best' Scottish ballads to the daughter of Sir Charles Halket of Pitfirran, he comments that 'this is a goodly bunch of flowers to lay on the grave of Lady Wardlaw – wild flowers no longer, if the new theory be correct, but hot-house plants of little or no fragrance'.[5] And the theory was a bit of an about face for Chambers who had earlier believed in the antiquity of the ballads 'as genuine relics of the old minstrelsy of Scotland'. Finally, Clyne refutes Chambers's 'dream of a female authorship for these Romantic Ballads', suggesting that the use of similar criteria 'would extend the same authorship indefinitely over the ballad literature of Scotland'.[6] Among other things, Chambers's theory of ballad authorship is uninformed about oral channels of transmission: the very qualities he had come to believe served as evidence of single authorship – similar scenes, phraseology, rhymes – have subsequently been identified as stylistic qualities characteristic of oral literature – especially in the seventeenth and eighteenth centuries – reflecting a particular aesthetic taste or alternatively resulting from oral formulation. And the ballads created and transmitted anew in each performance may bear those marks even when memorised and sung by later performers, those marks distinguishing certain ballads and versions from later versions which bear the mark of writing and the effects of widespread literacy or a different aesthetic sensibility.

Yet Robert Chambers was on to something and he gave to a woman authorship of some of the most renowned examples of Scottish balladry, however erroneously; and rightly, however innocently, affirmed that ballads were originally individually authored. In fact, the wife of Sir Henry Wardlaw of Pitreavie was not an anomaly in writing – or imitating – ballads and songs: the vogue for this kind of literature stimulated numerous women – some highly placed like Lady Wardlaw and Carolina Oliphant, Lady Nairne – to write verses; and early in the eighteenth century a number of Edinburgh women seem to have been dedicated to this pursuit, suggesting how widespread was the taste for these relics of Scotland. In fact the preface to *The Edinburgh Miscellany* of 1720 makes clear the contribution of women:

> As for the Ladies, who have generously contributed to make up this Work, we are proud to declare, that, tho they have sent us few of their Composures, they have sent nothing that is refuse. And therefore, while we publickly thank them for the Assistance already receiv'd, we beg they will continue to shine like the brighter Constellations amongst Luminaries of a dimmer Aspect. The rest of that Delicate Sex, will excuse us, tho we particularly thank the FAIR INTELLECTUAL CLUB for the Poems they have been pleas'd to favour us with for publick Use. And we presume the ingenious Readers of their Performances will allow us to intreat them to send more to bespangle the second volume.[7]

Yet Chambers, in looking for an author or the authors, was grappling with one of the enigmas of traditional balladry and song: for the most part, THE author cannot be discovered, having ceased to be relevant when her/his work was accepted and learned and sometimes recreated and transmitted by others. Thus THE author is irrelevant, for such ballads and songs exist not in a definitive text, but in multiple texts, that very multiplicity affirming the materials' traditional status. And those variable texts were performed by individuals, bearers of tradition, and sometimes bore marks of those individuals' creativity. Many of their names could be recovered from the manuscripts and discussions which lay behind the anonymous, unattributed texts in published collections. This is especially true when editions of ballads became based on fieldwork, on actual contact with singers of songs, rather than on earlier printed and manuscript materials. One of the exciting results of the collecting process, then and now, was the discovery of an individual with an extensive repertoire, an individual who might be called a specialist in oral balladry and song. Many – perhaps even a preponderance, if we accept Peter Buchan's statement that the 'ancient Ballads of Caledonia' were 'said or sung in the enchanting voice of their fair countrywomen' – of the specialists were women. One of the first performers of ballads to be singled out was Anna Gordon or Mrs Brown of Falkland – like Elizabeth Halket, Lady Wardlaw, before her, necessarily known by two names – that of her birth and the one acquired through marriage.[8]

Daughter of Professor Thomas Gordon, of the Chair of Humanity and then Greek at King's College, Aberdeen; wife of the Rev. Andrew Brown, minister of the parish at Falkland in Fife and later Tranent, Mrs Brown – born 1747 and died 1810 – is known for balladry she learned, largely as a child, from women in her family or connected with her family. Her contact with traditional balladry came through an aunt, Anne Forbes, who became Mrs Farquhar from Braemar; her mother Lillias Forbes; and a maidservant who had long been a Forbes family retainer. Robert Chambers had mentioned her in his essay on Lady Wardlaw because Mrs Brown performed some of the very materials he was attributing to Elizabeth Halket, those romantic ballads which he said have 'one marked feature – the pathos of deep female affections – the sacrifice and the suffering which these so often involve'.[9] Rather unwittingly then, Chambers may well have been among the first to articulate the close connection of women and balladry – as both authors and performers of a material particularly suited to women's concerns and feelings, a connection more implicit than explicit in Motherwell's category 'old singing women'.

Behind the published collections then lie the singers of ballads and songs; and many of them were women, a given accepted by the editor of the monumental collection, *The English and Scottish Popular Ballads*, when he was preparing the final work for publication.[10] In urging contemporary collecting of even the barest fragment, Francis James Child – whose name and numbering system continue to be identifying markers for the 305 entries canonised in his work – wrote:

> Something also must still be left in the memory of men, or better, of *women*, who have been the chief preservers of ballad-poetry. May I entreat the aid of gentlewomen in Scotland, or elsewhere, who remember ballads that they have heard repeated by their grandmothers or nurses?[11]

More familiarly, in congratulating his friend James Russell Lowell upon his election by the students as Rector of St Andrews University – a position he did not take up – Child humorously writes, 'thou art naturally lord of all Scotland'. And then, 'Let thy first decree be that every ballad known to any lady, maidservant, fishwife, dairywoman or nurse be given up under penalties of misprision & praemunire to all that shall be art & part in the withholding of the same'.[12] One senses his frustration at the state of ballad studies and his desire to expand scholarly understanding of the genre so associated with his name when he writes in *The Nation*:

> Where is the manuscript of Mrs. Brown of Falkland, to which Jamieson and Scott owe so much? At Aberdeen, very likely. Where is Herd's Manuscript, where the Glenriddell Manuscript, lent Scott by Mr. Jollie of Carlisle? And next, where are the Mrs. Farquhars, the Mrs. Browns, the Mrs. Arnots, the Miss Rutherfords themselves, and the nurses who taught them ballads? Small hope, we acknowledge, of finding such nurses any more, or such foster-children, and yet it cannot be that the diffusion of useful knowledge, the intrusion of railroads, and the general progress of society, have quite driven all the old songs out of country-women's heads – for it will be noted that it is mainly through women everywhere –
> 'The spinsters and the knitters in the sun,
> And the free maids that weave their thread with bones' –
> that ballads have been preserved.[13]

Child recognised then that women were fundamentally connected to the ballad; and the headnotes to the versions printed in *The English and Scottish Popular Ballads* amply attest to the role of women in preserving this species of popular literature. Child himself played a significant role in discovering their identities in his careful study of the manuscripts that lay behind the printed collections which were often silent on their sources.

If one cannot prove that Lady Wardlaw authored Scottish ballads, one can, however, affirm the connection of women to traditional balladry and song, genres that we are led to believe were once widely shared and performed in domestic environments in that sometimes romanticised period before the printed and electronic media began to dominate. So to explore women, ballads, and oral tradition, one must seek out the women who have remembered the songs, whose names are recorded as singers or reciters, beginning first with those who have been the subject of extensive study. Mrs Brown of Falkland provides the obligatory beginning.

How and why she was identified as a singer of songs seems lost to history. What we do know is that the Scottish antiquarian and historian William Tytler requested a copy of her ballads some time in 1783. Her fifty-one versions of thirty-eight ballad stories, thirty-three of which appear in the Child collection, make her repertoire one of the largest available for scrutiny. Child identified her and singled out her versions in the initial volume of his great study: 'No Scottish ballads are superior in kind to those recited in the last century by Mrs. Brown, of Falkland'.[14] Mrs Brown's repertoire was recorded in a series of manuscripts, which have continued to interest students of the ballad to this day, for reasons that have nothing to do with gender. Two manuscripts were completed in 1783 and were prepared at the request of William Tytler. The first, containing twenty texts, was put aside when Tytler requested copies of tunes, and eventually became the possession of Robert Jamieson; now bearing his name – the Jamieson Brown Manuscript – it also includes texts he collected from Mrs Brown in 1800 and others she subsequently sent him in a letter. The second and somewhat shorter manuscript, containing fifteen texts and tunes, is referred to as the Tytler Brown Manuscript. In 1800, William's son Alexander Fraser Tytler, serving as intermediary for Walter Scott, requested additional materials; those nine texts are known as the Fraser Tytler Brown Manuscript. Scott used both the Tytler Brown and Fraser Tytler Brown manuscripts in preparing the *Minstrelsy of the Scottish Border*;[15] and Jamieson printed those not used by Scott in his own 1806 collection *Popular Ballads and Songs, from Tradition, Manuscripts, and Scarce Traditions*.[16] Together the manuscripts contain sixteen texts in two versions and one in three, providing evidence which has been analysed in support of various theories and perspectives.

Ballad enthusiasts have been particularly interested in Anna Gordon's texts, their variations, and the reasons for differences between versions. Bertrand Bronson dealt with those questions in a 1945 article, concluding that conscious artistry on her part was responsible for the quality of her texts and suggesting that her literacy led to 'false notes, artificial touches, pretty sentimentalities, and a specious neatness'.[17] Holger Nygard took a different tack in comparing the multiple texts, finding that they are 'near verbatim texts, memorial in nature, departing from the earlier only in limited ways, primarily in the understood ranges of variant pronunciation . . . Mrs. Brown's ballads are essentially repetitions of a text, not recreations of a story maintained in fluid solution subject to a free variation in successive singings'.[18] Yet a third perspective is taken by David Buchan in *The Ballad and the Folk*:[19] he suggests that Mrs Brown orally recreated her ballads at each performance, utilizing oral structuring devices learned in her childhood, a so-called ballad architectonics with a preference for binary, trinary, and annular patternings of characters, stanzas, scenes, and even lines. In fact his study hinges on Mrs Brown's role as active re-creator of ballads, as inheritor of the techniques of oral formulaic composition, first promulgated by Milman Parry and Albert B. Lord in examining the Yugoslavian epics and their ancient progenitors, *The Iliad* and *The Odyssey*. How Mrs Brown, an educated woman who was familiar with Percy's *Reliques*, could have done this is explained with reference to the bi-cameral mind, parallel to the Scottish cultural dualism: the split between the Scottish perceptual framework and the formal, literate world of English – what David Daiches distinguishes as a presumed 'division between the language of the heart and the language of the head'.[20] This theory would have us believe that Mrs Brown held her oral and literate capacities separate; and the literate Anna Gordon Brown was not anxious to see her name associated with those songs she had learned to sing orally as a child. Her name and her texts, however, have become almost 'household' words to lovers of ballads and songs; and her versions have been almost universally praised for their completeness and aesthetic qualities.

David Buchan suggests that hers was a woman's repertoire, learned from women; in fact he implicitly faults her repertoire suggesting that it does not offer the full range of subject matters, which he suggests are three – magical and marvellous, romantic and tragic, historical and semi-historical. Her texts are predominantly in the former two as he explains: 'This imbalance presumably resulted from her sources of all being women, and therefore constitutionally more inclined to the marvellous than the martial.'[21] He goes on to suggest that women may well have continued the old patterns of re-creation of the ballads because they received less education than men. Other commentators have pointed to the overwhelming interest in romantic love exhibited in the versions Anna Gordon Brown is credited with having sung. But her gender and her gendered experience have not figured further or prominently in the analysis of her works. The same can be said for another study of a ballad repertoire of a nineteenth-century Scottish woman, one of Motherwell's 'old singing women', Agnes Lyle of Kilbarchan.

In an extended study of Lyle's repertoire, William McCarthy's *The Ballad Matrix: Personality, Milieu, and the Oral Tradition* explores the societal environment and context of Paisley and Kilbarchan early in the nineteenth century. An industrial area with a long history of textile manufacturing, the region's economy had fallen on hard times. An oversupply of labour, lack of unionisation, diminished demand for the textile products, together with the institution of factory manufacturing had altered the artisan culture of independent and educated hand-loom weavers, leading many of them to become vocal activists for improved working and living conditions. This was the milieu of Agnes Lyle, one of Kilbarchan's 4,213 inhabitants.

A woman of probably fifty when Motherwell collected from her in 1825, she had learned the majority of her songs from her father, a weaver, who had died at eighty some fourteen years earlier. Agnes's repertoire of twenty-one full texts, one nearly complete and seven fragments, is a mix of ballads and songs – a typical mix belied by the heavy focus on ballads in many collections and repertoires. Lyle's repertoire includes a weaving song, some materials bearing the marks of long oral tradition, and other texts undoubtedly originating from printed broadsides. We know relatively little about her: McCarthy tells us she may never have married, but was certainly minimally educated, being able to read and write. However, he surmises that her choice of ballads can tell us a great deal about her and her concerns – that she chose to sing the songs she did because they helped her, even implicitly, to articulate her own responses to the economic upheavals of the day; her materials reveal a 'single set of political and social attitudes, personal prejudices, ethical values, and aesthetic standards'.[22] McCarthy points out the frequency of texts which describe individuals involved with persons above them in social class and their abandonment – issues surrounding social difference, the violation or trust, human perfidy – treachery, malice, or faithlessness'.[23] Marriage in the ballads often equals death. His analysis is based on two premises – the first that because there were strong class tensions at this period of time, her texts must certainly reflect that; and the second, that the texts themselves contain certain markers, inherent conventions like the hunt being a prelude to love or death, the idea of a game suggesting love, of clothes indicating beauty and so on – in other words, meaning resides in the text. These interpretative suggestions fill the vacuum of Agnes Lyle: we do not have any real idea what she might have to say, why she might have chosen certain texts, what those texts meant to her. In addition to affirming the political-social nature of her repertoire, McCarthy also uses a close analysis of her texts to affirm that they, like Mrs Brown's according to David Buchan, were orally formulated. He separates her texts into the various meters employed and suggests that her oral formulaic capabilities were most successful in recreating texts using the so-called ballad stanza, rhyming abcb, and carrying a 4343 stress pattern. Texts using other metrical patterns were less successful.

As interesting as this analysis is, it remains a study of one woman's repertoire in isolation not only from her specific life and concerns, which we cannot really know, but also from comparison with other women's and men's repertoires which might suggest in a more definitive way whether there were indeed differences, and if so, what those differences might suggest, in general, about women's and men's choices of songs, about gender-related repertoires. As yet there have been so few extended repertoire studies, which ideally link individuals, their lives and times, with texts and tunes, that it is difficult to make even these tentative kinds of conclusions. I shall return to this issue.

One of the collectors who was inspired by William Motherwell was a disabled doctor, Andrew Crawfurd, who occupied himself for a number of years in collecting the ballads and songs of his native village, Lochwinnoch. Crawfurd gathered three volumes of song material – in addition to other antiquarian matters, especially on the Scots language, which make up a forty-six volume manuscript compilation, *The Cairn of Lochunyoch Matters*. His ballad and song collecting took place between 1826 and 1828 and provided Motherwell with materials for the musical appendix and the introduction to his *Minstrelsy Ancient and Modern* (1827). Publications which are derived from Crawfurd's collection began to appear in 1975 with Emily Lyle's preliminary volume of his work, *Publications of the Scottish Text Society*, 4th series, no. 9.[24] Lyle's edition offers the repertoires of two men and two women – with the bulk of the volume devoted to the repertoires of Mary Macqueen, Mrs Storie and Meg Walker, Mrs Caldwell. Crawfurd's Cairn provides scant information on the informants, less for the women than for the men: Crawfurd probably found it easier to elicit information from the men who served as informants. Of John Smith, he records that he is 'a very thirsty man'; no such insightful 'tidbits' describe the women.

Mary Macqueen Storie, the wife of William, a labourer, was from a traveller background and learned her ballads and songs from a great-grandmother, a grandmother, her mother and brothers. Emily Lyle arranges her extensive repertoire of forty-six texts according to their sources, providing thereby an implicit chronology. Motherwell paid to bring Mrs Storie to Paisley in order to record some of her tunes for inclusion in his *Minstrelsy* Meg Walker Caldwell was sixty-four when Crawfurd collected her songs which contain a number of local references. A widow living then at Bridgend, Lochwinnoch, she had no children and had learned her songs from many sources, including books. Seventeen items are printed, like Mrs Storie's and Agnes Lyle's a mixture of song and ballad, old and new. What is particularly striking is the fact that the individuals with the most extensive repertoires were women. Yet this study offers no explanation for that and does not broach the subject of possible gender-determination.

Other ballad and song scholars have provided lists of informants, bearers of tradition, and the songs which have been attributed to them – the beginning point for more extensive studies reconstructing their lives and times. Motherwell's list of 'old singing women' and other materials in his notebook and manuscripts provide this kind of data. Kenneth Thigpen offers a preliminary list of repertoires from Child's collection, including, of course, men and women, from Scotland and elsewhere in the English-speaking world.[25] Cumulatively, the prevalence, if not predominance of women's names in connection with ballads and songs certainly suggests the significance of ballads and songs to women and women's importance in studying the ballads and songs.

Women's names then have long been associated with traditional Scottish balladry and song – as possible author, certainly as tradition bearers, repositories of material which has some claim to being particularly Scottish. Mrs Brown's repertoire of material was singled out as having been a woman's repertoire – presumably because she learned the material from women. On the other hand, Agnes Lyle learned her material from her father. Does that make her repertoire any less a woman's repertoire? I would like to assume that 'gender' is a relevant category, that ballad and song singers chose/choose their materials for a variety of reasons – and that their gender and gendered experiences have something to do with their repertoires.

Students of balladry and song have come late to the consideration of 'gender', but recent studies have illustrated the salience of this dimension of analysis, recognising that 'gender' may influence the genres known and performed, the subject matter chosen, the style and venue of performance, and the meaning/significance of the material.[26] In terms of women and the ballad, I believe there is ample evidence to suggest that women have been among the primary performers and consumers of the form, and further, I believe, that gender – and more particularly, gendered life experiences – have had something to do with the choices of songs – both to know and to perform, as well as to hear. This is an easier proposition to explore when dealing wit contemporary performers and their repertoires. When dealing, as I am, with eighteenth- and nineteenth-century materials, there are a number of unknowables: for the most part we have a few women's names and lists of their texts. Sometimes we know something about the women and have their specific texts in front of us. We do not know whether these repertoires are those of passive or active tradition bearers – whether they actively performed the materials, or whether they were passive, remembering only what they had heard, but not actively performing or selecting. We do not know whether the materials really resonated with their lives or whether the texts were dredged up for the collector. We cannot ask them about their lives or surmise the structures of feeling which might well have affected their selections of materials for performance or hearing. We cannot hear them sing. And yet, we do have some limited, general data for the past: we know that women were extremely active as singers and hearers of ballads and songs; and we can assume that they selected the genre and particular examples because they spoke to their human, perhaps gendered, condition. Thus a preliminary reading of repertoires of several women may well offer some kind of window into their collective interests, revealing as well something about the presumed roles and fates of women.

Anna Gordon/Mrs Brown of Falkland's repertoire was presumably learned from women in her family when she was herself a child. This suggests a homosocial environment in which kinswomen shared such materials and, presumably, conversation topics on these and related subjects. A reading of the texts attributed to her reveals a number of recurrent topics, including Scottish chauvinism, virtue rewarded, class distinctions. Yet the preponderence of texts deal with women's life situations – especially with love and marriage, with obstacles to love and marriage, with family conflicts – especially between the wife and the mother-in-law, and with childbirth and children. It is tempting then to suggest that these topics figure in the songs because they were real life issues; if the ballad stories do not always resolve the issue ideally, at least the stories offer possible scenarios with potential relevance to women's lives.

Traditionally, women's roles have been restricted to being a wife and a mother, essential roles for the reproduction of the species – a non-individuated capacity that has been identified as enormously limiting to women as individuals in such classic texts as Simone de Beauvoir's *The Second Sex*.[27] Mrs Brown's ballads, however, do not interrogate these roles, but rather deal with them as given, offering theme and variation as support and consolation. Take the issue of marriage as a case in point. Marriage, the ballads suggest, should be for love; but there are powerful counter forces to that emotion which would control and limit women's choices – and men's too, of course; but the ballads seem to explore the topic with the potential wife and her family's concerns – that is the reproduction of and continuation of the family – as principal issues. In 'Lady Maisry' (Child 65), the heroine refuses all suitors but an English lord. A kitchen boy reveals her love object and her pregnant state to her brother who is furious – at her inappropriate choice of mate, perhaps at her premarital coupling – and burns her as a whore. While the Englishman arrives too late to save her, he will revenge her death. But, from the family perspective, she has been kept from mating with an inappropriate person, even if it has meant her death. The family, represented by a male member – here the brother, if this text is to be trusted – has rights in selecting appropriate husbands: and Englishmen aren't! Neither are kitchen boys or presumably low-born persons until or unless they rise in position. In 'Lady Elspat' (Child 247) the offendingly low-class person, opposed here by the mother, turns out in fact to be a judge's nephew; in a telling stanza the prejudice against the young man's presumed class location is articulated:

> But tho he was my first true love,
>   An tho I had sworn to be his bride,
> Caus he had not a great estate,
>   She would this way our loves divide.

In 'The Kitchie Boy' (Child 252C) the hopeful bride and wife outfits the kitchen boy with a ship and sends him off to return in disguise, knowing that her father will then presume he is wealthy and an acceptable husband. Her initial stanza sets the scene:

> O there was a ladie, a noble ladie,
>   She was a ladie of birth and fame,
> But she fell in love wi her father's foot-boy,
>   I wis she was the mair to blame.

The daughter's ruse works and only later is the father told. Women make independent decisions about whom to love and marry, but those decisions are often rescinded by family priorities, tied to nationalism or class position, the latter perhaps suggesting that class distinctions were more salient in Scotland than some commentators have suggested. But what may be revealed here is a contested area – who has the choice of a woman's mate, her family or her own sentiments. Sometimes she wins only to die; sometimes she wins and, we assume, lives happily ever after having made a love match – something other texts tell us is hard to achieve and sustain; sometimes, as in 'The Cruel Brother' (Child 11) she loses because all the appropriate family members have not approved of the match. I think it is possible to suggest that women, and Mrs Brown's circle in particular here, might well choose to sing songs which enter into the dialogue about appropriate mates and the right of choice, a question with some pertinence in their own lives.

Likewise, when they sang of tensions between women and their mothers-in-law, they may well have been fictively airing their own concerns. The competition of a man's mother and his wife for affective dominance in his life takes numerous forms in the ballads preserved in Mrs Brown's repertoire: in 'Willie's Lady' (Child 6), the mother-in-law puts a hex on her daughter-in-law making it impossible for her to be delivered of her child, so jealous is she of her daughter-in-law's youth and reproductive capacity, presumably lost to her. The mother in 'The Mother's Malison, or, Clyde's Water' (Child 216) puts a curse on her son when he decides to go visit his lady love; as a result he drowns – death being better than an inappropriate mate or, in this case, another woman competing for his affections.

Other texts deal with childbirth, a dangerous aspect of the reproductive imperative. The mother in 'Fair Mary of Wellington' (Child 91) forces all her daughters to marry even knowing they will die in childbirth; and statistically many women did. Cumulatively, in fact, Mrs Brown's ballad texts discuss, from multiple perspectives and with multiple outcomes, women's concerns – most particularly around the question of relations between men and women. Seduction figures frequently: in 'Gil Brenton' (Child 5), a woman is impregnated by a stranger against her will; in 'Bonny Baby Livingston' (Child 222) a man steals a woman against her will, a woman who loves another with whom she is finally united. Certainly seductions happened, perhaps even forced. The ballads may well then have provided the women's family circle with a way of discussing and dealing with very real possibilities facing women. It would be surprising if the songs did not have some relevance to their lives, however oblique.

Agnes Lyle learned her ballads and songs mostly from her father; McCarthy suggests they reflect her perspective on the politics of the time. One might just as easily, and perhaps more realistically, suggest that she selected those texts of her father's which spoke to her position as a woman, possibly unmarried. In reading the texts attributed to her, I was overwhelmed with the fact that there are very strong women characters in the majority of her ballads, women who take control of situations; women who are steadfast in their love despite seemingly insurmountable obstacles; strong-willed women who sometimes are perceived negatively; women, who because of their qualities, evoke strong love attachments from men. Agnes Lyle's 'Mary Hamilton' (Child 173B) exhibits a kind of strength in accepting her fate, taking personal responsibility for the actions that brought her to her death, in a repeated stanza:

> 'Gie never alace for me,' she said,
> 'Gie never alace for me;
> It's all for the sake of my poor babe,
> This death that I maun die.

Many of her women are active: they do things to effect their situations, or refuse to do things. In her 'The Eastmure King and the Westmure King' (Child 89B), the woman marries to save herself, though she is already pregnant by the man her husband has murdered. And she manages to swap her son for a daughter, insuring that on his maturity he can revenge his father's death. But she must make decisions, within a range of possibilities, showing a pragmatic strength. In 'Babylon; or, the Bonnie Banks O Fordie' (Child 14D), the third woman ignores his questions – Wiltow twinn with thy maidenhead, or thy sweet life? – and speaks up:

> 'If my three breathren they were here,
> Such questions as these thou durst nae speer.'

Admittedly, these examples are not unique to Agnes Lyle, but are versions which fall centrally in the regional tradition of which she was a part. Nor do these examples suggest that she was questioning women's role. Rather the texts seem to offer an exploration of women in traditional roles, as mothers, wives, lovers, but genuine players – sometimes positive, sometimes negative – in the action. The central woman in her version of 'The Baffled Knight' (Child 112E) might be taken as a paradigm for the women in the texts she chose to perform for Crawfurd/William Motherwell: she is appealing, clever, and finally gets the last word –

> 'But when eer you meet a pretty maid,
> And two miles from a town, sir,
> You may lay her down,' she said,
> 'And never mind her gown, sir.'

It is tempting, and I think justifiable, to suggest that her repertoire unconsciously projects a vision of women she personally found worthy of emulation, women of character, women of action, women who saw themselves as connected with men. Gender, I suggest, is a more potent lens than politics – especially when selecting ballads and songs to know and sing. But we will never know what Agnes Lyle would have said.

She was one of Motherwell's 'old singing women', having the largest repertoire of the eleven women so identified: Mrs Thomson – 14, Widow Nicol – 15, Widow McCormick – 7, Mrs King – 2, Mrs Gentles – 8, Agnes Laird – 10, Janet Holmes – 1, Mrs Rule – 6, Mrs Notman – 12, Widow Michael – 3.[28] For whatever reason, Motherwell did his most extensive collecting from women: women make up three-quarters of his sources, and women, on average, have more extensive repertoires than the men from whom he collected. Perhaps they were more available to talk with the strange young man from Paisley. Perhaps they were less educated and thus retained an interest in and facility for remembering ballads and songs longer than men who had more access to formal education. Perhaps ballads spoke particularly to women's experiences and might even be called a women's genre.

In examining the repertoires of Motherwell's 'old singing women', it is surprising to discover that there is very little overlap in their repertoires. Of the more than eighty texts known by them, only seven texts are repeated at all. Six ballads appear in the repertoires of three women: 'Hind Horn' (Child 17), 'Sir Patrick Spens' (Child 58), 'Child Maurice' (Child 83), 'Tam Lin' (Child 39), 'Mary Hamilton' (Child 173), and 'Lord Jamie Douglas' (Child 204). All but 'Sir Patrick Spens' feature women prominently in the plot: women as prospective mates (Child 17 and 39), women as mothers – both good and bad ones (Child 83 and 173), women as wives – here scorned (Child 204). But clearly these ballad stories are not exclusively found in women's repertoires. Yet it is tempting to suggest that their repetition across the repertoires of several women may suggest that the issues being dealt with in these particular items were of particular interest to women, dealing as they do with aspects of women's traditional role. 'Lord Jamie Douglas' (Child 204) deals poignantly with women's lot, her need to be under male protection. Dealing with a rejected woman – rejected because she had received a male visitor when she was ill, or because her husband was told she was unfaithful, or he himself was – she is unable to get her husband to listen to her side of the story. Stanzas from two versions of the ballad express, on the one hand, his adamant refusal to hear her perspective and, on the other, illustrate the kinds of variations so frequent in this kind of oral, popular literatature.

Child 204 I
When sea and sands turns foreign land,
  And mussels grow on every tree,
When cockle-shells turn silver bells,
I'll drink the Orange wine with thee.

Child 204 K
When cockle-shells grow siller bells,
  And mussels grow on ilka tree,
When frost and snaw turns out fire-bombs,
Then I'll come doun and drink wine wi thee.

The lines also express the kind of irretrievable breakdown that married relationships can have. She returns to her father, who promises both to get her a divorce and a new husband, to which she adamantly responds no, for she loves the man who rejected her: 'They're far awa that I luve best'. And the J version offers a somewhat jaded reverie on love:

Oh Johnie, Johnie, but love is bonnie
  A little while, when it is new;
But when love grows aulder, it grows mair caulder,
  And it fades awa like the mornin dew.

Presumably, it is men's love that fades, if the message of this text is to be accepted. Certainly one can read the text from a woman's perspective; and I suggest that the particular salience of these texts had something to do with their content. But it would be wrong to say much more: we simply do not have enough historical evidence to support any firm conclusions.

One of William Motherwell's male singers, Thomas Risk Smith, knew – or at least sang – eight songs for Motherwell. And it may be interesting to comment that there was but one overlap with the 'old singing women' – 'Johnie Scot' (Child 99). Five of the women also knew it, as did Mrs Brown. The ballad tells the story of a Scotsman who goes to England, with a company of soldiers provided by his father, uncle, or the king, to rescue his love; she is imprisoned because she is pregnant and loves a Scot. Her father intends to hang Johnie, but agrees to allow one-on-one combat with his champion. Johnie, of course, wins; immediately weds his love; and – refusing to take the Englishman's dowry – returns to Scotland. Reading this text now, it is easy to suggest its importance and interest to Scots singers, men and women: it is frankly chauvinistic; but it is also a love story. Perhaps the expression of national pride and national prowess, together with the love interest, make this ballad appeal to women, accounting for its redundancy in their repertoires, David Buchan had commented earlier on the absence of many martial ballads in women's repertoires, those texts presumably found in the men's repertoires. It is possible that 'Johnie Scot' might be one marginal example that spans the repertoires of both men and women, offering for the men a touch of the martial. And it is also possible that aspects of nationalism, when coupled with a love interest, provide a subject matter of highest appeal, certainly to the women, accounting for the appearance of 'Johnie Scot' in so many of their repertoires.

Yet, these interpretative comments are just that, preliminary attempts to begin the process of looking at women and ballads with gender as a central lens and focus. We cannot say definitively that women chose certain songs to sing and perform because of their gendered concerns. We can say, however, that women have long been conceptually associated with ballads: Lady Wardlaw certainly wrote 'Hardyknute' if not 'Sir Patrick Spens'. The record amply confirms that women have been among the most prolific and artistic singers, and presumably hearers, of balladry: Anna Gordon Brown, Agnes Lyle, Mary MacQueen Storie, Meg Walker Caldwell, and the rest of Motherwell's 'old singing women' are worthy performers. And we can certainly say that women's willingness to sing and recite for male collectors has done much to enrich our cultural heritage.

Notes

1.   William Motherwell, Ballad Manuscript, n.d., Manuscript Murray 501, Glasgow University Library; copy: Manuscript 25241.20, Houghton Library, Harvard University; *Minstrelsy Ancient and Modern* (John Wylie, Glasgow, 1827); Notebook, n.d., copy: Manuscript 2542.16, Houghton Library, Harvard University.
2.   David Daiches, *The Paradox of Scottish Culture: The Eighteenth Century Experience*, (Oxford University Press, Oxford, 1964), p. 28. Daiches suggests that antiquarianism was an acceptable form of nationalism while overt protests against the Union were politically 'incorrect' expressions of national sentiment.
3.   Peter Buchan, *Gleanings of Scarce Old Ballads* (Aberdeen, 1891), preface.
4.   Norval Clyne, *The Romantic Scottish Ballads and the Lady Wardlaw Heresy*, (A. Brown, Aberdeen, 1859), p. 5.
5.   Clyne, p. 6.
6.   Clyne, p. 6.
7.   *The Edinburgh Miscellany*, 2nd edn (J. M'Euen, Edinburgh, 1720), vol. 1, pp. ii–iii. I am particularly indebted to Sigrid Rieuwerts for this reference, for several pointed quotations from Francis James Child, and for her generosity in making available to me materials that were inaccessible when I began to draft this paper. The dialogue we have had has enriched my view of the ballad and my thoughts on its relationship to women.
8.   Ursula K. Le Guin, *Dancing at the Edge of the World* (Harper & Row, New York, 1990), p. 231, makes a similar, telling point about her own mother: 'Her maiden name was Theodora Kracaw; her first married name was Brown; her second married name, Kroeber, was the one she used on her books; her third married name was Quinn. This sort of many-namedness doesn't happen to men; it's inconvenient, and yet its very cumbersomeness reveals, perhaps, the being of a woman writer as not one simple thing – the author – but a multiple, complex process of being, with various responsibilities, one of which is to her writing'.
9.   Robert Chambers, *The Romantic Scottish Ballads: Their Epoch and Authorship* (1849), p. 35.
10.   Francis James Child, *The English and Scottish Popular Ballads* (Houghton, Mifflin, Boston, 1882–98).
11.   Francis James Child, 'Old Ballads: Professor Child's Appeal', 'Notes and Queries', *The Nation*, 12 (1873).

12. *The Scholar Friends*, ed. M. A. Dewolfe Howe and G. W. Cottrel (Harvard University Press, Cambridge, Mass., 1952), p. 57.
13. Francis James Child, 'Ballad Books', *The Nation*, 7 (1868), 192–3.
14. Francis James Child, *The English and Scottish Popular Ballads*, vol. 1, vii.
15. Sir Walter Scott, *The Minstrelsy of the Scottish Border* (1802).
16. Robert Jamieson, *Popular Ballads and Songs* (Edinburgh, 1806).
17. Bertrand Harris Bronson, *The Ballad as Song* (University of California Press, Berkeley, 1969), p. 72.
18. Holger Olof Nygard, 'Mrs Brown's Recollected Ballads', in Patricia Conroy, *Ballads and Ballad Research* (University of Washington Press, Seattle, 1978), pp. 68–87.
19. David Buchan, *The Ballad and the Folk* (Routledge & Kegan Paul, London, 1972), Part II 'The Oral Tradition: The Ballads', pp. 51–173.
20. Daiches, *The Paradox of Scottish Culture*, p. 65.
21. Buchan, *The Ballad and the Folk*, p. 76.
22. William McCarthy, *The Ballad Matrix* (Indiana University Press, Bloomington, 1990), p. 13.
23. McCarthy, *The Ballad Matrix*, p. 133.
24. *Andrew Crawfurd's Collection of Ballads and Songs*, ed. Emily B. Lyle (The Scottish Text Society, Edinburgh, 1975), 4th series, no. 9.
25. Kenneth Thigpen, 'An Index to the Known Oral Sources of the Child Collection', *Folklore Forum* 5: pp. 55–69.
26. Several review articles offer an avenue into this material: see particularly Rosan Jordan and Frank A. de Caro, 'Women and the Study of Folklore', SIGNS 2–3 (1986) 500–18 and Mary Ellen Brown, 'Women, Folklore, and Feminism', *Journal of Folklore Research* 26:3 (1989), 259–64. Two recent anthologies are also worthy of note: Joan Newlon Radner (ed). *Feminist Messages: Coding in Women's Folk Culture* (University of Illinois Press, Urbana, 1993) and Susan Tower Hollis, Linda Pershing, M. Jane Young, *Feminist Theory and the Study of Folklore* (University of Illinois Press, Urbana, 1993).
27. Simone de Beauvoir, *Le Deuxième Sex* (Gallimard, Paris, 1949).
28. It is interesting to note what items are in the repertoires of the various 'old singing women': Mrs Thomson ('Lady Marjory', 'Lambert-Linkin', 'Catherine Johnson', 'King William going a hunting', 'Rob's Bridal', 'Earl Robert', 'Skipper Patrick', 'Chield Morice', 'There was a May and a bonnie May', 'Susie Cleland', 'Lord Sanders', 'Johnnie Scott', 'Lord Brangwill', 'E down & oh Down') Widow Nicol ('The Loyal Lovers', 'The Young Laird o' Kelty', 'Old Row Down a Derry', 'The Tropper', 'Somebody', 'Robes of Brown', 'Captain Kid', 'The Bonnie Lass of Newport', 'I'll tell thee the true reason', 'Its braw sailing here', 'The Buss o'Bonnie Broom', 'Earl of Aboyne' or 'Bonny Peggy Irvine', 'Johnie Scot', 'Kempy Kane', 'Charcoal Jenny'); Widow McCormick ('Tamaline'/'Tam lin', 'The Knight and the Shepherd's daughters', 'Child Noryce'/'Child Norice', 'The Cruel Brother', 'Marjorie & William'/'Wm & Marjorie', 'The Brown girl', 'May Colean'); Mrs King ('There were three Sisters lived in a bouir', 'Hind horn'); Mrs Gentles ('Sir Patrick/Spens', 'Mary Hamilton', 'Sir James the Rose', 'The Young Johnstone', 'Isbel', 'Child Norice', 'The Elphin Knight', 'Lord Ronald'); Agnes Laird ('The Brown Bride and Lord Thomas', 'The Wee Wee Man', 'Johnie Scot', 'Lord Robert & Mary Florence', 'There was a Knight in Jessamay', 'The Cruel Mother', 'Willie of Winsberye/-berry'/'Lord Thomas of Winsbury', 'The King had only one daughter', 'There was a lady brisk and smart', 'Gay Goss hawk'); Janet Holmes ('Fair Annie'); Mrs Rule ('Fair Annie', 'Geordie Lukelie', 'The Turkish Galley', 'Jamie Douglas', 'I have a sister Lord Clifford says', 'Young Tamlin'); Mrs Notman ('Sir Patrick Spens', 'Willie the Widow's Son', 'Jamie Douglas', 'Lord Douglas', 'Tamlin', 'Mary Hamilton', 'Wallace', 'My love he's young but he's growin yet', 'Hynd Horne', 'Lord Gregory', 'Johnie the Valiant Scot', 'Johnie Scot' or 'McNachton'); Widow Michael ('The Jews Daughter', 'Child Nourice', 'Gill Morice'). For Agnes Lyle, see McCarthy, *The Ballad Matrix*.

4

Women and Song 1750–1850

Kirsteen McCue

> Who can tell the power of music and of song? Although the essence of time, they transcend
> time. As the wind or as the sunshine, their influence is everywhere, yet undefined.[1]

At the turn of this century Scottish songs and songwriters were in European vogue. The
pioneering work of Sarah Tytler and J. L. Watson,[2] and the biographies and editions
produced by Henry Lonsdale[3] and Charles Rogers,[4] have left us with a comprehensive
catalogue of views and opinions about songs and songwriters in Scotland from the 1840s
until the early 1900s. From then until recently there has been little interest in the genre
of Scottish song; in its influence on Scottish writing in general; or in the large group of
writers, both male and female, whose work clearly illustrates the importance of song as a
literary and musical form throughout the eighteenth and nineteenth centuries. Scottish
writers, both musically literate and illiterate, dabbled in songwriting because song held
a special place in Scottish society. Its popularity is simply revealed by the number
of publications produced with unending enthusiasm for well over a century from the
early 1700s.

A natural consequence of Scotland's publishing boom in the eighteenth century was
the development of a thriving music publishing industry, which had been virtually non-
existent prior to the 1700s. By the 1770s and '80s the turnover in musical publications
in Edinburgh alone was impressive, with at least thirty booksellers in the city dealing in
music in addition to other publications,[5] but music publishers also became established in
Glasgow, Perth, Stirling and Aberdeen. Although some orchestral and chamber music
was published, most of the musical publications produced in eighteenth-century Scotland
were connected with traditional Scottish music. There was an interest in national songs
and tunes elsewhere in the British Isles, but the number of publications of this sort in
Scotland far surpassed those produced in England, Wales or Ireland at this time. Scottish
song books were also varied, ranging from psalm tunes and hymns of the Church of
Scotland to fiddle or bagpipe tunes arranged for voice and pianoforte, with newly created
lyrics. Some song books appeared with melody lines, or with elaborate accompaniments
for small ensemble. Others, beginning with Allan Ramsay's *Scots Songs* (1718), appeared
with no music, but with the name of the melody and lyrics alone.

This outburst of song publications arguably stimulated writers of the period. But the
general respect for and interest in the genre of song in Scotland was also inspirational.

The place of music in Scottish society in the eighteenth century was a complex one. The restrictions of the Church of Scotland from the Reformation, and the departure of the Court in 1603, had resulted in a dearth of musical activity. The only genres which had continued to develop from the mid-sixteenth century were those of song, fiddle and bagpipe music. While many of the songs produced in Scotland during the 1700s were indistinguishable from their English counterparts,[6] many were written in the Scots language or were preoccupied with Scottish issues. The Union of 1707 arguably provided the perfect stimulus to exploit these specifically national traditions. Many Scots were keen to emphasise the elements of their society and/or history which characterised them as unique and independent. Scottish song, above all other musical genres, assumed an almost sacred quality among the Scots, regardless of their social or political standing. These songs emanated from an oral tradition of the nation's working people, yet apparently they spoke equally directly to her professional classes. Even those educated Scots who relished the new orchestral music of the contemporary European composers were deeply affected by the Scots songs which they continued to programme in their 'classical' concerts.[7] Moreover, the Scots language, which such ladies and gentlemen worked hard to eradicate, was also acceptable when dressed with a 'Scotch air'.

It is thus little surprise that the songs of well over 100 Scottish writers appeared in publications, both with and without music, from the beginning of the 1700s until around 1830. Robert Burns, Walter Scott, James Hogg,[8] and their influential predecessor Allan Ramsay,[9] presented readers with literally hundreds of songs and ballads. Their work includes the largest single collections of songs of the period and, at least in the case of Burns, the most important. However, there are numerous other writers examination of whose work allows a more comprehensive view of the subject. Amongst them is a large group of over thirty Scottish women.

As already discussed by Catherine Kerrigan in the Introduction to her *Anthology of Scottish Women Poets*,[10] the importance of women's role in the dissemination of the ballad tradition through performance is now undisputed.[11] Burns, who wrote more songs than any other individual at this time, was clearly influenced by a close friend of his mother's, who had 'the largest collection in the county of tales and songs'.[12] His mother was a fine singer, and his wife, Jean Armour, was also renowned for her singing voice.[13] Indeed, Burns was inspired to write his first song by, amongst other things, the beauty of Nelly Kilpatrick's singing.[14] The group of Scottish women who began to write songs during the eighteenth century were also frequently inspired by renditions of folk songs or ballads which were most often performed by other women, such as grandmothers, aunts, mothers and nannies. Yet, following Burns's example, they were often equally affected by published songs of the period.

Though some were professional writers – the playwright Joanna Baillie (1762–1851); the novelist Elizabeth Hamilton (1758–1816); the lady of letters and essayist Anne Grant of Laggan (1755–1838) – the majority of these songwriters were daughters or wives of lawyers, ministers and military or medical men. Joanna Baillie's father was a Church of Scotland minister in the Parish of Bothwell and also Professor of Divinity at the University of Glasgow. Anne Grant was the daughter of a Highland officer who fought in America during the Seven Years' War. She ultimately married the Reverend James Grant, an army chaplain based in the barracks at Fort Augustus. Alison Cockburn (*née* Rutherford, 1712–94) was a close friend of Walter Scott, came from a titled family, and married the lawyer Patrick Cockburn, son of Lord Ormiston, the Lord Justice Clerk. Lady

Ann Barnard (*née* Lindsay, 1750–1825) was the eldest daughter of James Lindsay, 5th Earl of Balcarres in Fife, was a close friend of Henry Dundas, and eventually married an ex-army officer, son of the Bishop of Limerick. In 1796 Andrew Barnard became the first Secretary of the newly acquired Cape Colony in South Africa, where the couple lived for five years. Carolina Oliphant, Lady Nairne (1766–1845), the most prolific of this group of songwriters, came from a distinguished Scottish family like Lady Anne Lindsay, and also married a military man, William Nairne, who was her cousin.[15]

Published songwriters were rarely women who stood low on the social ladder or who were self-taught. Burns was, of course, read by many educated women, including Anna Barbauld and Helen Maria Williams, but it is also thought that he influenced several Ayrshire working women who produced pastoral love lyrics during the period.[16] Jean Glover (1758–1801) was a weaver's daughter from Kilmarnock, who eventually disappeared from her home with a band of strolling players. Burns alerted James Johnson to the existence of 'O'er the Moor amang the Heather', a song performed by Glover, which Johnson included in his Scots Musical Museum.[17] Isobel Pagan (1741–1821), spent most of her life near Muirkirk in Ayrshire where she wrote poetry and songs and 'kept a kind of low tippling house'.[18] Her best-known published songs were, like Glover's piece, pastoral love songs concerning shepherds and shepherdesses. 'The Crook and the Plaid' employs the popular idea of the gentle shepherd, for the lover here spends his summer, while herding his flocks, reading 'books of history that learns him meikle skill'.[19] Pagan's connection with Burns was most probably founded on the fact that she was said to be the creator of 'Ca' the Yowes to the Knowes', also published by James Johnson in his *Scots Musical Museum*.[20] However, there is no reference to Pagan's lyric in Burns's correspondence, and indeed he appears to take the credit for both printed versions of the song.[21] Burns claimed that he noted down the song initially from a clergyman called Clunzie.[22] It is quite possible that Clunzie sang the lyric he had heard elsewhere, perhaps Pagan's song, but there is no evidence of this. Many collections published in this century quote this song in its first form ('As I gaed down the waterside,/There I met a shepherd lad') as Pagan's lyric. 'Ca' the Yowes' exemplifies two important aspects of songs of the period. Firstly, they commonly hailed from an oral tradition and consequently appeared in numerous different versions. Secondly, there was often difficulty in distinguishing lyrics written by men and women.[23]

Few women of Glover's or Pagan's social standing wrote songs which appeared in print. They undoubtedly learned their songs from local singers and the parish schools where most of them were educated. In contrast the daughters of the professional classes were taught privately at home by a governess or tutor, or attended schools which catered for their needs, both academic and social. They spent much of their time learning the 'ornamental accomplishments' of French, dancing, music and drawing, which along with reading, writing and arithmetic were regarded as essential requirements for such women, especially for married life.[24] Many of them, like Susan Ferrier's Mrs Douglas and her granddaughter Mary in *Marriage* (1818), showed an aptitude for playing the pianoforte, harp or guitar, and for singing. They also commonly displayed a special interest in Scotch airs or Highland laments. The lure of the Highlands was a powerful one. Susanna Blamire (1747–94), who was born and lived near Carlisle, wrote a large number of Scots songs, apparently inspired by frequent visits to her sister who married Colonel Graham of Gartmore in 1767 and settled in the Highlands.[25]

Many of the educated women were thus musically skilled. Blamire played the guitar and spent many hours writing her songs while strumming Border tunes which she particularly liked.[26] Lady Grisell Baillie (1655–1746), as revealed in her famous *Household Book*,[27] placed a great deal of emphasis on her own musical education and that of her two daughters.[28] They regularly attended the opera and concerts when they were in London, and often paid for musicians to visit the house to give concerts and to teach. Joanna Baillie refers to concerts in her home in Hampstead where frequently 'some young Lady or other is desired to sing Scotch songs with an accompaniment and everyone says O how beautiful!'[29] She apparently also excelled 'in vocal and instrumental music' and 'learned to play her own accompaniments on the guitar'.[30] Lady John Scott (*née* Alicia Spottiswoode, 1810–1900), who was writing songs from an early age, played the harp and sang, and 'was always making tunes, or recalling old ones'.[31] These women in particular were influenced and guided by song publications of the period, most of which were created specifically for them. Allan Ramsay's dedication in his *Tea-Table Miscellany*, which first appeared in 1724, read as follows:

> To ilka lovely British lass,
> Frae Ladies Charlotte, Anne, and Jean,
> Down to ilk bonny singing Bess,
> Wha dances barefoot on the green.

Likewise George Thomson, editor of numerous sophisticated volumes of songs, which were published with musical arrangements by composers including Haydn and Beethoven, stated clearly that he was a 'Song-broker' for the ladies.[32]

It is apparent from any study of the song collections produced between the late 1700s and 1830 that all editors adhered closely to set pieces and subject areas. The majority of the songs were love songs: some tragic, some comic, some celebratory, some sarcastic. Not surprisingly many of the songs produced by women were also concerned with love. Lyrics in a pastoral style, which either gloried in or despaired of love, proved the immortality of true love through absence and death, or glanced philosophically at the journey of life, were all most acceptable because they usually exhibited sound moral principles.

It is noticeable that women's celebrations of love were rarely the soft, gentle pastoral lyrics which were so common of the male song writers of the period. Women were certainly not incapable of writing songs in this vein, but for more common were excited, rhythmic, more physical love lyrics such as Joanna Baillie's versions of 'Woo'd and Married and a" (beginning 'The bride she was winsome and bonny') or her 'Fy, Let's a' to the Wedding'. Though educated in social etiquette, these women were happy to grasp the physical immediacy of many of the lyrics which came directly from an oral tradition. Baillie describes 'Fy, Let's a' to the Wedding' as 'An auld sang, new buskit',[33] and there are many songs of hers, and of Carolina Nairne's, which took their titles, melodies and often an aspect of their content from traditional, most commonly anonymous, lyrics published in other song books. Nairne's famous song 'The Laird o' Cockpen', is another fine example of this. In this lyric the Laird o' Cockpen decides to find himself a wife and settles on 'McClish's ae daughter o'Clavers-ha'Lee,/A penniless lass wi' a lang pedigree'. He dresses in his Sunday best and calls upon her. Exhibiting that independence of mind which characterises many of Burns's women, she confidently refuses his proposal. Cockpen's arrogance is rather crudely undermined by Nairne in Miss McClish's refusal, when in the middle of the dignified meeting, and between his bowing and her low curtsy, she gives the answer 'Na' to rhyme with 'awa':

Mistress Jean was makin' the elder-flower wine;
'An' what brings the Laird at sic a like time?'
She put aff her apron, and on her silk gown,
Her mutch wi' red ribbons, and gaed awa' down.

An' when she cam ben he bowed fu' low,
An' what was his errand he soon let her know;
Amazed was the Laird when the lady said 'Na',
And wi' a laigh curtsie she turned awa'.

Dumfounder'd was he, nae sigh did he gie,
He mounted his mare – he rade cannily;
An' aften he thought, as he gaed through the glen,
She's daft to refuse the Laird o' Cockpen.[34]

In some collections the song ended here, though in editions of Nairne's work there were usually a further two verses in which Miss McClish reconsidered the proposal and finally accepted the Laird's hand in marriage.[35] It is difficult to date the song, but it is almost certain that Nairne wrote it after the appearance of 'When She Cam ben She Bobbit' in 1792 in Johnson's *Scots Musical Museum*.[36] Though written earlier, this anonymous song was set after the marriage of Cockpen and Miss McClish. Cockpen, who was in real life a friend of Charles II, was accused in this song of an extra-marital affair. Such subject matter was not acceptable for most song collections of the period because it presented a model of behaviour which was not encouraged amongst British young ladies. Interestingly this lyric, which is a description of the Laird wooing the collier lassie, does show the distinct roles of women. Lady Jean as wife and mother, whose chief role was to produce the heir; and the collier lassie as mistress, who was there for 'companionship and sexual pleasure' alone.[37] Furthermore it describes the facility of the crossing of social barriers for men – from the aristocratic Lady Jean, to whom Cockpen was married, to the common collier lassie. Nairne clearly kept an affiliation with this traditional song by using the same melody and by incorporating its first line in her story, though she changed it so that it was the Laird who bowed and not the lady who curtsied: 'An' when she cam ben he bowed fu' law'. While some women were keen to adhere closely to the traditional lyric, Nairne was clearly intent on presenting a more respectable view of the Laird and his wife.

Women's love songs were varied in content. Some, like Nairne's 'The Lass o' Gowrie', or Joanna Baillie's Irish song beginning 'The morning air plays on my face', celebrated women's beauty and described their suitability for marriage. Jean Glover's 'O'er the Moor amang the Heather' displayed the manipulative power of women: the beauty of Glover's heroine, and more especially her singing, ultimately induces her suitor to declare undying love for her.[38] 'The Laird o' Cockpen' gave a glimpse of women's independence of mind, but tied this ultimately to social respectability. Others took this independence one step further. Roy's wife in Mrs Grant of Carron's (1745–1814) 'Roy's Wife of Aldivalloch' is described as a 'faithless quean' who leaves her husband for another man. This song was popular because Roy's wife is criticised for her action. Her independence is seen as a negative characteristic as it was with Miss McClish. While Nairne and Grant were keen on upholding the institution of marriage, some, including Joanna Baillie, were derisive. Her version of the traditional song 'Hooly and Fairly' was a bitter, sarcastic attack on the state of marriage. Beginning with the line 'Oh, neighbours! what had I a-do for to marry!', it concluded,

> I wish I were single, I wish I were freed;
> I wish I were doited, I wish I were dead,
> Or she in the mouls, to dement me nae mair, lay!
> What does it 'vail to cry hooly and fairly!
> Hooly and fairly, hooly and fairly,
> Wasting my breath to cry hooly and fairly!

Such powerful anti-marriage sentiments were the exception to the rule. Love and partnership were clearly what the majority of women sought. Most of their love songs spoke of the power of love which continued through the absence and even the death of the lover: the lesser-known Jane C. Simpson's (née Bell) 'Good-night', and 'He Loved Her for Her Merry Eye';[39] and Mrs Dugald Stewart's 'The Tears I Shed Must Ever Fall';[40] and the better-known Lady Nairne's 'Oh Never, Thou'lt Meet Me Again!; Joanna Baillie's 'The Gowan Glitters on the Sward', also known as 'The Shepherd's Song'; Lady Grisell Baillie's 'Werena my Heart Licht I Would Dee'; Lady John Scott's 'Durisdeer' or 'Ettrick'; Anne Grant's 'Oh, My Love, Leave Me Not!'; and Susanna Blamire's 'What Ails This Heart o' Mine' and her 'And Ye Shall Walk in Silk Attire' are just some of the examples. Lady Anne Barnard's famous 'Auld Robin Gray' was particularly popular because it too emphasised the power of true love in difficult circumstances. Though the narrator is betrothed to Jamie, she is compelled to marry Auld Robin Gray for financial stability as her parents have fallen ill. Jamie is at sea, and returns to find her already married. However, Robin Gray repents and promises release to his young wife:

> 'I've wronged her', he said, 'but I kent it o'er late;
> I've wronged her, and sorrow is speeding my date.
> But a's for the best, since my death will soon free,
> A faithfu' young heart, that was ill match'd wi' me.'[41]

Many of the songs connected with death were deeply spiritual. Mrs Agnes Lyon's (1762–1840) 'My Son George's Departure' thanks God for her son's existence rather than weighing heavily on his death, and Lady John Scott's 'Durisdeer' ends on a note of optimism, since she expresses her belief that she will meet her lover in heaven. The vogue for writing hymns and spiritual songs was stronger amongst the Scottish women songwriters of this period than it appears to have been amongst the men. Although hymns and devotional songs did not appear in general Scots song collections, nearly all the song books of individual writers – Carolina Nairne, Joanna Baillie, Lady John Scott – published in the nineteenth century had a special section for religious or sacred lyrics. The Glasgow poet Marion Paul Aird, who published her first collections of poetry in the 1840s, concentrated closely on religious lyrics.[42] Moreover Charles Rogers's edition entitled *The Sacred Minstrel* (1859) included the work of several other Scottish women: Isabella Craig, Margaret Crawford, Jane B. Simpson, Lady Flora Hastings and Mrs Margaret Inglis.

Religious lyrics such as Margaret Crawford's 'Day-dreams of Other Years', which looked philosophically at the span of woman's life, also spoke nostalgically of the home and child-hood. Songs of this nature were also common amongst women's songs of the period, and some, like Carolina Nairne's 'The Rowan Tree', have retained their popularity since they were first published. The majority of such lyrics hailed sentimentally from a childhood 'strewn with flowers'.[43] Nairne's coy references, in 'The Auld House', to the 'bairnies fu' o' glee', the 'wee dear auld house', 'the voices sweet, the wee bit feet', can be seen as anticipating nineteenth-century Kailyard sentimentality, and are typical of collections of such lyrics which proliferate at the turn of the century. The migration of families from country to city, or to foreign lands, naturally encouraged this highly charged emotional view of the home and the nation, and songs of this nature appeared in collections from the first decades of the nineteenth century: Mary Macarthur's 'The Missionary';[44] Carolina Nairne's 'Songs of My Native Land', or 'Her Home She is Leaving'; Margaret Crawford's 'The Emigrant's Farewell' or 'My Native Land'.[45]

There was one other genre of song which attracted several of the women songwriters and which became increasingly popular as the end of the eighteenth century approached. William Donaldson has stated that by the 1820s 'Jacobite song was confirmed as second only to the great body of love-song in the national canon and it maintained this position throughout the nineteenth century'.[46] Carolina Nairne, more than the other women songwriters of the period, was steeped in Jacobitism from her birth. Prince Charles Edward Stuart had visited her family house in Gask, Perthshire, her father had been actively involved in the '45 and her mother had even, as we are told in 'The Auld House', 'clipt a lock wi' her ain hand' from the Prince's 'lang yellow hair'. The profound effect of an upbringing in a Jacobite household, an experience which Nairne also shared with Lady Anne Barnard, was greatly emphasised by her biographers at the turn of the century, and it is clearly shown in the number of Jacobite songs she wrote. They ranged from the still popular 'Charlie is My Darling', 'The Hundred Pipers' and 'Will Ye no Come Back Again' to 'Charlie's Landing', 'Wha'll be King but Charlie', 'My Bonnie Hieland Laddie', 'Gathering Song' and 'He's Owre the Hills that I Lo'e Best'. As was the case with many of the Jacobite songs of the period, written by both men and women, the focus of the lyric was rarely, if ever, political. Nairne's 'Charlie's Landing' and 'Gathering Song' for example, set out to rouse a positive feeling for the Prince and his soldiers, but the majority of her songs, and those of others, were love songs concerned with Highlandry rather than Jacobitism. By the 1780s and '90s the physical threat of the Jacobites had dwindled and Jacobitism became the strongest outlet for Scottish national feeling. Women were generally uninterested in the nationalist element of Jacobitism, but they were clearly attracted by the idea of the Highland soldier and the Prince himself. Nairne, in 'Charlie's Landing', was surprisingly keen to roll the King in 'a tartan plaid' and give him 'Scotland's greeting'. This was perhaps naive for a woman keen to display good moral behaviour in her songs, for the tartan plaidie was commonly employed as a sexual symbol in literature of the period. Anne Grant of Laggan's 'Blue Bell of Scotland', also known as 'The Marquis of Huntly's Departure for the Continent with his Regiment', in 1799 ('Oh, where, tell me where, is your Highland Laddie gone?') was as popular in Europe as in Scotland.[47] Grant was also obviously in love with her hero who wore 'A bonnet with a lofty plume, the gallant badge of war,/And a plaid across the manly breast that yet shall wear a star'.[48] These songs were some of the most exciting of the canon, primarily due to their short, emphatic phrases, the descriptions of the Highlanders who were always larger than life and colourful, and their rhythmically rousing melodies. A fine example is Margaret Inglis's (1774–1843) 'Charlie's Bonnet's Down, Laddie' set to the tune 'Tullymet':

> Let Highland lads wi' belted plaids,
> And bonnets blue and white cockades,
> Put on their shields, unsheath their blades,
> And conquest fell begin;

> And let the word be Scotland's heir;
> And when their swords can do nae mair,
> Lang bowstrings o'their yellow hair
>   Let Hieland lasses spin, laddie,
>   Charlie's bonnet's down, laddie,
>   Kilt yer plaid and scour the heather;
>   Charlie's bonnet's down laddie,
>   Draw yer dirk and rin.[49]

One area which is missing from women's published songs of the period is the working song. Nairne's early lyric 'The Pleughman' and more especially her lively and descriptive, yet tragically evocative, 'Caller Herrin' go somewhere towards the tradition of rhythmic songs created specifically to accompany a physical task. Alison Cockburn's 'Poem on a Ball at Selkirk',[50] or Nairne's 'Kitty Reid's House', and 'The County Meeting', or Joanna Baillie's 'Hooly and Fairly' and 'Fy, Let's a' to the Wedding' are fast, spirited lyrics in the vernacular, which give the feeling of bustling activity, and they may indeed have some link with the oral tradition of working songs. But they are the exception to the majority of women's published songs. Jean Adam's 'The Song of the Mariner's Wife' (also known as 'There's nae Luck about the House') is more obviously connected with working women. Adam (1710–65) was the daughter of a shipmaster from Greenock, but was orphaned at an early age. Educated at a parish school, she became governess to a local minister where, in addition to her domestic duties, she read her way through the works of Shakespeare, Milton, and Samuel Richardson, and in 1734 produced her only publication entitled *Miscellany Poems*.[51]

Her only published song clearly called on her youth as a shipmaster's daughter. Written to match a spikey and rhythmic melody, 'The Song of the Mariner's Wife' exhibits a feeling of chaotic excitement expressed at the surprise return of the 'gudeman' from a long period at sea. With so little biographical material it is often impossible to discover the inspiration behind the songs themselves, unless the lyric is simply a variation on another published song. But this piece is so rigid in its rhythm that it may well be associated with women's work of some sort, and Adam does make a reference to spinning in the first verse:

> And are ye sure the news is true?
>   And are ye sure he's weel?
> Is this the time to think o' wark?
>   Ye jauds, fling by your wheel.
> Is this a time to think o'wark,
>   When Colin's at the door?
> Rax me my cloak, I'll to the quay,
>   And see him come ashore.
> For there's nae luck about the house,
>   There's nae luck at a';
> There's little pleasure in the house
>   When our gudeman's awa'.

At a time when several women novelists found themselves able to earn a living almost exclusively from their work,[52] it is interesting to note that the majority of them wrote songs for pleasure and most certainly not for financial gain. Many single songs, or groups of songs, were picked up by an editor who was looking for attractive pieces to include in a song collection. Such was the case with James Johnson in his *Scots Musical Museum* (1787–1803), or Charles Rogers in his *The Modern Scottish Minstrel* (1855–8). Consequently some women became famous for only one song: Jean (sometimes known as Jane) Elliot ('The Flowers of the Forest'); Jean Glover ('O'er the Moor amang the Heather'); Jean Adam ('The Song of the Mariner's Wife'); or Mrs Grant of Carron ('Roy's Wife of Aldivalloch'). Some editors approached writers to produce songs for specific publications. George Thomson commissioned Joanna Baillie, Anne Grant and Amelia Opie, amongst others, to produce new lyrics for traditional tunes to be included in his *Select Collection* of Scottish, Welsh and Irish airs (1793–1841). Likewise Robert Archibald Smith included several specially composed lyrics in his *Scottish Minstrel* (1821–4). This was the collection which included the first songs of Mrs Bogan of Bogan, the pseudonym of Carolina Nairne. While some women were unwilling to sell their creations for money, some were unwilling even to advertise themselves as the creator. Carolina Nairne managed to keep the authorship of many of her songs secret from her family as well as the public. As explained so vividly by Tytler and Watson, Nairne was part of a 'select circle' or lady songwriters, including the daughters of Baron Hume, who wrote songs for Smith's *Scottish Minstrel*. She was serious about her alter-ego and dressed as Mrs Bogan of Bogan, a 'country lady of a former generation', for her meetings with Purdie, the publisher of the collection. She wrote her manuscripts in different hands and apparently tried to conceal from the committee who read them that they were the work of a woman.[53]

Nairne was keen to avoid public recognition, but was happy to see her songs in print. Others tried to keep their songs for private use only, as Lady Anne Barnard explained:

> Happening to sing it ['Auld Robin Gray'] one day at Dalkeith-House, with more feeling perhaps than belonged to a common ballad, OUR friend Lady Frances Scott smiled, and, fixing her eyes on me, said, '*You* wrote this song yourself'. The blush that followed confirmed my *guilt*. Perhaps I blushed the more (being very young) from the recollection of the coarse words from which I borrowed the tune, and was afraid of the raillery which might have taken place if it had been discovered I had ever heard such.[54]

It was Sir Walter Scott who finally published the song through The Bannatyne Club when Lady Anne Barnard died in 1825. Like Lady Anne, Lady John Scott was generally highly sceptical about making her lyrics accessible to the public. Lady Scott allowed one or two songs, including 'Annie Laurie', to be published in aid of the widows and orphans of soldiers killed in the Crimean War, but the first collection of her songs appeared posthumously. Many of these women regarded their songs in the same personal light as the contents of a diary, and they could only be published if they were presented under a different name or when the author was dead. Many of Lady John Scott's songs were written for members of her family, or in memory of siblings, and so were undoubtedly circulated only amongst her close relatives.

This purposeful avoidance of public recognition may then mean that many of the anonymous songs included in collections of this period were also written by women. Jean Elliot's 'The Flowers of the Forest' and Susanna Blamire's 'And Ye Shall Walk in Silk Attire' were sometimes published without the author's name.[55] Anonymity lent these songs, the former of which was concerned with the battle of Flodden, a specially mysterious and timeless quality. Editors, like songwriters of the period, liked to believe that they were presenting genuine songs of the people. The educated Scots, who were wholly responsible for Scots song in its published form, were attracted by the idea that these songs were shared by all people. Eliza Cook in her long article on Scottish song published in 1852 expressed their sentiments exactly:

> Scotch songs are not 'pretty'. Though they have been the rage in drawing-rooms, they are yet born of the people. They were not meant to be merely ornamental; they were the growth of simple taste, of true feeling, often of intense passion: Love, joy and patriotism are their inspiration; not an *affected* feeling of things, but real, earnest, genuine feeling. Their power seizes hold of you.[56]

Though Cook's statement was the widely accepted view of the educated classes, the published songs of the period were not always the simplest expressions of human emotion. Song had became a highly complex art form by the eighteenth century. While some writers absorbed traditional songs as they were, and believed that they contained invaluable messages from previous generations, most writers grasped the traditional folk songs and ballads as templates which were to be altered and improved in order to educate the present generations. Under the auspices of this simple and 'genuine' form, there were complicated and detailed messages which set moral standards and laid down accepted patterns of behaviour.

In attempts to find the 'authentic' in song and lyrical poetry during the twentieth century, these writers have been discarded by many as representing an 'artificial' tradition. It cannot be denied that songwriters of this period stole from an oral tradition and moulded their swag into something new, supposedly less genuine and often variable in quality. But their songs nevertheless paint a vivid picture of personal, and thus social and political preoccupations. Present research suggests that the work of these writers deserves attention not simply because of the quantity of material, but, more importantly, because these songs, taken with the great Scottish Ballad tradition, make a crucial contribution to the renaissance of the lyric tradition in the early twentieth century.

Notes

1. Margaret Stewart Simpson, *The Scottish Songstress: Caroline Baroness Nairne*, (Anderson & Ferrier, Edinburgh and London, 1894) p. 7.
2. S. Tytler & J. L. Watson, *The Songstresses of Scotland*, 2 vols (Strahan & Co., London, 1871). These volumes include general essays on Lady Grisell Baillie, Jean Adam, Mrs Cockburn, Jean Elliot, Susanna Blamire, Jean Glover, Elizabeth Hamilton, Lady Anne Barnard, Carolina Baroness Nairne and Joanna Baillie.
3. H. Lonsdale edited *The Poetical Works* of Susanna Blamire (John Menzies, Edinburgh, 1842). Its preface, memoir and notes were prepared by Patrick Maxwell. The Woodstock Facsimile series edited by Jonathan Wordsworth produced a facsimile of this edition in 1994.
4. Rogers produced *The Life and Songs of the Baroness Nairne: With a Memoir and poems of Caroline Oliphant the younger* (J. Grant, London, 1869). He also edited two large collections of songs: *The Modern Scottish Minstrel: or the Songs of Scotland of the Past Century*, 6 vols (A. & C. Black, Edinburgh, 1855–8), and *The Sacred Minstrel: a Collection of Spiritual Songs with Biographical Sketches of the Authors* (Hulston & Wright, London, 1859).
5. This number estimate is based primarily on those sellers listed in C. Humphries & W. C. Smith, *Music Publishing in the British Isles from the Beginning until the Middle of the Nineteenth Centuries*, 2nd edn (Blackwell, Oxford, 1970), and F. Kidson, *British Music Publishers, Printers and Engravers* (W. & E. Hill and Sons, London, 1900).
6. T. Crawford, *Society and the Lyric* (Scottish Academic Press, Edinburgh, 1979), ix. Crawford stated: 'the lyric strand in eighteenth-century Scottish culture was not narrowly or

parochially Scottish, but a part of a general, all-British lyric culture'. See also *Love, Labour and Liberty: The Eighteenth-Century Scottish Lyic,* ed. T. Crawford, (Carcanet, Manchester, 1976).

7.   For discussion of the conflict between Scottish national music and compositions from the European mainstream see G. F. Graham, *An Account of the First Edinburgh Musical Festival* (William Blackwood, Edinburgh and London, 1816). See also W. Tytler, 'Dissertation on the Scottish Music', *Transactions of the Society of Antiquaries of Scotland* (Edinburgh and London), 1792, 469–510.

8.   The three most important publications were *Scots Musical Museum* (J. Johnson, Edinburgh, 1787–1803), the *Minstrelsy of the Scottish Border* (J. Ballantyne for Longman & Rees, Kelso, 1802–3) and the *Jacobite Relics of Scotland* (William Blackwood, 1819–21).

9.   Including his *Scots Songs* (1718), *The Ever Green* (Ruddiman, Edinburgh, 1724) and the *Tea-Table Miscellany* (Ruddiman, Edinburgh, 1724).

10.   C. Kerrigan, *Anthology of Scottish Women's Poets,* (Edinburgh University Press, Edinburgh, 1991) p. 2. Kerrigan writes that 'women played such a significant role as tradition bearers and transmitters that it can be claimed that the ballad tradition is one of the most readily identifiable areas of literary performance by women'.

11.   While ballads were frequently long and always detailed in their narrative content they were almost always performed with music. The literary terms used to describe songs in this period were ballad, lay and lyric. In fact all of them were intended to be sung, though the ballad usually related to people or places, the lay to history and romance, and the lyric to expressing the poet's own thoughts or sentiments. Both the lay and the lyric were described as short pieces.

12.   *The Letters of Robert Burns,* ed. J. De Lancey Ferguson & G. Ross Roy, (Clarendon Press, Oxford, 1985), I, p. 135 (no. 125).

13.   *The Songs of Robert Burns,* ed. D. A. Low, (Routledge, London, 1993), pp. 4–11.

14.   *The Letters of Robert Burns,* I, pp. 137–8 (no. 125).

15.   In 1824 she became Baroness. She is often referred to as 'Lady Nairne' and her Christian name appears both as Caroline and Carolina.

16.   *The Poets of Ayrshire from the Fourteenth Century Till the Present Day,* ed. J. Macintosh, (T. Hunter, Dumfries, 1910).

17.   J. Johnson, *The Scots Musical Museum,* ed. D. A. Low (Scolar Press, Aldershot, 1991), IV, p. 338 (no. 328). See also 'Notes on Scottish Songs by Robert Burns', published in the above, or separately edited by James C. Dick (London and Edinburgh, 1908), p. 57. Burns wrote that he 'took the song down from her [Glover's] singing, as she was strolling through the country, with a sleight-of-hand blackguard'.

18.   W. Stenhouse, *Illustrations of the Lyric Poetry and Music of Scotland* (William Blackwood, Edinburgh and London, 1853), pp. 315–6. Pagan, known as 'Tibbie', was disabled from youth and was estranged from her family. She lived alone, though had many visitors to sample her whisky and her apparently beautiful singing.

19.   *Scottish Poetry of the Eighteenth Century,* ed. G. Eyre-Todd, (W. Hodge, Glasgow, 1896), II, pp. 38–9. Eyre-Todd noted that this song subsequently appeared in two other versions, one written by Rev. Henry S. Riddell and the other by Hamilton Nimmo.

20.   Johnson, *Scots Musical Museum,* III, p. 273 (no. 264).

21.   *The Songs of Robert Burns,* nos 64 and 260. Low notes that no 64, which is the version supposedly written by Pagan, is found also in the Hastie MS, and that the second version, which is more commonly known now, was found in the Dalhousie MS.

22.   *The Songs of Robert Burns,* nos 64 and 260.

23.   A debate raged for decades over the authorship of 'The Land o' the Leal', which many believed was written by Burns, but which was always included in collections of songs of Carolina Nairne. See G. Henderson, *Lady Nairne and her Songs* (Gardner, Paisley & London, 1905), p. 51. See also A. Crichton, *The Land o' the Leal: The Deathbed Valediction of Robert Burns* (Edinburgh, 1919). Nairne wrote many songs which were inspired by the same melodies as Burns: 'The Lea-rig', 'Down the Burn Davie', 'Comin' thro' the Rye', 'Here's a Health to Ane I lo'e Dear' etc.

24.   *Eighteenth Century Women: An Anthology,* ed. B. Hill (Routledge, London, 1987), p. 45. Hill states that these subjects also formed the curriculum of most girls' schools. See 'Part Three: Female Education', pp. 44–68.

25.   There is no evidence that she knew Scots songs, or the work of any of the popular Scottish writers before her visits to Gartmore. Blamire was often referred to as 'The Muse of Cumberland' and while writing in Scots and standard English, she also wrote in a Cumberland dialect which is very similar to Scots. See *The Songs and Ballads of Cumberland*, ed. Sidney Gilpin (G. Routledge, London, 1866). See also S. Blamire, *The Poetical Works*, ed. H. Lonsdale & P. Maxwell (Edinburgh, 1842), xxviii.

26.   Blamire, *The Poetical Works*, xxii–xxxiii. See also *Susanna Blamire 'The Muse of Cumberland': A Tribute with Selections from her Work* (Carlisle, 1994), p. 6. This pamphlet contains many essays and commentaries and was produced by the Lakeland Dialect Society for the bicentenary of Blamire's death.

27.   *The Household Book of Lady Grisell Baillie 1692–1733*, ed. R. Scott-Moncrieff (T. & A. Constable for the Scottish History Society, Edinburgh, 1911), xli, xlviii, xxviii.

28.   Her daughter Grisell (known as 'Grisie'), later Lady Murray of Stanhope, was famous in both London and Edinburgh for her singing. See *ibid.*, xxviii. See also Lady Murray of Stanhope, *Memoirs of the Lives and Characters of the Right Honourable George Baillie of Jerviswood and of Lady Grisell Baillie* (printed at Edinburgh, 1822).

29.   Joanna Baillie's letter to George Thomson, December 1836: British Library Add. MS 35265, ff. 249–50.

30.   Margaret S. Carhart, *The Life and Work of Joanna Baillie* (Yale University Press, Yale & Oxford, 1923), p. 7.

31.   Lady John Scott, *Poems and Songs* (D. Douglas, Edinburgh, 1904), p. xv. This volume has an introductory memoir Lady John Scott written by her grand-niece, Margaret Warrender. Though she was writing from the 1830s, this was the first major publication of her works.

32.   George Thomson's letter to David Vedder, 21 December 1829. British Library Add. MS 35269, ff. 9–10.

33.   J. Baillie, *Fugitive Verses* (E. Moxon, London, 1840), p. 275.

34.   *Life and songs of the Baroness Nairne*, pp. 170–1.

35.   George Thomson, who published Nairne's song in 1824, and again in the 1840s, stated that the song was frequently made more respectable in performance by this coda: 'The Editor hopes the Author will pardon him for thus terminating the courtship, to which he was induced by having observed that the song, as generally sung, rarely escapes without some sort of postscript matrimonial'. See Thomson's *Select Collection of Original Scottish Airs*, vol. V (Muir Wood, Edinburgh, 1843), no. 250.

36.   Johnson, *Scots Musical Museum*, IV, pp. 364–5 (no. 353).

37.   L. Stone, *The Family, Sex and Marriage in England 1500–1800* (Weidenfeld & Nicolson, London, 1977; Penguin, Harmondsworth, 1979), p. 338.

38.   Johnson, *Scots Musical Museum*, IV, p. 338 (no. 328).

39.   *The Modern Scottish Minstrel*, ed. C. Rogers (Edinburgh, 1855–8), V, pp. 241–7.

40.   *The Modern Scottish Minstrel*, I, pp. 167–71.

41.   *Lays of the Lindsays; being Poems by the Ladies of the House of Balcarres* (Edinburgh, 1824), pp. 3–14.

42.   *The Modern Scottish Minstrel*, ed. C. Rogers (Edinburgh, 1855–8), V, pp. 258–62.

43.   Margaret Crawford's 'Day-Dreams of Other Years', *ibid.*, VI, pp. 209–11.

44.   *The Modern Scottish Minstrel*, V, p. 111.

45.   *The Modern Scottish Minstrel*, VI, pp. 206–7.

46.   W. Donaldson, *The Jacobite Song: Political Myth and National Identity* (Aberdeen University Press, Aberdeen, 1988), p. 109.

47.   A copy of this song exists in a handwritten songbook belonging to Ulrica von Pogwisch and now kept at the Goethe-Schiller-Archiv in Weimar (GNM 942). Haydn also wrote variations on the melody, and he set several of Anne Hunter's lyrics for his *English Canzonettas* published in London in 1794 and 1795.

48.   Anne Grant, *Poems* (Longman & Co., Edinburgh, 1803), pp. 407–9.

49.   *The Modern Scottish Minstrel*, ed. C. Rogers, IV, pp. 77–8.

50.   *Letters and Memoir of her own life by Mrs Alison Rutherford or Cockburn*, ed. T. Craig-Brown (printed for D. Douglas, Edinburgh, 1900), pp. 268–9.

51.   She founded a girl's school in Greenock, but this venture was unsuccessful and she died in a Glasgow poorhouse in 1765.

52.   Cheryl Turner, *Living by the Pen: Women writers in the Eighteen Century* (Routledge, London, 1992). Also *Living by the Pen: Early British Women Writers*, ed. Dale Spender (Teachers' College Press, London and New York, 1992).

53.   Tytler & Watson, *Songstresses*, II, pp. 134–7. See also *Life and Songs of the Baroness Nairne*, ed. C, Rogers (Edinburgh, 1896), pp. 43–8.

54.   *Lays of the Lindsays; being Poems by the Ladies of the House of Balcarres* (Edinburgh, 1824), p. 4.

55.   George Thomson, *Select Collection of Original Scottish Airs* (Edinburgh, 1801), II, p. 81 and I, p. 44 respectively.

56.   E. Cook, *Eliza Cook's Journal*, no. 174, VII (John Owen Clarke, London, 1852), p. 276.

5

Selves and Others:
Non-fiction Writing in the Eighteenth
and Early Nineteenth Centuries

Dorothy McMillan

The eighteenth century was for Scotland the kind of period that makes sense of the Chinese curse, 'May you live in interesting times'. It was a time neither comfortable nor stable and yet it moved, admittedly at great cost to some, toward the great intellectual flourishing of the turn of the century and beyond, and in its course, the way was paved for the commercial successes of Victorian Scotland. It is framed at one end by the 'killing time' of the 1680s and at the other by the economic upheavals and radical troubles of the early years of the nineteenth century. In between, Scotland saw the Union of 1707, the Jacobite Risings of 1715 and 1745 and the resultant reprisals, followed by the romanticisation of the Highlands. But it is equally the time of the Scottish Enlightenment working toward the intellectual ascendancy of the end of the century. It is, of course, possible to vary both the frame and the picture but it is not easy to avoid the evidence of a confused mixture of suffering and disaster with achievement and optimism.[1] Much shaping activity was proceeding as part of both conscious and unconscious national definition – and national here may be taken to mean both the notion of Scotland and that of Britain. The second half of the eighteenth century in particular was a time of consolidation of meanings of Scottishness and a time of construction of ways of Britishness.[2]

It certainly seems easier to demonstrate the ways in which non-fictional writing responds to and helps to shape the ideologies of its time than with fiction, poetry and drama. In some cases women's writing is a direct result of political pressures, might not indeed have existed at all but for specific historical circumstances. I am thinking of letters written to absent family or memoirs of people and places arising from unavoidable travel. All the early letters from women in the Dunlop family papers fall into these categories.[3] The women of the Dunlop family stayed at home and wrote to absent husbands or brothers: the letters of Sarah Carstares to her husband, William Dunlop, 'My dearst and desirable heart', in exile from the 'killing times' in Carolina, are particularly moving in their combination of practicality and affection.[4] Margaret Calderwood, on the other hand, was later given the opportunity herself to be a travel writer by the aftermath of the 'Forty-five Jacobite Rising. Her brother, Sir James Stewart, had assisted the Jacobites and deemed it prudent to flee to the Continent. His sister, worried about his welfare, travelled to Brussels through the Low Countries, keeping a diary as she went. Her lively anti-English prejudices and indeed a general unwillingness to be impressed by 'abroad' make her a more delightful female Smollett:

We used to laugh at the English for being so soon afraid when there was any danger in state affairs, but now I do excuse them. For we, at a distance, think the wisdom of our governors will prevent all these things; but those who know and see our ministers every day see there is no wisdom in them, and that they are a parcell of old, ignorant, senseless bodies, who mind nothing but eating and drinking, and rolling about in Hyde Park, and know no more of the country, or the situation of it, than they never had been in it; or how should they, when London, and twenty miles round it, is the extent ever they saw of it.[5]

Biography too is often conditioned by political pressures. When Lady Murray came to write the life of her mother, Lady Grisell Baillie, she found, as I shall show, that the plot of the memoir was governed by the political events which shaped her mother's early life.[6]

Selves and Others

The female non-fictional writing of the eighteenth and early nineteenth century falls into the categories one would expect. There is a great deal of work of primarily domestic origin like household books or letters and memoirs often privately circulated, although not printed. Biographies of family and friends belong to a wider but still mainly private community. Travel writing also usually consists of letters to family and friends, although by the early nineteenth century more publicly conceived travel writing was becoming commoner. Didactic writing was usually educationally slanted but by the early nineteen century became increasingly feminist in import, even when otherwise politically conservative. Indeed it can be argued that even the didactic writing that upheld the concept of the woman's sphere was based on a feminism no less aggressive for seeming to know its place.

These categories of non-fictional writing are not exclusive to Scottish women's writing and although the political situations differed for the three countries, other conditions under which Scottish women produced non-fictional writing before about the middle of the nineteenth century were probably not significantly different from those of their English, Welsh or even Irish sisterhood. Such writing was most likely to be generated and certainly preserved by the aristocracy, the gentry or the upper middle-class. It seldom addressed itself too contentiously to notions of nation partly because, given the social and political conditions of its production, it came out of a society which often crossed borders; sometimes, especially after the middle of the eighteenth century, had actual familial relations across the border or across the Irish Channel. For example Lady Murray of Stanhope who wrote the life of her mother, the Scottish heroine, Lady Grisell Baillie, lived for most of her life in London. Similarly *The Letters and Works of Lady Mary Wortley Montagu* edited by Lord Wharncliffe, themselves not published until nearly three-quarters of century after that most remarkable woman's death, are prefaced by 'Introductory Anecdotes' written by her granddaughter, Lady Louisa Stuart, Lord Wharncliffe's aunt. Lady Louisa may easily be claimed as a Scottish woman writer but she was brought up largely at Luton Hoo outside London. This tribute to her grandmother was the only time Lady Louisa Stuart sanctioned printed publication but she essayed poems and letters, of course, and wrote for private circulation a memoir of her friend, Frances, Lady Douglas, as a tribute to her friend and an offering to Frances Douglas's daughter, Caroline Scott.

This kind of writing, then, derived from familial and class interests and can seldom be felt as coloured principally by national prejudice or predilection. Indeed insofar as the women themselves may have lived for substantial periods outside Scottish boundaries, it is hard to see Scottish women's private writing, in the eighteenth century at least, as a distinctively national phenomenon. And yet some of this writing may seem to us now, as it did to some contemporaries, to demand interrogation as the product of a peculiarly place-engendered or place-conscious vision. Sometimes we are alerted to the significance of place by contemporary comment as when Scott compares the social life established by Edinburgh hostesses like Alison Cockburn to Paris rather than London.[7] Sometimes, however, we find ourselves peculiarly discoverers of a previously unavailable culture of place, enabled by distance to make pronouncements about the conditionings of place and cultivation which could, because of the refusal of print, only have been available to contemporary coteries. And these coteries might in any case have taken as norms, linguistic and social traces that we now find significant, indicative or even exceptional.

What we are able to discern from this non-fictional work is a habit of writing, consistent, conventional even, which refuses, however, to become a tradition available to posterity, because extensive publication never occurred. Yet in spite of this reticence, a kind of subterranean tradition existed which was at least partially known to, and drawn upon by, some of its practitioners. The circulation of private writing was often greater than is suggested by its initial addressees. This circulation was again, of course, not an exclusively Scottish phenomenon: circulation of private writing depended more on class than on place and hence occurred in London as well as Edinburgh. Lady Louisa Stuart's biographical anecdotes of Lady Mary Wortley Montagu make it clear that Lady Mary effectively published letters which included journal extracts, although she never communicated the whole of her diary to any other individual:

> It seemed her custom to note everything down without a moment's delay; and then, when she wrote a letter, to transcribe from the journal the passages she thought fittest to be communicated to her friends, or, one may say, to the world. For, although she did not design the correspondence for publication while she was living, she had it copied, and allowed many people to read it. The diary of course contained further details; but the cream having been skimmed for the letters, the rest was not very interesting or important.[8]

There was then generally a tradition of 'publicity' in private correspondence even where print was eschewed. More specifically, in the biographical memoir, where women celebrated the lives of other women, it is possible to discern a female tradition motivated by piety, love and a sense of shared values. And these values were often cross-generational, linking women with their real or spiritual mothers and sisters. Among the most moving of such biographical tributes is the memoir of her mother, Lady Grisel Baillie, by Lady Murray of Stanhope to which I have referred. The memoir was published in 1824 from Lady Murray's papers but was originally written in 1749 and, as the Preface indicates, 'plainly not intended for the public eye ... drawn up only for the gratification and instruction of [Lady Murray's] own relatives' (*Memoirs*, p. vii). Mrs Anne Grant of Laggan (discussed in detail in Chapter 8) who read and commented on everything, admired the memoir, noting the superiority of its 'living' qualities to the fictionalised version of Grisel Baillie's later and less close descendant: 'I feel more interested by her [Lady Murray's] unadorned prose than by Miss Baillie's metrical sketch from it'.[9] Lady Murray's literary modesty is, of course, the very stamp of the memoir's authenticity. She is insistent both on the significance of her task and her inadequacy to perform it:

> I am desirous of nothing so much as to preserve, and make known to her family, what I have observed in my dear mother's life and character; and also those things I well remember to have often heard her tell of, which passed in her younger years. Though it has often been in my thoughts, my unfitness to do it has hindered my setting about it . . . all I can remember must be trifling, compared to what a judicious observer might relate, that had access to know her well. (*Memoirs*, p. 32)

It is, of course, in what is 'trifling' that character in general, and the character of women in particular, may often be discerned. Lady Murray is the source of most of the information about her mother that Joanna Baillie later used in her 'Metrical Legend'.[10] Lady Murray charts her mother's childhood heroism during the troubles of Charles II's time when she visited her grandfather in prison and later ministered to her father who was in hiding in a vault of Polwarth church. Lady Murray neglects to comment on the wider political scene which necessitated her mother's heroism: this is a wholly personal memoir. Yet the social and political pressures on Lady Grisell and her unfailing subordination of self to country and family emerge in a manner that makes both mother and daughter seem peculiarly unself-pitying, although perfectly aware of both the circumscription and the compensatory powers of their women's lives. Lady Grisell Baillie's commitment to the family from her earliest days is largely the reason why her most substantial literary monument is her *Household Book* and not her songs.[11] Her daughter describes the interruption of her compositions during the family's exile in Utrecht: 'I have now a book of songs of her writing when there; many of them interrupted, half writ, some broke off in the middle of a sentence' (*Memoirs*, p. 49). But these are the days that Lady Grisell later described to her children as 'the happiest and most delightful of her life'. Paradoxically they were also days of exile when traditionally we might feel that loss would overbear enjoyment. But Lady Grisell's future husband was also there in exile and Lady Murray gives the sense of a lively group living on wit and ingenious making-do with that kind of solidarity that actually depends on loss rather than possession.

This kind of private writing which is designed for familial or coterie reading is, of course, difficult to discuss in aesthetic terms – revision by its original author would be almost a violation of its conditions of production, arguing a kind of insincerity which might entail generic invalidation, since the kind of shaping and polish that would be looked for in declared fiction might well be felt suspicious in the unvarnished 'truth' of letter and memoir. Hence, perhaps, the critical tendency to find as much interest in private writing in what seems to be accidentally revealed as in what is overtly claimed. It can, of course, be argued that this critical method is usefully employable for all writing, but it must have a peculiar point for writing which is not designed for the aesthetic fixity of novel or poem, which might even be perpetuated against, as it were, its own will.

At the same time in these familial memoirs the conditions of fiction do sometimes obtrude themselves. The eulogy of Lady Grisell Baillie by her daughter moves forwards with a sense of destiny. The destiny is a domestic rather than a public one but it is reached because other possibilities are set aside in the interests of a greater good. Fictional convention was already likely to chart the movement of hero or heroine from obscurity to fame and so the plot of Grisell Baillie's life from heroine to wife and mother peculiarly reverses and obliquely comments upon the fictional norm. Lady Murray's artless sincerity may be more insinuating than it at first appears.

Lady Louisa Stuart's memoir of her dear friend, Lady Frances Scott, written for Lady Scott's daughter, Caroline, is motivated like Lady Murray's memoir, by love, but even more clearly betrays the shaping drive of the novelist, especially in its construction of its minor characters. Lady Louisa seems to have been endowed with the satiric and observational skills peculiar to the kind of fiction which was developing at the turn of the century and, while she is anxious to protect the pure authenticity of her beloved subject, she exercises these skills on the surrounding cast, preserving Lady Frances as a woman in the midst of monstrous caricatures. Thus Lady Greenwich becomes the villain of the story but a new and interesting kind of villain in that she, the natural mother of the subject, exhibits all the traditional characteristics of the wicked stepmother, or, as Lady Louisa calls her, the bad fairy:

> You were forewarned, dear Car, that Lady Greenwich's portrait would be reserved for your private perusal. I fear I cannot sketch it with tolerable impartiality. She always does and will present herself to my mind as a wicked witch, a malignant fairy, the Carabosse or Fanfreluche of the tales that amused my childhood.[12]

Lady Louisa's instinct then is to write Lady Greenwich in the public mode of tale or novel, while the private mode of intimate memoirs allows her to get away with it.

But let us pause a little to chart where Lady Louisa fits in to the larger story of women's writing of the period. Lady Louisa Stuart (1757–1851), the eleventh and youngest child of the third Earl of Bute, briefly George III's Prime Minister, and Mary, daughter of Lady Mary Wortley Montagu, is descended, therefore, from the first Duke of Argyll, belonging to one of the great Scottish houses but brought up primarily in and around London, principally at Luton Hoo which Lady Louisa disliked. She came, partly through her friend and subject, Lady Frances Scott, to love Scotland and to spend as much time there as possible. Here she speaks of her first flight to Scotland with her newly married friend:

> You know, I believe, that I went down with them, and as it was my first flight from the nest you will conceive how the journey And every other novelty delighted me – Dalkeith and it's [sic], environs, Rosline castle, Hawthornden, Leith races, Edinburgh, Holyrood, Dr Robertson, Dr Blair, all the places and all the people I had been many a day longing to behold. (*Memoire of Lady Douglas*, p. 95)

Lady Louisa later collaborated with Sir Walter Scott on the unfinished 'Private Letters of the Seventeenth Century'. Scott praised highly both her literary and personal qualities: 'Lady Louisa unites what are rarely found together, a perfect tact such as few even in the highest classes attain with an uncommon portion of that rare quality which is called genius'.[13] It is in connection with Sir Walter Scott's praise of Lady Louisa Stuart's taste and judgement that her Scottishness is usually remarked but it is also the case that she herself never speaks of Scotland negatively, it is constantly a place of emotional sustenance.

Lady Louisa wrote a great deal, allowed some of her work to circulate among her intimates and sanctioned the publication in print of her biographical memoirs of her notorious grandmother, Lady Mary Wortley Montagu, although she was furious with the exposure of her authorship in a rather unkind review by John Wilson Croker in the February 1837 issue of the *Quarterly Review*. Lady Louisa wrote to Lady Louisa Bromley:

> Yes truly, in my opinion Croker has outdone even himself in impertinence. I confess my fingers itch to give him a suitable reply; he has laid himself open to it repeatedly. What

provoked *me* – me personally – the most, is his naming me outright, which as Lord
Wharncliffe [the editor of Lady Mary's works] had not done, nobody else had a right to do;
and only a blackguard like him would have done. (Montagu, *Essays and Poems*, p. 55)

This must strike the modern reader as an almost pathological fear of publicity, even for
the time, and especially when what is at issue is not poetry (which she did essay) or
fiction but biography. J. Steven Watson and Jill Rubenstein write sensitively about the
forces that fuelled Lady Louisa's fear of acknowledged authorship in print. In her youth
she had been warned off writing because of the increasing notoriety of her grandmother
in a later, more genteel period. When this is added to her aristocratic hauteur and her,
perhaps gendered, literary timidity, then something of the reason for her detestation of
publicity may emerge.[14] Jill Rubenstein stresses her fears that print inevitably brought loss
of caste, even where publication was anonymous:

> Lamenting the anonymous publication of *Trevelyan* by Lady Caroline Scott [for whom she
> wrote the *Memoire*], Lady Louisa wrote: *Trevelyan* is as much blown, I am afraid, as if the
> name were affixed to it. I say 'I am afraid,' for I will own to your private ear that I cannot
> get over my old – perhaps *aristocratic* – prejudices, which make it a loss of caste'. She used
> that same telling phrase – 'loss of caste' – to deplore Maria Edgeworth's published fiction.
> (*Memoire of Lady Douglas*, Introduction, pp. 5–6)

It was probably, then, generous concern for her nephew Lord Wharncliffe, Lady Mary's
editor, that persuaded her to allow publication of the 'Biographical Anecdotes' and she
was certainly right to fear that her cover would be quickly blown. The 'Anecdotes'
remain a most valuable source of information about Lady Mary, not that Lady Louisa
knew her – she was only five when her grandmother died – but Lady Mary formed part
of the mythology of her family life and what is believed about the famous by those
close to them is often as revealing as what is true. Lady Louisa in terms of 'truth' did,
however, have access to Lady Mary's diary before it was destroyed by Lady Bute and
she read the correspondence before it was edited (Montagu, *Essays and Poems*, p. 6).
Lady Louisa is the only source for such stories as the nomination of the eight-year-
old Lady Mary by her father as the toast of the Kit-cat club (he followed this up by
having her portrait painted to hang there). With a father like this what hope of self-
effacement? Lady Louisa is also the origin of the explanation of the feud with Pope
in Lady Mary's immoderate fit of laughter when Pope made passionate love to her
(Montagu, *Essays and Poems*, p. 9; p. 37). Lady Louisa has no difficulty in understanding
Pope's reaction, although even-handedly she recognises his meannesses too. Of more
interest than these fashionable stories, however, is her account of the persecution from
high and low that Lady Mary encountered during her courageous attempt to introduce
small-pox vaccination from the East. Lady Mary was wont to take her little daughter,
who had been innoculated, with her into sick-rooms, to prove her security from
infection:

> A child, especially a solitary child, if intelligent, attends to what passes before it, much earlier
> and more heedfully than people imagine. From six years old upwards, Lady Bute could see
> the significant shrugs of the nurses and servants, and observe the looks of dislike they cast at
> her mother. She also overheard anxious parents repeating to Lady Mary the arguments that
> had been used to deter them from venturing upon the trial; and aunts and grandmothers, in

the warmth of their zeal against it, quoting the opinion of this doctor or that apothecary. (Montagu, *Essays and Poems*, p. 36)

In such ways Lady Louisa neatly conveys Lady Mary but also what it must have been like to be her daughter.

An economy of means also informs the *Memoire of Frances, Lady Douglas* but its tone is modified by the love that is its motive force. I have suggested that Lady Louisa's method allows Frances Douglas to emerge as a woman among monsters in a way similar to Jane Austen's procedures with her Fanny except that Frances Douglas is less insipid. Lady Greenwich, the wicked mother, is wonderfully drawn with careless toughness:

> Now for the likeness – Lady Greenwich sallied every morning at the earliest visiting hour, entered the first house she found open, and there, in a voice rivalling the horn, published all the matches intrigues and divorces she had heard of; predicted as many more; descanted on the shameful behaviour of the women and the scandalous profligacy of the men; wondered what the world would come to – then bawled a little on public events, made war or peace; and, having emptied her whole budget, patched it afresh to carry it to another door, and another, and another, until dinner-time called her home. The rounds of the newspaper were not a bit more regular or certain. (*Memoire of Lady Douglas*, pp. 31–2)

But it is Lady Louisa's portrait of Charles Townshend, Frances Douglas's stepfather, and his relationship with his stepdaughter that is the triumph of the *Memoire*. Townshend married Frances's mother for primarily financial reasons and his infidelities were common knowledge. His attachment to his stepdaughter, however, was clearly deep if dangerous: he protected her from her unloving mother as far as he could but he also found in her youthful presence and conversation solace for his ruined public career. Lady Louisa's analysis of the bond between them is most subtle:

> Mr Townshend's partiality had itself given her unspeakable pain, by exciting continual uneasiness at it's excess, and terrifying apprehensions of it's nature. Do not mistake me however – he never was guilty of the least impropriety, never made the most distant approach to any personal freedom. He idolized her mind alone; seeming hardly to recollect she had a person: and perhaps the very consciousness that there was nothing sensual in his passion rendered him the less solicitous to put any curb upon it. But still *passion* it was – passion marked by it's engrossing tendency, it's overwhelming and uncontrollable force: in which she could not help feeling a something distinct from the paternal tenderness he used to show her. (*Memoire of Lady Douglas*, p. 46)

This seems a most intelligent grasp of what is *embodied* in an intellectual obsession which is in its own way abuse. Frances Douglas escaped from this net with Townshend's consent, since he sufficiently knew himself to comprehend her fears and when she did escape, she went to Scotland to Dalkeith House with her newly married brother and sister-in-law. There given her 'native genuine taste for all that was picturesque, romantic or poetical . . . the variety of rock, mountain torrent, waterfall, and sea-prospect, might fairly excite sensations approaching to rapture' (*Memoire of Lady Douglas*, p. 50).

Frances Douglas's story has a happy ending as she wins in gentle strength of character through all vicissitudes, including some turbulent property wrangles, to the age's ideal of happy, dutiful wife and mother. Jill Rubenstein guesses that the method of the narrative suggests the expectation of a wider audience than Frances's daughter, and hopes that Lady Louisa would have been happy to think of its eventual presentation to posterity: the guilt of editors, of course, necessarily engenders such hopes, but the absence of any injunctions against publication seems at least not to militate against Jill Rubenstein's case. And yet I am not sure: I think, at least, that in order to write in the first place, Lady Louisa had to persuade herself that any perusing eye would be a sympathetic one and one that would understand the issues of caste as well as morality that she engages with.

Alison Cockburn (1713–94)

The writing of Alison (Alicia) Rutherford Cockburn too is conditioned to a large extent by the audiences that it envisages. Alison Cockburn like Lady Anne Lindsay Barnard, who will be discussed in chapter 8, is celebrated for what we might now think of as her minor work. She is enshrined in literary history for her version of 'The Flowers o' the Forest', and this mood piece, first printed in *The Lark* (Edinburgh, 1765), stands in Scottish literary history in place of her more clearly social and intellectual writing. This to some extent reflects the contemporary popularity of the song: she came to be identified with it and was frequently asked for copies in her own hand.[15] But this contemporary opinion has certainly been reinforced by subsequent tendencies to privilege 'imaginative' writing over the workaday genres of letters and journals.[16] Of course, it has not merely been the work of women that has suffered from a critical bias in favour of fictions but since the work of women was, at least until the nineteenth century more often located in the 'private' realm, more of it has until recently so suffered.

As I have suggested a great deal of this private work was not really private, although it was clearly public only within specific classes or groups. The intellectual and social lives of eighteenth-century Scottish women of the upper classes were, unsurprisingly, intertwined. For example, Alison Cockburn was intimately connected with Lady Anne Barnard through her friendship with Lady Anne's mother, the Countess of Balcarres. Consequently the subject matter of their writing also overlaps: both Alison Cockburn and Anne Barnard write about the eccentric and sexually ambivalent Sophia (Soph) Johnstone brought up as 'a child of nature'.[17] And so once more, we find a literary tradition of a private sort, in this case more firmly Scottish, linking these women even though they did not put their work into print. Alison Cockburn indeed amusingly makes it clear from her letters that what was written by herself and her peers was seldom very private. Here she writes to her favourite correspondent, the Reverend Dr Douglas, about the fate of her birthday letter from him:

> A lady, a particular favourite was alone with me when I got it. You are right not to trust me with good letters. You might as well send me an ortolon [sic] to eat alone. That she heard me read the letter, that she put it in her pocket, is as certain as that many have read it, tho' it discovers my antiquity day and date. That it met with applause you will be sure; but (to mortify you and myself) I read it to one lady, no bad critick, and religious too. She stopd me and said it was a shame to treat sacred subjects in so ludicrous a manner! ... I put my letter halfway read in my pocket, and said I would not cast pearls befor swine, and askd her whether she worshipd God or the devil? (Letter to the Rev. Dr Douglas, Galashiels, 17 October 1784, *Letters and a Memoir*, p. 172)

Mrs Cockburn's letter allows us to see how private correspondence could function as a source of literary and intellectual interchange and controversy. Similarly private memoirs were constantly circulated and thus published if not printed. Again to Douglas she writes: 'I had hopes of sending you a read of interesting memoirs wrote by a friend of mine; but there is such a demand for them, I cannot this week' (18 January 1786, *Letters and a Memoir*, p. 180). But of print which is the only medium through which at last the work of these women will be made known, Alison Cockburn was, like her younger upper-class female compatriots, extremely suspicious. Although there is much half articulated evidence in her letters that she likes to think of herself as an author, she fears the déclassé imputation of print: 'As for printing, never fear. I hate print, and though I have been sung at wells to the flowers of the forrest, I never was in print that anybody but a street singer could decipher' (Letter to Douglas, 28 November 1775, *Letters and a Memoir*, p. 112).

The great advantage, however, in the eschewing of print is in the concomitant increase in the frankness encouraged by minute knowledge of the composition of one's audience, coupled with unwavering trust in its sympathetic interest. It is true that Alison Cockburn's biography of 'Felix', identified as Ambassador Keith, is alas, rather dull, perhaps because it seems to have been a response to a request rather than a spontaneous personal effusion, and because Keith had a somewhat too fortunate life for real interest. But her letters offer us Hume and Burns and Scott and Monboddo and Blair, all of whom attended her Edinburgh salon, in a forthright manner which speaks the woman as it reveals the men. Of Burns: 'The man will be spoiled, if he can spoil, but he keeps his simple manners and quite sober' (Letter to Douglas, 10 January 1787, p. 189); to Hume, who had quarrelled with Monboddo, she writes: 'Make ye friends with Lord Monboddo? no, that's out of my power: I have not now such influence with him as I have had; but I can teach you a way to bring it about when you come down' (Letter to David Hume, 16 December 1768, p. 72). Elsewhere she asks Hume to bring Rousseau to Scotland because the English will not appreciate him (neither, alas, did some of the Scots), opines that Sir Charles Grandison should be burnt by the hands of the hangman, expresses her scepticism about hell or complains about the contemporary folly of Balloon-madness. The letters everywhere entwine the gossipy and profound.

The refusal of print also enables in self-writing a directness about personal experience which dropped out of writing in later, more public periods. We have become in the course of feminism so determined to deprecate the suppression of women's writing that we have perhaps paid insufficient attention to the special advantages of private circulation over print and to the special characteristics of such writing. Alison Cockburn was often described by contemporaries as forthright and might to some extent, therefore, be a special case but it is hard not to feel that it is the peculiar relationship of writer and audience that gives her 'A Short Account of a Long Life' its remarkable character, a character established by refusal of self-disguise:

> Born in the year 1713, 29th September, old stile, the youngest of a numerous family, and coming unexpectedly seven years after my Mother had bore children, I was the little favourite of the family. My Mother dyed when I was ten years old. My Father and sisters doated on me. I was caressed in childhood, and indulged in youth. (*Letters and a Memoir*, p. 1)

Sixty-five years later we find Alison Cockburn writing again to Douglas that she thinks it 'the first of dutys to spread LOVE from heart to heart': indulging children may after all be a sound procedure. But perhaps even more moving is the unembellished rendering of suffering with no colour of fiction, no attempt to impress. Her nephew in a fit of melancholy attempted suicide by shooting himself in the head. When she was informed of the attempt and its failure she went directly to him:

> He ask'd my pardon, embrac'd me, and cry'd in my arms – dreadful was the scene altogether; and I thought I should have died of the pain he suffer'd in extracting the balls. (*Letters and a Memoir*, p. 16)

No less impressive is the wise compassion with which she tried to comfort him:

> Much discourse we had, and I endeavoured to prevent his looking on that fatal action as so very disgraceful as it appear'd to him. Such is the power of custom: what a Roman gloried in, a Briton thought most contemptible. (*Letters and a Memoir*, p. 17)

A year later her nephew made a second and successful attempt. This event, like the tragic early death of her own son, is rendered with a fortitude that never for a moment allows us to doubt the strength of the grief that she suffered. But it is in the account of her husband's death that Mrs Cockburn achieves a quality of writing which is made possible by a complete refusal of art. After 'twenty-two years of uncommon happiness' her husband fell victim to a never quite understood illness:

> Mr. Cockburn, on whom were the sweats of death, beg'd me to lie down with him. Wood [a young friend] was in the room, but I strip'd instantly and was embraced in his cold wet arms with such affection, dearer than the first embrace. Nature was worn out, and I fell asleep. – He watch'd some minutes, and then bade me go to my own bed: I did so, and sleep was allow'd me. About 8 o'clock I got up and apply'd the usual remedy. He found all was over. He look'd to me and said, 'Alice! it has seized my heart, while I can speak, I will pray.' His words were – 'O my God! I preserve the dearest and best of wives, and my dear Son! – help me, Alice! – Adam will be kind to you – go away'. (*Letters and a Memoir*, p. 9).

This purity of utterance does seem to be to some extent an effect of gendered perception. Alison Cockburn never questioned her husband's authority or superiority, he in turn never abused her trust. Explaining her acquiescence in his decision to send their son abroad, although she knows how she will miss him, she writes:

> I was full assured of his Father's tenderness being equal to mine, and his understanding much superior. I never in my life disputed a point but in sport, and to display my powers of argument on the wrong side of the question, a sort of sport he often led me into for his amusement. (*Letters and a Memoir*, p. 3)

But before we leap to the conclusion that here is a confirming example of female subordination, however willing, it is important to note that for Alison Cockburn this self-conception comes not out of weakness but out of proper pride and it is consequently empowering. For Alison Cockburn intellectual rigour eschews fussy self-assertion and thus enables the discourse of equality. Thus while recognising her friend David Hume's pre-eminence, she can still laugh at him as a creation of Nature, not God (*Letters and a Memoir*, p. 71) or tease him by remarking after a Highland expedition that 'these mountains, and torrents, and rocks, would almost convince one that it was some being of infinite power that had created them' (*Letters and a Memoir*, p. 45).

It is less clear, yet worth considering, whether Alison Cockburn's transparency of utterance is nationally conditioned. Scott whose mother was a close friend of Mrs Cockburn's suggests that Alison Cockburn's Edinburgh salon was French in style:

> My recollection is that her conversation brought her much nearer to a Frenchwoman than to a native of England; and, as I have the same impression with respect to ladies of the same period and the same rank in society, I am apt to think that the *vielle cour* of Edinburgh resembled that of Paris than that of St James's; and particularly that of the Scotch imitated the Parisians in laying aside much of the expensive form of these little parties, in which wit and good humour were allowed to supersede all occasions of display. The lodging where Mrs Cockburn received the best society of her time would not now offer accommodation to a very inferior person. (Quoted in *Letters and a Memoir*, pp. xxvii–xxviii)

This absence of display is equally an indication of proper pride specific, Scott would have it, to place and time. Alison Cockburn may then be seen both to enact and to portray the values of her time and place.

Alison Cockburn then alerts her readers to the problems of theorising private writing. For it has also become a cliché of the investigation of private writing, of the diaries, particularly of women, that we look within them for evidence of an explicit or covert process of self-construction, a kind of compensation for public powerlessness. But it turns out to be one of the dangers of feminist reading of autobiographical kinds that it has focused so firmly on these writings as constructions of or revelations of subjectivity.[18] It is hard to claim for some of the women with whom I am concerned that self-construction is a primary concern or even an oblique strategy; and it is not always interesting enough to read it as an unconscious aim. After all most texts can be made to provide consistent messages or traits if the reader is determined to find them; whereas the more sceptical reader might well go along with the more overt concerns of the writer. I want, therefore, to try to show in the rest of this chapter how excitingly various women's non-fictional writing can be. The didactic, political and philosophical writing of Elizabeth Hamilton is touched on by Carol Anderson and Aileen Riddell and Marion Reid's *A Plea for Woman* is referred to by Catriona Burness. I shall, therefore, conclude this chapter with a clutch of interesting and difficult to categorise women whose essays and memoirs have not attracted the attention now accorded to Elizabeth Grant of Rothiemurchus or Jane Welsh Carlyle but who in their different ways enrich the tradition of non-fictional prose of the nineteenth century.

Marjory Fleming (1803–11)

First, it would be churlish to exclude Marjory Fleming. Marjory Fleming is probably less famous now than she was when Frank Sidgwick produced the first transcription of her journals, letters and verses in 1934: contemporary readers are perhaps less uncomplicatedly susceptible to the charms, intensified by early death, of precocious little girls.[19] Marjory Fleming came from a solid Fife family well connected on both sides and acquainted with the circle of Sir Walter Scott. Marjory became very close to her older cousin Isabella Keith and spent 'most of her sixth, seventh and eighth years away from her home, at Edinburgh, Ravelstone or Braehead . . . under the wing of her aunt, Marianne

Keith, and under the immediate care and tuition of Isabella' (*Fleming*, p. xv). Isabella acted as her little cousin's teacher and the copybooks that have survived are the daily records of work done for and corrected by Isabella. The books would probably not have been so carefully preserved (adult women are seldom charmed by their own childish effusions) had it not been for the tragically early death of Marjory, possibly from meningitis as a complication of measles, when she was not quite nine years old. Here are a couple of extracts from the Journals. The first is from 1810 when Marjory was seven:

> Many people are hanged for Highway
> robbery Housebreking Murder &c&c
> Isabella teaches me everything I know
> and I am much indebted to her she is learn
> -en witty & sensible. – I can but make a
> poor reward for the servises she has
> done me if I can give her any but
> I doubt it. – repent & be wise saith the
> preacher before it is to late. – Regency
> bhnets are become very fashionable
> of late & every gets them save poor me
> but if I had one it would not become
> me. – A Mirtals is a beautifull plant
> & so is a Geramem & nettel Geramem
> Climbing is a talent which the bear
> excels in and so does monkeys apes &
> baboons. – I have been washing my
> dools cloths today & I like it very much.
> (Fleming, pp. 3–4)

In spite of the spelling mistakes we are likely to be struck by the charming range of reference of this little highly taught child and neither the charm nor the range disappears over the two years of the journals. But determining the focus of readers' concern at the present time is trickier. It might be deliciously tempting to find in the fluidity of the prose and the heterogeneity of its concerns some evidence of the closeness to the semiotic that Kristeva sometimes suggests might be the special characteristic of feminine writing by either sex.[20] But clearly if the characteristics of feminine writing are found in the exercises of a little girl then this might prove more embarrassing than illuminating. It seems likely that Marjory Fleming's exercises will be read now largely for historical information about a family and about the reading and learning practices of the gentry of the time. In this context it is remarkable to find the less than eight-year-old Marjory reading 'the misteris of udolpho' with Isabella and learning some of Pope's poems by heart (*Fleming*, p. 14). Less promising, however, is the early inscription of female worthlessness:

> Fighting is what ladies is not gua
> lyfied for they would not make a good
> figure in battle or in a dual Alas we fe-males are of little use to our country
> & to our friends, I remember to have
> read about a lady who dressed
> herselfe in mans cloths to fight for her

> father, wom<u>an</u> are not half so brave
> as her, but it is only a story out of Mo-
> thers Gooses <u>Fary</u> tales so I do not give
> it <u>cridit</u>, that is to say I do not belive
> the truth of it but it matters little
> or nothing. (<u>Fleming</u>, p. 126)

Yet even as Marjory Fleming repeats the formulas of prejudice, she does it with less conviction than informs her scepticism. Had she lived she might well have come to see that much of what passed for fact about women was also merely fairy story.

Ellen Johnston (?1835–73)

If Marjory Fleming's charming exercises warn us not to make too glib characterisations of feminine writing practices, the 'Autobiography' of Ellen Johnston in all its restrained pathos offers a moving example of the problems that self-educated writers encounter in finding models for their work. James Hogg, admittedly a writer of greater natural ability, solved the problem by sceptical generic manipulations which by confusing his would-be critics made him difficult to pigeonhole. In this way Hogg's writings both exploit and critique the models of his more educated predecessors and contemporaries. Ellen Johnston, conversely, becomes stuck, a fly in amber, in the narrative modes of the previous century. Johnston is becoming known again for her poetry: she is included in both Catherine Kerrigan's anthology and in Tom Leonard's *Radical Renfrew*.[21] The 'Autobiography' is a short piece of self-explanation which precedes the second edition of her poems.[22] Johnston's style is highly literary and declamatory so that the genuine sufferings of her situation are killed into a sentimental art in which the vigour, as it were, of Defoe is vitiated by the self-conscious pathos of Mackenzie. Her early childhood Johnston imagines must have been happy enough, her father a poetic stone mason dubbed Lord Byron by the Duke of Hamilton for whom he was working. But Ellen Johnston's troubles began when her mother refused to risk her child's life by accompanying her husband to America. When the father was reported dead in America Ellen's mother remarried a power-loom tenter and the eight-year-old girl's life was transformed from lowly idyll to persistent and drab misery. She is forced out to work as a power-loom weaver when only ten but the corrosive secret of her life which the reader requires no very sophisticated detective skill to work out is that she was sexually abused by her stepfather while she was still little more than thirteen. She tells her story of romantic longings fuelled by Scott's novels and Wilson's 'Tales of the Borders', of girlish desire to become an actress, of unhappiness at home, of running away and being beaten by her mother 'till I felt as if my brain were on fire', in a most fragmented way, the manner itself mimicking her confused sense of an identity fractured by desire and suffering. Her repeated references to the '*mystery*' of her life authenticate her shame but her appropriation of a second-hand literary discourse fights rather than aids the validation of her experience:

> Yes, gentle reader, I have suffered trials and wrongs that have but rarely fallen to the lot of woman. Mine were not the common trials of every-day life, but like those strange romantic ordeals attributed to the imaginary heroines of 'Inglewood Forest'.
>   Like the Wandering Jew, I have mingled with the gay on the shores of France – I have feasted in the merry halls of England – I have danced on the shamrock soil of Erin's green

isle – and I have sung the songs of the brave and the free in the woods and glens of dear old Scotland.

I have waited and watched the sun-set hour to meet my lover, and then with him wandered by the banks of sweet, winding Clutha, when my muse has often been inspired when viewing the proud-waving thistle bending to the breeze, or when the calm twilight hour was casting a halo of glory around the enchanting scene; yet in all these wanderings I never enjoyed true happiness.

Like Rasselas, there was a dark history engraven on the tablet of my heart. Yes, dear reader, a dark shadow, as a pall, enshrouded my soul, shutting out life's gay sunshine from my bosom – a shadow which has haunted me like a vampire, but at least for the present must remain the mystery of my life.[23]

The sentimental literary models that Ellen Johnston draws on for her story cannot adequately render it because they are models that have been developed for the educated classes to demonstrate their sensibilities by sympathising with the sorrows of the low, rather than models that enable the direct presentation of these sorrows. Yet the reader's perception of that inadequacy may in the end work peculiarly to stress the pathos that the writer cannot quite express.

Janet Hamilton (1795–1873)

Like Ellen Johnston Janet Hamilton has resurfaced in Scottish letters largely because of her poetry. Janet Hamilton's vigorous poetry is discussed in this volume by Valentina Bold but her prose pieces are no less worthy of reassessment. She was born in 1795 at Carshill in Lanarkshire, the daughter of a shoemaker, Thomson, who worked also as a farm labourer before he settled with his family in Langloan, Old Monkland, Lanarkshire; Janet Thomson also married a shoemaker with whom she lived for sixty years giving birth to ten children. She is one of the few working class writers to invade the pages of the *DNB*, from which this biographical information is taken. She learned to read as a girl and read, of course, the Bible, Shakespeare and Milton as well as many of the principal (male) 18th-century writers including Ramsay, Fergusson and Burns, but, like James Hogg, she had to teach herself to write and she devised a strange hand 'of oriental aspect' as the *DNB* puts it. She began writing occasional pieces at an early age but unsurprisingly family duties kept her from extensive composition until at the age of fifty-four she began to write for Cassell's *Working Man's Friend*. She continued to compose even during the last eighteen years of her life when she was blind and her son James acted as amanuensis. She published three volumes of poetry and prose between 1863 and 1868, a selection from these with new work in 1870 and her son produced an edited volume in 1880.[24]

Janet Hamilton's prose, like much of her poetry, is explicitly didactic, addressing the working classes from their own level. Janet Hamilton was lucky that her life, unlike Ellen Johnston's, was richly familial and local even if hard. Where Ellen Johnston is wandering, Janet Hamilton is fixed, where Ellen Johnston works with the materials of unsatisfiable romantic desire, Janet Hamilton believes that happiness comes not from lamenting one's station or lot but by self-betterment within it. It is tempting to claim that it is precisely Janet Hamilton's conservatism that has guaranteed her commemoration in both the *DNB* and Irving's of *Book of Eminent Scotsmen*, where other working-class writers might have been passed over. Yet from the earliest stages of her publications, her prose exhibits an intellectual energy, confident of its own political diagnoses, that has no more need to truckle to local agitation than to knavery and incompetence in the central government. Her 'Reminiscences of the Radical Time in 1819–20' is a remarkable piece from her first collection which is still not properly recognised for its perception of the effects of central politics on local life. Janet Hamilton has no real sympathy with 'Radicalism', but like many working-class writers who refuse it, she has a simple, unaffected understanding of the grievances which generate it. Throughout her anatomy of the pathetic would-be insurgent in her village, provoked by poverty and existing

local enmities, and by *agents provocateurs*, she has a clear sense of both grievance and manipulation. The 'would-be insurgents', she says:

> with their lean, pale faces, unwashed, unshaved, and uncombed, thinly clad, and out at knees and elbows, with reckless and defiant looks, come trampling along to the sound of a couple of fifes, these frequently being their only musical accompaniments; and many a banner with a strange device was borne aloft by them in their disorderly marches through our village to their annual place of meeting. ('Reminiscences of the Radical Time in 1819–20', *PES*, p. 362)

In spite of the ironic allusion, Janet Hamilton's stance is egalitarian: she clearly is intellectually superior to her projected readership but she refuses so to present herself and always identifies herself with the group that she equally seeks to educate:

> I might, but I will not here denounce the principal actors (Government spies included) in this miserable drama, who moved the wires that made the poor puppets dance. (*PES*, p. 372)

But Janet Hamilton's sympathy does not desert the poor puppets who would not, she suggests, have been so easily led into rebellion had they enjoyed the 'privileges and the legitimate powers they now possess under our present paternal and enlightened government' (*PES*, p. 372).

Throughout her writing Janet Hamilton argues for the importance of education, spiritual, intellectual and moral, for her own working people. Hamilton never wavers in her conviction that reading, reading poetry in particular, civilizes and spritualises. We can see now, of course, how education can be used to dull the aspirations of the working classes but Janet Hamilton could only see the joys of literacy, for they were all that she had herself known. To read poetry is to be given access to 'these lands of song and story . . . the glowing scenes where all that is grand and beautiful in nature and art combine to trance the soul in admiration'. At the same time poetry is seen not so much as a creator of the ambitious mind as a consolation for constricted opportunities, as the reader imbibes 'the very spirit of courage, patience and resignation' from the 'sublime sentiments' of Thomas Campbell ('The Uses and Pleasures of Poetry for the Working Classes', *PES*, pp. 226–31; p. 231).

Hamilton will perhaps be most valued today for her sharp, humorous sketches of local worthies and of manners and customs: 'Auld Robin an' Tibbie', 'Auld Kirsty Dinsmore', 'Sketch of a Scottish Roadside Village Sixty Years Since', 'Sketches of Scottish Peasant Life and Character in Days of Auld Langsyne'.[25] But at the same time it is not inappropriate to see in the work of this redoubtable auto-didact something of that process of self-construction which is commonly now discerned in the writing of her higher-class sisters. Janet Hamilton writes about self-education, self-formation and she is not without pride in her own achievement of it. In the 'Preface' to *Poems, Essays, and Sketches* she offers a brief autobiography which reveals determination, guile and some egoism as the ingredients of her success. Her mother, she explains, did not approve of her daughter's 'ballad singing, poetry, and novel reading, and would often threaten to burn my precious store, but a good fit of crying, on my part, always saved them ('Preface', p. ix). To this cunning early grasp of the power of tears was later added the sheer determination that combines nursing a child with reading a book to produce a woman, who in spite of her seeming conservatism, nevertheless teaches an oblique message of feminist aggression. Her most stirring appeals are directed at her fellow working mothers and these do have a radical undercurrent that is missing from the work addressed to a more general audience. In her 'Address to Working Women' we can detect faint tones of contempt for the relegation of women to basic nurture. 'Let us', she cries, 'aim at being "fervent in spirit" as well as "diligent in business"'. She points out that ants and bees are industrious; wrens are tidy and hens watch over their chickens 'zealously and affectionately'. Such basic functions are necessary but insufficient for the formation of the mothers of the future who are urged to fight against that 'spirit of predominance and exclusiveness' which has worked against women to lower them in their own self-estimation (*PES*, pp. 283–4).

Mary Somerville (1780–1872)

Here are some passages from the life of Mary Somerville, born into the conservative Scottish upper middle class and brought up in a large house near Burntisland. At eleven she returns home from school in Musselburgh where remarkably little education has been received:

> I was like a wild animal escaped out of a cage. I was no longer amused in the gardens, but wandered about the country. When the tide was out I spent hours on the sands, looking at the star-fish and sea-urchins, or watching the children digging for sand-eels, cockles and the spouting razor-fish.[26]

Here at thirteen she return to Burntisland after a winter in Edinburgh: 'On returning to Burntisland, I spent four or five hours daily at the piano; and for the sake of having something to do, I taught myself Latin enough from such books as we had, to read Caesar's "Commentaries" (*Personal Recollections*, p. 36). Still in her early teens she is reading a fashion magazine with a friend when she was "surprised to see strange looking lines mixed with latters, chiefly X'es and Y's, and asked; "What is that?" "Oh," said Miss Ogilvie, "it is a kind of arithmetic: they call it Algebra; but I can tell you nothing about it."' (*Personal Recollections*, p. 47). And here is the reaction of her father, a brave (and Tory) naval officer, to the news that his daughter, building on the revelation of the 'X'es and the Y's' had got through the first six books of Euclid:

> 'Peg [his wife], we must put a stop to this, or we shall have Mary in a strait jacket one of these days. There was X., who went raving mad about the longitude!' (*Personal Recollections*, p. 54)

It is, of course, notorious that it was almost as difficult for some middle-class women to get an adequate education as for their working-class sisters. And this was particularly the case in the classics, mathematics and the sciences. It is hard, given all that was stacked against her, to speak too highly of Mary Somerville's achievement in becoming a mathematician admired as an equal by the greatest mathematicians and scientists of her time on both sides of the Channel, honoured by the introduction into the University of Cambridge of her *Mechanism of the Heavens* as a text 'essential to those students who aspire to the highest places in the examinations'.[27]

The distinction of Mary Somerville, as the reviewer of her *Recollections* in *Nature* points out, provides ammunition to feminists and anti-feminists alike. If on the one hand 'such powers as hers had been more generally granted to women, why is she the only woman on record amongst us who has exhibited them?'[28] We need not, however, require women to be more accomplished than most men in order to grant them educational equality and Mary Somerville also manages gently to give the lie to 19th-century male fears that education made women unwomanly. Her daughter remarks that 'it would be almost incredible were I do describe how much my mother contrived to do in the course of the day'. she wrote for the press, taught her own small children, read newspapers and books and freely visited her friends, being very fond of society (*Personal Recollections*, p. 5). Mary Somerville qualifies for a 'Girls' Book of Heroines' but what qualifies her for this chapter is something additional. Her life and her opinions impeccably support any valorisation of women, indeed into extreme old age she remained tart about any assumption of female inferiority: her own politics were Liberal from an early stage, she advocated female education, supported female suffrage, knew the notable men and women of her age in letters as well as in science – Maria Edgeworth, Joanna Baillie, John Stuart Mill and the feminist philanthropist Frances Power Cobbe. But the arguments for reading her *Recollections* reside in her wit and her perceptions as well as her worth. Her accounts of local community, manners and habits in her childhood are often very funny and are authenticated by a precise and uncondescending use of the vernacular. Her account of the childhood game 'Scotch and English', a game which represented a raid on the debatable land, or Border between Scotland and England, suggests endemic national tensions by the end of the 18th century for the little children were always compelled to be English, since the bigger ones thought it too degrading (*Personal Recollections*, p. 23). The *Recollections* are throughout informed by a remarkable love for the beauty and specificity of the visible universe and its creatures which might be felt to underpin the work of all great mathematicians even as they seek for the invisible and abstract. The area round Sorrento where she spent the end of her life is rendered with a vision as fresh as scanned the shore at Burntisland. The love of birds which she felt intensely perhaps makes it understandable that she never allowed the discoveries of science to shake her simple religious belief:

> My love of birds has continued through life, for only two years ago, in my extreme old age, I lost a pet mountain sparrow, which for eight years was my constant companion: sitting on my shoulder, pecking at my papers, and eating out of my mouth; and I am not ashamed to say I felt its accidental death very much. (*Personal Recollections*, p. 16)

Christian Watt (1833–1923)

This chapter and the others on the non-fiction writing of individuals and groups show, of course, merely the tip of an iceberg. Many other women have written in the various categories of non-fictional prose during the period, some of them published their work, some of them have been subsequently published, some have had their memoirs and diaries preserved in libraries and some of this writing is almost certainly lying in chests and in attics in the dwellings of the high and the low all over the country. The remarkable Christian Watt papers edited by David Fraser are a relatively recent example of the kind of recovery that remains possible. Fraser explains Christian Watt's production of the memoirs that he has been permitted to publish:

> In 1880 Christian Watt, a woman of 47 who was to be a patient for many years in Cornhill, the Aberdeen Infirmary for those suffering from mental disorders, started to write down the recollections of her life . . . Her memory was encyclopaedic, her gift of narration superb. Before she died in 1923, she had recorded the principal events and impressions of a life of ninety years, describing folk and incident of the mid-19th century in a way which, a further six decades later, brings both vividly before our eyes.[29]

Christian Watt came from Broadsea in Buchan; her life was hard in ways that strike us as quite intolerable – 'My first job I was 8½ as skiffie to Mrs Lawson, the Banker's wife. It was 3 months of drudgery and half starvation. I resented being called all the time by my surname' (*Watt Papers*, p. 17). Christian's life took her to various parts of Scotland including Shetland and Lewis and she spent time too in America where the sight of bullied negroes provokes some sharp nationalist feeling:

> In America I had come face to face with reality, and the bitterness that burns in coloured folks hearts towards those who brought them there; the African Chiefs who sold their own people for gold are equally guilty as the purchasers. As a subjugated Scot I could sympathise, for a handful of greedy blockhead peers should never have had the power to vote to sell an independent minded nation for English gold. (*Watt Papers*, p. 62)

The fierce pride that generates such remarks survives the terrible spiritual and material sufferings of a life in which brothers, parents, husband and children die before their time, taken by illness or the sea, and poverty is a constant companion. Christian eventually needed the rest that Aberdeen Infirmary gave her but in the end her sufferings moulded an identity and she ended her days at the centre of a kind of salon within the Infirmary:

> I don't work much now. My three sons are very generous to me but I like to feel independent. I do a teacloth (but not often) for I must earn a penny to put a stamp on a letter to many friends. I have a steady stream of visitors. Students ask me about subjects to write theses, at 90 I have taken up the teaching job I started at 16. It is most enjoyable and I have happiness and peace. I can ask my guests to stay to lunch if they came in the morning. A lass who used to be a maid in Cairness House works here. She does my shopping, so I am like a lady of leisure. (*Watt Papers*, p. 154)

The Watt papers are certainly exceptional but the area of non-fictional prose remains one of the most fruitful areas for further research in Scottish women's writing. In it we will continue to discover how women negotiated private and public problems, how they responded to their families, their friends, their country and the lands they travelled to. We will by continuing to discover it and to read it, enlarge our notions of women in time and place and of the whole intimate, social and political life of Scotland at home as well as its implications abroad.

Notes

1.   Any attempt to sum up the history of a century is doomed to the superficially smart. Michael Lynch's *Scotland: A New History* (Century, London, 1991) with its bibliographies

has been most useful for me. The important history of Scottish women is Rosalind Marshall's *Virgins and Viragos* (Academy Chicago, Chicago, 1983). This study which remains the principal source of Scottish female experience for Olwen Hufton's *The Prospect Before Her: A History of Women in Western Europe*, vol. 1 1500–1800 (Harper Collins, London, 1995) is ironically out of print in Britain but not in America.

2.   The indispensable account of these processes is given by Linda Colley in her *Britons: Forging the Nation 1707–1837* (Yale University Press, New Haven, 1992; Pimlico, London, 1994). Historians do take issue with Colley but it is impossible to ignore her work. I have also found helpful David Cannadine's 'The Making of the British Upper Class' in his *Aspects of Aristocracy* (Yale University Press, New Haven, 1994; Penguin, Harmondsworth, 1995). For the notion of Britain in writing and the arts see the different, but not incompatible, approaches of Robert Crawford in his *Devolving English Literature* (Clarendon Press, Oxford, 1992) and Howard D. Weinbrot's *Britannia's Issue: The Rise of British Literature from Dryden to Ossian* (Cambridge University Press, Cambridge, 1995). There are also brief but suggestive considerations of the meaning of the Scottish Highlands for the eighteenth century in Simon Schama's *Landscape and Memory* (Harper Collins, London, 1995).

3.   *The Dunlop Papers: Vol. Three: Letters and Journals 1663–1889*, selected and annotated by J. G. Dunlop (privately printed by Butler & Tanner, Frome and London, 1953).

4.   Dunlop, *Letters*, p. 36.

5.   'Margaret Calderwood' in J. G. Fyfe (ed.), *Scottish Diaries and Memoirs 1746–1843* with introduction by J. D. Mackie (Eneas Mackay, Stirling, 1942). Fyfe's collection is an excellent one which includes the writing of a number of women: Elizabeth Mure of Caldwell's splendid observations on the changing manners of her time from just before her birth in 1714 to five years before her death in 1795; Lady Anne Barnard who is discussed at length in chapter 8; Mrs Fletcher, an Englishwoman who settled in Edinburgh and numbered the 'giants of the age' – Scott, Jeffrey, Brougham, Henry Mackenzie and Playfair – among her friends; Elizabeth Grant of Rothiemurchus, discussed by Peter Butter in this volume.

6.   Lady Murray of Stanhope, *Memoirs of the Lives and Characters of the Right Honourable George Baillie of Jerviswood and of Lady Grisell Baillie by their Daughter Lady Murray of Stanhope* (printed at Edinburgh, 1824). Further references in the text are to *Memoirs*.

7.   *Letters and a Memoir of Her Own Life by Mrs Alison Rutherford or Cockburn; also 'Felix', a Biographical Sketch and Various Songs*; notes by T. Craig-Brown (printed for David Douglas, Edinburgh, 1900) quoted in the Introductory Notes, pp. xxvii–xxviii. This opinion of Scott's is discussed in more detail later in the chapter.

8.   Lady Mary Wortley Montagu, *Essays and Poems*, edited by Robert Halsband and Isobel Grundy; includes 'Biographical Anecdotes of Lady Mary Wortley Montagu' by Lady Louisa Stuart (Clarendon Press, Oxford, 1977), p. 32. Further references in the text are to Montagu, *Essays and Poems*.

9.   .Anne Grant, *Memoir and Correspondence of Mrs Grant of Laggan*, edited by J. P. Grant, 3 vols (Longman, Brown, Green and Longmans, London, 1844) vol. III, p. 41.

10.   Joanna Baillie, 'Lady Grisell Baillie', *Metrical Legends* (Longman, Hurst etc, London, 1821).

11.   Lady Grisell Baillie, *The Household Book of Lady Grisell Baillie* (); Lady Grisell was the author of 'Werena my Heart Licht I Would dee'.

12.   Lady Louisa Stuart, *Memoire of Frances, Lady Douglas*, edited and introduced by Jill Rubenstein, with a preface by J. Steven Watson (Scottish Academic Press, Edinburgh, 1985), p. 29. Further references in the text are to *Memoire of Frances Lady Douglas*.

13.   Stuart, *Memoire of Frances, Lady Douglas*, quoted p. 14.

14.   Stuart, *Memoire of Frances, Lady Douglas*, Preface and Introduction throughout.

15.   *Letters and a Memoir of Her Own Life by Mrs Alison Rutherford or Cockburn*, p. 113. I am wholly indebted to this edition and have taken most of my biographical information from it. Further references in the text are to this edition.

16.   It would be untrue to claim that memoirs, letters, diaries and so on were neglected until the recent steady interest in them. Craig-Brown's edition is in itself an indication of this and J. G. Fyfe's two volumes of Scottish diaries are an indispensable printed source: *Scottish Diaries and Memoirs 1550–1746*, ed. J. G. Fyfe; *Scottish Diaries and Memoirs 1746–1843*, ed. J. G. Fyfe, with introduction by J. D. Mackie (Eneas Mackay, Stirling, 1942). Nevertheless Craig-Brown makes it clear that although the famous verses are not the most interesting

literary productions of Mrs Cockburn, without their fame she probably would not be deemed a suitable subject for his volume. And today, if she is known at all, it will normally be for these verses.

17.   The note to p. 79 of *Letters and a Memoir* includes Lady Anne Lindsay's portrait of Sophia.

18.   This is the governing theoretical premise of for example Sidonie Smith's *A Poetics of Women's Autobiography* (Indiana University Press, Bloomington, 1987). I give Smith as my example because she seems to do most with the position but she has been much followed.

19.   *The Complete Marjory Fleming, Her Journals, Letters & Verses*, transcribed and edited by Frank Sidgwick (Sidgwick & Jackson, London, 1934). Further references in the text are to *Fleming*.

20.   See Julia Kristeva, 'Revolution in Poetic Language' in *The Kristeva Reader*, ed. Toril Moi (Blackwell, Oxford, 1986).

21.   Catherine Kerrigan, *An Anthology of Scottish Women Poets* (Edinburgh University Press, Edinburgh, 1991); Tom Leonard, *Radical Renfrew* (Polygon, Edinburgh, 1990).

22.   Ellen Johnston, *Autobiography, Poems and Songs of Ellen Johnston, the Factory Girl*, (William Love, Glasgow, 1869).

23.   Johnston, *Autobiography*, p. xxii.

24.   Janet Hamilton, *Poems and Essays of a Miscellaneous Character on Subjects of General Interest* (Thomas Murray, Glasgow, 1863); *Poems of Purpose and Sketches in Prose of Scottish Peasant Life and Character in Auld Langsyne* (Thomas Murray, Glasgow, 1865); *Poems and Ballads* (Thomas Murray, Glasgow, 1868); *Poems, Essays, and Sketches* (Maclehose, Glasgow, 1870). Further references in the text are to *PES*.

25.   All these essays are reprinted in *Poems, Essays, and Sketches*.

26.   Mary Somerville, *Personal Recollections from Early Life to Old Age* with selections of her correspondence by her daughter, Martha Somerville (John Murray, London, 1873), p. 30. Further references in the text are to *Personal Recollections*.

27.   *Review of Personal Recollections* in *Nature: a Weekly Journal of Science*, vol. IX, November 1873 to April 1874, pp. 417–18.

28.   *Nature*, p. 418.

29.   *The Christian Watt Papers*, edited and with an Introduction by David Fraser, 2nd edn (Caledonian Books, Collieston, Aberdeenshire, 1988). The Infirmary is the same institution which later sheltered the poet, Olive Fraser: it seems to have been a remarkable institution. Further references in the text are to *Watt Papers*.

6

Burns's Sister

Robert Crawford

On Monday, 17 November 1862, with the backing of several St Andrews professors, aspiring medical student Elizabeth Garrett challenged the male domain of Scottish university education by walking towards a lecture theatre in St Andrews University to attend the eleven o'clock chemistry lecture. Her path was blocked by Susan Ferrier's nephew, Professor James Frederick Ferrier, the philosopher who invented the word 'epistemology', who stood in the doorway and asked Miss Garrett to turn back. She did.

This is in several ways an emblematic moment. It carries a secret dark irony since, about a decade before he blocked Miss Garrett's way, Ferrier had tried to learn something of chemistry when he realised that he had caught syphilis, probably from a London prostitute.[1] On a more public level, it is an incident that brings together considerations of epistemology and gender, suggesting subtle and less subtle ways in which knowledge might be gendered. Miss Garrett could be seen as the victim of a masculinist epistemology underlying the university system. One suspects that the act of carnal knowledge which destroyed Ferrier might make him all the more keen to deny the respectable Miss Garrett access to the intellectual and practical knowledge of chemistry. For Ferrier, the apparently respectable family man, both private and institutional knowledge were to be guarded for fear of scandal. The presence of Miss Garrett was an epistemological challenge and he acted to control what she knew. By the standards of the age, not least in Scotland, it could be argued that it was unladylike of Miss Garrett to wish to attend the chemistry lectures, and that Professor Ferrier and the others who opposed her did so out of punctilious regard. Oppressive regard, we might argue nowadays. Such oppressive regard has often been crucial in the development of male attitudes to women in Scotland and has frequently conditioned women's behaviour. This chapter examines in the context of Scottish literature several instances of oppressive regard which seem to me suggestive and useful to ponder in the context of the history of Scottish women's writing. It focuses on oppressive regard as figured in literary brother-sister relationships, and it argues that, however tempting the search might be, the articulation of the history of Scottish women's writing must be something more than the simple search for emblematic precursors of modern feminism. No human being, no writer, is simply an emblem.

For all that, Isobel Burns is a lost icon. While Virginia Woolf in *A Room of One's Own* made Shakespeare's imaginary sister a feminist emblem, the youngest sister of the Scottish bard, partly because she actually existed, has drifted into obscurity. It would be tempting to suggest that she should become a Scottish feminist icon, but to make her that would risk losing touch with the details of her historical existence, and with their significance. For a time at least, Isobel (sometimes Isabella) Burns was accorded iconic status as a living link to the dead bard, her brother. In examining the implications of that, I am not seeking to remodel her as a more acceptably modern feminist totem; instead, I am starting to look at the risks and pressures, as well as the attractions of iconisation. Supernatural or imagined figures are suited to being icons, but where largely ordinary human beings are treated as such, they become involved in a process of oppressive regard.

To begin to develop such a topic and to situate Isobel Burns within contemporary Scottish thinking about gender, it is worth turning to the most widely-read Scottish Enlightenment work on that subject, William Alexander's two-volume *The History of Women*, first published in 1779, and translated into French in 1791. Displayed on the title page, Alexander's Edinburgh medical degree gives him the authority of the all-male profession which knows most about women. His attitude to his audience is revealing. Advertising the third (1782) edition, he states that the work 'was composed solely for the amusement and instruction of the Fair Sex', for which reason he has 'avoided any technical term' and has 'entirely omitted' any system of references since 'we persuade ourselves, that nothing would be less attended to by the sex'.[2] So, in educating women about their own history, Alexander denies them access to the sources of that history; laziness about precise references is excused as suited to the intended audience. The world of scholarly authority, detail, and 'technical terms' is not their world.

In practice, though, Alexander often assumes a male audience, since he talks about women as 'the other sex' as opposed to 'ourselves'.[3] So, the reader of this work about women's history is treated by the author as if she were male, except when Alexander wants to excuse his lack of references, when his reader can be revealed as an untechnical female. Alexander is keen that women should have some education, but not too much: 'While our warmest wishes are, that female education were an object more considered by the legislature, and better planned by parents and guardians, we would not have it understood as our opinion, that women should pore out their fair eyes in becoming adepts in literature.' Alexander jokes awkwardly that men might grudge successful literary women 'the laurels of fame, as much as we do the breeches,' adding that the strain involved would rob women of many of their charms.[4] Woman is seen principally as a moulder of men. What is most interesting, and worth quoting at length, is the way, though he does not regret what has happened, Alexander sees gender as to a large degree socially constructed rather than decreed by nature. This means that, particularly in the developed world, women have come to be characterised by kinds of attractive timorousness and weakness. Early in his second volume, in a section flagged 'Difference of the sexes in civil life accounted for', he sets out his position clearly:

> We have just now seen, that, in savage life, the sexual difference, as far as it regards strength and activity of body, is not very considerable; as society advances, this difference becomes more perceptible; and in countries the most polished, is so conspicuous as to appear even to the slightest observer. In such countries, the women are, in general, weak and delicate; but these qualities are only the result of art, otherwise they would uniformly mark the sex, however circumstanced; but as this is not the case, we may attribute them to a sedentary life, a low abstemious diet, and exclusion from the fresh air; nor do these causes stop here; their influence reaches farther, and is productive of that laxity of the female fibres, and sensitivity of nerves; which, while it gives birth to half their foibles, is the source also of many of the

finer and more delicate feelings, for which we value and admire them; and of which, bodies of a firmer texture, and stronger nerves are entirely destitute. However paradoxical this may appear to those who have not attended to the subject, we scruple not to affirm that want of exercise, confined air, and low diet, will soon reduce, not only the most robust body, but the most resolute mind, to a set of weaknesses and feelings similar to these of the most delicate and timorous female. This being the case, we lay it down as a general rule, that the difference of education, and of the mode of living, are the principal causes of the corporeal and mental differences, which distinguish the sexes from each other; and we persuade ourselves, that nature, in forming the bodies and the minds of both sexes, has been nearly alike liberal to each; and that any apparent difference in the exertions of the strength of the one, or the reasonings of the other, are much more the work of art than of nature.[5]

This is an important passage since it points forward towards later feminist arguments, though it should not be seen as part of those. It is all the more striking, given Alexander's medical authority, that he should make such a statement about the relativity of gender roles in different societies. Indeed there are moments, as in a section from his thirty-first chapter giving 'A short view of the most material Laws and Customs, concerning the Women of Great Britain', where he perhaps seems to plead a feminist cause that counters his tone elsewhere. In those passages he emphasises the way in which women in his own society have been largely limited to the domestic in ways that are likely to have wide reverberations for the modern reader of this present history of Scottish women's writing, at the same time as having a sometimes ironic bearing on the life and public image of Isobel Burns. Again, I think it worth quoting Alexander at length, since few eighteenth-century Scottish books communicate so effectively the prevailing view of women in that society:

> In Britain, we allow a woman to sway our sceptre, but by law and custom we debar her from every other government but that of her own family, as if there were not a public employment between that of superintending the kingdom, and the affairs of her own kitchen, which could be managed by the genius and capacity of woman. We neither allow women to officiate at our altars, to debate in our councils, nor to fight for us in the field; we suffer them not to be members of our senate, to practise any of the learned professions, nor to concern themselves much with our trades and occupations. We exercise nearly a perpetual guardianship over them, both in their virgin and their married state; and she who, having laid a husband in the grave, enjoys an independent fortune, is almost the only woman among us who can be called free. Thus excluded from everything which can give them consequence, they derive the greater power which they enjoy, from their charms; and these, when joined to sensibility, often fully compensate, in this respect, for all the disadvantages they are laid under by law and custom.[6]

As a lower-class woman, Isobel Burns eludes Alexander's largely middle-class view to some extent, but only just. When attention centres on her in the late eighteenth century, and in the nineteenth century, not least in her grandson's 1891 *Memoir*, she is shown as a paragon of domestic virtue which goes some distance towards reshaping her brother's career, and which goes a greater distance in counterbalancing it. Though she is hardy and enduring, rather than delicate and vaporous, this working-class woman becomes, because of her brother's fame, the subject of an oppressive regard which, sometimes retrospectively, governs her life and its representation.

Isobel Burns (1771–1858) grew up as a working woman with a taste for poetry absorbed largely through oral culture. Robert Chambers, who interviewed her for his capacious *Life and Works of Robert Burns* (1850), recorded that 'Agnes, as she sat with her two sisters, Annabella and Isabella, milking the cows, would delight them by reciting the poetry with which her mind was stored – as the ballad of "Sir James the Rose", the "Flowers of the Forest", or the second version of the 145th psalm in the Scottish translation.'[7] Married to an agricultural worker and widowed early, Isobel reared nine children through her own efforts as a village schoolmistress, despite her lack of formal education. Her letters to her children and other relatives, several of which are reprinted in her grandson's *Memoir*, show her as articulate, resolute, above all concerned with her often harsh domestic situation and the wellbeing of her family. Her grandson makes a good deal of the qualities she shared with her famous brother:

> She seems in her youth to have attained to remarkable discrimination of thought and considerable cultivation of intellect; and in her more mature years she displayed traits of elevated sentiment, and of native force and felicity of expression, which may almost be regarded as akin to that with which her poet brother was so prodigally endowed. This formed a strongly-marked feature, not in her conversation alone, but also, and more especially, in her epistolary correspondence . . . In this respect, as well as in the unwavering independence of spirit and undaunted energy which she displayed, her life and character form a not uninteresting psychological study, illustrating as it does the principle of heredity . . . [8]

Ironically, in presenting Isobel's independence, Robert Burns Begg makes her all the more dependent on her brother, since it is surely his phrase 'the man of independent mind' which is alluded to. There are hints that, while she felt genuine love and admiration for the poet, Isobel was also aware of a need to establish her own, separate identity, protecting herself for as long as she could from his inquisitive admirers. So, for instance, when in middle life she stayed at Ormiston and Tranent, 'few even of Burns' admirers in that immediate neighbourhood knew until she had removed to Ayrshire that they had for so many years had a sister of Burns resident among them' (Burns Begg, p. 68). Writing to her son in 1834, in a (successful) attempt to secure a charitable annuity from a Mid-Lothian endowment, she makes no play on her relationship to the poet, and indeed points out that she remembers that her family name is actually '*Burness*' (her italics) (Burns Begg, p. 55).

The more time that passed, however, the more Isobel was known, and, indeed, could live only as Robert Burns's surviving sister. Her grandson quotes the whole of 'Marriage of Robin Redbreast and Jenny Wren', a Scots beast tale which appears to be a retelling of a folk story and which was one of Isobel's 'numerous stories for children' (Burns Begg, pp. 60–2). This narrative, in a lively Scots, seems to be the only one of Isobel's stories to have been written down and to have found its way into print. Yet, though recited by Isobel, it is presented as a work by Burns because she had originally heard him recite it, and had become convinced that he had composed it. One might contrast the way Burns's own revoicings of folk material have come to be known as Burns's works with the way Isobel's retelling of this folktale is seen as in no way hers, belonging instead to her brother. Only by being attributed retrospectively to Robert does the story gain circulation.

Isobel, certainly, is seen as a domestic authority, one from whom those with intimate access may hope to winkle out new Burns anecdotes, as her grandson (whose motives are torn between filial loyalty and the wish to impress readers of his book) suggests when, before revealing details of the time when she shared a house with the poet, he writes that, 'Her reminiscences of this period of her life were of too sacred a character to be alluded to except within the limits of her own family circle, or to some specially favoured and sympathetic listener' (Burns Begg, p. 17). Yet though she may have the dignity of domestic authority, like the women of William Alexander's *History*, she can have no position of public authority other than that of exhibit. The oral 'authorities' were such men as William Chambers, who might cite Isobel in their text or footnotes when writing about her brother for public consumption. Isobel's intimate authority is confined to the fireside and the oral; in the dominant, middle-class public sphere of scholarly print she exists only at the very margins. Men like Chambers owed a good deal of their reputation to the fact they were perceived as Burns 'experts'. Isobel's peculiar expertise (her contact with the poet had been far closer than that of any of his biographers) reaches the public only through the mediation of these men's words.

The longer she lived, the more Isobel came to be seen only as a Burns icon, what Sara Stevenson has called a 'living relic of her brother'.[9] Her grandson records, without ironic awareness, the translation of the ageing Isobel from an independent woman living in Tranent to a figure dependent utterly for her comfort and very survival on her brother's reputation:

> The undaunted mother and her two daughters continued to maintain themselves by their own unaided industry until the year 1842, when, by the efforts of Lord Houghton (then Mr Monkton Milnes), Thomas Carlyle, Dr Robert Chambers, and others, a fund was provided by the admirers of Burns, which, with the addition of a pension granted by the Queen at the solicitation of Lady Peel, secured for Mrs Begg an income sufficient to provide for the comfort of her old age. Carlyle's letter to Mrs Begg, dated 7th June 1842, announcing the successful issue of their efforts, is highly characteristic of the writer, and evinces the heartiness with which he had espoused the claims of Burns' sister to public recognition. 'Properly, however,' he says, 'you do not owe this to anybody but to your own illustrious brother, whose noble life, wasted tragically away, pleads now aloud to men of every rank and place for some humanity to his last surviving sister . . . ' (Burns Begg, pp. 66–7)

This letter seems generous in denying Carlyle's own efforts, but it is also (unintentionally) insulting in suggesting that no merits of Isobel's own may deserve support, and that she owes everything only to her 'illustrious brother'. This position of utter dependency brought Isobel some comfort late in her life, since she was 'accorded the use for her lifetime of a picturesque cottage near the banks of the Doon, and immediately adjoining the public road leading from Ayr to the poet's monument'. This had come about through a suggestion by William Chambers to his brother Robert 'that there was a great wish to have Mrs Begg planted somewhere about the spot of her brother's nativity' (Burns Begg, p. 67). The word 'planted' is dashingly insensitive here, suggesting that Isobel may be uprooted and resited like some sort of memorial tree. She appears to cease to be a woman and becomes an object – a Burns icon. The poet's sister, like the poet's home, becomes a worshipful curiosity.

So Robert Burns Begg recalls that his grandmother 'was for the last sixteen years of her existence regarded with much public interest and veneration, simply because she was the youngest sister of Burns'. As a 'last survivor', she represents the poet's family which 'has for more than a century concentrated so much of the kindly scrutiny of the Scottish people' (Burns Begg, pp. 1–2). It is hard for the modern reader not to feel that this 'kindly scrutiny' must have been a peculiarly oppressive regard for the old lady so 'planted' and exhibited along with the 'sons of Burns' on a platform before a crowd estimated at around 80,000 people at a great festival parade on 6 August 1844. This again is Isobel the Burns icon.

Writers who met Isobel were struck by her strong personality, yet even in recording this, they tend to see her only as a screen through which her more famous brother can be perceived. A wish to celebrate her individuality is overcome by the sense of her as a Burns icon in this obituary of 1858:

> At her house she received visitors of all grades and from all parts, and with all she was perfectly at her ease. Hundreds upon hundreds from every corner of the United Kingdom and from the Continent and America came every year to the little cottage at Belleisle to see the sister of the poet, and none went away without a higher respect for him and all belonging to him. They saw in her and in her two daughters very much of what they could well fancy the poet in his happier hours would have – frank openness, tempered with that dignified self-respect which repelled and checked vulgarity, no matter whether it assumed the air of patronising self-importance or of rude impertinence. Hers was the natural manner which art cannot communicate, and which is beyond convention. Mrs Begg was quite a lady without attempting it, just because she was every inch a woman; and the propriety of carriage, which in the case of her brother astonished the refined circles of Edinburgh three-quarters of a century ago, was not less remarkable in her.[10]

Much of this is a critical essay on Burns manifesting itself as an appreciation of his sister. She is made to show the poet at his best, implicitly counterbalancing any suggestions of his dissipation. Her style of life, 'the natural manner which art cannot communicate', is his style of writing as it was seen at the time. Even as her own individuality is praised, it is clear that she has been written by her brother.

Such is the fate of Isobel the Burns icon. She became more iconic still when photographed by Hill and Adamson in the 1840s. Unusually for their individual sitters, she confronts the camera absolutely directly, staring hard at the viewer. Sara Stevenson, whose 1986 sentences on this calotype first drew my attention to Isobel Burns Begg, writes that, 'This portrait is an expression of Hill's own enthusiasm for the poet. It is also a powerful portrait of an individual.'[11] Again here we have a balance between Isobel as herself and Isobel as Burns's sister. She seems to have accepted her fate as an icon, yet the patient, self-possessed way that the old woman stares at the camera suggests less acquiescence than powerful, enigmatic determination.

If the life and experience of Burns's sister represents anything, it is surely the dangers of turning a human being into an icon. For us to re-view Isobel retrospectively as a Scottish feminist icon would be to apply to her life pressures just as distorting as those of the Burns-worshippers. Her fate warns us not only of the constricting pressures of the bardolatrous male gaze, but also of the risks of icon-making in general. It may be that we feel a certain compulsion to identify Scottish feminist icons as part of a reorientation of our cultural history, just as those involved in the struggle for Scottish self-government may seek Scottish nationalist icons. Yet each of these searches is likely to lead to a naive and constricting essentialism in which the complexities and dignities of life are too readily airbrushed away. When we remember Isobel Burns Begg, we are duty-bound to consider the oppressive regard focused on her and to see something suspect in her iconisation. That note of suspicion might qualify our contemporary wish for icons of our own.

Our modern icons are likely to be far more virago-like than Isobel Burns. It is no accident that the pioneering and most widely known British feminist publishing house, to whom Scottish readers are grateful not least for the republishing of Catherine Carswell's fiction, is called Virago. Though that publisher's list includes such authors as Rose Macaulay whose work it is hard to label 'feminist' without immediate qualification, the list is in general based on authors whose work is feminist in its orientation. Virago has done powerful work in changing the culture of British publishing, while popular and scholarly feminism has helped reshape, to some degree at least, the teaching of literature (including Scottish literature) in British academia. There is an eminently justifiable temptation in revising our ideas of modern Scottish literature to add to the syllabuses which help construct notions of an academic literary canon works which conform to what might be caricatured as the Virago icon, that is books which clearly articulate a feminist consciousness. Yet if we are considering the history of Scottish women's writing, such an emphasis on iconic viragos is likely to produce considerable distortions, marginalising even some of those who were among the most popular and interesting women authors. Just as in Scottish writing as a whole we need to be aware of, and at times resist, the tendency to create a canon which, implicitly or explicitly, is based on nationalist political correctness or essentialist 'Scottishness', so I would argue that it is important to remember in the history of Scottish women's writing those writers who may possess few or no feminist credentials, or whose achievement seems in some way alien to contemporary taste. What I am arguing for is a broad church.

In one of the pews of this church sits the minister's daughter Anna Buchan (1877–1948), a Scottish novelist widely popular in the Scotland of the first half of the twentieth century, yet one who, because of the great fame of her brother John, was placed in a position that in some sense is comparable with that of Burns's sister. Isobel Burns did not write for publication; Anna Buchan did. Yet each felt the intimate pressure of a famous male writer to whom she was bonded by love and admiration, as well as by public perception. Anna Buchan tried to swerve away from simply being set beside her brother, and that action shaped both her independence and her consciousness of dependence in establishing the literary identity by which she was best known, the name under which she wrote: O. Douglas.

Throughout Buchan's writing there is a constant awareness of herself in relation to her brother:

> I did not want to use my name as (in my opinion) John had given lustre to the name of Buchan which any literary efforts of mine would not be likely to add to, so I called myself 'O. Douglas'.
>
> Before leaving for our holiday I had finished my book about India, and John read it and thought perhaps it might find a publisher. I urged him to try Messrs. Hodder and Stoughton, and it was accepted by that firm.[12]

The dedication of O. Douglas's late novel *The House that is Our Own* (London, 1940) is only one of several places in which it is made apparent that John 'corrected' his sister's work:

> To you, J. B., who, with little liking for mild domestic fiction, read patiently my works, blue-pencilling when you had to, praising when you could, encouraging always, I dedicate this story, which you are not here to read, of places you knew and loved.

As a young director of the firm of Thomas Nelson & Sons, John Buchan gave his sister an allowance of £100 a year which, she wrote, 'made all the difference in the world' to her.[13] Soon many works by both Anna and John Buchan were appearing on the Nelson Novels 'Select list of some of the most famous modern novels'. In 1929, for instance, that list included twenty books by John Buchan and ten by O. Douglas.[14] John was the financial enabler, role model, reader, and publisher of his sister's literary work which itself drew heavily for its material on events in the recent history of the Buchan family, not least on the life of brother John. Here again it is impossible to separate the literary career of O. Douglas from the issue of oppressive fraternal regard.

Yet to turn Anna Buchan into a feminist icon would be mistaken. In the more than semi-autobiographical *Ann and her Mother* (1922), O. Douglas has Ann, who is writing her mother's *Life*, state that 'It's a very hard thing, I should think, to write a book that is pleasant without being mawkish.' It is just such novels that O. Douglas attempts, writing a bourgeois fiction for those sophisticated enough to denote a hint of authorial mockery behind a character's announcing, 'I've brought you one of Annie Swan's – she's *capital* for a confinement.' Yet Anna Buchan was happy to hear her own fiction had been chosen by a pregnant woman, and her characters are not so adventurous as to crave the satisfactions of 'advanced' fiction produced by authors described by one of her speakers slightingly as 'Virginia Woolf and other highbrows'.[15] In the age of Lytton Strachey Anna Buchan sympathises with those who admire many aspects of Victorian life. Several times her works include discussions of fiction which are designed to defend what are seen as decent middle-class, middlebrow values:

> . . . 'Ella, I read that book you recommended, but I must say I thought it very queer. The mother going on like that! Such notions writers have now, hardly one of them can write a decent, straightforward story.'
>
> 'Well,' Peggy explained, 'they're not writing for you or your friends. They'd scorn to . . . If they think of you at all it's only to wish you were out of the world.'
>
> 'Well, I never!' said Mrs Lithgow, looking round helplessly. 'Peggy, what a way to talk! What have I ever done to writers? The only one I ever met was that brother of Mrs Warwick's, and I never thought he was right in the head, but I'm sure I've done nothing to deserve – '
>
> 'The fact that you exist is enough,' said Peggy inexorably. 'You're middle-class and middle-aged, two of the things the bright young writers hate most . . . and you're decent and clean-minded and you can't expect them to pardon *that*.'[16]

This passage gives as good a flavour as any of the world of O. Douglas's fiction. There is a deliberate and principled limiting of horizons, and a concentration on the pleasurable domestic details of bourgeois existence. Illness and death occur, politics is touched on in passing, but the focus is always on the decent minutiae of home life. Even the titles of some of the novels announce this – *The Day of Small Things*, *The Proper Place*, *The House that is Our Own*. Some of O. Douglas's people go to India, others to Switzerland, and each of these places is described, but none is loved as much as the domestic interior. The modern writers praised in these novels include Chesterton and Violet Jacob, whose *Flemington* is a 'delicate silver-point of a tale' which could be seen 'to hold all Scotland in its slender bulk'; Stevenson, Bunyan, Jane Austen are admired, no mention is made of Joyce or Huxley; there is much allusion to the life and work of John Buchan.[17]

It might be too easy to scorn O. Douglas's world with its avoidance of deep, dark emotions and its idealisation of the demesne of high tea. But just as MacDiarmid during the Second World War declared 'I'm the civilisation you're fighting for', so this writer whose beloved brother Alastair died in World War One, and who was no stranger to suffering, maintains that domestic life and all its routines are at the heart of her civilisation, whatever its more publicly acclaimed grand narratives. In its origins and development her own storytelling style can be seen as one that is consciously feminist and formed in contradistinction to the masculinist fictions of her brother John. So, in her autobiography *Unforgettable, Unforgotten*, Anna Buchan recalled of her childhood in Glasgow with her brother and her younger sister Violet (who was to die in infancy):

> The boys would never look into shop-windows unless there were books to see, or mechanical toys, or guns and fishing-tackle, but Violet would stand contentedly beside me as long as I pleased, to study the wares offered for sale.
>
> It was our game to choose what hats we liked best, what dresses, coats, and shoes, and when that palled she would say, 'Now go on with our story.'
>
> It was a story without beginning or end, added to every time we were alone together, all about what we would do 'some day'. We were going to live, Violet and I, in a vague place, very much like Broughton but with the sea as well as hills and moors, in a very small cottage . . . We often got so excited about this blissful future that we forgot where we were and bumped into passers-by, who must have wondered what made us so 'hiloarious'.
>
> On occasion Willie and Walter were not above listening to this family chronicle and contributing to it, though they always preferred the tales John told them, yarns of breathless adventure.[18]

This 'family chronicle' is born out of sisterly communion and geared to feminine taste though it does not absolutely exclude a male audience. Contrasting with John Buchan's masculine 'yarns of breathless adventure', it might be a description of O. Douglas's adult fiction. Compared with Catherine Carswell's novels, for instance, those of O. Douglas avoid deep emotional engagement. They are 'feminine' in a way that modern feminists might find frustrating and frustrated. Yet their popularity suggests that they represent an authentic view of the aspirations and imaginings of a substantial number of (not least Scottish) female readers of the earlier part of the century. They were reprinted regularly, sometimes more than once a year. Inscriptions on many of the copies I have seen, and the memories of women in my own family, indicate that these books were often given as presents between women. Anna Buchan's autobiography mentions in passing that she was a popular public lecturer, a celebrity in considerable demand. Yet this aspect of her work is downplayed, to make her appear all the more domestic in her pursuits. Her own emotional life is largely masked in her book, though the reader is aware of a constant focus on her famous brother and his work. Nevertheless, Anna, devoted to her own mother, makes the point that Mrs Buchan found John Buchan's work 'confusing' and full of 'rough people' while

> mine delighted her heart. They were as pure and almost as sweet as home-made toffee, their pages unsullied by swear-words, and they were about happy comfortable people. Like Dr John Brown's sister she might have said, 'They are very nice people – so like ourselves.'[19]

Here for a moment we sense that while she was all too aware of being John Buchan's sister (a fate in which she often delighted), Anna Buchan rejoiced nonetheless in her ability to be intimate with a treasured female audience. Unlike Isobel Burns, whose only writing took the form of private letters, O. Douglas was able to publish well-received and still enjoyable fiction. Her writing negotiated round the fame of her brother and his

writings by thriving on the conventionally circumscribed nature of the Scottish middle-
class woman's life and successfully seeking a largely female audience very different from
the more influential one targeted by that consummately successful public figure, her
brother. It is surely important that, rather than editing her out of the script, we attend to
Anna Buchan and her fiction, not least because it is likely to tell us a good deal about the
female readership of early-to-mid twentieth-century Scotland. It has an aromatic sense of
circumscribed decency.

O. Douglas's novels frequently present the figure of the impressive older brother whom
his stay-at-home sister admires. In *Eliza for Common* (1928), this figure is clearly John
Buchan, though elsewhere he may be translated into a fiancé or other beloved. Clearly
Anna Buchan was prepared to remain in and write out of this position, so that it may
seem to modern readers that she allowed and indeed encouraged herself to be limited
by her regard for her brother and by the public regard in which she knew he was held.
Particularly as the twentieth century developed it was unlikely that other women writers
would set such a position as acceptable. I wish to turn now to a contemporary novelist
whose striking first novel presents women as victims of their own oppressive regard for a
brother, suggesting a need to break out of just such a situation of subservience.

Naomi May's *At Home* is a minor classic of Scottish fiction. Published in 1969 it is
the claustrophobic story of the domestic life of three women in a London house, and an
absent man. Andrew is a successful British diplomat in Washington whose wife, Juliet,
is convalescing in her husband's Hampstead house, now occupied by his sisters, the
overbearing Anthea and the smart journalist Frances. The way in which the three women
jealously guard their images of and access to the distant husband/brother is a strikingly
stylised figuring of male-female power relations which uses the brother-sister bond to
powerful effect, and presents domesticity as an oppressively charged trap. Like Naomi
May's other fiction, *At Home* is drawn with a fine sense of ironic emotional geometry and
an accessible yet impressive use of her chosen resources. As the roles of wife and sister
blur, May's novel replays for the modern reader some of the issues present (but never quite
faced up to) in the situation of Anna Buchan. Early on in *At Home* one of the sisters puts
the position directly:

> 'Wish-fulfilment,' Frances said lightly, 'we need him, all of us. He compensates for something
> which we all lack – life,' she smilingly whispered in Juliet's ears, 'Andrew has life!'[20]

The novel's conclusion, revealing the vicious hypocrisy not only of the absent man but
also of several of the female protagonists, is both convincing and ironically subtle. The
book can be seen as carrying a feminist charge, but its emotional and ethical colouring
is not restricted to a black and white view of life. May likes a sting or twist in the
tail of her novels, as is clear in *The Adventurer* (1970) whose Ayrshire girl turns out,
unexpectedly, to be the title character, breaking spectacularly and adventurously free of
the young man who for most of the story seemed its eponymous hero. The scope of May's
fiction develops confidently with *Troubles* (1976), set in Northern Ireland and dealing
with the politics and domestic repercussions of events there, once more through ironic
emotional geometries and a sense of intimate betrayals. Her heroine's conviction, after
a near suicide, that 'it was through trivialities that she would survive' might recall the
convictions of O. Douglas, but May's fiction is both more daring and more convincing
in its emotional spectrum and its thematic range.[21] In terms of this chapter, one might
say that, in some ways at least, May's first novel marks the revenge of Burns's sister and

that her later fiction, while still preoccupied with entrapment and betrayal, builds on the attempt at painful liberation which is the first book.

Yet no more than Isobel Burns or Anna Buchan is Naomi May likely to be held up as a simply iconic 'Scottish Woman Writer'. Isobel Burns wrote too little; Anna Buchan was hardly a virago, and Naomi May not only writes about what is in contemporary Scottish fiction an unfashionable milieu – the upper middle-class – but is also a Scottish writer who has lived much of her life out of Scotland, both in Northern Ireland and in London. Though born in Glasgow in 1934, and later a good friend of the well-known Glasgow journalist Jack House, May is seldom or never discussed in Scottish literary circles. I became aware of her work only recently while compiling my 1994 introductory bibliography of twentieth-century Scottish literature. We are now most accustomed to thinking of Muriel Spark as in some important sense a Scottish writer; Carol Ann Duffy is included in Scottish as well as English anthologies. It is surely time that we looked more widely at other writers who, like Naomi May, might describe themselves as 'ex-pat' Scots.[22] This present chapter is attempting to make some generally feminist points in examining three women who, in different literary ways, were brought face to face with problems of oppressive regard figured through sisterly relations with brothers. But it is also arguing the case for a wide and generous spirit in future criticism, research, and history of Scottish women's writing. Such work may be in tune with the recent idea of 'Scotlands' rather than a monolithic 'Scotland', for it will encourage a pluralism of approach to Scottish women's writing which attends not only to past or present writers who conform to a prevailing contemporary ideology, but also to the whole spectrum of writing produced by women, as well as to the ways in which Scottish women may have been conditioned by writing. If such a broad and open approach can be established in pioneering volumes such as the present one, the rewards of future criticism and scholarship are likely to be the richer in ways which none of us may yet be able to predict.

Notes

1. All information about Ferrier comes from Arthur Thomson, *Ferrier of St Andrews: An Academic Tragedy* (Scottish Academic Press, Edinburgh, 1985).
2. William Alexander, *The History of Women from the Earliest Antiquity to the Present Time*, 3rd edn, 2 vols (printed for C. Dilly and R. Christopher, London, 1782), I, Advertisement.
3. Alexander, I, p. 1.
4. Alexander, I, pp. 87–8.
5. Alexander, II, pp. 57–8
6. Alexander, II, pp. 505–6.
7. Robert Chambers (ed.), *The Life and Work of Robert Burns*, Library Edition, 4 vols (W. & R. Chambers, Edinburgh and London, 1856), I, p. 36.
8. [Robert Burns Begg], *Isobel Burns (Mrs Begg): A Memoir by her Grandson* (privately printed, 1891), p. 4. Henceforth Burns Begg.
9. John Ward and Sara Stevenson, *Printed Light: The Scientific Art of William Henry Fox Talbot and David Octavius Hill with Robert Adamson* (HMSO for the Scottish National Portrait Gallery, Edinburgh, 1986), p. 137.
10. Quoted in Burns Begg, pp. 2–3.
11. Ward and Stevenson, p. 137. The photograph is reproduced in this exhibition catalogue.
12. Anna Buchan, *Unforgettable, Unforgotten* (Hodder & Stoughton, London, 1945), pp. 138, 131.
13. Buchan, *Unforgettable*, p. 102.
14. 'Nelson Novels' list appended to O. Douglas, *Olivia*, Nelson Novels edition (Nelson, London, 1929).

15.   O. Douglas, *Ann and her Mother* (Hodder & Stoughton, London, 1913), pp. 208, 104; Buchan, *Unforgettable*, p. 178; O. Douglas, *Taken by the Hand* (Hodder & Stoughton, London, 1935), p. 203.
16.   O. Douglas, *Taken*, p. 38.
17.   O. Douglas, *Eliza for Common* (Hodder & Stoughton, London, 1928), p. 274.
18.   Buchan, *Unforgettable*, pp. 51–2.
19.   Buchan, *Unforgettable*, p. 159.
20.   Naomi May, *At Home* (Calder & Boyars, London, 1969), p. 31.
21.   Naomi May, *Troubles* (Calder & Boyars, London, 1976), p. 218.
22.   Naomi May, autobiographical letter to the present writer, 14 August 1994, from which other biographical details in this chapter are drawn.

7

'Kept some steps behind him': Women in Scotland 1780–1920

Catriona Burness

This chapter aims to give a brief introductory account of the position of women in Scottish society between the early years of industrialisation and the aftermath of the First World War. This period has been described as 'littered with images and stereotypes of women: "Angel in the house", "the downtrodden factory worker", "the hapless Magdalen", and "the strident middle-class suffragette"'.[1] The stereotypes are familiar yet offer rather cardboard cut-out images than a nuanced understanding of what life was like for women in Scotland. The ideology of 'domesticity' profoundly influenced and confined women's lives. Yet in many thousands of individual ways women expanded their lives beyond the bounds of home and family. This chapter will explore some of the understandings of 'woman's sphere', alongside what Lady Frances Balfour referred to as the 'three great fights' of the Women's Movement in Scotland: 'First Education, then Medicine, then the Suffrage for Women'.[2] The contemporary analysis of the position of women in early Victorian society offered by the Scotswoman, Marion Reid, in her *A Plea for Woman*, will also be highlighted. Yet from the outset it seems vital to set this into the context of some discussion of the treatment of Scottish women's history to date. This involves recognising the interplay of what might be called the amazing, disappearing woman factor.

The Amazing, Disappearing Woman Factor

For instance, when I tell anyone that I am working on a history of women in Scottish politics since the 1880s, an all-too-familiar response is, 'Oh, that won't take long!', or 'Were there/are there – any?' Joy Hendry found similar reactions in 1980. She quotes a male Scottish poet, who greeted the news that *Chapman* intended the publication of a landmark double edition, *Woven by Women*, devoted to the work of Scottish women poets, with the cry 'Scottish women poets! Do you mean there *are* any?[3] MacDiarmid's famous remark that 'Scottish women of any historical interest are curiously rare'[4] apparently reflects widely held assumptions.

These assumptions have been challenged – in the past as well as in the present. Some of the earlier challenges took the form of highlighting the contributions of prominent women. In 1901 the social historian Henry Grey Graham included a chapter on 'Women of Letters' in his *Scottish Men of Letters in the Eighteenth Century*; and in 1908 Harry

Graham claimed that Scotland could lay claim to a generous share of the world's women who have ranked as celebrities:

> Scottish queens, from the sainted Margaret – who was, however, Scots only by adoption – to the ill-starred Mary; great ladies and leaders of society, from the Duchess of Buccleuch and Lady Stairs to Lady Eglinton and Gainsborough's Mrs Graham; writers and novelists, from Susan Ferrier, Catherine Sinclair, Lady Halkett, Mrs Brunton, and Mrs Hamilton to Mrs Grant of Laggan; poets and songstresses, from Joanna Baillie to Lady Nairne; they have inscribed their names indelibly upon the pages of the national history.[5]

These contributions appeared at a point when as Graham put it, 'Whether the hand that rocks the cradle is competent to rule the world is one of the controversial questions of the moment'.[6] Other histories were written by women active in various campaigns, such as Eunice Murray, the women's suffrage campaigner and propagandist. This earlier work is a reminder of the tendency for publications to appear at times when women are seeking to enlarge their roles. Yet many of these publications slipped from view this century to be rediscovered during the so-called 'second wave of feminism' unleashed by the women's liberation movement from the 1960s.

The publication of Sheila Rowbotham's *Hidden from History* in 1973 is generally seen as stimulating the development of women's history in Britain – although the process has been considerably slower in Scotland than in England. Writing recently on 'the manufacture of Scottish history', Joy Hendry commented that 'the pun "man-made" is irresistible',[7] and that attempting to write her essay on women's history in Scotland in 1982 rather than in 1992 would have given her 'a malicious sort of pleasure', as 'for an age women had been almost totally ignored by historians in Scotland'.[8] Recent years have seen a historical recovery operation initiated in 1983 by the publication of Rosalind Marshall's *Virgins and Viragos* and the Glasgow Women's Studies Group's *Uncharted Lives*. These were followed by the volumes co-edited by Eleanor Gordon and Esther Breitenbach, *The World is Ill Divided: Women's Work in Scotland in the Nineteenth and Early Twentieth Centuries* (1990) and *Out of Bounds: Women in Scottish Society, 1800–1945* (1992); and other works including Leah Leneman, *A Guid Cause: The Women's Suffrage Movement in Scotland* (1991); Lindy Moore, *Bajanellas and Semilinas: Aberdeen University and the Education of Women, 1860–1920* (1991); and Elspeth King, *The Hidden History of Glasgow's Women: The Thenew Factor* (1993).[9]

Some male historians have contributed to this important task of historical excavation – for instance, Rab Houston's exploratory essay on women in early modern Scotland[10] and Christopher Whatley's valuable study of the part played by women in the early stages of industrialisation in Scotland[11] – but it is clear that women have played the major roles. Yet some of those who have written key recent texts – Rosalind Marshall, Elspeth King, Lindy Moore – are not employed as academic historians; and many of the female academics engaged in the process of recovering Scottish women's history do so from the insecurity of temporary contracts. In Scotland, as elsewhere, the relationship between women's history and the mainstream of historical study has been indirect; few women are employed on permanent contracts within history departments at the Scottish universities (this is not to suggest that female historians *must* teach women's history!); the subject area is not securely established in Scotland, with few undergraduate courses and limited opportunities for research supervision despite the wide-ranging and ground-breaking nature of the subject.[12]

Scottish women's history remains at a pioneering stage. This tends to create a focus on basic research which may well have been likely to be present anyway given the strength of the empirical tradition in Scottish historical studies. The work undertaken, however, is not separate from international developments in the study of women in society. Expanding secondary literature elsewhere, particularly in western Europe and North America, has led to a lively debate about the purpose, methodology and theory of women's history.[13] The subject area has been perceived as loaded with emotional and ideological baggage, as 'at best . . . concerned with "women's issues" such as sex and the family; or at worst thought to be for feminists whose historical subjectivity is assumed'.[14] Much of the debate has focused on the desirability or otherwise of incorporating women's history into mainstream history. One approach to this question has been to place an emphasis on gender as a tool of analysis. This involves recognising the socially-conditioned behaviour of men and women, examining 'masculinity' and 'femininity', 'so that the new perspective turns out to be not just about women and women's issues but about all historical issues'.[15]

Gender history has been recognised as having a good deal to offer. Some European historians, such as Gisela Bock, have seen no inherent division between 'women's history' and 'gender history', viewing women's history as gender history *par excellence*.[16] The focus on gender, however, has not proved a final solution and has itself opened up new areas of debate. Gender history has proved particularly influential in the United States where its development has been strongly influenced by post-structuralist literary theory. One of its leading advocates, Joan Scott, argues that history 'is no longer about the things that have happened to women and men and how they have related to them; instead it is about how the subjective and collective meanings of women and men as categories of identity have been constructed'.[17] Yet the Scott approach, centred on textual deconstruction, has met with something of a European backlash. A range of criticisms have been made by historians of women. Among the most serious is the concern, summarised by Jane Purvis, that 'Scott's emphasis on the study of gender in history . . . decentres the study of women *as* women' and runs risks including once again subsuming women within a dominant male frame of reference, and the danger of 'a deconstructive death of the subject' via intellectualising and abstracting the inequalities between the sexes.[18] Discussing women's history in Ireland, MacCurtain and O'Dowd have commented that 'Theoretical arguments cultivated in the context of American historiography may not necessarily be helpful in studying the history of women in other countries, particularly, when, as in Ireland, much basic research still needs to be done'.[19] There seem to be clear parallels between the position in Scotland and in Ireland, although Irish women historians have gone further in questioning the relevance of Irish historical writing to the study of women, arriving at scathing conclusions:

> But perhaps the primary conclusion should be that most current Irish historical writing has little to contribute to the study of women in the past, and, therefore, that the position of women's history within it should not be a major concern. The most important task for writers of Irish women's history is the publication of research on all aspects of Irish women in the past. The international discussion on women's history has more relevance for the history of women in Ireland than the debate on the nature of Irish historical writing.[20]

From a Scottish perspective it is difficult to disagree with this commentary – although it might be remarked that Scottish history is itself generally under-researched and contributions on women's history should shape a fuller understanding of Scotland. For historians of women in Scotland, however, the current priority is research on all aspects of women's lives hitherto 'hidden from history'.

'Woman's Sphere': Society, Family and Work

There can be little doubt of the low status of women in the eighteenth and nineteenth centuries. Writing in 1930 and referring to eighteenth-century Scotland, Eunice Murray, a former speaker and propagandist for the pro-women's suffrage Freedom League, commented that 'the wonder is not that women were slow to demand rights, but that they had the courage to do so at all'.[21] In assessing the period 1500–1800, Rab Houston concluded that although 'there is no significant sense in which women enjoyed equality with men', some improvements did take place.[22] These might be summarised as growing literacy; new opportunities for employment, notably in industrial work; steady participation in Scottish agriculture; and marginal improvements in legal status. Yet there are qualifications attached to each of these factors; and within significant areas of continuity over the period, while women retained a central position in the family, 'They were denied a full voice in government, being the subjects of the forces of authority rather than wielders of its power'.[23] Women were specifically excluded from the parliamentary franchise by the 1832 Reform Act and Leah Leneman has commented that the emergence of what might be termed 'a women's movement', a grouping together of women to demand rights in the 1850s, 'began at a time when women's status . . . was about as low as it could get'.[24]

Leneman relates this low status to the operation of the cult of domesticity in its Victorian context. There was little new in the link between women and domesticity but the division between the home and work inherent in the process of industrialisation gave rise to an ideology of 'separate spheres'. This strongly prescriptive ideology allocated a public and active role to men, and a domestic, passive and submissive role to women. The impact upon women's status as workers was complex, but mainly negative – 'next to a certain loss of caste'[25] – as Marion Reid pointed out in 1843:

> If all woman's duties are to be considered as so strictly domestic, and if God and nature have really circumscribed her sphere of action – What are we to think of the dreadful depravity of thousands upon thousands of unprotected females, who actually prefer leaving their only proper sphere, and working for their own subsistence – to starvation? . . . These prejudices have also had the very bad effect of limiting woman's choice of occupations to a few, and those the most tiresome and unhealthy of all the avocations which exist in the world. (*Plea*, pp. 14–15)

Household poverty ensured that work remained a reality for many women at some stage of their lives – for instance, the average age of marriage in Scotland was relatively late at 26–7 years over the period from 1780 to 1920, creating a pool of available female labour. Indeed, as Whatley has shown, female and child labour played a crucial role in the first phase of Scottish industrialisation.[26] Women were a constant presence within the Scottish workforce over the nineteenth century, according to the census, fluctuating between 36 per cent and 29 per cent from 1841 to 1911. The census is notorious for its under-recording of women's work, particularly that of married women, but it underlines the concentration of females in some categories of employment, chiefly domestic service, agriculture, clothing and textiles. These sectors employed 90 per cent of the female workforce in 1841 and still accounted for 65 per cent of employed women in 1911.[27]

Low pay remained characteristic of women's work over the century; the average wage for a woman in Britain in 1900 was 42 per cent of the male average, and even within the 'skilled' profession of teaching women were paid only half the equivalent male salary between 1872 and 1900.[28] As Gordon has noted, women's low pay was often justified by statements such as 'it takes so much less to keep a woman than a man'.[29] This also reflects the assumption that women would be (or should be) dependants rather than providers, and that marriage was woman's destiny, within which she would come under the umbrella of the 'family wage'. Although there were significant exceptions such as the traditions of women's mill work in Dundee, there appears to have been a tendency for women to give up work on marriage, becoming more marked in the later Victorian period, reflecting the pressure of the cult of domesticity upon the working classes. After marriage too, although many married women undertook some kind of paid employment, the pressures of child-bearing and rearing aside from social pressures, were likely to constrain women's ability to take up work outside the home.

Child-bearing was an experience common to married women of all classes. Scotland also had a distinctive geographic distribution of bastardy ratios during the nineteenth century; in 1855 'a teenage girl in Banff was 20 times more likely to have a bastard as one in Ross'.[30] Fertility rates declined during the nineteenth century, however; the crude birth rate fell from around 35 per thousand in the 1870s to about 25 per thousand by 1911.[31] By the end of the nineteenth century the average family size for the population as a whole was 5.82, 4.84 for domestic servants, and under four for many professional groupings.[32] Explanations for the decline in family size have ranged from increased knowledge of and more systematic use of traditional methods of family planning such as coitus interruptus, the introduction and increased availability of new methods of contraception, and the practical and economic advantages of the small family to the bourgeoisie. The trend towards smaller families was led in Scotland, as in England, by the middle classes which already enjoyed an experience of home and hearth which was 'a far cry from that of the working class family without the material comforts or respite from domestic labour which only money could buy'.[33] Yet in some respects, as Holtby observed:

> While fashion dictated idleness to the well-to-do the new industrial system made it possible. The cleavage between the overworked factory woman and the underworked lady widened; both suffered. But they had one bond in common. Both, under the law, were in a state of servitude. The property alike of heiress-bride or half-stripped nail-maker belonged not to her but to her husband.[34]

The later nineteenth century saw some significant extensions to women's civil rights. These included the Married Women's Property (Scotland) Acts of 1877 and 1881 which introduced protection of the earnings of married women. Among the most significant of the campaigns waged by women to extend their spheres were those for access to education, the medical profession, and the suffrage. These campaigns were anticipated and the concept of 'woman's sphere' itself challenged as early as 1843 by Marion Reid who wrote:

> There is at present, we believe, almost every variety of sentiment on this subject, from the narrowest and most bigoted to the most extended and liberal . . . As long as opinions are so various on that point, it is not very philosophical to use the phrase as if its meaning were quite undisputed. (Plea, p. 8, pp. 10–11)

Politics and a Plea for Woman

Marion Reid is one of many women whose lives have been 'hidden from history'. Little is known about her life; the daughter of a Glasgow merchant, Marion Kirkland married Hugo Reid in 1839 and went to live in Edinburgh. She moved in progressive circles and attended the international anti-slavery convention which met in London in 1840. Like many other women, she was shocked by the exclusion of female delegates from the convention, and this may well have influenced her decision to write A *Plea for Woman*. Although she was apparently uninvolved in the later mid-Victorian women's suffrage movement her book was influential, and was 'something of a best-seller in its day . . . read by women on both sides of the Atlantic'.[35]

First published in Edinburgh in 1843, the *Plea* was reprinted in 1845, and 1850. It attracted even more interest in America where it was issued in 1845, and reprinted in 1847, 1848, 1851 and 1852 under the new title, *Woman, her Education and Influence*. According to Susanne Ferguson, 'it seems certain . . . that many American women read the *Plea* in the years when the American suffrage movement began' and that this influenced the call for women's suffrage made at the first women's rights convention held in the US in 1848 at Seneca Falls, although this is not mentioned in the most authoritative historical accounts of the movement. The relevance of the book was apparently overtaken by other publications in America by 1852, and the *Plea* was to remain out of print in Britain from 1850 until the publication of a Polygon reprint in 1988. The fate of the reprint shows something of the transience which threatens much of the present efforts to rediscover the efforts made by women in the past, as the reprint is now itself out of print in 1996.

Reid's work deserves consideration, however, as a landmark publication. The central emphasis on the need for women's suffrage and the clarity of her analysis is distinctive, although she acknowledged ' . . . this is by no means the first time that similar opinions have been given to the world' (*Plea*, ix). 'Scotland had no Mary Wollstonecraft,[36] but the French revolution gave some impetus to discussion of the question of civil rights for women. Women were involved in food, militia, and church patronage riots, accounting for 28, 6 and 46 per cent of identified rioters in these disturbances between 1780 and 1815.[37] Women also played a role in the political reform movement in the years leading up to 1820. Elspeth King noted that 'Reporters from the conservative press in the west of Scotland were continuously surprised and disgusted by the active and unexpected part played by women in reform meetings', providing a sample of outraged indignation from the *Glasgow Courier* in 1819:

> The exhibition of females, not only regularly formed in various of the processions, but actually bearing standards and mounting the hustings to invest the fellow who acted as president with the revolutionary cap. We know nothing of the characters of these women, but there was a time when the most abandoned of the sex in this part of the country would have blushed at such an exposure.[38]

Women's participation seems to have moved backstage after the failure of the 1820 radical uprising. According to King, 'One of the other side effects was that it wiped out the direct participation of women in political meetings, and indeed, the very memory of that participation' as the campaign for parliamentary reform endeavoured to appear more respectable than revolutionary. Generally linked with the Chartist movement, female political unions existed during the 1830s and 1840s – for instance, four in the east of Scotland, in Dunfermline, Perth, Forfar, and Kirriemuir – but were considered to be very much in a support role, to help their male relations to win the adult male suffrage. The Gorbals Female Universal Suffrage Association was told that women were forced to become beasts of burden and that the purpose of the Association should be 'to aid us [the male association] to emancipate the working classes from bondage'.[39] Equality of the sexes, however, was a key goal of Owenite socialism, and women such as Agnes Walker and Emma Martin acted as lecturers and missionaries for the Owenite cause.

At the same time women were involved in the anti-slavery campaign, and this appears to have been the campaign which particularly influenced Marion Reid. She declined to be drawn into lengthy consideration of the question of male suffrage, simply commenting that, 'It has already been ably discussed, and answered in the affirmative, by many of the greatest men of modern times: of these, Jeremy Bentham may be mentioned as the chief' (*Plea*, p. 23). Instead Reid was driven by 'scornful sneers – the more scornful in exact proportion to the want of anything like a reasonable argument' (*Plea*, ix), to focus upon the position of women:

> It is now high time – and we are glad to see that many efforts are being made – to call the attention of society, especially of woman herself, to the degraded rank which she holds among the human race . . . While in lands like our own, which have made considerable progress in civilisation, though she has won for herself many privileges, she is still very far from being allowed legal and social equality. Thus we see that the subjugation of the sex is general and undoubted . . . even in this country, her condition, though positively improved, is not much, if at all, improved in relation to that of her lord. Even here she is kept behind – still regarded too much as a mere appendage of man. She advances, it is true, when he advances; but it is no less true that she is always kept some steps behind him, and that not by any necessity of her nature, but by barriers which he erects to interrupt her progress. (*Plea*, pp. 1–2)

Reid clearly identified

> the disadvantages which, in this country, we conceive woman in general labours under. The principal of these seem to be:
> I. Want of equal civil rights.
> II. Enforcement of unjust laws.
> III. Want of means for obtaining a good substantial education.
> The second and the third of these grievances are, in themselves, and essentially, evil and unjust. The first is, perhaps, principally of importance, because without it there are no sure means of obtaining and securing the others. (*Plea*, p. 22)

The priority given to the suffrage places Reid ahead of her time. Yet she offered an interpretation of the impact of civil equality which reflects her times, and to some extent, her class status. Reid viewed women's natural, and she hoped, most frequent condition, as that 'of a happy wife and mother', and the argument for women's civil liberties was linked to an elevation and enlargement of women's domestic roles:

> But although we are convinced that no elevation of the position of woman can ever withdraw domestic occupations and pleasures from forming a part, and perhaps even the chief part of

her sphere, yet we are quite unable to see either the right or the reason which confines her to those occupations and pleasures. (*Plea*, pp. 14–15)

It is likely that other contemporary reformers found the claim that civil rights were compatible with woman's domestic roles helpful. This position was later extended into identifying areas of policy – education, health, and housing, for instance – to which women might bring a special perspective and knowledge. Ferguson notes that Reid anticipated many points later made both by Harriet Taylor Mill in the *Enfranchisement of Women*, and John Stuart Mill in *The Subjection of Women*.[40] Her vision of men and women co-operating in the advancement of society while retaining a traditional household structure and a gender division of labour seems close to that of J. S. Mill. Perhaps this reflected some need to reassure her contemporary audience; the fundamental message of the *Plea* is challenging and she opposed any restraint upon women entering any sphere of activity:

> The idea of any irruption being the consequence of the removal of these barriers is absurd. The dread of petticoated generals, ministers and legislators, is one with which we have so little sympathy, as to have some difficulty in believing in its existence. We would have every object of ambition as open to woman as to man, perfectly secure that the natural distinctions of the sexes are quite sufficient to maintain each in its proper place, without any of the artificial restraints which man is so fond of imposing, and which tend only to shackle and debilitate those who are bound by them. (*Plea*, pp. 39–40)

The arguments made in support of women's suffrage echo those made by the later suffrage campaign. She debunked the notion that women were virtually represented in parliament as their interests were identical to those of men, pointing to 'the many laws which have been obliged to be passed to protect them from their nearest male relatives . . . Those laws, then, are in themselves a convincing proof, first, that woman requires representation, and, second, that she is not represented'. She attacked existing inconsistencies which allowed women who met the property qualifications to vote for an East India Director or for a local Commissioner of Police, concluding 'Now, since no inconvenience has been found to result from allowing her to vote, for instance, for a commissioner of police – and since, in theory, it seems no more than justice – why not allow her right of voting for other local authorities, or any authorities whatever?' She also drew attention to the anomaly of taxation without representation, 'Does the tax-gatherer pass the door of the self-dependent and solitary female? . . . If she must pay, why cannot she also vote?' (*Plea*, pp. 26–7).

Opponents of women's suffrage sometimes suggested that women knew too little – 'But the great mass of voters do not possess, nor do they require, any very deep knowledge of political science' (*Plea*, p. 39) – or that women should not know too much, as an *Edinburgh Review* contributor protested:

> 'Subjects must sometimes come under discussion which could not be mooted before a female audience . . . it is not right that any one should be subjected to a painful struggle between the refined and decorous feelings of a British gentleman and the solemn and imperative duties of a British Legislator.' . . . It will be seen, in the passage I have quoted, that it is not the wounding of female delicacy that is feared. No: it is the pain that would be inflicted on the 'refined and decorous' feelings of our present 'British Legislators'. Now we cannot but think

that there is considerable affectation in absorbing such feelings to such persons; confusion they would be likely to feel, – but it is more probable that it would proceed from a guilty conscience than from true modesty. (*Plea*, p. 37)

Reid did not entertain many illusions about the immediate acceptability of her views, acknowledging that 'Many people – we are afraid the majority of the middle classes – think that woman's duties are comprised in good humour and attention to her husband, keeping her children neat and clean, and attending to domestic arrangements' (*Plea*, pp. 10–11). The value of her publication for sympathetic contemporaries, however, was a case argued with wit, clarity, logic and hope. Her conclusions were positive, and she suggested maximalist and minimalist positions:

If the subject is not allowed to rest, but, on the contrary, kept before the public by constant discussion, it will soon cease to be so startling as it is at present; and truth and right will be sure to prevail in the end.

Should prejudice still, however, be too strong to allow woman all the privileges of a rational creature, – if the age is not yet far enough advanced to admit of her having a voice in legislating for herself; at least it may be loudly demanded that justice be done her as to education and the laws, these being the results for which powers of legislation are most desirable. (*Plea*, pp. 40–2).

'Three Great Fights': Education, Medicine and Women's Suffrage

The limited scope of educational opportunities for girls and women was a major form of cultural confinement, attacked by Defoe as 'one of the most barbarous customs in the world' in 1697 – 'Their youth is spent to teach them to stitch and sew and make baubles. They are taught to read, indeed, and perhaps to write their names or so; and that is the height of a woman's education'.[41] Education was held to threaten the feminine charms of docility, modesty and delicacy – 'The softness of their nature, the delicacy of their frame, the timidity of their disposition, and the modesty of their sex, absolutely disqualified them for such exertions',[42] wrote one Scottish writer. According to Eunice Murray, 'Men believed these things; women said them, so afraid were they that if they possessed a well-developed brain they would be doomed to remain old maids'.[43] In consequence, in the mid-eighteenth century while 35 per cent of Lowland men were illiterate, the illiteracy rate of their womenfolk was 70 per cent; nine out of ten Highland women were then illiterate.[44] By the nineteenth century literacy rates had improved. In 1855 on the introduction of civil registration of marriages, it was found that 89 per cent of Scotsmen could sign the marriage register, as compared with 70 per cent in England and Wales. For women the figures were 77 per cent and 70 per cent respectively.[45] Yet girls remained on the periphery of educational provision – 'an academic schooling was generally seen as irrelevant to, even irreconcilable with, the woman's role – not least by mothers and daughters themselves. Consequently, fewer girls than boys went to school and those who did stayed a shorter time and learnt fewer subjects'.[46]

Nonetheless the notion of a democratic and egalitarian meritocracy is an enduring myth within Scottish society. Defoe referred to England as 'a land full of ignorance', while in Scotland, 'the poorest people have their children taught and instructed'. The level of educational provision in Scotland, however, was a matter of debate. In 1834 George Lewis found that only one in twelve of the population attended day schools, and that Scottish provision lagged behind that of France, Prussia, and parts of the United States, and was only marginally higher than that in England: 9 per cent attended day school in England; 9.6 per cent in Scotland. Such concerns were reiterated by the Argyll Commission of 1867 which claimed, (probably over-pessimistically), that just over half of children of school age in Glasgow appeared on school rolls.[47]

Lindy Moore probed more deeply into the extent of the Scottish 'democratic tradition' by investigating how far the pre-1872 system of parochial education 'provided sufficient teaching in the "higher branches" for talented and persevering children to advance, whatever their social origins'. She found that the subjects of Latin, maths and modern languages were available in a larger proportion of schools in Scotland than in England, but that there was little difference in the proportion of girls actually studying the subjects, and that the relatively greater number of Scottish boys studying classics meant that girls formed a smaller proportion of the total number of classics pupils: 5.7 per cent in Scotland compared with 6.5 per cent in England and Wales. This, she concluded, 'encapsulated on the one hand, the democratic tradition of Scottish education, which encouraged easier access to the higher branches of education, and, on the other, a presbyterian tradition which stamped women as second-class citizens'.[48]

This wider and older tradition of open access to the higher branches of learning probably accounted for the initial resistance within the Scottish educational establishment and its classrooms to the introduction of domestic subjects for girls into the Scottish curriculum. These moves from the 1850s apparently drew upon 'the combined influence of the English Committee of Council, the school inspectors, and the Scottish upper classes'.[49] This reflects both the pressures of the cult of domesticity, and the paradox, commented upon elsewhere by Linda Mahood, in the context of child-saving institutions, that philanthropic work (or educational work) 'emancipated middle-class women from the domestic routine of their own homes . . . in order to persuade working-class women to remain in theirs'.[50] From the 1870s, a domestic curriculum for girls appeared to also win the support of Scottish feminists who believed that it 'would raise the status of domesticity'.[51] The effect was to create an increasingly class- and sex-specific education which confined girls (and female teachers) within a limited curriculum. At the teacher training colleges only domestic subjects were open to the women students. As Lindy Moore remarks, it is surprising that even half-a-dozen schoolmistresses were reported to be teaching Latin or maths before 1872.[52]

The 'domestication' of the curriculum for girls underlined their exclusion from university education, closely linked to preparatory courses in Latin, maths and languages. The introduction of compulsory elementary education in 1872, albeit with exemptions, increased basic educational provision for girls. Secondary education remained, however, a middle-class and mainly male preserve: Scotland did not see an equivalent development to the spread of the English girls' schools. The founding of St Leonard's in St Andrews in 1877 under the headship of Miss Louisa Lumsden was exceptional rather than typical. The potential for female (and for male working-class) pupils to receive secondary education was improved after 1892 when all elementary education and some secondary education became free. Still, the priority for most working-class pupils, male and female, was to leave school for the workplace between the ages of twelve to fourteen. In the circumstances it is not surprising that the campaign for women's access to university, and to the medical profession, drew heavily upon middle-class activity, and the desire to extend the limited range of 'suitable' employment for middle-class women.

The 1850s and '60s saw the grouping together of women and sympathetic men in a variety of societies aiming at women's advancement. In England a key circle of women came together to found the Ladies Institute at Langham Place, London, in 1857, going on to publish the *English Woman's Journal* (subsequently the *Englishwoman's Review*) for much of the rest of the century. In 1860 the *Journal* reported upon special meetings of the National Association for the Promotion of Social Science held in Edinburgh and Glasgow, to which women were admitted 'as associates and members on equal terms with the men'.[53] The chief focus was on discussion of 'the opening up of new employments to women, and their more extensive admission into those branches of business already open to them'; identifying 'suitable' occupations, for instance, 'The Committee were desirous of extending the employment of women as book-keepers and cashiers in shops', and of 'finding an outlet for the emigration of a class of educated women'. The meeting also discussed the merits of 'lady doctors' – 'science and morality would alike be served by the general introduction of women as practitioners for their own sex', and concluded with the intention of setting up societies in Glasgow and Edinburgh.[54]

The fate of these committees is unknown but many later stalwarts of the Scottish women's movement attended, including Duncan McLaren MP, Prof. Blackie, Miss Emily Faithfull, and Miss Bessie Rayner Parkes. A small elite society, the Edinburgh Literary Society or Essay Society (later the Ladies Edinburgh Literary Society, and from 1880 the Ladies Edinburgh Debating Society) followed in 1865, initiated by nineteen-year-old Sarah Elizabeth Siddons Mair, bringing together 'a galaxy of youthful maidens eager on self-improvement'.[55] The Edinburgh Essay Society laid claim to being 'the first debating society in Scotland, and it is believed in all Britain, to hold a debate on the need for women to have a Parliamentary vote' (only five out of twenty were then in favour).[56] Its membership was small but drew in many who played significant roles in extending women's spheres. Over the years, these included, for instance, the young Marie Stopes, the birth control pioneer, and Mary Cornelius, founder of the Edinburgh Ladies Educational Association. To an extent it displayed the overlapping of membership in a range of societies typical of the Scottish women's movement.

The emergence of Ladies Educational Associations (LEAs) played an important role in the development of women's higher education. The LEAs set up in Edinburgh and St Andrews over 1867–9 ran university-style courses. The Edinburgh LEA offered courses given by sympathetic academics at Edinburgh University, effectively 'becoming an extra-mural arts department for women'.[57] Other LEAs formed in Aberdeen, Glasgow, Perth, and Dundee, took on wider roles, pressing for improvements in girls' schooling, pushing for women's admission to the Scottish universities, and running university-style courses. The provision of such courses led naturally to the desire for recognition of completion via certificates. A range of certificates were offered but the best-known and most sought-after title was that of the Lady Literate in Arts (LLA), a diploma after private study awarded by the University of St Andrews. In 1883 Glasgow University created a separate college for women, Queen Margaret's, while University College, Dundee, was open to women from its foundation.

The aim was to create opportunities and evidence of women's capacity for study. The campaign for women's entry to universities was closely linked to that for entry to a medical education for women. The unsuccessful attempts of Elizabeth Garrett (later Elizabeth Garrett Anderson) and Sophia Jex-Blake to enter medical degrees at the universities of St Andrews and Edinburgh during the 1860s were crucial test cases. The Surgeon's Hall riot in Edinburgh in 1870 vividly revealed the extent of entrenched male resistance to female medical students. The reactions of hostile university staff and a series of court decisons to establish the legal position in the 1870s ensured that Scotland did not pioneer the path for women's medical education in Britain. Women were denied entrance to the Scottish universities until 1892, much later than in the United States, Ireland, France, and Switzerland, although ahead of most English institutions, save for the trail-blazing University of London which opened its doors to women in 1878. Even after 1892, women were not admitted to university on equal terms with men. Resistance to women's entry into medicine remained, in terms of arrangements for teaching female students, and in attitudes. Elizabeth Bryson, one of the early medical graduates of St Andrews University, commented,

> It was the 'No, not a doctor!' from older, friendly, thoughtful men that I found hard to bear. They didn't like the idea of a woman doctor. Why? They feared the loss of something – delicacy? – modesty? – women should be protected from the harsh things, the sordid facts of life. What facts? Sex? What was modesty? Can real modesty be harmed by knowledge?[58]

Aberdeen was the only university to allow women access to mixed classes (which were cheaper) for graduation in *all* its faculties by 1900.

Alongside the campaign for improved educational opportunities ran that for women's suffrage. The defeat of John Stuart Mill's amendment which would have added women to the new electorate created by the 1867 Reform Act promoted the development of women's suffrage societies across Britain. The first Scottish society was formed in Edinburgh in 1867. The emphasis in the first stage of the mid-Victorian campaign lay in petitions – over two million signatures in support of women's suffrage were collected in Scotland between 1867 and 1876[59] – and in meetings, both public, and more private 'drawing room' meetings which raised the awareness of middle- and upper-class women. The failure to extend the parliamentary franchise to women on the passing of the Third Reform Act in 1884 dealt a blow to morale although suffrage societies continued their activity.

Progress had, however, been made in other areas. From 1881 qualified women could vote in local elections in Scotland while the creation of School Boards under the 1872 Education (Scotland) Act opened up a new forum of public activity for women. School Board elections probably provided some women with their first experience of canvassing electors and at the first School Board elections in Scotland in 1873 two women were elected, Jane Glen Arthur in Paisley and Flora Stevenson in Edinburgh. Other areas such as poor law and sanitary work also drew women into public roles. When Flora Stevenson's sister, Louisa, was appointed Convener of a Committee of the Parochial Board, one of its male members objected strongly: 'I object to Miss Stev'son because she's a wumman. Now you'll be telling me that Queen Victoria's a wumman, but the Queen is only a kind o' a figureheid. But Miss Stev'son's no a figureheid, she gangs into everything'.[60]

By the 1890s too, all of the political parties – Conservative, Liberal Unionist, Liberal, and the Independent Labour Party (ILP) – had women's organisations. The enlarged electorate after 1884 and the passing of the Corrupt Practices Act in 1883 created an environment in which parties were increasingly to depend on the efforts of voluntary helpers. The Primrose League, in particular, played a major role in drawing women into politics. Formed in England and Wales in 1883, and in Scotland in 1885, the League brought socialising into politics and by 1885 'many thousands of canvassers were furnished by the Primrose League'.[61] In Scotland, however, the Grand Council urged in 1905 that the tracing of removals was 'very suitable work for ladies, as they are not brought into contact with the electors at all'![62] Activity linked to the political parties was an important development but more influential in terms of creating the basis of post-1918 party organisation and membership than in furthering the cause of women's suffrage.

The suffrage movement entered a crucial new phase on the formation of the Women's Social and Political Union (WSPU) in Manchester in 1903; a Scottish branch was set up in 1906. The WSPU adopted militant tactics to grab publicity for 'The Cause', and after the 1906 election to put pressure upon the Liberal government. Scotland was important within this campaign as it was a bastion of parliamentary Liberalism; two successive Prime Ministers sat for Scottish seats as did several senior Cabinet ministers. In its early stages 'militancy' meant heckling at public meetings (not ladylike!) but in its later stages it encompassed window-breaking, and arson attacks upon property, and the famous tactic of hunger-striking adopted by arrested suffragettes. The more militant phase opened later in Scotland than in England, the so-called 'Scottish Outrages' dating from autumn 1912. The WSPU tactics were controversial and continued unabated until war broke out in 1914. Elspeth King underlines the value of the militant campaign, remarking that 'Until the outbreak of the first World War, the suffragettes were in the news every other day, and were putting their lives in danger so that women could have a future. Many historians have ignored this, and others have had the cheek to say that the militancy alienated the government and inhibited the women's cause. Women might still be waiting for the vote if it had been left to the men'.[63] The course of events makes it difficult to say what might have happened had war not broken out in 1914. Non-militant suffrage campaigning continued during the war itself, to ensure that women were not left out of any post-war extension of the suffrage, and the prospect of a renewed militant suffrage campaign after the war seems to have also influenced some cabinet ministers in favour of a compromise.[64]

What is clear is that the suffrage campaign involved the support of women of all classes across generations. Working-class activity is evident in the female political lodges of the 1830s and '40s, while the Scottish Women's Co-operative Guild offered consistent support for votes for women from 1893; and the close links between the ILP and the WSPU in cities such as Glasgow involved women not only in the suffrage campaign but in the early development of the Labour party. In concluding her history of the Scottish women's suffrage movement Leneman wrote, 'They have almost all been forgotten; yet never has any other cause mobilised so many women the length and breadth of Scotland in the way that "Votes for Women" did before World War 1'.[65]

Conclusions

Overall, women's experiences from 1780–1920 varied considerably, linked to factors such as class and locality, as well as gender, but by the 1920s women had made considerable advances. Winning the vote marked a major breakthrough towards citizenship as did the removal of legal barriers to women's entry into higher education and to a range of professions. Yet continuities qualify the extent of progress. Despite the removal of legal barriers women effectively found themselves excluded from areas of work briefly opened to them during the First World War. The gender division of labour stamped some occupations as 'women's work', characterised by low pay and low status. Equal pay had not been won and marriage bars remained in place in many jobs, including the Civil Service and teaching. The emphasis on 'woman's place is in the home' persisted throughout the inter-war years. Women had won the vote but the Heavens did not fall and there was no irruption of 'petticoated generals, ministers, and legislators'. In fact, only five women were returned to Westminster from Scotland between 1918 and 1939 and the first Scottish woman MP, the Duchess of Atholl, had opposed votes for women before 1918 and in the 1920s was the only woman MP to vote against giving women the vote at the age of 21.[66]

Her actions serve as a reminder that women were not unanimous on their new directions, and that the women's movement had to overcome the resistance of some women as well as deeply entrenched male opposition. By the 1930s, Winifred Holtby was among those who wrote of the dawning and reluctant recognition that hard-won gains might not be secure:

> The economic slump has reopened the question of women's right to earn. The political doctrine of the corporative state in Italy and Germany has inspired new pronouncements upon the function of the woman citizen. Psychological fashions arouse old controversies about the capacity of the female individual . . . Have we to readjust our ideas all over again? And whither, in 1934, are women going?[67]

Meanwhile the contribution of the women pioneers was already receding into 'the past'. Later in her life Elizabeth Bryson acknowledged that 'I was so busy living in my own present that I had little interest in the past' and that she had enjoyed entry to medicine 'as a free gift from the fighting pioneers . . . So short a time it takes the pioneer to be forgotten – or, worse than forgotten, slightly regarded. Youth, inheriting the accumulated riches, does not care much about those who gathered the store'.[68] A Whiggish, ever-onwards-ever-upwards view of historical developments, is questionable on many counts but it is particularly inappropriate in assessing the advance of women, as Holtby concluded:

> The march of the women is never regular, consistent nor universal. It advances in one place while it retreats in others. One individual looks forward, another backward, and the notions of which is 'forward' and which is 'backward' differ as widely as the directions followed.[69]

Notes

1.   Eleanor Gordon, 'Women's Spheres', in W. H. Fraser and R. J. Morris (eds), *People and Society in Scotland, Volume 2, 1830–1914*, (Edinburgh University Press, Edinburgh, 1990), p. 206.
2.   Lady Frances Balfour, *Ne Obliviscaris*, vol. II, (Hodder & Stoughton, London, 1930), p. 120.
3.   Joy Hendry, Editorial, 'The Women's Forum: Women in Scottish Literature', *Chapman* 74–5 (Autumn/Winter 1993), 3.
4.   Hugh MacDiarmid, *Scottish Eccentrics* (Routledge, London, 1936; 1972 edition), p. 160.
5.   Harry Graham, *A Group of Scottish Women* (Methuen, London, 1908), viii.
6.   Graham, vii.
7.   Joy Hendry, 'Snug in the Asylum of Taciturnity: Women's History in Scotland', in I. Donnachie and C. Whatley (eds), *The Manufacture of Scottish History*, (Polygon, Edinburgh, 1992), p. 126.
8.   Hendry, 'Snug in the Asylum', p. 126.
9.   Rosalind Marshall, *Virgins and Viragos: A History of Women in Scotland from 1080* (Collins, London, 1980); Glasgow Women's Studies Group, *Uncharted Lives* (Pressdram, Glasgow, 1983); Esther Breitenbach and Eleanor Gordon (eds). *The World is Ill Divided: Women's Work in Scotland in the Nineteenth and Early Twentieth Centuries* (Edinburgh University Press, Edinburgh, 1990) and (eds) *Out of Bounds: Women in Scottish Society, 1800–1945* (Edinburgh University Press, Edinburgh, 1992); Leah Leneman, *A Guid Cause*

The Women's Suffrage Movement in Scotland (Aberdeen University Press, Aberdeen, 1991); Lindy Moore, *Bajanellas and Semilinas: Aberdeen University and the Education of Women, 1860–1920* (Aberdeen University Press, Aberdeen, 1991); Elspeth King, *The Hidden History of Glasgow's Women: The Thenew Factor* (Mainstream, Edinburgh, 1993).

10. R. A. Houston, 'Women in the economy and society of Scotland, 1500–1800', in R. A. Houston and I. D. Whyte (eds), *Scottish Society, 1500–1800*, (Cambridge University Press, Cambridge, 1989), pp. 118–47.

11. Christopher A. Whatley, 'Women and the Economic Transformation of Scotland c.1740–1830', *Scottish Economic and Social History*, vol. 14 (1994), 19–41.

12. See Phyllis Stock-Morton, 'Finding our ways: different paths to women's history in the United States', in Karen Offen, Ruth Roach Pierson and Jane Rendall (eds), *Writing Women's History: International Perspectives* (Macmillan, London, 1991), p. 70; Mary Cullen, 'Women's history in Ireland', *ibid.*, pp. 429–30.

13. See Jane Purvis, 'From "women worthies" to poststructuralism? Debate and controversy in women's history in Britain', in Jane Purvis (ed.), *Women's History: Britain, 1850–1945* (UCL Press, London, 1995); Offen, Pierson and Rendall, *Writing Women's History*; Gisela Bock, 'Women's history and gender history: aspects of an international debate', in *Gender and History*, I, no. 1 (Spring 1989), 7–30; Joan Scott, *Gender and the Politics of History* (Columbia University, New York, 1988).

14. Margaret MacCurtain and Mary O'Dowd, 'An agenda for women's history in Ireland, 1500–1900', in *Irish Historical Studies*, vol. XXVIII, no. 109 (May 1992), 1–2.

15. Bock, p. 10.

16. Bock, p. 16.

17. Scott, p. 6.

18. Purvis, pp. 12–13.

19. MacCurtain and O'Dowd, p. 2.

20. MacCurtain and O'Dowd, p. 5.

21. Eunice Murray, *Scottish Women in Bygone Days* (Gowans & Gray, Glasgow and London, 1930), p. 172.

22. Houston, p. 47.

23. Houston, p. 47.

24. Leah Leneman, 'Two steps forward, one step back: the women's movement, 1850–1979', in Historical Association Committee for Scotland and the Historical Association, *Britain, 1850–1979: Politics and Social Change* (Edinburgh, 1995), p. 21.

25. Marion Reid, *A Plea for Woman* (Edinburgh, 1843; Polygon reprint, Edinburgh, 1988), pp. 14–15. Henceforth *Plea*.

26. See Whatley, 'Women and the Economic Transformation of Scotland c.1740–1830', pp. 19–41.

27. Figures cited in Eleanor Gordon, 'Women's Spheres', in Fraser and Morris, p. 209.

28. Gordon, in Fraser and Morris, p. 214.

29. Gordon, in Fraser and Morris, p. 214.

30. M. W. Flinn, J. Gillespie, N. Hill, A. Maxwell, R. Mitchison and C. Smout, *Scottish Population History from the Seventeenth Century to the 1930s* (Cambridge, 1977), p. 353. See also Andrew Blaikie, *Illegitimacy, Sex, and Society: Northeast Scotland, 1750–1900* (Clarendon Press, Oxford, 1993); and Andrew Blaikie, 'A Kind of Loving: Illegitimacy, Grandparents and the Rural Economy of North East Scotland, 1750–1900', in *Scottish Economic and Social History*, vol. 14 (1994), *passim*.

31. Debbie Kemmer, 'Victorian Values and the Fertility Decline: The case of Scotland', in *Critical Social Research* (1986), pp. 13–15.

32. Kemmer, p. 15.

33. Kemmer, p. 27.

34. Winifred Holtby, *Women and a Changing Civilisation* (Longmans, Green, London, 1936), p. 38.

35. Susanne Ferguson, 'Introduction', *Plea*, v.

36. King, *Hidden History*, p. 63.

37. Kenneth Logue, *Popular Disturbances in Scotland* (Donald, Edinburgh, 1979), p. 199.

38. *Glasgow Courier*, 2 November 1819, cited in King, *Hidden History*, p. 64.

39.   *Scottish Patriot*, 21 December 1839, cited in Elspeth King, 'Scottish Women's Suffrage Movement', in Breitenback and Gordon, *Out of Bounds*, p. 127.
40.   Susanne Ferguson, 'Introduction', *Plea*, vii.
41.   Daniel Defoe, *Essays upon Projects* (London, 1697), cited in Eunice Murray, *Scottish Women*, p. 166.
42.   Cited in Murray, *Scottish Women*, p. 171.
43.   Murray, *Scottish Women*, p. 171.
44.   R. A. Houston, 'Women in the economy', p. 134.
45.   Figures given in Helen Corr, 'An Exploration into Scottish Education', in W. H. Fraser and R. J. Morris, *People and Society in Scotland, Volume 2, 1830–1914)*, p. 294.
46.   Lindy Moore, 'Invisible Scholars: Girls learning Latin and mathematics in the elementary public schools of Scotland before 1872', in *History of Education*, vol. 13, no. 2 (1984), p. 121.
47.   Defoe quoted in Corr, 'An Exploration etc', p. 290; figures, Corr, 'An Exploration', p. 293.
48.   Lindy Moore, 'Invisible Scholars', p. 121, and p. 131.
49.   Moore, 'Invisible Scholars', p. 131.
50.   Linda Mahood, 'Family Ties: Lady Child-Savers and Girls of the Street', in Breitenbach and Gordon, *Out of Bounds*, p. 59.
51.   Lindy Moore, 'Educating for the "Woman's Sphere": Domestic Training versus Intellectual Discipline', in Breitenbach and Gordon, *Out of Bounds*, p. 32.
52.   Lindy Moore, 'Invisible Scholars', p. 131.
53.   *The English Woman's Journal*, vol. VI, no. 33 (1 November 1860), 145.
54.   *The English Woman's Journal*, vol. VI, no. 33, 147–50.
55.   Lettice Milne Rae, *Ladies in Debate: being a history of the Ladies' Edinburgh Debating Society, 1865–1935*, (Oliver & Boyd, London and Edinburgh, 1936), pp. 19–23. *passim*.
56.   Rae, *Ladies in Debate*, p. 33.
57.   Lindy Moore, 'The Scottish Universities and Women Students, 1862–1892', in Jennifer J Carter and Donald J Withrington (eds), *Scottish Universities: Distinctiveness and Diversity* (Donald, Edinburgh, 1992), p. 140.
58.   Elizabeth Bryson, *Look Back in Wonder* (D. Winter, Dundee, 1967), p. 161.
59.   Eleanor Gordon, 'Woman's Sphere', p. 228.
60.   Cited in Rae, *Ladies in Debate*, p. 42.
61.   Beatrix Campbell, *The Iron Ladies: Why do Women Vote Tory?* (Virago, London, 1987), p. 18.
62.   National Library of Scotland; Primrose League Grand Council Minutes, 16 December 1905.
63.   Elspeth King, 'Scottish Women's Suffrage Movement', in Breitenbach and Gordon, *Out of Bounds*, p. 146.
64.   See discussion of this point in Penny Summerfield, 'Women and war in the twentieth century', in Jane Purvis, *Women's History*, pp. 317–18.
65.   Leah Leneman, *A Guid Cause: The Women's Suffrage Movement in Scotland* (Aberdeen University Press, Aberdeen, 1991; rev. ed. Mercat Press, 1995), p. 217.
66.   See Catriona Burness, 'The long, slow march: Scottish women MPs, 1918–45', in Breitenbach and Gordon, *Out of Bounds*, pp. 151–73, *passim*.
67.   Holtby, *Women and a Changing Civilisation*, pp. 5–7.
68.   Bryson, *Look Back in Wonder*, p. 139.
69.   Holtby, *Women and a Changing Civilisation*, p. 182.

8

Some Early Travellers

Dorothy McMillan

In this chapter I take as my starting point that all literature of travel operates between notions of 'here' and 'there' and the audience for such writing may sometimes be in both places at the same time, just as the writer too may shift positions in significant ways. The four women that I deal with – Janet Schaw, Lady Anne Lindsay Barnard, Anne Grant of Laggan and Frances Wright – could all be discussed under different headings, but they all at some point in their lives fill my category of 'here' and 'there' writers. They can also be used to show the transition from eighteenth-century pragmatism (sometimes even callousness) in Janet Schaw through the humanised enlightenment attitudes of Anne Barnard to the romantic idealism of Anne Grant, albeit controlled by her stern evangelicalism, and finally to the post-French Revolution commitment to love and liberty that informs the work of Frances Wright.

Janet Schaw (?1737–?1801)

Janet Schaw's *Journal of a Lady of Quality* written probably between 1774 and 1776 during her journeys from Scotland to the West Indies, North Carolina and Portugal, was not published until 1921 after it had been serendipitously discovered in the course of a search for other material.[1] This accident of female authorial visibility is made yet more ironic by what is signalled by the volume's frontispiece, for opposite the title page proclaiming the 'Lady of Quality' is a portrait by Raeburn of Alexander Schaw, Janet's brother: the face of the author remains invisible, shadowed only by its possible likeness to the public face of Alexander and to that of her mother whose portrait is given later in the text. The voyages that Janet Schaw charts in this *Journal* were made at first in the company of her brother, Alexander Schaw, who had been appointed searcher of customs at St Christopher, and of the children, Fanny (18), John (11) and William, 'Billie' (9), of John Rutherford of North Carolina whose sister, Anne, had been the first wife of Janet's second brother Robert Schaw, himself settled in America. The group was also accompanied by Janet's 'abigail', Mrs Mary Miller, who becomes the comic villainess of the first half of the journey. Janet was then the only one of the group who did not have to travel, who made the arduous journey apparently out of family solidarity and perhaps sheer desire for the adventure. The editors explain that the journal seems to have been written for her own amusement and that of the supposed female friend to whom it is addressed, although obviously from the existence of several copies, it may be assumed that it circulated at least among a family group. Whatever the extent of the audience, the *Journal* was clearly a private document written without any sense that it could become, as it has, 'a document of rare interest and importance, one which, as far as we know, and especially as it bears on the Scottish phase of American colonial history, is unique' (*Journal*, Introduction, p. 6). What began in the personal and private sphere has become a public source in which the personal is in danger of being lost. The Andrews' meticulously researched edition has almost 100 pages of Appendices in the course of which Janet herself is scarcely mentioned: the dates of her birth and death are approximate. Presumably had she married (or killed someone, or published even one poem) the detail of her life would have become more available.

But, of course, Janet is in another sense not really lost, for it is possible to seek a self in the texture of the account itself. It is a teasing search. Elizabeth Bohls writing about the 'aesthetics of colonialism', that is, the ways in which the language of aesthetic discourse can be used to cover up the uglinesses of slavery, chooses Janet Schaw's journal as her central text partly because she finds it 'eminently readable, at times gripping, with a distinctive narrative voice'.[2] Questions remain, however, about whether this 'voice' ever quite crystallises into a woman.

Janet Schaw possibly makes her self most intensely felt in the early part of her *Journal* when she is dealing with the hair-raising outward journey in the frigate, *The Jamaica Packet*, under its almost unbelievably incompetent and venal captain, Thomas Smith. It is here that she establishes both her authority and her mode: what she writes is remarkably like the preface to a work of fiction setting out to shape a narrative voice and explain the rationale of selection:

> I propose writing you every day, but you must not expect a regular Journal. I will not fail to write whatever can amuse myself; and whether you find it entertaining or not, I know you will not refuse it a reading, as every subject will be guided by my own immediate feelings. My opinions and descriptions will depend on the health and the humour of the Moment in which I write; from which cause my Sentiments will often appear to differ on the same subject. (*Journal*, p. 20)

She clearly conceives of her narrative too in a self-consciously literary way which suggests that it is composed, that it is seldom rushed down in the hurly-burly of the actual events it describes:

> My going will cheer the Travils of the best of Brothers, and once more give me the other, lost from childhood. Time will restore me to you, perhaps to my dear Native land, on which may Heaven shower its choicest blessings. But farewell, my spirits are quite worn out, and my fatigues require rest, tho' I fear my narrow bed will be no great inducement to the drowsy powers. Adieu, sound and peaceful be the slumbers of my friend, whatever Mine prove. (*Journal*, p. 22)

And in truth between storm and sickness and appalling food and other vicissitudes, which include the ship turning on its side with concomitant loss of masts, it is hard to see how the *Journal* could be other than a largely retrospectively composed account. It is an account, however, which depends on Janet Schaw's skill in writing dialogue, in creating a sense of the characters around her and in being prepared to offer herself as a comic spectacle. After the ship has turned on its side, resulting miraculously in no more serious injury than her own cut forehead, John's leg being bruised and 'a poor duck, squeezed as flat as a pancake', a ridiculous scene is revealed by the return of light:

> The two state rooms had sent forth their contents, and the one occupied by the Captain, being a sort of store room, amongst many other things a barrel of Molasses pitched directly on me, as did also a box of small candles, so I appeared as if tarred and feathered, stuck all over with farthing candles. (*Journal*, p. 52)

Janet Schaw's fate here comically prefigures what is to be her persistent alleged fear in North Carolina, as the tensions mount towards rebellion against Britain, that she will in fact be tarred and feathered. Although in truth she seems never to have encountered more than the fear, she makes frequent reference to the practice and when she eventually escapes from the growing agitation she describes herself as having 'fled from the tar-pot' (*Journal*, p. 211). Yet perhaps this conjunction of comic incident and future fear is more than a happy coincidence.

But our sense of a rounded Janet Schaw on this outward voyage is given also by the information we get about her reading habits, her knowledge of Swift and Lord Kames, and her sense of Scotland as both special in itself, yet also part of a Britain of which she is proud. She uses English as an epithet of approbation quite as freely as Scotch but she has an important awareness that one's native land is both smaller and dearer than the larger unit to which it belongs. It is this, that in spite of her sometimes rather unthinking conservatism, arouses her sympathy for the wretched group of island emigrants who are being transported by the greedy Captain under ghastly living conditions. When she first sees these unfortunates, she remarks tartly: 'They looked like a Cargo of Dean Swift's Yahoos newly caught'. It would be hard to forgive this perception were it not almost immediately mitigated by her sympathy for the Islanders' grief when the ship passes their islands (the Orkneys or Shetlands):

> 'The rude scene before us, with its wild rocks and snow-cover'd mountains, was dear to them, far more dear than the most fertile plains will ever appear. It was their native land, and how much is contained in that short Sentence, none but those who have parted with their own can be judge of. (*Journal*, p. 28; pp. 33–4)

The Islanders' attachment to their native place enables Janet Schaw to move into a sentimental idiom of approval which associates them with herself and removes from them the stigma of the inhuman.

Janet Schaw's sympathies are not, however, lively enough to encompass the negro slaves of the West Indies or the Carolinas. She is less emotionally susceptible as she herself moves further away from her native place, her real sentimental anchors are removed and she allows herself more frequently to be persuaded by the prejudices of others; nor does it ever seem to occur to her that the nature of the slave trade inevitably removes the softening possibility of native place from its victims. Her comments on the treatment of the slaves in the West Indies may not be worse than what we find elsewhere but they are frighteningly at odds with what we might have wished from an otherwise lively emotional sense. And so the passages about the slaves constantly challenge a modern sensibility: we must be constantly alert to the anachronistic desire to assess Janet Schaw too harshly. What we do find, however, is that Janet Schaw finds it much more difficult to sustain her callous view of the sufferings of the slaves when she moves from the exotic paradise of the West Indies to North Carolina where also she finds political attitudes among the whites which are more challenging to her own.

As she approaches her lodgings in St John's shortly after her arrival Janet Schaw writes: 'Just as we got into the lane, a number of pigs run out at a door, and after them a parcel of monkeys. This not a little surprised me, but I found what I took for monkeys were negro children, naked as they were born' (*Journal*, p. 78). We are not, of course, dealing here with a problem of the eyes: Janet Schaw is making a joke, no great offence but a kind of preparation for the more serious ability to perceive the negro as a lower species of animal. The most chilling passage occurs on St Christopher (which Janet Schaw reaches from Antigua in a boat 'no larger than a Kinghorn boat' just after a eulogy on the beauty and natural profusion of the country):

> The Negroes who are all in troops are sorted so as to match each other in size and strength. Every ten Negroes have a driver, who walks behind them, holding in his hand a short whip and a long one. You will too easily guess the use of these weapons; a circumstance of all others the most horrid. They are naked, male and female, down to the girdle and you constantly observe where the application has been made. But however dreadful this must appear to a humane European, I will do the creoles the justice to say, they would be as averse to it as we are, could it be avoided, which has often been tried to no purpose. When one becomes better acquainted with the nature of the Negroes, the horror of it must wear off. It is the suffering of the human mind that constitutes the greatest misery of punishment, but with them it is merely corporeal. (*Journal*, p. 127)

Incomprehensible behaviour on the part of the slaves is always interpreted in the least favourable terms. Here she describes the responses of a family just off a slave ship and about to be sold (although it is unclear if they have any notion of what is likely to happen to them):

> They stood up to be looked at with perfect unconcern. The husband was to be divided from the wife, the infant from the mother; but the most perfect indifference ran thro' the whole. They were laughing and jumping, making faces at each other, and not caring a single farthing for their fate. (*Journal*, p. 128)

Nevertheless Janet Schaw is uneasily superior to the worst of her perceptions. When she gets to North Carolina, she comes constantly and finally dangerously up against the anti-British pre-independence spirit which leaves even her own family split and produces some tart remarks from her: the Ladies burn 'their tea in solemn procession' but they delay 'till the sacrifice [is] not very considerable, as I do not think any one offered above a quarter of a pound' (p. 155). Disquiet about the treatment of slaves is less firmly suppressed in this part of the journal. The negroes are still 'brutal hands' to leave children in (p. 157), still have 'yelping, discordant voices' (p. 169), but they also become 'stout' oarsmen (p. 177) or 'a noble troop' (p. 171). It is not, however, Janet Schaw's pro-British political conservatism that pushes her towards a more rationally based view of the negro population – after all the approved Loyalists do not treat their slaves differently from the 'rebels'; it is rather the radicalism of her beliefs about farming. She fancies herself, not it would seem without some justification, as a bit of an expert on the virtues of Scottish farming methods. And she is appalled by the primitive and unproductive methods she sees all around her. When Janet Schaw gets going on the wilful backwardness she observes even on her brother's estate, our sense of a real personality once again becomes strong:

> In the course of sixteen miles which is the distance between these places and the town, there is but one plantation, and the condition it is in shows, if not the poverty, at least the indolence of its owner. My brother indeed is in some degree an exception to this reflection. Indolent he is not; his industry is visible in everything round him, yet he is also culpable in adhering to the prejudices of this part of the world, and in using only the American methods of cultivating his plantation. Had he followed the style of an East Lothian farmer, with the same attention and care, it would now have been an Estate worth double what it is. Yet he has done more in the time he has had it than any of his neighbours, and even in their slow way, his industry has brought it to a wonderful length. (*Journal*, pp. 159–60)

The protectiveness of the older sister who knows better but who is also aware that her brother has not had the full advantages of Scotland is as pleasing as it is comic. Her brother's wife is more benighted: she is shocked by the idea of manuring the ground recommended by both Janet and Alexander and declares that she could never eat corn 'that grew through dirt'. But 'she is a most excellent wife and a fond mother . . . her person is agreeable, and if she would pay it a little more attention, it would be lovely' (p. 161).

Out of this combination of sisterly superiority and unsisterly bitchiness comes a more reflective attitude to the possible merits of the negroes, some of whom are credited with a more utilitarian approach to the natural riches of the land than their white masters:

> The Negroes are the only people that seem to pay any attention to the various uses that the wild vegetables may be put to. For example, I have sent you also a paper of their vegetable pins made from the prickly pear, also molds for buttons made from the calabash, which likewise serves to hold their victuals. The allowance for a Negro is a quart of Indian corn per day, and a little piece of land which they cultivate much better than the poorer white people with us. They steal whatever they can come at, and even intercept the cows and milk them. They are indeed the constant plague of their tyrants, whose severity or mildness is equally regarded by them in these Matters. (*Journal*, pp. 176–7)

Even the thefts of the negroes here seem to be attracting covert approval and their masters are turned into tyrants within a few lines. It is not, of course, surprising that the best as well as the worst of Janet Schaw's opinions come out of prejudices derived from her attachment to her native place. And as she makes her escape from an increasingly hostile America she anticipates her return with a fervour that indicates that it is at home that she is able to be herself without affectation or pretence: 'Our cabins and state-rooms are large and commodious, our provisions excellent and our liquor tolerable; but I long for a drink of Scotch two penny, and will salute the first pint-stoup I meet and kiss the first Scotch earth I touch' (p. 218).

But in spite of all the individualising and placing touches there remain peculiar question marks over Janet Schaw's journal. So much does our notion of the individual subjectivity seem to depend on our grasp of its external history that a full self cannot finally be made known to us by writing alone. In the case of a self in history we seem to need more evidence than is supplied by the text so that we can feel that our interpretation of the text's codes is at least colourably plausible. Elizabeth Bohls adduces Janet Schaw's refusal to protect herself obsessively from the bronzing power of the sun as the creole women in the West Indies do, as evidence of a proto-feminist distancing of herself from the gender codes of the society she is visiting even while she has accepted the racial codes; in addition since the gender codes depend on absolute difference between the colour of the creoles and of the slaves, Janet Schaw's rebellion here a little undermines the racial codes themselves – thus Schaw situates herself neither with the slaves nor with the creoles.[3] This seems a fair point, Janet Schaw's very praise of the creole women as exemplary wives and mothers clearly separates them from herself. But Bohls does not go on to consider, nor is it part of her aim to do so, the difference that it makes if Janet Schaw's addressee is a man. Why should the editors be so confident that Janet Schaw writes to a woman? Is it perhaps because of a feeling, not necessarily endorsed by the period itself, that what they take to be the proprieties of the time would be violated by such a lengthy correspondence with a man? But why not even imagine her writing to a man for whom she felt something more than the friendship of acquaintance? In such a context a number of her remarks would gain in piquancy what they lost in modesty. Remarks about the appearance and behaviour of men begin to take on the appearance of mild flirtation rather than feminine solidarity and the call to approve 'a brown beauty' becomes more strongly personal than political. Writing about the attractions of St Christopher's (St Kitt's) Janet Schaw concludes:

> They are a people I like vastly, and were there nothing to make me wish otherwise, I would desire to live for ever with them. But, oh, my friend! I again repeat that in the midst of these inchanting scenes and amongst a most agreeable people, I would prefer a habitation under a snow-cover'd mountain, were that habitation even a cottage. Do not suppose however that I repent, or in the least regret what I have done – that is far from the case. My heart approves my conduct and that merciful power who has guarded and supported me thro' numberless trials will at last reward that patience and fortitude he has himself inspired. At whatever time we meet, I am certain we will meet with unabated regard, and sufferings past are pleasant on recollection when properly supported. (*Journal*, p. 130)

This sounds much more like a lover left behind than a friend. Similarly at the end of this section of the Journal she entrusts to the care of her correspondent, 'sweet meats for your Sisters' and concludes: 'Oh thou envied paper! would I could enclose myself within you; my body I cannot, but there goes my soul in that, and that and that kiss' (p. 133). More seems to be implied here than routine wish for her return to Scotland: Janet Schaw's desire for fuller embodiment mirrors that of her modern reader.

Lady Anne Lindsay Barnard (1750–1825)

The recipients of the correspondence of Lady Anne Lindsay Barnard, travelling this time because of the needs of her husband's position, albeit a position she had largely secured for him, are well known: she wrote principally to Henry Dundas, Secretary of State for War in Pitt's first administration (Dundas had also been the suitor of Lady Frances Douglas and Lady Louisa Stuart and probably of Lady Anne), to McCartney, the first Governor of the Cape Province, and to her family. Our reading of the letters is made more confident by our knowledge of their destination. This does not mean that all their stories may be read on the surface but we can have some security in testing their apparently involuntary revelations. Her published letters to Dundas, published incidentally towards the end of the Boer War, tell the most complete story of her residence in the Cape between 1797 and 1802. They are very clearly the letters of a woman writing to a man and of a private individual, placed in a position of public trust, writing to a great public figure. In them Anne Barnard characterises herself as 'a poor weak woman', but patently does not believe her own characterisation. And although we cannot be sure how much attention Henry Dundas paid to her advice and political analysis we can, with hindsight, see how much of her policy was good policy. We can also see how peculiarly gendered her perceptions are: indeed some of her most acute analyses either come out of transactions with her own 'feminine' bitchiness or self-protectiveness, or are generated by the gendered discourse of the housewife.

Anne Barnard, in comparison with Janet Schaw, is remarkably free of racial or colour prejudice. Of course, direct comparisons are not fair because the countries they visited had wholly different conditions: in the West Indies there were only systematically degraded slaves, in the Cape the black people, even when enslaved, were not yet being treated with the contempt of later days and in the interior, wars had been fought with tribes that were free people and had to be treated with fear if not always respect. Nevertheless, Anne Barnard, although still sometimes taking the common alternative position to disgust, which was treating the blacks as if they were children, has a strong sense of the need to consider the specifics of every relationship whether personal or political. Sometimes, however, her fairness to the blacks, including the presumed ugly Hottentots (Khoikhoi), derives from the rather less pleasant trait of disparagement of the Dutch women.

The disparagement itself probably comes out of peculiar susceptibilities in Anne Barnard. She had, after all, married Andrew Barnard in 1793, apparently at the last gasp of possibility; he was twenty-eight and she was forty-three; neither of them had the financial sufficiency for comfortable living. Lady Anne's pleas to Dundas on her husband's behalf are easily readable as calling in obligations to herself. She must have been ever conscious of the need to keep in with Dundas and the parallel need to keep young for her husband. In circumstances like this even strong women turn to wiles. In the Dutch women of the Cape, and even of the interior, where it was harder to ignore their solid virtues, Anne Barnard found a constant source of validation in their grossness for her own slighter beauty: one of the first stories she tells Dundas is about the size of the Dutch female foot. It is a good story and well told:

> A tradesman in London, hearing their feet were so large, sent a box of shoes on speculation, which almost put the Colony in a blaze, so angry were the Beauties. But day by day a pair was sent for by a slave in the dark, until at last all the shoes vanished.[4]

The letters are spattered with references to the Dutch 'Glundalclitches' – Swift has a lot to answer for in the formulation of eighteenth-century prejudice. Even the vindication of her policy of conciliation of the Dutch through attentions to their women is couched in metaphor which emphasises the physical grossness of the women: 'I have given a most capital party . . . the mothers and daughters came, and to plough with heifers has always been reckoned a good means to improve reluctant soil' (*LCGH*, p. 84). But in spite of the size of the Dutch women, which makes 'Dutch doll' a peculiarly ironic appellation, the Cape *vrowes* are also notorious for infidelity: 'Amongst the Dutch women [three or four flirtations are] nothing – each one has her lover, and, if more, it only the more proves her charms (*LCGH*, p. 73).

But if the Dutch have their lovers, they also have their children, and Anne Barnard is vulnerable on this front. In Stellenbosch she says ruefully that so pitiable is it felt to be to have no family that she thinks of giving herself 'credit for half a dozen left at school' (*LCGH*, p. 117). And with a family in Rondebosch after failing to nurse an eleven-month child which was 'such a porpoise' in her arms she once more is tempted to claim some boys in England, but not girls, for 'I will not enact the girls' mother and leave my girls behind' (*LCGH*, pp. 159–60).

It is in such a context of mingled disparagement and desire that we must read Anne Barnard's celebration of black comeliness and dexterity and intelligence. The Hottentots she finds not ugly as the Boers would have them: 'their features are small and their cheek-bones immense, but they have a kind expression of countenance' (*LCGH*, p. 66). The Kaffir chief who visits the Castle where the Barnards live in the Cape with his train of wives and dogs 'was as fine a morsel of bronze as I ever saw, and there ought to be a pair of them with candlesticks in their hands' (*LCGH*, p. 79). The diminishing aestheticising of the Kaffir (Nguni) chief has its own dangers but is an advance on seeing him as a lower animal. When Anne Barnard sees a troop of slave children in the household of the Landdrost of Stellenbosch, she sees not monkeys, but 'eight little naked mice that run about the gardens and offices just as they came into the world, without being ashamed' (*LCGH*, p. 112). Her account of her meeting with a Hottentot girl is shaped by admiration for her beauty and youth:

> My good genius presented me Pharaoh's daughter in the very brook before me, washing her royal robes, one of the most picturesque creatures it was possible to see. From afar I saw my copper-coloured princess seated on a stone and all over ornaments, and making the waggon go on I slipped out and went across to her. She let me make a little sketch of her, none of the gentlemen being by, and in the return I gave her some old silver lace which I had in my workbag. Her transport on seeing it passed all bounds; she clasped her hands to adore it, tied it round her head, and then took it off and spread it on the bushes. She was really a very gallant-looking girl of eighteen, and most good-natured. (*LCGH*, p. 179)

Of course, the story of this encounter is also coloured by the willingness of the Western traveller to turn natives into aesthetic tour sites but this perception is mitigated by that telling 'really' where Anne Barnard recognises the dignity of the ordinary girl. And when she explains that on the following day she and her sister-in-law, lacking water to wash, 'went to a spring and bathed as nature meant us to do' (*LCGH*, p. 180), she seems to be eliding otherness, to be claiming kinship with the Hottentot girl.

If Anne Barnard's freedom from vulgar racism is inextricably bound up with her threatened female position, her political perceptions are equally rooted in a gendered self-deprecation which acts as a kind of decent cover for real assertiveness. From the beginning she assumes a role with Dundas that permits some titillating near flirtation. When she climbs Table Mountain with John Barrow, whose official reports on the state of the Cape Province are still read where hers are neglected, she makes sure that Dundas understands that her climb is an act of female assertion, yet simultaneously she invites him to speculate on its potentially embarrassing and teasing characteristics: 'If it was difficult to ascend the hill, it was much more so to descend. The ladies were dressed for the occasion, else – I need not say more after the word "else"' (*LCGH*, p. 71). She says no more but clearly wishes to tease his imagination with versions of her nearly exposed femininity. There is a telling difference here between the letter which she writes to Dundas about her garb for her climb and the letter she writes to her sisters. It is unsurprisingly a consistent feature of the letters to her sisters that they dwell more on domestic and personal detail than on social and political commentary but even when they relate the same personal exploits they vary in indicative ways. Here she describes her husband watching her leap away from him into the rocks:

> I had stolen a part of Barnard's wardrobe for precaution, which I found was eminently useful, but which made him, as I bounded up the rocks, laugh and call out, 'Hey-day, Anne, what are these?' – 'Yours! *myne lieve vriende*, my dear friend!' said I – 'You must acknowledge it is the first time you were ever conscious of my wearing them'.[5]

Clearly Anne Barnard wants to remind Dundas about what might have been seen had she not worn trousers while at the same time she refrains from drawing attention to her intimacy with her husband.

Elsewhere Anne Barnard is less coy about femininity but still persistently uneasy about the status of her public position. There can be little doubt that her consistent policy of conciliation of the disaffected Dutch through unselective sociability (a kind of 'democratic' behaviour at which aristocrats are adept) was both politic and effective in protecting the difficult British position in the Cape, difficult particularly with the background of French Wars. There can be little doubt too that at the time it was a policy that could be most effectively executed by a female public hostess. But, of course, Anne Barnard could not fail to recognise that outside this arena her role could only be modestly advisory. Her letters are peppered with references to 'miserable female notions' (*LCGH*, p. 45); a 'woman's opinion' (*LCGH*, p. 90); 'the geese called women' (*LCGH*, p. 145). Yet this self-effacement goes along with an occasionally irritable knowledge that she is right because she can see much that men, in their failure to attend to the particular and the personal, often miss.

Consequently she appropriates the discourse of the household to define the political. She is, she frequently says, 'a Martha' (*LCGH*, p. 72; p. 147) and as such she can see that good housewifery might save more than families. 'Women', she remarks, 'may say anything without presumption' and so she presumes to tell Admiral Pringle that he should conciliate the seamen in the Cape by anticipating in his speech to them concessions rumoured to be being made back home but not yet officially announced. He is not sufficiently daring to do so:

> Of course he must be right, as he is a clever man and knows his business; but how often have I not seen (to use a vulgar proverb) 'a stitch in time save nine'! (*LCGH*, p. 99)

It is not the only time that she uses this homely expression and when she does she is always proved right by events – of course, it is true that she is telling the story. Hostilities with the Kaffirs she also presumes to comment upon while apologising for 'having presumed to take up your attention by my poor details on what is so much out of my walk as this war, its commencement, or duration' (*LCGH*, p. 228). It is precisely in this housewifely attention to detail that Anne Barnard's strengths as a political commentator lie and it is this which marks her letters out from the official reports of John Barrow. It also enables her to critique Barrow's accounts in terms much more personally well-informed than those of twentieth-century post-colonial discourse.

John Barrow was a career diplomat appointed as personal secretary to Lord McCartney. McCartney made Barrow his official representative in the interior into which Barrow made several lengthy journeys. Barrow's task was to investigate relations between the

Dutch East India Company and the Afrikaners and between these and the native people. Mary Louise Pratt describes Barrow's narrative as 'a strange, highly attenuated kind of narrative that seems to do everything possible to minimize the human presence'; Barrow's account, she says, 'by and large separates Africans from Africa (and Europeans from Africans) by relegating the latter to objectified ethnographic portraits set off from the narrative of the journey'.[6]

Barrow had a chequered relationship with Anne Barnard: when they climbed Table Mountain together they were obviously in a sense 'mates' but the subsequent complicated political and personal relationships of the Cape resulted in a fight with Anne's husband which prevented the wives meeting on friendly terms. This is the kind of 'kitchen' detail that Anne Barnard can offer us and the kind which is usually omitted from assessments of public reports. Barrow's report is discussed by Anne Barnard in a letter to Lord Macartney after he had left the Cape. By this point, October 1800, Barrow had married Anna Maria Truter and Anne Barnard considers among other things the possible effect a prospective marriage might have had upon his official reports:

> I long to see Barrow's publication – you say that [it is said to have] very great merit. I am convinced it will in all respects where science, & knowledge, & information on his subject can shine; but I should doubt if the account of the place & people could be given with the disengaged honesty a man is likely to write with, who is here to-day & away to-morrow, & whether a lurking uncertainty whether he might not spend a lump of his life here, by marrying the Dutchwoman he was in love with, might not very naturally shackle his pen.[7]

What Anne Barnard is able to predict is what Mary Louise Pratt fails to investigate: Barrow is likely to distance himself from the people and the landscape since he cannot be quite sure where in the future he will be required to situate himself within it. Lady Anne, however, already knows how to gauge her gendered position and knows too how to draw upon her early experience of another allegedly difficult country to validate her point. Here she is speaking what she calls 'her nonsense' about conciliation with the Kaffirs:

> Well, were we to give up to the Kaffirs that part of the country I mention, supposing they stipulate for it, and supposing that we can according to our treaty with the Dutch, where would be the harm? The farms are already plundered and destroyed, the implements of husbandry burnt. The cattle are 'lifted', as they say in Scotland, and the farmers fled. (*LCGH*, p. 232)

It is not merely the situation of the Kaffirs that she assesses sympathetically; the ill-treatment of Hottentots – the 'free natives of the woods' – and Bushmen also attracts her attention. And always she responds from her experience. Even in her early excursions into the interior, into Hottentot Holland, she envisages the possibility of a free society:

> In Hottentot Holland there seemed to be a house and farm every mile, or mile and a-half, but no hamlet or village. As the land is cultivated by slaves, and as they are the property of the master, his house has generally a slave-house belonging to it, which, alas! is in the place of that happier cottage at home where each Englishman has his wife, his child, his pig, and his cat or dog, as great within its four walls as any emperor within his palace. Until we see here hamlets also raising up their humble heads, and the artificer receiving his shilling

or two a day for his work, and spending it as he pleases, unlashed by any rattan, or without chastisement but his wife's tongue if he has spent too much in porter, we will not see this a flourishing country. At present unwilling drudgery toils, unthanked, for indolent apathy! (*LCGH*, pp. 118–19)

Lady Anne Barnard obviously here derives her models for an ideal productive society from an idealised version of rural life wherever in the country she envisages the hamlets to be, and fictional and documentary versions of that society well into the nineteenth century, make it clear that this version of the cottage kingdom was more honoured in the breach than the observance. Yet it seems clear that to appeal to this model was a social advance on what was actually happening in the Cape then and later.

When John Barrow writes to Anne Barnard about the Kaffirs, he is admittedly giving the kind of ethnographic portrait that Mary Pratt deprecates but it is humanised in various ways and it clarifies itself by reference to the kind of unsophisticated society which he assumes her to be familiar with and which in spite of its lack of sophistication might still be an example of a high culture:

> The real Kaffirs I admire exceedingly. They lead a true pastoral life, are united in Clans exactly like those of the Highlands of Scotland, and in each clan everything – *except the ladies* – seems to be in common . . . I never met with such chearful good-tempered creatures as the women, and getting over the prejudices of color, they are really handsome, if an elegant form, a regular set of features enlivened by good humor, a skin smooth as velvet, eyes of a dark brown and full of fire, teeth white as ivory, are to be considered as ingredients that enter into the composition of a beauty. (Fairbridge, pp. 47–8)

Barrow goes on to praise the appearance and behaviour of the King, Gaika, and remarks that 'Mrs Gaika is a very affable and a very rational woman – I had a long confab with her' (Fairbridge, p. 46). But perhaps more significantly it is in his letters to Anne Barnard that Barrow explains the practical problems of his journey and the time spent in merely getting about. He is also aware that his method of travelling is at odds with what the country seems to demand and that his companions deprecate his refusal of the easy and tranquil movements to which they are more accustomed. He, like a modern tourist, is uneasily aware that he may never get another chance to see as much.

Lady Anne Barnard is then herself an exceptional commentator and additionally elicits exceptional commentary from others. There is no sense in overstating the actual influence she exerted in the Cape but if her combination of political astuteness and domestic goodwill is too simple a mixture for professional politicians then so much the worse for them. Let us give her the last word: 'To me the joy and comfort of society consists of loving and of being beloved by those one lives amongst, whether Britons or Hottentots' (Fairbridge, p. 293).

Anne Grant, Mrs Grant of Laggan (1755–1838)

Anne Barnard's sense of the important life being the private one would have been heartily echoed by Anne Macvicar Grant, yet Anne Grant became a public literary figure in a way that would have horrified Lady Anne. Of all the writers that I am considering in this section Anne Grant seems to me the most intelligent, the most likely to produce commentary on her age that can stand against the most serious reflections of the stalwarts of Edinburgh as well as the sages of the Lakes. Certainly Anne Grant within her own time offers perspectives that could possibly only be produced by a writer who worked towards but not within the centre, a writer who valued privacy but was obliged by economic motives to court publicity, in other words by a Scottish woman.

The review of her posthumously published correspondence in *Fraser's Magazine* is titled 'Mrs Grant of Laggan and Her Contemporaries'.[8] Here Anne Grant occupies the centre as it were and her commentaries on the great and the good of her time are clustered round her. And certainly it is hard to find well-known or even not very well-known figures of the period that escape Anne Grant's commentary. But the traffic was not all in one direction. The great and the good also made the effort to meet Anne Grant. Certainly her *Memoirs of an American Lady* were read during the summer of 1813 by Dorothy Wordsworth who borrowed the two volumes from Southey.[9] Anne Grant herself breakfasted with Southey and so much did her writing chime with the ethos of the period that a little known Lake poet, Isabella Lickbarrow, composed a poem based on an incident recorded in *Letters from the Mountains*.[10] Anne Grant knew Jeffrey (founder and editor of *The Edinburgh Review* and scourge of the Lake poets and Joanna Baillie) and idolised Scott, who was not always kind about her;[11] met Joanna Baillie and her sister when they were in Edinburgh and was most impressed by Mrs Hemans; one could go on.[12] One way of explaining this contemporary fame is to suggest that she wrung no withers and indeed her conservatism and forgiving evangelicalism made her acceptable to diverse shades of political opinion. For while she is tart about Wollstonecraft and L. E. L. (Letitia Elizabeth Landon) and Fanny Wright she is never lacking in generosity even towards those of whose opinions she disapproves. And that generosity was surely the result of the interplay of primitive and sophisticated, simple and complex, here and there in the pattern of her life. Particularly the generosity derives from her passionate attachment to the Highlands of Scotland.

John Barrow adduces Highland society to explain the apparently more alien society of the Kaffirs. Highland society for a number of commentators was becoming a paradigm for values that had been insuffiently understood before they were destroyed or undermined. Some kind of appreciation of Highland culture can be said to inform much of the understanding of other more distant cultures during the early nineteenth century. No one writing in Scotland in the Romantic period worked harder to make Highland culture valued and understood before it was swept away or corrupted than Anne Grant, Mrs Grant of Laggan. The perspectives that Anne Grant brings to bear on the Highlands, which were her home for thirty years, are more complex than those that either Barrow or Lady Anne Barnard were able to appropriate for their understanding of 'primitive' cultures. For Anne Grant had encountered another primitive society before her life in Laggan. She was an exceptionally early traveller, even, she jokingly suggests in her brief personal memoir, a natural one.[13]

Anne Macvicar [Grant] was born in Glasgow: both her parents had Highland connections, her father, Duncan, farmed early in life in Fort William, her mother was a Stewart from Argyll. Her father went to America in 1757 with a commission in the regiment of the Earl Eglinton. When Anne Grant was nearly three, she and her mother joined the father and Anne Grant's next ten years were spent in and around Albany on the River Hudson. But she had, she explains, made an early attempt at travelling to join her father. Having heard from her mother that America was in the west she set out when only about two and a half from the eastern edge of the town where the family lived and 'walked deliberately . . . very nearly a mile to the western extremity of the Trongate' before she was intercepted by a friendly lady to whom she explained that she was 'going to America to seek papa' (*Memoir*, p. 4). In telling this story Anne Grant is clearly anxious to establish both her determination and her precosity: 'My age and the expressed intention of my journey alone made the performance of this early exploit remarkable' (*Memoir*, p. 4).

Anne Grant's stay in America among the originally Dutch settlers in Albany, New England, introduced her to a society in the early stages of cultural development but yet in many ways a high culture of friendship and civility; it introduced her too to the civilisation of the Mohawks. Less happily it gave her some experience of the functioning of slavery, although not, of course, of its worst aspects. Her life there was not a particularly protected one and her experiences included journeys into the 'trackless wildernesses' of the country round Lake Ontario.

After the end of the war in Canada, her father retired from the army and was granted an allotment of land which he worked for three years before deciding in 1768 to return to Scotland eventually to take up the post of Barrack-Master of Fort Augustus. The family accompanied him to enter that Highland culture that came to mean so much to Anne Grant. Her entry was, however, confirmed by her marriage in 1779, when she was twenty-four, to the Rev. James Grant, a former army chaplain who had been settled for some years in the parish of Laggan. Anne Grant became the loving, although not uncritical, interpreter to the wider world of the culture she found in Laggan. Perhaps remembering from her experience in Albany, where she observed that traders with the Native Americans learned their languages to facilitate commercial success, Anne Grant learned Gaelic to promote cultural understanding, a noble aim but perhaps not wholly unrelated to the acquisition of some power, or at least standing, in the community.

She subsequently published both on Highland culture and on the societies she remembered in America. On the one hand her experience as a young adolescent in America seems to have equipped her to comprehend the community she later found in Laggan; at the same time her experience in Laggan feeds back into her reading of Albany, hence the sophistication and the unusual diversity of range of her perceptions.[14] She has a peculiar position as insider/outsider in both places, both participant and observer.

Clearly it was to some extent her experience of the communities and customs she encountered as a young adolescent in Albany that made it possible for her to come to terms with the community she later found herself in in the Highlands: 'I know nothing so silly', she writes from Fort William to her Glasgow friend, Harriet Reid, 'as the disgust and wonder your cockney misses show at any custom or dress they are not used to. I now think plaids and faltans (fillets) just as becoming as I once did the furs and wampum of the Mohawks, whom I always remember with kindness' (*L from M*, vol. 1, p. 48). Anne Grant has already found in simpler societies sources of strength and culture which on her return to the older, more sophisticated civilisation she has perceived to be lacking. Just as Albany aids an understanding of Laggan, so Laggan enables her perspective on both Madame Schuyler, the American Lady of the *Memoirs of an American Lady*, and on the social and political structures of Albany.[15] Her position as a 'travel writer' is then the reverse of the norm. Customarily travellers take a baggage of cultural assumptions to the new societies that they are exploring. Anne Grant *returns* from Albany, armed with its culture, only to discover as she becomes acquainted with Britain, that much of what must have seemed natural to her is far from being so by old world standards. And so in order to write about Albany after forty years she has to learn to see, not just as is the case with all memoirs of childhood, with an adult eye endeavouring to recapture the sensations of childhood, but also with a culturally re-equipped sense of what her childhood and early adolescence must have been like to her then, and an acute awareness of how it will seem to her readers now.

This generally works very well Anne Grant is aware of what will seem eccentric, if charming, in her descriptions of the social practices of what she calls the 'infant society' of Albany and its neighborhood (MAL, vol. 1, p. iv). She is able to clarify what is valuable in the naive sociability of the small, enterprising Pennsylvania community with its Dutch origins and to assess the social virtues that may reprove the vices of politer cultures. But at the same time she is aware that her readers would scarcely wish to live within the constrictions such a society necessarily imposes. Little privacy is available except that achieved by entering the wild, hence privacy is usually gendered since only the men become traders. Conformity is demanded and enforced, not by cruel means but simply by the inexorable pressure that the need to survive, and hence conform, exacts. Her description of the education and early habits of the Albanians has a kind of chilling charm. The children were divided into companies from the age of about five or six and remained attached to these companies until of marriageable age; children from the same family were generally in different companies and roughly equal numbers of boys and girls belonged to each. Once a year the groups went berry-picking, using baskets made by the Indians and 'there was great rivalry about these and about the quantity of berries picked'. Every child entertained the whole company on birthdays and on one other occasion every year. It was 'a sort of apostasy to marry out of one's company' (MAL, vol. 1, p. 60). The usefulness of these customs as socialising practices is clear but equally the pressure to conformity, the need for the suppression of eccentricity must have been acute.

Anne Grant insists on the superiority of the Mohawks of the original 'Five Nations'. Colonel Philip Schuyler, an ancestor of the American Lady, had persuaded four Sachems or chiefs of the Mohawks to accompany him to London where they were entertained at the court of Queen Anne. While stressing the nobility and eloquence of these earlier Mohawks, Anne Grant admits that the once powerful tribes are in a depressed and diminished state but she refuses careless prejudice in her discussion of the present day Indians. It is uninformed nonsense that they are lazy. It is true that with the Indians 'revenge is a virtue and retaliation a duty' but 'while faith was kept with these people they never became aggressors'. Although the Europeans 'by bad example and drink have seduced them from their former probity', they are still truly a noble people and Indian traders on their return from the interior are often influenced to become more like the Indians; 'lofty, sedate and collected . . . masters of themselves, and independent of others'. Of these social Indians, she says eloquently, 'let us judge from the traders who know their language and customs, and from the adopted prisoners who have spent years among them. How unequivocal, how consistent is the testimony they bear to their humanity, friendship, fortitude, fidelity and generosity' (MAL, vol. 1, pp. 84–6).

The Dutch settlers and the Indians are then admirable people whose social practices have much to teach the sophisticated and degenerate European. But the slaves are more problematic. To pronounce the keeping of slaves barbaric would seem to involve the condemnation of her friends. She is awkward about the matter. 'Let me not', she implores, be 'detested as an advocate of slavery when I say that I have never seen a people so happy in servitude as the domestics of the Albanians'. The bond between master and slave, who may have shared a cradle, was often closer than between brothers; mothers had a say in the transfer of children from one household to another and had considerable authority and freedom of speech. Nevertheless mothers taught their own children to be good *servants* and slaves guilty of drunkenness and levity were sold to Jamaica when they often had to be stopped from committing suicide. Nor had the Albanians, Grant admits, any 'philosophy, or knowledge of the generality of law' to allow them to question their belief that the negroes were 'a hapless race condemned to perpetual slavery'. Furthermore they regarded miscegenation with horror and its products as a 'dangerous, because degraded part of the community'. One such product was married off to a white woman from the older colonies and given a well-stocked and fertile farm '*in the depth of the wood*'. Anne Grant admits that when she visited this man, ironically named Chalk, she could not but regard him as a 'mysterious and anomalous being' (*MAL*, vol. 1, pp. 55–9).

Three years after these *Memoirs* Anne Grant published the work for which she is now best known, *Essays on the Superstitions of the Highlanders of Scotland* (1811): it is the only one of her published works to have been given a modern reprint.[16] Yet to come to this work after the American memoirs is a disappointment and one which is somewhat tartly registered by the reviewer in the *Monthly Review*. The charm of the *Memoirs* is largely, I have suggested, in its detail. It is not without intellectual interest but this is supported by masses of social specificity and the reader might be forgiven for expecting this kind of particularity from a work that seems to promise lots of folk lore and tale. But the *Monthly* reviewer complains: 'We are presented with some nicely-trimmed sentences on particular stages in the progress of human society, and with something like the good lady's displeasure at philosophers and men of science, for neglecting the delightful occupation of studying the Erse language: but not a single ghost or fairy even beckons in the distance.'[17] Anne Grant has some perfectly sharp, if somewhat partisan, things to say about the culture of the Highlands, about superstition as a civilising and religion-inducing force and about loyalty and simplicity as virtues to chasten the sophisticated but perhaps her best work on the people of the Highlands had already been done before she had settled into thinking of herself so explicitly as an explicator.

For Anne Grant began her publishing career not as a travel writer or a cultural interpreter but with a volume of poems, the expressed aim of which in some ways remained the purpose of Anne Grant's writings throughout her long life:

> Go artless records of a life obscure,
> Memorials dear of loves and friendships past,
> Of blameless minds from strife and envy pure;
> Go scatter'd by *Affliction's* bitter blast,
> And tell the proud the busy and the gay,
> How rural peace consumes the quiet day.[18]

Accordingly the principal poem of the volume, 'The Highlanders', celebrates Highland scenery and Highland manners. Anne Grant includes translations from the Gaelic and publishes a defence of Macpherson's *Ossian*.[19]

But the practical aim of the volume also informed the subsequent publications of Anne Grant – quite simply she needed the money. When Anne Grant reluctantly left her beloved Laggan in 1803, she had already lost three children in infancy, her eldest son, John Lauchlan, of consumption at sixteen and her husband eighteen months after the birth of her last child, John. (John was the only child to survive her. In this respect Anne Grant was just a little luckier than Margaret Oliphant, all of whose children predeceased her.) She was forty-eight and had eight children still to bring up on a small pension from the War Office, a consequence of her husband's few years as chaplain to Lord Lynedoch's regiment: it seems a good enough excuse for repairing to print. She is insistent, however, as is her son and later editor, that both the poems and the subsequently published *Letters from the Mountains* were published 'by the advice of her friends'. Anne Grant continued to need money and indeed took pupils after she had moved to Edinburgh in 1810, but we cannot quite imagine that there were not other motives both selfless and self-concerned. The selfless motive derived from her love for the people she had lived among while she was young and full of hope, the self-concerned from a never expressed, but yet often evident, belief that she and her opinions were after all worth something and that although she was a private person, her experiences might have something to offer those who had lived more in the light.

Anne Grant, then, illustrates in her writing most of the features usually identified as characteristic of non-fiction writing, of letters and memoirs. She is significantly a travel writer, an interpreter of other cultures and hence a critic of her own; she comments widely on the intellectual and social life of her times; and she gives insights into the more intimate aspects of family life. Perhaps modern readers will find the more intimate side the most attractive, at least as it is revealed in the earlier collections of letters. This is certainly what the contemporary reviewer in the *Monthly Review* found appealing, against the period's sense of what would normally justify publication of private letters:

> When we first glanced at the title of this work, we had not a very high anticipation of its claims: for in what respect the private correspondence of a lady placed in an obscure situation might be interesting or instructive, we could scarely form a conjecture.[20]

The merits of the work made themselves apparent, however, in spite of initial prejudice against their conception:

> The engaging volatility of youth apparent in the early part of the correspondence, and the good sense of more ripened years, which prevails in the latter part, equally pleased us. The sentiments of the author, when occupying the various relative situations of a daughter, a wife, a mother, and a protégée, are truly praiseworthy.[21]

The reviewer then recognises that the value of the volume lies in the very characteristics that he had originally deprecated: the charting of an ordinary, virtuous and hence possibly exemplary life.

By the time Anne Grant left Laggan in 1803 she had already shaped a life and it is that life that remains delightful to us still; it is, as her son says, 'an unconscious biography of the thirty years of her residence in the Highland'.[22] And given that Anne Grant herself prepared the letters for publication, it may not be wholly unconscious: we may believe that she wanted to present herself in as good a light as the Highlands. As far as the descriptions of the people and customs of the Highlands are concerned, these have a vivacity and specificity which is lacking in the later discursive *Essays*. The object is always to bring as vividly as possible before her correspondents the particularity of Highland life. Writing to Mrs Smith of Linthouse, Glasgow, in 1787, she offers the diary of one July Monday, Monday being the day that all dwellers in the glens come down for the supplies. The sketch, with its meticulous detail, is done, she says, 'between fancy and memory' as is the exuberant picture of the Highland wedding feast for which 'four fat sheep' died (*L from M*, vol. 1, pp. 230–1; vol. 2, pp. 115–16).

Anne Grant's own life emerges with the same sharpness of delineation, chiefly because of that dual perspective I have spoken of. She is always an implicated spectator, always within the society she describes and so it illuminates her even as she anatomises it. Woman and place consistently explicate each other. And there is a discernible passage from early sprightliness to later sober sense. When Anne Grant was a pretty eighteen-year-old, she merrily poked fun at a young college student who travelled complainingly with her father and herself. There is, one imagines, a half-secret narrative in which Anne Grant teases and flirts with the sulky young man (*L from M*, vol. 11, pp. 11–12). There is such a story too in her description of her marriage three months after the event. While on the one hand assuring her correspondent that their happiness is rational, not the 'ideal felicity of romances', another and much more romantic tale is readable out of her discovery of 'more of the complacency and attention of the lover in the husband than ever [she] expected', of generosity and impetuosity and of 'as nice and jealous a sense of honour as any Spaniard whatever' (*L from M*, vol. 1, p. 191). It is a much subdued, although not extinguished spirit that writes after the death of her husband that 'were [she] to choose so long a period to live over again, at any time of my life, I think it would be the very half year, the close of which swallowed up my hopes of earthly happiness' (*L from M*, vol. 1, p. 172).

After this point Anne Grant's life is in certain ways complete. Much sorrow still awaited her as one after another of her children died: it is unsurprising that her memoir of her own life breaks off after the death of her daughter, Charlotte, at the age of seventeen in 1807. She lived for many years after this and perhaps her opinions increased to compensate in a sense for the loss of that part of her life that was invested in the lives of her children. But it would never have occurred to Anne Grant to give up or to murmur the Lord; to love and to endure were her modes.

Frances Wright (1795–1852)

I want to conclude this section on travelling women with two of Frances Wright D'Arusmont's early works, *Views of Society and Manners in America* (1821)[23] and *A Few Days in Athens*, published in 1822,[24] although written rather earlier. Frances Wright is by far the most famous now of these four women. This is, of course, mainly because she courted the publicity that the others either refused or shunned but it is also, I think, because she can be claimed for the United States as well or perhaps more firmly than for Scotland. She became for America a powerful icon of radicalism whose name evoked conservative fears that went far beyond those that might have been justified by her actual writing or behaviour; she was by others, including Walt Whitman, greatly loved and admired.

Unlike the other women I have been discussing her travels were independently conceived rather than made possible because of the circumstances of a father or brother or husband. She lost both father and mother before she was two and a half; her brother was killed when she was still a girl and she did not marry D'Arusmont until she was thirty-five and already pregnant by him. Her closest companion, until her death a few months before Fanny Wright's marriage, was her sister, Camilla.[25] In spite of this, Scotland and ideas that had been nurtured in Scotland did much to form Fanny Wright. She was born in Dundee where her father was a wealthy merchant; his money and a subsequent inheritance from her uncle Major William Campbell made both Fanny and Camilla modest heiresses, a useful prelude to independence of body and mind. But wealth in itself does not secure a radical conscience and when that conscience came it owed a great deal to her Scottish origins, although her childhood and early adolescence was passed outside the country of her birth.

It also probably owed a great deal to early emotional deprivation, for Fanny was separated after the death of her parents from both Camilla, who went to a foster family in

Dundee, and her brother who was brought up among the family of his uncle James Mylne in Glasgow. Fanny herself was sent off to her maternal grandfather in London and after his death moved with her aunt Frances Campbell to Dawlish. The wealthy and indolent existence of her grandfather and later her aunt presented that contrast with the suffering poor that fuelled Fanny's radicalism but perhaps even more importantly the loss of her childhood, and the love that might have attended it, did much to form that identification of innocence and freedom that characterised her early social and political thought. Fanny Wright perhaps confirmed the romantic poets' sense of the significance of childhood through her own lack. Her later tendency to identify with such potential father figures as Jeremy Bentham and, in Europe and America, the Marquis de Lafayette, must be in part explicable as a need to access her own father. Her friendship with Mrs Millar to whom she wrote the letters that form her *Views of Society and Manners in America* gave her a mother substitute. At the same time she obviously throughout her life found universal benevolence an easier matter than personal relationships. She pushed relationships to their limit, trying the patience of those who loved her in ways that only a mother could perhaps have forgiven.

But her never known father nevertheless reinforced her own radicalism when it developed. James Wright, educated at Trinity College, Dublin, had been a correspondent of Adam Smith and more significantly a supporter of the ideas of Tom Paine to the extent of sponsoring an inexpensive edition of *The Rights of Man*. When his daughter later discovered some of his papers she was struck by 'a somewhat singular coincidence in views between a father and daughter, separated by death when the first had not reached the age of twenty-nine, and when the latter was in infancy'.[26] Fanny Wright refers several times in *Views* to the impact in America of Paine's *Common Sense*. But it is after all not perhaps wholly coincidence for Fanny, disgusted by the conspicuous consumption combined with the oppressive intellectual constraint of her feminine life with her aunt in Dawlish, quarrelled with her aunt and removed herself and Camilla, who had also joined her aunt's household, to the home of their great-uncle, James Mylne, professor of Moral Philosophy in the University of Glasgow (Glasgow College) the chair of which had, of course, been occupied by Adam Smith. Mylne himself was one of the ornaments of the Scottish philosophical tradition, known to his students as 'Old Sensation', an allusion to his philosophical position that knowledge reaches us through our senses. Through Mylne the eighteen-year-old Fanny had access to the College Library where she consolidated an interest in America, sparked off two years previously by her accidental discovery of Botta's history of America's fight for independence.[27] Mylne's wife, Agnes, was the daughter of James Millar, friend of both Smith and David Hume, professor of jurisprudence and civil law, supporter of the American Revolution, repudiator of the slave trade. Agnes's sister-in-law, Robina Craig Millar, who had lived with her husband in Pennsylvania until his death, became Fanny Wright's close friend and surrogate mother. Fanny Wright certainly spent most of her formative years in England acquiring the negative equipment for radical social and political thought but it was undoubtedly her three years in Glasgow before her journey to America that gave shape and intellectual rigour to her emotional positions.

She also interestingly spent summers during these Scottish years in the Highlands of Scotland. Anne Grant took her memory of pre-revolutionary America with her to the Scottish Highlands and then took her experience of the Scottish Highlands with her as she recollected Albany. Fanny Wright took the Highlands of Scotland among her intellectual and emotional baggage to America. But, of course, she had available to her nothing comparable to Anne Grant's participatory experience of a settled if threatened culture. The most telling Highland event of Fanny Wright's young life actually occurred in the Lowlands, when she saw an emigrant ship in the Clyde packed with Highlanders dispossessed during the period of the Enclosures. Her sense of their misery and helplessness, she later affirmed, made her pronounce 'to herself a solemn oath, to wear ever in her heart the cause of the poor and the helpless; and to aid in all she could in redressing the grievous wrongs which seemed to prevail in society'.[28] This experience obviously fed her desire to see the country for which they were bound, to find out whether it was in truth the land of opportunity and equality that she wanted to find it. There can be little doubt that Scottish thought and Scottish suffering fuelled the departure of Frances Wright with her faithful sister to America, provided with letters of introduction from Mrs Millar and warnings from Professor Mylne whose male chivalric sense overcame his intellectual daring in his parting advice that Italy would be a far more suitable destination for two young ladies.

But just as Frances Wright's deprived family life deeply affected her subsequent relationships, so the absence of that sense of community which so influenced Anne Grant, affected her subsequent political judgements and behaviour. She understood the message of the Highland emigrants only partially: she responded to human suffering finally in an abstract way and consequently imagined that it could be wholly rationally alleviated. Throughout her record of her first travels in America she tended, therefore, to take the abstract principle as apology for the specific practice, a tendency that she herself later admitted as seeing America under a 'Claude Lorraine tint'. The British journals were mostly outraged by her eulogies of American practice which carried with them explicit or implicit condemnation of British policy during and after the Wars of Independence. *Views of Manners and Society in America* was published as 'by an Englishwoman' and *The Quarterly Review* believes or pretends that 'Englishwoman' is an unconvincing pseudonym certainly for a man, probably for a chauvinistic American. Unfortunately *The Quarterly* is able to cite real errors of fact along with disagreements of taste and feeling where the advantage is usually with Fanny Wright. Even American journals worried about the fulsomeness of the compliments Wright paid to the new country: the *North American Review* felt that the whole book could better serve 'as the model toward which [the citizen] should strive to bring his country, rather than as a tablet of actual perfections'.[29] And later after she committed herself to America and to the amelioration of the problems of the negro slaves her altruistic and to herself costly establishment of 'Nashoba', a free slave community in Tennessee, was disastrous mainly because she understood impersonal compassion without really understanding how communities might work as organic entities. Anne Grant might never have had the free-thinking courage to be ahead of her time in the manner of Frances Wright but equally she would never have miscalculated the way people might interact in artificially constructed groups, free from communal history.

Yet the virtues of Fanny Wright's *Views* lies less in their strict accuracy than in the extraordinary vivacity of the descriptive and anecdotal writing, particularly when one considers how young she was when she wrote. The intellectuality of her approach, which she owes in part to a classical education unusual in a girl, is beyond question but the purely reflective passages of *Views* are of less value to the twentieth-century reader than those observations that bring to life the trivial but vitally important detail of life in the new country. It is in these seemingly casual passages that Fanny Wright reveals herself not merely as apologist and polemicist but writer. When she relates her little stories of passing life she does employ fictional models but her stories deliver a different message from the eighteenth-century narrative exemplars she chooses. When she arrives in New York she is struck in her first few days by the friendliness of its inhabitants. In illustration she tells a tale borrowed as it were from *Moll Flanders* with its ending reversed. She asks a woman carrying a heavy basket to direct her. The woman insists on taking her part of the way and lays down her basket on a step confident that it will come to no harm. Fanny Wright accepts the woman's company as far as the next street corner, partly out of a desire to test the honesty of New York: 'I waited to trace her back with my eye through the crowd of moving passengers and soon saw her in the distance crossing the street with her basket on her arm' (*VSMA*, p. 17) Notwithstanding the literary model for its narrative mode, this little tale has the stamp of authenticity, delivered particularly by that long look at the woman's receding back.

It is perhaps most shocking for modern readers to find that Fanny Wright for all her universal benvolence, for all her enthusiasm for the land of the free, does not sufficiently count the cost to the indigenous people of the 'Great Experiment'. Here she shows herself almost wholly a child of her time; the terms in which she discusses the native American differ very little from those that Patrick Sellar and his like had used of the persecuted Highlanders. Although Fanny Wright does to some extent recognise that the condition of the 'savage' Indians is the result of a clash of peoples, she cannot any more than most of her contemporaries see it as a clash of cultures. The only culture that she imagines for the Indian is the solitary wildness of the savage hunter. Faithful to her general refusal to find fault with American procedures she judges the often damaging procedures of government humane and equally often takes the policy for the practice, although she concedes the horrible results of the introduction of liquor and firearms (*VSMA*, p. 109).

Concessive as much of what she writes about the Indian is, it is impossible to miss the tones of contempt that lurk not very far from the surface of her concern:

> The falling greatness of this people, disappearing from the face of their native soil, at first strikes mournfully on the imagination; but such regrets are scarcely rational. The savage, with all his virtues, and he has some virtues, is still a savage . . . The increase and spread of the white population at the expense of the red, is, as it were, the triumph of peace over violence. (*VSMA*, p. 106)

Perhaps for all of us there must always be an 'Other', a group excluded from our full sympathy, felt to be not quite human or at least not quite human yet, and not worth waiting for. Yet occasionally her sense of her early self as a lonely alien in a strange culture moves her to comprehend something of the plight of the alienated young Indian: 'I know not if the circumstances of my own early life have tended to make me sympathize peculiarly with such a situation, but the position of the Indian youth, as an alien and an orphan, among his American guardians and playmates, strikes me as singularly affecting' (*VSMA*, p. 112).

Fanny Wright subsequently published widely and it is impossible here to consider all her activities or all her writing but it would, I think, be a pity not to take notice of another early work that might be felt still to have been written under some Scottish pressure. This is her curiosity, *A Few Days in Athens*, published in 1822. This purports to be 'The Translation of a Greek Manuscript discovered in Herculaneum' and is a fanciful defence of Epicurean philosophy. Given the attacks she suffered in her later life on both her politics and her morals we might well read this little romance as a proleptic *apologia pro vita sua*.

The felicity of the writing in the unexpanded version of *A Few Days* lies as much in its imagination of a loving community, of disinterested friendship and regard, as it does in the philosophical ideas which underpin it, although Fanny Wright was never seriously to part company with the moral materialism which it posits. One of the greatest compliments to the quality of her writing comes from the imitation of it by Walt Whitman. Whitman attended her lectures in America during her later years as an orator and reformer, read her writings and hugely admired her person and her moral energy.[30] Whitman's 'Pictures' uses Wright's description of the Stoic Zeno among his disciples; the word parallels are most striking: he lifts phrases, vocabulary and cadences from Wright's version, although interestingly he transfers the scene from the Portico which was Zeno's place to the Garden which was the teaching space of Epicurus.

Reading these two early publications of Fanny Wright it is tempting to feel that she missed her real vocation of writer in the fervour of her reformism which expressed itself in her public lectures as well, or course, as in her social experiments. Fanny Wright published her lectures but the force of oratory does not translate wholly to the printed page and there is a loss of the specificity that gives authenticity to her *Views* and to the figures who people her *Few Days*. Probably Fanny Wright's fame depends on her position as admired and feared public figure but we might now feel a sense of loss that the ability to be particular which fuels her early writing has been lost in the political visionary's need to be general.[31]

For all of these very different women who wrote about their experiences of other places and cultures Scotland itself, but more specifically the Highlands, played some part in their construction of the meaning and significance of other lives in more remote or primitive places. This might have been oblique as in the case of Janet Schaw whose compassion was stirred by the longing of the emigrants for their native place or centrally formative as in the case of Anne Grant of Laggan. In many ways this is unsurprising since the impact of the Scottish Highlands, its scenery and its people, on the Romantic imagination is widely acknowledged and documented, as is the effect of the Highland and Island emigrations on the New World.[32] Nevertheless it remains worth noting that some kind of affective response to the Scottish Highlands is consistently observable among women who wrote and women who travelled from the mid-eighteenth to the end of the nineteenth century, even though the Highlands themselves had, of course, undergone significant changes, upheavals even, during this time. Elizabeth Hamilton (1758–1816), born in Ireland, and brought up by her aunt in Stirlingshire, began her prolific and various writing career with a journal of a Highland tour. Mary Brunton hopes in a letter to Joanna Baillie in November 1813 that she 'will be so natural as to let me say, that a pretty little English knoll is not half so exhilarating as the top of a Scotch hill'.[33] And to her brother she remarks a little ruefully that her own special relationship with the Highlands is disappearing into fashion: 'As for the *Highlands*, you know they are quite the rage. All the novel-reading Misses have seen and admired them in the verdure and sunshine of July'.[34] And at the other end of the nineteenth century the celebrated Anglo-Scottish traveller, Isabella Bird Bishop (1831–1904), although born and educated in England, made her home with her mother and sister in Edinburgh from 1858 and maintained throughout her life a relationship with Scotland and particularly with the people of Mull where her sister had a cottage at Tobermory. Isabella Bird was the first woman to be admitted fellow of the Royal Geographical Society in 1892 after an extraordinary lifetime of travel and writing which continued until a few years before her death. In spite of a lifetime of precarious health she travelled to and wrote about Japan, Korea, Kurdistan, Persia and, as every schoolgirl knows, rode in the Rockies in 1873.[35] Isabella Bird was, of course, a missionary as well as a traveller but she believed in the efficacy of medical missions and in respecting native customs. In this tactful interventionism it seems likely that she was influenced by her experience of the West Highlands where she had already involved herself in the spiritual and material welfare of the people, co-operating with Lady Gordon Cathcart in crofter emigration to Canada where in 1866 she herself visited some of the emigrants. And the Highland experience continued to offer her isolation, sometimes excessive, and the opportunity for anthropological observation. In December 1880 she wrote to John Murray, her publisher:

> The great drawback of Mull in the winter is the irregular and often suspended post, as, for instance, there have been two days within a week in which the post-boat has been unable to cross, and almost always when that occurs the gale has been severe enough to prostrate a number of Mull telegraph poles. Thus, amidst howling storms, without letters, newspapers, or telegraph possibilities, the isolation is very trying; but my nerves are so shattered that I need complete rest, and that I have here, with sufficient amount of human interest to make the endurance of solitude wholesome. The Highlanders have some very charming qualities, but in cunning, moral timidity, and plausibility they remind me of savages of rather a low type.[36]

Yet it is clear that in her own way Isabella Bird is attached to her savages of rather a low type. But, although she would not be without them, unlike Anne Grant she would probably rather not be always with them. 'Here' and 'there' have changed places in the hierarchy of the desirable.

Notes

1. *Journal of a Lady of Quality; Being the Narrative of a Journey from Scotland to the West Indies, North Carolina and Portugal, in the Years 1774 to 1776*; edited by Evangeline Walker Andrews in collaboration with Charles McLean Andrews (Yale University Press, New Haven, 1921). A second edition was published in 1934 and a third with additional material in 1939. Three copies of the journal are known: the manuscript Egerton 2423 from which the printed text is taken; a copy in the same handwriting with only minor differences purchased by Vere Langford Oliver, an historian of Antigua, which gives the name of its author and has a dedication to her brother, Alexander, and a third copy owned by Colonel R. H. Vetch, a connection of the Schaw and Rutherford families. The third edition of the *Journal* contains material, including illustrations and a family tree, which are taken from a typescript of the Vetch manuscript, eventually made available to the editors by Vetch's inheritors. All quotations are from the third, 1939 edition. Further references in the text are given as *Journal*.
2. Elizabeth A. Bohls, 'The Aesthetics of Colonialism: Janet Schaw in the West Indies, 1774–1775', *Eighteenth Century Studies* 27 (Spring 1994), 363–90 (p. 365).
3. Bohls, p. 387.
4. *South Africa a Century Ago: Letters Written from the Cape of Good Hope (1797–1801)* by Lady Anne Barnard; edited with a memoir and brief notes by W. H. Wilkins (London: Smith, Elder, & Co., 1901), p. 56. Further references in the text are given as *LCGH*.
5. *Lives of the Lindsays; or, A Memoir of the Houses of Crawford and Balcarres*, ed. Lord Lindsay, 3 vols (London, John Murray, 1849), vol. iii, p. 384. Further references in the text are given as *LL*. It is also worth noting that in this account Anne Barnard is also pleased by her 'most intellectual slave', Mentor, calling her a '*braave vrow*, a rare wife'.
6. Mary Louise Pratt, *Imperial Eyes: Travel Writing and Transculturation* (Routledge, London, 1992), p. 59. John Barrow, *An Account of Travels into the Interior of Southern Africa in the Years 1797 and 1798* (Cadell & Davies, London, 1801; reprint Johnson Reprint Corporation, New York, 1968).
7. Dorothea Fairbridge, *Lady Anne Barnard at the Cape of Good Hope, 1797–1802*; illustrated by a series of sketches made by Lady Anne Barnard Clarendon Press, Oxford, 1924), pp. 228–9. Further references in the text are given as Fairbridge.

8.   Review of *Memoir and Correspondence of Mrs Grant of Laggan*, ed. J. P. Grant, 3 vols (Longman, Brown, Green and Longmans, 1844), in *Fraser's Magazine* 29 (April 1844) pp. 411–18.

9.   *The Letters of William and Dorothy Wordsworth*, ed. de Selincourt, 2nd edn, (Clarendon Press, Oxford, 1970), vol. III, pp. 121–2.

10.   Anne Grant, *Letters from the Mountains; being Correspondence with her Intimate Friends, between the Years 1773 and 1803*, 3 vols (Longman, Brown, Green and Longmans, London, 1806; all quotations are from the 6th edn, edited by her son, J. P. Grant). The poem 'Oh! happy lone retreat!' was published in Isabella Lickbarrow's *Poetical Effusions* (1814) to which Wordsworth subscribed. It has the following explanatory note: 'The following Stanzas were occasioned by reading in Mrs Grant's Letters from the Mountains, an account of a small island, which was supposed to be the burying place of a family. The person who speaks them is supposed to be a young Highland lady in distress, and within view of the island. The young lady seems to have been abandoned by a lover and to seek peace from pleasure, calumny and treachery.'

11.   In a letter to Maria Edgeworth, Scott insists that he never could have confessed the secret of his authorship of *Waverley* to Anne Grant. She is he says, 'so very cerulean . . . and the maintainer of such an unmerciful correspondence' that he 'should be afraid to be very intimate with a woman whose tongue and pen are rather overpowering'. Rather less kind was his later remark on hearing that she was minded to refuse the offer of a £50 pension as rather less than her deserts: Scott called her 'proud as a Highland-woman, vain as a poetess, and absurd as a blue-stocking' and predicted that she would, however, take the money, 'for your scornful dog will always eat your dirty pudding': she did. (Lockhart's *The Life of Sir Walter Scott* [1837–8]; quoted from the New Popular Edition, Adam & Charles Black, London, 1893, p. 517 and p. 582).

12.   Most of these meetings are described in *Memoir and Correspondence*.

13.   Most of the information about Anne Grant comes from her own biographical memoir and the account by her son which follows it. These form the preface to *Memoir and Correspondence of Mrs Grant of Laggan*, ed. by her son J. P. Grant, 3 vols (Longman, Brown, Green and Longmans, London, 1844). Further references in the text are given as *Memoir*.

14.   Anne Grant's published works are as follows: [Anne Grant] Mrs Grant, Laggan, *Poems on Various Subjects* (Longman and Co., Edinburgh and London, 1803); [Anne Grant], *Letters from the Mountains; being the Correspondence with her intimate Friends, between the Years 1773 and 1803*, 3 vols (Longman and Co., London, 1806; edited in 2 vols, with notes and additions, by J. P. Grant, Longman, Brown, Green and Longmans, London, 1845), quotations are from Grant's edition and references in the text are given as *L from M*; *Memoirs of an American Lady with Sketches of Manners and Scenery in America as They Existed Previous to the Revolution*, 2 vols (Longman and Co., London, 1808), references in text given as *MAL*; *Essays on the Superstitions of the Highlanders of Scotland, with Translations from the Gaelic*, 2 vols (Longman and Co., London, 1811); *Eighteen Hundred and Thirteen: A Poem* (1814). After her death her son, John, published the *Memoir and Correspondence* already referred to.

15.   The title of the *Memoirs* might lead the reader to expect a principal focus on Margarita Schuyler but for both the contemporary and the modern reader the chief interest of the work must lie in its delineation of customs and its sensitive rendering of the wild, romantic scenery of the area. The Albany hostess, Margarita Schuyler, unquestionably was, however, a formative influence on Anne Grant, and her memoir is still used as a biographical source.

16.   Norwood Editions, 1975.

17.   Review of *Essays and Superstitions*, in *Monthly Review*, LXIX (September–December, 1812, 251–9 (p. 251).

18.   *Poems on Various Subjects* (1803).

19.   A contemporary remarked that had Anne Grant been obliged to relinquish belief in either Ossian or the Lord, it would have been a near-run thing, which given her well-known piety, is a strong comment. Anne Grant met Macpherson after he bought the estate at Belleville and had some reservations about the man but she always believed in the fragments from Ossian. Her contribution to the debate is discussed in Fiona Stafford, *The Sublime Savage: A Study of James Macpherson and the Poems of Ossian* (Edinburgh University Press, Edinburgh, 1988).

20.   Review of *L from M*, in *Monthly Review*, XLIV (May–August 1808), p. 444.

21.   Review of *L from M*, p. 445.

22.   J. P. Grant, Preface to the sixth edition (Longman, Brown, Green and Longmans, London, 1845), p.v.

23.   *Views of Society and Manners in America* By an Englishwoman, (London, 1821); Frances Wright *Views of Society and Manners in America*, ed. Paul Baker (The Bellknap Press of Harvard University Press, Cambridge, Mass., 1963). All page references are to Baker's edition and references are given as VSMA.

24.   Frances Wright, *A Few Days in Athens, being the Translation of a Greek Manuscript discovered in Herculaneum* (Longman, Hurst, Rees, Orme, and Brown, London, 1822). References are given as FDA.

25.   Most of the biographical information about Fanny Wright is taken from the Introduction to Frances Wright, *Views of Society and Manners in America*, ed. Baker; from William Randall Waterman, *Frances Wright* (Columbia University, New York, 1924); from A. J. G. Perkins and Theresa Wolfson, *Frances Wright Free Enquirer: The Study of a Temperament* (Harper New York, 1939; 1972 Porcupine Press reprint); from Celia Morris Eckhardt, *Fanny Wright: Rebel in America* (Harvard University Press Cambridge & London, 1984); from Margaret Lane, *Frances Wright and the 'Great Experiment'* Manchester University Press, Manchester, 1972) and the *DNB*. The *DNB* typically lists Fanny Wright under her married name, although it is granted that she was better known under her maiden name. These biographies are all of interest but some are not always wholly reliable in broad historical terms – Eckhardt, for example, speaks of a man executed for treason being hanged, drawn and quartered in 1817, and so I have tried to use them with proper caution. Fanny Wright probably still needs a fully scholarly biography which is also of general interest.

26.   *Biography, Notes and Political Letters of Frances Wright D'Arusmont* (J. Myles, Dundee, 1844), p. 4. The biography was derived from an interview published in the Dundee newspaper, *The Northern Star*, 1844; printed in Boston by J. P. Mendun, 1849. The text was according to the *Northern Star* reporter revised by Frances Wright during a business visit to Dundee concerning an inheritance in 1844.

27.   Carlo Giuseppe Gugliemo Botta, *Storia della guerra dell'independenza dogli Stati Uniti d'America* (Parigi, 1809).

28.   Lane p. 7.

29.   *North American Review*, xiv (January 1822), p. 19; quoted in Baker, p. xiv.

30.   I am indebted for the information about Whitman's interest and his borrowings to David Goodale, 'Some of Walt Whitman's Borrowings', *American Literature*, 6 (May 1938), pp. 202–13.

31.   Fanny Wright's other published work includes: *Altorf, a Tragedy* (Philadelphia, 1819; London, 1822) discussed by Adrienne Scullion in this volume; *A Course of Popular Lectures* (New York, 1829; 1831, with additional material; vol. 2, Philadelphia, 1836); *Fables* (New York, 1830), various addresses and tracts.

32.   See for example James Hunter, *A Dance Called America: The Scottish Highlands, the United States and Canada* (Mainstream Publishing, Edinburgh & London, 1994). Hunter speaks of some affinity in the other direction too, as early as 1750 it was reported that a Highland regiment arriving in New York was particularly well received by the Indians, p. 236.

33.   Mary Brunton, *Emmeline with Some Other Pieces*, ed. Caroline Franklin (Routledge/Thoemmes Press, London, 1992), p. lxii.

34.   Brunton, *Emmeline*, lxxx.

35.   Isabella Bird Bishop's works include: *The Englishwoman in America* (John Murray, London, 1856); *The Hawdiian Archipelago: Six Months among the Palm Groves, Coral Reefs and Volcanoes of the Sandwich Islands* (John Murray, London, 1875); *A Lady's Life in the Rocky Mountains* (John Murray, London, 1879).

36.   Isabella Bird Bishop, letter to Mr Murray, December 1880, quoted in Anna M. Stoddart, *The Life of Isabella Bird (Mrs Bishop)* (John Murray, London, 1906), p. 141.

9

From Here to Alterity: The Geography of Femininity in the Poetry of Joanna Baillie

Amanda Gilroy

I

The course of Joanna Baillie's long poetic career, from the late 1790s to the middle of the nineteenth century, corresponds with an increasingly rigid gender ideology, grounded in the doctrine of separate spheres, an ideology by which she, like other women poets, is both constrained and empowered. She inhabits a dominant paradigm of the 'poetess', for she stays at home, literally and poetically, writing, as she puts it, about 'homely subjects'.[1] The author of the 'Life' that prefaces her *Complete Works* of 1851 tells us that '[s]he lived in retirement from the first hour to the last' (Baillie, v). Neither her Scottish dialect nor her English poems normally stray outside the parameters of the domestic and the devotional. However, I want here to explore three poems in which the female figures move outside the British domestic circle. In order to place these poems in the context of their cultural terrain, I will examine a number of other discourses which speak to the ideology of femininity, notably reviews of Baillie's poetry, conduct literature, and Frederick Rowton's 1848 anthology of women poets (in which Baillie has a prominent place).[2] These texts share a number of discursive features which help to show how Joanna Baillie negotiates the boundaries of the space allotted to femininity in the first half of the nineteenth century.

Feminist critics in recent years have been careful to analyse gender differences in conjunction with other socio-cultural differences, such as race, religion, class, sexual preference. I want to invoke at the outset Baillie's nationality, her Scottishness, for this would seem the most obvious 'other' difference for the feminist critic to analyse along with that of gender. The signposts to 'double marginalization' are securely in place. The poems to look at on this route would be the dialect poems and the poetic representations of rural Scotland, both of which often have a thematic focus on sexual politics. These poems would certainly repay further attention, not least for the factoring in of class that any analysis would have to undertake, for the dialect poems remain writing about the people from a position of class superiority. We are aware of the separation between Baillie's voice and her material, in much the same way that we notice the gap between William Wordsworth and his idiot boys and mad mothers. What is problematic is the ease with which these poems encourage the placing of Baillie within a masculine tradition which limits Scottishness to the purely local. This cultural delimitation is demonstrated by the way Baillie is represented in Jennifer Breen's influential anthology, *Women Romantic Poets*. She includes nine poems from Baillie's expanded *Fugitive Verses* of 1840, though six of these are from the 1790 volume. The longest pieces are 'A Summer's Day' and its companion piece 'A Winter's Day', which are naturalistic descriptions of the people and places of Lowland Scotland. Breen argues that 'these poems are as distinctive as any poem by Burns or Wordsworth, her nearest rivals in subject matter and form'.[3] Baillie's use of the Scottish vernacular in 'Hooly and Fairly' is part of the widespread attempt to break away from the formality of eighteenth-century poetic diction, but Breen also points out that 'her adaptation of the ballad for literary purposes, . . . echoes Robert Burns's literary treatment of Scottish songs' (Breen, p. xxvi). Baillie is placed in a secondary position, both female and Scottish, her work a belated echo of Burns's.

I would like to suggest that perhaps Baillie's 'Scottishness' rests, paradoxically, in her going away – from Scotland to London, of course (where she lived from 1784–1851), but also away from the pastoral and the local. The tradition of leaving Scotland might be seen as endemic to the Scottish psyche; one of Scotland's most successful exports has always been its people. Frequently this exile is a response to socio-political constraints, such as the Highland Clearances, but it also has to do with a less tangible sense of what is beyond the specificities of the here and now. The question of Scottish identity is displaced to the margins in this chapter; indeed, in locating Baillie within the parameters of gender ideology, I attend to the 'rhetoric of place' rather than the particularities of local context (though national difference turns up in a different frame in the later sections).

II

The first poem I want to consider is 'The Legend of Lady Griseld Baillie' published in *Metrical Legends* in 1821. The legend is, significantly, part of Baillie's own family history, and it constructs a politics of the family, centred on the notion that helpful daughters make happy homes. The family domain is doubly emphasised for Baillie tells us that 'the account we have of her [Griseld] is given by her own children' (Baillie, p. 708). Even the reader's attention is predicated on the identification of women with their familial, domestic roles: those readers who have tender memories of their mother, wife, sister or daughter are apostrophised to read or listen to the following 'short and faithful lay'. The Preface to this volume emphasises separate gender spheres – there may be some cross-over of masculine and feminine characteristics, but reversal carries the threat of deformity. The poem itself opens with a eulogy to 'Woman', who is defined by her difference from man. While man acts, she waits. She is malleable – 'of gentler nature, softer, dearer' – but not mobile: 'With generous bosom, age or childhood shielding,/And in the storms of life, though moved, unyielding'.[4]

After this build-up, it comes as no surprise to find that Griseld is a 'damsel sweet' (st. II), and her journey through life an 'unwearied course of gentle deeds'.[5] Visiting imprisoned father-figures, Griseld brings 'sweet' tales of home into alien spaces, familiarising Gothic surroundings; the years between her visits to Mr Baillie in prison and those to her father, in hiding in a burial vault, are passed in 'useful toil'. After the execution of Mr Baillie, Griseld's father flees to Holland, where he is joined by his family. Griseld bravely returns to Scotland to collect her ailing sister and is 'sweetly . . . repaid' by parental blessings. All this travel does not change her. Though the family are 'outlaws' in '[a] stranger's land', she sets about making 'a humble home' out of their 'alter'd lot': we find her sewing, cooking, looking after the children, 'with ready hand and heart,/Each task of toilsome duty taking' (st. XXXI). She 'clings' to her family (st. XLIV), and after their return to Britain declines the offer to become a maid of honour to the Queen. She also declines the hand of a wealthy neighbour to wait until it is possible to marry Jerviswood, the son of the man she visited in prison as a girl. The duties of a daughter are not erased by those of a wife and mother, and she remains 'subject to his [her father's] will' (st. XLIX) in a relationship of paternal monogamy. She goes abroad one last time, hoping to see the 'homely house' (st. LI) where her family resided during their exile, prompted, we are told, by '[m]aternal love,/Active and warm, which nothing might restrain,/Led her once more, in years advanced, to rove / To distant southern climes' (st. L).[6]

This short tour of the landmarks of the legend demonstrates Griseld's place in the gender ideology of Baillie's time. Even when she goes abroad, our heroine takes with her so much cultural baggage that travelling is just like staying at home. For an ideal woman, to go away is not to experience otherness, but to confirm the continuity of the same, the 'homely merit' of a 'helpful Maid'.

Reviewers of *Metrical Legends* pick the story of Griseld Baillie (rather than those of Columbus or William Wallace) as 'the most pleasing tale in the book', and confirm, in various ways, the hegemony of a certain pattern of femininity.[7] Moreover, the rhetoric of the reviews places this poem in the sphere of what is appropriate for a woman to write. The *Monthly Review* takes issue with what it perceives as Baillie's attempt, 'to reconcile the *literal* record' of heroic deeds 'with *poetical* effect'; according to the reviewer, this is 'to rob from *prose* . . . its own implicit *truth*; and to gain the effect, without paying the tax, of the essential decorations of verse'.[8] Though 'Griseld Baillie' is not exempt from this criticism, this strange discourse of economics – implicitly off-limits to a lady, and perhaps betraying subliminal anxiety about women in the literary marketplace – is replaced by a chivalric attitude to the female character and female poet. The reviewer quotes two passages, one which displays Griseld in her role as wife, and the other as daughter; these lines are 'most delightful' to the writer 'for they present an endearing image of affection, sense, and virtue'.[9] He concludes with a chivalric flourish:

> We . . . make our most courteous bow to the distinguished authoress whose work we have been examining; assuring her that, whatever unwelcome remarks our duty may have inflicted on her 'Metrical Legends', she has few more firm and decided admirers than ourselves.[10]

Polite censure and chivalry inscribe the superiority of the reviewer and limit the domain of the woman poet. Significantly, the reviewer observes that 'the manner in which Miss Baillie has related the . . . most touching instances of filial affection, in this her family-heroine, does infinite credit to her heart as well as to her poetical genius.'[11] It is crucial that poetical genius is enmeshed in the domestic affections.

This latter point is made at greater length in the *Scots Magazine* of the same year, with the reviewer making a characteristic elision between the woman writer's life and her text. The positing of this symbiotic relationship, which recurs again and again in reviews of women poets, is part of the apparatus of ideology – it marks a set of parameters for the woman and the poet, enforcing ideals of femininity both at home and on the page. The *Scots Magazine* confirms that both Baillie and her heroine are models of domestic virtue. The latter is described as a woman who,

> meek, unassuming, perfectly feminine, and little dreaming of celebrity, was, nevertheless, a bright example and ornament to her sex, possessing, in a pre-eminent degree, those humble virtues, and those fond and faithful relative affections, which render duties delightful, and hardships and difficulties tolerable, if not easy.[12]

The review includes a long quotation from the introductory verses which sketch 'the true feminine character'. Significantly, we are told that '[i]n the pleasing task of recording congenial virtues, Miss Baillie seems quite at home, and peculiarly inspired by her subject'. She is poetically at home because her own character mirrors that of her heroine. Indeed, the reviewer theorises that the poetic production implicitly depends on the private life of the writer – 'a negligent, or, . . . a fashionable daughter' could not have drawn this portrait. The review continues,

> It gives us pleasure to add, . . . that our admirable authoress, . . . was herself a pattern of filial duty, exalted, tender, and devoted, like that of her heroine . . . We could not, possessed of this knowledge, withhold such a lesson, we may add, such a triumph from the sex. To know that, the object of general admiration for powerful and original genius has, in the quietest seclusion, practised in their full extent all those homebred and homefelt virtues that she knows so well to describe, is praise beyond what genius itself could either deserve or bestow.[13]

A number of important points are made here. The rhetorical emphasis on 'home' ('homebred and homefelt virtues') picks up on the earlier comment that 'Miss Baillie seems quite at home' with her subject, so that home becomes both the place where virtue is engendered (and where [female] gender is contingent on virtue) and the locus of the poetic text: the text of the poem is home. The life of the poetess, as purveyed to us by the reviewer who peeks into 'the sacred recesses of domestic privacy', is a 'lesson' to other women, just as the textualised life of her heroine is a 'pattern' to be followed: at the end of the poem, Baillie's speaker addresses the 'polish'd fair of modern times' – the woman reader is clearly meant to identify herself, in terms of nationality and gender, with the 'British fair' who show 'kindred sympathy' with the 'modest worth' of the heroine.[14] Thus, Baillie plays a role in mediating the ideology of femininity, her public text celebrating and perpetuating private virtues. I will return later to the significance of this point.

The most extensive account of this volume is by Carlyle in the *Edinburgh Review* (October 1821). His use of tropes of spatiality reveals some of the implications of the 'placing' of the woman poet. Where the critic in the *Monthly Review* objected to the mixing of verse and prose, Carlyle argues that Baillie unsuccessfully invades the 'debateable ground' between two genres, history and poetry. Her material is the stuff of history, but she fails to attain 'a sublime view of mental greatness', for 'her store of imagery, [and] her range of feeling, are both circumscribed'.[15] Though Carlyle does not explicitly invoke a gender agenda, it is the portraits of Christopher Columbus, and especially, of William Wallace, to which he objects. Carlyle finds the single legend which tells a woman's story 'by far the most successful in the volume': Baillie's 'matter-of-fact poetry is here in its proper place'.[16] In the course of his review of this poem, Carlyle includes two substantial quotations: the first is from the picture of ideal womanhood in the introductory stanzas, the second is the account of Griseld's household tasks in Holland. This ideal figure has no place in history and her mind and situation are the stuff of Miss Baillie's 'every-day thoughts . . . and such as afforded room for employing the most valuable and uncontested faculties of her genius'.[17] This limited literary space is the best place for the woman poet, who details the 'simple doings' of 'a meek, unambitious creature'.[18] Again, there is a slippage between life and text, so that Griseld and Joanna Baillie become almost interchangeable, and Carlyle regards both with 'affectionate admiration'.[19] Baillie's poetry does not work by 'inflaming our hearts or expanding our imaginations' – it does not transport us anywhere – but it 'brighten[s] . . . our common existence'.[20] In legislating the terms on which women's writing will be valued, the reviewers annotate the geopolitical realities of women's lives: the good woman, the poetess, and her text, are denied a passport to the wider sphere of life and literature. The poetess is circumscribed within the parameters of the home, the space of domesticity and femininity, but, crucially, this circumscription is the key to public success.

III

The second poem, 'Sir Maurice: A Ballad', published in *Fugitive Verses* (1840),[21] is more exotic; the narrative departs from the narrow domestic circle into inappropriate spaces. The heroine seems initially to embody the transgressive agenda of much recent feminist criticism, her cross-dressing and exotic travel may be read as emblematic of an attempt to escape from the constrictions of bourgeois society. But the movements across cultural boundaries enacted in this poem need to be charted in some detail in order to assess how far they subvert the ideology of femininity. The poem opens with Sir Maurice gathering his troops for departure to the Holy Land; he notices a band from 'Moorham's lordless hall' led by the ancient Seneschal. Moorham's lord has been supposed killed in battle. Sir Maurice advises them to return home to 'defend' their castle and their lady, but a 'gentle page' insists that Moorham's lord is still alive. Sir Maurice quickly sees through the page's disguise, and is keen for the cross-dressed page to return to her proper sphere, explicitly linking movement away from home with sexual impropriety:

> To thine own home return, fair youth!
>   To thine own home return; . . .
>
> War suits thee not if boy thou art;
>   And if a sweeter name
> Befit thee, do not lightly part
>   With maiden's honour'd fame. (st. 17, 18)[22]

By the time he has convinced himself that 'a stripling's garb,/Betrays not wanton will', and acknowledged 'a maiden's pride' in '[a] daughter's love', the 'page' and her band have departed.

The scene then moves to Syria: Sir Maurice after much fighting is dangerously wounded and faints away. He awakes to find himself in a Saracen castle where he sees in turn the 'ancient Seneschal', Moorham's lord and finally the Saracen chief. The Saracen chief explains that since he has 'wedded an English dame', he will not keep an Englishman captive. Moorham's lord now appears again to explain his presence in the Saracen's castle. His daughter, dressed as a boy, 'boldly' crossed the sea with wealth to buy her father's freedom. Captured herself, she sought out her father, and her grief betrayed her sex. The Saracen chief then fell in love with her – and she married him to save her father.

Curiously, if the page's grief betrays her sex, it also betrays the textuality of sex: the woman who 'sorely wept' mimics Sir Maurice himself, who 'sigh'd and wept full sore', while he, of course, in an act of linguistic transvestism, echoes Keats's 'Belle Dame Sans Merci'. The tearful mimicry going on here is more than a sign that the legacy of sensibility facilitated the sympathetic tears of Romanticism's 'new men'. To add one more layer to all this dressing-up, we might note that the *Quarterly Review* calls Baillie 'the mistress of a masculine style of thought and diction'.[23] For a brief moment, then, the poem holds open some alternatives to the homely demarcations of gender.

The limitations of this other space should be apparent: girls can pass as boys only in a foreign place, and only until they cry, while the fluid femininity of all this weeping takes place in the context of imprisonment. Indeed, the metaphors of the prison and of slavery are traditional for the condition of womanhood, so that the floating femininity I have described is as much a function of bondage as of the deconstruction of essence. In any case, more traditional distinctions soon reassert themselves. Moorham's daughter, who remains unnamed, in marrying the Moslem lord to secure her father's freedom, pays a 'fearful price' (st. 52) – not the traditional currency of sexual virtue, but racial and religious purity (though it is hard to see this as completely disengaged from the inscription of sexuality). Consequently, she refuses to marry Sir Maurice after the death of her husband. Sir Maurice dons his 'warlike mail' and goes off to prove his 'prowess', while she becomes a nun.

Baillie's cross-dressed page is not an unfamiliar figure in Victorian women's writing. Elizabeth Barrett Browning and George Sand, amongst others, expressed the desire to be Lord Byron's page. Byron's heroine Kaled in *Lara* provided a model of emancipated androgyny, though importantly any hints of eroticism are effaced: as Caroline Franklin points out, Kaled's unwomanly behaviour is in 'the service of the "feminine" virtue of selfless devotion'.[24] Elizabeth Barrett Browning's 'The Romaunt of the Page' rescripts *Lara* from the page's perspective; in 1838 she writes that 'My ballad containing a ladye dressed up like a page and galloping off to Palestine in manner that would scandalise you, went to Miss Mitford this morning'.[25] Her page is a married woman in pursuit of her Crusader husband. She dies fighting to save him from enemy Turks, but not before her husband has rejected her displaced self-representation – she tells him her story as though it were her sister's – as 'Unwomaned'; the wife he mythologises is an angelic creature, not a cross-dressed fighter. Barrett Browning debunks Byron's glamour: Byron's Kaled succumbs to the female malady – madness – while Barrett Browning's heroine is sacrificed to Victorian bourgeois ideology. Baillie's heroine does not die, but her journey perhaps displays most clearly the circumscriptions of ideals of femininity, for here it is the woman, not the man, who articulates the platitudes of propriety. Though the heroine of 'Sir Maurice' has a more complex relation to the domestic than Griseld Baillie, she remains within a patriarchal plot: she moves from north to south, crossing the boundaries of gender, race and religion for her father's sake, and even her refusal of a romantic plot is generated by the ideals of domestic ideology. As a nun, she moves outside the home, in a role which suggests a possible alternative to being a wife or a page, but the poem does not emphasise sisterhood; rather, it charts a place for her that is made accessible through the idiom of separate spheres: she is enshrined as a type of angel in the house, tending the 'helpless', serving in her 'separate . . . state' – more as dutiful daughter than bride of Christ – the ultimate patriarchal authority (st. 67 and 68). At the end of the poem, what is emphasised is 'her meek worth' (st. 68).

'Sir Maurice' functions as a confirmation of 'woman's sphere' and the hegemony of female virtue. But the poem also works as a more oblique comment on the social place of the woman writer. The discourses of fame and of economics locate the text in an ideological marketplace in which the relation between public and private spheres, and gender, is at issue. I want to suggest that there is an analogy between the concerns of the text and concerns about the public display of the woman writer (and her text). The problem for Baillie's heroine is that in moving out of her proper sphere, she becomes the object of the gaze, 'scann'd' from 'top to toe' by Sir Maurice (st. 15), and she subsequently trades her feminine 'fame' for her father's life. Because her motives are unsullied, the narrative trajectory is recuperative, and she is replaced in an appropriate sphere. For nineteenth-century women writers, fame and femininity exist in an uneasy relationship. The 'public' act of representation threatens to undermine gender and class identity by making a spectacle of the writer, and figuratively forging links between poetesses and prostitutes, both of whom display their wares in a marketplace ordered by men. The question, then, is how to negotiate the crossing from private to public, to write within the geography of the feminine.

For writers such as Mary Robinson and L. E. L. (Letitia Elizabeth Landon), putting themselves on display is a risky marketing strategy – they both write poems in which women artists are the object of the male gaze, and their own lives are the stuff of gossip columns. Baillie travels a different route. Her exemplary public poetic status depends on the perception of her unviolated privacy. The overlap of the discursive domains of female virtue and public success, the two meanings of 'fame', is made clear in an *Athenaeum* review of 1841:

> Though residing within reach of the metropolis, the flattery of the coteries has never tarnished the freshness of her inspirations; nor could accumulated and increasing honours tempt her to leave the peaceful quiet of her home circle; she is personally scarcely known in the literary world, though with a fame and reputation on the strength of which any woman, less *womanly* in the best sense of the word, would have stared in effigy out of every print-shop window, and figured in the diary of every superficial Prince Puckler, or sprightly American, who thought fit to publish his fathomings of our literature, or his pencillings of our distinguished authors.[26]

Baillie's untarnished 'reputation', her standing as a virtuous woman, grounds her poetic reputation (even if her poetry was less good than it is, she would 'rank high' as an 'example'). She retreats from any compromising display of herself, a display that would make her a shopworn commodity. As the prejudices of the passage reveal, such display would compromise not only her gender identity but also her class and national status. For the 'womanly' woman (the tautology makes clear, for late twentieth-century readers, that this is a cultural construct), the personal cannot be public, except within the textual parameters already indicated (home as the subject of the poetic text). But this ideology is not simply constraining: Baillie's 'womanly' behaviour means that she resists being appropriated as the object of the gaze and being written into a (foreign) script that she cannot control.

Contemporary critics emphasise Baillie's conformity to a very limited private and poetic space – Baillie takes to heart her own lessons about woman's place in the home. In 1851, *The Athenaeum* declares: 'Never has woman more honourably adorned womanhood by the unobtrusive privacy of her life, and by the noble forms and features of her poetical creations'.[27] The *Dublin University Magazine* reflects that 'living in the seclusion of a quiet, narrow, domestic circle, without practical experience of the world's doings, "she kept the noiseless tenor of her way," unchequered by stirring incidents to disturb or excite a tranquil, uniform course of life'.[28] There are references elsewhere to her 'serene seclusion'; a 'life ... passed in tranquillity and seclusion'; a 'domestic circle of the highest moral purity' in which Baillie's most binding relationships are with her mother and her sister

(Baillie pp. v, x, xii). Another critic supposes Baillie's library as circumscribed as her life: 'Out of the fulness of a true heart her works have been written, rather than from any vast or precious store of book-learning'.[29] With this writing from the heart, Baillie conforms to a model of inner- not inter-textuality which limits her poetic horizons.

Other women poets (in particular Felicia Hemans) are praised in similar terms to Baillie. A *Blackwood's* reviewer writes that only Joanna Baillie disputes pre-eminence with Hemans. Hemans's 'attachment to the privacy of life, her wise dislike and avoidance of the *éclat* of literary renown, and the dull, dry, fever-heat of fashionable circles, tend to complete her qualifications as a fitting representative of her fair countrywomen'.[30] The review shows how discourses of gender are always inflected by other discourses, especially that of nationality: Hemans's virtues 'all speak of the cultivated woman bred under English skies, and in English homes'[31] (significantly, Hemans writes a poem entitled 'The Homes of England'). As the trope of travel suggests, this is also an issue in Baillie's poem: what happens there, I think, is that the question of sexual (im)propriety is displaced onto that of racial miscegenation, and this problem is then recuperated within a conservative gender ideology (though it is significant that the heroine' remains displaced – she does not literally return home).

IV

The separate gender spheres, emphasised at the end of 'Sir Maurice', are the explicit theme of Frederick Rowton's Introduction to *The Female Poets of Great Britain* (1848), and the principle that structures his selection of poems. Of the ninety-odd poets represented in this influential anthology, those allocated the highest number of poems are: Joanna Baillie, Mary Russell Mitford, Mary Howitt and L. E. L. (revealingly listed under her married name, Laetitia Elizabeth Maclean).[32] Rowton's Introduction is worth examining in detail, for it suggests a solidifying of the cultural terrain, a stricter drawing of the boundaries of gender, of the demarcation between public and private spheres. He demonstrates the production of a woman's world that provides the complement and the cure to the public, political, inherently male, sphere. Arguing against '[t]he doctrine of woman's intellectual inferiority', Rowton claims, however, 'that the sphere of woman's duty requires powers altogether dissimilar from those which are needed by man'.[33] Her sphere is defined by 'INFLUENCE' (man's by 'FORCE'), and is characterised as follows:

> Her province is to soften, round off, smooth down, the angularities of life and conduct . . . Home is her empire, and affection her sceptre. It is hers . . . to inspirit, to reinvigorate, to sustain . . . [Man] comes in contact with villainy and selfishness: it is hers to keep alive in his bosom the generous flame of virtue.[34]

He goes on for some time in this vein, and then sums up in a number of 'broad distinctions', or, as we would say today, binary oppositions: 'Man is self-relying and self-possessed; woman timid, clinging, and dependent . . . He thinks; she feels . . . Intellect is his; heart is hers'.[35]

Rowton's notion of male self-possession recapitulates the contours of Romantic ideology, an ideology of masculine (self-)mastery which is predicated on the figurative silencing of women, who function as muse or as mute poetic object in so many Romantic poems. The paradox is that the very existence of the anthology speaks to speaking rather than silent women. There is no space here to discuss the legacies of Romanticism; more important in the present context is Rowton's figurative expansion of woman's domain to an 'empire', so that the trope of the limited circle of femininity takes on global resonances. Woman's 'influence' is far-flung. Judith Newton posits that there is a shift from eighteenth-century conduct texts such as John Gregory's *A Father's Legacy to His Daughters* (1774) which aestheticise femininity in the service of a male consumer to those from the latter part of the century onwards wherein there is a new type of reference to women's influence. James Fordyce's *Sermons to Young Women* (1766) speak of 'an influence ... an empire which belongs to you ... I mean that which has the heart as its object'; as Newton argues, by the nineteenth century women's 'separate sphere is important less as a realm in which they may demonstrate good taste than as a dominion in which they exercise a special potency'.[36] This trend culminates, she argues, with Sarah Ellis's declaration of the social significance of women's influence at the beginning of *The Women of England* (1839): 'You have deep responsibilities; you have urgent claims; a nation's moral worth is in your keeping'.[37]

The implications of this domestic imperialism may be focused by a closer look at the image and ideology of the domestic circle, within which Baillie is so frequently located. This figure places the woman at the centre of the private sphere; for the woman writer, it is an image of the ideological constraints on the production and reception of women's texts. But the question of female 'influence' rearticulates the significance of this trope, widens the parameters, so to speak. Sarah Ellis in *The Wives of England* (1843) proposes that 'the English wife should ... regard her position as a central one'; 'it is not so much our private precepts which have weight', she argues, 'and perhaps still less our public ones, so much as the influence of individual character upon a surrounding circle, and through that circle upon the world at large'.[38] There is a ripple-effect whereby one good example inspires others to create their own circle, each one with a woman as its moral centre. The domestic woman, without leaving the sanctity of the home and the concerns of the heart, spreads her influence 'from heart to heart, into a never-ending future'.[39] In other words, at the same time that gender oppositions are becoming more rigid and woman's role increasingly circumscribed (at least rhetorically, for one must allow for the gap between theory and practice), a new type of power accrues to women, which might constitute an early version of female 'networking'.

The work of the ideal woman writer displays a similar circular logic. In the words of Mary Russell Mitford, in a pair of essays on Joanna Baillie and Catherine Fanshawe, the 'pattern of what a literary lady should be ... abstain[s] from the wider sphere of authorship', but from her domestic literary sphere she circulates 'sympathy'.[40] Women's role in literary production, as Mary Jean Corbett has recently demonstrated in her reading of Victorian womens' autobiographies, is to nurture the values of society.[41] Rather than producing wide-ranging texts, Mitford's model writer reproduces leisured, middle-class existence (this woman does not have to write for a living), she reproduces the bourgeois sensibility that has its roots in aristocratic gentility (remember the disdain of many eighteenth-century aristocratic women for publication). More significantly, the woman writer, and her circulating texts, inspire women to preserve their realm of tranquil domesticity, each woman, as in Ellis's example, creating her own circle, and reinvigorating men after their experiences in the public arena. Within this seemingly constraining patriarchal model, women are empowered as cultural producers, for they reproduce cultural values (this is a subtle modulation and expansion of earlier figurings of the woman writer and her relation to public and private discourses).

The metaphor of reproduction has further resonances, given the idealisation of motherhood, from Ann Taylor's tracts of the second decade of the century through to Harriet Beecher Stowe's invocation to the 'mothers of America' in *Uncle Tom's Cabin* (to cite a text published the year after Baillie's *Complete Works*).⁴² The ideal Victorian mother is Victoria herself; as Elizabeth Barrett Browning's poems 'The Young Queen' and 'Victoria's Tears' reveal, Victoria's command of her 'grateful isles' is predicated on her feminine sympathy. Joanna Baillie, of course, is not literally a 'wife of England' (or of Scotland, for that matter), nor is she a mother, though she functions as a poetic mother for a generation of women poets – Felicia Hemans's 1828 volume *Records of Woman* is dedicated to Baillie. Rowton foregrounds Baillie's status as honorary mother, as the reproducer of domestic ideology, by placing at the head of his selection the poems entitled 'To a Child' and 'A Mother to Her Waking Infant'. Both are popular texts, already in circulation: 'To a Child' was published in the *New Monthly Magazine* in 1821, and reprinted in *Fugitive Verses* in 1840; in the preface to that volume, Baillie tells us that 'A Mother to Her Waking Infant' (published in the 1790 edition) had found a place in Mrs Barbauld's *Choice Poetical Extracts* (1820). The circumstances of publication mean that both are likely to have been reproduced elsewhere, at least in commonplace books. The poems demonstrate Baillie's 'natural sentiments' and 'womanly tenderness of feeling'.⁴³ Rowton continues with a 'sweetly plaintive' song,⁴⁴ before turning to Columbus and extracts from the plays. But Baillie's sphere of influence is clearly signalled.

V

Before I turn finally to *Ahalya Baee*, a poem printed for private circulation in 1849 and published for the first time in the *Collected Works* of 1851, I want to make a brief detour to a text which appeared between these two dates, and which speaks with succinct eloquence to the issues I have been discussing: fame, femininity and maternity, and the social significance of separate spheres; what is also exposed is the colonial subtext of the metaphor of 'Empire'. In the first volume of *Harper's New Monthly Magazine*, a publication full of fashion plates and good advice for the women of America (though its paradigms of femininity were modelled on the women of England), one article (on the writer Jane Porter) begins thus:

> The frequent observation of foreigners is, that in England we have few 'celebrated women.' Perhaps they mean that we have few who are 'notorious;' but let us admit that in either case they are right; and may we not express our belief in its being better for women and for the community that such is the case. '[C]elebrity' rarely adds to the happiness of a woman, and almost as rarely increases her usefulness. The time and attention required to attain 'celebrity,' must . . . interfere with the faithful discharge of those feminine duties upon which the well-doing of society depends, and which shed so pure a halo around our English homes . . . The strength and glory of England are in the keeping of the wives and mothers of its men; . . . Happy is the country where the laws of God and nature are held in reverence – where each sex fulfills its peculiar duties, and renders its sphere a sanctuary! and surely such harmony is blessed by the Almighty – for while other nations writhe in anarchy and poverty, our own spreads wide her arms to receive all who seek protection or need repose.⁴⁵

It is no coincidence that it is foreigners – here represented as undifferentiated 'others' – who note the paucity of celebrated (or notorious) women in England. In a quite common manoeuvre (it is a staple of travel-writing, for example), national identity is asserted and confirmed in opposition to cultural otherness. But what is most interesting here is the marriage of the discourses of gender and nationality: the geography of femininity, that hallowed space of domesticity, is mapped on to, and secures, national boundaries. Happy homes are equivalent to a happy country. National peace and prosperity are predicated on the ideology of separate spheres, which function in gracious harmony. In this national idyll, England functions ultimately as a maternal figure, nurturing the orphans of those dark places where the light of domestic ideology never shines. Though *Harper's* is an American publication, all the fiction in the first number is British: the high cultural value attached to the deposed imperial power enables British domestic ideology to cross the Atlantic and recolonise the new country. A similar expansionist mode implicitly shadows the movements of Baillie's heroines in the poems I have considered above, for they take with them the manners and the mindset of British domestic ideology into other places.[46]

Ahalya Baee constitutes, I suggest, a type of counter-discourse to English imperialism and the accepted geography of gender. Baillie chooses to work in a gender-specific genre, for since the heyday of Byron and Southey, the oriental tale was associated with sexual politics. In the two other poems I have looked at in detail, the heroines' voyages out are ultimately voyages in, which reinscribe the female self within the definitions of the poet's own national culture; Baillie's heroines are always the women, wives and daughters of nineteenth-century Britain, though what they advertise is the transcultural 'essence' of femininity. For the first time, we have a non-British heroine, the narrative being based on Sir John Malcolm's account of the life of an Indian queen in his *Memoirs of Central India* (1823), an authority that Baillie invokes throughout her text, both in the preface and the extensive footnotes to the poem. The overdetermined emphasis on national and religious difference (Ahalya Baee arms herself for battle, she is a worshipper of Brahma, and attempts to exorcise a malevolent spirit from her son) – and the extreme situations in which she is placed (she witnesses her daughter's suttee at a time when British 'women were beginning to be considered too delicate to bear the public rituals of death')[47] – constitute the frame within which Baillie examines the construction of the feminine.

The heroine is not, however, simply an exotic 'other' to Baillie's home-loving girls.[48] Rather, this poem, written near the end of her career, poses an alternative to her earlier texts, testing out their plots of femininity and questioning Western cultural attitudes by going outside their parameters. The reinscription, or rescripting of the familiar, of home, is made possible within the inscription of difference. Ahalya Baee's first act transgresses the boundaries of gender: she refuses inducements to give up her sovereignty, and gives a 'display of warlike preparation' to her enemies (Baillie, p. 841). However, as the footnote to this section points out, she 'sent him [her opponent, the venal chief, Ragobah Duda] a message not to make war on a woman, from which he might incur disgrace, but could never derive honour' (p. 841). In other words, she manipulates the characteristics of masculinity and femininity, both arming for war and disarming her enemies through 'a politic display' of womanliness. This is an altered pattern of femininity.

It is crucially Ahalya Baee's role as a mother that is subversive. Normatively, the mother is the figure at the centre of domestic ideology which radiates out from her as 'influence'. Ahalya Baee is a biological mother with recognisable responses to her children, but she is also the mother of her country. Her most significant act displaces the discourse of maternity and of familial politics current in Britain, and has far-reaching implications for the allocation of gender spheres. In Britain, the familial relations of the monarch were replicated in the political sphere – in the wake of the Queen Caroline affair, the royals were expected to be caring mothers and fathers in their own homes

(Victoria was the model of wife and mother for the middle classes) as a type of personal guarantee for their political role as mothers and fathers of the nation (the ultimate paradigm of this expansionist rhetoric is Britain as the 'mother' of the Empire). Ahalya Baee inverts this movement from the literal to the figurative family. She begins with the figurative role, and fabricates an appropriate family for the political scenario. 'She must adopt another son and heir' to succeed her dead child, and she nobly chooses 'a soldier tried and brave' (pp. 841–2). She is much younger than her new son, an unnatural mother for whom the personal political: 'They were a state-constructed Son and Mother' (p. 842). At a time when 'motherhood was regarded as the most valuable and natural component of woman's mission', when all the ideological state apparatuses operated so that this 'specific historical construction of femininity was made to seem natural and universal', Baillie reveals the making of the maternal.[49]

Reconstructing the maternal puts pressure on the prescriptiveness of nineteenth-century gender ideology. Baillie's figures maintain separate spheres, 'distinct, and, . . . distant spheres of action', according to the footnote (p. 841), but these are separate spheres with a difference: Ahalya Baee and her 'son' are 'United firmly to their native land,/She the considerate head, and he the ready hand' (p. 842). He goes away to deal with wars on 'distant frontiers' and she stays at home, but the hierarchical valuation of these acts is reversed. The traditional (Western) dichotomy of mind over matter remains in place, but the coordinates of gender onto which this is mapped are inverted.

This odd couple represent a potential alterity at the heart of British domestic ideology. That Baillie is testing out her own culture's account of the feminine is confirmed by her reworking of the notion of separate spheres and her revision of the familiar figure of the circle, which, as we have seen, is a central trope of domestic ideology. Ahalya Baee 'dispens[es] justice with impartial skill' from 'her seat of sway' which is located within 'a charmed circle' (p. 842).[50] Here the woman wields direct public power, not indirect influence. Woman's empire is no longer confined to the heart and the home, but spreads out to form a wider circle, the feminine topography of the country itself which lies within a 'guarded girdle' (p. 844).

This is as far as Joanna Baillie ever travels in her exploration of the geography of femininity, and her evocation of difference has implications for the women back home. In conclusion, I return to the issue of female 'influence' and to the separate spheres posited in the *Harper's* article. We recall that the stability of a whole series of oppositions – foreign / domestic, public/private, stability/anarchy – are contingent upon women's 'faithful discharge' of 'feminine duties'. The imperialist agenda that is implicit in the writer's idealisation of England's embrace and assimilation of other nations rests on domestic security in a type of international version of separate spheres. Joanna Baillie is at home in this historical moment: her texts, and the cultural terrain within which they find a place, are complicit with the intertwined ideologies of gender and imperialism. Indeed, two of Baillie's closet dramas, *The Martyr* and *The Bride*, are produced in Ceylon and translated into Singhalese under the patronage of the Chief Justice, Sir Alexander Johnston, in an evangelical attempt to eradicate the vices of the natives.[51] *Ahalya Baee*, however, provides the material for a detour from the hegemony of home, allowing me to end with a post-colonial fantasy: Baillie's poem, set in India, the heart of the British Empire, comes into English homes to be read by the wives and mothers of England, and thus its alternative paradigm of the feminine may be reproduced through the network of female circles of influence. This reversal of British colonialism potentially casts the shadow of sexual-political anarchy on the pure halo around our English homes.[52]

Notes

1.   Joanna Baillie, *The Dramatical and Poetical Works of Joanna Baillie*, 2nd edn (Longman, Brown, Green and Longmans, London, 1853), p. 771. All subsequent references to Baillie's work (including the 'Life of Joanna Baillie') are to this edition, cited as Baillie, followed by page number(s); references to 'The Legend of Lady Griseld Baillie' and 'Sir Maurice: A Ballad' are to stanza numbers.

2.   Frederick Rowton, *Female Poets of Great Britain* (Longman, Brown, Green and Longmans, London, 1848).

3.   Jennifer Breen (ed.), *Women Romantic Poets, 1785–1832* (Dent, London, London, 1992), p. xxii.

4.   The prefatory stanzas are unnumbered; references to the poem 'proper' are to stanza numbers.

5.   The quote comes from the last stanza of the poem, which forms part of a concluding address to British women.

6.   For details of the journey undertaken by the family, see Robert Scott-Moncrieff ed, *The Household Book of Lady Grisell Baillie 1692–1733* (printed by T. & A. Constable for the Scottish History Society, Edinburgh, 1911).

7.   Article XII: Miss Baillie's *Metrical Legends*', *Monthly Review* 96 N. S. (1821), pp. 72–81 (p. 78).

8.   *Monthly Review*, 96, p. 78 (italics in original).

9.   *MR*, p. 80.

10.   *MR*, p. 81.

11.   *MR*, p. 79.

12.   'Remarks on Miss Baillie's Metrical Legends', *Scots Magazine* 8 N. S. (1821), pp. 260–5 (p. 263). The comment is placed in a national context: 'Of this character our Scottish maids and matrons have been allowed to partake in no common degree' (pp. 263–4).

13.   *SM*, p. 264.

14.   Though they are rejected, the fact that alternative models, including a caricature of the Blue-stocking, are represented, demonstrates that this legend of a good woman is not the only possible narrative of femininity.

15.   Carlyle, 'Article V: Miss Baillie's *Metrical Legends*', *Edinburgh Review* 2 (1821), pp. 393–414 (pp. 401, 393).

16.   *ER*, p. 410.

17.   *ER*, p. 412.

18.   *ER*, p. 411.

19.   *ER*, p. 412.

20.   *ER*, pp. 412–13. Carlyle shifts briefly to another model of the poetess when he speaks of Baillie's language displaying 'a witching coquetry . . . which it is as impossible to resist as to describe' (p. 413). It is hard to see Baillie as anything other than a supporter of domestic ideology. The only possible escape route for the contemporary feminist reader is that the gender oppositions are so fixed – in 'Wallace' and 'Columbus' the men are so manly and the women are so marginal, while Griseld's bravery seems merely another household task (Baillie's retelling of the legend suppresses Griseld's heroism) – as to prompt the question whether Baillie is espousing or exposing gender ideology.

21.   This is a revised and expanded edition of *Fugitive Verses* (1790); 'Sir Maurice' does not appear in the earlier edition. Typically, reviewers of the 1840 volume find the 'affectionately familiar' mode of Baillie's poem to her sister ('Lines to Agnes Baillie on her Birthday') makes it 'the happiest composition in the book' (see, *The Athenaeum* 691 [1841], pp. 69–70 [p. 69], and *The Quarterly Review* 67 [1841], pp. 437–52 [p. 449]). Other poems in this volume in a similarly affectionate mould include: 'Recollections of a Dear and Steady Friend', 'Two Brothers', 'Verses Sent to Mrs Baillie on Her Birthday, 1813'. 'On the Death of a Very Dear Friend' locates the friend (Justina Milligan) in 'her home of rest,/Where inmates dear were ever found/And sisterly affection sweetly fenced her round' (Baillie, p. 832).

22.   The stanzas are unnumbered in the text; I have numbered them to aid easy reference.

23.   p. 437.

24.   Caroline Franklin, *Byron's Heroines* (Oxford, 1992), p. 86.

25.   *The Letters of Elizabeth Barrett Browning*, 2 vols (London, 1897), I, p. 62.
26.   *Athenaeum* 691, (1841), p. 69.
27.   *The Athenaeum* 1211 (1851), p. 41.
28.   *Dublin University Magazine* 37 (1851), pp. 529–36 (p. 529).
29.   *Athenaeum* 691, p. 69.
30.   'Mrs Hemans,' *Blackwood's Edinburgh Magazine* 64 (1848), pp. 641–58 (p. 641).
31.   *BEM*, p. 641.
32.   Howitt has ten poems, and the others nine each; Mitford is allocated the most pages.
33.   Frederick Rowton, *Female Poets of Great Britain* (London, 1848), pp. xxi, xxii.
34.   xxiii. Rowton's model implicitly suggests that male authorship is dependent on the spiritual sustenance of a woman in the home (quite apart, one might add, from more mundane domestic economy).
35.   pp. xxiv–xxv. Rowton does not live up to his proto-Derridean claim that '[he is] not at all prepared to say that "difference" means "inferiority"' (p. xxii).
36.   Judith Lowder Newton, 'Power and the Ideology of "Woman's Sphere"', *Feminisms: An Anthology of Literary Theory and Criticism*, ed. Robyn R. Warhol and Diane Price Herndl (Rutgers University Press, New Brunswick, N.J., 1991; Macmillan, London, 1992), pp. 765–80 (p. 766; Fordyce cited on this page).
37.   Quoted in Newton, p. 766.
38.   Sarah Stickney Ellis, *The Wives of England* (Fisher, Son & Co., London, 1843), pp. 344, 345.
39.   Ellis, *Wives*, p. 342.
40.   Mary Russell Mitford, 'Female Poets: Joanna Baillie – Catherine Fanshawe', *Recollections of a Literary Life; or, Books, Places, and People*, 3 vols (R. Bentley, London, 1852), I, pp. 241–65 (pp. 242, 249). Those of Fanshawe's poems included in Mitford's essay were originally published in a volume of poems edited by Baillie in 1823.
41.   Mary Jean Corbett, 'Feminine Authorship and Spiritual Autobiography in Victorian Women Writers' Autobiographies', *Women's Studies: An Interdisciplinary Journal* 18 (1990), pp. 13–29. I am indebted to Corbett's analysis of women's reproduction of dominant ideologies.
42.   On Victorian ideals of motherhood, see, especially, Leonore Davidoff and Catherine Hall, *Family Fortunes: Men and Women of the English Middle Class, 1780–1850* (Hutchison, London, 1987), and Lynda Nead, *Myths of Sexuality: Representations of Women in Victorian Britain* (Blackwell, Oxford, 1988).
43.   Rowton, pp. 297, 298. Other poems addressing infants are: 'To Sophia J. Baillie' and 'To James B. Baillie' (see Baillie, pp. 804, 821).
44.   Rowton, p. 301.
45.   'Memories of Miss Jane Porter', *Harper's New Monthly Magazine* 1 (1850), pp. 433–8 (p. 433).
46.   Equally, foreignness is to be kept out of Britain: Baillie's patriotic 'Volunteer's Song, Written in 1803' asserts that 'Nor fiend nor hero from a foreign strand,/Shall lord it in our land' (p. 823).
47.   Davidoff and Hall, *Family Fortunes*, p. 408.
48.   A colonial discourse reading might choose to foreground Baillie's domestication of the 'other', her imposition of sameness onto cultural difference. We first encounter the heroine as the iconic object of the gaze: 'Behold that female form so meekly bending/O'er a pale youth'. She is 'of gentle mind', and spends much womanly time alleviating 'Woe, want, and suff'ring'; even the lowliest of her subjects can depend on their claim '[u]pon her heart'. Her religion, which may seem 'strange . . . to those/Who in a better, purer faith were born', nevertheless demonstrates her piety and her role as a 'humble daughter' (to Brahma). It would be possible to argue that these details gesture towards a global femininity that transcends geographical differences.
49.   Nead, *Myths of Sexuality*, pp. 26–7.
50.   Baillie's note from Malcolm confirms that this public transaction of affairs is not improper for Hindoo women, for they are not confined or compelled to wear veils.

51.   See Baillie, xvii. *Fugitive Verses* (E. Moxon, London, 1840) also includes school rhymes and devotional songs for negro children, who are idealised as happy and carefree, basking in God's love.

52.   My anglocentric references are allusions to the *Harper's* article; in today's political climate one would, of course, be careful not to make England a synecdoche for Britain, thus consigning Scotland, for example, to invisibility.

10

Some Women of the Nineteenth-century Scottish Theatre: Joanna Baillie, Frances Wright and Helen MacGregor

Adrienne Scullion

John Any-Body would have stood higher with the critics than Joanna Baillie.[1]

The women of the nineteenth-century Scottish stage are varied, little known and under-valued. Yet it is, of course, the case that women populated all aspects of this vital phase in Scottish theatre history. As actresses, managers and playwrights they were most influential, but they also occupied the stage as singers, dancers, musicians and acrobats, as well as being engaged as historians and critics and they were, of course, consumers of theatre as members of the audience and as readers of plays. This chapter can only begin the process of recovering the particular influence effected by women on the Scottish theatre in the nineteenth century and, in the context of a study of Scottish women's writing, the focus must be on the playwright – although I will also consider some of the dominant representations of women on stage in contemporary drama.[2]

The study of Scottish theatre can be a frustrating thing, equally neglected by theatre scholarship and by Scottish studies. However, influenced by Alasdair Cameron's ground-breaking historical scholarship (as well as his endless enthusiasm for the subject), its depth, its complexity and its social, cultural and economic influences are finally being recognised and studied, and the nineteenth century is proving to be one of the richest of seams for new researchers. Cameron, Christopher Worth and Barbara Bell have all argued for the National Drama as *the* Scottish genre of the period, each convinced of its centrality in any understanding of the period's theatre. In addition, the significance of the popular tradition is generally agreed upon and has begun to be interrogated seriously in some recent work in the field.[3] While much remains virgin territory a key point seems won: that the nineteenth-century Scottish theatre is by no means homogeneous; that it can neither be reduced solely to the National Drama nor just to the popular tradition; that it has many diverse guises, which together create a unique and fertile environment for exciting theatre activity. Throughout the century Scottish theatre is an important part of the infrastructure of British touring theatre, with fine Theatres Royal in the major centres of population; vital minor houses in smaller towns, in addition to those competing directly with the patent houses of Glasgow and Edinburgh, producing a strong local tradition of performance in the illegitimate theatres; a remarkable popular voice in the tradition of the geggy theatres;[4] and the rising phenomenon of the music hall. And this as well as the uniquely indigenous form of the National Drama, which produces a remarkable series of popular plays and memorable characters, employing local performers and allowing some to maintain a high profile and equally profitable career based wholly in Scotland. Scottish theatre is, unquestionably, a busy, vibrant, commercially successful enterprise, although one increasingly pressurised by the expansive praxis and aggressive market-pace economics of later-century touring systems and the cultural influence of London. Nevertheless, and despite the vitality and popularity one can find in the industry, this theatre (so much of it 'popular' and hence ephemeral and transitory) did not produce the highly specific type of documentary heritage which gives legitimacy to the theatre, and one is faced with the perennial and inescapable problem of the lack of play texts, and must acknowledge another in the series of missing links in the history of Scottish theatre.[5]

This position is no longer the critical impasse it once was. Where it exists at all the study of Scottish theatre has traditionally been a literary one, finding focus and legitimacy around several key texts – Sir David Lindsay's *Ane Pleasant Satyre of the Thrie Estaitis* (1552), Allan Ramsay's *The Gentle Shepherd* (1729), John Home's *Douglas* (1756) – and latterly expanding somewhat to allow for the phenomenon of the National Drama, although this too is generally justified in connection with literary values and the canonical Sir Walter Scott. It hardly needs to be said that within this procession of literary milestones the voices and even the images of women are typically marginalised and sometimes effaced completely. Whilst one has no intention to replace this antique Leavisite 'Great Men' version of history with an equally ill-suited roll call of 'Great Women', it is important to take every opportunity to celebrate the contributions made by women to a theatre culture that is so easily (and so often) written as patriarchal and even misogynist.

The relative lack of existing critical and academic engagements makes the study of Scottish theatre a particularly potent one for cultural historians. Scottish theatre history, as an incomplete narrative, full of gaps and inconsistencies, needs to be told with a different agenda and may be newly formed within a definition (or, at least, a discourse) of history that can both expand and contract as the critical agenda and the object of enquiry require. Scottish theatre has a long tradition but an ostensibly limited history, still less observable heritage. There are long periods where there is little written evidence: until the nineteenth century there are relatively few actual play texts. There is, however, oral and anecdotal evidence of a rich popular tradition and ultimately the relative riches of the twentieth-century theatre culture interdependent on a complex media industry. In such a context the nature of the object of enquiry is constantly changing, constantly redefining itself, shifting between and across the generic certainties of critical traditions, flitting with remarkable ease between 'legitimacy' and the popular. The historian attempting to record and to interpret this diffuse past must project a parallel repertoire of interdisciplinary methodological discourses. It is in accepting the critical ambiguity of Scottish theatre, and responding to this ambiguity, that the female past can most constructively be described and analysed.

The nineteenth-century theatre industry existed within a number of socio-economic and cultural-aesthetic systems. To account for this environment the historian is constantly refocusing her/his critical gaze across, between and within these systems. In so doing the interpretative vocabulary employed will not merely be in flux but, ideally, will develop an adaptable, interdisciplinary aspect. It seems important, therefore, to see Scottish theatre in structural terms, as an institution, and a series of institutions or socio-cultural junctures. The recovery of a lost herstory is an explicitly political act that must employ different historiographical strategies – and the strategies that appear most potent are interdisciplinary discourses which acknowledge and can make use of a particular political, or socio-cultural, commitment.

The most important playwright in nineteenth-century Scotland is Joanna Baillie.[6] She is the one woman whose name has remained at least passing-familiar within literary scholarship, even if her work has been forgotten within practising theatre. Baillie wrote, published and had produced some of the key plays of the Romantic theatre, was author of a significant piece of theatre criticism and was universally celebrated as *the* playwright of her generation.[7]

Joanna Baillie was born a daughter of the manse in Bothwell, Lanarkshire, Scotland, in 1762. Her mother was Dorothea Hunter Baillie, whose brothers, William and John Hunter, were the pre-eminent physicians of the age. Although her younger brother, Matthew, was set for a career in medicine, such an option was inconceivable for Joanna Baillie and her sister, and lifelong companion, Agnes. Nonetheless she was educated in the literatures and philosophies of the day and the depth and quality of this training is reflected in the tone and the scope of her own prose, poetry and drama which typically encompass mythological, classical and religious reference, philosophical discourse and contemporary commentary. In this her drama is typical of the age's commitment to complex prose and verse, dense with ideas and debate, social analysis and imaginative fantasy.

Baillie was already at a boarding school in Glasgow when, in 1776, her father was appointed Professor of Divinity at the University of Glasgow. The family moved from Hamilton to the environs and society of Glasgow's High Street, but two years later the professor was dead and the family left the precincts of the university. While her brother Matthew went to Balliol College, Joanna Baillie, her mother and sister retired to Long Calderwood, the Hunter estate outside Glasgow. There they remained until 1783 when William Hunter's death left Matthew heir to his School of Anatomy on Windmill Street, London, and the family moved to the metropolis. In the early 1790s, shortly after the anonymous publication of Joanna's first volume of poetry, the female Baillies moved to Hampstead where they resided for the rest of their lives.

Her first volume of plays, *A Series of Plays; in which it is attempted to delineate the stronger passions of the mind*, was published in 1798 and contains some of Baillie's best-known pieces, principally *De Monfort* and *Count Basil* as well as the influential preface or 'Introductory Discourse'. A second volume followed in 1802; her *Miscellaneous Plays* was published in 1804 and a third volume of the so-called *Plays on the Passions* appeared in 1812. Although she did again publish plays in the 1830s, it is on these early publications that Baillie's reputation as a dramatist rests, a reputation which Stuart Curran finds uniquely strong, arguing that

> aside from the authority of its preface, her three-volume *Series of Plays* ... was hailed in comparison to Shakespeare and, of all contemporary influences, exerted the most direct practical and theoretical force on serious drama written in the Romantic period.[8]

Baillie's first play to be produced for the theatre, and the play which receives most interest from critics and historians, was *De Monfort*, which premiered on 29 April 1800 at Drury Lane with the age's leading tragedians, Sarah Siddons and John Philip Kemble. It is a somewhat stilted heroic verse-tragedy whose stage success was rather limited. Nevertheless, it remained, on and off, in the Kemble repertoire, and was part of John

Philip Kemble's farewell tour in 1817, when it achieved particular success in Edinburgh, a city with close ties to the Kemble dynasty. The Theatre Royal was something of an outpost of the Kemble empire, being managed by Sarah Siddons's son Henry and, after his death, by his widow Harriet and her brother W. H. Murray, who was later influential in the development of the National Drama.

Edinburgh was also a loyal supporter of Baillie. Although so long resident in London, she was celebrated as a Scottish woman of letters, an identity which flourished through her friendship with Sir Walter Scott. Scott promoted and sponsored her work both in the Scottish capital and in London. Baillie first met the age's most popular novelist and storyteller in 1806 and a friendship began that was to last until Scott's death in 1832. When the Baillie sisters toured the north (the Lakes, Glasgow and the Highlands) in 1808, they were guests of Scott in Edinburgh. Perhaps inspired by this Highland excursion Baillie's next play was *The Family Legend*, which became, along with *De Monfort*, one of her most successful pieces for the theatre. It was produced, at the insistence of Scott, at the Theatre Royal Edinburgh in 1810,[9] and was subsequently revived in Newcastle with William Charles Macready, in Bath in 1811 and at Drury Lane, first in 1815 and again in 1821 when the lead was played by Edmund Kean. Its first production was particularly celebrated.

Walter Scott had been influential in winning the Edinburgh patent for Henry Siddons. Along with Henry Mackenzie, William Erskine, the two Robert Dundases and others prominent in literary Edinburgh, Scott proposed a theatre of higher and more literary quality than that which had operated under the Jackson patenteeship, with active and informed trustees whose influence and expertise would free the manager to concentrate on the quality of work on stage.[10] Prolonged negotiations and the payment of substantial compensation to the Jacksons (this debt resulted in long-term financial problems for the theatre) culminated in Henry Siddons's first season, beginning on 14 November 1809. *The Family Legend* was in rehearsal by the close of the year. Baillie's play was to lead the way in terms of new writing (and, in particular, new writing with a distinctive and Scottish theme) and its heroically Ossianic tone coincided with the patriotic mood of Edinburgh. It is an eventful tale of clan rivalry, deceit, revenge and retribution, lost loves, innocence at risk, concealed identity and espionage. Its several climaxes – which include the leading lady being abandoned on a rocky islet to await certain drowning and a dramatic and bloody duel – assure a spectacular entertainment but little by way of mature character development or sophisticated denouement. Sir Walter, however, knew the value of playing-to-the-balcony and realised the play's potential for sensational staging. Alasdair Cameron notes that for this first production Scott 'had insisted that authentic tartans (green for the Campbells contrasting with red for the Macleans) be used'.[11] However, Scott's involvement went further than mere costume consultant – although he took the job seriously.[12] He attended rehearsals, commented upon script and casting, and even went so far as to engage his brother's militia company to appear as extras in the final act.[13]

The enthusiasm of the period for what appears on the page to be monotonous versification begins to be explained by such spectacular and energetic stage presentations which transformed the exaggerated drama of verse tragedy through the *élan* of production.[14] Nevertheless, and despite the extravagances of production, *The Family Legend* remains an interesting and significant play, not a great one.[15] The plot is easily criticised for melodramatic excess, and Baillie seems to present a cast of characters drawn from central casting. Certainly they are readily divided into the evil and the worthy. Helen, daughter of Campbell, Earl of Argyll [*sic*], is the good and noble leading lady. Despite her love for her father's ally, Sir Hubert de Grey, she has made a politically expedient but loveless match with a rival clan chief, Maclean. With the marriage, and the birth of a son, an uneasy peace has been won. However, Maclean's lieutenants Benlora, Lochtarish and Glenfadden find such a peace shameful and the match dishonourable, setting upon a plot to murder Helen and throw the two clans back into war. Maclean is inexperienced and weak-willed, easily influenced by his vassals' scheming. Benlora tries to convince Maclean that the match, which he sees as an abomination against the traditions he values, is cursed:

> Helen the Campbell, foster'd in your bosom,
> A serpent is, who wears a hidden sting
> For thee and all thy name . . .
> A witch of deep seduction. – Cast her forth.
> The strange, unnatural union of two bloods,
> Adverse and hostile, most abhorred is.
> The heart of every warrior of your name
> Rises against it. Yea, the grave calls out,
> And says it may not be. (*The Family Legend*, II, ii)[16]

Benlora, Lochtarish and Glenfadden are, on one level, archetypal stage heavies, eager for battle, duping their chief as to their true nature and settling upon a cruel plot, whereby Helen will not just be banished but murdered. They threaten Maclean with insurrection if he will not submit:

> Decide – decide, Maclean: the choice is thine
> To be our chieftain, leading forth thy bands,
> As heretofore thy valiant father did,
> Against our ancient foe, or be the husband,
> Despised, forsaken, cursed, of her thou prizest
> More than thy clan and kindred. (*The Family Legend*, V, iv)

Duplicitous and mutinous they may be but their motivation is surely more complex than sheer blood-lust or mere personal ambition. Baillie presents them as characters who are out of time. They are old-fashioned warriors who cannot contemplate an age in which old hatreds must be put aside in favour of the political solution and social co-operation. Baillie shows that they must, in fact, rethink how they understand and define the authority of the clan, how they understand and define their community. Such a problem is typical of the Romantic age, and one which women writers of the period found particularly perplexing.

The political crises of the Romantic period, the 'Age of Revolutions', find common ground in the transition from one kind of society to a new, modern one – this being effected by revolutionary upheavals and processes of industrialisation, monitored in socio-economics and discussed in philosophy and cultural theory. Edmund Burke is the principle theorist of the organic society and the organic nation, suggesting that the authority of the state in fact derived from the model and ubiquity of the patriarchal family, that the nation is ordered by the hegemony of patriarchy extending easily and logically from the familial context into the public spheres of community and nation. He argued that:

> We procure reverence to our civil institutions on the principle upon which nature teaches us to revere individual men; on account of their age; and on account of those from whom they are descended.[17]

These are, of course, exactly the principles of patriarchy, authority and social order which are the key thematic concerns of *The Family Legend* – the principles which have allowed Helen to be sold as a pawn in a male plot and which are abused by Benlora and his co-conspirators.

Most influentially, and in direct response to Burke, Mary Wollstonecraft offered a feminist interpretation of society, acknowledging revolutionary process and founded upon radical hermeneutic reassessment.[18] She developed a model of society which like Edmund Burke's acknowledges the structural importance of the familial. However, her model was not founded on Burke's patriarchal family but on the egalitarian family which she developed as the essence of good government and, by extension, democracy. Her reinterpretation of Burke 'deliberately inverted her society's construction of gender and imagined a male political community grounded on the domestic affections usually attributed to women.'[19] Wollstonecraft's is a radical position of which Baillie's play is certainly no exemplar. Nevertheless, her clear interest in the actual and metaphoric function of the family as a point of social and economic organisation contributes to the central debates of the Romantic identity. Having recognised the idea of the individual within a new social order as a philosophical and practical concern, Baillie is compromised in further analysis by the generic restrictions of the theatre, and her dramaturgical commitment to 'delineate the stronger passions of the mind'. These limit her investigations into the ideological complexities of the Romantic identity.

Helen is fixed in her role as damsel in distress and Argyll is certainly a typical good father, the play's noble patriarch and the moral centre of his society. The conspirators, however, are more than villainous malcontents and similar complexity may be seen in several others of Baillie's characters. Most unusual is her correlation of John of Lorne, Helen's younger brother, and Sir Hubert de Grey. Neither is himself the archetypal stage hero but instead *together* they combine the attributes of the daring man-of-action and the thoughtful romantic lover. Structurally, John's role is that of the juvenile lead. He is devoted to Helen, travelling in disguise into the centre of Maclean's power to warn her of the potential danger of her situation. While John appears as the bold, heroic adventurer – he is brave but rash, keen to draw his sword against Maclean and Benlora – Sir Hubert comes closest to being the romantic lead. His adventurousness is no less than John's (Sir Hubert accompanies John throughout his foray into Maclean's territory and returns unaccompanied to rescue Helen's baby) but is restrained within a particular and conservative morality. John Genest makes a pertinent point:

> Miss Baillie says that she received the story [of *The Family Legend*] from the Hon. Mrs Damer, as a legend long preserved in the family of her maternal ancestors – according to the legend Helen was united to her first love – Miss Baillie could not well introduce this circumstance, but the play concludes in such a manner as to make the future union of Helen and Sir Hubert highly probable.[20]

It is certainly revealing of the morality imposed upon women in the late eighteenth and early nineteenth centuries that the traditionally romantic 'happy' ending is curtailed. The seeming censoring of Sir Hubert's heroism (always overshadowed by John and, in any case, off-stage) fits well with the restrained celebrations at the close of the play. There is no tableau of united lovers, no anticipation of wedding celebrations; instead merely a declamatory prayer from Argyll. Baillie's use of two characters, John of Lorne and Sir Hubert, to complete the structural demands of 'hero' successfully side-steps this very practical problem in adapting the source material to the Romantic stage. It is pertinent that in production the theatre's leading men (Siddons, Macready, Kean) generally opted for the more visibly dashing role of John.

While the story may be commonplace, the stage craft suggested by the play is in some measure assured. The stage pictures are certainly strong – bleak Scottish castles, the leading lady awaiting a watery fate, great pageantry, bloody duels and stirring epilogue – but perhaps not powerful enough to distract attention away from a generally formulaic storyline. Although the scenario contains few great surprises, there are at least one or two moments of sound plotting. No sooner has Helen been returned safely to her father's castle than a messenger arrives from Maclean with news of her death. John is intent upon immediate and bloody revenge but Argyll and Sir Hubert, thinking of the infant child, still in the care of the Macleans, counsel caution.[21] While Sir Hubert secretly returns to Mull to rescue the infant, Maclean and his entourage arrive at Argyll's castle to mourn Helen. Insisting that she was carried off by a sudden illness, and that she died in his embrace, Maclean is lured into Argyll's trap so that when Helen appears in the company there is a dramatic moment of confusion and a bold release of tension, with Maclean damned by his own words.

The finale of the play is a duel in which Lorne kills Maclean. Benlora attacks his captors, is mortally wounded and dies. Determined to negotiate his escape, Lochtarish says that if he and his men fail to return to Mull within the week Helen's son will be murdered. Just as Helen begs Argyll to release the Macleans, Sir Hubert arrives having rescued the infant. While Argyll condemns treachery he looks forward to an era of peace and reconciliation in which:

> . . . , men
> In blood so near, in country, and in valour,
> Should spend in petty broils their manly strength,
> That might, united for the public weal,
> On foreign foes such noble service do! (*The Family Legend*, V, iv)

Genest is, perhaps, too harsh when he calls this final speech 'contemptible'.[22] It should not be dismissed so completely. Its patriotic tone is directed as much to the audience as it is to the characters on stage. It offers a complex of potential 'countries', 'nations' and 'enemies' (although Argyll's enemy is certainly glimpsed when 'gazing southron') and reaffirms the new order of co-operation threatened by Benlora's machinations. Argyll describes an expeditionary force ambitious not to conquer and defeat but merely to defend 'the rights and freedoms of our native land'. This is by no means an inflammatory claim. Argyll's justification parallels the legitimacy claimed by British imperial expansion and so is at ease with a North British identity and politics. Nevertheless, Baillie is certainly allowing her (Scottish) audience a moment of patriotic release. This must have been particularly appropriate for her first-night audience, a group hand-picked by Walter Scott. Worth records that 'taking great pains that the text should not insult any particular clan, he [Scott] . . . wrote to a number of the Scottish clan chiefs to invite them to see the performance.'[23] The reviewer of the *Correspondent* recognised the 'national' appeal of the play and its production, but found such chauvinism distasteful:

> Its success here was evidently owing to this nationality . . . Applause was conferred almost entirely upon those parts in which high compliments were paid to the Scotch; the inhabitants of Edinburgh entirely forgot that there was nothing more ludicrous than that people should applaud praise given to themselves.[24]

The response of the audience surely signals a desire to see representations of themselves on stage, a desire that the National Drama was aimed at meeting.

While most of Joanna Baillie's drama is written in verse, a lively alternative may be found in *Witchcraft* (1836), a play of a surprisingly different tone and type, though like *The Family Legend* set in Scotland. The play is one of Baillie's most unusual, notable for a distinctive and sustained attempt at linguistic realism and a very different use of drama than her usual employment of the poetic-tragic mode allowed.[25] Although ponderously plotted it is unexpectedly intriguing, something of a psychological thriller set against a backdrop of religious intolerance and the fear of hellish witchcraft. The play offers a remarkably bleak vision of character and community. There are none of the heroics of *De Monfort*, *Count Basil* or *The Family Legend* and characters are generally unsympathetic, with dark and often guilty secrets, and demonstrate little by way of tolerance or humanity. At the play's close the townspeople of Paisley are baying for blood, the community being depicted as both paranoid and gullible. Grizeld Bane the 'witch' is to be burnt:

> Ay, there she comes, and the de'il raging within her. – The blackest witch of a'. – Let her be burnt at the stake . . . – Hurra! hurra! mair fagots and a fiercer fire for Grizeld! – Hurra! and defiance to Satan and his agents! (*Witchcraft*, V, ii)

Despite the limited depiction of women in *The Family Legend* – the good Helen, the loyal servant Rosa and the truly hospitable fish-wife[26] – with *Witchcraft* Baillie has a cast of complex and multifaceted women, and almost all with an 'unken't' dark aspect. While Violet has all the appearances of the virtuous and good love interest, she is socially damned because her father has been judged a murderer. During the play she conceals from everyone the truth about his disappearance, secretly visiting him in his close concealment on the moor. Nevertheless, her 'transgression' is temporary, and being motivated purely by love of her father it is essentially patriarchal and so she is easily and completely re-integrated into the hegemonic social order. Annabella, on the other hand, is the play's *femme fatale*, who lusts after the hero and spins a vicious plot to have Violet named a witch: she must be punished. Seduced by Grizeld's stories of devils and magic, she cannot be recovered by the play's morality and is murdered by an increasingly distracted Grizeld. The play's most overt malevolents, Grizeld, Elspy Low and Mary MacMurren, certainly try to indulge in black magic, from casting spells to conjuring up evil spirits and terrorising the local populace with their threats. However, they are, of course, no witches. Like Annabella, Elspy and Mary are in thrall to Grizeld who, it is revealed at the play's end, is but 'A miserable woman whose husband was hanged for murder at Inverness . . . and who thereupon became distracted' (*Witchcraft*, V, ii).

In 1836 Joanna Baillie's career writing drama ended with the productions of *The Homicide* at Drury Lane and *The Separation* at Covent Garden and the publication of some later works in a three-volume edition of *Dramas* (a volume which includes *Witchcraft*). Although only a minority of her plays were ever performed, her position as *grande dame de lettres* during the early and middle decades of the nineteenth century was secure. The majority of her plays were certainly written to be read, being closer to the genre of 'closet' plays that the era allowed for and celebrated, than to active engagements in the theatre industry. After her death on 23 February 1851 some of her works did hold the stage, but it rested with her substantial publications to assure her a place in the public's imagination.

It is perhaps unfortunate that when Baillie's drama is remembered at all it is in connection with the patronage of Walter Scott and as his *protégée*. His support for 'the best dramatic writer' in Britain since the Jacobeans[27] did secure stage production and access to Scottish literary circles, but Joanna Baillie's oeuvre is large enough and strong enough for her reputation to be considered on its own merits. During her lifetime she was celebrated as *the* female writer of the age, eclipsing the reputations of Hannah More, Anne Yearsley and Felicia Hemans. Byron described her as 'our only dramatist since Otway and Southerne; I don't except Home',[28] concluding that 'Women (save Joanna Baillie) cannot write tragedy; they have not seen enough nor felt enough of life for it.'[29] The summation reached by Genest is among the shrewdest of her contemporary critics. He considered that:

> Two things are required to make a good dramatic poet – genius and a knowledge of the stage . . . Miss Baillie possessed in a very high degree the first and more essential of these qualifications – she was very deficient in the second – the consequence has been, that she has presented to the public much fine poetry in dramatic shape, without having written a single play which is well calculated for representation . . . [30]

Certainly it is the case today that her work is neither remembered nor celebrated, nor is it likely to be revived. It is a type of drama that, despite its heroic intent and assured poesie, is in essence a form of the early nineteenth century. Nevertheless, for those employed in the historiography of the stage and the history of stage theory, her introduction to the *Plays on the Passions* is a remarkably engaging, insightful and salient commentary on the role of the drama. It evidences serious thought and reflection on a genre that the coming century would often dismiss as either tedious and portentous versification or mere and vulgar sensationalism.

Recent scholarship has had to work hard to claim for her any substantial reputation, but those willing to attempt the struggle are increasingly convincing. It is certainly the case, however, that such critics who do consider Baillie tend to be more interested in her contribution to and engagement with Romanticism and there is a relative scarcity of critical material relating to her career as it connects to the nineteeth-century stage. However, her plays do engage with some of the typical themes of the Romantic stage, including the 'representation of the passions, of national and local character, as well as the representation of the monstrous and extraordinary.'[31] This is developed by Daniel P. Watkins who suggests that Baillie used the drama with deliberate and political intent:

> She chooses drama to reveal, in ways lyric poetry cannot, the ideological conflicts disturbing and shaping the passions that constitute her primary thematic and psychological interest. As a genre in decline, drama in the romantic age is at once weighted with nostalgia and desire for the once-powerful and stable social world that had brought it to prominence, and, at the same time, pressured by the confidence, individualism, and

sheer defiance of the social energies struggling to assert ... their new found power and authority.[32]

A particularly radical analysis is suggested in Anne K. Mellor's ongoing reassessment of women within Romanticism. In her recent *Romanticism and Gender* she posits existing versions of Romanticism as masculine, thus excluding the work undertaken by the era's many female writers, who she suggests have a distinctive understanding of and use for Romanticism. Part of her project is to counter traditional canonical versions of Romanticism with a more inclusive intent. 'What happens to our interpretation of Romanticism', she asks, 'if we focus our attention on the numerous women writers who produced at least half the literature published in England between 1780 and 1830?'[33]

This is, of course, a necessary aspect of all feminist historical methodologies, but it has proved particularly effective within Romance studies. Mellor certainly builds an intriguing case for the distinctiveness of 'feminine Romanticism':

> Even a cursory, introductory study reveals significant differences between the thematic concerns, formal practices, and ideological positionings of male and female Romantic writers ... women Romantic writers tended to celebrate, not the achievements of the imagination nor the overflow of powerful feelings, but rather the workings of the rational mind, a mind relocated – in a gesture of revolutionary gender implications – in the female as well as the male body. They thus insisted upon the fundamental equality of women and men. They typically endorsed a commitment to a construction of subjectivity based on alterity, and based their moral systems on what Carol Gilligan has recently taught us to call an ethic of care which insists on the primacy of the family or the community and their attendant practical responsibilities. They grounded their notion of community in a cooperative rather than possessive interaction with a Nature troped as a female friend or sister, and promoted a politics of gradual rather than violent social change, a social change that extends the values of domesticity into the public realm.[34]

Whilst Baillie's conservative politics do not galvanise this discourse into the overt feminism of Wollstonecraft, her work shows that she was particularly aware of and in tune with Romantic *zeitgeist*, or at least Mellor's sense of the female and political aspects of that discourse. In passing, it is important to remember the origins of the story of *The Family Legend* as recorded by Genest. He says that 'Miss Baillie says that she received the story from the Hon. Mrs Damer, as a legend long preserved in the family of her maternal ancestors ...'[35] *The Family Legend*, then, is a story about a woman passed down through generations of women and finally made public through the pen of another woman.[36]

Mellor's analysis (reminding us of the importance of family as the basis of societal structures and again highlighting women writers' use of this image in particular and distinctive ways) insists that Baillie be recognised as a writer at the heart of Romantic practice. Nevertheless, it does seem important not only to see Baillie as a Romantic dramatist but as contributing significantly to the development of Scottish drama. In Baillie's work – and specifically the productions of her work at the Edinburgh Theatre Royal, productions which continued through the 1810s – are influential and immediate antecedents to the National Drama. *The Family Legend* anticipates some of the features recurrent in the National Drama. It is set in a mythologised-version of the Scottish Highlands and the Scottish past, where the clan system is still dominant and clan rivalry tangible and dangerous. It is heroic in tone, but with strong romantic undercurrents, and the beginnings of an interest in 'low' characters (servants and peasants) which the National Drama would develop into a tradition of 'Scotch types'. However, *The Family Legend* is an original play, not an adaptation, literary in its conception of what drama should achieve, with none of the set-piece songs or comedy which were part of the Scott (melo)dramas. It is, however, strongly narrative and tangibly patriotic, simultaneously escapist fantasy and culturally familiar, evincing strong emotion and determinedly moral – all important features of the National Drama.[37] The influence of Scott's Romantic diegesis is reworked across Baillie's drama. Set in isolated castles and against barren countryside, her dramatic milieu is typically Gothic. The role of the Gothic in first Baillie's drama and subsequently the National Drama is not part of the present project; however, it might be evocative to offer Michael R. Booth's list of some of the characteristics of this genre as it was adapted to the stage. He describes a drama peopled by:

> awful tyrants dwelling in gloomy castle fastness, robber bands lurking in forests and caves, fearful heroines fleeing villainy, humble cottagers, loyal comic servants, fearful spectres, much thunder, desperate combats and the triumph of virtue.[38]

For the nineteenth-century stage the idea and the image of 'Scotland' was predominantly such a mythic space as this in which Scottish characters were increasingly reduced to the broad categories of melodrama.

Although several of Baillie's plays are set in shadowy Scottish castles and against wild Scottish countryside, she attempts to mark this as significant not just picturesque. In *The Family Legend* the Highland/Lowland (or at least island/mainland) dichotomy is the source of dramatic tension and is played out in terms of scene shifts. It is also influential in a metaphorical way and in the characters' psychology. Significantly, in *The Family Legend*, Sir Hubert is, not just a Lowlander, but English. His humanity, depicted in his integrity, suggests that he be read as the most civilised of the characters – even the codes of hospitality embodied in Argyll seem old-fashioned and perhaps a little uncouth beside this perfect and refined nobility. Unlike the other men he does not engage in a battle of physical strength, but is active off-stage, away from public view. He is a kind of Romantic new man. While pretending to leave Scotland to be with his ailing father, he actually dashes off to Mull to rescue Helen's infant son. Contemporary codes of propriety apart, the play's end not only promises his reunion with the widowed Helen but equally a reformation of the 'family' with Sir Hubert as the 'good' father. Nevertheless, in their own terms (to which Baillie is scrupulously fair) the clansmen too are valorous and honourable. However (and here is an issue which anticipates some of the problems of characterisation associated with the National Drama), they do edge towards the figure of the 'noble savage' we see replayed in Scott's own work.

When it is all too easy to reduce the Romantic experience in Scotland to the one towering figure of Scott, it is crucial that we recover Baillie as a hugely significant figure. Her cultural credentials are impeccable, her poetry and drama literate and popular, patriotic but not nationalist. Instead of turning to prose (perhaps she saw that Scott cast too long a shadow) she commits herself to a career in poetry and emerges as the age's most assured dramatist and central figure in the development of Scottish theatre and drama in the nineteenth century. It was an identity which *Blackwood's*, that bastion of the North British sensibility, was keen to promote:

We [are] delighted with the opportunity afforded us of offering our tribute of admiration to one, who, in point of genius, is inferior to no individual on the roles of modern celebrity – whose labours have given a tone and character to the poetic literature of our nation – whose works were the manuals of our earliest years . . . whose deep and affecting morals, illustrated by the moving examples of her scenes, touched the heart and mind, and improved the understanding by the delightful means of an excited imagination – and whose pages we have never returned to, in our days of more matured judgement, without reviving the fading tints of admiration, and justifying our early estimate of her high intellectual superiority.[39]

Frances Wright

While Baillie's career was limited to Britain and she spent much of her life within a close domestic circle, the nineteenth century brought unprecedented opportunities for education, travel and exploration to women. Furth of Scotland, and away from the hierarchies and orthodoxies of the British stage, the burgeoning theatre culture of the United States of America offered new scope and different kinds of careers for actors, managers and writers. One Scottish woman who grasped the opportunities of the New World with unbound and dogged (not to say stubborn) enthusiasm was Frances Wright. Born in Dundee in 1795, Wright, who is remembered as an early and leading Owenite socialist, was considered 'the most notorious feminist radical in America'.[40] She wrote and had produced one full-length play, Altorf, a capable romantic drama made more significant by its clear and deliberate parallels to contemporary politics, the author's passion for democracy and, what we might now term, human rights.

Orphaned in early childhood Wright was raised in the care of several relatives before, at the age of eighteen, she entered the household of James Mylne, her uncle and one of Scotland's leading new philosophers. In his household she entered a radical intellectual culture the influence of which was to remain strong throughout her life. In 1818 she and her devoted younger sister Camilla travelled across America. She was immediately and completely fascinated by the potential of the New World, publishing her impressions in Views of Society and Manners in America, a book full of her praise for America and its constitutional principles. This same commitment to the ideal and the ideas of democracy are the central themes of her play Altorf, premiered (initially anonymously) at the Park Theatre, New York, on 19 February 1819.[41] Its cast consisted of that theatre's leading players including Henry Wallack, Edmund Simpson and, particularly notably, Mary Barnes, one of the country's leading actresses.[42] It was received warmly by audience and press alike:

> That the expectations of the audience were highly gratified was manifested by a greater share of applause than we recollect to have ever witnessed. At every fall of the curtain between the acts peals of approbation resounded through the house, at the end of the play loud cries of bravo! author! Altorf! were heard from box, pit and gallery.[43]

Influenced by Friedrich von Schiller, and his commitment to drama as a form of and vehicle for truth, Wright makes early and determined use of the drama, not just as a medium for escapist fiction and romance, but as a political document, a conduit for her socialist principles and her enthusiasm for the freedoms, rights and values of the youthful United States. Just this advocacy was acknowledged by one reviewer who supported Wright in her dedication of the play to 'the people of America'[44] by arguing that the author had:

trusted his [sic] work . . . to the unprejudiced liberality of an American audience. He trusted a tale of freedom to the feelings of the only nation where that cause of freedom dare be asserted.[45]

The plot, with its grand backdrop of forests and mountains, is characteristically Romantic and not dissimilar to the milieu of mountains, glens and lochs associated with the vision of Highland Scotland in Scott's prose and poetry and Baillie's drama, and which is a popular scenic feature of so much of the National Drama.[46] That the play is heavily influenced by Schiller's *Wilhelm Tell* (1804) suggests links with European Romanticism as well as a political use of drama. Wright's play is similarly set in fourteenth-century Switzerland and tells of the Swiss states' battles for independence over the dominion of Austria – a plot which offers clear parallels with the United States' own War of Independence with the United Kingdom.[47] The play, while not explicitly nationalist, is an allegory of democracy, recounting the frustrations of personal and national bondage and insisting upon the integrity of the individual within society. Nevertheless, the play proposes a version of nationalism which is certainly familiar from the Romanticism of Schiller:

> Oh, my country!
> Remain but simple, frugal, and content.
> Hold thy honour still the plough and distaff.
> Still think the shepherd's crook more worthy honour
> Than idle sceptres of more idle kings!
> Then shall your hearts be pure, your conscience proud,
> Your store be plenty, and your hearth set round
> With smiling children and with grateful guests;
> Then shall the blessing of your god be with you,
> The love, the envy, and the praise of men!
>
> (*Altorf*, 1)

This paean to native values is equally a favoured discourse within contemporary American culture. Typically the social values and cultural products of Europe were seen as base, profligate and corrupting, while America was simple, pure and good. Wright's 'Preface' to *Altorf* sets this ideological trope as a central aspect of her work. She not only dedicates her play to the spirit of democracy she so admired but draws wider conclusions about the importance of personal freedom within society and the failings of older cultural values. Her chosen example is the state of contemporary theatre. Although her comments are no doubt prejudiced by her devoted enthusiasm for America, they are nonetheless interesting, particularly in parallel with Baillie's similar criticism of theatre organisation in her introduction to the *Plays on the Passions* published two decades earlier:

> I know not if my wishes influence my judgement, but I cannot help believing that this country [the United States] will one day revive the sinking honour of the drama. It is I believe, generally felt and acknowledged, by the public of Great Britain as of America, that the dignity of English Tragedy has now degenerated into pantomime; and that rapid movements, stage tricks and fine scenery have filled the place of poetry, character, and passion. The construction as well as the management of the London Theatres perhaps present insurmountable obstacles to any who might there ambition to correct the fashion of the stage. No such difficulties exist here. But this is not all: America is the land of liberty. Here

is a country where Truth may lift her voice without fear; – where the words of Freedom may not only be read in the closet, but heard from the stage. England pretends to an unshackled press: but there is not a stage in England from which the dramatist might breath the sentiments of enlightened patriotism and republican liberty. In America alone might such a stage be formed; a stage that should be, like that of Greece, a school of virtue; – where all that is noble in sentiment, generous and heroic in action should speak to the hearts of free people, and inspire each rising generation with all the better and noble feelings of human nature.[48]

Altorf is indeed a noble tragedy, with a strong ethical core and heightened emotional debate – although its central conceit is, of course, that of a love triangle.

The hero is a young soldier, Eberard de Altorf, facing a moral dilemma between personal duty and national loyalty. The crisis is embodied in the characters of two women, Giovanna and Rosina. Altorf loved Rosina, daughter of the Count de Rossberg, a leading supporter of the Austrian royalists. Altorf's father Erlach insisted that he break his match with Rosina and instead marry Giovanna, the sister of de Rheinthal, like Erlach, a prominent Swiss Republican. Although Altorf consented and wed Giovanna the marriage is a mockery as he is still devoted to Rosina. In the coldness of the relationship de Rheinthal suspects Altorf's allegiance in battle as in love. Giovanna understands that Altorf has no love for her, but she commits herself to him, asking only his friendship and his constancy in his country's cause:

> I ask not – I do not wish your love;
> I ask only your confidence and friendship.
> Do not refuse me these! Unload your heart.
> I know it's nigh to burst. Here, turn to me!
> Tell me you will forget I am your wife,
> And make me as your sister.
>
>   . . .
>
> I do not ask thy love; but this I ask,
> By all the debt of gratitude thou ow'st me
> To guard thy honour! Start, but hear me, Altorf!
> Look to thy honour! As thou art a man,
> As thou art a soldier, as thou art a patriot,
> As thou art a husband – guard thy honour!
>
> (*Altorf*, II, IV)

Determined to reclaim Altorf's love, Rosina appears outside the camp disguised as a pilgrim. She is ill and wasted, broken-hearted at being abandoned by Altorf, Altorf sees her and, guilt-stricken, falls at her feet. In comparison to Giovanna's shrewd understanding of her political role, not only are Rosina's demands purely personal but she disavows any broader, social responsibilities:

> What ask I more, then? Why, my Altorf's love
> Is all I seek on earth or ask of heaven.
> Wrong not our love, to say it mocks at honour.
> I know but nothing of these public quarrels . . .
>
> (*Altorf*, III)

The 'public quarrels', however, inevitably impinge upon Altorf and the two women. De Rheinthal's suspicions grow with news that Rossberg has been seen close by. Altorf and Rosina meet but are discovered first by Rossberg, who convinces Altorf that de Rheinthal is determined to oust him, and then by de Rheinthal himself who sees in the tryst evidence of Altorf's perfidy. After a brief skirmish Altorf, Rosina and Rossberg flee. However, just as Rossberg planned, Altorf's flight is interpreted as desertion and gross treachery by the Swiss forces who, along with Erlach, pursue the lovers. They are found in Rossberg's castle, where Erlach curses his son and dies. Rosina finally understands that she has been used by her father:

> ROSSBERG The father gone, the son is fixed our friend.
> Austria now gains his sword, we his alliance.
> Himself, his lands, his title – all are ours.
> ROSINA   What hear I? Holy heaven is this the cause?
> Is this the cause why thou hast wooed him here?
> Have I been made the tool in such foul dealings?
> (*Altorf*, V)

The woman's true, if emotional, love has been subverted and again the woman is little more than a pawn in a male power struggle. Rosina kills herself with Altorf's dagger. Altorf kills himself. With his dying breath Rossberg makes clear his part in Altorf's demise, this redeeming the young hero from the taint of national disloyalty. Giovanna and de Rheinthal are left to survey the horror and mourn friends and enemies alike.

In this bald summary there may appear little opportunity for Wright to express anything by way of political debate or analysis, but characters continually explain their actions within a broad socio-political context as much as they justify them as the consequence of passionate love, jealousy or ambition. When Rossberg tries to persuade Erlach to join with him in supporting the Austrians, Erlach is quick to call on his republican principles:

> Rebellion? Treason? Thou'rt the rebel, Rossberg!
> Thou, who prefer'st the interest of one man,
> And that a base and mean and sordid interest,
> Unto the weal of thousands. Thou, who stoop'st
> A servile knee unto a thirsty tyrant,
> Whose hands are dropping with thy country's gore,
> And his vile coffers filled with plunder of its poor.
> (*Altorf*, I)

Primarily, the contrasting views of love described by the two women personify two extremes of the Romantic imagination and the Rational sensibility. The romantic Rosina is a typical tragic heroine lying dead at the play's close. Giovanna is politically aware and socially responsible but the cost of such understanding is not just to be unloved but to be rendered sexless. Either way the 'woman' is destroyed. It seems as if Wright (at least in the drama if not in society generally) sees no way for a woman to be both a sexual being and socially and politically active. Certainly in her own life these two demands were, if not conflicting opposites, then a source of tension and concern. Her notoriety, occasionally writ as 'godless immoralism', was confirmed by her attacks on the church as a citadel of conservatism, particularly sexual conservatism, her advocacy of the total abolition of marriage in favour of liberated liaisons. After her early success in America

Wright continued a high-profile public career which included the establishment in 1826 of a utopian community, Nashoba, in Tennessee, planned to be a model of sexual and racial equality. Its failure cost Wright much of her fortune. In 1828 she became editor of the *New Harmony Gazette*, a newspaper founded by Robert Owen at his New Harmony community in Indiana. The paper was renamed the *Free Enquirer* and Wright developed in its pages her feminist and socialist ideas. Despite her advocacy of total abolition of marriage on finding herself pregnant to the French Owenite Phiquepal D'Arusmont she quickly married him. The match was unhappy and she spent much of her later years in a tangle of legal process in which D'Arusmont managed to gain control over her entire property, including earnings from lectures and writing. In an attempt to win custody of her daughter and reclaim her property she divorced him but died, in 1852, before a settlement was achieved.[49]

Scott, Pocock and Helen MacGregor

Many of the female characters of nineteenth-century drama are constrained by social convention and generic formulae which prescribe their actions and limit their ambition. Despite the importance of Baillie and Wright as female Scottish playwrights none of their female characters achieved the popular recognition of possibly the most famous and certainly the boldest woman of nineteenth-century Scottish drama. This woman's first appearance on stage is greeted, neither with polite compliments nor declarations of love, but with the shocked and shocking exclamation that:

> By the soul of my father, it's Rob's wife, Helen! there'll be broken heads among us in three minutes. (*Rob Roy*, III, i)

This is the reaction of one of Walter Scott's most popular male characters (Bailie Nicol Jarvie himself) to the appearance of Helen MacGregor. Like some harpie-*deus ex machina* she appears at the opening of Act III of Isaac Pocock's *Rob Roy MacGregor; or, Auld Lang Syne* (1818)[50] as the action shifts from urban Glasgow to the paradigmatic Scotch-Romantic milieu of the Trossachs. Pocock's stage directions describe the moment:

> Helen Macgregor appears on the point of a projecting rock with claymore and target, a brace of pistols in her belt, and wearing a man's bonnet and tartan plaid. (*Rob Roy*, III, i)

The explicit request for a 'man's bonnet' aside, the image is of powerful, active and, in the context of other female characters, transgressive femininity. Pocock presents a bold and unexpected image of a physically strong and utterly assured woman. She is given lines quite unlike those of Giovanna's self-sacrificing verses and is set upon bloody revenge if anything untoward should happen to her lover:

> Remember my injunctions; for, as sure as that sun shall sink beneath the mountain, my words shall be fulfilled. If I wail, other shall wail with me, there's not a Lady in the Lennox, but shall cry the Coronach for them she will be loath to lose; – there's not a Farmer but shall sing, Weel awa' over a burnt barn-yard and an empty byre; – there's not a Laird shall lay his head on the pillow at night, with the assurance of being a live man in the morning. (*Rob Roy*, III, i)

Far from being ignorant of 'public quarrels' she is an active participant in politics, assuming full authority over the clan in Rob's absence, an authority she forcefully maintains. When Dougal intervenes for Frank and the Bailie she is typically assertive:

> Dog! do you dispute my commands! should I order you to tear out their hearts, and place them in each other's breasts, to see which there could best plot treason against Macgregor – would you dispute my orders? (*Rob Roy*, III, i)

One might argue that this image is merely the female equivalent of the age's fascination with the noble savage but this is to cast *Rob Roy* as a simplistic fairy tale of the Romantic imagination rather than the complex debate between a traditional social structure and a new political hegemony played out through a series of oppositions paradigmatic within Scottish cultural representation – the rural and the urban, the indigenous and the imported – that is presented by both Scott and Pocock.

While Helen MacGregor is certainly the pre-eminent example, the National Drama is full of such powerfully drawn figures, providing actresses with substantial and demanding roles. From Meg Merrilies in *Guy Mannering* and Madge Wildfire and Jeannie Deans in *The Heart of Midlothian*, the National Drama presents the actress with a remarkable repertoire of characters. Significantly, such strength of character is also to be found in the adaptations' more traditionally romantic characters, such as Diana Vernon.[51] She is certainly the play's centre in terms of the love story but she refuses the objectification (perhaps even victimisation) that this role can connote:

> The bride of Rashleigh! never, never! any lot rather than that – the convent, the jail, the grave – I must act as becomes the descendant of a noble ancestry! Yet how preferable is the lot of those, whose birth and situation neither renders them meanly dependant, nor raises them to the difficulties and dangers that too often accompany wealth and grandeur. (*Rob Roy*, I, ii)

Remarkably, she herself undertakes the transformative journey to the Highlands usually reserved for the romantic hero and she is no mere spectator of the tangled politics of the Osbaldistone family. It is certainly the case that much of her strength is derived from her loyalty to her father, and the play's conclusion is her union with her true love, Frank. Unlike Helen in *The Family Legend* or Giovanna and Rosina in *Altorf*, she has been active in the narrative, refusing to be the prize in a male-run political game and setting her own terms. Thomas Crawford usefully identifies such heroines as a feature typical of Walter Scott's novels and which we might see as being particularly apt for transfer to the stage. He writes of Scott's female characters that:

> The type of novel he chose to write – the adventurous novel of action; and the type of tradition in which he felt most at home – the tradition of folk and popular art – inevitably forced him to place his womenfolk in situations of danger, or circumstances where they could aid their lovers by bold and resolute action. His plots and his reading public alike demanded that his heroines should be faced with a certain type of decision; and the attempt to give them psychological verisimilitude within that framework inevitably led him to portray, not the drawing-room ladies of Jane Austen or the husband-hunting social climbers of Richardson, but women who, in the exceptional circumstances of the novels, act for one or two brief moments like the women of the future.[52]

It is, perhaps, ironic that these 'women of the future' are to be found in the National Drama and not in the drama written by contemporary Scottish women playwrights. However, perhaps in the lives of the writers themselves is to be found this bold and outward-looking independence of spirit. Certainly Fanny Wright's life is a model of social and political experimentation – such 'immorality' would certainly have been censored and suppressed by the Lord Chamberlain before it ever got near a paying audience. And Joanna Baillie, for all her retiring domesticity, built and maintained a career as a professional writer (winning both critical acclaim and popular success) without parallel in her lifetime.

If Helen MacGregor is the most visible of the early century's theatrical women, the recovery and the reassessment of contemporary women playwrights and managers and actresses reveal that she was by no means the only assertive and strong and memorable woman connected with the nineteenth-century Scottish theatre industry, an industry which was generously populated with women leading remarkable, exciting and independent lives.

Notes

1. Letter from Joanna Baillie to Sir Walter Scott, c.1825. Held in the National Library of Scotland, MS 3903, f. 131. This letter is quoted by kind permission of the Trustees of the National Library of Scotland.
2. It is very easy to imagine a companion piece to the present essay which would highlight the work of actresses and managers in Scottish theatre. After all, the manager of the first regular theatre in Edinburgh was the actress Sarah Ward. Ward was in Edinburgh from at least 1746 to join the company of actors at Taylor's Hall. She led a breakaway group consisting, according to James C. Dibdin, of that company's best actors, to the new theatre in the Canongate opening in 1747. Jessie Jackson was prominent in operating the Edinburgh Theatre Royal in the first decade of the nineteenth century after which Henry Siddons became manager. The actress Mrs Henry Siddons (*née* Harriet Murray) was as influential as any woman in the development of the Scottish theatre being joint lessee first with her husband and then, after his death, with her brother W. H. Murray. See Dibdin's *The Annals of the Edinburgh Stage: with an account of the rise and progress of dramatic writing in Scotland* (Cameron, Edinburgh, 1888), p. 100ff.
3. The nineteenth-century Scottish stage and, in particular, the National Drama, is introduced in Alasdair Cameron, 'Scottish drama in the nineteenth century', *The History of Scottish Literature*, vol. 3 ed. Douglas Gifford (Aberdeen UP, Aberdeen, 1988): pp. 429–41; Christopher Worth, '"A very nice theatre at Edinr.": Sir Walter Scott and the control of the Theatre Royal', *Theatre Research International* 17.2 (Summer 1992), pp. 86–95; Barbara Bell, 'Nineteenth-century stage adaptations of the works of Sir Walter Scott on the Scottish stage: 1810–1900' (Unpublished PhD thesis, University of Glasgow, 1991), partially distilled in her 'The National Drama', *Theatre Research International* 17.2 (Summer 1992), pp. 96–108; and catalogued in H. Philip Bolton, *Scott Dramatized* (Mansell, New York, 1992).
   The popular tradition is discussed in Elspeth King, 'Popular Culture in Glasgow', *The Working Class in Glasgow, 1750–1914*, ed R. A. Cage (Croom Helm, London, 1987), pp. 142–87; and in two essays in Alasdair Cameron and Adrienne Scullion's *Scottish Popular Theatre and Entertainment: historical and critical approaches to theatre and film in Scotland* (University of Glasgow Library Studies, Glasgow, 1996), Bill Findlay's 'Scots Language and Popular Entertainment in Victorian Scotland: the case of James Houston' pp. 15–38; and the editors' 'W. F. Frame and the Scottish popular theatre tradition' pp. 39–61.
4. The geggy was the particularly Scottish version of the booth or fit-up theatres which strolling companies used to perform in. Like circus tents, they were made from wood and canvas, were easily dismantled and stored between performances. Some geggies could hold up to 400 of an audience and were heated by charcoal braziers.
5. While the present project is more concerned with the 'legitimate' part of the entertainments environment, it should be stressed that the popular tradition is fundamental

to any understanding of the nation's cultural heritage. In passing, I would merely say that, just as women were active in all aspects of the legitimate stage, so women were high-profile and popular performers within this popular sector. A handful of examples merely point the way to further investigations. Towards the end of the century Ruth Stanley (a comedian), Helen Kirk (a singer) and subsequently Florrie Ford (a pantomime favourite and leading lady at the Beach Pavilion, Aberdeen) were music hall stars, and the Scotia on Stockwell Street, Glasgow, arguably the country's best-known music hall, was managed by the infamous Mrs Baylis who so notoriously told the young Harry Lauder to 'Gang hame an' practise'.

6. This is the case despite the significance of Isaac Pocock and his adaptations of Scott, to which this essay will return.

7. The first substantial account of her work is Margaret S. Carhart's 1923 study of *The Life and Work of Joanna Baillie* (Yale University Press and Humphrey Milford and Oxford University Press, New Haven & London, 1923). In this she mentions the opinions of some more of Baillie's notable admirers: 'If I had to present any one to a foreigner as a model of an English Gentlewoman,' said William Wordsworth, 'it would be Joanna Baillie.'

W. Davenport Adams, in an uncompleted biographical guide to the drama, has Mary Russell Mitford ascribe to Baillie's tragedies 'a boldness and grasp of mind, a firmness of hand, and resonance of cadence that scarcely seem within the reach of a female writer.' To this he adds Hazlitt's opinion that 'Miss Baillie 'has much of the power and dramatic spirit of dramatic writing, and not the less because, as a woman, she has been placed out of the vortex of philosophical and political extravagances.' W. Davenport Adams, *A Dictionary of the Drama* vol. 1 (Chatto and Windus, London, 1904), p. 100.

8. Stuart Curran, 'Romantic Poetry: the altered "I", in *Romanticism and Feminism* ed Anne K. Mellor (Indiana UP, Bloomington and Indianapolis, 1988) pp. 185–207 (p. 186).

9. The production is catalogued, with Scott's account of the opening night, in Dibdin's *The Annals of the Edinburgh Stage*, pp. 261–2.

10. Scott's involvement with the negotiations for the patent and the subsequent operations of the Theatre Royal are discussed in full in Christopher Worth's splendid essay '"A very nice theatre at Edinr." . . . ', *Theatre Research International* 17.2 (Summer 1992), 86–95.

11. Cameron, 'Scottish drama in the nineteenth century', *The History of Scottish Literature*, vol. 3, p. 430.

12. Letter from Scott to Joanna Baillie, 13 June 1809 in *The Letters of Walter Scott*, ed H. J. C. Grierson, in twelve volumes (Constable, London, 1932–6), vol. 2, pp. 196–7.

13. See Scott, *Letters*, vol. 2, pp. 253–5 (letter to Joanna Baillie, 13 October 1809); pp. 287–9 (letter to Joanna Baillie, 22 January 1810); pp. 290–2 (letter to Joanna Baillie, 30 January 1810).

14. Sir Walter Scott describes the scene in the Edinburgh Theatre Royal on the opening night of *The Family Legend* in a letter written to the author:

> My Dear Miss Baillie, – You have only to imagine all that you could wish to give success to a play, and your conceptions will still fall short of the complete and decided triumph of the *Family Legend*. The house was crowded to a most extravagant degree; many people had come from your native capital of the West [Glasgow]; everything that pretended to distinction, whether from rank or literature, was in the boxes, and in the pit such an aggregate mass of humanity as I have seldom if ever witnessed in the same space. It was quite obvious from the beginning, that the cause was to be very fairly tried before the public, and that if anything went wrong no effort, even of your numerous and zealous friends, could have had much influence in guiding or restraining the general feeling. Some good-natured persons had been kind enough to propagate reports of a strong opposition, which, though I considered them as totally groundless, did not by any means lessen the extreme anxiety with which I waited the rise of the curtain. But in a short time I saw there was no ground whatever for apprehension, and yet I sat the whole time shaking for fear a scene shifter, or a carpenter, or some of the subaltern actors should make some blunder. The scene on the rock struck the utmost possible effect into the audience, and you heard nothing but sobs on all sides. The banquet scene was equally impressive, and so was the combat. [Henry] Siddons announced the play *for the rest of the week*, which was received not only with a thunder of applause, but with cheering and throwing up

of hats and handkerchiefs. Mrs Siddons supported her part incomparably, Siddons himself played Lorn [sic] very well indeed, and moved and looked with great spirit. A Mr Terry, who promises to be a fine performer, went through the part of the Old Earl with great taste and effect.

Letter from Walter Scott to Joanna Baillie, 30 January 1810. Reproduced by Dibdin, *The Annals of the Edinburgh Stage*, pp. 261–2.

15.   John Genest, chronicler of theatre activities of the period, catalogues *The Family Legend* in his *Account of the English Stage*, concluding that 'on the whole this is a good play – the language is frequently beautiful, and the plot is interesting . . . '. John Genest, *Some Account of the English Stage from the Restoration in 1660 to 1830* (Carrington, Bath, 1832), vol. 8, pp. 459–60.

16.   Joanna Baillie, *The Family Legend* (Ballantyne, Edinburgh, 1810).

17.   Edmund Burke, *Reflections on the Revolution in France* (1790), quoted by Anne K. Mellor, *Romanticism and Gender* (Routledge, London 1993), p. 67.

18.   See her *A Vindication of the Rights of Man in a letter to the Right Honourable Edmund Burke* (1790) and *A Vindication of the Rights of Women* (1792).

19.   Mellor, *Romanticism and Gender*, p. 68.

20.   Genest, *Account of the English Stage*, vol. 8, p. 459.

21.   However, even here Genest finds fault with Baillie's structure: 'In the 4th act, Argyle [sic] retires to his chamber to compose himself, and to gain strength to hear the story of Helen's sufferings – he returns to the stage *immediately*, yet he is supposed to have heard the story in the mean time – this is contrary to the laws of the Drama that there can be no excuse made for it . . . '. *Account of the English Stage*, vol. 8, p. 459.

22.   Genest, *Account of the English Stage*, vol. 8, p. 459.

23.   Worth, '"A very nice theatre at Edinr." . . . ', *Theatre Research International* 17.2 (Summer 1992), 92.

24.   *Correspondent* (12 March, 1810) quoted by Carhart, *The Life and Work of Joanna Baillie*, p. 146; and Worth, '"A very nice theatre at Edinr." . . . ', p. 92.

25.   In a preface to the play Baillie claims that: 'The language made use of, both as regards the lower and higher characters, is pretty nearly that which prevailed in the West of Scotland about the period assigned to the event or at least soon after it . . . '. 'Introduction' to *Witchcraft* in *The Dramatic and Poetical Works of Joanna Baillie, complete in one volume*, (2nd edn, Longman, Brown, Green and Longmans London, 1853). This second edition contains useful notes as to the 'Life of Joanna Baillie' not included in the first edition of 1851. *Witchcraft* was first published in *Dramas* (Longman, London 1836) but this edition does not contain the 'Introduction' quoted above.

26.   There is, however, another woman mentioned in *The Family Legend* and that is Lochtarish's mother. He threatens the Argylls that, should he and his company not return home inside a week, Helen's infant son will be killed and the killing will be done by his mother. For as Lochtarish explains to Helen: 'My aged mother, lady, loves her son/As thou dost thine; and she has sworn to do it.' Helen replies: 'Has sworn to do it! Oh! her ruthless nature/Too well I know.' (*The Family Legend*, V.iv).

27.   Sir Walter Scott thought her: 'certainly the best dramatic writer whom Britain has produced since the days of Shakespeare and Massinger . . . ' *Letters* vol. 2, p. 29.

28.   Letter quoted by Carhart, *The Life and Work of Joanna Baillie*, pp. 38–9.

29.   Letter to Moore (1815) quoted by Timothy Webb, 'The Romantic poet and the stage: a short sad, history', in *The Romantic Theatre: an international symposium*, ed. Richard Allen Cave (Gerrards Cross, Smythe, 1986), pp. 9–46, (p. 41). It is also the case that Byron tried to sponsor Baillie in London, and specifically at Drury Lane, just as Scott had championed her plays in Edinburgh. See Terence Hoagwood, 'Prolegomenon for a theory of Romantic drama', *The Wordsworth Circle* 32.3 (Spring 1992), (p. 49–64, p. 50).

30.   Genest, *Account of the English Stage*, vol. 8, p. 333.

31.   Worth, '"A very nice theatre at Edinr." . . . ', p. 87.

32.   Daniel P. Watkins, 'Class, gender and social motion in Joanna Baillie's *De Montford*', *The Wordsworth Circle* 23.2 (Spring 1992), 109–17, (p. 109).

33.   Mellor, *Romanticism and Gender*, p. 1.

34. Mellor, *Romanticism and Gender*, p. 2–3. She refers to Carol Gilligan, *In a Different Voice: psychological theory and women's development* (Harvard UP, Cambridge, Mass.). See also Mellor's 'On Romanticism and Feminism' in her *Romanticism and Feminism*, pp. 3–9, (p. 4).

35. Genest, *Account of the English Stage*, vol. 8, p. 459.

36. An interesting parallel may be drawn between this and a similar tradition of storytelling which Mellor highlights as contributing to the development of the novel. One might also suggest that in Scotland the ballad and other storytelling forms were not restricted to the lower-class but circulated throughout society: 'As students of the history of the novel are now coming to accept, the English novel probably originated in those modes of writing we associate primarily with upper- and middle-class women – letters, journals, diaries – with an oral tradition sustained by lower-class women – ballads, folk-tales, fairy tales, 'old wives' tales', and gossip.' Mellor, *Romanticism and Gender*, p. 5.

37. It might be useful to see the National Drama as a crucial middle ground between the theatrical impossibility of Romantic drama and the Victorian theatre's investment in melodrama and a more domestic, familial drama. Melodrama, after all, is a genre in which the family is overburdened with metaphor and symbolism, the narratives are concerned with the morality and action of the individual self and yet, like the National Drama, is founded on clear plot and strong characterisation with music and scenic design fundamental to the creation of meaning.

38. This is Michael R. Booth's definition of Gothic melodrama in his *Theatre in the Victorian Age* (Cambridge UP, Cambridge, 1991), p. 152.

39. [William Harness], *Blackwood's*, 16 (1824), 162.

40. This according to Barbara Taylor in *Eve and the New Jerusalem: socialism and feminism in the nineteenth century* (1983; Virago, London, 1991), p. 66.

41. *Altorf* was revived in 1829 in New York and published both in New York and London.

42. Mary Barnes is the mother of the playwright Charlotte Mary Sanford Barnes (Mrs E. S. Conner Barnes), author of a number of significant mid-century plays, including *Octavia Bragaldi; or, The Confession* (1837) and *Charlotte Corday* (1851).

43. Review from *New York Evening Post*, 20 February 1819, quoted by Celia Morris Eckhardt in *Frances Wright: rebel in America* (Harvard UP, Cambridge, Mass. 1984), p. 28.

44. Frances Wright, 'Preface', *Altorf* (M Carey and Son, Philadelphia, 1819).

45. Quoted by Eckhardt, *Frances Wright*, p. 28.

46. Henry Adelbert White emphasises the importance of stage effects and scenic painting to the success of the National Drama in *Scott's Novels on the Stage* (Yale UP, New Haven, 1927), pp. 4–5, 213–14.

47. Mercy Otis Warren had, of course, written a bold satire on the politics of the War of Independence with her play *The Adulateur* (1772), which is a much more overt piece of political drama than Wright's *Altorf*. Her later play *The Ladies of Castile* (1790) is a closer parallel, similarly allegorical and with two contrasting women being central to the drama.

48. Wright, 'Preface', *Altorf*.

49. See Taylor, *Eve and the New Jerusalem*, pp. 65–70.

50. Scott's novel *Rob Roy* was published in 1817, Pocock's adaptation of *Rob Roy* premiered at Covent Garden on 12 March 1818 with William Charles Macready in the title role. It was first produced at the Edinburgh Theatre Royal on 15 February 1819. All quotes come from Pocock's *Rob Roy MacGregor; or, Auld Lang Syne* (John Miller, London, 1818).

51. In his *Account of the English Stage* Genest disagrees with this interpretation of Pocock's Diana. Cataloguing the first production at Covent Garden he concludes that: 'This is musical Drama, in 3 acts, is a very pleasing piece in representation – Pocock has dramatized the popular novel *Rob Roy* in a creditable manner on the whole, but he has committed one gross and unpardonable fault – he has reduced the interesting and spirited character of Diana Vernon to a mere singing girl.' *Account of the English Stage*, vol. 8, p. 657.

52. Thomas Crawford, *Walter Scott* (Scottish Academic Press, Edinburgh, 1982), p. 77.

11

The Other Great Unknowns: Women Fiction Writers of the Early Nineteenth Century

Carol Anderson and Aileen M. Riddell

Elizabeth Hamilton (1758–1816), Jane Porter (1776–1850), Mary Brunton (1778–1818), Christian Isobel Johnstone (1781–1857) and Susan Ferrier (1782–1854) were among the most interesting women writing in the early nineteenth century. Like the work of a number of other once popular novelists who have now largely sunk from sight, their fiction and other writings were widely read, admired and influential in their own time, and, in some cases, continued to be so until later in the nineteenth century.[1]

These writers are varied in their attitudes and interests, diverse in their styles and techniques, and we do not wish to suggest they form a 'group' or reduce them to fit some preconceived pattern. Nevertheless, working as they did around the same time, and often with an awareness of each other's work, they show some shared concerns. These writers were all working, too, in a period when there were particular pressures on them both as women and as Scottish writers. The strains and paradoxes that shape their fiction do not result in 'flawed' work, however; rather, we suggest, their writings are unusually interesting and rich for the modern reader.

The early nineteenth century was a period of cultural vitality: the years following the French and American Revolutions saw political ferment and important intellectual debates in Britain, which fed into the literature of the time. Despite the diaspora created by both colonialism and Clearances, Scotland, and in particular post-Enlightenment Edinburgh, where many of the writers discussed here lived at least for a time, remained a hive of intellectual activity Sir Walter Scott, the 'Great Unknown' novelist who dominates the period, tends to be presented as the key figure in the development of the historical and 'national' novel at this time. Yet women writers played an important role in the evolution not only of historical fiction, but of so-called 'regional' writing;[2] and writers like Porter and Hamilton contributed to a general interest in nationalism in the period.

This was also, though, a period of some self-doubt in Scotland. The effects of the 1707 Union continued to manifest themselves in various ways. It is important to recognise the extent to which writers were working within a British framework; with considerable pressure from London, economic as well as cultural, even those writers who continued to live mainly in Scotland were affected. The Union influences the themes, plots and structures of such writers' novels, as well as their attitudes, for instance to language, as suggested in Brunton's *Self Control*: 'To Scotish [sic] ears, the accents of the higher ranks of English conveys an idea of smartness, as well as of gentility'.[3] A concern with 'Scottishness' is often highly self conscious in early nineteenth-century fiction. Several of our writers refer, apparently approvingly, to Ossian, the largely spurious 'Highland poet', invented by James Macpherson, whose Romantic representations of Scotland were popular across Europe. At the same time, a scene set in a fashionable English literary salon in Susan Ferrier's *Marriage* suggests the author's ironic awareness of the marketability of Romantic Scotland: 'Two ladies from Scotland, the land of poetry and romance, were consequently hailed as new stars in Mrs Bluemits' horizon'.[4] Several of the women novelists pre-date Scott in their interest in the Highlands and in rural life generally, and 'Romantic' representations of the Highlands in their work go alongside attempts to represent a more 'realistic', sometimes 'anti-Romantic' view of Highland life. Such tensions are typical of this time of uncertain identity in Scotland.

The literary traditions upon which the writers discussed here draw in their novels also underline their 'double identity' as Scots and Britons. Most are influenced by English and Anglo-Irish, as well as Scottish traditions: Brunton builds on the work of Samuel Richardson, in some respects, while Ferrier alludes to many earlier and contemporary English writers. The relationships between women writers are also important; involving much complex cross-referencing and intertextuality. Jane Austen apparently used the work of the earlier Scottish writer Mary Hamilton as a source for names;[5] she also admired Mary Brunton. Austen's work, in turn, is clearly known to Susan Ferrier (the opening of *The Inheritance* echoes the opening of *Pride and Prejudice*). Mary Brunton pays tribute to Joanna Baillie in the dedication to *Self Control*, and admitted to the influence of Maria Edgeworth upon her writing.[6] Jane Porter refers to Joanna Baillie's work in *The Scottish Chiefs* (1810) and Elizabeth Hamilton admired Hannah More's writing. Ferrier read the work of More, too, as well as that of Edgeworth, Brunton and Elizabeth Hamilton.

Seeing women writers in terms of a female tradition can lead to a better understanding of their work. Mary Brunton expressed the difficulties of being a woman writer in a letter to her friend Mrs Izett:

> I would rather, as you well know, glide through the world unknown, than have (I will not call it *enjoy*) fame, however brilliant. To be pointed at – to be noticed and commented upon – to be suspected of literary airs – to be shunned as literary women are, by the more unpretending of my own sex; and abhorred as literary women are; by the pretending of the other! – My dear, I would sooner exhibit as a rope dancer – I would a great deal rather take up my abode by that lone loch on the hill, to which Mr I, carried my husband on the day when the mosquitoes were so victorious against him.[7]

Brunton published her first novel anonymously, but her name leaked out, and she commented that 'of course all the excellences of the book are attributed to Mr B, while I am left to answer for all its defects'.[8] Ferrier, like Brunton, tried to avoid trouble by publishing anonymously.

Women, when they did publish, were expected to be moral or didactic in their fiction. Male writers were also affected by this imperative, for the novel form still had uncertain status, but the pressures were especially intense on women. Eighteenth-century conduct books for women, with their didactic and moral aims, underlie common genres adopted by women, such as the 'novel of manners', characteristically treating matters of social conduct in polite society. Traces of the conduct book tradition are especially obvious in the work of Hamilton, Brunton and Ferrier. Many middle-class women were exposed to the work of eighteenth-century Scottish religious writers such as James Fordyce (*Sermons* to *Young Women*, 1766) and John Gregory (*A Father's Legacy to his Daughters*, 1774) whose works instructed 'ladies' how to behave, and were widely influential in Scotland and beyond.[9] The religious culture of Scotland was strong, and Presbyterianism in some ways repressive towards women; interestingly, though, it could also have the effect of feeding a radical social awareness and even a form of feminism.[10]

For all the pressures of convention on women, the early nineteenth century was also a period of feminist awareness. Several of the writers discussed here appear to have read Mary Wollstonecraft or to hold ideas similar to hers, and contribute to the debates about education evident in much fiction published at this time. In some cases, they hold progressive or even subversive views on education and cognate matters. Most of them, unsurprisingly, are middle or upper class, for these were the women who had access to some kind of education, and the leisure and opportunity to write and consequently the concerns and viewpoints of their social class dominate. Some writers, nevertheless, are extremely critical of the upper classes, and even the work of those more 'conservative' in their professed political views, such as Hamilton, a noted anti-Jacobin, may be seen as having some radical implications as well.

All of the writers discussed here show concern with a range of contemporary issues, both at home and abroad. Social decay, and attempts at 'improvements' in the Highlands, are concerns of Johnstone and Ferrier; the colonies (from Canada to the West Indies) haunt several novels, while slavery appears in Brunton's fiction, and occupied Ferrier's attention in later life.[11] All these writers were copious correspondents or essayists, and their non-fiction further illustrates the range of their opinions and the breadth of their reading.

Elizabeth Hamilton

Born in Belfast to a Scottish father and Irish mother, Elizabeth Hamilton (1758–1816) lived from an early age with close relatives in Stirlingshire, and, from the evidence of her published correspondence, as an adult strongly identified with the Scottish element of her heritage.[12] In one of her letters, she refers to the Scots as 'my good country folks' (Benger, II, p. 73); in another, she argues for the institution of Scots language as a school subject, lamenting the passing of her native '*gude braid Scotch*'. She writes to her friend, the poet Hector MacNeil that, 'It is a shame in our own country to find how few can read their *native* tongue with any ease or propriety' (Benger, II, p. 20).

Her aunt, no doubt conscious of the ignominy often attached to one achieving the status of a 'learned lady', had in Hamilton's youth 'quietly advised her to avoid any display of superior knowledge, by which she might be subjected to the imputation of pedantry' (Benger, I, p. 50), advice illustrative of current attitudes to female education, a topic on which Hamilton was to publish more than one volume.[13] Nevertheless, Hamilton took her aunt's advice to heart as a young woman: in a letter she remembers 'hiding *Kaim's* [Sic] *Elements of Criticism*, under the cover of an easy chair, whenever [she] heard the approach of a footstep, well knowing the ridicule to which [she] should have been exposed, had [she] been detected in the act of looking into such a book' (Benger, II, p. 31).

During Hamilton's career as a writer, she contributed to the whole range of publishing in the Romantic age. She produced both non-fiction (including essays in journals and treatises on education and religion), and fiction; among her three novels, was her 'black baby',[14] *Translation of the Letters of a Hindoo Rajah* (1796). She also wrote what Gary Kelly has called a 'quasi-novel',[15] her *Memoirs of the Life of Agrippina, the Wife of Germanicus* (1804), as well as poetry and songs. One of her novels, *Memoirs of Modern*

Philosophers (1800),[16] in which she satirises the Jacobin philosophies of Godwin and his group (including Mary Wollstonecraft), enjoyed enough success in its own day for a commentator in the *Gentleman's Magazine* (1816) to remark of its stridently feminist anti-heroine, Bridgetina Botherim, that she had become 'a proverbial point in conversation'.[17] Similarly, a frequently uttered phrase in her most successful work, *The Cottagers of Glenburnie* (1808), 'I canna be fashed' (though according to Sarah Tytler 'linger[ing] chiefly as a tradition of darker ages'),[18] became a very popular maxim in its day, as did other Scottish phrases used by Hamilton in this last novel.[19] Her way of dealing with the competing claims of the Scots and English language varieties within *The Cottagers of Glenburnie* is one of that novel's most interesting features.

Hamilton's love of the Scots language is evident from her letters, and from her best-remembered poems, such as 'My Ain Fireside'. Yet as Emma Letley has noted, Scots language in *The Cottagers of Glenburnie* is used exclusively by lower-class, uneducated characters, whilst English is the preserve of the omniscient narrative voice, as well as the heroine, Mrs Mason.[20] Since members of Edinburgh polite society, throughout the eighteenth century and well into the nineteenth century, were obsessed with ridding themselves of Scotticisms in their writing, in order to get ahead in the new British society, Hamilton's ambivalence towards the Scots language is hardly surprising. What is perhaps surprising is her use of this language variety at all; the energy and vividness of some of the Scots in this novel is worth remarking also, especially as it appears earlier than the major fiction of writers such as Scott, Galt and Hogg, noted for their use of Scots.

Another surprising feature of *The Cottagers of Glenburnie* lies in the character of its masterful heroine, Mrs Mason, whose self-imposed mission, to improve and rebuild the unfulfilled lives of the Glenburnie residents, is indicated in her name. Elements of similarity between this novel and Mary Wollstonecraft's earlier *Original Stories* (1788) – which has a frame narrative involving two young ladies being kindly instructed by a relative, named Mrs Mason – suggest that Hamilton, despite her anti-Jacobinism, shared certain interests with her revolutionary predecessor.

In *The Cottagers of Glenburnie*, Mrs Mason's social position – as a *Mrs*, but importantly, without a husband – is one she could not have achieved had she married, even if she had been widowed. Without father or husband to submit to, she is afforded an independence and status rare for a woman in the early nineteenth century, and probably impossible for a wife. Spinsterhood, thus characterised, is not a pitiable state for a woman, as it is shown for instance by Jane Austen throughout her works, from *Sense and Sensibility* (1811) to *Persuasion* (1818), but an empowering one. Mrs Mason may fail with the irredeemable MacClartys, but not for want of trying, and she singlehandedly brings about a revolution of sorts in Glenburnie, in health, hygiene and education. Far removed from the real-life revolution in France, non-violent action in Glenburnie nevertheless results in the reformation of almost all the inhabitants' lives. Conservative perhaps, but thematically interesting and genuinely funny, Elizabeth Hamilton is by no means simply the 'soup and sanitation' author of David Craig's description.[21]

Among her achievements in *The Cottagers of Glenburnie* is a description of Highland landscape that in some ways prefigures Scott's *Waverly* (1814). Hamilton's depiction of the natural beauty of the rugged landscape around Glenburnie is striking, but suffused with moral symbolic meaning, and always tempered by a concern for practical matters, as when a party sets off for Glenburnie:

> They were struck with admiration at the uncommon wildness of the scene which now opened
> to their view . . . Mrs Mason and Mary were so enchanted by the change of scenery which
> was incessantly unfolding to their view, that they made no complaints of the slowness of
> their progress. (p. 99)

No sooner is the romantic scene set, than Hamilton reduces its conventional appeal by
diverting the reader's attention to the much more down-to-earth subject of the state of
repair of the road.

Jane Porter

The underlying quotidian interests here contrast with the romanticism of her near
contemporary, Jane Porter (1776–1850), author of *The Scottish Chiefs* (1810). Jane Porter
wrote a good deal, novels as well as shorter fiction, sometimes collaborating with her
equally prodigious writing sister, Anna Maria (1780–1832), for instance with *Tales round
a Winter Hearth* (1826) and *Coming Out* (1828). Like Hamilton, she was the author of at
least one 'quasi-novel', *Sir Edward Seaward's Narrative . . .* ;[22] she was also a contributor
to the *Gentleman's Magazine* and other periodicals. But it was her first two novels which
were most successful.

Like Hamilton, Jane Porter was born outside Scotland, to just one Scottish parent, in
this case her mother, but her formative years were spent in Edinburgh, where the young
Walter Scott was an early childhood friend.[23] Some years later, in a conversation with
George IV, Scott apparently credited her novel *The Scottish Chiefs* with being 'the parent,
in his mind, of the Waverley Novels'.[24] This anecdote may be apocryphal, but Porter's first
two highly successful novels did predate the publication of Scott's first, *Waverley* (1814).

Her first novel, *Thaddeus of Warsaw* (1803), was based upon real-life figures in recent
Polish history, including the nationalist General Kosciuszko (about whom her brother,
a well-travelled historical painter, supplied vital information). By 1810 this novel had
gone through nine editions, and Porter had received tributes for it from all over Europe,
including a letter from the patriot General Kosciuszko himself. Mary Brunton's heroine,
Laura Montreville (of *Self-Control*, 1811), chooses Porter's Thaddeus as her favourite
hero.[25] With *The Scottish Chiefs*, set in Scotland in the time of William Wallace and
Robert the Bruce, Porter's fame was established. The 'burning of the Barns of Ayr, and
of Wallace's appearance in the conflagration' was deemed by Joanna Baillie to be 'one
of the sublimest descriptions she had ever read',[26] and according to James Hogg, Sir
Walter Scott, whose feelings about the novel were rather mixed, nevertheless declared it
'a work of genius'.[27] Both this and Porter's first novel enjoyed various translations, and
the writer was elevated to the status of 'a lady of the chapter of St Joachim by the King of
Wurtemberg' (*Dictionary of National Biography*) in recognition of her writing talents; more
sensationally still perhaps, according to a postscript to the third edition of *The Scottish
Chiefs* in 1816, the novel had been proscribed by the Emperor Napoleon himself.[28]

Though many of the Porter sisters' works are partly concerned with Scottish affairs,
The Scottish Chiefs is the only one of their novels to deal with an exclusively Scottish
theme. In this, Porter, unlike Elizabeth Hamilton, allows no mundane business to cloud
the mythic appearance of the Scottish landscape:

> He struck into a defile between two prodigious craggy mountains; whose brown cheeks
> trickling with ten thousand rills, seemed to weep over the deep gloom of the valley beneath.

> Scattered fragments of rock, from the cliffs above, covered with their huge and almost impassable masses the surface of the ground. Not an herb was to be seen; all was black, barren, and terrific.[29]

And of her hero, she writes:

> Wallace stood on the cliff, like the newly-aroused genius of his country. His long plaid floated afar; and his glittering hair, streaming on the blast, seemed to mingle with the golden fires which shot from the heavens. (I, p. 50–1).

The great success of *The Scottish Chiefs* was no doubt at least partly attributable to the vogue for all things Scottish with the reading public, in the wake of Macpherson's Ossianic tales. Porter's taste for Ossian – shared with Brunton and Ferrier – is clear; indeed, at one point in the novel Robert the Bruce quotes to Wallace 'many passages apposite to his own heroic sentiments, from Ossian and other Scottish bards' (II, p. xv).[30]

Set deep in the past, with a central figure, Wallace, already established as a Scottish national hero in numerous chapbook versions of his life, the subject matter of *The Scottish Chiefs* lends itself to the kind of romantic glorification at which Jane Porter excels, and she states in the first of a series of prefaces to successive reprints of her novel 'my history [is] intended to be within the bounds of modern romance'; yet in the same preface she also expresses, in some detail, her debt to tradition and history.[31] Elsewhere she cites her childhood nurse, Luckie Forbes, as one of her major sources of information concerning 'the wonderful deeds of William Wallace';[32] another and more important source, acknowledged in the first edition, was Blind Harry's *The Wallace*.[33] Drawing on the genre of romance as she does, it is nevertheless worth noting Jane Porter's insistence upon the traditional and historical basis for her novel, claims which demanded that the novel be read seriously. At the very least this novel takes its place as a vital link between older Scottish literature and the rise of the historical novel after Scott's *Waverley*.

Certainly, an aspect of *The Scottish Chiefs* which probably added to its interest when it appeared is the resemblance of the events related in the novel to more recent events in Scottish history – the Jacobite uprisings of the preceding century. This connection can hardly have escaped the notice of the contemporary reading public, affording a certain extra *frisson* of excitement. (Readers of *Waverley* were to be reminded in its sub-title that 'Tis Sixty Years Since'). Perhaps wary that her novel might be seen to promote rebellious nationalism, though, Porter writes an ending which may have had its message for her own times; *The Scottish Chiefs* closes with the words, 'and a lasting tranquillity spread prosperity and happiness throughout the land'.

All the same, there may be a hint of subversion in the novel. Though Porter mainly focuses attention in *The Scottish Chiefs* on the male characters, the 'makers' of the public history of which she writes, her characterisation of the principal females is worth attention. A recent critic finds something lacking in many of the characters, but writes of Joanna, Lady Mar, that she 'is one of the most believable characters in the novel . . . her actions are reasonably motivated, her inward struggle is recognised, and, while wicked, she is complex enough to feel remorse'.[34]

Joanna first appears as a teenage houseguest of the Earl of Mar, who seduces her during his wife Isabella's confinement, and having made her pregnant, takes her as little more than a child bride, when Isabella dies in childbirth. Joanna's tragic life story is fraught with desperation; in the reader's final glimpse of her at the close of the novel, she is confined as a lunatic, having been driven out of her mind by remorse. She is presented as an incoherent, dangerous madwoman, enveloped in scarlet velvet; this figuring can be seen as anticipating the repressed female anger discerned by Gilbert and Gubar below the surface of later fiction by writers such as the Brontë sisters and George Eliot.[35]

Mary Brunton

Mary Brunton's fiction at first glance might seem very different, despite the fact that where it deals with Scotland, it favours Highland settings in common with the work of Hamilton and Porter. Brunton herself, born Mary Balfour in 1778, grew up on the Orkney island of Burra. She married Alexander Brunton, a minister, who seems to have been an encouraging, supportive husband. They lived in Bolton and then Edinburgh, until Mary Brunton died in childbirth in 1818, having published two novels, *Self-control* (1810–11) and *Discipline* (1815), and started a third, *Emmeline* (1819), which remains in fragment form; to this, Alexander Brunton added a useful *Memoir* of his wife.

Brunton's work, like that of her contemporaries, is circumscribed by the limitations on the woman writer of the period. The titles of the two complete novels signal their moral and didactic ends; Christian beliefs underlie them, and both contain conventional messages about, for instance, the need to contain passion through self-control. Both have plots featuring heroines who must resist onslaughts on their virtue from ignoble noblemen, and who learn to recognise the appropriate suitor. Both *Self-Control*, and especially *Discipline*, however, are more interesting to the modern reader than they might at first seem.

Brunton's letters sometimes sound an ironic note: 'It is alleged that no virtuous woman would continue to love a man who makes such a debut as Hargrave [the libertine in *Self-Control*]. All I say is, that I wish all the affections of virtuous persons were so *very* obedient to reason . . . '.[36] In her novels Brunton shows, as one critic remarks, 'resistance to the usual literary patterns supplied for identificatory readers'.[37] Her fiction expresses scepticism regarding the clichés of fiction; Laura Montreville in *Self-Control* 'had no ambition for the dangerous glory of reforming a rake into a good husband' (p. 91). Likewise there are ironic reflections on the literary representation of death-bed scenes (*Self-Control*, p. 399).[38]

Laura herself is in some ways a subversive figure. Judith Lowder Newton argues that some nineteenth-century women novelists, discontented with the prevailing ideology that women should be content with 'influence', subverted masculine authority by 'quietly giving emphasis to female capability'.[39] These writers may not have felt able to give their female characters 'such traditionally masculine power as the power of control', but they managed to make women *seem* powerful 'by giving emphasis and value to power as capacity'. Brunton's heroines (not discussed by Newton) show striking 'ability', and attempt to 'take control' at least of their own lives. In a letter to Laura, the Scottish-born heroine of *Self-Control*, her friend the good Mrs Douglas remarks '"All male writers, on the subject of love, so far as my little knowledge extends, represent possession as the infallible cure of passion"' (p. 234). *Self-Control* shows both Warren, and more especially Hargrave, attempting to 'possess' Laura, literally to capture her. Laura, however, is an active heroine who illustrates more than passive resistance to male attempts at possession; she demonstrates female 'self-possession'.

From the start, Laura is described as having 'an active mind, a strong sense of duty, and the habit of meeting and of overcoming adverse circumstances' (p. 1). She is also, significantly, a 'reasonable and reasoning creature' (p. 3). Later in the novel, she studies mathematics, a science 'so little in favour with a sex who reserve cultivation for faculties where it is least wanting' (p. 255). The emphasis on reason, and on the woman's access to education and ideas, echo the work of Mary Wollstonecraft. Laura seems all the stronger when compared with the weak men in the novel, such as Hargrave or her widower father, who finds 'in her enduring spirit a support to the weakness of his own' (p. 112). He dies in London, a bankrupt, leaving Laura to fend for herself, although not before she has already attempted to provide financially for both of them by selling her paintings. This involves trudging round London dealers trying to sell her work during which she is even mistaken for a prostitute. *Self-Control* highlights the economic realities of life, a realism attributed by Sarah Smith[40] to Brunton's religious background. Exact details of the rent payment are given (p. 137), and Laura, no sheltered heroine, is shown staring poverty in the face.

It is significant, too, that De Courcy, the hero, is shown paying for the support of Hargrave's illegitimate child by a poor, proud serving-girl who had returned her seducer's attempts at 'payment' before her premature death; Hargrave's 'possession' of her brought not only the death of passion, but also the end of her will to live. Brunton's work arguably has a radical edge not only in its attention to financial matters, but in its sympathy for the 'lower' characters, who struggle for survival, often with dignity. There is also an implied critique of the upper classes embodied in characters such as Lady Pelham (see p. 216, for instance), which prefigures the work of Susan Ferrier.

Self-Control, now attracting some critical attention again, is usually viewed as 'uneven'. Certainly it does have a rather unlikely episode in which Laura, abducted to Canada by a crazed Hargrave, hurtles to freedom down a river on a canoe! However, her journey suggests Laura's capacity for survival in an almost Romantic symbolic way that points ahead to the greater exploration of subjectivity in Brunton's second novel, *Discipline*.

Brunton expressed mild impatience with her first heroine: 'If ever I undertake another lady, I will manage her in a very different manner. Laura is so decently kerchiefed, like our grandmothers, that to dress her is a work of time and pains'.[41] In *Discipline*, the heroine, Ellen Percy, is initially flawed, suffering from 'dastardly habits of self-indulgence' (p. 84), and the novel records her process of learning. The first person narrative technique makes the spirited Ellen a more accessible, engaging and 'modern' heroine than Laura.

Again, the novel is firmly focused on the social and economic aspects of existence; Ellen's father, 'who began the world with very slender advantages' (p. 2), is a self-made merchant of the new commercial classes treated with disdain by the established aristocracy. At first the women's roles, including Ellen's, appear traditional; her friend Juliet Arnold is 'educated to be married' (p. 57), and Ellen herself contemplates marriage, possibly to the worthless Frederick De Burgh, as a route to status and wealth (p. 46). Again, however, the death of a financially ruined father forces the heroine out of security and dependence. Poverty and loneliness loom large. Ellen's alienation and despair are powerfully conveyed: 'A long forgetfulness was varied only by dim recollections, which came and went like the fitful dreams of delirium' (p. 163). But we see her adopt the role of self-reliant individual, taking herself from London to Edinburgh on the promise of employment; though here, too, she has difficulty in obtaining work, 'for Edinburgh, at that time, contained no market for the fruits of feminine ingenuity' (p. 244).

Again, there is an ironic undercutting of literary formulae: 'Heroines of romance often show a marvellous contempt for the common necessaries of life; from whence I am obliged to infer that their biographers never knew the real evils of penury' (p. 252). *Discipline* shows Ellen's daily struggles: 'I had neither home, property nor friends. That which gives independence – the only real independence – to the poorest menial, was wanting to me' (p. 278). The importance and dignity of work are stressed here; the depiction of the dreadful Mrs Boswell also implies the outcome of female dependency in particular.

It is Mrs Boswell who is responsible for the sane and innocent Ellen enduring a spell in an asylum. In this powerful and disturbing section of the novel, Ellen witnesses various kinds of insanity: 'Each scorned or pitied every form of madness but his own' (p. 294). Among those she encounters is a benign-looking old man, whose visionary speech is decidedly Romantic in tone. He, too, is presumably mad; but this section of the novel implicitly questions social judgements about madness and sanity. Ellen's own joy when she is liberated, the rapture of the prisoner delivered into freedom (p. 300), draws on fashionable expressions of liberty in the poetry and fiction of the time.

Similar themes recur in the representation of the 'hero', Maitland. Like Ellen's father he is involved in commerce; he is also, however, an idealist: 'Himself a West India merchant, and interested, of course, in the continuation of the slave-trade, he opposed, with all the zeal of honour and humanity, this vilest traffic that ever degraded the name and character of man. In the senate of his country he lifted up his testimony against this foul blot upon her fame' (p. 117). For all his wealth, he lives frugally, and his attitude to marriage shows his strikingly egalitarian outlook (p. 140).

Significantly, Maitland is Scottish; in fact, he turns out to be 'really' Henry Douglas, a Highland Chieftain. As in *Self-Control*, much of the action of the novel is set in London, but happiness and moral worth are associated with Scotland, specifically the Highlands (again anticipating the work of Susan Ferrier). *Discipline*, through the introduction of Scottish characters such as the gardener Campbell and his family who play small but important parts, prepares the way for the concluding section with its descriptions of Highland life. Both realist and Romantic, conventional and radical, like the other writers we examine, Mary Brunton defies easy categorisation. It is only a pity she died so young, and wrote so little.

Christian Isobel Johnstone

Not much is known of the early life of Christian Isobel Johnstone (1781–1857), who, of all the writers under consideration here, was probably the most prolific. Her career in journalism began when in 1812 she and her husband took over the *Inverness Courier*, and from that time onwards Johnstone actively pursued a literary life through journalism and creative writing. Later, together with her husband, Johnstone founded a number of cheap periodicals in Edinburgh – including the *Edinburgh Weekly Chronicle*, the weekly *The Schoolmaster* and the monthly *Johnstone's Magazine* which was in 1834 amalgamated with *Tait's Edinburgh Magazine*. Johnstone had been writing for *Tait's* for some time prior to the merger, at which point, however, her role changed significantly, when she more or less assumed the editorship. According to one commentator,

> She now formed a permanent connexion with [*Tait's Edinburgh Magazine*], and although not, strictly speaking, the editor, she had entire charge of the literary department, and was a large and regular contributor. She was to *Tait* what Professor Wilson was to *Blackwood*; the ostensible always, and, indeed, the real editors, being the respective publishers.[42]

Apart from her formidable career in journalism, Johnstone was noted for the interest she took in new and upcoming writing talents, such as the radical poet Robert Nicoll

(1814–37), whose work was first published under her auspices.[43] Over and above all this, Johnstone wrote a number of books for young people as well as a number of novels for adults including *Clan-Albin* (1815) and *Elizabeth de Bruce* (1827) – and enjoyed her greatest success with a very popular cookery book, *The Cook and Housewife's Manual* (1826).[44] In his essay about Wordsworth, Thomas de Quincey sets Johnstone apart from other women writers of the time, like Joanna Baillie and Mary Russell Mitford, who, he claims, wrote mainly for pleasure, and for whom he (rather patronisingly) had 'no doubt that the little cares of correcting proofs . . . would be numbered amongst the minor pleasures of life'. However, he considers that 'Mrs Johnstone of Edinburgh has pursued the profession of literature – the noblest of professions, and the only one open to both sexes alike – with even more assiduity, and as a daily occupation'.[45] In this respect, Johnstone differs from the other writers considered in this chapter. She did not turn to writing as an intellectually stimulating pastime but as a remunerative concern, by which it was possible for a woman to earn a decent living. Johnstone's mildly feminist liberal-mindedness is in evidence thoughout both her novels, though discussion here is limited to her first, *Clan-Albin*.[46]

Clan-Albin opens like a conventional folk-tale, with the arrival of a mysterious young woman in a highland village; she gives birth to a son and then dies. Throughout the novel, romance motifs abound. The early action takes place on the island of Eleenalin, the burial place of the chiefs of Clan Albin in former times where 'dreadful screams had been heard to issue from the island, and often a pale blue light had been seen playing there, amid surrounding darkness'.[47] Later locations are castles and a Spanish convent; important letters are intercepted; and characters include staples of romance fiction such as the wandering musician.

Yet under the guise of romance, by setting the action in the very recent past (from the 1780s to the early 1800s), Johnstone succeeds in drawing the reader's attention to a number of live political issues. By the time of the publication of *Clan-Albin* in 1815, for instance, some of the worst atrocities of the Highland Clearances (at Strathnaver in Sutherland) had just taken place, and Johnstone leaves no room for doubt in the reader's mind as to the rights and wrongs of this when she writes of a similar event at Glenalbin:

> The banishment of the last of the clan was now fixed and inevitable; and the tears and shrieks of the women, the deep and hopeless grief of the men, the wailings of feeble age, and helpless infancy . . . formed a spectacle of woe which might have touched even the cold heart of him whose selfish luxury had produced misery so wide spreading and extreme. (I, p. 126)

Johnstone also takes the opportunity to comment on other so-called improvements, satirising the pointless efforts of one landowner, whose feeble picket fence 'formed a strange contrast with the massive pile it meant to enclose' (I, p. 270), and whose next equally preposterous plan is to whitewash his castle.

Like many women writers contemporary with her, Johnstone was deeply interested in the topic of education, and she brought this together with another live political issue – the degradation experienced by troops in the new Highland regiments – in *Clan-Albin*. The hero Norman McAlbin spends much time during the early weeks of army life on his endeavours to educate and enlighten the men in his regiment, thereby hoping to make their lives more bearable. This enterprise is obstructed and finally prohibited by his superiors. 'How should *scholars* and *philosophers* condescend to observe the trifling minutiae of regimental orders?' (II, p. 309), one pompous superior officer enquires.

Johnstone also explores wider social and political issues. McAlbin is deeply affected by some of the more distressing scenes of the workers in the industrial Midlands:

> . . . Numerous smoky manufactures . . . rose in this prosaic region, . . . every stream polluted by the dirty puddle of some dye-vat or filling-mill . . . at the warning of a bell, they marched to labour or refreshment, – a Highland feeling of contemptuous pity took possession of his mind . . . he recalled all he had formerly heard of the 'division of labour' and the 'wealth of nations' with an asperity which succeeding years softened down, but never wholly removed. (II, p. 187)

Though Christian Isobel Johnstone's novels undoubtedly contain large elements of romance, they deal seriously with Scottish (and sometimes British) current affairs, and for this reason make peculiarly stimulating reading for modern readers.

Susan Ferrier

Less prolific than Christian Isobel Johnstone, Susan Ferrier is, nevertheless, one of the most significant and achieved novelists of the period. Of her three novels, the first, *Marriage* (1818) is best known but the two others, *The Inheritance* (1824) and *Destiny* (1831), also make a special contribution to nineteenth-century fiction. Their titles suggest some of the issues, familiar from many other nineteenth-century novels, that appear, intertwined, in all her work. It is too easy, however, to see Ferrier as merely conventional. Like Johnstone, she shows social engagement and 'progressive' attitudes; her novels are interesting, too, for the insights they provide into the Scotland and Britain of their time (she lived all her life in Edinburgh but spent time at Inveraray Castle, where she sharply observed the life of the Highland gentry). Above all her work is vivid, vigorous, and in its acerbic social satire, often extremely funny.

Ferrier's novels have been treated primarily as 'novels about courtship, marriage and female education in the line established by Richardson, Burney and Austen',[48] the line of 'novels of manners and sentiment'.[49] Her work does indeed deal with social *mores*; Scott admired her work along with that of other 'ladies . . . gifted by nature with keen powers of observation and light satire'.[50] Ferrier's satire, though, is often pungent and stinging, the product of what Anne Grant of Laggan calls 'a clever caustic mind'.[51] Within a Christian and moral framework, her work criticises most robustly, among other targets, superficiality, greed and selfishness, especially in 'worldly' wealthy society. In *Marriage*, for instance, the rather eighteenth-century 'type' figure of 'Mr Brittle' sells his china wares to Lady Juliana, pressing on her

> 'this choice piece – it represents a Chinese cripple, squat on the ground, with his legs crossed. Your Ladyship may observe the head and chin advance forwards, as in the act of begging. The tea pours from the open mouth; and till your Ladyship tries, you can have no idea of the elegant effect it produces.'
>   That is really droll,' cried Lady Juliana, with a laugh of delight; 'and I must have the dear sick beggar, he is so deliciously hideous.' (p. 132)

The satire is all the sharper because Juliana is spending money her husband does not have; bankrupt, the weak Henry Douglas is forced to avoid prison by going to India. Juliana's self-absorption is complete, however: 'She knew she could not live without him – she was sure she should die; and Harry would be sea-sick, and grow so yellow and so ugly, that, when he came back, she should never have any comfort in him again' (p. 154).

Juliana is not only selfish but misguided, shown by Ferrier to have married for the 'wrong' reasons. *Marriage* uses the strategy of antithesis common at the time, to contrast Juliana with the dutiful and sensible Alicia Malcolm, and to compare Juliana's two daughters, Mary and Adelaide. Mary Cullinan notes that *Marriage* attempts to illustrate 'the ideal qualities a woman should possess and the ideal type of marriage which she should enter'.[52] Mary, who has been brought up by Alicia Malcolm, marries happily at the end, unlike her foolish sister. True love and its values are distinguished from infatuation, and from alliances based on the desire for money or status. But if there is a didactic element here, the message is transmitted with sharp humour, as in *The Inheritance*, where the upwardly-aspiring Bell Black marries an elderly military man who has been in India: 'Mrs Major Waddell played the Nabob's lady as though she had been born a Nabobess; she talked much and well of curry and rice, and old Madeira, and the liver . . . '[53]

There is also an element of social comment; the pressures of the 'marriage market' on women are revealed here, and again in the same novel when Gertrude is expected to marry Mr Delmour to further his political career. The limitations in the lives of unmarried women are also exposed, notably in the grotesque figures of the Glenfern aunts in *Marriage*. Significantly, these single women have received only a slight and superficial education, as have the women who make foolish marriages. By contrast, the 'wise' women, Alicia Malcolm and Mary Douglas, have been educated in a fuller sense, and have learned how to think rationally, as well as to feel for others. Anne Mellor points out that Ferrier's *Marriage* has a radical edge to it; it 'can be read as a fictional translation of Wollstonecraft's *Vindication [of the Rights of Woman]*'.[54]

Various ironic references to the conservative and didactic writers of the eighteenth century, such as John Gregory and James Fordyce, suggest Ferrier's impatience with traditional views of female roles voiced by unsympathetic characters like the tyrannical old laird in *Marriage*: '"If a woman can nurse her bairns, mak their claes, and manage her hooss, what mair need she do?"' (pp. 68–9); or Lord Rossville in *The Inheritance*, who lectures Gertrude more than once on how women should behave, but, it is implied, illustrates through his own person that a narrow life and 'weak contracted mind' (p. 20), are not the prerogatives of women.

A scene in *Marriage* implies a defence of the right of women to intellectual development. Mary attends a literary party at the home of Mrs Bluemits, which parodies the eighteenth-century English Bluestocking group of women writers and thinkers. The women gathered hold hilariously pretentious and trivial conversations about literary topics. However, the satire here is not directed against genuinely educated women: 'Next to goodness, Mary most ardently admired talents. She knew there were many of her own sex who were justly entitled to the distinction of literary fame. Her introduction to the circle at Mrs Bluemits' had disappointed her; but they were mere pretenders to the name' (p. 424). Mary adduces Hannah More's comments in *Coelebs in Search of a Wife* (1809) to contrast Mrs Bluemits's group with truly learned women like Elizabeth Carter, one of the original Bluestockings, and the scholar and translator, Elizabeth Smith, who combined learning and domestic virtue.[55] Like some other women writers, Ferrier slips in her radical ideas alongside the more conventional ones.[56] But Susan Ferrier's learning did not stop at her female contemporaries; as Anne Mellor remarks,

Ferrier is 'well acquainted with the Enlightenment thinkers of late eighteenth-century Edinburgh'.[57]

Ferrier's witty and spirited correspondence too shows that she was far from being stuffily conventional. In one of her letters she dwells ironically on the 'moral' of *Marriage*: 'I expect it will be the first book every wise matron will put into the hand of her daughter, and even the reviewers will relax their severity in favour of the morality of this little work'.[58] In another letter, she asks Charlotte Clavering if she has read Maria Edgeworth's 'Fashionable Tales', and comments 'I like the two first, but none of the others. It is high time all *good ladies* and *grateful little girls* should be returned to their gilt boards, and as for sentimental weavers and moralising glovers, I recommend them as penny ware for the pedlar' (pp. 65–6).

Ferrier knew that as a woman she had to work within a given framework, yet she is in her own ways subversive. She presents some morally worthy 'good ladies' in her fiction, but others, among the peripheral characters, are subversive in their eccentricity or sharpness of insight, suggesting a covert attack on conventional ideas of femininity. In *Marriage*, these are the awful but powerful Lady MacLaughlan and the witty but naughty Emily; in *The Inheritance*, the prattling Miss Pratt who is considered absurd by most of the characters in the novel, and described as 'often wrong' by the narrator, but 'a person from whom nothing could be hid' (p. 63). Significantly she first appears in company with the paragon, Mr Lyndsey, and is the first character to notice that he is in love with Gertrude, whom she very acutely observes as resembling the portrait of the absent but important figure of Lizzie Lundie.

In its representation of women, Ferrier's work demonstrates, and sometimes exploits, the tensions which affected the Scottish woman writer at this time. The representation of Scottish culture in her novels, too, is complex. Her work is satirical, seemingly anti-Romantic. There are many self-conscious references to the differences between Scottish and English culture; *Marriage*, most famously, is structured on the contrasts between them. English prejudice is exposed in the superbly drawn Dr Redgill, a gluttonous physician 'with a projecting front' (p. 231) who has followed in Dr Johnson's footsteps in making a '*tower* through the Highlands' (p. 235), and who has little time for Scotland: 'The people I give up – they are dirty and greedy – the country, too, is a perfect mass of rubbish . . . But the breakfasts! that's what redeems the land . . . ' (p. 237). The Scots are often satirically treated as well. All Ferrier's novels show weak or degenerate Chiefs; the ironically named Sir Sampson in *Marriage* is a shrunken parody of the Highland warriors of Jane Porter or Scott, or the dashing heroes of Joanna Baillie or Byron.

Ferrier's work, however, has a Romantic aspect especially when it comes to her native land. Various characters seem to suggest the superior moral worth of the 'untainted' Scot as with the gruff, Scots-speaking Adam Ramsay in *The Inheritance*: '"what are the eyes of the warld, and whar do they stand? For muckle I ha'e heard of the eyes of the warld, but I ha'e never been able to see them yet"' (p. 158). He sees through the surfaces of genteel society, and embodies deeper, older values, like Molly Macauley in *Destiny*, who is a singer of old Scots songs and a native Gaelic speaker, music and song being important bearers of Scottish culture in Ferrier's work.

Landscape is also significant. Anne Mellor suggests that, like other Scottish, Irish and Welsh women writers, Ferrier represents landscape in specifically feminine Romantic terms. Whereas in the work of male Romantics sublimity is associated with power and terror (and Ferrier makes reference to Wordsworth several times in her novels), landscape inspires in her female protagonists 'a heightened sensibility, not of anxiety, but of love, reverence, and mutual relationship', what Mellor calls 'the feminine sublime'.[59] Highland landscape also acts as a touchstone of character; those who fail to respond positively are shown to be deficient: Juliana in *Marriage*, Florinda in *Destiny*, Lady St Clair in *The Inheritance*, or Lord Rossville who essays 'improvement' but suffers from 'a mental darkness', so that for him nature's works 'were a sort of account-book, in which were registered all his own petty doings' (p. 44). The use of the economic metaphor there is strikingly effective; Ferrier's feminine Romanticism has a tough side.

Ferrier, like Mary Brunton, is alert to matters of money, class and property. Although her later novels, *The Inheritance* and *Destiny*, have been critically neglected, both are interesting for their 'sombre depiction of the social hierarchy and its workings, or non-workings, which was most unusual among novelists of courtship and manners in her time'.[60] In *The Inheritance*, class attitudes are probed. Colonel Delmour, discussing Lizzie Lundie's portrait, pronounces beauty wasted on the lower classes. He could never marry a huntsman's daughter, however beautiful: '"there is degradation in the very idea"' (p. 78). Lyndsey argues humanely against such snobbery: '"why may not a noble mind be conferred on a peasant as well as on a prince?"' (p. 77). Ideas about property and expansion are also compared. Lyndsey declines office and status in the British Empire offered through the family connections of Lord Rossville, '"giving as his sole reason, that he was satisfied with what he already had, and meant to devote himself to the management and improvement of his own estate"' (p. 26). Lyndsey's views may not seem especially radical to the modern reader, but Lord Rossville's utter incomprehension sharpens the scene's impact.

Destiny, Ferrier's last novel, is often held to be overly pious; it is certainly uncomfortably bleak, and this rather than its piety may account for its neglect. It attacks Patronage in the church through the fiercely comic depiction of the minister McDow who has an undeservedly comfortable living (his gluttony echoes that of Dr Redgill in *Marriage*), but who is finally ejected from his church and from the novel. Ferrier's Presbyterian radicalism appears, too, when the spendthrift Lady Waldegrave fails to pay a workman, arguing that '"there is nobody so poor that cannot get credit somewhere"'[61]. Edith rebukes her with '"the poor are most to be pitied when their sufferings are occasioned by the thoughtlessness and extravagance of the great"' (II, p. 292).

Ferrier's satirical representation of society does not fade in her later work; rather, it darkens. Loraine Fletcher argues that Ferrier 'introduces into the novel form a sceptical attitude to rank and money that is Victorian rather than eighteenth century or Regency'.[62] Susan Ferrier's work, both satirical and Romantic, with its conventional aspects and feminist elements, echoes much in the work of other Scottish women writers of her time; it may also be seen as a bridge to Victorian fiction.

Elizabeth Hamilton, Jane Porter, Mary Brunton, Christian Isobel Johnstone and Susan Ferrier are a disparate group; but writers such as these all explore a range of topical issues in their novels, albeit retaining their requisite 'femininity' by indicating political messages only in a covert fashion. Their works may sometimes show the strain of the competing claims of convention and the desire to speak out; what cannot be denied is that, from questions of women's rights to education, through the injustices of the Highland Clearances, the nature of history, the slave trade, class conflict and certain unfair practices of the Scottish church, these early nineteenth-century writers address a host of public matters. Their novels comprise 'the Great Unknown' literature of their time, a rich and hitherto largely unexplored legacy.[63]

Notes

1.   Ann H. Jones in *Ideas and Innovations – Best Sellers of Jane Austen's Age* (AMS Press, New York, 1986) lists the nine most popular novelists of the period 1800–20; these include (besides Walter Scott) Elizabeth Hamilton, Mary Brunton, Jane Porter and Anna Maria Porter; cited by Anne K. Mellor, *Romanticism and Gender* (London, 1993), p. 214.

2.   See Gary Kelly, *English Fiction of the Romantic Period 1789–1830* (Longman, London, 1989), especially chapters 3 and 6.

3.   *Self-Control* (Pandora Press, London, 1986), p. 2. All references are to this edition. For publication details of the first edition, see bibliography at end of book.

4.   *Marriage* (Oxford, 1986), p. 414. All references are to this edition. For details of first publication, see bibliography.

5.   See Mellor, *Romanticism and Gender*, p. 53.

6.   See Dale Spender, *Mothers of the Novel* (Routledge, London, 1986), p. 336.

7.   Alexander Brunton, 'A Memoir of Mary Brunton', in Mary Brunton, *Discipline* (London, 1842), pp. 2–56 (pp. 7–8); quoted by Spender, *Mothers of the Novel*, p. 332.

8.   Alexander Brunton, p. 23, quoted by Spender, p. 333.

9.   See Vivien Jones, *Women in the Eighteenth Century* (Routledge, London, 1990) for extracts from these writers; also Judith Lowder Newton, *Women, Power and Subversion: Social Strategies in British Fiction 1778–1860* (University of Georgia Press, Athens, Georgia, 1981).

10.   As argued by Sarah Smith in 'Men, Women and Money: The Case of Mary Brunton', in *Fetter'd or Free?: British Women Novelists, 1670–1815* ed. Mary Anne Schofield and Cecilia Macheski (Ohio University Press, Athens and London, 1986), pp. 41–58; and Loraine Fletcher, 'Great Expectations: Wealth and Inheritance in the Novels of Susan Ferrier', in *Scottish Literary Journal* 16.2 (1989), 60–77.

11.   Noted by James Irvine, 'A Glimpse of Susan Ferrier' in *Susan Ferrier 1782–1854* (National Library of Scotland, Edinburgh, 1982), pp. 5–8 (p. 7); and see her letters in John Doyle (ed.), *Memoir and Correspondence of Susan Ferrier* (J. Murray, London, 1898). A letter of 1852 remarks her enthusiasm for *Uncle Tom's Cabin*.

12.   Hamilton's letters are published in Elizabeth Benger, *Memoirs of the Late Mrs Elizabeth Hamilton. With a Selection from her Correspondence and Other Unpublished Writings*, 2 vols, (Longman, Hurst, Rees, Orme & Brown, London, 1818). Further references to this are given in the text as Benger.

13.   A full list of Hamilton's published books is given in the bibliography.

14.   See Benger, *Memoirs etc*, vol. 2, p. 126.

15.   See Gary Kelly, 'Revolutionary and Romantic Feminism: Women, Writing, and Cultural Revolution', in Keith Hanley and Raman Selden (eds), *Revolution and English Romanticism: Politics and Rhetoric* (Harvester, London, 1990, pp. 107–30 (p. 123).

16.   See the reprint of Elizabeth Hamilton's *Memoirs of Modern Philosophers* (London, 1992), with an introduction by Peter Garside, p. xi.

17.   Quoted in *Dictionary of British Women Writers* ed. Janet Todd, (Methuen, London, 1989) p. 312.

18.   'Sarah Tytler' is the pen-name of the Scottish novelist, Henrietta Keddie (1826?–1914), quoted in Jean L. Watson's 'Prefatory Note' to *The Cottagers of Glenburnie* (Dunn & Wright, Glasgow, n.d.), p. 9. All subsequent page references, however, are to the 1832 Edinburgh edition of the novel.

19.   See Kelly, *English Fiction of the Romantic Period*, p. 91.

20.   See Emma Letley, *From Galt to Douglas Brown: Nineteenth-Century Fiction and Scots Language* (Scottish Academic Press, Edinburgh, 1988), p. 3.

21.   The 'soup and sanitation' phrase belongs to David Craig, in his *Scottish Literature and the Scottish People, 1680–1830* (Chatto & Windus, London, 1961), p. 214.

22.   The full title of this, and all Porter's published books, is given in the bibliography.

23.   In Jane Porter's entry in *The Dictionary of National Biography*, ed. Sidney Lee (London, 1896), vol. XLVI, pp. 182–4, the writer comments, 'Walter Scott . . . was a frequent visitor at their house, and he . . . delighted them with fairy tales or stories of the borders.'

24.   Quoted from *The National Portrait Gallery of Illustrious and Eminent Personages of the*

Nineteenth Century; with Memoirs, 5 vols, (London, 1834), vol. 5, p. 5. Of some 175 'portraits' in this series, only eight are of women, two of which are the Porter sisters.

25.   See *Self-Control* (London, 1986), p. 66.

26.   Footnote in *The Scottish Chiefs* (1839), vol. 1, ch. 29. In the same footnote, Porter also directs the reader to 'Baillie's historical volume of "Metrical Legends" [1821] in which 'the reader may find her eloquent words on the subject'. All subsequent page references are to the 1839 edition of *The Scottish Chiefs*.

27.   James Hogg, *Domestic Manners of Sir Walter Scott* (J. Reid, Glasgow, 1834; reprinted E. Mackay, Stirling, 1909), p. 212.

28.   In *The National Portrait Gallery* (1834), the biographer suggests that 'the Emperor Napoleon felt particularly jealous of all references to past lawful *regimes*, and examples of patriotic loyalty, and of the genuine spirit of freedom . . . ' (p. 5) such as those expressed in *The Scottish Chiefs*.

29.   *The Scottish Chiefs*, I, p. 126.

30.   It seems unlikely the implicit anachronism (Porter's use of Macpherson's 'translations of Ossian') was intended.

31.   From the 'Preface to the First Edition', reprinted in the Standard Novels edition (1839), xxxiii; xxv.

32.   From the 'Retrospective Introduction' to the Standard Novels edition of *The Scottish Chiefs* (London, 1831), viii.

33.   'Blind Harry' or Henry the Minstrel (?1440–?1492) was the half-legendary author of *The Wallace*, an epic poem extolling Wallace's martial feats. Enormously influential for later generations of Scottish writers such as Burns, it probably came to Jane Porter through the popular rewriting in 1722 of William Hamilton of Gilbertfield.

34.   Hannah Hinson Jones, 'Jane Austen and Eight Minor Contemporaries: A Study in the Novel 1800–1820' (Unpublished doctoral thesis, University of Newcastle upon Tyne, 1979), p. 223.

35.   See Sandra M. Gilbert and Susan Gubar, *The Madwoman in the Attic: The Woman Writer and the Nineteenth Century Literary Imagination* (Yale University Press, New Haven/London, 1979).

36.   Alexander Brunton, pp. 25–6, quoted by Spender, p. 334.

37.   Katherine Sobba Green, *The Courtship Novel 1740–1820: A Feminized Genre* (University of Kentucky Press, Kentucky, 1991), pp. 120–34 (p. 121).

38.   See also *Discipline* (London, 1986), p. 252, p. 328. All references are to this edition. For details of first publication, see bibliography.

39.   Newton, *Women, Power and Subversion*, p. 6.

40.   Smith, 'Men, Women and Money', p. 44.

41.   Alexander Brunton, p. 16, quoted by Spender, p. 331.

42.   William Anderson, *The Scottish Nation; or the Surnames, Families, Literature, Honours, and Biographical History of the People of Scotland*, 3 vols, (Edinburgh, 1863), III, p. 713.

43.   See the Centenary Edition of Robert Nicoll, *Poems and Lyrics: with a Memoir of the Author* (William Tait, Edinburgh, 1835; Centenary Edition, A. Gardner, Paisley, 1914), in which a 'Sketch of the Life of Robert Nicoll' by Christian Johnstone, first published in 1842, is also reprinted. For details of other novels see *The Edinburgh Tales* (William Tait, Edinburgh, 1845–6).

44.   Published under the pseudonym, 'Mrs Margaret Dods, of the Cleikum Inn, St Ronans' – after the character in Scott's *St Ronan's Well* (1823). By 1858 some ten editions of this book had appeared, and its popularity continued for a considerable time after that. The most recent edition of the book was published in London by Rosters (1988).

45.   Quoted from *De Quincey's Works, Vol II: Recollections of the Lakes and the Lake Poets: Coleridge, Wordsworth, and Southey* (A. C. Black, Edinburgh, 1862), p. 209.

46.   Christian Johnstone's politics (shared with her husband) were serious enough to instigate the end of at least one business partnership: according to her entry in *A Biographical Dictionary of Eminent Scotsmen* (originally edited by Robert Chambers; revised throughout and continued by the Rev. Thomas Thomson, London, 1855), the Johnstones sold their half of the *Edinburgh Weekly Chronicle* because their political views were irreconcilable with

those of their co-proprietor, William Blackwood, who was 'heart and soul with the Tories' (p. 406).

47.   Christian Johnstone, *Clan-Albin: A National Tale*, 4 vols (Edinburgh, 1815), I, p. 40. All subsequent references are to this edition.

48.   As summarised by Loraine Fletcher, 'Great Expectations', p. 60.

49.   Kelly, *English Fiction of the Romantic Period*, p. 299.

50.   Introduction to *St Ronan's Well* (1823), quoted in Ioan Williams (ed.), *Sir Walter Scott on Novelists and Fiction* (Routledge & Kegan Paul, London and New York, 1968), p. 428.

51.   Quoted in *Memoir and Correspondence of Susan Ferrier*, p. 207.

52.   Mary Cullinan, *Susan Ferrier* (Twayne, Boston, 1984), p. 47.

53.   Susan Ferrier, *The Inheritance* (Three Rivers Books, Mill Green, 1984), p. 425. Further references are to this edition. For details of first publication, see the bibliography.

54.   Mellor, *Romanticism and Gender*, p. 49.

55.   This scene is noted by Sylvia Myers, *The Bluestocking Circle: Women, Friendship and the Life of the Mind in Eighteenth Century England* (Clarendon Press, Oxford, 1990), p. 293.

56.   This is argued at greater length by Nancy L. Paxton, 'Subversive Feminism: A Reassessment of Susan Ferrier's *Marriage*' in *Women and Literature* 4 (1976), 18–29.

57.   Mellor, *Romanticism and Gender*, p. 49.

58.   *Memoir and Correspondence*, p. 76.

59.   Mellor, *Romanticism and Gender*, pp. 85–106 (p. 97).

60.   Fletcher, 'Great Expectations', p. 60.

61.   *Destiny or The Chief's Daughter*, 2 vols (London, 1882, II, p. 291. Further references are to the same edition.

62.   'Great Expectations', p. 61.

63.   *Suggested Further Reading*: helpful material may be found in the following: Nancy Armstrong, *Desire and Domestic Fiction: A Political History of the Novel* (Oxford University Press, London and New York, 1987); N. S. Bushnell, 'Susan Ferrier's *Marriage* as a Novel of Manners', in *Studies in Scottish Literature* 5 (1968), pp. 216–28; Jenni Calder, 'Heroes and Hero-Makers: Women in Nineteenth-Century Scottish Fiction', in Douglas Gifford (ed.), *The History of Scottish Literature* vol. 3 (Aberdeen University Press, Aberdeen, 1988), pp. 261–74; Wendy Craik, 'Susan Ferrier', in Alan Bell (ed.), *Scott Bicentenary Essays* (Edinburgh, 1973), pp. 322–31; Stuart Curran, 'Women readers, women writers', in *The Cambridge Companion to British Romanticism*, ed. Stuart Curran (Cambridge University Press, Cambridge, 1993), pp. 177–95; Douglas Gifford, 'Myth, Parody and Dissociation: Scottish Fiction 1814–1914', in *The History of Scottish Literature* vol. 3, pp. 217–59; A. M. Hall, 'Memories of Miss Jane Porter', *Art Journal* 12 (1850); Andrew D. Hook, 'Jane Porter, Sir Walter Scott, and the Historical Novel', *Clio* 5 (1976), pp. 181–92; Gary Kelly, 'Elizabeth Hamilton: Domestic Woman and National Reconstruction', in *Women, Writing and Revolution 1790–1827* (Clarendon Press, Oxford, 1993), pp. 265–304; Gary Kelly, 'Romantic Fiction', in *The Cambridge Companion to British Romanticism*, ed. Stuart Curran (Cambridge University Press, Cambridge, 1993), pp. 196–215; Dorothy Porter, McMillan 'Heroines and Writers', in Caroline Gonda (ed.), *Tea and Leg-Irons: New Feminist Readings from Scotland* (Open Letters, London, 1992), pp. 17–30; Aileen M. Riddell 'What happened to the tales of our grandmothers?', *Chapman* 74–5 (Autumn/Winter 1993), 5–10.

12

Rediscovering Scottish Women's Fiction in the Nineteenth Century

Moira Burgess

Though we know that the nineteenth century in Scottish fiction has until recently been a neglected period, 'neglected' hardly seems a strong enough term to apply to the women writers of that time. Some advance has certainly been made. Susan Ferrier, Mary Brunton, Margaret Oliphant and the Findlater sisters, for instance, are now well enough known, and other chapters in this volume testify to the attention which their work is beginning to receive.

But they are the tip of an iceberg. A comprehensive directory or index covering Scottish writing of the period will yield the names of literally scores of nineteenth-century women novelists,[1] and to many researchers they are likely to be nothing but names. Amelia Edith Barr, who began novel-writing at the age of fifty and published forty-seven novels in the next thirty-five years? Grace Kennedy, a retiring lady who published all her 'religious tales' anonymously?[2] Mary Cross, described by an admittedly enthusiastic critic as 'someone whose name must be familiar . . . to readers of current Scottish fiction'?[3] Sarah Macnaughtan? Felicia Skene? Who are these women? Ought we to know?

Because they have been so largely forgotten, this of course is the problem: are they forgotten because they deserve to be? They may have been the merest scribblers making pin-money from casual and ill-considered romantic tales. (Though if this was so, their lists of editions and translations indicate that they fooled a lot of the people a lot of the time; a consideration of popular taste of the day might want to ask how this was done.) Much more study is needed to establish the value of their work and their place in the canon of Scottish writing.

The present chapter makes a tentative beginning on such a study. The writers I consider here may perhaps stand as representatives of the group. Their lives span the whole of the nineteenth century, extending in fact well into the twentieth; Flora Annie Steel in her ripe old age could have read Catherine Carswell's *Open the Door!* (and would have enjoyed it, we may hazard a guess, after learning about the robust exploits of Mrs Steel). Among them, too, they spanned the genres. They wrote historical, romantic and religious fiction, children's books, non-fiction, and a great deal of journalism. They also, however, wrote 'serious' novels; serious in their own estimation (as, in several cases, we know from their memoirs), and for that reason, I would suggest, deserve serious consideration.[4]

Catherine Sinclair

Catherine Sinclair (1800–64) was born in Edinburgh, the fourth of six daughters of Sir John Sinclair of Ulbster, who also had several sons by his two marriages. There is an attractive picture of the large, affectionate Sinclair family in the memoirs of Lucy Bethia Walford, Catherine Sinclair's great-niece and herself a writer whom I discuss later.[5] The Sinclairs were tall, handsome, gifted and sociable – 'they did everything, went everywhere, and knew everybody', the young Lucy Walford believed – though Catherine and some of her sisters were pockmarked from smallpox inoculations. 'I believe she felt it keenly,' remarks Walford, 'though . . . her charm of manner and witty conversation made her a universal favourite.' The unmarried Sinclair brothers and sisters, fond of entertaining, welcomed visitors on whom to 'warm up their powers of conversation . . . These really clever talkers,' reports Walford, 'were sadly given to puns.'

From this cheerful family circle came *Holiday House* (1839), generally regarded as one of the first children's books, in the sense that we use the term today. Catherine Sinclair had acted as her father's secretary from the age of fourteen until he died when she was thirty-five, and only then began her writing life. Remaining unmarried, she was very fond of her small nephew George Boyle, son of the Earl of Glasgow, and so *Holiday House*, like other famous children's books, was probably written with a particular child in mind. (She explains in a preface that she had told versions of the stories to young friends and relations over many years.)

Holiday House – which was still being reprinted, and evidently enjoyed, seventy years after its publication – must have been a bright light in the monotonous landscape of moral and religious tales intended to improve rather than entertain. Sinclair saw contemporary children as 'carefully prompted what to say, and what to think, and how to look, and how to feel'.[6] Walter Scott himself had remarked to her that in the rising generation there would be no poets, wits or orators, because all 'play of the imagination' was so carefully discouraged. In *Holiday House* the prompting is certainly there, but imagination, humour and story-telling skill practically disguise the didactic purpose. 'In these pages,' Sinclair remarks, 'the author has endeavoured to paint that species of noisy, frolicsome, mischievous children, now almost extinct'.

And Laura and Harry – based, as Walford confirms, on Catherine Sinclair and her brother Archie – are attractive little tearaways. They are 'heedless, lively romps', but truthful, honest, never greedy or cruel, and unfailingly considerate of one another, if of nobody else. They are motherless, with their father abroad, and their guardians are their kindly uncle and grandmother, though they live under the stern rule of the dragon nurse Mrs Crabtree. Sinclair makes the point very strongly that Laura and Harry respond much better to the methods of joking Uncle David and gentle Grandmamma than to Mrs Crabtree and her tawse.

They cannot be left on their own for an instant without disaster. In a moment of inspiration they write notes inviting all their friends and relations to tea (not, of course, informing Mrs Crabtree, who refuses to give them any food for the party). Laura cuts off all her hair (she only meant to trim it), while Harry, playing with candles, sets the nursery ablaze. Laura falls into the river in her last clean frock; Harry naughtily locks himself into a room and manages to break the key. It is all marvellous fun, wittily exaggerating all the terrible things that children might do, or are told not to do, or wish they dared to do.

In its closing chapters *Holiday House* draws near to the conventional children's book of its day, as elder brother Frank, the flower of the flock, dies a lingering death by consumption. (His character and his death, Sinclair tells us, are based on those of her brother James.) This sorrow, it is carefully explained, is what causes Harry and Laura to grow up into sensible people, where neither punishment nor kindness had quite succeeded. Have young readers over the years skipped that bit, and gone back to read again how Harry and Laura are chased by the mad bull?

Before publishing *Holiday House*, however – and even before her father's death, since she tells us that he 'revised and corrected' the work – Sinclair wrote *Modern Accomplishments* (1836). In a dedication to the then Princess Victoria she specifies that she is 'venturing to write on the subject of female education and character', and in a preface she expands on this:

> Actual hypocrisy is not the subject treated of . . . It is intended rather to separate the essentials of religious conduct from its excrescences . . . [and] to illustrate the pernicious consequences of an undue prominence in education given to ornamental above useful acquirements. (*Modern Accomplishments*, pp. x–x1)

All this sounds very dull, but in fact Sinclair breathes life into her theme by way of her characters, who are coolly and wittily outlined. Lady Fitz-Patrick is, or was, a society beauty: 'She still maintained an opinion, that to feel young was the same as to be young; therefore her costume was as juvenile as ever' (*Modern Accomplishments*, p. 2). She is bringing up her beautiful daughter Eleanor to value appearance above everything else. Her sister Lady Howard, on the other hand, is a blue-stocking: 'Nobody could conjecture what number of languages Lady Howard knew, and there was even a report that she had been convicted of Greek and Latin' (*Modern Accomplishments*, pp. 8–9). Lady Howard subjects her equally beautiful daughter Matilda to a series of educational plans, even though she 'had already lost several of her family, who were successively the wonders of the day. Each of them knew his letters at three years old, sung and repeated hymns at four, spoke French at five, and died at six' (*Modern Accomplishments*, p. 12).

A third sister, Miss Barbara Neville, is a professed Christian, but does not impress her family as being really religious: she could be a martyr or a nun, but, observes one of her sisters, '"to sit soberly down in peaceful insignificance, and consistently fulfil the simple duties of your own station, is a piece of religious heroism that you are quite unequal to"' (*Modern Accomplishments*, p. 17). Neither Lady Fitz-Patrick nor Lady Howard goes in much for peaceful insignificance, but then they do not claim to be religious. In contrast to these three sisters is their sister-in-law Lady Olivia Neville, who, before her angelic death, has brought most of her in-laws and the world around to acknowledge that she is a *true* Christian.

As promised in the preface, there is a further contrast between heedless Eleanor and thoughtful Matilda. Eleanor is being educated in 'accomplishments' only. Matilda, having had enough stamina to survive her mother's earlier experiments, is now being properly educated, and loves it. The novel has unusual strength as a voice supporting the education of women. But the main theme of *Modern Accomplishments* is Christianity, true and false, which should prepare us – but does not quite – for what we find in Sinclair's later novel *Beatrice*.

Beatrice (1852) is a very different strand in Sinclair's writing, and, after the wit and precise observation of *Modern Accomplishments*, comes as something of a shock. Lucy Walford considers it Sinclair's most ambitious and ingenious novel; so it may be, but it has a higher purpose, as the thirty-page preface takes pains to make clear:

The object of this narrative is to portray, for the consideration of young girls now first emerging into society, the enlightened happiness derived from the religion of England, founded on the Bible, contrasted with the misery arising from the superstition of Italy, founded on the Breviary. (*Beatrice*, v)

The setting of *Beatrice* (in spite of the preface's references to England) is the fictional Inverness-shire village of Clanmarina. As the book opens, the village has two lairds, the 'proud, cold and obstinate' (and Roman Catholic) Earl of Eaglescairn, and Sir Allan McAlpine, 'rich, old, and childless, [and] a miser', but Protestant. A flurry of disinherited heirs and unexpected deaths leads to the point where younger relations have succeeded to the titles, maintaining, however, their respective religious affiliations. A shipwreck introduces the beautiful child Beatrice. There is a mystery about Beatrice, to which the novel's sub-title, 'or the Unknown Relatives', provides a clue.

The main thrust of the book, however, is the attempt by the wicked Lord Eaglescairn and his troop of Jesuits to convert Clanmarina's honest peasantry, and the young McAlpine laird, and all his relations, and the vicar, to the Popish faith. So relentlessly is this theme pursued, and so broad a brush is used, that we are tempted to wonder whether the witty and urbane Catherine Sinclair is here writing tongue-in-cheek.

Other evidence, however, suggests that this is not so. In the same year as *Beatrice*, Sinclair published a non-fiction work, *Popish Legends and Bible Truths*, dedicated to her nieces. An undated letter from her asks for a friend's help to settle a young minister in a living in Largs: 'For my nephew's sake, I am most anxious to keep a man of such anti-Romanizing views amongst us.'[7] (Sinclair evidently felt that she could defend herself against the Pope with ease, but was less sure about the younger generation.) So *Beatrice* remains as a seriously intended, if polemical, novel, an unexpected side of Sinclair's writing which we must take into account. Perhaps we have to conclude that, in those disturbing mid-century years of industrial revolution and sudden Irish immigration, in spite of her easy manners and dinner-table puns, Catherine Sinclair felt an unwelcome wind of change and withdrew into the persona and values of a conventional Scotswoman of her time, in a way somewhat similar to Susan Ferrier before her.

Henrietta Keddie ('Sarah Tytler')

Henrietta Keddie (1827–1914), who published most of her work as 'Sarah Tytler', came from a background very different from the privileged Sinclair circle. In her autobiography *Three Generations* she traces her mother's family back to the distant figure of 'Dauvit Gib, tenant in Blebo', who died in the year of the 1745 rebellion.[8] Tenant farmers and millers, and their wives, are prominent among her more immediate relatives; those, that is, who survived to follow any trade at all. Her family history presents us with the quiet and chilling, if not untypical, information that seven of her mother's nine brothers and sisters died untimely of consumption.

Those who did survive had large families, and the book contains warm scenes of many young cousins in farmhouses and country towns. We learn too that, as Keddie's father's circumstances 'grew less and less hopeful', his daughters had to earn their own living.

My elder sisters had already been governesses for several years. Eventually, we young women combined forces, and began a school for girls in the little town of our birth [Cupar] which we knew so well. (*Three Generations*, p. 232)

The school opened in 1848, when Henrietta was twenty-one, and continued until 1870, when, having already published several novels, Henrietta Keddie went south to London with her sister Margaret, thereafter living by her literary work.

Three Generations, true enough to its title, does not tell us nearly as much about Henrietta Keddie's writing as we would like to know. Her first and second novels, she informs us, fell flat, and she was not paid for them, since 'remuneration . . . was conditional on a certain sale, which was not achieved'. She was already, however, a professional writer in outlook:

> I got a sudden alarming request to supply another chapter, as the material was not sufficient to fill the regulation three volumes. I saved the situation by the simple device of inflicting some of the principal characters with a sharp, but not fatal, attack of fever. (*Three Generations*, p. 254)

Her writing career began in earnest a few years later, when she sent a version of the traditional Borders story 'Muckle Mou'ed Meg' to *Fraser's Magazine*. It was accepted, and she found the confidence to move on to 'inventions', short stories of her own. She was an author, and began to move in literary circles. Unfortunately she tells us little about her own work in *Three Generations*, although she is worth reading on her friend, Mrs Craik, on Jane Ann Cupples 'drawing down upon herself more attention than she cared for' at a fancy dress ball, or on Mrs Oliphant: 'She was not tall, and she had a tendency to the stoutness which she was apt to describe in her mature women characters under the style of "matronly bountifulness"' (*Three Generations*, pp. 289–90).

From another source we learn that Henrietta Keddie did not actually choose the pen-name Sarah Tytler, which 'was put upon her, without connivance of her own, by the publisher to whom she intrusted her early publishing business'. Publishers, she may have begun to think, are like that. Keddie and her friend Jeannie Watson, editing a book on Scottish women songwriters, wanted to give it the suitably euphonious and Scottish title *The Linties*. 'Business counsels prevailed' and it appeared more prosaically as *The Songstresses of Scotland*.[9]

Henrietta Keddie, like Margaret Oliphant, was an extremely prolific writer, and even an admirer must admit the element of hackwork in much of her production. She knew the difference herself: 'I think those [novels] which got most of such praise as I prized were *The Nut Brown Maids*, *Citoyenne Jacqueline*, *St Mungo's City*, *Kincaid's Widow*, and *Miss Nanse*' (*Three Generations*, p. 344). Most of her work is now forgotten, although Francis Russell Hart does consider two of Keddie's novels worth mentioning in his survey of the Scottish novel: *St Mungo's City* (1884) and *Logie Town* (1887).[10]

St Mungo's City is the story of two Glasgow families. In the first family, the three Miss Mackinnons are great-granddaughters of a tobacco lord. They have come down in the world, though they still regard the *nouveaux riches* as 'the cotton and iron dirt'. They are indeed reduced to utter poverty, hanging on from day to day in expectation of a long-delayed legacy. When the will is eventually made public, it does not please them. It cannot be right. There is only one thing to do:

> 'It's twa shirra-officers, I think,' [reports Miss Bethia] 'come in a cab, sayin' they have a warrant for us.'
>
> 'A warrant!' cried Eneas [their grand-nephew] horrified . . . 'There must be some huge blunder . . . These are my aunts – the Miss Mackinnons – who have lived here for more than

half a century . . . You may as well accuse them of setting fire to his house as of burning his will. What do you say, Aunt Janet?' asked Eneas, almost cheerfully, his confidence reestablished by the incredibility of the charge.

'That we brunt it, sure enough, and what for no?' demanded the undaunted woman. (*St Mungo's City*, pp. 211–12)

In Tam Drysdale, head of the second family, we have a notable character in Glasgow fiction. A contemporary reviewer appreciated this:

Any citizen of Glasgow will recognise at once as typical of the self-made man of the past generation the picture of the sturdy old dyer, with his faith in himself and in his money, his quick wit and commonsense in the city and his magnificent vulgarity at home.[11]

Keddie delightfully mocks his party manners: "'I believe the takes of salmon are not promising well, Sir Hughie; every fish costs five pounds to this day. Let mother help you to another slice, Leddy Semple. The lamb ought to be first-rate, Sir Jeames, from what it fetches.'" (*St Mungo's City*, p. 137).

If the Drysdale daughters are rather typical Victorian novel heroines, there is a distinct spark of originality in her presentation of the son, young Tam. When we first meet him he is a somewhat dour, awkward young man, college-educated but unwilling to take his place in society or at business, or to do anything definite with his life. His problem is that he has a social conscience, dismissed impatiently by 'auld Tam' with the words "'We're not here to mend the whole economy of things'", but a conscience recognised, though hardly understood, by his mother: "'He's no easy about the rich and the poor, though I'm clear the Bible owns them baith'" (*St Mungo's City*, p. 37).

However, young Tam's fellow-feeling for the working classes is sadly shaken when he joins them on a Clyde steamer trip 'doon the watter' at the Glasgow Fair. The chapter is an impressive piece of keen observation, from the sunny freshness of the morning, through the refreshments, the broadening jests, the quarrels, to the jaded, wearisome return trip. Tam is eager to take part in the people's holiday, and has taken care to dress like the rest of the company (in a frock-coat and a chimney-pot hat); but no one wants him there. No one talks to him. He is even regarded as some kind of spy. It is not long before we find him buckling down to his father's business and taking part in the mild social whirl available in city and county. Tam is himself again.

St Mungo's City, then, is a novel of manners; but it is also a fairly detailed picture – and a valuable one, as something rare in contemporary Scottish fiction – of a bustling, enthusiastic, attractively naive Victorian Glasgow. How this was achieved, since Keddie, a Fifer, appears to have had minimal connections with the west, is something of a mystery. She may have picked up hints from exiled natives whom she knew in London: 'There was Charles Gibbon, who came up to London with William Black, a pair of bold adventurers from old "St Mungo's City" (*Three Generations*, p. 340). The reviewer in *The Scots Pictorial*, however, probably puts his finger on it:

The impression given . . . is that the author has pretty thoroughly explored modern Glasgow, always keeping a watchful eye on its antiquities, and that she has carefully studied the section of its past social life in which she has embedded her clever and ingenious romance.

And it is typical of her fictional practice that she researches carefully backgrounds of which she has no intimate experience:

When Miss Keddie wrote *Citoyenne Jacqueline*, a tale of the Great Revolution, she had never
been in France, but founded her book upon a close and sympathetic study of the best literature
of the period, deriving her knowledge of French character from the various French teachers
who had come under her observation.[12]

But she must at least have sailed 'doon the watter' herself or taken very detailed notes
from some of her Glasgow friends.

In *Logie Town*, however, she is at home. Hart does not hesitate to call it a better novel
than *St Mungo's City*.[13] Logie is Cupar, and Keddie views her native town 'with wholeness
and urbane compassion, with a finely balanced sense of its values and deficiencies'. Town
and central character are closely identified at the novel's opening: 'A good many years
ago, young Lizzie Lindesay looked out of her open window, up and down the High-gate,
the main street of Logie' (*Logie Town*, p. 1). The High-gate is Lizzie's book, and she reads
it with interest, knowledge and love. She is not looking out for Adam Lauder, of course,
but, while not looking for him, she sees

> [the houses] all of gray stone, with roofs for the most part of cold blue slate, though here and
> there the warm red tiles lingered . . . As a rule the houses were without pretension, rigidly
> plain in their height and breadth, blinking out from formal rows of narrow windows on the
> causeway for the most part. (*Logie Town*, p. 9)

The main thread of the story is a simple enough romance, in which Lizzie comes to marry
not Adam Lauder but a much less likely person, an exiled French nobleman who comes
into his estate in time to sweep her off to his chateau in Gascony. (Keddie by now knew
what her readers liked.) But the true heart and soul of the novel is its picture of Logie.

> Some of those houses . . . were old town houses which the neighbouring gentry had occupied
> in the winter, when the little town figured as a miniature Edinburgh. The whole place was
> of far greater antiquity than might have been imagined from its general aspect . . . Logie had
> been the scene of courts and national parliaments in its day. (*Logie Town*, pp. 9–10)

What we have is a loving portrait of the town past and present; its houses, Lauder's paper-
mill (the only industry), its school, its great spring market, and its people, old, middle-aged
and young.

> As Logie was not a manufacturing town . . . it was the more select and aristocratic, in its
> higher strata of widows and maiden ladies, female representatives of neighbouring laird's
> families, retired naval and military officers, clergymen, bankers, lawyers or 'writers', and
> doctors. Its inferior strata ranged from substantial unpretending tradesmen down to jobbing
> gardeners, day labourers, and a few hand-loom weavers. (*Logie Town*, p. 2)

Logie Town knows them all and brings all these to life in a Scottish novel which deserves
to be rediscovered.

Lucy Walford (1845–1915)

With Lucy Bethia Walford we are back in the world of the Scottish gentry. Walford
was the seventh of nine children of John Colquhoun, a younger son of the laird of Luss.

Her father rented a Highland home each summer for his leisured pursuits of shooting and fishing (and nature study, though, in the custom of the time, a lot of the rarities he observed ended up stuffed in his private museum). Lucy and her brothers and sisters spent idyllic months walking, rowing and swimming in what were then fairly remote parts of Scotland, like Mull and the Kyles of Bute. Her autobiography *Recollections of a Scottish Novelist* (1910) gives a lively picture of that cosy, curiously sheltered way of life. But *Recollections*, unlike Henrietta Keddie's *Three Generations*, also gives quite a full account of Walford's earlier writing days. Like many authors she began early, writing a massive historical romance (now fortunately lost, she herself admits), in 'high-flown *Scottese* of the most blatant type', at the age of thirteen. A more successful attempt four years later resulted in her first published story.

Her first novel *Mr Smith* (1874) was written in the early years of her marriage; 'as my husband was obliged to be absent for the greater part of each day, I had much time to myself'. She had just heard news of the death of 'the real Mr Smith', a local hero from Port Bannatyne on the Isle of Bute, whom she and her family had known years before:

> Would it be possible to make a hero out of this 'short, stout, grey man' who was externally nothing, internally everything? Could anything of a romance be constructed around such an unromantic figure? His personality might be all that I and others knew it to be; but could I depict it – could I make anything of it? (*Recollections*, p. 148)

She tried to, and *Mr Smith*, when finished, was accepted by John Blackwood, to whom Margaret Oliphant and George Eliot were also indebted for the publication of their earliest fiction. (In contrast to Henrietta Keddie's publisher, Blackwood persuaded the diffident Walford *not* to use a pseudonym.) It was followed by over thirty more novels, many of them serialised in *Blackwood's Magazine* and *Longman's Magazine*, and by much other writing:

> I was then [1890] at my busiest. I was pouring out at one and the same time novels, magazine stories, essays, poems, anything and everything. Referring to my literary record . . . I find that I have produced forty-five full-sized books, and may add that there are two smaller ones in the press at the present moment [1910] . . . In addition to other work, I was for four years London Correspondent of the New York *Critic*, for which I wrote a fortnightly budget of literary news . . . The articles had to be sent in punctually, and it will always be a source of triumph to me that such a born free-lance as myself should have faithfully fulfilled this binding engagement. (*Recollections*, p. 193)

What did all this industry amount to? Walford is probably the lightest of the novelists discussed here, but – as *Recollections* suggests and her novels confirm – a gifted and lively writer nevertheless. Compared to the turgid run-up of the stereotypical 'Victorian novel', the opening lines of *Mr Smith* have remarkable confidence and style:

> A short, stout, grey man.
> Mr Smith.
> The butcher was disappointed that he wasn't a family. (*Mr. Smith*, p. 2)

Not just the butcher but everyone in the small town of Eastworld has formed an advance opinion of this incomer who has built a new house on the Hill.

'They do say he has twenty thousand a-year' [says Mrs Hunt, the doctor's wife].
'No, Polly, it's ten [says her husband]. It has come down to ten since he arrived.'
(*Mr Smith*, p. 14)

He doesn't fit any of their preconceptions, but he is a well-off bachelor, just turned fifty, and Mrs Hunt is desperate to catch him for one of her daughters. It is likely however that the bold Tolleton girls will get in first. (The brash *nouveau riche* Mr Tolleton, in fact, has nipped in and become the first to call on the newcomer, even as debate rages about whether this honour should go to the rector or the doctor.)

Helen Tolleton wants a rich husband and makes a determined play for Mr Smith. He appears to be attracted to her; has he been taken in by this hussy? No, it seems that he sees a gentler, nicer Helen behind the bold facade, and, almost in spite of herself, Helen begins to appreciate his true worth. It is a delicate, understated process, so unobtrusive that, when Mr Smith dies suddenly and an engagement ring is found in his pocket, no one – not even Helen – is quite sure who was to have received it. In the wake of his death people learn much more about Mr Smith. 'They did not want him when he came, as the postmaster said, but they knew what he was when he was gone' (*Mr Smith*, p. 273).

The ring was indeed for Helen and she acknowledges the difference his life and death have made to her. She is now the Helen he alone saw, and she marries an equally nice young man (who happily comes into a title). A small-scale novel, then, but unexpectedly sensitive; one can see why John Blackwood snapped it up, and how Walford went on to gain her undoubted contemporary popularity.

Innes Adair remarks in 1898 in *The Scots Pictorial* that 'Mrs Walford's novels seem to have a firm hold on all classes of readers'.[14] (*Recollections* tells us that these readers included Mr Gladstone and Queen Victoria herself. The Queen loved *Pauline* and wept over *Leddy Marget*, though Walford suspected she could not quite take on board the over-sprightly heroine of *The Baby's Grandmother*.) Adair approvingly observes of Walford:

> In the fair British matron with her children [of whom she had seven] growing up to manhood and womanhood around her, you will look in vain for the attributes of the 'New Woman' . . .
> [Her books] may not addle your brains on questions difficult to name and as difficult to understand as some of our female writers do . . .

He does not specify the writers he means, but if he had discovered the work of Walford's near-contemporary Flora Annie Steel, then or a few years later, some salutary addling might well have occurred.

Flora Annie Steel (1847–1929)

Flora Annie Steel was born in Harrow, but moved at the age of nine to Forfar, where her father was sheriff clerk. Flora was one of eleven children, 'all healthy, strong Scottish children, half Lowland and half Highland', as she wrote in her self-aware autobiography *The Garden of Fidelity* at the very end of her long life. Her mother, in the intervals between defusing her father's quick temper, taught all the children to play cards so that they would not lose money at the table in later life. 'My children may be rooks, but they shall never be pigeons,' this gifted and charming lady would declare.[15]

Flora was more conventionally educated by governesses (one of whom told her later that she had as a child 'quite appalling energy') and at a private school in Brussels, where she was declared '*diligente mais point gracieuse*'. She had made up her mind to be a doctor (Elizabeth Garrett Anderson having qualified in 1865), but instead married at twenty. She deals briskly with that:

> Why I married I cannot say: I never have been able to say. I do not think either of us was in love. I know I was not; I never have been. That is a sad fact, but it has to be faced. It has not made life any the less entrancing. (*The Garden of Fidelity*, p. 27)

(Though her daughter, completing Steel's autobiography for the press, added a postscript: 'To [my father] my mother was the one entirely right thing in this world.')

Her husband was in the Indian Civil Service, and they sailed for Madras immediately after the wedding. She was teasingly called 'Steel's baby bride', but we may feel that those who thus teased her did not know her very well: 'Many many women of my ignorantly-kept generation have told me that their honeymoon was spent in tears and fears. Mine was not. I simply stared' (*The Garden of Fidelity*, p. 28).

And on the Indian stations, where she was sometimes the only European woman, she rode with her husband through his district, becoming intimately acquainted with the life and customs of what was then northern India (now partly Pakistan). Later she met women in purdah, and – armed with information not available to men – took up the cause of the education of Indian women, with the far-off goal of emancipation in view.

When, aged forty-two, she returned to Britain, she approached a writing career with all her customary energy. Her early story 'Lal' was rewritten and rejected several times, but: 'Having made up my mind it was worth printing, I determined it should be so, and having exhausted all the minor magazines I tried the major ones, beginning with *Macmillan's*' (*The Garden of Fidelity*, p. 193). They accepted it and asked for more. Macmillan then published her first novel *Miss Stuart's Legacy* (not her chosen title, she points out, but she seems to have let it go for once). Mowbray Morris of *Macmillan's Magazine* – who thought for three years that his correspondent F. A. Steel was a man – was 'kindness itself', though 'He told me once in after years that he had never been set upon so fiercely as he was by me when he ventured to make a slight alteration in my work' (*The Garden of Fidelity*, p. 194).

Steel set some of her novels in Scotland, but her distinctive contribution probably lies in her series of Indian novels, among them *The Potter's Thumb* (1894) and *The Hosts of the Lord* (1900). She won the recognition of her time with *On the Face of the Waters* (1896), her novel of the Indian Mutiny, which had been in her thoughts 'for many long years – in a way ever since I came out to India'. The Northern India she knew had not changed greatly since 1857, and she had heard tales of the Mutiny from both the Punjabi and the British sides. In 1894 she returned to India to read through boxes of documents and meet descendants of the Mogul dynasty in Delhi.

In the preface to *On the Face of the Waters* Steel declares with characteristic vigour that she has not allowed fiction to interfere with fact 'to the slightest degree'. Every incident in the Mutiny has been reported exactly, right down to the weather on the day, and everything said by historical characters is based on their own writings or on eyewitness reports. There is a fictional story, of course, but we are not to think its events overdrawn: 'An Englishwoman *was* concealed in Delhi, in the house of an Afghan, and succeeded in escaping to the Ridge just before the siege. I have imagined another, that is all' (*On the Face of the Waters*, p. vi). As to the title, which had come to her at a very early stage:

When you ask an uneducated native of India why the Great Rebellion came to pass, he will, in nine cases out of ten, reply: 'God knows! He sent a Breath into the World'. From this to a Spirit moving on the face of the waters is not far. (*On the Face of the Waters*, p. viii)

The result is a fine, thoughtful, eventful novel, quite as full of authentic colour as any Kipling work. Perhaps Buchan too is foreshadowed in one of the central characters, Jim Douglas, an ex-army officer, cashiered through no fault of his own, and now a spy. But the female characters too play a full part in the story. Through flighty, clever Alice Gissing, and quieter Kate Erlton who undergoes the concealment-and-escape adventure, we gain a woman's experience as we seldom do in Buchan.

Above all, Steel, thanks to her knowledge of India, is understanding and considerate of both races involved in the Mutiny. Her purpose as outlined in the preface is clear and beautifully expressed:

I have tried to give a photograph – that is, a picture in which the differentiation caused by colour is left out – of a time which neither the fair race nor the dark one is ever likely quite to forget or to forgive. (*On the Face of the Waters*, p. viii)

Throughout, as her autobiography makes clear, Flora Annie Steel retained her interest in social problems, particularly those affecting women. She comes across to us as something of a Naomi Mitchison fifty years ahead of her time. Though not militant in the cause, she was, of course, a supporter of women's suffrage: 'All my life I have been keen, not so much on the rights, as on the wrongs of women' (*The Garden of Fidelity*, p. 265). As she grew older, she began to enquire more and more deeply into the position of women, looking for the reasons behind their assignation to inferior status in both historical and contemporary times. She published a book on the subject, *The Curse of Eve*. Underpinning her research was a strong sense of her own individuality, 'the ultimate Self', a personality she acknowledged and valued.

But – like Mitchison, and like Margaret Oliphant – she acknowledged also the operation of forces beyond herself, beyond the rational world. One 'pouring wet day in Aberdeenshire' she sat down to work on a story which wasn't going well.

While I was considering I became conscious of a figure beside me, conscious, not with the physical, but with the mind's eye. A figure in the white uniform of an Indian railway guard. The uniform was soiled and crumpled, the brass buttons tarnished; the man middle-aged, middle-sized, stoutish, with a corn-coloured beard, a red face, and clear blue eyes. I often fancy I should know him again if I saw him. (*The Garden of Fidelity*, p. 197)

With the uncanny verisimilitude found in dreams, he introduced himself as Nathaniel James Craddock, and proceeded to tell Steel, word for word, a story called 'The Permanent Way'. She was told later that it was one of the best she had done.

Nathaniel returned twice to tell her other stories, also 'good ones, better than most I turn out'. She knew no one of his name or appearance, but did have a solution for the puzzle. 'For the present, I keep that to myself', she says, and unfortunately never did reveal it. She died just before her autobiography was published in 1929; ninety years after *Holiday House* and nine years after *Open the Door!*

These are merely four of the Scottish women fiction writers of the nineteenth century whose work has by and large been forgotten. The *Scottish Fiction Reserve Directory* lists innumerable names of writers whose fiction is held in Scottish libraries. Clearly, there is a massive task of reassessment to be undertaken by a future generation of scholars.

Notes

1. See, for example, Moira Burgess, *Scottish Fiction Reserve Directory*, 2nd edn (National Library of Scotland, Edinburgh, 1986) and the *Wellesley Index to Victorian Periodicals*.
2. See entry for Barr in *Who Was Who 1916–1928* and for Kennedy in the *Dictionary of National Biography (DNB)*.
3. D. Walker Brown, *Clydeside Litterateurs* (Carter & Pratt, Glasgow, 1897), pp. 33–8.
4. The writers discussed in this chapter were prolific: other work not referred to in this chapter is contained in the general bibliography.
5. Lucy Bethia Walford, *Recollections of a Scottish Novelist* (Williams & Hargate, London, 1910; reissued Kylin Press, Waddesdon, Bucks, 1984), pp. 15–18.
6. See her preface to *Holiday House* from which the other quotations in this paragraph also come.
7. Literary Manuscripts Collection, The Mitchell Library, Glasgow, AL4, p. 161.
8. Henrietta Keddie, *Three Generations* (John Murray, London, 1911).
9. Both anecdotes are found in 'Henrietta Keddie ("Sarah Tytler")', *Scots Pictorial* 1 (January 1898), 354–5.
10. Francis Russell Hart, *The Scottish Novel: A Critical Survey* (John Murray, London, 1978), pp. 109–13.
11. 'Dogberry', 'Under the Reading Lamp: *St Mungo's City*', *Quiz*, 15 August 1884, p. 230.
12. *The Scots Pictorial*, 1 January 1898.
13. Hart, *The Scottish Novel*, p. 112.
14. Innes Adair, 'Mrs L. B. Walford', *The Scots Pictorial*, 19 November 1898, pp. 271–2.
15. Flora Annie Steel, *The Garden of Fidelity* (Macmillan, London, 1929).

13

Elizabeth Grant

Peter Butter

I

'It's the good girls who keep the diaries; the bad girls never have the time.' Elizabeth Grant (1797–1885) was not a bad girl, though a wilful one; but it seems that she had not the time to keep a diary regularly until 1845 when she was a good middle-aged lady. For she says that when compiling her *Memoirs of a Highland Lady* she had 'no memoranda of any sort to guide me' (M, I, p. 234).[1] If, as there is no reason to doubt, this is true, she had an extraordinary capacity for visual recall – of large numbers of persons, their characters, appearance, clothes, and of scenes, especially interiors. She is, however, no Boswell; she remembers, or cares to tell, comparatively little of what people said, even when in her Irish journal she is writing about current happenings. In general she is more concerned with what can be seen than with the inner life. 'These Memoirs are but the fair outside, after all, a deal is hid, both as regards myself and others, that it would be painful to record and worse than useless to remember' (M, II, p. 245). Fortunately she sometimes transcends this limitation.

Though having no memoranda for the *Memoirs* she does tell of having written, at about the age of seventeen, a journal of daily doings great and small to send to an aunt in England to show the happiness of life in the Highlands. When her father read it he was so bewildered, 'unused to that poetick or portraitick style of writing, it was not known at that period, that he judged the wisest thing to be done with so imaginative a brain was to square it a bit by rule and compass'. He began to teach her mathematics, 'an entrancing study', in order to 'strengthen the understanding sufficiently to give it power over the fancy' (M, I, p. 331). The flights of fancy in these adolescent writings were chastened, but the imaginative brain lived on, complementing memory. Like all the best autobiographies the *Memoirs* at their best are imaginative recreations of the past, not just feats of memory.

Though she published little, and that only to raise money in hard times, Elizabeth Grant was a lifelong writer. Apart from the adolescent journal for her aunt, during her early life she often started journals for her mother or sisters when separated from them, and regretted that she had not continued them. In her early twenties during an illness she wrote 'essays, short tales, and at length a novel. I don't suppose they were intrinsically worth much, and I am sure I do not know what has become of them, but the venture was invaluable. I tried higher flights afterwards with success when help was more wanted' (M,

I, p. 168). Help was certainly wanted during her final winter at the Doune (1826–7) with her mother and sister Mary. They had hardly any money, lived mainly off the land, and had to sell things to buy groceries. By the light of bits of candle stuck on a nail she and Mary wrote during the long nights, and made over £40 from *Fraser's Magazine* and *The Inspector*, enough to pay some debts and enable them to travel to London on the way to India. I do not know whether she wrote anything from then until the beginning of 1840, when she began her Irish journal which was continued, with gaps, until her death in 1885. Two selections from this journal have been published, both from the period 1840–50.[2] During another period of hardship during the Irish potato famine she contributed about a score of articles, descriptions of travel and sketches of Scottish and Irish life to *Chambers' Edinburgh Journal* (1846–7), and *Howitt's Journal* (1850). In 1850 she planned to write a novel, and thought of rubbing up and republishing her sketches of the Highlands, written earlier for *The Inspector*. Most important, between 1846 and 1854, concurrently with describing her present life in the Irish journal, she compiled her account of her early life up to 1830.[3]

II

The *Memoirs* is much her best work. Both it and the *Irish Journal* have a spontaneity and sparkle lacking in the works written for publication; and the *Memoirs* has the advantage of dealing with her times of most intense experience in youth and of that experience having been matured over the years without losing its freshness. The best parts of the *Memoirs* are those about the Highlands, 'that dear home of all our hearts'. It is not, as in many autobiographies, the child that comes across to us most vividly, but the sharp-eyed young lady. The years of infancy in Edinburgh, where she was born in 1797, left little trace; and during the time in London and the south of England between 1802 and 1812 she was not so much at home and part of a community as in the Highlands; there was less to appeal to her imagination. It was not until 1812 that the family settled at the Doune of Rothiemurchus, though the place was already familiar from several summer holidays and a long stay in 1808–9. It is with the eyes of the adolescent girl, complemented by the intelligence of the middle-aged writer, that we see the life of the Doune and of the surrounding community.

Both are shown unsentimentally, with realism as well as affection. The children were subjected to quite unnecessary hardships, and the deficiencies of their education and of their parents are unsparingly criticised. In winter they rose at half past six

> without candle, or fire, or warm water . . . and really in the highland winters, when the breath froze on the sheets, and the water in the jugs became cakes of ice, washing was a cruel necessity . . . As we could play our scales well in the dark, the two pianofortes and the harp began the day's work. How very near crying was the one whose turn set her at the harp I will not speak of; the strings cut the poor cold fingers so that the blisters often bled. (M, I, p. 221)

Their governess was an ignorant woman 'totally unfitted to try to direct us'. Their mother was often ill and bad-tempered, and did not show the children much affection. 'She never much cared for me', thought Elizabeth. The father on the other hand did love the children, and could be a charming companion. 'He was the King of all our romping plays', and his 'voice was the herald of joy to us'. Elizabeth loved him; but even before his financial irresponsibility was revealed was able to see some of his defects. He was despotic, impatient, unperceptive of her character and needs, sometimes even cruel as when he whipped the children to make them drink their milk at breakfast. A characteristic mixture of an almost ruthless realism with sensibility is shown in a passage on what happened after she heard of the death of a cousin, Patrick Grant:

> I, all unthinking, and very sorry, for Patrick had been very kind to us, went straight to the drawing room with my sad news. My Mother immediately went off into hysterics, was carried to bed, and lost her baby – all which was represented to me by my father as a consequence of my extreme want of consideration . . . I was very much grieved at my thoughtlessness . . . and with many tears promised to be for ever more cautious in all cases. We had none of us an idea that another baby was expected and the affliction in the schoolroom was quite distressing at the disappointment – for a day. (M, I, pp. 255–6)

This affliction lasted but a day; and all the descriptions of the young Grants' afflictions do not destroy, rather authenticate, the overall impression of happiness conveyed – the delight in freedom, in the beauty of the country, above all in people. In her experience of nature Elizabeth was no Wordsworth (I do not remember any reference to Wordsworth in her writings), her love not moving on from the 'glad animal movements' of youth to any 'sense sublime' of mystical presence or moral influence. Her best descriptions are not of the beautiful scenes round the Doune, certainly not of the mountains, but of houses, especially interiors, and of people. I was about to say that she was more a Jane Austen than a Wordsworth; and that would be partly true. The ingredients for a Jane Austenish novel are present in her portrayal of the home life of the Doune – irony, wit, intelligence, firm moral judgements with sympathy, strong sensibilities in the main kept in check, the charm of young girls, picnics, theatricals and the like. But the surroundings of the Doune were very different from those of Chawton, and Elizabeth's sympathies had a wider social range. Her sense of human dignity in her poorer neighbours has more in common with Wordsworth than with Jane Austen. For instance, she tells of 'the only child of a poor widow, Christian Grant, a fine young man named Allan', who was sent to open the Loch Ennich sluice gates for the timber floating:

> It was a wild night, wind and hail changing to snow, and he had eleven or twelve miles to go through the forest full of paths, and across the heath that was trackless. Poor old Christy. She gave him a hot supper, put up a bannock and a little whiskey for him, and wrapped his plaid well round him. She looked after him in the driving sleet as he left the warm house. Such risks were common, no one thought about them. Early in the morning down came the water . . . and the floating went merrily on, but Allan did not return . . . When evening came on and no word of him, a party set out in search, and they found him at his post, asleep seemingly, a bit of bannock and the empty flask beside him. He was quite dead. The mother never recovered her reason. The shock brought on brain fever, and that left her strangely excited for a while. After that she calmed . . . The first sensible action she did after her long months of darkness was to arrive at the Doune one morning and set herself to pluck the fowl. Every one was of course kind to her, so she came next day, and from that time never failed to arrive regularly when the family was at home . . . She never would remain all night, preferring her little cabin on Druieside, to which she returned cheerfully except on stormy nights, when she would shake her head very sadly, and sometimes let fall

tears. She never mentioned her son. My Mother never let her want for anything. (M, I, pp. 274–5)

If this were not so good as it is, in its directness and economy, one would say that it would form the basis for a Wordsworth poem. Wordsworthian also is the story of a young shepherd lost in the snow on a winter night:

> It was not till late autumn when our gamekeeper was on the Braeriach shooting grouse, that he saw seated on a shelf of rock midway down a precipice a plaided figure. It was all that was left of the missing shepherd . . . and his Colly dead beside him . . . His widow was past all knowledge of his fate; her anxiety had brought on premature childbirth, fever ensued, and though she recovered her strength in a degree, her mind was quite gone. She lived in the belief of the speedy return of her husband, went cheerfully about her usual work, preparing all things for him . . . Sometime towards evening she would look wearily round and sigh heavily, and wander a little in her talk, but in the morning she was early up and busy as ever. She was never in want, for every one helped her; but though she was so much pitied, she was in their sober way much blamed. The highlanders are fatalists . . . We must 'dree our weird', all of us, and 'tis a 'flying in the face of providence' to break the heart for God's inflictions. They feel keenly too; all their affections are very warm and deep; still, they are not to be paraded. A tranquil manner is a part of their good breeding, composure under all circumstances essential to the dignity of character common to all of the race. (M, I, pp. 277–8)

In telling these and similar stories Elizabeth is more than the witty observer of outsides; she enters imaginatively into what she has seen or been told.

Her picture of the surrounding society has the same combination of realism and affection as her portrayal of her home and family. She shows the poverty, the hardships, the excessive dram-drinking, the prevalence of illegitimacy; and, more prominently, the dignity of character, the sense of community – the bereaved mother and widow are looked after, the products of irregular unions uncensoriously called 'accidentals'. There was a strong sense of class, but also more mingling of classes than later. Feudal hospitality was offered to all at the clan chief's at Castle Grant, and on a humbler scale at the laird's at the Doune. 'A few candles lighted up bare walls at short warning, fiddles and whiskey punch were always at hand, and then gentles and simples reeled away in company . . . a highlander never forgets his place, never loses his inborn politeness, never presumes upon favour' (M, I, p. 48).

Apart from the hall and the dance floor another place where all met was the kirk. The Minister came to the kirk near the Doune only once in three weeks – which was just as well, since he had only two sermons, one on charity, the other on undue regard for the vanities of life. Yet he was a learned man, and liked. 'On the day he was expected, the people began gathering early, forming little knots moving slowly on, visiting . . . stopping to talk.' First there was a service in Gaelic (how many Gaelic speakers are there in that area now?), after which the laird's family entered for the English service beginning with a psalm:

> serious severe screaming quite beyond the natural pitch of the voice, a wandering search after the air by many who never caught it . . . The dogs seized the occasion to bark, for they always came to the kirk with the rest of the family, and the babies to cry . . . When the

minister could bear the din no longer he popt up, touched the precentor's head, and instantly all sound ceased.' (M, I, pp. 248, 249–50)

Then there was a prayer during which the congregation stood; then one of the two sermons, during which Elizabeth could give her attention to the well-dressed girls and the men and old women taking snuff. She does not mean to mock the proceedings; but the value of what she shows is social – the gathering of all the people in a communal act – more than religious. She says that her neighbours were not much troubled by the kittle theological questions which had so vexed the puritanic south:

> Our mountains were full of fairy legends, old clan tales, forebodings, prophecies, and other superstitions, quite as much believed in as the Bible. The shorter catechism and the fairy stories were mixed up somehow together to form the innermost faith of the highlander, a much gayer and less metaphysical character than his Saxon tainted countryman. (M, I, p. 253)

This was before the fragmentation of the Church of Scotland, which contributed, along with social and economic changes, to the destruction of the sense of community. Visiting the Doune in 1846 Elizabeth felt that 'the whole condition of our once united district' had been altered. The few Grandees shut themselves rigorously up, and each class did not notice the one above or below. She writes, less vividly, about the social and economic changes in three articles in *Chambers Journal* in 1846–7; 'My Father the Laird', 'My Brother the Laird' and 'My Nephew the Laird'. The third of these is probably the only place where she deals with the Clearances, the process which affected Highlanders more than any other in her lifetime. Presumably they had not affected her area before she left the Doune in 1827. Nevertheless it is odd that she does not show any awareness of them in *Memoirs*; one suspects some wilful blindness (she must have heard talk about them in Edinburgh? Or perhaps not much? Was golden age Edinburgh oblivious of the social changes taking place around it – of the effects of the industrial revolution as well as of the Clearances?). In 'My Nephew the Laird' the nephew (not corresponding exactly to any one in her life) has in some ways made great improvements on the estate. It is more efficiently run, and those who remain on it are more prosperous; but one effect has been that some families have lost their small holdings and emigrated to America. She regrets this, and the passing of the old ways, the old gaieties; but she cannot be too indignant about the emigration because she and her husband were acting in a similar way in Ireland.

III

The Grants moved to Edinburgh in 1814, and were based there until 1820. Place and dates make us think of Edinburgh's golden age, the New Town, Scott, a man of genius at every street corner, the *Edinburgh Review*, *Blackwood's Magazine*, and Tory dominance even after the death of Dundas in 1811. We should not be disappointed that the young Elizabeth was not centrally interested in any of these. She lived in a succession of houses in the New Town, but says little about its architecture or about the contrast with the Old. At her age she was naturally mainly concerned with whether the houses were comfortable and well adapted for giving parties. Scott she was never in company with; 'he went very little out, and when he did go he was not agreeable, generally sitting very silent, looking dull and listless, unless an occasional flash lighted up his heavy countenance'. But Mrs Scott was much in evidence, driving about in her Barouche and at parties, where she often appeared the worse for drink (more likely, opium). The general inferiority of Scott's family (young Walter a 'good-natured goose', Anne 'very ugly and very pretending') accounted, Elizabeth thought, for the 'insipidity of his ideal gentlemen and ladies' (M, II, pp. 73–4). These comments are prejudiced – Whig against Tory, old landed family against new. But her unfashionable dislike of *Waverley* perhaps has some validity – 'the hero contemptible, the two heroines unnatural and disagreeable, and the whole idea given of the highlands so utterly at variance with truth' (M, II, p. 72). She may well have thought her own portrayal of a Highland society – albeit in a different place and time – more authentic than Scott's. On the other hand one might say she is unperceptive about the effect Scott intends by use of his narrator.

She knew some of the notable people of the time, and heard, and no doubt contributed to, much intelligent and witty talk, but does not convey much sense of it. She does not show much interest in politics except when they impinged directly on the family, as when their house was stoned because of her father's support of Protection. The difference between Whig and Tory is treated as a social one, dividing Edinburgh into factions. If one wants discussion of larger themes one can go to Cockburn's *Memorials* (1856). The qualities of this part of *Memoirs* are different – spontaneity, directness, sharpness of observation and in the writing, a vivid picture of the excitement and boredom of an active social life among a wide variety of characters. But in comparison with the Highland chapters, there is some narrowness of focus and superficiality. There is not a sense of a whole society, only of particular groups. Though the many sharply-etched portraits are well-executed and entertaining, they are, one feels, a bit over-confident and lacking in nuance. But there was one incident in these years that compelled Elizabeth to go, briefly and reluctantly, beneath 'the fair outside'. She fell in love with a perfectly suitable young man and he with her, and was induced to break off the engagement for the absurdly inadequate reason that the fathers had quarrelled long ago. She submitted, with justifiable resentment; and to punish her mother embarked on a series of 'heartless flirtations, entered on purposely to end in disappointment'. When at the end of their time in Edinburgh the results of her father's imprudence began to be revealed and bailiffs came to the house, she was struck with guilt 'for that vile flippancy which had hurt my own character and my own reputation while it tortured my poor mother . . . Then it seemed as if a veil fell from between my giddy spirits and real life, and the lesson I read began my education' (M, II, p. 151). It is like *Persuasion*, but without the happy ending – or rather, without the same happy ending. The story continued into marriage in India with elderly, asthmatic Colonel Smith, and her on the whole happy life with him in Ireland – an ending Jane Austen would have approved, as she would approve Elizabeth's elegant handling of the unromantic courtship. Cupid 'threw shafts and bolts away as unsuitable to a staid Brigadier and a maiden past her prime. His object was to touch the lady's reason, which he did . . . and the parents too, a matter affected principally by the Irish acres, warranted not to be bog. Who would have thought a marriage thus systematically arranged could have turned out so well' (M, II, p. 244).

IV

The Irish acres turned out to be a bit boggy after all, and not worth the £1200 a year expected. Elizabeth settled bravely to work through difficult times for her often ailing colonel, her children and the tenants and workers on the estate. Emma had accepted a less prosperous Mr Knightley (a comparison she herself makes – *IJ*, p. 101) in a less attractive environment; loved him, and was on the whole content. 'I have sobered myself down to be quite happy with "good home brewed ale" and to think of Highland days as a glass of champaign not often attainable' (*IJ*, p. 15).

There is still sparkle, however, in her writing – on a wide range of topics, of which I have space to comment on only a few. For the historian there is great interest in her detailed account of life on the estate during the potato famine of 1845–9. She and her husband did their best, as they saw it, for their people – providing food and clothing, keeping as many people as possible in employment, draining, improving methods of farming, etc. She resumed periodical writing to support her giving, and sometimes had hardly any money in hand for her own household's necessary expenses. But David Thomson in the Introduction to his edition of the *Journals* criticises her for joining in the landlords' policy of eviction. 'We determined', she writes, 'to get rid of all the little tenants and to encrease the larger farms – and we did it – but not at once – just watched for opportunities and managed this delicate business without annoying anyone' (*IJ*, p. x). Thomson acknowledges that the evictions on the Smith estate were conducted more humanely than most, but blames them for insensitivity to peoples' attachment to their land and for turning a blind eye to the bad conditions on emigrant boats and to the small chance of the emigrants' getting work at their destination. I cannot judge of their actions; but it is true that she does not in the *Journal* show the affection and respect for her neighbours that she did for the Highlanders. In the 'busy practical present instead of the poetick past' she walks round the estate, visiting and helping every one as well as she can; but there is not the imaginative entering into the lives and feelings of others that was present in *Memoirs*. In her dialogues 'Mrs Wright's Conversations with her Irish Acquaintance', Mrs Wright appears as a bossy lady patronising her inferiors.[4] The name might suggest irony, but she comes through as simply, irritatingly 'right'.

In her comments on politics in the *Journal* Elizabeth shows the contradictions often found in the aristocratic radical. Some of her opinions are surprisingly radical. Not only was she scornful of 'our little Queen' and her husband ('a sad stick'), but also opposed to monarchy. 'When we are fit for further equality this magnificent remnant of barbarism will be laid aside like other worn out institutions' (*IJ*, p. 95). She thought that great changes must come slowly, for the world is not ready for them. 'But come they must as intelligence progresses, the present aristocracy must fall as the feudal system fell when its power is no longer wanted' (*IJ*, pp. 232–3). The defects of upper-class families, including her own, she attributes largely to bad education. 'Eton, Harrow, and other celebrated publick schools nurse the vices which are matured at Oxford, Cambridge, Edinburgh . . . When I think of my brothers I tremble for my son. I would not have him wade through the mud that nearly choked both' (*IJ*, p. 209). At about the same time as these comments she contributed an article to the very radical *Howitt's Journal*,[5] to which her aunt Mary Gillies also contributed an article on the misery of the London poor. This was the decade of *Past and Present*, *Shirley*, and *Mary Barton*; and from a distance Elizabeth shared the worries about the condition of England question. But in her own domain she remained the benevolent patrician, determined that her children should take their proper place in society and make suitable marriages.

Like the *Memoirs*, the *Journal* is concerned mainly with the fair (and dark) outside; but in some moving passages she allows herself to touch on what was usually hidden, painful to record and to remember. Her parents had deprived her, without the slightest good reason, of her early lover; her father, by his irresponsibility, of her early home. In 1849 it became clear that these were not all their ill-doings. At the time of the financial crash in 1827 Elizabeth and sister Mary were induced by falsehood into signing a document which might have left them penniless. After 1827 their father had not remitted, out of his large Indian income, the money to pay the interest on a loan: 'I can excuse all this from his bad education and the unprincipled society he had been thrown amongst. But I won't agree to call all the chicanery and all the deception and all the careless disregard of others . . . as only a "pity"' (as sister Jane had done). Brother William had 'behaved just as ill as father'. He had not taken care of his sisters' interests, and had involved himself in massive debts as a result of the failure of the Calcutta Bank of which he was a Director. 'It makes the heart ache to think of what these two talented men might have been' (*IJ*, p. 443). This forthrightness is admirable, as is her ability to endure without becoming embittered. When William came to stay he was kindly received and helped; and she continued to think of her father with gratitude for 'the value of early constant intercourse with such a mind as his' (*IJ*, p. 16). An intense internal drama of conflicting emotions is hinted at. The opportunity to vent these emotions in the *Journal* was perhaps her salvation.

Does one's heart ache when one thinks of what this talented lady might have been? If so, the old lady looking serenely out of a late portrait rebukes one. She has made a success of her unromantic marriage and her boggy acres, and repels pity as impertinence. She has left a large amount of writing which is always entertaining, always well written, occasionally moving; has left authentic pictures of three different societies and sharply-observed sketches of a large number of people; has brought us close to her own honest, brave, caustic yet affectionate self. And yet one feels that there were capacities in the vivacious young lady and in the writer of the stories of the Highlanders lost in the mountains that were not fully developed. The keen eye and the quick intelligence endured, but the needs of the practical present blunted the imagination.

Notes

1. References to *Memoirs of a Highland Lady* (M) and to *The Highland Lady in Ireland* (IJ) are to the Canongate Classics editions.
2. *The Irish Journals of Elizabeth Smith 1840–1850*, ed. Thomson and McGusty (Oxford University Press, London, 1980); *The Highland Lady in Ireland*, ed. Pelly and Tod (Canongate, Edinburgh, 1991). The longer, Canongate, selection contains about a quarter of the whole.
3. *Memoirs of a Highland Lady* was published complete for the first time in 1988, edited by Tod (Canongate, Edinburgh, 1988). Her niece, Lady Strachey's, abridged editions (privately printed in Edinburgh, 1897; published by John Murray in 1898) contain most that the ordinary reader will want, but the Victorian lady imposes some censorship on the Georgian one. The 1911 edition is reduced by the omission of most of the Dutch and Indian material, as is the 1950 Albemarle Library edition edited by Angus Davidson.
4. *Chambers Edinburgh Journal*, XIV (1850), pp. 251–2, 261–3, 333–5, 396–8.
5. *Howitt's Journal* 26 (June 1847), 362–3.

14

Viragos of the Periodical Press: Constance Gordon-Cumming, Charlotte Dempster, Margaret Oliphant, Christian Isobel Johnstone

Ralph Jessop

The works of the critic are of their nature fugitive and ephemeral.[1]

Countless shelves of nineteenth-century periodical literature contain a vast range of disparate subjects providing windows onto a world at once familiar and strange, distinct and occult. The periodicals played important roles in informing the thought, general knowledge, political views, and literary tastes of nineteenth-century Britain. A large proportion of the many periodical writers were women who have been forgotten, their biographies unwritten and likely to remain so. A great many Scottish names appear in *The Wellesley Index to Victorian Periodicals* but as yet relatively few of these have even been positively identified as Scottish women.[2] We do know, however, that several Scots made substantial contributions to nineteenth-century periodical literature and, through their many writings, to the literary culture and society of Britain. Though some were better known as novelists, these workers in words all plied the trades of the periodicals: journalism, literary criticism, travel writing, and reviews of a diverse range of books across several subject boundaries. Such work is all too easily submerged by other literature and forgotten, a testament not to its limitations alone, but to our own. Among the most notable Scottish viragos of the periodical press were Christian Isobel Johnstone, Margaret Oliphant, Charlotte Dempster, and Constance Gordon-Cumming. It is the journalism of these women that I want to introduce and celebrate. I have chosen to discuss them by starting with the most recent first.

Constance Gordon-Cumming

Little seems to be known about Constance Frederica Gordon-Cumming (1837–1924), a Scottish traveller involved with the Church Missionary Society who published some sixteen books and pamphlets concerning her travels. She also contributed some thirty-six articles to *Blackwood's Magazine* (Maga) and other journals. With considerable journalistic skill she investigated religious practices, customs, history, work, and at times cast a romantic haze of adventure and scenic splendour over the places she visited in Japan, China, America, Ceylon, India, Scotland, and several other countries. In her 1882 article, 'Across the Yellow Sea', she recounts an adventurous journey from Peking to Nagasaki. After telling of her dangerous voyage she gives a brief account of the rise of Christianity in Japan during the sixteenth and seventeenth centuries, bloody in persecutions and martyrdoms.[3] In 'The Offerings of the Dead', she explores ancestor-worship in China and India, discussing Chinese customs, at times with evident disgust, claiming, for example, 'that Ancestor-worship lies at the root of the appalling female infanticide of China – a practice about which there is no concealment' with the provision of 'Baby-towers for the reception of the bodies'.[4]

In 'Wolves and Were-Wolves' she relates some tales of Russian peasant heroism in grappling with rabid wolves and gives an account of 'slaying the last wolf' in late seventeenth-century Scotland. Interestingly, she also claims that 'Breton peasants still believe implicitly in the real existence of the *Loup-Garou* – the demon Were-wolf' which she then continues to describe and characterise through discussing Were-wolf mythology.[5] Her fascination with the mysterious can also be detected in her rather credulous, selectively detailed report of a visit to a female spiritualist medium in Boston Massachusetts. She concludes the article by warning that those who pursue the subject of spiritualism 'soon find themselves plunged in an intricate . . . labyrinth in which light becomes darkness'.[6]

In sharp contrast to these interests in religious practices, customs, tales of adventure and the mysterious, Gordon-Cumming's 1884 article, 'The World's Oil Supply in the Nineteenth Century' rather surprisingly advocates, as a method for preventing shipwreck, literally pouring oil on stormy seas. She explains that 'pouring oil on troubled waters' is no mere metaphor. A certain Mr Shields had attempted in vain 'to stir up the authorities of Aberdeen to lay the oil apparatus, so as to guard the mouth of their most dangerous harbour'.[7] While this may sound quite far-fetched, Gordon-Cumming informs the reader that the practice was used at Folkestone and reported on favourably in the London papers. Her chief concern in this article, however, is with discovering sources of oil. An oil spot in the Gulf of Mexico, various oil-springs and petroleum fountains, a Pitch Lake on the island of Trinidad, a wide variety of oil sources and types, and American oil-drilling ventures and 'oil-cities' are described, prices and profits given in what turns out to be a thoroughly researched account of a fairly recent phenomenon, the late nineteenth century's quest for oil.

While this article clearly draws from her experiences as a traveller many of her articles fall more surely under the genre of travel-writing. In 'Notes of a Wanderer in Skye' Gordon-Cumming attempts in several places to eke out of otherwise dreary scenes of island poverty and abject hardship something of the picturesque for the artist-traveller equipped, like herself, with sketch pad. After some brief descriptions of the islanders' bothies, the article becomes more concerned with geological curiosities. The rock formations of basalt and oolite are depicted and recede behind mention of Skye's inevitable romantic mists, island tales and legends.[8] Her geological interests find fuller treatment in 'Granite Crags' which recalls her knowledge of the Moray Firth region, of the Inner Hebrides, the Cuillins of Skye, Arran's Goatfell, Orkney, Shetland, Northumbria, Cornwall, 'delightful months of pleasant gipsying' beneath the foothills of the Himalayas, ambitious journeys mountaineering, and travels in the Californian canyons.[9] Apart from her work as a travel writer, Gordon-Cumming also dabbled in book reviewing in her 1891 article, 'Musical Instruments and their Homes' which also drew on her knowledge of China.[10] Though Gordon-Cumming's travel-writing and journalism may have been fragmentary and ephemeral she was often a powerfully evocative writer whose extensive travels were tightly compressed into accounts that displayed a talent for research and the skill of subtly blending romance with reportage.

Charlotte Dempster

Charlotte Louisa Hawkins Dempster (1835–1913) was born at Forfar and educated at home by several masters including a professor of anatomy. After spending her late teens in Paris, she travelled to Italy, settling at Cannes in 1880.[11] She wrote several novels and published some thirty-nine articles mainly in the *Edinburgh Review*. Dempster's first article for the July 1861 number of the *Edinburgh* reviews with sure-footed competence and critical restraint three German works on Albrecht Dürer, emphasising the hardships of his life and resilience of his spirit though contradicting romantic claims concerning his death as a pauper.[12] In 'French Anti-Clerical Novels' she reviews two politically-motivated French novels, *Le Maudit* and *La Religieuse*, subversive in their anti-clericalism. Although Dempster sympathises with the anonymous author (Jean Hippolyte Michon), she disputes the moral rectitude of his inclusion of 'gross incidents, and still grosser innuendos' within the letters of one of his female characters, concluding of the author that 'He has either graduated in the worst class of French novels, or we must suppose that in constantly touching pitch his own mind has not escaped defilement'. With an eye for rhetorical strategies and for political import, Dempster claims that his 'objectionable vulgarity' is 'a powerful weapon in the hands of his enemies' and goes on to link the author's work to religious tendencies for reform 'in every European country'.[13]

Some eight years later in 1872, Dempster reviewed eleven recent books on the art of lace-making, arguing for its status as one of the Fine Arts. The article is concerned with categorising the several kinds of lace by describing the methods of production, discussing the problems of identifying its origin, and outlining certain details of the history of the art in relation to its production and fashions. Referring to Matthew Arnold, Dempster laments and argues against British philistinism with regard to the art.[14] Beyond such aesthetic topics, implicitly connected with political questions concerning the status of women, her historiographical and scholarly interests are evident in such reviews as 'The Fall of the House of Stuart'.[15]

A cultivated intellectual, a scholar, and as all such women of the time, entirely off-campus and anonymous (as were most reviewers), she had a fair degree of intellectual freedom. This is evident in her 1883 article, 'Persecution of the Jews', in which she writes against the barbarity of anti-Semitic persecution. Though she attempts a rational explanation of the phenomenon, she denounces propositions and practices of genocide and 'Jew-baiting' as 'not only a monstrous injustice, but . . . an outrage on decency, a darkening of the fair face of Christendom'. But, as one might expect of many a Victorian writer, she goes on to reveal her view of Christian superiority, Judaism being 'a step to the knowledge of Him', and she advocates an alternative way of eradicating the Jewish faith: 'The conversion of the Jews . . . must be the result of the words and deeds of the whole Christian world. Equality before the law, charity, and good will are solvents which nothing can resist'.[16] In her assumption of Christian superiority, she did not entirely expunge the germ of anti-Semitic prejudice from her own Christian perspective though she condemns it in others. However, Dempster was a subtle thinker and may have been tonguing her cheek at the extreme improbability of 'The Conversion of the Jews' – if so, encouraging the bigot and anti-Semite to treat the Jew with 'Equality before the law, charity, and good will' was perhaps a nice way to seduce some Christians into unintended good actions.

Margaret Oliphant

Margaret Oliphant (1828–97) is gradually becoming one of the better-known Victorian women novelists. Her name appears in all of the relevant biographical dictionaries, several of her novels are available in paperback editions, and during the last thirty years there has been a revival of interest in her life and work.[17] Within a prolific output of contributions to the periodical press, she wrote reviews of fiction, poetry, biographies, popular theology and science, art criticism, histories, discussions on the woman question. According to Elizabeth Jay she wrote more than 400 articles.[18] It should therefore come as no surprise that she was reluctant to define the term 'literature', claiming that 'To confine its meaning . . . is about as exclusive and limited a notion as it is to confine that other term society to the fashionable world'.[19] Inheriting the encyclopedic enlightenment intellect of so many Scotch periodical reviewers and no doubt regarding herself as belonging to that breed of spirited and outspoken Scottish women she celebrated, Oliphant reviewed a diverse range of texts with confidence and pugnacity. In her 1855 article, 'Modern Light Literature', she writes: 'The art of criticism is essentially an art of fault-finding', going on to claim that 'we like the crash and the dust of genuine demolishment'.[20]

In this article John Ruskin receives severe censure. Popularly supposed 'a great authority and influence in art' criticism, Oliphant 'cannot for a moment consent that he is so', denouncing him on almost every page of her review for his pretensions, contrasted with the favoured humility, and 'clearer insight' of another critic, Mrs Jameson ('MLL', p. 702). Enjoying the cut and thrust of her criticism, Oliphant denounces Ruskin for having 'no true satisfaction in another man's reputation, unless he himself had a hand in making it' and she outrightly accuses him of plagiarising the work of Augustus Welby Pugin ('MLL', p. 707; p. 716). In a later article, Oliphant criticises the simplistic idealism of Ruskin's utopian prescriptions for men and women in his *Ethics of Dust*.[21]

She scores many hits against John Stuart Mill, some of which are casually thrown off, such as her gibe at his notorious early education, describing him as 'a little monster', and, never missing an opportunity, her quotation from Lord Neaves's satirical poem 'Stuart Mill on Mind and Matter'.[22] A later, wittily argumentative article provides a more sustained attack on Mill's advocacy of extending the franchise to women, displaying Oliphant's scepticism concerning the value of the vote and her distrust of Mill's championing of women's rights. She claims to speak for the majority of women but if her views against extending the franchise to women have become an anathema, this article seems to mark something of a change in her thinking as she begins to insist more strongly on the distinct nature of women and their separate sphere of work and to attack with a sneering sarcasm the prejudices of men, unimpressed by their weak abilities and need for female support.[23]

But although her periodical articles are often sharply critical and denunciatory she had favourites and could also give balanced appraisal. Walter Scott, repeatedly praised in Oliphant's reviews, was regarded as the paradigm and paragon of fictional prose writers against whom she measured many others such as Edward Bulwer Lytton, calling Scott 'the greatest of all fictionists, past or present'.[24] In a much later article she writes, 'Miss Edgeworth was not so great as Sir Walter – who was?'[25] In 1855 Bulwer Lytton, the author of silver-fork novels famous in their day, particularly *Pelham* (1828), received Mrs Oliphant's somewhat qualified praise and was hailed some eighteen years later as 'the minstrel of the Gentleman'.[26] She recognised the great talents of Charles Dickens but could make some pointed criticisms of his work. She labels him 'a *class* writer, the historian and representative of one circle in the many ranks of our social scale . . . It is the air and the breath of middle-class respectability which fills the books of Mr Dickens'.[27]

Later praising the middle class as 'the strength of our country', this was by no means an entirely derogatory remark though it hints at his limitations and ties in nicely with some of her many complaints about his work ('CD', p. 452). For example, she is suspicious of Dickens's remedies for social ills, perhaps regarding his underlying middle-class biases as weakening his political philosophy and his art. *Hard Times* is detested for being theory-driven and is flawed by Dickens's 'lame and impotent conclusion', itself a failure to address 'the great question between the "hands" and their employers' ('CD', p. 456). She also complains about Dickens's tendency to caricature and make characters interesting merely by endowing them 'with some exaggerated peculiarity', a point she elaborates in a later article in which Wilkie Collins's *The Woman in White* is preferred to *Great Expectations* ('CD', p. 457; cf. p. 463).[28] But if Scott is supreme, Lytton great, Dickens undoubtedly a master yet capable of gross errors and suspicious as a champion of the poor, Oliphant is interestingly divided about the work of Charlotte Brontë. Clearly appalled by its declaration of sexual warfare, Oliphant nevertheless recognises and warms to the revolutionary power of Brontë's *Jane Eyre*, that 'fierce little incendiary', 'one of the most remarkable works of modern times'.[29]

Oliphant deals with several Scottish subjects in her reviews. Reconciled to and a supporter of the union between Scotland and England, she does not lend her support to Victorian Scottish nationalists' calls for Home Rule. However, her nationalist sympathies are evident in, for example, her 1867 review, 'The History of Scotland', in which she gives a lengthy quotation from the famous Declaration of Arbroath.[30] She views Scotland with a mixture of realism and sentimental pride as a picturesque theatre of tragedy and indomitability, mirth and agony, intellectual excellence and spirited physical adventure.[31] Her romance with Scotland was inextricably blended with her several attacks on English ignorance and misinterpretation of Scottish life and culture.

At times Oliphant resents English ignorance when it results in serious misrepresentation or misinterpretation.[32] She highlights some of the differences between England and Scotland, particularly the differences between their respective national churches.[33] English imitators of Scotch dialect, 'our native Doric' – the novelists Reade and Kingsley – are criticised for being '*too* Scotch to be genuine', their pretensions set against the work of Galt and Scott.[34] She was angered by English misinterpretations of the Carlyles' married life. In reviewing Jane Welsh Carlyle's posthumously published letters she argues against Froude's 'mistake and misconception of the most fundamental kind' of assuming Jane's 'immeasurable social superiority' over Thomas.[35] Reviewing Dean Ramsay's *Reminiscences of Scottish Life and Character*, Oliphant contradicts the 'southern heresy' of describing 'the Scotch character' as 'supernaturally reserved' by celebrating the 'outspoken, effusive, and humorous old maids of Scotland, quick of wit and of wrath, fearing nothing and nobody, dealing in the broadest sarcasms and sharpest repartees'.[36] However, though she values the distinctive outspokenness of Scottish women, in another article she dismisses as somewhat 'comic' seventeenth-century Scotland's 'paternal government' and its use of 'the joogs and branks' for punishing witches and scolds.[37] But if her sympathies lie with the wronged Countess of Buchan (whose horrific torture she condemns in her 1867 review 'The History of Scotland')[38] and not with the lot of ordinary women (the witches and scolds who revolted against 'paternal government' and had their tongues bridled by the branks), in an earlier review written in 1860 she celebrates ordinary Scottish womankind, though somewhat at the expense of their more outstanding figures:

> Scotland has or had a peculiar faculty in the production of womankind – womankind not of genius, but *character* – working not at the Fine Arts, or other money-making or fame-acquiring business, but mighty in the grand and ancient vocation of life! ('SNC', p. 722)

She relishes the picturesque scenes of Scottish life found in the rich, healthful gossiping and humour after church, '"the crack i' the kirkyard"' being valued by such women of *character* above the Kirk minister's sermon ('SNC', p. 726).

In this article Oliphant contradicts some other southern heresies including the still-current prejudice about Scottish meanness ('SNC', p. 727).[39] More importantly, she recounts several anecdotes illustrating Scottish humour along with some nice analyses of its peculiar nature as distinct from that of the English and French. Scottish humour, according to Oliphant, was spontaneous; no mere play on words, it 'breaks unexpectedly into the soberest discussions', relies on the auditor's imagination and the joke 'is delivered commonly with a dry quietness which makes it irresistible to those who can see, but betrays nothing to those who cannot' ('SNC', p. 729; p. 730). It is worth quoting just one of the anecdotes presented by Oliphant: an old aunt, annoyed by her nephew's dandyish fuss in dressing himself, asked the young man, '"Whaur's this ye're gaun, Robbie, that ye make sic a grand wark about your claes?" The young man lost temper, and pettishly replied, "I'm going to the devil!" – "Deed, Robbie, then," was the quiet answer, "ye needna be sae nice, *he'll just tak ye as ye are!*"' ('SNC', p. 729).

Against 'the uprooting of our old institutions' and the reforming *zeitgeist* her politics generally may be described as conservative in her adherence to the status quo, and, much in keeping with the political bias of Maga, High Tory in denouncing reformers.[40] In a sensitive short biography of the tragic life of the one-time famous charismatic Scottish preacher Edward Irving, her anti-democratic views find vent in her argument against the popular belief 'that the Church of Scotland is the most democratic of all corporations'.[41] Like so many Scots in the nineteenth century she was a keen royalist ardently captivated by Queen Victoria. Flattered by the Queen's love of the Highlands and enshrinement of the family, Oliphant can see no flaw in Victoria's reign over Britain and the empire.[42] Though imperialist, when reflecting on the causes of the Indian Mutiny and how to prevent such future atrocities, she expresses regret at Britain's 'very little understanding of the mind, and thoughts, and meaning of [the Empire's] inhabitants'.[43] Imbued with a strong sense of the unassailable superiority of Christian doctrine and its value to humanity yet decidedly sceptical about the possibilities and worth of attempting to force trade links with the colonies, her imperialism is comparatively beneficent. Opposition to slavery is indicated in several articles, Dr Livingston's missionary 'enterprise' in Africa recruited to the cause as 'a directly Anti-slavery expedition'.[44]

Her moral views on the portrayal of evil in fiction and on sexuality are also conservative and provide a good preface to her views on sexual politics. She is highly sceptical about Dickens's portrayal of 'childish suffering', a scepticism that betrays her tendencies to glide over, ignore, or refuse to discuss in print the sordid abuses inherent in Victorian society.[45] But her concern about the dangers of over-emphasising societal evils in fiction seems to arise from a belief that fictive and non-fictive representations of a prevalent viciousness misrepresented human nature. Oliphant consistently opposes what might be termed the 'vicious fallacy': 'It is better to tell the story of the much-tried milkmaid, which is visibly a fiction, than to preach philosophical suggestions of universal wickedness, which are supposed to be true'.[46] She despises what she describes as Thackeray's theory that young men must be purged by passing through a phase of vice, a point she reiterated and elaborated in condemning the heterodox theology of Frederick Denison Maurice.[47]

She frequently casts a nostalgic eye back to vaguely described halcyon days of politeness, reserve, decorum, and political stability. Compared with the earlier and more radical writer, Christian Isobel Johnstone, Oliphant is conspicuously circumspect when touching on sexual morality or any issue relating to sex, as is evident in her veiled suggestions that the owners of those notorious hens which so plagued Thomas Carlyle with their cackle in Cheyne Row were some neighbouring prostitutes.[48] She can however be somewhat more blunt about sex, in particular when outraged at the depravity of a work such as Thomas Hardy's *Jude the Obscure*, which, in her 1896 article, 'The Anti-Marriage League', she regards 'as an assault on the stronghold of marriage'.[49] And yet she could deal with sensitivity and kindness towards those who, like Mary Ann Evans (George Eliot) and her lover G. H. Lewes, clearly broke Oliphant's code of sexual morality.[50]

Many of her views on the woman question and sexual politics generally may be discerned in her frequent remarks on the portrayal of women in literature – fictional and non-fictional. Oliphant always keeps a watchful eye on presentations of women and is quick to pounce on a depiction that degrades, insults, or deals in stereotypes. She thinks Walter Scott comes close to producing 'an individual woman' in Jeanie Deans; but Dickens, she feels, doesn't achieve his ambition to create a comparable heroine.[51] Thackeray's Blanche Amory, on the other hand, was, she felt, a gross insult to womankind ('T and HN', p. 90). Concerned that young women might emulate his characters, she condemns Thackeray for creating 'tender pretty fools' instead of 'rational creatures'. ('T and HN', p. 95). And yet in life she was clearly suspicious of some celebrated female intellectuals. Reviewing Harriet Martineau's autobiography in 1877, Oliphant repeatedly calls in question Martineau's honesty and concluded that 'she has been very much overrated as a writer; and . . . we find it very difficult to understand on what her great reputation was founded'.[52]

Discussing Charlotte Brontë's *Jane Eyre* in 1855, Oliphant declares that:

> It is but a mere vulgar boiling over of the political cauldron, which tosses your French monarch into chaos, and makes a new one in his stead. Here is your true revolution. France is but one of the Western Powers; woman is half of the world . . . Here is a battle which must always be going forward.[53]

Though such sentiments seem worthy of a radical feminist this is more by way of elucidation of Brontë's text, with its implicit declaration of the 'Rights of Woman', and its influence on other novelists and society than a sentiment which Oliphant wholeheartedly endorses. Yet she recognises the value of *Jane Eyre*'s reversal of so many confining assumptions concerning heroines and the portrayal of women in fiction.[54] Nostalgically recalling more genteel wooing than the rough manner of *Jane Eyre*'s Rochester, the 'chivalrous true-love which consecrated all womankind', Oliphant arguably wavers over the issue.[55] But she clearly deprecates some of the narrative practices of Brontë's imitators – such as Julia Kavanagh and Mrs Gaskell.[56] She later speaks out against fictional works that portray love as merely 'a certain act common to men and beasts' since such redescription confines love's endlessness, variety, and beauty.[57]

In attempting to understand Oliphant's position with regard to the woman question, one has to read her articles, 'The Laws Concerning Women' (1856), 'The Condition of Women' (1858), 'The Great Unrepresented' (1866), 'Mill *on the Subjection of Women*'

(1869), and 'The Grievances of Women' (1880). Drawing upon these articles and informed by her many remarks about gender in other articles, one can provide an outline of her views on several key issues relating to the woman question. In her brief discussion of the subject Merryn Williams suggests that Oliphant's views are more complex than the simply anti-feminist standpoint she could too easily be accused of taking.[58] Elaborating this thesis in her longer treatment of the problem of Oliphant's position with regard to gender politics, Williams concludes that 'Oliphant is a complex figure, typecast as antifeminist, yet concerned throughout her life with the problems of women and the author of several novels that are rooted in this concern.'[59] However, such apologies aside, Oliphant's anti-feminism is evident even in the very complexity of her ideas on the issue as promulgated in her periodical articles.

Oliphant admired indomitable women, capable of dealing with particular injustices – her ideal female was inviolable.[60] She was vehemently opposed to making changes to the laws affecting women with particular reference to marriage and divorce and believed that woman's natural role was that of mother.[61] She supported a biologically-determined gender division of labour and therefore opposed opening the professions and trades to women as unnatural, extravagant, and, considered as something which would bring about equality, chimerical.[62] She did, however, support the admission of women to the medical profession and did make some suggestions about a 'Celibate Class' of female tradeswomen.[63] Extending the franchise to include married women she believed was unnecessary ('GW', p. 709). However, with regard to single women, Oliphant eventually came to the opinion 'that I think it is highly absurd that I should not have a vote, if I want one – a point upon which I am much more uncertain' ('GW', p. 708). Her views on the relationship between men and women were fundamental to all of these views on the woman question. She believed that as men and women were physically distinct, their work was also distinct. But this physical distinction and sexually-determined division of labour starkly contradicted her view that intellectually, morally, and spiritually men and women were as one and shared in the same existence.[64] Advancing both unity and disunity between men and women, her views on the woman question were therefore fundamentally self-contradictory. Furthermore, she used this notion of unification in the one domain coupled with division in the other to mitigate the obvious injustices resulting from sharply distinct spheres of work for men and women.

As this basic self-contradiction (between her theoretical principle of male/female sameness and a practical difference of sexually-determined duties and roles) was never resolved in her writing and as she so explicitly condemned attempts to change the position of women radically, she was at least implicitly biased in favour of the patriarchal misogynies of the status quo irrespective of how many of her novels were rooted in the concerns of women. Taken collectively, her views on the woman question are more con-fused than complex. Though modifications and certain shifts in her ideas may be traced and described as developments in her thought and though she celebrated woman's work and the nobility of motherhood, she was no advocate of women's rights nor of the drive to ameliorate the condition of women even although she clearly insisted on their high social and moral value. However her position does deserve greater elucidation than is possible here if only to explain where she was mistaken and to indicate the potential virtue of her notion of a sameness or correlation between the intellectual, moral, and spiritual existence of men and women, a notion which arguably suggests a much more radical position than Oliphant's bourgeois and Tory political sympathies could ever have allowed her to endorse.

Christian Isobel Johnstone

The novelist and journalist Christian Isobel Johnstone (1781–1857) was co-editor with her husband John Johnstone of the *Inverness Courier*, the *Edinburgh Chronicle* and *The Schoolmaster*, which became *Johnstone's Edinburgh Magazine* and later merged into *Tait's Edinburgh Magazine*.[65] Throughout the various strands of her work Johnstone was concerned with aspects of female experience. She wrote a variety of novels which included an instructional children's novel *Diversions of Hollycot, or The Mother's Art of Thinking*, playfully parodying Horne Tooke's heavily speculative *Diversions of Purley*. Part of the book is devoted to the mother recounting to her children the story of that famous Scottish heroine 'Grisell Baillie'.[66] Another of her novels, *Clan-Albin* (1815), reveals something of the robust, worldly nature of her writing, a novel which begins with the death of a woman shortly after giving birth and with the down-to-earth concern about arranging to have a recently bereaved mother suckle the new-born infant – nothing as frank as this in the contemporary works of Jane Austen![67] She also contributed a very large number of interesting articles to the periodicals, mainly to the radical journal *Tait's*, the political opponents of Mrs Oliphant's Tory outlet, *Blackwood's*. Writing to William Tait in 1834 from Cheyne Row in London, Carlyle said of her that 'Mrs J., we often say here, would make half a dozen Cockney "famed women."'[68] Four years later in another letter from his London home to Tait, Carlyle again drew a broad comparison between London and Scottish authors in praising Johnstone's *True Tales of the Irish Peasantry*: 'Pray offer the good brave-hearted lady my hearty remembrances, good-wishes and applauses. – Radicalism, I grieve to say, has but few such practical adherents! Radicalism, when one looks at it here, is – a thing one had rather not give a name to!'[69]

Her first periodical article was for *Blackwood's*, a short piece which records 'an *old usage* which still exists, and which to me was as novel as it was delightful', namely, Mothering Sunday.[70] With romantic nostalgia she recounts the idyll of a rural English family gathering, including Church service, for this hitherto unknown old custom that venerated the family's mother. As with so many nineteenth-century women writers, women would come to have a special place in her work but the subject by no means formed the boundary of her interests. Johnstone's second and last article for *Blackwood's* is a highly allusive, literary-philosophical musing on day-dreams and presentiments and 'the universality of the feeling of preternatural influences glancing back into the dark abyss of time, or forward into the undiscovered depths of futurity'.[71]

Her career with *Tait's Edinburgh Magazine* saw her move away from philosophical musings and reminiscences and into the realm of literary criticism. In one of her early articles for *Tait's* she attacks the Irish novelist Maria Edgeworth for writing respectable fashionable novels to a bourgeois, unromantic pattern of female decency, triviality, and sexual safety[72] She also argues that Edgeworth, in failing to capture the 'true raciness' of the Irish, and in several other ways cannot properly be regarded as an Irish author: 'Neither her feelings, mind, nor imagination . . . are Irish', and even *Castle Rackrent* could not 'establish Miss Edgeworth's title of a national writer'.[73] Johnstone would later produce many short reviews of contemporary authors and several notably long reviews of works dealing with a variety of biographical and historical subjects such as her articles, 'Life of Mrs Siddons', 'The Life and Writings of William Cobbett', and 'Lockhart's Life of Sir Walter Scott'.[74]

But if Johnstone began writing for *Tait's* as a literary critic, like so many of her contemporaries she was by no means limited to this single specialism. Her quasi-philosophical musings, evident in her earlier articles, re-emerge later in such articles as 'Marriages are made in Heaven' in which she explores love as 'a deluding guide to matrimony', problematises the possible motivations to marry, raises and dismisses the virtues of arranged marriages, and concludes that love or sexual passion, though fallible, is nevertheless the only guide we have.[75] The veil-of-illusion and stoical scepticism of the following passage is advanced as a protection against the inevitability of a torment of burning passion and its frustration and suggests not only that Johnstone has a Pauline awareness of the fierce power of sexual desire but also of its imperfect enjoyment within so many marriages. She writes as a romantic and fearless existentialist, grappling with a consciousness of angst, the problem of the fundamental reality of madness or chaos, the false idols of poetic and idle depictions of love, and the self-consuming nature of self-absorption in leisured idleness:

> Marry then for love, in God's name, all who are fools enough to marry! Love is the only apology for such an absurd step. Burning, over-mastering passion, fusing two beings into one; satisfied with nothing short of a perpetual struggle to attain such an intermixture of soul, body, and interests as nature has rendered unattainable; this alone can justify the tying of the knot which may not be unloosed. It is madness, but it is a madness which is in the order of nature, and must be undergone. The only advice that can be given to those unfortunates who stagger hither and thither beneath the load of the tempest, is to keep their reeling wits as sober as possible, – to speak and act as like rational beings as they can, – to remind themselves, perpetually, that they are living in a world of dreams, out of which they must one day awake, in order that the fading of their garish fancies may be as gradual, and their *exit* into the world of reality, accompanied with as slight a shock as may be . . . There is a period of life, when leisure to brood over one's own thoughts is dangerous and unnerving; the period when those throbbings and longings, vague and undefined, but mighty and bewildering, which form the buoyant and surging couch and canopy of love, are awakening into existence. Lack of such employment as leads the mind out of itself, is then all but inevitable destruction. The tone of our literature, the general tendency of daily conversation, increases the danger. ('MMH', pp. 186–7)

As this and her concluding comment makes clear, for Johnstone, 'MARRIAGE IS NO JOKE!', a warning she adds to stern and sound advice against marrying 'a sentimental man':

> He is a selfish voluptuary: he would take without giving. He has lived over in fancy all that gives happiness in reality, and the edge of his feelings have been blunted. Devoted exclusively to such trains of thought, his mind is empty and without resources. Shrinking from the labours and contests of life, his thoughts are devoid of that manliness and vigour which exercise alone can give. Dull, inane, feeble, loveless, he can feel for no one; protect, support, or cherish no one; cheer the dull path of life to no one. In the prime of life, he will be at best but a negative; and in old age he will sit moping and snivelling by the chimney corner,
>
> > Clownish and malcontent,
> > Peevish, impertinent,
> > Dashing the merriment;
>
> a clog, a log, a nuisance, and an incumbrance ('MMH', p. 188)

Johnstone boxes the ears of the sentimentalist with joyous and robust vigour. That said, her serious advice to women is that sentimentality is a form of greed and moreover the cause of positive harm to the wife of a sentimental man. There is probably more to this advice than its evident wisdom concerning companionship. Johnstone's condemnation may also extend to the idle day-dreamer, the drunkard, the drug addict, the sexually selfish, all 'voluptuaries' who take without giving. Such wider condemnation could, of course, only be articulated by way of carefully disguised hints.

Her interest in and knowledge of sex can also be glimpsed by looking at another article, 'Customs and Manners of Persian Women'. This is a review of a book translated by James Atkinson.[76] In Johnstone's review she emphasises the particular privileges and powers of Persian women and quotes Atkinson's work describing, for example, the women's pleasures at the bath which included 'embellishing their beautiful forms', an embellishment which was described in fairly graphic and sensual detail.[77] But Johnstone also quotes a description of the rituals of the nuptial night which, for an article published in 1833, is unusually explicit, including details of the undressing of the bride and the placing of each of her legs in turn against her husband's. What is more interesting than such comparative sexual frankness, however, is Johnstone's teasing complaint at having to end her quotation at this stage of the ritual: 'We regret that the prudery of European Manners will not permit us to proceed farther'. Perhaps tantalised nineteenth-century readers would have rushed out to buy the book. If so they must have been disappointed since, apart from a slightly erotic drawing of a large-eyed and exotically bejewelled Persian woman and some advice about pregnancy and childbirth, Johnstone's article had already included most of the more suggestive material. If her readers were teased into reading Atkinson's translation perhaps all she was doing was a throroughly good marketing job. Whatever she was up to, and although to our more jaundiced eyes her writing may seem sexually coy, it is fairly clear that Johnstone was neither sexually naive nor a prude.

If, by comparison with contemporary and later writers, she was relatively fearless in her treatment of sexual matters, fearlessness was carried over into her political concerns, in particular in arguing against the slave trade. As she was later to remark when reviewing Carlyle's published lectures *On Heroes*, 'there is moral courage [in Carlyle's lectures], though it requires more courage in our society to attack one social abuse than fifty doctrinal systems'.[78] The courage to attack social abuse is perhaps never more evident in Johnstone's work for *Tait's* than in her articles concerning the slave trade. In one article on the subject published in 1833, she declares that 'till the Slave Trade is effectually annihilated, no progress can be made in civilization'.[79] In the same article and in one published some five years later she is uncompromising in illustrating the atrocities of slavery as reported by eye witnesses.[80] Writing against Barbados planters and the system of apprenticeship, adopted after the British abolition of slavery proper, she even names some of the bad absentee planters such as a certain 'Mr Ewing' from Glasgow on whose estate 'the people are ill cared for'.[81] In another article also from 1838, she writes warmly on Lord Brougham's speech against slavery.[82] She also 'puffed' the work of the anti-slavery poet Thomas Pringle.[83] But her enthusiasm for the anti-slavery movement did not extend to one of its earliest adherents, William Wilberforce, whose bill to abolish slavery finally received royal assent in 1807. Rejecting the popular claim that Wilberforce was the founding father of the anti-slavery movement, in 1838 Johnstone wrote a revealing article in which, partly through quoting other writers, she charges Wilberforce with being a hypocrite or moral equivocator. Johnstone's Wilberforce might almost have provided Dickens some five years later with a model for *Martin Chuzzlewit's* Pecksniff. Her concluding remarks include the comment that Wilberforce's 'faults were often more detrimental than those of his most corrupt contemporaries . . . If not always the advocate or apologist of oppression and abuse, he was their frequent abettor'.[84]

The strong sense of justice evident in her articles attacking slavery is also evident in at least two of her articles on Scottish issues. In 'Memoirs and Trials of the Political Martyrs of Scotland' Johnstone describes the scandalously unjust trials of Thomas Muir, William Skirving, Thomas Fyshe Palmer, Joseph Gerrald, and Maurice Margarot in late eighteenth-century Scotland. Muir has recently been described as a 'Scottish Republican and Revolutionary'.[85] Johnstone pointed out that 'One of Muir's greatest alleged crimes against the state, was lending a copy of Paine's "Rights of Man"', a crime for which Muir was to suffer transportation to Australia. Though she somewhat heroises these agitators for political reform, Johnstone is careful to indicate the political context in which the trials occurred:

> This incipient agitation [for Reform] was especially active in Scotland, where an intelligent and thoughtful population had attained considerable political knowledge and no correspond-ing degree of political power . . . A people at peace, and possessing full knowledge of their rights and interests, without any direct and powerful control over their own affairs, is a condition which, of all others, may alarm a bad government. The people of England and Scotland had reached this stage. Ireland was still in a state of strong excitement; and the shock of the French Revolution – the crash of the tumbling walls of the Bastile – of 'the King's castle' – shook the old despotisms of Europe to their deepest foundations. In the words of a popular Tory song of the day –
> [The Devil had entered the swine;]
> and the power and consternation of 'the better classes of society,' was commensurate to the 'madness' of the 'swinish multitude'.[86]

Johnstone's article bristles with many such comments and quotations, the selection of which may attest to her views of Tory ideology and her stance on the issues of political reform and independence for Scotland.

But while this article is concerned with political freedom and the burgeoning demand for reform, a later lengthly and detailed study written at the beginning of the 'hungry forties', squarely addresses the condition of the poor in Scotland. Drawing a moral lesson from the work of William Alison and his *Observations on the Management of the Poor in Scotland* (1840), Johnstone writes of the destitution and consequent high mortality rate from fever in Scotland's cities: 'Fever has one good effect, in somewhat quickening the apprehensions of the more affluent classes, and teaching them, from their own danger, to take greater interest in the sufferings of their less fortunate fellow-creatures'.[87] Some three years later this moral lesson would be given more colourful embellishment in Carlyle's famous re-telling in *Past and Present* of the poor Irish Widow who died from typhus.[88]

Though declaring herself no admirer 'of poor laws, and still less of workhouses and compulsory assessments', Johnstone admits their usefulness and even 'in the present condition of society, their absolute necessity' ('CLP', p. 685). Her article is concerned with advocating a poor law in Scotland similar to that of England which she regards as providing better conditions for the unemployed poor than the inadequately managed and meanly funded feudal and clerical arrangements in Scotland. According to Johnstone, 'a well-considered poor law is meant to prevent or alleviate . . . extensive and extreme destitution among the innocent as well as the improvident and profligate; mendicancy, vagrancy, recklessness of all moral restraint, juvenile delinquency, disease, and crime' ('CLP', p. 760) Her article sets out to establish that such prevention and alleviation in the Scotland of the 1840s was urgently needed. She is once again tough-spirited enough to name names, citing appallingly unjust distributions of wealth on certain estates, such as that of the Duchess of Sutherland:

> We include one more Sutherlandshire parish, Assynt, where, out of a population of 1760, about sixty are admitted as permanent or occasional paupers, and have £14 a-year divided among them, or, on the average, about a penny a-week. ('CLP', p. 691)

Letting such statistics speak for themselves, her article champions the cause of the poor against the Kirk sessions, landowners, and the Tory ideology as supported by that famous Scottish Churchman, Thomas Chalmers. Though she advances a mere utilitarian reason for providing the poor in Scotland with State assistance, Johnstone makes their plight all the more threatening by suggesting the more sophisticated view that such deprivation within a society must affect even those most removed from this deprivation through implying their own inhumanity and selfishness – as other classes cease to care, hardened or corrupted they condemn themselves to moral poverty and their own degradation. Though this argument would provide small comfort to the poor and would be unlikely to make any difference to the views and actions of the hard-hearted, selfish egoist, Johnstone is surely correct, her argument and her message chillingly prescient of our own times:

> Poor Laws are auxiliaries of the march of improvement, as they form the preventative of the perpetuated hereditary debasement of a large and valuable portion of the community, who, without their sustaining power, remain a down-draught on social progress, while their suffering condition hardens or corrupts every other class. Slavery is to be condemned, not alone for the misery and degradation which it entails on the slave, but also for the deadening of the moral feelings, and the actual cruelty and profligacy which the unnatural condition of the slave engenders in his master. In like manner, the mischievous consequences of unrelieved misery and destitution, existing in the bosom of an otherwise prosperous society, cannot long be confined to the actual sufferers, were the luxurious portion of society so selfish and inhuman as to disregard all suffering which did not immediately affect themselves. ('CLP', p. 749).

Notes

1. Margaret Oliphant, 'Sydney Smith', *Blackwood's Magazine* (March 1856), 350–61 (p. 350).
2. *The Wellesley Index to Victorian Periodicals: 1824–1900*, ed. Walter E. Houghton and others, 5 vols (University of Toronto Press Toronto; Routledge & Kegan Paul, London 1966–89).
3. 'Across the Yellow Sea', *Blackwood's Magazine* (May 1882), 623–34. Her perilous voyage from Peking to Nagasaki was re-told in greater detail in 'Some Eventful Voyages', *Blackwood's Magazine* (March 1890), 372–83 (pp. 378–80).
4. '"The Offerings of the Dead"', *British Quarterly Review* (January 1885), 47–76 (p. 62).
5. See 'Wolves and Were-Wolves', *Temple Bar* (November 1890), 351–68 (pp. 351–2; pp. 357–8; pp. 360–2).
6. '"Unfathomed mysteries"', *Blackwood's Magazine* (May 1883), 628–42 (p. 642).
7. 'The World's Oil-Supply in the Nineteenth Century', *Blackwood's Magazine* (September

1884), 336–62 (p. 337). The dangers of Aberdeen's harbour were indicated in Gordon-Cumming's account of the sinking of *The Duke of Sutherland* in 1853 (see 'Some Eventful Voyages', p. 376).

8.   'Notes of a Wanderer in Skye', *Temple Bar* (September 1883), 75–92.
9.   'Granite Crags', *Temple Bar* (October 1883), 244–61 (p. 249).
10. 'Musical Instruments and their Homes', *Blackwood's Magazine* (April 1891), 527–45.
11. Virginia Blain, Patricia Clements and Isobel Grundy (eds), *The Feminist Companion to Literature in English: Women Writers from the Middle Ages to the Present* (Batsford, London, 1990). Hereafter cited as *FCL*.
12. 'Literary Remains of Albert Dürer', *Edinburgh Review* (July 1861), 39–64.
13. 'French Anti-Clerical Novels', *Edinburgh Review* (October 1864), 437–63 (pp. 447–8; p. 460).
14. See 'Lace-making as a Fine Art', *Edinburgh Review* (January 1872), 37–55 (pp. 54–5).
15. 'The Fall of the House of Stuart', *Edinburgh Review* (April 1882), 291–321.
16. 'Persecution of the Jews', *Edinburgh Review* (April 1883), 291–320 (p. 319),
17. For example, Vineta Colby and Robert A. Colby, *The Equivocal Virtue: Mrs Oliphant and the Victorian Literary Market Place* (Archon, Hamden, 1966); 'Mrs Oliphant's Scotland: The Romance of Reality', in Ian Campbell (ed.), *Nineteenth-Century Scottish Fiction: Critical Essays* (Barnes & Noble, Totowa, N. J., 1979, pp. 89–104; John Stock Clarke, *Margaret Oliphant: A Bibliography*, Victorian Fiction Research Guides Series: 11 (University of Queensland Press, St Lucia, 1986); Jenni Calder, 'Heroes and Hero-Makers: Women in Nineteenth-Century Scottish Fiction', in Douglas Gifford and Cairns Craig (eds), *The History of Scottish Literature*, 4 vols (Aberdeen University Press, Aberdeen, 1988), III: *Nineteenth Century*, pp. 261–74; D. J. Trela (ed.), *Margaret Oliphant: Critical Essays on a Gentle Subversive* (Susquehanna University Press, Selinsgrove; Associated University Presses, London, 1995).
18. Margaret Oliphant, *The Autobiography of Margaret Oliphant: The Complete Text*, edited and introduced by Elizabeth Jay (Oxford University Press, Oxford, 1990), vii.
19. 'The Byways of Literature', *Blackwood's Magazine* (August 1858), 200–16 (p. 203).
20. 'Modern Light Literature' ['MLL'], *Blackwood's Magazine* (December 1855), 702–17, (p. 702).
21. See 'The Latest Lawgiver', *Blackwood's Magazine* (June 1868), 675–91.
22. 'Macaulay', *Blackwood's Magazine* (May 1876), 614–37 (p. 615); see 'Lord Neaves', *Blackwood's Magazine* (March 1877), 380–90 (pp. 387–8); see [Charles Neaves], *Songs and Verses Social and Scientific* (Blackwood, Edinburgh and London, 1868), pp. 18–21.
23. See 'The Great Unrepresented', *Blackwood's Magazine* (September 1866), 367–79 (p. 379; p. 368; p. 372).
24. 'Bulwer', *Blackwood's Magazine* (February 1855), 221–33 (p. 223).
25. 'Men and Women', *Blackwood's Magazine* (April 1895), 620–50, (p. 642). For some examples of Oliphant's encomiums on Scott, see 'Scottish National Character', *Blackwood's Magazine* ['SNC'] (June 1860), 715–31 (p. 717); 'A Few French Novels', *Blackwood's Magazine* (December 1881), 703–23 (p. 703); 'The Letters of Sir Walter Scott', *Blackwood's Magazine* (January 1864), 15–26.
26. See 'Bulwer', p. 223; 'Kenelm Chillingly', *Blackwood's Magazine* (May 1873), 615–30 (p. 630).
27. 'Charles Dickens', *Blackwood's Magazine* ['CD'] (April 1855), 451–66 (p. 451).
28. See also 'Sensation Novels', *Blackwood's Magazine* (May 1862), 564–84 (p. 574).
29. 'Modern Novelists – Great and Small', *Blackwood's Magazine* (May 1855), 554–68 (p. 557; p. 558; and see p. 568).
30. See 'The History of Scotland', *Blackwood's Magazine* (March 1867), 317–37 (p. 332; pp. 329–30); cf. 'Scotland and her Accusers', *Blackwood's Magazine* (September 1861), 267–83.
31. For example, see 'A Scotch Physician', *Blackwood's Magazine* (November 1885), 669–90.
32. Cf. Robert and Vineta Colby, 'Mrs Oliphant's Scotland: The Romance of Reality', in Ian Campbell (ed.), *Nineteenth-Century Scottish Fiction: Critical Essays* (Barnes & Noble, Totowa, N. J., 1979), pp. 89–104 (p. 93).
33. For example, see 'Clerical Life in Scotland', *Macmillans* (July 1863), 208–19.
34. 'Modern Novelists – Great and Small', p. 567. Also see 'Scottish National Character', p. 731.

35. 'Mrs Carlyle', *Contemporary Review* (May 1883), 609–28 (p. 611). Cf. Simon Heffer, *Moral Desperado: A Life of Thomas Carlyle* (Weidenfeld and Nicolson, London, 1995), p. 56: 'the social gap between Jane and [Carlyle] was vast'.

36. 'Scottish National Character', p. 722. Oliphant may have had in mind remarks made by the historian Henry Thomas Buckle (see 'Among the Lochs', *Blackwood's Magazine* (October 1861), 479–98; p. 489).

37. 'Scotch Local History', *Blackwood's Magazine* (March 1886), 375–97 (p. 395; p. 388).

38. See 'The History of Scotland', p. 328.

39. Other, more serious, misrepresentations of Scotland were severely criticised in Oliphant's nationalistic and rousing article condemning the historian Henry Thomas Buckle, 'Scotland and her Accusers', *Blackwood's Magazine* (September 1861), 267–83.

40. 'Light Literature for the Holidays', *Blackwood's Magazine* (September 1855), 362–74 (p. 365).

41. 'Edward Irving', *Blackwood's Magazine* (November 1858), 567–86 (p. 571).

42. See 'The Queen of the Highlands', *Blackwood's Magazine* (February 1868), 242–50.

43. 'The Indian Mutiny: Sir Hope Grant', *Blackwood's Magazine* (January 1874), 102–20 (p. 119).

44. For example, see 'Social Science', *Blackwood's Magazine* (December 1860), 698–9. 'The Missionary Explorer', *Blackwood's Magazine* (April 1858), 385–401 (p. 400).

45. See 'Charles Dickens', p. 457.

46. 'The Condition of Women', *Blackwood's Magazine* (February 1858), 139–54 (p. 151). Cf. 'Novels [1]', *Blackwood's Magazine* (August 1863), 168–83 (p. 179): 'he is a greater benefactor to us who teaches us to think better of our kind, than he whose endeavour it is to direct our eyes to the worst side of human nature'; and also, 'Novels [2]', *Blackwood's Magazine* (September 1863), 257–80 (pp. 259–60).

47. See 'Thackeray and his Novels' ['T and HN'], *Blackwood's Magazine* (January 1855), 86–96 (p. 95; cf. p. 96); 'Modern Light Literature – Theology', *Blackwood's Magazine* (July 1855), 72–86 (p. 86). Thackeray received kinder treatment in 'Thackeray's Sketches', *Blackwood's Magazine* (February 1876), 232–43.

48. See 'Thomas Carlyle', *Macmillan's Magazine* (April 1881), 482–96 (pp. 487–8). For another example of this delicate treatment of sexual matters, see 'Miss Austen and Miss Mitford', *Blackwood's Magazine* (March 1870), 290–313 (p. 298).

49. 'The Anti-Marriage League', *Blackwood's Magazine* (January 1896), 134–49 (p. 141; and see pp. 139–40). Cf. Merryn Williams, *Margaret Oliphant: A Critical Biography* (Macmillan, Basingstoke, 1986), p. 179, where Hardy's response is quoted; and see Norman Page, 'Hardy, Mrs Oliphant, and *Jude the Obscure*', *Victorian Newsletter* 46 (1974), 22–4.

50. See 'Life and Letters of George Eliot', *Edinburgh Review* (April 1885), 514–53 (pp. 535–8).

51. See 'Charles Dickens', pp. 464–5. According to Oliphant, unlike Shakespeare, Tennyson also 'had no skill . . . to make us women wonderful in their womanhood' ('Tennyson', *Blackwood's Magazine*, November 1892, 748–66; p. 761).

52. 'Harriet Martineau', *Blackwood's Magazine* (April 1877), 472–96 (p. 496). Earlier in the century Christian Isobel Johnstone warmly supported Martineau, claiming that 'The sentiments and opinions contained in her books shew how lovely a thing the mind of woman may become, when allowed fairly to develope [*sic*] itself' ('Miss Martineau's Illustrations of Political Economy', *Tait's*, August 1832, 612–18; p. 613).

53. 'Modern Novelists – Great and Small', p. 558.

54. 'Modern Novelists – Great and Small', p. 558.

55. 'Modern Novelists – Great and Small', p. 557.

56. See 'Modern Novelists – Great and Small', p. 559.

57. 'The Anti-Marriage League', p. 145.

58. Williams, *Margaret Oliphant*, pp. 106–12.

59. Merryn Williams, 'Feminist or Antifeminist? Oliphant and the Woman Question', in Trela (ed.) *Margaret Oliphant: Critical Essays on a Gentle Subversive*, 165–80 (p. 179).

60. For example, see 'The Laws Concerning Women', *Blackwood's Magazine* (April 1856), 379–87 (p. 387).

61. 'The Laws Concerning Women', p. 384; 'The Condition of Women', p. 152; 'The Grievances of Women', *Fraser's Magazine* (May 1880), 698–710 (p. 701).
62. 'Social Science', p. 714; p. 712; 'The Condition of Women', p. 145.
63. 'Social Science', p. 714; p. 712; 'The Grievances of Women' ['GW'], p. 709.
64. 'The Condition of Women', p. 144; p. 145.
65. FCL. I am indebted to Aileen Riddell for information about Johnstone.
66. [Christian Isobel Johnstone], *Diversions of Hollycot, or The Mother's Art of Thinking* (Oliver and Boyd, Edinburgh, 1828), pp. 70–88.
67. [Christian Isobel Johnstone], *Clan-Albin: A National Tale*, 4 vols (Macreadie & others, Edinburgh; Longman & others London; Cumming, Dublin, 1815).
68. William Tait was the editor of *Tait's* for its first two years before the Johnstones took over the editorship. *The Collected Letters of Thomas and Jane Welsh Carlyle*, 25 vols, ed. C. R. Sanders, K. J. Fielding, C. de L. Ryals *et al.* (Duke University Press, Durham, N.C., 1970–97), 7, p. 311.
69. *Collected Letters of Thomas and Jane Welsh Carlyle*, XI, p. 234.
70. 'Old Usages: Mothering Sunday', *Blackwood's Magazine* (November 1827), 595–602 (p. 597).
71. 'Day-Dreams', *Blackwood's Magazine* (December 1827), 724–9 (p. 729).
72. See 'Miss Edgeworth's Works', *Tait's* (June 1832), 279–85 (p. 280; see also p. 283).
73. 'Miss Edgeworth's Works', p. 282; p. 285.
74. 'Life of Mrs Siddons', *Tait's* (August 1834), 467–79; 'The Life and Writings of William Cobbett', *Tait's* (August–September 1835), 491–506, 583–97; 'Lockhart's Life of Sir Walter Scott', *Tait's* (April 1837–May 1838), 205–29, 469–87, 557–66; see also 'Sir James Mackintosh's History of the Revolution of 1688', *Tait's* (May 1834), 247–58.
75. 'Marriages are made in Heaven', ['MMH'] *Tait's* (November 1832), 184–9 (p. 185; see also p. 186).
76. *Customs and Manners of the Women of Persia and their Domestic Superstitions*, translated from the original manuscript, by James Atkinson (Oriental Translation Fund, London, 1832).
77. 'Customs and Manners of Persian Women', *Tait's* (March 1833), 738–45 (p. 740).
78. 'Carlyle's Lectures on Heroes and Hero-Worship', *Tait's* (June 1841), 379–83 (p. 383).
79. 'The Slave Trade – Voyage to Western Africa', *Tait's* (March 1833), 789–99 (p. 789).
80. See 'The Slave Trade', p. 796; 'Abolition of Negro Apprenticeships – Sturge and Harvey's Tour in the West Indies in 1837', *Tait's* (March 1838), 135–48 (pp. 144–5).
81. See, 'Abolition of Negro Apprenticeships', p. 142; p. 147.
82. 'Lord Brougham's Speeches on Slavery', *Tait's* (April 1838), 203–9 (see p. 208).
83. 'The Poetical Works of Thomas Pringle', *Tait's* (May 1838), 280–3.
84. 'Life of Wilberforce', *Tait's* (June 1838), 337–54 (p. 354; and see p. 343; pp. 349–51).
85. M. Donnelly, *Thomas Muir of Huntershill, 1765–99* (Bishopbriggs Town Council, Tillicoultry, 1975), p. 1.
86. 'Memoirs and Trials of the Political Martyrs of Scotland; Persecuted during the Years 1793–4–5', *Tait's* (January 1837), 1–20 (p. 2; p. 4).
87. 'Condition of the Labouring Poor, and the Management of Paupers in Scotland', ['CLP'] *Tait's* (November and December 1840), 681–96, 749–60 (p. 682).
88. See *The Works of Thomas Carlyle*, centenary edition, 30 vols, ed. H. D. Traill (Chapman and Hall, London, 1896–9), *Past and Present*, III.ii, p. 186. Carlyle also referred to Alison's work.

15

Jane Welsh Carlyle's Private Writing Career

Aileen Christianson

Jane Welsh Carlyle (1801–66) published nothing in her lifetime.[1] She left no unpublished novels, short stories or essays to be discovered and published after her death. Why, therefore, should she be considered in a volume on the writing of Scottish women? The reason is that she was an incomparable writer of letters of which more than 3,000 have survived. Her private writing career, for all its apparent spontaneous unintended nature, has been considerable. However private this mode of literary output, as part of the genre of life-writing, it is now as open to critical approaches as any other genre.

After her death Thomas Carlyle collected her surviving letters, providing explanatory notes to many. In response to reading them he wrote, 8 July 1866:

> The whole of yesterday I spent in reading and arranging the <u>letters</u> of 1857; such a day's <u>reading</u> as I perhaps never had in my life before. What a piercing radiancy of meaning to me in those dear records . . . Constantly there is such an electric shower of all-illuminating brilliancy, penetration, recognition, wise discernment, just enthusiasm, humour, grace, patience, courage, love, – and in fine of spontaneous nobleness of mind and intellect, – as I know not where to parallel![2]

The tone of this passage is representative of that sustained by Carlyle throughout his *Reminiscences* of Welsh Carlyle: grief-stricken and guilt-stricken in equal measure, exaggerated and hyperbolic in its estimation of her character and talents.[3] He continued with an estimation of her writing talents which was to become the basis of claims that Welsh Carlyle should or might have been a novelist if only she had not married Thomas Carlyle:

> As to 'talent', epistolary and other, these <u>Letters</u> . . . equal and surpass whatever of best I know to exist in that kind; for 'talent', 'genius', or whatever we may call it, what an evidence, if my little woman needed that to me! Not all the <u>Sands and Elliots</u> and babbling *cohue* [mob] of 'celebrated scribbling women' that have strutted over the world, in my time, could . . . , if all boiled down and distilled to essence, make one such woman.[4]

What is interesting about this passage is the manner in which he both exaggerates and patronises Welsh Carlyle's talents; they equal or surpass the 'best' he knows; George Sand

and George Eliot are both reduced and contained within a babbling mob of 'celebrated scribbling women'. 'Babbling and scribbling': the alliteration conjures up the Victorian man's view of women writers. 'Strutted over the world' demeans them with its implication of an arrogant and inappropriate (in Carlyle's view) imitation of the male gait striding over the world of letters. The underlying male fear of the threat of independent women is expressed in the image of these two prolific and distinguished writers being 'boiled down and distilled to essence'. Reduced to their essence by boiling, they still could not equal Welsh Carlyle. But the woman who is above them in talent, 'epistolary and other', is contained by Carlyle within the phrase 'my little woman'. This lays claim both to his ownership of her and to his superior status. What Carlyle does here is prepare us for the foregrounding of his grief in the *Reminiscences*. In these he details his grief, his memories as much as Welsh Carlyle's life. Elizabeth Hardwick, who coined the phrase 'private writing career' for those writers such as Welsh Carlyle who wrote personal records in letters or diaries but who never published formally, points out how this passage works: 'With this exaggeration and lack of precision, the excellence of the letters fades. They have not been defined, thought about, carefully placed.'[5]

Welsh Carlyle explores a double life in her letters. There was a conflict in this double life between the public Mrs Carlyle, wife of Thomas Carlyle, and the private Welsh Carlyle, her own self. The public self was the wife of the 'genius', patient, thrifty, clever, self-denying, gallantly suffering illness. The private self, just as visible in the letters, is vigorous, ironic, humorous and egotistical. This self has a hidden core, invisible to Carlyle when he constructed his reminiscences of Welsh Carlyle. He based these around her public self, the self which was most flattering to his grief-stricken ego. But when the letters are read closely, Welsh Carlyle's core of self-confidence and self-assertion becomes apparent.

It is necessary to start with Carlyle. Without his collecting of Welsh Carlyle's letters there would have been no evidence, other than anecdotal, of her talents. Whatever nineteenth-century attitudes he betrays in the diminutives that unconsciously denigrate and control his 'little woman', his 'Goody', his 'Goodikin',[6] the task which he completed to assuage his grief was a major one. No assessment of Welsh Carlyle's writing would be possible without it. Once the letters were sent by her, they went out of her control. It was Carlyle, who by collecting them, attempted to bring them into his control. Carlyle in this way laid the ground work for future versions of her life and career, versions which, though they may challenge and re-define his view of his wife's character and abilities, are still largely dependent on Carlyle's collection.[7]

But how do we approach her as a writer, however many of her letters have survived and however fine her epistolary talents are? We have been accustomed to assess writers on the works they have chosen to publish. But the widening of the canon into a more inclusive approach as to what constitutes 'literature' means that material such as letters can be assessed for its literary content, not just for its historical, factual, or personal interest. Welsh Carlyle's work comes into the genre of life-writing, a more encompassing term than autobiography (itself from the Greek for self-life-writing). Letters, journals, and diaries can now be considered as a legitimate part of literary output. As Sidonie Smith, in her consideration of 'the relationship of gender to genre to formal autobiography', theorises:

> Since all gesture and rhetoric is revealing of the subject, autobiography can be defined as any written or verbal communication. More narrowly it can be defined as written or verbal

communication that takes the speaking 'I' as the subject of the narrative, rendering the 'I' both subject and object.[8]

Thus, in letters, the self writing, the 'I', is the subject but also the object of her own letters, narrating herself but also narrated by herself. One of Smith's concerns is that women 'may write autobiographically, choosing other languages of self-writing – letters, diaries, journals, biography. Even so, their stories remain private, their storytelling culturally muted, albeit persistent'.[9] This idea of the culturally muted but persistent output is similar to that of the private writing career that chose no public outlet. This provides the framework for considering Welsh Carlyle's work.

The letter writer must consciously construct each individual letter for a particular audience, the recipient of that letter. This demands flexibility in construction of different letters; journals or diaries intended for private, personal consolation can be more unstructured, registering feelings and events of the moment without the need to tailor or modify for the recipient, the recipient being the writer herself. They can be used to record fact but also feelings as they are felt and understood at the moment of recording. With letters there has always to be some sense of the reader reading as well as the self writing. This evidence of the reader is particularly clear in Welsh Carlyle who frequently repeats the same material in different letters written at the same time, framing it appropriately for each recipient. 'Every life contains within it multiple discourses on discourses, stories on stories.'[10] Welsh Carlyle's epistolary output was so extensive that it is particularly open to an analytic approach through its multiplying narratives. 'Discourses on discourses, stories on stories' are what the totality of Welsh Carlyle's letters become. Interlinked by coterie speech, stories, references, they comment and cross-comment on each other, on her interpretations of self.[11] Read separately, they are miniaturised, skilled, created individual narratives. Read together, they provide evidence of a life lived, organised, and constructed for consumption by her public, the particular recipients of her letters; telling 'the story she wants to tell about herself, she is seduced into a tantalizing and yet elusive adventure that makes her both creator and creation, writer and that which is written about'.[12]

Welsh Carlyle was an only child, better educated than most middle-class girls in Latin and mathematics, encouraged to believe that she had special talents, first by her father, then Edward Irving and Carlyle.[13] The sudden death of her father in 1818 ended the safe childhood world of boundless possibilities. She entered the world of the young woman constricted by her mother's and society's expectations of appropriate young-ladyish behaviour and of marriage. She mythologised her childhood as tomboyish, scholarly, unconventional, the Eden before her father died. But she could also be critical of her intense education:

> She talked of . . . the mistake of over-educating people. She believes that her health has been injured for life by beginning Latin with a little tutor at five or six years old, then going to the Rector's school to continue it, then having a tutor at home, and being very ambitious she learnt eagerly. Irving, being her tutor, and of equally excitable intellect, was delighted to push her through every study; then he introduced her to Carlyle, and for years they had a literary intimacy, and she would be writing constantly and consulting him about everything.[14]

This was in 1847 when she was suffering from illness and depression. But in 1849, she visited Haddington for the first time in many years. Under the emotional impact of her visit, she took a less critical view:

> Passing my dear old schoolhouse, I observed the door a little a-jar, walked in and sat down in my old seat ... <u>Ach gott! our</u> maps and Geometrical Figures had given place to <u>Texts from Scripture</u> and the foolishest <u>half-penny pictures</u>! it was become an <u>Infant School</u> ... Miss A[lexander] and her Infants were not, it seemed early risers; their schoolroom after eight o'clock was only <u>being swept</u>, it was at <u>seven</u> of the morning that James Brown once found <u>me</u> asleep there[15] – after two hours hard study – asleep betwixt the leaves of <u>the Great Atlas</u>, like a <u>keep-lesson</u>![16]

The difference between this humorous, apparently spontaneous response to the experience of revisiting her old school and her sombre, depressed assessment of over-education stems from their contexts. The first was part of a long discussion of illness and morbid dreams with a young Quaker woman to whom Welsh Carlyle would present herself as serious; the second is part of a letter written to herself which records an interplay between the present of her experiences that day and the past of her memories. What it does is frame her past in the present, containing the pain she felt at this clash of her past and present within her customary epistolary style.

One of the ways that Welsh Carlyle constructed herself as an adult was to define herself typically as the spoilt child, as a basis for her assumption of centrality in her life or letters, even when she felt edged out by her own, societal or her husband's expectations that Carlyle as husband should be central. She used this idea to draw attention to herself as somehow abandoned in adulthood by the expectations she had been encouraged to have in childhood:

> 15th April, 1856. – I am very feeble and ailing at present; and my ailment is of a sort that I understand neither the ways nor outlooks of; so that the positive suffering is complicated with dark apprehensions. Alas, alas, and there is nobody I care to tell about it, – not one, – poor ex-spoilt child that I am![17]

This is a passage from Welsh Carlyle's journal, kept intermittently, 1855–6. It is generally more sober in tone and less prone to the ironic gloss of most of her letters; yet here is the self-conscious addition of 'poor ex-spoilt child that I am!' Even with no reader other than herself, she inserts an ironic self-reference. She uses the same image to tease Carlyle later that year for some oblique complaint of his:

> Aren't you a spoiled child, without the childness and the spoiling, to go and write in that plaintive, solemn way about 'help of some connexions of Jane's in Glasgow', as if you were a desolate orphan 'thrown out <u>sang froid</u> to charity'. If you weren't satisfied with the <u>duffle</u> you got, why couldn't you have said so straightforwardly, and told me you wished me to choose another?[18]

Here there is a sense of the child who was herself indulged, admired and encouraged, trapped into nurturing and sustaining the other child, the male child who legally owned all that had been hers, including her sense of herself. While recognising the state as a material fact in her character, her 'I-ity' tendency,[19] she also saw it as something defining for others as well:

> From them I went to the Marine-Store woman ... I asked her to tea last night, and she came – except for the dash of over-graciosity in her manners – quite natural when one considers

the contradiction of her position, I like her very much – She is an only child as well as myself and we made a great deal of good talk from comparing notes about the disadvantages entailed on only children from the beginning. (TC, [22 April 1841] *CL*, 13, p. 109)

This fellow feeling with Clara Balfour, whose husband was a marine-store keeper and also a temperance missionary, is a rare example of Welsh Carlyle expressing solidarity firmly with another woman.[20] It is noticeable that it was her 'only child' status (with no hint of 'spoilt' here, her lower-class position and her upbringing having been less privileged and secure than Welsh Carlyle's), not her status as a woman, that Welsh Carlyle responds to. Balfour is interesting as she had an independent life as a lecturer on temperance, a reminder that not all Victorian women were constrained by social expectations into private lives with no public manifestations.

The style of Welsh Carlyle's letters is remarkably consistent from the beginning. There is a sense of an artistic consciousness at work, choosing to write with the apparent spontaneity of dashes, underlinings, breathless constructions, the rhythm of speech rather than the formality of nineteenth-century published writing, giving the whole an air of intimacy and immediacy; a stream of consciousness, inviting the reader into sympathetic complicit understanding with the writer. Margaret Oliphant in her *Autobiography* describes her own style as a novelist in a way which is illuminating of Welsh Carlyle's:

> I have always had my sing-song, guided by no sort of law, but by my ear, which was in its way fastidious to the cadence and measure that pleased me.[21]

This 'cadence and measure' of writing that gives the appearance of speech, imitating the best oral story-telling, is precisely the effect that Welsh Carlyle achieves in her letter writing. It was assumed by the Carlyles that letters would be shared by families, read aloud as well as passed around. The rhythms of a complete letter of Welsh Carlyle's indicate a controlling awareness of how structure as well as cadence and measure work to please the ear. Oliphant continues with a reference to her 'perfectly artless art'. This is a phrase that encapsulates what Welsh Carlyle did with her style of studied, casual simplicity. Apparently artless, these are 'only' letters, dashed off quickly for the entertainment of husband, relatives, friends. But through her 'artless art', Welsh Carlyle constructs a record of her life which controls and defines it for herself, while ensuring that her recipients respond to just as much of her discourse as she chooses. She enacts in her letters the tension between her acculturated sense of what it is to be a middle-class woman in nineteenth-century British society and her specific and conflicting sense of what it is to be herself, individual, unconstricted by gender and marital expectations.

On 19 and 20 November 1847, Welsh Carlyle wrote two letters which cover mainly the same material. The first is to her cousin, Helen Welsh, one of two sisters to whom she expressed most about her own feelings. The other is to John Forster, the recipient of many casual notes, good examples of the kind of semi-flirtatious tone that Welsh Carlyle adopts with many of her male correspondents. The themes of the letters include suicide, illness, the importance of Carlyle's bust compared with Carlyle's wife, the proofs of Geraldine Jewsbury's new novel, *The Half Sisters*, and the 'new ideas' about marriage in Germany.[22] First the letter to Helen Welsh:

> For two weeks we had been living in that extraordinary <u>substance</u> called <u>November-London fog</u>, which, not being <u>born</u> to it, I can never reconcile my mind to . . . I am determined to

take all possible care of myself this winter having not yet forgotten the horrors of the last, – so yesterday instead of going to Notting Hill to see a <u>bust</u> of my Husband which Weigall had finished, and appointed four o'clock for showing me – I lay on the sofa, wrapt in a horse-cloth – and so soon as tea was over went to bed – It looked shockingly <u>unfeeling</u> not to rush off in omnibuses to see my husbands bust, under the condition of having to return thro' the cold dark night – but it would have been still more unfeeling to have thrown my Husbands wife into an inflamation of the chest, under which no woman however well disposed can discharge her household duties – . . . We dined with Forster <u>in chambers</u> one day last week, and I selected from his large most miscellaneous Library a great cargo of books – as it were in the spirit of divination; that I might have reading enough for a whole <u>shut up</u> winter! Among the rest <u>Antidotes against the Causes that abridge human Life</u> (which Forster read as <u>Means of abridging human Life</u>) . . . At the same moment yesterday that a '<u>Devil</u>' came to the door with a <u>proof</u> for C . . . , another <u>Devil</u> handed in a <u>proof</u> addressed to <u>me</u>! The first sheet of Geraldines <u>Half Sisters</u>. Forster who has kindly charged himself with the getting out of this book for her, insisted that if <u>I</u> would not absolutely correct all the <u>proofs</u> for her myself I would at least read them carefully over and 'score out or alter any <u>exceptionable passages</u> as my own <u>great good sense</u> (!) should suggest.' – Bother! – . . . Bolte is returned from Germany[23] – all agog with <u>something</u> that she calls '<u>the new ideas</u>' – above all quite rabid against <u>marriage</u>. Varnhagen, Bettina [von Arnim], all the <u>Thinkers</u> of Germany she says have arrived at the conclusion that marriage is a highly <u>immoral</u> Institution as well as a dreadfully disagreeable one and that the only possible . . . (HW, [19 November 1847], *CL* 22, pp. 162–3)

The letter ends abruptly here as the lower half of the page has been torn off, possibly because of further comments on marriage. By the next day, in the letter to Forster, the faint reference to suicide ('*Means of abridging human Life*') has been made explicit, Carlyle has objected to Welsh Carlyle being involved in Jewsbury's proofs at all, which leads her to refer to the 'new ideas' as not just Bölte's latest enthusiasm but as having 'much truth'. The tone of the whole is suitably ironic and humorous for sending to a bachelor:

Sure enough we are in 'the gloomy month of November when the people of England commit suicide" – under 'attenuating circumstances'! The <u>expediency</u>, nay necessity of <u>suiciding myself</u> is no longer a question with me; I am only uncertain as to <u>the manner</u>! // On Thursday I was appointed to go to Notting Hill to see my Husbands <u>Bust</u>, and had to break my appointment. <u>Unfeeling</u> as it looked to let myself be withheld by any weather from going to see my Husbands bust; I thought it would be more <u>really</u> unfeeling to risk an inflamation in my Husband's Wife's chest, which makes my Husband's wife such a nuisance as you, an unmarried man, can hardly figure. // Since then, I have mostly lain on the sofa – under the horse-cloth – 'reading with one eye shut, and the other eye not open' (as poor Darley used to say) some of those divine volumes you lent me – . . . // You perceive whither all this is tending and wish that I would hasten at once to the catastrophe – Well the catastrophe is – I write it with tears in my eyes – that I cannot venture to the Play on Monday night. Even if I did not, as is almost certain I should, bring on my <u>cough</u> I should pass for <u>capricious insane</u> . . . // I am also bothered about these proofs – C has got some furious objection to my meddling with them – even declares that I 'do not know bad grammar when I see it any better than <u>she</u> does' – that 'if I <u>had</u> any faculty I might find better employment for it' &c &c – So after having written to her that I would do what you wished I must write again, that I am not permitted – // I do think there is much truth in the <u>young german</u> idea that Marriage is a <u>shockingly immoral Institution</u> as well as what we have long known it for an extremely disagreeable one – Please countermand the proofs – for every one that comes occasions a <u>row</u> Ever affectionately/Your J C ([20 November 1847]; *CL*, 22, pp. 164–5)

The letter to Helen is more guarded as it would be read or heard by Welsh Carlyle's uncle, Helen's father, John Welsh. It is necessary to read letters like this with the double perception that Helen or her sister, Jeannie, would use. There would be humorous stories to amuse their father with underlying references to pain and illness that the cousins could interpret. So, in this letter, there is the specific reference to London fog for the non-Londoners; the humour of the equivalence of the 'Husbands bust' and the 'Husbands wife'; and the 'new ideas' are safely labelled Bölte's. The Welshes knew Jewsbury so would be amused that Welsh Carlyle was to work on the proofs and would all understand the reference to 'exceptionable passages' as Jewsbury's first novel *Zoe* had been considered shocking in 1846 reviews.[24] The letter to Forster includes more quotations; an example of coterie speech; a hint that Forster as an unmarried man could not understand the role and duties of a wife and how illness interfered with that; explicit connections between illness and suicide, expressed ironically. It concludes with an admission that Carlyle and she were fighting over her involvement in Jewsbury's proofs, not because of the grammar, as he claimed, but because the possibility of 'exceptionable passages' put him on his dignity as a husband about what was respectable for *his* wife (as Welsh Carlyle's equivalence of 'bust' and 'wife' makes clear) to be involved in. Welsh Carlyle articulates it explicitly to Forster in February 1848 when *The Half Sisters* was about to appear with a dedication to her:

> I neither positively accorded to, nor positively declined at the time, meaning to revise the question when the book was <u>ready</u> for being <u>dedicated</u>, and to be guided by my Husbands authentic feelings in the matter – Knowing his dislike to be connected in people's minds, by even the slightest spider-thread, with what he calls 'George Sandism and all that accursed sort of thing' I was not at all sure that the <u>half-toleration</u> he gave when asked about it would not be changed into <u>prohibition</u> if he found it likely to be acted upon . . . If <u>anything</u> of the last Chapters I read be left in it, not only would <u>he</u> detest a dedication to <u>his</u> wife but his wife herself would detest it . . . You see how I am situated – wishing <u>not</u> to give pain to Geraldine – still less to give offence to my Husband and least of all to promenade myself as an 'emancipated' woman – ([26? February 1848]; *CL* 22, p. 225)

The problem with George Sand was that she was a radical and a sexually emancipated woman, and Jewsbury was identified with her; even though her own behaviour as a single woman was unexceptionable, she had an intellectual and emotional passion that both Carlyles found by turns threatening and tiresome. There were ideas in the novel that challenged the current status of women that Carlyle held to, and that Welsh Carlyle apparently accepted. It was concerned with the need for middle-class women to be properly educated so that they would not be like 'grown children'; one character, as Jewsbury and Welsh Carlyle also did, disclaimed interest in the 'rights of women', but said that the rights women really want are 'not to have their lives and souls frittered into a shape to meet the notion of a "truly feminine character"' (*The Half Sisters* 2, p. 32).

   Welsh Carlyle's attitudes, to women, to marriage, to men, were not imposed by Carlyle: they had been internalised in her childhood and youth, and operated from within her own deepest self. The fact that they meshed with Carlyle's social attitudes meant that they were reinforced into a constrictive pattern from which she could not escape. What she could do was illuminate them by conscious ironic tales about the way her society worked and unconscious uneasiness expressed in her illnesses. Jewsbury's energetic reactions to similar constraints were an affront, an irritation and a stimulant to her. Her surface response to women's issues was consistently sceptical; they were as much material for satire as any other 'issue' was. In a letter to Martha MacDonald Lamont about Lamont's recently published novel, *The Fortunes of Women*, she wrote:

> I hope it wont be to write up what they call 'The rights of Women' at all rates – I am so weary of hearing about these <u>rights</u> of ours – and always to the tune of 'don't you wish you may get them'?

But she continued with:

> Your '<u>life</u>' looks useful and satisfactory – I wish I could say the same of mine – which has been for long standing still, and looking out into the Vague. I have had ideas about breaking out into <u>insurrection</u>, for the sake of the excitement of the thing, and joining Garibaldi and Mazzini, or latterly the more successful Hungarians![25] – but have carried them no further into practice than by showing myself on the platform at a meeting for 'Roman Liberty' which came off the other day at Bradford. (1 August [1849]; *CL* 24, p. 157)

The underlying response here to her own restrictive role and life indicates an awareness of the constrictions on women as a whole, but she expresses it in terms of the individual, equating it with the fight for national liberty in Italy and Hungary, rather than in relation to women. She also uses it as part of her standard satirical rhetoric, teasing Carlyle for his hostility to these issues:

> I have been on a platform at a public meeting for Liberty – Roman – thank your stars it was not for 'the <u>rights of women</u> – '. ([19 July 1849]; *CL* 24, p. 135)

For all her disclaimers about interest in the 'rights of women', we have already seen how she was aware of the application of the 'new ideas' about marriage to her own marriage. She refers to them as making sentimental novels seem old-fashioned after reading Dinah Mulock's novel *The Ogilvies*:[26]

> curious as being written by a young Irish girl – twenty years old – with little knowledge of <u>anything</u>, society included – but it is full of Love 'as an egg's full of meat' – the old highflown romantic circulating Library sort of love – which one looks at in these days of 'the new ideas' as one would look at a pair of peaked shoes or a ruff out of the reign of Elizabeth – and the plot goes ahead famously –. (HW, [2 December 1849]; *CL* 24, p. 304)

Welsh Carlyle shows an astute sense of the way new ideas can make even recent attitudes seem interestingly quaint, expressing her critical insight in terms of a fashion become historically curious rather than simply old-fashioned.

Welsh Carlyle externalises herself through the letters, hinting that there is a well of pain and misery behind the controlled social exterior; at a visit to the Macreadys, when for 'days and weeks not a cheerful feeling' had been in her mind, she

> talked talked . . . and they laughed till their tears ran down. <u>I</u> could not <u>laugh</u> – but no matter – perhaps my own gravity made the things I was saying only more amusing by contrast.

As they discussed depression, Welsh Carlyle remarking that 'everyone I suppose has their own fits of depression to bear up against if the truth were told', her auditors refused to accept this:

> 'Oh no surely! some people are never out of spirits – <u>yourself</u> for example, I really believe you do not know what it is to be ever sad for a minute!!! one never sees you that you do not keep one in fits of laughter!' I made no answer – but congratulated myself on having played my part so well. (HW, [19 May 1846]; *CL* 20, p. 194)

This illustrates both Welsh Carlyle's awareness of the construction of her social persona and her own technique for presenting herself in letters as a brave soul soldiering on under illness and depression. Her discussion of herself is embedded always in a narrative of daily events orchestrated to be accessible and entertaining to the recipient.[27] When she refers to suicide in a letter to her other cousin, Jeannie, it is in the context of an excuse for a delay in writing which admits how ill she has felt and yet weaves it into a rhetoric of rueful bravery:

> I have been putting off writing from day to day, in expectation of having either to notify to you my final death and burial, or some energetic resolution taken to deliver myself 'out of this' – You are to know that with the first warm days back came my <u>sickness</u> with all its hideous accompaniments, depression of spirits, incapacity of exertion, &c &c &c – enough to make a woman poison herself if she had only the courage; for I can never join in with the high flown twaddle about killing oneself being '<u>a piece of cowardice</u>' –. (JW, [15 June 1849]; *CL* 24, pp. 65–6)

She was particularly inclined to discuss her method of functioning in society with Jeannie and Helen because they knew her well, and knew the hidden story behind some of her depressions: Carlyle's devotion to Lady Ashburton which seemed to supplant Welsh Carlyle as the emotional centre of his life, leaving her only the technical role of orchestrating his comfort and household.

To Carlyle's sister Jean, married to a painter in Dumfries with several children, Welsh Carlyle would write:

> I have little to tell you worth even a penny stamp – <u>oneself</u> – at least <u>myself</u> is a sort of irish-bog-subject in which one is in danger of sinking overhead – common prudence commands therefore to 'keep out of <u>that</u>,' whatever else – and my days do not pass amidst people and things so interesting in themselves, as to be worth writing about to one safe and sound on the outside of <u>all that</u> as you are. (JCA, [?10 March 1850]; Froude *LM* 2, p. 105; *CL* 25, p. 45)

The idea of a woman full of hidden feeling and pain, implicit in the image of the woman sinking beyond her depths in a peat bog, might be missed by her recipient. But her cousins could read the double meaning when she described her state during a visit to Lady Ashburton in the country:

> I have not been so well latterly as in the first week – the sickness or more properly a sense of suffocation has given me many bad hours – but it is wonderful how one gets used by long endurance to sufferings which in the first moments of them drive one beside oneself – To see

me here nobody I am sure would suspect that I am not quite healthy and content – I know better – but the less one meditates on one's own miseries the better. (JW, [28 September 1848]; *CL* 23, p. 125)

The illness hidden behind the social facade is felt as 'suffocation'; this image seems an indicator to the cousins of Welsh Carlyle's unhappiness at being in the social space of someone about whom they knew she felt ambiguously; to us it is emblematic of the intensity of her reaction to the threat posed to her own precarious sense of self by the aristocratic surroundings controlled by her hostess.

Welsh Carlyle lived a life both extraordinary and ordinary. It was extraordinary in that she married and lived for nearly forty years with an irascible, writing 'genius' whose whole soul was devoted to himself and his gifts, and who expected the same devotion from her. She sustained a relationship with him, carving a role for herself, apparently in his shadow but, in fact, in their own house, his equal. It was ordinary, however, in that after her intense education in girlhood and her normal adolescent assumptions of 'specialness' and fame to come, she became as dutiful a housekeeper and wife as any other Victorian middle-class wife, constrained and moulded by her husband's, her own, and societal expectations of what she might or might not do. Welsh Carlyle wrote about duty often, believing in a 'sense of *duty*, of *self-denial*' that was 'stronger' than 'low, human appetite', as she wrote of Sir Philip Sidney depriving himself of water to give to a dying soldier (HW, c.4 February 1843; *CL* 16, p. 45). She wrote to Mary Smith in 1857 about her shock in 1828 on removal to Craigenputtoch. The letter enacts the ironic clash of expectations for the young Welsh Carlyle in its vivid description of her epiphany over the baking of bread:

> We were very <u>poor</u> and, further and worse, being an only child, and brought up to 'great prospects,' I was sublimely ignorant of every branch of useful knowledge, though a capital Latin scholar and a very fair mathematician!! It behoved me in these astonishing circumstances to learn – to sew! . . . Also, it behoved me to learn <u>to cook</u>! . . . So I sent for Cobbett's '<u>Cottage Economy</u>' and fell to work at a loaf of bread. But knowing nothing of the process of fermentation or the heat of ovens, it came to pass that my loaf got put into the oven at the time myself ought to have put into bed, and I remained the only person not asleep, in a house in the middle of a desert! One o'clock struck, and then two and then three; and still I was sitting there in an intense solitude, my whole body aching with weariness, my heart aching with a sense of forlorness and <u>degradation</u>. 'That I who had been so petted at home, whose comfort had been studied by everybody in the house, who had never been required to <u>do</u> anything but <u>cultivate my mind</u>, should have to pass all those hours of the night watching <u>a loaf of bread</u>! which mightn't turn out bread after all! // Such thoughts maddened me, till I laid my head on the table and sobbed aloud. It was then that somehow the idea of Benvenuto Cellini's sitting up all night watching his Perseus in the oven, came into my head; and suddenly I asked myself, 'After all, in the sight of the upper powers, what is the mighty difference between a statue of Perseus and a loaf of bread, so that each be the thing one's hand hath found to do? The man's determined will, his energy, his patience, his resource, were the really admirable things, of which the statue of Perseus was the mere chance expression. If he had been a woman living at Craigenputtoch, with a dyspeptic husband, sixteen miles from a baker, <u>and he a bad one</u>, all these same qualities would have come out most fitting in a <u>good</u> loaf of bread!' // I cannot express what consolation this germ of an idea spread over an uncongenial life, during five years we lived at that savage place. (Bliss, pp. 256–7)

This letter is quoted by Valerie Sanders in *The Private Lives of Victorian Women* and Norma Clarke[28] as emblematic of Welsh Carlyle's life purpose: in place of writing formal autobiography or a more articulated public writing career, she substitutes a passionate acceptance of and commitment to her life's work of housewifery – whether through baking bread, as in this letter, or the years of earthquakes in the house. When Carlyle was away she would vigorously recreate the home through painting, upholstery, and encounters with builders, joiners and plasterers. Clarke makes an analytic comparison between the two Carlyles' lifeworks:

> Throughout her life, Jane Carlyle worked hard to convince herself that making bread was equal to making a statue of Perseus, that running a house was essentially the same as writing a book. This projection of her subjective experience on to a culture which quite clearly did not agree, took its logic from Thomas Carlyle's unique position and the dissemination of his ideas – which originated in the life he shared with Jane Carlyle – through that culture. The outward similarity of his life to hers, the uncomfortable congruence in writing and housekeeping, blurred important differences. Each had to find the means within to endure a deal of uncongeniality, but while his endurance answered to the meanings of existence (and took him outwards), hers answered to the dissimulations of domesticity (and drove her inward).[29]

This interpretation of the letter is convincing as an approach to Welsh Carlyle's psychology of survival in spite of stress. But it omits acknowledgement that this powerful letter was written in retrospect (over twenty years) to encourage a younger woman. It begins by congratulating Mary Smith for having stayed in a position that was uncongenial to her:

> So many talents are wasted, so many enthusiasms turned to smoke, so many lives blighted for want of a little patience and endurance, for want of understanding and laying to heart that which you have so well expressed in these verses – the meaning of <u>the Present</u> – for want of recognising that it is not the greatness or littleness of 'the duty nearest to hand,' but the spirit in which one does it, that makes one's doing noble or mean!

The tale of the loaf of bread and Cellini follows this moral precept. As in all tales of moral instruction, the ilustration is emblematic of the moral, and constructed in this way to appeal to the recipient, a governess and teacher. The tale is drawn carefully to indicate Welsh Carlyle's educated knowledge of Cellini (mentioned by Carlyle in contemporary letters, not Welsh Carlyle), to emphasise her own fortitude, to underline the epiphany of the moment which implicitly has sustained her through the intervening years. It is a sophisticated piece of self-writing and Smith could be expected to respond to the pathos of the circumstances of the young Welsh Carlyle, as educated as herself, shown learning to come to terms with circumstances.

There is a gap between Welsh Carlyle's self-critical statements and her assertiveness of her own individuality, her 'I-ity', which leads the reader to question not just the presentation of herself for the recipients of her letters, but also her presentation of herself for her own consumption. It has been assumed by most interpreters that the ironic self of her letters contains an unexpressed pain about her life. But it seems possible, given her skill at constructing herself, that it was rather another construction of a self which could contain her pain and which was then preferred for the admiration of the recipients. This assumes that she was as aware and self-conscious of her writing processes as Carlyle of his.

Virginia Woolf's assessment of her was that her 'genius ... was positive, direct and practical. Her letters owe their incomparable brilliancy to the hawk-like swoop and descent of her mind upon facts. Nothing escapes her. She sees through clear water down to the rocks at the bottom.'[30] Woolf is responding to Welsh Carlyle's clarity but also to the intelligence that could produce her sharp and ironic style. Oliphant described the same stylistic characteristics in her 'wonderful talk': 'the power of narration which I never heard equalled except in my mother, the flashes of keen wit and sarcasm, occasionally even a little sharpness, and always the modifying sense of humour under all.'[31] These two professional writers identify the powerful technique that Welsh Carlyle exhibits in all her letters. She herself, commenting that a letter from her cousin had 'a certain sly sarcasm', saw it as 'peculiar to the family' (JW, 18 August 1842, *CL* 15, p. 28), thus imputing to Jeannie the stylistic mode at which she herself excels.

It is inevitable that Welsh Carlyle's letters and journals should be analysed for subtexts of discontent and critiques of women's position and of her own life. But it does a disservice to her considerable skill in the art of writing letters to ignore the achievement of letter after letter in which she creates supreme comic moments. The letters are a presentation of life through an ironic prism; irony at the expense of all, herself included. She chose to write in a private, muted form. This allowed her to conform to her sense, however culturally pre-determined, of what women should be, while constructing her own analysis of her life and self through the vast body of her letters. In the end her choice was not to seek fame, to publish, or to challenge social constraints. It was to accept the dictates of a conventional 'wifely' life of duty, of repression; and, in sarcastic and humorous counterpoint to that life, to weave her continuous web of commentary on her life and the lives surrounding her. It is appropriate that Dickens, the novelist who wrote narratives of savage comedy, full of unconscious images of pain and sexuality, should have particularly admired Welsh Carlyle for her story-telling skills – the recognition of like for like. Welsh Carlyle's claim to literary production does not rest on her meagre poems or journals, but on her astonishing collection of letters which record, comment on and create an unrivalled store of specific, artful, and controlled narratives. These are a rich field for analysis for insights into a complex, ambiguous, private woman, and for assessment of what she said and did not say about her condition as a nineteenth-century woman, constrained and limited in her possibilities. But if that is all they are used for then the full success of her achievements as a writer, the controlled performance of each letter, measured, self-conscious and skilled, remains unrecognised. In these letters we find an unequalled record of Welsh Carlyle's success as a life-writer.[32]

Notes

1.   Born Jane Baillie Welsh, Haddington, East Lothian, 1801; married 1826, Thomas Carlyle (1795–1881; *DNB*, essayist, historian); died London, 1866. The punctuation and spelling in all quotations are Jane Welsh Carlyle's. References to the letters are to *The Collected Letters of Thomas and Jane Welsh Carlyle*, 25 vols, ed. C. R. Sanders, K. J. Fielding, C. de L. Ryals, W. Bell, I. Campbell, A. Christianson, J. Clubbe, H. Smith (Duke University Press, Durham, N.C., 1970–97).
2.   Thomas Carlyle, 'Jane Welsh Carlyle', *Reminiscences*, ed. Ian Campbell (Dent, London, 1972).
3.   When two writers have the same surname, it is cumbersome identifying them by their full names. To call them 'Jane' and 'Thomas', however, is to continue the over-personalised tone of many analyses of their letters and relationship. Before marriage JWC's signature

was Jane Baillie Welsh; after marriage Jane Welsh Carlyle. In the text of the chapter she is, therefore, identified as Welsh Carlyle; in the notes as JWC and Thomas Carlyle as TC.

4. *Reminiscences*, p. 138.

5. Elizabeth Hardwick, *Seduction and Betrayal* (Weidenfeld & Nicholson, London, 1974), pp. 174, 172–3.

6. TC's nicknames for JWC, diminutives of Good, her nickname for him (e.g. *Collected Letters* 24, pp. 175, 177).

7. Editions of JWC's letters are not neutral. The choice of letters and excerpts of letters by editors define JWC according to their ideas of her. For a description of the controversy between Froude and A. Carlyle over the interpretation of TC's and JWC's relationship and characters, see T. Bliss (ed.), *Jane Welsh Carlyle: A New Selection of Her Letters* (Gollancz, London, 1950). Even *The Collected Letters of Thomas and Jane Welsh Carlyle* which is publishing her letters complete, defines her by enshrining her as one half of the definitive nineteenth-century letter-producing pair.

8. Sidonie Smith, *A Poetics of Women's Autobiography* (Indiana University Press, Bloomington, 1987), p. 19.

9. Smith, *A Poetics*, p. 44.

10. Smith, *A Poetics*, p. 46.

11. TC wrote that her letters 'abound in allusions very full of meaning in this circle, but perfectly dark and void in all others: "*Coterie-Sprache*", as the Germans call it, "family circle dialect" occurs every line or two; nobody ever so *rich* in that kind as she; ready to pick up every diamond spark, out of the common floor-dust, and keep it brightly available', *Reminiscences*, p. 52.

12. Smith, *A Poetics*, p. 46.

13. Irving (1792–1834; *DNB*) introduced JWC and TC to each other in Haddington, 1821; see *CL* 1, p. 359 and *Reminiscences*, p. 52.

14. Caroline Fox, *Memories of Old Friends* (Smith Elder & Co., London, 1882), p. 220. Cited in *CL*, 21, p. 219.

15. James Brown was Irving's successor, 1813.

16. 'Much Ado About Nothing', 2 August 1849, J. A. Froude (ed.), *Letters and Memorials of Jane Welsh Carlyle*, 3 vols (Longmans, Green & Co., London, 1883) 2, p. 53; Bliss, pp. 195–200; A. and M. Simpson (eds), *I Too Am Here: Selections from the Letters of Jane Welsh Carlyle* (Cambridge University Press, Cambridge, 1977), pp. 185–97; *CL* 24, p. 166.

17. A. Carlyle, *New Letters and Memorials of Jane Welsh Carlyle* (John Lane, London, 1903) 2, p. 88.

18. Froude, *LM* 2, p. 289.

19. 'You did kindly to send the little separate note: the least bit "*all to myself*", (as the children say) was sure to give me a livelier pleasure than any number of sheets in which I had but a secondary interest. For in spite of the honestest efforts to annihilate my *I-ity*, or merge it in what the world doubtless considers my better half; I still find myself a self-subsisting and alas! selfseeking *Me*. Little Felix, in the Wanderjahre, when … he pulls Theresa's gown, and calls out, "*Mama Theresa I too am here!*" only speaks out, with the charming trustfulness of a child, what I am perpetually feeling, tho' too sophisticated to pull people's skirts, or exclaim in so many words; Mr Sterling "*I too am here!*" JWC to John Sterling, [4 June 1835], *CL* 8, p. 138.

20. Clara Lucas Balfour, b.Liddell (1808–78; *DNB*); lecturer and writer on temperance; brought up and educated by her mother after her father's death.

21. Margaret Oliphant, *The Autobiography of Margaret Oliphant*, ed. Elisabeth Jay (Oxford University Press, Oxford, 1990), p. 104.

22. Geraldine Endsor Jewsbury (1812–80; *DNB*), novelist; *The Half Sisters* (Chapman & Hall, 1848). For more on the challenging and passionate Jewsbury/Welsh Carlyle friendship, see Aileen Christianson, 'Jane Welsh Carlyle and her Friendships with Women in the 1840s', *Prose Studies* 10 (1987), 283–95; and Norma Clarke, *Ambitious Heights: Writing, Friendship, Love – The Jewsbury Sisters, Felicia Hemans and Jane Carlyle* (Routledge, London, 1990).

23. Amalie Bölte (1811–91), German feminist who was working in London as a governess.

24. Published 1845; for reactions to its publication, see *CL* 19, pp. 24–5, 41.

25.   Giuseppe Garibaldi (1807–82) and Giuseppe Mazzini (1805–72); the latter was a close friend of JWC's; the Roman Republican forces had been defeated by the French and Garibaldi and Mazzini fled Rome in July. The Hungarians had begun an insurrection against Austria and Russia in April 1849 but were about to be defeated.
26.   Dinah Mulock Craik (1826–87; *DNB*).
27.   For further discussion of how JWC constructed herself in her letters, see Aileen Christianson, 'Rewriting Herself: Jane Welsh Carlyle's Letters', *Scotlands* 2 (1994), pp. 47–52.
28.   Valerie Sanders, *The Private Lives of Victorian Women: Autobiography in Nineteenth-century England* (Harvester Wheatsheaf, Brighton, 1989), ix and p. 168, and Clarke, *Ambitious Heights*, pp. 121–3.
29.   Clarke, *Ambitious Heights*, p. 123.
30.   Virginia Woolf, 'Geraldine and Jane', *The Common Reader Second Series* (Hogarth Press, London, 1932), p. 198.
31.   Oliphant, *Autobiography*, p. 98.
32.   Further primary and secondary material not already mentioned in text or notes includes: L. Huxley (ed.), *Jane Welsh Carlyle's Letters to her Family: 1839–1863* (John Murray, London, 1924); R. L. Tarr, 'Jane Welsh Carlyle's Publications', *Thomas Carlyle: A Descriptive Bibliography* (Clarendon Press, Oxford, 1989), pp. 470–509; R. L. Tarr & F. McClelland (eds), *The Collected Poems of Thomas and Jane Welsh Carlyle* (Penkevill Publishing Co., Greenwood, Florida, 1986); P. Rose, *Parallel Lives of Five Victorian Marriages* (Penguin, London, 1983); see D. J. Trela, 'Jane Welsh Carlyle and Margaret Oliphant: An Unsung Friendship', *Carlyle Annual* 11 (Spring 1990), 31–40. N. Clarke, 'Jane Welsh Carlyle: Letters, the Self, and the Literary,' and A. Christianson, 'Constructing Reality: Jane Welsh Carlyle's Epistolary Narratives', *Carlyle Studies Annual* 16 (1996) pp. 7–14, 15–24.

16

Beyond 'The Empire of the Gentle Heart': Scottish Women Poets of the Nineteenth Century

Valentina Bold

> Let loftier minstrels sway the lordly brain –
> Be mine the empire of the gentle heart.
> (Elizabeth Jane Irving, *Fireside Lays*, 1872)

Nineteenth-century poetry by women is often equated with Irving's 'Empire of the gentle heart'. According to received wisdom, ladies and ministers' daughters dominated a secluded literary scene, composing stilted rhymes focusing on family and faith. Certainly this was a strand in nineteenth-century poetry, exemplified by the cautious compositions of women like Lady Nairne, Caroline Oliphant the Younger, and Joanna Baillie. However, an alternative tradition of vigorous verse was present albeit neglected by contemporaries. The most exciting poetry of the period went beyond 'the empire of the gentle heart' into uncharted territories: personal, social and political. The majority of the second type of poetry was composed by women dismissed, because they lacked formal education, as 'self-taught'. Autodidacts, paradoxically, produced the most exciting verse of the nineteenth century.[1]

Autodidactic woman wrote primarily for self-expression, when they could, with conviction, passion and skill. Isobel Pagan (1741–1821), for instance, wrote poetry at the same time as running a howff from her home at Muirkirk. Remembered as vivacious, she has been described as a woman of 'a very unearthy appearance': she had a squint, a large tumour on her side and a deformed foot. She had a child by a man called Campbell who deserted her. Although Pagan could not write, the tailor William Gemmell transcribed on her behalf. She outlines her education, and boisterous present, in *A Collection of Poems and Songs* (c. 1805). Typically for an autodidact, she had only occasional lessons but was a voracious reader:

> I was born near four miles from Nith-head,
> Where fourteen years I got my bread;
> My learning it can soon be told,
> Ten weeks, when I was seven years old . . .
> And when I grew a wee thought mair,
> I read when I had time to spare;
> But a' the whole tract of my time,

> I found myself inclined to rhyme,
> When I see merry company,
> I sing a song with mirth and glee,
> I sing a song with mirth and glee,
> And sometimes I the whisky pree,
> But 'deed it's best to let it be.

Pagan was one of a number of poets writing in the early part of the century, who reinterpreted vernacular traditions. Her lyric experiments include 'Ca' the yowes to the knowes', which appears in Johnson's *Scots Musical Museum* (1787–1803) set to a plaintive air. Conventionally, it features a 'shepherd lad' who 'rowed me sweetly in his plaid' by 'the water side' yet this pastoral frame conceals subversive elements. Pagan was no proto-feminist, but her heroine is attractively canny in the tradition of the cautious lover Jenny, of *The Gentle Shepherd* (1725): 'I was bred up at nae sic schule,/My shepherd lad, to play the fule'. Pagan's woman complies with her lover's demands only when assured of gaining 'gowns and ribbons meet,/Cawf-leather shoon'. 'Wicked Tibbie' was, moreover, a skilled satirist, sharp as her younger compatriot Burns. Her concisely dismissive pieces are exemplified by the following:

> Mr –, in the Kyle,
>   Ca'd me a common –:
> But if he had not tried himsel',
>   He wadna been sae sure!

This is symptomatic of a persistently robust strain among Scottish women poets; parallels include Jean Glover (1758–1801), a travelling performer from Townhead of Kilmarnock and supposedly bad lot, represented in the Museum by a near-bawdy lyric about a rendezvous 'O'er the muir amang the heather'.[2]

Comparisons can be drawn between Pagan, Glover and Janet Little (1759–1813), 'The Scotch Milkmaid'. The finest woman vernacular poet of her time, Little was born in the same year as Burns, at Nether Bogside, Ecclefechan. She worked as a domestic for the Reverend Johnstone, accompanying his family to Glasgow. Later she served Mrs Dunlop, Burns's patron, who passed Little on to her daughter, Susan Henri, to become head dairymaid of Loudon estate. Dunlop proved an active, if ambivalent patron, admiring her 'rustic poetess' with the qualification 'she writes blank verse, which I don't like'. Stepmother to five children, the Milkmaid had considerable physical presence despite being lame from 1790.

Little's extensive range is evident in *The Poetical Works* (1792). Romantic formulae and formal English pieces abound. 'Upon a Young Lady's leaving Loudon Castle' laments: 'What means this silent, solitary gloom?/All nature in her dishabille appears'. Additional examples of this style include Little's pensive 'On Happiness' and mournful 'To a Lady, A Patroness of the Muse on her Recovery from Sickness'. Little was making a concerted bid for patronage, dedicating her Poetical Works to 'The Countess of Loudon' and drawing attention to 'moral lessons' learnt in the workplace. Despite such placatory and refined pieces the Milkmaid is at her best when drawing on the precedents of Ramsay and Fergusson. Her dishonest trader Rab, in 'On Seeing Mr – baking cakes', is kin to the cynical madam of Ramsay's 'Lucky Spence's Last Advice' and 'browster wives' of Fergusson's 'Leith Races'. Rab complains:

> My cakes are good, none can object;
>   The maids will ca' me thrifty.
> To save a sixpence on the peck
>   Is just an honest shifty.

Ramsay's additions to 'Christis Kirk on the Green' and Fergussons's ebullient 'Hallow Fair' are recalled by Little's 'On Hallowe'en'. Then there is the pseudo-Burnsian 'From Snipe, A Favourite Dog, to his Master' and the spirited Scots 'To My Aunty': 'Wha ne'er o' wit nor lear was vaunty'. 'Given to a Lady who asked me to write a poem' is hilariously reductive, highlighting the double standards women poets faced. Burns, a 'ploughman chiel', was acclaimed:

> But then a rustic country quean
> To write – was e're the like o't seen?
> A milk maid poem books to print;
> Mair fit she wad her dairy tent.[3]

As Little suggests, autodidacts were treated solely as social peculiarities. In contrast, poets of a higher social standing were tolerated, and even admitted to the literary canon. And while modesty meant that ladies often published anonymously, their rank was usually implied. Carolina Oliphant (1766–1845), Lady Nairne, used a respectable-sounding pseudonym, Mrs Bogan of Bogan, for Robert Purdie's *The Scotish Minstrel* (1821–4) and her work is of a similarly unthreatening character. The collected works of Oliphant, 'The Strathearn Poetess', were posthumously published under her own name, as *Lays from Strathearn* (1846). Evocative airs enhance the mainly melancholic lyrics here. Family Jacobite allegiances, after the event, are evident in songs like 'Will ye no come back again?'. It finely captures the characteristic, late-Jacobite, elegiac and tearful qualities which pervade James Hogg's seminal *The Jacobite Relics of Scotland* (1819–21). Nairne mournfully wishes for the Stuarts' return, emphasising her sentiments with a skilfully matched, poignant air:

> Bonnie Charlie's now awa,
> Safely owre the friendly main;
> Mony a heart will break in twa,
> Should he ne'er come back again.

Oliphant is equally soulful regarding intimate matters. 'The Land of the Leal', set to 'Hey tutti tatti', consoles Mrs Campbell Colquhoun on the death of her 'bonnie bairn'.[4] Lady Nairne portrays a woman piously bereaved, 'wearin' awa' . . . /Like snaw-wreaths in thaw', and joyfully anticipating joining her child in the desirable 'land o' the leal'.

The self-styled refined were prone to the excesses of nineteenth-century 'good taste', epitomised in work from 'the female Wordsworth', John Wilson, and his excessively influential *The Isle of Palms* (1812). But Oliphant was capable of producing credible, if sanitised, oral-style songs like 'The Pleughman'. Generally the attempt to charm her reader makes for a lack of verisimilitude. 'The Boat Song o' the Clyde', for instance, delights the reader with a joyous vision of holidaying 'doun the water'. The breathless Scots-English, though, is slightly jarring; unpleasant aspects of city life are minimised: 'An' oh! how sweet in flow'ry June,/To leave auld Glasgow's smoky toun'. 'Caller Herrin' attempts to profile the dangers implicit in fishing, strikingly and movingly equating fish with 'lives o' men'. However, this is a somewhat gutted fish-wife's cry, designed for an audience who did not desire to hear about life in the raw:

> When ye were sleepin' on your pillows,
> Dream'd ye aught o' our puir fellows,
> Darkling as they faced the billows,
> A' to fill the woven willows?
>
> Buy my caller herrin',
> New drawn fraw the Forth.

The well-bred wistfulness of 'Caller Herrin' was later to be parodied by Robert Tannahill.[5]

Upper- and middle-class poets coyly professed their relish for situations of humble domesticity, even if its details were unfamiliar. Elizabeth Hamilton (1758–1816), the novelist of *The Cottagers of Glenburnie* (1808), preferred 'My Ain fireside' to 'great ha's'. Lady Charlotte Campbell, in 'Yes, I Will Go With Thee, My Love', rejected 'courtly scenes' for a 'lonely cott'. Dorothea Maria Ogilvy of Clova (1823–1895) is more believable in 'The Weary Spinnin O't'. Her protagonist, at least, bewails her life: 'Sittin spinnin, sittin spinnin/A' the lea-lang day'. Ogilvy was more experimental than most of her peer group: writing a dramatic comedy, *Willie Wabster's Wooing and Wedding on the Braes of Angus* (1868) as well as *My Thoughts* (1870) and *Poems* (1873). Lady Anne Barnard (née Lindsay; 1750–1825), ironically chose to set 'Auld Robin Gray' to 'The bridegroom greets when the sun gangs down'. Anne Barnard's bride is resigned to a marriage of convenience (unlike the woman in a similar situation in Burns's 'What can a young lassie do wi' an auld man'): 'I'll do my best a gude wife to be,/For Auld Robin Gray, he is kind to me'.[6]

Of course there were honourable exceptions among the generally unchallenging ranks of lady poets. Some women, while examining life at home, looked outside Scotland for exotic inspiration. *The Poems* (1802) of Anne Hunter (née Home; 1742–1842), range from 'Birthday odes' for members of her family to a topical 'Cherokee Indian Death Song'. Anne Grant of Laggan (née McVicar; 1755–1838), was born in Glasgow, raised in America, and married a Highland minister. Grant of Laggan is best known for her prose: *Letters from the Mountains* (1806) and *Essays on the Superstitions of the Highlanders* (1811). However, her poetry is equally insightful, from her ethnographic *The Highlanders and other Poems* (1808) to the triumphalist *Eighteen Hundred and Thirteen* (1814). *Poems on Various Subjects* (1803) examines the exploitation of indigenous peoples both in Scotland and America. 'The Highlanders' is a romantic history of the Celts, attacking the causes of depopulation. 'An Ode: On reading one upon the same subject by Professor Richardson of Glasgow' expresses 'Indignant grief' at the treatment of Native Americans. Such pieces contrast with better known, sentimental pieces like 'On the Marquis of Huntly's Departure for the Continent with his regiment in 1799' (sometimes referred to from its opening as 'Oh where, tell me where, is your Highland Laddie gone?').[7]

While several Lady Poets deserve to be reassessed others were, perhaps, overrated. A case in point is Joanna Baillie (1762–1851) who, in addition to her dramas, published genteel verse (initially anonymously). The majority of her poems, in *Fugitive Pieces* (1790), *Metrical Legends* (1821), *A Collection of Poems* (1823) and *Fugitive Verses* (1840), are competent but constricted. There are hagiographies like 'A Metrical Legend of William Wallace' (eulogising a hero from whom Baillie claimed descent) and 'The Legend of

Lady Griseld Baillie' (treating another ancestor with reverence). Some items are more imaginative. 'The Elden Tree', a ballad imitation, is a tale of cruelty with an uneasy happy ending as a fratricide becomes a monk. However, the lure of convention prevented Baillie from developing such unsettling elements in her work. She was viewed, above all, as a beneficial moral influence on poetry. Baillie's simplistic hymns, exemplified by 'Second Devotional Song' ('Our heavenly Father sent his Son/From hateful sin to save us') won enthusiastic admiration.

Like Scott in *The Minstrelsy of the Scottish Border* (1802–3), Baillie specialised in making her 'traditional' songs conform to modern manners. 'Woo'd and Married and a' originally had a skittish bride reprimanded; Baillie's version has a woman reassured by her lover. 'Fy, let us a' to the Wedding (An Auld Sang, New Buskit)' makes William Scott of Thirlestane's abusive 'The Blythsome Bridal' genteel. Scott's 'sow-libber Patie' and 'fat-luggit Leesie' are removed, in favour of 'bonny sweet Nanny' and 'Laurie the laird'. Even the fare is refined from 'lapper-milk kebbucks' to 'veal florentines'. The metaphorical meat, thereby, is removed from the piece: a neutralising tendency typifying Baillie's poetry.[8]

The politeness which pleased contemporary critics was sustained by the next poetic generation. It included ladies like Caroline Oliphant the Younger (1807–31), Lady Nairne's niece, with her languid lyrics 'O Never! O Never' and 'Home in Heaven'. The compositions of Alicia Anne Spottiswoode, Lady John Scott (1810–1900), are of a similar tendency but much livelier. *Songs and Verses* (1904) includes spirited historical pieces such as the Jacobite 'We've Lookit for ye Lang', and imaginative reconstruction such as 'Darnley after Rizzio's Murder'. The latter opens, fittingly, lugubriously: 'O my Mary! humbled here before thee,/I do confess how great has been my sin.' Spottiswoode is, though, mainly remembered for 'Annie Laurie', skilfully reworking a buoyant traditional song attributed to William Douglas of Fingland, and set to the air of 'Kempie Kaye'. Spottiswoode's exuberant lyrics seem to look forward to Violet Jacob's *Songs of Angus* (1915). The elder writer, at her best, transcends the constrictive, domestic melancholia which plagued her contemporaries.[9]

Many women poets portrayed family life as blissfully compensating for lives which were humdrum or even miserable. This is especially true of those from working- or middle-class backgrounds. Mary Inglis cherished the transient 'sinless mirth' of infants, for example, in 'Let the Bairnies Play'. She was the daughter of a United Presbyterian minister, living near Glasgow from 1858. Jessie D. M. Morton (b.1824), a Dunfermline newsagent, celebrates 'My first-born' in *Clarkson Gray* (1866), which also includes comic pieces like 'Her Broken Bowl', directed against 'Ane o' the awfu' cleanin' kind'. Mrs Lindsay Carnegie (b.1844), from an Anniston military family, was influenced by the sickly English style of Mrs Opie. In *Children of Today* (1896) Carnegie praises 'My Daughter': 'Flower-gemmed like the month of May'. Isabella F. Darling (b.1861), who lived in Glasgow, immortalised 'Baby' in *Poems and Songs* (1889): 'Two lily lids, which fall and rise/O'er dewy violets, "baby's eyes"'. *The Poems* (1880) of Ellen Corbet Nicholson (b.1848), Mrs Snell, a teacher born in Strathaven, look back happily on 'puirtith's happy days' in 'The Ae Wee Room'. Less confidently, though, Nicholson expresses a suspicion of warfare (found frequently among nineteenth-century Scottish women poets), in 'For Fatherland'.[10]

The expression of suffering was much admired. For example the Dundee poet Jean Kyd (b.1858), 'Deborah' of *The People's Journal*, featured her trauma, as a two-times widow, in *Poems of the Hearth* (1869). Mourning poetry was commonplace, which is not to detract from the genuine grief it often conveyed. Multiple instances can be listed. Lydia Falconer

Fraser (d.1876), the wife of Hugh Miller, produced 'Thou'rt Awa' for the sake of dead children: 'angels are thy teachers now'. Anna Marie Maxwell (*née* Ainslie; 1793–1845), a governess before marriage, published *Letters from the Dead to the Living* (1820), and her dolorous poems include 'The Rose' and 'Edmund's Grave'. Maxwell published *The Young Lady's Monitor and Married Woman's Friend* (1840) and edited *The Renfrewshire Annual* (1841–2). Hannah Brown Mackenzie, a reviewer for *The Glasgow Herald*, offers gloomy 'Mementoes' of the dead in *Worthy of Trust* (1885). Margaret Thomson Laird (d.1869), later Mrs McLeod, a Paisley iron founder's daughter and wife of an Alloa Free Church minister, shows heartfelt emotion in her 'Anniversary Lines on the Death of My Only Son, Removed in Early Childhood'. The Paisley warehouse worker Jeannie Johnstone (b.c.1870, whose father was the gardener-poet Alexander Johnstone) expressed similar feelings while remembering a deceased three-year-old, 'In Loving Memory of Jane B. Johnstone'. Her only consolation is a deep-felt religious faith: 'Weep not, your darling rests secure/On a loving Saviour's breast'.[11]

Unquestioning religion pervaded nineteenth-century poetry. Women of the manse, as would be expected, excelled in treatments of pious themes. For instance, Mary Lundie Duncan (1814–40), a minister's wife from Cleish, wrote the uncomplicated hymn 'Jesus, tender Shepherd'. Jane Catherine Lundie (1821–84) from Kelso, wife of a Free Church minister, rejected the things of this world in favour of heavenly fulfilment in 'Pass Away Earthly Joy'. In Kilmarnock, Marion Paul Aird (1815–88), 'Marimonia', great-niece of the minister-poet Hamilton Paul, published *The Home of the Heart* (1846), *Heart Histories* (1853) and *Sun and Shade* (1860). 'The Violet', associated with faithfulness and early death, stands here for Divine truth. Aird's piece for children, 'Far Far Away', fervently seeks a better world: 'Had I the wings of a dove I would fly/Far, far away' to heaven.[12]

Faith was affirmed strenuously by the vast majority of nineteenth-century women poets. Mary Cross, from Glasgow, was scornful in dismissing atheists in 'To a Sceptic'. Alice Pringle, a United Presbyterian minister's daughter from Auchterarder, displayed her gushing devoutness in 'The Strongest Power' from *Greycliff Poems* (1878): 'Oh! many wondrous links there be/That bind us to infinity'. Pringle, who lived in England for most of her life, also wrote melodramatic verse. Elizabeth Cecilia Douglas Clephane (1830–69), daughter of the Sheriff of Fife, wrote 'The Ninety Nine' (or 'The Lost Sheep') which was appreciated by the American hymn collectors D. L. Moody and Ira Sankey. Reprinted as 'Breathings on the Border', this plaintively asks for 'Thy strength to do the work/My God hath set for me'. More judgementally, Catherine Napier's *The City of the World* (1845) condemns 'The Drunkard', 'The Felon', 'The Debtor' and 'The Hypocrite' with gusto. Poetic drama of a similar tenor includes Mrs Leckie's *The Guardian* (1843); her other works were *The Stepmother* (1842) and *The Dream of the Western Shepherd* (1847). A final example of this almost endless stream of religious versifiers is offered by Margaret Ballantyne, a Paisley weaver's daughter who was middle-aged in 1890. In 'Flowers and their Mission', she advocated that we 'carry bright sunshine', through faith, to others.[13]

Despite such confident religiosity though, undertones of uncertainty can be detected. Traces of doubt can be found in the work of women like Margaret Stewart Sandeman of Springland (1803–83). The niece of Lady Nairne, Sandeman was married to a descendant of the Glassite sect and suffered at first-hand the enormous upheavals and family dislocations following the Disruption of the Scottish Church in 1843. She describes her experiences with ambivalence in 'Quitting the Manse': 'We are leaving the scenes of our happiest hours', although 'the Church of our country is faithful and free'. Personal sacrifice might, it seems, be quietly resented. Sandeman's daughter, Mrs Margaret Fraser

Barbour (1823–92) of Bonskeid, was, incidentally, also a religious poet but one of a more conventional nature. Barbour forgives 'Death' freely: 'thou sett'st free/The prison'd bird'. The Christian poetry of Anne Ross Cousin (1824–1906), 'A. R. C.', who was married to a Free Church minister, is ostensibly dogmatic. 'Christ within the Veil', in Cousin's *Immanuel's Land* (1897), mistrusts religious representations in conformity to standard beliefs: 'Tis faith alone, with pencil of sweet light,/May trace the Unseen – and only on the heart'. However, 'The Double Search' is less confident, shifting uncomfortably between a lost Soul and the lost 'Lord of Light' who, eventually, 'shall timely meet'. Mary A. Mackay, from Caithness, is enigmatic in the manner of the great Dundee sceptic James Young Geddes in *The New Jerusalem* (1879). Her 'Shadows of Long Ago' cries out: 'You come to me – bruised and alone –/The heart I used to know'. 'A Retrospect', ostensibly recommending fulfilment through faith, whispers 'I did not crown one grand desire'.[14]

Dissatisfaction with the status quo in society was expressed by autodidactic women in particular. Three similar poets, worthy of especial attention, are Mary Pyper, Maria Bell and Isabella Craig-Knox. Pyper (1795–1870) was born in Greenock. Too sickly to attend school, she was raised in Edinburgh and studied literature at home with her mother, a single parent. Pyper's favourite poet was Dryden; she thought Burns 'rather coarse'. She worked for fifteen years in a trimming shop, then as a seamstress, but was prevented from working after losing her sight. Latterly she lived on the charity of St Columba's congregation, Edinburgh. There is a great deal of wry humour in Pyper's work, given her circumstances. This is particularly true of *Select Pieces* (1847). 'On Asking a Lady to Subscribe' offers bitter observations on a mean-spirited patron who is metaphorically blind to the poet's merits. 'Epitaph – A Life' is economically poignant:

> I came at Morn – 'twas Spring, I smiled,
>   The fields with green were clad;
> I walked abroad at Noon – and lo!
>   'Twas Summer – I was glad.
> I sate me down – 'twas Autumn eve,
>   And I with sadness wept;
> I laid me down at Night, and then
>   'Twas Winter – and I slept.

Pyper's later work is habitually resigned and may strike modern tastes as unsavoury. *Sacred Poems* (1865), for example, features 'Lines Written on the Death of a Little Child': 'Scarce hadst thou felt the parting pang/Till death had set thee free'. Pyper glosses over unsavoury aspects of the present and the past. 'Thanksgiving. For the Removal of Cholera' has sickness presented as God's pestilence. 'Negro Emancipation. Written on the Morning of August 1, 1836' credits Britain with having 'strain'd each nerve' to help the 'injured children' of Africa.[15]

The succinctness of Pyper's early poems resembles that of Maria Bell's (d.1899). Bell is elegantly terse in *Songs of Two Homes* (1899). 'Life' sums up the human condition as a wearying journey to Christ: 'A busy way of life that goes/Past many graves that gape and close'. 'An Empty House' recalls Emily Dickinson's 'There is another sky' in which the narrator begs 'Prithee my brother,/Into my garden come'. In Bell's poem, a heart is offered to God – 'no man may crave it' – so 'the great King may enter/To take His pleasure'.

'The Weary Land' takes an apparently comforting theme (the afterlife) and turns it into a ghastly prospect. This poem is like a dreary coda to Stevenson's 'Requiem':

> There is a weary land afar
>   Beyond a weary sea,
> And Scottish lads go sailing there,
>   Go sailing out so free;
> But back they come as weary men
>   A weary life to dree,
> Or find their graves with outland folk
>   Beyond the outland sea.

Although little is known about Bell's circumstances, it is likely she was an autodidact. Her desire 'Just to be all alone and quiet lie/Upon my bed', expressed in 'Peace', suggests she knew the rigours of labour well. Certainly her disturbing poetry is a far cry from the 'empire of the gentle heart'.[16]

The third member of this untypical trio is Isabella Craig-Knox, 'Isa' (1831–1903), of *The Scotsman*. Craig-Knox was an Edinburgh hosier's daughter who spent a great deal of her life in London. There she served as Secretary to the National Association for the Promotion of Social Science, publishing fiction in *The Quiver* and campaigning for women's rights. The preface to *Poems* (1856), though, draws attention mainly to Craig-Knox's desire for 'the approval of persons of taste and education' which would increase her 'appreciation of the class to which she belongs, and whose elevation and refinement she most earnestly desires'.

Much of Craig-Knox's work is quietistic, such as 'Live and Let Live'. An old man, in 'The Workman to his Sons', accepts the labourer's lot gladly: 'Bearing my burden all the way'. Some of Craig-Knox's Scots poetry verges on the sickly. 'My Mary and Me', for example, pass mildly from courtship to auld biddieship together. There are, though, glimpses of real originality, especially in reframing Biblical and apocryphal stories. 'The Poor Old Jew' recycles the legend of the Wandering Jew, calming prejudice with reason. 'Martha and Mary' reworks the Biblical sisters of Bethany into an industrial parable, framed by the city's 'smoky vapour'. Craig-Knox asserts the need for upholding working people's sense of community; friendship between men prefiguring sisterly solidarity. While Martha and Mary are not related by blood, their fathers ploughed together:

> Poverty, pain and labour,
>   They shrank not to endure –
> The stay and the strength of a nation
>   Are the strong and the patient poor.

Martha and Mary become temporary love rivals, indirectly resulting in Martha being blinded in an industrial accident. They reject the divisive town and end up in a country cottage where they are, macabrely, bound as if by a 'wedding vow'.

Craig-Knox is keenly aware of the relentlessness of manual labour. 'Rest', in *Duchess Agnes* (1864), opposes the powerful evocations of industrial strength which characterised poetry by some Victorian men, such as the representation of the railway engine in the work of Alexander Anderson ('Surfaceman'). And Craig-Knox's depiction of the hideousness of factory life anticipates the bleak townscapes of John Davidson:

With grind and groan,
    With clank and moan,
Their task the prisoned forces ply; –
    The great wheels fly
As if they wove the web of Fate;
And to and fro, amid the roar,
Squalid creatures pace the floor;
Slaves of those iron wheels that they,
Bound their impulse to obey,
And upon their bidding wait;
While to their service dumb,
    Not only men are given,
    But childish troops are driven,
And women come,
Till every heart with weariness is numb.

Such discomfort with nineteenth-century experiences is sustained in poems about military life like 'They Died at Alma', which has points in common with 'The Attack on the Great Redan, and Fall of the Malakhoff' in Elizabeth Campbell's *Poems* (1862). Proceeds from the sale of Craig-Knox's *Poems: an offering to Lancashire* (1863) were intended to aid the distressed Cotton districts. But her political vigour declined in her late work, like the insipid *Songs of Consolation* (1874). (Craig-Knox should not be confused with 'Isa' [Cowan], poet of Newton Stewart and author of of *The Banks o' Cree*, 1882.)[17]

Hostility to urban life bore fruit, elsewhere, in a strain of pastoral poetry following the tradition of *The Gentle Shepherd*. Anna McGowan (1812–65), a minister's daughter born in Galloway who died in Kirkcudbright, wrote cheerful nature *Poems* (1855). Mary Anne Shaw from Paisley, daughter of the poet John Shaw, extolled 'The Summer Breeze' and, 'In Sparkling Melody', 'Mother Earth'. Elizabeth Jane Irving (b.1842), a teacher who lived in Castle Douglas, then Amsterdam, wrote rustic *Fireside Lays* (1872) like 'Nut Gathering'. Excepting the anti-war poem 'Faithful in Death', Irving's poetry is self-confessedly 'less of mind than soul'. Margaret Wallace Thomson, a music teacher from Paisley, composed an 'Autumn Song' which is joyful as Hogg's 'Boy's Song': friends seek 'Hip and haw, and nut and rasp,/Ripened ready to our grasp'. Increasingly nature poems were contemplative. Thomson's 'In the Woods' evokes unknown natural truths, symptomatic of a shift towards autumnal poetry like Annie S. Swan's (1859–1943) 'Nae Rest till we Win Home' and 'Harvest Days'.[18]

Elizabeth Hartley (b.1844), a gardener's daughter from Dumbarton, was experimental in her poems about nature. A sickly child, Hartley left school at eight years old. As a committed reader, at ten she had memorised most of *The Lady of the Lake* (1810). At the early age of sixteen she produced *Evening Thoughts* (1862), later reissued as *The Prairie Flower* (1870). Contemporaries like Alexander Murdoch in *Recent and Living Scottish Poets* (1883) considered that 'Mrs Hartley . . . writes with much beauty, power and purity of feeling'. *The Prairie Flower* is a Transatlantic adventure with Emersonian overtones and similarities to Whittier's 'Song of Slaves in the Desert'. Like Craig-Knox's rustic idyll in 'Martha and Mary', Hartley creates a strange, allegorical landscape. The Prairie is an imagined place where self-fulfilment is possible, although Hartley's women are more isolated than Craig-Knox's. Unlikely connections abound in this quasi-Biblical wasteland:

The golden light of morning is awaking in the East,
And dispelling twilight's shadows, with their hazy
    wreaths of mist.
It tinges now the forest with its changeful verdure
    bright,
And it dances on the streamlet in its floods of
    bursting light,
And it breaks upon the prairie as it stretches far
    away,
Till it meets the dim horizon in a line of misty
    grey.
O'er its lakes, where floats the lotus, and its
    snow-white blossoms weaves,
While the Ibis stalks amongst them, and seems whiter
    than their leaves.

The desert, in this context, becomes a place for exploration and development, rewarded by fruitful love.

Hartley relishes unusual associations. 'The Violets. An Incident of the Battle of the Wilderness' has a dying soldier consoled by the ubiquitous Victorian image of the single flower. 'The Child and the Sunbeam', distastefully for modern audiences, parallels a sunbeam on a child on its mother's knee, and that which will touch its grave. There are quirky pieces, like 'An Auld Wive's Soliloquy on Velocipeding', in Scots, and the 'Address to Dunbarton Castle': 'O mighty mass of frowning rock!/Long has thou brav'd the tempest's shock', sees the rock as timelessly associated with the Wallace and his 'Despising Southern slavery there'. 'The Right of Way' treats a current debate, contrasting the brutality of the rich with gentle 'green glades'. Striving for originality, Hartley was sometimes unsuccessful but in her attempt to find an original voice can be compared with writers like Browning and Clough.[19]

Women frequently wrote about those who defied convention, from necessity or choice. Agnes Marchbank (Mrs Marshall; b.1846) from Edinburgh wrote *Songs of Labour* (1872), *Home and Country* (1892), *A Swatch of Hamespun* (1895) and *Some Edinburgh Bohemians* (1891). Her 'Tina-Tit' opens with 'Wee, wee Tina-tit / . . . Tumbling ower the Pussie-cat' bravely. As the poem progresses, Tina-Tit is 'Crushed in all her womanhood' by the 'love of gold'. She finishes as 'Puir, reckless Tina Tit' at 'the very brink/O' madness and despair'. Marchbank's 'Limpin' Kate' is equally an outsider. Realising suitors desire her 'siller', she stays single. Joanna Picken (1798–1859), 'Alpha', daughter of Burns's contemporary Ebenezer Picken, presents a similar message in Scots in her powerful and reductive critique of marriage in 'An Auld Friend Wi' a New Face'. Picken, who worked as a music teacher and moved to Canada in 1842, presented spinsterhood as highly preferable to marriage.[20]

An independence of spirit is splendidly evident in the work of Janet Hamilton (née Thomson; 1795–1873). There is some truth in the patronising remarks of George Eyre-Todd, who called Hamilton 'one of those remarkable women in humble life of whom Scotland has produced so strong a crop' in his *The Glasgow Poets* (1906). Hamilton worked from the age of seven, 'Slave in all but name', like her subjects in 'A Lay of the Tambour Frame'. Hamilton's experiences can fruitfully be compared with William Thom's, described in *Rhymes and Recollections of a Handloom Weaver* (1844). Married at thirteen, Hamilton raised ten children and lived in Langloan, Coatbridge. She was blind from 1855.

Sympathy for fellow workers, at home and abroad, is constantly evident in Hamilton's work. *Poems and Essays* (1863), *Poems of Purpose and Sketches in Prose* (1865), *Poems and Ballads* (1868) and *Poems, Essays and Sketches* (1880) range from local and personal to national and international issues. 'Luggie Past and Present' treats the river earlier celebrated for its beauty by David Gray, but now a 'molten river' of industry. There is a pervasive morality in Hamilton's work. In poems like 'The Fruits of the Spirit' she suggests faith compensates for weariness. Even so, she energetically hated all forms of exploitation. 'Oor Location' is primarily a temperance poem, but anticipates Thomson and Davidson in its depiction of urban nightmare:

> A hunner funnels bleezin', reekin',
> Coal an' ironstane, charrin', smeekin';
> Navvies, miners, keepers, fillers,
> Puddlers, rollers, iron millers . . .
> Thick and thrang we see them gaun,
> First the dram-shop, then the pawn;
> Owre a' kin's o' ruination,
> Drink's the king in oor location.[21]

Hamilton espouses a variety of causes. Although eloquent in Scots, and defending the language of 'Wallace the wicht', Burns and Hogg in 'A Plea for the Doric', she was a true Briton. Hamilton's admiration for her monarch informs 'Lines. Suggested by Seeing the Train Containing the Queen and Suite pass through Coatbridge, on the Caledonian Railway, on her way to the North, May 1, 1862'. (Victoria was a popular poetic figure celebrated, for instance, by the Paisley writers such as Jean Clerk in 'Victoria' (1840), and Isabella Ledgerwood (b. 1866) in 'The Jubilee Year'.) Hamilton is outspoken in her support of liberty abroad. She advises supporting 'The Spanish Revolution', 'Pray for Poland' and 'Freedom for Italy – 1867':

> 'He is the freeman whom the Truth makes free;
> All else are slaves,' I cry aloud to thee,
> O Garibaldi! in the fateful hour.

Despite her militarism in defence of liberty, Hamilton is ambivalent regarding warfare. 'Night Scene at the Fall of Sebastopol' uses imagery drawn from *The Iliad* to sketch out a terrible scene: 'Like leaves in autumn, drenched in pools of blood,/Lie dead and dying'.[22]

Doubts about establishment ethics were often expressed by nineteenth-century poets, from Mrs Gordon's defence of animal rights in *Man and the Animals* (1840), to Agnes Stewart Mabon's suspicion of Jedburgh politicians in *Hamely Rhymes* (1887). The Glasgow poet and piano teacher, Marion Bernstein, in *Mirren's Musings* (1876) refused to tolerate dismissals of 'The Wetched Sex'. A poet of some power and anger, Bernstein was enraged by callous assertions like that in *The Weekly Mail* (to which she contributed): 'Kicking never degrades a woman, however much it may injure her physically. Now, if she had what some call her rights, she would be very seriously degraded indeed'. 'A Woman's Logic', Bernstein's response, ironically remarks, that if violence 'cannot degrade' then 'I am tempted to using/This weapon against you today'. Much of *Musings* was written from Bernstein's sickbed but her weak constitution is not reflected in the poetry. 'Wanted a Husband' attacks the conventional expectation that wives should 'Be a cheerful companion, whenever desired,/And contentedly toil day and night if required'. In contrast the ideal man is defined, with a biting coda:

> Wanted a husband who's tender and true,
> Who will stick to his duty, and never get 'fou,'
> But when all his day's work he has blithely gone
>   through,
> Help his wife, 'set to rights,' till her work is
>   done too . . .
> Now, if such a lad you should happen to see,
> He's wanted by many, but yet – not by me!

'Wanted in Glasgow' wryly demands relief 'From the factory chimneys on every side,/By which folks in Glasgow like herrings are dried'. 'An Appeal' condemns the law of the time whereby sailors had to turn over escaped slaves to their owners; it wishes that 'every Tory chief/Fall from his misused power'. Such pieces recall the work of the Glasgow radical Alexander Rodger (at once ferocious social critic and editor of the reactionary *Whistle Binkie*; 2nd to 5th series, 1839–46). Bernstein's radical streak is sustained through pieces like 'A Dream' which reworks the visionary tradition of Ramsay, Burns and Hogg from a woman's perspective. She provides an ambitious programme for righting contemporary wrongs, imagining women in control of the House of Commons and the abolition of the House of Lords; female judges would ensure that truth became 'The fashion'. Heartfelt religious beliefs underpinned Bernstein's desire for social change. Her piety is apparent in the Messianic 'The Great Passover' and additions to the Kirk's 'First Paraphrase'. 'To an Atheist' bewails the unbeliever's plight: 'And is this world thy only hope?'.[23]

Women poets were often reluctant radicals, attempting to reconcile piety, and a desire for respectability, with an acute awareness of injustices. Jessie Russell (b. 1850), in *The Blinkin' o' the Fire and other Poems* (1877), describes herself as 'A Poetess, with lowly lot,/Whose verse to fame can ne'er aspire'. An orphan, she was raised by Cameronian grandparents in Dumfriesshire, becoming a dressmaker in Glasgow and marrying a ship's carpenter. On the one hand, she wrote conservative pieces like 'A Temperance Lay'. 'Sleep', too, is a docile piece: the 'wearied labourer', summoned by a bell to 'rough-shod labour', finds consolation only in the knowledge of eternal rest with Christ. On a similar level, 'Love's labour light' claims family pleasures make domestic drudgery sweet. On the other hand, powerful, simply expressed pieces like 'Woman's Rights versus Woman's Wrongs' highlight the desparate plight of working women:

> Woman struggling for daily bread to keep body
>   and soul together.
> Trudging to work, on a scanty meal, through all
>   kinds of wintry weather,
> Pacing behind the shop counter, braving a
>   thousand ills,
> Stitching away at the sewing machines, or
>   weaving the web in the mills.

Russell recommends 'the lash' to punish, 'the man who kicks or strikes a defenceless woman'. Bernstein's response to this, moreover, provoked Russell to go further and, in 'A Recantation', demand female suffrage. In 'A Domestic Dirge' she incites 'wives o' working men' to "strike" tae git the feck o't'. Russell's politics were not generally violent; 'Intimidation. An Incident of the late "Shipwright's Dispute" on the Clyde' shows her ready to support the side of law and order. However, she was outraged when natural justice was violated. 'The Carpenter's Wife's Advice' condemns the treatment of the 'kindly sin' of a Glasgow joiner, William McKenzie, jailed for thirty days for giving his employer's rotten wood for an old woman's fire. Russell's moral outrage here typifies a recurrent voice of Scottish autodidactic women.[24]

There are similarities in the work of Hamilton, Russell and Ellen Johnston, 'The Factory Girl' (c. 1835–73). Born in Hamilton, Johnston led a singularly hard life. Her mother was unintentionally bigamous. Johnston raised a beloved illegitimate daughter and suffered frequent bouts of illness. She worked in weaving mills in Glasgow, Ireland, Manchester and Dundee, where she was blacklisted for subversiveness, and died in the Barony Poorhouse in Glasgow. The 'Testimonial' from the Reverend George Gilfillan, prefacing Johnston's *Autobiography, Poems and Songs* (1867), shows the prejudices Janet Little faced, almost a hundred years before, still alive and strong: 'subtracting all the signs of an imperfect education, her rhymes are highly creditable to her heart and head too. . . . I hope she will be encouraged by this . . . to read to correct the faults in her style'. Johnston celebrates the factory environment, perhaps, overzealously, regretting her time as 'The Factory Exile', outwith 'Thou lovely verdant Factory'. 'Galbraith's Trip' and 'Kennedy's Factory for Ever' portray happy work outings and 'Address to the Factory of Messrs. J and W. I. Scott & Co., John Street, Bridgeton' enthuses: 'HAIL! Royal Sovereign of the Factory race, / . . . Thy worth is matchless as it is unknown'. A less attractive side to factory life, though, is suggested in 'Lines. On Behalf of the Boatbuilders and Boilermakers of Great Britain and Ireland': 'Ye rich! who gained fortune's heart,/How greedy your selfish souls' are decried for offering 'sixpence a day,/For work that is well worth a pound'. In proclaiming, 'Be your watchword – "Union for ever"', Johnston loses the 'sweetness' Gilfillan attributed to her. Johnston is often outspoken on behalf of social and political victims, from 'The Drunkard's Wife', stripped of dignity by her husband, to 'The Exile of Poland'. There is an attractively defiant streak in her work; 'Welcome, Garibaldi', for instance, hails the foreign hero as Wallace's spiritual descendant. Johnston's work offers a curious blend of peace-making and incitement to rebellion.[25]

Despite sporadic appearances of such assertive poets in the later nineteenth century, the 'empire of the gentle heart' retained many subjects. Lizzie Hunter, from Clackmannanshire, limply celebrates 'Memories of the Past'. Lady Lindsay's *A String of Beads* (1892) is full of insipid pieces like 'The New Doll' and 'Busy fairies' although *The Apostle of the Ardennes* (1899) is racier, featuring lust, a palmer, a prelate and, ultimately, a reformed reprobate. More skilfully, there are the translations of Mary Gray (b. 1853), a telegraph clerk from Huntly, Aberdeenshire, educated in England and Germany. She earned a degree from St Andrews University, translated into English and Scots and published *Lyrics and Epigrams after Goethe and other German Poets* (n.d.). 'The Violet', from Goethe's 'Elwin and Elmire', is a *carpe diem* piece with a twist. A 'heedless maid' steps on a violet: '"Oh, sweet," it said, "is sic a death,/Through her, through her I dee."'.[26]

At the end of the century, some poets still used traditional elements to invigorate their work. Jessie Margaret King, 'Marguerite', (b. 1862) is a case in point. Born in Bankfoot (and not to be confused with the illustrator Jessie M[arion] King (1875–1949), King worked in *The Dundee Advertiser and Evening Telegraph* offices. 'A Midsummer Night's Dream' describes an otherworldly gathering, in the delightfully grotesque tradition of Hogg's 'Witch of Fife':

> Ae e'enin' I laid mysel' doon to sleep
> 'Mang the moss that cushioned a burnie's brim,
> An' some eldrich pooer 'gan my senses steep,
> An' the munelicht was thrangit wi' shapes fu' grim.

King's gleeful supernaturalism is wholly refreshing. Alice Werner's work is just as strong; the influence of oral lyrics, and Stevenson, can be discerned in her pensive poems of the 1890s, such as 'The Edge of the Links':

> Years ago, you were walking
> Here by the Northern Sea;
> You heard the curlews calling
> As now they are calling me,
> And your soul was glad of the whin-blooms
> And the salt winds strong and free.

Such enigmatic feelings anticipate Marion Angus at her best.[27]

Nineteenth-century poetry by women was, as a whole, characterised by tremendous thematic and stylistic diversity. Historical and contemporary topics were addressed, from Jacobitism to industrialism, urban life and political change. Devotional matters were recurrently treated and, despite professions of faith, traces of religious doubt are evident. Refined ladies represent the polite end of a spectrum which, at the other extremity, incorporates a great deal of challenging material by working women. The 'Empire of the Gentle Heart' was undoubtedly an inhibiting force, restraining writers like Lady Nairne and Joanna Baillie. Nonetheless, its domination was sometimes resisted, especially by autodidactic writers, from Janet Little to Janet Hamilton to Jessie Russell. The latter group offered a vibrant and exciting challenge to the formal and derivative poetry which Irving identified as desirable. The poets discussed are representative of a rich and varied tradition which deserves further and detailed reassessment.[28]

Notes

1. See Tom Leonard, *Radical Renfrew* (Polygon, Edinburgh, 1990) and William Finlay, 'Reclaiming Local Literature: William Thom and Janet Hamilton', Douglas Gifford (ed.), *The History of Scottish Literature*, vol. 3, (Aberdeen University Press, Aberdeen, 1988), ch. 19
2. [James Paterson], *The Contemporaries of Burns, and the More Recent Poets of Ayrshire*, (Hugh Paton, Carver & Gilder, Edinburgh, 1840) discusses Pagan, pp. 113–23 and Glover, pp. 35–7. On Glover see *The Ballads and Songs of Ayr* (John Dick for the editor, James Paterson, Ayr, 1846), pp. 56–9. On Pagan see *The Ballads and Songs of Ayrshire* (T. G. Stevenson, Edinburgh, 1847), pp. 63–6.
3. See Valentina Bold, 'Janet Little "The Scotch Milkmaid" and "Peasant Poetry"', *Scottish Literary Journal* 20 (November 1993), 21–30. Quoted in *Robert Burns and Mrs Dunlop*, ed. William Wallace (Hodder & Stoughton, London, 1888), pp. 288–9. *The Poetical Works of Janet Little, The Scotch Milkmaid* (Ayr, 1792), pp. 37–9, 42–4, 25–8, 171–2, 167–70, 129–32, 164–6, 113–16. *The Works of Allan Ramsay*, ed. B. Martin and

J. W. Oliver (Scottish Text Society, Edinburgh, 1945–6), I, pp. 22–6. *The Poems of Robert Fergusson*, ed. M. P. McDiarmid (Scottish Text Society, Edinburgh, 1956), II, pp. 160–7.

4.   Caroline Oliphant, *Life and Songs of the Baroness Nairne*, with a memoir and poems of Caroline Oliphant the Younger, ed. Charles Rogers (C. Griffin, London, 1869), pp. 135–6, 3–4. See too George Henderson, *Lady Nairne and Her Songs*, 3rd edn, (A. Gardner, Paisley, 1905).

5.   Oliphant, pp. 113–16, 5–6. See Robert Tannahill, *The Poems and Songs*, ed. David Semple (A. Gardner, Paisley, 1900), p. 169.

6.   Hamilton, see Catherine Kerrigan (ed.), *An Anthology of Scottish Women Poets* (Edinburgh University Press, Edinburgh, 1991), p. 170. Campbell, see CLX, *The Harp of Renfrewshire*, 1819 (A. Gardner, Paisley, 1872). Ogilvy, see Kerrigan, p. 188. Lady Anne Barnard, see Kerrigan, p. 167. Robert Burns, *Poems and Songs*, ed. James Kinsley, (Oxford University Press, London, 1969), no. 347.

7.   Mrs John Hunter [Anne Hunter], *Poems* (London, 1802), pp. 23–33, 63, 214; see also James Beveridge (ed.), *The Poets of Clackmannanshire*, (J. S. Wilson, Glasgow, 1885). Mrs Grant, Laggan, *Poems on Various Subjects* (printed for the author by J. Moir, sold by Longman & Rees, Edinburgh, 1803), pp. 21–109, 298–302, 407–9. See Allan Cunningham, *The Songs of Scotland* (London, 1825), IV, pp. 156–7; Anne Grant, *Memoir and Correspondence*, ed. J. P. Grant (Longman, Brown, Green & Longmans, London, 1844); George Eyre-Todd (ed.), *The Glasgow Poets*, 2nd edn (A. Gardner, Paisley, 1906), pp. 51–60. Native Americans were popular artistic subjects. Mrs Siddons was a 'Wild Indian Girl' in Edinburgh in 1815: see Donald Mackenzie, *Scotland's First National Theatre* (Edinburgh, 1963), p. 17; the Irish poet Sydney Owenson (Lady Morgan) used *The Mohawks* (London, 1822) for political satire.

8.   See Joanna Baillie, *The Dramatic and Poetical Works*, 2nd edn, (London, 1853), pp. 710–30, 748–61, 765–7, 807, 817, 818–19. On Baillie's high moral standing see 'Celebrated Female Writers' in *Blackwood's Edinburgh Magazine* 16 (August 1824), p. 162. See too Eyre-Todd, pp. 93–103 and Kerrigan, pp. 172–6. 'Woo'd an' Married', David Herd, *Ancient and Modern Scottish Songs*, 1776 (printed by J. Wotherspoon for J. Dickson and C. Elliot, Edinburgh, 1869), II, p. 115 and James Johnson, *The Scots Musical Museum* (1787–1803), ed. Donald A. Low (Scolar, Aldershot, 1991), I, no. 10. On 'The Blythsome Bridal' see Robert Chambers (ed.), *The Songs of Scotland* (Edinburgh, 1862), pp. 146–50.

9.   See 'Memoir and Poems of Oliphant the Younger', in Oliphant, *Life and Songs of the Baroness Nairne*; Kerrigan, pp. 185–6. Lady John Scott, *Songs and Verses* (Edinburgh, 1904), pp. 51–3, 37–8; see Kerrigan, pp. 186–7. On 'Annie Laurie' see Chambers, pp. 309–10.

10.   Mary Inglis, see Robert Ford (ed.), *Ballads of Bairnhood*, 2nd edn (A. Gardner, Paisley, 1913), p. 129 and Kerrigan, p. 209. *Ballads of Bairnhood*, p. 136 mentions Inglis's *Croonings* which I have been unable to trace. On Jessie D. M. Morton see Alexander G. Murdoch, *Recent and Living Scottish Poets* (T. D. Morrison, Glasgow & London, 1883), pp. 337–43 and *Ballads of Bairnhood*, p. 187, 353. Lindsay Carnegie, see Kerrigan, p. 198. On Isabella F. Darling see *Ballads of Bairnhood*, pp. 79–81. On Ellen C. Nicholson see Murdoch, pp. 345–8. James and Ellen C. Nicholson, *Poems* (Hamilton, Adams, London, 1880), pp. 147–8.

11.   Lydia Falconer Fraser, see Kerrigan, p. 192; on Anna Maria Maxwell see Robert Brown (ed.), *Paisley Poets*, 2 vols, (J. & J. Cook, Paisley, 1890), I, pp. 357–60; Hannah Brown Mackenzie, Kerrigan, p. 212. On Margaret Thomson Laird, Leonard, pp. 239–40; see too Brown, II, pp. 167–9. On Jeannie Johnstone see Brown, II, pp. 526–8.

12.   On Mary Lundie Duncan see Duncan Campbell, *Hymns and Hymn Makers*, 5th edn (Black, London and Edinburgh, 1912), pp. 109–10. On Jane Catherine Lundie see Kerrigan, p. 193; Marion Paul Aird, *Heart Histories and Violets from the Greenwood* (Johnstone & Hunter, London, Edinburgh, Glasgow and Kilmarnock, 1853) v, pp. 103–4. On Aird see Eyre-Todd, pp. 322–5 and *The Ballads and Songs of Ayrshire*, pp. 59–62.

13.   On Mary Cross see Murdoch, pp. 348–52. Alice Pringle, *Greycliffe Hall*, (Glasgow, 1878), pp. 317–19; see too Robert Ford (ed.), *The Harp of Perthshire* (A. Gardner, Paisley, 1893), pp. 356–8. See Elizabeth Cecilia Douglas Clephane in *Hymns and Hymn Makers*, pp. 135–6. Catherine Napier, *The City of the World* (London, 1845, pp. 14–16; 24–34. On Margaret Ballantyne see Brown, II, pp. 382–5.

14.   Margaret Stewart Sandeman, see *The Harp of Perthshire*, pp. 186–8; M. F. Barbour, see

The Harp of Perthshire, pp. 260–2. Anne Ross Cousin, see Kerrigan pp. 189–90. On Mary
A. Mackay see John Horne (ed.), *Some Present-Day Songs and Singers of Caithness* (William
Rae, Wick, Thurso, 1899), p. 79, pp. 81–2.
15.   Mary Pyper, *Select Pieces* (Edinburgh, 1847), reprinted as *Sacred Poems*, ed. E. B. Ramsay
(A. Elliot, Edinburgh, 1865), p. 68, pp. 70–1, pp. 50–2, p. 74.
16.   Maria Bell, *Songs of Two Homes* (Oliphant, Anderson & Ferrier, Edinburgh and London,
1899), 1, pp. 8–9, 24, 139. Emily Dickinson, *The Complete Poems*, ed. Thomas H. Johnson
(London, 1975), p. 2. Robert Louis Stevenson, 'Requiem', from 'Underwoods' (1887), in
Collected Poems, ed. Janet Adam Smith, 2nd edn (Hart Davis, London, 1971), p. 130.
17.   Isabella Craig-Knox, *Poems* (Edinburgh, 1856), 'Preface', pp. 1–5, 10–13, 54–6, 6–9,
163–72, 141–3. *Duchess Agnes* etc., (A. Strahan, London, 1864), pp. 89–73; see Kerrigan,
pp. 96–7. Alexander Anderson, *Songs of the Rail*, 3rd ed (Edinburgh, 1881); Elizabeth
Campbell, *Poems* (Arbroath, 1862), pp. 3–4. See *The Poems of John Davidson*, ed. Andrew
Turnbull (Scottish Academic Press with the Association for Scottish Literary Studies,
Edinburgh, 1973), 2 vols.
18.   On Mary Anne Shaw see Brown, II, pp. 479–82. On Elizabeth Jane Irving see Malcolm
McLachlan Harper (ed.), *The Bards of Galloway*, (T. Fraser, Dalbeattie, 1889), pp. 12–15,
68–86. Elizabeth Jane Irving, *Fireside Lays* (printed by Robert Anderson, Glasgow, 1872),
pp. 68–86, 235–8. On Margaret Wallace Thomson see Brown, I, pp. 556–62. Annie S.
Swan, see Kerrigan, pp. 213–14.
19.   See Murdoch, pp. 343–5. Elizabeth Hartley, *The Prairie Flower and Other Poems*
(Dumbarton, 1870), pp. 9–34, 75–7, 131–3, 54–6, 59–62, 79–81. John Greenleaf Whittier,
see F. O. Mathiessen (ed.), *The Oxford Book of American Verse* (New York, 1950), pp. 156–8.
See Robert Buchanan, *The Poetical Works* (Chatto & Windus, London, 1884).
20.   Agnes Marchbank, see *Ballads of Bairnhood*, pp. 167–8, Kerrigan, pp. 200–1. Joanna
Picken, see Leonard, pp. 188–91.
21.   Eyre-Todd, pp. 226–7. James Hamilton (ed.), *Poems, Essays and Sketches by Janet Hamilton*,
(Glasgow, 1880); J. Young (ed.), *Pictures in Prose and Verse, or, Personal Recollections of the late
Janet Hamilton*, (Glasgow, 1877). Hamilton, pp. 233–4, 137–9, 316–17, 59–60. David Gray,
The Poetical Works, ed. Henry Glassford Bell (Glasgow, 1874), pp. 1–62; James Thomson,
The City of Dreadful Night (1880), ed. Edwin Morgan (Canongate, Edinburgh, 1993).
22.   Hamilton, pp. 161–2, 36–7, 33–4, 116–17, 263–4, 52–3. See Alexander G. Murdoch,
The Scottish Poets (Glasgow, 1887), pp. 334–7. Sketch of the late Mrs Hamilton, (Glasgow,
1873). See Edwin Morgan, 'Scottish Poetry in the Nineteenth Century', and William
Finlay, 'Reclaiming Local Literature: William Thom and Janet Hamilton', both in Gifford,
chapters 18, 19; Kerrigan, pp. 181–3. On Jean Clerk, see Brown, II, p. 120. On Isabella
Ledgerwood, see Brown, II, pp. 516–17.
23.   On Agnes Stewart Mabon see Kerrigan, pp. 202–5. Marion Bernstein, *Mirren's Musings*
(Glasgow, 1876), pp. 9, 53, 7, 112–13, 101–2, 91, 18–23, 60–3, 46. See Leonard, pp. 296–305.
Alexander Rodger, *Poems and Songs* (Glasgow, 1838). *The Works of Robert Tannahill*, ed.
Philip A. Ramsay (London, n.d.), no. 91.
24.   Jessie Russell, *The Blinkin' o' the Fire and Other Poems*, (Cossar, Fotheringham & Co.,
Glasgow, 1877); see also Leonard, pp. 306–9.
25.   Ellen Johnston, *Autobiography, Poems and Songs* (W. Love, Glasgow, 1867). This
volume won £50 from the Royal Bounty Fund.
26.   Lizzie Hunter, *The Poets of Clackmannanshire*, ed. James Beveridge (J. S. Wilson, Glasgow,
1885), pp. 172–4. Lady Lindsay, *A String of Beads, Verses for Children* (Adam & Charles
Black, London and Edinburgh, 1892), pp. 32–3, p. 22. Mary Gray, see Kerrigan, p. 208.
27.   Jessie Margaret King, in *The Harp of Perthshire*, pp. 371–2. James Hogg, *The Queen's
Wake*, 1813, 6th edn (Edinburgh and London, 1819), pp. 70–95. Alice Werner, *Echoes Re-
Echoed* (W. C. Henderson, St Andrews, 1934), XLVIII.
28.   All anthologies which include these poets are quoted in the footnotes. Readers are
advised to consult the Scottish Poetry Collection in the Mitchell Library, Glasgow.

17

What a Voice!
Women, Repertoire and
Loss in the Singing Tradition

Elaine Petrie

It is convenient to refer to folksong collections by the names of the collectors rather than those of the contributors but this means that, while James B. Duncan and Gavin Greig willingly acknowledged their great debt to Duncan's sister, Mrs Margaret Gillespie, to Miss Bell Robertson from New Pitsligo and their other contributors, the scholars are still better known than the sources whose voices have been subsumed into the collection. The collection (3,050 song texts and 3,100 tune records) compiled by Greig and Duncan in Aberdeenshire between 1904 and 1917, is indebted to a long list of informants but the most prolific correspondents were women like Bell Robertson, Margaret Gillespie, Annie Shirer and Margaret Harper.[1]

Before the twentieth century, collections focused on tragic and historical narrative ballads, culminating in Francis J. Child's *English and Scottish Popular Ballads*, completed in 1898, which brought together all the principal manuscript records of narrative ballad stories and, in doing so, established its 305 texts as a standard reference point. Singers' voices were thus lost in other ways: significant parts of their repertoires were ignored and little information was gleaned about any actual performance. Greig and Duncan were in some ways ahead of their time, for they recorded whatever the people sang and found a rich brew of lyric songs, shanties, work and bothy songs, Irish songs, music hall songs alongside ballads and narrative songs taken from broadsides and chapbooks or linked to older traditions through the process of oral transmission.

Their most prolific respondent, Bell (Isabella) Robertson (born 1841), is reckoned to have contributed material for almost 400 songs.[2] From her earliest girlhood she demonstrated a passionate interest in songs and avidly sought out new songs and variants. She also took an active interest in dialect and the conservation of Buchan terminology and proverbial sayings. A neighbour noted that she was 'a perfect mine of local traditions, and many a tale she told me and my children of smugglers and pirates, and strange happenings in days gone by, which have never found their way into print'.[3]

It is perhaps significant that her audience was a domestic one made up of women and children. Towards the close of her life she summed up her family role in a way that will still find an echo with many women: 'I was the eldest of five, and the only girl. That partly accounts for my me[a]gre education. I could never be spared to go to school.' Bell did spend some time learning to with Janet Taylor, a local woman, who 'never stopt spinning for lessons, but we laid the book on top of the meal barrel, and read while she spun, but I was so dense she had to come, and she couldn't do with that, so she put me away telling mother I would never learn'. Bell determined to write 'in spite o' her' and succeeded even if her large awkward handwriting and idiosyncratic spelling are in contrast with the intelligence and sensitivity her letters reveal, perhaps confirming that Janet Taylor's aspirations for her pupils were extremely limited: 'she never made us spell, we read our lesson, that was all'. The loneliness and sense of frustration that Bell often experienced in later life were already very real to her as a small child denied self-expression: 'I was so lonely. Everyone laughed at me when I asked questions or told any idea, and would tell it as a joke, so I stopped telling'. She found some outlet in teaching the three youngest brothers to read; they 'got all the home instruction they ever got from me' since her mother 'had little time and was glad I did it'.[4] In addition, Janet Taylor did keep a collection of chapbooks in which Bell found songs like 'The Bonnie House o' Airlie' (233F) and 'Sir James the Rose' (235P).[5]

Bell's role as homeworker and carer became formalised. She spent five and a half years 'in the Sist[e]r bus[i]nes[s]' as housekeeper to her brothers, while one studied for the ministry in Glasgow.[6] The first of these years was the happiest of her life but in personal terms the experience was ultimately frustrating: 'I had aspirations but there were obsticles' [sic]. She returned to the northeast to care for her mother, after which she became a housekeeper again, finding some outlet in her study of dialect words and in writing mainly devotional poetry, some of which found its way into print, so that at the time she began corresponding with Gavin Greig in response to his column on folksong in a local newspaper, he was able to describe her as 'our well-known Buchan poetess'.[7]

Bell's main source for songs and inspiration was her mother, Jean Gall (born 1804), whose family all came from Strichen. Her maternal grandmother, Isobel Stephen, 'was a fine folk singer I am told and had a lot of Ballads. Mother learned them from her and passed them on through me.'[8] Bell was always adamant that all her mother's songs came from singers and that consequently many were very old. She compares her grandmother's version of 'Fair Ellen' (1229B) against that in Child 63B:

> The book says it is from Mrs Brown's recitation in 1800 but my Grandmother had had [it] long before that time as she was married long before that and though she might [have] and doubtles[s] learn[e]d songs after she was a Wife, I know from my Mother that she had a large store of songs and ballads when she was a lass. She would have had, at least, at the time given as the date of vers[i]on A from Mrs Brown's recitation before 1783.[9]

Bell learned other songs and fragments from a variety of sources such as her Aunt Bell ('Sweet Willie and Fair Annie' 212); Janet Taylor (mostly fragments); Mary Scott, a girl of Bell's own age ('The Mermaid' 27H); Meggie Johnstone, a servant with the family, who sang as she milked every night; a girl who came to hoe when Bell was 14; a woman called Annie Gray who was her mother's age; John Johnstone, a neighbour ('The False Bride' 1198T); the sisters and daughters of Willie Ross ('The Laird of Drum' 835Q); a tinker boy ('The Bonnie Banks o' Airdrie' 199B); James Ross, a local singer ('Down in Yon Valley' 1199X); Mrs Mutch, Bell's landlady, and at least one ploughman at a 'meal an ale' (a harvest supper). Additionally, her father had once been in the habit of buying chapbooks and Bell heard him recite 'bits of King John and the Bishop' which he had got in this way.[10]

David Buchan points to her significance as a member of a village folksong tradition but sees her as a passive recorder, typical of the literate stage of transmission. Unlike a recreative performer who retained the narrative core of the text and might expand it by using stock phrases, floating verses and standard structural patterning devices such as repetition, mirroring, dual and triple parallels, Bell was at pains to give the texts exactly as she heard them, preserving phrases and words she knew to be flawed. Her scrupulousness in giving the texts as she received them was in good part due to her understanding of the scholarly nature of the work undertaken by Greig and Duncan and did not stem from ignorance or lack of curiosity about the material. Letters show that her views were knowledgeable and perceptive when sought.[11]

The great puzzle is why, despite her marvellous recall of the words, Bell did not sing and left no tunes. She had a good enough ear to recognise a pretty tune and she retained the rhythm of 'The Harpin' Mannie' (270), learned as a nursery song, well enough to help Greig recognise the tune type. Performance was important to her – she speaks disparagingly of the imperfect 'kind of chant' of the tinker boy[12] – and yet she did not sing herself. Nowhere does she say that she was tone deaf or unable to carry a tune and in fact the presence of a tune helped her to learn a song quickly while book texts had to be read over and over.[13] She makes no reference to reciting in public either. Her only recorded 'performance' was the subject of some family amusement: 'Bessie Bell and Mary Gray [1256B] had been one of the first songs I tried to lisp. I had been too young to have any rememberance of it but I remember my Mother telling me and mimicking my Baby attempts to sing it and funny it had been'.[14]

> Bessie Bell and Mary Gray
> They were twa bonny lasses
> They bigger a bower on yon burn brae
> And thicket it owre wi' rashes.
>
> Oh Bessie Bell I loed yestreen
> And thocht I neer wad alter
> But Mary Gray's twa pawky e'n
> Made a' my courage falter.

Bell's songs were clearly treasured by her but her secluded life and the changing social structure of the northeast offered decreasing access to what she called 'the song environment'. It seems possible that despite her avid desire to acquire the ballads and folksongs that represented her culture and heritage – in a sense her identity – her pious disposition and her life experiences, which customarily thrust her into a role of serving others without seeking notice, stole the voice that would have passed her heritage on as a complete and living form.

Margaret Gillespie (*née* Duncan) was born like Bell in 1841 and together they resemble twin pillars supporting the great collection in which their songs are preserved. James Duncan estimated that he had got 330 tunes and 'the words reasonably complete' of about 230 songs from his older sister.[15] A large part of her repertoire was learned in girlhood from her parents, Elizabeth Birnie and William Duncan, who both sang. Elizabeth Birnie contributed assorted lyrics and ballads: 'The Soldier Maid' (182D); 'My He'rt it is Sair' (1165A) and 'Clyde's Waters' (1231A) while 'The Herd Laddie' (429B) came from her father. Margaret also learned songs from her father's stepmother, Mrs Duncan of Craigculter, and from the journeymen carpenters who came to work for her father, who was a wheelwright and carpenter. Schoolmates, a washerwoman and her mother's dressmaker, Katy Steven, are also cited as early sources.

Younger brothers such as James and George were able to train for professions, the ministry and teaching respectively, but Margaret, an older child and a daughter, followed local practice and went into domestic service at the age of twelve. As a consequence she was able to widen the range of sources from whom she picked up songs, tunes and fragments. Initial terms may have been spent with members of her extended family such as her step-grandmother at Craigculter, and the Birnie family at Artamford, who were perhaps also related. She also stayed at Mains of Elrick, Auchnagatt, in 1857 and at Ardo of Belhelvie in 1862. During this time she learned songs from other farm and domestic workers, men and women.

Although she did acquire some additional songs after her marriage and during her time in Glasgow, where, following her husband's death, she kept lodgers, her repertoire was probably substantially completed during the first twenty five years of her life. Margaret Gillespie's repertoire therefore consisted of a core of songs she – and her siblings – had known since early childhood. George, the youngest brother, who was born almost twenty years after his sister, copied down some of his parents' songs in his teens, thereby confirming that his parents were still actively rehearsing their songs. This family tradition, transmitted to Margaret when she was as young as five or six years old, was augmented by a more diverse regional or village tradition where ballads and popular lyrics were sung alongside songs made up round recent local events or characters. Bell Robertson's mother told her that 'when anything notisable happ[e]ned they had mad[e] a song about it to keep it'.[16] One such local song, 'Jock Scott' (1096 B and C), was known to some of the Duncan men but is not recorded from Margaret. Brothers John, William and James all learned it from their father who recollected seeing the lovers being separated as in the song: 'And forcin' her on horseback high, from me she was torn away;/Her little hands was stretched out for tears she couldna see'. It may be that James Duncan simply did not request a version from his sister since it was well recorded by others who shared the same source but it may have been associated in the family with the menfolk. Evidence from the Stewart family (discussed later) suggests some demarcation of repertoire is possible.

It has been suggested that 'almost the entire stock' of Margaret Gillespie's ballad texts 'derived from broadsheet or hapbook' (Buchan, p. 248) and if so this probably reflects the diversity of her sources and may give a more accurate portrait of the nature of the singing community in the northeast than Bell's more restricted circle. Study of the ballads has often adopted conventional literary standards and looked for complete, artistically satisfying narratives, sometimes imagining that they would point to a tradition of oral transmission leading back to a pure undefined proto-form. Too often there has been little effort to discover why songs matter to the people who sing them. Singers, as the Greig-Duncan archive ably demonstrates, welcomed songs of all descriptions from those by music-hall performers like Harry Clifton ('Pretty Polly Perkins of Paddington Green' 1212 and 'On Board of the Kangaroo' 1211, both published by him in 1856) to the work of local songmakers such as George Bruce Thomson whose 'Pirn-Taed Jockie' (1220) and 'Macfarlan' o' the Sprotts' (1221) have retained their popularity to the present day. With Margaret Gillespie and Bell Robertson we have, for the first time, informants whose repertoire was extensively mined. Their editors were not only interested in the big ballads, nor even simply in their informants' active repertoire, but systematically trawled their memories for information on songs they might have heard but did not necessarily perform complete. They acquired information on these informants' sources and this helps to provide a clearer picture of the rural or village song culture to which Buchan points (p. 249).

   The twin circles of home and community defined the world for women like Margaret and Bell, growing up in the 1850s. With farms scattered round the Buchan hinterland, school, church, markets, hiring fairs and occasional communal activity such as harvesting, with its attendant supper, may have presented the only regular opportunities for coming together in song. It was an environment that could foster exceptional creative talents as demonstrated by the flowering of the ploughman songs or bothy ballads. But that is in many respects a male-orientated genre since the bothies accommodated the male workers (women were lodged in the farmhouse under the eye of the farmer and his wife) and even as late as the mid-1980s it was still a matter for debate whether women could enter Bothy Ballad singing competitions at Folk Festivals. Even in the heyday of the bothies, singing was not a universal experience. After all, it was Bell Robertson's view that her mother was 'out of the song atmosphere' by her twenties by reason of working 'at the back of beyont'[17] and in households where 'there was no songs'.[18] Not every place would have gifted singers and while larger fermtouns might require a range of ploughmen and cattlemen, the mere presence of a number of young unmarried men and women meant that many farmers and their wives saw their task as imposing order and restraint rather than encouraging regular merry-making.[19] For many women, marriage and its attendant domestic ties, must have marked a withdrawal from or at least restricted access to communal singing. Their audience, as we have seen with Bell, was often provided by children, their own or others', and this must account for the frequent citing of women as first sources of songs. In the case of Margaret Gillespie, her removal to Glasgow in connection with her husband's work displaced her from the social and geographical setting in which her songs were learned. It may have made them all the more significant to her while removing the opportunity to relate them. That dislocation was rendered the more absolute by her departure in 1910 for South Africa where both her sons were farming. Her granddaughter Ursula who was around seven at the time of Margaret's arrival remembers that she had a pleasant voice and that she 'used to love singing her songs as she worked at her sewing-machine.'[20] Margaret's son, William, had also inherited some musical talent and had sung in a choir in Scotland but though he sang Scottish songs for his children they have not been passed on.[21] Even within a musical family, something more than talent and interest is required to maintain a traditional repertoire from one generation to the next.

   Ballads which had been thought to be dying out in the 1800s were recorded in the early 1900s; but with a series of extended wars, greater mobility and the gradual fracturing of small communities as people sought jobs or an education in the bigger towns, there was a recognition that traditional pastimes were under increasing threat from organised concert parties and pre-recorded music available on record and on radio. In 1925, Alexander Keith edited the ballad texts from the Greig-Duncan papers as *Last Leaves of Traditional Ballads and Ballad Airs*. As usual, obituary notices for traditional song were premature.

   Following in the footsteps of Greig and Duncan, an American researcher, James M. Carpenter, brought new technology to bear on tradition when he took his cylinder recording machine to Scotland in the early 1930s. In a series of visits, he recorded some of the Greig-Duncan contributors but he also spent one summer copying down '300 songs and ballads, amounting to 400 seven-stanza pages'[22] from one woman who had escaped the earlier editors' exhaustive trawl. Little is known of Bell Duncan of Lambhill, by Insch, who was in her eighties when Carpenter recorded her. Her repertoire, which included tunes, ran to around sixty-five Child ballads, mostly in fairly full versions, and other items which she had learned from her mother as a girl.

Still later, in the 1950s, fieldworkers of the School of Scottish Studies revealed that a community still existed for whom traditional ballads, and indeed a whole range of folksong and folktales, were an integral part of life, thus clearly demonstrating the significance of an appropriate social context or function for the preservation and organic transmission of folk song and narrative.

Even as Greig and Duncan were busy recording the song tradition they feared was about to be lost, the woman whom many now regard as the queen of Scottish ballads[23] was growing up in the very countryside in which they collected. Jeannie Robertson (aptly and regally named Regina Christina by her parents), was born in 1908 to a family of northeast travellers, or tinkers, whose nomadic lifestyle frequently brought them into conflict with the settled community. In Jeannie's childhood she spent six months of the year settled in Aberdeen and the summer months in a caravan, travelling round Deeside and Donside, mostly in company with other families, leading a life that was in but not of the village and farm communities mined by Greig and Duncan.

It was from her mother, Maria Stewart, that Jeannie first heard the ballads that came to distinguish her repertoire:

> I learned all my big ballads at nicht. My mother cudnae sleep as her two sons and her husband was oot in the First World War and she cudnae sleep because she was worried. And she used to set up till aboot two in the mornin'. Her and her brother used to sing the songs togither, and I used to listen, and I got interested in the ballads and the folksongs. I started to learn them at that time. The auld sangs went from mouth tae mouth in these days. They never learned them off of paper, that's certain.[24]

Jeannie has described how, at the age of nine, she got her mother to sing songs over till she got the words and tune right, then Jeannie would practise as she did household chores.[25] Jeannie's repertoire, recorded over a period of years by fieldworkers such as Herschel Gower, James Porter and Hamish Henderson (who 'discovered' her in 1953), confirms the eclectic tastes of a traditional performer. The archive comprises 'approximately twenty Child ballads, an equal number of ballads originating from Broadsides, bothy songs, scores of lyrics, children's songs and verses and a variety of extended tales and anecdotes' including extensive sections of personal reminiscence, or *memorat*.[26] Perhaps most exciting of all, she contributed items which, despite the comprehensive efforts of Greig and Duncan, had not been found by them in the northeast. 'Edward' ('Son David' Child 23) and 'The Twa Brothers' (Child 49) are powerful songs and it may be that their themes of family rivalry held their relevance in the traveller community precisely because of its complex web of relationships and the need for travellers to help each other in the face of hostility from the establishment and the settled community.

Jeannie's dramatic presence as a performer made a strong impact on her hearers and transcended the characteristic traveller style of singing; what Belle Stewart calls 'the richt auld way o' singin' things, the auld Tinkie-tone, the twangy kind o' singin'.[27] James Porter has listed Jeannie's characteristic performance techniques as: an expansive delivery, fluid rhythm with both an internal and external pulse, idiomatic enunciation, *portamenti* and *appoggiature*, careful phrasing and a sense of drama and characterisation.[28] Jeannie herself laid stress on personal conviction in performance, describing her mother as 'a guid singer and a *true* singer'.[29] Singers who learned songs directly from Jeannie have described her insistence that they learn to 'tak' it oot right'. Her nephew, Stanley Robertson, who sings many of her songs, recalled, 'If you did not sing it *exactly* as she told you, you were in trouble', but her concern was not simply to preserve an idiosyncratic style. She wished to ensure conviction and commitment to the song itself: 'I'll learn you this song, but I want you to sing it right, sing it proper, and sing it real'.[30] This insistence on engagement with the song is confirmed by her daughter, Lizzie Higgins, who was told by her mother in early life that she had not suffered enough to be a great singer. Later describing her own mature performance Lizzie was able to say: 'I *have* been through it, I know what I'm singing about and I can put my whole soul into the song'.[31]

This identification with the song stems in part from the association of the song with the singer from whom it was learned and the close personal and family ties that this often represents. Lizzie explained that 'every one o' these songs, ballads and pipe tunes we sing, they mean something to us privately'. In her own case, 'I dinna see my audience, I see her [Jeannie] an me a wee kid lang afore the war. An as Am singing Am hearin' her singing'.[32]

Lizzie (1930–93), learned songs from both her mother, Jeannie, and her grandmother, Maria Stewart. The process seems to have been less systematic than that by which Jeannie learned from Maria. Jeannie made no effort to teach her and Lizzie simply picked them up from her mother's singing. Lizzie's recordings are not facsimile copies of her mother's renditions. She had a striking, husky voice and her pacing and ornamentation are distinctive but there are also variations in the text ranging from different verse order (and thereby story construction) to simple word switches.[33] Another important influence was the piping of her father, Donald Higgins. Lizzie identified this as her first love and the source of her style of ornamentation. Her development as a singer was clearly coloured by a wish to have been a piper but, with the exception of the MacPhee family, piping in traveller circles has been the preserve of men.

Initially Lizzie was reluctant to perform publicly, which may account for a bias towards lyric song in her repertoire. There is some evidence that her brother, Jeemsie, was seen as the promising singer among the children. He 'was a bonnie singer. He sung like Jeannie. Traditional ballad, classical ballad style though he was a wee boy . . . An' I'd be staundin' back, I was always the shy one, like'.[34] It is clear that she avoided for a time the muckle sangs that were identified with Jeannie and she did not come out as a public performer till Jeannie had retired due to ill health. Before this time she had sung at home and at work, among her fellow fishworkers, introducing what she called 'auld fashioned' songs alongside contemporary popular favourites as she was 'Elvis Presley mad' and 'a bonny pop singer and a bonny blues – American ballad blues – singer' with a gift for yodelling.[35] Among the ballads Lizzie sang was 'Lord Lovel' ('Lord Lovat' Child 75). She only sang it when 'in top form'[36] by reason of its special significance to her: her mother sang it nightly as a lullaby till Lizzie was eleven or so. This private identification of songs with early experiences and family members is surely a powerful factor in the conservation of songs and related traditions.

The songs that figured regularly in her appearances at Aberdeen Folk Club in the 1970s confirm a leaning towards the lyric: ballads such as 'The Cruel Mither' (193) and 'Lady Mary Ann' ('Still Growing' 1222) are balanced by 'Up and Awa wi' the Laverock' (written by Andy Hunter to a traditional tune), 'A Auld Man Came Coorting Me', 'Tammie Toddles' and 'A Beggar A Beggar'. Of these, the first two have a strong female focus, the first dealing with infanticide, the second with a young woman married, for dynastic reasons, to a boy many years her junior. By contrast, her cousin, Stanley Robertson, who also learned many of his songs from Jeannie (his aunt) and Maria Stewart (his grandmother), has made 'Clyde's Water' (1223) a signature piece. In this song, the narrative focus is on a young man (Willie), whose death and that of his sweetheart, who exercises great fortitude in searching for his body, are incurred as the result of the malign interference of both mothers. The version Stanley sings seems to be substantially broadside in origin though thematic motifs in this ballad have ancient roots.

That there may be some evidence for gender affecting understanding and performance of songs is confirmed by comparative work done by Ailie Munro. She studied different renditions of the same song from both traditional and revival singers (that is those who have consciously acquired songs from printed sources or the recorded performance of others rather than by oral transmission). Striking differences are demonstrable in the performance of 'The Banks o' Red Roses', a lyric concerning a young woman who is murdered by her lover. For women performers, such as Sheila Douglas and Heather Heywood, it relates the tragic betrayal of a girl who has been seduced; for Stanley Robertson, a thoughtful and articulate performer, the girl is loose morally, and is seeking to trap her lover with her pregnancy. It is her nagging persistence that causes him to snap.[37] On the other hand it must be noted that 'Johnie My Man', a dialogue between a downtrodden wife and her drunkard husband who finally turns his back on the tavern for her sake, seems extremely popular with male singers despite its largely unflattering picture of what is often interpreted as a favourite masculine pastime.

Some gender demarcation can be discerned in the family of Belle Stewart of Blairgowrie.[38] While many members of the extended family are fine storytellers, it is the women, Belle and her daughters Cathie and Sheila, who are the singers. The daughters have learned their songs not only from Belle but from a range of relatives. MacColl and Seeger find that the Stewarts' repertoires were largely fixed by 1960 and that there is a high degree of stability in subsequent recordings of the same text. There is a degree of demarcation in who sings what, despite a considerable overlap in the latent repertoire of each singer. Sheila and Cathie clearly recognise certain titles as their 'mither's sangs'. Belle and Sheila share a preference for ballads and love songs while Irish broadside songs are a speciality of Sheila's. Cathie favours sentimental and love songs. Belle also has a number of bothy, cant and comic songs as well as some examples of *canntaireachd* (vocal representation of pipe music).

This wide-ranging repertoire is extended by examples from other traditional genres. The Stewarts all know a range of children's songs and games as well as folktales and riddles. Where the family is apparently novel is in the love of making new songs, often based on domestic gatherings. The best known of these is Belle's 'The Berry Fields of Blair' which is widely known. However, despite this creativity, none is sanguine about the future of the traditions they uphold. The need for a community with shared values and regular singing opportunities as a foundation for the conservation of song and other traditions has not diminished and traveller ways are now under pressure from mass culture conveyed by the all-pervasive influence of television: 'I think it's because o' television that the cant and things like it are goin' to die oot wi' the bairns, because they're no' takin' the same interest that we did'.[39]

All of which leads back in a circle since reports of the frailty of folk tradition and its imminent demise have usually been the stimulus for collecting. Certainly the precise nature of the repertoire changes down the generations as one might expect of an organic process reflecting a society that itself endures change. Nevertheless the passing on of traditional folk beliefs, tales and songs continues. Urban myths abound, 'friendship' cakes, which have to be divided and passed to an acquaintance, keep appearing, and playground games are substantially those of twenty years ago. This last area of folk transmission, which includes playground songs, skipping and clapping games, is nowadays almost exclusively female. The exhaustive work of the Opies has shown the remarkable persistence of this aspect of folklife, despite the longstanding presence of television and radio in other quarters of the children's lives.[40] Some games, perhaps the ring and line dances ('The Grand Old Duke of York', 'Here we go round the Mulberry Bush', 'In and Out the Dusty Bluebells'), seem to be actively encouraged by adults at parties; others, particularly the clapping games ('Under the Bramble Bushes', 'A Sailor Went to Sea'), have a life of their own among children. There is evidence of continued creativity as contemporary objects such as cans of Coke are now appearing in playground songs. The functions of the songs are changing in other ways. Just as Revival singers picked up and recycled folk songs, an increasing number of children's entertainers are appropriating children's traditions and giving them a polished gloss. The extremely popular children's television and concert entertainers, 'The Singing Kettle', whose Cilla Fisher and Artie Trezise are well known as folksingers, have incorporated many traditional items into their performances so that, for example, 'Have You Ever Ever Ever in Your Long Legged Life?', a clapping game, is now expanded into a stage participation song. It will be interesting to monitor what effect, if any, this has upon the playground performers.

Catherine Kerrigan has outlined an appealing but ultimately unprovable case for the ballads as effectively a women's tradition waiting to be reclaimed and reinterpreted.[41] The problems of appropriating balladry as a predominantly female expression of experience are complicated by the complexity of a singer's response to a song: what makes her want to learn it and what it means to her once it has been absorbed. Jeannie Robertson learned 'Lord Donald' in response to her audiences who frequently asked for it since it bore some connection to her 'My Son David' but she learned it quickly because, 'it appealed to me as a guid story'.[42] The singer's perception of a song may change over time. American singer, Almeida Riddle, remembered a woman called Fanny Barber who sang 'Barbara Allan' with tears running down her face. She had sung the ballad from girlhood, when its tragic outcome must have seemed romantic, and had named her only daughter Barbara as a consequence. That daughter's death at the age of fourteen must have transformed the resonances of the song.[43]

This complexity in response levels has been explored by James Porter in his study of a range of Jeannie's performances of 'My Son David'. Variations in pitch and *tempi* were affected by Jeannie's relationship with her audience and her changing perception of herself as a 'folksinger', an internationally-regarded performer rather than an Aberdeen housewife. Jeannie interpreted the song as the result of a fair fight between an elder son, David, and a younger brother, John, who attempted to usurp the elder's authority and position. At the end, David is atoning for the fratricide by committing suicide: 'Well, it's very plain to be seen what he meant. If he was gang awa' in a bottomless boat – well he was gang to droon himsel'. He wad never come back. He was gang to destroy his ain sel'.[44] There is no suggestion, as is sometimes assumed, that David has killed his brother at his mother's behest. As Porter suggests, an element of Jeannie's commitment to the song, which, as her title shows, concerns a mother who loses a child, may have stemmed from the loss of Jeemsie, who died of meningitis, aged eight.

Perhaps it is through the lyric songs that we may hear the woman's voice speak out less equivocally, as in 'O Haud Your Tongue, Dear Sally'.[45] This song, seemingly Irish in origin, subverts the conventional May–December device for although the standard complaint of the old man's sexual inadequacy remains, the final verse shows the price to be paid for a passionate relationship:

> But now I've got a young man
> Withoot a penny ava.
> Now I've got a young man
> Tae roll me fae the waa.
> He broke my china cups and saucers,
> He lay an broke them aa.
> And he's killt my little wee lap dog
> That follet my jauntin-car.

The cautionary impact of the song seems simple but, set in the context of travelling society where violence towards women was apparently accepted, even in some circumstances applauded, the reading may be more complex than at first anticipated.[46] The harsh realism of the song's ending transcends the broader humour of a song like 'A Auld man came coortin me' with its warning, 'Maids when you're young never wed an auld man'.[47] Both songs were frequently performed by Lizzie Higgins and, in many respects they seem ideal 'woman's' songs, although Jeannie Robertson learned the latter from a young man when she was twelve years of age.[48]

With Jeannie Robertson and Lizzie Higgins, as again with Belle Stewart and her daughters Cathie and Sheila, it is possible to observe something of the oral transmission process in action. Two points clearly emerge: that the living tradition embraces more than the narrative ballads privileged in literary study and there is no simple women's tradition.[49] We know that men and women become equally good performers and that women learn songs from fathers as well as mothers and grandmothers, just as men learn from female relatives. One great difficulty in reclaiming the older ballads as women's expression is that their world view seems to serve the dominant male tradition rather than questioning or providing any kind of counter strand. It is contemporary women's songwriting such as the work of Sheena Wellington that provides a clearer more assertive voice.[50] Yes, there are strong women in the ballads, women who demonstrate heroic feats of endurance, but their role is normally to suffer, to endure like 'Fair Annie' (1161) – and possibly to die ('Bonnie Annie' 1225; 'The Lass of Roch Royal' 1226). Jeannie of Bethelnie ('Glenlogie' 973) and The Laird of Drum's spirited young wife (835) are exceptional – but titles of the songs in which they appear commonly commemorate their male partners. Even ballads which might hint at origins in a society where matrilineal descent meant that the issue of who a woman married would directly affect the destination of her family's lands, ultimately show the isolation of women. Thus a sister is murdered on a brother's whim because she has not sought his permission to marry ('The Cruel Brother' Child 11). Sisters and notably mothers are shown to be anything but allies – because their position is likewise dependent on the good will of a man. One response is that the ballads show their historical context, realistically recording women's position as chattels or dynastic pawns, and what we are learning about contemporary cases of domestic violence and incest shows that this cautionary, archetypal portrayal is not necessarily redundant. The tragedy is relieved by the defiant female voice characteristic of the lighter song tradition, audible in outpourings of lost love like 'Mormond Braes' (1142) ('I'll cast my line and try again') and 'Go and Leave Me if You Wish It', through the humorous songs of street-wise women tricking country-soft men to the complaint of 'Betsy Bell': 'I wonder what's a-dae wi' a' the men'.[51] On the other hand, sung by men, these songs can be read as showing women's perfidy. What the ballad transcriptions cannot convey but what rings through the audio recordings now available is the emotional sincerity which Jeannie, Lizzie and other traditional singers insist on. Their passionate conviction and the moving tones in which they sing perhaps provide echoes of the lost voices of those earlier singers.[52]

Notes

1.   *The Greig-Duncan Folk Song Collection*, ed. Patrick Shuldham-Shaw, Emily B. Lyle, Peter A. Hall, Andrew R. Hunter, Adam McNaughtan, Elaine Petrie and Sheila Douglas, 8 vols (Aberdeen University Press in association with the Universities of Aberdeen and Edinburgh, 1981–).

2.   Alexander Keith attributes 383 ballad and folk song contributions to Bell. See *Last Leaves of Traditional Ballads and Airs* (The Buchan Club, Aberdeen, 1925) p. 290.

3.   Mrs Frank Russell, *Fragments of Auld Lang Syne* (Hutchinson & Co., London, 1925), pp. 316–7. See David Buchan, *The Ballad and the Folk* (Routledge & Kegan Paul, London & Boston, 1972), p. 249.

4.   Letter to William Walker, 21 November 1921, Aberdeen University Library (AUL) MS 2732/23/1, f. 58a. I am grateful to the University of Aberdeen and to Mr Paul Duncan for permission to quote from manuscripts contained in the Greig-Duncan archive.

5.   Unless otherwise stated the reference numbers are to the song numbers in the Greig-Duncan Folk Song Collection.

6.   Letter to James B. Duncan, 16 September 1915, AUL MS 998/15/27.

7.   Gavin Greig, 'Folk Song of the North East', no. 6, in *The Buchan Observer* (7 January 1908), reprinted in Gavin Greig, *Folk-Song in Buchan and Folk-Song of the North East*, eds Kenneth S. Goldstein and Arthur Argo (Folklore Associates, Hatboro, Pennsylvania, 1963).

8.   Letter to William Walker, 8 December 1921, AUL MS 2732/23/1, f. 64v. The MS is a copy in Walker's hand.

9.   Letter to James B. Duncan, 1 June 1915, AUL MS 998/15/17. The punctuation is editorial.

10.   Letter to James B. Duncan, 11 May 1915, AUL MS 998/15/16a.

11.   Letter to James B. Duncan, 25 August 1916, AUL MS 998/15/25. For example Robertson discusses a range of queries raised by Duncan, as in the case of 'The Lass of Loch Royal'.

12.   See notes to 'The Bonnie Banks o' Airdrie' (199B), *The Greig-Duncan Folk-Song Collection*, 2, 521.

13.   Letter to James B. Duncan, 22 January 1917, AUL MS 998/15/50.

14.   Letter to James B. Duncan, 19 [August] 1915, AUL MS 998/15/24c.

15.   'Folk-Song in the North-East: J. B. Duncan's Lecture to the Aberdeen Wagner Society, 1908', ed. P. N. Shuldnam Shaw and E. B. Lyle, *Scottish Studies* 18 (1973), p. 7.

16.   Letter to James B. Duncan, 3 October 1914, AUL MS 998/53/4.

17.   Letter to James B. Duncan, 5 October 1915, AUL MS 998/15/28.

18.   Letter to James B. Duncan, 2 August 1915, AUL MS 998/15/22.

19.   Peter Hall, *Greig-Duncan Folk Song Collection*, 3, xxvii.

20.   Letter from Ursula Gillespie to Dr Emily B. Lyle, 27 January 1981. It is worth noting that Margaret Gillespie transmitted more than songs. She passed on many aspects of material culture such as recipes for Scottish food and 'all I know about sewing, knitting and crochet work was taught to me by Grandma'.

21.   Letter from Robin Giles (great-grandson of Margaret Gillespie) to Elaine Petrie, 13 August 1994. Professor Giles indicates that his grandfather William's songs 'have not survived to my generation'. His aunt, Ursula Gillespie, did maintain an interest in Scots song through her grandmother's books.

22.   Transcript of an interview with James Madison Carpenter by Alan Jabbour, 27 May 1972, Library of Congress, AFS 14762–14765 LW06918, p. 7. I am grateful to Dr Ian Olson for drawing my attention to this extract. Little work has been done on Bell Duncan's repertoire, partly due to the lack of adequate cataloguing in this collection.

23.   See Fred Woods, cited in Herschel Gower, 'Analyzing the Revival: The Influence of Jeannie Robertson' in *The Ballad Image: Essays Presented to Betrand Harris Bronson*, ed. James Porter (Centre for the Study of Comparative Folklore and Mythology, Los Angeles, 1983), pp. 131–47 (p. 131).

24.   Herschel Gower, 'Jeannie Robertson: Portrait of a Traditional Singer', *Scottish Studies* 12/2 (1968), 113–26 (p. 126)

25.   The School of Scottish Studies Sound Archive, recorded 19 October 1972 by Hamish Henderson and James Porter, SA/1972/221/B4.

26.   Gower, 'Portrait', p. 113

27.   Ewan MacColl and Peggy Seeger, *Till Doomsday in the Afternoon: The Folklore of a Family of Scots Travellers, the Stewarts of Blairgowrie* (Manchester University Press, Manchester, 1986), p. 163.

28.   Paraphrased from Gower, 'Analyzing the Revival', p. 136.

29.   Gower, 'Analyzing the Revival', p. 134.

30.   Gower, 'Analyzing the Revival', p. 145.

31.   Ailie Munro, 'Lizzie Higgins and the Oral transmission of Ten Child Ballads', *Scottish Studies* 14/2 (1970), 156.

32.   School of Scottish Studies Sound Archive, SA 1972/22/B.

33.   Compare 'What a Voice' on Lizzie Higgins, *What a Voice* (Lismor LIFC 7004) and Jeannie Robertson, *The Great Scots Ballad Singer* (Springthyme SPRC 1025). Lizzie sings 'if I had wings like that swallow high' where Jeannie sings 'swallow fly'. Ailie Munro gives more detailed comparisons in 'Lizzie Higgins', pp. 155–87.

34.   Stephanie Smith, 'A Study of Lizzie Higgins as a Transitional Figure in the Oral Tradition of the Northeast of Scotland', M.Litt. thesis, University of Edinburgh, 1975), p. 22, cited in Gower, 'Portrait', p. 140.

35.   School of Scottish Studies Archive, SA 1972/221/B4.

36.   Munro, 'Lizzie Higgins', p. 160.

37.   Ailie Munro, *The Folk Music Revival in Scotland* (Kahn & Averill, London, 1984), p. 289. Revised as *The Democratic Muse* (Scottish Cultural Press, Aberdeen, 1996).

38.   MacColl and Seeger, *Till Doomsday in the Afternoon*, pp. 162–5.

39.   Sheila McGregor, quoted by MacColl and Seeger, p. 35.

40.   Iona and Peter Opie, *Children's Games in Street and Playground* (Oxford University Press, Oxford, 1969); *The Lore and Language of Children* (Clarendon Press, 1959, Oxford); *The Singing Game* (Oxford University Press, Oxford, 1985).

41.   Catherine Kerrigan, *An Anthology of Scottish Women Poets* (Edinburgh University Press, Edinburgh, 1991), p. 4.

42.   Gower, 'Portrait', p. 138.

43.   Almeida Riddle, *A Singer and Her Songs: Almeida Riddle's Book of Ballads*, ed. Roger D. Abrahams (Baton Rouge, Louisiana, 1970), p. 87.

44.   James Porter, 'Jeannie Robertson's My Son David: A Conceptual Performance Model', *Journal of American Folklore* 89 (1976), p. 19.

45.   Herschel Gower and James Porter, 'Jeannie Robertson: The "Other" Ballads', *Scottish Studies* 16/2 (1972), 144–5.

46.   See Ailie Munro, *The Folk Music Revival in Scotland*, p. 230, note 24. Betsy Whyte, *The Yellow on the Broom* (London, 1986), p. 1, shows the strict standards of behaviour imposed by traveller men on their wives. Duncan Williamson in *The Horsieman* (Canongate, Edinburgh, 1994), pp. 153–4 explains that couples wishing to marry were expected to elope, this symbolic act of force showing the seriousness of the man's intentions.

47.   Gower and Porter, '"Other" Ballads, pp. 147–8.

48.   Gower and Porter, '"Other" Ballads, p. 148.

49.   For an interesting expression of this point see Willa Muir, *Living with Ballads* (Oxford University Press, London, 1965), p. 196.

50.   See for example the confident tone of 'The Women o' Dundee' or 'Beirut' on Sheena Wellington, *Clearsong*, Dunkeld Records, DUNC 012.

51.   MacColl and Seeger, pp. 265–6.

52.   Other useful work on the oral tradition not already cited includes: David Buchan, *A Book of Scottish Ballads* (Routledge & Kegan Paul, London, 1985); Dave Harker, *Fake Song: The Manufacture of British Folk Song, 1700 to the Present day* (Open University Press, Milton Keynes and Philadelphia, 1985); Emily Lyle, *Scottish Ballads* (Canongate, Edinburgh, 1994).

18

Margaret Oliphant

Merryn Williams

Last term he had not even gone along to see if there was any audience for some of his later lectures – 'Charles Reade, an unjustly neglected novelist', and 'Mrs Oliphant – a lesser Trollope'. Perhaps it was better that the latter lecture never got delivered these days. How strange that the revival in Mrs Oliphant's reputation which he had been predicting all these years had never actually come about! Why, he wondered? It must be something to do with the modern world. (Robert Barnard, *Death of an Old Goat* (1974))

The speaker is a ridiculous elderly academic, his mind still stuck in the Victorian age, whose admiration for Mrs Oliphant is a sign of his absurdity. Yet in the twenty years since that was written, there has indeed been a revival in her reputation. A modest revival; she is still unfairly bracketed with Trollope who was a very different and much cruder writer, and there are hardly any critical studies or dramatic adaptations (while fresh tributes to Charlotte Brontë and George Eliot appear all the time). But several of her novels and short stories got back into print in the 1980s and readers were startled to discover how good they were. Why, then, did she remain obscure for nearly ninety years?

Margaret Oliphant was born in 1828 and died in 1897. We know the outlines of her story, from the unfinished *Autobiography* which was published in a mangled form after her death. A scribbler from her teens, she brought out her first novel, *Margaret Maitland*, at the age of twenty-one and thereafter wrote on average two books a year. She was always short of money and always having to support her relations – first an alcoholic brother, then a husband whose stained-glass business failed and who died young, then her three surviving children, then a second brother and his family after he had somehow come to grief. Throughout her long life she kept the pot boiling by turning out whatever the public wanted – romances, melodramas, religious works, articles for *Blackwood's Magazine*. She never gave herself time to work 'with an artist's fervour and concentration to produce a masterpiece – I don't think I have ever had two hours undisturbed (except at night, when everybody is in bed) during my whole literary life'.[1] By a final brutal irony, the children for whom she had sacrificed so much all died before her.

Yet it would be a mistake to think that this great mass of work is rubbish. 'Her best work was of a very high order of merit', wrote the novelist Howard Sturgis. 'The harm that she did to her literary reputation seems rather the surrounding of her best with so much which she knew to be of inferior quality'.[2] Contemporaries, while acknowledging that she over-produced, still believed her to be a great writer. 'Had Mrs Oliphant concentrated her powers', one of them wrote in 1883, 'what might she not have done?'[3] And in *The Victorian Age of English Literature* (1892), which she wrote with her son, one or other of them noted:

> We can do no more than mention . . . the name of Mrs Oliphant, for reasons which the reader will easily understand. It would be false modesty to leave it out of a record of the novelists of the Victorian age.[4]

Yet within ten years, she had been all but wiped off the record: anti-Victorianism and then the Great War had altered the literary landscape permanently. Her name survived for the wrong reasons and in the footnotes to literature; Hardy, annoyed by her review of *Jude the Obscure*, referred in 1912 to 'the screaming of a poor lady in *Blackwood's*',[5] and Hardy's biographer claimed her as a member of the lunatic fringe.[6] 'Victorian prude', 'anti-suffragist', these are the images of her which have come down to posterity. In 1938 Virginia Woolf, who knew about her from her father and from Anne Thackeray, gave what must have seemed the final summing-up:

> She wrote books of all kinds. Novels, biographies, histories, handbooks of Florence and Rome, reviews, newspaper articles innumerable came from her pen. With the proceeds she earned her living and educated her children. But how far did she protect culture and intellectual liberty? That you can judge for yourself by reading first a few of her novels; *The Duke's Daughter, Diana Trelawney, Harry Jocelyn*, say; continue with the lives of Sheridan and Cervantes; go on to the *Makers of Florence and Rome*: conclude by sousing yourself in the innumerable faded articles, reviews, sketches of one kind or another which she contributed to literary papers. When you have done, examine the state of your own mind, and ask yourself whether that reading has led you to respect disinterested culture and intellectual liberty. Has it not on the contrary smeared your mind and dejected your imagination, and led you to deplore the fact that Mrs Oliphant sold her brain, her very admirable brain, prostituted her culture and enslaved her intellectual liberty in order that she might earn her living and educate her children?[7]

Some of this is true. Most of her articles have dated (the enthusiasm for the British Empire, current in her day, seems particularly alien) and the novels mentioned above are not her best. The three-volume system was against her, so that many of her books are too long and many others are pot-boilers. Yet if her work is sifted we shall find excellent reviews and essays, penetrating historical sketches, and a number of novels and stories – realistic and 'supernatural' – which deserve to survive. We do not feel, when we read this work, that she is at all out of tune with 'the modern world'. Indeed, she is often disturbingly un-Victorian.

She reviewed many of the century's great novels as they came out and had her own opinion of them. Like most of her contemporaries, she ranked Thackeray above Dickens. It was an 'age of female novelists',[8] as she put it, and her thoughts on most of them survive. George Eliot – great but too solemn; Charlotte Brontë – great, but obsessed with love; Emily Brontë – welcomed with reserve, although some of her own ghost stories show the influence of *Wuthering Heights*. In the 1890s, conscious that her kind of novel was going out of fashion, she acknowledged Hardy's genius but damned his 'grossness', saying that she preferred 'a world which is round and contains everything, not "the relations between the sexes" alone'.[9] On the other hand she quite warmly admired a new generation of writers like Stevenson, Barrie and Kipling.

There were novelists from an earlier age whom she admired too; Susan Ferrier, Jane Austen, and Scott was the great wizard who had interpreted Scotland to the outside world – which knew little of its special virtues and traditions. The tough-minded, anti-romantic Jane Austen was undoubtedly the novelist most like herself. Writing in 1870, she paid tribute to her 'fine vein of feminine cynicism':

> It is the soft and silent disbelief of a spectator who has to look at a great many things without showing any outward discomposure, and who has learned to give up any moral classification of social sins, and to place them instead on the level or absurdities. She is not surprised or offended, much less horror-stricken or indignant, when her people show vulgar or mean traits of character, when they make it evident how selfish and self-absorbed they are, or even when they fall into those social cruelties which selfish and stupid people are so often guilty of, not without intention, but yet without the power of realising half the pain they inflict . . . This position of mind is essentially feminine.[10]

It is the position of mind we find in her own mature novels, and here it helps to know that she had been a very idealistic girl, but had become more cynical as she grew up. She was aware that many other people had lower standards than herself, but, in her novels at least, she was beyond being surprised. She believed that Jane Austen too had had to conceal her work from her family and behave as if it was not particularly important. And although she earned a living from her books, she felt that she never quite achieved the status of a professional.

She remains a paradoxical figure. A Scot who made her name with a series about life in the Home Counties; a realist who is celebrated for her ghost stories; a woman who wrote marvellous fiction about the war between the sexes remembered as an outraged Victorian matron. The real Margaret Oliphant had many dimensions and was a far greater writer than has been thought.

The Autobiography: Significant Silences

One of her best-known works, and it is more vivid than many of her novels, is the book first published as *The Autobiography and Letters of Mrs M. O. W. Oliphant* (1899). Vivid, but flawed; we know that she worked on 'this pitiful little record of my life'[11] in the 1880s and '90s with the idea that it should be published posthumously to make money for her niece and to clear off her debts. But it is in no sense a full record of her life, even granted that few autobiographies tell the whole truth. It breaks off abruptly, 'And now here I am all alone. I cannot write any more.', and there are several other gaps in the story.

Her first editor – Annie Coghill, a cousin who had lived with and perhaps off her for years – wrote in the preface to the first edition:

> But when those to whom she had intrusted it came to examine the manuscript, a great disappointment befell them. It had no beginning; scraps had been written at long intervals and by no means consecutively. The first entry in her book was written in 1860, and mentions, rather than records, the struggles of her early widowhood. The second, in 1864, is the outpouring of her grief for the loss of her one daughter, her little Maggie, suddenly

snatched from her in Rome. After this is the long gap of twenty-one years, till the time when in her bright house at Windsor with both her sons still left to her, and her two adopted daughters about her, she was moved to write down a more connected and less sad record.

So far, then, there is narrative in her own writing. After 1892 there is nothing, and it seemed impossible to allow the late years of her life – full of work, full of varying scenes and interests – to remain altogether unrecorded. The best thing that could be done, therefore, was to supplement her manuscript with letters, and to connect these with the slightest possible thread of story . . .

Mrs Harry Coghill, as she called herself, was a sentimental woman without much literary judgement. Her aim was to portray her friend as 'noble, loving and womanly in the highest sense' and to tell an edifying story. She left out whole chunks of what Margaret had written, removed several barbed remarks about Leslie Stephen, G. H. Lewes and others, and added a choice of letters which, in some cases, did nothing for her reputation. A note to her publisher of 16 August 1866 – 'I send you a little paper I have just finished about Stuart Mill and his mad notion of the franchise for women' – caught the attention of several modern readers, who naturally concluded that Margaret Oliphant had been anti-emancipation. Some of them decided that in that case she could not be worth reading. Yet if Annie had looked more closely she would have found other letters and articles which showed that her friend had changed her mind on the 'woman question' within ten years. Another letter which might have been better left out was one from Margaret's younger son, Cecco (F. R. Oliphant), written on 30 October 1887:

> Many people think that the unemployed are not bad fellows on the whole, as long as you don't ask them to work, but they are certainly an abominable nuisance.

Annie clearly had no idea that some readers might find this offensive. On the contrary, she described Cecco as 'gifted', 'much beloved', and altogether a fine character, and Margaret's record also suggests that he and she lived in perfect harmony. The truth is more complicated and more interesting.

Happily, the full text of the *Autobiography* became available in the 1970s, and has now been published. But, even with this in front of us, there are several significant gaps.

The most obvious is her reluctance to say much about Frank, her husband. She tells us she refused his first proposal 'but in six months or so things changed. It is not a matter into which I can enter here'. Later she describes being 'torn in two' during the early years of her marriage because he and her mother did not get on. We often have to turn to her novels to supplement what she says or does not say in the *Autobiography*, and there is a fuller description of their conflict in *The Quiet Heart* (1854). Probably she never felt quite the same about Frank afterwards. There are other hints in her novel *Agnes* (1865), which, although she denied it, is strongly autobiographical:

> She was no longer able to admire Roger, however much she tried, nor to look up to him, nor even to trust him much . . . Though she had never said it to herself, she knew very well in her heart that she had lost the perfect life for which everybody hopes, and that never on earth, if even in heaven, there could be between herself and her husband that marriage of true minds, which is the highest ideal of human existence. But this knowledge did not make Agnes fall off from him, or even grow indifferent. (Ch. 30)

The *Autobiography* contains haunting, intensely memorable pictures of her early life with Frank and her last journey with him to Italy (where he had gone to recover his health but only succeeded in making her pregnant with a posthumous child):

> The garden was gay with flowers, quantities of brilliant poppies of all colours I remember, which I liked for the colour and hated for the heavy ill odour of them, and the sensation as of evil flowers. (p. 36)

Or:

> The mere sight of the place was enough to freeze the tired traveller, so ill and languid to begin with. I feel still the chill that went into my heart at the sight of this room, so unfit for him; but we soon got a blazing fire. I remember kneeling by it lighting it with the great pine cones, which blazed up so quickly, and all the reflections, as if in water, in the dark polished marble of the floor. (p. 68)

Yet there is a hole at the centre, and we do not possess even a photograph of Frank, or a description by some third person, to fill it. She seems to have decided early on that she did not want to talk about him and it is obvious from the *Autobiography* that while his death made a deep impression, it did not totally devastate her like the loss of her daughter Maggie four years later.

There are other important things which are not discussed. She mentions a friendship after Frank's death with R. H. Story, later Principal of Glasgow University – 'good fellow, good friend, though we have drifted so far apart since then' (p. 95). It has been suggested that he fell in love with her; this must remain speculation, since it would have been inconceivable for either of them to say so. Yet we can see from *A Country Gentleman* and the short story, 'A Widow's Tale', that she shares the feelings of a young widow who is attracted to another man, while thinking that a second marriage would be unwise. She is also silent, or almost silent, about some of her immediate family.

There is a great deal in the early part of the *Autobiography* about her mother, who influenced her strongly. Her father, Francis Wilson, is 'a very dim figure', though a cancelled sentence describes the Wilsonian temperament as 'a compound of vitriol and vinegar' (p. 22). She does not, as we might expect, tell us when or how he died, but his death certificate states that it was in 1858 'by the visitation of God'. This is reminiscent of the sudden death of Dr Marjoribanks, which so appals his daughter, so perhaps he had something in common with that dour but sympathetic figure. On the other hand, where did she find the inspiration for the violent and frightening husbands and fathers in her great novels of the 1880s, *The Ladies Lindores, A Country Gentleman, Kirsteen*? What is the basis for her reported statement, which we can quite believe, 'that while she knew something of the human brute, she knew little of men who were at once good and strong'?[12]

Then there were her two brothers, Frank and Willie, whom she supported for much of their adult lives. Willie, an alcoholic who could never hold down a job, appears in many of her early novels and in *The Doctor's Family* (1863). Yet in those days Margaret would never have talked about him openly; Mrs Gaskell's *Life of Charlotte Brontë* (1857) shocked her because she believed that Branwell's problems should not have been made public. Writing the *Autobiography*, to be published after both she and Willie were dead, she felt able to tell part, but not all of the story. She was even more tight-lipped about the other brother, Frank. In 1868 something happened which ended his career and made him and his children completely dependent on her; this was why she took the 'great decision, to give up what hopes I might have had of doing now my very best, and to set myself steadily to make as much money as I could' (p. 132). She does not tell us exactly what brought on the crisis, saying first 'it is not likely that such family details would be of interest to the public' and then adding with a flash of insight:

> And yet, as a matter of fact, it is exactly those family details that are interesting, – the human story in all its chapters. I have often said, however, that none of us with any of the strong sense of family credit which used to be so general, but is not so, I think, now, could ever really tell what were perhaps the best and most creditable things in our own life, since by the strange fate which attends us human creatures, what is most creditable to one is often least creditable to another. These things steal out; they are divined in most cases, and then forgotten. Therefore all can never be told of any family story, except at the cost of family honour, and that pride which is the most pardonable of all pride, the determination to keep unsullied a family name. (p. 130)

She was careful, then, to say as little as possible about why her second brother came to grief. He worked in a bank, and a novel of 1887 (*The Son of his Father*, ch. 4) suggests that some money was missing, but, again, in her own person, she never said so.

She was reticent, too, about the children she had brought up. Her nieces, Madge and Denny, are scarcely mentioned in the *Autobiography*, though surviving letters show them to have been very important in her later years. (She channelled her negative feelings about them and their father into *The Curate in Charge*.) Only a little is said, and then only after his death, about her long struggle with her elder son Cyril. The *Autobiography* virtually stops after 1875 – 'With that year began a new life, one of which I cannot speak much' (p. 151). His friend Howard Sturgis also refused to discuss Cyril's behaviour: 'It is very difficult to write of these things without saying what she would never have wished said'.[13] This is certainly more dignified than the modern tendency to tell all, but it is infuriating for the biographer.

Cyril's relationship with his mother (he drank, and was content to live off her) is shown vividly in the first chapters of *The Wizard's Son* (1884). For her younger son Cecco, she and Annie Coghill had nothing but praise. But his letters and those of other members of the family tell a different story, and I believe that, in *A Country Gentleman*, she gave a more honest picture of his character.

It is always difficult to tell how much of a creative writer's work is based on events in his or her own life, but in the case of Margaret Oliphant, there are certain clues. Throughout her long career she turned to fiction to discuss painful and complicated events and emotions, which she believed it would be wrong to speak of in relation to herself. A late and impressive example is 'Mr Sandford', published anonymously in 1888, the story of an elderly, successful artist (supporting four expensive young people just as she was doing) who suddenly finds that the public no longer wants his work. In the last year of her life she reprinted it under her own name with a revealing preface:

> The moment when we first perceive that our individual tide has turned is one which few persons will find it possible to forget. We look on with a piteous surprise to see our little triumphs, our no-little hopes, the future we had still believed in, the past in which we thought our name and fame would still be to the good, whatever happened, all floating out to sea to be lost there, out of sight of men.[14]

As she had feared, she was in much the same position as her fictional painter. In her late sixties, she was still living from hand to mouth; the three-volume system on which she had depended was dying, and she was unable to provide the kind of 'sex-question' novels the public seemed to want. There is also a hint, in this moving story, that the artist has been known to prostitute his talent:

> There was very little fault to be found with the picture . . . except, perhaps, that, had not this been Mr Sandford's profession, there was no occasion for its existence at all.

In her *Autobiography*, too, she brooded over the artist's calling and the choice she had had to make when she was younger:

> I have been tempted to begin writing by George Eliot's life . . . I wonder if I am a little envious of her? . . . How I have been handicapped in life! Should I have done better if I had been kept, like her, in a mental greenhouse and taken care of? . . . (pp. 14–15)

We have seen that there are great silences in this book; it has no conclusion, and it is not a substitute for a conventional biography. It remains a classic for other reasons. Considering the repeated tragedies in her life, it is remarkable that the *Autobiography* is so humorous, so bracing and free from self-pity. 'I have lived a laborious life, incessant work, incessant anxiety . . . and yet so strange, so capricious is this human being, that I would not say I have had an unhappy life (p. 14). 'Werena my heart licht I wad dee', she quoted from Grizel Hume [Lady Grisell Baillie, 1665–1746]. It is this quality which makes her novels, at their best, not at all depressing, but full of wit, zest, sharp insight, wicked humour.

Novels Without a Hero

'I have learned to take perhaps more a man's view of mortal affairs', Margaret Oliphant wrote, 'to feel that the love between men and women, the marrying and giving in marriage, occupy in fact so small a portion of either existence or thought'.[15] She was thinking of *Jane Eyre*, which had made its author famous and founded a whole school of romantic fiction by women. Unlike Charlotte Brontë and George Eliot, she married early, had several children, and had written all her good work after she became a single mother. Although the demands of the market forced her to write some romance, she was bored by it as early as 1865 when she wrote in the preface to *Agnes*:

> Life . . . lacks altogether the unity of the regularly constructed fiction, which confines itself to the graceful task of conducting two virtuous young persons through a labyrinth of difficulties to a happy marriage . . . yet at the same time everybody knows that there are many lives which only begin after that first fair chapter of youthful existence is completed.

Agnes has an imperfect marriage, but neither dies of a broken heart nor takes a lover; this, the author suggests, is the stuff of real life. Consider, too, the last paragraph of *Hester* (1883), one of the first novels to be reprinted in modern times:

> And as for Hester, all that can be said for her is that there are two men whom she may choose between, and marry either if she pleases – good men both, who will never wring her heart.

> Old Mrs Morgan desires one match, Mrs John another. What can a young woman desire more than to have such a possibility of choice?

How disappointing for readers who had been waiting to see whom the heroine would marry! In this novel, the central figure is not young Hester but the elderly, unmarried Catherine, who runs the family bank and whose heart is broken when her adopted son deserts her. Margaret was always drawn to women who were not heroines of romance, to spinsters, mothers of grown-up children and those who were simply too intelligent for the men they met. These women, even if surrounded by relatives, tend to be very much on their own.

Her experiences with the men in her own family had made her cease to believe in the myth of the man as provider. She did not dislike them, exactly, but she treated them, as one observer noted, 'with habitual tolerant good-humoured contempt'.[16] In her biographies, such as *The Life of Edward Irving* (1862), a man may take a heroic role, but her attitude to the men she actually knew is reflected in *At his Gates* (1872), about an artist's wife who is disappointed that her husband is not Michelangelo. The high ideals she had cherished as a young woman had taken a terrible beating. In her fiction, men are sometimes innocent youths, whom she treats with a certain tenderness, sometimes 'human brutes'; more often, they are simply commonplace.

It is women who hold families together, and although she is well aware of 'the wounds which people closely connected in life so often give to each other', she does not believe that the family can be walked away from. Women have responsibilities to their kinsfolk, far and near, and society, too, has its claims. In *Kirsteen* (1890), the two young people who become engaged in the Scotland of 1812 know they cannot ignore the conventions:

> In those days there was no thought of the constant communications we have now, no weekly mails, no rapid courses overland, no telegraph for an emergency. When a young man went away he went for good – away; every trace of him obliterated as if he had not been . . . She was very well aware of the fact, and raised no thought of rebellion against it. When she gave that promise she meant waiting for interminable years – waiting without a glimpse or a word . . . He would be as if he were dead to her for years and years. Silence would fall between them like the grave. And yet all the time she would be waiting for him and he would be coming to her. (ch. 3)

The weak and smug use the conventions for their own advantage while the strong rebel against them, but no one can escape completely.

The *Chronicles of Carlingford* are her most famous work, unfortunately. Margaret Oliphant has been called a minor Trollope because he too wrote a loosely linked series of novels set in an imaginary part of southern England and dealing mainly with the problems of clergymen. But while she took advantage of the public's appetite for religious novels, she had been raised north of the border in a different tradition and found the schisms in the Church of England absurd. She was seriously interested in the status of the priest, the man who attempts to guide others, and studied this in a fine short story, 'The Rector' (1861). But the two Carlingford novels which centre on clergymen, *Salem Chapel* (1863) and *The Perpetual Curate* (1864), are arguably not her best. The enduring novels in this series, *The Doctor's Family* (1863) and *Miss Marjoribanks* (1866), have nothing whatever to do with church politics.

Margaret Oliphant sometimes said that men would prefer to marry women with no families so that they could claim their entire attention. One such man, and he is no worse than others, is Dr Rider who in 'The Executor' (1861) slides out of marrying a girl who has elderly parents, and in *The Doctor's Family* falls hopelessly in love with a tough young woman who is coping single-handed with five helpless people, including his own brother. Nobody expects him to take on these responsibilities himself because he is 'only a man'. These stories, her first mature work, set the pattern for what was to come.

The good later books can all be described in the same way; novels without a hero. (Or when there is a hero, as in the interesting Scottish novel *A Son of the Soil*, published in 1866, there is no heroine and he had to marry a weak incompetent girl.) *Miss Marjoribanks*, which Q. D. Leavis saw at the link between *Emma* and *Middlemarch*, is about a woman of superlative talents who manipulates those around her for their own good. Most of the men she meets do not fall in love with her precisely because she is their superior, preferring more 'womanly' types who will look up to them. The author is well aware that men's feelings for women include contempt and aggression:

> He would have liked to have knocked Miss Marjoribanks down, though she was a woman. And yet, as she was a woman, he dared not make any demonstration of his fury.

This is brutally expressed in an interesting story, 'The Scientific Gentleman', from *Neighbours on the Green* (1889). 'Why should I trouble more for a woman – an old woman – than for a man? . . . You are plain; you are old. You have lost what charms. Therefore, what right have you to be considered?' Men are self-centred, sometimes violent, although these truths are concealed by the placidity of middle-class life in the Home Counties. A great deal of *Miss Marjoribanks* may seem trivial because it is about Lucilla's efforts to get a civilised social life going in the small town of Carlingford (under the quizzical eye of her father, who happens to be a Scot). But the point is made that other careers are closed to her; she can neither take over her father's practice nor go into Parliament like many far less intelligent men. The novel improves dramatically when Dr Marjoribanks dies and she realises that she has lost her male protector and much of her income, and is nearly thirty. It is necessary for her to marry and find a new sphere of activity if she is not to 'drop down into worsted-work and tea-parties like any other single woman' (ch. 42).

The hero of this novel, Tom Marjoribanks, is absent for most of it; he goes to India after Lucilla rejects him in the first volume and comes back to marry her years later when her name has been linked with several other men. There is no suggestion that Lucilla made a mistake by not marrying him in the first place. Like many modern women, she wants to spend her twenties exploring what she can do before settling down; her conventional language about 'being a comfort to papa' is understood to be a polite fiction. Tom is likeable and convincing, but, unlike her, a one-dimensional character. The final love-scene between them works precisely because it is comic.

Barbara Lake, a 'passionate and somewhat sullen brunette' whose world revolves around getting married, is contrasted unfavourably with Lucilla because she has no self-control or self-respect. She is quite prepared to spoil her sister's life because she has had a disappointment – 'dead selfishness and folly', the author says with unusual seriousness, are 'the two most invincible forces in the world' (ch. 35). Margaret Oliphant disapproved of fiction written by women who were, in her opinion, obsessed with sex. But she saw no reason to punish Barbara, as most writers would have done, by denying her what she most wants, a man. She succeeds in marrying Mr Cavendish at the end of the novel, and he is quite good enough for her.

Miss Marjoribanks has a 'hardness of tone', as the publisher perceived when it was being written, and the great novels of the 1880s are harder-toned still. They usually centre on women who are surrounded by their families but whose 'being is an undiscovered country':

> She had no one to anchor to ... with all the relationships of life still round her, mother and wife, she, for all solace and support, was like most of us virtually alone.

This is from *The Ladies Lindores* (1883), where a woman is unable to protect her daughter from a nightmarish marriage into which she is pushed by the men of the family. The daughter, Caroline, is too gentle and civilised to resist and endures years of misery, comforting herself by reflecting on Wordsworth's 'noble philosophy of sorrow' and by the belief that she is doing her duty. Her husband is a coarse man, as virile as she is ladylike, who outrages her by his sexual demands. He is finally killed by a fall from his horse – significantly, a 'powerful black horse', flecked with foam (which reappears as a symbol of sexual passion in *A Country Gentleman*). This leads to a murder mystery which is believable (though the author was not normally happy with melodrama) because he is obviously a man likely to come to a bad end. But the scene which everyone remembers is the one where Caroline appalls her mother by saying hysterically that she is glad to be a widow: '"to think I shall never be subject to all *that* any more – that he can never come here again – that I am free – that I can be alone"' (ch. 29). 'That it was a shame and outrage upon nature was no fault of poor Carry', the author comments. Having been 'so dutiful all her life', she breaks free and insists on marrying the man who had been her first choice. Indeed, the novel argues that women must find the courage to defy parents and husbands rather than outrage their own natures. But there is no prospect of happiness for Caroline, who is heading for trouble at the end of the book because she has chosen a weak man and because her two children are little replicas of her husband. In the sequel, *Lady Car* (1889), she dies, disillusioned with her new family. Second marriages, in Oliphant novels, rarely work.

This is also the theme of *A Country Gentleman and his Family* (1886). The central character, Theo Warrender, has a disappointing career at Oxford University because his 'fine and fastidious mind' is not adapted to passing examinations and scorns the 'opinion of the common mass'. 'Don't despise the tools we must all work with', his tutor warns him (ch. 1), but the intolerant young man will not listen. If this sounds like Cecco, his mother, who is a freer spirit than any of her children, sounds like Margaret.

> The woman who has not found in her husband that dearest friend, whose companionship can alone make life happy, when she discovers after a while that the children in whom she has placed her last hope are his children, and not hers – what is to become of her? She is thrown back upon her own individuality with a shock which is often more than flesh and blood can bear. (ch. 4)

Mothers cannot change the characters of their adult children or prevent them from coming to grief. Mrs Warrender reflects wryly that 'to think of Theo as cheerful was beyond the power of mortal imagination' (ch. 14), and this is significant. His inability to be 'cheerful', like more commonplace people, his intolerance of 'the usual conditions of humanity', means that he will wreak the same havoc in his private relationships as in his

Finals. He falls in love with a young widow who has a much-loved child, batters down her feeling that remarriage would be wrong, and then is miserable because he resents the child's existence. It is clear that he is the kind of man whom no woman will satisfy, but Margaret Oliphant also wishes to make the general point that mature women who seek for romance are deluding themselves. Inevitably Theo dislikes the boy and in the end is violent to him; inevitably the mother refuses to reject her child and the marriage breaks up. But by this time she has had two more babies and is left feeling 'she had awakened suddenly from a strange dream, a dream full of fever and unrest, of fugitive happiness but lasting trouble' (ch. 52).

The characters of Theo, his wife Frances and the impish little boy are extremely subtle and convincing, and the study of an intolerant temperament which is at the heart of *A Country Gentleman* has extraordinary power. There is also a sub-plot, included to pad out the three volumes, which is less remarkable but still interesting. Theo's sister is a conventionally good, pure girl whose admirer, Dick, has a previous 'entanglement' which has to be kept secret from her family. This happened in America, where young men apparently go to sow their wild oats. In Oliphant novels, most males are a disruptive force while women only wish to live quietly, and they and their children are often happier on their own.

The Scottish dimension, present in much of her best fiction, is absent from this novel. It takes place in a small English hamlet where life centres around the village shop and society is 'limited, dull and commonplace', expressed through dank and claustrophobic imagery. The book is in part a satire on the conservative and narrow-minded. Everything a county family does is governed by the most absurd rules, laid down by the vicar's wife and Theo's prim and proper sister; yet beneath this dull surface run currents of violence and sexuality which cannot always be kept down. Theo, who is 'not to be spoken to on ordinary subjects', is blamed for his moral absolutism, yet this backwater is so suffocating that inevitably people will break out. The author concludes, tongue in cheek, that only the self-satisfied are truly happy.

Both these remarkable novels have been out of print for over a century. *Kirsteen* (1890), though, was reprinted in 1984, and has all the force which they lack. In some ways it is a peculiarly Scottish story about a vanished society which Margaret Oliphant, born in 1828, could just remember. Windows are blocked up because of the Window Tax; London seems as remote as America. Yet at the same time it is her most modern novel.

There is a love story in it, yet, like the rest, it is a novel without a hero. Kirsteen pledges herself in the first chapter to Ronald, who will remain the only man in her life, but he appears just once and speaks only a few words. He is going to India, and the reader imagines he will be kept there in cold storage, like Tom Marjoribanks, until the end of the novel. Meanwhile she gets on with making the fortune which is to support them when he comes back. But Ronald is killed and the pledge turns out to be 'for death instead of life'. There is a touching, and perhaps ironic picture of the young officer dying on a foreign field with his fiancée's handkerchief pressed to his lips: 'all to the increase and consideration of our great Indian territory, and the greatness of Great Britain in that empire upon which the sun never sets' (ch. 31).

But, however this is read, it does not alter the fact that this is basically a hard-edged novel. Kirsteen's feeling for Ronald is 'the golden thread that runs through all the years', but by far the greater proportion of her life is spent in unromantic work and duty. She is a 'dry tree' (like Catherine Vernon in *Hester*) and founds no family of her own, but her life is dominated by her birth family from the first chapters, when she is a drudge without a free moment, to the last, when as the elderly and wealthy Miss Douglas she is surrounded 'by hordes of nephews and nieces, her advice, which meant her help, continually demanded from one side or other of a large and widely extended family' (ch. 46). These are not idealised beings like Ronald, but convincingly flawed. Her father is a despot and a bully; her mother (though she idealises her) weak and spiteful; there is a crowd of brothers who take more than they give and three sisters who are all very different from Kirsteen. She herself is slightly despised by everybody – and this makes the novel unique in Victorian literature – because she has no man. Her sisters all get married, and take the conventional view that any man is better than none. Anne is absorbed in 'her own little circle of existence', over-dependent on her husband and unwilling to acknowledge 'bonds of older date or wider reach' (ch. 35). Mary, who appears in some very skilful and funny scenes, flatters her elderly admirer by pretending to be helpless when she is actually selfish and calculating. And Jeanie, who has a 'passionate superficial nature', is ready to run away and become a kept woman if she cannot get the man she likes best. It is particularly difficult for Kirsteen, and for her creator, to understand this temperament. She has a 'one-ideated soul', believing fervently in true love which is 'never to be obliterated by baser contact':

> It cost her a painful effort to bring herself even to the threshold of Jeanie's confused mind . . .
> And yet she could not forsake her little sister even though the circumstances were such as
> she did not understand. (ch. 40)

Central to Margaret Oliphant's conception of life is the belief that one's family must not be abandoned. Kirsteen has left home, under extreme pressure, but she is 'not prepared to blaspheme her father's house'. This is why she makes her sister Anne visit their dying mother and is reluctant to take Jeanie away. Even her relationship with her father, Drumcarro – who, not Ronald, is the central male character in this novel – is not entirely hostile.

Drumcarro is known in the neighbourhood as an 'auld slave-driver' because he has made his money in the West Indies. At first we are left in doubt about whether he has committed crimes against slaves:

> Whether these supposed cruelties and horrors were all or almost all . . . exaggerations . . .
> belonging like many similar atrocities in America to the Abolitionist imagination, is a
> question unnecessary to discuss. (ch. 5)

This is the kind of language habitually used by *Blackwood's* which sided with the South in the Civil War and never troubled itself much about the rights of non-white races. But at the end of the novel, after Drumcarro has committed a murder, we are told that it is not his first. 'Old scenes far off and gone' haunt him, 'cries and sounds of the lash' (ch. 44). We have already seen how he brutally bullies his family, pushing his sons out as soon as possible, treating the girls as servants unless they can make an advantageous marriage, and caring only for the recovery of his ancestral lands. In the conversation in Chapter 40 Oliphant makes it clear that his views on public affairs are intolerant and that he does not rule out torture 'with the ignorant'. In both domestic and social roles, he is a slave-driver. Yet at the end of the novel it is important for Kirsteen, still unaware that he has killed a man to protect the family name, to promise she will help him buy back the family land. He is forced to acknowledge that she is the highest achiever among his children: 'a lass – and all my fine lads that I sent out for honour and for gain!' (ch. 46). And she, on her side, agrees with him that the family comes first: 'there was a fine strain of tradition in Kirsteen's veins'.

It was highly unusual, as has been said, for a Victorian heroine to remain unmarried, but Margaret Oliphant habitually looked back beyond the Victorians to the novelist she most admired, Scott. The dauntless Kirsteen has much in common with Jeanie Deans, who also makes her way alone to London, and her fate resembles that of his unmarried heroines – Flora Macdonald, Rebecca, Minna – who are morally better and more interesting than the women who get their man. Her idealised concept of love and honour is too extreme for most people, and she is 'a help to everyone that bore her name even though they are imperfect and ungrateful. Kirsteen was a rare and not very welcome visitor in the house she had redeemed. They all deplored the miserable way of life she had chosen, and that she had no man' (ch. 46). The author quietly notes the limitations of these people, and pays tribute to the Scottish single women – including the mantua-maker Jean Brown and the housekeeper Marg'ret – who 'make a story for themselves' (ch. 5).

Her shorter pieces, especially those collected in the posthumous *Widow's Tale* (1898) also show a distinctly unconventional mind. The title story is about a young mother who is almost destroyed by a 'coarse-minded man' because she gives way to passion – 'not of love, of shame, of horror, of self-disgust'. In 'A Story of a Wedding-Tour' a bride runs away from her husband, because his brutality disgusts her, and finds a quiet haven for herself and her child. (This is also the theme of *The Marriage of Elinor*, 1892) And in the remarkable 'Queen Eleanor and Fair Rosamond', a middle-aged wife finds she can get on very well without her businessman husband:

> It was rather a relief to them all when the father went away again. They did not say so indeed in so many words, still keeping up the amiable domestic fiction that the house was not at all like itself when papa was away. But as a matter of fact there could be little doubt that the atmosphere was clear after he was gone.

Later she learns to do without him permanently when she stumbles into his suburban love-nest and finds out that he is a bigamist. The vices of middle-aged men are treated with a resigned tolerance: 'It seems as if they must break out – as if common life and duty became insupportable'. (Was she thinking of her brother, who had also 'broken out' at fifty with disastrous results?) There is nothing romantic about his behaviour and he ends up 'elderly, stout . . . oh so commonplace'. Women have to hold the family together, for no one else will.

Many other novels, major and minor, have a 'happy ending' with a prospect of wedding bells. The reading public in those days would hardly have tolerated anything else. Yet Margaret Oliphant was actually at her best when writing about family breakdown, problems with stepchildren, independent women pursuing careers. Out of touch with 'the modern world'? Hardly.

The Scottish and the Supernatural

Most admirers of Margaret Oliphant would argue that she was a realist, one who looked below the surface of behaviour and exposed the hollowness of many Victorian clichés. Yet in her own day she was well known as the author of some unusual anti-realist, or at least non-realist fiction – her 'stories of the seen and the unseen'. They were written between 1879 and 1895 and she did not churn them out mechanically like so many other things: 'I can produce them only when they come to me'.[17] Some of them, particularly the 'Little Pilgrim' group, are not worth reading. But her once-famous novel, *A Beleaguered City* (1879), and a few short stories, are of enduring value and have never quite lost their appeal.

The first thing to note is that, although these stories were popular with religious readers, they are not pious. Up to the age of about twenty-five she had been an ardent Free Presbyterian; her teenage years were dominated by the Disruption of 1843. She continued to call herself a believer throughout her life. But she outgrew the rigid dogmas in which she had been raised, and after the death of her beloved daughter in 1864 she found it very hard to accept the goodness, if not the existence, of God. She was haunted by the problem of why so many people died before their time, especially children. She made the narrator of *A Beleaguered City* a sceptic because she was more attracted to this position than she would admit. So although these stories are concerned with what happens to the human personality after death, they raise more questions than they answer.

It is also interesting that they are at the opposite extreme from the *Chronicles of Carlingford*. Except for 'Old Lady Mary', which will be discussed below, none of them is connected with that padded, comfortable Home Counties world. 'The Open Door' and 'The Library Window' are set in Scotland; *A Beleaguered City* in a French cathedral town. (Margaret Oliphant felt at home in France, and noted in the charming love story 'Mademoiselle' that 'the old Scotch stock' was 'never uncongenial with the French'.) 'The Land of Darkness' is wholly metaphysical and takes place in an underworld where names and social status are irrelevant.

This group of one short novel and four stories needs to be read together. They are all about the intense wish of the living to make contact with the dead (and vice versa) and they are all, in their strange way, realistic. The man who has just entered hell in 'The Land of Darkness' is greeted by a peevish voice saying 'This is my corner'. The citizens of Semur (*A Beleaguered City*) are sunk in materialism and believe 'there is no God but money'. Ostentatiously religious persons behave no better than anyone else. Those who can perceive what the author calls 'the real meaning of life' are the narrator, who is Mayor of Semur and sees himself as a public servant, and his wife, who is a bereaved mother. When they are pushed out of their city because some supernatural force wishes to teach them a lesson, they are among the few responsible people who forget their own needs and think first of the public good. Something extraordinary happens, and the dead almost manage to contact the living and jolt them into a deeper awareness. But the Mayor notes sadly that, afterwards, they go back to their old ways:

> The wonderful manifestation which interrupted our existence has passed absolutely as if it had never been. We had not been twelve hours in our houses ere we had forgotten, or practically forgotten, our expulsion from them . . . Everything, I say, is as it was – everything goes on as if it would endure for ever. We know this cannot be, yet it does not move us . . . A little time, we are aware, and we, too, shall be as they are – as shadows, and unseen. But neither has the one changed us, and neither does the other. (ch. 10)

Other novels also comment on the transience of deep feelings, and in her *Autobiography* Margaret had pondered the question of how a living person can disappear into 'the unseen' and send no message back. 'The Open Door' (1882) and 'Old Lady Mary' (1884) are both ghost stories, of a sort. In the former, a disembodied spirit is battering at a door which no longer exists with the words 'let me in', like the spirit of Catherine in *Wuthering Heights*. The author makes it clear that this ghost is not fun to have around ('some think it grand to have a ghost so long as they're no in the way of coming across it'), and its existence is not a matter of abstract interest, because its bizarre behaviour threatens the life of a child. We recall that she herself had lost several children; the narrator's son Roland is 'the only one left us of many', and this gives us a clue to her religious views, which are touched on near the end of the story. She was aware of the arguments against life after death, but could not bear to listen to them, because it was emotionally necessary for her to believe in a loving God who would reunite the dead and living. So the local doctor, a sceptic, cannot explain what has happened, while the clergyman – 'one of a class which is not so common in Scotland as it used to be' – gets rid of the ghost and saves Roland's life by invoking the moral law:

> 'Do ye think the Lord will close the door, ye faint-hearted creature? . . . Cry out no more to man. Go home ye wandering spirit! go home!'

What is being said here is that there is no such thing as eternal punishment (a doctrine which John Campbell of Rhu, whom she had met, had been expelled from the Church of Scotland for preaching). On one side, a dogmatic and loveless religion; on the other, agnostics (like her friend Leslie Stephen) who rejected religion totally. Margaret Oliphant did not wish to join either party but did insist, in this story and in *A Beleaguered City*, that a mother cannot be permanently separated from her child by death. However, she did not seek to prove anything. At the very end of the story, she touches on the possibility that 'human agency was at the bottom of it', and readers are left free to make up their own minds.

The central figure in 'Old Lady Mary' is the kind of woman who often appears in the *Chronicles of Carlingford* and other 'English' fiction. She is elderly, cushioned from life's harsher shocks, has always been treated with great respect and has reached a stage where her little pleasures 'just so much good wine, so many cups of tea' have become her main interest. Like all of us, she does not really believe that she can die and so has neglected to make provision for her young cousin. She does make a will, but hides it in a secret drawer – the stuff of innumerable bad novels – so that at first the reader expects this story to be about the hunt for the missing will.

But what it is really about is the primary duties of human beings, of which the old lady only becomes aware when she has reached the 'borders of the unseen'. The first hint she gets is when she is addressed without her title:

> She felt sure that some one had called her by her name, 'Mary'. Now all who could call her by her Christian name were dead years ago – therefore it must be a dream. However, in a short time it was repeated – 'Mary, Mary! get up; there is a great deal to do'.

Her instinct is to escape responsibility:

> 'To do', she said, 'for me?' and then she looked round upon them with that charming smile which had subjugated so many. 'I am afraid', she said, 'you will find me of very little use. I am too old now, if ever I could have done much, for work'.
> 'Oh no, you are not old – you will do very well', some one said.

This is the beginning of an agonising process in which she is deprived of the 'cares and attentions which had seemed necessary to existence' and made to see that she has 'played with the future of the child she had brought up, and abandoned to the hardest fate'. There is nothing she can do about it because her physical existence stopped at death (the will does eventually get found, but that is no longer important). She becomes another restless spirit who belongs nowhere; perhaps the author is suggesting that those who will not exert themselves on earth will have to do it in some other sphere. Although she finally escapes, she has lost her self-approval, which is 'more bitter than death'.

Agony is metaphysical; no one does anything to Lady Mary when she arrives in 'the unseen' but she is forced to think about her life and tortured by the 'intolerable recollection' of past failures. Hell is other people, as Sartre said, and it can also be found within oneself. The inhabitants of 'The Land of Darkness' – the Oliphant version of hell – are not tormented by demons in the old-fashioned way but torment each other, and when they are left alone are still miserable. In this dull landscape life bears a distinct resemblance to life on earth, drained of colour and meaning. People experiment with different ways of passing time but no future seems possible – 'do you know what manner of thing a child is? There are none in the land of darkness'. It is just hinted that hell need not be a permanent condition. But the story ends, not on a pious note but with the narrator still trapped.

In 'The Library Window', once again, Scottishness and the supernatural are brought together. The place, 'St Rule's', is a thinly disguised portrait of St Andrews, which Margaret had visited as a girl around 1850. The narrator is old now, but is looking back to a time when she was young and spent hours in the company of old people, who remember a still more distant past. There is talk of Sir Walter Scott, of the 'great new buildings' on the Mound in Edinburgh, and of 'these wicked window duties . . . when half the windows in our houses were blocked up'. We are conscious of looking back through a long stretch of time, and also that the window (like the open door in the story of that name) is a metaphor for human efforts to see into the unseen. The June evening in Scotland, when light goes on and on, suggests that we are in a twilight zone where the boundaries between the seen and unseen blur. The narrator glimpses a man through a window (perhaps Scott, perhaps the projection of her own romantic desires?). Yet for others this room does not exist or is mere illusion. Nothing is certain. The intensity of experience varies, as in *A Beleaguered City*, and although Margaret Oliphant claimed in public to be a believer, as an artist she is much more tentative.

'I cannot help thinking that much grain will be left when Time has winnowed out the chaff'.[8] That was Howard Sturgis's final judgement, and, a century later, many of us would agree. If you pick up a book by Margaret Oliphant casually, it is easy to think that she was an unimportant writer, but all the novels and stories discussed here deserve to survive. The *Autobiography*, too, has lasting value, for its picture of an artist who felt she had to choose 'perfection of the life or of the work'.[19]

Notes

1. Mrs Harry Coghill (ed.), *The Autobiography and Letters of Mrs M. O. W. Oliphant* (1899). References are to the more complete edition of Elizabeth Jay, *The Autobiography of Margaret Oliphant* (Oxford University Press, Oxford, 1990), p. 30.
2. Howard Sturgis, 'A Sketch from Memory', *Temple Bar*, September–December 1899.
3. John Skelton, 'A Little Chat about Mrs Oliphant', *Blackwood's*, January 1883.

4.   Mrs Oliphant and F. R. Oliphant, *The Victorian Age of English Literature* (Percival and Co., London, 1892), vol. 2, p. 201.
5.   Thomas Hardy, *Jude the Obscure*, (1912), Postscript.
6.   Robert Gittings, *The Older Hardy* (Heinemann, London, 1978), pp. 82–3.
7.   Virginia Woolf, *Three Guineas* (Hogarth Press, London, 1938), pp. 166–7.
8.   'Modern Novelists, Great and Small', *Blackwood's*, May 1855.
9.   'The Old Saloon', *Blackwood's*, March 1892.
10. 'Miss Austen and Miss Mitford', *Blackwood's*, March 1870.
11. *Autobiography*, p. 60.
12. Meredith Townsend, 'Mrs Oliphant', *Cornhill*, June 1899.
13. Sturgis, 'A Sketch'.
14. 'On the Ebb Tide', Preface to *The Ways of Life* (Smith & Elder, London, 1897), p. 9.
15. *Autobiography*, p. 10.
16. Skelton, 'A Little Chat'.
17. Margaret Oliphant to William Blackwood, *Autobiography and Letters* (1899), 13 November 1884.
18. Sturgis, 'A Sketch'.
19. Margaret Oliphant authored over 100 works. Some additional titles are given in the general bibliography. See also John Stock Clarke, *Margaret Oliphant: A Bibliography*, Victorian Research Guides, 11 (University of Queensland Press, 1986).

   Useful secondary material includes: Vineta and Robert A Colby, *The Equivocal Virtue: Mrs Oliphant and the Victorian Market Place* (Archon Books, Hamden, Conn., 1966); Merryn Williams, *Margaret Oliphant: A Critical Biography* (Macmillan, London, 1986); D. J. Trela, *Margaret Oliphant: Critical Essays on a Gentle Subversive* (Associated University Presses, London, 1995).

19

Caught Between Worlds:
The Fiction of Jane and Mary Findlater

Douglas Gifford

The achievement of the Findlater sisters deserves reassessment on two grounds. Firstly, the quality of their work is remarkably high, and at best as good as anything written by the finest women fiction writers from Ferrier and Oliphant to Carswell and the modern revival of Scottish women's fiction; and secondly, they represent with unusual clarity and articulation their awareness of their predicament, and their paradoxical response to it. Their particular problems were those of the intelligent upper-class woman writer in Scotland at a very significant juncture, the transition from the social and personal values of the Victorian eras to the post-Great War. They exemplify the profound and paralysing internal debate concerning sexual and gender freedoms more strongly than any other woman writer in Scotland from the period of Margaret Oliphant to that of the modern 'Scottish Renaissance'. Sometimes this exemplification is conscious and successfully ironic, with a wit that can capture the ridiculous moment or pretentious pomposity with a sardonic penetration or a joyful hilarity. At other times they reveal how deep their social conditioning has been in their rhetoric of propriety and acceptance of conventional boundaries. At all times, however, their writing holds a strong and clear sense of the suffocation of the personality and personal development of women through their subjection to domestic hierarchies and duties, and through the expectation and acceptance of their female and male peers of circumscribed possibilities of sexual expression. This clear sense of circumscription is regularly conveyed in recurrent and powerful images and premonitions of the grave, of ghostliness, of ghastly dreariness, and of suffocation; often set against equally powerful representations of figures of rebellion, not often located in the main protagonists, but in off-centre figures, sometimes Bohemian or gypsy, who are viewed with a complex mixture of attraction and dissociation. They are writers caught between two different worlds, between the nineteenth and the twentieth centuries; but at the same time writers who catch and describe the tensions of their own dilemma.[1]

In order to understand where their ambivalence of response originates, it is necessary to appreciate their strange, yet very Scottish background. They were daughters of the Free Church minister at Lochearnhead, but they were also closely related to the ancient and titled Scottish family of the Borthwicks. Thus the two elements of religious fundamentalism and aristocratic sensibility combined in ways which might seem unusual outside Scotland, but which not infrequently work behind the writing of Scots connected with church and traditional family, like Susan Ferrier, Stevenson, Barrie, Carswell and Buchan – to name but a few. Poverty and family pride co-existed uneasily for the Findlaters, especially in the days after their father's death, when they had to move to Prestonpans. This move ended what had been for them a singularly 'out of the world' childhood and adolescence, in which they had very much to rely on each other, and in which the dreariness of their austere lives was enlivened by the beauty of the landscape around them on one hand, and being taken to village deathbeds on the other. The move south exchanged the austerity of the manse for the comparative poverty of the large but draughty mansion of Harlawhill. The cheapness of coal at Prestonpans was a consideration in heating its icy Adam drawing-room. Such a conjunction of high social status and low means was not uncommon in nineteenth-century Scotland, especially after the Disruption in the Church of Scotland in 1843. Many principled ministers (including the Findlaters' grandfather) left comfortable livings to join the Free Church.

The sisters were surrounded by genteel and morally exhortative aunts and a strange climate of conventionality and independence. From this genteel poverty they were, through their fiction, however, to become comfortably off and well-known figures in Scottish and English distinguished society. They were friends of Sir Edward and Lady Grey of Falloden, of Lady Frances Balfour, of Ellen Terry, and admired by William Gladstone, and they moved in literary circles which included Rudyard Kipling and Walter de la Mare. An American tour in 1905 introduced them to William James, Amy Lowell and the Emerson family; Henry James was to become a close friend and admirer when they settled in their various homes on the south coast of England. But their sense of their original poverty, which had forced them into society in embarrassingly outmoded dress, never left them; awareness of the need for the wherewithal to sustain a life-style above the middle-class 'vulgar' (one of their most frequent words, used to distance themselves from crass behaviour of whatever class) is everywhere in their work. To be fair, this sense is always alongside a Carlylean stress on duty and the spiritual quality of experience as opposed to material wealth; but it must be admitted from the outset that the sisters do not radically attempt to probe the possibility that wealth, taste, and 'breeding' might be interrelated, perhaps because their own austere beginnings convinced them that force of character could triumph over all. Jane's strongest statement of this belief emerges in her picture of Miriam Pillar, the lower-middle-class girl of vulgar family whose sheer fundamentalism of intelligence triumphs in *The Ladder to the Stars* (1906); it will surprise modern readers that the novel enraged *The Scotsman* reviewer of 1906, who found the implicit suggestions of freedoms due to women, and its 'egotistical' heroine, with her interest in books on democracy, dangerously encouraging of self-culture.[2]

Jane Findlater and Mary Findlater are each successful novelists in their own right. Too often their work is conceived as the product of a curiously inextricable and lifelong relationship, as though as 'the Findlaters' they somehow become a single author in all they do, so that even when they write separately their work is located within a common corpus. They did collaborate successfully in several works, and there is astonishing similarity in many of their themes and attitudes. But each had a distinctive voice, and the warmth and closeness of their sisterhood, while remarkable, should not prevent the reader from seeing the clear difference between Jane's wider range of social and human sympathies and Mary's drier, caustic and more focused approach to middle- and upper-class dilemmas.

Jane Findlater

Between 1896 and 1921 Jane Findlater produced seven novels and two volumes of short stories, in addition to a volume of literary essays, four novels with her sister, and two slighter collaborations with Mary, Kate Douglas Wiggin and Allan McAuley. Jane Findlater was a more uneven writer than her sister; her attempts at English historical melodrama, as in *A Daughter of Strife* (1897), or at writing for children, as in *All That Happened in a Week* (1905), were marked by self-consciousness and artificiality; these were not the worlds she knew (although by the time she wrote *The Ladder to the Stars* in 1906 she had acclimatised so well to southern English society she could mock its middle-class pretensions with deadly accuracy). Four of her novels, and her volumes of stories, are the achievement on which she should be reassessed as an important turn-of-century fiction writer.

The *Green Graves of Balgowrie* gained great praise when it appeared in 1896. In that year, as guests of Lady Frances Balfour at London dinners, they began to meet pillars of English state and society who would become their admirers. Mary describes how Jane looked 'so small between the Prime Minister and the Chancellor of the Exchequer', and her pride in Jane when a Cabinet minister asked her which of them was 'the distinguished authoress of *The Green Graves*'.[3] Something of the essential paradox of the Findlaters is realised in the conjunction of these sensitive young women, so aware of the narrowness of their background and experience, with the glittering world to which their family connections had introduced them. The paradox is heightened when one considers that the central themes of Jane's *The Green Graves* (and Mary's early novel, *A Narrow Way*, 1901) are to do with isolation, loneliness and complete failure to relate to the larger world beyond rural immolation; subject matter very much drawn from their own experiences of being out of the world and enclosed by the repressive conventionality of middle-class piety, from immediate family and the innumerable Borthwick spinster aunts who were to reappear endlessly in their fiction. All their novels are about women trapped in variations of the same predicament, in which they feel their confinement the more keenly since they are all too aware that it is their own acceptance of the rules of conventional society which imprisons them. Caught between the dictates of an older age and perception of the new freedoms of modernity, the sisters express their deep sense of being trapped, carrying the duties of the past beside their awareness of new possibilities to which they cannot aspire, and which they therefore portray in ambivalent terms of traditional condemnation on one hand and of fascination and admiration on the other.

The *Green Graves of Balgowrie* expresses Jane's divided vision in a curiously slow, cumulative and powerful movement which simply tells of waste – the waste of the lives and intelligence of two sisters, Henrietta and Lucy Marjorybanks, who literally and metaphorically waste away in the dreary chill of their ramshackle mansion of Balgowrie and their austere mother's half-mad and tyrannical devotion to ancient conventionality. Set in the eighteenth century, its commentary on the banal and crippling effect of excessive attention to etiquette and social ritual fits all ages, and especially that of the Findlaters themselves. There is a grim and elegiac poetry in the scenes of the two girls posturing politely to imagined lords and ladies for hour after hour in winter evenings in the frozen hall of their draughty country house. Findlater reinforces this with an echoing motif of graves, burials, and a sense of time which sets the quiet agony of her sisters amidst a beautiful, timeless and uncaring Scottish landscape. This is of course a traditional aspect of Scottish fiction from Scott's *Old Mortality* (1816), down to the work of Grassic Gibbon, and it will be found, possibly inherited from Jane Findlater, in Nancy Brysson Morrison's *The Gowk Storm* (1933) and *The Winnowing Years* (1949).

   Findlater's canvas may be narrow, but there is depth and psychological subtlety in her portrayal of the grim and eccentric mother, who is not so much cruel as warped in her selfish idealism, and a genuine pathos in the way the sisters care for each other in their loneliness. Something of Hardy's sense of the blindness of fate merges with the Findlater sense of isolation, and the novel's remorseless, if understated movement towards their unfulfilled deaths, brought about by their mother's diseased sense of propriety and social obligation. If she is a version of the wicked stepmother of fable, the more unnatural for being their real mother, then Dr Hallijohn, the worldly country physician whose fault is his excessive drinking, is the novel's unlikely guardian, and friend to the children. His attempts to save them are – again, in contradiction of folk-tale – doomed. Findlater handles his gentle love affair with the older Henrietta, wise beyond her years, with delicacy and a degree of role reversal. It is the unworldly girl whose intuition, moral sense and, ultimately, death, ruins Hallijohn's happiness, but saves him as a human being and devoted servant to his community. This lesson of the triumph of simple goodness over worldly degradation is part of the tradition of nineteenth-century Scottish fiction's inheritance of the Scottish Enlightenment's belief in that instinctive faculty, possessed by every human being, great or humble, for discerning Good. The Scottish philosophy of Common Sense helped create Scott's Jeanie Deans, and after her a long line of humble agents of communal good. Not surprisingly, given their background, the Findlaters perpetuate this tradition in their central figures, those gentle, intuitive women who, like Jeanie, trust in 'nature's voice' and God when society betrays them.

   To become successful in fiction, such an ambitious, yet simple emphasis clearly depends on unusual talents in authorial control of narrative, tone, and metaphor to make the moments of epiphany convincing and poetic rather than melodramatic. The Findlaters are not always successful; Jane's next venture in *A Daughter of Strife* (1898) is a melodrama, derivative and only occasionally attaining that powerful simplicity which is the mark of her finest work. She sets the tragic story of Anne Champion in London in 1710. Anne, a poor straw-plaiter, is betrayed by her lover's friend, who lies to her that her fiancé, a surgeon working in Flanders, has married another. The wickedness of Richard Meadowes is impressive, with some convincing psychological insight; but the historical background is thin, a stage set for a world Findlater does not know in the way she knows her lonely rural places. All too soon the novel illustrates the dangers of working in alien traditions, as it descends to Victorian skulduggery and revenge.

   The return to known territory in *Rachel* (1899) is significantly much more successful, an attempt to present the mind and career of a Victorian evangelist (whose progress bears many resemblances to that of the meteoric career of the early nineteenth-century charismatic preacher Edward Irving, the friend of Thomas Chalmers, who went on to hear voices from beyond and to see apocalyptic visions – and to destroy himself in the eyes of his public through the increasing grandiloquence of his claims). Michael Fletcher is an astonishing and disturbing presence in this story of enormous and tragic talent; once again, the reader is reminded of Hardy, in the story's conjunctions of dreams and fate, ambition and tragedy – with something of Hardy's hints of the rural supernatural in the portentous figure of Michael's gypsy mother, who has abandoned him yet comments on his career at choric intervals. Rachel is the daughter of the old minister who first takes Michael as assistant in his lonely Lothian parish. Lively and mocking, she is tantalised by this dreaming giant, whose visions are a mixture of genuine second sight and indulgent mysticism. For his part, Michael sees through her mockery, making contact with her deeper and more serious personality. Their inevitable drawing together is spoiled, ironically by Michael's greatness of heart; he has pledged himself to marry an Edinburgh girl, in order to rescue her and her mother from the streets.

In this Findlater works in a tradition of examination of naive idealism which since Scott and Galt has been a feature of Scottish fiction. Scottish novelists frequently focus on the incongruities of real goodness when confronted with the fallen world. The outstanding modern exponent of this is Robin Jenkins, in novels like *A Would-Be Saint* (1978) and *The Awakening of George Darroch* (1985); Jane Findlater's novel stands comparison with Jenkins's best. She captures perfectly the massive honesty of Michael, but also his subtle degeneration into self-deception and tricks of theatrical presentation. There are no melodramatic happy endings; neither does Rachel, after Michael's harrowing death, fulfil conventional expectation by allowing her wry and devoted New Town cousin to comfort her in a marriage of friendship.

The Story of a Mother (1902) is not of this quality. It has interest, perhaps, in that it works around a fascinating piece of Findlater family history. The Duchess of Sutherland told their friend Lady Grey that their father was not the son of the Durness minister, but of 'a Spanish pirate', and that their grandmother (by all accounts a striking and beautiful woman, the subject of much gossip in Sutherland) used to visit him on his ship. This shocked the sisters, and perhaps it is not surprising to find them later recasting this story, so that, struck on viewing portraits of the Sutherland aristocrats, the Reays, they discovered a more socially acceptable paternity for their father by identifying his features in Eric, seventh Lord Reay, on the basis that he had been a constant visitor to their mother, and had instructed the child to be named after himself. The story once again reflects the divided response of the sisters to the conventions of polite society; they are at once intrigued and dismayed.[4]

The novel has neither pirate nor peer as father to the beautiful wife of the pedantic minister. What is striking, however, is the way in which Findlater exploits the conventions of romance to raise, but not fulfil, the reader's expectations that either the old or the young Lord Ruxton (the novel's version of Reay) has been involved with Helen Hoseason. Son Zachary is the young lord's name-son, and his particular protégé; he is raised to be an aristocrat. The reader is constantly teased with possibilities, but in the end made to accept that Lord Ruxton has simply admired a truly loyal and good woman from afar. Thus once again Findlater plays with her fascination for the Byronic and forbidden, while simultaneously drawing back from commitment to such subversive behaviour. The novel suffers from Findlater's ambivalent inclinations, since fear of having gone too far pushes her back to conventional happy endings; Lord Ruxton gains his humble Griselda, and Zachary, presumed lost at sea, turns up sixteen years later – having endured slavery under a Spanish pirate. Melodramas of aristocracy and piracy sit awkwardly together; and the novel's strange movements of plot and place, from a vividly realised far north of Scotland to conventional society London, mirror its author's unease concerning her family's history and uncertain status, as well as the divided loyalties of both Findlater sisters.

By 1902 the health of their mother had led the sisters to spend winters in the south of England. Their web of eminent friends was steadily growing, and the connection with Scotland increasingly attenuated to summer visits. After their highly successful American tour of 1905 their series of homes were in the south-west of England. From this period by far the most successful work Jane produced is in *The Ladder to the Stars* (1906). By now she knew her English society, its classes and its subtleties of speech and manner, and by now, after a volume of remarkably perceptive critical essays on modern fiction and poetry, *Stones From a Glass House* (1904), and the slight but charming children's story, *All that Happened in a Week* (1905), she had acquired much of her sister's caustic social bite, so that *The Ladder to the Stars* fuses her visionary aspirations towards Carlylean spiritual truth with trenchant irony on the upwardly ambitious lower middle classes of English small towns.

This is also the most questioning and challenging of the Findlaters' novels, separately or jointly written. Miriam Sadler's unwillingness to conform to the stereotypical behaviour of her extended family in Hindcup-in-the-Fields singles her out for gossip and disapproval. Her unspoken rejection of their Wesleyan sanctimony and hypocritical materialism, her refusal to follow the advice of the family chief, the formidably vulgar Aunt Pillar with her family of Pillars in their small, inbred society, earns her indulgent disapproval which gradually turns to vicious condemnation and ostracisation. Miriam's crime is to want to think for herself. She is a female Jude; highly intelligent, suffering silently in her sense of her own inability to fit in with family and society, devouring the books that the famous writer Alan Gore lends her, yearning desperately for something which she cannot express to herself. Findlater does not make her the New Woman, like Jude's Sue; she is less rebellious, and her desires are purely to do with mind, as she struggles with ideas of democracy and freedom, to the jeering of her relatives. Their mockery, malice and mean-spiritedness is the most striking aspect of this novel, as Findlater applies all the satirical bite of Ferrier and Oliphant to this new world of the Victorian mercantile class, capturing their arrogance and cultural philistinism. The reader may suspect that her descriptions are sometimes less than fair, and that once again too much respect is paid to breeding and aristocratic qualities which later writers will deconstruct as products of privilege and exploitation of others, but the overall effect, that of sympathy for the lonely traveller between cultures, is strong and clear. Miriam wins some of her battles; she becomes a respected writer for the intellectual journals, and in the end she looks set to marry Alan Gore, to the intense astonishment of her feckless mother and socially-climbing relatives. But again, before her limited success in climbing her ladder to spiritual fulfilment, here is again that Findlater ambivalence concerning morality; Miriam falls for the young, utterly unconventional Polish violinist, Herman, symbol of untrammelled and genuinely artistic worth – but unfortunately and irredeemably foreign and therefore suspect. It is as if Jane Findlater yearns for Miriam to find him, but having brought them together, just cannot break the conventions which insist on a very British fulfilment. Herman turns out to be unhappily married, but contemptuous of convention, and Miriam for a brief moment stands tempted to deny all traditional ideas of propriety and duty and throw in her lot with him in Europe. This is a genuine moment of exploration of morality for Findlater; her intellect allows the validity of choice, but – without explanation other than simple assertion of the impossibility – Miriam *knows* that this cannot work for her; British manners are to remain intolerant of foreign excess, however attractively presented. Here perhaps is the essence of the Findlaters' predicament – to see the new choices, to admit their attractions, but in the end to realise that the immense weight of Free Church and family tradition cannot be overturned.

The situation of the Findlaters reminds us that they were creatures of their time; we must wait fourteen years till Catherine Carswell insists on Joanna Bannerman's right to take a married lover, and twenty-five years till Willa Muir's Lizzie Shand returns to her little Scottish east-coast town, having scandalised them by living with a married German professor for many years – only to go off again, this time with a younger woman.

After this Jane wrote no more novels on her own; short stories and collaboration with Mary were to follow. She had collaborated in 1901 with Mary in *Tales That are Told*, and would again in 1916 in *Seen and Heard Before and After 1914* (although, significantly, Mary contributed there only one novella to Jane's five stories). They would write three novels together from 1908, novels which would conjoin her sense of the impossibility of giving rein to attractive and vividly imagined possibilities of emotional and sexual choice with Mary's even deeper and ever more ironic sense of emotional and social imprisonment.

Jane's short stories and novellas are unusually wide-ranging and sympathetic, often being centred on the lives of tinkers and gypsies, as well as those of farm servants and social misfits. The two novellas occur in collections of short stories: *Charlie Over the Water* in *Seven Scots Stories* (1912), and the title story of *A Green Grass Widow* (1921). The first is no Jacobite tale, but a sombre account of how an old island woman is manoeuvred into leaving her beloved croft by her youngest son, Hector, desperate to escape the stifling monotony of labour and scenery for some glimpse of life. All the other children of the widow are dead, from war or childbirth in slums, except for Hector and an older son, Charlie, a farmer in Cypress Creek, Memphis, Tennessee. Once again the tension between rural seclusion and the attractions of the big world works on protagonists ill-equipped to handle transition. Findlater's descriptions of industrial Glasgow and the emigrant ships on the Clyde are succinct and effective, as are her accounts of Hector and his mother's meetings with the irrepressible New York family, the Kosters, their great railway journey, and their wonder – and the widow's growing unhappiness – in the New World. The Findlaters' American tour is clearly the source of the rich contrasts of territory in this poignant tale of innocence abroad.[5] But here the American experience is imaginatively redeployed to allow each side of the Atlantic to work on the other, so that even the headstrong Hector comes to realise, in the misery of their seemingly endless steerage-class journeys, the truth of one of the Findlaters' most typically Victorian and Scottish creeds – that life is, at dark times, best met with resigned endurance. Endurance is, perhaps, what the Findlaters and their women protagonists do best.

Equally surprising and striking as a departure from what readers expect from the Findlaters is the novella, *A Green Grass Widow*. Jane's ability to empathise with all kinds of humanity is nowhere seen to better effect than in her tales of the lives of the travelling folk, tinkers and gypsies; she knows and represents vividly their private language, and tries, with remarkable success for her period and background (and without George Borrow's experience of living-in), to give an accurate picture of their otherness. 'They are more like savages than people who have been dwellers in a civilised country for generations', she claims in her introduction. This locates her as working within the perspective of Scott in, for example, 'The Two Drovers', with that nineteenth-century detachment and whiff of condescension which separates the anthropological attitudes of the Scottish Enlightenment from twentieth-century recognition of cultural relativism. Once again, the Findlaters are in between eras; for Jane treats her tinkers with an ironic feminism which firmly locates the men, with their drunken wife-beating and feckless swaggering, as the 'savages', while their wives are allowed to dream – pointlessly, as they know – of settling, of dry beds and schooled bairns. The novella tells of Ran Reid and his wife and their five children. With typical ambivalence, Jane at once celebrates their harmony with rough nature, while showing that within the tinker culture, peer group envy and jealousy mirror that of so-called civilised society. The Great War takes Ran off to fight, and regular payments via the post office give Mrs Ran undreamed of wealth – which she immediately knows will have to be hidden from Ran on his return, for he will certainly use it for drink – with all that that entails. She's right; when he returns, he well-nigh kills her, until daughter Flora fells him. Mother and daugher, in a poignant, deeply ironic moment, burn their accumulated wealth, since to keep it risks disaster. Findlater presents the tinker men with clear-eyed understatement, with something of the matter-of-fact accounting of violence typical of the 1914 saga of Irish immigrant labourers in Scotland, Patrick McGill's *Children of the Dead End*. The Ran children witness the aftermath of the horrific murder of a tinker wife – and its concealment from police – by her drunken husband; no one questions the cover-up. For all its rural setting, the story anticipates much of the social realism of later Scottish fiction.

These, and the short stories alongside them, should not be identified as belonging to the Kailyard. They draw, indeed, from contemporary short stories like those of Neil Munro and James Barrie, and their ambivalent treatment of Highland and Lowland rural life and character, in which pathos and sceptical realism go hand in hand. Modern criticism is recognising that the work of these writers needs to be re-assessed as frequently deeply parodic of the Kailyard tradition.[6] With the recognition now given to writers like Jacob, Carswell, and Willa Muir, we need to accord the Findlaters, and Jane outstandingly, an important place in developing that early twentieth-century realignment of Victorian sentimental realism. Stories in these collections, like 'The Bairnkeeper' (a thirteen-year-old is shamelessly exploited by a drunken and miserly farmer's wife) and 'The Tattie-Bogle' (a natural is similarly exploited by a deceitful wife, so nastily that she brings about his death through exposure), can savagely strip away the veneer of social respectability from women as well as men, while 'The Deil's Money' and 'The Love Bairn' show human nature at its very worst, the first telling how the village idiot is cheated of his money, the second of the utter degradation of a wife by her appalling husband. Yet there is grace and humour; in 'The Love Bairn' the wife will buy her husband's illegitimate child from its grandmother, and often hilarity moves alongside tragedy. These stories are from *Seven Scots Stories*; similar tragi-comedy is found in *A Green Grass Widow*. An Edinburgh slum war-widow, who loses her two sons to war, but soldiers on with astonishing humour and smeddum; a handicapped island servant who breaks her heart because she can't get to see 'the pictures', when the mobile cinema comes around; and a child who has to feed his drunken father's abandoned family – these outcasts and misfits, as well as tinkers and maltreated women, are Jane Findlater's concern, and some of her finest achievement lies in these all-too-neglected stories. Hugh MacDiarmid (writing as C. M. Grieve), generally ungenerous and unappreciative in his assessment of Scotland's women writers, places the Findlater short stories amongst those of Stevenson, Munro, Buchan and Cunninghame-Graham as the finest from Scotland.[7]

Mary Findlater

Mary Findlater began as a poet with two volumes, *Songs and Sonnets* (1895) and *Over the Hills* (1897), with poems of nostalgia and exile which anticipate the finer work of Marion Angus and Violet Jacob. Between 1899 and 1914 she wrote five novels, all of which are significant in their understanding and exploration of the many different ways in which women of the period could be emotionally and developmentally trapped. The three novels which focus on Scottish women and situations are particularly intelligent, perceptive, and ironic analyses of situations only too familiar to the Findlaters.

Like her sister, Mary tried early to work within English traditions of fiction. In *Betty*

Musgrave (1899) the Musgraves come from the Borders; but after a brief use of Border landscape and ruins, the narrative moves to London, taking Betty and her alcoholic mother to increasingly degraded lodgings, which allow Mary to present assorted landladies and fallen lodgers in the manner of Trollope and Thackeray. But it is the work of Margaret Oliphant and her recurrent figure of the enduring heroine which clearly influences this novel, with its unremitting emphasis on the dire straits of the central figure, Betty, and her traumatic relationship with her appalling mother. The Findlaters are of a later generation than Oliphant, however, and their use of her supporting figures, such as the Woman of Feeling, the saintly Mrs Wentworth, or the wayward but ultimately loyal lover Oliver, seem anachronistically unconvincing.

Mary Findlater's perception of the role and possible assertions of women is more restricted than her sister's, for all her satiric bite. She was continually to place singularly unassertive women in passive roles, while, paradoxically, seeing clearly and ironically the agents of their circumscription (mothers, relatives, lovers, husbands) together with the social codes which operated behind them. *A Narrow Way* (1901) is set in Edinburgh's easily recognisable posh 'Morningsfield' (a nice amalgam of Morningside and Bruntsfield) and with the move to a setting so familiar to the author there is an instant access of ironic authority. Nothing in the tradition of Ferrier and Oliphant excels the portrait here of old Miss Cameron, a merciless anatomisation of what in reality exists beneath the conventional appearance of the sweet and genteel old spinster. Miss Cameron is the female equivalent of Mr Woodhouse, but subjected to a novel-long deconstruction which reveals her utter selfishness, the shallowness of all her ideas, and the petty authoritarianism with which she rules her niece Kitty, who has endless trivial tasks, church attendance, and ludicrous curfews imposed upon her by this mission-, health- and propriety-obsessed martinet.

It is this wicked satire on Miss Cameron as representative of legions of such prolonged lives of undeserved wealth and status which is outstandingly successful in the story; the narratives which move around her are conventional enough. The Edinburgh backwater of old spinsters and maids with prams is visited by widower Dr Marks, back from India, and a delicate love story unfolds beneath the suspicious nose of the old lady who, although she doesn't approve of suttee, thinks widows and widowers should stay as such, and wants Kitty to marry the wimpish rector's son, a fine wet specimen, wickedly – and yet sometimes surprisingly sympathetically – observed. And a subplot on a theme recurrent throughout the Findlaters' work (culminating in their last joint novel, the powerfully tragic *Beneath the Visiting Moon*, 1923), concerning the exploitation of a lowly, lonely and vulnerable young governess, which moves between perceptive satire on middle-class selfish insensitivity and conventional melodrama, allows Mary to present some delightfully selfish female dragons of different conventionalities. But the real success lies in the way in which Miss Cameron is identified as the ultimate embodiment of Mrs McGrundy in Edinburgh, and that claustrophobic Victorian stuffiness of rooms and rules. Kitty's sense of suffocation well nigh destroys her as a person, just as in reality many such dependants were destroyed. But Mary refuses to leave her as a conventional victim; Kitty may be passive, but – again, so characteristic of the Findlaters' contradictory vision – she can comment with wit and even anger on Miss Cameron's social uselessness and total lack of fulfilment. As always, Mary draws back from the final implications of her criticism, however, letting Miss Cameron off the hook on which she's impaled her, and allowing a somewhat unjustified tranquillity for the old lady in Kitty's married happiness, in a way which recalls how Mary and Jane anatomised their Borthwick aunts, but allowed after their deaths that they had a worth which reflection and time had revealed. Arguably what reflection and time had in fact revealed was that the hold of older proprieties on the Findlaters was, for all their ironic awareness of its decrepitude, and for all their instinctive sense of the possibilities open through rebellion, just too strongly ingrained.

Mary's greatest public success was with *The Rose of Joy* in 1903. As often in the Findlaters' fiction, imagery is used in a combination of motif and symbol which at best is a powerful and atmospheric enhancement of their main themes. In this case, rose imagery – which could so easily have degenerated into conventionality – is developed from Emerson's famous image of the rose of joy as ideal thought and 'immortal hilarity', in contrast with the 'care, canker and sorrow' of this world of time and chance. The rose imagery will move in strange ways in this novel, from actual white roses in a garden, suggesting early innocence, to more daring usages, such as the sultry rose-red sky, 'like the sky above Flodden Field' as Susan's sister ominously suggests. It is finally the image of Neo-Platonic idealism crucial to both Findlaters, in their life-long move towards fulfilment in mind rather than body.

In this novel Mary balances Neo-Platonic idealism against her sense of the tragic destiny she and Jane find so often in the lives of their women. The very opening – the visit of a soldier to his now faded and out-of-the-way love of twenty years ago – enforces the dominant sense of loss, cross-purpose and mismatch which haunts the book, as well as the fair observation that most hopeful loves and marriages peter out in mundane middle-age disappointment (a view which both Findlaters increasingly present, perhaps for obvious reasons, in their fiction). Susan Crawford is this old love's daughter; a poor and plain girl, whose intensity of response to nature and art lights up her plainness with sudden beauty. Juliet Clephane, the full-blown red rose, is a real beauty, but without Susan's spiritual dimension, her belief in Emerson's transcendental 'rose of joy'. Yet they become close friends, amidst a richly idiosyncratic and well-realised web of East Lothian relatives – the novel captures well the isolation, malice and envies of these rural and coastal communities, with the great road to Edinburgh and the outside world by-passing them. These are kind, if sometimes grotesque families; but kindness cannot prevent Susan marrying the wilful, ugly, imaginative and charming Darnley Stair, appropriately called 'Dally' – for his feckless if captivating impulsiveness, and his genuine understanding of Susan's talent in painting, conceal from her what Archie Hamilton sees is the veneer hiding a dangerously irresponsible man.

Findlater avoids romantic melodrama in showing how the wrong pairings emerge through wrong timings, misunderstandings, and Dally's superbly presented mixture of genuine feeling and manipulation of Susan and his relatives so that he can pay off debts. There is a striking anticipation of the betrayal of Elizabeth Shand by her husband Hector in Willa Muir's *Imagined Corners* (1935) in the genuinely embarrassing revelation that Dally is already married, and the Findlaters capture the shock and outrage of surrounding relatives and society with a ferocity which stems directly from their own uprbringing and inherited values. Susan has committed the mistake of Henry James's Isobel Archer in *The Portrait of a Lady* (1881), in that she has allowed herself to be manoeuvred into inventing value for Dally, just as Isobel did with Gilbert Osmond (and just as Carswell's Joanna will do with the philanderer Pender in *Open the Door!*, 1920); but her final situation will be that of making a mature person from the tragic wreckage of her life.

If Findlater's ending lacks the ambiguities of James's, it has its own strength in the portrayal of Dally as a complex figure who feels real love for Susan but whose wayward feelings – and indeed his very insights and talents – have destroyed him more than any calculated badness. Dally's remorse is real – just as Susan still feels real love for him. Susan may not have the regenerative function of Scott's Jeanie Deans, but she carries on something of that tradition in her endurance of the loss of child and husband, in her simple loyalty and her redemptive forgiveness. This is a mature, effective novel with the tragic inevitability of Hardy at his best; yet, with its literary echoes of ideas and images drawn from Burns, Mackenzie, Carlyle and James Thomson (*The City of Dreadful Night*, 1875), with its modern versions of Scottish traditional Men and Women of Feeling in Colonel Hamilton and Lady Agnes, and above all, with its sensitive realisation of the Lothian weather, land and seascape, it takes its place within a very Scottish tradition of fiction. Mary's deep love of the Lothians is revealed in an astonishing three-page-long epiphany towards the end of the novel, in which Susan rediscovers her rose of joy, with, significantly, a commitment to the celibate life of friendship, culture and the pleasures of the mind through her – and Mary's – vision of the harbours, fields, red-roofed fisher-dwellings, the moonlights, the winters, and the morning light of this, the Findlaters' dearest territory. (It is, however, typical of Mary that she should allow this epiphany to be mixed in Susan's mind with her memories of Dally's observations and insights.)

What discussion so far has not revealed is Mary's effective use of an ironic and often very funny running commentary on manners and affectation amongst her upwardly (and downwardly) mobile middle-class burghers and impoverished gentry. This is a prominent and effective counterpointing to her presentation of quiet tragedy. It can dart out amidst family gloom, with Susan's ponderously ineffectual mother's description of a suitor ('the doctor, quite a young man, though his name is Tollemache'), or the hilarious description of Susan's impoverished wedding, with its burnt porridge, grotesque melted jellies, 'chaos of custard', and where 'hens rush in where angels fear to tread' among the guests for rice. It's part of the complexity of the ugly-distinguished Dally that he's often very funny; introducing Susan to his fallen aristocratic family, he typically remarks that 'the home of my fathers . . . is closely surrounded by turnips'.

Such humour is set against tragedy in *A Blind Bird's Nest* (1907), and more exuberantly indulged in *Tents of a Night* (1914), Mary's last two novels. The first reflects the long residence of the Findlaters in the south-west of England after the American tour, with its splendid recreation of the creeks and coves, the sleepy overgrown villages of another of their beloved territories. Their best work needs such an organic and imaginatively realised setting, whether it be the Orkney islands, the Highlands of Perthshire, the Lothians or, as in *Tents of a Night*, the haunted fields and shores of Brittany. Here Mary lovingly evokes this overgrown, sea-edged, time-and-weather-beaten part of England, so close to Hardy's Wessex. Once again Mary's protagonist is one who, unlike Jane's more active women, endures rather than initiates. Agnes Sorel's father is a murderer – albeit one who has killed to defend the honour of his useless drone of a sister. (As so often with social disgrace in the Findlaters' work, the stigma attached to it by the judgement of peers seems disproportionate to the crime, as though disgrace is crime enough, and blots out all consideration of the hows and whys of the misdeed, such as Darnley Stair's bigamy, or – as will be seen in *Penny Monypenny* – Lorin Weir's involvement with a scarlet woman in Paris. Significantly, comparable misdeeds will be treated far more leniently by author and characters in, for example, the slightly later novels of Carswell and Muir.) Agnes has to carry the stigma for her father, and Mary captures well the condescending pseudo-tolerance of relatives and community, contrasting this sharply with the bleak but honest and deep relationship (another frequent Findlater creation) with her austere grandmother, and – a new development in her fiction – the attitudes of the Americans who are living in the district, with their fresh vitality and frank assessment of morality. This contrast of old world-new world attitudes, with a concomitant respect for the new which is nevertheless restricted to fascinated observation, becomes a feature of much of the Findlaters' fiction from now on.

Yet again the influence of Hardy can be read, in setting, character and tragic narrative. There is a discrepancy, however, between the depth of the theme involving Agnes, her father, his sister and his mother, and their generally hypocritical relatives, on one hand, and on the other Mary's increasing reliance on a God-given providence which allows the shallower romantic interest of Agnes's mature English lover and her young American saviour to come to a happy ending – as though Mary had begun to divide her response to life between a sense of tragic horror and a palliative faith (for which there may well be good reasons, as discussed below). According to the title-page epigraph, 'God builds the nest of the blind bird'; this move to a more affirmative faith tends to reduce some of the power found in her earlier fiction, which came from its grim realisation of the ways in which society confined poor and single women.

But Mary had by no means given up all engagement with contemporary issues. *Tents of a Night* (1914) is a fine comedy of international manners, which, in its sharp observation of Scottish travellers in France, most surprisingly anticipates the humour of Jacques Tati in his delightful film parody of the European summer holiday at the coast in *Les Vacances de Monsieur Hulot* – and, closer to home and the present, the ironic travel commentary of Janice Galloway in *Foreign Parts* (1995). If tragedy is now avoided, the eye for grotesque detail and human folly is sharper than ever, in this picture of Anne Hepburn in Brittany with her kindly but staid uncle and aunt from Polmont in Scotland, Anne seeking and her relatives seeking to avoid her Bulgarian lover, Dragotin Voinovich. It cannot be denied that the Findlaters are of their time in their instinctive suspicion of foreignness and non-whites. Yet few travel novels can have captured the petty irritations and triumphs of the new European tourism as well as Mary does here. She combines her insights and witty commentary with a balanced respect for native Breton dignity and culture, and, through the changing perspective of Anne Hepburn, simultaneously indulges and mocks her own prejudices; the novel is a constant oscillation between distrust of the travellers and the hotels Anne and her relatives encounter, with their noise and smells of eternal omelettes and garlic, their brashness and otherness, and Anne's discovery that a well-dressed Frenchwoman can put any British woman in the shade, and her affectionate realisation of the insularity of her Scottish friends and relatives. The joyousness of Breton churchgoing is compared with the grimness of the Scottish sabbath; the plight of the village idiot is seen as common to both, and in the endless repetitive birdcry of the natural, Mary finds a dark poetry shared by the Celtic nations, 'his plaint to the Unknown about the unintelligible world'. The Scottish supernatural finds its parallels here too; around these darkened villages and tumuli the revenants, those shadowy ghosts who must return to their earthly places, are all too credible to Anne Hepburn.

Most impressive, however, is the way the itinerary finds its spiritual centre in ancient Breton culture, in the standing stones, the menhirs and dolmens of Carnac, which reach through all the superficiality of the new motor cars, the dusty countryside, the shallow ebb and flow of holiday infatuations, to suggest something of the mystery and permanence of Grassic Gibbon's standing stones in *Sunset Song* (1932). And Anne will find, at the heart of the novel, a powerful symbol for the vanity of earthly desires in the skeleton of the prehistoric man, huddled in the very position in which he died, surrounded by his weapons. Here Mary anticipates the Scottish Renaissance movement of the 1920s, with its quest for spiritual significance in the immemorial past, in its remains and its mythology; Gibbon's short story 'Clay' will use this moment of breakthrough to the past, as will the novels of Neil Gunn. This communion with the dead is appropriately a turning point for Anne – and, indeed, a turning point for Mary, as she turns ever-increasingly to Emerson and his belief that the mature soul must eventually turn away from earthly loves, from 'home in another heart', to leave such toys for vast and universal truth. Around the time of the Great War both Findlaters, by now in their fifties, divide their vision, as in this novel. On one hand, just as Mary leaves Anne with neither of her lovers, seeking something more than ties of sexual love, they turn their seeking women towards the spiritual and eternal; but on the other, just as with Mary's presentation of the New Woman, frank, cheerful and unashamedly physical young Barbara, Anne's cousin, they are undoubtedly envious of the New World which is unattainable to them.

The wit, lightness of touch, and satire on modern tourism should not therefore distract from the underlying seriousness of the main theme, that of Anne's eventual ridding herself of her 'blue spectacles', her romantically envisioned quest for the perfect earthly relationship and the perfect lover. The novel is thus about Anne's movement from this immaturity to a higher idealism and her shamed realisation of the virtues of those she has seen as drones and bores, and the complex nature of human goodness and appearance. She has perceived that the holiday lifting and laying of tents of a night is a heightened version of human relationships and their impermanence; the image of the great liner aglow with lights, seen at night by Anne as it moves on a darkened sea, is Mary's other image for the transience of modern rites of passage, ships which pass in the night. Anne joins those other impressive Findlater women who choose to find their freedoms within their private imaginations, outside relationships of male–female love and marriage. It is perhaps a choice which avoids the engagements of later women with society and politics; but it is an honourable choice nevertheless, and one which their joint novels would impressively endorse.

Mary and Jane Findlater

It is significant that Mary's work falls away in quantity, if not quality, after the American tour of 1905; the America that her diaries capture so well perhaps arrested her confidence, just as for both the Findlaters the impact of the Great War would affect them with the growing realisation that they were of the old world, and now powerless to realise themselves in the new, however much they might gaze across at it with fascination and envy. Mary perhaps had another reason for losing confidence; Eileen Mackenzie describes (without realising the true importance of the event?) how in Torquay in 1902 Mary was attacked by a lunatic who tried to throw her off the cliff-edge, and how, with Jane petrified with fear, only good luck saved her life. This event surely deserves more understanding than Mackenzie's somewhat casual 'existence in Torquay was not wholly monotonous'.[7] Both Findlaters, as girls and women, suffered all their lives from moments of blank metaphysical terror; one can only speculate as to the profound effect of this savagery on such sensitive and protected women.[8]

It is clear that, after the turn of the century, the two sisters increasingly relied on each other for support in a changing and violent world. Their first collaboration was a volume of stories, *Tales That are Told*, in 1901. Yet here Mary takes the lead with four stories to Jane's two; her confidence not yet impaired. That said, it is an uneven collaboration. Mary opens with 'My Little Hester', a ghost story in the manner of Margaret Oliphant's 'The

Library Window' and 'The Open Door', classic mergings of the traditional supernatural working within old aristocratic families of Scotland, with their long memories of betrayal and hatred. She handles the ambiguities which go with this genre, and the open-ended possibilities of interpretation, with an assurance which places her midway between Oliphant and the Barrie of the magnificent *Farewell Miss Julie Logan* (1932). If the story has a flaw, it is in the way it splits its focus between sad young Hester, a descendant of the girls of *The Green Graves*, and the retributive haunting, which has little to do with Hester's story, other than straining her already overwrought nerves. 'The Red Shepherd' is likewise unsure in its attempt to bring together its two episodes in the life of tragic Anne MacFarlane; her disastrous marriage to a drunken, failed dominie doesn't fit with her marriage to the red shepherd, and her tragic end, though immensely powerful, seems contrived. Mary's short stories don't have the authority and wit of her longer fiction; indeed, in her sad little tale 'Void of Understanding', in which an idiot dies saving his brother in a snowstorm, she writes more in the manner of her sister, and her final tale is a curious over-clever piece, 'The Incident of Helen Walker', where a famous politician goes to ground in disguise and falls in love with a woman doing likewise. Are they already married, and playing a game of reinvigoration? Should we recognise them as real figures of history?

These were the sisters' first attempts at short fiction, so perhaps they were feeling their way through different genres and modes. Jane's stories seem unsure also: a conventional smuggler's tale set in Cornwall, 'Life's Deceitful Morning' draws unsuccessfully on the tradition of *Lorna Doone* (1869); 'In Hopefield Square' recasts the situation of so many Findlater novels, that of the dutiful girl serving an old martinet, so that the well-observed genteel Edinburgh setting is broken, unconvincingly, by the visit of the Czar of Russia, who comes to see the selfish old lady because her brother is his physician. Never before or after did the Findlaters allow a fairy-tale ending like this, in which the downtrodden young woman gets to marry the Czar's physician, escaping from grim Edinburgh to exotic St Petersburg.

There were other collaborations soon after this – in 1904 and in 1911 the sisters worked with their friends Kate Douglas Wiggin and Allan McAuley to produce two four-handed fictions, *The Affair at the Inn* and *Robinetta*. These light, unpretentious exercises in popular entertainment, for all they have recognisable Findlater creations in their old lady drones and stiff-lipped Englishmen, are trivial, however, compared to the wholly successful *Crossriggs* of 1908. Here, as perhaps only on one other occasion, in their last novel, *Beneath the Visiting Moon* (1923), their different kinds of wit and insight merged seamlessly. It is probably their best-known work, since its reissue by Virago Press in 1986, and I have discussed its important place in the development of Scottish women's fiction in my chapter 'Contemporary Women's Fiction I: Tradition and Continuity'. The novel takes up the theme of Margaret Oliphant's *Kirsteen* (1890), which must have been well-known to the sisters, in its presentation of the vivid, if hardly beautiful daughter who is imprisoned as the mainstay of a large, impoverished, aristocratic family who depend totally upon her. The Findlaters move Oliphant's more dramatic Argyllshire and London location down in scale, deliberately deromanticising any post-Scott echoes, so that their familiar out-of-the-world settings here become the sleepy village of Crossriggs, somewhere imprecisely located in the Lothians. Alexandra Hope is to discover that the furrows of her life are indeed crossed, as she battles to achieve some articulation of her identity and talents amidst her endless domestic duties, looking after, as she says with a shade of bitterness, everybody else's children but her own – the 'children' including her widowed father, the fruitarian eccentric 'Old Hopeful', a gentle tyrant once again descended from Mr Woodhouse. It is ironically, her own generous love which betrays and smothers Alex; her love for her gentle, feckless sister, her dotty father, her nieces and nephews and her community, her only escape from family duties coming in her evening readings to the local, crusty and infinitely narrow-minded Admiral, her shamefaced way of making money to feed endlessly hungry mouths. Alex is strong; but in her strength, as with the Findlaters themselves, lies her weakness. She has suitors; but she will not marry recommended local worthies, nor, on account of his being seven years younger than her, will she marry Van Cassilis, the Admiral's nephew, who genuinely loves her, having seen through the trauchled exterior to the quality beneath.

Here the Findlaters sustain some powerful ambiguities; the reader has to read through Alex's denial of Van to see perhaps veiled criticism of her fearful self – for after all, seven years is hardly an insurmountable age difference. Do the Findlaters parody their own situations here? It's tempting to read it so, since by refusing Van, Alex leaves him to the voracious Dolly, the finest of a line of wanton, selfish, yet undoubtedly alive ladies that the sisters love and hate to create, fascinated by their unconventionality, their sexual honesty, their blowsy dresses, their essential vulgarity. Vulgarity comes dangerously close here, and in the wanton woman of *Penny Monypenny*, to being more impressive and attractive than good taste – although, of course, the Findlaters draw back from the implications of their own instinctive creativity – but not before the ensnared Van, realising too late his terrible rebound mistake, commits suicide. (It is not made obvious that his drowning is a deliberate act, but Alex's sickness of heart and the narrative context strongly suggests this; ambiguity typically being allowed to linger.)

A dangerously conventional situation has been slowly revealing itself, behind Alex's maternal involvement with Van Cassilis. She loves Maitland, the famous writer who lives in the village with his cold and selfish wife. Yet the Findlaters manage this well, avoiding the pitfalls of melodrama and sentiment, so that Maitland's wife convinces as a beautiful but shallow, detached and almost inhuman figure, and Alex's repressed passion for Maitland becomes an image of her suppressed desire for sexuality and life. This novel takes Oliphant's Victorian implications into the open; but the Findlaters are once again then caught between generations, as Alex and Maitland, alone together on a glorious morning in the country outside Crossriggs, come close to sexual passion – but retreat after realising their mutual attraction into duty and self-abnegation. After this, Alex's discovery that, following her readings to the Admiral, she has a great talent for public readings for which people will pay good money, seems a symbolic way of allowing her utterance of herself, but of a circumscribed and unfulfilled self, who accepts a marriage of family duty and modest public success in place of a fulfilment which has been seen and wanted, but – by Alex and authors – avoided. Alex would cease to be the Alex who lives within a framework of conventions, which she sees clearly and mocks cleverly, if she broke out, just as the Findlaters would cease to be the women writers who capture their own predicament in the crossrigs of their fictions if they allowed their heroines the liberties of the new age. The gentle rhythms of the seasons, beautifully evoked, the quiet, yet appealing melancholy of the village settings, the sense of elegy which hangs over these sad lives – all these work to such a profound effect precisely because the Findlaters are objectifying an inner as well as an outer landscape, a mental world of sad and witty little mutinies against conformity which they know are doomed to failure.

Penny Monypenny (1911) combines Mary's scathing observations on middle-class Scottish and Edinburgh gentry with a picture of wasted talent such as Jane described in

Rachel. If the figure of Penny herself, young, innocent and with everything to look forward to, is somewhat too naive a version of the New Woman, this sweet idealism is balanced with the acidity of the Findlaters' picture of the Carter family, Edinburgh New Town period manners at their zenith. The Carters are outraged by their son Henry's marrying of Josephine in the West Indies ('Why, she's almost black!) and Josephine is the last in that line of wayward women that the Findlaters love to hate, fascinated by their creations' disregard for stuffy propriety, and their insistence on going their own way. They presented some men like this too – Darnley Stair was one, and here Lorin Weir (perhaps modelled, in his skinny elegance and Bohemian charm, on Robert Louis Stevenson?), unwelcome heir to the old brothers Monypenny, because he hasn't got the Monypenny name, is a delightfully frank speaker who cuts through Edinburgh manners to say just what he thinks, suggesting that the Findlaters are using him to express what they are too inhibited to profess explicitly. Lorin and Penny are in love, but opposed by all relatives; Lorin, possibly from the knowledge that consumption will kill him soon, possibly from sheer self-destructiveness, takes up with Henry's wife in Paris. Josephine's relationship with him is intriguing; her sleazy sexuality and sloppy personal habits, together with her alien origin, allow the Findlaters to come out in the end against her, but not before showing that they clearly admire her zest and sexuality, and showing her fidelity in nursing the cynical and dying Lorin. The influence of Henry James is by now very clear; Penny is a less successful Maisie, Josephine a tattier Madam Merle; and there are complex and successfully realised modern relationships in this strong novel.

As the war went on, the Findlaters were becoming tired, and uncertain of their place in the new fiction and literature. *Stones From a Glass House* had shown as early as 1904, for all its sensible insights into literature, that Jane didn't like the new realism of *The House With the Green Shutters* (1901); the sisters were to become increasingly unhappy about new trends. *Content With Flies* (1916) was their war effort, purporting to show the sisters making do with very little during the years of austerity. 'As cats when they can get no mice/content themselves with catching flies' is how they introduce their amusing account of their humble and economical ways of making-do in a country cottage. Yet the book reveals more than they intend, in its picture of withdrawal from a world of bombs and badness; and a volume of short stories in the same year, *Seen and Heard Before and After 1914*, confirms that the Findlaters were unsure in their responses to the developments of wartime. Mary has only one contribution here, the novella *Real Estate*, subtitled 'An Unromantic Story', about two old ladies who suffer a declension in money and living standards, and find themselves having to fend for themselves, *almost* without servants. Mary is in good form as far as her usual waspishness about elderly drones is concerned; but the frequent repetition of Emerson's views has become intrusive, and young Miss Fairfax, the whirlwind New Woman who blows the dust of their self-pitying lives by teaching them the basics of modern survival, is an unconvincing *dea ex machina*, a too-obvious symbol of the future. What redeems this story is its ruthless avoidance of self-pity, as though the Findlaters had determined to show through their writing that they were unbowed.

And Jane's stories here still have power – 'The Little Tinker' being one of her best stories of the kind, with an astonishing central image in the figure of the hundred-year-old matriarch of the travellers carried by her menfolk to administer her wrath on a backsliding woman who has been taken in by farmers to have her child, and has found a taste for the settled life. An older Scotland speaks ferociously here, before 1914, and it is noticeable that the two other stories placed in that category are stronger in their rural realism than the stories placed 'After 1914', which are to a great extent overt propaganda for the war effort, with much of the unpleasant moral superiority of the White Feather movement, as they contrive to present slouching ne'er-do-weels avoiding the war, in contrast with the brave endeavours of those who had to stay at home. Clearly the Findlaters were losing sympathy with the present.

It is then all the more impressive and satisfying that their last novel, *Beneath the Visiting Moon*, as late as 1923 (though Jane was not to die till 1946, having endured another war, and Mary lived till 1963), is one of their finest. It is ambitious in its scope of time and place and beautifully arranged in terms of its running allusion to Shakespeare and its sustained symbolism of the enchantment of the moon, signifying the delusions of mortals in love and ambition. It sets the tragic story of Barry Lovell, the daughter of another of these shoddy women the Findlaters could present so effectively, an innocent girl cruelly endowed with nothing but astonishing beauty, which becomes the snare for her destruction. The Findlaters never created a more grotesque and sordid family group than the fallen aristocrats, the Mauchlynes of that Ilk, living in haughty squalor in an Edinburgh slum. The grasping, gaunt mother is sternly magnificent, redeemed in the end by her grim love for Barry's child; her fey daughter in her tattered finery is a harmless Madge Wildfire; and Steenie Mauchlyne, pacing the darkened streets in quest of women of the night, arrogant and vulpine, utterly selfish and amoral, is quite simply one of their finest characters. Here again is the influence of James and *Portrait of a Lady*. There was nothing to stop Isobel Archer falling in love with Gilbert Osmond if she looked at him in a certain way; and the simple Barry sees in Steenie a romantic and fallen aristocrat whose dour reticence she takes as powerful feeling for herself. She swallows the bait laid by a charlatan whose instinctive talent for the hunt enables him, despite his essential stupidity, to catch her as his prey. He does not escape justice; on the positive side the Findlaters create a range of decent protectors in Mr Black the self-made Edinburgh merchant, the cynical but essentially decent Cyrus, his secretary, and – last and best of their Women of Feeling – Sybilla Erskine, a figure of real presence and nobility, set in her home in the northern isles as a beacon of true light, four years before Virginia Woolf's Mrs Ramsay in *To the Lighthouse*.

All through this novel the false light of the moon enchants poor mortals with the deceits of Shakespeare's Midsummer Night; even out of season moon imagery plays its part, as when Steenie slips the poisonous plant, Moonwort, under Barry's door. Legend has if that this is the key to all doors, at night – and it is the key to love-deluded Barry's undoing, and to her final tragedy. The novel has a second, triumphant movement to balance this tragedy. Steenie had been forced to marry Barry; after her death, pleading poverty, he denied responsibility for his dead wife's child, Belle. In their picture of Belle, adopted by Sybilla Erskine, the Findlaters succeed in placing a young woman on the threshold of a New Age, with the repressions and snobberies of the past behind her.

Sad though it may be that these two gifted ladies should abandon fiction hereafter, disillusioned with a twentieth century so utterly different from the Victorian repressions, duties, and certainties amidst which they had grown, it is deeply satisfying to leave their achievement with one of their finest expressions of tragedy and hope in the lives of women.

Notes

1.   For biographical information on the sisters the only relatively full source is Eileen Mackenzie's *The Findlater Sisters: Literature and Friendship* (John Murray, London, 1964); hereafter *Mackenzie*. Paul Binding's introduction to *Crossriggs* (Virago Press, London, 1986,

vii–xiv) is a useful brief summary of their life and ideas. For critical discussion of these novels (and for several other women novelists of the early twentieth-century) I am indebted to the original and perceptive discussion of Alan Freeman in his as yet unpublished PhD thesis, *Scotland's Missing Zolas: Fiction by Women 1900–1940* (Edinburgh University, 1992). The novels themselves, with the exception of *Crossriggs*, are now out of print and hard to obtain. For a more detailed account of where the work of the Findlaters places in the tradition of Scottish women's fiction, see my chapter later in this volume 'Contemporary Fiction I: Tradition and Continuity'.

2. *The Scotsman*, 24 September 1906.
3. *Mackenzie*, p. 35.
4. *Mackenzie*, p. 47.
5. From Eileen Mackenzie's account of this, Mary's American Diary is a fascinating, perceptive and important account of cultural relations between Britain and America at the turn of the century. Cf. *Mackenzie* pp. 49–78.
6. See Douglas Gifford, 'Myth, Parody and Dissociation', in Gifford (ed.), *The History of Scottish Literature*, vol. 3 (Aberdeen University Press, Aberdeen, 1988), pp. 217–58.
7. C. M. Grieve, *Contemporary Scottish Studies: First Series* Leonard Parsons, 1926), p. 34.
8. Mackenzie notes the recurrence of moments of horror and unaccountable terror from childhood to maturity: cf. *Mackenzie*, pp. 10, 15, 115, 124, and the Torquay attack, p. 45.

20

Scottish Women Writers Abroad: The Canadian Experience

Elizabeth Waterston

In many countries, the work of women writers has been excluded from or only selectively admitted to the canon – those books included in school reading lists, analysed by students of literature at universities, and alluded to with respect by critics. In Canada, however, any history of the national literature would certainly include many women writers, from Susanna Moodie, Isabella Valancy Crawford and Sara Jeannette Duncan, to Margaret Laurence, Alice Munro and Margaret Atwood.[1] Many of these 'canonised' women were of Scottish descent, and virtually all of them were very heavily influenced by Scottish writers from Scott to Spark. Perhaps the hint of heather had much to do with the relative ease with which these writers leapt over the prejudices of male teachers, editors, publishers and critics, since a colonial devotion to the old country persisted long after Scots no longer predominated in the demographic mix in Canada.

But in Canada, as elsewhere, there was an equally interesting group of women whose work has not survived as part of the canon, in spite of their enormous popularity and the respect they aroused in their own time.[2] This group would include Margaret Murray Robertson, May Agnes Fleming, L. M. Montgomery, Marshall Saunders, Nellie McClung, Marian Keith and Grace Campbell – again mostly of Scottish descent and again heavily indebted to Scottish writers, though unfortunately for their ultimate reputation, they modelled their work on Scottish writers who have also slipped from prominence: Catherine Sinclair, Mrs Oliphant, and the Kailyard novelists, especially J. M. Barrie.

Both groups transplanted and naturalised Scottish themes, techniques and topics; then they hybridised the work of the Scots by adding a female twist to stories devised by men. In *Tradition in Exile*, John Matthews compared the process of new country growth from old country roots to the development of a banyan tree.[3] In Canada, the new growth not only came up Canadian, it also came up feminine.

Let me illustrate this hybridising process first by looking at a woman who was not Scottish but who responded to Scottish literary material. Susanna Moodie emigrated from England in 1832. She came to Canada with an already well-established reputation as a writer of romances and histories; but *Roughing it up in the Bush* (1852; 1988)[4] shows a radical change in manner and tone, partly in response to the new life, but partly also I believe because of the influence of John Galt. Mrs Moodie's brother, Samuel Strickland, had worked for and with John Galt in Upper Canada in the 1820s and wrote with great admiration of the novelist in *Twenty-Seven Years in Canada West* (1853). Galt's *Lawrie*

Todd or the Settlers in the Woods (1830) was still a best seller in 1832 when the Moodies emigrated; and although *Bogle Corbet or the Emigrants* (1831), Galt's book set in Ontario, was less well known, I suspect that it too was well read in the Strickland-Moodie-Traill circle. At any rate, Mrs Moodie's *Roughing it up in the Bush* present the annals of her new parish in a tone very close to Galt's. Here is the same dry enumerating of details, the same desire to write not romance but fictional autobiography. Susanna Moodie's experience and perspective, however, are both feminine. From the first moment when she is left in the malaria-stricken port of Montreal, 'alone with my babe in the boat' (1988, p. 16), to the final triumph of her emerging from the bush into the small but civilised town of Belleville, to a 'pretty green cottage' (p. 518), with a fine china tea-service, she presents the woman's view of pioneering.

Susanna Moodie's work has been deservedly admired, studied, criticised, reissued. Margaret Murray Robertson's, on the contrary, has been sneeringly dismissed as Sunday School fiction. Nevertheless her novels, and particularly *Shenac's Work at Home* (1866, 1993)[5] are interesting products of the period between Scott's death and Stevenson's emergence, when according to critics' assumptions there was a hiatus in the novel in Scotland and Canada. New criticism has urged a revision of that assumption: those 'empty' years were in fact filled in most English-speaking countries with successful and influential work – which happened to be written by and for women. Mrs Oliphant's *Margaret Maitland* (1849) has been credited by Francis Hart with being a remarkably successful account of the Great Disruption of the church;[6] Margaret Robertson in Canada should be credited with an equally important tracing of religious developments in Canadian communities just before the Dominion's Confederation. The Scottish strain in her work is indicated by selected titles: *The Bairns, Christie Redfern's Troubles, The Twa Miss Dawsons, The Orphans of Glen Elder: A Tale of Scottish Life.*

Born in Stewartfield in 1823, daughter of a clergyman, sister and niece of other ministers, Margaret Robertson was brought by her family to a parish in Vermont when she was nine. The Reverend James Robertson again moved after four years, when Margaret was thirteen, to Sherbrooke, Quebec. At twenty-four she was sent to prestigious Mount Holyoke Female Seminary, in Massachusetts – where one of her classmates was Emily Dickinson. Margaret Robertson's sister Mary was so gifted academically that she was later offered the post of Principal of Mount Holyoke College. She turned down this opportunity in order to marry a Presbyterian minister and to accompany him to a parish in the bush in Glengarry County, Ontario. Eventually her son, writing as 'Ralph Connor', portrayed her as a central figure in his bestsellers, *The Man From Glengarry* (1901) and *Glengarry Schooldays* (1902). Hers is a poignant version of the recurring story of brilliant women, over-qualified for the job of minister's wife. L. M. Montgomery, Marian Keith and Grace Campbell are others of the kind.

In *Shenac's Work at Home*, later republished as *Shenac: The Story of a Highland Family in Canada*, valiant Shenac MacIvor saves the steading that has been wrested from the bush by her family. She also cultivates her own soul. She undergoes a profound conversion during the Presbyterian revival of 1864–5. This exploitation of actual religious history recalls Mrs Oliphant's much-admired *Passages in the Life of Margaret Maitland* (1849). Robertson's work was mocked in the *Oxford Companion to Canadian Literature* (Toronto: 1983) as having 'sanctified trouble' (p. 712). She did indeed believe that sorrow is sent to help us find salvation; but her novels are far more than mere religious tracts. Nevertheless, although she was already the author of eight published and popular books, the Montreal census of 1871 lists Margaret Robertson as having 'no occupation'.

To return to the canonical list, we find a more complex case of Scottish influence in the work of Irish-born Isabella Valancy Crawford. She was so steeped in the work of Walter Scott that in her best-known poem she chose to extend and Canadianise the story of *The Lady of the Lake*, adapting Scott's story of Ellen Douglas and her three suitors, the disguised King James, the powerful Roderick Dhu, and the handsome young chieftain Malcolm Graeme. In Scott, of course, the focus is on the battles between these powerful men, and on the political significance of the defeat of Roderick Dhu. In Crawford's poem *Malcolm's Katie* (1884) Malcolm Graeme reappears as the father of Katie, a Canadian lady of the lake.[7] In the pioneer Canadian community, Malcolm's Katie re-enacts some of Scott's story. One of her suitors bears the kingly name of Alfred, the other is a young axeman named Maxwell Gordon. There is no Roderick Dhu in the Canadian forest – but that forest is itself described by Crawford in terms reminiscent of Scott's descriptions of the fiery cross:

> In the shrill moon the scouts of Winter ran
> From the ice-belted north, and whistling shafts
> Struck maple and struck sumach and a blaze
> Ran swift from leaf to leaf, from bough to bough,
> Till round the forest flashed a belt of flame. (1972, p. 199)

There are no battles in *Malcolm's Katie*, only the march against the forest by men like Max, and the quiet fight on Katie's part (like Ellen's, in *The Lady of the Lake*) to determine her own fate.

It was Walter Scott's historical fiction rather than his poetry, however, that had the greater impact on Canadian readers and writers. Among the successful novels in the manner of Scott at the turn of the twentieth century were Agnes Laut's *Lords of the North* (1900), mythologising the Canadian heroes, McTavish, Mackenzie, and Simon Fraser, and Jean McIlwraith's swashbuckling *The Curious Career of Roderick Campbell* (1901). McIlwraith carried the Scott influence from the genre of historical fiction (already considered rather outdated) to the further marginalised sub-genre of children's literature with *The Little Admiral* (1924) set in the time of General James Wolfe.

Children's literature at the turn of the century was of course doubly influenced by the Scots: George Macdonald and Robert Louis Stevenson dominated both the sentimental and adventurous varieties. Margaret Marshall Saunders, who as a girl in an Edinburgh finishing school 'almost' met Macdonald – to her regret he cancelled a tea-time invitation – published in 1894 the first Canadian world bestseller. *Beautiful Joe* shows the influence of *At the Back of the North Wind* as well as of Anna Sewell's *Black Beauty*. In *Beautiful Joe*, a tender-hearted story that reaches out to many a 'cowrin', tim'rous beastie', Saunders also shows a debt to Burns, and a continuation of affection for domestic and farm animals.

With Sarah Jeannette Duncan, we return to human – all too human – characters, and to regional realism in the Galt manner. As annalist of the small Ontario town, which she calls Elgin, Duncan in *The Imperialist* (1904) traces the minute changes in social patterns and business practices, as well as politics, very much in the dry documentary fashion of Galt.[8] She adds however a mocking tribute to a more recent Scottish fashion. The sentimental Kailyard novelists had focused on Presbyterian ministers as protagonists. Duncan draws into her Canadian town the archetypal Reverend Hugh Finlay. With a sly and feminine eye she observes him in the pulpit:

He was a passionate romantic, and his body had shot up into a fitting temple for such an inhabitant as his soul. He was a great long fellow with a shock of black hair and deep dreams in his eyes . . . His face bore a confusion of ideals; he had the brow of a Covenanter and the mouth of Adonais, the flame of religious ardour in his eyes and the composure of perceived philosophy on his lips. He was fettered by an impenetrable shyness; it was in the pulpit alone that he could expand, and then only upon written lines, with hardly a gesture, and the most perfunctory glances, at conscientious intervals, toward his hearers. A poor creature, in this respect Dr Drummond thought him – Dr Drummond, who wore an intrammelled surplice which filled like an agitated sail in his quick tacks from right to left. 'The man loses half his points,' said Dr Drummond. I doubt whether he did, people followed so closely, though Sandy MacQuhot was of the general opinion that it would do nobody any harm if Mr Finlay would lift his head oftener from the book.

Advena Murchison thought him the probable type of an Oxford don. She had never seen an Oxford don, but Mr Finlay wore the characteristics these schoolmen were dressed in by novelists; and Advena noted with delight the ingenuity of fate in casting such a person into the pulpit of a Presbyterian Church in a young country. She had her perception of comedy in life; till Finlay came she had found nothing so interesting. With his arrival, however, other preoccupations fell into their proper places. (1961, p. 69)

Sarah Jeanette Duncan is rightly admired by all critics of Canadian literature. Her wit sparkles, her characterisation is deft, and her voice is pleasant to follow. The dissection of a Canadian town – or at least of the Scots-Canadian part of it – is neatly done. Plotting is nicely worked out on two levels. A traditional critic might say that Duncan provides politics for her male readers and romance for the women. The only major flaw is in the resolution: Mr Finlay's unwelcome Scottish fiancée, who has followed him to Elgin, is disposed of by Dr Drummond. Like the judge in Gilbert and Sullivan, Dr Drummond announces, 'I will marry her myself' – an unlikely decision by such a canny and comfortable divine. Most of Duncan's eighteen other novels are more neatly resolved, but unfortunately for Canadian nationalists the others are set in India or England, where she spent most of her married life.

L. M. Montgomery follows the Kailyard school in a more subtle way. If there is irony in her treatment of villages, ministers, briar bushes, or sunbonnets, the irony is tucked into subtexts little perceived by her early readers. Today there is a revival of interest in the thorns and thistles in Montgomery's garden.[9] There is no doubt, however, about the influence on her work of a spectrum of Scottish writers, from Burns, Scott and Stevenson to Barrie, MacLaren and Crockett. One less obvious influence is indicated in the title of one of her earliest stories, *Kilmeny of the Orchard* (1910).[10] Something of James Hogg's perception of the grotesque quality in Presbyterian communities appears in many of her works. Kilmeny is a girl blasted into voicelessness by her mother's sin of pride. Because the mother refused to speak to her own father, the young Kilmeny cannot speak at all. Until love comes into her life in the person of a young Nova Scotian, she can express herself only through her violin. Other examples of abnormal psychology abound in Montgomery's novels from *Anne of Green Gables* (1908) on, village grotesques glossed over in a tone of whimsy. The Canadian Kailyard grows strange weeds.

Montgomery has never lost her devoted following. Many other once-popular women writing in the early twentieth century, however, have disappeared, excluded from college reading lists and not saved by drifting to the children's shelves (where favourite books are lovingly handed down from grandmother to mother to daughter). Nina Moore Jamieson is one of the undeservedly forgotten. Jamieson's *The Hickory Stick* (1924) is based on the experiences of a very young teacher in the Bruce County, an area remote enough from Toronto for some of the qualities of a pioneer Scottish-Canadian community to be preserved into the days after the First World War. This is Hogg territory too, country gothic, grotesque in the perverse application of ideals.

Margaret Wemyss Laurence catches some of that unforgiving harshness in her novels. Set in western Canadian prairie town, her *Stone Angel* (1964) and the other 'Manawaka' novels portray the Scots pioneers and their descendants as 'fire-dwellers' in the Carlylean sense of living in the Rue St Thomas de l'Enfer. I do not know how closely Margaret Laurence read Carlyle when she was at college in Winnipeg, but I hear echoes of his tumultuous prose as her characters face their own versions of Carlyle's EVERLASTING NO of frustration and despair. Rachel Cameron in *A Jest of God* (1966), her sister Stacey Cameron MacAindra in *The Fire-Dwellers* (1969), and their classmate Vanessa MacLeod in *A Bird in the House* (1970) work out their lives in Carlylean ways converting the details of everyday living into apocalyptic symbols. They reach a YEA which is perhaps less firm, clear and everlasting than Carlyle's affirmation of work and duty. But the old Scottish austerities of courage and endurance are not far from the solutions each of Laurence's women works out for herself. In the last major novel, *The Diviners* (1974), Laurence's protagonist finally travels to Scotland to find the source of her own beliefs, tensions, and ardours. The trip settles ancestral ghosts, and convinces her that she is rooted not in a dream of Scottish history but in a new Canadian reality.[11] This theme of moving out of Scottish shadows is expressed again more directly in an essay, 'The Road From the Isles', in *Heart of a Stranger* (1974).[12] Just before returning home to Canada, Laurence visited Jane Duncan in Ross-shire. It seems to me that Laurence shares the tough, independent spirit of Duncan, though her Carlylean prose style seems richer and her conception of character more complex.

Something more closely cognate to Jane Duncan's treatment of her 'friends' is found in the stories of Alice Laidlaw Munro. Here I find the same magic realism, in which remembered scenes and people emerge with a gloss of suggested meanings. The facts remembered by Alice Munro and converted into her incisive tales have the same mythic quality, the same sense of being drenched in truth, that I feel when I read Jane Duncan. Duncan's 'Jean Robertson' stories in particular have the same gritty angular quality of unpretty experience, keenly recalled, and polished into crystal clarity. Jane Duncan is not, I believe, particularly revered in Scotland by the critics, although she has an enormous popular readership; Alice Munro is the darling of both critics and general public. Even her titles, such as *Who do you think You Are?* (1978), *Something I've Been Meaning to Tell You* (1974), or *Friend of My Youth* (1988), mix vernacular appeal with an expectation of irony and subtext. Born in 1931, just six years after Margaret Laurence, Alice Munro also comes from the same kind of small town, dominated by memories of Scottish pioneers, including her own forebears.

In *Lives of Girls and Women* (1971), Munro tells a story like that unfolded in Sarah Jeannette Duncan's *The Imperialist*, of an ambitious, passionate, intelligent young woman. Like Duncan, Munro strains that story through her experiences of the day, the local environment, and her sense of her own status as a woman and a writer. Duncan and Munro are separated by sixty years of history, both literary and political. The socio-economic milieu and the geographic and climatic setting show few changes. There are however some major differences. The relationship between mother and daughter has shifted dramatically. Advena's mother cannot understand her daughter: 'I pity the man that marries her!' she says. Munro presents a fierce, over-concentrated mother, essentially like her daughter in rebelliousness, though less able to put her resistance into force. In place of the Reverend Hugh Finlay, a sympathetic character in spite of his self-delusion, Munro presents Garnet French, a fanatical Baptist, and a travesty of all the devout domineering young men in Kailyard stories. Munro is not interested in politics, Duncan is not interested in budding sexuality – or at least is too trammelled by the conventions of her day to suggest it. The endings are indicative of the changes between 1904 and 1971. Like Munro's Del, Duncan's Advena leaves a society which has no interest in her; but she leaves with her husband, ready to take up a self-subordinating life as a minister's wife in a prairie town. Good luck to her! But we feel more confident of the luck of the modern girl, who mounts a bus alone, and heads for the city. Munro, like her Del, broke from the bonds of her small town, not the least of which bonds was a Scottish patriarchal attitude to women.

Munro has been influenced by the short-story tradition of the Southern writers such as Eudora Welty and Flannery O'Connor; but she also strikes a tone and introduces a range of experience comparable to John Galt's. Not that Munro necessarily read Galt; but there is something about the characters in a desiccated smalltown life of appearances and eccentricities that stirs memories of Mrs Balwhidder, of Leddy Grippy. Her ease and accuracy in handling the junctures between the apparently normal flow of events and the sudden tensions or surprises of change create annals of a parish very much like Galt's.

Nowadays Laurence and Munro as well as Margaret Atwood and Carol Shields and Marian Engel and other talented women are firmly established as major Canadian writers, as well as being genuinely popular writers with a very wide following. Perhaps the academy, no longer as heavily male-dominated, has become ready to take note of the popular opinion which from the beginning accepted these writers as names to be revered. These women all continue to thread into their work memories of the Scottish strand so closely woven into the fabric of Canadian life. I note as a tiny but significant detail that Atwood named the hero of *The Edible Woman* (1969) Marian McAlpine. McAlpine is also the name of the girl in Morley Callaghan's *The Loved and the Lost* (1951): there it is used to place the young woman as part of the Montreal Scottish oligarchy. Sinclair Ross gives the same suggestively dynastic Scottish name to the protagonist of his short story 'The Outlaw' and again to the protagonist of his novel *The Whir of Gold* (1970). By such hints and devices, many Canadian novelists suggest the continuing dominance of Scottishness in Canadian life.

I do not think however that any of our writers, male or female, respond to Scottish writers with the kind of eagerness once accorded to Burns or Scott or Carlyle or Stevenson. The Scottish strain appears rather as the product of dominance of Scottish traditions in schools, publishing houses and literary reviews, lingering long after demographic change in Canada had moved the balance away from the predominant Scottishness of early days.

Notes

1.   See for example William Herbert New, A *History of Canadian Literature* (Macmillan, London, 1989). For a wider context see J. K. Galbraith, *The Scotch* (Macmillan, Toronto, 1964).
2.   See Carrie MacMillan, Lorraine McMullen and Elizabeth Waterston, *Silenced Sextet: Six Nineteenth Century Canadian Women Novelists* (McGill-Queen's University Press, Montreal, 1993).
3.   John Matthews, *Tradition in Exile* (Toronto University Press, Toronto, 1971).

4.   Susanna Moodie, *Roughing It in the Bush, or Life in Canada*, ed. Carl Ballstadt (1852; Carleton University Press, Ottawa, 1988).

5.   Susanna Moodie, *Shenac's Work at Home: A Story of Canadian Life* (American Sunday School Union, Philadelphia, 1866).

6.   Francis Hart, *The Scottish Novel: A Critical Survey* (John Murray, London, 1978), pp. 93–7.

7.   Isabella Valancy Crawford, *Malcolm's Katie* in *Collected Poems of Isabella Valancy Crawford*, ed. James Reaney (University of Toronto Press, Toronto, 1972).

8.   Sarah Jeannette Duncan, *The Imperialist* ed. Claude Bissell (McClelland & Stewart, Toronto, 1961).

9.   See *Harvesting Thistles: the Textual Garden of L. M. Montgomery*, ed. Mary Rubio (Canadian Children's Press, Guelph, 1994).

10. L. M. Montgomery, *Kilmeny of the Orchard* (McClelland & Stewart, Toronto, 1910).

11. See Colin Nicholson's chapter in Colin Nicholson (ed.), *Margaret Laurence: Reappraisals* (Macmillan, London, 1989).

12. Margaret Laurence, *Heart of a Stranger* (McClelland & Stewart, Toronto, 1974).

21

Women and Nation

Susanne Hagemann

What does it mean to speak of 'women and nation'? To illustrate a possible spectrum of answers, here are three voices from outside Scotland. First, Virginia Woolf's anonymous daughter of an educated man in *Three Guineas*, according to whom nations are made by and for men:

> 'Our country' . . . throughout the greater part of its history has treated me as a slave; it has denied me education or any share in its possessions. 'Our' country still ceases to be mine if I marry a foreigner . . . in fact, as a woman, I have no country. As a woman I want no country. As a woman my country is the whole world.[1]

Second, Frances Bellman in Iris Murdoch's *The Red and the Green*, who perceives a parallel between women and small nations: 'I think being a woman is like being Irish . . . Everyone says you're important and nice, but you take second place all the same.'[2]

Third, Sally Roberts Jones, whose explicitly anti-English poem 'Tryweryn' is inspired by Liverpool Corporation's construction of a reservoir in North Wales:

> Nothing's gone that matters – a dozen farms,
> A hollow of no great beauty, scabby sheep,
> A gloomy Bethel and a field where sleep
> A few dead peasants. There are finer charms
> Observed in rising water, as its arms
> Circle and meet above the walls; in cheap
> Power and growing profits. Who could reap
> Harvests as rich as this in ploughmen's palms?
> All's for the best – rehoused, these natives, too,
> Should bless us for sanitation and good health.
> Later, from English cities, see the view
> Misty with hiraeth – and their new-built wealth.
>
> All of our wealth's in men – and their life's blood
> Drawn from the land this water drowns in mud.[3]

This poem, written by a woman, asserts the validity of national identification by contrasting English and Welsh attitudes and interests. Questions of gender do not arise here.

Examples such as these indicate that there is no obvious connection between women and nationhood. This is not to be wondered at, given that even the terms *woman* and *nation* as such are fuzzy. *Woman* can be defined by referring either to biological sex or to socially constructed gender.[4] In the field of literature, a sex-based definition leaves the theorist or critic with the difficult task of establishing a link between anatomy and writing – a link which, whatever form it takes, will of necessity be highly metaphorical, and may consequently cast some doubt on the advisability of using women as a category in the first place. Shifting emphasis from sex to gender obviates this problem but creates another one instead. What women as a gender have in common in modern European societies is their subordination by patriarchy; turning this into a focal point of literary analysis has as a rule meant stressing the importance of authorship and experience, an approach whose disadvantages have been detailed in many recent feminist publications.[5] As Elizabeth Grosz points out, 'the mere *sexual identity*[6] of an author is no guarantee of the text's position regarding women or femininity.'[7] Nor, for that matter, is it a guarantee of the text's position regarding nationhood.

There have been innumerable attempts to define the term *nation*. They fall into two categories. Some refer to 'objective' criteria such as race or language, others – less concretely, but more comprehensively – to subjective identification. One of the classic statements of subjectivity is provided by Ernest Renan. After showing that 'la race, la langue, les intérêts, l'affinité religieuse, la géographie, les nécessités militaires' are not sufficient to create a nation, he goes on to say:

> Une nation est une âme, un principe spirituel. Deux choses qui, à vrai dire, n'en font qu'une, constituent cette âme, ce principe spirituel. L'une est dans le passé, l'autre dans le présent. L'une est la possession en commun d'un riche legs de souvenirs; l'autre est le consentement actuel, le désir de vivre ensemble, la volonté de continuer à faire valoir l'héritage qu'on a reçu indivis . . .
>   . . . L'existence d'une nation est (pardonnez-moi cette métaphore) un plébiscite de tous les jours . . . [8]

This view is still current among social scientists today, partly on its own, partly as a complement to the search for 'objective' characteristics.[9] Like genders, nations are constructs.

All this considered, what – to repeat the question asked at the beginning – can be meaningfully said about the relationship between women and nation in twentieth-century Scottish literature? Several ways of approaching the subject seem possible. First, an images-of-women type of criticism, dealing with the relevance of women to the idea of nationhood in literature written from a patriarchal point of view. (Classic images-of-women criticism concentrates on male authors; however, I prefer to avoid the suggestion that texts by men are necessarily patriarchal and texts by women necessarily subversive.) Second, an argument in the manner of *Three Guineas*, according to which women for historical reasons can have no interest in nations. In order to escape focusing on authors' experience, it would again be advisable to start with texts – feminist ones in this case, as the premise is feminist. The perspective here would be the converse of the images-of-women one, the subject under discussion being not the relevance of women to nationhood but the relevance of nationhood to women. Third, an analysis of reception: how have 'women and nation' been dealt with by literary critics? Fourth, a Bellman/Murdoch-style comparison between the discursive construction of women and that of small nations such as Ireland and Scotland. Fifth, an exploration of the national dimension of women's writing in general. This author-centred approach would draw its justification not from an assumption that there is an identifiable women's tradition in literature,[10] but from the long neglect of texts by women, and in particular of their treatment of national identity; it would thus be an attempt to redress the balance, a version of gynocritics (Showalter's term)[11] 'unified' by patriarchal critics' silence rather than by intrinsic characteristics. This would in essence widen the Woolf-based interpretation.

This is obviously not a closed list. Other ways of dealing with the problem include experience-based criticism, for those who find such an approach fruitful, and comparative studies looking both at and beyond Scotland. However, for reasons of space I shall confine myself to the first five possibilities mentioned, and give a few brief examples of how these lines of thought might be explored. I do not aim to provide a comprehensive analysis of the relevant sections of twentieth-century Scottish literature.

I shall discuss the connection between female characters and national identity using three disparate texts which, in very different ways, can be regarded as patriarchal: Hugh MacDiarmid's *A Drunk Man Looks at the Thistle* (1926), R. S. Silver's *The Bruce: Robert I King o Scots* (written between 1948 and 1951), and Rosamunde Pilcher's popular romance, *Wild Mountain Thyme* (1978).[12]

In the *Drunk Man*, the relationship between femininity and Scottishness can be analysed on different levels, from the divine to the everyday one. I shall focus on the gender aspect of the moon/thistle imagery. As Kenneth Buthlay points out in his introduction to the 1987 edition, the moon 'is associated with the "eternal feminine" which [MacDiarmid] tended to link with Sophia, the divine wisdom (God's "Other", in feminine form)' (xlii), and the thistle symbolises both 'the barrenness and perversity of Scottish life' and 'the puzzle of the nature of life which confronts all mankind' (xliii). The thistle is also identified with the Drunk Man himself: 'The munelicht's like a lookin'-glass,/The thistle's like mysel'', he says at an early stage (p. 22), and later: 'The munelicht is my knowledge o' mysel',/Mysel' the thistle in the munelicht seen' (p. 74). This imagery recurs in connection with the Drunk Man's wife, Jean, who is thus linked with the moon:

> O Jean, in whom my spirit sees,
> Clearer than through whisky or disease,
> Its dernin' nature, wad the searchin' licht
> Oor union raises poor'd owre me the nicht . . .
> Be thou the licht in which I stand
> Entire, in thistle-shape, as planned . . .
>
> (p. 148)

The feminine, embodied by the moon and Jean, helps the Drunk Man, who claims a likeness to the thistle, to know himself. In so far as the thistle can be regarded as a Scottish emblem, these statements of selfhood and otherness place femininity outside the national sphere.

The moon is of course also said to be the mother of the bastard thistle (p. 54),[13] and the Drunk Man accuses a woman (according to Buthlay's interpretation she is 'the Unknown Goddess' [p. 25]) of making a thistle of him, of preventing him from being as happy and free as the moonlight by pressing morality on him (p. 24). Femininity thus produces the thistle and all it stands for, but remains extraneous to it. The moon is located outside or above the world of the thistle (pp. 100–1, 136). The thistle is the stronger of the two, though: its shape withstands the moon's attempt to transform it into pure light (p. 138–42), whereas in its turn it is capable of choking both sunlight and moonlight (p. 160). The dichotomy between moon and thistle is reminiscent of that between nature and culture, which plays an important role in images-of-women criticism: nature, with which women are stereotypically associated, is (deconstructionist moves apart) seen as both anterior and subordinate to culture. Critique of culture/the thistle may entail an idealisation of nature/the moon; but the Drunk Man clearly focuses on the former, assigning a position beyond the realities of Scottish life, beyond nationhood, to the latter and, by implication, to femininity.

R. S. Silver's historical play *The Bruce* does not give much room to women – predictably, in view of its subject matter. Out of the six female characters who come on stage, four (Bruce's sister Christina, his wife Elizabeth, a commoner called Jean and a nameless serving woman), while being loyal to Bruce as a person, do not evince any commitment to the idea of national freedom. In contrast, the two remaining female characters, Bruce's sister Mary and the Countess of Buchan, show considerable awareness of this concept. Mary, asserting the Countess's right to crown the King of Scots in default of her imprisoned brother, the Earl of Fife, argues the priority of national over marital allegiances; and the Countess, performing the coronation, speaks of 'Scotland's richt' (p. 23). However, whereas men such as the Bishop of Glasgow or his servant James are given the chance of fully explaining why they support Bruce, the Countess's compliance is taken for granted, even though it brings her into conflict with her husband as well as the English. Moreover, the very next scene shows her shut up in a cage by English soldiers, and it is mentioned that the same fate has befallen Mary (while Elizabeth, also captured, has been given a more comfortable prison). The two women, who have spoken out for the Scottish nation like some of the men, are thus forced into extreme passivity and confinement – that is into a situation typical of women as represented in literature.[14] In short, women are allowed or even expected to share in the fight for independence but incur sanctions when they identify with the construct of Scottishness. Furthermore, although captivity and death at the hands of the English are often talked about, the Countess's is the only case actually shown on stage, so that national victimisation acquires feminine connotations.

The term *Scottish author* is as vague as *woman* and *nation*. However, in an article which concentrates on texts rather than authors it seems legitimate to include *Wild Mountain Thyme* on the strength of its predominantly Scottish setting, without considering the issue of Rosamunde Pilcher's cultural affiliations. The novel tells the story of a London girl, Victoria Bradshaw, who goes to Sutherland with one man and returns with another. The place she visits, Benchoile, is dominated by men: the owner Jock Dunbeath, a childless widower who dies early on in the novel, his bachelor brother Roddy, and their divorced nephew John, to whom Jock leaves the estate. The only woman who has traditional associations with Benchoile is the housekeeper, Ellen Tarbat. Roddy describes her as an integral part of the place, almost its personification (a picture which is borne out by the narrator):

> God knows what would happen to Benchoile if [Ellen had a heart attack]. She's been here for ever, longer than most people can remember. She arrived in the first instance, fresh from some remote Highland croft, to look after my younger brother, and she's remained,

immovable as a rock, ever since. You'll meet her, but don't expect a devoted, smiling, gentle old dear. Ellen is as tough as old boots and can be twice as unpleasant! (pp. 147–8)

The 'frailness' and 'lack of substance' which John notices in Ellen (p. 177) correspond to the precarious situation of Benchoile itself, left to a half-American, London-based banker who intends to sell it. And like the estate, Ellen mainly exists; she hardly reflects (or, more precisely, the narrator does not show her reflecting). She is not present at the only discussion concerning Scotland and its problems in general. Victoria is; but only as a silent listener to whom Roddy apologises at the end: 'We're behaving abominably. I am sorry. We should have saved it for later.' (p. 186) On a more local level, Victoria is allowed to discuss the future of Benchoile with John (pp. 201–4); but when he finally does decide to keep it, exactly as she asked him a hundred pages earlier, the decision appears to be the result of his own solitary cogitations rather than her suggestion (300–2). The Scottish nation and its heritage are essentially the concern of men. Given this bias, it is not surprising that the narrative, centring as it does on a woman and her search for a husband, should fail to represent the taking over of a Sutherland estate by an absentee landlord as a cause of foreboding.

Lewis Grassic Gibbon's *A Scots Quair* (1932–4) can be interpreted both as a patriarchal and as a feminist text. Women and nationhood prove to be connected in highly ambiguous ways. On the one hand, Chris Guthrie is of course explicitly identified with Scotland both by Robert Colquhoun and, strangely enough, by the fascist laird Stephen Mowat in *Cloud Howe*.[15] However, when Mowat speaks of restoring the Scottish nation, Chris is quick to contradict him: '*Was there ever the kind of Scotland you preach? – Happy, at ease, the folk on the land well-fed, the folk in the pulpits well-feared, the gentry doing great deeds? It's just a gab and a tale, no more.*' (p. 275). Scottishness for Chris does not lie in history or culture, which is why political nationalism leaves her unmoved. She regards nations mainly as structures serving to exercise power over the people (p. 408). In contrast for instance to her brother Will, who thinks of Scotland in terms of human beings and their activities, Chris equates it with the land, with nature. On Will's remark that Scotland is '*dead or . . . dying – and a damned good job!*', Chris reflects:

> Daft of Will to say that: Scotland lived, she could never die, the land would outlast them all, . . . and the winds come sailing over the Grampians still with their storms and rain and the dew that ripened the crops – long and long after all their little vexings in the evening light were dead and done. (p. 165)

Will's attitude, though negative, is compatible with received concepts of national identity; his sister's is not. Chris takes a presocial view of Scotland, a view which harmonises with her general distrust of political creeds and contributes to placing her outside the discourses, institutions, and practices of nationhood. The patriarchal stereotype linking women with nature and men with culture remains intact here; what gives *A Scots Quair* a feminist potential is its revaluation of nature and, concomitantly, of women. This revaluation, however, does not make women nation-minded but merely downgrades nations as political and cultural entities.

In a study of the post-1918 Scottish Renaissance published in 1992, I argued that if the central characteristic of the Renaissance movement is the search for a new national identity, then novels such as Catherine Carswell's *Open the Door!*, Nan Shepherd's *The Quarry Wood*, or Willa Muir's *Imagined Corners* do not form part of its core, since they focus on the self-realisation of a gender rather than a nation.[16] This statement was based on a 'Woolfian' notion of women being indifferent to the claims of 'their' country; but I now feel that it should be modified. I would still maintain that at the centre of *The Quarry Wood*, for instance, is a woman's development rather than the question of Scottishness. However, on the one hand, the same might be said about Neil Gunn's *Highland River* and on the other, *The Quarry Wood* certainly does have a pronounced Scottish dimension. To give only one example, the protagonist, Martha Ironside, clearly is a lass o pairts, a variation on a common Scottish motif. In contrast to several of her male contemporaries or near contemporaries, from young John Gourlay in George Douglas Brown's *The House with the Green Shutters* to Murdo Anderson in Fionn Mac Colla's *The Albannach*, Martha successfully completes her university studies and settles down as a teacher – a Kailyard career par excellence. What distances *The Quarry Wood* from the Kailyard is the fact that the talented youth is female and in the course of the novel learns to be (to use a cliché of modern feminism) a strong and independent woman.[17] This, however, does not detract from the Scottishness of the novel, unless Scottishness is restrictively defined as masculine.

An anthology clearly revealing of the notion that women's writing is incompatible with a foregrounding of national identity is Moira Burgess's *The Other Voice* (1987). In her introduction, the editor claims that 'there is a music, or tone of voice, peculiar to Scottish women's writing, which . . . tends . . . to an ironic detachment, particularly perhaps when the writer is observing other women.'[18] Burgess's attempt to provide examples of this 'tone of voice' consequently involves focusing on the 'observation' of women, that is on women's personal experience; and if the personal is political in the texts selected, it is so in a feminist rather than a national(ist) sense. If short stories such as Nancy Brysson Morrison's 'No Letters, Please' and Janet Caird's 'The Deprived' – the former concerning the life and death of a doctor's wife as seen through the eyes of her self-absorbed husband, the latter, an old people's home in which all references to death are suppressed, with questionable consequences – are typical, then Scottishness does not hold much interest for women writers. If this is the case, however, the editorial purpose indicated by the word *Scottish* in the collection's subtitle, *Scottish Women's Writing Since 1808*, is self-defeating. Generally speaking, it is of course possible to demonstrate a lack of national consciousness in some works by women writers;[19] however, adopting a 'Woolfian' approach with regard to the gender as a whole would amount to considerable oversimplification.

Questions of reception have already surfaced in my foregoing remarks on *The Quarry Wood* and *The Other Voice*. I shall now expand on this aspect of the women/nation relationship, first of all by looking at two possible readings of Alanna Knight's novel *Colla's Children* (1982). The blurb of the 1983 Futura edition emphasises the protagonist's femininity at the expense of her involvement in history:

> Morag Macdonald is a child of the Hebrides, spirited, strong, and steeped in the magic and the traditions of the windswept, ancient isles.
>
> A true daughter of Clan Donald, 'Colla's Children', Morag makes her way to the Isle of Lewis and there embarks on a loveless marriage and the rigours of a crofting life, as unchanging as the surrounding hills. Until Sergei Svenson, a Norwegian sea captain, sweeps briefly, but tempestuously into her life . . .
>
> COLLA'S CHILDREN

A haunting and powerful tale of the Hebrides and its rich, turbulent history – and of Morag, who seeks the key to her own history, a woman before her time.

To be sure, the novel does describe Morag Macdonald's life and loves; but it also tells a story of the Outer Hebrides from the Clearances to the First World War. Tradition and change shape the characters' lives. Tradition means remote Hebridean communities which regard not only the English but also Lowland Scots as foreigners; it means black houses, ceilidhs, fairs, and illicit whisky stills as well as relics of the past such as the Standing Stones of Callanish, and supernatural visions which later come true. The crofting and fishing economy exemplifies both continuity and transformation, the latter particularly through the land agitation of the 1880s. Change can be sudden and brutal, as in the case of the Clearances or the sinking of the *Iolaire* off Stornoway harbour in 1919, the two catastrophes with which the book opens and closes respectively, or it can be gradual: emigration, the pull of Glasgow, which is portrayed as a 'monster' that swallows up the Hebridean folk,[20] and the decline of Gaelic are motifs which recur throughout the novel. The Hebridean panorama is held together by Morag, who experiences or at least witnesses the events in question. In this sense, *Colla's Children* establishes a close connection between the female protagonist and the history of the Hebrides; and in so far as Hebridean history is part of Scottish history, this is at the same time a close connection between women and nation. This aspect is very imperfectly covered by the blurb's brief reference to the 'rich, turbulent history' of the Hebrides. A text which might well be read as a historical novel is thus marketed exclusively as a romance.

In contrast, in an essay on the prose work of Violet Jacob, Carol Anderson attempts to retrieve an undervalued woman writer precisely by stressing her Scottishness. Starting from Hugh MacDiarmid's reaction to Jacob – 'what irks MacDiarmid is that although her imagination was stirred by Scotland, she doesn't *assert* Scottishness'[21] – Anderson argues that 'a general preoccupation with Scottish culture' (p. 34) is in fact one of Jacob's strong points:

> More specifically, some of what I see as Violet Jacob's most interesting (and radical) fiction deals with the experience of women in Scottish society. This is not her only, or even her central concern, perhaps, but in her handling of such themes in her neglected short stories particularly, Jacob becomes a writer really to reckon with. MacDiarmid, with his masculine concept of Scottishness (the one that has prevailed) appears blind to this aspect of her work, and probably it would not in any case have been congenial to him; Jacob has been underestimated in part because she was a woman, and a writer with particular kinds of interest. (p. 34)

From Anderson's subsequent discussion of prose texts such as 'The Debatable Land' or 'Thievie', Jacob emerges as a writer whose 'remarkably "modern" engagement with issues of gender and power' (p. 40) in a Scottish context is at odds with her standing in 'the' Scottish literary tradition.

Going beyond individual cases, Marilyn Reizbaum prefaces an examination of Scottish and Irish women's writing with a discussion of the fact that literary and cultural critics rarely establish a link between feminism and nationalism, between gender identity and national identity:

> The feminist call in Scotland and Ireland for the reformulation of the canon of Scottish and Irish works parallels the challenge to the mainstream Anglo-American establishment

presented by Scotland, Ireland, and other countries or cultures like them – former colonies who retain a marginalized standing in relation to the former colonizer. For example, while British anthologies often ignore Scottish and Irish authors, anthologies and critical works of Scottish and Irish writing typically treat women writers with the same disregard . . . when we speak about opening the canon to literature from marginalized cultures, the issue of gender is subsumed by the cultural imperative, and . . . the response of feminists from within and from without may be to lump all cultures under the rubric of patriarchy.[22]

Women in Scotland and Ireland, according to Reizbaum, 'have sought to alter this dynamic, seeing on the one hand the paternalistic nature of cultural marginalization (their identification with the nationalist cause) and, on the other, the patriarchal dimension of their own cultures' nationalist movements (their exclusion from it)' (p. 168). Reizbaum represents 'the creation of a discourse between culture and gender' (p. 181) as a very recent phenomenon, the only Scottish example she cites being Liz Lochhead. She thus ignores the precedent set by earlier writers such as Shepherd, and overplays women's difficulty in dealing with the Scottish nation. However, the parallel she draws between the two types of marginalization is a valid one: women and small nations, as Frances Bellman observes with regard to the Irish in *The Red and the Green*, do present notable resemblances. Like women, the Scots have frequently been defined as Other by a dominant group claiming to set a universal norm. In the sphere of literature, women and Scots have suffered from similar methods of peripheralisation and expressed their protest along similar lines. This applies not only to the question of canonicity addressed by Reizbaum but also to aspects of writing such as the stereotypes associated with women and Scots, or more particularly Gaels, the endeavour to construct unbroken feminine and Scottish literary histories largely independent of masculine and English traditions respectively, or the search for a literary language which adequately expresses the subordinate group's sense of identity.[23] Beyond their historically specific situation, women and Scots are paradigms of marginality.

Bearing in mind the overt Welshness of the poem 'Tryweryn' quoted above, I shall now examine the Scottishness of four texts by women: Nannie K. Wells's 'A Prayer',[24] Naomi Mitchison's *The Bull Calves* (1947), Jackie Kay's 'So You Think I'm a Mule?' (1988) and A. L. Kennedy's 'The Role of Notable Silences in Scottish History' (1990).[25] Nannie K. Wells's poem 'A Prayer' combines nationalism with religion:

> God, give us the grace to hate
> our unemancipated state,
> and to wipe from Scotland's face
> her intellectual disgrace.

In the following stanzas, the Scots are exhorted to abandon canniness, self-interest, conformity, and fear of others; they are to reach for the stars, to 'utter prophecy', and, with the help of God, to throw the 'foreign yoke' off their minds and take delight in their own country. Nationhood is then linked with Scotland's soil, wind, rivers, and mountains, the suggestion being that nationalism is natural and dependence on England perverse. Finally, the Deity is invoked once more:

> God, now to us the vision give
> to know for what we ought to live.

The poem dates from mid-century, but stylistically it stands in an older tradition of nationalist rhetoric. It has affinities with the writings of Lewis Spence (who in fact was born in 1874, only a year before Wells) rather than with those of MacDiarmid and his circle. As for its vision of Scotland, both the present unsatisfactory state of the nation and the possible better future remain vague. The tenor seems ambiguous. The nationalist strain of the poem is evident; but the prayer form can either be taken at its face value, as an expression of a religious faith which permeates everything, including politics, or it can be read as an ironic intimation that nothing short of a miracle can save Scotland. As far as 'authorial intention' is concerned, the irony is presumably unconscious; but it is this ambiguity which gives Wells's otherwise undistinguished poem a certain complexity.

Naomi Mitchison's historical novel *The Bull Calves*, set in the Haldane family territory of Gleneagles in 1747, in the aftermath of the Jacobite rebellions, is remarkable for its constant subversion of seemingly clear-cut categories. For example, the characters in their conversations set considerable store by the distinction between Highlands and Lowlands; but William Macintosh of Borlum, the main representative of the Highlands, is in fact half English. When Duncan Forbes of Culloden accuses the English, as typified by the Duke of Cumberland, of despising the Scots, William relativises the traditional opposition by reminding him that the royal family are 'incomers from Germany' (p. 388). In religion, William officially belongs to the Episcopalian Church, but his actual practices range widely, including Quaker and Roman Catholic elements. In view of this indeterminacy, of which many more examples might be adduced, what can be the meaning of Scottishness in *The Bull Calves*? In her extensive notes on the novel, Mitchison (or the narrator?) describes her vision of a future Scotland in terms of a Scottish 'soul' but does not flesh this concept out in any way:

> The new Scotland will be away different from the old Scotland, at least in looks. It may drop everything, the language, the music, the dances, the kilt and the plaid, the memories and stories, the remaining crafts of the countryside, aye and the kirk sessions in with the rest. Yet the soul does not die and it returns in its right shape. (p. 486)

In the narrative itself, the marriage of the central female character, Kirstie Haldane, to William Macintosh can be read as symbolising the union of Lowlands and Highlands. The union is miraculously fruitful, since the couple have a child, born to Kirstie at the age of well over forty. Little Elizabeth, however, is not present at the family gathering in the Ochils which her parents have come to attend; she remains hidden in the narrative, as does the soul of Scotland in the notes. Interestingly, Elizabeth is one of the few entirely fictitious characters in the novel (cf. p. 407): the utopian, feminine Scotland she embodies lies outside the realm of history. In a sense, the same is true of Scottishness, which the passage quoted above divorces from historical phenomena such as language, culture, tradition, and religion. Scottishness from this point of view is an ahistorical fiction.

Jackie Kay's poem 'So You Think I'm a Mule?' focuses on definitions of identity. The main speaker is a Black Scottish woman whose Scottishness is questioned on account of her Blackness:

> 'Where do you come from?'
> 'I'm from Glasgow.'
> 'Glasgow?'
> 'Uh huh, Glasgow.'

The white face hesitates
the eyebrows raise
the mouth opens
then snaps shut
incredulous
yet too polite to say outright
liar
she tries another manoeuvre
'And your parents?'
'Glasgow and Fife.'
'Oh?'
'Yes. Oh.'

(p. 127)

To the questioner's either/or logic, the woman opposes her both/and. Later she rejects her interlocutor's classification of herself as a 'mulatto', stating that she is Black and 'at home with that', (p. 128). The woman thus claims the right to a multiplicity of identities, but only in so far as she can live them out to the full. Defining herself as both Black and Scottish is no contradiction in terms, which is why she can assume both identities without diminishing either; by contrast, defining herself as half Black and half White (a 'mulatto') would be tantamount to saying that she is neither. Identity in this poem is to a large extent a matter of language. The woman had a White mother and a Black father and grew up in Glasgow – these are the facts, about which there is no dispute. What is at issue is whether these facts are compatible with her regarding herself as Black and Scottish. In other words, the problem is the meaning of Blackness and Scottishness. The woman's solution to the problem is essentially performative: in the last analysis, she is Black because she says so.

A. L. Kennedy's short story 'The Role of Notable Silences in Scottish History' offers an even more explicitly constructionist view of Scottishness than Kay's poem. It reduces not only history but also geography to a text. The grid formed by the streets of Glasgow, for instance, is described as follows:

The roads come together, cross and go on and little strands of history follow them. In some places, many lines will cross: what has been, what is and what will be and you can walk from one coincidence to another, not step on a crack. It's like strolling across a book, something big and Victorian with plenty of plots. It makes you wonder who's reading you. (p. 67)

Existence, too, is textual, since persons whose lives are not recorded disappear from history without trace. Significantly, textuality does not imply truth. In her very first sentence, the narrator introduces herself as a compulsive liar: 'I find it very hard to tell the truth.' (p. 62). She again and again draws attention to the dichotomy between truth and falsehood, but at the same time suggests that the two are impossible to distinguish. When a friend of hers is stabbed by a stranger in a pub, her interpretation of the event is that 'because the stranger believed in lies about blood loyalty and city violence, he came to the pub to make them true' (p. 71). What matters is the text, which produces reality – in so far as reality can be said to exist at all. Scottish identity is thus created by telling stories – for example about 'the dreadful Massacre of the McIvers' (p. 63) or about a recent book entitled *Killing Time: Seven Centuries of Scottish Slaughter*, which, as the narrator predicts, 'will join the distinguished ranks of Scottish Classic Literature, alongside *Bonnie Charlie's Glasgow Cookbook* and *Fish of the Outer Hebrides*' (p. 69). The stories, once written, can be rewritten at will: if Shylock's 'If you prick us do we not bleed?' can be attributed to a 'Viennese moneylender' (p. 68), then presumably no aspect of any text can be regarded as permanent. Scottishness, like any other type of identity, basically consists in nothing but the ability to 'make up your past as you go along' (p. 64). A more extreme approach to Scottishness as a construct is difficult to imagine.

My aim in this chapter has been to illustrate the variety of possible answers to the question implicit in my title. The stance I have adopted in evaluating them is a feminist anti-essentialist one. The only general statement that can be made about women and nation is the paradoxical one that no general statement can be made about them. Both women and nations are constructs, and any interpretation of the relationship between them depends to a considerable extent on the political interest which motivates it. My own discussion of Mitchison, Kay, and Kennedy provides a pertinent example of this. In order to argue the case against the assumption to be found both in some patriarchal and in some feminist writing, that the idea of nationhood is essentially alien to women, I have referred to three texts by women which subvert the notion of Scottishness as pregiven or definable. The selection might at first seem a strange one, since it could be polemically read as a confirmation of the very idea it is supposed to refute. However, these texts can also serve to demonstrate the degree of sophistication to be found in women's representations of the Scottish nation (without simplistically attributing either sophistication in general or subversion in particular to the authors' sex or gender). In other words, the patterns which emerge in an analysis of women and nation in twentieth-century Scottish literature are basically those of the various contrasting discourses of femininity – discourses which can thus be seen to perpetuate and validate themselves.

Notes

1. Virginia Woolf, *Three Guineas* (The Hogarth Press, London, 1938 and 1952), p. 197.
2. Iris Murdoch, *The Red and the Green* (1965; Penguin, Harmondsworth, 1967), pp. 31–2.
3. The poem, which first appeared in *Turning Away* (Gomer Press, 1969), is reproduced from Tony Curtis (ed.), *The Poetry of Snowdonia* (Seren Books, Bridgend, Mid Glamorgan, 1989), p. 67, by kind permission of the author. For the national significance of the 'scandal of Tryweryn' cf. Gwyn A. Williams, *When Was Wales? A History of the Welsh* (1985; Penguin, Harmondsworth, 1991), p. 291: 'It was the powerlessness of Wales which was exposed here. Liverpool corporation decided to build a reservoir at Tryweryn in northern Merioneth and to drown a Welsh-speaking community of peculiar cultural significance to Welsh speakers in the process. There was no authority anywhere in Wales which could challenge the decision . . . A campaign of protest and opposition built up . . . To no avail. It was at this point that violence entered Welsh nationalist politics . . . Control over its own water became and has remained an inflammatory issue in Wales.'
4. According to Judith Butler, even sex is not prediscursive but merely culturally constructed as prediscursive. See e.g. *Gender Trouble: Feminism and the Subversion of Identity* (Routledge, London, 1990), p. 109, p. 148.
5. See for example Sara Mills, 'Authentic Realism', in *Feminist Readings/Feminists Reading*, by Sara Mills and others (Harvester Wheatsheaf, Hemel Hempstead, 1989), pp. 51–82 (pp. 77–9); Pam Morris, *Literature and Feminism: An Introduction* (Blackwell, Oxford, 1993), pp. 64–5, 85–6; Sue Spaull, 'Gynocriticism', in *Feminist Readings/Feminists Reading*, pp. 83–121 (pp. 116–18); Chris Weedon, *Feminist Practice and Poststructuralist Theory* (Blackwell, Oxford, 1987), pp. 152–3, 167–8.
6. According to feminist theory, sexual identity 'is culturally rather than biologically determined' and is thus not to be confused with biological sex. (Maggie Humm, *The Dictionary of Feminist Theory*, Harvester Wheatsheaf, Hemel Hempstead, 1989, p. 205).

7. Elizabeth Grosz, 'Feminism and Anti-Humanism', in *Discourse and Difference: Post-Structuralism, Feminism and the Moment of History*, ed Andrew Milner and Chris Worth (Centre for General and Comparative Literature, Monash University, Clayton, Victoria, 1990), pp. 63–75 (p. 73).

8. Ernest Renan, 'Qu'est-ce qu'une nation?' (1882), in *Oeuvres complètes* ed. Henriette Psichari, 10 vols (Calmann-Lévy, Paris, 1947–58), I: *Questions contemporaines – la réforme intellectuelle et morale – dialogues et fragments philosophiques – discours et conférences* (1947), pp. 887–906 (pp. 903–4).

9. I am indebted to Dr Ruth Drost for drawing my attention to Renan and his lasting influence.

10. Cf. for example, Elaine Showalter, *A Literature of their Own: British Women Novelists from Brontë to Lessing* (Princeton UP, Princeton, N.J., 1977), p. 11.

11. See Elaine Showalter, 'Towards a Feminist Poetics', in Mary Jacobus (ed.), *Women Writing and Writing about Women*, The Oxford Women's Series, 3 (Croom Helm in association with Oxford University Women's Studies Committee, London, 1979), pp. 22–41 (pp. 25–6).

12. Hugh MacDiarmid, *A Drunk Man Looks at the Thistle* (1926), ed. Kenneth Buthlay, The Association for Scottish Literary Studies Annual Volumes, 17 (Scottish Academic Press, Edinburgh, 1987); R. S. Silver, *The Bruce: Robert I King o Scots* (The Saltire Society, Edinburgh, 1986); Rosamunde Pilcher, *Wild Mountain Thyme* (1978), in 2 vols (Coronet, London, 1991–2), II (1992), pp. 1–304.

13. W. N. Herbert distinguishes between moon as mother and moonlight as wife; but since both are feminine symbols, they may be conflated for my purposes. (*To Circumjack MacDiarmid: The Poetry and Prose of Hugh MacDiarmid*, Clarendon Press, Oxford, 1992, pp. 52–5.)

14. See Mary Ellmann, *Thinking about Women* (Macmillan, London, 1968), pp. 79–82, 87–9.

15. Lewis Grassic Gibbon, *A Scots Quair: A Trilogy of Novels. Sunset Song – Cloud Howe – Grey Granite* (1932–4), foreword by Ivor Brown (Hutchinson, London, 1950), pp. 273, 298.

16. Susanne Hagemann, *Die Schottische Renaissance: Literatur und Nation im 20. Jahrhundert*, Scottish Studies 13 (Lang, Frankfurt am Main, 1992), p. 53.

17. Nan Shepherd, *The Quarry Wood* (1928), introduction by Roderick Watson, Canongate Classics 4 (Canongate, Edinburgh, 1987). In contrast to my 'optimistic' reading of *The Quarry Wood*, Margaret Elphinstone argues that 'the ending . . . leaves the reader frustrated, as Martha never does reconcile the elements which make her who she is'. ('Four Pioneering Novels', *Chapman 74–5: The Women's Forum: Women in Scottish Literature* (Autumn/Winter 1993), 23–39 (pp. 30–31). I do not find this argument convincing, for although the final scene does show Martha 'in a domestic interior' (Elphinstone, p. 34), an earlier passage in the novel, pointing beyond this ending towards Martha's later teaching career (p. 179), suggests that Martha has in fact come to terms with both her social background and her education. Her decision not to sail '*beyond the Pillars of Hercules*' (p. 210), which Elphinstone interprets as a denial of 'the possibility of wider horizons' (p. 34), can also be regarded as an expression of her commitment to Scotland and her local community, particularly since it is contrasted with Luke Cromar's search for a meaningful life in Liverpool. It may be worth remembering in this context that Dante (whom Martha has read; p. 76) shows the most famous literary figure to venture beyond the Pillars, Ulysses, telling of his fatal exploit in Hell (Canto 26).

18. *The Other Voice: Scottish Women's Writing since 1808*, ed. Moira Burgess (Polygon, Edinburgh, 1987), i.

19. And a certain opposition to national ideals in others. For instance, Willa Muir's short story 'Clock-a-doodle-doo', which tells of a Clever Clock's aspirations to bring about a Horological Renaissance, can be read as a satire on Hugh MacDiarmid. (The story was first published in *The Other Voice*.)

20. Alanna Knight, *Colla's Children* (1982; Futura, London, 1983), p. 84.

21. Carol Anderson, 'Debateable Land: The Prose Work of Violet Jacob', in *Tea and Leg-Irons: New Feminist Readings from Scotland*, ed. Caroline Gonda (Open Letters, London, 1992), pp. 31–44 (p. 33).

22. Marilyn Reizbaum, 'Canonical Double Cross: Scottish and Irish Women's Writing', in *Decolonizing Tradition: New Views of Twentieth-Century 'British' Literary Canons*,

ed. Karen R. Lawrence (University of Illinois Press, Urbana 1992), pp. 165–90 (p. 166).

23.   I have explored the parallels between discourses of femininity and Scottishness or Celtitude in two papers read at Bordeaux (September 1993) and Budmerice (July 1994). See the conference proceedings for further discussion, examples, and references. ('A Feminist Interpretation of Scottish Identity', in *Proceedings of the Scottish Workshop of the E. S. S. E. Conference/Actes de l'atelier écossais de la conférence de l'E. S. S. E. [European Society for the Study of English], Bordeaux, 1993*, ed. Horst W. Drescher and Pierre Morère, Scottish Studies/*Études écossaises*, special issue (G. D. R. *Études écossaises*, Université Stendhal/Scottish Studies Centre, Johannes Gutenberg-Universität Mainz, Grenoble/Germersheim, 1994), pp. 79–91; 'The Omnific Word: Language, Literature and Otherness in Scotland', in *Proceedings of the Fifth International Conference on the Literature of Region and Nation, Budmerice 1994*, ed. Igor Navrátil [Bratislava: forthcoming]).

24.   Nannie K. Wells, 'A Prayer', in *An Anthology of Scottish Women Poets*, ed. Catherine Kerrigan, with Gaelic translations by Meg Bateman (Edinburgh University Press, Edinburgh, 1991), p. 228. It is not clear from Kerrigan's anthology when the poem was first written, although it was published in her collection *Twentieth Century Mother, and Other Poems* (1953). Internal evidence suggests that the date is 1939 or later: Wells prefaces the poem with 'acknowledgements to W. H. Auden'; the allusion appears to be to the third part of 'In Memory of W. B. Yeats', which provides both the verse form and some words and phrases. See W. H. Auden, *Collected Shorter Poems 1930–1944* (Faber and Faber, London, 1950), pp. 66–7.

25.   Naomi Mitchison, *The Bull Calves* (1947), The Scottish Collection (Richard Drew Publishing Glasgow, 1985); Jackie Kay, 'So You Think I'm a Mule?' (1988), quoted in *Sleeping with Monsters: Conversations with Scottish and Irish Women Poets*, ed. Gillean Somerville-Arjat and Rebecca E. Wilson, research and interviews by Rebecca E. Wilson (Polygon, Edinburgh, 1990), pp. 127–9; A. L. Kennedy, 'The Role of Notable Silences in Scottish History', in *Night Geometry and the Garscadden Trains: Short Stories* (Polygon, Edinburgh, 1990), pp. 62–72.

22

Annie S. Swan and O. Douglas:
Legacies of the Kailyard

Beth Dickson

Annie S. Swan (Mrs Burnett-Smith) was one of the most commercially successful popular novelists of the later nineteenth and early twentieth centuries. She wrote 162 novels under her own name and at least forty under the male pseudonym David Lyall, as well as numerous journalistic articles throughout a literary career which began with the publication of *Aldersyde* in 1883 and ended with the author's death in 1943.[1] It is probable that of all women writers included in this volume, she had the largest readership. *Annie Swan's Penny Stories*, for example, sold 140,000 copies in the first week.[2] Her autobiography *My Life* (1934), written at the zenith of her popularity, was reprinted six times within the first year of publication.[3] Its readers, who came from all social classes, included Queen Mary and Mr E. Laffray, a prisoner in Pentonville jail.[4] Much of this popularity was due to the development of mass literacy during her lifetime. Nothwithstanding her popularity she was comprehensively dismissed by most Scottish literary critics including Mrs Oliphant, J. H. Millar and Hugh MacDiarmid. Her work was seen as belonging to the 'Kailyard' school which presented a falsely sentimental image of Scotland. Swan's work brings into sharp focus the legacy of continuing confusions about the Kailyard in Scottish criticism which does not always distinguish effectively between popular and literary writing. Swan was part of the Kailyard, but she must be understood in wider contexts. In her writing, she shows herself to be a woman of her day strongly supporting conventional notions of womanhood. This has led to criticism from sociologists and historians that her books were instruments of social control. Yet, despite holding these conventional opinions, she used the economic power her earnings brought her to retain a degree of individual freedom in her own life which she felt no need to accord to her fictional creations. Annie S. Swan's novels are straightforward works of popular fiction – she herself never claimed anything more for them – but the issues she highlights in literary history and the choices she made as a woman writer are complex. After setting the historical context, this essay will discuss her relationship with Kailyard fiction and her significance as a woman writer.

The Education Act of 1872 (the relevant Act for England and Wales had been passed in 1870) together with the abolition of Newspaper Stamp Duty in 1855 and the abolition of Paper Duty in 1861, made possible significant changes in popular culture. The provision of education produced a new readership of lower middle-class and working people eager both to improve and entertain themselves through reading, newspapers and magazines proving popular because they met that demand. The *Daily Mail*, founded by Alfred

Harmondsworth in 1896, was a key product developed for this market. William Robertson Nicoll (1851–1923), a former Free Church of Scotland minister turned editor, was just as aware of the potential of this emerging market as Harmondsworth. Among the newly literate were a large number of women. In 1893 at Nicoll's invitation Swan became the chief contributor, and lent her marketable name to *The Woman at Home*, subtitled *Annie Swan's Magazine*, which included fiction, features on dress, cookery, the lives of the rich and famous and a problem page.

Swan was well-placed to take advantage of these developments in mass literary culture. Her father was a committed member of a church in Leith which belonged to the Evangelical Union – a denomination noted for its break with Calvinist teaching.[5] Knowing Evangelicalism from the inside meant that Swan was familiar with its religious journals. Indeed, she began writing for Howie Wylie's *Christian Leader*. It also meant that she knew what the group believed, not merely about Christianity but also about such issues as the position of women. Most importantly, she knew what such people aspired to, what their attitudes were and what they would and would not tolerate in fiction. Swan herself had little formal education – she went to a Dame's school and Queen Street Ladies' College (*ML*, p. 18). However, she read any books or magazines which came her way from Jane Porter's novels such as *The Scottish Chiefs* (1810) to *The Penny Encyclopaedia*, *Good Words*, *Chambers' Journal*, *The Sunday Magazine*, *The People's Friend*, *The People's Journal* (*ML*, pp. 25–30). She also knew where her talents as a writer lay:

> I have scrupulously observed the rules of the game, so far as editors are concerned. They know they can depend on me to deliver the goods in time, preferably before they are needed . . . And I have honestly tried to give them what they want, realising that he who pays the piper calls the tune . . . I have never had any illusions about the place accorded to me in the world of letters. Judged by some canons it is a very low place. (*ML*, p. 289)

Annie Swan wrote this in 1934 towards the end of her career, when it was clearer, at least to her, that the forces which shaped her writing were quite different from those which shaped, say, the work of Thomas Hardy, who was pointed out to her once at a social gathering by Nicoll as the only writer of fiction present who would still be read a century later.

William Robertson Nicoll was an Aberdeenshire Free Church minister who resigned his charge on health grounds and took up a career in journalism. In 1886, ten years before the appearance of the *Daily Mail*, Nicoll had begun a weekly newspaper, *The British Weekly*, which was developed not for the newly literate but for those just finding their way into the world of culture – English Nonconformists. Although they were educated, many of them would not read fiction because they thought of it as 'lies'. (Although Nonconformity is not a Scottish phenomenon, similar attitudes to fiction can be seen in various Scottish denominations.) Valentine Cunningham has shown how attitudes to fiction changed amongst Nonconformists throughout the nineteenth century. Sectarian attitudes to culture relaxed: fiction, previously regarded as sinful, began to be tolerated especially if it was considered to be of a morally improving nature. Different denominations went through this process at different times. Nicoll was anxious to transform attitudes to culture and exploit this market simultaneously:

> I thought that much more might be done in the way of uniting religion with literature, believing that Non-conformists had too long behaved as exiles from the world of culture.[6]

He also commented that for *The British Weekly* to be successful, he 'must have 20,000 intelligent subscribers'.[7] In a letter to Annie Swan, S. R. Crockett jokingly remarked on how much money he was making out of his 'lies' – a joke, however, which showed that the memory or experience of how this issue had exercised many consciences was still real (*ML*, p. 87).

It was the fiction written about Scotland by the Scottish writers – J. M. Barrie, Ian MacLaren, S. R. Crockett and Annie S. Swan – for the specific market demands of this publication, many of whose readers were English, which earned the lasting opprobrium of the Scottish literary establishment who damned it as 'Kailyard'. At that time the distinction between popular and literary fiction was unclear. Then Swan's fiction could be noticed by Mrs Oliphant in *Blackwood's Magazine*, which also reviewed fiction by Thomas Hardy and Robert Louis Stevenson. In 1889, in a review of J. M. Barrie's *A Window in Thrums* (1889), which includes the brief reference to Annie Swan, Mrs Oliphant grapples with the new phenomenon of popular literary culture and sets the pattern of Scottish intellectual response to it for some time to come. Mrs Oliphant is struck by Barrie's realism and psychological insight but is concerned by the parochial setting, 'this poor little local separateness', because it misrepresents the Scottish nation which she argues 'contributed to the greatness of the empire' and through Sir Walter Scott gave 'the laws of noble fiction to all the world'. She argues that because 'so great a proportion of the educated classes have drifted away from their original firm standing on the soil', 'those who are lower in the scale of intelligence and knowledge ' have located Scottish identity in superficial local phenomenon rather than in larger national considerations:

> If this is so, as we are much inclined to suspect, then it is doubtless the fault of those who ought to know better, but who have in so many ways dissociated themselves from the 'masses', and broken the old unity of feeling. The books called 'Carlowrie,' 'Aldersyde,' 'Blinkbonny,' 'Glenairlie,' &c., are cheap books, and perfectly well-adapted, with their mild love-stories and abundant marriages, for the simpler classes, especially of women, whose visions are bounded by the parish, who know nothing higher in society than the minister and his wife and believe that all the world lieth in wickedness except Scotland. To cultivate this spirit is, however, pernicious in the highest degree, though the little books in question are all amiable, simple, and virtuous beyond reproof – and silly.[8]

Mrs Oliphant is aware that there is a lucrative market for cheap books provided they contain the sort of material the readers want. Valentine Cunningham has shown that she herself included populist elements in her fiction in order to enhance its sales.[9] Despite using these methods, Mrs Oliphant distances herself intellectually from the phenomenon as seen in the fiction of Barrie and Swan. Her paternalistic attitude to popular readers means that she sees them as socially restricted and ignorant of the world. Though she blames the educated cohort of Scottish society for such developments, she cannot resist a cutting dismissal of mass taste which is also a declaration of her own superiority. Mrs Oliphant was not alone in holding these attitudes. Her insult was mild compared with what followed. W. H. Henley, who coined the term 'Kailyard' in 1895, coined it as an insult, one of which his friend J. H. Millar, who was thought to have invented it, thoroughly approved. And W. R. Nicoll, even when guardedly acknowledging a difference between popular and literary fiction, would not use the term precisely because it was an insult.[10] But the most violent language came from Walter Raleigh, then Professor of

English Literature at the University of Glasgow, when praising *The House with the Green Shutters*: 'I love the book for just this – it sticks the Kailyarders like pigs'.[11]

Leading figures of the Scottish Literary Renaissance continued the invective. George Blake described J. M. Barrie's *A Window in Thrums* as 'a debauch of sentimentality' and Hugh MacDiarmid had this to say of the Kailyard:

> The disease has never been properly diagnosed, and although its evil effects have been recognised and certain steps have been taken successfully to abate them, it is still working widespread if more subterranean mischief.[12]

One way of accounting for the strength of the language used to describe the Kailyard would be to note the similarity between reactions in Scotland and England to popular literary culture. In *The Intellectuals and the Masses* John Carey argues that the English literary intelligentsia were hostile to the reading public created by nineteenth-century educational reforms and that the purpose of modernist literature was to exclude such readers from high culture.[13] The fact that Mrs Oliphant characterises the two parties in the Scottish debate as the 'educated' and the 'masses' (and her placing of 'masses' in quotation marks suggests that she is uncertain of the term or it is perhaps new to her) are very similar to the attitudes displayed by contemporary English literary intellectuals when they made their response to mass culture. Carey also notes that two metaphors consistently used to describe mass culture were of the herd and of the spread of viruses or bacteria.[14] In the quotation above, MacDiarmid demonstrates the latter usage while the former may be implicit in Raleigh's remark.

Not only do Scottish intellectuals show a hostile response to popular literature but Swan herself vividly illustrates the other side of Carey's argument that for many, reading the modernist poetry of Yeats, T. S. Eliot, Ezra Pound and the Sitwells was an experience of exclusion. Swan's verdict on these writers is that 'they have, with strange insistence and mysterious, dynamic force, clothed their meaning in imagery the simple-minded find it difficult to grasp'.[15]

When Swan takes issue with Scottish Modernists, however, she does not accuse them of being too difficult. Swan's volume of Scottish history, observation and fiction, *The Land I Love* (1935), is a retort to David Cleghorn Thomson's *Scotland in Quest of Her Youth* (1932) in which most of the Scottish writers associated with the 'Literary and Cultural Renaissance' argue for greater honesty in addressing Scottish cultural issues and for jettisoning the religious and political outlook of nineteenth-century Scotland which, they argued, had obscured the 'real' nature of Scotland.[16] To counter Naomi Mitchison's contribution, Swan argues:

> Naomi Mitcheson [*sic*] says that the books are being written right enough, but asks who is reading them? The people who matter in Scotland, the workers by hand and brain, can't afford seven and sixpenny books. She also asserts that 'the real muse of Scotland was always crude, vigorous, unashamed of speech and acts. Scotland must learn not to be ashamed of her own youth and vigour'. There are plenty of critics of Scotland. Indeed, sometimes one has the depressing conviction that her foes are those of her own household. (*TLIL*, p. 9)

Swan, though she makes little of it, is aware that the cost of literature is part of the argument, but mainly she is happy to argue over that bone of contention between the

Kailyarders and Modernists – the question of the representation of the 'real' nature of Scotland.

However, it is here that Scottish and English intellectual attitudes diverge. First of all, MacDiarmid and the other Renaissance writers took issue with Kailyard writers on their own terms. Much of the debate about the Kailyard is a Scottish expression of a wider British debate about the nature of the 'real'. MacDiarmid can be related to writers south of the border such as Gissing and Hardy in wanting to show 'things as they are', and not ignoring, perhaps even emphasising, the unpleasant or disturbing. On the other hand, Thomas Knowles has shown, writers such as J. M. Barrie argue that life is bad enough, and that there is no need to dwell on its sordid side in fiction.[17]

Although in *The Land I Love* Swan includes fictional descriptions of the difficulties of urban life, the values she promotes are those of the nineteenth-century Christian and Liberal middle class and consequently conflict with the secular and Leftist or Nationalist views of younger writers. But these younger writers do not simply dismiss conservative views of the previous generation. Unlike English Modernist literature Scottish Modernist literature is not – with the exception of MacDiarmid – particularly obscure or difficult. This is because rather than wishing to exclude popular writers and their readership, Scottish Modernists had a point to prove and thus remained in dialogue and debate with popular writers. They wanted to create a new vision of Scotland but as much as that they wanted it to be *understood* by those who proclaimed its opposite.

In some ways this debate was a pseudo-debate. As Swan pointed out the readers who read her books were unlikely to read works of high literature because they cost too much. And while the readerships of popular and literary fiction might overlap, they also had significant differences. Some readers of popular literature did not want to read literary fiction because it did not provide that instant, reliable formula of escapism they were looking for. Further, even if Swan had written about the 'real' as critics wanted, it would not have made her fiction imaginatively authentic, it would only have produced melodrama. Among the participants in this debate about the 'real', the actual nature of the debate between the relative significance of literary and popular culture was only intermittently grasped. While on the one hand the debate provoked Modernists into writing some of the finest works of twentieth-century Scottish literature, their work in the end did little to check the industry that before and since has profited from stereotypical images of Scotland in fiction, which large sections of Scottish society as well as a broader British audience find attractive.

The second divergence between Scots and English intellectuals was political. The Scots saw popular culture as reactionary, rather than subversive. For them the Kailyard was closely related to the British state. *The British Weekly* was published in London primarily for an English audience and reaffirmed attitudes to Scotland which allowed Scottish difference to be expressed in a quaint and politically unthreatening manner. As Christopher Harvie has argued:

> [The Kailyard] acted to mollify social tensions, facilitate moderate reform, and uphold the authority of a centralist, welfarist political system. The Kailyard writers were therefore more than a forgotten tribe of sentimentalists: they and their successors have been an important part of the British political establishment.[18]

William Robertson Nicoll in particular was close to Lloyd George during the First World War. Letters between Nicoll and leaders of Nonconformist denominations show

Nicoll defending Lloyd George in an attempt to keep this considerable sector of political support loyal.[19] Annie Swan moved in these circles too. She took up Liberal politics in later life and it was not until Lord Roseberry told her that it was politically damaging that she stopped using North Britain as part of her address (*ML*, p. 254). This older Victorian Scottish attitude to national identity celebrated British Imperialism, rather than a separate Scottishness. Swan contrasts this position with the 'rabid nationalism' of the younger writers of the 1930s whose work the Kailyarders saw as threatening the status quo.

Until relatively recently Scottish literary critics have usually been embarrassed or outraged by the Kailyard. Valuable attempts have been made by Ian Campbell and Roderick Watson to trace elements in Kailyard fiction back to older habits of Scottish writing or thinking.[20] However, if we think about what is new and different about Kailyard fiction and see it primarily as a limited historical phenomenon (while properly acknowledging ancestors and descendents) and use Carey's arguments to foreground the debate between the popular and the literary, we can cut the Gordian knot of the Kailyard. The legacy of the Kailyard can be seen as a strength, not a weakness. If we understand the significance of the Kailyard as *popular* literature, we can validate the success of the Modernists, while repudiating the snobbery which has been expressed towards popular readers. Then at last we can see the Kailyard for what it is – an outright Scottish success.

It took some time, therefore, for the distinctions between popular and literary culture to become clear to those involved in both areas. It is likely that Swan herself was confused about her status, particularly at the beginning of her career. She writes that her early novels were modelled on those of Mrs Oliphant and that Oliphant's review in *Blackwood's* caused her some pain (*ML*, p. 40). *Aldersyde* (1883) is sub-titled 'A Border Story of Seventy Years Ago', producing a faint echo of the subtitle of *Waverley*, ''Tis Sixty Years Since'. *Aldersyde* is not a conventional love story, since the central female character does not marry. Although it does deal with middle-class characters and manners, the resemblance to Oliphant's fiction is only superficial. Swan never wrote with Oliphant's psychological and social insight. Novels such as *The Gates of Eden* (1887) and particularly *Maitland of Laurieston* (1891) show Swan dealing with serious issues, but always in a popular manner. By the late nineteenth century, Swan had settled down to write the pious unremarkable fiction demanded by her large, newly literate and often religious readership.

Mrs Oliphant, whose review caused disappointment, is important for Annie Swan in another way because she provided an example of an author's life. Swan records that reading Mrs Oliphant's biography 'gave me such a strange sensation, almost as if I read my own life, written by another hand. Of course the facts are all different, and she was much abler in every way than I, but her point of view regarding many things was quite the same as mine.' (*Letters*, p. 45). Both women wrote professionally to earn a living. They also combined writing and domestic life in a manner reminiscent of that earlier model for women writers, Mrs Gaskell, who left detailed records of her daily routine. In a manner typical of a number of previous women writers, including Mrs Oliphant herself, Swan was always careful in her public utterances to subordinate her writing to her domestic responsibility:

> I never obtruded my writing – it was done mostly in the early morning, while others were asleep. I seldom talked about it, and I gave the most meticulous attention to household affairs . . . (*ML*, p. 273)

Although Swan carefully upholds domestic values in her fiction, it is also clear that her writing gave her, as it gave Mrs Gaskell and Mrs Oliphant, an unusual degree of individual freedom. Swan's earning power probably allowed her the freedom to marry. In 1883 she earned £50 for *Aldersyde* and was married in the same year. It gave her the ability to support her husband's medical studies. This fulfilled his professional ambitions, and also perhaps her ambitions for a higher social standing. Writing increased her income, bringing such an ambition within reach, and a husband who was a doctor, rather than a school-teacher, as James Burnett-Smith was when she married him, was more suitable:

> I felt sure I was going to succeed as a writer, and that such success must mean a wider sphere and different surroundings from the little schoolhouse on the edge of Star Moss. Obviously the husband I loved must not lag behind. (ML, p. 46)

Her earning power also enabled her to achieve a London lifestyle consistent with her ambition, which would not have been within the power of a doctor's income alone:

> I worked hard with my pen during those early years in London. It was necessary, for though my husband was soon earning a substantial income, our expenses were constantly increasing. We were both lavish spenders. We loved beautiful things, and Jim's taste in pictures and furniture led him into all sorts of extravagances. (ML, p. 77)

Finally her earning power enabled her to maintain control of her financial independence:

> Never in all the years we lived together, did he ask how much money I had made or what I had done with it. He earned enough for the upkeep of his home and the family needs. What I had made provided the frills and the adventures. We had, from the beginning to the end, separate banking accounts. (ML, p. 275)

It should not be supposed from this that the Burnett-Smiths thought themselves involved in anything other than a conventional marriage. Elsewhere Swan, knowing it would be thought 'antiquated', unhesitatingly describes James Burnett-Smith as 'the head of the house' (ML, p. 273). Like Mrs Gaskell, Swan found much of her happiness within the accepted notions of middle-class femininity, modified substantially though these were by considerations of temperament and the dynamics of her marriage. Terry Lovell's comment on the attraction for many women of the ideology of domesticity in the context of Mrs Gaskell's life is valuable here:

> It is simply not plausible to present domesticity as always and uniformly an oppressive imposition upon women. As feminists we need to be able to register the extent to which domestic life has had and continues to have a compelling attraction for many women.[21]

Certainly this ideology of domesticity is everywhere in Swan's fiction. *Adam Hepburn's Vow: A Tale of Kirk and Covenant* [AHV] (1885) is an early novel in which she was drawn to weighty historical themes – Adam Hepburn's increasing instability is somewhat remi-niscent of the mental deterioration of John Galt's Covenanting zealot Ringan Gilhaize. What is striking about Swan's novel, however, is the way in which nineteenth-century ideology revises that of the seventeenth century. Although there are short accounts given of the points at issue in the Covenanting struggle, the most gripping scenes in the book are those in which government forces offend not merely against religious freedom but against the ideology of domesticity. In the opening chapter which describes the signing of the National Covenant, an Ayrshire minister and his family travel to his sister's house in Edinburgh. The sister is nursing a baby, to which the minister's daughter is drawn 'as if the babe were a magnet from which she could not separate herself' (AHV, p. 8). Though this metaphor is basic its use is instructive. Swan rarely uses figurative language and its use here alerts us to the necessity of women forging relationships with children with all the power of a natural force. Bridget Fowler's study of popular 1930s magazines leads her to the observation that 'the use of figures of speech, complex vocabulary and syntax and literary allusions' is not common in this kind of writing.[22] More generally it seems tenable that the use of figurative language is, in popular fiction, either clichéd or reserved for moments of high drama, or both.

Agnes grows up to be a blameless wife of a Covenanting husband who is killed by a Government soldier. Later on a boy in his teens is shot within earshot of his mother, and later still a family home is burned down leaving the three women homeless. Though in this novel the seventeenth-century struggle was over religious freedom, the offenders can be read as those nineteenth-century destroyers of domestic bliss – drunken and foul-mouthed men – whose enemies are the mother, the child and the home.

For Swan ideology is not only a means of interpreting history it is also a means by which contemporary life should be regulated. In her study of Sunday School prizes, Dorothy Entwhistle found that Swan's Mark Desborough's Vow [MDV] came eleventh out of the thirteen novels most commonly presented as Sunday School prizes to children in north-west England between 1870 and 1914. The novel sometimes reads like a handbook of advice for young adolescent males. Entwhistle argues such books were a way of 'socializing children into appropriate attitudes and behaviour'.[23] The hero, Mark Desborough, is enjoined by his 'angel-mother', who dies in the opening chapter, to look after his brother, Wilfred. Mark works hard for a firm of woollen manufacturers where his assiduity is eventually rewarded. 'It's only work, Mark, – hard honest conscientious work, which brings in the guineas,' his employer tells him (MDV, p. 54). Mark's brother is a painter who has little talent and squanders what he has. To show how clearly Wilfred fails to achieve true masculinity because of his laziness, he is continually described as 'womanish' and 'effeminate'. Wilfred drinks too much and is friendly with atheists. The girl with whom Mark is in love falls in love with Wilfred. Mark takes this disappointment stoically and is glad when Lucy brings Wilfred to a Christian commitment. Wilfred dies soon after this and Lucy is free to marry Mark who has made enough money from business to buy back his family home, lost through his father's debts. Mark is the ideal man, who affirms such values as family loyalty, industry, self-help, respect for women, and sexual probity.

Although Swan espouses conventional attitudes to women she is also aware of the problems they face which men do not. The difficulties faced by the central character in Aldersyde arise because she cannot inherit property. Women are also disadvantaged because of the domestic roles assigned to them. Sisters who manage a brother's household will no longer be needed when the brother marries. One mother's dying request to her daughter is that she stay single in order to look after her father. Because of untimely deaths single women often beome surrogate mothers without the legal, biological or social compensations of motherhood. Either such characters think that these arrangements are perfectly proper or they are rewarded either by a turn of the plot which marries them off or provides for them financially, or they feel rewarded because female self-sacrifice is one of the highest values in their belief system. In general Swan is dismissive of women who do not assume a conventional role. In *We Travel Home* [*WTH*] she discusses this in the context of a wife entertaining her husband's business guests:

> That is part of a wife's duty, and when she shirks it, as I have known some women to do, her partner has the right to call her to task for it. There are many decent men compelled, through the inefficiency or laziness of their wives, to entertain their business friends at hotels or restaurants. It is a grievance with them, and engenders resentment, which is not healthy in family life. The women who incur it are fools for themselves. Most men have pride in their homes, and it is up to the wife to respect that pride and maintain it. (*WTH*, pp. 89–90)

Often for Swan considerations of class outweigh considerations of gender. Although in another chapter in *We Travel Home* she acknowledges that the lives of domestic servants before 1914 were oppressive and were in need of reform, the chapter soon becomes a complaint against women who think themselves too good for service:

> The girls being trained in our elementary and secondary schools have no use for domestic service, even though their mothers would like them to settle down to it. They have other ideas. They all want to be teachers, secretaries, or – if nothing better offers – shop assistants. (*WTH*, p. 66)

Such strands in Swan's thinking show how she assumed the values of the class into which her own ambition for freedom and wealth had taken her.

While the ideology of domesticity provides a pervasive context for Swan's fiction, Providence and work are its organising themes. Providence, or Destiny, as she sometimes calls it, is the expression of the belief that ultimately the suffering of the good will be rewarded and evil will be punished. Providence is often linked with heredity. Work raises a cluster of related issues surrounding debt, the aristocracy and poverty. Many of Swan's characters endure periods of considerable hardship. Often this pain is one they cannot share, but the books insist that if they submit to their burden, Destiny will eventually release them from their suffering.

Swan's novels are no strangers to work. Memorably *Aldersyde* opens with a servant ironing a pile of damp linen. Hard physical work has its own dignity. Sandy in *The Gates of Eden* (1887) is roundly condemned for being ashamed of his father, a humble farmer who made the money to send him to University. Swan is, however, also aware of the sheer boredom which poverty often entails. Rosamund in *The Luck of the Livingstones* (1932) declares that she is 'so dreadfully tired of being poor', and in Uncle Peter in *The Gates of Eden*, Swan shows how persistent poverty can lead to obsessive habits of miserliness. Sometimes however, hard work is the means of achieving status and wealth. Often heroes or heroines are born into aristocratic families saddled by debt. It is usually her indictment of the aristocracy, and here they contrast with those whose hard work does not raise them out of poverty, that they squander their wealth and despise work. They are stereotypically the 'idle rich'. At the same time, heroes such as Mark Desborough show the value of work as by it he is enabled to regain his aristocratic status by merit.

Women who are not afforded the same opportunities to work often have to make strategic marriages to ensure their family's financial well-being. If such a marriage is only a marriage of convenience, then the heroine, no matter how much she tries to accept her lot, will never succeed. *Meg Hamilton* (1914), Meg tells her father 'I'm not a creature for sale', (*MH*, p. 27). However, sex is a saleable commodity: Meg refuses the suitor her father chooses, but in the end she does in a sense marry for money, although she is also genuinely in love. In contrast to this restriction of women's possibilities, her brother is able to go abroad and begin a career. The only way Swan allows a woman to combine work and family security is through writing. Ursula Vivian in the novel of that name is a female version of Mark Desborough. Her father has spent the family money and is in debt to all local shops. Both Ursula's mother and father die quite soon after she has finished her education. Ursula retrieves the situation by writing novels. She also becomes a mother to her brothers. Only when she has restored the family's wealth independently, does she marry Laurence Abbott, a rich and appropriate suitor.

These themes of Providence and work link Swan closely with older and sterner Scottish habits of thought. As these are usually expressed in Swan's work through prevailing attitudes to domesticity they are thus softened from their expression in earlier novels such as John Wilson's ('Christopher North' of *Blackwood's*) *The Trials of Margaret Lindsay* (1823). The overwhelming insistence in Swan's novels that women should submit and endure, and that they will be rewarded if they do, has led Bridget Fowler to cite these novels as works of social control:

> At its most conscious, such social control is exerted by editorial selection on the basis of practical rules of thumb about the genre and 'what the audience wants' which filter out any ideologically or stylistically alien product. Part of the success of the dominant class lies in the creation of the tacit assumptions that this selection process is routine and has been cut off from the area perceived as ideology and propaganda. It is consequently not seen as a form of class cultural control but as *axiomatically* following from the nature of the genre.[24]

In this regard it is instructive to look at the the case of *The Pendulum* more closely. Swan explains:

> After the war, the late Sir Ernest Hodder Williams, who had great respect for my work, kept on urging me to write a story dealing with the effect of war on family life. I did not particularly want to write such a book . . . (ML, 281)

This is the only case I can find of Swan ever mentioning that someone from the literary establishment directed her to write. Although the novel is perhaps her most striking, from the point of view of commercial success she was to find the suggestion a bad one. While reviewers regarded *The Pendulum* favourably (either they thought it an honest account of the pressure put on family relationships in wartime or they found it a perceptive account of the attitudes of the Wesleyan Methodist family with which the novel is concerned) Swan noted, however, that 'its effect on my usual public was very curious, in some respects disastrous' (ML, p. 281).

The novel is unique in Swan's oeuvre. She must have been concerned that the book would disturb her readership for she begins by claiming that it is a 'true record', knowing that this was the only ground on which some Christian readers would tolerate the adultery at the heart of the novel (TP, foreword). The tone of the novel is tarter than usual and the incidents much livelier, rather bearing out the claim that they have been taken from life, as Swan's imagination did not usually produce incidents of such calibre. As the novel progresses it becomes obvious that it is a critique of the 'Nonconformist conscience' – the phrase is used more than once – and in the novel Swan criticises many aspects of the ideology of domesticity on which she had built her literary reputation.

Many of these traits are personified in the character of Granny Champney, the matriarchal mother-in-law who upholds family dignity and promotes family success. 'You couldn't move in Granny Champney's rooms without hitting against something. There was neither space for your legs nor your mind in them.' (*TP*, p. 39) Her more open-minded daughter-in-law, Magda, says that talk about God's will leaves her cold (*TP*, p. 36). When her husband, Owen, gets on in business Magda does not see him as supporting the Empire but rather as making 'mean bargains with natives, ruthless exploiting of people who could not help themselves' (*TP*, p. 50). Owen's neglect of Magda leaves her open to the charms of one of his friends, George Mallison. Throughout, though she admits to 'restless, rebellious thoughts', she still believes that if she commits adultery God will punish her for it (*TP*, p. 38). Magda is confused with religious doubt; Mallison, on the other hand, presents a thoroughly secular view, and given Swan's previous books and the profile of her readership, the attitudes that he gives voice to are among the most surprising in the novel. In the first place he disputes Magda's claim that their attraction is a result of the exigencies of war: '"That's got nothing to do with you or me. It began that day on the lawn under the cedars. The chief thing is that *we* should be happy."' (*TP*, p. 156). He rejects her claim that what they feel is a temporary aberration: '"All rot! I never was more normal. I know what I want and I mean to have it", (*TP*, p. 161). He challenges the Champneys' claim to sound social standards, wanting instead '"the full life, not the starved Champneys' concept of duty and obligation and self-repression"' (*TP*, pp. 159–60).

George represents the attraction of desire before duty. But it is not duty which stops Magda from succumbing but fear of retribution. She interprets her daughter's experience of sex before marriage as a punishment on herself for flirting with temptation. While Magda's temptation is presented as a personal struggle at the end of the novel, it appears that Magda's struggle is primarily the result of heredity. It is revealed that her true father is an aristocrat. The significance of this is not merely that Magda belongs 'naturally' to the great and the good and thus has found her proper place in life. What is also significant is that she was born outside of marriage. She considers that this 'roving blood' explains the illicit sexual desires of herself and her daughter: they have not had free choice (*TP*, p. 331).

The novel also includes references to contraception, sex education for teenagers, as well as the double standard, sex before marriage, sex outside marriage, doubts about Providence, religious hypocrisy, shady business dealings – it is hard to think of much else Swan could have included which would have shocked her readership more: 'It more than shocked; it alarmed my public, and they were not slow in expressing their strong disapproval.' (*ML*, p. 282).

Swan elsewhere writes about the strong 'bond' which grew up between her and her readership, something she prized greatly for itself and as compensation for the dismissive remarks of literary critics. *The Pendulum* put this bond at risk. It seems clear from this that Swan was not so much writing to control her readers but rather being controlled by their approval or disapproval. Joseph McAleer makes a similar point in his *Popular Reading and Publishing 1914–1950* (1992) when discussing the religious publishing firm, Lutterworth, whose bankruptcy came about because it wished to propagate a religious message in an outdated style:

It is unlikely, however, that popular publishers cast themselves – or could cast themselves – as agents in a master plan for social control and domination, as Bridget Fowler has suggested they did . . . financial misfortune could lay waste to even the holiest of intentions, as Lutterworth Periodicals discovered after the Second World War. Lutterworth, moreover, could not make such an 'archaic element' as religion sell papers.[25]

For Swan *The Pendulum* was an unhappy and salutary experience. She never wrote another book like it.

In conclusion, Annie Swan was what she claimed to be – a popular novelist. Her vast popularity was due to the developments in mass literary culture which she capitalised on through her relationship with William Robertson Nicoll and *The British Weekly* and latterly with John Leng and *The People's Friend*. *The British Weekly* was the first home of the Kailyard school of which Swan was part. The debate between the Kailyarders and the critics, is, I have argued, a part of the debate engendered by the development of mass culture. Though there is a strand of anti-populism in some Scottish Renaissance writing, politically and creatively the Renaissance writers reacted differently from their English contemporaries, finding popular versions of Scotland reactionary, but not feeling so threatened by them that they divorced themselves from them by cultivating an exclusive formal complexity. Rather, Scottish Modernists, provoked by the Kailyard, embarked on a imaginative programme of literary redefinition. Like most of the participants in the debate, Swan shows signs of confusion about its true nature. Occasionally the sociological realities predominate over the literary ones, but not always and not consistently. To designate Swan exclusively as a 'Kailyard' writer is to fail to recognise the full significance of her popular appeal. As a woman writer she behaved in many ways like women writers of greater literary significance, such as Mrs Gaskell and Mrs Oliphant. And this seems to show that women faced similar problems because of their gender whether they were writing in high or popular culture. Swan's novels clearly affirm some of the core values of womanhood and identity of her day. Given the scandal of *The Pendulum*, however, it is clear that she could only exert control within certain limits. The relationship between Swan and the readers she wrote for worked to the advantage of both. She was rewarded financially, while her readers of whatever class enjoyed the popular fiction which made their circumscribed or even hard lives briefly more tolerable. She also felt particularly rewarded by the response of her working-class readership. Swan records a talk she gave to women in the East End of Glasgow:

> Leaving the building, I had to pass through a large crowd to reach my car. Many toil-worn hands were thrust out to grasp mine, and one woman, with a shawl over her head, said unsteadily: 'Ye canna dee yet, for *we* couldna dae withoot ye'. (ML, p. 297)

Anna Buchan ('O. Douglas')

If in her fiction Annie S. Swan sometimes lets slip some unease about nineteenth-century prescriptions for women's lives, O. Douglas's novels are evidence that a thoughtful and sensitive woman could take the potentially stultifying conventions and values of popular fiction and, convinced of their rightness, exploit them in an altogether more sophisticated way and offer them as an expression of a humanly satisfying life. We are used to novels written by women from a pre-feminist era anticipating feminism, or paying lip service to conventional female roles while demonstrating restiveness or outright rebellion in subtexts. What is unusual is that in Anna Buchan's work text and subtext do not conflict. There are only the merest glimmers that other lives for women are possible. I will outline the kind of life which O. Douglas admires as well as looking at the shadowy alternatives which present themselves. Firstly, though, the nature of her relationship with the Kailyard should be explained.

One of a number of confusions with which the term Kailyard has left us is that it is over-readily applied to too many different kinds of popular Scottish fiction, and too often when that fiction is not chiefly concerned with stereotypical views of Scotland made humorously attractive for a readership which comprises many non-Scots. In *Edinburgh Essays on Scots Literature* Angus MacDonald demonstrates this confusion when trying to categorise O. Douglas and the Findlater sisters (perhaps somewhat oddly grouped together):

> They can write well and often shrewdly (Miss Buchan in a style which reminds me of her brother), and they have had the good taste to see that the tradition must be modified and to some extent purged of its sentimentality. Yet even they are overweighted by the tradition; and while the 'Kailyard' type can offer a refuge from the overgrown commercialism of our 'lives', we feel that it is too 'precious' and too narrow in scope ever to make a national novel.[26]

Yet O. Douglas's works cannot truly be called Kailyard. They have some elements in them which are commonly identified as Kailyard: notably in the presentation of the Scots dialogue of servant women, which, together with an ironic view of their attitudes, is offered for the reader's amusement. O. Douglas was familiar with Barrie's work which she admired for its irony and observation but criticised for its 'pawkiness' (*Unforgettable, Unforgotten*, p. 74).[27] In her books she tries to render her specifically small-town-and-rural, upper middle-class background sympathetically and valuable in itself. She avoids Barrie's sentimentality and Swan's woodenness.

Her first novel, *Olivia*, was published in 1913 on the eve of the disruption of the society that it portrays. Her novels are usually thought of as romantic fiction, although sometimes the absence of plot makes them hard to categorise. There is something of a mismatch between Douglas's talents and the form in which she chose to express herself. On two occasions she compares Priorsford, the town based on Peebles in which some of her fiction is set, to Mrs Gaskell's Cranford. It is probably therefore more accurate to describe her work as a set of observations on society expressed as romantic fiction – a form chosen, presumably, because it was financially remunerative.

The overarching theme of this fiction is well expressed in the title of her eighth novel *The Day of Small Things* (1930). This novel is set, as so often, in a small Scottish community, viewed mainly from the perspective of the upper middle class. When women are not looking after their families, they run Nursing Homes, attend Sales of Work, expect their daughters to take up Guides or engage in amateur dramatics. They also visit each other for informal chats, formal dinners or extended stays. The ethos of the nineteenth-century Free Church is much in evidence. In *Penny Plain* (1920) the heroine, Jean, admits that she had been brought up by her Aunt Alison to make every moral decision as though she were on her death-bed. Women in these places know that the small things of their lives may not seem adventurous or momentous, but as Nicole, the heroine of *The Day of Small Things*, says:

> 'The small things keep you going wonderfully: the kindness of friends; the fact of being needed; nice meals; books; interesting plays; the funny people in the world; the sea and the space and the wind – not very small, are they, after all?' (*DST*, p. 31)

Nicole's statement is made in response to her mother's feeling that her daughter, whose fiancé was killed on an expedition to Everest, has missed out on happiness. Nicole's restricted life is strikingly compared with her fiancé's death in undertaking one of the most exacting physical challenges the world has to offer; but as in the fiction of Annie S. Swan, triumph in adversity was an important component of this world view. 'The fact of being needed' alerts the reader to another of its strands – the necessity for charitable activity, further evidence of the religious impetus behind these attitudes. This emphasis on the virtues of contentment within a small community, endurance and philanthropy are repeated throughout O. Douglas's work – famously in *Penny Plain* and *Priorsford* (1932).

While it is perfectly easy to understand what O. Douglas believes, it is much harder to understand why she believes it. At times it seems that nothing happens at all. In *Priorsford*, Miss Teenie, one of the cast of community characters, expands on the kindness of one of her neighbours who gave her a bowl of fruit as a Christmas gift and told her to keep the bowl: 'I think that was so thoughtful, for if you've got a bowl to return it's always on your mind.' (*P*, p. 274). Even the most straightforward of enterprises were shrouded in difficulty. Men were expected to go off to the extremes of the Empire without a second thought but women found it hard to get on the train to London. Beatrice in *Taken by the Hand* (1935) is surprised when the lady in her compartment says that a day on the train is such a rest:

> 'This was a new light on travelling. Beatrice had been in the habit of hearing people make rather a fuss about it. Kind Mrs Lithgow had urged her that morning to eat more breakfast 'because, you know, you've a journey before you,' and she had been sent early to bed the night before for the same reason. (*TBH*, p. 57)

This swaddling of mature human beings which incapacitates them, making them unable to grasp the joys of human maturity, leads inevitably to the development of the inner life described by Mrs Hope, a mother-figure to Jean in *Priorsford*:

> We just sit here, Augusta and I, day in and day out; read *The Scotsman* and *The Times*, sometimes play patience, sew a little, read a little, talk a little, and think a lot. (*P* p. 93)

Does the 'O' in O. Douglas's pseudonym stand for 'nothing' – nothing to do, nothing to say, woman degree zero?

Alternative lives cannot be recommended in this fiction but they can be explored. This exploration is conducted in several ways: through unhappy characters; travel; the impulse to drama; work; writing and money. There are women who are manifestly unhappy with their lot. Muriel Duff-Whalley in *Priorsford* feels that she lacks intelligence or determination or any virtue which would make her remarkable and allow her to carve out a life apart from convention. Unless she marries she will wither away in Priorsford, 'this dead-alive place', 'this spinster-haunted place' (*P*, pp. 54–5). (Muriel is found a suitable husband by the good offices of her author.) Esmé Jameson in *The Day of Small Things* lost her husband in World War I. Her anger and grief are hinted at but left undeveloped. She comes to Kirkmeikle to recover herself in peaceful surroundings and the setting effects a recuperation. The setting has the same restorative effect on Althea, the jaded, young society girl who comes to stay with Nicole and develops into a mature and satisfied woman, having been re-educated in true and permanent values. Betty Barton, who acts as secretary to Jean in *Priorsford*, is not a society girl, but a New Woman. Because her parents died early, Betty had to earn her living. This has made her efficient but somewhat ruthless. In conversation with her employer, Betty says that though she wants a home because she has never had one, if she had had a home, she would probably have wanted her freedom. "'I think you would,'" says Jean, gently condemning her contrariness, her refusal to accept things as they are. When later on she receives and refuses a proposal of marriage from Jean's brother, who is generally thought a bit conceited, Betty enjoys the knowledge that the rejection will have dented his confidence. However, the author comments, 'Hers seemed a singularly barren triumph.' (*P*, pp. 356). Although O. Douglas acknowledges that women face difficulties, her narrative strategies usually work to ensure that the difficulties are overcome where her characters are permitted to share her values. And where the characters' values differ the author distances herself from her characters.

Travel away from the Priorsford community tends to strengthen characters' self-confidence. Beatrice's journey to England helps her to take decisions for herself. Where she was a psychological child at the time of the death of her own mother, she has matured to the point where she can nurse an old lady in her dying illness and accept her death in an adult fashion. A much more indicative example of the effect of travel occurs in *Olivia in India*, Anna Buchan's first novel which, therefore, signals the birth of O. Douglas. It is on her trip to India to visit her brother who works in the Indian civil service that Olivia declares '*I am going to write a book*. You are surprised? But why? I read in a review lately that John has great distinction of style, so perhaps I have too.' (*OII*, p. 134). Olivia's question 'why not I?' is remarkable for being one of the few times a heroine, with the permission of the author, takes a decision to alter significantly the conditions of her life. Perhaps the 'O' in O. Douglas stands for Olivia, the name of the heroine of *Twelfth Night*, but ironically in this case, one whose fullness of experience is inhibited not by the death of her brother but perhaps by his living success. Anna Buchan quotes often from this play and in her memoir in *Unforgettable, Unforgotten* tells of how her passion for Shakespeare was sensed by Walter Raleigh and led to a spirited conversation at dinner from a girl who felt herself shy in company (*UU*, p. 85). As O. Douglas, she recognises in her fiction that drama enables people to 'try out' a range of personalities and forms of expression otherwise unavailable to them. Most of the fiction includes characters who read plays or engage in amateur dramatics. In *Jane's Parlour*, Caroline gets as far as persuading her father to allow her to go to Drama School in London. However, Caroline realises that her talent is limited and she eventually returns to the marriage proposed for her in chapter one.

None of O. Douglas's heroines work. None of them needs to. Each has sufficient money to live without taking a job. Beatrice in *Taken by the Hand* sees the importance of work and wishes she was going to London to take up a job, not simply to stay with relations. The satisfaction of work would be to be purposeful. And there does seem to be in the novels a feeling that domestic work – looking after children or managing a household – are in some way insufficient means of channelling the full range of human energies. Indeed looking after children is closely related to ideas of sacrifice; it is here, as in Swan, one of the highest ideals to which women can aspire. In *Penny Plain* Jean refuses Lord Bidborough because she feels she has to look after her brothers. He puts to her the dangers of self-sacrifice, that hers is a strategy for avoiding choice and decision, a selfish refusal to will or to determine:

> Do you know Penny-plain, I believe it is all the fault of Great-aunt Alison. You are thinking that on your deathbed you will like to feel that you sacrificed yourself to others. (*PP*, p. 185)

Although she does not use the language of sacrifice, Jean is deeply influenced by it, as her lover suggests. When discussing how she would like to bring up her own daughters, she says:

> 'It all amounts to this, bring up a girl to think of others and she won't have time to worry about herself and her feelings. But it's' – Jean sighed – 'it's a counsel of perfection.' (PP, p. 185)

The beginnings of a recognition that such self-sacrifice might not be the only way of life to which women might aspire is implied by the minute description of the social round and of philanthropic activity – both activities which take up the time of women who do not need to work. It is commonly argued by historians of the nineteenth century that middle-class women engaged in philanthropy to avoid boredom but also to avoid the stigma of work.[28] However, it is only possible to be philanthropic if you have enough money to given away but Jean Jardine, O. Douglas's quintessential heroine, has enough, but only enough, to live on. However, because of an act of kindness to a passing stranger, Jean inherits a huge fortune: 'Penny Plain' is 'buried under bullion' – her friend's phrase (PP, p. 217). This twist of the plot is rather like Olivia's declaration that she is going to write. As in the case of giving Olivia the motivation to write, Anna Buchan by an act of imagination wills a significant change of circumstance for her heroine – albeit in a very different way.

As soon as it happens it is immediately hedged about with a financial responsibility of suitably Presbyterian proportions. The inheritance is divided into four and each quarter is tithed. The boys will not receive their share until they are twenty-five – the intervening interest having been added to the original tithe. The local minister is then consulted on what the tithed money may properly be spent on. In the sequel, *Priorsford*, Jean has to hire a secretary to administer a philanthropic enterprise which has developed into a cottage industry. But despite these admirable expressions of virtue, the inescapable significance of this inheritance means that Jean, like Jane Eyre before her, is made financially self-sufficient and marries Lord Bidborough as a woman of substance, and not as a dependent. It is noteworthy that Beatrice of *Taken by the Hand* also marries from a similar financial position – indeed her husband will be financially dependent on her:

> 'On the other hand, I'd have like to feel –' he hesitated. 'That I was dependent on you,' cried Beatrice. 'But I am, Christopher. I am dependent on you for everything that matters – for all my life.' (TBH p. 358)

The other socially acceptable work which the nineteenth century permitted women was writing. There are a number of lady writers scattered throughout O. Douglas's work. They all declare (Mirren Strang in *Priorsford*, Jane Naesmyth in *Taken by the Hand* and Kathryn Eliot in *Jane's Parlour*) that they write for money. (For Mirren and Kathryn this is actually a form of self-deprecation – they believe they have no talent and churn out fiction merely to earn.) Jane Naesmyth, Beatrice's guide in *Taken by The Hand*, is the editor of a woman's magazine. She went into journalism because she had to earn her living but she is not found wanting as was Betty Barton in *Priorford*. Jane is self-supporting, and although she is single, there is no implication that this is seen as a failure or a less than human state. She is wise enough to be able to advise Beatrice and to provide her with the friendships necessary for her growth. Although the main spotlight falls on Beatrice and her growth to maturity and marriage, the cameo of Jane Naesmyth, the single, self-sufficient career woman, is not undercut by the governing virtues of acceptance, endurance and philanthropy.

While on a first reading O. Douglas's fiction seems so much a product of its time, with its lack of critical engagement with the repressed position of women in nineteenth-century society, this judgement is not sufficient as an assessment of the novels. Their popularity must be due in part to the articulation of womens' feelings about their lives: their time taken up with domestic and social matters; their feelings of inadequacy in social situations; their fear of the new or unfamiliar. Many characters are described as shy, not particularly gifted or distinguished in any way – a more realistic representation and a respite perhaps from the galaxy of nineteenth-century fictional heroines with dazzling conversation, formidable intelligence and the presence of mind to cope with all the implications of mad women in the garret? Within this restricted but nonetheless lovingly embraced lifestyle, whose main characteristic is an acceptance of circumstance, Olivia decides to write and O. Douglas decides to bestow an inheritance. These decisions reject life-as-it-is for life-as-it-might-be. Work may mainly be philanthropic or it may result in an embittered person, but it also becomes an admirable means of self-development in the character of Jane Naesmyth. However, it is the possession of independent financial means which secures for two of these heroines the individual personal dignity they need to be able to enter equally into marriage with the man they love. The refusal to locate a woman's worth in a husband or family, but to give it – literally – a cash value controlled entirely by the woman, so that the money is the symbol of her internal worth, makes O. Douglas's fiction in this respect at least, quite unconventional.

Notes

1. Annie S. Swan, *Aldersyde* (London and Edinburgh, 1883). No exhaustive bibliography of the works of Annie S. Swan exists. These figures are taken from a simple count of the holdings of her work in the National Library of Scotland. As a rule Swan's fiction will not be footnoted. Titles additional to those referred to in the text may be found in the general bibliography.

2. *The Letters of Annie S. Swan*, ed. Mildred Robertson Nicoll (Hodder & Stoughton, London, 1945), p. 30. Further references are to *Letters*.

3. Annie S. Swan, *My Life* (Hodder & Stoughton, London, 1934). Further references are to *ML*.

4. See Letter from Gerald Chichester, Assistant Private Secretary to Queen Mary, to Mrs Burnett-Smith, 8 July 1931 (National Library of Scotland, Accession 6003, Box 1, Folder 1a); Letter from E. Laffray to Mrs Burnett-Smith, 29 October 1936 (National Library of Scotland, Accession 6003, Box 1, Folder 1d).

5. A detailed historical account of this group and of Annie S. Swan and her father as representatives of it can be found in R. Q. Gray, 'Religion, Culture and Social Class in Late Nineteenth and Early Twentieth Century Edinburgh', in Geoffrey Crossick (ed.), *The Lower Middle Class in Britain 1870–1914* (Croom Helm, London, 1977).

6. Quoted in Valentine Cunningham, *Everywhere Spoken Against: Dissent in the Victorian Novel* (Clarendon Press, Oxford, 1975), p. 62.

7. T. H. Darlow, *William Robertson Nicoll: Life and Letters* (London, 1925), p. 70.

8. Mrs Oliphant, 'The Old Saloon', *Blackwood's Magazine* 146 (1889), 254–75 (p. 266).

9. Cunningham, *Everywhere Spoken Against*, p. 233.

10. J. H. Millar, *A Literary History of Scotland* (T F Unwin, London, 1903), p. 511. W. R. Nicoll, 'Farewell Sermons Yesterday', *Manchester Guardian*, 16 October 1905.

11. Quoted in George Blake, *Barrie and the Kailyard School* (A. Barker, London, 1951), p. 100.

12. Blake, p. 72. Hugh MacDiarmid, 'Newer Scottish Fiction (I)', in *Contemporary Scottish Studies* 25.6.26 (Edinburgh, 1976), p. 109.

13.   John Carey, *The Intellectuals and the Masses: Pride and Prejudice among the Literary Intelligentsia* (Faber & Faber, London, 1992).
14.   Carey, pp. 24–5.
15.   Annie S. Swan, *We Travel Home* (Ivor, Nicholson and Watson, London, 1934), p. 258. Further references are to *WTH*.
16.   Annie S. Swan, *The Land I Love* (Ivor Nicholson and Watson, London, 1934). Further references are to *TLIL*. David Cleghorn Thomson, *Scotland in Quest of Her Youth* (Oliver & Boyd, Edinburgh and London, 1932).
17.   Thomas Knowles, *Ideology, Art and Commerce: Aspects of Literary Sociology in the Late Victorian Kailyard* (Acta Universitatis Gothoburgensis, Goetborg, 1983), p. 46.
18.   Christopher Harvie, 'Behind the Bonnie Briar Bush: The "Kailyard" Revisited', in *Proteus* 3 (1978), 55–69 (p. 69).
19.   Darlow, pp. 249–51.
20.   Ian Campbell, *Kailyard: A New Assessment* (Ramsay Head, Edinburgh, 1981). Roderick Watson, '"Oor Ain Folk?": National Types and Stereotypes in Arcadia', in Horst Drescher and Herman Volkel (eds), *Nationalism and Literature: Third International Scottish Studies Symposium* (Scottish Studies 8 Peter Lang, Frankfurt, 1989), 131–42.
21.   Terry Lovell, *Consuming Fiction* (Verso, London, 1987), p. 91.
22.   Bridget Fowler, 'True to Me Always: An Analysis of Women's Magazine Fiction', in Christopher Pawling (ed.), *Popular Fiction and Social Change* (Macmillan, London, 1984), pp. 99–126 (p. 109).
23.   Dorothy Entwhistle, 'Sunday-school Book Prizes for Children: Rewards and Socialization', in Diana Wood (ed.), *The Church and Childhood* (Blackwell, Oxford, 1994), pp. 405–16 (p. 416).
24.   Fowler, p. 105.
25.   Joseph McAleer, *Popular Reading and Publishing in Britain 1914–1950* (Clarendon Press, Oxford, 1992), p. 253.
26.   Angus MacDonald, 'Modern Scots Novelists', in Edinburgh Essays on Scots Literature (Edinburgh, 1933), pp. 149–173 (p. 163).
27.   Anna Buchan, *Unforgettable, Unforgotten* (Hodder & Stoughton, London, 1945).
28.   F. K. Prochaska, *Women in Philanthropy in Nineteenth Century England* (Clarendon Press, Oxford, 1980), pp. 149–73 (p. 163).

23

Tales of Her Own Countries: Violet Jacob

Carol Anderson

Violet Jacob (1863–1946), born Violet Kennedy-Erskine, enjoyed some success in the early twentieth century with her novels and short stories, and her poetry in the Lowland Scots tongue. Her books were widely reviewed both north and south of the border, and she had a recognised place in the literary scene of her time.[1] For many years, however, Jacob was represented only by a bare handful of poems in anthologies, until her prose work started reappearing in print in the 1980s and '90s. Now it is possible to see that her output is more diverse than has sometimes been assumed.

'The spirit of place drew her mightily', it is written of a character in her novel *The History of Aythan Waring*,[2] and the same might be said of Jacob herself, much of whose work is based self-consciously in the various territories which were her 'Own Country'.[3] 'Regional' literature was popular in her time; it has not always been in favour since, but as Linda Hutcheon remarks of contemporary literature, 'the local, the regional, the non-totalising are reasserted as the center becomes a fiction'.[4] The time may be ripe for a revaluation of a writer like Jacob, whose work evokes physical place but also location in other senses.

Most of Jacob's significant work was written between the 1890s and the 1920s. She began working at the *fin-de-siècle*, in what Elaine Showalter has identified as a period of borderline battles, a time of cultural insecurity characterised by 'fears of regression and degeneration', when 'the longing for strict border controls around the definition of gender, as well as race, class, and nationality, becomes especially intense'.[5] Jacob, however, is located on borderlines of various kinds: her work explores borderlands, challenging boundaries, enacting 'border crossing'.[6]

Jacob grew up in Angus, on the east coast of Scotland, at her landed family's home at Dun, but first began writing seriously when, in the 1890s, she accompanied her Irish husband, Arthur, an army officer, to India, and recorded her life there in diaries and letters. Although she was also writing her first novel *The Sheepstealers* at this time, she expresses doubts about the value of her fiction in her diaries.[7] The diary as a form 'poised ambivalently between private and public statement'[8] allowed Jacob, like other women, to write without the necessary anxiety caused by publication. We learn little of Jacob's inner life – she is of her time and of her class in her personal reticence – but while, like autobiographical forms, women's travel writing has often been regarded as 'trivial or marginal to the mainstream',[9] the Indian letters and diaries, unpublished in her lifetime, are interesting for various reasons.

The Jacobs were stationed at Mhow, in central India, a region which Violet explored when she went riding 'up the country',[10] alone, and described to her mother, commenting that the hot, rather bare, flat landscape 'appeals to me more and more as time goes on'. 'How anyone but a dolt can call such a weird country dull, I don't know', she says, 'And yet there are people who see nothing interesting in it. One comfort is that they all congregate together and so can be easily avoided' (p. 28). She continues:

> The weirdness of this whole country appeals to me like nothing ever has yet; it is impossible for anyone who cannot see it to have an idea of it, and there are enough and to spare of those who can have none either. I keep thanking God, like the Pharisee in the parable, that I am not as other men, and certainly not as other women, in this matter. There are vast stretches, intense silences, sudden, odd-shaped hills, a night that swoops down with no twilight, heavy, hot, sweet smells; after dark, stifling air and little fires lit all over the country; and, one may add, the knowledge of the presence of these idols and Hindu shrines and Mohammedan graves lurking in the waste places. Above all, there are no footfalls in a land where man and beast go unshod. I have grown to love it passionately. That Indian life that one reads of in books, made up of clubs and what passes for society, the only India that most people know anything about, never touches one, or one would die of boredom; . . . (p. 39)

Despite Jacob's use of the quasi-impersonal 'one' here (which hints at her aristocratic background) there are underlying assumptions: 'most people' are British, for instance. Violet Jacob was a member of the colonial expatriate community in India, and she measures her own responses to the landscape and its people from within, and against, the responses of that community. India is, for Jacob, 'weird', undeniably 'other'.

At the same time, she declares her love for Central India, and her accounts of the country are sensuous, richly detailed, often humorous. She makes efforts to cross cultural boundaries, learning some Hindustani and taking great interest in all the people she meets, of various classes and religions. She especially notes Hindu superstitions and legends, telling the tales to her young son, Harry. Like Stevenson around the same time, who wrote that the tales and legends of Polynesia bore resemblance to those of Scotland,[11] Jacob may have been sympathetic because she knew so well the superstitions of her own culture.

Jacob's writing shows tensions, but then, like other women travellers writing in the nineteenth and twentieth centuries, she was writing from within various, sometimes conflicting, discourses relating to both colonialism and 'femininity', resulting in the presentation of 'a self which transgresses and which conforms both to patriarchal and imperial discourses'. Her lack of attention to political matters, for instance, may be understood in the context of the traditional 'feminine' discourse which determines that 'women writers are more likely to describe their interactions with people' than with 'larger colonial issues or strategies'.[12] But Jacob challenges the rules of her own society for women in her conduct, as is shown both explicitly and implicitly in her writing. There are dangers of measuring Jacob against stereotyped images of the 'memsahib', but she clearly felt 'different', and by her own account was unusual in her behaviour, dressing mannishly for her trips (*Diaries and Letters*, p. 66), and smoking (p. 73), thus acting in some ways like the 'New Woman' of the time.[13] Riding alone in wild places, as she did, was to usurp the role of the adventurous male. Michelene Wandor comments that

Jacob 'slowly and surely knocks the cliché about Victorian passive womanhood on the head'.[14]

Collecting and painting plants and flowers was a conventionally feminine activity for Victorian women, but while plants were the excuse for Jacob's jaunts, they were by no means their sole end: 'I don't suppose I shall ever find anything rare, but that doesn't matter to me though I should dearly love to do it. The delight of a new wide country is enough for me and plants that I have never seen are the crowning part of it' she says (p. 44). Jacob's delight in her 'new wide country' suggests that for her, as for some other women, life in the colonies offered 'a release from the constraints of Victorian culture'.[15] Furthermore, many of Jacob's paintings of plants and flowers (some reproduced in the modern edition of the diaries) are extremely bold; huge, richly coloured blooms push out beyond their frames, the composition suggesting an eye impatient with constraint and convention.

In her writing, too, she sometimes surprises. While there are 'certain subjects which women are not supposed to know or write about' in the nineteenth century 'sex being the most obvious',[16] Jacob, as some critics have noted of her other work, is occasionally unusually frank.[17] In a letter to her mother in 1897 (p. 95) she calmly records an amusing sexual anecdote, and she herself has an irreverent sense of humour. Few people are spared her irony, whatever their race or gender; she is adept at deflating pomposity and pretension. Susan Tweedsmuir comments that when Violet Jacob was living in Egypt a few years later, the fact that she had published a small volume of poetry 'made her a little suspect to the military society of Cairo'.[18] In various ways, as an artist, a woman and a Scot of aristocratic background in colonial society, Jacob had a kind of insider-outsider status that fed into her growing interest in life on the margins and in the 'in between' places.

This kind of interest is apparent in her first novel, which draws on her own mixed family background. Jacob's mother was Welsh, and *The Sheepstealers*, published in 1902, is set in the Anglo-Welsh borderlands, exploring 'two communities living close together on the borders of two nations'.[19] Like Hardy, with whom she was compared,[20] Jacob examines what the Anglo-Welsh critic and writer Raymond Williams describes as (both literal and metaphorical) 'border country'.[21] The territory of the novel is isolated land at the foot of the Black Mountain; suggestively described as 'a kind of intermediate stage' (p. 3) between the high peaks and the valley, 'that region of neither yesterday nor today' (p. 4). This is a rural world in transition, its culture lovingly evoked but not uncritically viewed.

The 'hill-people' who occupy this border region 'were neither entirely mountain nor entirely valley bred, though retaining something of each locality, and something of the struggle between nature and civilization seemed to have entered into them, giving them that strenuousness which all transition must bring with it' (p. 4). The novel examines the struggles of the community and of individuals, with a plot revolving around a real episode in Welsh history in which the rural poor rose up to protest against increased tolls on roads. This protest is portrayed with sympathy, as are the title figures including George Williams: 'in the eye of the law, he was a hedger and ditcher by occupation; on its blind side, he was something else as well' (p. 64). The handling of the various kinds of 'borderline' characters in this novel looks ahead to Jacob's later work. Rhys Walters, for instance, becomes an outsider in his own community when he is mistakenly believed to be responsible for a man's death; like several other characters, including his mother, Rhys is neither wholly sympathetic nor wholly despicable, and the reader is invited to see both from within and without. *The Sheepstealers* was well-received when it appeared in 1902, and Jacob wrote some other mainly minor fictions set in the Welsh borders.[22]

Many of Jacob's short stories also foreground specificity of place, with a volume of 1922 titled *Tales of My Own Country*, which imaginatively claims her Angus territory. The 'country' of these tales is in one sense Scotland. The story 'The Fiddler', like a number of others in the collection, has a historical setting, and, like *Flemington*, explores the effects, though some twenty years on, of the 1745 Jacobite rebellion, 'that convulsion of Scotland'.[23] A visiting Englishman hears fiddle-music, and 'the love of country, which was a passion in the race around him, which, unexpressed in mere words, poured out of the violin, was revealed to him, though he could only grasp it vicariously' (p. 107). The story suggests that the musician, Neil Gow (a historical figure here given imaginative life), with his great humanity, and his ability to draw all classes together, can heal old wounds and create a degree of national harmony.

'Country' in the title of this volume more significantly, though, perhaps, denotes a specific region, Angus, and Jacob's note to the collection remarks that the scenes in it are all 'portraits of places'. A story like 'The Watchtower' (p. 217), with painterly care delineates a physical terrain both highland and lowland, and primarily rural – for Jacob's 'country' is also 'countryside'. Her people are mainly farmers, shepherds, working women in remote communities; the English visitor in 'The Fiddler' 'felt a stirring of pity in him for the dwellers in this lost, strange backwater' (p. 104). Some critics have assumed that Jacob occupies the Kailyard,[24] (Angus was the home-ground of the influential, if complicated 'Kailyarder', J. M. Barrie), but in her own time, Jacob's short fiction was compared to that of Guy de Maupassant,[25] and several short stories demonstrate her capacity for unflinching unsentimentality in her treatment of rural life.

'Thievie', for instance, is intensely realist about the physical hardship of rural life, and about women's status in society; this tautly written tale, with its evocation of the 'sullen' elements, and the flood-waters rising symbolically around a claustrophobic small town, also suggests a tide in human affairs. The title refers to a miserly old man who drowns in a flood rather than let his unmarried, ageing daughter, Janet, have the money (received from a son in Canada) which he has hoarded; she knows her chances of marriage, without money behind her, are slight and sees her father as having stolen her rightful inheritance, that of a full life. Janet herself is not a particularly sympathetic character, but the story shows how she is embittered by her exclusion from power and happiness in a patriarchal society.

Jacob's frank exposure of power structures and the struggles of those marginalised by society, women and others, can be seen again in another story 'The Debatable Land'. Robert Louis Stevenson remarked in an essay that he had, in imagination, 'shaken a spear in the Debatable Land',[26] the historically 'debated' borderland between Scotland and England. The story thus implicitly recalls national struggles, and appears in a volume claiming place ('my country'); but it simultaneously undermines any idea of 'possession' of place or people. Jessie-Mary, an orphan girl of whose birth and origin 'no one in the parish knew anything definite' (p. 67), working as a servant and virtually a prisoner of her uncaring employers, escapes the rough unwanted sexual advances of her employer's son by escaping into 'the debatable land'. Literally, this is a piece of wild, uncultivated land not owned by the local landowner, and it is graphically described. It is also, however, metaphorical: a place of freedom, no-man's land, the young woman's place of refuge, 'the wild zone' in several senses.[27] Douglas Dunn comments that this story 'is remarkable for its valiant breaking of barriers. This is exactly the kind of story of which the kailyarders were incapable'.[28]

It is significant that the girl escapes with the aid of a gypsy man; the story subtly implies she is still not entirely free. But he is, like her, a marginal, landless figure: 'When evening fell on the debatable land, it found him sitting at his transitory threshold, as he mended his rabbit snare' (p. 83). Jacob's personal motto, on her bookplates, was 'to be and not to have'. Those who own little and live nowhere, gypsies, the dispossessed and vagrants, move through her fiction, posing a challenge to the settled and the staid, to the idea of ownership; while lawbreakers are presented without judgement, or with sympathy. The figure of the sheepstealer (like those in the novel of that name) who appears in 'The Watchtower', for instance, is seen from the perspective of a man who knows and likes him.

Unconventional, transgressive women, in particular, recur in Jacob's work. The comic tale 'The Disgracefulness of Auntie Thompson' paints an interesting portrait of a strong woman despised by the aspiring snobs of her neighbourhood. Jacob's Aunty Thompson prefigures Meg Menzies in Lewis Grassic Gibbon's short story 'Smeddum':[29]

> Her appearance, which was intensely plebeian; her tongue, which was very outspoken; and her circumstances, which were a deal better than her habits warranted – all these disagreed in some undefined way with the ideas of her small world. A woman who had laid by as much as she was reported to own had no business to keep no servant and to speak her mind on all subjects to those who did, as if she were on the same social level as themselves. She was unabashed and disgraceful; she did not deride convention, because she seemed to be unaware that it existed. (p. 40)

Also sympathetically presented are the 'marginal' women in these stories, who have suffered loss, frustration or ill treatment. Phemie Moir in the story 'The Fiddler', for example, once loved dancing, but now, as the minister tells his English visitor, '"the bairns are feared of her, and some of the more foolish of my congregation take her for a witch"'. She is not mad, he says, '"She is thrawn, that's all – twisted, I suppose you might say in England"' (p. 93). The choice of adjective recalls Stevenson's story 'Thrawn Janet', but the story is one of wholly human suffering. There is nothing supernatural here as there is in 'Annie Cargill', Jacob's ghostly tale about a gypsy girl abandoned by a member of the ruling classes.

Outsiders and rebels are not her only subject: in her subtle novella, 'The Lum Hat',[30] Jacob focuses on a conventional character, Christina Mills, a smalltown bank manager's daughter, who gains her idea of love from 'the decorous books of her day' (p. 8). Her marriage to a worldly sea captain shocks her, and she leaves him; on his death she again refuses the wider experience offered by marriage with the suggestively named Aeneas. The story is finely tuned and symbolically suggestive, even if Jacob's own more natural sympathies lie with those who have an appetite for life, or who defy their community: like Willa Muir, in her later novel *Imagined Corners*, set in a fictional version of Montrose, Jacob is especially interested in those who leave, and return as outsiders. The young man in 'The Figurehead', for instance, Tom Falconer, has been to sea, and, back on land, cannot finally settle with a rather limited young woman who does not share his vision, represented by the ship's figurehead.

There is a more extended exploration of the insider-outsider experience in *The Interloper* (1904). The novel's central character, Gilbert Speid, has grown up in Spain, but returns to Scotland, the land of his parents, when he inherits the estate of Whanland. The effects of his arrival on the small town of Kaims (Montrose, again), are examined, along with the discoveries he makes about his own identity, provoked by a miniature painting of his dead mother, who turns out to have been another transgressive woman.

The Interloper, like Jacob's first novel, again illustrates Jacob's interest in characters of different social backgrounds, and relationships that cross class boundaries. There is an especially memorable and sympathetically drawn upper-class figure in Lady Eliza, a spirited, but unfulfilled older woman whose personal suffering is quite movingly evoked,[31] although her faults are also made plain. The rural and small town 'vernacular' speakers are vividly characterised, too, notably Granny Stirk, 'The Queen of the Cadgers' who makes a heroic horseride across country to save the day for the star-crossed lovers, Gilbert and Cecilia. There are many fine examples of vernacular dialogue here and throughout Jacob's short fiction and novels.

Although she herself came of an aristocratic, landowning family, whose history she recorded in *The Lairds of Dun* (1931), in childhood Jacob played among the ploughmen on the estate farm, and drew on the social and literary resources of different worlds, a crossing of class and cultural borders not unprecedented in Scotland. In her use of Scots, and of the song and ballad traditions, Jacob, as various critics have observed, is in a long and honourable line of women poets and songwriters. The anonymous ballads (many of them, as Catherine Kerrigan has suggested, probably created by women in the oral tradition) fed into the work of the aristocratic women of the eighteenth and nineteenth centuries, such as Carolina Oliphant, Lady Nairne, who may be seen as Jacob's poetic forebears.[32]

Her own poetry draws strongly on the oral and folk traditions, her language reflecting the continued strength of local dialect in north-east Scotland, a region rich in folk song and balladry. Jacob's titles often suggest the importance of a place and its language and culture, (*Songs of Angus, More Songs of Angus*), and she uses Angus Scots in almost all her best poetry. Colin Milton argues that Jacob and the other north-east poets should not be judged by criteria established by MacDiarmid for instance, appropriate to modernist poetry, but should be placed in the context of an older tradition, with which Jacob worked in a freshly self-conscious way.[33] Milton points out that Jacob, along with Mary Symon, Charles Murray and Marion Angus, born in the 1860s, worked at a time when vernacular culture was still strong but a growing anglicisation was reaching north-east Scotland because of developments in education. Thus these poets were creating along a linguistic borderline.

Jacob's poetry is frequently in the first person, adopting the vernacular voices mainly of farming folk and vagrants, both male and female, who are economically characterised. One poem is much-anthologised, 'Tam i' the Kirk', in the voice of a male speaker, a love-poem in which Dorothy Porter notes fascinating echoes of *Jane Eyre*.[34] But Jacob is not a one-poem poet. As Kerrigan points out, 'From Browning onwards, the use of a persona has been a major device of modern poetry, and Violet Jacob in using this device was clearly effecting a new synthesis of old and new'.[35] Although some of her adopted voices are more convincing than others, Jacob's use of masks allows exploration of a range of experiences and emotions.

Some of her speakers are wandering outsider figures such as recur in her fiction, permitting the expression of radical sentiments not, perhaps, expected of a woman of her class and time. The poem 'The Gangrel' has a fine rousing opening:

It's ye maun whustle for a breeze
Until the sails be fu';
They bigg yon ships that ride the seas
To pleasure fowk like you.

For ye hae siller i' yer hand
And a' that gowd can buy,
But weary, in a weary land,
A gangrel-loon am I.[36]

The speaker in 'The Poacher to Orion' similarly has an egalitarian sense, addressing the hunter in the sky as an equal:

November-month is wearin' by,
The leaves is nearly doon;
I watch ye stride alang the sky
O' nichts, my beltit loon.

(p. 32)

The use of the singular verb with the plural noun in the second line ('The leaves is . . .') shows Jacob's care in rendering the oral usage of her region. In a poem like 'The Tramp to the Tattie-Dulie' the vernacular, appropriately, becomes particularly dense and vigorous.

There are some spirited and tough female voices, as in 'A Change o' Deils' and 'The Helpmate', and several poems sympathetically explore women's experience. 'The Jaud' is in the form of a dialogue between two speakers, one of them a respectable 'auld wife' who betrays her envy of the beautiful dead 'jade', and

'the warld she had that was no for me
And the kingdom that ne'er was mine!'

(p. 67)

Jacob implicitly questions society's view of the woman who transgresses, yet also implies sympathy for the woman who has never known excitement, or, perhaps, sexual pleasure. Another poem, 'The End o't' gives voice to a young pregnant woman anxiously mourning her fate, and makes interesting use of the thistle as a metaphor:

There's a fine braw thistle that lifts its croon
By the river-bank whaur the ashes stand
An' the swirl o' water comes whisp'rin' doon
Past birk an' bramble an' grazin' land.
But simmer's flittit an' time's no heedin'
A feckless lass nor a pridefu' flow'r;
The dark to hide me's the grace I'm needin'.
An' the thistle's seedin',
An' my day's owre.

Many of Jacob's poems, in the folk tradition, are songlike, and some, including 'The Wild Geese', have been put to music in modern times.[37] Others, such as the cradle song, 'The

Tinkler's Baloo', might be compared with the 'bairn sangs' of William Soutar. Jacob wrote both poems and stories explicitly for children, yet could also produce a fine drinking-song, 'Faur ye weel'.

Jacob's poetry, following the ballad and the folk tradition generally, often evokes the supernatural, the other world that lies beyond the borders of our own, what, in 'The Neebor' the speaker calls the 'dairk side o' the windy-pane' (p. 26). Born in the Victorian age, and like many others acutely aware of death and suffering through her own experience, Jacob explores what her compatriot Margaret Oliphant calls 'the seen and the unseen'.[38] This sense of the liminal is present in poems such as 'The Rowan' and 'The Brig', the latter drawing on the motif of the 'bridge of dread'. In others, like 'The Cross Roads', there is an effective use of dialogue, drawn from the ballad tradition, and perhaps most touching and chilling when it is between child and adult, as in two fine poems, 'The Northern Lichts' and 'The Baltic'.

Certainly, Jacob is not always 'safe' in her concerns. Many of her poems were popular because they appealed to love of country at the time of the First World War; but some deal with the war itself, and although mixed in quality, a few, written after the death of her only son, Harry, at the Battle of the Somme in 1918, including 'The Field i' the Lirk o' the Hill', and the English poem, 'Prison',[39] movingly express a dry, controlled grief. Jacob's English poetry is generally ignored, but a few interesting, almost Pre-Raphaelite pieces, such as 'The Scarlet Lilies',[40] evoke passion and sexuality.

Many of Jacob's vernacular poems may be judged as sentimental or 'couthy'; the best, however, can be very affecting. In 'The Water Hen' a male speaker is haunted by the voice of a bird bidding him keep faith with the lover from whom he has separated in anger. The wind assures him as he leaves, 'there's mony a load on shore that may be skailed at sea' (p. 39), but the end poignantly hints at regrets for love denied and lost through silence. This deceptively simple poem gains power from its unobtrusive 'echo' effects, created through repetition with variation in the structure, and subtle use of alliteration and assonance.

It is true that much of Jacob's work creates an atmosphere of melancholy and longing, which, 'like all the poetry of exiles', says John Buchan, 'finds comfort in the memory of old unhappy things'.[41] But some poems, notably 'Craigo Woods', arguably go beyond mere nostalgia, to explore memory and loss:

> Craigo Woods, wi' the splash o' the cauld rain beatin'
>   I' the back end o' the year,
> When the clouds hang laigh wi' the weicht o' their load
>   o' greetin'
>   And the autumn wind's asteer;
> Ye may stand like ghaists, ye may fa' i' the blast that's
>   cleft ye
>   To rot i' the chilly dew,
> But when will I mind on aucht since the day I left ye
>   Like I mind on you – on you?

This carefully crafted poem exploits the onomatopoeic resources of Scots, using 'plangent repetitions'[42] and syntax to create a heavy, brooding atmosphere ('laigh wi' the weicht o' their load o' greetin'"); there are some vivid images, too, like that of the 'braw reid puddock stules . . . like jewels' in the second stanza.

In her poetry, Jacob was operating along the borders of tradition, looking both to local dialect and folk traditions, and also to written literary traditions. Robert Crawford comments that the poems in Liz Lochhead's volume *Dreaming Frankenstein* 'are constantly animated by their situation in a 'debatable land' between speech and writing, so that they partake of energies that come from both'.[43] In this respect Jacob's poetry also inhabits such a space.

Jacob's most substantial achievement, however, is almost certainly *Flemington*, a complex and powerful novel first published in 1911. Drawing on the fictional tradition of Scott, it is set in Scotland around the time of the 1745 Jacobite rebellion, and the battle of Culloden in 1746, and is named after Archie Flemington, its central character, a young artist born in France to Jacobite parents. His French mother and Scottish father are remembered only as 'vague people who were ceaselessly playing cards';[44] orphaned in childhood, as a young man Archie is still in the powerful grip of his grandmother, Christian Flemington, an embittered Jacobite turned Whig. His occupation as a portrait painter provides cover for work as a government agent; but when Archie comes to spy on the Jacobite Logie brothers, David, a judge, and his younger brother, James, at their home, Balnillo, he finds himself torn by divided loyalties.

Flemington is tightly written, with a strong narrative drive lightened by flashes of wit and humour; and, like Stevenson (another influence), Jacob is good at involving the reader sensuously in the world she creates. The vividly created setting is mainly Angus, in and around Montrose; this really is Jacob's 'Own Country' (the mansion of Balnillo is modelled on her own family house at Dun), and it is used to powerful symbolic effect. From early on, trouble is foreshadowed in a dialogue between the Logie brothers, who are to be so important in Archie's life:

> 'The bar is very loud tonight, Jamie,' said Lord Balnillo. 'I doubt but there's bad weather coming, and I am loth to lose more trees.'
> 'I see that the old beech by the stables wants a limb,' observed the other.
> 'That's the only change about the place that I notice.'
> 'There'll be more yet,' said the judge. (p. 13)

And indeed much change – and damage – lie ahead. At the end, the image of the mutilated tree reappears, this time outside a house in Holland. The bar separating the harbour from the open sea, as in Tennyson's poem, 'Crossing the Bar' (1889), is evoked again in the novel, too, where sea metaphors recur, generally to disturbing effect.

Much of the action of *Flemington* takes place in a dark, troubled landscape, and there is no glorification of the conflicts shown; Jacob shows above all the bitterness of war, and the complicated interrelationship of public and private life. Even for James Logie, an 'honourable soldier' (p. 59), war is not just about high ideals, but is a means of escaping personal pain: '"I have turned to it for consolation as a man may turn to his religion,"' he says (p. 62), and, on losing his wife, Diane, '"Fighting was all I wanted . . . I did not want to be killed, but to kill"' (p. 67). Diane's death, significantly, is caused by the violent intervention of her father, '"a rich man – a hard, old, pinched Frenchman"' (p. 64), who cannot accept Logie because he is poor and Protestant. Love, it is implied, crosses the boundaries of religion, nationality and economic status; the destructive forces are intolerance, rigidity, a greedy desire to control.

The novel's frame of reference is wider than just Scotland itself, and while there *is* a concern with Scottish identity, there is no simple celebration of national pride. The spirit of the 'folk' is embodied ambiguously in the figure of the beggar, Skirling Wattie, who has a sweet singing voice but is cunning and self-seeking; and the community is shown as narrow and suspicious in its attitudes to 'foreigners' (significant given that Archie is half-French). A key scene takes place in an inn doubling as a brothel, called 'The Happy Land', and the ironic resonances are clear. This is a '"tormented country"' (p. 59); after Culloden 'The country smelt of blood; reeked of it' (p. 171). Those who survive, like David, the Jacobite judge, do so by means of compromise and expediency. Power is in the hands of the incoming 'Butcher' Cumberland, who shows little humanity either to Scotland or to to Archie. *Flemington* can be seen as a form of the adventure romance; but it is a complex reworking of a form sometimes used to express an imperialistic vision.[45]

The adventure is also a form mainly developed by male writers; following in this tradition, *Flemington* depicts public conflict, explores the bonds chiefly between men, and matters of male honour, and has few female characters. For these reasons John Buchan saw it as a 'masculine book'.[46] It is terse and understated (qualities which were considered 'masculine' at the time).[47] Yet again, this novel reinterprets a genre. When Madam Flemington leaves her interview with Cumberland, his last remark is telling: '"Damn me, but I hate old women! they should have their tongues cut out"' (p. 225). If some male-authored romances of the time were 'deeply misogynistic', as Lyn Pykett suggests (p. 67), Jacob seems here to offer a critical rejoinder. Reading the novel very differently from Buchan, Joy Hendry describes *Flemington* as offering a 'very female vision'.[48]

When the novel is placed against the background of the 'crisis of gender definition' manifest by the 1890s,[49] an implicit concern with gender roles and their boundaries can be detected. It is interesting that Archie has 'the refinement of a woman' (p. 37), for instance. There is also a strong mutual attraction between Archie and James, echoed in that between Archie and Captain Callander; as events unfold, Archie, thinking of James, feels 'regret for the friend who might have been his, who, in his secret heart, would be his always' (p. 72). There may be homoerotic undercurrents here; Caroline Bingham remarks the 'ambiguous attraction, justified in the text by Flemington's resemblance to Logie's dead wife, a literary convention of the period which permitted an attraction between two men to be mentioned'.[50]

Certainly, the relationship between Archie and James Logie gives the novel much of its emotional power. In one scene, Archie finds himself listening to the other man's tragic history, and sees with horror that:

> The power in his face seemed to have given way, revealing for a moment, a defencelessness like the defencelessness of a child looking upon the dark; and it told Archie that there was something that even Logie dreaded and that that something was memory.
>
> The deep places he had guessed in James's soul were deep indeed, and again Flemington was struck with humility, for his own unimportance in contrast with this experienced man seemed little less than pitiful. The feeling closed his lips, and he looked round at the shortening shadows and into the stir of coming sunlight as a man looks round for a door through which to escape from impending stress. (p. 62)

The moral dilemmas involved, and the emotional conflicts evoked, in this novel that explores debatable lands of several kinds, are extremely moving.

Neither side in the political conflict is portrayed as straightforwardly 'right'. Each of the major characters is compassionately presented, for all their manifest faults, and the novel's narrative strategies invite the reader to sympathise with those of both Whig and Jacobite persuasion. James Logie is bigoted, yet generous; Christian Flemington is inflexible and snobbish, yet also a strong, charismatic woman. Archie Flemington himself is on the traditionally unpopular side as a Whig and a spy, but is a sympathetic figure whose perspective the reader often shares; the psychology of his relationship with the manipulative Christian Flemington is subtly presented. No simple estimations emerge: *Flemington* explores borders not only physical and metaphorical, but moral, the borderlands of judgement.

Flemington offers a tragic, in some ways very modern, vision; the novel is full of random happenings and the workings of fickle 'Chance', suggested by the card-playing and the symbolic, ironic Ace on which Archie sketches during his captivity. The innocent suffer, and justice is not seen to be done. Archie reflects on 'the ironic futility of things in general' (p. 62), and the events of the novel essentially bear out this view, although there are lighter moments, in the portrayal of the splendidly vain David Logie, or when Christian Flemington meets Skirling Wattie, the beggar who has lost both his legs and is pulled around the Angus countryside on a cart by a team of dogs:

> 'You are one of the few persons in these parts who can afford to keep a coach,' she remarked.
>   A broad smile overspread his ribald countenance, like the sun irradiating a public house.
>   'Dod, ma leddy, a'd think shame to visit ye on fut,' said he, with a wag of his head.
>   'You have better reasons than that,' she replied rather grimly.
>   'Aye, aye, they're baith awa',' said he, looking at the place where his legs should have been. 'A'm an ill sicht for the sutors!' [shoemakers] (p. 145)

These two characters here show a respect for 'difference', but such moments are fleeting. Human beings 'only connect'[51] briefly, and then again communication breaks down. Jacob's work, however, expresses great humanity, inviting understanding and sympathy for the fallibility of characters stumbling along moral borderlines through a dark, often bewildering, unpredictable world.

Violet Jacob was herself a traveller in many lands, real and fictional, yet she still has not found a secure place on the literary maps, perhaps because of some of the very qualities which make her work potentially alive for us today. Much of her work deals with areas and subjects far from the centres of power; she examines lives 'out on the borderlands, . . . lives for which the central interpretive devices of culture don't quite work',[52] and her chosen genres are of debatable status: historical fiction, romances, diaries and letters, short stories, poems in Scots. The recovery or reassessment of writers like Jacob may require an adjustment of critical boundaries, a recognition of the wider issues at stake: questions of national identity, class, and gender, for instance. Edward Said has written: 'Criticism cannot assume that its province is merely the text, not even the great literary text. It must see itself, with other discourses, inhabiting a much contested cultural space'.[53] There is still, in Scotland, as elsewhere, a need for critics to enter the debatable land.[54]

Notes

1. Hugh MacDiarmid, for example, published some of her poems in *Northern Numbers*, and commented on her work in *Scottish Educational Journal*, 17 July 1925. Edinburgh University awarded her an honorary degree in 1936.
2. *The History of Aythan Waring* (William Heinemann, London, 1908), p. 97.
3. A reference to the title of Jacob's short story collection *Tales of My Own Country* (John Murray, London, 1922).

4.   Linda Hutcheon, *A Poetics of Postmodernism* (Routledge, London, 1988), p. 58.
5.   Elaine Showalter, *Sexual Anarchy: Gender and Culture at the Fin de Siècle* (first published, Viking, New York, 1991; references here to the Virago edition of 1992), p. 4.
6.   See Maggie Humm, *Border Traffic: Strategies of Contemporary Women Writers* (Manchester University Press, Manchester, 1991), p. 9.
7.   *Diaries and Letters from India 1895–1900*, ed. Carol Anderson (Canongate, Edinburgh, 1990); see p. 134, p. 159. Further page references are given after quotations in the text.
8.   Linda Anderson, 'At the Threshold of Self: women and autobiography', in *Women's Writing: A Challenge to Theory*, ed. Moira Menteith (Harvester, Brighton, 1987), pp. 54–71 (p. 60).
9.   Sara Mills, *Discourses of Difference: An Analysis of Women's Travel Writing and Colonialism* (Routledge, London, 1991), p. 61. Further references are given after quotations in the text.
10.   The title of Emily Eden's record of her time in India, first published in 1866.
11.   Stevenson, *In the South Seas: The Marquesas, Paumotus and Gilbert Islands* (first published 1900; see *Island Landfalls*, ed. Jenni Calder, Canongate, Edinburgh, 1987, pp. 34–8).
12.   Mills, *Discourses of Differences*, p. 106.
13.   Some useful insights into the 'New Woman' can be found in *The New Woman*, ed. Juliet Gardiner (Collins & Brown, London, 1993).
14.   In a review of the *Diaries and Letters* in *The Sunday Times*, 15 July 1990.
15.   Sandra Gilbert and Susan Gubar, *No Man's Land: The Place of the Woman Writer in the Twentieth Century*, vol. 2 (Yale University Press, New Haven and London, 1989), p. 66.
16.   Mills, p. 81.
17.   For instance, Joy Hendry comments on this in 'Twentieth Century Women's Writing', in *The History of Scottish Literature*, vol. 4, Twentieth Century, ed. Cairns Craig, (Aberdeen University Press, Aberdeen, 1987), p. 294.
18.   Susan Tweedsmuir, *The Lilac and the Rose* (Duckworth, London, 1952), p. 34.
19.   *The Sheepstealers*, (William Heinemann, London, 1902), p. 5. Further references are given after quotations in the text.
20.   For instance, in a review in *The Spectator*, 13 September 1902, p. 368.
21.   Raymond Williams, *The Country and the City* (first published The Hogarth Press, London, 1973; references here to the Paladin edition of 1975), p. 239.
22.   For example, *Irresolute Catherine* (John Murray, London, 1908), *The History of Aythan Waring*, (William Heinemann, London, 1908) and some stories.
23.   *Tales of My Own Country*, p. 50. Further references are given after quotations in the text.
24.   Trevor Royle in *The Mainstream Companion to Scottish Literature* (Mainstream, Edinburgh and London, 1993), p. 158, refers to the 'rural sentimentality' of Jacob's short fiction.
25.   For example by a sympathetic French reviewer in *Journal de Seciève*, 26 March 1923 (included among papers in National Library of Scotland Acc. 6686).
26.   In 'The Manse', collected in *Memories and Portraits*, 1887. See Robert Louis Stevenson, *The Scottish Stories and Essays*, ed. Kenneth Gelder (Edinburgh University Press, Edinburgh, 1989), p. 253.
27.   See Elaine Showalter, 'Feminist Criticism in the Wilderness', in *The New Feminist Criticism: Essays on Women, Literature and Theory* (Virago, London, New York, 1985), ed. Elaine Showalter, pp. 262–3 (essay also reprinted elsewhere), on the wild zone as 'female space'.
28.   In his introduction to *The Oxford Book of Scottish Short Stories* (Oxford University Press, Oxford, 1995), xix.
29.   First published in *The Scots Magazine*, January 1933, pp. 248–56, and reproduced many times since.
30.   First published in *The Lum Hat and other stories: Last Tales of Violet Jacob*, ed. Ronald Garden (Aberdeen University Press, Aberdeen, 1982).
31.   See *The Interloper* (William Heinemann, London, 1904), pp. 42–3.
32.   See the introduction to *An Anthology of Scottish Women Poets*, ed. Catherine Kerrigan (Edinburgh University Press, Edinburgh, 1991), pp. 8–9.
33.   In *The Literature of the North*, ed. David Hewitt and Michael Spiller (Aberdeen, 1983), p. 82. Further references are given after quotations in the text. See also Colin Milton, 'Modern Poetry in Scots Before MacDiarmid', in Cairns Craig (ed.), *The History of Scottish Literature*, vol. 4 (Aberdeen University Press, Aberdeen, 1987), pp. 11–36 (pp. 32–3).

34.   Dorothy Porter [McMillan], 'Scotland's Songstresses', *Cencrastus* (Spring 1987), 48–52 (p. 49).

35.   Kerrigan, p. 9.

36.   *The Scottish Poems of Violet Jacob* (Oliver & Boyd, Edinburgh and London, 1944), p. 22. Further references, given after quotations in the text, are to this edition. The poems were previously published in various volumes of poetry.

37.   For instance, by Jim Reed in *I saw the Wild Geese Flee* (Springthyme Records, 1984).

38.   Some of Oliphant's short fiction was published in *Tales of the Seen and the Unseen* (Edinburgh and London, 1902).

39.   In *More Songs of Angus and Others* (Country Life, George Newnes, London, 1918), p. 41.

40.   In *More Songs of Angus and Others*, pp. 48–50.

41.   In the introduction to *Songs of Angus* (John Murray, London, 1915), ix.

42.   Janet Caird, 'The Poetry of Violet Jacob and Helen Cruickshank', *Cencrastus* (Winter 1984), 32–4 (p. 32).

43.   'The Two-faced Language of Lochhead's Poetry', in *Liz Lochhead's Voices*, ed. Robert Crawford and Anne Varty (Edinburgh University Press, Edinburgh, 1993), p. 67.

44.   *Flemington*, ed. Carol Anderson (Association for Scottish Literary Studies, Aberdeen, 1994), p. 59. Further references, to this edition, are given after quotations in the text.

45.   See Peter Keating, *The Haunted Study: A Social History of the English Novel 1875–1914* (Secker & Warburg, London, 1989); reference here to the Fontana edition of 1991, pp. 354–6.

46.   In a letter, 31 December 1911, National Library of Scotland Acc. 6686.

47.   See, for instance, Lyn Pykett, *Engendering Fictions: The English Novel in the Early Twentieth Century* (Edward Arnold, London and New York, 1995), pp. 64–6. Further references are given after quotations in the text.

48.   Hendry, 'Twentieth Century Women's Writing', p. 294.

49.   Pykett, *Engendering Fictions*, p. 16.

50.   In a review of *Flemington*, *Times Literary Supplement*, December 9, 1994, p. 22.

51.   The reference here is to E. M. Forster's phrase in *Howard's End* (1910).

52.   Caroline Steedman, *Landscape for a Good Woman: A Story of Two Lives* (London, 1986), p. 5. quoted by Pam Morris, *Literature and Feminism*, (Oxford, 1993), p. 166. Steedman is referring to working-class lives, but there is still a point to be made here.

53.   Edward Said, *The World, the Text, and the Critic* (Harvard University Press, Cambridge, Mass., 1983), p. 225, quoted by Linda Hutcheon, *A Poetics of Postmodernism*, p. 69.

54.   See general bibliography for primary texts. An early work is *The Baillie MacPhee* (a poem), by Walter Douglas Campbell and Violet Kennedy-Erskine, with illustrations by Violet Kennedy-Erskine (William Blackwood, Edinburgh and London, 1888). Modern reprints of 'Thievie' and 'The Debateable Land', both stories from *Tales of My Own Country*, are in, respectively, *The Other Voice: Scottish Women's Writing Since 1808*, ed. Moira Burgess (Polygon, Edinburgh, 1987), pp. 123–39, and *The Oxford Book of Scottish Short Stories*, ed. Douglas Dunn (Oxford University Press, Oxford, 1995), pp. 152–60.

Suggested Further Reading: In addition to the works already cited in the notes the following contain useful material: Carol Anderson, 'Debateable Land: The Prose Work of Violet Jacob', in Caroline Gonda (ed.), *Tea and Leg Irons: New Feminist Readings from Scotland* (Open Letters, London, 1992), pp. 31–44; Carol Anderson, '*Flemington* and its portraits', *ScotLit* 11 (Autumn 1994), 1–2; Sarah Bing, 'Autobiography in the Work of Violet Jacob', *Chapman* 74–5 (Autumn/Winter 1993): *The Women's Forum*, 98–109; Ronald Garden, 'Violet Jacob in India', *Scottish Literary Journal* 13, no. 2 (November 1986), 48–64; Douglas Gifford, 'Myth, Parody and Dissociation: Scottish Fiction 1814–1914', in *The History of Scottish Literature*, vol. 3, ed. Douglas Gifford (Aberdeen University Press, Aberdeen, 1988), pp. 217–59 (pp. 242–3); Marion Lochhead 'Feminine Quartet', *Chapman* 27–8: *Woven by Women*, vol. 6, no. 3–4 (Summer 1980), pp. 21–31; Isobel Murray, 'The Forgotten Violet Jacob', in *Cencrastus* 19 (1983), p. 54 (a review of *The Lum Hat and Other Stories*). This chapter is a greatly extended and reworked version of a paper originally given at the 1993 MLA Conference in Toronto.

24

Fictions of Development 1920–1970

Margery Palmer McCulloch

This chapter takes its impulse from what Germaine Greer has termed 'the phenomenon of the transience of female literary fame'.[1] Its aim is twofold: to make a start on the reclamation and re-presentation of women novelists writing in Scotland between 1920 and 1970, and in particular those of the inter-war period, and to demonstrate how these writers explored female experience, becoming makers of their own images in ways which frequently ran counter to the often stereotypical depiction of women and their roles in the Scottish male-authored fiction of the times. In the 1920s and '30s these women wrote alongside but outwith the predominantly male Scottish Renaissance movement, in a way which reflected the marginalisation of women in a society still strongly patriarchal, notwithstanding the recognition given to their war work and the expansion of the franchise to include women in 1918 and 1928. Nevertheless, despite the dominant ideology of the times, the optimism about prospects for change and advancement in the inter-war period is reflected in the significant amount of writing by women in the 1920s and '30s and by the feminist nature of much of this work. The new Scottish women writers honestly depict the subordinate roles allotted to women in personal and social life. But not content merely to mirror the status quo, they also challenge this situation, either explicitly or obliquely, and chart the attempts of their female protagonists to lead a different, personally determined life, often in the face of family or social disapproval.

Inevitably the choice of authors and texts for discussion has involved a degree of personal choice. The period span is a wide one and I am aware that there may be writers of interest whom I have overlooked or individual works which may deserve more attention than they receive here. I have selected texts which seem to me to offer an ideological awareness of the situation of women in their time together with a satisfying fictional form. Mary Cleland's *The Sure Traveller* and Dot Allan's *Makeshift* are therefore featured as opposed to less challenging novels by O. Douglas; and the fiction of Nancy Brysson Morrison rather than what seem to me the more theatrically conceived novels of her sister Peggy, who wrote under the name of March Cost.[2] I have divided the chapter into two sections: 1920 to 1939, its central focus, followed by a more general account of the post-Second World War period. With the exception of Naomi Mitchison's *The Bull Calves*,[3] historical fiction has been left to the chapter on that topic. On the other hand, some writers whose work has been allocated an individual chapter will be represented here also because of their contribution to fictions of development.

Although neglected for many years, Catherine Carswell is now one of the most appreciated of these early twentieth-century writers and her two novels *Open the Door!* (1920) and *The Camomile* (1922) are among the first to challenge stereotypes of women's experience.[4] What gives Carswell's first novel its extraordinary vitality is the fluidity of her narrative form and her sharp eye for the ironic comedy of social pretensions and psychological delusion. Fresh, too, in the Scottish context, is the way in which women are the true subjects of her novels, as opposed to being seen from outside. *Open the Door!*, for example, is iconoclastic in the way female sexuality is foregrounded in the narrative. Its heroine grows to womanhood in the early years of the new century before the outbreak of the First World War, a time when the Victorian oppositions of Madonna and Magdalen still prevailed and women were conventionally expected to fulfil the roles of wives and mothers without acknowledging sexual awakening. Juley, Joanna's mother, is one such woman: 'With her husband she had a measure of happiness. To the end she idealised him; to the end hid her hunger under self-censure . . . When she felt the stirrings of passion in herself she was dimly ashamed'. (p. 15) Joanna is different, although she shares her mother's capacity for self-sacrifice. From her childhood years we are made aware of her sexuality, felt but not understood in her idealisation of her older cousin Gerald, coming to awareness in her first love affair with the conventional Bob, and first given expression in her short-lived marriage to the Italian Mario:

> Now she thought of the coming night with awakening senses . . . But was it right: Did all wives feel and behave like this? She thought of her mother, of Mrs Boyd, of Aunt Georgina, of the teaching and traditions in which she had been nourished. Which was right – these traditions or this abandonment? (p. 109)

On the other hand, it could be argued that the feminist challenge of *Open the Door!* is limited to this depiction of female sexuality and that in many respects the novel conforms to Toril Moi's definition of a socially constructed 'feminine' work.[5] Joanna may rebel against the restrictive mores of her Scottish Presbyterian upbringing, but her flight is principally a sexual one. She enters the world of work as an artist, but in keeping with the conventions of the time in relation to women and the arts, she becomes a sketcher of fashion designs, not a painter like her lover. Here Carswell does not challenge the convention of women being directed into what were considered the minor arts, but endorses it through her depiction of Joanna. In addition, although both author and heroine lived through the period of the struggle for women's enfranchisement, the discourse does not include the question of women's rights; and while Joanna's insistence that her mother's identity should not be distorted after death by the disguising of her lack of achievements – 'For failure might be one's word' (p. 337) – this insight is not accompanied by any recognition that her 'failure' might not have been personal and essential, but one brought about by constricting social mores and the lack of opportunity for self-determining experience. Whether or not the ending of this novel is distorted by its autobiographical nature, one notices that its heroine consistently defines herself in relation to her male lovers, thus throwing doubt upon the degree of liberation afforded by sexual freedom. The world of work becomes less and less substantiated as the setting moves to London and the denouement predicts a marriage ending which was the staple of romantic fiction. Splendid novel though it is, *Open the Door!* is ideologically ambivalent so far as a wider concept of women's emancipation is concerned.

This is not the case with Carswell's *The Camomile* or with Willa Muir's *Imagined Corners* (1931),[6] both among the strongest of these inter-war novels. Despite a limiting epistolary form, in which Ellen is the sole correspondent, *The Camomile* ranges widely in its depiction of female ambitions and criticism of social conventions. The formative relationship for the heroine, Ellen, is still with a man, Don John, but here the relationship and growing experience are intellectual as opposed to sexual. It is Don John who gives Ellen the courage to pursue her writing ambitions, an activity frowned upon by her family and associated with the failure and mental instability of her dead mother, and it is the realisation that her self-image is intrinsically bound up with her commitment to writing which leads her in the end to break off her engagement with Duncan, a doctor in the Indian Colonial Service, and to leave Scotland for London where she and a female friend will together pursue their individual careers. The theme of sexual exploration recurs here: in the healthy acceptance of her sexual feelings by Ellen in contrast to the convention-bound attitudes of her fiancé; and in both the criticism of the trivial social formalities surrounding marriage and the lack of honesty in relationships. Carswell's representation of Duncan and his Anglo-Indian colleagues anticipates Forster's satirical portraits in *A Passage to India* (1924), while it gives the first of several depictions in these early novels of the hostility and patronising attitude directed towards women who attempt seriously to make a career as writers. Warning Ellen not to 'speak of anything abstract or "superior", or of "high-brow works of art"' in case she is regarded as 'a bore and a blue-stocking', Duncan continues: 'Life . . . is a bigger affair than books, and life is pre-eminently your business. Wait till your hands are full of life, and I doubt if you will have the time or the wish to add to the mass of feminine writings already in the world' (pp. 236, 250) – exactly the same attitude as that of the hostile fiancé in Dot Allan's *Makeshift* and one in part responsible for the literary 'silences' which have made this historical study necessary.

Willa Muir's *Imagined Corners* is similarly critical of the limited roles allotted to women in Scottish society. While Carswell's handling of narrative form and characterisation are perhaps her outstanding qualities as novelist, Willa Muir's novel impresses by the intellectual variety of its discourses and by her sure grasp of the conventions and restrictions of Scottish smalltown life. In Elizabeth Shand she creates a credible portrait of a young, university-educated woman experiencing her first passionate love affair and finding that her true intellectual and emotional awakening begins only after marriage and her realisation of the extent to which she has subordinated her intellectuality and sense of self to the role of dutiful wife demanded by society. While Muir's ironic narrative and dialogue catch the meanness and petty rivalries of the women of Calderwick, she communicates also the sterility of lives which are allowed no useful, independent public role, but have to play the parts allocated by social and religious convention. Her depiction of the tortured but ineffectual minister and his family is an acute post-Freudian representation of different kinds of psychological breakdown. Her variation of the notion of the *doppelgänger* in the complementary characterisation of Elizabeth Shand and her older sister-in-law Lizzie, now returned as the sophisticated Frau Elise Mütze, enables her to explore the processes of self-discovery and self-determination in her female characters, at the same time offering external perspectives on Scottish society. One can only regret that in her own life Muir subordinated her considerable talents and ambitions to the development of her husband's career as poet. Her second and only other published novel, *Mrs Ritchie* (1933), develops the sketches of personal frustration among the minor female characters of *Imagined Corners* in its portrayal of the tragedy of a woman denied the education and self-determination her nature and intellectual abilities demand.

Although both have a limited fictional output, Carswell and Muir are outstanding figures in early twentieth-century women's writing. The themes which preoccupied them in relation to women's lives, however, recur in several neglected novels of the period which deserve to be better known. *The Sure Traveller* (1923) by Mary Cleland (Margot Wells) – the frequent use of a pseudonym by women writers seems to substantiate the hostility shown in their fiction towards the professional female writer – and Dot Allan's *Makeshift* (1928), are both good 'Glasgow novels' as well as challenging representations of women's experience. Cleland's heroine Catherine anticipates Virginia Woolf's 1929 protest in *A Room of One's Own* when she strikes the keynote in the early chapters of *The Sure Traveller*: 'I know how it hurts to be baulked and thrust for life into a mould that isn't yours. A girl can't break away unless she has money of her own or training; and I have neither' (p. 11).[7] Middle-class Catherine has arrived home in Glasgow in December 1889 from her boarding school in the south where she has been encouraged by her headmistress to entertain ambitions of entering Girton. Like Muir's Frau Elise Mütze, she finds that while returning to her native environment may demonstrate how much she herself has changed, life in Glasgow, and in her family in particular, continues as before. Catherine's mother, sister in spirit to Jane Austen's Mrs Bennet, will have none of her daughter's ambitions and has exchanged Catherine's preferred 'room of her own', an ascetically furnished turret room, for a properly 'feminine' bedroom, romantically decorated by spinster aunt Beenie. For this socially-conscious and houseproud mother, Catherine's intellectual aspirations promise future spinsterhood: 'the men don't like college-bred women for wives, and if you got left, later on, you'd be blaming me in your heart' (p. 19): a view echoed by her aunts, her conventional brother and potential suitors among his friends. Only her withdrawn father seems to understand and sympathise with her ambitions, but he will not overrule his wife in this matter of a daughter's education. That the girls are their mother's affair, while the father pursues his ambitions through his sons, is a recurring motif in this and other novels of the time.

Catherine, however, is not depicted as a victim heroine, and although thwarted in her principal ambition, she pursues her rebel road, refusing to join her grandfather's church or teach in the Sunday School as has been the family custom and refusing also to conform to the social expectations of her mother and her friends with regard to making herself attractive and available for a proposal of marriage. She regains her tower room and there pursues her interest in poetry, while becoming involved outside her home with Glasgow's slum-dwellers. Having begun to learn Gaelic, her Highland father's first language, she visits his island home and the grandmother she has never met and there discovers the secret which has kept her father absent for so many years: his abandonment in youth of the girl who bore his child, in favour of a good Glasgow marriage with business prospects. In the end, Catherine herself proposes marriage to a childhood friend who has been forced by his father to take up a business career for which he is unsuited, and together they leave for the islands to regenerate land which has fallen into disuse and lead the kind of life her father had abandoned.

The Sure Traveller is one of two complementary books written by Mary Cleland in the early 1920s which share some characters and themes. The first of these, *The Two Windows* of 1922, is much less successful, and this is to a large extent the consequence of its predominantly working-class setting. However sympathetic one is to her attempts to show that beauty and innocence and intelligence can be found in such an environment, and in the children in particular, she herself did not have the insider's experience or technical capacity to carry this through successfully. *The Sure Traveller*, on the other hand, succeeds because it is written with sympathy and understanding within both class and gender categories, yet at the same time it extends these to show how class discrimination and unthinking adherence to restrictive social convention can warp the lives of all. Even Catherine's mother, who at the outset evokes little sympathy, is seen ultimately as a somewhat tragic figure, emotionally unfulfilled and wronged in the face of her husband's withdrawal and lack of genuine love for her.

In Dot Allan's *Makeshift*, it is the workworn mother who unwittingly inspires her young daughter with her lament of 'second best': 'That's what my life has been made up of, Jacqueline; makeshift all the time . . . I've missed it somehow, but there's more in life than that' (p. vii). As with Carswell's Ellen and to a lesser extent Cleland's Catherine, it is the determination to be a successful writer which helps this girl hold firm in the face of social pressures to conform to an acceptable female role: 'Words – words – words . . . she sat plying her pencil, creating for herself a new heaven and earth . . . a kingdom whose key none could wrest from her' (pp. 12–13).

Makeshift offers one of the most overt critiques among these novels of the limited opportunities afforded women in the early decades of the century. Unlike *The Sure Traveller*, its setting is not precisely dated but the frequent references to 'surplus women' and its heroine's employment as a typist – 'a cog in the wheel of commerce that whirs unceasingly from the granite steeps of Maryhill to the many-storied buildings that cluster round the Clyde' (p. 32) – suggest the post-1918 period. Alongside the depiction of its heroine's tenacity, this novel provides several sketches of maimed and maiming women: Jacqueline's mother and the undemonstrative, houseproud aunt with whom she lives after her mother's death; Miss Price, one of the elderly 'surplus women' typists, who lodges poorly in a bedsitting room; the middle-class mother of Jacqueline's explorer friend, Owen, who, he tells her, 'smothered me in devotion, shut me in on affectation of delicate health, from the world'. He reports his doctor's advice: '"Get out, my lad," he said. "Take the bit between your teeth and go . . . She's no more ill than you or I . . . Her only disease is selfishness, heart selfishness. And it's no life for you here if you're to remain whole."' (pp. 124–5). There is no understanding in this male response that the mother too may have been denied the ability to 'remain whole', that her 'selfishness' may be as a result of her own limited life opportunities and her fear of losing the only role open to her. The noted writer and womaniser, Torrance, who takes an interest in Jacqueline's literary ambitions – and also in her youthful attractiveness – is 'violently opposed to all forms of women's rights. The mind of woman was not that of a normal human being, he was wont to declare, but of one warped by reason of her sex'. (p. 56).

Here, and throughout many of these fictional scenarios, we have the representation of woman as what Simone de Beauvoir called 'the other',[8] marginalised in society, treated as something abnormal because she does not conform to male values, hunted for her sexual attractiveness but when caught confined within the conventions of marriage which allow her no independent role. 'Do you suppose women never get bitten with the desire for freedom?' Jacqueline asks Owen. 'I thought instinct bade the average woman walk softly, eschew danger,' is his reply, 'There's danger in breaking loose, you know' (p. 109). In Allan's scenario, however, marriage seems to present greater potential dangers for Jacqueline. Caught up in her emotional involvement with Owen, she puts aside her poetry as an immature activity while after his sudden death she becomes pressurised into an engagement with the ambitious and predatory son of a well-to-do neighbour. Like Duncan in Carswell's *The Camomile*, William sees no way forward for a wife with writing ambitions: 'What the blazes did the man mean jawing away about Jacqueline's poetry, puffing up the poor kid she could write?', is his response to a chance meeting between Jacqueline and her former mentor Torrance who reawakens her interest in her early ambitions. 'Didn't he realize she was going to be married – married? Wasn't that a sight more worth talking about than this "modern movement", this "rhythmic feeling", and all the rest?' (p. 215). The novel has an optimistic ending in that Torrance's visit brings Jacqueline's hesitations about her intended marriage into the open. An unexpected legacy from an old friend of her father arrives just at the right moment and the night before her wedding she boards the London train with her cheque and poetry file and her mother's words about 'makeshift' ringing in her ears, leaving behind wedding presents, new clothes and prospective bridegroom. Allan's novel is an important critique of women's experiences and ambitions in the 1920s as her *Hunger March* (1934) is of working-class deprivation in the Depression of the 1930s.

The settings of novels by Lorna Moon, Nan Shepherd and Nancy Brysson Morrison may be primarily rural as opposed to urban, but the same kinds of ambitions and restrictions in relation to women's lives are manifested. Like Nan Shepherd, Lorna Moon (Helen Wilson Nora Low) was born in Aberdeenshire. She left Scotland in adult life, however, becoming a successful Hollywood scriptwriter in the 1920s before dying of tuberculosis in 1930 at the age of forty-four. She wrote only two books of fiction: a collection of short stories *Doorways in Drumorty* (1926) and *Dark Star*, published a year before her death. Both books are marked by a lively use of Scots language and, like Willa Muir's *Imagined Corners*, a caustic, penetrating eye for the foibles of Scottish smalltown life. Just as Lewis Grassic Gibbon's treatment of the Mearns and its people outraged his family and society, Moon's characterisations of Strichen so outraged her family that her father rejected her first book as 'unacceptable'.[9]

Dark Star, with its fateful title, is less naturalistically conceived than the representations of Glasgow life by Carswell, Cleland and Allan. Divided into three parts, the novel's first section gives a vivid characterisation of the child Nancy, abandoned by her unmarried mother and brought up by a now ailing grandmother. As in her short stories, Moon's narrative method is close to caricature at times, with a fast pace and the creation of scenes which have all the colour and liveliness of a fairground. The fair is a recurring motif in the novel, for it is there that the child's earliest memories are centred and where her mother met the negro medicine man for whom she abandoned her daughter. The active characters are principally women, but the men, although apparently colourless and unassertive, hold the economic and therefore the ultimate power. As she notices how people's lives are ordered, Nancy's wish in childhood and adulthood is for her 'personal door' (pp. 36, 285) and the freedom which goes with it. Alongside Moon's imagistic and satiric characterisation, there is in her plotting a melodramatic element which at times heightens narrative tension, at others renders the happenings less credible. Next in importance to her wish for a 'personal door' – perhaps even taking precedence – is Nancy's overwhelming need to find out who her real father is: the son of the aristocratic Fassefern family for whom her mother worked, or the family's groom. Much of her childhood imaginative energy is taken up with this search for her father and when in adult life she is abandoned by the man she loves, she fulfils the dark legend of the fated Fasseferns by throwing herself into the sea from a high cliff, in the process identifying herself as one of them.

Despite such melodramatic moments, this is a fine book which tells with perception and humour of imagination and innocence, of commitment to ideals and the social conventions and personal ambition which can thwart and distort such ideals. In the end the sexual theme becomes a theme of betrayal and the opposition is once again that between the public world of the man and female creativity domesticated through childbearing. For the musician with whom Nancy falls in love, new experiences and new loves are necessary to his art. On the other hand, as far as women are concerned, in his view 'new life is their business' (p. 194). What predominates, however, is the novel's linguistic and imaginative vitality in its depiction of the girl's growth to maturity and the social context in which she lives her life.

Published one year before Moon's novel, Nan Shepherd's *The Quarry Wood* has a similarly idealistic and imaginative heroine and lively use of the Scots language.[10] Books and learning provide Martha's escape from the roughness of farming life and an argumentative mother who has no understanding of her daughter's ambitions. Yet the girl's love is for the countryside also, and the novel is a sensitive account of her attempts to balance the world of university and country home, her idealistic love of learning and her naivety and vulnerability in matters of sexual love and social relations. She is seen as an intellectual and therefore a pure, unsexual being by her friend's husband, Luke, who feels free to play with her feelings, little realising the passions being stirred within her. These novels by Shepherd and Moon predate Grassic Gibbon's portrayal of Chris Guthrie and her north-east environment and deserve to have their place alongside *A Scots Quair* in the canon of twentieth-century Scottish fiction.

In all the books discussed so far, a consistent element has been the friction or lack of solidarity between mothers and daughters. Older women in these narratives are marginalised in a public sense, despite the domestic power they wield. Some, like Carswell's Juley, are clearly incapable without a male figure to guide and organise their lives. So far as their daughters are concerned, then, there are no progressive role models, no recognised route to independent adult status as there is for their brothers, who move into the male world of work and power in the footsteps of their fathers. It is little wonder, then, that daughters of intelligence and imagination should look towards education as a route to independence and should reject the confined domestic world offered by their mothers. The overwhelming evidence from these novels of the 1920s and '30s, however, and from social and economic records of the times, is that a society organised on patriarchal principles has no means whereby young women can enter into adulthood alongside their brothers as *human beings*; they are instead categorised and constricted by biological function and by the perception of marriage as their essential goal. Even entry into the world of work, when it is allowed, is considered a low-grade, temporary affair, filling in the time before marriage – which may be why the choice of writing as a profession and the commitment which that vocation involves provokes such a hostile response from the men in these narratives. Yet marriage as conventionally perceived is in fact a return to a childish state for the women, a giving up of any awakened sense of self and ambition in return for the care and protection of a husband and a domestic life lived with and for children. 'Every child-woman must have her doll' (p. 56), as the writer Torrance tells Jacqueline in *Makeshift*, despite his encouragement of her talent. It is little wonder that many of the narratives here are what have been described as counter-narratives, where from their early days these female protagonists characterise themselves as rebels against set conventions and the feminine, ladylike behaviour expected of them. What is perhaps surprising is the representation of the attitudes of the mothers and substitute mothers of these fictional daughters. In almost every case depicted, the mother attempts to thwart her daughter's ambitions for education and emancipation and to shape her instead in her own mould. Like long-term prisoners these unsatisfied older women seem to have internalised their subjection and lost the capacity to imagine living another kind of life.

As we have seen, Catherine Carswell is the writer who most openly and memorably explores sexual relationships in her fiction, but the preoccupation with awakening female sexuality and sexual relationships generally is a significant element in these counter-narratives, where the taboos and hypocrisy of existing sexual mores are uncovered and challenged. In Lorna Moon's *Dark Star* and Dot Allan's *Makeshift*, for example, the heroines are the objects of attempted rape by men who are known to them. In the case of Moon's Nancy, a young teenager becoming conscious of but not yet understanding her developing sexual feelings, the assailant is the brother of the minister's wife in whose house she lodges. Allan's older heroine is attacked by her employer, who considers that his rights extend to her body as well as to her typing skills. In both cases what strikes one is the innocence of the girls involved, an innocence which involves ignorance of the details of the sexual act. In both cases, too, there is a point in the attack where the victims seem temporarily frozen in a kind of fascinated trance at what is happening, as if they were powerless to defend themselves. Here one sees how the innocent girl may so easily and through no fault of her own become the 'fallen woman' in society's eyes. This theme is further developed by Moon in her rehabilitation of Divot Meg in *Dark Star*. Betrayed by the first young man she went out with, Divot Meg has adopted a mien of coarse negligence as an alternative to the role of victim and outcast expected by society. Moon chooses also to draw a relationship between female sexual repression or frigidity, and vicious, spiteful and socially conforming female behaviour.

Such themes of sexual betrayal, illegitimacy and rebellion against accepted sexual conventions occur so frequently in these novels that they provide evidence, I believe, of the concern felt by women of the period about the unsatisfactory nature of sexual relationships between men and women and the hypocrisy which underpinned social codes with regard to marriage, prostitution and illegitimacy. Nor is this concern related to the situation of lower-class women only. In Nancy Brysson Morrison's first novel *Breakers*, it is the young daughter of a country minister who is despatched to an east-coast village to have her baby in secrecy and she returns home alone to a manse where the father remains in ignorance of his daughter's 'fall from grace'. The matter is never mentioned until retribution comes in later years with the appearance of the discarded son and his seduction of his mother's niece. In Mary Cleland's *The Sure Traveller* it is the Highland father whose youthful betrayal is uncovered. On the other hand, in Muir's *Imagined Corners* and Carswell's *Open the Door!* it is the educated, middle-class woman who consciously breaks the social code with regard to sexuality, becoming an emigrée in the case of Muir's Frau Mütze, and in the case of Carswell's Joanna remaining within society, but in a relationship for long kept silent and subordinate.

Just as the discourse of Dot Allan's *Makeshift* is probably the most explicitly challenging with regard to the social and sexual roles allotted to women, so that of Nancy Brysson Morrison's fiction is perhaps the most oblique, the theme being rendered through images which create a sense of claustrophobic oppression in her rural, edge-of-the-Highlands settings and through intimations of deterministic outcomes in her plots. Although in *Breakers* (1930), it is the illegitimate son Callum who ultimately becomes the tortured protagonist of the novel, it is here that we find the first sketch of the oppressive minister's household, with its three youthful, lively daughters, trapped in a manse in a rural area far from other social contacts, in a dank, darkly wooded setting.[11] The manse and the same specific country setting recur in some of her later novels, of which *The Gowk Storm* (1933) is the finest.[12] All tell of female vitality left to fade in obscurity; of patriarchal control in the form of ineffectual fathers who nevertheless hold power over their daughters and of male suitors who are the only hope of escape.

Breakers is interesting also for its creation of the kind of fatalistic scenario familiar in Scottish literature and for its depiction of a Highland Clearance episode which predates Neil M. Gunn's *Butcher's Broom* (1934) and Fionn MacColla's *And the Cock Crew* (1945). Like Gunn, Morrison calls on the detail of Alexander Mackenzie's *The History of the Highland Clearances* in her vivid account of the burnings at Inchbuigh, and her novel should be recognised for its contribution to the fictional representations of these events.[13] *The Gowk Storm*, too, has a deterministic context, but its private sorrow is conveyed in a taut first-person narrative form which has the economy, poetry and fateful suspense of a traditional ballad, its symbolic, imagistic language working against the surface realism of the social conventions depicted to produce a deeply tragic story of destroyed lives. Morrison shows hostility to the warping influence of Scottish Calvinism and to the similarly destructive effect of narrow social prejudices. 'Do you believe, Nannie ... in leaving everything with God, or do you think we should make efforts to change things?' (p. 92), asks Emmy, the most rebellious of the daughters, as they sit storm-bound in the kitchen after their minister father has put an end to the love affair of the eldest, Julia. The Scots language, when used here, is not associated so much with intimacy, as with the narrowness and prejudice of the dry old Nannie who curbs the girls' questioning, and with the most ignorant and vicious members of the community who hound Julia's Catholic schoolmaster lover from his charge.

Finally, in this group of inter-war novels, there is Catherine Gavin's *Clyde Valley*, published in 1938.[14] Like Nan Shepherd's Martha, Lennie, a similarly imaginative child, has a difficult relationship with her dominant rural mother. On the other hand, unlike Shepherd's heroine, who seems to lose the will to pursue her intellectual ambitions after university, Lennie follows her degree with success both as creative writer and personal assistant to a parliamentary candidate. With the possible exception of Muir's *Imagined Corners*, this novel comes closest to the Scottish Renaissance critique of the moribund nature of Scottish political and social life. Gavin, whose own diverse career pattern was that of university lecturer, journalist and historical novelist, and who emigrated to America after marriage in the post-war period, would appear to have had little sympathy with the ambitions of either nationalists or socialists. Hypocrisy in politics, in the mores of west-end artistic dilettantes, in the male-dominated universities, comes under attack alongside the negative portrayal of the mother's jealousy and narrow religious morality which warps her family relationships and in the end brings about the death of her daughter's lover. The representation of the love interest between Lennie and her politician employer is perhaps the least satisfactory element in this novel, being over-romanticised and with the girl being saved from 'fallen woman' status by the drowning of the man. There are fine, intelligent representations of both urban and rural life, however, with convincing linguistic flexibility as the narrative moves between them.

What a study of these inter-war novels demonstrates – and the reason for the major focus on them in this chapter – is the artificially limited nature of the early twentieth-century fiction revival as it has settled in our perspectives of the Scottish Renaissance. In their time, these women writers demonstrated an intelligent, modern, iconoclastic spirit which fulfilled the demands of the Renaissance manifesto, often in areas not tackled by the male writers. Many pursued urban themes when the literary revival was predominantly rural in context and imagery. Nan Shepherd and Lorna Moon deployed a strong, revitalised and unsentimental Scots language which complemented MacDiarmid's Scots language credo and compared favourably with Grassic Gibbon's language experiments in his fiction. They tackled the taboos of the representation of sexuality, especially of female sexuality, a subject mostly ignored or handled unconvincingly in the male fiction of the time. And most importantly, they challenged the man-made stereotypes of women, endorsed in Renaissance poetry and fiction in the symbolism of the woman as the poet's muse, the spirit of Scotland, the essentialist female spirit of goodness who makes sure that 'the moon is properly trimmed and not smoking and that all the stars are lit'.[15] Nationalism, on the other hand, is not a preoccupation of these women, despite the strength of feeling for countryside and sea-coast evinced in many of the novels. Shut out from public life as they were in the early decades of the century, identification with country is not their concern. Carswell's Ellen and the heroines of Allan, Muir and Gavin all leave Scotland. Virginia Woolf's comment: 'as a woman my country is the whole world', is echoed by Dot Allan in her criticism of the Scottish Renaissance movement and other such movements which 'tend to cut us off from the rest of the world instead of making us one with it'.[16]

As in other areas of life, the outbreak of the Second World War disrupted the development of women's writing, and the nature and perspectives of the fiction which emerged in the post-1945 period differed from that of the 1920s and '30s. There is something of a lull in the early post-war years, a diminution in the authors listed, accompanied by the disappearance of several names prominent in the early period or their continuation in a less challenging form. Nancy Brysson Morrison and her sister March Cost continued to publish as did Dot Allan. Morrison's *The Winnowing Years* (1949) and *The Hidden Fairing* (1951) attracted positive attention, but neither repeated the fine achievement of *The Gowk Storm*. Other writers from this early post-war period include Elisabeth Kyle (Agnes Mary Robertson Dunlop), a prolific writer of novels and books for children who profiled writers such as Nan Shepherd and Mary Cleland in the *Scots Observer* of 1931; Dorothy K. Haynes, Margaret Hamilton and Elizabeth Mackintosh, who wrote plays under the pseudonym of Gordon Daviot and detective novels under the name of Josephine Tey, her popular *The Daughter of Time* being published in 1951.

The most significant novel to come out of this interim period is Naomi Mitchison's *The Bull Calves* (1947). Mitchison is consciously ideological, but not narrowly feminist in this historical novel. She attacks the oppression of women in her account of the limited opportunities open to her female characters and the lack of support for her heroine, Kirstie, when her marriage to a clearly unsuitable minister goes disastrously wrong, but this gender focus is widened to include other marginalised groups: the slave mineworkers of Ayrshire, where Kirstie's husband is called to serve; Roman Catholics; the Highlanders, treated harshly and with suspicion after the '45 rebellion. Having been born into a privileged family, Mitchison's public life style enabled her to explore the theme of national renewal usually absent from the novels of female development and, as with the depiction of Chris Guthrie in *Sunset Song*, Kirstie at times seems symbolic of Scotland herself, a Scotland marginalised in relation to English power and ideology. In relation to the feminist perspective, the quasi-autobiographical narrative form, drawing on family papers and life-stories, is the kind of personal record usually treated with caution by professional historians, but one increasingly relevant in the representation of unrecorded women's experience, while the discourse includes the rhythms of the speaking voice in its conversations between women, a process of initiation through the older Kirstie's relations with her young cousin. At a more sinister level the novel also deals with the initiation of women by women into the evil of the witches' coven, a fate which befalls the young Kirstie in her despair during her wretched marriage. This historical novel interacts with the central theme of fictions of development in that its demonstration of change through time has meaning for a contemporary generation who also seek to reorder the way their lives are lived.

There is an intellectual confidence and sophisticated self-consciousness in the manipulation of form and material which marks Mitchison as outstanding in any account of Scottish fiction, but a confident handling of fictional form is increasingly evident in the new writers making their first appearance in the late 1950s and early 1960s. What seems most noticeable is the retreat of the 'woman question' from the foreground of these new novels. Although the representation of women's lives is still present, this appears more in the form of a subtext. The thematic and formal focus has shifted.

Jessie Kesson's *The White Bird Passes* (1958) and *Glitter of Mica* (1963) and Jane Duncan's 'My Friends' series of novels are probably closest to the inter-war developmental novels. Yet there is a difference even here. Jessie Kesson's Janey is discriminated against not primarily because she is a girl, but because of her mother's outcast and deprived situation as a single parent. Janey's fortunes become one with all those who live in run-down, economically destitute areas of large cities and she would have been similarly deprived if she had been 'John' not 'Janey'. The death of Helen Riddel in *Glitter of Mica*, although linked to an unsatisfactory love relationship, is a more complex affair than the suicide of the innocent, idealistic Nancy in Moon's *Dark Star*. These differences point forward to Kesson's *Another Time, Another Place* (1983)[17], where, although the nameless 'young woman' finds herself trapped by marriage, it is in fact the whole community which is trapped by its farming traditions and economic hardship, and the Italian 'prisoners' who, ironically, are the ones with the freedom of wider horizons. Jane Duncan's books depict the modern world of emancipated women and ambitious life styles, notwithstanding their heroine's roots in the simple Highland community of Reachfar. Despite the confident narrative style, however, and its knowing intellectual and social references, Duncan's novels are in my view less satisfying than the earlier representations of female experience. There is a complacent lack of distancing between author and first-person narrator/heroine here which makes the experiences depicted much less objective and rounded than those in Carswell's *The Camomile*, for example, where the equally dangerous epistolary form is used with wit, self-awareness and self-criticism.

More innovative formally and thematically are the early novels of Muriel Spark, with *The Ballad of Peckham Rye* (1960) and *The Prime of Miss Jean Brodie* (1961) especially relevant to the Scottish literary tradition. In these novels Spark plays ironically with Scottish Calvinistic determinism as a fictional tool, ordering her narrative and preparing nasty surprises for her characters as if she were a Calvinist God.[18] Nevertheless, in *The Prime of Miss Jean Brodie*, she simultaneously communicates, below the surface comedy of her ironic representation, that same problem of 'surplus women' treated more directly in Dot Allan's *Makeshift*. However ludicrous they may appear, 'the vigorous daughters of dead or enfeebled merchants, of ministers of religion, University professors, doctors . . . seen leaning over the democratic counters of Edinburgh grocers' shops arguing with the Manager at three in the afternoon' (p. 42), together with Miss Brodie herself, are stand-ins for the many women still looking for an outlet for talents unrecognised and unused in the authoritarian, patriarchal society of the late 1930s. Other authors who began to publish in the 1960s include Joan Lingard, Elspeth Davie and Shena Mackay. Like Spark, Mackay is stylistically innovative, her self-consciously macabre or surrealistic scenarios quite unlike the more 'innocently' melodramatic passages in the earlier Lorna Moon. Davie brings a painter's eye to her narratives, while Lingard extends her exploration of young women's love relationships to include contexts such as that of the Irish Troubles.

While, then, there is still in these later novels a preoccupation with the way women lead their lives or are forced by circumstances beyond their control to lead their lives, it is this expanded scenario, accompanied in some authors by a distancing from the conventions of the novels of realism and romance and a perception of fiction as literary performance, which marks them out as harbingers of the contemporary novel. Whether or not the literary success of present-day female authors and the continuing emancipation of women in the social and public worlds will ultimately come together to make an end of the novel of female development has yet to be seen. For the fiction writers of the 1920–1970 period, however, and for the writers of the inter-war years in particular, it was a form of the utmost relevance.[19]

Notes

1.   Germaine Greer, 'Flying Pigs and Double Standards', *Times Literary Supplement*, 26 July 1974, p. 784.
2.   Mary Cleland, *The Sure Traveller* (Hodder & Stoughton, London, 1923); Dot Allan, *Makeshift* (Melrose, London, 1928).
3.   Naomi Mitchison, *The Bull Calves* (Jonathan Cape, London, 1947; reprinted Richard Drew Publishing, Glasgow, 1985). All page references are to the reprint.
4.   Catherine Carswell, *Open the Door!* (Melrose, London, 1920; reprinted Virago, London, 1986; Canongate, Edinburgh, 1996); *The Camomile* (Chatto & Windus, London, 1922; reprinted Virago, London, 1987). All page references are to the reprints.
5.   See Toril Moi, 'Feminist, Female, Feminine', in *The Feminist Reader*, ed. Catherine Belsey and Jane Moore (Macmillan, London, 1989), pp. 117–132. My use of these terms here accords with Moi's definitions.
6.   Willa Muir, *Imagined Corners* (Secker, London, 1931; reprinted Canongate, Edinburgh, 1987 and 1996). All page references are to the reprint.
7.   See Virginia Woolf, *A Room of One's Own* (Hogarth Press, London, 1929).
8.   Simone de Beauvoir, 'Women and the Other', from 'Introduction', *The Second Sex* (1949), reprinted in Dennis Walder (ed.), *Literature and the Modern World* (Oxford University Press, Oxford, 1990), pp. 305–10.
9.   David Toulmin, Introduction to Lorna Moon, *Dark Star* (1929; reprinted Gourdas House, Aberdeen, 1980). All references are to the reprint.
10.   Nan Shepherd, *The Quarry Wood* (Constable, London, 1928; reprinted Canongate, Edinburgh, 1987). All references are to the reprint.
11.   Nancy Brysson Morrison, *Breakers* (Collins, London, 1930).
12.   Nancy Brysson Morrison, *The Gowk Storm* (Collins, London, 1933; reprinted Canongate, Edinburgh, 1988). All references are to the reprint,
13.   Alexander Mackenzie, *The History of the Highland Clearances* (A. & W. Mackenzie, Inverness, 1883; reprinted Mercat Press, Edinburgh, 1991).
14.   Catherine Gavin, *Clyde Valley* (Arthur Barker, London, 1938).
15.   Neil M. Gunn, *The Shadow* (Faber & Faber, London, 1948), p. 75.
16.   Virginia Woolf, 'Women and Nationalism', in Walder, *Literature and the Modern World*, p. 199. Dot Allan, quoted by Elizabeth Kyle, 'Modern Women Authors 3', *Scots Observer*, 25 June 1931, p. 4.
17.   Jessie Kesson, *The White Bird Passes* (Chatto & Windus, London, 1958; reprinted B & W Publishing, Edinburgh, 1996); *The Glitter of Mica* (Chatto & Windus, London, 1963); *Another Time, Another Place* (Chatto & Windus, London, 1983). The three novels are reprinted in *The Jessie Kesson Omnibus* (Chatto & Windus, London, 1991).
18.   Muriel Spark, *The Ballad of Peckham Rye* (Macmillan, London, 1960); *The Prime of Miss Jean Brodie* (Macmillan, London, 1961; Penguin, Harmondsworth, 1965).
19.   Additional titles by the writers discussed in the chapter and by writers briefly mentioned

are either discussed elsewhere in this volume or are included in the Bibliography. Information about the Glasgow Novel can be found in Moira Burgess, *The Glasgow Novel*, 2nd edn (Glasgow District Libraries, Glasgow, 1986).

I am grateful for the help afforded by the unpublished 'Bibliography of Twentieth-Century Women Writers' by Karen Stewart. This bibliography, which forms the basis for the 'Twentieth Century' Bibliography in this volume, was prepared by Karen Stewart for an exhibition of women's writing to celebrate the Glasgow 'Year of Culture, 1990'. It also contains brief biographical and critical remarks. A copy of it is deposited in Glasgow University Library.

25

Marion Angus and the Boundaries of Self

Christopher Whyte

A lively portrait of Marion Angus emerges from the letters she wrote to Mairi Campbell Ireland between November 1929 and the summer of 1931.[1] The years in question marked a major turning point in her life. Her first volume, *The Lilt*, containing only twelve poems, had appeared in 1922. Nine of these poems were reprinted with seventeen new poems as *The Tinker's Road* in 1924. Twenty-five new poems came out as *Sun and Candlelight* in 1927 and a further twenty-four as *The Singin' Lass* in 1929. *The Turn of the Day* dates from 1931. As will be seen, Angus looked on this book with some trepidation. It was in the nature of a retrospective, with only six new poems and substantial extracts from *The Lilt* and *The Tinker's Road*. One further book appeared in the remaining fifteen years of her life, *Lost Country* in 1937, containing twenty-nine poems, many of which had already appeared in periodicals.[2]

So the rhythm of one volume every two or three years which Angus had established during the 1920s was broken at the start of the new decade. This interruption can in large measure be attributed to the traumatic events of 1930. In early April the poet's younger sister suffered a complete mental breakdown and was taken into care in Glasgow. The cottage at Hazelhead, Aberdeen, which had been their home, had to be sold and Angus effectively became a nomad. She writes from the home of her other sister, a minister's wife in Greenock; from a house at Crawfurd, Lasswade, south of Edinburgh, where she temporarily found refuge; and from Inchdowrie in Glen Clova, Angus, a favoured holiday destination. In 1931 her ailing sister emerged briefly from care but the experiment proved to be a mistake. Visits had subsequently to be restricted even if 'I see always before me her savaged face and emaciated form' (6 May 1931). Angus wondered if the breakdown would mark the end of her career as a poet, since 'all the emotions, hopes, aspirations which might possibly at another time have found their way into poetry are for the present absorbed and used up in anxious care for my poor sister' (16 February 1930). She presumed that 'most people take it my little song is sung' (May 1930) and assured Ireland that 'it is only your outgoing gracious appreciation that has kept in my mind the very idea of writing again' (June 1929).

In this fashion Angus lost both what would appear to have been the central relationship of her life and any prospect of a permanent home. At times the letters make heartrending reading. She begs Ireland to 'Forgive me all my disappointing failures and don't judge me just now seeing that the waves are going over my head and the waters are very deep'

(October 1930). Angus considers herself 'a homeless vagrant' (June 1930), 'my roots all torn up out of their soil' (?July 1930) and complains that 'I never seem to alight on a branch but I must be off again' (15 November 1930). She reflects that one 'has to go where one is led (or driven) and I feel like a leaf before the wind – only a leaf has no business worries, nor sleepless nights, nor human feelings of anxiety or grief' (9 May 1930). Under such depressing circumstances, it is hardly surprising that the imminent appearance of *The Turn of the Day* filled her with foreboding: 'It is almost all old stuff . . . I tremble already when I think of the scathing remarks of reviewers and their quite natural assumption that having nothing more to give I palm off old things . . . the book will be a dismal failure . . .' (23 March 1931).

The tone of the correspondence is not uniformly plangent. Angus took on the role of mentor and counsellor, encouraging Ireland and offering suggestions as to where she might place her work. On occasions the roles were reversed. Praise for one of Angus's radio broadcasts elicited the request that her friend should write to the BBC as a disinterested listener expressing her enthusiasm, in the hope that Angus would receive further offers of work (14 September 1930). And indeed these were years of intense activity for her. She gave frequent lectures and broadcast talks on Scottish poetry, saw Neil Gunn at a literary dinner, John Masefield at a verse speaking competition and spent an exhausting day striding round Edinburgh's Old Town in the company of Patrick Geddes. The two women did not meet face to face until their correspondence was almost a year old. Ireland's rueful assertion of how plain she is reeks of coquetry and provoked a spirited response: 'if you were as beautiful as Helen of Troy or Cleopatra it would have no effect on me – in fact you would certainly be a bore – all beautiful women (almost) are' (27 May 1930). Ireland's husband intercepted a letter and penned an indignant complaint at the omission of any reference to himself therein. He also appears to have indulged in ungracious reflections on Angus's poetry. Addressing him as 'Mrs Ireland's *Supreme* Lord and Master', she replied in kind: 'you think my poems (to call them so) are incomprehensible! You have thus revenged yourself to a great extent for the slight received from me. Only one thing I can say in return, to show how forgiveness exceeds cruelty, that *I shall never explain them to you*' (6 March 1930).

Angus had forthright views on cultural and political matters which she did not hesitate to voice. The movement for Scottish independence inspired little sympathy in her, disgusted as she was by what she saw as the disunity and amateurishness of its members: 'I come in contact sometimes with the Nationalist people. They have no leader or such spokesman or woman and they are at odds with one another and none of them seem to know what they want' (July or August 1930). Her alienation from their objectives is given even stronger expression in a letter written the following year: 'What a colossal blunder Home Rule would be! At least in the present state of Scotland . . . They are all just babblers with no deep convictions, no earnest seeking after the highest good of Scotland and no foresight or even knowledge of political economy!' (23 March 1931).

Ireland's husband was not the only person she had to defend her poems from. Ireland showed some to a friend and made the mistake of relaying her adverse comments to the author. Angus rounded on her: 'As for me why should she think me anything but an amateur? Amateur means lover and I love poetry. And what does she mean by local? Everyone is local, even Milton, Tennyson, Wordsworth etc.' (17 April 1930). That litany of magical names is an indication of how far Angus's pride had been wounded. In calmer moments she gave a more cautious evaluation of her own achievement: 'the small people in poetry by which I mean the Rachel Annand Taylors, the C. M. Grieves, the Marion

Anguses – even the Ronald Campbell MacFies – *need* approbation, whereas the *great ones* [are] set apart beyond the praise of men, tranquil and blessed and serene. Would we were like them!' (January 1931). She had little faith in or fondness for reviewers. Presenting one of her books to Hugh MacDiarmid she commented ruefully that it 'does not deserve much recognition. (Anyhow it won't get it)'.[3] Relieved to find in Neil Gunn at least 'one reviewer who is not puzzled by something obscure in my efforts' she reiterated that 'they are not obscure'.[4]

Her views on literature were no less forthright than those on politics: 'Realistic pictures I think tend so often to become sordid' (December 1929–January 1930). Her own preference was for an art of transcendence, for 'life is a queer business and I think only worth while at all if one can look beyond it' (18 February 1930). In one who had written such a Housmanesque poem as 'Anemones' (SL, p. 30) an admiration for the Classical scholar and wistful Georgian homosexual comes as no surprise. Indeed, wistfulness is a quality Angus's readers have often attributed to her own verse. He pleased her because of his 'perfect technique' and 'melancholy pessimistic mind' (27 May 1930). Her enthusiasm for Donne and Crashaw shows her to have been abreast of a change in literary taste that did not become general until she was well past her fiftieth year: they 'are *the real thing*. Beside them most moderns seem like tinkling cymbals when they touch on the things of the soul' (9 February 1930). While confessing to a weakness for the work of Fiona MacLeod and 'a great longing to see those Islands of Dream and Beauty', she found 'a lack of depth' in Celtic poetry. It has, in the last analysis 'little to touch the mind and soul' (9 March 1930).

Such selective quotations sketch in a possible context for reading Marion Angus's poetry: the Celtic Twilight in its Scottish manifestation, the chaste pastoralism of the English Georgians and its Scottish transmutation in the work of William Soutar (a useful point of comparison for Angus[5]) and the renewed interest in English poetry of the early seventeenth century with its cerebral elaboration, the cultivation of shorter forms and a strong attraction towards the baroque. Yet in order to gain a measure of Marion Angus's radicalism it is necessary to set her love poetry against that of a much younger poet. 'If I gave you immortality' ('Ma thug mise dhut biothbhuantachd') is one of the poems from his 1943 *Dàin do Eimhir* which Sorley MacLean chose never to reprint.[6] It is numbered nineteen in the original sequence, placing it roughly one-third of the way through the cycle. Like so many of its companion poems, it is rooted in a convention of love poetry which can be traced back as far as the Provençal troubadours. MacLean was familiar with their work through Pound's creative imitations.[7] The speaker wants the woman he loves to have a sexual relationship with him. In order to persuade her to agree, he reminds her that her physical beauty is, like all earthly beauty, destined to fade. Readers may be familiar with the *topos* from Marvell. Baudelaire had exasperated the convention almost sadistically by discoursing to his mistress on the rotting carcass of a sheep.[8] MacLean gives it a further twist:

> is ged bhios tusa aig fear-pòsda
> is tu gun eòl air mo strì-sa,
> 's e do ghlòir-sa mo bhàrdachd
> an déidh cnàmhachd do lithe

> *and, though you will be married to another and ignorant of my struggle,*
> *your glory is my poetry after the slow rotting of your beauty.*

The woman the poet loves has already announced her intention of marrying another man. So it would not make sense to urge her to yield her body to him. She can never belong to him physically but she does belong to him in his verse. And his possession of her is more essential and lasting than her husband's for, while her beauty will decay as part of a process that is as relentless as it is gradual, his poetry is subject to no such law of transience. She is most truly herself there thanks to a vicarous appropriation which requires no civil or religious ceremony. The rejected lover makes a claim to power based on his prerogative of access to language, to creative achievement and the permanence it offers. She can benefit from these only at one remove, through him. Here is Angus's treatment of the same theme entitled 'The Sang' (SC, p. 12):

> The auld folks praised his glancin' e'en,
> Tae ilka bairn he was a frien',
> A likelier lad ye wadna see,
> But – he was nae the lad fur me.
>
> He brocht me troots frae lochans clear,
> A skep o' bees, a skin o' deer;
> There's nane s'uld tak' wha canna gie,
> An' he was nae the lad fur me.
>
> He luiket aince, he luiket lang,
> He pit his hert-brak in a sang;
> He heard the soondin' o' the sea,
> An' a' wis bye wi' him an' me.
>
> The tune gaed soughin' thro' the air,
> The shepherds sang't at Lammas fair,
> It ran ower a' the braes o' Dee,
> The bonnie sang he made fur me.
>
> Sae lang 'twill last as mithers croon
> And sweetherts seek the simmer's moon;
> Oh, I hae gaen wha wadna gie,
> For it s'all live when I maun dee.

Angus lets us see the conventional situation from a different viewpoint. The female speaker asserts her individuality by means of a refusal which is emphasised at the end of the first two verses and formalised at the end of the third. It has no rational basis and cannot be justified by external considerations. The man wooing her is good-looking and has the makings of a fine father. The gifts he brings have a purity which is redolent of an imagined folk world. However, her own principles stop her from accepting them: 'nane s'uld tak' wha canna gie'. Her lover makes a song which has an independent life and will survive her. She has given in spite of refusing to give. One could even go so far as to say that a part of herself has been stolen. Angus does not attempt to undermine the convention she is dealing with by reminding us that she, a woman, has made this poem. The speaker is explicitly gendered, the writer is not. The sense that a boundary has been violated remains.

A part of the speaker's self has gone from her. She has given birth against her will, not to a child, but to a still more wayward, uncontrollable and durable entity, a song. In 'The Fiddler' (*TR*, p. 29) music once again has the ability to embody an individual:

> A fine player was he . . .
> 'Twas the heather at my knee,
> The Lang Hill o'Fare
> An' a reid rose tree,
> A bonnie dryin' green,
> Wind fae aff the braes,
> Liftin' and shiftin'
> The clear-bleached claes.
>
> Syne he played again . . .
> 'Twas dreep, dreep o' rain,
> A bairn at the breist
> An' a warm hearth-stane,
> Fire o' the peat,
> Scones o' barley meal
> An' the whirr, whirr, whirr,
> O' a spinnin-wheel.
>
> Bit aye, wae's me!
> The hindmaist tune he made . . .
> 'Twas juist a dune wife
> Greetin' in her plaid,
> Winds o' a' the years,
> Naked wa's atween,
> And heather creep, creepin'
> Ower the bonnie dryin' green.

The fiddler evokes in turn the three ages of woman: Artemis, Demeter and Hecate, young girl, mother and hag. They flash before the speaker like cameos. She is entirely passive. She has no control over each picture, how long it will linger, or what will come next, no ability to accelerate or slow down the passage from one to the other. It is not clear whether her own memories are being evoked or not. Is she each of the three women presented? Is the last verse a prophecy or a recognition? Are these three different selves only possibilities or have they been realised? And why is the speaker a witness rather than a protagonist, given that the fiddler remains in control throughout?

It is characteristic of Angus's verse to reduce the three ages of woman to two, eliminating the figure of the mother or projecting it onto other women so as to leave a direct confrontation between the young girl and the hag. The interval that separates them is telescoped and the transition from one to the other bewilders the speaker. She is unable to clarify how, when or why it came to pass. The change is independent of her control or volition. She is aware of it, not as a process, but as a result. 'At Candlemas' (*TR*, p. 24) is a characteristic example:

Lang syne at Candlemas
At first cam o' the mune,
I, a bit lassie,
Hame-gaun fae the toon,
Fell in wi' a stranger
Frail as ony reed,
Wi' a green mantle
Hapt aboot her heid.

Haste, I wad haste me,
The whinny road along,
Whinny, crookit road
Whaur the grey ghaists gang.
Wi' her een fu' o' spells,
Her broo runkled sair,
She micht weel be the witch
O' the Braid Hill o' Fare.

Here cams Candlemas,
A wan deein' mune,
Eh! bit I'm weary.
Cauldrife wis the toon!

Yon's a blythe bairnie
Soople as a reed,
Rinnin' wi' a hankey
Tied aboot her heid,
Hastin', hastin',
Limber-licht fit,
Doon the crookit road
Whaur the grey moths flit.

Quo' she, 'Ye're sma'-bookit,
Yer broo's runkled sair,
Er' ye the auld witch
O' the Braid Hill o' Fare?'

Two almost identical meetings are distinguished only by the vague qualifiers 'Lang syne' and 'Here'. In each a young girl encounters an old woman on a lonely road. The old woman is both sinister and pathetic. The same doubt torments the young girl in each case. The speaker plays first one part, then another. There is only the slightest of divisions between the two and language tends to blur it. The words thought by the speaker in the first scene are spoken by the girl in the second. The effect is to emphasise the impression of bewilderment, of uncertainty about the change of roles. The speaker seems to be asking, 'How could I have moved so rapidly from one side of the exchange to the other? Which is truly me? Am I still the young, frightened girl? How have I become that which I was so frightened of only a moment ago? And might I change again just as unpredictably?'

The other woman functions as another self in this encounter of young girl and hag.

She both may and may not be a separate person. The encounter with a former self is more explicit (and perhaps more conventional) in 'Hogmanay' (*SL*, p. 11):

> What knocks at my door this Hogmanay?
> A cannie young lassie, limber and gay.
> Lips o' mine, e'en o' mine –
> Come ben, come ben tho' ye're deid lang syne.
>
> Whaur ha'e ye tint yir Sabbath shoon?
> The fiddles is tuned and a' the toon
> Is kissin' and courtin' and dancin'-fey
> Tae the screich o' the reels on Hogmanay.
>
> When the stars blaw oot an' the mune grauws wan,
> It's ower the hills wi' a bonny young man
> Whaur the floo'er o' love springs thorny an' sweet –
> And tho' an auld wife maun awhilie greet
> Ye'll aye gang limber an' licht an' free –
> Canny bit lassie that aince wis me.

The boundaries of the self fluctuate throughout this lyric. The stranger who knocks on the door has long since died. Again the problem of transition, of continuity is raised. If the girl has indeed died, she cannot be identical with the old woman, the hag. They are presented as two separate people rather than aspects of a single life. The status of the dallying in the second and third verses is uncertain. Is it a memory? Is the girl who will engage in it truly dead, now only a ghost? Is the speaker addressing a living girl actually distinct from herself who will have a living lover? And if so, how can the girl once have been herself ('that aince wis me')?

Dorothy Porter McMillan has written that Angus 'exploits shifts in person and tense to confuse present and past and sometimes upsettingly to fragment experience', adding that, by showing us 'women who are both themselves and observers of themselves', she conveys 'peculiarly female difficulties in maintaining an integrated notion of self'.[9] The insight is precious, yet by gendering the 'difficulties' Porter McMillan risks setting them against an implicitly masculine standard of integration by which women are found wanting. The elision of Demeter, of childbirth and motherhood, in most of Angus's verse tends to make its world 'socially' rather than 'ontologically' feminine. Rather than offering verbal texts where both genders are present, so that the difference between them requires foundation and explanation, it repeatedly excises the male presence from social reality. After all, what links the young girl before puberty and the old woman is the absence of menstruation, the inability to conceive and nurture another body (potentially of a different gender) within one's own. The reason for this weaker gendering may well be that Angus privileges in her poetry a relationship which is intragender rather than intergender, between members of the same gender rather than across a gender boundary. The other in her poetry is primarily another woman, if indeed it is another person at all and not a different, temporarily lost or separated aspect of the self.

Relating to a differently gendered other is a minor issue in her work. Indeed, the position for which she has been typecast, that of the faithful lover who is jilted or ignored, is attributed to a male speaker in a number of poems.[10] Its flexibility is clearly demonstrated in 'The Faithful Heart' (*LC*, p. 34), where a man arrives with news 'from Brig o' Feugh,/Whaur I was wild and young'. The relationship of the past tenses in lines 1 and 2 is unclear. Is the speaker no longer 'wild and young'? Angus characteristically keeps the crucial information from us until the last couplet. The visitor brings news of all and sundry yet what matters is silence rather than communication: 'But I socht nae news o' my auld love/Nor named her bonny name'. Until the third word from the end the speaker could be a woman and the news perhaps even a form of wooing. We are confronted with a self-suppression presented as an extreme form of fidelity.

This rueful yet eloquent silence recurs in 'Two is Company' (*LC*, p. 10)[11], where

> We gaed and gaed to the ha'thorn tree
> That hings by the weepin' well,
> Jean and Nelly o' Upper Stanehive
> And the third ane was mysel'.

Jean boasts about the fine gown she had when young and Nellie recalls her glorious corn-coloured hair. The person who speaks or thinks the poem is silent:

> And never a sough, as we sat and sat
> By the weary, weary well,
> O' the braws I had lang syne, or hoo
> I wasna' ill-faured mysel'.

She claims she was not ill-looking in an understatement that brings her confidence and anger powerfully home.

I have already said that Angus's unmarried younger sister would appear to have been the most significant other throughout her adult life. One can only speculate as to whether this explains the gender patterns in her poetry. 'Lost Things' can be read as a lament for her, although as it was printed in *The Turn of the Day* (p. 16) it probably antedates her definitive mental collapse:

> But since that summer morning
> On which I woke to weep,
> The rose has claimed her loveliness,
> The hills her beauty keep.
>
> While high among the uplands
> Or down the forest path
> I long for her lost foolishness
> Her quick impatient wrath.

One can, of course, posit a male speaker for this poem, dispelling any possibility that it illuminates the relationship between two women. Yet the solitary wanderer on the moors is a typical self-projection of Angus's[12] and one has the feeling that, although the speaker 'woke to weep', the lamented woman was perhaps not in bed beside her.

One of Angus's most disturbing poems, 'The Blue Jacket' (*TD*, p. 48), explicitly concerns two sisters:

> When there comes a flower to the stingless nettle,
>   To the hazel bushes, bees,
> I think I can see my little sister
>   Rocking herself by the hazel trees.
>
> Rocking her arms for very pleasure
>   That every leaf so sweet can smell,
> And that she has on her the warm blue jacket
>   Of mine, she liked so well.
>
> Oh to win near you, little sister!
>   To hear your soft lips say –
> 'I'll never tak' up wi' lads or lovers,
>   But a baby I maun hae.
>
> 'A baby in a cradle rocking,
>   Like a nut, in a hazel shell,
> And a new blue jacket, like this o' Annie's,
>   It sets me aye sae well.'

What disturbs one here is the element of fantasy. Artemis and Demeter are conflated and the young girl dreams of becoming a mother without any need for participation from a male. The nut and the hazel shell could hardly be further from the realities of human conception and birth. Here motherhood coexists with immaturity and the baby becomes an inanimate possession like a piece of clothing. While it may be intrusive to push what is unspoken too far, the third verse implies that the two have been close enough for the speaker to observe that her sister's lips are 'soft', and to hear a whispered rejection of the male sex which has the ring of a vow of fidelity or complicity.

In 'Waater o' Dye' (SC, p. 9) two women become as one. Wandering beyond the moor, the speaker enters into symbiosis with a female ancestor whose experience comes to function as her own. The result is one of Angus's finest, most explicit and uncompromising poems:

> Waater o' Dye, whaur ye rin clear
> I hear the cry – sae aft I hear –
> O' ane wha lauched and lo'ed and sinned
> And noo gangs sheda'less as wind.
>
> Wi' her I traivel, straucht an' sure,
> To the grey clachan yont the muir,
> Hapt in the breckan and the whin,
> Whaur dwalt the forebears o' my kin [. . .]
>
> Waater o' Dye, whaur ye rin still
> On me she warks her auncient will;
> What I hae niver kent, I ken –
> The feel o' babes, the luve o' men [. . .]

> An' aye she hauds me for her ain,
> Flesh o' her flesh, bane o' her bane –
> Some lang-deid wumman o' my kin –
> Waater o' Dye, hoo still ye rin.

The speaker feels closer to a dead woman than to any of the living. She learns what it is like to have a child not by having intercourse with a man but by merging with another woman. Even if her purpose were to experience sexual love from a man, it is achieved through identification with another woman rather than the search for a male partner. So fluid are the boundaries of Angus's self that she can cross them and unite with the dead. As in 'The Fiddler', this fluidity is experienced passively. But where the man's playing had provoked dismay and dissociation, here the effect is profoundly affirmative and pleasurable. The two female figures in 'Hogmanay' might just have been the same person at different stages in her life. Now there is no doubt that Angus's symbiosis is with a woman whose life, at least in terms of chronological time, had absolutely no overlap with hers.

The other woman is not infrequently one of the travelling folk and may, like the woman in 'Waater o' Dye', have had the experience of love and childbirth unknown to so many of the speakers in Angus's poems. In 'Welcome' (*SL*, p. 13) an old man from the glens and a girl with ragged shoes turn up at the door of a house. They are welcomed in by a woman who reflects that the girl could well be the child she had dreamed of holding in her arms the night before. The speaker in 'Fairy Tales' (*LC*, p. 33) assures her listener that the tinker mother with a plaid so thin it offered her 'nameless bairn' hardly any protection was nevertheless more blessed than any of the fairy folk. Angus's most striking tinker woman appears in one of the few new poems in *Turn of the Day*, 'The Broken Brig' (p. 10):

> Twa o' us met whaur the waters spring
> This ae nicht o' a',
> Ane to rage and ane to sing
> At onding o' the snaw.
>
> The twain o' us wi' never a moon
> In the blin-drift and the sleet,
> Ane wha gaed like thistle doon,
> Ane wi' silly feet.
>
> Me wi' a he'rt o' fear and dreid
> Whaur the burns was rinnin' big,
> Her to gang forrit wi' lifted heid
> First ower the broken brig.
>
> The twain o' us by the reid fire flame
> Oot o' the mirk and snaw—
> Oh wha' is this that lands me hame
> This ae nicht o' a'?
>
> A tinker wife wi' a dreepin' plaid
> The candle stalks atween,
> A whey-faced wife wi' a dreepin' plaid
> And twa sichtless e'en.

The poem tells a story in an ordered, sequential fashion unusual for Angus. On the other hand, she characteristically withholds the crucial detail until the very end. Here the echoes of the ballads which can be heard throughout her verse are particularly strong in the repeated refrain, the formulaic parallelism encouraged by the presence of two protagonists, and the rhetorical question of verse 4. It is impossible to gender the speaker, who could as well be female as male. During a snowstorm, with all the streams swollen, two people meet at a broken bridge. The moon is blotted out so that the speaker cannot tell just who is acting as a sure-footed guide. By the time he or she realises the danger, it is too late. And, of course, a moment's reflection tells us that a blind woman would be much less incapacitated in these extreme conditions than a seeing one. Angus asked Campbell Ireland 'will you understand I wonder the meaning of the "Broken Brig". To me it is quite clear so I shall not *explain* it to you. "Simply faith without sight"' (2 July 1930). Her interpretation significantly shifts the poem from an interaction between separate individuals to a spiritual process within a single person, the choice being to remain paralysed or to accept an unknown inner guide although the circumstances and possible consequences of action are entirely uncertain. Even in this simplest of poems the boundaries of self and other are unstable.

Angus's poetry cannot be reduced to a rigid binary opposition of self and other. Indeed it is the instability of the terms on either side, the way they constantly threaten to change places or blend into one another, that gives her poetry that 'obscurity' or difficulty which is its distinguishing feature. Angus achieves extremely complex effects using the simplest means. In her work folk poetry undergoes a change of function from narrative to inner psychological vocabulary. The change is so subtle as to leave the surface repertory practically unaltered. The unstable dichotomies that underpin her writing can be variously expressed as self versus other; living versus dead; respectable woman versus tinker; virgin versus hag; childless virgin versus woman with knowledge of sex and childbirth, and woman with a home versus vagrant, homeless woman.

The house functions as an image of the self where the door has a major significance, not in a crudely sexual sense, but as the point of transition between what is me and what is not me, the place where the boundaries of self are liable to infringement. 'The Eerie Hoose' (*SL*, p. 14) presents the image with extraordinary richness and clarity:

> Says she: – It is an eerie place
> This hoose I ca' ma hame
> Wi' wa's baith stooter than the hills,
> An' frailer than the faem.
>
> Says she: – It is an eerie hoose,
> Wi' chaumers braid and blue,
> Whaur I gang wi' a fearsome step,
> A han' afore ma mou'.
>
> Sin' thir's ae word gin I suld speak
> Hoo saft so e'er it fa' –
> Wad gar its very stoops to rock,
> Syne melt like simmer snaw.

> Says she: – It is an eerie hoose,
> Clear lichted wast an' east,
> Whaur I gang wi' twa shakin' airms
> Close gruppit to ma breist.
>
> Sin, thir's ae steekit door whase latch,
> Gin I tuik thocht to lift,
> The corner-stanes wad slip awa'
> Like weeds in winter's drift.
>
> Says she: – 'Twad be a dowie hoose
> An' weary lang the day
> Wis thir nae door I daurna try,
> Nae word I daurna say.

The lyric falls into four sections, emphasised by the repetition of 'Says she' at the start of stanzas 1, 2, 4 and 6. An opening and a closing stanza frame two pairs of stanzas. If the supposition that the 'hoose I ca' ma hame' (and which by implication may not be) is the self is justified, then its boundaries, the walls, are both impenetrable and insubstantial. The experience is either of extreme separation from others or of unpredictable flowing into them ('frailer than the faem'). Both pairs of verses are concerned with a prohibition whose infringement would lead the structure of the self to dissolve entirely, one connected with the mouth, the other with the arms. In the first case this is a word which must not be spoken, in the second a door which must not be opened. The persistence of the self is dependent on the observation of these taboos (and it may not be improper to see a sexual symbolism in that 'steekit door' whose latch must not be lifted). The double negatives of the last verse induce a disturbing ambivalence. It might just be a brave declaration of the speaker's intention to defy these taboos. But a different conclusion emerges from a more literal and faithful reading. Only the acknowledgement of the prohibitions can make living within the house bearable. If they were absent to remain there would have no sense. The self depends for its stability on prohibition.

An interpretation of this kind gives a context for the recurring figure of the tinker woman. She passes on the road outside, perhaps with a child, with or without a male partner. Her experience is shut out from the circle of the self and yet by inviting her inside for rest and sustenance the speaker can achieve a temporary identification with her. The contrast between the restricting house and the open moorland to which Angus so often returns would then represent an alternation between self as confinement, as prison, and a liberated state where the boundaries of self dissolve and the speaker can become, for example, the forgotten ancestor of 'Waater o' Dye'. 'The Seaward Toon' (*TR*, p. 9) supports such a reading. The poem is a reproach to one who has 'barred yer painted door . . . steekit sae fast yer door . . . steekit yer painted door' and in consequence will never reach the magical town by the sea not 'biggit by mortal hand' where everything is 'hapt in a droosy air/That's naither cauld nor heat'.

The house is not always tenanted. One may knock at the door and find nobody there. When boundaries are so fluid one will at times subsist outside one's body, outside, as it were, oneself. 'The Bridge' (*L*, no page number) is redolent of late Romantic poetry. In spite of the Scottish setting, its English diction gives it a derivative ring. However, the content is significant. The woman described does not love 'this dark street of stone' with its 'windows high'. With the help of memory she creates a bridge taking her to Invereye where she weaves a crown of cherry blossom and wades in the green waters of the brook. Even if her feet were fettered inside the house, her heart would escape to this beloved place. Her body might be trapped but her self would be absent, elsewhere. In 'Invitation' (*SL*, p. 16) a girl invites a lad to hold her in his arms while insisting that he 'can never win . . . the white soul o' me'. 'Huntlie Hill' (*SL*, p. 23) has a similar ambivalence, more chilling because the poem is projected into the time after the speaker's death. If her lover longs for her he can seek her in 'a bonnie birk'. Yet his possession will still be an illusion, for the 'pipin' bird' that 'gangs moontin' ower the plain' far out of reach might be 'the liltin' hert o' me/Ye never socht to gain'. He can hold her body in the fair birch tree, but her soul will be elsewhere.

'The Lane Kirkyaird' (*TK*, p. 31) can be usefully read as a counterpoint to MacDiarmid's 'Crowdieknowe'.[13] Both poems make use of the Christian iconography of the resurrection of the body. It conforms to a certain stereotype that the male poet reproduces the quoted ideology (while redirecting it) whereas the female poet dissolves it entirely. MacDiarmid envisioned the sturdy Border farmers railing against God for daring to waken them while their womenfolk urge them to be more diplomatic. When the last trumpet sounds in Angus's churchyard, the nearby sea replies that those it is seeking to wake are no longer there. They have long since gained release for both body and soul:

> 'The auld kith an' kin
> They hae lang won free,
> Far abune the whin
> An' the spindrift thin
> An' the cauld fine smell o' the whin.'

The terms of the critical debate around Marion Angus's poetry had already been fixed at the time of her death in 1946. Her obituarist in *The Scotsman* comments:

> She possessed the gift of 'natural magic' which Matthew Arnold regarded as the chief contribution of the Celt to English poetry; and she understood what Mr de la Mare has called 'poor mortal longingness', especially the longingness of aged and forsaken women, and expressed it in verse of rare subtlety, tenderness, and sweetness.[14]

The tribute blends three factors: race, gender and age, all of them tending to assign Angus a marginal position at the edge of 'English' poetry. Malcolm Chapman has examined in detail the 'feminisation' of the image of the Celt in France and England during the latter part of the nineteenth century.[15] It is part of a complex rhetoric of imperialist appropriation of the defeated races in cultural rather than purely economic terms. In so far as the Celts are intrinsically feminine they face a destiny of military defeat and subordination while retaining the apparent privileges of closeness to nature and a highly developed spirituality. The attribution of a typically 'Celtic' quality to Angus's verse turns it into yet another of the 'idiosyncratic excrescences' (the phrase is MacDiarmid's)[16] with which defeated races can decorate the culture of the conqueror. As we have seen, she would hardly have agreed to having her work characterised in this way. There is a parallel between the perception of Celtic culture as 'ancient' (and marked out for imminent demise) and the way Angus's age (her first volume appeared in her fifty-sixth year) has fundamentally coloured the reception of her poetry. Had she been a teenager, the longing for a male partner which was seen as its dominant theme would have had a less elegiac quality. But then, the foregoing discussion has shown the theme of unrequited love to be something of a red herring. Other women, rather than any male figure, constitute the principal focus of her work.

Two years before her death Herbert Grierson and J. C. Smith placed Angus at the head of a group of Scots poets faithful to the tradition of Ramsay, Burns and Stevenson (as opposed to the innovative, 'synthetic' approach of MacDiarmid). Helen Cruickshank was so impressed by the accolade that she asked Nan Shepherd to give the poet a copy of the passage.[17] A modern reader might be less enthusiastic about Grierson and Smith's judgement. Grierson and Smith use terms remarkably similar to those of the obituary. None of the poets who came after Stevenson 'attempted anything big; most of them struck the familiar notes of humour, pathos, patriotism (deepened by the war), domesticity, and theology'. Angus is therefore very definitely one of a cohort of minor figures, 'the sweetest singer of them all [with] that touch of natural magic, and that tragical undertone which, rightly or wrongly, we associate with Celtic blood'.[18] Reviewing Maurice Lindsay's edition of Angus's *Selected Poems*, Robert Kemp saw Angus as 'more a woman's poet than a man's', lacking 'some of the robust health of her sister poetess of Angus' (the reference is to Violet Jacob). Kemp's equivalent of 'natural magic' is the 'distrust of anything blunt and outright' in Angus's work (the avoidance of too masculine a directness?).[19] Lindsay's preface confronts a deeper mystery. Aware that 'love (or sex, if you are a Freudian) is the stimulus which makes most young men attempt to relieve themselves in bad verse round about their twentieth year' he wonders 'what the stimulus may have been which suddenly turned [Angus] from a desultory versifier into a gentle lyric poet when she was over fifty years of age'.[20] Kemp also touches on the issue but decides that 'it is not long before one feels that one is prying and withdraws'. He is echoed some twenty-seven years later by Dorothy Porter McMillan for whom the 'drive to detect the covert narratives along with the sense that such a desire is tactless is what makes some of the poems truly disturbing'.[21]

One could argue that readings of Angus's verse have until now been disproportionately coloured by her life, which has an undeniably opaque quality (especially for male readers). Violet Jacob's life can be conjugated with relative ease according to the familiar patterns of a male-dominated society (marriage to a cavalry officer, travel overseas in the service of the Empire, childbirth and the tragic loss of an only son in the First World War). Her role as a female scion of the Kennedy Erskines of Mar unable to pass on the family name gives her a precise place as an outsider in traditional patterns of kinship and inheritance. The same cannot be said for Angus. She was the daughter, granddaughter and sister-in-law of ministers, by their nature a vagrant breed unlikely to establish family connections with a particular location or to accumulate significant material possessions.[22] Her constant companion as an adult, we have seen, was an unmarried sister. If male readers have been unable to interpret this predicament as anything other than tragic, the poet played into their hands in lines such as these from 'Cotton Grasses' (SC, p. 32):

> Of joyful tears unwept,
> Of tenderness unwist,
> Of lovers' lips unkissed
> And promised trysts unkept.

Each line ends with a participle prefixed 'un-', implying that hers is a poetry of gestures missed, of events failing to occur, much as a spinster's life can appear to be a gap, a failure, the absence of a gesture only a man could make.

In the introduction to her *Anthology of Scottish Women Poets* Catherine Kerrigan confesses publicly to her mistake in treating the work of Jacob, Angus and Cruickshank as 'minor ripples in the modern literary revival' even if, when 'compared with the work of MacDiarmid, the arch-modernist, they are seen as deficient'.[23] What matters is that 'their work is traditional within female, not male, writing'. Their poems must be read 'in terms of women's work and women's experience'. Porter McMillan might not agree. For her 'a literary tradition has no meaning unless writers are conscious of belonging to it and working with it whether to reinforce or to subvert'.[24] The customary bracketing together of Jacob, Angus and Cruickshank may prove to be a further manifestation of their disadvantaged position as women writing within a male-dominated culture rather than a means of overcoming it. Even the suggestion that their adoption of vernacular modes was a mask allowing the expression of otherwise unacceptable contents is ambivalent. Any poetic speech is speech using a mask. Poetry is always written in a species of code which makes equal demands on writers of both genders. As we have seen, the obscurities of Angus's verse do not admit of easy solution. The urge to resolve them, to break the code, may well be inappropriate. It would be a violation, not of her feminine *pudeur*, but of the nature of the medium itself.

No male critic can participate in the retrospective construction of a female tradition which serves as a springboard for subsequent (women) writers. But he can engage in a kind of *cross-reading* which is equivalent to the *cross-writing* practised by the vast majority of writers, both women and men. The creative imagination has scant regard for gender boundaries. It is part of the daily experience of many of us not just to think ourselves into, but at times to think of ourselves as the other sex. Poetic texts are incorrigibly promiscuous, whatever the intentions or prescriptions of their authors. Their sole desire is that we should read them and their determination to seduce us is indifferent to gender, race or age. They impose one single condition: that no encounter with them should be the last.

Notes

1. Now deposited in the National Library of Scotland MS 19328.
2. See *The Lilt and Other Verses* [L] (D. Wylie and Sons, Aberdeen, 1922), no page numbers; *The Tinker's Road and Other Verses* [TR] (Gowans and Gray, Glasgow and London, 1924); *Sun and Candlelight* [SC] (Porpoise Press, Edinburgh, 1927); *The Singin' Lass* [SL] (Porpoise Press, Edinburgh, 1929); *The Turn o' the Day* [TD] (Porpoise Press, Edinburgh; Faber & Faber, London, 1931); *The Lost Country and Other Verses* [LC] (Gowans and Gray, Glasgow, 1937). For quotations in the body of the essay, the initials of the volume and a page number are supplied.
3. Edinburgh University Library Special Collections MS 2942.5.
4. NLS Deposit 209 Box 17: undated letter.
5. Joy Hendry indicates some possible influences of Angus on Soutar in 'Twentieth Century Women's Writing: The Nest of Singing Birds' in Cairns Craig (ed.), *The History of Scottish Literature*, vol. 4 (Aberdeen University Press, Aberdeen, 1987), p. 294.
6. Somhairle MacGhill Eathain, *Dàin do Eimhir agus Dàin eile* (William MacLellan, Glasgow, 1943), p. 20. I quote MacLean's English prose translation from p. 98.
7. See Christopher Whyte, 'A Note on *Dàin do Eimhir* XIII', in *Scottish Gaelic Studies* 17 (1996) pp. 383–92.
8. See 'La Charogne' in Charles Baudelaire, *Les Fleurs du Mal*, ed. A. A. Adam, (Garnier, Paris, 1961), pp. 35–6.
9. Dorothy Porter [McMillan], 'Scotland's Songstresses', *Cencrastus* 25 (Spring 1987), 48–52 (pp. 49–50).

10.   See 'This Woman', *SL*, p. 17 and 'The Doors of Sleep', *TD*, p. 12.

11.   Yeats's 'The Secrets of the Old' appeared in *The Tower* in 1928 so Angus could have read it before writing this poem. See W. B. Yeats, *The Poems: A New Edition*, ed. Richard J. Finneran (Macmillan, London, 1984), p. 225.

12.   See 'Penchrise', *TR*, p. 21; 'Lost Country', *LC*, p. 7.

13.   Hugh MacDiarmid, *Complete Poems 1920–1976*, ed. Michael Grieve and W. R. Aitken, 2 vols (Martin, Brian & O'Keefe, London, 1978), I, pp. 26–7.

14.   'Death of Marion Angus: Scots Vernacular Poet', in *The Scotsman*, 20 August 1946.

15.   Malcolm Chapman, *The Gaelic Vision in Scottish Culture* (Croom Helm, London; McGill-Queens University Press, Montreal, 1978). See especially Chapter 4, 'Ernest Renan and Matthew Arnold', pp. 81–112. The influence of this feminisation can still be detected in Colin Milton's observation that Angus 'uses the supernatural elements of the folk tradition . . . to create a sense of kinds of experience which are beyond the routine, rational and explicable, moments of contact with the numinous'. See 'Modern Poetry in Scots before MacDiarmid', in *The History of Scottish Literature*, vol. 4, p. 34.

16.   Hugh MacDiarmid, *Contemporary Scottish Studies* (Scottish Educational Journal, Edinburgh, 1976), p. 11

17.   Helen B. Cruickshank, 'A Personal Note', in Maurice Lindsay (ed.), *Selected Poems of Marion Angus* (Serif Books, Edinburgh, 1950), xv–xxi (xviii).

18.   Herbert J. Grierson and J. C. Smith, *A Critical History of English Poetry*, 2nd rev. edn (Chatto & Windus, London, 1947), p. 515.

19.   Robert Kemp, 'The Wershness of Love', in *The New Alliance and Scots Review*, vol. II, no. 2 (May 1950), p. 31.

20.   *Selected Poems*, xii, xi.

21.   Porter, p. 50.

22.   Her father Henry, son of the Rev. Henry Angus of Aberdeen, was United Presbyterian minister of the Erskine Church in Arbroath from 1876 until his death in 1902. As his first charge was Sunderland Trinity church in 1859, it is just possible that Marion was born there rather than in Scotland. Her sister married William Service in June 1904. He had been ordained to Arbroath in February 1899 and the pair moved to Greenock West Parish of the Church of Scotland in September 1904. (The Rev. Alexander Lamb, *The Fasti of the United Free Church of Scotland 1900–1929*, Oliver & Boyd, Edinburgh & London, 1956, pp. 394–5; *Fasti Ecclesiae Scoticanae*, new edn, vol. III, Oliver & Boyd, Edinburgh, 1920, p. 209).

23.   Catherine Kerrigan (ed.), *An Anthology of Scottish Women Poets*, with translations from the Gaelic by Meg Bateman (Edinburgh University Press, Edinburgh, 1991), p. 8.

24.   Porter, p. 48.

26

Catherine Carswell: *Open the Door!*

Glenda Norquay

As its dynamic title suggests, *Open the Door!* is a novel about movement and space, concerned with exploring and crossing the boundaries of identity, gender and aesthetics.[1] This traversing and transgressing of space is manifested in various ways: first in the novel's preoccupation with different locations – Glasgow, Italy, London – and their symbolic significance; secondly in the challenges it poses to women's existing roles and spheres; and, perhaps most importantly, in its attempt to understand and redefine the formation of a gendered identity, 'opening the door' to a new perspective on the self.

Carswell's project, then, is clearly an ambitious one. In this chapter I want to examine the strategies used to achieve such a 'breaking through', and in so doing to give a sense both of the novel's achievements and of its inherent tensions. *Open the Door!*, although ostensibly using the format of romance, is a dense and complex text, wide-ranging in the issues it considers and fascinating in the interconnections established between them. My focus in this chapter, therefore, will be on formal elements of the novel, including its heavy use of symbolism and literary allusion, its shifts between nineteenth-century realism and twentieth-century experimentalism, and its reworking of a romance motif, all considered in relation to the novel's wider thematic concerns with the emergence of a gendered self.

Catherine Carswell was born in 1879, brought up in Glasgow by prosperous and religious middle-class parents she later described as a 'simple and philistine family'.[2] From an early age Carswell perceived herself – and her family because of their evangelical fervour – as alien to their environment. Like the heroines of both *Open the Door!* and *The Camomile*, her early life reads as a search for escape from the moral and cultural confines of Glasgow.[3] She attended English Literature classes at Glasgow University (at a time when women couldn't sit for a degree), visited Italy, and studied music at the Frankfurt Conservatory. Her first marriage, to Herbert Jackson in 1904, ended in disaster when he attempted to kill her and was declared insane. She then had to fight a long legal battle to have her marriage annulled. Her second marriage, to the journalist and writer Donald Carswell, was a successful partnership both professionally and personally. She also enjoyed friendships with D. H. Lawrence, Hugh MacDiarmid, Rebecca West, and Edwin and Willa Muir. Most famously, she was sacked from her job as reviewer with *The Glasgow Herald* in 1915, after writing a favourable account of Lawrence's novel, *The Rainbow*.[4] Lawrence himself commented in detail on the first draft of *Open the Door!* and was a major influence on its development.

Open the Door! was Carswell's first novel and, as her son suggests, is based to a large extent upon her own experiences.[5] Written over five years, it was published in 1920 yet remains very much a book of the pre-war era, marking in itself a transition from nineteenth-century realism to the more fragmented and introspective style characteristic of early twentieth-century fiction. The novel opens in Glasgow in the late nineteenth century. Significantly, however, it begins with a departure from that city as the central character, Joanna, leaves for a holiday in Edinburgh with her mother, brothers and sister. As they leave Glasgow, Joanna is enthralled by sunlight on the Jamaica bridge which strikes off a ship on the river underneath:

> This picture ... appealed not so much to the little girl's untrained eye, as symbolically through her eye to her heart which leapt in response. The sunshine on that outgoing vessel and the great, glistening current of brown water, filled her with painful yet exquisite longings. She did not know what ailed her, nor what she desired.[6]

This is an important moment in two respects. This powerful yet unarticulated and undefined desire becomes characteristic of Joanna's emotional life. Brought about by the crossing of space, over the ribbon of the river, it marks a desire for change and movement, but the nature and source of such fulfilment are unclear. The structure of the story that follows is determined by this quest for satisfaction, and the novel itself becomes an exploration of the drives and constraints that shape women's lives.

The brief moment on the bridge also marks another change in the novel, signalling a transition from the solid and detailed realism with which the family's departure from the railway station had been described, into an epiphanic moment characteristic of modernism both in its focus upon the subconscious of the character and its weighting of significant symbolism upon an apparently trivial moment. At this point the reader realises that the novel will offer and demand more than a conventional tale of family life in a specific social context: like Joanna, the writing itself is involved in a struggle to express the inexpressible and will draw upon symbolism, literary allusion, and such moments of interiority to trace the course of indefinable longings. In the first book of the novel, we see Joanna moving from one avenue of escape to another, in a quest for self-fulfilment and self-discovery, and are given clear indications of how to judge the trials she undergoes.

The early stages of the novel set up the first of several locational contrasts, between Glasgow, which is seen mainly as a place of loss and darkness, full of religious and sexual tensions, and Duntarvie, the family's holiday home in the Perthshire countryside, which offers freedom and physical release. Here Joanna finds one of her first and abiding avenues of escape – the world of nature: 'it came to her that she might make of her rapture a place of retreat for future days' (p. 32). The novel will explore various places of retreat – both real and symbolic – but 'Nature' as embodied in Duntarvie, is one of the least problematic and most abiding. But Duntarvie also serves as an initiation for Joanna into the two different kinds of sexuality which run through the book. One is embodied by her older cousin Gerald Bird, whose hairy ankles she finds both exciting and alarming. Her sense of his erotic otherness emerges in a scene where he is skinning and stuffing small birds he has shot. Joanna becomes aware that she too would like to be slit and skinned by Gerald. This moment offers the first hint of that link between dangerous sexuality and masochistic desire which features so strongly in the novel's romantic scenarios. It also introduces the bird symbolism which will later dominate the text.

A different kind of sexuality is represented by Alec Peddie, a boy from the nearby farm, who offers to show Joanna 'what lads is for'. His offer, preceded by the appreciative, 'You look awful bonny, Jo', is rejected but the moment is presented as one of warm reciprocity. 'But the thrill of the boy's touch remained with the girl and the shameless young pagan look he had given her took its place also in her dreams' (p. 37). The alternative to the erotic and predatory relationship offered by Gerald is, it appears, one of mutual and 'natural' desire – an opposition which will become highly significant as the novel develops.

Another area of potential escape, again established in Joanna's early years, is that of physical activity, whether running across the moors, performing daring feats on the nursery trapeze, or climbing trees: 'At such moments she was the queen of her own body, and not of her body alone, but of a whole system of laws she could not even begin to formulate' (p. 38). She is, however, afraid of jumping and this again becomes a symbolic key to her character. At one point she forces herself to perform a leap from the parlour window of which she is terrified. Offering an image of the combined attractions and terror of flight, the action also illustrates Joanna's belief that to find and prove herself she must launch into the unknown. With characteristic Carswell symbolism, a simple incident from childhood prefigures subsequent events and offers a key to Joanna's evolving sense of self.

By her late teens Joanna's desire for escape formulates itself into longing for a lover. The first suitor to present himself is Bob Ranken, a family friend, who fails to meet the passion of her demands. Initially Joanna is disappointed that he initiates so little, appearing both hesitant and demanding. One of his demands, however, that she 'wait' for him while he makes his fortune in South Africa, does fulfil an aspect of her own needs: the desire for a vocation: 'She was gluttonous for sacrifice' (p. 63). But with Bob she fails to find the predatory sexuality of Gerald Bird: 'She would like him to have beaten her and made her his but instead he was crying now in expectation of punishment' (p. 72). Reinforcing an emerging pattern in Joanna's politics of identity, this desire shows her dependent upon possession by a stronger, more powerful masculine force, against whom her self can be defined.

Following the failure of this relationship, Joanna's next flight of escape is through place: into the dream of Italy. Spurred on by a letter from an Aunt who lives there, she decides to learn Italian and experiences another epiphanic moment before she enters the class: 'The desire came upon her for liberated movement – the deep-set human longing for wings' (p. 87). Ironically, the classes do not offer the release she expects, but through a friend she makes there she is introduced to Mario Rasponi, an Italian inventor specialising in flying: a man who 'was energy itself, but energy pent not radiant' (p. 90). Even without this association of his vocation with the prevalent bird imagery, the reader recognises that Rasponi offers what Joanna failed to find in her relationship with Bob Ranken. Again the heavy-handed symbolism and oppositions of this first book work against the novel's apparent realism, adding a schematic quality to events and giving the reader clear directives as to interpretation.

Rasponi, a Lawrentian character of 'narrow rapacious lips' and a 'delicate glittering quality' and the one figure in the novel with no autobiographical antecedents, is weakly characterised but serves his function which is to indicate the failure of yet another avenue of escape. He offers Joanna life in a cage: 'a cage full of sunshine and beauty and delight, a cage of which the man you love held the key' (p. 98). Realising from the outset that such a cage might become a prison, Joanna nevertheless marries him and leaves for Italy. At this point Carswell directs our interpretation through another textual device, as the novel becomes redolent with literary allusion to Elizabeth Barrett Browning's *Aurora Leigh*. In that epic verse-novel, Italy represents a land of passion, sexual freedom, and love, while England is seen in terms of coldness, restraint, the law and language of the father.[7] Indeed, Aurora describes the life of women in England, embodied by her strait-laced aunt, as 'a cage-bird's life':

> She had lived
> A sort of cage-bird life, born in a cage,
> Accounting that to leap from perch to perch
> Was act and joy enough for any bird.
> . . . I, alas,
> A wild-bird scarcely fledged, was brought to her cage,
> And she was there to meet me. Very kind.
> Bring the clean water, give out the fresh seed.[8]

The bird imagery, so noticeable from the first appearance of Gerald Bird, can now be seen as a link with the English verse novel. Carswell's text enters into dialogue with Barrett Browning's, interrogating the imagery and oppositions established by the poem. The nineteenth-century epic suggests that emotional release may be brought about through the warmth and passion of Italy. For Joanna, however, life in Italy is one of constrictions and imprisonment, both physically in her isolation and emotionally in the obsessive passion and jealousy of Rasponi. Ironically echoing the words of Romney to Aurora, where he suggests that women are all heart and men driven by the head, Rasponi accuses Joanna of drawing with 'your head alone . . . one must draw with one's heart, one's blood'.[9] Release through 'womanly' warmth appears insufficient as a source of fulfilment. Finding his physical domination arousing, Joanna's sexuality is conventionally 'awakened' by her Latin lover, but this passion also becomes a prison because of his desire to posses her totally.[10] For the reader, Rasponi serves as a warning against Joanna's romantic desire to be an object of possession.

Marriage to Rasponi also strengthens Joanna's sense of her cultural and national identity. His jealousy is particularly aroused by her unspoken assumption that one day she will 'go back' to Scotland. Her rootedness in Scottish identity, an important element in the novel's dialogue between places, becomes a means of questioning the romantic myth of Italy. Italy serves as a catalyst for her sexual evolution but in terms of her spiritual development, it only promotes ambiguities. When in Italy she finds herself longing for Glasgow and Scotland, but also recognises that when there she had not felt at home. Through this dichotomy another element in Joanna's psychic formation is introduced: she feels other and alien wherever she may be. Another element of her quest, therefore, becomes the search for a 'homeland'.

While the Italian scenario proves structurally useful in reinforcing the novel's themes, a certain unease can be detected in the mechanical and melodramatic resolution to Joanna's unhappiness. Rasponi's death by an accident upon his velocipede neatly ensures Joanna's return to Scotland, with questions raised by the relationship unresolved. Likewise in the Italian setting, textual uncertainty can be noted in the heavy reliance on the novel's schematic symbolism. Joanna, in her brightly coloured clothes, is described as 'looking like some gay-coloured shy bird' (p. 114). When Rasponi is dead, her freedom is epitomised by the release of a bunch of swallows that have been captured that morning. The novel reinforces the message unhesitatingly:

> As each took flight, Joanna's heart went with it. Had not she too been snared? Snared indeed by her own desire; but still more by her own desire set free. And each bird, as it went from her, was, as a thank-offering for freedom. (p. 135)

While such an incident may be consistent with the novel's departures from realism, it is again heavily directive of the reader's sympathies. It also postpones central questions about what constitututes liberation and its relationship to Joanna's masochistic desires.

What appears as weaknesses within this first book can, however, be better understood in relation to the development of the novel as a whole. In Italy the 'door' of the title is actualised when Joanna notices a little door in the garden wall of a villa known as 'La Porziuncola' where a woman celebrated for her lovers allowed them to enter. But the symbolism of the door has already been flagged by the epigraph to the first section, a quotation from the Second Book of Kings, 9:3, 'Open the door and flee'. In the first book, therefore, the door stands for flight and escape, but the door in the garden wall remains as an alternative symbol of openness to pleasure and feelings. By combining the symbols we can see the early part of the novel as a search for escape through the process of defining and awakening to pleasure. The second book, introduced by a quotation, from Colossians, 4:3, 'Open a door of utterance', is much more concerned with finding a voice, with ways of giving expression to feeling. The third and final book, in which a radical shift in perspective takes place for Joanna, opens with Revelations, 21:5; 'Behold, I make all things new'. This final epigraph gives the most accurate indicator of what the book is striving towards: not escape, not entry, but revaluation. It aims to bring characters, places and events together in new and illuminating juxtapositions. It would have been too easy to show Joanna finding herself sexually in Italy, or realising her true love is Scotland. Instead, through plot device and symbolism which could be described as dream-like, the Italian period is depicted as only one phase of the character's evolving identity. In a brave artistic move, the second book opens with Joanna back in Scotland three years later, still enmeshed in the same problematic relationship with her mother and still suffering the moral and cultural constraints of life in Glasgow.

With increasing sophistication, the second part of the novel explores the nature of the constraints surrounding Joanna, offering a more complex representation of the limitations she experiences. Although the bird imagery is still there, the novel is less heavily schematised in its later sections, the symbols used with greater flexibility. And in the second section Joanna is presented as possessing a new consciousness of the world around her, which makes the earlier sections appear justifiable in their dream life quality: back in Glasgow, Joanna describes herself as 'not merely a woman reprieved but a woman awakened' and it appears that both character and text have 'woken up'. New perceptions are brought to difficult relationships in her life although she also begins to appreciate that solutions are not easily found. In the most significant areas of tension – the representation of the mother/daughter relationship, and in Joanna's new love affair with the artist, Louis Pender – resolution only comes in the third book.

Joanna's relationship with her mother, Juley, provides one of the novel's strongest themes. Juley, with her idiosyncratic religious convictions, appears to possess the vocation, that sense of purpose, which Joanna herself lacks, but Juley also imposes intolerable pressures upon her. Admiring Juley's goodness and zeal, deeply responsive to the love she showers upon them, the whole family are nevertheless irritated by her habits, her enthusiasms, her morality. On her return to Scotland Joanna despairs. In spite of the recognition of similarities between herself and her mother which came in Italy, she is still practising the same deceits and evasions, still attempting to save her mother's feelings yet maintain her own existence. Within this classic mother/daughter dynamic, Juley represents what Joanna must reject, in order both to attain adult sexuality and to challenge her mother's image of dutiful womanhood. Yet to turn away from what she represents also involves a rejection of the whole-hearted love the mother offers. Again the novel draws upon symbolism to convey complex emotional tensions: Joanna's symbolic movement away from her mother is depicted when Juley's illness forces her daughter to tidy out the hitherto secret central drawer in her mother's vast wardrobe, a moment described as the severance of the umbilical cord.[11] It is only on Juley's death in the third section of the novel that Joanna recognises that all her mother had sought was that simple declaration of love from her daughter – which had always proved too difficult and had been left perhaps too late. But even after her death Joanna refuses to join with her sister in a sentimentalising of her mother's happiness and good nature, believing that an admission of Juley's struggles, failures, and dissatisfactions shows more respect for the woman. For Joanna, to see Juley only in the role of mother, and to think of motherhood as an all-fulfilling promise for the future, is in itself reductive of human aspirations. Juley's death is not only movingly presented but is also deeply significant in terms of the wider themes the novel seeks to explore. If it frees Joanna, it also allows the reader to make retrospective assessment of one of the most powerfully delineated and influential relationships in the novel.

More important in terms of the romance plot, but lacking the resonance and detail of the mother/daughter relationship, is Joanna's long affair with the married and older artist, Louis Pender. When she first becomes enamoured of Pender he brings to her mind an image of that Italian door in the wall, which stands for 'unacknowledged, all unsatisfied desire' (p. 167). Strongly linked with the sexual bird imagery of the novel – there is something of the hawk in his face – Louis develops in Joanna a new awareness of her own capacity to be both dove and hawk, possessed and possessor. Yet while he is presented as extremely important in Joanna's sexual and emotional development, meeting her need for sacrifice by providing her with a relationship which can never come to anything, the descriptions of Louis show an unhappy man, curiously lacking in life. And soon Joanna realises that this relationship cannot meet all her longings:

> Dimly she realised that such a union as she desired beyond all desires was what her mother had in vain craved from her father through all the years of a marriage physically fruitful. Was it something that only women desire? Did men fear and avoid the consummation of spirit it was bound to bring? Or was it, whispered the sceptic in her, a lovely delusion? There were, one must believe, certain false dreams – will o' the wisps – which could lead the spirit disastrously astray. Was this such a dream? (p. 254)

As with the Italian escape, dream imagery is used to suggest that Joanna's aspirations have still not found shape or articulation.

Joanna's ability to survive the traumatic end of her relationship with Pender is only one of several personal 'revelations' that are brought about in the third book. Another arises through the death of her mother. A third comes through her direct involvement with the real suffering of the Moon family from whom she rents rooms. The death of their child,

Joanna's favourite, forces her to confront genuine troubles which put into perspective the emotional fluctuations characterising her life. Each of these events is presented as a step towards maturity for Joanna. The final revelation in the book is the realisation of her love for her quiet Scottish friend, Lawrence Urquhart. Throughout the second and third books Lawrence has represented an alternative to the power dynamics found in Joanna's other relationships with men. At the beginning of her passionate affair with Louis, in which they battle and hate as well as love, Joanna briefly encourages Lawrence and they are engaged for two days before Louis reclaims her. The moment of her coming together with Lawrence is described in noticeably different language from that of her other sexual encounters:

> 'I do mean it,' Joanna answered, looking at his hands, and though she was fighting hard for steadiness, her voice went wavering pathetically like a lost child's. 'I wish I could know you were my friend. I think I need you –'
>
> Not one other word could she speak. But there was no need, for the next moment Lawrence's black head was against her knees, against the knees that even now he dared not picture as a woman's. He had dropped crouching on the floor before her, burying his face in her skirts, and his arms clasped her with trembling determination. (p. 224)

They describe each other as friends, the language is one of 'need'; and they are both seen as childlike, hesitant, trembling, unsteady in the expression of their feelings. Overcome with emotion, Lawrence falls to his knees and burying his head in her lap clasps her, as a child would its mother. This image is re-enacted in the ending of the novel when Joanna, at Duntarvie and like a girl again, runs over the heather in desperate pursuit of him: 'With the tears pouring down her scarlet cheeks and all her features convulsed like a frantic lost child's, she got somehow over the brow of the hill and looked for him' (p. 396). When they come together the embrace is again childlike. Lawrence appears to offer the mutuality which has, in the early pages of the novel, been suggested as ideal through the encounter with Alec Peddie. The language, which has become increasingly abstract throughout the third book, now speaks of their relationship in terms of seeds, rebirth and new life.

The moment at which Joanna and Lawrence come together unites many of the themes and images of the novel. In a burst of physical activity she runs, as she describes it, for 'life'. In the embrace with Lawrence she finds the maternal role that has eluded her and creates a mutuality of need unacknowledged in the relationship with her own mother. In all her other relationships she had sought dominance from her partner, forcing the man to play a patriarchal role in relation to her submission. The discovery, made within the final pages of the novel, that she is two years older than Lawrence reinforces the alternative nature of the relationship, while the absence of bird imagery in the conclusion also suggests that a new pattern of identity has been established. Joanna's opting for Lawrence also suggests an essentially Scottish resolution to her dilemmas: the scene of their reconciliation, taking place near her old refuge, Duntarvie, appears to contain an integrity and innocence lacking in Italy, in London, and in the previous love affairs. It would seem that only now can Joanna accept a kind of Scottish identity, where before she has felt the need to define herself through exile, or the active embrace of other cultures. In this relationship with her native land she appears freed from patriarchal structures and finds a 'motherland'.[12]

In its conclusion the novel's symbolism is therefore heavily weighted towards presenting Lawrence as the solution to Joanna's unfulfilled desires. And yet, certain questions remain to be asked, both about the implications of this solution and the idea of 'unidentifiable longings' with which the novel began. Although the novel follows a romance format, as Joanna faces the trials of wrong relationships before finding the right man, other questions about a world outside romance have been raised, although rarely fully addressed or answered. Joanna's resentment at Lawrence's ability to lose himself in the world of men acknowledges the social and cultural constraints acting upon her, as does her increasing irritation at the way in which other women, in particular her sister and cousin, feel their lives are fulfilled by having children. Her artistic aspirations, initially a source of strength and rebellion, diminish disappointingly as the novel progresses. So, while the novel may appear to move towards personal resolution – with an almost Lawrentian celebration of the union of spiritual and sexual fulfilment, the finding of 'life' – it also has an undercurrent of larger social and psychological questioning.

One of the novel's underlying concerns is with role and vocation. Juley in many ways embodies the last of a breed of Victorian women who found an outlet for their energies in religion and philanthropy. Lacking her mother's faith, such an avenue is not open to Joanna, but she nevertheless seeks a purpose in the world. She is shown to be pleased when able to earn some income but this is never seen to be particularly important and instead her vocational energies go into relationships, all of which demand sacrifice and, except for Louis, a certain degree of dependency. With the latter, although not financially dependent, she is still not seen as his equal since moral laws demand that she be a shadowy figure on the sidelines of his social world. Some social concerns about a woman's place are therefore voiced in the novel.

It could be argued, however, that in respect of women's roles the novel evades and ignores much that was happening at the time of writing. In a novel purporting to explore new opportunities and forces for change, the silence about the growth of the Independent Labour Party, women's agitation for the Vote, and the range of new employment opportunities created towards the end of the century, is striking.[13] In the face of such activities Italian classes, artistic talents, an unfortunate marriage and an adulterous affair all seem rather weak responses to a new world.[14] And yet, in defence of the novel, it is worth recalling the argument of the writer, suffragette and feminist Cicely Hamilton who, in her strongly argued polemic of 1909, *Marriage as a Trade*, suggests that women should not be blamed for seeing the world in terms of romance and personal relationships as for many this represented a hard economic necessity which dominated and structured their view of the world:

> To her a woman in love is not only a woman swayed by emotion, but a human being engaged in carving for herself a career or securing for herself a means of livelihood. Her interest in a love story is, therefore, much more complex than a man's interest therein, and the appreciation which she brings to it is of a very different quality.[15]

While the sidelining of Joanna's artistic aspirations may diminish the novel's explicitly feminist message, it nevertheless offers insights into the economic and ideological determinants of female consciousness at the time which led women to channel their aspirations and energies into a search for self through sexual fufilment.

The novel is at its most radical, however, in exploring the construction of women's gendered identity. Although the romance plot may offer an overly-neat image of progression in the development of a young woman towards romantic happiness, the novel's tense and introspective quality points towards more complex psychological patterns. In its return to Scotland, to nature, to Duntarvie, and to Lawrence's childlike embrace, the text's circularity of structure suggests a psychic inevitability to Joanna's longings, which questions the possibility of ever fully articulating or fufilling one's desires. In this respect Carswell's novel engages with issues of women's psychic formation which now preoccupy feminism.

The romance pattern, and the importance of family background to the novel, allow us to see Joanna in a range of different scenarios, each of which determines her sense of self in relation to place, to a sexual partner, and to a different phase of her development. But even more striking is the fluidity which allows her to respond to people and circumstances. Although her search for a fixed identity suggests that Joanna perceives this fluidity as a weakness in her character, it might also be interpreted as a product of her gendered identity. In her autobiography Carswell speculates on what she sees as a particularly feminine characteristic:

> Why are men so much more afraid than women of losing their identities? Does nature provide for the more striking physical changes through which every normal woman has to pass – i.e. when she bears a child? How would men tolerate the change in their very shape? Although the shape is restored (more or less) after childbirth, the woman has had her lesson that nothing is static, including herself. With men the illusion of their own firmness persists much longer . . . [16]

The sense of female fluidity expressed here accords with much theoretical work on gendered identity and the mother/daughter relationship, which suggests that being mothered by someone of the same gender creates different relational capacities in boys and girls, leading girls to develop more fluid ego boundaries and to evolve a sense of self that is continuous with and empathetic to others.[17] In both loving and rejecting her mother Joanna shows an ambivalent relationship to Juley's emotional dominance. To acquire a new 'identity' she must move away from that empathy with the mother, but can only do so through definitional relationships with men, in which she submits to their power and possession. Until she meets Lawrence Urquhart this process is a destructive one, crushing her in relation to masculine 'firmness': with Gerald, Bob and above all, Louis, Joanna re-enacts a father/daughter relationship in which she is dominated by a patriarchal force. But in the friendship with Lawrence, she escapes from the female masochism characteristic of her other relationships. In this respect the final romance appears to symbolise a possibility of bringing maternal empathy to a relationship outside the same-sex nexus.

Moreover, in its depiction of the Juley/Joanna relationship and in the maternal dimension to the final sexual partnering, the novel moves towards a recognition of the dyadic mother/daughter relationship as central to the identity formation of women. Here Carswell anticipates the thinking of French feminist, Luce Irigaray, who asks 'But how, as daughters, can we have a personal relationship with or construct a personal identity in relation to someone who is no more than a function?'[18] In its depiction of Juley's spiritual anguish, the physical and emotional dimensions of her marriage, her personal habits, hesitancies and disappointments, the novel goes some way to making the character much more than a 'function of motherhood'. And the characterisation of Juley becomes an important determining factor in our understanding of Joanna's sense of herself, establishing a new configuration of relationships between women which both acknowledges and problematises what Irigaray has called 'the matrilinear debt' ('The Bodily Encounter with the Mother').[19]

Once again we can see how *Open the Door!* remains in dialogue with *Aurora Leigh*, extending that poem's debate about a woman's role and female fulfilment. Carswell makes her own task more difficult, her explorations of gendered identity more complex, by filling the empty space of motherhood so noticeable in *Aurora Leigh*, in which the poet is brought up by her widowed father until adolescence:

> As it was, indeed,
> I felt a mother-want about the world,
> And still went seeking, like a bleating lamb
> Left out at night in shutting up the fold, –
> As restless as a nest-deserted bird
> Grown chill through something being away, though what,
> It knows not.[20]

Cora Kaplan has suggested that through this device Aurora 'foregoes an early and desirable experience of loving . . . she also avoids, if we adopt a Freudian scheme for the socialisation of children, the full conflict of the Oedipal crisis . . . since she does not have to 'give up' her father to her mother and identify with the weaker sex.'[21] Carswell faces up to the implications and problematics of this process by foregrounding the mother/daughter relationship and interpreting it in conjunction with sexual relationships in the text. Read in this way the romance plot is not so much a distraction from the novel's deeper concerns but rather a recognisable language in which to articulate a more complex analysis of the formation of a gendered identity within a specific cultural context. Writing in 1909, Cicely Hamilton had asked the question: 'From woman's art and woman's literature what does one learn of the essential difference between the masculine and feminine fashion of regarding the closest of all relations – the relation of mother and child?' and had found women's literature lacking both in terms of its depiction of love and of the maternal.[22] While *Open the Door!* may appear to rely upon the conventions of romance, in its narrative of female development it succeeds in offering a new perspective on the mother/daughter relationship which translates into a sophisticated analysis of gendered identity and which places the novel firmly within a tradition of women's writing.

Notes

1. Catherine Carswell, *Open the Door!* (Andrew Melrose, London, 1920; Virago, London, 1986).
2. Catherine Carswell, *Lying Awake: An Unfinished Autobiography and Other Posthumous Papers*, edited and with an introduction by John Carswell (Secker & Warburg, London, 1950), p. 29.
3. Catherine Carswell, *The Camomile* (Chatto & Windus, London, 1922; Virago, London, 1987).
4. Catherine Carswell, 'New Novels', *The Glasgow Herald*, 4 November 1915.
5. John Carswell, Introduction to Virago edition, *Open the Door!*.
6. *Open the Door!* (Virago, London, 1986), p. 9. All subsequent page references are to the Virago edition.
7. Elizabeth Barrett Browning, *Aurora Leigh* (London, 1857). The Women's Press edition (London, 1978) contains an excellent introduction by Cora Kaplan.
8. *Aurora Leigh*, I, ll. 303–12.
9. None of all these things
Can women understand. You generalise
Oh, nothing, – not even grief!
Aurora Leigh, II, ll. 182–4

10. 'She had tried her best and rejoiced that he had beaten her. He had made her his anew and she longed for him.' *Open the Door!*, p. 116.

11. *Open the Door!*, p. 242.

12. See Glenda Norquay, 'Welcome O Mine Own Rugged Scotland!': Gender and Landscape in Scottish Fiction', *Regional Europe: Voice and Form: Conference Proceedings* (Vitoria, 1994).

13. Ironically, one of the groups established by feminists in the inter-war period, to campaign for equal rights, pay and opportunities for women, called itself the Open Door group.

14. For a critique of the novel in these terms see Pam Morris, *Literature and Feminism* (Blackwell, Oxford, 1993), pp. 142–3.

15. Cicely Hamilton, *Marriage as a Trade* (Chapman & Hall, London, 1909; The Women's Press, London, 1981), p. 117.

16. *Lying Awake*, p. 128.

17. In particular the work of Nancy Chodorow has been influential in this area. She writes: 'Mothers tend to experience their daughters as more like and more continuous with themselves. Correspondingly girls tend to remain part of the dyadic primary mother-child relationship itself. This means that a girl continues to experience herself as involved in issues of merging and separation . . . By contrast, mothers experience their sons as a male opposite. Boys are more likely to have been pushed out of the pre-oedipal relationship, and to have had to curtail their primary love and sense of empathic tie with their mother. . . . Girls emerge from this period with a basis for 'empathy' that boys do not. . . . Furthermore, girls do not define themselves in terms of the denial of pre-oedipal relational modes to the same extent as do boys. Therefore, a regression to these modes tends not to feel as much a basic threat to the ego.' *The Reproduction of Mothering: Psychoanalysis and the Sociology of Gender* (University of California Press, Berkeley, 1978), pp. 166–7.

18. Luce Irigaray, 'Women-Mothers, the Silent Substratum of the Social Order', *The Irigaray Reader*, ed. M. Whitford (Blackwell, Oxford, 1991), p. 50.

19. 'The Bodily Encounter with the Mother', *The Irigaray Reader* p. 44.

20. *Aurora Leigh*, I, 11.39–45.

21. Cora Kaplan, Introduction to *Aurora Leigh*, p. 19.

22. Hamilton, *Marriage as a Trade*, p. 113.

27

Willa Muir: Crossing the Genres

Margaret Elphinstone

Willa Muir's autobiography is an elusive text; ostensibly it was never actually written, but that need be no deterrent to making it the starting point of this examination of self, gender and society in her work. On the contrary, the location of autobiography as a hidden subtext, both in the novels and in the late works *Belonging* and *Living with Ballads*, is exemplary of Muir's analysis of marginality and identity.[1]

It seems appropriate to begin with two autobiographical incidents embedded in the two non-fiction texts, even though these books, appearing at the end of her writing career, might not seem at first to be the obvious place to start. Lumir Soukup describes Muir's struggle to sustain her output at this late stage, and is aware of the limitations of time and old age:

> It was a pity that Willa felt morally obliged to write *Living With Ballads* . . . [It] had far too complicated and vast a range for one person to encompass alone, the more so since Willa was hurt, ill, in constant pain and of advanced age . . . When it came to the actual continuous writing of *Belonging*, age, the efforts of past years, constant pain and ill health all took their toll . . . [2]

Belonging (1968) is explicitly a memoir of Edwin; *Living with Ballads* (1965), a book Edwin was commissioned to write, and that Willa wrote after his death, is an examination of the significance of the ballad as expression of a culture and a society. Both books fulfil their stated purpose more than adequately. They also engage with that major theme in all Muir's writing: the issue of identity in relation to belonging. Belonging is represented in both, as I hope to show, in terms of an Edenic state of both unity of self and union with what Muir calls 'the universe'; lapse from this state of belonging is marked by a sense of dislocation, and of entrapment in a maze of misconceptions and dead ends.

Both Edenic and labyrinthine images will be familiar to anyone who knows the poetry of Edwin Muir. A study of either Willa or Edwin Muir constantly uncovers evidence of a fruitful exchange of not only the ideas that belong in both Muirs' construct of the conscious world, but also the images that reflect the unconscious. Willa is the one who frankly acknowledges the depth of the relationship between Edwin and herself: 'I had discovered that if Edwin and I did not Belong together, I now Belonged nowhere' (*Belonging*, p. 84).

It is interesting that Edwin and Willa Muir shared a language – Orcadian and Shetland dialect – which in every place (except Orkney, where they stayed briefly) emphasised their mutual difference from their surrounding community. The shared imagery can be related not only to shared lives and thoughts, but also to their shared immersion in European literature, particularly the joint translations of Kafka's work which they undertook between 1930 and 1962. Willa Muir's autobiographical writing (unlike Edwin's) focuses overtly upon the dynamic of this central relationship. However, although the predicament of the isolated self is therefore examined obliquely rather than directly, it nonetheless informs both her non-fictional as well as her fictional writing.

Janice Morgan examines autobiography in terms of a textual construction of an identity, an 'evolving self', an identity which consists precisely in a negotiation between the actual and the imaginary, between text and lived experience. In women's writing particularly, she argues for 'the specificity of this writing, for what we might call a poetics of women's selfhood'.[3]

Moreover, she places this analysis of women's autobiography within the context of the deconstruction of the boundaries between genres, in particular those of autobiography and fiction. This removal of genre boundaries seems especially helpful in examining Muir's *œuvre*, since here we have an apparent multiplicity of genres – political pamphlet, essay, novel, memoir, sociological/literary study which, as I shall argue, all use similar literary devices to examine the theme of the evolving self. In each form, the same dynamic is at work, that of the reconstruction of identity within the text, in terms of negotiation with a society, or tradition, in which that identity has been hidden and marginalised.

The two autobiographical incidents that Muir describes at the end of her life relate precisely to an initiation into awareness of self, in terms of either belonging, or not belonging, to the culture in which she finds herself. The earlier incident is described in *Belonging*, in the context of her explaining herself to another outsider in mainland Scotland, Edwin Muir. This first chapter encapsulates the tension in *Belonging* between overt narrative and subversive subtext. Willa never wrote an autobiography. Edwin Muir's autobiography achieves almost mythic status in its evocation of the author's Orkney childhood, a state of innocence shattered by the expulsion from Wyre, and the confrontation with the city and with death.[4] He barely mentions Willa. Like Edwin Muir's poetry, his autobiography synthesises the specific and the mythic, in terms of a relationship between man and place. Willa Muir's story of their joint lives is presented as a memoir of him; the fact that it is also the record of her own married life is on the face of it incidental. And yet what the text offers is not quite what it purports to be. Certainly it is about Edwin, but one could argue that the main character is the first-person narrator, Willa. One could go further and say there is a dialogue at the centre of the book between narrator and character. The 'I' of the narration is looking back and textually constructing not only Edwin, but also herself in the past.

Willa Muir says very little about her own childhood, but the one passage in which she reconstructs her childhood self relates directly to the title of the memoir: *Belonging*. Muir has a good deal to say in the book about her preoccupation with Belonging to the Universe, but it is in this short passage that the theory first becomes embodied, according to the conventions of fiction, in the creation of a character. Edwin Muir created one myth about the meaning of belonging, in terms of place. Here, we find Willa Muir offering another version. The overt text makes this brief excursion into her past marginal to the real purpose of the Memoir; however, in terms of thematic unity, this early incident would seem to be absolutely central:

'Do you feel now that you belong to Glasgow,' I asked. The question of 'belonging' had preoccupied me nearly as far back as I could remember.

Edwin hesitated and said that if he belonged anywhere it must be to Orkney.

I did not feel that I belonged whole-heartedly to Montrose. Well before I was three, I explained, I had discovered that I did not really belong to the Montrose way of life. My people spoke Shetland at home, so my first words were in the Norse dialect of Shetland, which was not valid outside our front door. I remembered standing in Bridge Street, where we lived, fingering my pinafore, dumb with embarrassment, while four or five older girls squealed in delighted mockery of what I had said and urged me to say it again. (*Belonging* p. 19)

It seems that the genesis of the informing principle of the book is not founded on any memory of Edwin, but in a perception of her *self* at a critical moment in early childhood. The subsequent discussion in the text between her and Edwin relates her myth of the fall to his. For Edwin, the transition from Orkney to Glasgow was the descent from the primeval childhood world into a fallen culture. Willa finds a parallel experience – what she calls 'that kind of shock' – in the girl who realises for the first time that she does not belong.

It is hardly surprising then, that the images in this passage reflect the major themes of the novels. There is the issue of location: the small Scottish east-coast town where the line between belonging and not belonging is sharply delineated and rigidly enforced, and, within that town, the boundary between indoors and outdoors. The three-year-old Willa, who is here a character in a text, framed by a discussion about location and belonging, has, up until this point, found an unquestioned identity, a place to belong, 'at home'. The shock of discovery here is the shock of identifying the threshold. There is a boundary to identity; the edges of the unproblematic self are the walls of the house. This is the beginning of a dynamic negotiation of an identity that, in Muir's novels, both Elizabeths have to engage with in Calderwick, and is the threat and the challenge that drives Annie Ritchie back into the four walls of her house as into a self-destructive prison.

Furthermore, the issue of not belonging beyond that threshold is a linguistic one. What makes this child in the regulation pinafore different from the other girls is the way she speaks. When that is defined for her as 'not belonging', she is literally 'struck dumb'. The innocence of the child at home is Edenic (or semiotic, perhaps: there are possibilities here for a psychoanalytic interpretation) in its unconsciousness. Expulsion means self-awareness, and the child's realisation of the dislocation between self and other comes in terms of speech – in mythic terms she moves from Eden to the Tower of Babel. Conscious identity is founded upon this first shocking awareness of not belonging in the world in which she finds herself. The difference in language is a source of pain and alienation, and yet, paradoxically, it is language that allows the experience of separation to be transformed. Muir in adult life became a writer and translator – as she says here to Edwin 'I was always good at languages'. By means of language the subject who is first constructed in this passage through painful awareness of difference, can achieve a voice of her own – many voices of her own. Through language the adult narrator can give form and meaning to the pain of the inarticulate three-year-old.

At the beginning of *Living With Ballads* we have another autobiographical incident. Muir is discussing the singing games that she played at her school in Montrose:

These singing games were not made for solitary performers; they needed to be set going by a social group . . . We eleven-year-olds were proud to be included in the singing games.

Admission to them was a promotion, a step towards being grown-up, which meant for us chiefly being mated and married. The rhythms of puberty, already stirring in us, directed our attention to the future bliss of choosing and being chosen by a sweetheart, but until invited to join the ring of senior girls we had to make do with solitary attempts to divine that future by skipping-rope, a frenzy of skipping which was merely self-made magic, not to be compared with the communal choosing practised in the singing games. These games left us all satisfied and happy. (*Living With Ballads*, p. 14)

The movement here is from the separation of childhood into a communal world. The experience of puberty, the desire and curiosity about a future mate, can now be integrated into a shared experience. This second recollection of a childhood incident, like the first memory of alienation, is expressed through language. In this case it is language in a heightened form – song, not speech, accompanied by shared actions which are the basis of dance. The emphasis in the first incident was on differences in language; here, the words of the song are sung quite literally in unison. The solitary skipping, on the other hand, is merely 'self-made magic' – there are no words to it. In the singing games, the first thing the younger girls have to do is to learn the words and the actions, in other words, to inherit a tradition. Moreover, Muir explains how these are not the words of everyday speech in Montrose, and so the girls at once 'set a good distance between our ordinary world and that of the song'. Later she uses the phrase 'a magic circle'. Muir is to develop this argument in relation to the ballads throughout the book: the shared, communal world is a liberation from isolation. It becomes a temporary, or perhaps a fantasised, solution to the problems of isolation and marginality; during the fantasy social belonging can be achieved without paying the price of repressing individual desire or imagination, and conversely, the community does not have to be rejected in order to create a 'self-made magic'. When she later (ch. 2) compares two singers of ballads, she demonstrates how the ballads, properly rendered, offer a direct route into a communal tradition, in which specificity of time, place or character no longer prevents entry into the collective tradition, or 'magic' world.

These incidents, written by Muir at the end of her life, about her experience at the beginning of it, frame the novels in other ways than the merely chronological. One could see them as epitomising for Muir the difficulties and paradoxes of belonging. An autobiographical reading might suggest that these experiences played their part in formulating the concept that was to become a crucial issue in all her writing. A more textual reading might take them as an exposition of the basic paradigm of all her work, an image that provides a suitable conclusion to her whole *œuvre*.

Muir's writing about her past self is in both texts marginal and transgressive of genre. It seems highly ironic that she consistently returns to the theme of identity and belonging, and yet within her own texts she makes her self marginal. In *Living With Ballads* she brings in her self-in-the-past only to efface her. The experience described is that of merging of self into other, of truly belonging in a shared imaginative experience. But we are specifically told that the game is 'not for grown-ups'. The adult author creates a self-in-the-past that is now beyond her own reach. The self-conscious author, who names her own work, is engaged in a different act of creation. She belongs in the solitary, fallen world of the isolated individual.

In Muir's novels too we see characters imprisoned in the isolation of their subjective worlds. In both published novels the world of superficial social intercourse is a restricted one that offers little ultimate hope. Partial escape only becomes possible in the dream world, the world of the unconscious, where the individual merges with what Muir calls the 'universe'. In both *Imagined Corners* and *Mrs Ritchie* dreams are crucial, and the dream world continually subverts the appearance of social realism. However, although the impulse to freedom may arise from the unconscious, it remains a mere possibility unless it is physically realised in the conscious, external world.[5]

So the seat of belonging is located in the other, magical world. In the ordinary everyday world, where people try to talk to one another in ordinary, everyday language, there are barriers to communication. In Muir's delineations of the external social world, there are always walls, blind alleys, shut doors, closed windows. Each character in a Muir novel is enclosed within a private, individual world that also becomes a prison. But there is another world; another possibility is open even to an Annie Ritchie, and both Elizabeth Shands actively seek the freedom that the other world offers. But, just as for the singers of the ballads, isolated selfhood is a limitation, and the expression of that separation is a travesty of the communication that language might potentially be. The two Elizabeth Shands 'together might make one whole woman', but separately, neither can entirely liberate herself from the restrictions of Calderwick.

Muir was a psychologist by training, and she very deliberately brings psychological paradigms to her construction of fictional characters. She uses tensions between the conscious and the unconscious in fiction, by aligning them with tensions between the actual and the imaginary. One might say that she integrates Freudian psychoanalysis with one of the traditional tenets of Scottish literature: the polarity of the ordinary and the marvellous, the inner world inhabited by ghosts and dreams, and the outer world of appearances which seem to be real. Hence Muir's insistence on the importance of dreams in her fiction. In her discussion of singing games she relates the symbolism of the games to the symbols in dreams, and concludes:

> The foundations were being laid for a bridge between unconscious feelings and conscious personalities; there was not yet much traffic to cross the bridge and the territory beyond it was largely unexplored, but the lines of communication were being kept open. (*Living With Ballads*, p. 20)

The division between conscious and unconscious here is to be reconciled through communal expression: a shared language that voices the shared unconscious world. Moreover, it is the language, the song, that makes the unconscious magical. The 'self-made' magic of solitary skipping does not do the trick; experience is not transfigured by it. It is the common tradition that is needed, the long-established words that have to be learned by the initiates. They have to learn to belong in that tradition, in order to experience the Belonging which is a liberation from the non-magic world of the separated self.

Muir discusses the significance of Belonging explicitly and frequently in *Belonging*. Belonging, she reiterates, is located in the unconscious self, and conscious awareness of it comes in terms of language, at the point of loss. (And yet, as she goes on to demonstrate, language can become the basis for forging a new sense of social belonging.) Muir extends the scope of the discussion by examining her and Edwin's marginal status in terms of nationality, in Scotland, in England, and in Europe. She is never simplistic about nationality; her relationship with every place is complex, marginal and full of creative, if difficult, tensions. On the one hand she can record the simple relief of understanding the language in Britain, or the pleasure of 'our sense of belonging to the historic Rome' (p. 256). On the other hand she considers her and Edwin's chosen status of 'non-joiners' of nations, groups, and political parties (pp. 165–6), and painfully uncovers feelings of dislocation in her childhood home on the east-coast of Scotland (e.g. pp. 114, 207). It is in Scotland that the feelings of alienation in the social world strike agonising chords in the inner world too, for example at St Andrews in 1940:

> I had been lost in a bleak region where there was no living thing, not even a microscopic insect on a minute speck of lichen, nothing but ice, deep clefts and high ridges of blueish ice, with jagged peaks of ice rising beyond them that I knew I had to climb. (*Belonging*, p. 207)

It is in Scotland, where the issue for Muir herself is most acute, that the two published novels are set, in versions of Muir's childhood home of Montrose. It seems a strange irony that Muir's unpublished novels are now shelved, literally and metaphorically, in St Andrews, where Muir herself engaged in the most acute struggle of her adult life with issues of identity and marginality. For Muir, as for the two Elizabeths in *Imagined Corners*, Europe represents an equivocal kind of freedom. For a Scottish woman, it seems, the issue of Belonging is most painful when it relates to Scotland, and yet it is in relation to Scotland that it must be resolved.

It might seem at first that this duality of belonging and not belonging, as an essential part of the construct of self, is a long way from the genre of social comment or political pamphlet. However, deconstruction of genre is a particularly useful approach to Muir's work, as the subversive content of her political writing lies precisely in her refusal to be bound by the accepted paradigms of a genre that explicitly deals solely with the outer world of organised societies. Muir's political writing transgresses that convention in its persistent analysis of the evolving self.

Muir most successfully constructs identity in terms of belonging or not belonging through creation of characters within texts. Ironically, she says herself in *Women: An Inquiry* (1925) that a woman who attempts to be 'formal and abstract' has 'killed herself spiritually'.[6] This pamphlet is the most formal and abstract of all Muir's work – and the most deeply inconsistent in its paradoxical definitions of gender difference as both essential, and socially constructed. I was relieved to find a general comment by Patricia Mudge which confirmed my own uneasiness about this particular text:

> While [Muir] detested the male dominance she saw all around her, championing the feminist cause wasn't her primary concern. Even if it had been, Willa's opinions were too inconsistent to be taken seriously.[7]

Women: An Inquiry is an uncomfortable text. Muir's assertion that women are essentially different 'in spirit' from men sometimes takes on a momentum that carries determinism to conclusions which Muir herself feels obliged to qualify apologetically. If, she argues, women's creative energy is naturally directed to the 'creation of human beings' rather than ideas, then it follows that they belong naturally in the home, the private sphere; they are intuitive rather than intellectual; in art they are better at the lesser genres, as they lack the wide vision required for anything of epic proportions; belonging to the world of the unconscious, they deal with the concrete and specific, not the universals or abstractions of the conscious intellect. Muir tells us this from the standpoint of the omniscient didactic author, and this early text seems strangely conservative and 'masculine' in precisely the way that Muir herself defines that term. Her essentialist stance, her eschewal of dream and metaphor for an apparently logical rationale seems to only prove her case: that this 'masculine' form and narrative point of view do not suit her. Her vehement objections to the inferior status of women in a male world seem to contradict her determinist argument. She begins with an analysis of the 'slave mentality' of all inferior groups, and suggests that gender too may be socially constructed. She makes a radical analysis of the textual status of woman as object rather than subject, the power structure of the marriage contract, and the political rationale for the repression of female sexuality, and yet in this article the generic woman remains unliberated. I suggest that this is because this figure has no character. She is abstract and generic, and the universalist assumptions, along with the lack of a self as subject, make uneasy reading in this post-colonial age. They also contrast strikingly with Woolf's essay in the same series: *Mr Bennett and Mrs Brown* (1923), in which Woolf insists on specific time, place and character, in the manner which makes all her political essays so challenging of genre and gender.[8] Occasionally Muir gives herself away completely: 'women display the same passionate interest in other people ... neighbours, servants and children are their dearest topics.' (*Women: an Inquiry*, p. 22). It is easy to criticise the unconscious subjectivity of seventy years ago, but my point is that Muir in her later political writing finds ways to avoid the pitfalls of assumed omniscience and universality.

The published novels are more consistently radical: after all, when Muir set out to write fiction, she was able to employ the literary construction of the inner self that Modernism offered her, and the psychoanalytical model of identity that her academic training had given her, in order to bring the plural, fragmented and radically subversive subject into the written text. In *Women: An Inquiry* she does offer a paradigm of the unsubdued unconscious that can be related to the search for Belonging, undertaken by characters in the novels such as Elizabeth Shand and William Murray, and a paradigm of its opposite, the utterly subdued unconscious, that is to achieve full focus in the characters of Annie Ritchie and Mrs Grundy.

Imagined Corners was described by Muir herself as two novels contracted into one (*Belonging*, p. 163). She does herself less than justice here, as the plot lines relating to the Murray and the Shand families are thematically linked to create the dynamic tension that informs the novel. Elizabeth Shand and William Murray face essentially the same dilemma, which is expressed in parallel images of the dual worlds that they encounter both in waking life and in dream. Moreover, the fate of Ned Murray is a sword that hangs over all the characters who are aware of the fragmented nature of their own consciousness. Elise too, as another outsider whom Calderwick has rejected, stands in opposition to all those who outwardly conform, not merely her own family. Although these are not the only connecting links between the two families, they perhaps embody most fully the paradoxical nature of identity and belonging.

The contradictions within which the characters strive to create themselves are multiple, and fragmented. Muir takes us beyond the binary poles of inner/outer lives, nature/culture, freedom/imprisonment, feminine/masculine. I have examined elsewhere the effect of these dualities on constructions of gender within the novel.[9] Elizabeth Shand has a private, inner world, reflected in the wilderness of moor and sea that surrounds the social construct which is Calderwick. But she is also faced with the restrictive role that Calderwick offers her for being a woman. William Murray has his dream world: 'that remote sea on which he had been cradled, unstirred by desire or regret, at one with his God' (*Imagined Corners*)' p. 5). He also has the role Calderwick offers him. As Elizabeth has assumed the additional burden of being not only a wife, but a Noble Wife (e.g., p. 35), so William has to be not only a man, but also the Minister (p. 106). That is to say, unlike the other characters, they not only have to accept the roles a punitive society has dealt them, they have also voluntarily undertaken an extra burden. They must not only manage to conform outwardly (which for them is not the point), they must be noble, or ministerial, in spirit. A kind of hubris, perhaps? What most horrifies William about his brother Ned is the likeness between them. Ned mirrors that part of William that William would like to imagine does not exist. Elizabeth too finds herself reflected, not in any exemplary Calderwick wife, but in a 'fallen woman' (p. 164), which is the role assigned to Elise by Calderwick. Elizabeth's escape becomes possible when she acknowledges her spiritual connection with Elise. William, on the other hand, betrays Ned in a way which amounts to a betrayal of himself, and so in becoming spiritually isolated, both Ned and William are destroyed.

It is Elizabeth's awareness of connections rooted in the unconscious mind, and her striving after a sense of unity with creation, that aligns her with William Murray. However, as Muir makes clear, the unconscious, where the belonging that Elizabeth seeks can become manifest, is embodied in physical life. Both Elizabeth and William consistently ignore, or misinterpret, the physical world, as if it were not part of the self. At the bazaar they seem not to notice when their feet touch, although everyone else is agog with awareness. Elizabeth misinterprets the sexual feelings she has for Hector for spiritual love, because she cannot acknowledge her bodily self. Her need to deceive herself shows that she is, ironically, more prudish than Mabel, who reads the meaning of sex with acute, if limited, clarity.

This reading of the denial of the body amounting to a denial of the unconscious self would seem to support Alison Smith's assertion that there is a liberation both in terms of sexuality and identity in the final partnership and flight of the two Elizabeths.[10] Such a relationship would seem to be a logical resolution of Elizabeth's earlier evasions. However, I think there is an ambiguity about Elizabeth and Elise's journey at the end. France is not the wilderness that has always represented spiritual freedom for Elizabeth. On the contrary, the very landscape echoes the imprisonment of soul that has tormented Elizabeth in Calderwick: 'this dry bright landscape with those gnarled little trees, that looked as if they had been maimed and tortured . . . crippled, like herself' (p. 281).

William Murray's progress towards death by drowning, prefigured in dreams and images, is accompanied by his persistent denial of bodily reality, and so, ironically, the drowning in the end becomes physical. The tortuous alleys in which William has been mentally and physically wandering finally lead him to his death in the stagnant imprisoned water of the corner of the harbour. As Hector Shand realises earlier, 'Better to drown in the open sea than in that stagnant muck' (p. 44).

William Murray returns to the sea he dreamed of, but not to its infinite possibilities; the space he drowns in is restricted and polluted. In the final analysis I would argue that Elizabeth and Elise are not really free either. Although they have escaped Calderwick, they carry its crippling effects with them, and so they will meet manifestations of it wherever they go. Even their transgressions against Calderwick's social code are mirrored in the geography of the place. Calderwick is the map of their inner worlds, or, conversely, their inner world is made in the image of Calderwick. The novel begins with the meticulous location of Calderwick within the Universe, and also within Scotland. The narrator of *Imagined Corners* makes one thing clear: belonging to the universe, if one happens to be Scottish, means coming to terms with belonging, or not belonging, to Scotland. Elise and Elizabeth are Scottish women, and it is in terms of an idea of Scotland that their identity is constructed. This is the case both within the world of the novel, and in terms of the nature of the text in which they are written. If Elizabeth thinks she is separate from society, with a unique relationship to a private universe, she is shown to be mistaken:

> So Elizabeth, shutting her front door behind her, thought herself alone in her castle, but if she was alone anywhere it was in a castle in Spain. (p. 264)

Even as she thinks this, she is the uppermost thought in every mind in Calderwick. Her struggle towards an inner identity, and towards belonging to the universe, cannot be a journey into isolation. It would seem to be no accident that girls playing singing games, like those in *Living With Ballads*, do appear in this novel, when William Murray goes to visit Annie Watson. Calderwick, as much a fallen world as ever Brown's Barbie was,[11] is a restricted and divided society externally, but the way to the freedom of the unconscious, towards a true collective belonging, is physically present and open to all. Wind and water from sea and moor force their way into the High Street, and beat upon closed doors and windows. Everyone in Calderwick is perforce involved in a relationship with these dangerous elements. The rejection of Ned, whose incarceration in the lunatic asylum is the epitome of all the spiritual imprisonments in the novel, is a *communal* rejection of the unruly unconscious. Calderwick is a society, and every character belongs to it, and that makes it what it is. No one can escape simply by running away.

In *Mrs Ritchie* the battle against the dangerous unconscious becomes even more sharply focused, especially in the first part of the novel (which Muir herself felt was more controlled than the second half; *Belonging*, p. 163). The extraordinary achievement of *Mrs Ritchie* is the portrayal of a battle of cosmic proportions which takes place in the mind of the apparently insignificant Annie Ritchie: the images of Heaven and hell, God and devil, make the conflict Miltonic in its symbolic weight, while at the same time the trivial discourse of smalltown life is meticulously exposed. *Mrs Ritchie* is a curious book. Written at the height of the Modernist period, it is in its focus upon the inner life of a character a Modernist text; yet the narrator remains firmly outside the struggle, even though one might expect the images of death and judgement to make the individual predicament universal. But there is nothing Joycean about the revelation of the inner world of Annie Ritchie. We do not so much enter into her consciousness as examine it under a microscope. As in *Imagined Corners*, Muir's own standpoint is made quite explicit. The Calderwick God is shown to be created in the image of repression and conscious judgement. He is the antithesis of Belonging to the Universe. He stands for the ironically diabolical doctrines of original sin and predestination, which are instruments to torture and destroy the innocent self, and its collective expression.

Perhaps it is this peculiarly Scottish construct of God which makes Annie Ritchie not so much an Everywoman, but rather Mrs Grundy in Scotland. The construction of a negative image of female Scottish identity, which was present in *Imagined Corners*, has here become central. In Mrs Ritchie identity in terms of Scottishness and gender is not realised; it is only indicated by the rigorous repression which is needed to eliminate its possibilities.

If we turn back to *Women: An Inquiry* the dynamic is clearly set out. There, Muir explains that the negation of women's identity is as powerful a force as its fulfilment, but its perverted strength is turned inwards towards repression, and outwards to the suppression of everybody else: 'Creative power', she tells us, 'is, of course, the obverse of an equal power for destruction' (*Women: An Inquiryr*, p. 17). Similarly, if we turn to *Mrs Grundy in Scotland*, published shortly after *Mrs Ritchie*, when clearly the themes of the novel were still active in Muir's mind, we find a social study of the effects of the repressed unconscious, as we shall see.

In *Imagined Corners* the unconscious self is shown to be repressed by being divided; the characters have to integrate the physical and spiritual aspects of their selves in order to be healed, and that is hard because they live in a society that insists on the hypocrisy of separation. Annie Ritchie identifies her physical, sexual self with the devil – she sees body hair as the mark of the devil that is signed on her body at puberty. Godliness, and therefore salvation, is only possible if she represses her diabolical sexuality. Love, therefore, is something she must deny both herself and her family. She never allows herself to respond sexually to her husband, and this enforced isolation reaches its extreme from when she stops speaking to him altogether. She beats her three-month-old son when he has an erection, and banishes him from the house when, as an infant, he dares to watch when she breastfeeds his young sister. It becomes her task to eradicate the physical form her children's lives. Throughout her life hair remains for her the devil's mark, and she habitually punishes her children's expressions of natural feeling by beating them with a hairbrush. It is such a beating that finally drives Sarah Annie, a woman in her twenties, from her mother's house.

Throughout the novel Annie's terror of unconscious feelings is expressed through images of savagery and of Africa. Young Annie Ritchie is strangely stirred by stories of savage tribes in Africa, and demonstrates her goodness throughout her life by her rigid organisation of mission work. As a child, savage drumbeats echo in her brain, and she flirts with magic practices among the other girls. She learns to despise her family because she fears them; they are a dangerous source of natural feeling. When Annie is forbidden to go on to the High School she is terrified at her own rage:

> This passion within Annie obliterated the neat scheme of rational activities which her mind had been following under Mr Boyd's guidance, submerging it as a volcanic flood might submerge an intricate system of linked waterways. (p. 33)

The chaos represented by Africa still menaces her when the Boer war breaks out: 'from the dark blot of Africa death might spread and spread until it came to Calderwick' (p. 176). Africa here is not only the dangerous unconscious, it is also death, for the social taboo that the repressed unconscious fully apprehends, being both of the body and of the soul, is death. Annie, who has banished such knowledge from her conscious world, lives in fear of death, while, of course, it comes closer to her all the time. Sleep, too, becomes a terror to her, as in sleep the unconscious rules, and she is troubled by nightmares.

She finds her own way to subdue these uprisings in her self: like the mission work, everything must be rigidly organised and delineated. She denies her own body, and instead she has a house, which becomes her self: 'Indeed, the house was Mrs Ritchie, and Mrs Ritchie was the house' (p. 192). Annie sees herself as having triumphed over her husband's sexuality on her wedding night as she has remained 'locked away and inaccessible' like 'the prim clean house', while Johnny 'could not find the key' (p. 158). The children recognise her identification with a house when they give her birthday presents that are for the house, never for herself. And again, when Samuel John, aged seventeen, demands a latch key, Annie taunts her husband with what she sees as unnatural acquiescence in a kind of incest, when she says he should be ashamed 'to ken that your son'll be trying the key in the lock o' your house' (p. 253). Later John Samuel, filthy with the mud of the trenches, desecrates his mother's clean bed as he collapses exhausted into it.

The railway too becomes an image of orderliness, running as it does on straight lines, and never deviating from its path. As a child Annie finds a way out of her fear and misery by contemplating its straight, unrelenting tracks (p. 55). Years later, John Samuel laughs at the comparison of his mother with the railway when he is drunk (p. 320). He sees how she defies death itself, she simply 'persists'. But it is his mother, embodied in the train, that kills him. In a sense she already has; in his mind, as he suffers from shellshock, she has become the Great War itself. The irony of all Annie's efforts to escape death is that death is exactly where she leads her family, because in her paradigm opposites have become reversed. Her husband Johnny, who ends up becoming a coffin maker, is driven into a spiritual imprisonment that is deathly. His actual death comes to him as a longed-for liberation:

> Annie was aye yattering about the life after death. Ay weel, maybe it was the one thing left to hope for. Imphm, many a man, no doubt, had been driven before him into the same corner, with the walls narrowing and narrowing until there was no way out except through the narrow gate of a coffin. (p. 205)

Annie denies her own mortality by the traditional Calvinist expedient, so well documented in Scottish literature, of electing herself to grace. Since she has never succumbed to human love or passion, her place in heaven is assured. Her struggle is to get her family there with her, and it is only because she fails to redeem them from common humanity that she feels sorry about her husband and son, in the last ghastly image of the book, when she sits patting their grave mounds. Like her predecessor James Hogg, Muir here shows us a monster created out of the doctrine of the elect. In the end Annie Ritchie has actually *become* the devil, as Sarah Annie realises (p. 332). The fundamental temptation that Annie has resisted is the temptation to belong – to be at one with other humans and the world she inhabits. Annie is diabolical in her successful separation of her self from love and life. Interestingly, Annie at her most devilish speaks in a different voice, a thin, weak voice behind which her power is veiled. Once again, language is a measure of belonging, or of dislocation. This kind of devil has appeared many times in Scottish literature. The innovation, in *Mrs Ritchie*, is that for the first time the devil is a woman.

Muir wrote two novels after *Mrs Ritchie*, neither of which has been published. Sadly, for Muir the relationship between fiction and autobiography seems to become a negative one after 1933. In terms of subject matter, the two novels are almost undisguised accounts of two periods in the Muirs' married life: the years in Prague, and the period in Hampstead just before Gavin Muir's accident. However, it would be simplistic and misleading to define these texts as either fictional or autobiographical on the basis of subject matter alone. The point is that as novels they lack subtlety in narrative point of view, resulting in an apparent lack of perspective in the world presented, in comparison with the two published works of fiction.

Mrs Muttoe and the Top Storey (1940) echoes, often verbatim, themes familiar from the rest of Muir's *oeuvre*.[12] The correlation between a woman's body and her house is carried forward from *Imagined Corners* and *Mrs Ritchie*, but in this text the ironic connotations have been replaced by a reiteration of the more suspect aspects of Muir's construct of woman as she was defined in *Women: An Enquiry*. Elizabeth's Shand's struggle, it seems now, has ended in her narrator's surrender to the notion of the biologically determined role of woman as nourisher of all those who inhabit her home, who descend in strict hierarchy from her husband to the dog. One reason for this surrender is the lack of tension between Alison Muttoe and her narrator. Only twice does the narrator shift to another character's point of view, and both instances strike a discordant note. This in itself would be immaterial, were it not for the lack of irony in the portrayal of both main character and narrator. Mrs Muttoe's struggle between the work of the intellect (her translating) and the work of the mother and all-provider is couched in terms of a laboured allegory of the Autocrat in the Top Storey and the nurturer and protector at the Centre (lower down), who seems usually to be the mother, but at one point is described as God. The realistic episodes make the point more succinctly, and it is not a new one: we are shown through repeated small defeats that it is impossible to fulfil both the role required of woman and the intellectual role of writer at the same time. The unremitting rearguard action that results from trying to do so is narrated in a manner in which irony seems to have been succeeded by a painful desperation. When at the end of the novel realistic narrative fragments into nightmare, the essay into the surreal does not expand any boundaries either of social role or genre, but merely reiterates the pain and isolation of defeat:

> She was being smothered by something, as if a hood had been put over her head; she struck out with her bound hands and kicked with her feet; her heart was hammering and she was sweating with fear. But she managed to push the smothering hood off her face and opened her eyes. She could see nothing. She was lying flat on her back. How had they got her down? (p. 283)

The loss of ironic distance also leads to a loss of the acute social analysis that Muir displays in the published novels. The Top Storey motif takes on the disturbing connotation that middle-class intellectuals alone live the life of the mind (at the top of the house), and the servants are only capable of dealing with bodily functions (in the basement). This is borne out by a narrative in which characters who are servants lack any kind of inner life. The gaps in *Women: An Enquiry* concerning class in relation to gender roles have here widened into chasms, as Muir represents Mrs Muttoe as embodying a universal, instinctively maternal role that finds its pre-ordained, natural environment as doyenne of the 1930s middle-class household. (The family is seen as 'an ultimate human value . . . father, mother, child: a fundamental pattern'; p. 161.) Mrs Muttoe is resented by her servants because she demands love and approval as well as service, and insists upon offering them love and support as well as money:

> And how difficult to admit a stranger – an outsider – into a private relationship. How difficult to let a servant enter your home circle, so that she could live in your home without feeling an outsider. But if you didn't do it, if you made your servant a permanent outsider, it was no home that you offered her. (p. 58)

The book begins with a confidence trick practised by an ostensible servant upon Mrs Muttoe, and throughout the book she is beset by servants who turn out to be sexually immoral, incompetent, bigoted, or engaged in stealing the silver. The servant Alice is explicitly compared to the dog in her stupidity, and in her need for care and attention (ch. 9). The potential irony is that Mrs Muttoe is the deceiver: in enacting the role of dispenser of 'loving-kindness' (p. 189), she demands an exorbitant emotional service from the women she pays to look after her house which is, as the imagery constantly reminds us, the symbolic extension of herself. The author of *Imagined Corners* and *Mrs Ritchie* might be expected to ruthlessly analyse this dynamic, but Muir seems to have identified herself so closely with Mrs Muttoe that the ironic perspective is dangerously lacking.

The Usurpers (c. 1952), also draws heavily on autobiographical material, to such an extent that it was feared to be potentially libellous.[13] The name Jamesina, which Muir chooses for her textual self, seems to foreground the identification of the text with real life, rather than its separate status. And yet this is the only novel written pseudonymously, by Alexander Croy, which would seem to suggest a change in the persona of the narrator. One is tempted to speculate as to whether Muir thought she might be more successful as a male writer when dealing with this subject matter, which is public and political rather than domestic and parochial. Certainly the narrator is ostensibly far more impersonal than the narrator of *Mrs Muttoe and the Top Storey*, and the focus of the action is not on one woman, but on the group employed in the Utopian (British) Mission to Slavomania (Czechoslovakia). The office reflects Europe in microcosm, and its individuals embody the politics of power, the struggle between communism and capitalism, and the threat of both to individualism. The tone is pessimistic, the vision one of social disintegration:

> 'It is a nightmare,' returned Russell, 'A nightmare spreading over most of the world, I think. Our office is well inside the nightmare by this time.' (p. 125)

However, the novel falls short of wide social panorama. There is a curious lack of focus on the political struggle, and the voice of the narrator seems more impassioned on the subject of discrimination over the office tearoom, and which of the British workers should have access to scarce family accommodation, than about arrests without trial, interrogation, or imprisonment under an increasingly totalitarian regime. Mr Bower, the incompetent and toad-eating head of the Cultural Mission, emerges as the real villain, and the narrative voice seems at times to assume the querulous tone of complaint about office politics rather than that of social or political analysis. The text presents a strange reversal of supposed priorities: instead of the office reflecting the politics of the larger world, the politics of the larger world seem to acquire meaning only in relation to what happens in the office. Inevitably this leads to a sense of trivialising potential tragedy, and so Vladimir's proposed escape to the west at the end lacks conviction or any real sense of urgency. Jamesina Russell comes close to a representative figure of woman as delineated in *Women: An Enquiry* (she can only count on her fingers), and, unfortunately, the narrator seems to be too closely created in her image to be able to transcend the limitations of this construct, or to fully enter the public sphere, even in the guise of a pseudonymous man.

Why should the later novels be so disappointing? It certainly appears as if Muir could no longer distance herself far enough from the material of her own life to shape it into satisfactory fiction. The autobiographical subject matter can perhaps be perceived as symptom rather than cause; it is not the origin but the way of telling the narrative that matters. Muir does in fact present plausible reasons for difficulty in the texts themselves: the desperate struggle of the intellectual woman to take her place in the public sphere while fulfilling her role in the private one, and her subsequent failure to engage fully with the wider world of politics and ideology. But the problem is that the narrator has become victim rather than analyst; many contemporaneous women writers in England and Scotland address, sometimes savagely, the same dilemma (one could cite for example Carswell, Woolf, Richardson, West, Sinclair, Radclyffe Hall), but usually they retain an ironic narrative control in their fiction, however bitter the struggle of their women characters.

Muir makes in clear in *Belonging* that she resented and felt oppressed by the dual role that seemed always to be demanded of her, but in her own writing about women, it does seem that she was at least partly entrapped by her own essentialist code. The closer she comes to analysing her own social origins and assumptions, the more ironic her narrative, and the less oppressed her narrator, seem to be. In other words, when she presents limiting and constricting constructions of gender as cultural, and in her case, Scottish, rather than as biological, the sharper the focus of her writing.

In *Mrs Ritchie*, Muir created a character who conforms to a Scottish construction of womanhood, and shows her to be diabolical. She never revisits Scottish cultural territory in her fiction, but she does continue to develop the theme in other genres. In a short article 'Woman in Scotland' (*Left Review*, no. 2) Muir summarises her blueprint for the Scottish woman who stands for the repression of the unconscious.[14] She does not allow herself to be an individual, a subject self, she must be, in Muir's favourite term, not self but 'environment': 'The mother as environment for her family is, so to speak, the basic diagram of womanhood' (p. 769). *Women: An Enquiry* also contrasts woman as individual, with a sense of her own identity, with woman as environment, who in denting her own identity becomes dangerously repressive of others. In *Mrs Muttoe and the Top Storey* the proposition that woman *is* environment seems to be accepted without question.

Mrs Grundy in Scotland extends the analysis, using the figure of Mrs Grundy, or MacGrundy, to embody in female form the repressive forces in Scottish society. Muir explains Mrs Grundy's origins in an English play, but goes on to define her specific place in Scottish society.[15] Through Mrs Grundy, Muir analyses how capitalism and anglicisation have induced a sense of inferiority in the Scots, which has been the root cause of social repression: 'the grimness with which these rural Scots repress each other is a measure of how far they distrust themselves' (p. 63). But Mrs Grundy, who, in Muir's parable, came to Scotland on the train with Queen Victoria, finds an ally which has been *in situ* in Scotland since the Reformation – the 'lawful authority of the Kirk Sessions' (p. 45). So Mrs Grundy becomes the emblem of hypocritical sabbatarianism, of dull, middle-class respectability, and of the virtue that lies entirely in appearances. Muir describes Mrs Grundy's habits and icons in images familiar from the Calderwick of the novels, right down to the ball-fringed tablecloths that hide the voluptuous legs of the furniture.

Mrs Grundy is in some ways an Annie Ritchie taken from the novel form and recast as a figure of speech in a political debate. One only has to look back to *Women: An Inquiry* to see how she infuses life into Muir's essay style. In this genre, we do not focus so much on her inner struggle as on her outward effect, but she derives from a fictional character, and in her, Muir's abstract argument becomes embodied and realised. Moreover, now that Mrs Grundy is specifically Scottish, Muir abandons the dubious universalism of her earlier article, for a practical analysis that makes a startling contribution to the issue of Scottish identity that informed the twentieth-century Scottish Renaissance.

Mrs Grundy in Scotland was published as part of a series instigated by Christopher Grieve and Leslie Mitchell, entitled *The Voice of Scotland*. The series seems an eminently fitting place for what is perhaps Muir's most overtly radical work, in so far as she tackles the combined issue of gender and nationality for the first time (I think) in the history of Scottish critical or political theory.

She does this by extending her earlier analysis of the negative powers of the repressed unconscious. Mrs Grundy exists because the possibilities of what one might designate the collective unconscious of Scottish life are suppressed and unrealised. Thus Muir describes the burial of pre-Reformation culture as 'a violent convulsion', which is similar to Annie

Ritchie's convulsive attempt to bury her personal imaginative feeling. Muir, for example, discusses Alexander Carmichael's description of the repression of Highland folk-tale, song and music which occurred over the generation when he collected the *Carmina Gadelica*. Just as the implicit tragedy of *Mrs Ritchie* is the loss of what Annie Ritchie might have been, so too the tragedy of a repressed and repressive nation lies in the possibilities which have never even been articulated.

Mrs Grundy is a philistine, for art, like the 'fine fume' of sex (p. 103), threatens her, because secretly it attracts her. Muir points out how the demand made upon the preachers of the Kirk is that they provide drama; through them their congregations demand the catharsis which is not open to them in any other form. The Kirk is art thwarted, and yet it is also art legitimised, because imprisoned within a suffocating doctrine. Thoughts, for Mrs Grundy, must never be free: 'a Scot who wanted to think new thoughts had to do it behind Mrs Grundy's back' (*Mrs Grundy* p. 163).

The two novels are about the constricted spirits of individual human beings, who are trapped in isolation and separation, and who search for, or, alternatively, reject, some way of 'belonging to the universe'. Their identity is wounded, the body is denied, and so the spirit, which belongs with the body, is imprisoned and perverted. Mrs Grundy is not a character in a novel; she lacks the necessary individuality; instead she is an emblem of repressed nationality, which is the sum and logical conclusion of the repressed individuals in the novels. The danger is that 'she may persuade the people that she is the national spirit of Scotland' (*Mrs Grundy*, p. 187).

In one sense she is indeed 'the national spirit of Scotland'. In *Women: An Inquiry* Muir argues that the very potential of woman makes her a more repressive force when she is negated. In *Mrs Grundy in Scotland* the repressed manifestation of Scottish womanhood suggests, paradoxically, just how far she could be the new liberating voice of Scotland. Muir concludes: 'If [this book] will help Scotland to make a new consciousness I shall not have written in vain.' (p. 185).

But Mrs Grundy is not a Britannia-like female figurehead. Although Mrs Grundy shares a common line of ancestry with this being, fathered as she is by the Punch cartoon, Mrs Grundy also has, one might say, a maternal parent, who is not emblematic of a patriarchally constructed nation, but who is a character in a novel. That is to say, in the Scottish case of unrealised national consciousness, Mrs Grundy is not merely the symbol of a tragedy; the tragedy is her own. It takes place in her inner world. Her tragedy is that of Annie Ritchie, her fate is what Elise and Elizabeth attempt to flee from. It is also, Muir implies, the tragedy of every Scottish woman, including, for example, Mary Watson, who is an apparently insignificant character common to both books. Mary Watson outwardly enacts the repression of the unconscious self, but she, like all the women in Muir's *oeuvre*, potentially inhabits an inner world which is a microcosm of a massive struggle centred upon the meaning of self, gender and society. This struggle is the inevitable consequence of Belonging, or rigidly repressing the impulse to Belong, in Scotland, and in the Universe.

Notes

1.   Willa Muir, *Living With Ballads* (The Hogarth Press, London, 1965); *Belonging: A Memoir* (The Hogarth Press, London, 1968).
2.   Lumir Soukup, 'Belonging', *Chapman* 71 (Winter 1992–3), 31.
3.   Janice Morgan and Colette T. Hall (eds), *Redefining Autobiography in Twentieth Century Women's Fiction: An Essay Collection* (Garland Publishing Inc., New York and London, 1991), p. 3.

4.   Edwin Muir, *An Autobiography* (The Hogarth Press, London, 1954).

5.   Willa Muir, *Imagined Corners* (Martin Secker, London, 1931; Canongate, Edinburgh, 1987); all references are to the Canongate edition. *Mrs Ritchie* (Martin Secker, London, 1933); all references are to this edition. Also published in Willa Muir, *Imagined Selves: Imagined Corners; Mrs Ritchie; Mrs Grundy in Scotland; Women: An Inquiry; 'Women in Scotland'*, ed. Kirsty Allen (Canongate, Edinburgh, 1996).

6.   Willa Muir, *Women: An Inquiry* (The Hogarth Press, London, 1925), p. 35.

7.   Patricia Mudge, 'A Quorum of Willas: another look at Willa Muir', *Chapman*, 71 (Winter 1992–3), 1–7 (p. 3)

8.   Virginia Woolf, *Mr Bennett and Mrs Brown* (The Hogarth Press, London, 1923)

9.   Margaret Elphinstone, 'Four Pioneering Novels: *Open the Door!*, *The Conquered*, *The Quarry Wood*, *Imagined Corners*', *Chapman* 74–5 (Autumn/Winter 1993), 23–9.

10.   Alison Smith, 'And Woman created Woman: Carswell, Shepherd and Muir, and the Self-Made Woman', in *Gendering the Nation: Studies in Modern Scottish Literature*, ed. Christopher Whyte (Edinburgh University Press, Edinburgh, 1995), pp. 25–47, pp. 41–3.

11.   George Douglas Brown, *The House with the Green Shutters* (Macqueen, London, 1901).

12.   Willa Muir, *Mrs Muttoe and the Top Storey* (typescript of unpublished novel dated 20 May 1940), 284pp. In St Andrews University Library.

13.   Willa Muir (Alexander Croy, pseudonym), *The Usurpers* (typescript of unpublished novel, c.1952), 377pp. In St Andrews University Library.

14.   Willa Muir, 'Women in Scotland', *Left Review*, no. 2 (1935–6).

15.   Willa Muir, *Mrs Grundy in Scotland* (George Routledge and Sons, London, 1936).

28

'To know Being': Substance and Spirit in the Work of Nan Shepherd

Roderick Watson

Nan Shepherd once remarked that with prose fiction she only wrote 'when I feel that there's something that simply must be written'. Her sense of what 'must be written' produced three novels within a five-year period and a collection of poetry called *In the Cairngorms* (1934). After this creative burst, undergone in her late thirties, she published no further fiction. Her last book, *The Living Mountain*, was written in the years towards the end of and after the Second World War, but it was not published until 1977. This volume celebrated the experience of climbing and hill-walking in the Cairngorms, one of Nan Shepherd's life-long pleasures, and here, as in her poems, it is possible to identify the passionately metaphysical strain which underlies her creative prose and her sense of the nature of existence itself. It is this aspect of Nan Shepherd's work which I want to explore in this chapter, but it will be helpful to consider first – if only to move beyond – the substantial social and biographical foundations to her fiction, and her acute sense of the life of women in rural Scotland during the first twenty years of this century.[1]

It is difficult not to make connections between Shepherd's personal history and some aspects of the lives of her characters. Her fiction displays a very strong feeling for the experiences of women, both young and old, who have learned to strike a balance between challenging and accepting the roles allocated to them by society. All three novels take this question on hand, and although none of them are entirely radical in their solutions at a social level, the final focus of the work goes beyond the social to discover a wider and more disturbing realm of absolute being – a realm which is wholly integrated with the material world, and yet one in which the familiar novelistic distinctions of character, place and gender seem to dissolve into insignificance. In particular this seems to me to be the final burden of Nan Shepherd's second novel, *The Weatherhouse* which is, I think, her finest book.

To begin at the beginning, however, let us start with the social world and *The Quarry Wood*. Published in 1928, this *Bildungsroman* draws on Nan Shepherd's own experience of Aberdeen University and Teachers' Training College and the countryside around Cults where she lived all her life. At a more fictional level the book describes how young Martha Ironside discovers the life of the body – sexual passion – and the life of the intellect at university. But she also discovers that her own roots have a claim on her too, and the novel ends with her returning to the community of her childhood to serve as a schoolteacher there.

After an absurdly idealised and painful affair with the husband of her best friend, and a blackly comic encounter with the male complacency of another suitor, Martha decides not to make her identity dependent on any man: "'Am I such a slave as that? Dependent on a man to complete me! I thought I couldn't be anything without him – I can be my own creator.'"[2] This position, and her sharp intelligent independence throughout the book, offers support for her role as something of a feminist hero, along with her Great Aunt Josephine and the many other tart and serene spinster figures in Shepherd's novels. (In this respect it is interesting to compare Nan Shepherd's protagonists with Grassic Gibbon's Chris Guthrie who takes three volumes and as many husbands to reach the same point, by which time she seems both spiritually and physically exhausted.) Certainly Martha's social courage and her human compassion are not in question, for she adopts little Robin (one of a succession of orphan children fostered by her slovenly mother) in the sure knowledge that most of the little community around her will assume, to her detriment, that he is her own bastard child. The book is set in the years before the Great War when even the rumour of scandal had the power to damage a career, especially that of a rural schoolteacher.

Martha has decided not to sail 'beyond the Pillars of Hercules'[3] – symbols of the gateway to new worlds, but pillars, too, which hold up this world – the world of home and the Quarry Wood where she played as a girl and met with her lover. Yet at least part of her university education has had everything to do with leaving the middle sea of her early life, everything to do with sailing beyond those metaphorical pillars, and it is possible to see her decision to stay at home, and not least her decision to take up a woman's traditional child-rearing role, as a kind of failure.

Once again an illuminating comparison suggests itself between Martha – the name has its own humble and dutiful connotations[4] – and the Chris Guthrie of *Sunset Song*, published four years later. Chris could have gone to university like Martha, but she chose the 'Scottish' Chris, which she identified with the land and the speak of the folk around her. Martha does go to university, but she never loses touch with the rugged Scots spoken by her family, and she comes to find through their homely good nature and the tough, careless, serene and sardonic spirit of her Great Aunt Josephine, that indeed 'man does not learn from books alone' (QW, p. 1). What Martha learns, what the novel tells us about, lies at the heart of how Nan Shepherd sees human relationships, and the social and sexual life of women in her time.

Disappointed in love when she was young, Miss Josephine Leggatt simply decided to live her own life, in the untidy and determined style that suited her, regardless of the opinion of her family and neighbours. She takes Martha in hand when she is a troublesome nine-year-old, and it is Martha in turn who looks after the old lady through a desperately long and painful illness before she dies 'aged seventy-nine and reluctant'. Martha's own mother was no stranger to scandal, having been ostracised by her respectable middle-class family (except Aunt Josephine) for marrying a ploughman considered to be 'beneath her'.

Martha, too, will learn something of her mother's experience, for her affair with Luke Cromar brings her to recognise the power of physical passion that lies within her, even if it does remain sexually unconsummated:

> She lived for the incidence of those cyclones of desire that lifted her and drove her far beyond herself, to dash her back bruised, her very flesh aching as though she had been trampled . . .

... She wanted Luke, his presence, his life, his laughing vitality; and it seemed to her, crouching mute upon the floor with the mood upon her, that reaching him she could draw his very life away and take it for her own. 'I mustn't, I mustn't,' she thought. It was like rape. And her exultant clutching was followed by an agony of shame. But next time the mood possessed her she clutched again. 'He is mine. I can hold him. I can have his life in me.' And she felt like a dabbler in black magic, the illicit arts. (*QW*, p. 126)

Compared to such frankness and such power we, the readers, see Luke as a shallower and less self-aware character, romanticising Martha as 'Beatrice among the pots' and more than half in love with his own self-appointed role as a superior Dante, the only person who can recognise her inner spirit. Martha's true education will be to understand herself beyond the confusions of desire, and to outgrow Luke, having finally seen him for what he is.

When she turns down another suitor, Roy Rory Foubister, no less than twice (for the novel projects a future moment when he returns after the 1914–18 war to propose again), Martha seems to have dedicated herself to a sexless future as the local schoolmistress. Indeed, Great Aunt Josephine's legacy has gone deeper than the house and the money she left her in her will, for Martha chooses to take on another bright and mischievous child, just as she herself was once taken in hand by her Great Aunt:

> Her mind rioted across the future. She meant to educate Robin. He was now two years and two months old, and already his mind was alert and his speech engaging. Another game for the gods was ahead of her.
> So she went home. (*QW*, p. 207)

If such a decision is not to be seen as a return to woman's traditional place – involved with childcare and 'home' – and even as a kind of defeat, we have to emphasise that Martha has certainly had the opportunity to do otherwise, and that her choice has been freely and consciously made. More than that, she has also joined a significant number of Nan Shepherd's characters who have chosen to live full and vigorous lives without men.

Nan Shepherd has no illusions about 'home', but the value of her fiction resides in the fact that she can recognise the narrowness and the failings of small Scottish communities without losing sight of their strengths as well. Her work never slips into mere anti-Kailyardism, or the gothic gloom of books such as *The House with the Green Shutters* (1901), *Gillespie* (1914), *The Grey Coast* (1926), *The Albannach* (1932) and others. On the other hand, Shepherd's novels do clearly recognise the heavy price that is paid by many women in our society, and she knows that that price can be exacted with equal harshness whether they seek to conform to, or to resist, the mores of the day. Thus it is that Shepherd's eye never fails to notice the downtrodden wives, aunts, mothers, sisters and servant girls standing patiently in the shadows at the edges of her main narrative concerns.[5] In *The Quarry Wood*, Martha is all too aware of the example set by her Aunt Sally, and little histories in much the same vein feature in each of Shepherd's novels:

> Sally Ironside's life, indeed, had demanded, or perhaps developed, gumption. For nine brief days she had been the speak of the place. She had left home at the age of thirty, with neither wealth nor looks to commend her, and gone through a marriage with the man whose taste in womankind had roused the astonishment of all Peterkirk and Corbieshaw and Crannochie ...

Eighteen months later, the sole addition to her worldly gear the bairn in her arms, Sally found herself on the street, her husband having given her to understand that their marriage was a form only and invalid. Sally disputed nothing; nor did she offer any interference – legal or moral – with his subsequent marriage to a lassie with siller. Ten years later she paid a brief visit to her old home at Peterkirk, in the garb of the Salvation Army. She was well-doing and self-respecting, but what sieges and stratagems she had carried on in the interval against a callous world only Sally herself could tell. She did not choose to tell too much. The bairn had died. 'Good thing,' said Sally briefly. (QW, p. 40)

The bittersweet and bleakly comic tone of this passage is characteristic of Shepherd's narrative voice, even to the submerged but potentially disruptive puns implicit in an idiomatic reading of the phrase 'aunt sally' and the popular term 'Sally Army' for the Salvation Army. In this respect Shepherd's tone is an exact match for the disinterested and ironically detached point of view which characterises the widowed Mrs Craigmyle ('Lang Leeb') in *The Weatherhouse*. A ninety-year-old lady who has long since withdrawn from the social and sexual complications of human life, Mrs Craigmyle sits in her corner observing the passing comedy of her daughters' and granddaughters' lives as if they were as distant from her as the sufferings in some old Scots ballad:

The old lady's was an intelligent indifference to life. She took no sides, an ironic commentator. Two and thirty years of Craigmyle wedlock had tamed her natural wildness of action to an impudence of thought that relished its own dainty morsels by itself. Her cruelties came from comprehension, not from lack of it.[6]

For such an observer, 'Life is an entertainment hard to beat when one's affections are not engaged.' (WH, p. 7)

'Lang Leeb' is a wonderful fictional creation, but there is something chilling and spider-like in her humour, too, and in this respect she may stand as a representative of the novelist herself, with something of George Eliot's witty, dry and judgemental tone. This is certainly the spirit which Shepherd adopts, once again with a wryly comic twist, in yet another reference to Sally's pain and her, and our, relationship to it as both author and readers:

'I've had a venturesome life,' said Sally.
A footnote to her life might have run: For *venturesome* read *betrayed, persecuted, forsaken, hampered and undaunted*: but the general public finds footnotes uncomfortable reading and leaves them alone. (QW, p. 182)

And yet, Aunt Sally, and Great Aunt Josephine and now Martha, too, all find that they can call on deep resources of life and energy to see them through their trials. And Martha's father, the ploughman Geordie Ironside, had the same capacity, too:

'She's come through the hards, yer aunt Sally,' Geordie had said to Martha. Sally had thriven on the hards. She had her brother's hearty capacity for life – a big eater and a big endurer, with power to exist spiritually for a long season on one joke or one idea.
Martha returned home the following evening. She felt happier than for long . . . She did not realize how much the lightening of her heart was due simply to the hurry and excitement of her journey, and to her contact with the vigorous personality of her aunt. (QW, p. 182)

For Nan Shepherd 'gumption' counts in the end. And it is precisely this appetite for life, however coarsely expressed, that Martha learns from Aunt Sally, and her Great Aunt Josephine, and finds within herself as the ability to be her 'own creator'. The same positive force can be recognised in the common life of the rural communities described in all three of Nan Shepherd's novels – and indeed we learn to value it as a human resource that isn't taught at universities, that cannot be learned from books alone.

Shepherd's third novel *A Pass in the Grampians* (1933) returns to the *Bildungsroman* format of her first, by describing young Jenny Kilgour's rite of passage as she learns to strike a balance between the dour virtues of her grandfather's life on a remote hill farm, and her fascination with the vulgar shallowness, but also the voracious and glorious energy of Bella Cassie, a local girl who has returned to her old neighbourhood to show off as a now successful and talented singer with money to spend on a flashy bungalow, noisy picnics and drinking parties to see the sunrise – much to the scandal of the country community. Conscious of a similar 'fury of being' within herself, and in the grip of a scarcely recognised physical infatuation for Bella, Jenny longs to go beyond the pass in the Grampian mountains (those pillars of Hercules again) which symbolises her grandfather's fine inheritance of stoic labour and silent consideration, to reach the ocean beyond, whose eternally fluid state, symbolised by water and fire, represents Bella Cassie and a whole new world of art and desire and generous gratification. (Nan Shepherd's writing is generally notable in this respect for its recognition of female sexuality, and the world of physical sensation.)

Andrew Kilgour and Bella Cassie, mountains and sea, continuity and change, substance and spirit, are all given their proper weight in the novel, and neither set of terms is privileged over the other. Bella herself sees it as a conflict between the divine imperatives of 'I LABOUR' versus 'I AM',[7] and while her own talent for singing seems closer to the latter term, singing is a kind of labour, too. Similarly, she recognises that work can have its rhythm, its joys and its spiritual release as well, even if, remembering her discontent as a child, she concedes it was not so for her:

> The rhythm of the saw would quicken. Then Bill took the long trunk, held together now by little more than the underside of the bark, and raising it in his strong hands rapped it sharply on the end of the saw-stalk – knock, knock, knock. At each knock, with a sharp crackle of sound, a log broke off and bumped to the floor; and Mary chopped them for kindling . . . Bella could hear the thud, and the sharp insistent crack of the kindling wood under Mary's axe. Mary wielded the axe with a quick sure movement of the wrist, on and on, silent for the most part, completely satisfied. But in the other corner of the shed, silent, too, but silent from a sense of powerlessness and despair, another child was crouched. Her sullen hands took the potatoes – an insane multitude of potatoes – one by one from the pail of water, and cut away the earthy skin, and gouged out the eyes, and one by one dropped them in the iron pot. On and on, on and on. She knew she was the one spot of discontent within the shed. (*PG*, p. 46)

Labour and being, substance and spirit – both are then given their due, and nor are they assigned gender-specific roles. The book ends with Jenny and her grandfather reconciled to parting, each carrying a little of the other in themselves, each recognising that things must change. 'Getting leave to live' in this sense characterises how Nan Shepherd's fiction manages to find positive value even in the harshest and narrowest of the rural communities she describes, and this opening up of symbolic creative space in a realistic tradition – without indulging in sentimental rusticity, gothic melodrama, Calvinist gloom, elegiac nostalgia or the spiritualisation of the feminine – is her greatest contribution to the portrayal of the social scene in modern Scottish fiction.

But there is another element of considerable note in Shepherd's writing – a metaphysical insight into the nature of being, or indeed the puzzle of being – that goes beyond the social scene, although it is, in fact, deeply rooted in realism and an understanding of the world which can be related to scientific materialism. Elements of this vision are very marked in Shepherd's poetry with its imagery of air, light, water, darkness and stone, and although the same features can be found in all three of her novels, they are most strikingly present in *The Weatherhouse* (1930). In this respect Nan Shepherd's writing can be aligned with aspects of MacDiarmid's muse in the 1930s, and indeed with the prevailingly 'scientific' tenor of the literature of the period. And yet, on the surface at least, *The Weatherhouse* would seem to be only another story about a small rural community woven out of a complex web of family ties, old stories and new gossip.

The Weatherhouse is not a 'development' novel in the same style as Shepherd's first and third books, for although the plot does revolve around nineteen-year-old Lindsey Lorimer's engagement to Garry Forbes, Lindsey remains a relatively minor figure on the margins of a tale which is far more complex than just an account of her growing to maturity. Indeed, it is difficult to assess who the 'major' figures in this book might be, for the text involves them all in a Chekhovian web of inter-relationships which allows everyone in the book to have their own history, their own dignity, their own little tragedy.

The social foundations of Shepherd's fiction are as firm as ever, for she describes 'Fetter-Rothnie' as 'a land denuded of its men' during the First World War, and the petty problems of this little community 'inhabited by old-wives and ploughmen' are played out against that background. The war is evoked only indirectly, but its most particular impact comes to us through Garry Forbes's nightmare memories of the Front where he suffered a mental breakdown under the impression that he was rescuing himself when he dragged a noisome corpse from a shell hole back to safety.

Garry's idealism thinks that Fetter-Rothnie has little to tell him when it comes to the 'reconstruction of the universe' after the war, but it is Shepherd's triumph that gradually he, and we too, come to see how wrong he is. That stressful moment's identification with the body of another person becomes a metaphor for what we all share with each other, and it haunts Garry as an experience of 'dissolution – a dimension that won't remain stable . . . You people who live in a three-dimensional world don't know. You can't know.' (WH, p. 114). It leaves him with the determination 'to get past the appearance of things to their real nature' even if this insight should turn out to be deeply disturbing, or seem to make a fool of him:

> 'That's what they said about me: beside himself, cracked. I was in a fever, you see. But I'm convinced I saw clearer than in my right mind . . . I wasn't rightly sure which was myself, you understand. And it's like that all the time. You do things, and you're not sure after they're done if it is yourself or someone else you've done them to.' (WH, p. 115)

This is a crucial insight for Garry, for in the name of 'truth' and 'honour' he has exposed Louisa Morgan's supposed secret engagement to his dead friend David Grey for the pathetic pretence that it is, and this exposure tips a nature already prone to fantasy into despair and the escape of full-blown delusion. It is ironic that the final unmasking is not made by Garry himself – who has learned compassion in the meantime – but by Ellen Falconer, a woman of sixty, who has been recruited to 'truth' through her own scarcely concealed infatuation with the gaunt and intense young man, and the belief that here at last is a noble cause worthy of her own dreamy nature – tragically unfulfilled and uncommitted for the most part of a long and empty widowhood. In a sense Louie Morgan in her mid-thirties and elderly Ellen Falconer are sisters under the skin, and if *The Weatherhouse* is a *Bildungsroman* at all, then it is their story it tells – a story about the central importance of the inner imaginative life, and yet a terrible warning about its pitfalls, too, balanced by Garry Forbes's story, and his recognition that life is not susceptible to the clear-cut definitions and solutions of his training as an engineer.

Time and again the novel evokes the unknowability of things – how much we need one another, and yet how little we know each other and even ourselves – and this, the book's true theme, is a much vaster issue than the slender plot of Louisa Morgan's fantasy engagement, and Garry Forbes's early certitude that it is his duty to deliver a blow 'against falsehood' in 'a small but definite engagement in the war against evil'. (*WH*, p. 66). Garry's moment of insight, when it comes, is quite specific:

> The complexity of human motive and desire had not come home to him, and he supposed, without thinking much about it, that right and wrong were as separate as the bridges he helped to build and the waters over which he built them. But in . . . his discovery in the dissolution of the solid land of a new dimension by which experience must be multiplied, he was only giving articulate expression to thoughts that had for some time been worrying his brain. Limits had shifted, boundaries been dissolved. Nothing ended in itself, but flowed over into something else . . . (*WH*, p. 118)

Nan Shepherd finds a variety of thematic and symbolic forms for conveying this 'new dimension' in which everything flows over into something else, and this is especially evident in her treatment of landscape and weather. Shepherd's novels, and her poems, too, are full of striking natural description, for landscape and weather provide an inexhaustible store of images to evoke both solidity and fluidity, substance and spirit, as well as the moments when these oppositions are dissolved. Thus, for example, Ellen Falconer's commitment to Garry's cause – described as her 'second spring' – is evoked by the image of seeing a bird as if for the first time, as if it were 'a flake of earth, loosened and blown into the air' which then manages somehow to 'change shape and rise, and poise, and speed far off, beyond the power of eye to follow' (*WH*, p. 77).

Garry's own 'second spring' comes about when he undergoes the same transfiguration, marked by three distinct stages in how he experiences Fetter-Rothnie in the course of the novel. In the first instance, all he can see is an empty and cheerless land (there is a war-time blackout in force), a desolate, lumpen place, without fire or light:

> It seemed as though out of the primal darkness the earth once more were taking form: an empty world, older than man, silent. In a while Garry became acutely aware of the silence. It burdened him. He stood to listen. A bird was stirring, dead dry leaves rustled in the beech hedge; far off, a dog barked. The lonely echo died, there was no wind, the world was still as dream. Life had not yet begun to be, man had not troubled the primordial peace. Strange stagnant world – he hated its complacency. Standing there on the ridge, dimly aware of miles of dark and silent land, Garry felt a sort of scorn for its quietude: earth, and men made from earth, dumb, graceless, burdened as itself.

'This place is dead,' he thought. The world he had come from was alive. Its incessant din, the movement, the vibration that never ceased from end to end of the war-swept territory, were earnest of a human activity so enormous that the mind spun with thinking of it. Over there one felt oneself part of something big. One was making the earth. (WH, pp. 55–6)

This passage is replete with literary echoes, from the Romantic ethos of Coleridge's 'Dejection' ode to the organicism of D. H. Lawrence, and certainly Lawrence was equally sensitive to the seductions of modernism, experienced by Garry as the hubristic scale of the First War, and the thrills of 'incessant din', 'movement' and 'vibration'. Later in the novel, however, Garry has another vision of the place:

Strange how the land could be transfigured! A blue April morning, the shimmer of light, a breath, a passing air, and it was no longer a harsh and stubborn country, its hard-won fields beleaguered by moor and whin, its stones heaped together in dyke and cairn, marking the land like lines upon a weathered countenance, whose past must stay upon it to the end; but a dream, wiling men's hearts . . . Below the hills blue floated in the hollows, all but tangible, like a distillation that light had set free from the earth . . .

Garry's thought went back upon the evening when he had seen the land emerge and take form slowly from primordial dark. Now its form was on the point of dissolution into light. And the people whom the land had made – they too, had been shaped from a stuff as hard and intractable as their rock, through weathers as rude as stormed upon their heights; they too (he thought) at moments were dissolved in light, had their hours of transfiguration. In his aunt dancing her wilful reel on the kitchen floor, in Lindsay grieving for Louie's hurt, he had seen life essentialised. (WH, pp. 112–13)

Garry's dancing aunt, Miss Barbara (Bawbie) Paterson, is another of Shepherd's characters given over to the indomitable spirit of vulgar life, and in The Weatherhouse she is regularly associated with the land and indeed specifically with the earth. This is how she first appears to Lindsay Lorimer, Garry's fiancée:

She had a feeling as though some huge elemental mass were towering over her, rock and earth, earthen smelling. Miss Barbara's tweeds had been sodden so long with the rains and matted with the dusts of her land, that they too seemed elemental. Her face was tufted with coarse black hairs, her naked hands that clutched the fabric of Lindsay's dress were hard, ingrained with black from wet wood and earth. 'She's not like a person, she's a thing,' Lindsay thought. (WH, p. 27)

At a social level, Lindsay and Garry will learn to look beyond appearances to see the transfiguring spirit beneath the eccentric behaviour of folk such as Bawbie Paterson, or in the marginalised travelling tinker, Johnnie Rogie (who accidentally sets fire to Knapperley, Paterson's house), or in the ineffectual good nature of Francie Ferguson, bullied by his wife and despised by his neighbours. At a deeper level however, the transfiguration is much more than a matter of manners, mores, or having a good heart, and Garry glimpses this more profound perspective as he remembers the night he caught Bawbie by surprise, 'a hard-knit woman of fifty five . . . dancing alone on her kitchen floor in the middle of a world war, for no other reason than that she wanted to!' (WH, p. 57):

In time he went to bed, but sleep did not come. Instead came fever and a new throng of disordered visions. He saw the solid granite earth, on which these established houses, the

Weatherhouse and Knapperley, were built (less real, as he had said to Mrs Falconer, than the dissolution and mud of the war-swept country), melt and float and change its nature; and the people fashioned out of it, hard-featured, hard-headed, with granite frames and life-bitten faces, rude tongues and gestures, changed too, melted into forms he could not recognise. Then he perceived a boulder, earthy and enormous, a giant block of the unbridled crag, and behold! as he looked the boulder was his aunt. 'You won't touch me,' she seemed to say. 'I won't be cut and shaped and civilised.' But in an instant she began to move, treading ever more quickly and lightly, until he saw that she was dancing as he had caught her dancing on the night of his return. Faster and faster she spun, lighter of foot and more ethereal, and the rhythm of her dance was a phrase in the tune that had eluded him. And now she seemed to spurn the earth and float, and in the swiftness of her motion he could see no form nor substance, only a shining light, and he knew that what he watched was a dancing star. (*WH*, p. 119)

Thus *The Weatherhouse* sets out to challenge the genre of Scottish rural realism in fiction, and indeed the usual distinctions between substance and spirit. In its outlook it is closer to the more metaphysical focus of, say, MacDiarmid's poetry with (in David Daiches's memorable phrase) 'the midden heap linked to the stars, and *both equally there*'. Garry's vision, after all, is no more than a material fact, for indeed we are all made from the stuff of stars, and Shepherd's visions of 'dissolution' at the heart of the novel are profoundly and scientifically sustainable. And this is the third and final insight that comes to Garry:

He looked again at the wide leagues of land. And a curious thing happened. He saw everything he looked at not as substance, but as energy. All was life. Life pulsed in the clods of earth that the ploughshares were breaking, in the shares, the men. Substance, no matter what its form, was rare and fine.

    The moment of perception passed. He had learned all that in college. But only now had it become real. Every substance had its own secret nature, exquisite, mysterious. Twice already this country sweeping out before him had ceased to be the agglomeration of woods, fields, roads, farms; mysterious as a star at dusk, with the same ease and thoroughness, had become visible as an entity: once when he had seen it taking form from the dark, solid, crass, mere bulk; once irradiated by the light until its substance all but vanished. Now in the cold April dawn, he saw it neither crass nor rare, but both in one. (*WH*, pp. 175–6)

Garry's education (in what cannot be learned from books) is complete, and his vision – both social and metaphysical – is central to all Nan Shepherd's fiction for it informs her creative use of weather and landscape, as it does her interest in small rural communities, and her Chekhovian compassion even for dullards and fools.

    Yet this insight has its own dangers, and *The Weatherhouse* contains a counter-text on dissolution and the oneness of all things, for if the merging of spirit and substance occludes the borders between the immaterial and the material, it can do the same between imagination and fact until, as Louie Morgan finds in explaining her fictitious engagement: 'Things are true and right in one relationship, and quite false in another' (*WH*, p. 105). And yet pathetic Louisa Morgan is also correct, for her story is not so much about someone who cannot tell the difference between the truth and a lie, as it is about the possibility that we may never know the truth of ourselves, nor what is in the heart of others. Equally tragic is the plight of Ellen Falconer, who always thought of herself as an imaginative and sensitive being, deeply in touch with the physical world (although incapable of naming a single bird or plant) who has to recognise in the end that her 'sensitivity' has blinded her to actual people, even her own daughter, and led her to waste her life.

The ambiguous borders between spirit and substance, as indeed between prose fiction and 'reality', are evoked again at the very end of the novel when Lindsay remembers Demon, Louie Morgan's dog when they were girls together, only to be told that there was no such animal:

> I know she pretended about a lot of things. But Demon –? He seems so real when I look back. Did she only make me think I saw him? He used to go our walks with us. We called to him – *Demon, Demon* – loud, I know that.
>
> She pondered. The dog, bounding among the pines, had in her memory the compelling insistence of imaginative art. He was a symbol of swiftness, the divine joy of motion. But Lindsey preferred reality to symbol.
>
> 'Queer, isn't it?' she said, coming out of her reverie. 'I remembered Demon was a real dog.' (*WH*, p. 199)

Demon, of course, is as real to us as Garry and Bawbie Paterson and Lindsay herself, and this little vignette says a lot about the nature of art with its capacity to show us symbols in the real and reality in the imagination.

All three of Nan Shepherd's novels deal with the specific substance of life in the rural north-east of Scotland, and all three have a vivid sense of the material and social realities faced by women in these small communities. At the same time they display a potent sense of spiritual being, a transcendent reality glimpsed through and evoked by Shepherd's extended passages of natural description. Writing in *The Living Mountain* about the delight she finds in the natural world, Nan Shepherd asked herself why 'some blocks of stone, hacked into violent and tortured shapes, should so profoundly tranquillise the mind'.[8] She came to the conclusion that it was a matter of conscious willing – an act of love, in effect, beyond all questions of sexuality, which is what makes us most truly human:

> It is, as with all creation, matter impregnated with mind . . . It is something snatched from non-being, that shadow which creeps in on us continuously and can be held off by continuous creative act. So, simply to look on anything, such as a mountain, with the love that penetrates to its essence, is to widen the domain of being in the vastness of non-being. Man has no other reason for his existence. (*LM*, pp. 79–80)

At this level of being what we encounter is no less than Garry Forbes's 'dissolution' – a not necessarily comfortable experience which can challenge our stability and our own sense of identity. On the other hand, if sexual and social differences fall away in the face of this experience, they fall away into a sense of unity with the material universe and with each other as fellow living beings which is entirely affirmative. (By comparison, the 'many Chrisses' in Grassic Gibbon's *Scots Quair* fade back into the land in a gesture which is darkly elegiac and fatalistic in its spirit.) Shepherd's sense of affirmation, however, is no easy or sentimental act of spiritual abstraction, for Garry Forbes's final vision contained both the light *and* the earth – 'neither crass, nor rare, but both in one' – just as Nan Shepherd's final vision never loses its roots in the real, the local and the contingent; the very foundations of those pillars of Hercules where spirit and substance meet.

The closing words of Nan Shepherd's last book, *The Living Mountain*, say it all:

So my journey into experience began. It was a journey always for fun, with no motive beyond that I wanted it. But at first I was seeking only sensuous gratification – the sensation of height, the sensation of movement, the sensation of speed, the sensation of distance, the sensation of effort, the sensation of ease: the lust of the flesh, the lust of the eyes, the pride of life. I was not interested in the mountain for itself, but for its effect upon me, as puss caresses not the man but herself against the man's trouser leg. But as I grew older, and less self-sufficient, I began to discover the mountain in itself. Everything became good to me, its contours, its colours, its waters and rock, flowers and birds. This process has taken many years, and is not yet complete. Knowing another is endless. And I have discovered that man's experience of them enlarges rock, flower and bird. The thing to be known grows with the knowing.

I believe that I now understand in some small measure why the Buddhist goes on pilgrimage to a mountain. The journey is itself part of the technique by which the god is sought. It is a journey into Being; for as I penetrate more deeply into the mountain's life, I penetrate also into my own. For an hour I am beyond desire. It is not ecstasy, that leap out of the self that makes man like a god. I am not out of myself, but in myself. I am. To know Being, this is the final grace accorded from the mountain. (*LM*, p. 84)

A novelist may well come to question her craft if 'knowing another is endless', and especially if 'the thing to be known grows with the knowing'. Perhaps it is not surprising that after such insights, after such grace, there were no more novels that 'simply must be written'.[9]

Notes

1. Anna Shepherd (1893–1981) was educated, worked and lived in the family house in Aberdeen all her life. An outstanding student at Aberdeen University, she went on to lecture in English at the Aberdeen Training Centre for Teachers; on retirement she edited the *Aberdeen University Review* to which she had earlier contributed articles. She was an enthusiast for north-east writers: she edited *The Last Poems* of Charles Murray and established the Charles Murray Trust, admired the work of Marion Angus and encouraged younger writers like Jessie Kesson, as well as writing perceptively as early as 1938 on Hugh MacDiarmid's later poetry at a time when many readers did not understand what he was trying to do. Nan Shepherd did not marry; she looked after her mother and Mary Lawson, a family servant (with her forthright personality and broad Scots, a model for a number of Shepherd's fictional characters) until the deaths of both. When Mary died at the age of ninety-two, Nan was eighty years old herself. Additional biographical information can be found in Vivienne Forrest in 'In Search of Nan Shepherd', *The Leopard Magazine* (December 1986–January 1987), 17–19. See also review of *A Pass in the Grampians*, *New York Times Book Review*, 3 September 1933.
2. Nan Shepherd, *The Quarry Wood* (Constable, Edinburgh and London, 1928; Nan Shepherd, *The Grampian Quartet*, Canongate Classics, introduced by Roderick Watson, Canongate, Edinburgh, 1996), p. 184. Henceforth *QW*.
3. Two mountains located on either side of the straits of Gibraltar, the 'pillars of Hercules' marked the Western limits of the ancient Mediterranean world, and the gateway to the new. 'Scota' the mythical progenitrix of the Scots sailed through these pillars to start the race.
4. See Luke 10:38–42.
5. For a fuller discussion of this aspect of Shepherd's work in all three novels see Roderick Watson, '" . . . to get leave to live." Patterns of Identity, Freedom and Defeat in the Fiction of Nan Shepherd', in Joachim Schwend and Horst W. Drescher (eds), *Studies in Scottish Fiction: Twentieth Century* (Peter Lang, Frankfurt, 1990), esp. pp. 213–15.
6. Nan Shepherd, *The Weatherhouse* (Constable, Edinburgh and London, 1930; in *The Grampian Quartet*, p. 13. Henceforth *WH*.
7. Nan Shepherd, *A Pass in the Grampians* (Constable, London, 1933 in *The Grampian Quartet*, p. 45), p. 97. Henceforth *PG*.
8. Nan Shepherd, *The Living Mountain* (Aberdeen, 1977); in *The Grampian Quartet*, p. 79. Henceforth *LM*.

9.   Further helpful material can be found in: Mairi-Ann Cullen, 'Creating Ourselves: The Poetry of Nan Shepherd', *Chapman* 74–5 (Autumn/Winter 1993), 115–18; Alison Smith, 'And Woman Created Woman: Carswell, Shepherd and Muir, and the Self-Made Woman', in Christopher Whyte (ed.), *Gendering the Nation* (Edinburgh University Press, Edinburgh, 1995); Jessie Kesson, 'Nan Shepherd: In Recollection', *Aberdeen University Review*, LII, 3, no. 183 (Spring 1990), 187–91; Louise Donald, 'Nan Shepherd', *The Leopard Magazine* (October 1977), 20–2; Joy Hendry, 'Twentieth-century Women's Writing', in *The History of Scottish Literature*, vol. 4, ed. Cairns Craig (Aberdeen University Press, Aberdeen, 1987).

29

Twentieth-century Poetry I:
Rachel Annand Taylor to
Veronica Forrest-Thomson

Dorothy McMillan

I

Liz Lochhead is the first fully professional Scottish woman poet of the modern period, perhaps of any period of Scottish women's writing. Before her, Marion Angus is alone among twentieth-century women poets in being remarkable for the quality, quantity and priority of her verse. Many of the writers dealt with elsewhere in this volume tried their hand at poetry but are not famous for it. Violet Jacob might be an exception to this, yet it is hard to feel that she would benefit from the publication of her collected poems as Marion Angus would. Catherine Carswell, Nan Shepherd, Naomi Mitchison and Muriel Spark all wrote poems, but it is not for their verse that these writers are chiefly remembered. Nor do I want to pretend to comprehensive coverage by merely romping through a list of names – the bibliography can do that – and some service has been done to women poets by the various anthologies now available.[1]

I should like, however, to look in some detail at three poets from the earlier part of the century who might be felt to be exemplary cases of women's experience in poetry. The first, Rachel Annand Taylor, is a kind of heroine, frequently the self-conceived heroine of her own verse; the second, Olive Fraser, was regarded, and regarded herself for most of her life, as mentally ill: after appropriate treatment she enjoyed a brief re-awakening, sadly too late, into a fuller life; the third, Helen Cruickshank, despite her lifelong activity in and for poetry, was a self-submerged and generous handmaiden to a male-dominated poetic movement. That these are oversimplifications will emerge but they will do as preliminary characterisations and they certainly suggest roles which female poets have to confront and transcend in their path towards professional autonomy.

Rachel Annand Taylor (1876–1960)

Of the Scottish women poets who began writing at the end of the nineteenth century, and who might be labelled Edwardian, the most prolific and possibly the most enduring, is Rachel Annand Taylor. I say 'possibly' most enduring because although her verse still pops up in anthologies, the lushness of Taylor's poetic imagination seemed cloying and effusive even to some of her contemporaries. Her great champion was Herbert Grierson who in his *A Critical History of English Poetry* praises her more highly than any other Edwardian woman poet:

> The rich colouring of Mrs Taylor's *Rose and Vine* (1909) shows the influence of Rossetti; in *The Hours of Fiametta* she recaptures the subtle ardours of the Italian Renaissance; the rich sense-material of *The Dryad* is transfigured in the flame of her vivid Celtic spirit to a masterpiece of symbolism.[2]

There is, of course, something already troublingly vague and gushing in Grierson's praise. Rachel Annand Taylor was, it turns out, one of Grierson's students at Aberdeen University. In the *Aberdeen University Review* he pays tribute to her in a way which seems to explain the damaging woolliness of his criticism. Grierson recalls that he made his entrance as professor at Aberdeen University in the same year as the University conferred a number of honorary degrees on women graduates to mark the fiftieth anniversary of the admission of women with full legal rights. For him in this atmosphere of celebration of female achievement the most memorable event was, he explains, 'the appearance, among the first group of the new entrants, of a young woman with a startling shock of red hair whom, when an essay came to be read, I placed alone in the first class'.[3] Later in his article Grierson remarks Rachel Annand Taylor's indebtedness to the 'Pre-Raphaelite poets, Rossetti, Morris and Swinburne' but he has already let slip that the Pre-Raphaelite qualities of her hair interested him as much as those of her poetry. Grierson suffered for his praise of Taylor. René Wellek, appraising Grierson as an academic critic, complains of his unsympathetic attitude to the modern poets of his time like Yeats: 'instead we get fulsome praise of Laurence Binyon and hear even of the Rev. Andrew Young, Mrs Rachel Annand Taylor, and Mrs Fredegonde Shove'.[4] Yet it would be impossible for Wellek to make his contempt so firmly felt if Rachel Annand Taylor had not helped him by being, along with Shove, a 'Mrs', an appellation evidently unpleasing to Wellek's male critical ear. Rachel Annand Taylor seems then to have suffered both uncritical admiration and uninformed dismissal (it seems unlikely that Wellek took the trouble to read her work) because of the way her female status was read by her male critics.

Ironically Rachel Annand Taylor seems herself to have found her marriage less than an advantage to her work. In a letter to Grierson ('My Dear Professor') in 1921 she remarks ruefully that Christina Rossetti, Emily Brontë and Sappho had 'the sense to avoid a perfectly unnecessary and undesired husband. Well! that was a bad mistake but I was only a girl when consent was wrung from me, and absolutely ignorant of many things, for all my reading'.[5] And she is also tartly critical of the way in which Wordsworth found his sense of his poetic self in the adoring mirror of female support:

> But the solemn self-content of W. W., the serene unquestioning way in which he battens on his harem of strict domesticities, – sister, wife, sister-in-law, daughter – makes me very sick.[6]

Taylor's own poetic voice is then a consciously feminine one. It is one which she seems to construct, however, more out of her encounters with her own wildly romanticised sense of the ethos of the Middle Ages and the Renaissance than out of her less ideal encounters with contemporary experience. Taylor's four volumes of poetry: *Poems* (1904), *Rose and Vine* (1909), *The Hours of Fiametta* (1910) and *The End of Fiametta* (1923) were all published before her historical and biographical studies: *Aspects of the Italian Renaissance* (1923), *Leonardo the Florentine* (1927) and *Dunbar, the Poet and His Period* (1931).[7] But she can be found pillaging Arthurian legend and what she conceived as Renaissance notions of love and beauty in her earliest verse. Her too willing belief that passion and the love of beauty constitute the soul of poetry is both the individualising note of her poems and their curse. But Taylor is sufficiently self-aware to recognise some of her poetic self-deceptions:

> How can I know if this be steeped indeed
> In those great hues my great Intentions need?
> For, as I toil, the Dream that I sustain
> For ever in the temple of my brain,
> Like a sweet story told on painted glass,
> O'erfloods my doing, till the glories pass
> All precious colour that was ever wrung
> Like wine from matter, that hath ever sprung,
> Sudden and unexplained and perfect flower,
> From the idle soul of some fair fortunate hour.
> So, in the light of what it ought to be,
> My longing imagery I must see
> As lovelier, lovelier, lovelier than it is.
> One day mine eyes unsealed may break my heart for this.
>
> ('The Fear of the Artist', *R and V*)

Yet even in this fear that the fictions of her verse may simply be lies Taylor damagingly goes for the aching repetitions of 'lovelier' rather than seeking the precision of differentiation.

I called Rachel Annand Taylor a heroine because she so consistently establishes that as her fictive personality. Chiefly she is identified with Fiametta, derived presumably from Boccaccio's supposed Beatrice, the lady who in *The Decameron* presides over the day devoted to stories of lovers who survive disaster or misfortune and attain happiness. Taylor is one of those who can easily imagine herself living within another period but cannot imagine herself as being other than significant within it; no anonymous Tuscan street girl for her. This self-conception makes her femininity a little less than feminism. True, she asserts a woman's right to fuller experience than her period would easily grant but she spins the justification out of a sense of a special self to whom she is most indulgent as in this sonnet inscribed 'To Another Woman':

> Well! I am tired, who fared to divers ends
>   And you are not, who kept the beaten path;
> But mystic Vintagers have been my friends,
>   Even Love and Death and Sin and Pride and Wrath.
> Wounded am I, you are immaculate;
>   But great Adventurers were my starry guides:
> From God's Pavilion to the Flaming Gate
>   Have I not ridden as an immortal rides?
> And your dry soul crumbles by dim degrees
>   To final dust quite happily, it appears,
> While all the sweetness of her nectaries
>   Can only stand within my heart like tears.
> O throbbing wounds, rich tears, and splendour spent, –
>   Ye are all my spoil, and I am well content.
>
> ('The Sum of Things', *H of F*)

I seem merely to have taken Rachel Annand Taylor out of relative obscurity to complain about her but it is rather the misdirection of her talent that we should lament, for her technical skill and her ear are often remarkable. MacDiarmid's estimate of Rachel Annand Taylor is hard to unsettle: 'an unprofitable prepossession with the Italian Renaissance has robbed the Scottish Renaissance of one whose true place should have been at its head'. MacDiarmid praises her Scottish poetry, written both in English and in Scots. She does write some exhilarating pieces on her native Aberdeen but her poems in Scots in *The End of Fiametta* – 'Lord Roland', 'Lady Isopel', 'The Return', 'The Kirkin' Goon' while distinguished by some felicitous phrases, are characterised by nostalgic evasion of the immediate. Even in her much anthologised 'The Princess of Scotland' romance overpowers observation:

> 'Who are you that so strangely woke,
>   And raised a fine hand?'
> *Poverty wears a scarlet cloke*
>   *In my land.*
>
> 'Duchies of dreamland, emerald, rose,
>   Lie at your command?'
> *Poverty like a princess goes*
>   *In my land.*
>
> 'Why do you softly, richly speak
>   Rhythm so sweetly-scanned?'
> *Poverty hath the Gaelic and Greek*
>   *In my land.*
>
> 'There's a far-off scent about you seems
>   Born in Samarkand.'
> *Poverty hath luxurious dream*
>   *In my land.*
>
> 'You have wounds that like passion-flowers you hide:
>   I cannot understand.'
> *Poverty hath one name with Pride*
>   *In my land.*
>
> 'Oh! Will you draw your last sad breath
>   'Mid bitter bent and sand?'
> *Poverty only begs from Death*
>   *In my land.*
>   ('The Princess of Scotland', *E of F*)

That Scottish poetry could have benefited from a perception modified by journeys, literal and metaphorical, into foreign place and time seems indisputable but Taylor's travel into the past cast a cheating light on her Scottish and later English experience making her an unreliable recorder of the present. Once more, sadly, she knows it. She writes to Patrick Geddes, indicatively by her always dubbed 'Merlin':

> But I'm not really good at 'social' poetry. It needs much more rhetorical quality than I possess.
> – And I am much too conscious of the tragedy of the unemployed to speak of it easily.[8]

Perhaps, however, she could have learned to speak of it difficultly had she not adhered so firmly to a soft *fin-de-siècle* belief in expressive poetic beauty at the expense of a more modern commitment to tough impersonality. In 'To a "Georgian"' (*E of F*) Taylor attacks her contemporaries for seeking for 'copy' in the streets and meeting only 'base inessentials':

> You take a perverse pleasure in the unsought
> And evil noise, the squalors that are fought
> With bitter gaiety by the scornful poor,
> The people that so mockingly endure.

It is possible, Taylor claims, to find essential, spiritual beauty 'up abominable stairs':

> Or, in the corner of a two-roomed place,
> A little child, locked fast in Shakespere's grace
> Of music and imagination – well! –
> Waking to the World-politic from that spell.
> (If that same child be of Apollo's clan,
> She'll never be a sordid 'Georgian.')
> Beauty is beauty, whether her white feet
> Go flickering down the dark dramatic street,
> Or on the violet, silver-hung hill-side
> She walk alone, the wild deer for her guide,
> Or in pierced palaces of long ago
> She finger her ball of amber. For I know
> Better than any what wild wonders be
> Within the Keeps of Lady Poverty.

While the criticism of Georgianism as a middle-class aesthetic may well be made to stick, the point is vitiated by Taylor's insertion of herself as heroic triumpher over the constraints of poverty. A contemporary review in *The Daily News* puts the case thus:

> If only she could put personal suffering more disinterestedly on the altar before which she bows, giving it some of the *im*personality which is essential even to what is called personal, or intimate poetry, her feeling, thought and appreciation of metre would result in moving poetry.[9]

A *Times Literary Supplement* reviewer of *The End of Fiametta* more brutally stresses the need for the poet to murder the heroine: 'We advise her [Fiametta's] creator to make perfectly sure that Fiametta is dead and buried before beginning another book of poems'.[10] After this volume Rachel Annand Taylor turned from poetry to history and biography: it seems to have proved easier to silence the poet than to kill Fiametta.

Olive Fraser (1909–77)

Olive Fraser was effectively silenced for much of her life by illness, mental and physical, and by the poverty and immurement in institutions that resulted from it. That we know so much of her work now is a tribute to the remarkable, energetic, sisterly persistence of

Helena Mennie Shire who knew Olive Fraser when they were students at Aberdeen University and whose sister Elma Mennie remained a friend and correspondent throughout her life. Helena Shire was largely responsible for the publication of thirty of Olive Fraser's poems in *The Pure Account* in 1981, and eight years later in *The Wrong Music* edited most of the available poems.[11] Olive Fraser's story then is an exemplary one, not merely about how the difficult-to-categorise case is in danger of slipping out of history, but also about the crusading generosity of a critic who has striven to fill the empty spaces in Scotland's literary map. Olive Fraser presents, of course, a problem of reading for it is impossible to spend most of one's life out of the world without having an eccentric approach to it. Nor do the lessons learned in reading, for example Clare, prove really helpful, since Olive Fraser was no uneducated genius but rather an educated intellectual whose misfortunes denied her both the integrated life of the mind and the companionship of fellow writers which one would have supposed to be her destiny.

It is hard to better the summation of her life's poetry given by Helena Shire:

> The early poetry needs to be described as an achievement of twenty years writing even though, in a sense, it never happened since poet and her whole range of poetry never encountered the eye, ear and mind of the general public of the time. It is there as a living process, preserved, as it were, in amber. On the other hand the poetry Olive Fraser wrote from the moment of even partial restoration to health when lyrics flowed abundantly from her pen is accessible to us, contemporary if strange. She writes in old-style poet's grammar and her thought is under discipline of stanza and rhyme. Her argument strides with swingeing power through a whole poem, sometimes in one sentence. But everywhere she shows 'the sense of musical delight' so seldom heard today. (WM, pp. 42–43)

Yet although that sense of musical delight may be what seems valuable about some of the earlier poems, particularly the nature poems like 'Tell the wild plantain' or 'The Tree' or 'Meadow Rain', it is a starker virtue that prises a plain, fierce pride out of the potential bitterness of the late poem, 'Nobody will come':

> Nobody will come, my love,
> In the winter's rain.
> In the dingy-sheeted bed
> Turn to me again
> Lie we close in silence bound
> 'Til we both are underground.
> Nobody will come tonight.
> Nobody will ever
> Step below the church's wall,
> Cross the flying river
> To separate yourself and me
> Desperate faithful poverty.
>
> 3rd August 1974
>   (WM, p. 194)

Annand Taylor's genteel 'Lady Poverty' is transformed to a deathly lover; but the dingy sheets both shelter and stifle what might have been a much louder voice in Scottish writing.

Helen Cruickshank (1886–1975)

Here is the last poem that Helen Cruickshank wrote before she died on 2 March 1975, a few weeks before her eighty-ninth birthday. It was published in 1978 in a slim volume *More Collected Poems;*[12] it is unfinished, although some of its roughness seems to me an effect of art rather than accident. And in its way it characterises Helen Cruickshank's lifetime of service to writers and writing; in published form it is called 'She Did' with retrospective irony:

> I cannot stay, the woman said,
> I've wool to spin and bread to bake
> And sheets to wash and clothes to pin,
> I cannot stay today.
>
> No tea today, the worker said,
> There's fruit to pick,
> And wood to break,
> I cannot spare the time.
>
> Then I must look up Mrs Bell,
> She's almost blind as well,
> She counts on me when she's not well,
> I cannot stay today.
>
> But Mors was on his rounds that day,
> And saw her rush and haste away,
> With ne'er a wish to stop and play,
> Still less to hear a prayer.
>
> Stop Stop! he said, but she said No!
> I have no time, away you go,
> Whereat he caught her untied lace,
> And tipped her over on her face.
>
> I cannot, with so much work to do,
> With beds to make and rugs to shake,
> And animals to feed,
> And get the cobbler man
> to mend my leaking shoe.
>
> You weary me, old Mors replied,
> You'll do as you are bid,
> You'll stop this fuss.
> Then he raised his mattock high,
> and battened down the lid.
>
> I cannot stay, she cried again,
> I've beds to make and rugs to shake
> And hay to toss and ted.

> O Mr Mors, now let me stay,
> You hinder me, she said,
> I cannot stay, please go away.
> With that he took his mattock out,
>   and battened down the lid.

> Now Mrs B –, Mors replied . . .

Helen Cruickshank's conception of her poetic role is of a piece with her version here of her social role. Her life was one of selfless devotion to poetry and its practitioners: 'I remember', Michael Grieve, Hugh MacDiarmid's son, said to me, 'that she was very good to us.' Her friends and Scottish letters profited from this devotion, her own poetry perhaps suffered from the self-abnegation that it implies. Her life tells a constant story of generous accommodation to circumstances that inhibited her own self-fulfilment. She left school at fifteen like many others deprived by financial circumstances of the university education from which she would undoubtedly have profited. After her father's death in 1924 she looked after her invalid mother for sixteen years thus denying herself the fulfilment of marriage. Yet in spite of these truncations of her full self, she remained a figure in the literary world of Edinburgh where she worked and lived for most of her life. She was active in nationalist politics and in the Scottish branch of PEN; her work includes poems dedicated to MacDiarmid (Christopher Murray Grieve), Grassic Gibbon, Wendy Wood. There is some evidence in both her life and work of the kind of tough assertiveness that characterised the male writers of the Scottish Renaissance who were both her associates and the beneficiaries of her struggles. For example she explains in her autobiography, still unpublished at her death, how she secured through protest her promotion in the Civil Service but the larger odds remained stacked against her as against other women because marriage would have involved her resignation from the Civil Service and she needed the money to support her mother. And so, she writes, 'I said goodbye to my hopes of being able to marry my penniless artist'.[13]

Her poem 'Beech Leaves' pinpoints the inhibition of daring by self-effacing compassion which figures Helen Cruickshank's social and poetic place. The middle-aged poet picks and blows a beech-leaf and is transported in Proustian manner to the childhood world in which she learned to make her leaf music. The issues of gender and class hover around her memories:

> And I saw myself, a sturdy lassie of six,
> Going to school with my two big brothers
> Down the hill to the village, where we were the 'gentry-kids'
> Among the rough-spoken children there.

In the most tender and unpolemic way possible Cruickshank reveals her ambivalent relationship to male pursuits and values:

> And once the boys found a wasps' byke in the bank,
> And gathering other boys from the school, attacked it
> With switches of broom,
> Sending me first, their protesting sister,
> Up the road away out of danger;

For I always wanted to do what the boys did,
And did, too.
But this time I felt on the side of the wasps,
For what had they done that their house should be harried and torn?
So I went up the road and watched, hoping the boys would get stung.
And hoping, too, that they wouldn't.[14]

Throughout her life in poetry Helen Cruickshank tended to enact repeatedly the dilemmas of these early relationships in which protective love usually overpowers indignation. Self and its sufferings is most often only an oblique presence in her verse. Writing in *Octobiography* of a difficult seven-year relationship with an artist whom she met at a musical party in Edinburgh she remarks that the association 'gave my pen its poetry', but the poems ('The Price o' Johnny', 'Heresy', 'There Was a Sang', 'Fause Friend' and 'Sae Lang has Sorrow') which she cites as 'evidence – none of it strictly factual – of my emotional confusion during this period' are remarkable either for obliquity of reference or sad self-effacement:

> There was a sang;
> But noo, I canna mind it.
> There was a star;
> But noo it disna shine.
> There was a luve that led me
> Thro' the shadows –
> And it *was* mine.
> ('There was a Sang', CP)

The stress on *was* simultaneously claims experience and places it in an irrecoverable past.

Of course, it would be ridiculous to claim that had Helen Cruickshank dumped her mother and married her penniless artist, kicked over the traces of love and responsibility, she would have been a more innovative poet. And as it is she remains an enduring voice in Scottish poetry and particularly in her poetry in Scots – 'The Ponnage Pool' and 'Sea Buckthorn' read the messages of the natural world in the tactful way that seems the mark of her talent. 'In Glenskenno Woods' (CP) compresses life's promise, mystery and sorrow in perfect miniature:

> Under an arch o' bramble
>   Saftly she goes,
> Dark broom een like velvet,
>   Cheeks like the rose.
>
> Ae lang branch o' the bramble
>   Dips ere she pass,
> Tethers wi' thorns the hair
>   O' the little lass.
>
> Ripe black fruit, an' blossom
>   White on the spray,
> Leaves o' russet an' crimson,
>   What wad ye say?

What wad ye say to the bairn
  That ye catch her snood,
Haudin' her there i' the hush
  O' Glenskenno Wood?

What wad ye say? The autumn
  O' life draws near.
Still she waits, an' listens,
  But canna hear.

II

The Middle Years

In 'Language and Liberty', his introduction to his anthology of twentieth-century Scottish poetry, Douglas Dunn remarks the difficulties of women poets between Helen Cruickshank and Liz Lochhead:

> Earlier in the century women poets were prominent – Rachel Annand Taylor, Violet Jacob, Marion Angus and Helen Cruickshank being the best known. Until the 1960s, however, literary women might have been discouraged by a conspicuously male-centred poetic country.[15]

And Douglas Dunn includes in his anthology only four poems by Muriel Spark and one by Elma Mitchell between Helen Cruickshank and Veronica Forrest-Thomson, a special case to whom I shall come shortly. Of course, as I have already suggested, the poetic landscape was not so empty of women as this suggests but perhaps Douglas Dunn feels that although there are poems to fill this emptiness, there are few poets. This is not what Helen Cruickshank believed in her last thoughts on the Scottish poetry scene: 'Of the future of the women poets I do not care to predict, Flora Garry, Edith Ann Robertson, Bessie McArthur, Dorothy Paulin, Alice C. [V.] Stuart already have sound work to their credit and we hope for more'.[16] But could we in the 1970s after the *deaths* of Sylvia Plath and Stevie Smith and only a few years before that of Elizabeth Bishop possibly hope for more from the poets that Helen Cruickshank names? To do so would, I fear, be to judge Scottish women's poetry by a whole different set of criteria that would not really be healthful. Catherine Kerrigan seems to me right to include poems by these writers in her anthology but to write about them in any more extensive way seems merely to invite quarrels with their literary conservatism. A closer look at Alice Vandocken Stuart might clarify my position. Alice Stuart was born in Rangoon in 1899, educated at St Hilda's School, Edinburgh and Somerville College, Oxford. She lived in Edinburgh where she worked as a teacher. She published four volumes of poetry at roughly ten-year intervals: *The Far Calling*, (1944), *The Dark Tarn* (1953), *The Door Between* (1963) and *The Unquiet Tide* (1971).[17] Apart from period indicators within some of the poems it would be more or less impossible to distinguish what she wrote in 1944 from what she wrote nearly thirty years later. In 1963 in 'A Wreath for E. B. B., 1806–1861' Stuart celebrates the few 'singing sisters' that have achieved the stature of Elizabeth Barrett Browning. A successor to Christina Rossetti ('consummate artist') and Alice Meynell ('polished purity') is sought:

What of this later age? One music only
Rises in fountain jets of power like these,
The New England voice of Edna St Vincent Millay
    Beyond Atlantic seas.
                                    'A Wreath for E. B. B.', *DB*)

It is a pity that the last poetic heroine had such a rhythmically recalcitrant name. But it is easy to savage this kind of writing and I do not want to take Stuart out of mothballs merely to sneer at her. But I do want to observe that to publish four volumes of verse is surely to think of oneself as a poet and it is interesting that Stuart does think about her poetic mothers. But she stops at Edna St Vincent Millay, a perfectly respectable if unadventurous choice, but Millay died in 1950 and Stuart's poem was written after Stevie Smith who was certainly not writing like this, after Sylvia Plath had started publishing and perhaps even more to the point well after Marianne Moore and Elizabeth Bishop had become famous. When one looks at a poem from Stuart's last collection one's sense of a literary time warp is even stronger:

> As the long reaches of the tide
> draw out, draw out, even so subside
> the unquiet urges of my heart
> poured to some infinite apart.
>   . . .
> Only, perhaps, with severing breath
> in the large benison of death
> shall my vexed heart, that unquiet tide
> stand silver-calm and sanctified.
>   [('The Unquiet Tide', *UT*)]

It is clear that the only possible justification for publishing this poem in 1971 is that poetry need only be 'poetic' for its essential niceness to carry the day.

But no one now is likely to think of poetry as nice. Until the end of the Second World War it might still have been possible to regard the writing of poetry as a kind of romantic option particularly for a woman who didn't have to earn her own living. But poetry is a hard choice now, not merely because of the virtual impossibility of making it pay without compromise or sideline, but also because poetry has been outed, as it were, as the difficult thing, the unromantically hard option.

Veronica Forrest-Thomson (1947–75)

Veronica Forrest-Thomson and Liz Lochhead were both born in 1947: Liz Lochhead has become the central Scottish woman of letters, Veronica Forrest-Thomson died tragically in 1975 before she was twenty-eight. Yet both in their own way mark a revolution in Scottish women's poetry the fruits of which we are still enjoying. It is perhaps inevitable that the way forward has been largely Liz Lochhead's way; indeed poetry in general has not followed the high formalist path of Veronica Forrest-Thomson's verse – the poems of her mentor at Cambridge, J. H. Prynne, are themselves known only to a somewhat elite audience but significantly usually an audience of practising poets.[18] We don't of course, know just what her path would have been had she lived but certainly in the late 1960s and early '70s she marked a possible future. In *Poetic Artifice* Forrest-Thomson tries to formulate a theoretical basis for modern poetry and to find a way of talking about those non-discursive aspects of poetry that we cannot simply subsume under such headings as subject and theme. She explains that the aim of the book is 'to talk about those aspects of poetry that are most difficult to articulate and which most clearly mark it as poetry': all those things in other words that much criticism is in flight from since the ratio of yield to enquiry is so uncertain. Responding to a weak reading of Plath's 'Daddy' in terms of theme, emotion and situation, she remarks tartly: 'Why she should have bothered to write poems if this was what she wanted to say is of course not explained; it is taken to be enough that she was a poet'.[19]

No one then could have been more excitedly aware of the sheer difficulty and difference of poetry than Veronica Forrest-Thomson. On the other hand the issues of gender and of nation may seem scarcely to have engaged her at all. Yet Edwin Morgan in the prelude to the *Unfinished Poems* that he wrote to commemorate her life and work suggests that she may be characterised as belonging in a sense to the Scottish poetic developments which were proceeding during her tragically short life. Edwin Morgan's introduction to his poems briefly and movingly explains the circumstances of Forrest-Thomson's life and work:

> The sequence of poems is written in tribute to Veronica Forrest-Thomson, a young poet from Glasgow who died in tragic circumstances in 1975. Studying and later teaching in Liverpool, Cambridge, Leicester, and Birmingham, she was probably better known in England than Scotland, but she can be seen as belonging – in her own strange and oblique way – to the revival of poetry that has taken place in Glasgow during the last decade or so. She was a spiky, difficult character of great intelligence and wit, engaging, vulnerable and lonely. I liked and admired her very much. She wrote both poetry and criticism, and the influences on her work were various and formidable: the French structuralists, Wittgenstein, John Ashberry, J. H. Prynne . . . but shot through with a raw, moving, almost ballad strain from time to time, and especially in her love poetry. A book of poetic theory, *Poetic Artifice*, was published in 1978 (Manchester University Press). Allardyce, Barnett have now published her *Collected Poems and Translations* (1990). She had an extraordinary talent, and her life and work, unfinished after so much promise, will be remembered.[20]

Here is how she described herself at a reading at the Bristol Arts Centre in 1967 – she seems to be crediting Scotland with something of her inheritance:

> Veronica Forrest was born in Malaya in 1947, but educated in Scotland with an early specialisation in Greek and Latin which had infected her with a, perhaps exaggerated, respect for impersonality and formal values in art. It was this which first aroused her interest in concrete poetry as an antidote to the formlessness and academicism of the Movement writers and the introversion of the so-called 'confessional poets'.[21]

She later found concrete poetry inadequate but in all her statements about the nature of her art she insists on it as artifice, and if the adventure with language remains its raison d'être, it is not a simple semantic adventure but one which co-operates with the non-referential, non-semantic potential of language itself, co-operates with 'all the rhythmic, phonetic, verbal and logical devices which make poetry different from prose and which we may group together under the heading of poetic artifice'.[22] Veronica Forrest-Thomson then experienced poetry in a different way from those who take refuge in simpler notions of meaning and communication. The sheer difficulty of language and of modes of communication exercised her throughout her short writing life. She was enormously influenced by Wittgenstein's linguistic philosophy – this was Cambridge in the 1960s – and, married to Jonathan Culler, she was early introduced to Structuralism and Deconstruction. She was a thoroughly intellectual poet who also felt deeply, although she herself would have said that feeling and the referential meaning that identifying feeling implies, should be the last features of her poetry to which the reader should come. She complained that it has been the tendency to criticism to defuse technical innovation by the normalising critical process which she calls 'Naturalisation': 'an attempt to reduce the strangeness of poetic language and poetic organisation by making it intelligible, by translating it into a statement about the non-verbal external world, by making the Artifice appear natural'.[23] It is not that Forrest-Thomson believed that Naturalisation should never occur but that it should be deferred until the formal strategies of the poem had done their work.

The poet Martin Harrison investigates the meaning of her 'deeply felt notion of art' for the contemporary poet's search for significant form;[24] Alison Mark reads her linguistic battles in parallel with the battles of hysteria for expression (the problem here is that this seems merely to replace one set of imponderables with another potentially more incoherent set);[25] the most sympathetic reading of her poetry, however, comes from Ian Gregson in *Verse*.[26] Gregson manages to do justice both to Forrest-Thomson's cerebral interests in language and linguistic philosophy and that 'raw, moving strain' that Edwin Morgan remarks: his reading of 'Richard II' as 'a kind of elegy for coherent meaning' which 'expresses what deconstruction means at a psychological level' helps us both with Forrest-Thomson's poem and with Shakespeare's character. Yet one cannot help feeling that sometimes Forrest-Thomson has a clearer design on her readers than she is quite prepared to admit. In her introduction to the poem which was commissioned to be read in Southwark Cathedral as part of the Shakespeare birthday celebrations on 26 April 1975 she writes: 'At the present time poetry must progress by deliberately trying to defeat the expectations that [readers] will be able to extract meaning from a poem' and, indeed, when readers/listeners encounter the opening of the poem, most will feel defeated:

> The wiring appears to be five years old
> and is in satisfactory condition.
> The insulation resistance is zero.
> This reading would be accounted for by the very damp condition of the building.[27]

Yet the reader senses immediately which lines of *Richard II* are in Forrest-Thomson's mind as she writes and her introductory note confirms that she did indeed choose V, v, 42–66, where Richard, having failed to discover or construct any coherent meaning in his experience, hears music which although incomprehensible to him, he takes as a *sign* of love.

Most of the poems in 'Language-Games' enact problems of language and perception and are unashamedly but not unamusingly erudite. 'Phrase-Book' hilariously exploits traditional jokes about linguistic muddles – 'words are a monstrous excrescence' – along with the fears of a pursued female tourist, 'Go away. I shall call a policeman', to indicate that language and meaning can be no more controlled and policed than the world that language is believed to give us access to: 'It is raining cats and allomorphs./"Where" is the British Embassy'. 'The Hyphen', for the centenary of Girton College, uses the signification of the hyphen, '1869–1969', to signal human need for connection in history to a comprehended past, yet also recognises that the hyphen acts to divide as well as to join:

> Portraits busts and books
> > the 'context in which we occur'
> that teaches us our meaning,
> > ignore the lacunae
> of a century
> > in their state-
> ment of our need to hyphenate.[28]

The poems in the later posthumously published collection, 'On the Periphery', have an explanatory preface which indicates that the periphery in question is that of traditional poetry. Forrest-Thomson affirms the deadly seriousness of her poetic quest to make art a 'new and serious opponent – perhaps even a successful alternative – to the awfulness of the modern world'. And yet even as the poems enact the confrontation of artifice and world, abstraction is often felt with an almost physical intensity which makes us re-comprehend Eliot's contention that for Donne thought had the odour of a rose: 'polythene buttercups strew our way/with images of "natural"/regeneration. inevitable' ('On the Periphery'); 'Exuberant pronouns flourish like baroque/cherubs in the spring air beckoning'; and the creatures of artifice are made to suffer real pain: 'The gentle foal linguistically wounded / Squeals like a car's brakes/Like our twisted words' ('Pastoral'). Here is what Veronica Forrest-Thomson says about the last poem in the sequence and the process that wins for her the 'right', as it were, to write it; her remarks also sadly recognise that writing, far from being a bulwark against personal loss, may rather intensify it:

> The last poem 'Sonnet' is the love poem I have tried throughout to write straight and have been held back from by . . . technical and sociological difficulties. For, as to theme, this book is the chart of three quests. The quest for a style, . . . the quest for a subject other than the difficulty of writing, and the quest for another human being. Indeed such equation of love with knowledge and the idea of style as their reconciliation is as old as the art itself, for the other person is the personification of the other, the unknown, the external world and all one's craft is necessary to catch him. And, of course, being caught as a poetic fiction, as a real person he is gone.[29]

This is her poem of art and loss:

> SONNET
> My love, if I write a song for you
> to that extent you are gone
> For, as everyone says, and I know it's true:
> We are all always alone.
>
> Never so separate trying to be two
> And the busy old fool is right.
> To try and finger myself from you
> Distinguishes day from night.

> If I say 'I love you' we can't but laugh
> Since irony knows what we'll say.
> If I try to free myself by my craft
> You vary as night from day.
>
> So, accept the wish for the deed my dear.
> Words were made to prevent us near.

That Veronica Forrest-Thomson was a serious and sometimes imperious poet is beyond question. It is equally true that hers is not a personal or confessional voice, although it is distinctive. It often moves its readers because of rather than in spite of its brave intellectuality. But it is also surely true that her austere art is not a product of happiness and her sad early death places her beside the very different Plath as a poet of suffering and truncated promise. Germaine Greer in the 'Epilogue' to her *Slip-shod Sibyls: Recognition, Rejection and the Woman Poet* remarks the problem for the contemporary woman poet of terrible precedents: 'too many of the most conspicuous figures in women's poetry of the twentieth century not only destroyed themselves in a variety of ways but are valued for poetry that documents the process'.[30] Self-destructive behaviour, *pace* Alvarez, is actually not a characteristic of twentieth-century male poets or indeed male poets in general. Greer quotes the poet Anne Stevenson who is also Sylvia Plath's biographer:

> And what's 'to make'?
>
> To be and to become words' passing
> weather; to serve a girl on terrible
> terms, embark on voyages over voices,
> evade the ego-hill, the misery-well,
> the siren hiss of *publish, success, publish,*
> *success, success, success.*
>   ('Making Poetry')

'The way that the woman poet avoids the ego-hill and the misery-well,' Greer claims, 'is by developing what male poets always instinctively gravitated towards, a community of poets, a school, so that the isolated poet does not disappear into solipsism and cannibalize herself.'[31] Well, Veronica Forrest-Thomson had other poets around her and it was not enough but it does seem plausible that community is both protective and inspiring for the writer and there is some case for arguing that a number of the most fully professional and artistically consistent of the contemporary Scottish women poets are public people who are generally involved in the life of letters.

Notes

1.   Catherine Kerrigan (ed.), *An Anthology of Scottish Women Poets* (Edinburgh University Press, Edinburgh, 1991); Douglas Dunn (ed.), *The Faber Book of Twentieth-Century Scottish Poetry* (Faber & Faber, London, 1992); Rory Watson (ed.), *The Poetry of Scotland: Gaelic, Scots and English, 1380–1980* (Edinburgh University Press, Edinburgh, 1995). Minor contemporary collections include: Tom Hubbard (ed.), *The New Makars: The Mercat Anthology of Contemporary Poetry in Scots* (The Mercat Press, Edinburgh, 1991).
2.   Herbert Grierson & J. C. Smith, *A Critical History of English Poetry* (Chatto & Windus, London, 1944), p. 466.

3. Herbert Grierson, 'Rachel Annand Taylor', *Aberdeen University Review*, xxx (1945–6), 152.

4. René Wellek, *A History of Modern Criticism, 1750–1950* (Cape, London, 1986), vol. 5: English Criticism, 1900–1950, p. 50.

5. Rachel Annand Taylor, unpublished letter, December 1921, in MS 9328, National Library of Scotland.

6. Rachel Annand Taylor, unpublished letter to Grierson, October 1909, MS 9328, NLS.

7. Rachel Annand Taylor, *Poems* (J. Lane, London, 1904); *Rose and Vine* [R and V] E. Mathews, London, 1909); *The Hours of Fiametta* [H of F] (E. Mathews, London, 1923); *The End of Fiametta* [E of F] (G. Richards, London, 1923); *Aspects of the Italian Renaissance* (G. Richards, London, 1923); *Leonardo the Florentine: A Study in Personality* (G. Richards, London, 1927); *Dunbar, the Poet and His Period* (Faber & Faber, London, 1931).

8. Rachel Annand Taylor, unpublished letter to Patrick Geddes, 20 May 1910, MS 10572, National Library of Scotland.

9. *The Daily News*, Friday, September 10 1910.

10. The *Times Literary Supplement*, 6 March 1924.

11. Olive Fraser, *The Pure Account* (Aberdeen University Press, Aberdeen, 1981); Olive Fraser, *The Wrong Music: The Poems of Olive Fraser, 1909–1977* [WM], ed. Helena M. Shire (Canongate, Edinburgh, 1989). The latter volume offers a biographical account of Olive Fraser from her student days in Aberdeen and Cambridge Universities (in both of which she won poetry prizes, in Cambridge the prestigious Chancellor's Medal), to her death in 1977 in the Royal Mental Hospital, Cornhill, Aberdeen, a death which released her poetry for publication. Helena Shire points out that also out of this hospital had come the poems of Christian Watt, an east-coast fisher wife whose papers, some now published, are referred to in Chapter 5 of this volume.

12. Helen Cruickshank, *More Collected Poems* (G. Wright, Edinburgh, 1978).

13. Helen Cruickshank, *Octobiography* (Standard Press, Montrose 1976), p. 60.

14. Helen Cruickshank, 'Beech Leaves', *Collected Poems* (Reprographia, Edinburgh, 1971).

15. Douglas Dunn (ed.), *The Faber Book of Twentieth-Century Scottish Poetry* (Faber & Faber, London, 1992), xliv.

16. *Octobiography*, p. 168.

17. Alice Vandocken Stuart, *The Far Calling* (The Poetry Lovers' Fellowship, London, 1944); *The Dark Tarn* (G. Ronald, Oxford, 1953); *The Door Between* [DB] (H. J. Macpherson, Dunfermline, 1963); *The Unquiet Tide* [UT] (Ramsay Head, Edinburgh, 1971).

18. J. H. Prynne, *Stars, Tigers and the Shape of Words: The William Matthews Lectures 1992* (Birkbeck College, London, 1993).

19. Veronica Forrest-Thomson, *Poetic Artifice: A Theory of Twentieth Century Poetry* (Manchester University Press, Manchester, 1978), p. 162.

20. Edwin Morgan, *Collected Poems* (Carcanet, Manchester, 1990), p. 373. 'Unfinished Poems' were first published in *The New Divan* (1977). Veronica Forrest-Thomson, *Collected Poems and Translations* (Agneau 2, Allardyce, Barnett, London; Lewes, Berkely, 1990). It is worth noting that this volume was published with the assistance of the Scottish Arts Council.

21. Forrest-Thomson, *Collected Poems*, 'An Impersonal Statement', p. 260.

22. Forrest-Thomson, *Poetic Artifice*, ix.

23. Forrest-Thomson, *Poetic Artifice*, xi.

24. Martin Harrison, 'An Introduction to Veronica Forrest-Thomson's Work', in Denise Riley (ed.), *Poets on Writing: Britain, 1970–1991* (Macmillan, London, 1992), pp. 216–22.

25. Alison Mark, 'Hysteria and Poetic Language: A Reading of the Work of Veronica Forrest-Thomson', *Women: A Cultural Review*, vol. 5, no. 3 (1994), pp. 264–77.

26. Ian Gregson, 'Lost Love and Deconstruction: the Poems of Veronica Forrest-Thomson', *Verse* 8.3/9.1 (Winter/Spring 1992), 113–16.

27. Forrest-Thomson, *Collected Poems*, 'Richard II', p. 110; p. 265.

28. Forrest-Thomson, *Collected Poems*, 'The Hyphen', p. 35.

29. Forrest-Thomson, *Collected Poems*, p. 264.

30. Germaine Greer, *Slip-shod Sibyls: Recognition, Rejection and the Woman Poet* (Viking, London, 1995), p. 390.

31. Greer, *Slip-shod Sibyls*, p. 422.

More Than Merely Ourselves:
Naomi Mitchison

Jenni Calder

By the time Naomi Mitchison's best-known novel, *The Corn King and the Spring Queen*, was published in 1931, she had a reputation as an unconventional and distinctive writer.[1] It was her third novel, and she had also published several volumes of her short stories, a volume of poetry, and books for children. Her fiction was set in the past, but the tone and approach she adopted were fresh and challenging. She was dealing in modern issues, and with situations and emotions that were very much a part of her own life. The distinctiveness of her fiction was partly the result of combining a sensitive feel for historical environments with an idiom that was entirely contemporary.

In 1939 on the eve of war, Mitchison was living in a remote part of Scotland, having up to that time spent most of her life in Oxford and London. Born in Edinburgh, she had never lost touch with her Scottish origins, but her intellectual roots appeared to be in Oxford. Her first books were concerned with the Classical world, with the clashes and confrontations of Ancient Greece, with the frontiers of the Roman Empire, with themes of aggression and power, the relations of friends and comrades, masters and servants, men and women. In the wake of the First World War, in which she lost many friends and nearly lost both her husband and her brother, she explored a world of raw violence and naked emotion, a distant world, but nevertheless vivid and clearly the same world as that which she was experiencing.

Her first novel, *The Conquered*, was published in 1923 when she was in her twenty-sixth year.[2] Its originality and its uncompromising treatment of confrontation, sacrifice and sex gave it considerable impact. Set in the time of the Roman conquest of Gaul, it gained the respect of Classical scholars as well as capturing readers with its vigorous, straightforward narrative. The stories and novels that followed investigated the entanglements of the personal and political, located in an old world, but very much informed by the realities of a threatening present. *The Conquered* contained a message about British involvement in Ireland. The reiteration in several of her stories of the clash between Athens and Sparta stems from her increasing awareness of the seductive attractions of totalitarianism in Europe.

Mitchison wrote fast, but *The Corn King and the Spring Queen*, a massive and complex novel, took her five years to complete. Bold and wide-ranging, skilfully narrated, it invents a country on the edge of the Black Sea, exposed to the influence of both the horsemen of the Asian steppes and the sophistication of Classical Greece. The key figure is a woman,

Erif Der, who takes on the depth and resonance of myth as she wrestles with her identity as queen and her role as a vessel of fertility. She travels the Mediterranean world, gaining in substance and maturity as she goes, but always with a tantalising aura of ambivalence. Mitchison had tested a number of ideas about the frontiers of female action in earlier stories. In *The Corn King* she gathers many of the threads together to create a memorable figure. If the plotting is uneven, the vitality of imagination, the sure handling of character and dialogue, and the powerful recreation of an intellectual, material and emotional climate are what make the novel impressive.

Erif Der carries with her an instinctual world empowered by contact with the seasons, the earth, fertility and growth. Given her role as Spring Queen, the natural cycles cannot turn without her. Although she encounters other worlds and other systems, some of which resist her, the essence of her magic survives and is reaffirmed. The intellect cannot control the future, which lies with Marob, Erif's homeland. At the end of the novel she says, 'After I come back, there will be a good season in Marob . . . and dancing and marriages and new songs and new things made. Everything will go on again' (CKSQ, p. 637).

The fictional territory of Marob had an emotional resonance for Mitchison that went far beyond the novel itself. It became the touchstone of an environment she herself longed to occupy, both in reality and imaginatively. Much of her fiction, whether set in prehistoric Scotland, Ancient Greece, or contemporary Africa, is part of a process of creating a world in which she herself has a position and a role. This is linked with her implicit, and sometimes explicit, belief that leadership is not only a legitimate but an essential task. One of the currents that runs through much of her writing, and is suggested by many of the subjects that engage her, is that groups, whether nations or small communities, need leaders.

She needed to locate herself in her real and fictional environments. Equally she required places where intellect and instinct could combine creatively. Her locations are much more than geography. They come with a social and cultural apparatus which has a psychological as well as a historical authenticity. She spent time researching artefacts as well as written records. It is the marriage of this research and a highly-charged, personal response that gives her fiction its particular flavour.

In the early 1930s Naomi Mitchison seemed confident of her identity as a writer to be taken seriously alongside her friend Aldous Huxley, her protégé W. H. Auden and other contemporaries. She wrote regular book reviews and articles. She experimented with the theatre. She travelled widely, to the United States, the Soviet Union, to Vienna in 1934, to France, Italy, Greece and Denmark, and wrote about her experiences. Hers was a voice that was listened to. But then in 1935 she wrote a contemporary political novel, *We Have Been Warned*, based on her growing involvement with left-wing politics and her 1932 trip to Russia. It is a ragged tale, too rawly based on personal experience, and was not well received.[3] Her next novel, *The Blood of the Martyrs* (1939), set in early Christian Rome, was criticised by those she thought of as her literary allies, notably in the *New Statesman*, for which she sometimes wrote (and would later write for frequently).[4] The criticism rankled, and disrupted her sense of belonging to the London literary scene.

By this time there was a physical divorce from London. She and her husband Dick Mitchison had bought Carradale House in Kintyre in 1937, and the outbreak of war caught and more or less kept her there. She had already begun the process of rediscovering her Scottish identity, to which her long poem 'The Alban Goes Out' is testimony. In the years that followed, she created a new role for herself, as a Scottish writer deeply embedded in Scotland's past and deeply committed to Scotland's present. It was a new phase of her career as a writer and also as a public person. It was to be productive in a number of ways.

In some respects *We Have Been Warned* can be seen as Mitchison's first 'Scottish' novel, although only a small part of the action takes place there. In it she articulates, through the sisters who are her two central characters, a response to contemporary Scotland. "'When I say Scotland,'" Phoebe, one of the main characters, muses, "'I mean the Gare Loch, I mean the coming together of Highland and Lowland with sparking and flaring and building of great ships full of engines, propellers turning slowly then faster and faster and faster. Only they are not building and turning now . . . Scotland is not functioning'" (*WHBW*, p. 14). The non-functioning of Scotland is a strand in the political theme of the novel, which explores the creative possibilities of socialism – and its limitations. "'We can only imagine a few years from now'" says Dione, the central character, "'we can only imagine easy things – tidying up the world, making it all as good as the best now. But not better, not different, not strange. That is the strength of the Labour Movement, it only imagines easy things. The strength and the weakness'" (*WHBW*, pp. 66–7).

The novel does not work. It is overreliant on a vein of melodrama and Mitchison has too personal an involvement in the characterisation. But it highlights a number of the driving forces of her fiction: her belief in community and co-operation, the coming together of the personal and political, the relationship between idealism and action. *The Blood of the Martyrs* focuses some of these aspects in a very different context, although it is clear why early Christian Rome had such a strong appeal. Her motley assortment of slaves and exiles are united by commitment and shared danger. *The New Statesman* reviewer felt that Mitchison had stepped out of her proper place as a 'teller of folk-tales' and missed its allegorical significance.[5] In fact Mitchison is much more convincing handling a political theme – and it is a political rather than a spiritual theme – in a historic setting than in the present. She needs that distance.

At the heart of *The Blood of the Martyrs* is the celebration of agape, the 'love-feast', the sharing of faith symbolised by the sharing of food together on an equal base. Agape was something Mitchison strove towards in her personal life, tried to create wherever she found herself but particularly when she settled in Carradale in Kintyre. She thought she found there an environment in which she could preside over 'a breaking of barriers and setting free of resentments and complexes', as she described it in *The Kingdom of Heaven* (1939).[6] Her setbacks and frustrations in this effort are reflected in her writing, particularly in the poem sequence, 'The Cleansing of the Knife', written between 1939 and 1947 and published in the volume, *The Cleansing of the Knife and Other Poems* in 1978.[7]

Her direct creative response to Carradale is expressed in the first poem of the sequence, 'The Alban Goes Out', a dynamic and often lyrical account of a night's ring-net fishing with the Carradale fleet. She combines precise observation with intensity. Above all, there is the communication of shared activity:

> Men and engines grunting and hauling,
> The nets dripping, the folds falling;
> The spring-ropes jerking to the winches' creaking
> Wind in the fathoms from their sea-deep seeking,
> Steady and long like a preacher speaking.
> But the flow of the net we must all lay hold on,
> The cork-strung backrope our hands are cold on,

> As we thrash at the net the dead fish falling
> Gleam and break from the tight mesh mauling . . .
>
> (CK, p. 6)

The poem is a celebration of her place in Carradale, perhaps encapsulated in a single line – 'How can we think of our neighbours except in a neighbourly way?' (CK, p. 5), which also echoes her preoccupation in *The Blood of the Martyrs*. Shared endeavour, comradeship: she aspired to these in her personal life and expressed them in much of her writing.

'The Cleansing of the Knife' looks at the other side of the Carradale coin. She worked on this long sequence through most of the war years. If 'The Alban Goes Out' reflects a sense of acceptance by the community, her Carradale honeymoon period, 'The Cleansing of the Knife' is about her growing ambivalence about Carradale in particular and the Highlands in general. It was an ambivalence that flavoured all her Highland concerns from that time on, and it arose from commitment on the one hand, frustration on the other.

The frustration was centred on what she identified as a Highland fickleness, which in turn was at least partly caused by an inability to confront history:

> Here is the problem set,
> Demanding a clear head:
> What can we do for Scotland?
> The past that must not be forgotten
> For all our wish to forget:
>   . . .
> Must we be thirled to the past
> To the mist and the unused sheiling?
> Over love and home and the Forty-Five
> Sham tunes and a sham feeling?
> Must we be less than alive,
> Must we lurk in the half light?
> Is this the best we can do?
>
> (CK, p. 45, p. 65)

In unravelling an answer to the question, Mitchison is addressing 'Donnachadh Ban', Duncan Munro, a Carradale forester, who was apt to retreat from reality into whisky. The sequence carries a highly-charged message, a statement of hope and aspiration, and of Mitchison's own perceived role in creating a new Scotland. Written into it is both a personal intimacy with people and place and the experience of war:

> Where are you, Donnachadh Ban,
> And what way are you minded?
> I cannot see you at all;
> My eyes are blinded
> By the grey plaster dust
> Of a smashed house in Partick
> Where a boy's body lay . . .
>
> (CK, p. 41)

The choice Mitchison presents is between escape – 'We can lift the glass and drink' (CK, p. 44) – and committed, communal action. The short lines and insistent rhythms of the poem convey a real sense of urgency as the answer emerges – 'We are more than merely ourselves' (CK, p. 51).

The poem blends the personal and the political with an intensity and a metaphorical power that her fiction sometimes lacks. As a poet, Mitchison is uneven. She can fall into slack rhythms and diction which suggest slack thought and feeling. But that is not the case here, or in 'The Alban Goes Out', or with many of the poems she writes about people and work at Carradale. When she can anchor her responses in the material and actual, for which she has an acute eye, she is a memorable and significant poet. Her courage and directness, her tendency to throw herself headlong into emotionally dangerous waters, can produce clumsy, ineffectual poetry. But when she carries it off successfully, the poetry that results has a challenging immediacy. The particular blend she achieves in 'The Cleansing of the Knife', with its unguarded expression of a need for a recognised role, provides a guide to understanding much of what she wrote later.

Through the war years she had two other major writing projects. Early in the war she embarked on writing *The Bull Calves*, a novel which she quite consciously conceived as part of the process of reiterating, if not reinventing, her Scottish identity.[8] She also undertook, from 1 September 1939, a diary for Mass-Observation, an organisation whose aim was to document the lives of ordinary people all over Britain in an attempt to piece together a picture of the way Britain lived and thought. Naomi Mitchison was clearly not an 'ordinary' Scot, but she kept, with only one significant gap, an extraordinarily detailed account, running to 1,600 pages of typescript, of all aspects of her life during the war years.

The diary, part of which has been published as *Among You Taking Notes* (ed. Dorothy Sheridan), has considerable documentary and historical value and, like her volumes of autobiography, is an important part of her output.[9] It illuminates many of the preoccupations that drove her poetry and fiction. She chronicles events and feelings as they unfold, writing in her characteristically unliterary, straightforward style, and wearing her honesty on her sleeve. It is more than a useful insight into a particularly resonant period of her own and Scotland's past. Its quality, capturing moment after moment of living and feeling, spontaneous, peppered with hasty responses and judgements, has its own value:

> I'm willing to give them a good deal, of time and energy and thought and love. Take, eat. But what good is it going to do? Mightn't they be better left alone? Is it possible to do anything from above? I have to sacrifice a good deal in order to live here: above all the privacy that a big town gives, the privacy of the crowd in the Underground, in which one can think one's own thoughts and let one's eyes cloud with any kind of imagining. Here I have to be good . . . all around are men and women waiting to catch me out. Sometimes I could scream. How can a writer work in these conditions? (*AYTN*, p. 58)

This passage captures the tone of the diary and also reveals something of Mitchison's contradictory feelings about her implantation in Scotland and her inherent sense of both noblesse and obligation. These are currents detectable in much of her writing.

The Bull Calves was Mitchison's first novel to be set in the relatively recent past and her first fully Scottish novel. Writing it was part of the process of re-establishing her Scottish roots. Initially, she was not sure whether fiction was the appropriate vehicle for what she wanted to say. 'I think the novel, as a form, is finished, at least for important things, yet I don't want exactly to write social history or biography,' she wrote in her diary during the early stages of gathering material for *The Bull Calves*.[10] But, as with her earlier novels, ultimately she found that fiction provided her with the most natural and appropriate means of focusing her views. She required a narrative, and she required characters who could both enact the past and throw light on the present. The fact that she peopled the book with her own ancestors, the Haldanes of Gleneagles, at the same time as drawing directly on her contemporary experience of Carradale, to the extent of virtually casting herself and local fisherman Denis Macintosh in the leading roles, accentuates the two-way reflexive nature of the book. A piece on 'Writing the Historical Novel' highlights this:

> There is a continuous mirroring back and forth of ancient and modern events and ways of thought, one throwing light on the other. And in order to think from the inside of your mirror of the past you find yourself imitating it, holding a coin of that period in your hand as though about to spend it, holding a sword as though about to strike with it, pinning a brooch as though it were new from the fashionable jeweller. Above all, you will get it into your tongue, or, being a writer, into your pen.[11]

The Bull Calves was also the result of an increasing engagement with politics, or rather the unavoidability of politics. 'I began to realise that politics was not a special kind of game for skilled players, but rather a whole aspect of life,' she had written in *The Moral Basis of Politics* (1938). Neither historian nor the historical novelist could avoid the political; equally, it was not legitimate for the political to exclude what she called the novelist's point of view, 'a wide, rough view, but a valuable one . . . the common-sense point of view on people, both as individuals and members of groups; but a view with slightly more detail and with rather more clarity than is usual'.[12]

The 'rather more detail' encompasses the tactile quality of Mitchison's relationship with the past, which is part of the distinctiveness of her historical fiction, part of the imagination's route to recreation. It helped her not only to bridge present and past, but to fashion a context which could accept an essentially contemporary idiom. She required the involvement of the contemporary in order to experience history: her wartime diary provides many clues to this and the novel itself is testimony to the process.

Did it succeed? For some, it did so triumphantly, but the book, much to Mitchison's disappointment, never struck the chord in Scotland which she hoped to sound. Although she was using the book in part to reinvent her own Scottish identity, she was also writing it 'for people here [Carradale] . . . to make them confident and happy' and added 'I don't want to write for the *New Statesman*, for the international culture of cities . . . if only I can do something for my own people in Scotland. I would like of course, just for once to be a best seller'.[13] *The Bull Calves* was not a bestseller in Scotland, and was not a part of either the literary establishment or the established anti-establishment. She often fretted at what seemed to be her lack of literary status.

Mitchison draws on her own family history, setting the novel at Gleneagles after the 1745 Jacobite Rising and using the central character, Kirstie Haldane, to give herself a Scottish voice. The relationship and past history of Kirstie and her husband William Macintosh of Borlum are the novel's centre. Kirstie has had an unhappy first marriage, William, a Jacobite, an eventful exile. The Haldanes of Gleneagles are poised to play a full part in an accelerating process of agricultural, industrial and economic development, a movement that had begun before the '45 and gathered force again after it. Mitchison identifies a social and political hub, and draws her characters into it. Characters are swept up by it; sometimes they can help to direct it; but they cannot escape it.

Although multi-layered and wordy, there is an essential dynamism in the novel provided by the characters themselves, their emotional vigour and political collisions, and the language Mitchison has distilled from listening carefully to and reworking the living language she heard in Kintyre. She tackles a wealth of historical detail and several focal issues, weaving together debate, environment and action, and the rhythms of folk history. This process is illuminated by the extensive notes at the end of the novel. What is important is that the novel itself catches a flavour of authenticity, however arrived at. This is Kirstie telling her niece Catherine of the burning of Aberuthven:

> 'And all these poor folk and plenty more, with every bit thing they had burnt over their heads and that in January. The seed-corn had been burnt with the meal. The bairnie's cradle, the weaver's loom, the joiner's and mason's tools, the surgeon's instruments, the Minister's books, the wee things the lassie had put by her wedding, all gone.' (BC, p. 68)

By concentrating the action in one place, the house and policies of Gleneagles, over a period of two days, Mitchison maintains a strong focus on the novel's pivotal relationship, between Kirstie and William. This allows her to range widely in time, space and ideas. Flashback and reminiscence build up the strata of narrative, without losing sight of the immediate locale.

There is an element of self-conscious seriousness about the book, underlined by the appended notes, which provide a fascinating gloss on the making of the novel. They also explore aspects of the relationship between history and fiction, a relationship which had absorbed Mitchison from the start of her writing career. She is above all a storyteller, but a storyteller with a powerful awareness of how tightly personality and behaviour are knotted into the social and cultural environment, Without history, there is no story, and vice versa.

In many respects *The Bull Calves* provided the foundation for the fiction that followed. It was a form of statement of intent, upbeat and forward-looking, implicitly identifying post-war Scotland as a place of political and social optimism. Yet, as her wartime diary reveals, she had few illusions about the nature of the task.

In the 1950s Mitchison was writing busily, for adults and children. *Lobsters on the Agenda* (1952) is probably her best Scottish novel with a contemporary setting.[14] Much less ambitious than *We Have Been Warned*, it deals in a gentler, more ironic way with some of Mitchison's ambivalence towards the Highlands which also provides the theme of 'The Cleansing of the Knife'. Kate Snow, the novel's heroine, is a partial incomer in a remote Highland community which she observes with mixed affection and impatience. The community is divided. The old co-operative ways of dealing with day-to-day life are vanishing. Mitchison uses the book to highlight some of the particular problems of remote rural communities that had become, through her work as an Argyll County Councillor and on the Highland Panel, virtually a professional concern. But although there is exasperation in her tone, there is also an affectionately relaxed handling of the narrative. The issues emerge organically. For all Kate's frustrations, there is a strong sense of the author's pleasure in the writing. Indeed, the author herself actually appears as one of the characters, in her role as member of the Highland Panel – 'this odd woman, Mrs Mitchison, sitting and talking and biting her nails, not what you'd expect from a Government Committee' (LA, p. 212).

The book has a message, that mutual loyalty and trust 'ought to make us together more able to achieve something than we could ever do separately' (*LA*, p. 253) – a reiteration of 'more than merely ourselves'. It is a simple message, and is as much about communality as *The Blood of the Martyrs*. Mitchison reaches out for something that will draw people together, some unifying force or idea, but doesn't find it in the Highlands. 'You could sum up the Highland way of life, if you were unkind, in four words' Kate muses: 'devilment, obligement, refreshment, buggerment' (*LA*, p. 213).

Another novel very much informed by Carradale pre-dates *Lobsters on the Agenda – The Big House* (1950).[15] It is written for children, but its central situation reflects Mitchison's perceptions of Highland life and her place in it as much as any of her Scottish fiction. It explores issues of inheritance and class stereotypes, centred on the relationship and adventures of Su, from 'the big house' and Winkie, son of a crofter. Su is trying to reach beyond the limited environment of 'Tigh Mhor' but feels out of place at the village school. Winkie is a bit of a loner, awkward in the initial encounters with Su. But he has the superior knowledge of the environment and that gives him confidence and almost reverses traditional class roles. It is a powerful story imbued with the atmosphere of Argyll's prehistory, a haunting feature of the area even today. Time-travelling adventures allow Sue and Winkie to share their aristocratic and humble experience and link themselves with their ancient roots.

Mitchison was writing a great deal for children at this time, ranging from reworkings of the Orkney sagas, such as *The Land the Ravens Found* (1955) to delightfully matter-of-fact fantasies, such as *Graeme and the Dragon* (1954), and more stories inspired by Carradale, for example *Little Boxes* (1956) and *The Far Harbour* (1957), which echoes some of the themes of *Lobsters on the Agenda*.[16] Many of these stories, with their relaxed and friendly tone of voice, suggest origins in tales Mitchison may well have been making up for her grandchildren. (Su and Graeme are both names 'borrowed' form her oldest grandchildren.) *Graeme and the Dragon*, in particular, strikes a note of improvisation and spontaneity which has survived forty years remarkably well.

Mitchison's engagement with contemporary Scotland was also expressed in her championship of particular causes. Her involvement in the herring fishing inspired the writing of the documentary *Men and Herring* (1950) and the play *Spindrift* (1951) with Denis Macintosh.[17] *Spindrift* was first performed by the Citizens Theatre in Glasgow and recently revived at Edinburgh's Festival Theatre. It highlights the effect of a diminishing industry on a dependent community and the conflict this inevitably brings to families. It is blunt about the realities, while at the same time capturing an almost romantic lyricism.

This was a productive period for Mitchison. Scotland, past and present, remained a major preoccupation, alongside some of her earlier interests. If it became more difficult for her to sustain a political optimism about Scotland's future, and if personal experience brought frustration, her commitment to Scotland continued. At the same time, the world of myth and legend and the relationship between mythic and historic versions of the past continued to feed her fiction. *Behold Your King* (1957) pursues some of the currents of *The Blood of the Martyrs*, weaving a tale from the events of the Crucifixion.[18] It gets off to a rather faltering start – by this time Mitchison was adept at employing a formula based on a concentrated focus on time and place and at first the reader is overly aware of this. But the drive of the narrative soon takes over, and indeed draws attention to the organic process by which a tale takes shape out of people and events.

Norse saga has proved an especially rich source for her. *The Swan's Road* (1954) is a non-fictional account of Norse voyagings, to Scotland, to other parts of Europe, to

Constantinople and the East to America. It provides the groundwork for *The Land the Ravens Found*, based on one aspect of the story, a voyage of Vikings and Scots to Iceland and their settlement there. One of her most striking and original pieces of fiction from this period is *Travel Light* (1952), a resonant allegorical tale concerning the adventures of Halla, cast out by a jealous stepmother to find her own way in the world.[19] Published as a book for children it is a subtle and deftly sustained narrative, resulting in a fresh, natural and effective blend of myth and history. It captures timeless rhythms of storytelling:

> Halla listened to them speak of Micklegard, and some had been there and some not. But it seemed that in the middle of the city there was a palace in which you might go from one hall into another all through a summer day and never come back again to the one from which you had started. And in these halls there was every imaginable thing. There were golden birds set with jewels that by some art opened their wings and sang. There were rare foods and delicious scents, strange animals held by golden chains, lamps that turned night into day. And in the innermost hall was the Purple-born, and on orders of the Purple-born was all done: by his word was feasting, was dancing, was racing with chariots or fighting of wild beasts or honey-sweet moving of smooth-smelling women. So this, thought Halla, sitting among hounds and hawks on the deck of the ship, listening, was the Master Dragon of Micklegard. (*TL*, pp. 60–1)

Mitchison has continued to draw on legend and early history as a source for her fiction, with *Early in Orcadia* (1987) demonstrating that her particular talent for the imaginative reconstruction of the past has not faded.[20] But the 1960s saw her fiction responding to another source of stimulus. In 1963 she made her first visit to Botswana, and for the next quarter of a century spent a great deal of time there, living in Mochudi at the invitation of Linchwe, chief of the Batgatla, and working with them on a range of community projects. Out of this stemmed a novel, *When We Become Men* (1965), many stories and several books on African history addressed to Africans, and records of her experiences there.[21] As always, her particular combination of practical and creative response had an immediate effect on her writing. Her hands-on application to her surroundings and her sensitivity to legend combine to enable her to adopt a heritage and traditions new to her, and to achieve an authentic-sounding tone of voice and projection of character and environment.

When We Become Men is an important novel, written very soon after Mitchison's first visit to Botswana. It illustrates the rapidity and skill with which Mitchison could grasp the social and political currents of territory that was new to her, and the way her approach manifests her continuing and consistent preoccupations, good and bad, of the modern, western world. In some respects she had been here before, for she is in frontier country again, looking at encounters not so different from those of the barbarian world with Athenian democracy, of Gaul with the Romans, of Scottish Highlanders with post-conflict (post-1745 and post-Second-World War) government and southern intrusion. She had often described the clash between a colonising power and native resistance. She had often contrasted, with sympathy, value systems that failed to mesh. If the territory was geographically and specifically new, psychologically she knew exactly where she was.

She is comfortable in Africa, and is able to express dramatically the issues that concern her. She conveys the benefits of tribalism by seeing them through the eyes of Isaac, an urban black South African political refugee. She is a scientist who is at home with people for whom magic is a reality: while the life of her other hero, Letlotse, is saved by penicillin, it is hinted that Isaac himself is saved by the touch and power of the chief. She recognises and articulates the dilemma caught at crossroads of change. Isaac accepts the traditions of the tribe which adopts him and allegiance to the chief. His friend Josh remonstrates: ' "You belong to Africa, not to any one man, even your chief . . . Africa, Isaac, Africa, all this we haven't seen but we know it's there once we get free" ' (*WWBM*, p. 207). Mitchison herself wanted to believe that it was possible to combine the community values of tribalism with the political structures of a modern state, just as she passionately hoped that an enlightened approach to the economy of the Highlands need not destroy social cohesion.

Just as she had drawn Carradale into the writing of *The Bull Calves* and collaborated with Denis Macintosh on *Men and Herring* and *Spindrift*, *When We Become Men* was written with the involvement and approval of her Botswana friends, almost as a collaboration. It underlines the way Mitchison saw her role, as a mouthpiece for a community, a traditional storyteller. To achieve this she had to become wholeheartedly a part of the chosen community – it is noticeable in all her writing how eager she is to participate in collective action, whether it is dancing, sharing food, hunting or building schools, how quickly she adopts the collective 'we'.

Her African writing can be seen as a third phase of her career, or as the pursuit of another route through the same territory as had always commanded her attention. The landscape is different, the details of tools and dress and ornament vary, but the psychological and emotional terrain is essentially the same. People and their environment, physical, political and cultural, are her concern. The way people relate, in families and communities, their identification of goals and their pursuit of action, the relationship between macro and micro arenas of behaviour – this continued to be the meat of Mitchison's fiction.

This was equally true of her experiments with science fiction. *Memoirs of a Spacewoman* (1962) and *Solution Three* (1975) show her exploring the interactions of individual experiment and communal benefit, sharply flavoured by her own scientific background – her father and brother were both distinguished scientists and she grew up in an environment of experiment and enquiry. *Memoirs of a Spacewoman* has an inward sensuality, released and intensified through a context in which women have control over their own lives, without dependence on men. It is a compelling piece of writing. *Solution Three* explores a world in which homosexuality is the norm, heterosexuality deviant. These novels unleash a significant current in Mitchison's interests, and also give play to an attractive vein of mischievousness, often present in her children's stories and her more journalistic pieces. Also set in the future is *Not By Bread Alone* (1983)[22] which posits a situation where science has solved the problem of feeding the world, and explores the cultural and psychological consequences on people's needs and perceptions.

Mitchison is a storyteller in both fiction and non-fiction. Every aspect of her intricate life has fuelled her stories. She has chronicled much of her life in diaries, volumes of autobiography and in articles, notably those published in the *New Statesman* during the 1950s and '60s which are filled with detail of life and work at Carradale. In some respects she has quite deliberately lived her life as a story, the drama sometimes self-induced, friends and family often drafted in to play out roles on a stage she herself has constructed. This instinctive feel for theatre is at the heart of her prose narratives and her best poetry. Sometimes it can lead her astray and unbalance her normally four-square command of action. Sometimes she allows emotion to skew the dynamic, but not often.

In over sixty years of writing, the nature of the dynamic has not really changed. Wherever she is, Mitchison homes in on the relationship between individuals and the events and forces that sweep through their lives. After the Second World War she travelled even more extensively, to India, Pakistan, the Middle East and Australia as well as to Africa, North America and many parts of Europe. Everywhere she was tuned to the possibilities of story. Her narrative skill is the result of her ability to illuminate the whole picture through a focus on detail. Her individuality comes from her application of a contemporary idiom, familiar, almost conversational, to cultures and periods that have often been distorted by attempts to construct an appropriate literary voice. Her best writing brings the distant and marginal to our attention: historically distant – the ancient world and the future; geographically distant – Africa; off the edge of centralised consciousness – the Scottish Highlands. She writes less well when she moves into the centre as in *We Have Been Warned* and some of her short stories. But in everything she has written it is the quality of her alert and questing intelligence that is the driving force. She is a natural storyteller. If she has never managed to fit that role entirely naturally to a chosen community and an attentive audience, the tension of her constant endeavour has produced a unique and commanding body of work.

There is a curious parallel between Naomi Mitchison and another Scottish woman writer, who died in 1897, the year in which Mitchison was born. Margaret Oliphant was also prolific, also widely travelled and wide-ranging in her interests and subjects. Both women have been strangely overlooked. The contemporaneous reputations of both of them have been dependent on readers and critics outside Scotland. It is tempting to suggest that Scotland is not only inhospitable to women writers, but inclined to penalise those who move out of a specifically Scottish frame. Yet Mitchison, like Oliphant, has made a distinguished contribution to Scottish literature.

She is also an innovator and has ploughed her own furrow. The metaphor is apt, for Mitchison has indeed ploughed, and got her hands dirty in a variety of ways. It shows in both the subjects she chooses to write about and the quality of her prose. She can move into apparently alien cultures because she looks with the eyes of a doer as well as a writer. There is no doubt that a degree of patrician confidence has helped. At the same time, her need for acceptance as a storyteller is honestly and nakedly expressed.

This gives us a guide as to how to place her, which the individuality of her voice otherwise makes difficult. She identifies herself with an ancient tradition. She is the mouth of the tribe, recording its past, telling its stories, articulating its needs, rehearsing its rituals. She recognises that much of the world is hostile to this role, especially to a woman occupying it. Neither Scotland nor England were comfortable with it. Perhaps she got closest to what she wanted in Botswana. It is certainly the case that only recently, after more than half a century of writing in Scotland, has she begun to be taken seriously as a Scottish writer. In a recent interview Naomi Mitchison was asked if she had intentionally set out, in her early novels, to bring a twentieth-century idiom to bear on the distant past. Was she a self-conscious innovator? 'I couldn't have done aught else,' she replied.[23] She has said on more than one occasion that her books directly reflect what was going on in her life at the time. She has used her life generously in her fiction, but perhaps not from choice. There is a sense in which her writing has been compelled, and is indelibly stamped with a closely meshed personal and social commitment. The result is a singular voice and a body of literature of a character and an independence quite unlike anything else in twentieth-century Scottish writing.[24]

Notes

1.   Naomi Mitchison, *The Corn King and the Spring Queen* (Cape, London, 1931; Canongate, Edinburgh, 1990). Further references are to *CKSQ* and to the Canongate edition.

2.   Naomi Mitchison, *The Conquered* (Cape, London, 1923).

3.   Naomi Mitchison, *We Have Been Warned* (Constable, London, 1935). Further references are to *WHBW*.

4.   Naomi Mitchison, *The Blood of the Martyrs* (Constable, London, 1939).

5.   John Mair, review of *The Blood of the Martyrs*, in *The New Statesman*, VXIII, p. 450.

6.   Naomi Mitchison, *The Kingdom of Heaven* (Heinemann, London, 1939), p. 119.

7.   Naomi Mitchison, *The Cleansing of the Knife and Other Poems* (Canongate, Edinburgh and Vancouver, 1978). Further references are to *CK*.

8.   Naomi Mitchison, *The Bull Calves* (Cape, London, 1947; Richard Drew, Glasgow, 1985). Further references are to *BC* and to the Drew edition.

9.   Naomi Mitchison, *Among You Taking Notes* [*AYTN*], ed. Dorothy Sheridan (Gollancz, London, 1989).

10.   Naomi Mitchison, Mass-Observation diary, unpublished, p. 623.

11.   Naomi Mitchison, 'Writing the Historical Novel', *Scotland*, 13, 61.

12.   Naomi Mitchison, *The Moral Basis of Politics* (Constable, London, 1938), xi.

13.   Mass-Observation diary, p. 661.

14.   Naomi Mitchison, *Lobsters on the Agenda* [*LA*] (Gollancz, London, 1952).

15.   Naomi Mitchison, *The Big House* (Faber & Faber, London, 1950).

16.   Naomi Mitchison, *The Land the Ravens Found* (Collins, London, 1955); *Graeme and the Dragon* (Faber & Faber, London, 1954); *Little Boxes* (Faber & Faber, London, 1956); *The Far Harbour* (Collins, London, 1957).

17.   Naomi Mitchison and Denis Macintosh, *Men and Herring: A Documentary* (Serif Books, Edinburgh, 1949); *Spindrift: A Play in Three Acts* (French, London, 1951).

18.   Naomi Mitchison, *Behold Your King* (Frederick Muller, London, 1957).

19.   Naomi Mitchison, *The Swan's Road* (Naldrett Press, London, 1954); *Travel Light* [*TL*] (Faber & Faber, London, 1952; Virago, London, 1985). Further references are to the Virago edition.

20.   Naomi Mitchison, *Early in Orcadia* (Richard Drew, Glasgow, 1987).

21.   Naomi Mitchison, *When We Become Men* [*WWBM*] (Collins, London, 1965).

22.   Naomi Mitchison, *Memoirs of a Spacewoman* (Gollancz, London, 1962); *Solution Three* (Dobson, London, 1975); *Not by Bread Alone* (Marion Boyars, London, 1983).

23.   Naomi Mitchison, interview with the author, 19 June 1994.

24.   Naomi Mitchison has published about seventy-five books, including novels, short stories, plays, poetry, fiction and non-fiction for children, travel writing, commentary on a wide range of subjects and autobiography. She has edited several more, and written innumerable articles.

A complete bibliography (excluding articles) can be found in Jenni Calder's biography, *The Nine Lives of Naomi Mitchison* (Virago, London, 1997). A fuller list is given in the general bibliography of this book.

31

The Modern Historical Tradition

Moira Burgess

It is a truth universally acknowledged that Scottish historical novels and women novelists go together. The axiom calls for closer examination, and not only because, like most such truths, it is at best half-true. We can easily list many male novelists who, at least sometimes, write historical novels (Neil Gunn, Nigel Tranter, George Mackay Brown, even Iain Crichton Smith) and, of course, many women novelists deal with contemporary concerns. More insidiously, however, the belief seems to come with a corollary: when considering contemporary Scottish literature, historical novels can safely be ignored. It is time to look at Scottish women historical novelists with a clear eye.

If mentioned at all in surveys of Scottish fiction, the historical genre is usually dismissed in a line or two. Alan Bold devotes a chapter in his *Modern Scottish Literature* to 'Women and history: Plaidy, Mitchison, Dunnett'.[1] He accepts (following Anthony Burgess) 'the pre-eminence of women in historical fiction', and comments that 'In Scotland, historical fiction tends to be produced with an energy that would overwhelm an industry'.

A few years earlier Francis Russell Hart in *The Scottish Novel* similarly titles a chapter 'Mitchison and later romancers', remarking:

> There have been few signs . . . that Scotland has lost its unique position as the stereotypical land of popular romance . . . But the garish covers often hide thoroughly researched fiction-alized histories and biographies. They are almost all by women, most of them non-Scots . . . It is too easy to pass off the phenomenon as merely exploitative or fraudulent; in fact, the talents are formidable and prolific and deserve far more than the glance accorded them here.[2]

Hart and Bold agree, then, that most twentieth-century Scottish historical novels are written by women (though both acknowledge the considerable presence of Nigel Tranter in this otherwise female field). We should note, however, that both – Hart more consciously perhaps than Bold – include in their survey writers who were not Scottish, either by birth or, in Muriel Spark's term, formation. Jean Plaidy was born in London, as was another popular if perhaps more serious chronicler, Margaret Irwin. Jane Lane and D. K. Broster, mentioned by Hart, were born respectively in Ruislip and Liverpool. All spent their long and prolific writing lives mainly, if not exclusively, in England. Ever since Jane Porter's *The Scottish Chiefs* (1810) Scottish history has been attractive to non-Scottish historical novelists.

In both Hart and Bold the category 'historical novel' seems to shade into 'historical romance'. In this sub-genre, certainly, the preponderance of women novelists becomes very marked. The historical romance, indeed, would seem to be, in the commercial (and usually pejorative) term, a 'woman's book', written by women for women. There is no particular need to belittle these writers, who are producing what they want to write and what many people want to read. (Curiously, the identification of historical romances as 'women's books' has given rise to the odd circumstance that two at least of the most popular names in the field, Jessica Stirling and Emma Blair, are in fact pseudonyms used by men – respectively Hugh C. Rae, b.1935, and Iain Blair, b.1942.)

But Douglas Gifford, writing of 'romancers . . . who set their tales of love in a [historical] period for colour and backcloth', has usefully pointed out that 'their characters seem "modern", their love stories the most important element, for all the research'.[3] This is probably a benchmark to bear in mind. If, then, we separate out and discard what are, by these criteria, historical romances – which in any case are too numerous, and rather too similar, to deal with at any length here – we begin to see more clearly the actual contribution made by women novelists to the Scottish historical novel.

I intend to treat four novelists in particular: Jane Oliver, Naomi Mitchison, Dorothy Dunnett, and Sian Hayton. They are not the only Scottish women writers who have attempted, with some success, the serious historical novel;[4] but as we consider their work, published over some eight decades, I think we may trace a development and deepening in the approach of Scottish women novelists to the writing of historical fiction, parallel perhaps to a similarly deepening interest in women's history on a wider scale.

Jane Oliver

Jane Oliver (1903–70) belongs to the school of women historical novelists already mentioned: the group praised by Hart, who flourished before and shortly after the Second World War. Unlike Plaidy, Irwin, Lane and Broster, Jane Oliver (a pseudonym for Helen Christina Easson) was Scottish, born in Liddesdale. She lived in England for many years, working in various occupations (bookshop assistant, physical education teacher and masseuse are among those listed on her book-jackets), but retained a love for Scotland. She has described how, as an ambulance driver in the London blitz, she achieved detachment during the hours of waiting for a call-out:

> As the ambulance station shuddered and a near miss came screaming down I deliberately steadied myself for an effort of will too definite to be considered mere daydream or reverie. In all but the material sense, I returned to the Borderland. My body remained, indeed, in the bare, brilliant room . . . but I myself, as nearly free from time, perhaps, as I shall ever be until the hour of my death, walked once again up the hill road that wound past the patchwork of little fields in Liddesdale to the fell and the moor beyond.[5]

This is in part the imagination of the writer at work, and Oliver was clearly a dedicated and diligent historical novelist. We learn, again from her book-jackets, that she embarked as a young woman (with *Mine is the Kingdom*, published in 1937) on an ambitious enterprise: 'a series of closely linked novels with which the author has planned to portray the whole course of Scottish history, not as periodic outcrops of romantic improbability, but as a coherent and vividly dramatic whole'.[6]

She pursued this aim over some thirty years. Today, however, twenty-five years after her death, her books are out of print (though they do appear in some numbers on the shelves of second-hand bookshops). Is this, as so often, due to a mere shift of taste, or are Oliver's novels lacking in some essential quality which would give them longer life?

Hart, as we have seen, commended the women historical novelists, Oliver among them, for their 'thoroughly researched fictionalized histories and biographies', and Oliver's research seems to have been extensive and intelligently applied. Her novels are supplied with bibliographies and with four- or five-page prefaces which lay out the known historical facts and explain how she has used them for her fictional purposes:

> No essential incident has been wholly invented. There is historical evidence or at least traditional ground for the whole dramatic story of Columba, and out of a list of forty chief characters, only eight unimportant fictitious individuals have been introduced.[7]

> Where I have presumed to build up a personality about which little is known, it has been only after examining all available foundations to ensure that the structure raised on them might be sound.[8]

Yet it is surely not to the point to praise a novel for the quality of its historical accuracy alone. Allan Massie, in a recent review of Joan Lingard's *After Colette*, remarks that 'this is a novel that would work even if the character of Colette had been wholly invented, surely the key test by which the use of "real figures" in fiction should be judged'. On this criterion, do Oliver's novels work? Are her 'real figures' – Columba, James VI, Queen Margaret, Queen Mary – real to her readers? They are certainly real to Jane Oliver. We have seen how she was able to detach herself from wartime London and walk, all but physically, in timeless Liddesdale. With a similar effort of imagination she places herself, when working on a novel, in sixth-century Iona or sixteenth-century Edinburgh, and finds there people with whom she is very much at home:

> [Columba's] voice, which had been high and sweet at the oratory, had broken now and was already steadying into a bass of tremendous range and power which, taken together with his great stature and increasing strength, made strangers take him for several years older than he actually was. (*IG*, p. 105)

Conventionally Columba is imagined as sweet and self-effacing; Jane Oliver startles the reader into a new perception of the saint's formidable presence.

Yet if we today do not mesh completely with Jane Oliver's carefully imagined historical worlds, several reasons may be suggested. Each novel centres on a famous historical figure: king, queen or saint as the case may be. We are given the Story of St Columba, the Story of Alexander III, greatest of the early Scottish kings. This approximates, of course, to a long-established method of teaching history, which is however out of favour now, but novels accommodate characters in ways that history textbooks do not.

Tied in with this approach is a certain stateliness of diction, in both narrative and dialogue. We see King Malcolm and Queen Margaret discussing the upbringing of their children:

> What could it matter [wonders Malcolm] if he picked them up, hushing them in his arms and giving them special titbits because they had pushed their supper aside? . . . 'Are you not too hard on them sometimes, sweetheart? . . . Would it not be better to give way, this once, and pick him up so that we might have peace?'

'If they are afterwards to have authority over others,' [Margaret says], 'then surely they must learn first to submit to authority themselves?' (SMS, p. 229)

The required point is made, and the opposing views are well in character. But can we believe that, alone in their apartments, over the cradle of a yelling baby, even medieval kings and queens addressed each other with such perfect syntax and grace?

In the same novel we find very clear signs that we are being told a story:

The other country with which [the kingdom of Scotia] was intermittently to do battle for the next six centuries. (p. 28)

It was as Edinburgh that its name was soon to pass into Scottish history. (p. 204)

Jane Oliver, writing in the mid-twentieth century, naturally knows the course which Scottish history has taken since the period in which her novel is set. Her contemporary readers perhaps had a good grounding in the matter, too, from school. Malcolm and Margaret hardly anticipate the nature of their future fame. Jane Oliver exploits the ironies of her characters' ignorance and her readers' knowledge. She perhaps underlines her points in a rather heavy-handed and old-fashioned manner but these technical flaws arise most likely from her very conscientiousness, her insistence on tying her story to well-grounded historical fact.

At other moments, throughout her novels, a different and supernatural emphasis makes itself known. A monk sees inexplicable light in the church where Columba is praying. Margaret's coffin becomes too heavy to carry until Malcolm's body is brought to join it. This sense of the magical comes from a writer who, as I have suggested, in the hell of the blitz could project herself in thought to 'the circle of the Border hills [where] the spirit was so safe that the fate of the body scarcely mattered'. At times in her writing Oliver achieves this magical fusion of the temporal and the spiritual; another and significant element in the work of later historical novelists.

Hart, in the chapter already cited, categorises Oliver's novels as 'informed, if conventional, fictionalized biographies of Scottish monarchs'. Before writing her down, however, as a worthy but uninspired chronicler of times long past, the reader should bear in mind *In No Strange Land* (1944), not strictly a historical novel, and therefore not dealt with here, but a painful and beautiful book arising from the death of Oliver's husband John Llewellyn Rhys in a wartime air-crash after only a year of marriage.[9]

Naomi Mitchison

Ten years before Jane Oliver began writing, Naomi Mitchison (b. 1897) had published her first novel, *The Conquered* (1923).[10] She was a young wife and mother at the time, and famously, as she tells us in one of her volumes of autobiography,

used to push the pram . . . I had a big notebook . . . and I used to have this opened out at my end of the pram so that I could write my book while I went on slowly pushing . . . I got a good deal written this way.[11]

In the same autobiographical work she explains why she began her writing career with historical novels:

> In my twenties I was having interesting, highly detailed dreams, which had only to be
> trimmed off and finished in order to turn into stories . . . Before that I had started two or
> three modern novels, but as I was completely without direct experience of the emotional or
> social situations I had got into my plots, they were very bad. (*YMWA*, p. 161)

She embarked on a course of reading, and then writing, about the ancient world: Greece,
Rome, Gaul, Britain.

So far, so conventional. Many historical novelists, no doubt, began for similar reasons,
though not all could describe their path with such detached clarity. But *The Conquered*
was immediately recognised on publication as something quite unconventional and re-
warding. It was frequently reprinted: the 1932 reissue was a 'Florin Edition', an indication
of its popularity. In this first attempt we can already see certain features which recur in
the historical novels which – among so much other writing – Mitchison has continued
to produce for some seventy years.

Most noticeable perhaps at the time of publication was the role of *The Conquered*
as a commentary on contemporary events, specifically the Irish situation of the time.
Mitchison records in *You May Well Ask* (pp. 162–3) that her publishers asked her if
she was Irish, and that her mother was 'somewhat shocked at my chapter headings from
'The Irish Volunteer' and 'The Croppy Boy'. This parallelism continues to be a strategy
in Mitchison's historical novels. *The Blood of the Martyrs*, published in 1939, while in its
own right an absorbing story of the persecution and martyrdom of first-century Christians
in Rome, clearly arises from Mitchison's concern with contemporary persecution in
Germany and Austria. Donald Smith considers that:

> *The Blood of the Martyrs* shows most directly the way in which she harnesses the popular
> format of the historical romance, and its close emotional identification with the reader, to
> moral and literary seriousness.[12]

And, underlying the many strands and complexities of *The Bull Calves* (1947), her great
novel of the eighteenth century, it has been observed that:

> The responsive reader will not miss the many correspondences between 1747 and 1947, the
> year of the novel's publication, including the fact that major wars have just finished in the
> period of the novel and in the author's time.[13]

Mitchison's novels unsurprisingly exploit the political potential of the historical in ways
that do not occur to Jane Oliver. And Mitchison's treatment of the sexual has a strength
which, if now somewhat dated (and politically incorrect!) derives in large part from her
easy use of 1930s colloquial idiom:

> He turned on her and kissed her as she'd never been kissed yet; he didn't care whether she
> liked it or not – but she did. She gasped and gave a few little cries – she didn't know what
> he mightn't do next, but she half hoped he'd do it all the same![14]

> 'Pick up my clothes,' he said.
>   'I won't!' said Erif Der, getting pinker.
>   'Yes you will,' said her brother, and got her by the two plaits . . .
>   'You beast, Berris!' she said, 'I'll make you sorry for that!'[15]

It is clear that this colloquial style in both narrative and dialogue derives from the upper-class family and the boarding school and is now rather dated, but it was in the current mode when the books were published and insofar as it permits the past and the present to reflect upon each other, it is one of Mitchison's contributions to historical fiction. She recognised this herself:

> Oddly enough I was the first to see that one could write historical novels in a modern idiom: in fact it was the only way I could write them. Now everybody does, so it is no longer interesting. (YMWA, p. 163–4)

(Though 'now' in this quote is the late 1970s, we may note that it did take some time before 'everybody' followed suit; Jane Oliver was still couching her stories in would-be period idiom twenty-five years after *The Conquered*.) And yet, of course, since the class-marked slang of Naomi Mitchison dates very quickly, Jane Oliver's may be as lasting an idiom.

Mitchison expounds her theory and practice concerning 'the question of language' at some length in the notes which follow *The Bull Calves*.[16] Always aware of what she is doing in her writing, she explains:

> In my novels of the ancient world I have transcribed Latin, Greek, or whatever it may be, into current English, using slang or debased forms when it seemed as though this was the best way of giving the reader the feel of how people were talking . . . On the whole this book [*The Bull Calves*] is in current West Coast speech, Kintyre speech – Carradale speech maybe – at any rate the kind of spoken Scots that comes most naturally to me . . . Of course none of this is what people in the eighteenth century actually spoke . . . I could have made my book people talk that way, but, because I was not actually thinking or imagining in it, that would have been artificial, *a barrier between myself and them, as also between them and the reader.* (BC, p. 408–10; my italics)

And, as Mitchison herself must have realised and the reader certainly does, there is no barrier at all impeding our understanding of the characters in her historical novels. Whether these characters have their being in Hellas, Rome or eighteenth-century Gleneagles, we are there and they are people we know. Mitchison's characters – ordinary people, underdogs, it may be noted, as often as kings and queens – are not 'modern' in the sense used by Gifford, quoted above; 'timeless' is perhaps the word, firmly based though they are in their historical or mythical setting. Undoubtedly they have timeless and rec-ognisable human motivations. After a tussle with her publisher over some unambiguously phrased passages in the contemporary novel *We Have Been Warned* (1935), Mitchison acknowledges this, just slightly tongue-in-cheek:

> In some of the stories in *The Delicate Fire* there is, I would have thought, far more overt sex than in *We Have Been Warned*, but apparently it's all right when people wear wolfskins and togas. (YMWA, p. 179)[17]

One final element in *The Conquered* remains to be mentioned, introduced there almost – apparently – as an afterthought, but clearly no such thing, since it returns and grows in importance throughout Mitchison's subsequent writing. Meromic in *The Conquered* is the son of Kormiac the Wolf, a Gallic chieftain, but is now a slave of the Roman conquerors, and as a punishment for insurrection has had his right hand cut off. Maimed and exhausted, he has reached the end of his tether, and we reach the last sentence of the book:

> On the paths and under the bushes there were tracks of wolves, and one wolf that went lame of the right fore-foot; the tracks went north. (*The Conquered*, p. 284)

Meromic has disappeared; we are to understand that he (son of the Wolf) has metamorphosed into a wolf. In the magical space so often present in Scottish literature – as we have seen in some of Jane Oliver's novels, but here to much greater effect – two worlds intersect.

The belief that this can and does happen surfaces again and again in Mitchison's writing. Her own childhood terrors – described in her first volume of autobiography, *Small Talk* (1973)[18] – and Kirstie's 'appearances' in *The Bull Calves* (pp. 164–5, in particular) run alongside the events of everyday life. Most striking is the situation in *The Corn King and the Spring Queen* (1931), her masterpiece in the opinion of many, though others would argue for *The Bull Calves*.

> Erif Der was sitting on a bank of shingle and throwing pebbles into the Black Sea . . . She was thinking a little about magic but mostly about nothing at all . . . She jumped down twelve feet on to another shingle bank, but she was not at all an easy person to hurt; air and water at least knew too much about her. (*CKSQ*, p. 21)

Erif Der is a witch (her brother is so angry with her, in the passage quoted above, because she has magicked him into taking all his clothes off), as are some of the other women in Marob, even if they only use their powers to keep the milk from turning. The country of Marob itself is fictional, but historical Sparta and Alexandria take their place in the rich, crowded book; Erif is fictional, but women like her took part (as Mitchison knew from Frazer's *The Golden Bough*) in the fertility rites which take place on Plowing Eve. History is connected with magic, and magic is connected with women; this perspective, which differs from that found in the more conventional historical novels of Jane Oliver, is also found in very recent Scottish historical fiction.[19]

Dorothy Dunnett

There is no direct line of descent to Dorothy Dunnett from either Oliver or Mitchison. If she looks back, it is perhaps to older models. Trevor Royle considers that '[her] cycle of novels [the "Lymond" series] is central to the tradition of the historical romance in Scottish fiction',[20] and Hart remarks that 'it is difficult to recall a single romantic or mythic topos that is not included' in Lymond's story.[21]

Dunnett's historical novels comprise the six-book sequence tracing the career of Francis Crawford of Lymond, *The Game of Kings* (1962), *Queens' Play* (1964), *The Disorderly Knights* (1966), *Pawn in Frankincense* (1969), *The Ringed Castle* (1971) and *Checkmate* (1975); a single novel, *King Hereafter* (1982) on the life of Earl Thorfinn of Orkney, also known (we discover) as Macbeth; and the House of Niccolo series, beginning with *Niccolo Rising* (1986).[22] Since the Niccolo series is still in progress – at the time of writing, six volumes of a projected eight having appeared – I shall deal here principally with the

Lymond books, mindful of the fact that not until *Checkmate*, the final Lymond novel, is the whole tapestry clearly seen.

A reader coming fresh to the Lymond novels must notice first of all the brilliant colours of their world. There is colour in the landscape:

> The next day, the autumn trumpets gave tongue, the sun shone like copper, and a flaming row was taking place in the Priory cloisters. To the north the hills of Ben Dearg reared empurpled, and soft airs shuddered on the blue water. On Inchmahome, Discord beat against the ancient pillars. (*GOK*, p. 79)

and in the background detail:

> the cloth-of-gold robe and the knives and daggers hilted with rubies, or the plated gold cap fringed with chained jewels. Around them rode the boyars in their furred brocades, on Turkish horses with necks curved each like a palm branch, coloured wolf grey, and the grey of lilac and starling, and red bay and gold-brown and russet. (*RC*, p. 176)

and above all in the people who crowd the pages:

> smooth as silk floss, the shining apricot hair fell back from the matt skin, flushed and speckled with sun. (*DK*, p. 27)

Dunnett's first career was as a portrait painter and this in part explains the strong visual element in her novels. The books are packed with period detail and the extent of her research is legendary:

> I have to go into all sides of life of the period. I find out as much as I can about every social aspect, clothes, houses, attitudes; I need to know what places looked like, what seasons were like, flowers, birds, all of that . . . As a historical novelist I have to look right across the scene, and bring together threads of information from all possible areas of scrutiny – manuscripts, archaeology, place names, literature and language, all have a bearing.[23]

Dunnett's dialogue has something of both Oliver's stateliness and Mitchison's occasional use of colloquial slang. In the end, however, it is essentially her own, a stylised mode of speech which suits the flamboyance of the books, though once again it is hard to believe that anyone, then or now, ever talked in quite this way. Appropriate Scots words occur (as do Latin, French, Italian, Russian, Arabic) and Francis Crawford of Lymond has the pleasant habit of quoting from the medieval makars, rather as Dorothy L. Sayers's Lord Peter Wimsey quotes the metaphysical poets, to indicate his culture and his mindset. His own particular style of rhetoric is individual and unmistakable, which is useful when, for the purposes of the story, he is operating incognito.

This often happens, since he is an adventurer, a charismatic hero, frequently battered by physical, mental and emotional assaults but never quite destroyed. Dunnett in the Renton interview describes him as 'a complicated, guarded man, whose dilemmas and crises confront him with himself and allow him to change'. For all that, and for all the swarming colour of the books, the reader may feel that there is a certain black-and-white quality, morally, about the Lymond series. Lymond performs actions which outrage the civilised society of his day, and may even give the modern reader pause, but he is basically good – we have no doubt of that – while his principal adversary Gabriel is wholeheartedly and irredeemably bad. (A distinctive feature of Dunnett's fiction – in the Lymond series, the Niccolo series, and her contemporary thrillers – is the appearance under various names of a big, handsome, fair, blue-eyed, bland-mannered man who is usually the villain of the piece.) There is a curious physical resemblance between hero and villain in the Lymond series which raises some intriguing questions regarding the traditional use of dualism in Scottish fiction.

But if there are strongly traditional element in Dunnett's historical fiction, there is also a strand which may be seen as something fairly unusual in the conventional historical novel (though Mitchison, of course, incorporates it in her work). It is the presence, centre stage but not necessarily in the role of heroine, of a strong woman – Sybilla, Philippa, Kate, Christian Stewart, Lady Buccleuch, Oonagh, Marthe, Kiaya Khatum – the list goes on.[24] Some are high-born, some sturdy yeowomen, some courtesans; all have minds of their own and good Scots (or Irish, or Arabic) tongues in their heads. They do not, generally, join in actual warfare – that would be an anachronism Dunnett could not allow – but they are seen to form a powerful and plausible force behind the men who do. They nearly all adore Lymond, but given a charismatic hero this is more or less obligatory. Otherwise these intelligent, independent women point forward to an interesting development in the work of Scottish women historical novelists.

Sian Hayton

This is best seen in the work of Sian Hayton (b.1944) who published her first novel, *Cells of Knowledge*, in 1989. *Cells of Knowledge* proved to be the first book of a trilogy which has since been completed by *Hidden Daughters* (1992) and *The Last Flight* (1993).[25] Obviously there has been little time for critics to evaluate this long and complex work, though John Burns has suggested that *Cells of Knowledge* 'seems [to be] concerned with exploration of religion and the roots of spiritual awareness'.[26]

This reading, while valid enough, tends, to underplay the issue of gender expressed by the author in the note on the jacket flap of *Cells of Knowledge*:

> Celtic folk-stories often give women credit for brains, initiative and courage. In tenth century Britain, as in Europe as a whole, the Church was gaining power rapidly and in the process eroding the status of women. I was interested to see what would happen when a Celtic heroine confronted the Church face to face.

We have a 'strong woman', Marighal, who appears, exhausted, at the door of the monastery of Rinstnoc (Portpatrick) on the night of a terrible storm. The monks take her in, noticing her fine clothing and her red hair, 'uncovered, even though she was of middle years'. This part of the story is told in the form of a letter from one of the monks to the Bishop of Alban, with marginal annotations by a more scholarly monk, of stricter inclinations, appointed to investigate the mystery of Marighal. The annotator leaves us in no doubt where he stands:

> He [the letter-writer] should not make so much of the woman's appearance. Such close study could lead to unchaste thoughts. Especially the hair. If it was not covered she must be a woman of dubious virtue. (CK, p. 18)

Marighal asks to be baptised and the monks are edified by her eagerness, remarking that women often come to the faith more readily than men. The conversation which follows is significant enough to be quoted at some length:

> 'Is this, perhaps, because a woman learns sooner what the faith will require of the faithful?' [Marighal suggests]
>   'Yes, but not from superior understanding,' [says Cadui, one of the monks] 'for a woman's understanding is inferior to a man's. It is rather because her life is more lowly and miserable so that she lives closer to the example of our Saviour . . . '
>   ' . . . But what if this is not the way of a woman's life? What if she is strong and clever and free? Will God's loving kindness be taken from her?' [asks Marighal]
>   'Most certainly,' [says Cadui] 'for then she would not be womanly, and God would turn his face from such a creature.' (CK, pp. 19–20)

Burns considers that 'this sharp contrast between male and female perspectives is a prominent theme in the novel'. It may even, I would suggest, be seen as the essential theme.

Though in the conversation quoted Marighal appears to be an ordinary woman – if intelligent and outspoken beyond the monks' expectations – she is soon revealed to have supernatural strength and powers, terrifying to them and quite too much for them to accept. Moreover, she is one of a number of sisters, the eponymous 'hidden daughters' or a giant who is himself an elemental spirit of earth and forest. We are approaching, surely, the territory of the earth-goddess whose cult predated Christianity and is still traceable in some Christian rituals and beliefs. It is no wonder that the monks find Marighal too hot to handle.

In Hayton's work, then, the element of magic in everyday life, the interface of history and myth, can be seen taking on full importance. It is by no means a new trend in Scottish literature; we may think of its use in the work of Neil Gunn and Lewis Grassic Gibbon, outstandingly in their use of ancient artefacts such as earth houses and standing stones, while, as I have said, the 'magical space' is hinted at by Jane Oliver and acknowledged by Naomi Mitchison. At present, however, there would appear to be a revival of magic and myth in the historical novel, to which other women novelists like Margaret Elphinstone and Ellen Galford are currently adding their distinctive contributions.

Dunnett, as we have seen, puts before us a parade of strong women who are resilient and resourceful in a perfectly explicable human way. Hayton goes farther, or farther back, to the idea of women supernaturally born and superhumanly gifted; but Marighal's part, as an apparently ordinary woman, in the conversation quoted above cannot help but have significance to modern ears.

Women, however 'strong and clever and free', do not generally, we have suggested, take centre stage in conventional historical novels (much less in conventional history itself) unless they are queens or saints. Of the novelists we have considered here, Oliver would seem to accept the convention. Mitchison and Dunnett, in different ways, have been seen testing it and pushing at its limitations.

Hayton has the courage to ignore it. In her novels, in mythic terms, history springs from deep female roots, and women, so largely absent from Scotland's history as written hitherto, come in from the margins of the page. It is a new kind of Scottish historical novel. Perhaps it is what Scottish women historical novelists should have been doing all along. Certainly it is what some of them are now doing, and will, let us hope, continue to do.[27]

Notes

1.   Alan Bold, *Modern Scottish Literature* (Longman, London, 1983), pp. 215–18.
2.   Francis Russell Hart, *The Scottish Novel: A Critical Survey* (John Murray, London, 1978) pp. 182–97 (p. 192).
3.   Douglas Gifford, 'Recent Scottish Fiction', *Books in Scotland* 1 (1978), 9–11 (p. 10).
4.   Others worth consideration might include Christine Orr, Marion Campbell and Eona Macnicol.
5.   Jane Oliver, 'Return to the Borderland', in Rhoda Spence (ed.), *The Scottish Companion: A Bedside Book of Delights* (R. Paterson, Edinburgh, 1955), pp. 41–6 (p. 42).
6.   Jacket of Jane Oliver, *Mine is the Kingdom* (Collins, London, 1937).
7.   Jane Oliver, *Isle of Glory* (Collins, London, 1947), p. 9. Further references are to IG.
8.   Jane Oliver, *Sing Morning Star* (Collins, London, 1949), p. 10. Further references are to SMS.
9.   Jane Oliver, *In No Strange Land* (Collins, London, 1944).
10.   Naomi Mitchison, *The Conquered* (Cape, London, 1923). All further references are to the Cape Florin edition, 1932.
11.   Naomi Mitchison, *You May Well Ask: A Memoir 1920–1940* (London, 1979); references are to the Fontana edition, here p. 162. The chapter 'Why Write?', pp. 161–81, sheds valuable light on Mitchison's work from this period.
12.   Donald Smith, 'Introduction', Naomi Mitchison, *The Blood of the Martyrs* (Canongate, Edinburgh, 1988) xiii.
13.   Douglas Gifford, 'Forgiving the Past: Naomi Mitchison's *The Bull Calves*', in Joachim Schwend and Horst W. Drescher (eds), *Studies in Scottish Fiction: Twentieth Century* (Peter Lang, Frankfurt, 1990), pp. 219–41 (p. 222).
14.   Naomi Mitchison, *The Blood of the Martyrs* (Constable, London, 1933); references are to the Canongate Classics edition, Edinburgh, 1988, here p. 189.
15.   Naomi Mitchison, *The Corn King and the Spring Queen* (Cape, London, 1931); references are to the Virago edition, London, 1983, here p. 26.
16.   Naomi Mitchison, *The Bull Calves* (Cape, London, 1947). Further references are to BC.
17.   Naomi Mitchison, *We Have Been Warned* (Cape, London, 1935); *The Delicate Fire* (Cape, London, 1933).
18.   Naomi Mitchison, *Small Talk* (Cape, London, 1973).
19.   Other historical novels by Naomi Mitchison not referred to in the text include: *When the Bough Breaks* (Cape, London, 1924), *Cloud Cuckoo Land* (Cape, London, 1925), *Black Sparta* (Cape, London, 1928), *Barbarian Stories* (Cape, London, 1929), *The Powers of Light* (Cape, London, 1932), *Travel Light* (Faber, London, 1952), *To the Chapel Perilous* (Allen & Unwin, London, 1955), *Behold Your King* (Muller, London, 1957), *Early in Orcadia* (Richard Drew, Glasgow, 1987), *The Oath-Takers* (Balnain Books, Nairn, 1991), *Sea-Green Ribbons* (Balnain Books, Nairn, 1991). Her *Among You Taking Notes: The Wartime Diary of Naomi Mitchison* (London, 1985) covers the period of composition of *The Bull Calves*.
20.   Trevor Royle, *The Mainstream Companion to Scottish Literature* (Mainstream, Edinburgh, 1993), p. 99.
21.   Hart, *The Scottish Novel*, p. 195.
22.   Dorothy Dunnett, 'The "Lymond" Series', all published by Cassell, London: *The Game of Kings* (1962) (GOK), *Queen's Play* (1964), *The Disorderly Knights* (1966) (DK), *Pawn in Frankencense* (1969), *The Ringed Castle* (1971) (RC), *Checkmate* (1975); *King Hereafter* (Michael Joseph, London, 1982); 'The "House of Niccolo" Series', all published by Michael Joseph, London: *Niccolo Rising* (1986), *The Spring of the Ram* (1987), *Race of Scorpions* (1989), *Scales of Gold* (1991), *The Unicorn Hunt* (1993), *To Lie with Lions* (1995).
23.   'Dorothy Dunnett interviewed by Jennie Renton', *Scottish Book Collector*, 12 (1989), 2–4 (p. 3).
24.   I am indebted to Kirsten Stirling for first drawing my attention to this.
25.   Sian Hayton, *Cells of Knowledge* (1989) (CK), *Hidden Daughters* (1992) (HD) and *The Last Flight* (1993) (LF) are all published by Polygon, Edinburgh. Sian Hayton has

also published a novel with a contemporary setting, *The Governors* (Balnain Books, Nairn, 1992).

26.   John Burns, 'Myths and Marvels', in Gavin Wallace and Randall Stevenson (eds), *The Scottish Novel in the Seventies* (Edinburgh University Press, Edinburgh, 1993), pp. 71–81 (p. 77).

27.   Jane Oliver, Naomi Mitchison and Dorothy Dunnett are all prolific writers. Other works by them not explicitly discussed are included in the general bibliography.

Other critical work not referred to in the text includes: Douglas Gifford, 'The New Internationalism', *Books in Scotland* 32 (1989), 7–14; 'Elusive Women, Elusive Landscapes', *Books in Scotland* 45 (1993), 17–22; 'Lonely Quests and Enchanted Woods', *Books in Scotland* 49 (1994), 19–25.

32

Jane Duncan:
The Homecoming of Imagination

Lorena Laing Hart and Francis Russell Hart

In 1972, Jane Duncan, our two daughters, and their mother stood in our New England kitchen reminiscing about a visit to Jane's Friendly Shop in Cromarty. The girls were remembering jellies and jams made by Jane and the local women for whom the tiny coffee shop provided pin money. This memory moved our daughters back in time to their grandmother's currant jelly, so translucently clear that it reminded them of rubies. Their grandmother's daughter took another memory step backward to a vivid image, in her childhood home, of a kettle with a tall, upright arm and ring, from which hung a mash of fruit in a funnel-shaped bag. As the essence of the fruit dripped slowly through the cloth, no one was to go near this contraption, to touch or, heaven forbid, to squeeze it, for then the final product would be cloudy. 'Sometimes,' said Jane with a mischievous smile, 'I squeeze the jelly bag'.

We have long puzzled over Jane Duncan's figurative squeezing of the jelly bag in her creative process. Along with her worldwide family of readers, we have wondered what is fact, fiction, or myth, particularly in the relation of her fictional 'I', Janet Sandison, to her actual life and self. Endless inquiries finally led Jane to clear this cloudiness in her autobiography *Letter from Reachfar* (1975).[1] She quotes Boris Pasternak: 'facts don't exist until man puts into them something of his own ... willful, human genius – of fairy tale or myth.' To this she adds: 'Well, my books are the "something of my own." ... All those people I knew were facts but I hope ... I have put something of my own into what I have written of them so that, now, they have something of the quality of myth.' Uncle George, her acknowledged inspiration as a storyteller, had his own name for it: 'In spite of George's pronouncement that I am the biggest liar in the country, I try not to "lie" in my writing ... I fictionalise my own experience' (*Letter*, pp. 140, 151, 108). In the three sections that follow, we hope to explore this process and discuss a few of its more striking results.

'Something of My Own'

The child Janet Sandison realises with astonishment that Big John the Blacksmith, who had sung 'the funniest song I had ever heard' and who 'threw the heavy hammer' far distances at the Highland games, was also the 'tame angel' at church, the precentor with a tuning fork that seemed much like Moses's staff (*Monica*, 1960, pp. 295–8; *Flora*, 1962, p. 9). Many people lived in Janet's grandmother: the infrequently seen granny with an instinctive sympathy and appropriate response to trouble and tragedy; the tall Mrs Sandison respected as a midwife and veterinarian; a mysterious 'Power' with the reputation of good witch; and the 'Law' who enforced a code of behaviour: 'it came home to me with a crash of thunder that there are all kinds of aristocracies – that Lady Lydia was of one kind and my grandmother of another kind, and that I was listening to a throne speaking to a throne' (*Muriel*, 1959, pp. 16–17). The 'two-or-three-peoplishness' of character was a recurring revelation to Jane Duncan.

She herself was 'many-peoplish.' Born in 1910 in Renton, Dunbartonshire, her 'real name' was Elizabeth Jane Cameron. To her family, she was Bet or Aunt Bet; on her accounts, she was Mrs Clapperton; to readers, she was Jane Duncan, and this is the name on her gravestone. 'By way of belated tribute to my dead parents,' she chose her father's first name, Duncan, as part of her pseudonym and named Janet Sandison after her mother (*Letter*, p. 107). Her publishers abetted the name game when, between 1969 and 1975, they issued four novels by Jane Duncan attributed to Janet Sandison, proclaiming that 'Janet Sandison *is* Jane Duncan' and even, 'Janet Sandison is author of the Jane Duncan books'! Behind this public masquerade lived an intensely private writer.

In 1959, 'always a late developer' (*Letter*, p. 88), she sprang from anonymity to fame with the bestseller, *The Miss Boyds*. Between 1956 and her death twenty years later, she wrote twenty-three novels, eight books for children, and *Letter from Reachfar*. She had been writing in secret since the early 1930s. Lacking confidence that any of it was worth publishing, she periodically consigned the manuscripts to bonfires. Years of service in Air Force Intelligence during the Second World War were, for the writer, a 'sterile' interlude. After the war, as a secretary near Glasgow, she fell in love with a Lowland engineer, Sandy Clapperton, an unhappily married man. When he went to work in Jamaica in 1949, Jane went as his wife. Their time together was short. By 1953, he was seriously ill with heart disease; by 1957, she knew he could not recover; in March, 1958, he died, leaving her alone in a place she found disturbingly unreal and socially intolerable for its antiquated racism. Nine months later, she sailed home to share a small cottage in Jemimaville with her Uncle George and to make her living as a writer.

There was little risk involved. Macmillan had accepted four novels before she left Jamaica, and upon her arrival in London, they accepted three more she had brought in her luggage, all seven secretly 'put on paper' in sixteen months while Sandy was ill.[2] The first, *Muriel*, was sent to a London agent as 'a desperate throw' amid mounting medical costs and anxiety (*Letter*, p. 24).[3] Then came Sandy's death and the midwinter voyage to the cottage by the Cromarty Firth. Here, on the first night in her icy bedroom, she began her most naturalistic Reachfar novel, *Flora*. Following *Flora* and the well-crafted 'detective' story, *Madame Zora* (1963), which suggests her discomfort with the modes of the 'popular novelist,' she reintroduced the antipathetic 'St Jago' (Jamaica) setting in a series of five novels, *Cousin Emmie* (1964), *The Mrs Millers* (1965), *Friends from Cairnton* (1965), *My Father* (1966), and *The Macleans* (1967). Only in the milieu of her Jamaican years could she correlate in fiction the essential facts of her adult life, her two pivotal rebellions: her 'marriage' and her 'secret sin' of writing.

Then, about 1966, came a rupture in imagination. Jane was feeling trapped in the myth she had created, 'tired of being totally identified with Janet Reachfar,' of being 'blown up into a romantic balloon by the Reachfar novels': 'It makes me feel that I can't write at all, only tell people about my operation like that woman I met in the train' (*Letter*, pp. 105,

116). This feeling occasioned *The Hungry Generation* (1968). In her final eight years, she alternated among the very different tetralogy of Jean Robertson,[4] the children's books, and the sometimes anguished, sometimes detached last Reachfar novels, *The Swallow* (1970), *Sashie* (1972), and *The Misses Kindness* (1974), centred on her husband's death and its aftermath, and *George and Tom* (1976), a contented, relaxed chronicle of home life in Ross-shire from 1959 to 1966. Jane had faced and transformed in fiction the losses and compensations that textured her life. Suddenly, on 20 October 1976 at the age of sixty-six, she died.

Eighteen years later, she is remembered chiefly for *The Miss Boyds*, an accident that would probably displease her. She had strongly objected when Macmillan published it first. She cited other reasons, but we suspect she did not want to be introduced and stereotyped as author of childhood idylls of croft life. She never wrote another novel quite like it. Some reviewers found *The Miss Boyds* 'charming,' 'enchanting,' but it is ultimately a story of disenchantment. The Black Isle village's traditional way of life is vividly, lovingly narrated, but with the First World War and depression, this way is in its twilight, and it is menaced by reckless, giggling, 'hot-arsed' invaders, six old maid sisters. The narrative surface, deceptively simple, confined to a perceptive child's consciousness, is dominated by wonderfully voiced and paced stories of memorable events, rich in ritual, slapstick, and ludicrous near disasters. But flowing beneath the surface is the sad trend of change and loss, historic and personal. As a recreation of childhood experience, *The Miss Boyds* is nearly perfect. But its mode largely precludes the dimensions of storytelling that most interested Jane: the mystery of adult relationships, the essential conditions – exile and dispossession – of her fictionalising, and the mythmaking power of memory.

It is tempting to suggest *The Miss Boyds* as an introduction to Jane Duncan's fiction. Here, however, it is fairer to appraise four later novels, chosen independently by both of us, which exemplify her sophisticated handling of a variety of narrative modes.

To Tell One's Own Story

Flora, begun on the homecoming night in 1959, is the most potent and credible of her earlier novels. While in parts it has some of the charm of *The Miss Boyds*, it is almost the obverse in its harsh realism. The main plot is a grim horror story. Despite an agreeable conclusion, the reader is left with the ominous feeling that the story may repeat itself. In form, *Flora* is based on a constant of all the novels: Janet's periodic returns, in fact or memory, to Reachfar, her ancestral croft.

The landscape is now blighted by the presence of Flora 'Bedamned' Smith and her family and by the 'bleak,' 'black,' 'sullen' hump of their house. The father, a mason, is a figure of hereditary gloom, drudgery, and avarice; the eldest son steals his money and flees to America, another dies in an accident, the remaining two are killed in the Second World War. 'Chorchie,' the little sister, whose mother died after delivering her, grows into a drooling, lustful idiot. The grotesquely misshapen creature with her 'horrible adoration of this hideous body,' treads the landscape with a 'crablike gait,' a 'frightful fiend' of daytime nightmare (*Flora*, pp. 120, 147, 179). She torments animals, tears up crops, and approaches men in a travesty of sexual invitation. Her bestiality leads Janet for the only time in the novels to think it 'desirable to get away from his place, Reachfar' (p. 122). A curious novel for Jane Duncan's homecoming!

Flora offers a unique perspective on four women who are central to the Reachfar story: Janet's grandmother, the matriarch, midwife, and kindly witch, who never looks backward; Janet's gentle, sickly mother, who, having laid aside her own dreams because of life's accidents, finds contentment in the present; and fiery, restive, proud Aunt Kate, who said 'no' to her suitor Malcolm out of a sense of duty to her ageing mother. The fourth, Janet, the first university-educated woman, is the anomaly. She must 'hammer out the pattern' of her life as she goes along.

These four strong women contrast sharply with the vapid Flora, who compulsively plays surrogate mother to 'Chorchie' and is the willingly victimised caretaker of all who live in the chaos and despair of Bedamned's Corner. Disgusted with Flora's passivity and Janet's contentment within the croft, the frustrated rebel Aunt Kate reacts with anger: 'You're as bad as FLORA BEDAMNED' staying on 'this godforsaken hill.' 'I feel like an old rag lying on the ground for people to tramp over . . . like Flora Bedamned,' who is 'enough to make you ashamed that women were ever born' (pp. 113–14, 130, 152, 262). But Janet (like her author Jane) is no simple rebel. She willingly forgets her own rage at Flora's passivity and blind thankfulness and comes at last to think of her as a survivor who has managed to live through her 'most appalling' story, saintlike in her selfless service, a 'sort of miracle' (pp. 226–8, 248).

Flora has no counterpart elsewhere in the Reachfar novels. Like the very different Marion of *The Macleans*, she transcends the antithetical typology of many of Jane's women characters. On one hand is the conventional parochial materialist who is bound by 'what people say or think,' best exemplified by the hated stepmother Jean in *Annie* (1961). On the other, as seen in the prostitute Annie herself, is the figure of innocent, ruthless autonomy, which takes many shapes in the novels. The figure appears in the frivolous Miss Boyds and their later dangerous avatars, the Misses Kindness, in the lovely half-breed Linda Lee, the obscene high-society tart Rose, and Percy, the elusive young woman in *The Swallow*, who arrives and departs as unpredictably as a bird following its own inner rhythms. They are 'a sort of innocence' and, menacing or appealing, they fascinate the moral imaginations of Janet and Jane. Flora and Marion Maclean subvert such extreme polarities.

Flora is marred only by the coincidental happy ending of the subplot, the revival after many years of Kate and Malcolm's romance. 'I could never write tragedy,' explained Jane in the sometimes misleading *Letter from Reachfar*, 'for I am, I think, an incurable optimist' (p. 138). In *The Macleans*, she proved herself mistaken. Her most ambitious social-psychological novel, *The Macleans* probes complex problems of unacknowledged racial injustice, the extremes of love and hate conjoined with the appetite for power, and the ambiguities of human relationship and identity. It is centred on three Scottish families in the alien, insular environment of Caribbean St Jago.

On the sugar plantation, Paradise, in the 1950s, the blazing sun, heat, humidity, tropical colour, and jungly bush have cast an evil spell. Whites, their leisure and lavish life-style supported by a black serving class, have too much time for ritualistic drink, gossip, and lies. In this artificial social structure, Janet does not trust her own responses and feels she is living amid the distortions of a house of mirrors. When her 'husband' Twice, the plantation's chief engineer, becomes ill and faces life as a semi-invalid, the dream of returning to Scotland is precluded. Janet can remain here only by recognising her own truth: 'Paradise . . . is . . . a big white lie in the middle of a black island' (*Macleans*, p. 21). The *Tempest*-like symbols on St Jago – the cloak of the Union Jack, the magic wand of the field marshal's baton, the book of the Bible and British law (pp. 149, 240) – are crumbling in the face of an urge for national emancipation. Few of the central characters are willing to recognise the inevitability of historic change. They are enchanted. Allusions to Prospero's enchanted isle are recurrent. A female Prospero, sitting at her high house on 'Olympus,' is Marion Maclean.

Janet has considered Marion a friend of long standing and admired her as part of a magic circle: the perfect lady-in-waiting to the ancient Madame Dulac, owner of the plantation; the always charmingly composed hostess-wife to Rob, its manager; and the ideal loving mother of seven sons. Unknown to Janet, beneath the public facade is a demonic will to control her husband, her sons, and their succession at Paradise. Marion and Rob, who dreams of being a Caribbean sugar baron, are obsessed with wealth and power. One son, the renegade Roddy, has deceived his parents by studying English and arts rather than engineering and has published a novel. When Janet helps Roddy flee the island and defends him, Rob is enraged and spreads lies about Janet. Marion, by contrast, reacts with distance and cold rejection to this interference 'in the discipline of *my* family'. Mystified and disillusioned, Janet sees the Marion of her imagination 'wither away,' but her sinister ambitions are so incredible that Janet cannot accept them as truth until late in the novel. She asks, do we love the images we project on people, formed from some 'aspect of ourselves'? 'What does anybody know of anybody, come to that?' (pp. 56, 156, 204).

Rob is being destroyed not only by his wife but by self-delusion, paranoia about a conspiracy to replace him, and Paradise itself, which is consuming him but cares nothing for him. Determined to rescue his father, the returned prodigal Roddy persuades Rob to retire to Scotland. Even Marion appears reconciled to the end of a dream of almost forty years. But the novel ends in catastrophe: the natural volcanic unpredictability of the island and its underlying societal instability merge. As Marion arrives on the porch of the Great House, the earth moves in convulsive shudders. Once more, thinks Janet, Marion seems to 'dominate the whole demented world,' 'radiating courage and pride in her control of herself and Rob' (p. 262). She calls. Rob runs from the lawn, shouting, 'Come into the open,' just before a stone pillar of the colonnade falls and kills both of them.

Woven through this tragedy of ruthless ambition and lies is the continuing plot of the later Reachfar novels: the effects on relationship of Twice's illness and Janet's secret commitment to writing. Twice withdraws to 'some far place'. His heart condition prevents any more 'grand rows,' any talk of what may excite or upset. An 'invisible but impenetrable screen' separates Janet and Twice. The 'moment of isolation . . . lying in wait', even for two so 'well attuned,' stretches over many months (*Macleans*, pp. 40, 103, 111, 113), like the bleak indifference and psychic exhaustion so compellingly evoked in *Monica* and to be evoked once more in *Sashie*. The effects of prolonged illness were well known to Jane Duncan, and their recreation in fiction remains one of her striking achievements.

Janet too is withdrawing. If St Jago is 'all lies,' she can find her own truth only in writing. She retreats more and more to the world of her private imagination, and here she is another aspiring Prospero. She escapes, by writing in secret in the spare bedroom, to a new world where 'never before, had I had such a feeling of being in complete control' (p. 191). It is ironic that, at the time when she was writing *The Macleans*, Jane Duncan was realising the negative side of the writer's power. She had lost control of her own myth, was feeling trapped by others in her counterself. This sense of entrapment partly precipitated her next novel.

The Hungry Generation, simple in plot and homely in setting, is an affectionate scrutiny of the dynamics of the living members of the Reachfar family, their connections to each other and to their pasts and futures. There are none of the devices – disappearances, catastrophes, extreme mental states, major illnesses and deaths – found in her other novels. Perhaps her finest work, this novel's distinctive quality is its evocation of the various 'realities' that slide in and out of the layers of consciousness, and of the thoughts – Janet likens them to herring and flounder – that swim below the flow of everyday, glinting briefly at the water's surface before they can ever be articulated. She senses these 'intimations of immortality' in her brother's children, 'the hungry generation'. The novel skilfully adapts Wordsworth's ode to the reality of modern childhood.

Following the earthquake in *The Macleans*, the childless Janet travels to her brother's home in Aberdeen for a holiday. The tensions and stresses of generational relationship play out among the lively, uninhibited children, the sensible and intuitive father, the mother at unquestioning ease in her role, the relaxed old great uncles George and Tom, and most particularly the unfamiliar aunt. By coincidence, much of the children's care is left to Aunt Janet. She discovers that they shift openly and unselfconsciously between their worlds of imagination and reality, hungry for fantasy, poetry, and Wordsworthian 'clouds and clouds of glory,' but also for porridge, elevenses, and chocolate cake with a 'glop' centre. In forty-six-year-old Janet, 'the homely nurse,' intimations of immortality have faded; too much experience has collapsed on itself. The imagined and the actual are disconnected.

She discovers something else. She had come to believe that the Reachfar of memory belonged to her in a way it could to no one else, for she had been a child there in a 'golden time,' and it was 'mine only and mine forever' (*Macleans*, p. 138). But now her mythic kingdom has been usurped by the children. They have given it physical form in the garden shrubbery, where they refuse to admit Aunt Janet, for they cannot accept her as the 'Channatt' of Reachfar story. If 'Channatt of Reachfar' steps out of the children's fantasy as Aunt Janet or if Aunt Janet steps into it, they fear the magic will disappear. They are trying, their father thinks, to actualise dream into fact, into a new reality, as an artist would.

Eight-year-old Liz, the only child who had visited the actual Reachfar, has used her memories and the tales of George and Tom to maintain a superiority over her younger brothers. But Aunt Janet, the best storyteller, becomes a challenge to Liz's authority. A grand battle erupts over an improvised worksong. Liz claims that she is entitled to sing Channatt's part but that the boys cannot sing the parts of George and Tom because those two 'Reachfar people' are just across the way in another bedroom. Janet points out that the two elderly gentlemen are not the original 'Reachfar people,' for the George and Tom of Reachfar are 'memory people' as much as Channatt is a memory person (*Generation*, pp. 71–2). The logical brother 'Dunk' calls his sister a fool for not recognising that Aunt Janet is the Channatt of long ago. But logic cannot fathom the mystery:

> It was sad but true and of the very essence of life that the 'Channatt' who had attended Achcraggan school and the old Aunt Janet who sat on the bed were not 'the same' . . . That you may once have been Channatt is . . . a thought that lies too deep for tears. (pp. 69, 206).

The climactic testing of Janet comes with Liz's question: does she remember the 'candle creatures' of Reachfar? Through the shadowy web of association, the memories of George and Tom, and a forgotten 'queer little book' of home magic, the mystified Janet finds her answer: hand shadows. In a bedtime ritual, with a candle in the darkened room, Janet creates 'candle creatures' on the wall. A skirmish ensues over whether 'they are only shadows' or '*are* creatures,' but it quickly dies away (pp. 94–109). Janet is beyond testing. She has given the children, proclaims Liz, 'the past history of our kingdom' (p. 241), and she is accepted in a little ceremony into their shrubbery Reachfar. She enters not as Channatt, however, but as the historian, the storyteller.

Read biographically, the intricate struggle between Janet and Liz over myth and reality is an intriguing instance of fictionalising. It obliquely reveals Jane Duncan the writer at a time when she was struggling both to control and to escape from her myth, which had been expropriated by 'hungry' readers (see the dedication to the novel). Read intrinsically, *The Hungry Generation* enacts a complex transition. The myth is no longer simply Janet's. She has transferred it to the children, her 'race future.' She has discovered the essential paradox in her identity as storyteller:

> I seemed to see what was mirrored in my memory reflected again in their eyes so that, while they received this dream which they desired and which I wanted to give to them, they were, at the same time, giving it back to me in a richer, deeper form. (p. 149).

This mystery of reciprocal transference is subtly played out on an adult level in *Sashie*.

Sashie is the most intimate of Jane's books, a prolonged therapeutic exchange, sequestered from society, between Janet and her ideal friend. At the end of *The Swallow*, Twice dies in bitter alienation, his last words to Janet a caustic put-down of her first recognition as a writer. In *Sashie*, guilt-stricken but numb, she is moved to Paradise Great House, where she slips into alcoholic indifference and deliberate disconnection, fearing her memory will release monsters she cannot overcome. Sashie, the flamboyant St Jago hotelier, persists in his visits in the face of her sullen rebuffs. When ancient Madame Dulac dies, he moves Janet to his beachhouse. There, she breaks down completely, then recovers under Sashie's wise guidance. The novel portrays the death and rebirth of memory and imagination.

The distance in mode that Jane Duncan had travelled from the witty hilarity of *Muriel* to the harrowing interior drama of *Sashie* is immense. Yet a single whimsical 'prop' reappears: a visored helmet separated from its bogus suit of armour. At the end of *Muriel*, in a gesture of outrage at her 'friend,' Janet kicks the helmet through a stained-glass window, and Twice, outside, retrieves it. They decide that it represents the non-existent 'Ordinary Person' without brains or heart. In St Jago, the helmet takes on a deeper meaning, tied to Janet's desire to write. When her father dies and she has yet to give him the book he longed for with her name on it, she burns her manuscripts. But on the following day, the helmet clonks to the floor from her closet and she immediately begins to write again, her papers weighted down by the helmet, her story seeming to flow out through the visor. The helmet has become custodian of her memory. When Twice dies, she is convinced that her writing has helped to kill him. Sashie asks for the helmet: 'Thank you, my sweet. I shall treasure it' (*Sashie*, p. 25). Now he will be the custodian of her memory. He directs without asking that her papers be put in Twice's coffin-like trunk and taken to his home. The medicine man in Sashie knows that one day Janet will have to remove the manuscripts from the trunk to free herself from their guilty association with the dead Twice.

For Jane Duncan, writing was always an intensely secretive act. The sense of her writing as a 'secret vice' (*Letter*, pp. 18, 96, 125) was fictionalised into Janet's guilt.[5] For Janet the child, writing was 'capers . . . chust for bairns and foolish ones,' such as the 'clown' George (*Boyds*, p. 75), yet it became 'some part of my essential self . . . actively seeking for and believing in its right to claim its own happiness' (*Annie*, p. 279). For the adolescent, it was a 'hard core of desire' in an awakening 'sense of personal privacy,' a 'singularity of personality' (*Father*, pp. 166–7). For the St Jago housewife, what seemed at first 'some furtive and disgraceful petty vice' (*Emmie*, p. 167) grew into an addictive escape from a repellent culture and then caused a frenzy of guilt over the deaths of her father and Twice. It is Sashie who helps Janet accept her identity as a storyteller and her vocation as a writer.

Jane once told us that Sashie was an amalgam of young Second World War pilots whom she knew, all at such risk of being maimed. The novel is dedicated to one of them, her friend Frederick Ashton, the choreographer. At the same time, Sashie may well be her most fully fictionalised character. He represents the ideal of the being that so preoccupied Jane over the years, the titular subject of her novels, the *friend*. With Sashie, Janet found 'more than a friendship in the accepted sense . . . in a curious way more intimate than any relationship I had ever known' (*Sashie*, p. 144).

In *George and Tom* (p. 247), Janet tries to define this ideal friend: 'I like him and admire him because he is the sort of person I would like to be . . . always on hand when my spine needs stiffening.' Instead of offering the pap of bland sympathy, he says, 'Your father is dead, Janet. You will never see him again' (*Macleans*, p. 181). Sashie 'bothers' with her as she slides into the abyss of uncaring hopelessness and guilt. When she hallucinates, his eyes appear everywhere, threatening to break 'the twilight of . . . mind' (p. 20). Then, just before her days of total oblivion, his eyes become the well of her Thinking Place at Reachfar, her own childhood reflection, and she will reach down into memory and slowly find herself.

Sashie had been a dancer-actor whose world of magic and beauty was reduced to ashes when his fighter plane was shot down. Like the bogus armour, he now has 'tin legs'. He affects a public shell of acerbic wit and charm and vivid clothing and disguises his disfigurement with a mincing 'faggot' walk. A show of sexual ambivalence masks his asexuality: 'One of the most comforting features of the years of my friendship with Sashie was its sexlessness' (*George and Tom*, p. 188).[6] He seems a symbol of disconnection, a cynical gadfly with few kin, rootless, isolated, and solitary. But to the few he cares about, he is a person of deep feeling, insight, and intelligence who has experienced many kinds of death. By listening quietly to her story that 'all began at Reachfar,' Sashie helps Janet heal herself by reawakening her memory. In the telling, the story is shared with, transferred to another.

And he is, however intimate, an *other*. At Janet's gentle prodding, he begins to recreate his own poignant life. He recalls rainy afternoons spent with his 'enchanting' mother at his puppet theatre, enacting many roles, singing and playing together, the true play of the child as Janet had known it only secretly with her 'playmates' George and Tom. He recalls his mother's term of endearment, *mon petit autre*, and her gesture of giving him a flower from her corsage as she bid him goodnight:

> She contrived to make me feel loved and secure and yet at the same time independent, with a place of my own that even she did not enter uninvited and the little ceremony of the flower seemed to symbolise the tie between us and at the same time our separateness. (*Sashie*, p. 204)

When he went to America in the late 1930s, she refused to go with him, for he was an adult and must *tell his own story*.

But Sashie cannot quite tell Janet the most important part of his story: his life as a dancer before losing his legs. Instead, he slips a letter and some photographs into her briefcase the night before her departure. Sashie is one, she finally learns, with the beautiful 'dancing young man' of the London theatre in the 1930s, about whom she was quite 'dotty' in his role as Ariel. Memory and myth coalesce. From the deck of the ship that will carry her home, Janet tosses a rosebud from her bouquet to Sashie on the dock below, a sign of their connection and their separateness. As he receives this last token of transference, his outstretched arms convey the grace of a curtain call, the elegant gesture of exchange between performer and audience, teller and listener. Sashie is still her Ariel. Over her dark recent past, 'the brilliant little figure . . . seemed to float . . . like the spirit of the future,' of freedom from the past (p. 186). And now, having served his Prospero well, he too is freed by the 'little death' of their parting.

In its dramatic intensity, the scene is characteristic of most of Jane's endings. In its wordless ritual and its seamless flow from the story, it is her most masterly.

'Going Down to Wick'

In telling one's story, writes Peter Brooks, 'only the end can finally determine meaning . . . everything is transformed by the structuring presence of the end to come.'[7] By 1956, when she began her novels in earnest, Jane Duncan had already experienced two ends: the sale of The Colony (Reachfar) and the death of her father. She began in the presence of another: her husband's imminent death.

When as a child Jane travelled alone by train from Glasgow to Inverness, Uncle George would meet her, they would collect the horse and trap at Fortrose, and George would say, 'We might take a notion and go down to Wick.' They both knew they would drive straight home, but 'he had indicated that we were free to take a notion and go down to Wick if we really wanted to. And behind his words, somehow, there was implied a gleeful mischief at the consternation of the family if we really did' (*Letter*, p. 42). This complex whimsy came to symbolise the two crucially autonomous acts of her life. When she decided to live unmarried with Sandy, her brother said, 'Well, at long last somebody is taking a notion and going down to Wick.' And when she became a writer, her good fortune proved that 'we all have the life-gift of the liberty to take a notion and go down to Wick' (*Letter*, pp. 124, 151). The notions proved fatefully linked. The transference of identity from wife to writer entailed a terrible bargain: the loss of Sandy. Linked to these was yet another end: the loss of home.

The early novels lead Janet to the end of meeting Twice and choosing to live with him. The middle novels move among temporary places to a 'home' in alien St Jago, where she is trapped when he becomes ill and Reachfar is sold. The later novels lead to his death, her emergence as a writer, and her homemaking within sight of Reachfar. The novels were conceived as chapters of a single life-story, yet each 'chapter' needed its own closure. To create one, Jane Duncan negotiated three related sets of polarities: intimacy and separateness, loss and recovery, and autonomy and belonging.[8]

The formulaic 'friendships' that plot the early novels are mostly lacking in true intimacy, and hence their ending in separation causes Janet no existential shock of separateness. Her true intimacies remain, with Twice and her family. The eccentric 'friends' from Muriel and the Miss Boyds through Martha's aunt and Madame Zora have lasting impact only as they threaten, sustain, or renew these intimacies. With *Cousin Emmie*, the tenth novel, comes a change. New conditions emerge. They are not accidental but intrinsic to character: Twice's illness, Janet's secret writing, Twice's opposition to this 'going where I can't follow' (*Swallow*, p. 133), and her resistance. Relationships form out of motives and needs in Janet's imaginative life and Twice's frustration as invalid husband and thwarted father. They develop intimacies: the Mrs Millers and Sashie are true friends; Roddy Maclean is a spiritual ally; Mackie and Percy are Twice's surrogate children.

The separateness caused by Twice's illness and Janet's secret is the groundwork of the novels from *Cousin Emmie* through *The Swallow*. In *The Macleans*, Janet must fight her own battles, internal and external, for control. In *The Hungry Generation*, she struggles for control of her own story and ends with a temporary but devastating feeling of 'cold apartness,' which, in *The Swallow*, becomes a contented, sometimes defiant detachment. Poignant interludes of renewed intimacy occur, but by the time of Twice's death, the separateness seems painfully complete. In *Sashie*, Janet withdraws from everyone and everything past and present and recovers through the friendship with Sashie, who teaches her the separateness even of intimacy. The little ceremony of the flower at shipside and the little ceremony of Janet's acceptance into the children's Reachfar, Jane Duncan's most subtle and evocative endings, convey the same message and illustrate how profoundly her later endings differ from the earlier ones.

As the earlier novels are plotted on coincidental friendships, so their endings are often arbitrary: the comic put-downs of Muriel and Jean; the tragic discovery of Violet Boyd's body; coincidental reunions with Rose; death, murder, and suicide in *Sandy and Martha's Aunt*; Aunt Kate's reunion with her long-lost lover; Madame Zora's fortuitous death and legacies. Beginning with *Cousin Emmie*, the endings are integral to intimacy and separateness and to the elegiac paradox of loss and recovery as well.

Many of the novels end with recoveries – of health, of relationships, of liberty or autonomy, of memory – in effect, of identity – through recovery of the past. But in later novels, the complexities of recovering the lost are explored. In *The Mrs Millers*, Janet outgrows her hatred of St Jago into a loving knowledge of the island's native culture. When Twice almost dies and is saved by black friends Janet has made, she promises God anything for his survival. When he recovers, she learns that Reachfar has been sold, the price of her bargain. In *Friends from Cairnton*, she recovers in memory the lovable side of the once-hated Cairnton, but out of the past appears the grim, hostile Maggie Drew, once Janet's Sunday School teacher, who embodies Cairnton's Old Testament religion with its vengeful deity. With the disintegration of Maggie, Janet overcomes the false idea of a bargaining God. She learns in reverie that what is loved cannot be lost. The bargaining *seems* renewed at the end of *My Father*. Janet nurses the black yard boy Caleb back from the edge of death, then receives word her father has died. Yet, by the mystery of loving transference, he lives on, for Caleb shares his love of the land and even improves his writing by imitating her father's 'copper plate hand' (*Father*, p. 228; *Sashie*, p. 161). In *Sashie*, Janet's own recovery begins through sharing the gardening with Caleb, 'a coal-black Reachfar Highlandman' (*Swallow*, p. 87).

The most suggestive instance of recovery through transference occurs at the end of *The Macleans*. Roddy, just returned from Scotland, tells Janet the story of his visit to a Black Isle village on the day of a momentous funeral. He is overwhelmed by the quiet, dignified intensity of the ritual and feels 'baptised into . . . the *human* family' (p. 225). Not until Janet tells him does he know whose village and whose funeral it was. He has transferred his experience into a unique gift for Janet, a memory of her father's burial. A similar transfer is made at the end of *George and Tom*. Janet will not revisit nearby Reachfar, but a fragile rowan sapling is brought down to her new home. It finally comes into bud on the day old Tom dies quietly in the garden.

But for Jane Duncan, a balance had to be struck between recovering the past and freeing oneself from it. The problem was how to remain rooted in one's place and code and yet forge one's own identity, tell one's own story. *The Miss Boyds* ends in nostalgic resignation: 'what was past was past' (p. 277). In *Monica*, the past is a commitment to be clung to; in *Rose*, it is a code to be broken. In *Annie*, freedom is forgetting the past. In *Sandy* (1961), the despotic past dies with grandmother Denholm; in *Flora*, it begins again with a nephew who is his grim grandfather reincarnate. But in later novels, the balancing grows personal. Reachfar and its family are gone. With Twice's death, Janet must make her own identity and her own home. One is autonomy, the other is belonging. To achieve one, she must achieve the other.

She must learn to be 'selective about life' (*George and Tom*, p. 35), decide which parts of the past to 'cast off'. The St Jago past is violently cast off with the deaths of the Macleans and Madame Dulac. In *The Hungry Generation*, some of the past is transferred to the children. In *Sashie*, during her illness, Janet rejects all that is past. After her recovery, Hugh Reid turns up from the past to propose marriage. Sashie's imagined 'mocking presence' saves her from slipping back into her old habit of acquiescence, and the 'ghosts of the past' are laid to rest (*Sashie*, p. 158). 'You had to be free to cast off what no longer belongs,' Sashie explains, and she replies, 'you will always belong, Sashie' (p. 155). She has come a long way from the helpless early Janet, creature of others' influences, to a sense of determining what belongs, controlling her own life, her story.

Casting off has an inverse side: adoption. Symbolic adoption is a motif of the late novels. Janet, the childless woman who had lost her only child, 'adopts' Roddy, Caleb, Sashie, Twice's son Mark, and the girl Helga (in *The Misses Kindness*). When, at the end of *George and Tom*, Tom dies, George reveals he was the love-child of Janet's grandfather and was adopted into the family by her grandmother. Janet, likened all her life to her grandmother, has replaced her as matriarch, and the matriarch-writer has formed her own extended family by adoption. This is the ultimate fiction of Jane Duncan's last novels, *Jean Towards Another Day* (1975)[9] and *George and Tom*. Janet's quest for belonging has ended in a converted storehouse by the shore. The Reachfar hill top is visible, but 'I would never want to go to Reachfar again,' for doing so 'would do nobody any good and it might harm my writing' (pp. 56, 58). Derelict houses are restored for a selected family, notably almost all male, who still belong. Most notable among them is the beloved, asexual Sashie.

George and Sashie become fast friends, and the imaginative linkage is meaningful. George is Jane's and Janet's muse. Clowning storyteller, wise counsellor, peaceable anarchist, and Lord of the Dance (*Letter*, p. 53), he is a fitting companion and counterpart to Sashie, the jester, the cynic in flamboyant mask, Janet's Ariel and beautiful dancing young man. These are Jane Duncan's free spirits. She has shared with them the homecoming of her imagination.

In *My Father* (p. 118), Duncan Sandison asks his daughter to keep 'home always fresh in your mind . . . never to forget the kind of people you belong to'. Jane Duncan was a 'peasant at heart,' of 'peasant blood' (*Letter*, p. 138; *Father*, p. 227). Her family were faithful sabbatarians, and her childhood experience of the Scottish Church's Old Testament emphasis adds rich texture to her work. New Testament precepts were followed on weekdays at The Colony. A clutch of eggs or a bit of jam went off to a poor widow or an ailing shepherd. Still, the real religion of The Colony was 'more primitive and pagan,' grounded in natural mysteries, best expressed in her priestess-witch grandmother's 'kinship . . . with all living things' (*Letter*, pp. 83, 87). Jane held close to her earthly roots; the cycle of the seasons dictated her writing schedule. A long gestation process went on as she built up 'a head of steam' during the gardening and the mundane domestic and social activity of spring and summer. Then, as autumn days drew in, she shut herself in her house for her own harvest, a 'debauch' of 'putting on paper'. Even in her imagination, she followed the practical utilitarian code of The Colony, using every thread of her experience.[10]

Though she herself does not make the connection, Jane's craft seems tied to her family history. The Colony, she explains (*Letter*, p. 12), was so called because at one time 'a colony of weavers lived on that ground'. They had 'gradually died off and drifted away, leaving mine as the last surviving family'. She saw herself as 'the custodian of that lost identity,' of the 'race memory' of her crofting, weaving ancestors (*Macleans*, p. 92). She commemorated that identity by making the fabric of story.

A long, dream-like reverie at the end of *Friends from Cairnton* recreates the goodness and fellowship intrinsic to The Colony. The reverie begins with an enabling memory of clarity and particularity. On a winter evening long ago, everyone inside the house is busy. The women are knitting and sewing. George, Tom, and Janet are hooking a rag rug out of strips cut from old clothes. The brown Clydesdale, Betsy, is to be the central image, but the curve of her shoulder will not come right. They decide instead to use the brown strips for a simpler, more linear shape, a depiction of the house. Janet's mother says this is fine, for even though the actual house is white, it can be identified by working in the word *Reachfar*. The rug is then remembered beneath the minister's feet at Janet's mother's funeral as he says, 'When we love, we cannot lose' (*Cairnton*, p. 365). When the adult Janet returns from her reverie, she has 'reclaimed' the lost Reachfar and the scene of her mother's funeral through the memory of making the hearth rug.

The form of this reverie is an emblem of Jane Duncan's narrative process. It is distinctively recursive, looping backward and forward, hooking the fabric together with the repeated re-entry of threads from the past, 'as if in obsessive reminder that we cannot really move ahead' without them.[11] Characters, like 'coloured threads . . . almost inextricably interwoven' (*Macleans*, p. 92), appear, disappear, reappear from novel to novel. Uncle George, a thread 'in the very fabric of all the years I have lived' (*George and Tom*, p. 248), is drawn at some point in every book to the topside of the fabric. The threads of places and homes move in and out, as Jane the weaver reaches back in time to 'that transcendent home,'[12] Reachfar, and carries it forward as a 'country of the mind' (*Letter*, p. 12).

She often uses the figure of the writer as weaver, spinner, or tapestry maker. 'My novels are spun like a thread out of some store of material that is inside of me' (*Letter*, p. 101), some 'memory tangle' (*Macleans*, p. 92). 'My current piece of tapestry . . . had a character resembling that of life . . . made up of many complexly interwoven strands . . . on the surface, less than a third of the coloured thread was to be seen, the remainder being concealed in and behind the basic canvas' (*Swallow*, pp. 144–5). So did Jane work her past 'like a great tapestry showing people, places, and events in every colour from sombre to gay, a huge experience' (*Generation*, p. 191).

On the day after she died, Jane's nephew Neil Cameron wrote to us: 'She had been slightly unwell for a few days, with the flu as we thought. In fact she was apparently suffering from some sort of inflammation of the heart, followed early Wednesday by a coronary thrombosis.' And two weeks later: 'Aunt Bet is buried in Kirkmichael Churchyard, just in front of my father's grave. There is that beautiful view over the firth to her house and the Colony hill beyond.' Janet Sandison's father once says to her, 'I am thinking that the everlasting life and Heaven is to be minded on in a good way by your friends' (*Father*, p. 59). So do we mind on Jane.

'Reachfar', *Hingham, Massachusetts*

Notes

1. Jane Duncan's adult books were all published by Macmillan: see the general bibliography. (All 'Reachfar' titles begin *My Friend(s)*; for brevity, in the text we give only the friend's name.) Page references are to original editions with a few exceptions where originals were not available to us: *Muriel* and *Cousin Emmie* in Pan paperback printings, and *Monica*, *Annie* and *Friends from Cairnton* in Ulverscroft large print editions.

2. The seven were written in the following order: *Muriel*, *Monica*, *Rose*, *Miss Boyds*, *Annie*, *Sandy*, and *Martha's Aunt*. The third, *Rose*, was delayed for publication until ninth quite possibly because it is Jane's 'unpleasant' novel, mildly 'shocking' in language and sexual frankness.

3. For sheer verbal energy, wit, and humour, *Muriel* is unequalled among Jane Duncan's books. Its acceptance by Macmillan as the first novel by an unknown author confirms our assessment of its talent. Together with *Rose* and parts of *Monica* at least, it probably represents the 'material [that] had been written down a number of times before between 1931 and 1956 and then destroyed' (*Letter*, p. 94). Our essay necessarily but regrettably slights the wit and humour of early novels, qualities that almost disappear from the serious, often melancholy later books.

4. Of the Jean Robertson novels 'by Janet Sandison', only *Jean in the Morning*, the first, remains well worth reading. In its gusty, roguish realism, one senses the liberation Jane felt in writing this story of a Lowland slum child who survives by lying, thieving, 'cheeky' defiance, and unsentimental charity. It contains some of Jane's best prose. The second and third are confused, overburdened with Dickensian plot and extravagant symbol and with polemics against wealth and materialism. For the fourth, see note 9 below. For an account of the four, see F. R. Hart, *The Scottish Novel* (John Murray, London, 1978), pp. 390–1.

5. There is no hint in *Letter* of guilt or conflict with Sandy Clapperton over Jane's secret writing. She simply never told him because of her 'long habit of secrecy' and her fear that, like her father (to whom she had mentioned her ambition once in the 1930s), he 'would think I was cherishing an unattainable dream' and would 'weaken further the already faint spark' (p. 125).

6. It is interesting to compare Sashie's asexuality with Jane Duncan's ideal of the writer (*Letter*, p. 41): 'I think the true writer is, in mind, a dichotomous creature, half-male, half-female, built on the Chinese principle of Yin and Yang.'

7. Peter Brooks, *Reading for the Plot: Design and Intention in Narrative* (Knopf, New York, 1984), p. 22.

8. We are aware that our analysis of the struggles of Janet (and perhaps Jane) for autonomy and individuality begs for the application of recent models of the distinctively female life cycle. Not qualified as developmental psychologists, we simply offer our analysis for others to interpret. See especially Carol Gilligan, 'Woman's Place in Man's Life Cycle,' *In a Different Voice* (Harvard University Press, Cambridge, Mass., and London, 1982), pp. 5–23.

9. In the final Jean novel, the rebellious urchin, now a mature housekeeper, becomes a wealthy heiress and gathers together into her expanding old ladies' home and her renovated village the good, kind people of her acquaintance. The little matriarch, refreshingly unlike her antecedent Esther Summerson of *Bleak House*, arranges marriages, uncovers hidden kinships, and presides over happy reunions and transformations. Read for the wish-fulfilment fairytale it is, *Jean Towards Another Day* is delightful.

10. A brief anecdote perfectly exemplifies how Jane used everything. During a visit to her in 1967, we tried unsuccessfully to remember all the lines of the rhyme that begins, 'Monday's child is fair of face,' and promised to send a complete copy when we arrived home. On 29 November 1967, Jane wrote, 'And thank you so much for the text of "Monday's Child". I have not yet decided how this is to be used but it certainly will be if I live long enough.' In *Sashie*, written four years later, Janet and Sashie find they were both born on Thursday, but she cannot remember the last line of the verse until just before her leavetaking. She goes to her briefcase to enter it in a manuscript and discovers what Sashie has hidden there, the letter and photographs identifying him as her Ariel.

11. Brooks, *Reading for the Plot*, p. 125.

12. Brooks, p. 111.

33

Jessie Kesson

Isobel Murray

Jessie Kesson died in September 1994 without having published an autobiography announced as forthcoming in 1981. What we know about her life is mainly gathered from her fictions, always a highly risky process, or from a number of interviews which tend to be full of meat but lacking in chronology. She was born illegitimate in the Workhouse in Inverness in 1916, and lived in Elgin with her mother, who was not the prostitute of popular myth but rather 'an enthusiastic amateur'.[1] She was separated from her mother who had fallen ill with a contracted disease, and sent to an orphanage at Skene, in Aberdeenshire, aged nine. After doing well at school she was not allowed to proceed to university, because the Orphanage Trustees thought education would be wasted on a girl. She never ceased to regret and resent this.

Subsequently she was diagnosed as neurasthenic, and she spent a year in a mental hospital, another of a series of gifted women, from Florence Nightingale and Beatrice Webb to her personal heroine Virginia Woolf, who suffered in the attempt to express their talents in the male-determined world they found themselves in.[2] She then met and married her husband Johnnie (who died in 1994). She began her first career, as cottar wife. Encouraged by novelist Nan Shepherd, she began to write for magazines, and features and plays for radio, for the BBC in Aberdeen and the Scottish Home Service. After she and Johnnie moved to London with their family, she had an extraordinary range of jobs. As well as writing radio plays for the newly instituted Third Programme, she cooked and cared for old folk, did psychodrama with disturbed teenagers, hoovered a cinema at Palmer's Green and cleaned a nurses' home at Colney Hatch. She was by turns teacher, social worker, artist's model and radio producer: small wonder she wryly called the projected autobiography *Mistress of None*.[3]

She published four volumes of fiction, all slim, at intervals of many years. None appeared before she was over forty: *The White Bird Passes* (1958), *Glitter of Mica* (1963), *Another Time, Another Place* (1983) and *Where the Apple Ripens*, published in 1985 and containing a novella first published in 1978 and a number of previously published short stories.[4] This is all of a large output of prose and verse that she chose to reprint in book form. She wrote some plays for television and more than forty for radio, and is described by Stewart Conn as 'one of the finest of for-radio practitioners'.[5] But they are unpublished. And so what emerges is a picture of a writer who published little, who honed and refined her material into the smallest effective space: 'No Padding . . . I pare to the essence'.[6]

While this is clearly in one sense true, it is also true that she taught herself to translate into different media, and, more importantly, to expand her instinctive concision and impose order on complex material.

To different degrees, almost all her fictional work is intimately concerned with her own life and the conditions which in part determined it. Indeed the reader must always be on guard not to accept the fictional composition as historical fact. The tension between autobiography and 'fiction' is best revealed in the case of her first novel, *The White Bird Passes*. Here she emerges as a marvellously sensitive prose writer, whose precision of language and structural skill belie the 'untutored' image of a cottar wife turned writer. Here too she has won the battle against the Kailyard writing urged on her by an early 'Editress',[7] and found her major subject matter, the search for identity and fulfilment, internal resistance to oppressive social and personal circumstances, especially in women's experience.

I suggest that Kesson was not miraculously endowed with all the gifts of great writing: she served a long, lonely apprenticeship in her craft. I will sketch the evolution of *The White Bird Passes*, from the first autobiographical account that I have found, in 1941, to the publication of the finished work in 1958. Kesson spent her rare leisure hours in the 1940s and '50s writing for papers, magazines and periodicals as well as radio. An examination of the *North-East Review* (NER) and the *Scots Magazine* (SM), and a number of miscellaneous scripts deposited by the BBC in the Scottish Theatre Archive at Glasgow University Library, reveals an author constantly experimenting with point of view, selection of material and modes of presentation. The practice of writing prentice pieces, trying out prose and verse, fiction and autobiography and subgenres like character 'profile', as well as her radio drama, is most evident as the author prepares her first and most directly 'true to life' book.

Between 'Railway Journey', an apparently factual, first-person account of the anonymous author's childhood, published in two parts in *NER* in October and November 1941, and *The White Bird Passes*, I have found fifteen other pieces which show the writer reworking and shaping parts of the material of the final novel.[8] But a comparison of 'Railway Journey' and *The White Bird Passes* shows how the process generally works. In a way, 'Railway Journey', which is some 1,500 words in all, covers the whole 'plot' of *The White Bird Passes* (approximately 37,000 words), and adds more, the implication that when Ness of Kelbie's Close finally returns to Elgin after her mother is dead and her schooldays are over, she finds no place, no people for her there any longer, and takes another train, back to Aberdeen, very much deracinated and on her own once more. The piece hinges on her memories of childhood during the journey from Aberdeenshire to Elgin.

Her mother here is instantly recognisable as the mother in the novel to come:

> I was crying for the mother who loved me in her own bitter way; I was crying for the good companion who could tell wonderful stories, for the woman who 'loved all beauteous things'.

Liza in *The White Bird Passes* is described in the third person, focalised through Janie, but the effect is clearly the same, as when 'Liza, in one of her rare, enchanting moods' sings and weaves stories of the Hangman's Tree (*WBP*, p. 65), or on the history of Elgin Cathedral: 'Liza was in the mood for telling . . . Liza gave it a vivid, personal life of its own' (*WBP*, pp. 82–3). The final choice of point of view in the novel allows occasional intervention from a narrator, perhaps an adult Janie, hinting at further emotional pain in years to come.

Those rare moods of communication between Janie and her Mother more than made up for the other things lacking in their relationship. And yet, if these moments had never existed, it would have been so much easier for Janie in the years to come (*WBP*, p. 66).

The young girl in 'Railway Journey' has an endless fascination with tinkers and their caravans, and she already identifies with them:

> Down to the caravan encampments which always fascinated me ... terribly interested in these uncouth, wandering folk, who like myself were just so much flotsam and jetsam ... We had no roots ... This was affinity

In *The White Bird Passes* the same identification occurs, and lasts – an identification which Kesson has come to recognise as the keynote of her fiction:

> Nor had she outgrown her affinity with what Grandmother would have called 'Ne'er do weels,' the Lane 'Riff Raff', and Skeyne 'Ootlins'. Skeyne's word was the best word. The most accurately descriptive. Ootlins. Queer folk who were 'oot' and who, perversely enough, never had any desire to be 'in'. (*WBP*, p. 118)

Interviewed by Isobel Murray and Bob Tait in 1985, Kesson quoted this, and continued:

> Every work I've ever written contains ae 'ootlin'. Lovely Aberdeenshire word. Somebody that never really fitted into the thing ... It's always aboot people who don't fit in! Now, I know mysel at last and it's just in one line in that book where fowk were oot who never had any desire to be in.[9]

So far, then, the summary of the early part of 'Railway Journey' sounds like an accurate summary of the equivalent part of the novel. But some crucial elements are missing, which will be developed separately or together and added to the mass of worked-over material before the final shaping of the novel.

There is no mention here, for example, of Annie Frigg. In *The White Bird Passes* the enchantment of this old 'witch's' perpetually unfulfilled promises of rewards for Janie's errands is what is stressed. It is only when Liza pays her one visit to the Orphanage that she brings news of Annie Frigg's death: here it becomes another example of the dissolution of the Lane community. In 'Anybody's Alley' (*NER*, December 1943), and most subsequent accounts, Annie's promises become a staple of childhood in the Lane, to which the protagonist is especially susceptible. But in this version it is the death of one of the heroine's own contemporaries, Dolly Mutch, that causes her to fear that her mother might die soon. The connection between death in the Lane and the protagonist's fears for her mother is spelt out more clearly in a radio adaptation of 'Anybody's Alley', broadcast from Aberdeen in 1947, with Kesson herself as narrator. Here we find Annie Frigg's promises, and more, and then her actual death:

> When Annie did die; it was skipping time; and death affects a bairn's skipping. It was my first realisation of death. I knew people died ... – but it was always other people who had died, not us – or ours – so, when Annie died death became real. I thought that if Annie could die my mother could die too. So I couldn't skip long – I was aye running up the Wynd into the lobby shouting up to my mother, (to the great amusement of the other tenants) 'Mam, wull you nae die soon! Say ye winna die soon'.

When the novel is finally crafted, it is not the natural death of a child, nor of Annie Frigg, that puts Janie in such real and lasting fear for her mother – it is the suicide of Mysie Walsh, her mother's warmer and more extrovert friend and contemporary, and like her, an 'old-fangled', if amateur, whore (*WBP*, p. 16). Liza's reaction to Mysie's suicide and funeral – 'Mysie Walsh's in the best place' – has her labelled by neighbours a 'hard-hearted bitch' (*WBP*, p. 36), but the reader is allowed greater latitude for emotional understanding, and is aware of the close kinship between Liza and Mysie. And when we look at the treatment of time in *The White Bird Passes*, we notice that it is handled with brilliant economy: the descriptions of life in the Lane (Chapters 1 to 6) contrive to give both an impression of habitual, daily life over years and an account of Janie's life over a mere seven days, from Chapter 1, where a depressed Mysie sends Janie for cheese, through the discovery of her corpse that evening, and her funeral, to the brief and futile escape of Liza and Janie to the Diddle Doddle (lodging house) exactly a week later. Mysie Walsh has become a tragic and ironic figure whose presence and absence bind the whole action together, analogous to the way in which the death after childbirth of Helen Mavor overhangs the whole action of the novella, *Where the Apple Ripens*.

One of the striking aspects of *The White Bird Passes* is the glamour and colour that young Janie's perception lends to the slum Lane and its range of poverty-stricken, variously crippled and drunken characters. 'Railway Journey' makes no mention of Lane characters like Poll Pyke, Battleaxe, and the Duchess, while the novel gives the impression of a densely populated arena, wholly alive for Janie: 'the Lane was home and wonderful' (*WBP*, p. 86). Words have a special magic for Janie. She loves the tinkers, with 'the magical facility of rolling far-sounding places round their tongues' (*WBP*, p. 46), and the joys of a special language of their own. Beulah the tinker is not to be found in 'Railway Journey', but she is a centrally important figure in Chapter 4 of *The White Bird Passes*, and there are sketches of her character in periodical and radio pieces.[10] This is all in stark contrast to 'Railway Journey', which lacks romance and excitement beyond Liza, and an ootlin other than the narrator, who claims: 'I was nine when I left it, but I'd never been young'. The Janie offered later with her contradictions and paradoxes is more complex, and convincing. In *The White Bird Passes*, Mrs Thane repeatedly points to the contradictions she finds in Janie, and she tries to explain to the Trustees:

> She's a puzzle. She can be as crude and knowing as they come. And, at the same time, she's less sophisticated and more sensitive than any of the other children, who haven't had such a deplorable background. (*WBP*, p. 149)

This more complex view of the protagonist begins to be evident by 1946, in a piece called 'Makar in Miniature'. Like 'Railway Journey', this concentrates on the protagonist, to the virtual exclusion of her mother. Its theme is her transforming imagination, so central to *The White Bird Passes*:

> The Makar in her asserted itself early . . . Making was the vivid-hued quality, the great coat of many colours that enveloped and sheltered her throughout the drabness of a slum childhood . . . The Makar was never herself, yet she never lost identity . . . 'Ye canna speak tae me the noo, Mam, I'm the hedgehog.' She crowded many lifetimes into the brevity of a day . . . When she was ten the Makar left the Wynd to live in a country orphanage. Two new elements began to have their influence upon her – words and Nature . . . With the approach of her teens, the Makar no longer consciously became, she simply was. She was

Spring, Summer, Autumn, Winter – each in its season. She could see them so vividly, hear them so acutely, smell them so intensely, become so immersed in them that she knew she was part of them.

This is an early and very effective portrayal of the writer-in-the-making. In the end, though, this treatment from outside, by turns loving and mocking and even a little condescending, is less effective than the focalisation through Janie in *The White Bird Passes*. And it is not until the novel that Kesson finds the perfect synthesis of the protagonist and her surroundings that makes Lady's Lane so memorable.

One final crucial figure absent from the early sketch of 'Railway Journey' and central to *The White Bird Passes* (and of course to 'Until Such Times', the short story in *Where the Apple Ripens*), is the grandmother. Kesson has made it clear that her own grandfather never came to terms with her illegitimacy, and refused ever to speak to her, but her own grandmother was clearly an important supportive figure for the young Kesson and her mother. The evolution of the Grandmother in Chapter 5 of *The White Bird Passes*, and in the short story, can be traced by any reader who compares them with 'Memory Portrait of a Grandmother' (*NER*, October 1944), 'The Shadow' (*SM*, vol. 46, 1946), and 'Grandmother' (*SM*, vol. 51, 1949). Grandmother's line, 'Sorrow be on shoes. The lark needs no shoes to climb to heaven', occurs in 1944, and 1949, and again in 'Until Such Times': as Kesson wrote in 1944: 'her very words and their intonation drift down the years because they transcended the commonplace.' Tributes to the Grandmother and her ability to enter the child's world are constant: 'Grandmother was the glow that kindled and lit up all my childhood in a slum' (1949).

A comparison of the treatment of the orphanage years in 'Railway Journey' and *The White Bird Passes* gives a fairly similar result to the slum years comparison: the outline is similar, but the novel is expanded to a fuller life and depth, without sacrificing any of Kesson's ambition to pare to the bone. The timespan in the novel has what was to become Kesson's characteristic concision: she concentrates only on the day of arrival and the final decisions about departure and destination.

Arrival at the orphanage is movingly described in 'Railway Journey', but again with less emotional complexity than in *The White Bird Passes*. The narrator thinks it 'the loveliest place I had ever seen', and a joy outside and in. Apart from asking if she can go home when she is fourteen, the girl's main problem is that all her hair has been cut off. In the novel, there is a conscious conflict: she misses her mother and her hair, but decides on her priorities:

> If I got one wish I'd just ask for all my hair back again. No, I wouldn't. I'd just ask to get home to my Mam again. Not having any hair wouldn't matter if I could just get home again. (*WBP*, p. 110)

In both accounts, the protagonist remains fascinated by poetry, and becomes increasingly interested in education, with the encouragement of a perceptive dominie. In 'Railway Journey,' despite the dominie's help, she is sent to work on a farm, which corresponds to Kesson's 'real life' experience, while in *The White Bird Passes* she may be on her way to 'Kingorm' (Aberdeen University), where, says the Mannie, 'They've decided to mak' a scholar oot o' her' (*WBP*, p. 154). So the ending of the novel is able to juxtapose this fragile hope with the physically uncomfortable experience of 'lowsing the sheaves' and the sexually suggestive talk of the men. But the passage from 'The Valley of White Poppies' by 'Fiona Macleod', from which Kesson took her final title, does not bode well: it speaks of 'the grave of dreams':

> A white bird floats there like a drifting leaf:
> It feeds upon faint sweet hopes and perishing dreams
> And the still breath of unremembering grief.
>
> And as a silent leaf the white bird passes.

The most striking feature of the treatment of the orphanage years in the novel that was absent from 'Railway Journey' is the ongoing concern with Janie's mother and the possibility that she might die, a thread that strongly connects both parts of the narrative. There is her one visit to Janie, suffused with irony, when she comes to ask for Janie to come home, because she has chronic syphilis and her sight is failing: she needs someone to take care of her. There is a touching scene where Liza and Janie try to re-establish contact after a long separation. Afterwards, Janie is characteristically divided between a naive triumph that Liza was not drunk, but ill, and a late realisation of how much Liza meant: 'But Liza had been beautiful . . . [She] had always leapt burnished, out of her surroundings. And in the leaping had made the dim world bright' (*WBP*, p. 125); and how much she owed her mother:

> All the things I know, she taught me, God. The good things, I mean . . . She put a singing seal in Loch Na Boune and a lament on the long, lonely winds . . . And I would myself be blind now, if she had never lent me her eyes. (*WBP*, p. 129)

This persistence of Liza, alive and dead, is a significant unifying feature in the novel, as well as adding emotional depth and resonance.

In the novel Mrs Thane's husband, 'the Mannie', becomes a major figure in Janie's life, like Beulah and Grandmother. He is the subject of a story, 'Judgment', published in *NER* in April 1946. The particulars of this story, where the children consume aging, broken biscuits intended for the hens, and go virtually unpunished, do not recur, but the story deals also with the bairns' general response to the Mannie, and much of this survives, verbatim, into Chapter 9 of *The White Bird Passes*. The girl's respect and affection for him, the nearest thing she has had to a father figure, are evident.

Trustees' Day, passed over with just the unfavourable verdict in 'Railway Journey,' is treated in effective detail in *The White Bird Passes*. As in the Lane years, the reader simultaneously gets the impression of years passing at the orphanage, and of the particular events of one conclusive day. The first account of this fateful day was given, again, in 'Makar in Miniature'. And again, although the account is effective enough, a comparison with the more accomplished treatment in the novel shows up the difficulties of rendering her subject from outside, while sometimes speaking over her head:

> The Makar didn't die on the day the orphanage trustees gathered round the dining-room table to decide her way of life . . . Eleven remembered years of life went by in seconds, each year vivid and colourful. Suddenly the Makar saw that those years hadn't made her, she had made the years. Their texture was too fragile ever to be displayed to middle-aged trustees. Somewhere within her mind the words beat thrawnly, But I being poor have only my dreams. The Makar felt choked and trapped. The words tore themselves up from inside

her: 'Bit I dinna wint tae dust and polish! I wint tae write poetry, great poetry, as great as Shakespeare!'

The Trustees' verdict is not recorded in this case, but the Makar is nonetheless victorious: 'Closing the dining-room door, the Makar came out – alive.'

Re-reading *The White Bird Passes* in the context of some of Kesson's output in the preceeding fourteen years, especially her early use of the same material, clearly does not change a purely qualitative judgement of the book. But it does stress some aspects of the book that it is easy to get wrong, or take for granted. Above all I hope to have shown by this account that Kesson does not simply warble her native wood-notes wild. Although she was well-taught by her Dominie, Kesson served a craft apprenticeship in which her teachers were her beloved books, and her own painstaking practice. This survey has convinced me more than ever of the success of the narrative method in *The White Bird Passes*, generally in the third person and usually focalised through Janie, although with occasional interventions (by an older Janie?) which go beyond what the child can understand at the time. It has stressed Liza's life and possible death throughout, particularly with the invention of Mysie Walsh, whose opting for self-destruction at the start balances the decline of Liza from chronic syphilis years later. And it has underlined the establishment of figures significant in different ways for young Janie, from Annie Frigg and the tinker Beulah to Grandmother and the Mannie, as well as a memorable set of minor characters who are celebrated by Janie's imagination and memory.

But I cannot leave *The White Bird Passes* without pausing on one other feature which this book has in common with the others, the marvellous control Kesson exercises in the rendering of emotional experience. Muriel Spark, whom Kesson much admired, often unobtrusively omits the emotions of her characters: 'I think it's bad manners to inflict a lot of emotional involvement on the reader – much nicer to make them laugh and keep it short.'[11] But Kesson's fiction by no means frees the reader from emotional involvement: instead, by a judicious mixture of understatement and silence, it has the very powerful emotional impact that Hemingway famously aimed for in *Death in the Afternoon*:

> If a writer of prose knows enough about what he is writing about he may omit things that he knows and the reader, if the writer is writing truly enough, will have a feeling of those things as strongly as though the writer had stated them. The dignity of movement of an iceberg is due to only one-eighth of it being above water.

I suggest that the success of *The White Bird Passes* is finally dependent most of all on the literary tact which encourages the reader to sense and share feelings that are not spelled out, and to be aware always of emotional depths that are the more powerful for being unplumbed. The twinned characters of Liza and Mysie Walsh, and the apparent limitation of their experience to what the child Janie understands, are relevant here.

This characteristic remains centrally important in *Glitter of Mica*, the novella *Where the Apple Ripens*, *Another Time, Another Place* and a number of the short stories. In many ways *Glitter of Mica* is more complex and more ambitious than *The White Bird Passes*. Here Kesson's interests are wider. She treats a number of major characters, most of them with understanding and sympathy, constantly indicating the constraints imposed on them by history, economic systems, tied houses and the feeing system, class, kirk and small community gossip. She chooses a very complex narrative structure, which interweaves and juxtaposes past and present and covers three generations of one family, as well as centring insistently on a single momentous day on which years of frustration and oppression found ugly expression in a brutal attack and a putative suicide.[12] Uniquely, she chooses here a male protagonist, and uniquely here varies the narrative from her customary focalisation through the main character to alternating that with omniscient narration, allowing other main characters to be presented by a strong, implicitly commenting voice, or briefly focalising through them. The book begins after the climactic attack, but before news of Helen's death. Events are given through Hugh Riddel's memories, and by a broad survey of Caldwell on the crucial Friday evening.

The scale of social analysis is new here. 'Caldwell is first and foremost the land of the farm-worker' (GM, p. 9). The exploitation of the farm-worker is a major topic, which is stressed to us through Darklands' Head Dairyman, Hugh Riddel, and his recollections of his father's career and working conditions, long before we understand the circumstances in which Hugh is now staring at 'the bleakest landscape in Scotland', and averting his eyes from Ambroggan House, 'asylum for the wealthy mentally ill of the land' (GM, pp. 12, 11). Indeed, the reader only appreciates the plot, timescale and structure on careful rereading.

An extraordinary amount of material, character and action is crammed economically into this short novel, but a summary would suggest that this is the unhappy story of Hugh Riddel (and his more oppressed and frustrated father before him), his unfulfilling marriage, his alienation from his daughter Helen, his affair with Sue Tatt, his years-long contempt for Charlie Anson and his final attack on Anson, when he discovers him with Helen, her apparent subsequent suicide, and eventual death in the mental asylum. This is challenging material, and presented so forcefully that a first-time reader may be too preoccupied with the dramatic events and the 'iceberg' sense of unarticulated emotion to give enough weight to the anatomy of the community, the evidence of the dehumanising pressures of ownership, status and class.

But they are insisted on, and basic to the novel. So much so that five years after the publication of the novel Kesson wrote another version, a play for radio, *And Barley Rigs*, which tells a story in which Hugh has no daughter Helen, in which Sue Tatt is only mentioned by gossip, and in which there is no antagonism between Hugh and Anson. But most of this play is still taken verbatim from the novel. There is still plenty of material in the study of Hugh's oppressive life conditions, and his father's, and in his sexual unhappiness, and his affronting the gossips by his open visits to Sue Tatt.[13]

All the main characters of the novel are to some extent crippled by circumstances, community, or each other, and vividly presented. As a cottar wife, Kesson was only too aware of the circumstances, but these characters are her own invention. All are to some extent ootlins, isolated, and unable to communicate meaningfully, whether or not they are ready with words: only Sue Tatt has a meaningful, if stormy, relationship with her daughter Fiona, 'one which gave [her life] wholeness' (GM, p. 131).

Hugh's peripatetic childhood has led to rootlessness. His strong sexuality has been baffled by his choosing for his wife a woman like his mother, passive and chaste – and frigid – who has come to fear him dumbly, while the wrinkles in her stockings can drive him to a murderous frenzy. He needs the release of his relationship with Sue Tatt, although there is no hint of its being any more than that. He is possessed by anger, and alienated from his daughter by the 'wall of words' which her vocation in social work applies to desperate realities. Perhaps, in his angry depths, his dislike for and rivalry with crofter Charlie Anson is his strongest emotion: certainly when he discovers Anson with Helen his response is immediate and brutal, his full attention on Anson. When Helen at last catches his attention he has nothing for her but a moment of disengaged pity, and the reader is left to wonder if he loves her at all, and whether he is concerned by his own possible part in her possible suicide: a neighbour insists that Helen was unaware of the oncoming brake, 'thinking it mattered', comments the narrator wryly (GM, p. 145).

Helen herself is very much an ootlin, cut off from her parents and community by her education, her very language, but unnourished by her job or her colleagues. She is humiliated by the fact that Charlie Anson discovered at the same time as she did (some three months before) the urgency of her sexual needs, and her own recognition that 'the flesh could have belonged to any man' (GM, p. 108). Pregnant, she has determined to marry Anson, but when her father interrupts their lovemaking Kesson's 'iceberg' technique leaves us, for the most part, to empathise with her humiliation over his total focus on Anson: if we are to see her as committing suicide, how far is her father's indifference to her the motive?

The pictures of Sue Tatt and Isa Riddel are both effective, and invite sympathy and understanding, never judgement, Sue is the ultimate ootlin, the community scapegoat, but a fascinating combination of personalities and roles, and a survivor less crippled by community pressures than the others, and much more on good terms with both her family and her sexuality. Isa is the downtrodden wife, who bathes in the reflected glory of her daughter's education, and rarely manages to act spontaneously, as she does on the train despite her feeling of 'outwithness' (GM, p. 82), or to answer Hugh back, as she does over the tinker Betsy Ann (GM, p. 153).

Anson is the exception. His cold, mean ambition and calculation are rendered by the narrator with distaste and from his own viewpoint without shame, and his manipulation of his status as a crofter is as inhuman as his attitude to women – 'the only warmth he could ever feel for them was the heat of rising lust' (GM, p. 119).

The lesser characters, of all classes, serve as a combination of Greek chorus and commenting 'bodies,' stressing the stifling conventions squeezing the lives of any individuals living in this bleak countryside, under this inequitable class and economic dispensation. Here is a fair resemblance to such Scottish classics as *The House with the Green Shutters*, although Kesson's novel is less negative than Brown's, with positive aspects of the community and a comic perspective both apparent, for example in the bus journey from the Town to Caldwell on the Friday evening.

Kesson first published the novella *Where the Apple Ripens* with John Calder in *New Writing and Writers* 15, in 1978. It was reprinted as the title story in a Chatto and Windus collection in 1985, with only very minor emendations, mainly a matter of toning down the emphases marked by capitalising common nouns, or printing words stressed by Isabel in block capitals. At some sixty pages, it is the shortest piece I will have room to discuss, and I have always considered it a minor miracle, or what Kesson aims at, 'the sma' perfect'.[14] It captures the moment when Isabel Emslie is on the brink of womanhood, poised between childish things and sexual curiosity and excitement, desperate for experience as the time comes to leave school, and partly chastened by the death of Helen Mavor, an older schoolmate, who has died after childbirth. She is saved from her own urgent response to the attentions of an experienced crofter-seducer only by the arrival of the postman, and the indignity of her situation causes Isabel to vow never to repeat the occasion of such humiliation. This seems a more powerful disincentive than the fate of Helen Mavor.

The novella is brilliantly and unobtrusively structured, so that the reader at least is always aware of the dangers of repeating Helen's fate. We are inside Isabel's head, experiencing or remembering vivid moments, hearing fragments of poetry and music, from traditional ballads to hymns, from playground songs to popular hits: this jumble of excitements highlights the way in which Isabel is caught between two worlds, childhood and womanhood, in a daze of adolescent feeling and fantasy. I found a few early sketches with details that survive, but the shock discovery was the scripts of two radio plays which predate the published novella by up to seven years.[15] Each play seems to me by itself 'sma' perfect,' but the way in which Kesson has crafted them together into the seamless novella, adapting radio techniques to literary uses and combining the two plots into one particularly resonant story, is quite extraordinary.

'In Memoriam' was recorded in March 1971. It begins with Helen Mavor's death notice and funeral, and Isabel's reactions, including her admitting, 'I was just so pleased to be alive, myself. That I kept forgetting all about Helen being dead.' Here is the source of the music so haunting in the novella, a ballad singer, 'used to interpret and extend Isabel's mood, or feelings, when she, herself, has no words for them'. The Alex Ewan character, here Jim Summers, was at Helen's funeral, and is much talked about as a seducer. He comes to ask for milk, and Isabel sets out on the journey. So far, all is in line with *Where the Apple Ripens*, and many lines and passages will survive into the novella. But in the play Jim Summers is only asking for a kiss when the postman interrupts them, and the play ends with Isabel volunteering to go back for the milk pail that night. Isabel has again forgotten Helen Mavor's fate, and Jim Summers's housekeeper, who has just been sacked, pregnant like her predecessors.

Kesson uses almost all this material in *Where the Apple Ripens*. But she also uses almost all the material from 'But Myrrh', recorded in December 1972. Here there is no Helen Mavor character, no Alex Ewan clone. Instead the play is much involved with Isabel (the same Isabel, clearly) and her family, and introduces her brother Davy and their relationship, and almost all he does or says in the novella. It is about Isabel's last day at school, becoming a woman, preparing to go away to work. It stresses her sexual curiosity, with vivid memories of the onset of menstruation and speculations about her parents' sex lives, and her own potential future, 'not under one Horseman, but under every horseman that ever was'. The late mention of a girl who died after her baby was born is used only to make Isabel's undemonstrative mother show how much she loves her, although she never kissed or hugged her. The slender 'plot' depends on the anticlimax of Last Day at School: because of a visitation by the School Board, there is a half day: Isabel's moment as centre of attention is lost: they forgot to give her her 'Bumps', and she had no solemn last words from the Dominie.

The novella combines the material and often the very words of these two plays, except for the endings, and goes on to develop some features more fully. The physical aspects of Isabel's young womanhood are stressed – indeed the whole novella seems sexually charged. But Isabel's case is central, and clearly her solitary sex life is well under way. When she reaches Alex Ewan's croft, he appears smaller than in her night-time fantasies, which were romantic, numerous, and drawn from both life and literature: she wonders if Else has similar experiences, 'in the hope that she might not be alone in such shameful delight and painful frustration' (*WAR*, p. 65). Sexual experience is dealt with here much more directly than in *Glitter of Mica*, and Isabel's experiences are more like those of the young woman in *Another Time, Another Place*, who refused sexual intercourse with Luigi in fact for a long time, but yielded in fancy: 'Turning away, she was unable to look on him in the clear light of day, for she had raped his privacy, had conjured up his every intimacy in fantasies covered by the night' (*ATAP*, p. 84).

In the novella, Kesson also expands the substance and significance of Isabel's central journey to Alex Ewan's croft with the pail of milk, already important in 'In Memoriam'. Now the journey becomes more symbolic: Letizia Accinelli has usefully compared its presentation to 'Little Red Riding Hood', and noted also that the characters who meet and often warn Isabel on her way effectively amount to a revisiting of her childhood so that she can put it behind her on the way to womanhood.[16] Thus in the novella she meets two sets of women and one of girls, 'the unbeliever's wife', the blacksmith's apprentice, the midwife who attended her birth, Alick Mearns the bachelor crofter. But on two occasions before she is 'saved by the bell', Isobel most significantly meets the Postman. First, she is on 'the kind of road that lured her into navigating it blind' (*WAR*, p. 55). She nearly unseats Postie, and he calls her 'A menace to other folk. As well as to yourself!' (*WAR*, p. 55). Later at the level crossing she sees Postie trundling his bike across. 'He never allowed anybody else to break the rules, did Postie ... And there he was, breaking the rules himself, taking the short cut that would have taken a mile off her own journey' (*WAR*, p. 61). Postie remains an ambiguous figure: although his arrival halts her seduction, he joins Alex Ewan in a sniggering male conspiracy from which Isabel is excluded.

Whereas in 'In Memoriam' the interruption in the seduction led to Isabel's return for more, in the novella she walks away with a new determination. The indignity of the incident in the byre remains with her:

> For never. Never again would she stand not knowing what to do. Crumpled and sticky and dirty, with her knickers dangling around her knees. And herself be told to 'tidy up'. (*WAR*, p. 68)

Helen Riddel had been doubly humiliated, by Anson's knowingness and her father's disregard. Isabel has been doubly humiliated, by 'the shamelessness of her urgent need' (*WAR*, p. 67) and by this public exposure. A double humiliation again climaxes the story of *Another Time, Another Place*: 'Twice she had lost the rudiments of dignity, that outward physical dignity that held the visible self together. Once in the heather with Luigi, and now on leaving the officer's room' (*ATAP*, p. 92). The young woman's case is perhaps the worst of all, because she will have to endure public disgrace and reaction for an indefinite period: 'It was the burden of shame within herself, and which would be extended to, and cast over her man, that was beyond enduring' (*ATAP*, p. 91).

Another Time, Another Place was hurried out in 1983, to coincide with the release of the film, on which Kesson collaborated with director Mike Radford. By this time we will not be surprised to find that the basic situation occurred in real life: Kesson as a cottar wife was required to help three Italian prisoners of war sent to work on the land. She wrote a vivid documentary account, 'Moments from Time', in *NER* in July 1944. But she fictionalised the story in a play for radio, 'Another Time, Another Place', in 1980.[17] Basically, this amounts to a sketch of what the novel will be: on the whole radio, like film, is a medium which can hold less narrative detail and structural complexity than fiction.

The play cannot hope to convey the isolation of the young woman as the novel does, even with 'voice overs' instead of constant focalising. The young woman is an alien in the unnamed community, with a town childhood and an orphanage background, not long married to a good older man not much given to speech, and as likely to identify with the children of her neighbours Kirsty and Meg as with these older women. 'It was as if the whole chapter of their youth had been torn from their book, and they had turned the page from childhood to middle age' (*ATAP*, p. 35). She is also by her marriage a prisoner there, with no expectation of release, and avid for wider horizons, excited at the thought of 'heroic men from far-flung places' (*ATAP*, p. 8).

The physical life of the novel is stronger too. Luigi's constant criticisms of wind and weather only underline a harsh working milieu with strenuous labour in inclement conditions. The class system is clarified: Elspeth, the crofter, is welcomed at the village flower show, while the cottar wives 'could have "dropped in" from another planet, to find themselves invisible, in a marquee' (*ATAP*, p. 28). At other times the young woman can find herself particularly an ootlin, with the two older cottar wives and mothers allied against her.

A significant short scene introduced into the novel is the young woman's memory of consulting the doctor and rejecting his hypothesis of pregnancy: 'You must know. When something important like that is happening . . . You must feel something. I never feel anything' (*ATAP*, p. 73). Her sexual awareness is transformed with the arrival of the Italians, Luigi's admiration, and her dreams of Paolo:

> A key which had opened a door that had never been unlocked. And herself becoming the prisoner, stumbling blind, into the light of a new awareness, bursting out of her body in response to Luigi's admiration. (*ATAP*, p. 23)

She dances with Luigi before an attentive Italian company, identifying with the waking Eve, and her subsequent realisation that Paolo is indifferent coincides with her first hesitation with Luigi: 'Maybe . . . some day' (*ATAP*, p. 63). Her eventual acceptance of Luigi's invitation into the bothy is marked both by sexual awakening and by guilt and fear: 'Her body that had taken her unaware, asserting a life of its own, clamouring for its needs, lay quiet now, cold with apprehension' (*ATAP*, p. 85). And after her second encounter with him in the heather she realises 'she would never truly know whether she had yielded to the instinct of her body or to a sense of long loss that the word "last" had evoked' (*ATAP* p. 88).

Her attempt to save Luigi from a false rape charge by confirming their intimacy paradoxically ensures his punishment as well as her disgrace. The prison metaphor has permeated the novel, leading up to the final realisation: 'So this was what it was like to be a prisoner' (*ATAP*, p. 91). Only two minor consolations are left her, the possibility of a renewed friendship with Elspeth, now that the Italians have gone, and the gifts they have left, 'con amore', which importantly include 'Dina', a name they have chosen for her, anonymous no more.[18]

Notes

1. See Joy Hendry, 'Jessie Kesson Country', *Scots Magazine* [SM], October 1989, 11–22 (p. 14).
2. See Elaine Showalter, *The Female Malady: Women, Madness and English Culture, 1830–1980* (Virago, London, 1987), esp. ch. 5, 'Nervous Women: Sex Roles and Sick Roles'.
3. Hendry; Hugh Macpherson, 'Scottish Writers: Jessie Kesson', *Scottish Book Collector 2*, Issue 8 (1990/91), 22–5; Isobel Murray (ed.), 'The Sma Perfect: Jessie Kesson', in *Scottish Writers Talking: Interviewed by Isobel Murray and Bob Tait* (Tuckwell Press, East Linton, 1996).
4. Page references will be made to Chatto & Windus editions: single-volume reprints by Paul Harris and Virago have the same pagination. Further references will be accompanied by abbreviated titles with page numbers in brackets: *WBP, GM, ATA, WAR*. Note also a short story, 'Cold in Coventry', in Aonghas MacNeacail (ed.), *A Writers' Ceilidh for Neil Gunn* (Balnain Books, Nairn, 1991), pp. 99–111.
5. *Cencrastus*, 6 (Autumn 1981), 37.

6. 'My Scotland', in *Scottish Review* 35 (1984), 39–41 (p. 41).

7. Murray, *Scottish Writers Talking*, p. 66.

8. In *North-East Review* (*NER*) and *SM*, and the Scottish Theatre Archive (STA) at Glasgow University Library. In most cases no line is drawn between 'truth' and 'fiction', and Kesson writes in English with Scots dialogue. 'The Years Between', *SM* 37 (1942), 14–18; 'Blaeberry Wood', (poem in English), *SM* 37 (1942), 204–5; 'Triumphant Day', *SM* 37 (1942), 387–90; 'Anybody's Alley', *NER* (December 1943), 8; 'Profile of Phemie', *NER* (April 1946), 5; 'Pilgrimage', *SM* 45 (1946), 167–70; 'Vagrant: A Scottish Profile', *NER* (August 1946), 7–8; 'Makar in Miniature', 'a beautiful portrayal of sensitive Scottish childhood', *NER* (September 1946), 5–8; 'Anybody's Alley', 'some memories of a Scottish childhood', (radio play for the Scottish Home Service, written and narrated by Jessie Kesson, October 1947), STA KazBox6/1, 1–11 (2pp. missing); 'The Shadow', *SM* 46 (1946), 71–4; 'Grandmother', *SM* 51 (1949), 21–5; 'Tuppence Coloured', *SM* (1950), 273–4.

9. Murray, *Scottish Writers Talking*, p. 50.

10. 'Sleeping Tinker' was the story with which Kesson won her first literary prize, in the 'Sangschaw for Makars' competition, 1942; a radio version from 1947 in which Kesson participated is in STA KJ Box 4/8. See also 'This Wasted Day' in *WAR*, pp. 148–59.

11. Quoted in Ruth Whittaker, *The Faith and Fiction of Muriel Spark* (Macmillan, London, 1982), p. 15.

12. The time scheme is on close inspection inconsistent: when his father came to Darklands in 1939, Hugh was a boy; but if the novel is set in 1962, Helen must then be at least 27, so born within a very few years of her father.

13. Perhaps Kesson's earliest public criticism of the short lets/tied houses system was voiced by her on radio, in 'The Cottar's Wife', on *Farm Forum* in 1949 (STA J.1 Box 5/1).

14. Murray, *Scottish Writers Talking*, p. 61.

15. See 'The Near Kingdom' in *SM* 44 (1946), 249–53, and 'May Melody', *NER* (May 1946), 7–8. 'In Memoriam' (28 pages) is in STA Kj Box 11/9, and 'But Myrrh' (28 pages) in STA J.m Box 9/1.

16. Maria Letizia Accinelli, 'The Role of Women in Jessie Kesson's Fiction and Kesson's Treatment of Female Characters' (unpublished M.Litt. thesis, University of Aberdeen, 1990), pp. 186–93.

17. 33 pages (STA J.K. Box 7/1).

18. For further useful material see: Elizabeth Adair, *North East Folk* (P. Harris Publications, Edinburgh, 1982), pp. 78–81; Carol Anderson, 'Listening to the Women Talk', in Gavin Wallace and Randall Stevenson (eds), *The Scottish Novel Since the Seventies* (Edinburgh University Press, Edinburgh, 1993), pp. 170–5 (*ATAP*); William Donaldson, review of *WBP*, *Cencrastus* 4 (Winter 1980–81), 47–8; William Donaldson, introduction to *GM* (Edinburgh, 1982); Douglas Dunn, Introduction to *WBP* (London, 1987); Douglas Gifford, review of *WAR*, *Books in Scotland* 23 (Winter 1986), 8–9; Cuthbert Graham, Introduction to *WBP* (Edinburgh, 1980); Isobel Murray 'Jessie Kesson: Writing Herself', in David Hewitt (ed.), *Northern Visions: Essays on The Literary Identity of Northern Scotland in the Twentieth Century* (Tuckwell Press, East Linton, 1995).

34

Scottish Women Dramatists Since 1945

Jan McDonald

There are many Scottish women dramatists but few plays by women have been published and few have been performed more than once. The texts most widely available are not necessarily always the most challenging in terms of imaginative insight or of dramaturgical innovation: they are, simply, those deemed by the controllers of production to be the most 'marketable'. Since the majority of publishers and of artistic directors is male (although the majority of theatregoers and performers is female) the dissemination of theatre pieces by women in the public arena is artificially restricted. I consider it important, therefore, to examine both unpublished and unperformed plays in the course of the chapter.

It is also important, albeit quite difficult, to avoid creating an alternative 'canon' in what is perforce a summary of Scottish women's achievements in playwriting over the last fifty years. It is for this reason that I have chosen to investigate the principal trends in women's writing for the theatre in the period rather than to take the easier course (perhaps) of providing a critical appraisal of the work of a select group of individual dramatists. I appreciate that, in the first place, my choice of 'trends' or 'issues' can only be subjective and secondly, that the inherent danger of this approach is that the distinctive creative individuality of each writer may become blurred. While subjectivity is unavoidable, I hope that by a judicious choice of topics, I shall obviate the latter.

The broad issues for discussion are, first, feminist re-visioning of history, of mythology and of existing literary and theatrical texts; secondly, the creation and definition of communities of women, including the significance of the concept of 'sisterhood', the nature of the bond between mothers and daughters, and that between lesbian women; thirdly, the exploration of Scottish national identity particularly with regard to its perceived impact on gender, stereotyping, sexual relationships and artistic expression and opportunity. The final sections deal with dramatic and theatrical language.

Revision of History, Literature and Legend

> Don't/let history frame you/in a pretty lie.
>
> Liz Lochhead, *Dreaming Frankenstein*

The purpose of 're-visioning' is to challenge the received opinions contained in the original text, and for feminist writers, it is to initiate a reinterpretation of the role of women as constructed and marginalised by history, mythology and the literary canon. It is a technique much favoured by late twentieth-century Scottish women writers.

Two plays which seek to reconfigure historical events by focusing on undocumented female characters are Ena Lamont Stewart's *Business in Edinburgh* and Sue Glover's *The Straw Chair*.[1] Both dramatists examine the plight of the abandoned wife of a celebrated husband, abandoned because each refuses to adhere to conventional notions of 'womanhood' and, in particular, refuses to be *silent*. Stewart's play concerns the sojourn in the Capital of Sarah Hazlitt, wife of the nineteenth-century essayist and critic, while she is waiting for a divorce under Scots law. A woman of independent mind who despised the mercenary 'husband hunting' that preoccupied ladies of her class, she was not a virgin on her marriage but attracted Hazlitt with her 'good sharp intellect and ready laugh'. It was after the birth of their son that Hazlitt 'became sickened at the thought she was not pure,' succumbing to the conventional morality of the Madonna myth, the mother as the vessel of unimpeachable domestic virtue. Paradoxically, however, the reason for the divorce is so that he can marry his mistress. The supposedly respectable Edinburgh lawyer, himself given to nasty sexual advances to women of all classes, excuses Hazlitt's conduct on account of his literary status. He is 'a great man'. Sarah retorts:

> And the wives of great men are of no account: We seldom read of them. Well, the world has never taken much account of women. Someday it may have to.

Sue Glover's protagonist is Lady Rachel of the Grange, wife of James Erskine, Lord Advocate in the 1730s and '40s, whose infidelities and brutal treatment led to her threatening to expose him as a secret Jacobite and traitor. When she refused to be silenced in her public campaign against him, he despatched her to the island of St Kilda or Hirta, where, isolated from her culture, class and language, she is considered crazy, devilish, intemperate. With obvious dramatic irony, her sole attendant, Oona, likens her to 'a skua, a wild, useless bird, the imp of hell. When they catch one, men take out its eyes, sew up its sockets and send it off to a slow death'. Lady Grange is last seen writing an imaginary letter on invisible paper in the futile hope of communicating with the absent men who have effected her exile. Clever, threatening, vocal women who transgress the male hegemony are condemned to isolation and silence, to a metaphoric 'scold's chair'.

Mary Shelley in Liz Lochhead's *Blood and Ice* is also in 'exile' as a result of her association with Shelley, social rebel, erratic genius and unfaithful sexual partner. The play, which Lochhead suggests is set in Mary's own consciousness, traces her development from being the passive 'creature' of her famous parents, William Godwin and Mary Wollstonecraft, and the disempowered sexual partner in Shelley's ('the dead man's') bed to being the active creator of the novel, *Frankenstein*, which, as she comes to realise, is her own story. She *is* 'Frankenstein', the creator who loves creation and hates its results and 'the monster, poor misunderstood creature, feared and hated by all mankind' and 'the female monster, gross, gashed . . . denied life, tied to the monster bed forever'. Finally, she recognises her true status, that of explorer and survivor – 'My own cool narrator.' By taking control of the means of communication, Mary Shelley (and coincidentally her author) takes the power to re-create her historically constructed image.[2]

Lochhead chose to critique a woman's story. Other women writers have turned their attention to men's stories, in which women have been relegated to playing minor parts. Joan Ure's companion pieces, *Something in it for Cordelia* and *Something in it for Ophelia*, were written to complement productions of *King Lear* and *Hamlet* at the

Edinburgh International Festival and are set in Waverley Station after the performance of Shakespeare's tragedies at the Assembly Hall. Ure's young women refuse to play their parts in prescribed male tragedies and are not content to be victims once-removed of a man's tragic disposition.[3]

Cordelia has forcibly transported her middle-aged father (he is only fifty-five not an 'ancient') to the Station on the handlebars of her bicycle, before the maunderings of the Fool and Lear's own partiality for applause entice him into participating in the tragic ending of the play. She distrusts inflexible male idealism which she believes will certainly lead to tragedy for everyone, and she has a better idea. She will set up her father (his throne reduced to a wheelchair) in a summerhouse in a Highland retreat, a sort of one-man heritage theme park, while she caters for the tourists – a practical young woman's interpretation of Shakespeare's vision of the reunited pair in prison, taking on themselves 'the mystery of things'.

Hannah Macnair, a bank clerk from Falkirk and practising member of the Church of Scotland, finds herself appalled at the behaviour of the characters in the production of *Hamlet* which she has just seen, in which 'everyone was showing off. Jumping about and carrying on!' She is particularly incensed about the characterisation of Ophelia, 'a simple, perhaps rather stupid girl, I suppose, poor thing,' who is positively dangerous as a role model not just for Hannah's sister's Sunday School class but for all the young women of Scotland who cannot afford to behave with such histrionic self-indulgence. 'Cordelia' and Hannah are young, strong, pragmatic and eminently capable of debunking the myths that society and literature have spun around 'femaleness'.

Ure's third Shakespearean revision, *Seven Characters out of the Dream*, owes, as its title implies, not a little to Pirandello, and, like much of her work explores the paradoxes of theatrical art, the ambiguities and interconnecting 'realities' of the stage and of life, of 'fiction' and 'fact', of the 'role' and the 'actor'. A group of seven actors who had performed in *A Midsummer Night's Dream* meet for a reunion party wearing their stage costumes. There are, therefore, several layers of performance: the 'real' actors who are playing actors, dressed for other parts, yet for the most part playing themselves – or are they? In fact, they glide in and out of their Shakespearean roles and their 'Urean' ones. The participants can be seen as operating within a 'fact/fiction' spectrum, from Puck, who remains Shakespeare's mischievous spirit, to the girl Lion, who always plays 'herself' and has the clearest conception of the distinction between stage 'truth' and everyday existence. This female Lion is also treble-cast as a stagehand, in the context of the production when she swept the stage, in the context of the party when she prepared the food and in 'real' life when she supports her family in caring for a mentally handicapped brother.[4] Between the two extremes is Oberon who laments, 'It's never my play I'm in', and Helena who has had too many parts to play. 'I didn't know who I was. All I did know was that I was . . . in flux'. Joan Ure's metadrama comments ironically on the predisposition of women to play as cast, recognising both the strengths and the dangers of fluidity.

Marcella Evaristi reassesses from a feminist standpoint the problematic tale of Troilus and Cressida, already revised by Chaucer, Henryson and Shakespeare. Her radio play, 'Troilus and Cressida and Da-Di-Da-Di-Da' questions the nature of sexual fidelity. The play opens with the lovers repeating oft-renewed vows, but the lyricism is spiked by the irony inherent in the intertextual references drawn from such disparate sources as the love 'duets' between Orlando and Rosalind in *As You Like It* and between Annie Oakley and Wild Bill Hickock in *Annie Get Your Gun*:

TROILUS: I've no problem about loving *you* forever and a day.
CRESSIDA: Oh, I need you to. I bank on that and what's more,
Anything-You-Can-Vow-I-Can-Vow-Better. I'll love
you forever and a fortnight, forever and a leap year,
forever and a forever.

Yet by morning Troilus has deserted her for the masculine values of *gloire*, honour in battle. The rest of the play is a juxtaposition of Troilus's love letters, in which his descriptions of his masturbatory love-making become less focused on the memory of Cressida and more on speedy self-gratification and scenes of Cressida's descent into prostitution, after the loss of her baby, her expulsion by Troilus's family and the ultimate sacrifice of her body to her father's seedy career. 'Thus war doth make pornographers of us all.' Evaristi leaves open the question, whose infidelity to what and to whom reduced the pair to prostitute themselves thus?

Arguably Evaristi's finest dramatic work, *The Hat*[5], another play for radio, may be viewed as a feminist pastiche of Wilde's *The Picture of Dorian Gray*, for she probes the relationship between a work of art and its subject, not to investigate the nature of youth and age, virtue and dissipation, but to contrast the ways in which a woman is represented in art and how she seeks to represent herself. The Surrealist collage made by Crispin Barker with his lover, Marianne, as model, depicts a woman in a brilliant hat, resplendent with a dead bird, feathers and jewels. He casts her out for a new model, Katya, and Marianne leaves, wearing a plain fawn cloche hat which Crispin has always despised. Under the tutelage of an Irish sculptor, a master of impermanence who creates statues of wax in summer and of snow in winter, she begins to decorate the plain hat. As she becomes closer to the image of the *Femme Sauvage* depicted in the work of art, so the collage changes to represent a naturalistic picture of a real woman in a plain fawn hat. Crispin, outraged by the mysterious desecration of his masterpiece, destroys the decorative accretions on the cloche and thus restores his picture. Marianne both is and is not the Hat, which speaks with a young male voice. She is both the *Femme Sauvage* and the shy girl in the fawn cloche. She is, in artistic terms, both a surrealistic and a naturalistic figure. She is both 'Dada' and 'Mamma'. The men cannot cope with such duality.

Liz Lochhead, in her dramatic reworking of another *fin-de-siècle* cult novel, Bram Stoker's *Dracula*, likewise seeks to destabilise the male concept of a single femaleness.[6] Jonathan Harker has 'captured' the 'likeness' of his fiancée, Mina, and her sister, Lucy, in a photograph, which is firmly in his possession. It represents two well-brought-up young women, prettily dressed for polite male consumption, yet both girls are re-presented shortly afterwards as vampires, explicit objects of his carnal lust. The victims of Dracula in Stoker's novel have been interpreted by post-Freudian critics as repressed women who, unable to acknowledge the existence of their sexuality, conjure up a fiendish 'other' who forces them into a physical relationship which they simultaneously loathe and enjoy. Submission to this 'alien' force brings weakness and death. Lochhead negates this interpretation by positing an alternative, namely, that Dracula liberated his victims from their sexual and psychological repressions induced by a patriarchal culture and its dominant religion, Christianity. Lochhead accepted the commission to adapt the novel when she read that Dracula could not enter *without invitation*. Both Lucy and Mina desire the intrusion of Dracula for it signals their empowerment, and their liberation from the dominant male culture that reduced them at best to two-dimensional icons and at worst to appetising comestibles.

It is, however, in their various reconfigurations of Scottish myths and legends that women dramatists have proved particularly adept. These are not used nostalgically to conjure up a lost Highland Utopia or a Gaelic never-never land in the manner of some male writers. On the contrary, the mythical world, particularly in Rona Munro's work, is invoked by features of the real landscape and interwoven into the contemporary world to create modern psychological thrillers, imbued with terrifying violence directed against women and, at times, instigated by them.

The 'character' of Helen in *Piper's Cave* is described in the stage directions as 'the place, the landscape', and in her sunbathing pose on the beach, she mirrors the shape of the mountain, Caileag-og.[7] She is passive but produces reactions of fear and pleasure in the 'humans', Alisdair and Jo. The same actress also 'plays' Jo's friend and would-be lover and Alisdair's temptress and victim. Munro identifies the hubristic piper of the legend who sought to conquer the underworld with his playing but who remains forever trapped in the cave with Alisdair, the derelict dropout, likewise a prisoner, fearful of the light outside and the dark inside his self-imposed cell.[8] Jo, on the other hand is linked to the sea, particularly to the seals, imagining herself at times to be a Selky, a seal who has become a woman. Her closing lines may imply a return to sea and/or the assumption of a new state:

> It's dark. Dark and warm. I'm floating, I'm floating in saltwater . . . I am sleek. I am silver. I
> am sleek. I am silver. Raise a whiskered muzzle out of the water, roll in disguised as a ripple,
> sing in a voice that makes you cry as though it reminded you of something you've lost . . .
> sleek and silver. Hanging in the dark, waiting . . . waiting. That's all.

The notion of mythological mutation from sea creature to woman and back again is also explored in Sue Glover's *The Seal Wife*, in which Rona (the name means Island of Seals) takes a human partner, bears his child, but, betrayed by the hunter who told her he loved his seal prey better than his fellow humans, returns to the sea only to die at his hand. If in *Piper's Cave* the sea creature/woman identification signifies the woman's ability to be part of, even to be, an ever mutable landscape, in *The Seal Wife*, Glover, ever preoccupied with the isolation of the 'rare' and the 'special', reiterates her favourite theme of the hounding of the 'strange' by the unexceptional, uncomprehending herd. In *The Straw Chair*, Isabel's fascination with the Hirta legend that human beings were originally born with scales but lost them with the loss of innocence, is associated with her acknowledgement of her own sexuality and her desire to consummate her 'rigidly pious' marriage:[9]

> Would you love me dressed in scales . . . Aneas? Would you hold me closer if we were both
> created new and innocent with scales? Would you slither in the sea, around me, with me?

The various mythical associations of women with the sea superimposes on a socially constructed fixed female identity an image of creative fluidity and dangerous mutability. Munro pursues this further in *The Maiden Stone*.[10] The Stone is a monolith shaped like a woman embedded in a dry-stone dyke and legend has it that the figure was a farmer's wife who, running from the Devil who had tempted her, prayed to God for salvation and was turned to stone. The tale signifies the fate of woman, calcified into eternal stasis by a patriarchal religion, but this reading is undermined by the action of the play in that all the women characters are identified, or identify themselves, with the Stone so that Munro resists a fixed perspective of 'eternal' womanhood while simultaneously recognising a common bond.

There is, in addition, the sense that the 'human' characters reconstruct myths by unconsciously or perhaps subconsciously reaffirming them, in that they role-play mythical characters or cast others in legendary roles thus perpetuating an old story. Deirdre in *Bold Girls*, for example, *is* Marie's husband's illegitimate daughter in terms of the narrative.[11] She is also variously seen by Marie as the ghost of herself as a young bride, her sexually vibrant alter ego, and the daughter she never had. She may also, as her name implies, be the spirit of Ireland debased by the Troubles. Her 'sorrows' lead not to tears for her lost realm but to stealing, wanton vandalism, a fascination with knives and an orgasmic enjoyment of violent scenes:

> DEIRDRE: Brick in your hand, hard in your hand, hit skin and it'll
> burst open and bleed, hit bones and they'll break. You
> can hear them break, hear the snap.
>
> Get a car, fast car, drive it till its wheels burn,
> leave it smoking, expanding, exploding.

In *Piper's Cave*, the description of violence is made all the more powerful by the uncertainty surrounding the identity of victim and attacker. Alisdair talks about the girl he followed from the bus (Jo and/or Helen or neither?), Jo tells of the assault on her by the impotent man who carved a 'J' on her arm, (Alisdair or not?), and describes finding Helen (or was it?) in bed cradling her abuser. The knives which Jo and Alisdair carry are tangible signs of a dangerous scarcely latent gender antagonism. Thus the physical violence and terror inherent in apparently fanciful legends is made explicit in a modern context.

In *Mary Queen of Scots Got Her Head Chopped Off* Liz Lochhead re-examines a myth of a different kind, a culturally constructed myth based on what might be regarded as verifiable facts. She offers the audience not a re-vision of Mary and Elizabeth, the closed historical characters, but of the accretions with which popular culture has surrounded them, crytallised in the final scene in the children's playground in which Catholic Marie is set upon by the 'Proddy' gang of Jock Tamson's bairns reaffirming four centuries of prejudice and mirroring the anarchic circus parade of animals and freaks that opens the play. Identification or empathy with the Queens is constantly challenged by a complex series of role-playing strategies and particularly by the ironic narrative commentary of La Corbie, so that Mary (Marion, Mairn) and Elizabeth (Bessie, Leezie) are exposed as social and theatrical constructs rather than as the romantic heroines of the Thistle and the Rose.[12]

Communities of Women

> The thing about Daddies, all the Daddies, is that they up and leave you, they go out with their friends, they go inside, they die, they leave you . . .
>
> Rona Munro, *Bold Girls*.

In her highly perceptive essay 'Feminine Pleasures and Masculine Indignities: Gender and Community in Scottish Drama',[13] Adrienne Scullion comments on the frequent use by Scottish dramatists of gender-specific communities and goes on to compare the codes and structures of masculine communities (usually work-related), which tend to be hierarchical and exclusive, with communities of women in which 'belonging is assumed and implicit in the simple acknowledgement of sisterhood'. While it is true that women generally do not require any rites of initiation of the neophyte and that a sense of harmony may be created by communal singing or dance, many of those communities represented in the plays being examined are the result not of deliberate choice by women but of the literal or metaphorical 'absence' of men. The dramatists are at pains to show that, however mutually supportive groups of women may be, those who are not present still wield the power and therefore have a disproportionate impact on the women's actions and relations.[14]

The week-long withdrawal of the Hirta women to neighbouring Boreray in *The Straw Chair* gives them liberty from unpaid domestic chores and allows them to talk, to sing and to create their own ballads evolving a new voice, a new female mythology. But on their return the men are eager to assert their marital rights and, Oona jokes, many babies are born nine months later – one week's liberty brings a lifetime's responsibility. In the same play, Rachel, Oona and Isabel bond together in the dance and find mutual sympathy and strength but the future of all three is controlled by the power of the absent male hierarchy.

Sue Glover's *Bondagers* had obvious connotations with both positive 'bonding' and negative 'bondage'.[15] The women are bonded together by shared work experience, shared knowledge of the local environment, shared acquaintances and shared pain and pleasure. Their 'uniform' which they wear to work also 'binds' them together, so that Ellen, bondager turned 'Maister's Lady', is distanced from the others by the restricting corset under her fine dress. So is Rachel, in *her* tattered finery, isolated from the Hirta women whose 'uniform' of rough blue skirts and bare feet, Isabel happily adopts.[16] But the women in *Bondagers* are also in bondage to the men who never appear on stage. While there may appear to be some liberation in their lifestyle in that they are not tied to domestic drudgery and child-rearing, their security is uncertain, their relationship with the 'hind' to whom they are bound and his family is problematic, and, in the face of the disintegration of the old agricultural system, itself male-controlled, their future is grim. In the final words of the play, Liza, the most independent spirit of the group, who vowed to eschew domesticity and housewifely skills, begs older Sara, to teach her to spin – a capitulation to traditional 'female values'. The absent men also exert considerable influence on the women's personal lives, the emigration to Canada of Sara's partner and Tottie's father, and Steenie, Liza's brother, leave the women vulnerable in a social group where they are accorded little value. Kello's 'macho' promiscuity has tragic results for Tottie and disrupts the lives of Liza, Bella and Sara. While, therefore, the physical and psychological withdrawal of men is seen to bond women together almost in self-defence, it rarely results in the creation of a lasting sisterhood.[17]

Sisterhood and Lost Girls

> Don't you think we are sisters? Are we not somewhat alike?
>
> Liz Lochhead, *Blood and Ice*

The representation of relationships between individual women, the exploration of the concept of a real or metaphoric sisterhood, is an issue which engages many of the writers. Joan Ure, in *The Lecturer and the Lady*, writing at a time before 'Women's Lib' became

'Feminism', challenges the preconceptions of the supposedly irreconcilable stereotypes of the 'liberated' woman and the suburban lady, complete with hat and handbag.[18]

The Lady (Susan) visits a distinguished woman lecturer (Jessie) in her hotel bedroom, the morning after the latter's talk to a woman's group – of the Women's Guild rather than of the radical feminist variety. The topic of their conversation is primarily women's freedom of choice. After a frosty beginning, the dialogue between these two apparent opposites accompanied by the sacramental wine (provided by the Lecturer) and the Fuller's Cake (provided by the Lady, to signify that 'she is conventional') evolves to elucidate the individuality of each woman. The initial ironic reference to a spurious kind of sisterhood platitudinously uttered by Jessie as she 'throws on a few clothes' in front of her well-groomed visitor, 'Still, we're all girls together, aren't we?' is problematised as Jessie admits that she personally acts in front of other women 'as if all eyes were alien and likely to be barbed.' The divide between the women of the world and the ladies of suburbia crumbles as each of the characters comes to call the other by her given name. They become Jessie and Susan – rather than the Lecturer and the Lady.

Susan chooses to return to her marriage. Jessie achieves a personal, rather than an ideological or clichéd, bonding with another woman. 'O Susan Fleming, née Cummings. I love you and your like. So help me. So help me.' Yet, there is no complacency in the conclusion. Each woman accepts the consequences of her choice but neither is entirely comfortable with the persona prescribed for her by society's preconceptions. Both remain 'lost girls'.

> JESSIE: Wendy was a lost girl too, except Peter Pan was too quick in convincing her she was there to comfort lost *boys*.
> SUSAN: And who's to comfort the lost boys when Wendy gives the job up?
> JESSIE: They'll remain uncomforted. As Wendy does. As you do.

In *Wedding Belles and Green Grasses* Marcella Evaristi traces the development of three women, Rita, Stephanie and Jo through adolescence to marriage and motherhood. They are bonded into sisterhood by blood and marriage but above all by their Catholic upbringing. Indeed the play may be seen as a case-study of the effects on female sexuality of single-sex Catholic education. Their obstensible role models and mentors, the 'Sisters' of a religious order, are found wanting and are replaced by the Agony Aunts of women's magazines and by the dictates of their peer group who allocate points (or penalties) for achieving (or succumbing to) specific levels of sexual foreplay. Pleasure and guilt in sex are inseparable: relationships are the stuff of romantic fiction. Young Jo, wearing her First Communion dress, not because she is religious but because 'she likes dressing up', roleplays a passionate love scene between the Emperor Napoleon and Josephine. She confuses 'crossing your heart' with making the sign of the cross. In a telling comic moment, the guilt of sex, the fear of pregnancy and the paradoxes of religion are dramatised:

> RITA: D'you remember that girl that got pregnant without having . . . you know . . . properly done it?
> STEPHANIE: Yes, I've got a statue of her over there![19]

Evaristi presents both in this play and in *Eve Set the Balls of Corruption Rolling* an acutely observed and on the whole a positive interpretation of female relationships.[20] Liz Lochhead is more ambivalent although the theme of sisterhood is pervasive throughout her work. There is a plethora of sisters in her plays but they are quite definitely not at all 'alike'. In *Blood and Ice*, Mary, her half-sister Claire and her maid, Elise, present an uneasy representation of similarities and opposites. Lochhead dramatises this through the use of mirror images and particularly of the puppet doll, that Elise made for Mary's son, William, which is Mary on the one side and Elise on the other. This toy made William 'screech and laugh – to see his mama, and how under the skirt, she was but a maid'. Elise makes it clear that the 'rights of women', as preached by Mary Wollstonecraft, certainly do not appear to apply to the servant class. Sisterhood relies on socio-economic factors rather than gender. Mary's later dream shows Elise sewing a lifesize doll, initially identified with Claire but revealed to be Mary herself. Mary, Claire and Elise are alike yet not alike. Lochhead questions the notion of women's experience being universal and destabilises a concept of sisterhood which transcends cultural and social divides.

In *Dracula*, Lochhead changes Stoker's characters, Mina and Lucy, from friends to sisters, the dramatist's fascination with sisterhood being no doubt as strong a motivation for the change as dramaturgical economy. These sisters are, however, as different as 'chalk and cheese' to Jonathan Harker and 'night and day' to Dracula. Mina is the conventional icon of Victorian womanhood: Lucy describes herself as 'crazy Lucy, mad sleepwalking skinny Lucy with her migraines and her over-vivid imagination'. Yet the perfect wife and the neurotic anorexic both seek the empowerment of Dracula. The maid, Florrie, completes the triad of sisters and maid, the prototype of which has been explored in *Blood and Ice*. Like Elise's, Florrie's status as a 'sister' is unstable and depends solely on the whim of Mina, her mistress.

Mary, Queen of Scots, and Queen Elizabeth were cousins in history but Lochhead chooses to represent them as 'sister' queens and dramatises the similarities in their situations as well as the contrast in their choices in coming to terms with their difficulties. Both women are deprived of their mothers in childhood, both are expected to marry for extrinsic political reasons, both favour a suitor who is a subject and each is fascinated by the other. Paradoxically, at the outset the Catholic 'whore' is a virgin and the Virgin Queen has a lover. The choices they face are the same but the decisions they make are quite different although ironically, these lead in each case to personal isolation and to historical idealisation.

Similarities and differences are likewise explored in *Quelques Fleurs* in which two real sisters defy their biological links and reveal a chasm of difference in their political and social responses to late twentieth-century materialistic culture. Verena cannot buy a child and her sister rejects the role of surrogate mother. Neither is capable of giving what the other really wants. In this, as in Lochhead's other plays, sisterhood is shown as being skindeep.[21]

Mothers and Daughters

> The long-suffering are not always kind.
> Joan Ure, 'My Year for Being Rich and Famous is Over'

Of all the relationships between women, that between mother and daughter is potentially both the closest and the most mutually destructive. Joan Ure's representation of this subject which permeates her dramas is comic, poignant and acutely observed. 'Mothers' are seen as revelling in self-sacrifice, self-abasement and self-effacement. The mother of Lion in *Seven Characters* 'saw herself as an instrument. She very nearly didn't see herself at all'. They burden their children with over-anxious attention – 'You know that woman never slept when I could possibly be awake', cries Jane in *Me Jane! You Elfie!* – and are so obsessed by being their daughters' 'handmaiden, best friend and everything else' that they create a 'tight uncomfortable bond'.[22]

Since the 'Urean' mother has negated all sense of personal worth, she exists only in her daughter's need for her and, therefore, her greatest pleasure comes when her child is ill, tired and dispirited. Fiona, in *Take Your Old Rib Back, Then*, admits:

> Lie down on the couch and look defeated and apologise for ever having aspired and Mama is a joy to be with.[23]

The obverse side of self-sacrifice is resentment and envy, and Ure's representation of motherhood includes an indictment of the mothers' jealousy of their adult daughters whom they see as enjoying freedom of choice in a lifestyle denied them. In *I See Myself As This Young Girl*, Zeeri, left to look after her daughter's baby, so envies Dahlia her career that she can only cope with her frustration by self-dramatisation in the role of an unmarried mother burning with an unfulfilled vocation.[24] A mother's envy produces pity in her daughter and destructive envy/pity axis precludes a nurturing bond as Fiona realises in *Take Your Old Rib Back, Then*, 'I pity my mother and that is terrible. I love her and she can't love me for envy'. The only way in which the mother's envy can be assuaged is by taking the daughter's achievements as her own, 'if she's made me. If she can be what she calls proud of me'. Ure, by implication, proffers the same advice as Rona gave in *The Seal Wife* when she is leaving her daughter in Agnes's care: 'Love and let go'.

Marcella Evaristi treats the topic of motherhood comically in *Scotia's Darlings* in which Abigail, uncertain and insecure, has never been able to stop talking to her mother (despite the decease of the latter) whose over-anxious interference she repeats in coping with her snobbish stepdaughter, and attacks it again much more seriously in *Commedia*. Elena's family has assumed that now she is a widow she will conform to the behavioural patterns of a *donnina*, a diminutive form of woman, 'positively shrunk, all in black'. Her elder son, Cesare, knows that his Mamma's place is in the *cucina* and he is enlarging her prison as the play opens. She, however, wants to be more than the construct of her conventional offspring and has a passionate affair with David, a man young enough to be her son. Neither the mother nor the children can escape mutual dependency: she dreams of herself as a whore, they congregate in the family home even in her absence, and follow her to Italy as they cannot imagine that she could be happy without them. Elena comes to realise that she *is* the subject of the song she composed for her children when they were little, 'Tin Mags the Kitchen Witch', who 'looks like Mummy for most of the week' but who can also license anarchy and misrule, until she sets the alarm to turn them into 'good little boys once again'. Ironically her children are equally anxious that *she* returns to being 'a good little mother,' her status as such being necessary not only for their emotional stability but for their social credibility.[25]

Ure and Evaristi investigate motherhood through an examination of the individual psychology of the mother/child bond. Rona Munro's *The Maiden Stone* is a metaphorical treatment. The character of Bidie is in part a kind of earth mother. She has a large, apparently fatherless brood, at times identified with small animals who form a throne for her and drag her in a cart; she has milk to feed Harriet's hungry babies; she 'mothers' the orphan, Mary, and even Harriet herself. She has wisdom but she is also dangerous and unfathomable and she is irrevocably linked to the devilish Nick. Harriet is the 'bad' mother, who abandons her children, forgets their names, exploits their talents, uses them as servants and is haunted by them until she becomes the Stone, for Harriet is an actress, creator of art rather than life.[26] Lochhead also explores the dilemma of woman as artist and as mother in *Blood and Ice*, in which Mary Shelley's 'hideous progeny', her novel and her 'monster' are inextricably linked with her real children and her guilt at their death.

Lesbian Relationships

> JANE: You are like Juno, Elfrida.
> ELFIE: Her measurements were Enormous.
> JANE: No, I mean, loving . . . mothering . . . all the world. Caring, considering, protective, encouraging. Not barren ground, you.
> ELFIE: You're embarrassing me. I don't like to be turned into an earth goddess or even a principle.
>
> Joan Ure, *Me Jane! You Elfie!*

Adrienne Rich in 'Compulsory Heterosexuality and Lesbian Existence' asks why women redirect the search for love and tenderness from the mother, 'the earliest source of emotional caring and physical nurture', to men?[27] One answer that she provides is that of societal pressure, a view which reinforces both Joan Ure's and Rona Munro's exposition of lesbian relationships in twentieth-century Scotland. The Woman in *Scarlet Mood*, who had 'not expected to be a lover of women', confesses that she hungers,

> as much as any man does
> for the nourishing breast
> of the good, the mother, the eternal female.
> The kind, the responsive
> giver of healing and comfort,
> cherisher and suckler of life.

But the 'hunger' of the lesbian is laughed at in this 'barren land', feared both by men and by heterosexual women who know nothing of it, 'except in literature, where nothing is *fact*'.[28]

The connection between lesbianism and essentialism is further developed in *Piper's Cave* and *Your Turn to Clean the Stair*. In the first play, Jo makes sexual overtures to her friend, the 'real' Helen, who responds ambivalently, but the former finds peace and satisfaction in her assumption into the metaphorical Helen, the landscape and the environment. Kay in *Your Turn to Clean the Stair* is, like Joan Ure's Elfie, given a procreative role in that she is a single mother, and her room, full of plants, is referred to as a garden, an appropriate environment for the nurturing female. As opposed to the alcohol and junk food consumed by other members of the tenement, Kay offers wholesome soup and bread. She provides temporary succour for Lisa who is afraid of the violence associated with her relationships with her husband and the macho Bobby. But Lisa sees Kay too as a sexual voyeur and rejects further overtures. Kay is left alone and lonely whereas Lisa, in resisting external construction, by both sexes, emerges as a positive strong force, but, as in Joan Ure's plays, lesbianism is perhaps too closely identified with 'motherliness' and essentialism.[29]

A more sensitive and subtle representation of the Scottish lesbian is presented by Munro's monologue, *Saturday Night at the Commodore*. The speaker, Lena, is inhibited from developing her friendship with Nora into sexual union because of the cruelty in young female peer group pressure. If she wants to stay one of the gang, she can't be a 'lezzie', but she is, although even as she speaks as a mature adult, she has not quite recognised the fact. The audience is made aware of her love for her friend through her fond descriptions of Nora's 'wee twisted grin' and her envy of Nora's vibrancy and happiness with her female partner, a contrast to Lena's own solitary existence as a schoolteacher finding companionship only in a night out with the 'girls', when they can leave their husbands and children.[30]

National Identity, Gender, and Art

> Dickless in Scotlen-s-no joke.
> Marcella Evaristi, *Terrestrial Extras*

In addressing the issue of national identity, the women dramatists set their work in a wide range of geographical areas within Scotland and critique a variety of social and cultural backgrounds. They do not portray Scottish society as homogeneous, nor do they, as many of their male colleagues do, suffer from 'the Slab Boys Syndrome', as Joyce McMillan succinctly called the tendency to focus on urban, working-class life, usually in the West of Scotland.[31]

While Ena Lamont Stewart's *Men Should Weep* (originally entitled *Poor Men's Riches*) which was commissioned by Glasgow Unity to give a woman's view of the social conditions depicted in its highly successful production, *The Gorbals Story*, and Aileen Ritchie's plays for Clyde Unity, an ideological offspring of the above company, have working-class or lower-class settings, other women writers cover a wide spectrum of locations and socio-economic groups.[32] Ure, when she is writing naturalistically, which is rare, focuses largely on fringe intellectuals and left-wing bohemians. Marcella Evaristi's middleclass Italian background, which includes a Jewish strain, allows her to comment with inside knowledge on the inward tensions that exist for those with dual nationality and culture, comically summed up by Stefano in the description of an Italian Hogmanay in *Commedia*:

> You get stuffed full of pasta and pollo alla cacciatore and wine, and then we all remember just in time and manage to down a finger of whisky before the bells.

The problem is also more seriously voiced by him: 'I feel like a refugee from a country that never existed'.

Her background as a partial outsider also allows her to critique the pretentions and follies of both Glasgow suburbia and Edinburgh's New Town. Rona Munro and Sue Glover often choose predominantly rural agricultural or fishing communities, the former being particularly inspired by her native north-east, while the latter favours lonely places, often islands where she can best explore her recurrent themes of isolation and social exile.

Despite the variety of backgrounds and settings, however, the women's plays consistently explore the relationship between national identity and culturally constructed codes of gender in which men and women are polarised into opposites and are arbitrarily allocated predetermined roles which inhibit fruitful relationships.

In Ure's *Scarlet Mood*, the Woman laments:

> No true woman of Scotland
> but she who suffers in love.
> For a true man of her land
> is separate, moral and hates all women
> for good religious reasons.

while the Man asks:

> Is it the oatmeal I take at my breakfast
> or the whisky on Saturday night, eh,
> that gars me grue at the wimmen
> as if the shape o' them would bite me?

He goes 'to the continang' for sexual fulfilment. He 'can't love a woman at home'. The Woman, summing up this section of the piece, asks (and answers):

> How do I love thee, my man, or my country?
> I love thee against my will.

'Maleness' is generally defined as being emotionally inhibited, physically powerful and preoccupied with the public world of work, preferably in dangerous occupations, rather than having interest in the personal or creative spheres.[33] Women collude in the perpetuation of the myth of 'the hard man' according to both Catherine Lucy Czerkawska and Rona Munro. In *O Flower of Scotland*, the former writer expresses the view. 'The whole bloody country idolises them. And mothers too. They're the worst. They encourage it'.[34] In the context of Northern Irish society (same difference in this respect!) Rona Munro gives Bold Girl Cassie a monologue expounding how gender divisions are handed down from one generation to the next.

> CASSIE: My Mummy taught me how to raise my family. How to love them, how to spoil them. Spoil the wee girls with housework and reproaches, the length of their skirts and the colour of their lips: how they sit, how they slouch, how they don't give their fathers peace, how they talk, how they talk back, how they'll come to no good if they carry on like that. They're bold and bad and broken at fourteen but you love them as you love yourself . . . that's why you hurt them so much.
>
> Ruin the boys, tell them they're noisy and big and bold and their boots are too muddy ('Clear that mess up for me Cassie.') Tell them to leave their fathers in peace and come to their Mummy for a cuddle, tell them they'll always be your own wee man, always your own bold wee man and you love them better than you love their Daddy, you love them best of all . . . that's why they hurt you so much.

It is in order to negotiate what she calls 'this macho culture' that Liz Lochhead wants to stay in Scotland to develop further the exposé of those 'isolating wares of Scottish nationhood: the drunk man, haggis, tartan, poverty, chauvinism'[35] that were introduced in *Mary Queen of Scots* and *Jock Tamson's Bairns*.

A common theme in the dramas is how women seek to re-present themselves and re-negotiate their societally determined roles. The women in Ena Lamont Stewart's *Men Should Weep* are not only the victims of bad housing, an inadequate diet and poor healthcare but also of the men who are shown to be brutalised, morally defeated or spirtually undermined by unemployment, signifying the loss of their predetermined 'identity'. Each of the major female characters is seen to change herself to survive the deprivation she suffers in her environment. These changes are not always positive. Pleasure-seeking Isa degenerates into drunkenness and infidelity; Jenny with social aspirations follows in the footsteps of Shaw's Kitty Warren and becomes a successful prostitute; most significantly, Maggie changes from devoted obedient wife to independent woman. In the closing scene, when the prodigal daughter, Jenny, returns with money to rehouse the family, John casts her 'whore's winnins' back in his daughter's face, an action which finally crystallises Maggie's growing self-realisation. Maggie points out that she herself has been John's 'whore' for years with much less remuneration:

> Aye, I wis your whore. An I'd nae winnins that I can mind o'. But mebbe, it's a' right to be a whore if ye've nae winnins. Is that the way it goes John?

To save herself and her family, she is forced to recognise and to represent herself as on a par with her prodigal daughter, finally ceasing to pay lip service to the false 'ideal' of her husband as breadwinner and master. 'I can manage him', she assures Jenny, 'I can aye manage him'.[36]

Other women characters who succeed in overthrowing a culturally conditioned role in the playing of which they have to an extent colluded, are Margie in Sue Glover's Home Front,[37] who finally refuses to be 'a gingerbread wife' in the domestic idyll she concocted in her letters, and Jess and Anna in Evaristi's Hard to Get.[38] Set in the immediate post-Women's Lib era of the mid 1970s, Hard to Get critiques the repercussions of the movement on the personal lives of two couples, each of whom pays lip service to its importance, but the men are as emotionally unconvinced as the women are destabilised, floundering between their old roles and their new. For Jonathan, a 'liberated' woman is a woman liberated to be a more amenable sexual partner. Luke assures Jess that she has become 'a woman' now that she has had sex with him, that he has, godlike, transformed her into a new being, that she, for a time, takes as her true 'self'. Only when each character negotiates his/her own self-representation can their relationships develop. A neat summing up occurs in Jonathan's patronising question to Anna, and her wise reply:

> JONATHAN: What on earth are you going to be when you grow up?
> ANNA: I don't know but I've a feeling I might have to invent it.

This culturally determined schism of gender is shown to have devastating results not only on individual relationships but also on the art of the country. It was Sherry Ortner who asked the question, 'Is Female to Male as Nature is to Culture?' suggesting that 'woman is being identified with – or, if you will, seems to be a symbol of – [Nature] something that every culture devalues, something that every culture defines as being of a lower order of existence than itself'.[39] Joan Ure equates 'culture' with 'fact', and 'nature' with 'fiction', expounding the thesis that in Scotland 'fiction'/'nature'/'woman' is relegated to the second division in the national league table. The breeding of sexual antagonism thus denies the nurturing co-existence of art and life creating the discord expressed in Scarlet Mood:

> A country makes the artists it deserves
> as it makes governments
> Our artists shriek in paranoic discords
> when they are not just havering.
> You hope they do not feel they speak for you.

She rails against the Scottish *Zeitgeist* which she finds symbolised on whisky bottles, tea cosies for Americans and The Military Tattoo yearly at the Festival and by the Scottish Soldier, who is for her 'an ambiguous image visually', being both 'male' in terms of his toughness, physical bravery and aggression and 'female' in his 'decorativeness', colourful skirt, velvet and lace and in the sentimental songs that he sings. But as a patron of the arts, she finds the Scottish male unpredictable, uncomprehending, more at home with 'fact' than 'fiction'.[40]

In Lochhead's *Mary Queen of Scots* John Knox is convinced that he is in full possession of the 'facts' –'God speaks plainly in his word' – and will admit no ambiguity of interpretation. La Corbie's speech explicates his denunciation of the Roman Catholic Church, of women as mothers and rulers and, by the nature of its rhetoric, of poetry and art:

> LA CORBIE: Knox has torn the Mother of God from oot the sky o' Scotland and has trampit
>   her celestial blue goon amang the muck and mire and has blotted oot every name
>   by which ye praise her – Stella Maris, Star of the Sea, Holy Mother, Notre Dame,
>   Oor Lady O' Perpetual Succour.

Joan Ure's twentieth-century theatrical equivalent of John Knox is 'Paisley Adams', the careful accountant who 'will do nothing that has not been guaranteed successful Somewhere Else'. The artificial polarisation of male, cerebral, 'culture' and female, creative, 'nature' is challenged by Scottish women dramatists in that the divide both inhibits productive gender relations and healthy artistic achievement.

Dramatic Language

> 'I am no longer afraid of this, my language'.
>
>   Joan Ure, *Scarlet Mood*

A multiplicity of social settings and geographical locations leads to considerable versatility in dramatic language, including the use of contemporary and historical Scots. Rarely does Joan Ure write in Scots and when she does it is for the purposes of ironic comment. 'The Scottishness [of my characters is] in their psychology and should show up in performance' (*A Play for Mac*). More recent dramatists, such as Lochhead, Glover and Munro have made both traditional Scots and the contemporary vernacular work well for them, for example, in Lochhead's translation of *Tartuffe* and, above all, the robust mixture of the prosaic and the poetic in *Mary Queen of Scots*.[41] In *The Straw Chair*, Sue Glover's creation of three distinct communities on Hirta is aided by the use of Gaelic by the islanders, Scots by Isabel and her husband, and Rachel's anglified more aristocratic register. The language of *Bondagers*, the result of thorough research, according to the writer emerged almost unconsciously: 'I didn't mean to write it in Scots at all. But the words just came. It certainly isn't authentic Scots like say Hector MacMillan.'[42]

Rona Munro's period play *The Maiden Stone* is also written in a language not historical but living but unlike Glover, she does have a conscious theoretical agenda, concerned to 'assert her place . . . in a distinctive Scottish culture and to explore the possibilities of writing in Scots as well as in English'.[43] All the dramatists quoted above, and indeed Evaristi and Czerkawska, eschew what Catherine Lockerbie called 'the debilitating Glasgow dominance', a rejection concomitant with their rejection of an urban male-dominated working-class ethos.[44]

A distinctive feature of the women writers is their success in bringing poetry into the theatre. Their language is replete with polyvalent imagery, intertextual reference and an almost physical celebration of the sound of words. While, of course, each dramatist has her own clutch of favourite images that recur throughout her work, one that permeates the women's writing in general is food.[45]

Rona Munro's article in *Theatre Scotland* was jokingly entitled 'Sex and Food' but her flippancy has a serious edge.[46] Women are preoccupied with food – they buy it, prepare it, cook it, serve it, eat it, every day of their lives. The kitchen is the hub of female activity, communion and drudgery. It is woman's sphere and her prison, a duality recognised by Elena, alias 'Tin Mags, the Kitchen Witch' in Evaristi's *Commedia*. The action in *Hard to Get* centres round a series of dinner parties, with Jess, a very bad cook, as hostess. Moving from her fear of eating artichokes, via putting a kebab skewer through her husband's hand, Jess learns that food need not be a social challenge, but something to be shared with friends.

Food dominates and polarises the characters in Munro's *Your Turn to Clean the Stair*. Lisa's pitiful attempts at upward social mobility come to grief when her planned meal of chilli con carne and avocadoes clashes with Brian's mundane desire for an omelette or egg and chips. Mrs Mackie has degenerated from doing her own baking to offering stale Garibaldi biscuits to her guests, while she feeds on seedless raspberry jam and 'lean cuisine' ready-made meals. In *Bold Girls*, the food, like the society, is debased by the Troubles: children indulge in crisps and raspberry ice-cream syrup, the absent men gorge themselves on pies, hamburgers and beer, while Cassie, on a diet, has half a grapefruit by day so that she can celebrate with six gins at the Club. Mothers use food to woo their sons while their daughters are, literally and metaphorically, 'chewed, swallowed and eaten alive by all that [they're] wanting and can't have'. Lochhead also uses the imagery of food and appetite to brilliant effect in *Dracula*, when the polite lunch party at Heartwood is held up for comparison with the meals of flies and sparrows enjoyed by the zoophagous Renfield and, equally tellingly, with Dracula's desire for human blood. Cold chicken is served. Jonathan, who has been fondling Mina's bosom, is offered 'a breast or a leg'. He chooses both. 'Saucy' Florrie flirts with him and he praises the 'sauce'. Lucy refuses the dead cold meat, linking herself unconsciously with Renfrew (and Dracula):

> Something inanimate
> Something on a plate
> Is something I hate
> . . .
> Now something blood heat . . . that's what I call sweet.

Hunger, the obverse image, dominates Rona Munro's *Fugue*. The real hunger of a healthy appetite is juxtaposed with Kay 1's hunger for physical, sexual and emotional fulfilment:

> Every bit of me, every cell of me's hungry – my mouth to be filled, my eyes to laugh or cry, all my skin itches to be touched, to move, to stretch . . . and nothing will ever be *enough*.[47]

The sun, that 'licks your flesh like a hot tongue', is likewise contrasted with the hungry licking Ghost Girl, 'the fear of violence and death' that haunts the Kays.[48]

Theatrical Language

'It is not possible to have a poem made out of theatre?'

[Joan Ure]

The use of imagistic language is merely one strand in a theatrical texture that for many of the women writers also includes the use of song, choral speaking, dance and movement. Joan Ure, for example, uses a variety of dramaturgical techniques which have subsequently become regular features in contemporary post-modern performance pieces. *Scarlet Mood* incorporates poetic monologues, stand-up comic routines, a long centrepiece narrative in prose, songs, dance and movement. Dance is the vehicle for the realisation of the theme in *Punctuated Rhythms*, inspired by the techniques of improvised jazz.[49] Dance is used by Sue Glover to signify 'harmony' in the medieval sense, albeit in her plays the cosmic reconciliations are more temporary than eternal. She also use folksongs to good theatrical effect, e.g. the recurrent chorus of 'The Carles O' Dysart' in *An Island in Largo*, signifying Selkirk's ambivalent attitude to his native land. Her device of opening a play either with a song (as in *Home Front*) or with informal choral speaking (as in *Bondagers*) at once establishes the 'atmosphere' she seeks to create, an encapsulation of the theme or ethos of the play, and provides a frame in which to set the ensuing dramatic action.

Glover, Munro and Ure use the playing space not only to indicate specific locations or naturalistic settings but symbolically to define spheres of psychological or metaphysical 'influence'. Joan Ure and Liz Lochhead in particular highlight the process of representation itself by consistently employing alienation devices that underline the theatricality rather than the mimetic realism of the drama. Characters comment to the audience on the way the production is progressing and on the dialogue provided by the dramatist, the supreme example being La Corbie's astringent interventions in *Mary Queen of Scots*.[50]

Conclusion

All the plays which have been discussed were written to be performed. The scripts are merely 'pre-texts' for the performance texts, each one of which will vary from one production to another. The dramatist, unlike the poet, the novelist or the painter, cannot see the full realisation of her work without a host of other artists or interpreters. The survival of these dramas is in part the result of the playwright's collaboration with theatre companies that were prepared to provide a supportive creative environment and take the financial risks necessary to promote new work. Glasgow Unity encouraged Ena Lamont Stewart, Glasgow University Arts Theatre Group promoted the surrealistic dramas of Joan Ure and the more recent writers have had benefit of working with Communicado, the Traverse, the Tron and the Royal Lyceum. The reason for a comparatively high number of successful radio plays by women is a direct result of the enlightened policy of three Radio Scotland drama producers in the 1970s and '80s, Stewart Conn, Gordon Emslie and Marilyn Ireland.

In the last few years a number of young companies have sprung up, many initiated by women, such as Stellar Quines, Diva and Chimera, which have as their primary aim the performance of women's work. Others such as Lookout, Factional Theatre and Crush were founded by women writers or devisers of performance art. These may prove to be ephemeral but the work that is being produced at present is innovative both in its subject matter and in its dramaturgy. The future for women's writing is brighter than it has been at any time for the past fifty years.

Notes

1. Ena Lamont Stewart, *Business in Edinburgh* (Scottish Society of Playwrights, Glasgow, 1977); Sue Glover, *The Straw Chair* (1980), unpublished, Traverse Theatre Collection, National Library of Scotland.
2. Liz Lochhead, *Blood and Ice*, in Michelene Wandor (ed.), *Plays by Women*, vol. 4 (Methuen, London, 1985). For further discussion of revisioning in Lochhead's plays, see Jan McDonald and Jennifer Harvie, 'Putting New Twists to Old Stories: Feminism and Lochhead's Drama', in Robert Crawford and Anne Varty (eds), *Liz Lochhead's Voices* (Edinburgh University Press, Edinburgh, 1994), pp. 124–47.
3. Joan Ure, *Five Short Plays: Something in It for Cordelia, Something in It for Ophelia, Seven Characters Out of the Dream, The Hard Case, Take Your Old Rib Back, Then* (Scottish Society of Playwrights, Glasgow, 1979).
4. This play is a particularly apt choice for such a revision as Shakespeare's text itself presents a series of 'play-within-play' scenarios.
5. Marcella Evaristi, *Troilus and Cressida and Da-Di-Da-Di-Da*, unpublished; *The Hat* (1988), unpublished; quotations from author's copies.
6. Liz Lochhead, '*Mary Queen of Scots Got Her Head Chopped Off*', and '*Dracula*' (Penguin, Harmondsworth, 1989). For a fuller discussion of Lochhead's adaptation see Jan McDonald, '*Dracula*: Freudian Novel to Feminist Drama', in Peter Reynolds (ed.), *Novel Images* (Routledge, London, 1993), pp. 80–104; and Jennifer Harvie, 'Desire and Difference in Liz Lochhead's *Dracula*', *Essays in Theatre/Études Théatrales* 11.2 (May 1993), 133–43.
7. Rona Munro, *Piper's Cave*, in Michelene Wandor and Mary Remnant (eds), *Plays by Women: Five* (Methuen, London, 1985).
8. There are many variations of this common legend of a human being trapped in the 'fairy world' and Rona Munro also evokes the story in *Fugue*.
9. Sue Glover, *The Seal Wife* (1980), unpublished, Scottish Theatre Archive, Special Collections, Glasgow University Library.
10. Rona Munro, *The Maiden Stone* (Nick Hern Books, London, 1995).
11. Rona Munro, *Bold Girls* (Samuel French, London, 1991; Hodder & Stoughton, London, 1995). For a recent discussion of *Bold Girls* see Douglas Gifford, 'Making them Bold and Breaking the Mould: Rona Munro's *Bold Girls*', *Laverock* 2 (1996)
12. For further discussion of self, nation and feminism see Colin Nicholson, 'Liz Lochhead: The Knucklebones of Irony', in Colin Nicholson (ed.), *Poem, Purpose and Place: Shaping Identity in Contemporary Scottish Verse* (Polygon, Edinburgh, 1992), pp. 203–23 and Ilona S. Koren-Deutsch, 'Feminist Nationalism in Scotland: *Mary Queen of Scots Got Her Head Chopped Off*', *Modern Drama* 35 (1992), 424–32.
13. Adrienne Scullion, 'Feminine Pleasures and Masculine Indignities: Gender and Community in Scottish Drama', in Christopher Whyte (ed.), *Gendering the Nation* (Edinburgh University Press, Edinburgh, 1995), pp. 169–203.
14. This view is also taken by Nina Auerbach, *Communities of Women: An Idea in Fiction* (Harvard University Press, Harvard, 1979), p. 3: 'A Community of women may suggest less the honor of fellowship than an anti-society, an austere banishment from both social power and biological rewards.'
15. Sue Glover, Bondagers, in *Theatre Scotland* 2.6 (Summer 1993).
16. The nurses' uniforms in Ena Lamont Stewart's *Starched Aprons* (1945), unpublished, (STA, Ar box 10/4) might be expected to fulfil a similar bonding function, but in fact the play rarely rises above a Mills & Boon 'Doctor/Nurse romance'.
17. Female friendships may, however, provide a temporary respite, for example that between Sarah, Mrs Pillans, and Biddy in *Business in Edinburgh*; Liz and Sharon in Munro's

The Way to Go Home (1987), unpublished (author's copy); and Maggie, Cassie and Nora in *Bold Girls*. See also Scullion's comments in *Gendering the Nation*, p. 173, on how Lamont Stewart demystifies female tenement solidarity in *Men Should Weep*.

18.   Joan Ure, *The Lecturer and the Lady*, unpublished (STA, Jg box 2/11).
19.   Marcella Evaristi, *Wedding Belles and Green Grasses* (1981), unpublished (STA, Hn box 9/6).
20.   Evaristi, *Eve Set the Balls of Corruption Rolling*, unpublished (author's copy).
21.   Liz Lochhead, *Quelques Fleurs*, unpublished; Verena's monologues, however, are presented as 'A Tale of Two Sisters' in *Bagpipe Muzak* (Penguin, Harmondsworth, 1991).
22.   Joan Ure, *Me Jane! You Elfie*, unpublished (author's copy).
23.   This desire to have a sick child so that one can fulfil a spurious maternal instinct by nursing it, known as the 'Munchhausen-by-Proxy Syndrome', is articulated by Martin in *Something in It for Ophelia*:

> What love means to mothers like mine is that you lie quite still in your bed while she turns down the clean sheets and sends for the doctor and serves you meals on a tray. Love to mothers like mine means you never do anything brave or anything generous or anything great because then she wouldn't know what to expect.

24.   Joan Ure, *I See Myself As This Young Girl* (1969), unpublished (STA, Jg box 2/10).
25.   Marcella Evaristi, *Scotia's Darlings* (1978), unpublished (STA, Hn box 9/3); *Commedia* (Salamander Press, Edinburgh, 1983).
26.   The character of Harriet is based on the actress, Charlotte Deans, who toured extensively in the north of England and in Scotland in the late eighteenth and early nineteenth centuries. See Charlotte Deans, *Charlotte Deans 1768–1839: A Travelling Actress in the North and Scotland*, first published 1937 with a commentary on the story of a Travelling Player by *Frances S. Marshall* (Titus Wilson, Kendal, 1984).
27.   Adrienne Rich, 'Compulsory Heterosexuality and Lesbian Existence', in Maggie Humm (ed), *Feminisms: A Reader* (Harvester Wheatsheaf, Manchester, 1992), p. 176.
28.   Joan Ure, *Scarlet Mood*, unpublished (author's copy).
29.   Rona Munro, *Your Turn to Clean the Stair* (Nick Hern Books, London, 1995).
30.   Rona Munro, *Saturday Night at the Commodore*, in Alasdair Cameron (ed.), *Scot Free* (Nick Hern Books, London, 1990).
31.   Joyce McMillan, 'Women Playwrights in Contemporary Scottish Theatre', *Chapman* 43–4 (Spring 1986), 69–75.
32.   Ena Lamont Stewart, *Men Should Weep* (Scottish Society of Playwrights, Glasgow, 1982).
33.   Alisdair in *Piper's Cave*, for example, seeks to establish his masculine credibility by citing the macho occupations in which he has supposedly been engaged: these include paratrooper, soldier, submariner, trawlerman, lorry driver, slaughterhouse employee and oil rig worker. Both Sue Glover in *Waiting Rooms* and Liz Lochhead in *Quelques Fleurs* use the oil rig worker as an emblem of roughneck maleness.
34.   Catherine Lucy Czerkawska, *O Flower of Scotland*, unpublished (author's copy).
35.   *Liz Lochhead's Voices*, p. 32 and p. 164.
36.   For an interesting new reading of *Men Should Weep* as reinventing the myth of the mother as Madonna in urban melodrama, see Scullion, in *Gendering the Nation*, pp. 171–3.
37.   Sue Glover, *Home Front* (1982), unpublished (STA, Hv box 5/7).
38.   Marcella Evaristi, *Hard to Get* (1980), unpublished (STA, Hn box 9/2–3).
39.   Sherry Ortner, 'Is Female to Male as Nature is to Culture', in Humm, *Feminisms: A Reader*, p. 253.
40.   Joan Ure, unpublished lecture, Personal Papers (Scottish Theatre Archive).
41.   Liz Lochhead, *Tartuffe: A Translation into Scots from the Original by Molière* (Third Eye Centre and Polygon, Glasgow and Edinburgh, 1986).
42.   Sue Glover interviewed by Catherine Lockerbie, *Theatre Scotland* 2.6 (Summer 1993), 31.
43.   Quoted in Lizbeth Goodman, 'Rona Munro', in Goodman (ed.), *Contemporary Women Dramatists* (St James's Press, London, 1994). This volume also contains essays on Marcella Evaristi by Ned Chaillet, pp. 78–81, and Liz Lochhead by Adrienne Scullion, pp. 147–51.

44.   Sue Glover interviewed by Catherine Lockerbie. See note 42.
45.   Personal systems of significant imagery include Joan Ure's use of theatrical metaphor, Lochhead's pervasive use of mirrors, flowers and blood, Sue Glover's islands and Rona Munro's ghosts and spirits.
46.   Rona Munro, 'Sex and Food', *Theatre Scotland* 1.3 (Autumn 1992), 15–21.
47.   Rona Munro, *Fugue*, in *Your Turn to Clean the Stair*.
48.   For useful comments on specifically female discourse in Scottish drama see Susan C. Triesman, 'Transformations and Transgressions: Women's Discourse on the Scottish Stage', in Trevor Griffiths and Margaret Llewellyn-Jones (eds), *British and Irish Women Dramatists since 1958: A Critical Handbook* (Open University Press, Buckingham and Philadelphia, 1993), pp. 124–34.
49.   Joan Ure, *Punctuated Rhythms* (1962), unpublished (STA, Jg box 3/6).
50.   Jennifer Harvie gives a detailed account of Lochhead's use of metatextuality in *Liz Lochhead's Voices*, pp. 135–46.

35

The Remarkable Fictions of Muriel Spark

Gerard Carruthers

In her most fantastic piece of fiction 'The Playhouse Called Remarkable', Muriel Spark offers a definition of art.[1] The story recounts the genesis of artistic sensibility on Earth shortly after the Flood when Moon Biglow and five companions arrive from the Moon and establish a theatre to present 'The Changing Drama of the Moon'. This is a performance which varies its words and music but always narrates the true adventures of a singing, acrobatic Moongirl who sets out to investigate the mysterious singing voice on a Moonmountain. The girl is trapped by the voice which spins her around throughout the night and mocks her in song while she responds with a defiant contrapuntal harmony. During the day, however, the girl is totally incapacitated as a ray from the Sun strikes the mountain and stabs her through the throat. Through the repetition of the daily cycle, she learns that the voice's inspiration is the Sunray and she communicates this knowledge, in song, to the Moonpeople at the foot of the mountain instructing them to take her story, as a drama, to the inhabitants of Earth. The ensuing 'art mission' of Moon Biglow and his colleagues locates itself in Hampstead and is at first a huge success, the Moonmen's theatre being hailed by the natives as 'The Remarkable'. Opposition comes, however, from local cultural leader Johnnie Heath who claims that the visitors are interfering with the 'native purity' of Hampstead and that the playhouse cannot be registered with the council as 'known as the Remarkable' since 'remarkable' is an adjective and not a noun. Through Johnnie's harassment, the people gradually return to the indigenous 'tum tum ya' chant and one night, in the stupor of this mantra, they sacrifice Moon's girlfriend Dolores. Disheartened, the missionaries, with the exception of Moon, leave Earth. A legacy is left behind however, as Moon explains:

> The absence of the Changing Drama of the Moon began to be felt. The sense of loss led to a tremendous movement of the human spirit. The race of the artist appeared on earth . . . whenever the tum tum ya movement gets afoot, and the monotony and horror start taking hold of people, the artists rise up and proclaim the virtue of the remarkable things that are missing from the earth.[2]

Despite its playful surrealism, 'The Playhouse Called Remarkable' presents the process of fiction in a way which has resonances throughout Muriel Spark's work. It paints art as an instrument bringing a special kind of truth which counters the mundanity and incompleteness of everyday existence. This is seen at a profound level in the tableau of 'The Changing Drama of the Moon' with its echoes of classical tragedy, opera, and ballet, as well as its overall function as allegorical narrative. The allegory, however, has no easy key. This is a deliberate ploy. Spark's intention is to emphasise the surface texture of the tale, its pure fictional means or its heavy and deliberate artistry found in its sweep of generic references, and this effect is compounded as Moon asserts the entire veracity of the Moongirl's adventures. Both implicitly and explicitly, then, there is an insistence on the significance of a story whose provenance is pointedly fictitious and through this on fiction or art as having its own autonomous or necessary reality. This magic or romantic formalism is urged again in the Earth-based part of the story, by the deviant elision of adjective into noun in the usage of 'remarkable', an elision to which Johnnie Heath (the unimaginative essence of Hampstead, as his name implies) objects, and which Moon invests with visionary significance as he eulogises 'the remarkable things that are missing from the earth'.

If 'The Playhouse Called Remarkable' shows the 'remarkable' process of art, or the imagination, changing the world in an ideal representation, Spark's fiction generally, both thematically and formally, is, however, much more ambiguous about this 'transfiguration of the commonplace'. Remarkable qualification of mundane reality is registered in her work in several ways which show a much less certain usage than in her short story. It is indicated in a frame of reference where the human world is set against the existence of God. It is also found in the ostentatious creation of fictions both by Spark herself and by her characters. In the case of Spark this involves stylistic and fabulistic flamboyance which frequently extends to intruding highly artificial or fictive devices into her settings and in the case of many of her characters to hatching elaborately selfish plots which exploit moral ambiguities. In Spark's oeuvre, however, it is not only the designs of her nefarious characters which are duplicitous; even the operations of God and the novelist herself sometimes appear in a sinister light. The net result in Muriel Spark's work is an epistemological complexity where textual mechanics and thematics collude and collide and where creative schemes become highly problematic. It is these characteristics above all which have made Spark one of the most enigmatic and compelling of twentieth-century novelists.[3]

Muriel Spark's career represents a long attempt to fuse her belief in artistic truth and her religious apprehension. She became a convert to Roman Catholicism in her thirties, arriving via membership of the Church of England and after an upbringing in Presbyterian Edinburgh where she was born in 1918 into a half-Jewish family.[4] Her Catholicism, Spark has often claimed, provided her with a system which enabled her to become a novelist, but it must be stressed that she explores doubts and tensions within her faith as much as she affirms it.[5] This is true of what is often taken to be her most 'Catholic' first phase as a novelist which lasts from her first novel *The Comforters* (1957) to *The Mandelbaum Gate* (1965). Within this period all her novels have to be read with regard to an explicitly invoked Catholic framework but, at the same time, there is within the sequence, especially as Spark reviews her own biography, a growing sensitivity to the complexity of the social and cultural particulars which impinge upon human existence.

The Comforters is a particularly ambiguous and confusing start to Spark's career as an anagogic novelist.[6] Religious uncertainty is explicitly registered by the central character Caroline Rose, a half-Jewish convert to Catholicism, as she attempts to square the notion of freewill with the concept of an omniscient God. In addition to struggling with this paradox, Caroline also has to negotiate with her co-religionist Georgina Hogg who exploits her faith to magnify her own importance and to interfere in the lives of others. In complex combination, the novel collides these theological and moral interests with an intrusive parodic fictiveness. Georgina's immorality (her lack of moral substance) is signalled by her disappearance, both in private and also in front of the eyes of several other characters. Conversely, Caroline, in her speculative and moral honesty, is rewarded by the apprehension of herself as a fictional character as she hears her thoughts being typed out moments after they have occurred. This striking metaphorical technique, however, sits awkwardly with the fact that considerable space is taken up in convincing the reader that Georgina is nasty and that Caroline is essentially good. It may suit the purposes of the agnostic writer of the *nouveau roman* to undercut moral realism with the exposure of the artifice of the text; but Spark is no agnostic and in utilising the analogy between God and the author rather might have been expected to be seeking corroboration of a valid moral scenario, and to be representing the perspective of a real God in whom she believes. Instead of corroboration, however, the result is an unsettling reading experience where the reader's co-operation in going along with the moral message of the novel is jolted by the sharp reminder that these characters are not real. This causes not only their deconstruction but the deconstruction of the Christian God who supposedly presides over their moral status. Spark herself is aware of the difficulty of her mode, keeping open the option that Caroline is inventing everything, and eventually has her decide to write a novel about 'characters in a novel', (p. 231), so confirming the indeterminacy of reality and the unreal in *The Comforters*.

In *The Comforters* the fictional process is remarkable in an extreme way. Any theological exposition it carries is untrustworthy, and indeed, at times, events in the novel seem to be under demonic control. Many of Spark's subsequent novels have this rather demonic perspective but manage more coherently to combine theme and form. Again, however, her second novel *Robinson* (1958), features another short-circuiting combination. Robinson is a moral catalyst as he fabricates the appearance of his own murder, so that three adults marooned on his isolated island fall under each other's suspicions of having committed the 'crime', and, through this pressure, reveal something of their deeper moral propensities. However, the moral scenario is somewhat overwhelmed by a complicated psychoallegorical setting (the island is shaped like a human being) and the strange, perhaps disturbed, behaviour of Robinson. These jarring aspects – the moral and the psychological – also sit uncomfortably with the novel's rather pale echoes of Defoe's classic work. In the end the whole situation can be read as the product of the disturbed and overactive literary imagination of its central character January Marlowe.[7]

After her first two novels, Spark's anagogic form and moral commentary emerge much more cleanly. This is seen first of all in her creation of remarkable fictions of a clearly defined supernatural kind which, even as they operate to bring about the effect of *contemptus mundi*, allow more credence into the social and moral situations where they intrude. *Memento Mori* (1959) is a modernised *danse macabre* where death takes on the persona of an anonymous telephone caller reminding a group of geriatrics that they 'must die'. Not entirely unreasonably, most of the old people interpret this warning as a threat and wonder whether any of their acquaintances might be the perpetrator. The opportunity is provided, then, for these individuals to examine their consciences after the manner of Christian discipline to see where they may have given offence. Most of them, however, perceive the warnings in terms of the continuing importance of their lives (though in actuality these lives have now become grotesque parodies of former vitality). It is in an attempt to puncture such self-deceiving and conceited fictions that Death, as an agent of the divine economy, has made an intervention in the first place. The effect of this intervention is double-sided as, according to their level of self-awareness, some of the geriatrics are driven to greater moral ruin and ignominious death while others are able to prepare themselves for their end with spiritual calmness. Into the first category falls Godfrey Colston, who amid the suspicion-charged atmosphere allows himself to be blackmailed over an extramarital affair which occurred several decades before (with a woman now dead), when what is called for is honesty with his wife as the couple approach the end of their lives. Similarly, his sister Dame Lettie Colston is battered to death when her fear over the telephone calls leads her to be so vigilant for her physical safety that she disturbs a burglar who is of course unconnected with the calls but who turns out in practice to be Death's instrument. Thus, with great ingenuity and 'economy' (a favourite term of Spark's), the opportunity for grace or violent poetic justice are provided in the text through the characters' potential responses to the one device.[8]

Spark's growing confidence as a theological satirist is to be seen in *The Ballad of Peckham Rye* (1960), and outstandingly with the character of Dougal Douglas who is at once a more ostentatious yet subtler supernatural agent than the telephone-using Death. He is the first of a number of 'cockeyed' characters in Spark's novels (if the less flamboyant and less surely focused Robinson is discounted) who apply their imaginative energies to the lives of others, bringing them both the potential for insight and chaos. Dougal, on his own admission 'one of the wicked spirits that wander through the world for the ruin of souls' (p. 106), becomes assistant personnel manager at a textiles factory and part-time ghost-writer of the biography of a retired actress. He is, then, if a demon, a highly modern one. At the factory, his role, as described in the fashionable vocabulary of industrial psychology, is 'to bring vision into the lives of the workers' (p. 15). His real role, however, is to bring into the open the consistent lack of (moral) vision in those with whom he deals. Two extremes give a good indication of Dougal's uncanny talents. His boss Mr Druce murders his mistress largely as a result of jealousy after Dougal also enters into a liaison with her; and his landlady is assured in her blindly obsessive tidiness as Dougal makes his bed so well that he elicits from her a note expressing her 'landlady's delight' (p. 48). As well as being very modern in his methods of ruin, then, Dougal obeys that particular set of ancient demonological rules which dictate that an evil spirit can work only as a catalyst.[9] The structure of the parable is clear. Wrong begets wrong and Dougal is brought into the lives of those who deserve him.

The next major shift in Spark's work sees the elimination of such ostentatious, if well-managed, supernatural devices and a move toward greater realism and the judicious utilisation of what might be termed the supranatural as distinct from the supernatural, as employed in the obtrusively fictive manipulations of the text for anagogic ends which were previously so disorientating in *The Comforters*. *The Bachelors* (1960), however, which appears immediately after Spark's supernatural phase, is an accomplished novel in its own right but is almost a stopgap in terms of Spark's evolving technical experimentation. The novel is one of her most jaundiced and disgusted perspectives on contemporary suburban society. Her previous contempt for the things of this world accelerates into an almost dystopian vision of the fallen world. The characters include a doctor who has killed a former lover in a bungled backstreet abortion, a lawyer who is guilty of the very confidence trickery with which he is prosecuting a crooked medium, and a false priest who uses his facade to pursue a licentious lifestyle. This extended inversion of society's role models produces yet another variation on Spark's vision of a demon-infested world, but on this occasion, with black comedy which is much less exuberantly pronounced than in her supernatural phase. The social naturalism of the novel is continued with a more forgiving emphasis in *The Prime of Miss Jean Brodie* (1961), *The Girls of Slender Means* (1963) and *The Mandelbaum Gate* (1965) which together form something like a trilogy of personal history for Spark.

Jean Brodie is one of Muriel Spark's most profound studies of the imagination. It explores the febrile brain of schoolmistress and demagogue Jean Brodie, within the strongly particularised setting of the Edinburgh which Spark had known in her interwar childhood years. Brodie designates what she takes to be the emergence of the most visionary period of her life, as her 'prime', and this self-identification registers her combination of wilful individualism and her pursuit of a normal personal development which is, to some extent, denied to her. Brodie's interaction with the world is carefully detailed through the pressures which operate on her as a 'schoolmarm' of her period and also through her attempts to refurbish the narrative of her own life and fabricate narratives in the lives of the girls she teaches. Brodie is located as one of the 'progressive spinsters' (p. 53) of Edinburgh who eclectically involve themselves in the numerous intellectual currents of the interwar years. This oxymoronic identity is explained by the fact that while such women might indulge in a degree of freethinking, their spinsterhood is thrust upon them by a combination of their Presbyterian background and the carnage of the Great War. They are essentially delineated as they 'lean over the democratic counters of Edinburgh grocer's shops at three in the afternoon arguing with the manager on every subject from the authenticity of the Scriptures to the question of what the word "guaranteed" on a jam-jar really meant' (p. 53).

Historical and social factors, then, are prominent in a way which is more pronounced than in Spark's previous novels. This extends to the very Scottish concern with education. Jean Brodie might almost be read as an exemplar of the 'democratic intellect' as she refuses to respect curricular boundaries and appropriates all school studies under the concern of experience. At the same time though, her sense of her experiential superiority over her girls leads to her totalitarian attempts to control her pupils' destinies. Her contrasting nature is visible too in the way she can be read as a representation of an ambivalent Scotland itself, as she identifies with Mary, Queen of Scots and abhors John Knox, and, at the same time, acts, in the perception of Sandy Stranger, 'Like the God of Calvin' (p. 161). But if her psychology is sociologically and culturally infused, it is also highly personal; she projects her interests into her own life, remoulding her dead lover Hugh, who has been killed in the war, into a cross between her ideal lover and Robert Burns, and elevating her rival lovers Teddy Lloyd and Gordon Lowther into something like principles of art and music, the subjects which they teach. Brodie, then, is not only denied life by circumstances beyond her control but can be read as either a classic schizophrenic, or a victim who denies life to herself, perhaps because of her 'vocation' to teach and the personal limitations this places her under. There is heavy irony in relation to the outcome of the novel as she claims descent from Deacon Brodie 'hanged on a gibbet of his own devising' (p. 117). In spite of Brodie's dismissal from her post for her avowal of Fascism, however, the final moral implications of the novel are not clear. As in all her novels, Spark refuses to offer readers secure conclusions. Spark's fiction presents a woman who cannot be judged with any complete certainty, who is on the one hand precisely located in social and cultural history, and on the other, functions within Spark's characteristic demonic framework.

Brodie's attempts to mould her chosen girls lie at the moral heart of the novel. Her effects on them are various. She encourages the persistent delinquent Joyce Emily

Hammond to run off to fight for the Falange in the Spanish Civil War where she is killed; Mary Macgregor, whom Jean Brodie has treated as a fool, afterwards regards her schooldays as the happiest of her life; Brodie's attempts to place Rose Stanley as her proxy in the bed of Teddy Lloyd fails; Sandy Stranger is driven to conversion to Rome and taking the veil in reaction against her teacher; and the rest of Brodie's chosen set are comparatively little affected, merely retaining vivid perceptions of their time with her. Brodie, then, to some extent operates like Dougal Douglas in magnifying existing propensities while, at the same time, having little effect on those whose natures are not amenable to her. This is not to argue that she is not morally culpable. She is clearly so, for example, in the case of Joyce Emily; but the implication is that she is not solely responsible for results.

Brodie's relationship with Sandy is the most ambiguous and the most resonant in the novel. Even before Brodie has begun to pronounce on her pupils' futures, Sandy is actually fictionalising her teacher's life when she composes 'The Mountain Eyrie' (based on Brodie's reminiscences of her dead lover) and when she forges a love letter between Brodie and Gordon Lowther. The point of course is that Sandy's imagination resembles her teacher's in its tendency to appropriation. Later, as a nun, Sandy writes her famous psychological treatise, *The Transfiguration of the Commonplace*, and this, it is implied, is based on observation of her teacher. The substance of this work is never revealed, but it is implied that it wrestles with the problem of discriminating between genuine vision (whether spiritual or artistic) and a state of mind which wilfully and in an introverted way distorts reality. Sandy has learnt the theoretical distinction between these categories through her involvement with Brodie, but, as she clutches her cell-bars, she realises that absolute discrimination between the two, at least for human beings, is impossible.

The dynamics of Spark's plot are equally ambiguous. The novel can be read as a critique of Calvinism, whose predestinationist doctrine Sandy associates with Brodie. Sandy comes to believe that a central idea of Calvinism is that it is 'God's pleasure to implant in certain people an erroneous sense of joy and salvation, so that their surprise at the end might be all the nastier' (p. 141). This of course is precisely what Spark has Brodie discover too. Her flash forward authorial intrusion (one of her most successful supranatural devices) informs the reader of the eventual thwarting of Brodie well before the unravelling of the plot, so that the moral dynamic of the action rather than simply the action itself is placed in the foreground. However, it also ironically confirms that Brodie's means of operation is not entirely dissimilar from those of her author. Spark of course is not meddling in the lives of real people but the implication is that the artist, even as she attempts to articulate a 'kind of truth', has to cast doubt on her own God-playing role, especially if she is a humble Christian in a fallen world.[10]

The Girls of Slender Means continues the strong autobiographical element in Spark's work as it features something of her experiences as a female involved in the war effort. Its focus is a hostel of women forced into close proximity by the Second World War. It is a less complex novel than *Jean Brodie*, featuring an emotionally spare world which, if it does not demonstrate Catholic certainty (none of Spark's novels does), locates clear-cut moral issues revolving around its characters in a way that *Jean Brodie* never does. This is perhaps no surprise since it deals with a time when Spark's own mature religious apprehensions were emerging. At the same time, it is certainly not a comfortable novel and has a dystopian quality akin to that of *The Bachelors* as feminine prettiness, the appearance of wartime togetherness and victory celebrations mask a horrible world of avarice and vice. The novel is one of Spark's most poised in its balance of social and moral scenarios.

Spark's fiction next moves to a greater degree of emotional and personal complexity (perhaps the high point in her entire canon) as she deals with another element of her early formation, her Judaism, in *The Mandelbaum Gate*. Spark has claimed that she does not feel particularly Jewish.[11] However, her short story 'The Gentile Jewesses' qualifies this statement by acting as a claim of right to her Jewish identity as, in semi-fictionalised form, it charts the narrator's lineage through a half-Jewish mother and grandmother, and so even as it acknowledges an unorthodoxy in identity, it charts inheritance according to the orthodox Jewish female transmission mechanism.[12] *The Mandelbaum Gate* operates similarly, registering the diffuse identity of another half-Jewish woman who has converted to Catholicism, Barbara Vaughan, who comes to realise that her uncertain identity is, in fact, a very accurate exemplar of the human condition. This uncertainty, then, becomes necessarily positive.

Barbara seeks relief from her teaching job at an all-girls school and the canonical problem of her love affair with a divorced Protestant in a trip to the Holy Land of Palestine and Jordan in the early 1960s. This is at once a setting of religious certainty and diversity, being the meeting place of Judaism, Christianity and Islam. Her situation has strong affiliations with that of Jean Brodie, but Barbara is in the more fortunate position of being 'gifted with an honest analytical intelligence, a sense of fidelity in the observing of observable things, and at the same time, with the beautiful and dangerous gift of faith which by definition of the Scriptures, is the sum of things hoped for and evidence of things unseen' (p. 18). She is at home with reality, then, and also with the metaphysical. She feels no need to fabricate a new identity as she wittily answers the hostile questions of a Zionistic tour-guide on the specifics of her Jewishness with, ' "I am what I am" ' (p. 23). Later she is located as 'a spinster of no fixed identity' (p. 45) which is at once an acknowledgement of the power and simultaneous inadequacy of society's labelling process. The mystery of identity is analogous to the mystery of faith, Barbara realises, while listening to a priest at the Holy Sepulchre preaching on the intangibility of faith, and his claim that ' "where doubts of historic authenticity exist, they are as thrilling in their potentialities for quest and discovery as a certainty would be" ' (p. 213). Barbara too is of 'doubtful authenticity', and the point is that human identity, in its necessarily feeble and fluid form, should not be taken for a certainty, or arrested as in some ways Jean Brodie attempts to do, but constantly questioned as it interacts in human relationships. This is the 'dangerous gift of faith' which Barbara discovers at the Holy Sepulchre.

Barbara's situation is complemented by that of archetypal English diplomat Freddy Hamilton. Together Freddy and Barbara are caught up in the volatile Palestinian troubles since as a Jew she journies too far into Jordan and becomes endangered, and he becomes accidentally caught up in espionage intrigue surrounding his diplomatic station. Environmental and external circumstances, then, press their identities on them; but what they both learn through these pressures in their lives is greater self-reliance. As a result, Barbara decides to resign from her school and to marry her lover no matter her church's position over this action, and Freddy risks his diplomatic status in helping to protect Barbara. Barbara's sense of the necessary instability of identity is counterpointed by her horror at the arguments of Adolf Eichmann, whose trial she attends. He claims to have been involved with the technical arrangements but not the actuality of the holocaust. Barbara finds herself nauseated as she finds that his 'actual discourse was a dead mechanical tick, while its subject, the massacre was living. She thought, it all feels like a familiar dream, and presently located the sensation as one that the anti-novelists induce' (p. 177). Eichmann is using an arid formalism to distance human and moral existence and suffering, and Barbara is appalled since she realises that life is morally involved even as it is messy.

The form of *The Mandelbaum Gate*, in its leisurely attention to Barbara's mental processes and experiences, reflects Barbara's apprehensions and marks Spark's most profound philosophical enquiry. In a sense it is a negative performance in its presentation of a generally negative theology. Spark dispenses with her usual textual trickery (and the unease expressed by Barbara over the anti-novel perhaps indicates a moment of reconsideration by Spark in relation to her past technical feats in the novel), to find that she can present a version of the remarkable where everyday normality and group identity is a thin crust which individuals have imaginatively to break through for themselves. Spark's next phase as a novelist, however, retreats from the formal implications of *The Mandelbaum Gate*. It is marked by five short novels, novellas even, which, in their pared emotion and tightness of form and fictiveness, are her purest and most ostentatious fictions. *The Public Image* (1968) begins the sequence as it documents the careers of Annabelle Christopher, an English actress working in Italy, and her husband, Frederick, as they are swamped by Annabelle's growing fame and film-image. Frederick attempts to counter this with his own dramatic fiction as he arranges for his wife to be at a party while he kills himself in order to escape their claustrophobic existence and ruin her reputation.

In her next four novels, Spark attains a fictional or claustrophobic intensity, and reaches the radical novelistic platform implicit in her development. The first of these, *The Driver's Seat* (1970), will arguably come to be seen as the greatest of all her novels. It features her most fluent technical manipulation to convey the shocking tragedy of a spiritually isolated woman who attempts to create a remarkable fiction around her life – and death. Ostensibly, Lise is on holiday in Southern Europe; and the reader is warned well in advance through Spark's characteristic flash forward technique that she will be found brutally done to death. Where in *Jean Brodie* this technique operates to forearm the reader, in this novel it obfuscates. The kind of trick played on the geriatrics of *Memento Mori* is here played upon the reader, who is led to look for clues to the eventual murderer. In the end however, the clues provided are reversible and have to be re-read as it transpires that Lise has all along been contriving her own death herself.[13] We first encounter Lise in a shop where she is trying on a dress which she tears off when the assistant informs her that it is stain-resistant. Lise claims to be insulted by the implication that she is a messy eater; but the reader realises at the end that the real reason for her behaviour is that she is selecting props which will make her death, and the events leading up to it, vividly memorable.

Lise continues to manipulate reality as she plays the role of a girl in search of a holiday romance. She reiterates to those she meets that she is looking for her 'type' and pretends to be a well-travelled polyglot. Ironically, as well as tragically, these roles indicate Lise's apprehensions of her failure in life. She is creating a parody of the life she wishes, even as she has given up searching for it. As with Jean Brodie, Lise's problems may be internal; but society's part in them is strongly suggested. Her place in a sexist office hierarchy and in wider society is recorded through what Peter Kemp calls the 'constant stress on externals' in the novel, externals which are signifiers of materialistic isolation in the contemporary world.[14] Lise's functional foldaway furniture in her flat has won prizes for its interior designer, it is reported, but the reader has to grasp that it has in fact been rewarded for its clinical creation of exteriors. It is as a protest against this coldly rational but disturbing world that Lise responds with her own 'externals' leaving behind in her holiday setting absurdist clues such as presents marked 'Olga' and 'Papa', along with a series of contradictory actions and stories which both highlight her disfunctionality in the world and amount to a scattering of her reason and motivation to the four winds. Her eventual selection of a rehabilitated sex offender for her slayer is a last sad attempt to confirm her own 'normality' to the world – and to cover the traces of her own actual victimisation by society which is ultimately more profound than physical abuse. The close alliance of themes with duplicitous narrative and plot structure makes *The Driver's Seat* Spark's most shocking and most accomplished work. In the end it leaves, in the words of the description of Lise, 'a garish effect on normal impressions' (p. 76), to the extent that contemporary 'normality' is rendered a highly questionable category for the reader.

Spark's subsequent three novels make even more explicit use of textual manipulation. If Lise's story posits the impoverished inclination towards surface appearances or materialism in modern-day life, these novels positively rejoice in their own materialistic formalism. *Not to Disturb* (1971) features a stage-managing butler and other servants who wait offstage planning the profitable media campaign which is to be mounted in the wake of the forthcoming violent deaths of decadent aristocrats Baron and Baroness Klopstock, and their male secretary. These are to bring about their own deaths in the library due to the ramifications of an eternal triangle. Gothic horror, Jacobean and Greek tragedy and a number of other heavily marked genre-references are exploited; the net effect is to bring down upon them a welter of determinism. The obliquely made moral is that the trio who have lived by immoral fictions are to die by the ironically similar means of shoddy, predictable fictionalised scenarios. Consummate fictiveness here registers the moral scenario much more effectively than in *The Comforters*, as it consumes an entirely corrupt cast whose characteristics draw on strong stereotypes of bad behaviour, which the reader can readily identify. These characters are 'not to be disturbed' in a novel which spectacularly features Spark's habitual trick of energising tired-out situations or clichés. This reinvestment with novelty, through the piling and colliding and the metaphorisation of stock scenarios, represents another remarkable transformation where familiar materials bring about a devastating pure poetic justice. *Not to Disturb* is a different kind of horror story in its formal claustrophobia as it succeeds as another comment on contemporary values and is, at the same time, an anagogic fiction as it conveys an image of Hell where human freedom is negated as a punishment for immorality.

The Hothouse by the East River (1973) is one of Spark's more confusing novels. Paul and Elsa Hazlett and their friends are killed during the Second World War but go on to live in the New York of the 1970s anyway. The reader gradually pieces this together and finds that the seemingly neurotic behaviour of the characters is not a result of their residence in a particularised setting of metropolitan madness, but more simply, because they are ghosts. Secular satire and the metaphysical (the attempted rendition of purgatory or Hell) thus decay into one another, in a misdirection of the technique of *The Driver's Seat* (where re-reading invests seemingly gratuitous behaviour with concrete reasons) and of *Not to Disturb* (where the fictive world is much more clearly defined from the start). Much more successful is *The Abbess of Crewe* (1974), Spark's abbatial parody of the Watergate scandal, which features Alexandra, who in her attempt to control life within a convent is a version of Jean Brodie, an inversion of Barbara Vaughan and a grotesque version of Richard Nixon. She rigs her own election as abbess by utilisation of the mass media and by replying to criticisms of her clearly corrupt behaviour with stylish but incoherent statements which succeed in disarming her critics. Alexandra feeds her nuns pet-food and keeps them under electronic surveillance. These novel, modern means of ensuring their immolation and supervision are in reality mechanisms for retaining comfort and power for herself. She is Spark's extreme realisation of a mind imaginatively dislocating itself from reality so as to conquer reality, and the most pointedly anagogic acknowledgement by Spark that the imagination can be dangerous. With its riotous farce, *The Abbess of Crewe* is, along with *Not to Disturb*, the most flamboyant example of this negative technique of Spark's where wilful fiction is both warned against and indulged. It is perhaps the novel that most signals her ambivalence concerning the imagination, and represents an inversion of her position in 'The Playhouse Called Remarkable'.

After *The Abbess of Crewe* Spark continues to observe and comment on comprehensive human deceit and hypocrisy. She reveals a maze of confidence trickery in the 1970s world of international finance, civil law and religious cults in *The Takeover* (1976), and she is even more condemnatory in *Territorial Rights* (1979) as she counterpoints the deceptions of suburban relationships and continental kidnapping crime. As is so often the case in Spark's work, the flawed man-made constructions she attacks are exploded through farce rather than being subjected to more reasoned critique. This self-sufficiency of Spark's imagination is wryly acknowledged in *Loitering with Intent* (1981) as she turns elements of her own early literary life in 1950s London into fiction. Fleur Talbot becomes secretary to Sir Quentin Oliver who runs the 'Autobiographical Association', which is actually a cover to extract blackmail material from its members. Fleur not only defeats her employer's criminal purposes but goes on to exploit him and his associates in her subsequent career as a novelist. ('In fact, under one form or another, whether I have liked it or not, I have written about them ever since, the straws from which I have made my bricks', Fleur confesses to the reader, p. 199.) Fleur's craftwomanship is both avenging and infernal, since she too is tampering with life stories for financial, as well as artistic, gain. Her final statement, 'And so, having entered the fullness of my years, from there by the grace of God I go on my way rejoicing' (p. 222), playfully acknowledges her vampirism, where 'fullness' refers to her successful appropriation of the lifeblood of her real-life studies. The resonance of this description in relation to Spark herself is, of course, clear. It becomes even clearer in *A Far Cry From Kensington* (1988) where, via her alter ego, Nancy Hawkins, she wreaks a fulsome revenge on her former literary collaborator, Derek Stanford, whom she has accused of producing wildly fabricated versions of her life and of being mythomanic.[15] Nancy repeatedly lambasts him in the character of Hector Bartlett as a 'pisseur de copie', thus framing Stanford in the kind of mythological position she feels he deserves. Again, then, on a very personal score, Spark operates in accordance with her cherished principle of poetic justice. At the same time, however, this intriguingly raises the question of how permissible such a manoeuvre actually is; a question raised in much of Spark's fiction.

Spark's most recent novel, her nineteenth, *Symposium* (1990), is a parable of the type found in her early fiction and a return to Scottish supernatural themes. Margaret Murchie, whose presence constantly attracts evil happenings, decides to embark upon a more wilful and concerted ordering of such events through blackmail and murder, only to find that other criminals outmanoeuvre her. The novel reaffirms Spark's essentially tragicomic vision of a world where the evil of humans is constantly defeated as it collides with yet more contending human evil. The divine moral economy, then, readjusts itself to counter human interference, and so remains somewhat impenetrable.

This impenetrability is dealt with in what has probably been Spark's most significant fictional gambit of recent years when she returns to a long-standing interest in the Book of Job in *The Only Problem* (1984). In *The Ballad of Peckham Rye*, Dougal Douglas, an agent of evil, had claimed that his life was licensed by Scripture, as indeed it is in terms of the Christian dynamic of the war between good and evil; and, in *The Mandelbaum*

Gate, Barbara Vaughan, in the culturally diverse setting of the Middle East, reflected that anything could be proved by Scripture. Spark has repeatedly remarked on what she takes to be the slipperiness of Scripture in the mimicry of what she considers to be its duplicitous quality in her novels and this is the hallmark of her unusual Christian vision. In *The Only Problem* Spark engages most directly with the question of Scripture, using the situation of Job to provide a structure for her novel. Rich Harvey Gotham retreats to a cottage in the south of France to write a monograph on the problem of suffering in Job. The irony is, of course, that as he does this, he is isolating himself from the human life in which he is ostensibly interested. He is similarly idiosyncratic in his pedantic researches into the Book of Job which extend to sending a friend to the zoo to observe the eyelids of the crocodiles to see if this helps identify the Book of Job's leviathan. Spark satirises Harvey's inappropriate attempts to employ human logic in reading the Book of Job. Ironically enough, however, like Job, he has apparently gratuitous trials visited upon him when his estranged wife, Effie, becomes implicated in French terrorism and his complicity is suspected. Harvey's complacency gradually, though never completely, breaks down as human suffering closes in around him. First of all he grasps that 'Job will never become clear. It doesn't matter; it's a poem' (p. 132). Secondly, he reasons that 'if the answers are valid then it is the questions that are all cock-eyed' (p. 180). Somewhat bathetically the sum of his conclusions is that God is ineffable but has created a colourful world. In the face of these facts he decides to 'live another hundred and forty years. I'll have three daughters, Clara, Jemima and Eye-paint' (p. 189). Harvey here is responding in celebration (though there remains a dark underside to this celebration) much as Spark has done throughout her work to the mysterious existence of God. The paradoxical conclusion to *The Only Problem*, that if there is a God, human life's only analogue for God's perception is to see itself as a poem, is an elucidation of a belief which creeps through Spark's fiction and provides her with yet another licence for her remarkable transformations of art. The standard response to the realisation of the higher ways of God is an acceptant quietism. Conversely, Spark in her flamboyant fictions reveals both herself and her characters responding with what might be termed 'noiseyism' or, in a favourite phrase of her own, 'rejoicing', in the face of the human absurdity which is part of the divine comedy.

Notes

1. 'The Playhouse Called Remarkable' was published in Muriel Spark's *Collected Stories*, *1* (Macmillan, London, 1967).
2. *Collected Stories, 1*, p. 146.
3. Good studies of Spark include: Peter Kemp, *Muriel Spark* (Paul Elek, London, 1974); Ruth Whittaker, *The Faith and Fiction of Muriel Spark* (Macmillan, London, 1982); Alan Bold, *Muriel Spark* (Methuen, London, 1986); Alan Massie, *Muriel Spark* (Ramsay Head, Edinburgh, 1979); Joseph Hynes, *Critical Essays on Muriel Spark* (Macmillan, London, 1992). Much exploration of Spark's work still needs to be done, notably concerning her place as arguably the most internationally successful Scottish writer of the twentieth century, her treatment of women and her place in contemporary fiction writing of the English-speaking world. At present there is only an account of her early career in Derek Stanford's *Muriel Spark: A Biographical and Critical. Study* (Centour Press, Edinburgh, 1963).
4. The most extensive source of information on Spark's life up to the beginning of her career as a novelist is in *Curriculum Vitae* (Constable, London, 1992), the first part of her unfinished autobiography.
5. For Spark's view of this relationship between her Catholicism and her fiction see 'How I Became a Novelist', *John O'London's Weekly* III, no. 61 (1 December 1960), 683; and 'My Conversion', *Twentieth Century* CLXX, (Autumn 1961), 58–63.

6.   Quotations from Muriel Spark's novels come from the Macmillan first editions with the exception of *Loitering with Intent* and *The Only Problem* which are published by The Bodley Head.

7.   A useful discussion of this most neglected of Spark's novels is in Carol Ohmann, 'Muriel Spark's *Robinson*', *Critique: Studies of Modern Fiction* VIII (Fall 1965), 70–84.

8.   This term recurs in Spark's fiction and statements she makes about her art. It has been a key concept for critics evaluating the formal, emotional and theological implications of her work.

9.   Spark would know well the seminal Scottish example of such supernatural rules, James Hogg's *The Private Memoirs and Confessions of a Justified Sinner* (1824).

10.   See 'The House of Fiction' (Muriel Spark interviewed by Frank Kermode in 1963), in Malcolm Bradbury (ed.), *The Novel Today: Contemporary Writers on Modern Fiction* (Collins/Fontana, London, 1977), p. 133.

11.   See Lynn Barber's interview with Spark, 'The Elusive Magician', *Independent on Sunday*, 23 September 1990, p. 8.

12.   'The Gentile Jewesses', *The Stories of Muriel Spark* (The Bodley Head, London, 1985).

13.   For a particularly illuminating study of the narrative technique of *The Driver's Seat* see Ian Rankine, 'Surface and Structure: Reading Muriel Spark's *The Driver's Seat*', *The Journal of Narrative Technique* 29 (1985), 146–55.

14.   Kemp, p. 123.

15.   See *Curriculum Vitae*, pp. 189–92; and Alan Taylor's interview with Spark, 'The Vital Spark', *Scotland on Sunday*, 'Spectrum Supplement' (16 September, 1990), 25.

36

Vision and Space in Elspeth Davie's Fiction

Valentina Poggi

Reading Elspeth Davie's stories and novels is like visiting a retrospective exhibition of paintings or drawings by the Bolognese artist Giorgio Morandi: in both cases the dominant impression is of sameness combined with variation, familiarity allied to strangeness; with Morandi it is simple household objects, with Davie it is commonplace settings and situations that come to be invested with symbolic and metaphysical meanings. It is not known whether Davie – a teacher and connoisseur of art, as any reader could surmise even in the absence of biographical data[1] – ever came across and liked Morandi's paintings, nor is it meant to suggest that he inspired her to write the way she did. However, an interesting affinity can be found between her aesthetic approach to reality and Morandi's peculiar blend of abstractism and realism. Wandering through a Morandi exhibition one sees on all sides homely shapes like vases, glasses, jars, and especially his celebrated bottles: squat or slim, lying or standing, isolated, grouped or scattered, their smooth rounded shapes, suffused with a mellow light that becomes one substance with their subdued colours, emanate an austere, contemplative stillness, like the pictures of a secularised, twentieth-century Piero della Francesca who had exchanged his Christs and Madonnas for these humbler still-life forms, carved, as it were, out of condensed light. A similar contemplative stillness emanates from the fiction of our author, the result in part of the repetition of themes and structures, characters and situations, in part of a style whose rhythm is rather one of articulate musing than of spoken language. Davie's austerely undramatic settings and unrealistic-sounding conversations, like Morandi's homely objects and Piero's ecstatically rigid angels and saints, deliberately give up all effort toward referential liveliness lest the viewer, concentrating on that, should miss the underlying meaning; they function as containers – bottles, indeed – for the refined essences that are distilled from the writer's deep sense of the emotional malaise of contemporary Western humanity, torn between the torment of self-repression and a naive or reckless striving after the impossibly elusive ideal of interpersonal communication.

Among the structuring devices employed in Davie's variations on this all-pervading theme, the one that most obviously displays its nature of container or frame is the duologue: two characters of the same sex, presumably friends of long standing, hold a conversation with the sole purpose of squeezing every ounce of meaning out of a generally trifling subject. The lack of references to the speakers' private lives, backgrounds and subsequent histories marks them as little more than props for the dramatisation of ideas.

In 'A Room of Photos' (*The Spark and Other Stories*), the duologue takes place in a photographer's shop, and its theme is the instinctive refusal of human beings to see themselves as others see them: both this theme and the formal, deliberate phrasing recall the dramas of Pirandello and his ironic or compassionate outsiders, so very competent in expressing their subtle perceptions through maieutic dialogue. 'A Conversation on Feet', in the same collection, centres on the analogy (suggested by a woman to an older friend who receives it with shocked perplexity) between the easeful sensation of walking barefoot in a ploughed field, and the sudden awareness that 'falling in love' means the experience of a union so intimate as to abolish all distinction between self and other: 'There was no division between earth and feet.'[2]

The referential and psychological context of the duologue is more clearly defined in 'Out of Hand' (*HTT*), where a boy and his sister interpret their grandfather's compulsive way of unfolding and rearranging his newspaper as the token of a progressive withdrawal from the 'poisonous world' that fills its pages with evils and frivolities; at the end, in the boy's deeper understanding of the old man, there is a sense of something achieved, not just of a theme canvassed. In the similarly titled 'Out of Order' (*TR*), where the dialogue alternates with third-person narrative, two young men reflect first on the absurdity of a mechanised world where machinery is made useless by vandalism or lack of care ('Kiosk Encounter' in the same collection has a similar duo consider the same subject); then on the delusion of the man in the street, who believes he is doing all he can to fight 'guns and bombs . . . poisonings and pollutions of sea and river' by the ritual reading of his newspaper. Finally, while one young man is clearing away bits of broken glass from a play-ground, the other limits himself to picking up a single splinter, in token of his scepticism about the use of such a 'ludicrous, totally useless, pointless, infinitesimal contribution to world order' (*TR*, pp. 72–5) thereby making explicit the symbolical overtones of the title.

The speakers of these duologues are deliberately denied any characterisation beyond the fact that one appears to be older, subtler, or more addicted to philosophising than the other. Sometimes, however, this framing device is enriched by the presence of the character-type whom Marina Spunta has defined, after the title-story of the earliest collection, 'the spark': a person endowed with peculiar sensitiveness and insight into other people's minds, whom complacent conformists tend to ignore or dismiss as threatening their self-importance, while diffident or repressed individuals shy away from them in jealous defence of their privacy.[3] Sparks are often children or adolescents, the very intensity of whose innocent gaze makes them more formidable to their adult antagonists. In 'A Private Room' (*S*) and 'A Visit to the Zoo' (*S*) two aunts reject the attempts of their young relatives to break the spiteful silence in which they nurse their bitter memories of men. The casually met 'spark' is more likely to be listened to, and can provide at least a moment of shared perplexity, as in 'Removal' (*S*) and 'Security' (*TR*), or even lead the interlocutor to take action, as when, in 'A Collection of Bones' (*S*), a window-cleaner persuades the protagonist to break, one after the other, his crazy collection of wishbones, in a grandiose and futile bid for good luck, which leaves him limp and flaccid ever after, as if 'every single bone in his body, big or little, had been cleanly and systematically snapped in two' (*S*, p. 189).

There are also cases, however, when the spark's insight is welcomed for what it is, no prying curiosity, but an urge to help. 'Counter Movement' (*DD*) is a very successful example of duologue, with a plausible situation deftly sketched and speech that sounds both imaginative and natural. Seated at the counter of an eating place a girl (who has just parted with her lover and heard his cool advice to 'start living [her] own life again', though at first it might be hard, 'like grasping a nettle') engages in conversation with the waiter who is busy mixing salads. His seemingly voluble talk about nettles being good in soups and salads, about customers wanting perfection, about his preference for the crisp and sharp over the oily in cooking, helps the girl turn her thoughts, from the 'tall order' she has received of 'living every minute to the full', to a saner, inspiriting involvement with the life that goes on all around her. Both the waiter's words and his quick, graceful dancer-like movements from counter to tables to kitchen, along with the vivid hues of the peppers and beetroot he is dressing, create a 'counter movement' to the dangerous proclivity, instilled in the girl by the heartless behaviour of her lover, to let 'everything melt and float gently past' her (*DD*, pp. 52, 57, 59).

The punning title ('counter' must obviously be read both as a noun and an adjective) is another recurrent feature in Davie's writing. The title story of *A Traveller's Room* hinges on a young girl's interpretation of 'traveller' in its broad sense, and on her imagining the habitual occupant of her temporary lodging as an explorer with the freedom of the whole world before him; when, however, he turns out to be just a commercial traveller, the anticlimax does not make this dream of freedom appear less, but more authentic. Less successful, in the same collection, is the story 'Bulbs', based on the confusion of vegetable and electrical bulbs. The device is used to better purpose in 'Connections' (*DD*) and 'The Stroke' (*DD*). The former, a ghost story set in a desolate railway station, plays on the broad as against the technical sense of the word, focusing on the deep though hardly conscious need for company of a man who on principle and from force of habit refuses to 'connect' with his fellow-beings. In the latter an Edinburgh banker, lying in his bed in hospital after a slight stroke, feels the night-nurse's hand lightly stroking his head, and broods on the manifold meanings of the word:

> The club, the sword, the hatchet stroke . . . the soft, full stroke of the painter's brush, the quick and fretful stroke of the pen . . . a sudden crisis in the body's blood . . . a single finger smoothing away fear . . .

in which last sense the word expresses

> the only touch most of them would wish to feel, the only voice they would choose to hear in the final moments of their life on earth. (*DD*, pp. 169–71, 174)

(Presumably written before Elspeth Davie's own stroke, this beautiful story has a sadly prophetic ring.)

A situation akin to the duologue is found in the grouping of people – whether friends as in 'The Eyelash' (*S*) and 'A Loaded Bag' (*S*) or, as in 'Bones and Bouquets' (*TR*) and 'Death of a Doctor' (*DD*), people of different age and status, casually meeting in a hospital ward or surgery waiting room – who, in the course of a seemingly trivial conversation, reveal their personal worries and idiosyncrasies, or (if they belong to the spark-type) a deeper-than-ordinary concern with other people's problems. Underlying this device is the awareness that the craving for communication, being seldom satisfied in the family, drives many people to try and indulge it among utter strangers; and also the persuasion that in such neutral environments an original utterance or gesture, being less expected, will leave a stronger impression on the mind. This can be seen in 'A Field in Space' (*TR*), a story that presents all the recurrent elements so far mentioned: there is the conversation, set within the duologue (the anecdote is told by a man to a friend), the punning title, the 'spark'. During a pause in a board meeting its members are invited to describe their fields – of activity or research, as they reasonably assume. But one of them understands the term literally, and describes first the actual patch of ground in one corner of which he has erected a small telescope, then the experience of looking through it at night; when, he says, 'you're shot out into the depths of space . . . It's an awful moment. Hair-raising! . . . some nights I'm almost thankful to be down to earth again and walking back home across the field in the dark.' Though they try to seem unconcerned, his listeners are made to feel nervously doubtful of the relevance of their own fields – be they economics, Christian ethics, physics or even human relationships. The ending of this story presents another recurrent trait of Davie's style: the language suddenly soars from matter-of-fact to lyrical in startling imagery, opening up new horizons of thought and feeling:

> We were hastening towards familiar cafés where we might find food and drink. But round Peterson's head it appeared to be still black night. For like a hollowed Hallowe'en turnip-head with its candle, his brow shone, transparent, as if – straight down through the first lights of the city – the uncanny stellar radiance had pierced inside his skull. (*TR*, pp. 52–3)

'A Field in Space', if not one of her best, could stand as the quintessential Davie story, in that it adds to all the elements so far listed a motif so central to her fiction as to be nearly obsessive: that is the primacy of space and vision in the perception of reality. The affinity with Morandi and Piero is just one aspect of kinship between Davie's mode of imagination and the visual arts in general. The sense of space – whether limited like a field or unlimited like the sky, actual or metaphorical, physical, psychological or metaphysical – is of far greater importance in her work than the concept of time, just as the building up of her effects depends more often on the sense of sight than on that of hearing or touch.[4] While some critics are repelled by the almost tone-deaf flatness of some dialogues and conversations, held by the most unlikely people in the most formal diction, others, like Gifford, Murray and Spence have praised the visionary and contemplative quality of her writing, and rightly suggested that the implausible articulateness of characters like the adolescents Brenda and Jane in the novel, *Creating a Scene*, is rather deliberate than casual.[5] This curious flatness of tone, like the repeated, cliché-like narrative situations, aim at thwarting expectations of realism, of articulate plot and 'natural' characterisation, so as to make them concentrate on an abstract, symbolical and surrealistic, as opposed to mimetic, vision of reality.

A kind of manifesto of this approach can be found in 'Space' (*S*), whose theme, proclaimed by the title, relates to opposing conceptions of the role of space in paintings. In it Mullen, a rich self-satisfied businessman, rather than reveal that he has spoiled a freshly painted watercolour by leaving it in the rain, pays what he considers an excessive price for a picture he dislikes:

> On the white paper were two interlinked shapes – a small oval, outlined in pale green and discreetly spotted with darker colour like an egg, and in front of it, in brown outline, a rectangular shape crossed with regular bands like a cage whose bars, on closer glance, were seen to resemble the thin, gnarled trunks of trees. A small, grey spiral, tightly wound, occupied the right-hand corner. (*S*, p. 143)

It might be called an abstract representation of the three dimensions: the tightly wound spiral seems ready to spring upwards, the bars/trees urge the eyes to look through and beyond them, the oval suggests at once the line of the horizon and an egg-like fullness, in contrast with the empty spiral and cage; the sense of a pent-up energy striving to break out and expand is enhanced by the hint at imprisonment – the cage – and by the opening of blank spaces in the picture. It is precisely in their views of these empty spaces that artist and philistine reveal their opposite attitudes to the visual arts – and to the world as well. When Mullen finds fault with 'the large spaces of untouched paper – these white patches', the painter replies:

> 'The white forms have a meaning as well as the coloured shapes. Would you rather I had filled them in with white paint?' (S, p. 144)

Exactly so: Mullen, the successful owner of a well-established firm, a thick wallet and a well-fed stomach, can see those empty patches only as evidence of unproductive laziness. He has made his money by filling fields with regular rows of fruit trees, and making the fruit into jams and preserves that fill miles of shelves in supermarkets all over the country; hence comic irony in his discomfiture at having to pay twenty guineas for a nearly empty sheet of paper. The painter, on the other hand, though he gets the price he wants, resents being denied a last glance at the picture, which to him was not merely an object for sale.

That jam-making is the source of money and pride for the unwilling picture-buyer is not irrelevant. Mullen is another representative of that rage to clutter the world with superfluous goods and unwanted sweetness already stigmatised in Davie's first novel, *Providings* (1965). The protagonist, a young man living on his own for the first time, is pestered by his mother with jar upon jar of homemade jam, which everyone else knows he has never liked. The jars and the jam function as punning symbols of claustrophobic parental love which strives to contain the developing personality and future of the child. The aim is not only to suggest the youth's inability to break away from the bonds of adolescence, but also to create a material image for the emotional vacuum that clamours to be filled with new relationships and connections. The importance of organising one's own personal space is emphasised in the second half of the novel, when the youth is in charge of turning a whole floor of a department store into an 'ideal home', complete with kitchen, bedroom and living-room furnishings. His attempt to match lines, volumes, colours and shapes to create a place fit for companionship and communication, an ideal offering to the girl he loves, suggests that the author sees interior decoration, like town-planning, as an art that if rightly practised can help the individual to fit into a community, without feeling either lonely or confined. But for the young man the space he must first of all share with his beloved is the blank space of freedom, a neutral place with no furniture, no atmosphere, no dimensions or responsibilities, away from a stifled and stifling home-life.

The jam-jars accumulating in his cupboard, the heaps of exotic souvenirs treasured by the girl's parents, can be seen as the antithesis of the empty patches that aroused Mullen's 'horror vacui' in 'The Space' (S). At the same time Davie's 'horror pleni' is at once aesthetic, moral and psychological. With her aesthetic preference for the spare and bare over the rich and ornate, she dislikes the consumer society that sets *having* above *being* and which in its insatiable appetite cannot have its fill of material goods. The claustrophobic atmosphere created by her long enumerations of objects of all kinds, whether handmade or mass-produced, suggests that identity and sanity are liable to be deranged by the multiplying of possessions like a stream banked up by boulders and mud. This fear is central in 'Family House' (S), where four brothers and sisters, who have devoted their lives to caring after their house and cramming it with beautiful, valuable furnishings and ornaments, realise as they pass middle age that they have neglected to live in themselves and begin to give or throw away their accumulated treasures. They are even overjoyed to discover that dry rot will soon make an end of the whole building. Even more sinister is 'The Siege' (S), where a newly widowed woman, perhaps from an obscure sense of always having been emotionally starved, becomes a compulsive buyer of foodstuffs, and sits at home behind a protective wall of family-size packets as if making provisions against a siege. What she wants is to shut out all possibility of escape from her own alienated self.

A more complex attempt to mediate between the search for an aesthetically satisfactory approach to reality, and the awareness of social issues, conflicts and crimes, is explored in 'Promise' (S): Carter, an art-teacher and amateur painter, exchanges the 'deadly smoothness' of his small land- and sea-scapes, painted on pure white canvasses, for the raw, rough surfaces of collage-like pictures whose paint is thickened and encrusted first with twigs, insects, seeds or the grit of city streets, then with scraps of newspapers reporting accidents and crimes, financial crashes and changes in fashion. Instead of 'the stripping of objects down to the abstract form, the human being to the bare bone', as Davie puts it in 'The Free Fur Coat' (*TR*, p. 94), art becomes for Carter a frenzied striving after inclusiveness, a dream of transferring the whole of reality into his pictures, perhaps to avoid the accusation of glossing over its dirt and social unrest. Paradoxically, it is a dream that the author herself seems to pursue, when she heaps her pages with lists of collectors' items and detailed descriptions of supermarkets, shoe-shops and restaurants filled to excess with consumer goods, even if the effect is generally a sense of disquiet at such multiplicity and proliferation. 'Promise' reaches an ironical climax when the artist outrages his friends by inserting real banknotes into his compositions, and is compelled to admit he is 'never going to change the economic outlook that way . . . the art maybe, but not the other . . .'. Leaving his attempt to let the picture paint itself by exposure to the atmosphere (it had all begun with seeds falling on a wet canvas), he peels the paper money away, and is confronted with white patches in the picture:

> These blanks were more than pale oblongs. They were holes which had to be filled up – gaping holes in space, letting through God knows what sights of emptiness and cold. No paper could patch these up. He loaded his heaviest brush with paint. (S, p. 125)

Here 'filling up' the blank spaces may not entail any encroachment on the vital space of the soul, but may rather represent an effort to introduce some order into the chaos of experience and achieve a measure of freedom. It is such personal involvement that paint and brush symbolise for Davie's professional or amateur painters, decorators and art-teachers.

The social role of art is the central issue in *Creating a Scene* (1971), Davie's second novel. The white paint described in the Prologue as in great demand among the pupils of an art-class in an Edinburgh Comprehensive School is an obvious symbol of their need for freedom, but may also stand for the creative imagination that is needed for real human relationships to be established in such alienating surroundings as the new housing schemes, whose inmates feel displaced and lonely. That it is difficult to achieve social cohesion through art becomes evident when the creation scene painted on the wall of a prospective 'social centre' is defaced, encrusted and overlaid with bits and fragments of all kinds, like Carter's pictures in 'Promise': but what seems at first mere vandalism, the underdog's protest against art of any distinction, is soon recognised as an oblique attempt at showing the life of a community, since now the defaced mural presents 'the relics of family life . . . horrors and pleasures . . . exorcised into patterns' (CS, p. 144). This kind of 'concrete' art is set against the other type where 'human beings [are] lost in an abstract pattern', the art practised by the young painter Joe, who honestly admits: 'One half of me is destructive.' (CS, pp. 105–6). Here Davie seems to be balancing, one against the other, the diverging tendencies in her own style: on the one hand austere minimalism and surreally symbolic atmospheres and on the other detailed, and even cluttered, settings of urban life in modern Scotland.

For indeed space in Davie's fiction is not just an abstract category, but can often be identified as place: the speeches in her dialogues may lack local inflections, but in many cases the physical and emotional background is easily recognised as Scottish, most prominently in *Climbers on a Stair* (1978) and *Coming to Light* (1989) where Davie's relationship with Edinburgh really comes to light as a lifelong love-affair, qualified by doubt and misgiving: there is love for the beauty of its ancient buildings, its celebrated skyline and variegated history; misgiving at the town-planning that threatens to destroy its character; irony about the coolly complacent attitude of its citizens, their condescension to incomers and strangers, and also their difficulty to commune with one another. 'The Stroke' has an intense passage on a typical

> beautiful, cold, lonely Edinburgh dining room . . . where, on first entering, guests didn't at once look at one another, but instead looked about them . . . first-time guests felt silenced, as though swept away down precipitous drops of stone . . . It was the combination of wild and formal in this city . . . these gulls and scraps of paper rising in the air in contrast to the tidy drawing room; all gave new guests an eerie sensation. (DD, p. 169)

Where specific geographical references are lacking, the attitudes of certain characters give them away as inheritors of a typical Scottish Presbyterian dourness. This is the case in 'Traveller' (S), where a woman is outraged at the idea that a pedlar is sitting outside her door, giving away for free the poor merchandise she has rejected. More explicit is 'Thorns and Gifts' (TR), where the boy narrator gives us a clue and passes a judgement on his country, when he speaks of his mother: 'brought up . . . in another country . . . speaking the same tongue with a different accent – she was thought almost a foreigner . . . my mother only asked to be allowed to charm people and not to harm them.' But 'Charm was not . . . liked or understood much in our part of the world.' (TR, pp. 129–30).

This is one of many short stories where the theme of women's oppression by rigid family structures and social conventions surfaces discreetly yet poignantly. Davie avoids a harsh militant tone when dealing with the question, but her characteristic mixture of low-keyed irony and compassion is only the more effective, and so is her deft use of imagery and symbolism, where again space and place play an important role: a thing not to be wondered at, seeing that women's grievances are so often caused by their being unjustly confined within the circle of house and home, and to a narrow range of physical, moral and emotional experience. Liberation is usually identified in Davie's women characters with the sudden discovery that they must have space to breathe, must leave the places where they lead a cramped life, and head not just towards other places, but virtually in all possible directions. The young girl dreaming of an imaginary explorer in *A Traveller's Room* is actually dreaming of her own escape, away from the already too familiar route that, on every holiday, takes her from South to North. The narrator of 'A Map of the World' (S) is another young girl, whose gender is at first left undefined, as is her attitude to her elder sister's obsessive interest in foreign countries; but when she sees the latter 'stretched . . . flat on her back . . . on the map' (S, p. 137), as if desperately trying to fit herself into a picture of the world, she takes charge of the situation and urges the other to decamp, leaving their invalid mother, alcoholic father and egocentric brother to fend for themselves. The idea that it is necessarily a woman's duty and glory to stay put in order to assist the sick and elderly, is rejected no less firmly in 'The Stroke' (DD), where the man in hospital overhears a 'powerful old woman' hectoring on the phone her meek middle-aged daughter, and wonders if the latter is 'a saint? . . . he decided no. She wasn't tough enough, and saints were . . . adventurers, explorers, leaders for the most part.' (DD, p. 171).

In *Climbers on a Stair* the urge to travel is at last fulfilled after long hesitation by Clara Kirk, a widow who, though she 'had never crossed a border', kept 'a great deal of luggage in the cupboards and wardrobes of her first floor flat' (CS, p. 74); those suitcases are props to her fantasy life and symptoms of alienation, not unlike the packs of food stored by the widow in 'The Siege' (S). If this woman, in the end, manages to leave fantasy for reality, it is also thanks to the fact that a genuine interpersonal relationship (though marked by truly Scottish restraint) has been gradually established among the various householders who, like her, go up and down the stair around which the novel is built:

> Viewed at an angle from the bottom the inside stair is a single sculptured spiral . . . To make up for the long, steep climb it gets lighter as it goes up, and in the roof there is a cupola of opaque, greenish glass. (CS, p. 1)

One is reminded of the spiral in the watercolour of 'Space' (S): the stair, in this most light-hearted of Davie's novels, represents both a symbol-instrument of connection between lonely people, and an invitation to look up for a way out of preoccupations that might easily become obsessions: the young man's shock at the sudden death of a friend, the town-planner's misgivings about his job, the piano-teacher's determination to inspire her pupils with perfectionist zeal. But it is also a diagram of the narrative structure, which winds from one point of view to another, then picks each one up again, and finally asks the reader to watch, from the vantage point of the top landing, through the eyes of the oldest and only resident left, the music teacher, a piano being heaved up the stair and the arrival of new people, with whom she is certain soon to make friends: the spiral design – approach, contact, parting – will thus continue.

Like this, most of Davie's fiction tends to an overall effect definable in starkly visual, pictorial terms: not Woolf's impressionistic 'luminous halo', but abstract systems of lines, patches of vivid colours, solid blocks of volume. The women at the piano in 'Accompanists' (TR) seem to come out of a cubist picture:

> The young girl who turns pages . . . is slim, pale, with . . . [a] startlingly straight back. The pianist . . . her feet firmly planted, strong hands spread out on her knees and her head bowed . . . is in black to her ankles. These two . . . have become welded together unawares like some medieval tableau carved out of solid black wood. (TR, p. 147)

Before the story ends this Cubist impassiveness has given way to near-surrealist strangeness: during the last part of the concert the two accompanists quit their 'place': leaving the tenor alone to find his way through the 'Songs of Love and Seeking', they start eating cherries out of a paper bag, share them amicably with women in the audience, and finally make a quiet exit; presumably to go, as one girl suggests to her boyfriend, 'off on the world-trip themselves', since 'they love running around the same as men'. The little act improbably staged by these women is a climax to the silent drama played out in the minds of the audience who listen to the romantic love songs: the men wondering if a protracted search in remote places might not have been better than their too quick choice of a partner; the women doubtful if the men in the songs would really have been happy to find the woman they sought for. 'Would they be prepared to sit down and actually talk to her instead of offering her a life-long devotion?' (*TR*, pp. 154, 148).

Female voices complaining of men who let women down are often heard in Davie: bitter, perhaps unfair, as when the widow in 'A Private Room' (*S*) remembers how her husband used to look at the stars rather than at herself; wryly ironical, as in 'Bones and Bouquets' (*TR*), where the patients in an orthopaedic ward discuss the two male visitors of a girl who has tried to commit suicide: her boyfriend ('Very kind, very helpful, very, very good to his mother. Not the marrying sort of course – not yet') and an older, married man ('An absolute gentleman of course'): 'God Almighty!' one of them comments: 'The mobs of kind men there are these days! . . . The world's so jammed up with them you can hardly get moving around.' (*TR*, p. 174).

If the diction in Davie's duologues at times sounds stilted, it is deliberately so, not out of inability to handle colloquial speech. As well as by the snatches of dialogue just quoted, evidence of the author's fine ear for the rhythms and inflections of deceptively trivial talk is afforded by the conversation between husband and wife in 'Oven Gloves' (*S*). She is just back from a walk in a totally new outfit; he vaguely perceives something unusual in her appearance, but cannot discover, nor really cares what it is, he is merely unpleasantly puzzled by her talk about the oven gloves her late mother-in-law used to give her for a present every Christmas. A delicate web of symbols and ironies, the story is an utterly convincing rendering of the kind of everyday scene that sums up the drama of a stale and unprofitable married life. The fed-up wife does not actually complain that her husband takes her so much for granted that he can no longer actually *see* her, but her restrained impatience is felt in the practised nature of her self-control. This is seen in a symbolic gesture like setting an empty flower-vase on the table (a reminder of loving homages now long unpaid), and above all in her slighting allusions to those cheap, unimaginative gifts from her mother-in-law, on whom her husband is still fixated enough to resent the implicit charge of meanness. Those oven gloves embodied the older woman's determination to bind her daughter-in-law to the role of housewife and the narrow circle of the kitchen: a role symbolically rejected, as the wife goes out to visit a neighbour who is sure to notice and praise the new outfit, bought 'after much thought and saving', and carefully chosen as a way of expressing her personality, subtly changing in time and yet the same, 'the same, yet miraculously different in every part' (*S*, p. 94). Her aesthetic satisfaction in the coat's colours, mingling 'pointilliste fashion' as in a painting by Seurat and discreetly echoed in hat, bag and shoes, represents for this woman what change of scene and travelling meant for the others: a way of asserting her identity, a sense of harmony with the world, a measure of freedom.

As the examples so far quoted indicate, the everyday dramas of human relationships are mostly enacted by Davie's characters against the unglamorous background of urban life lived in flats, shops, schools, restaurants, hospitals, or in even less exciting holiday resorts. The most impressive exception is represented by the title story of her third collection, *The Night of the Funny Hats* (1980), set in south-west Australia, among people travelling by bus from Perth to Adelaide. The experience of moving across a wide expanse of land not really modified by the presence of man (in spite of the tarmac and the pipeline snaking its way alongside the road), and the resulting weird feeling of living in an alien space, untouched by history and civilisation, runs through the whole story like an unquietly pulsing vein. The response to the natural scenery, uncanny in the glaring light, feels like agoraphobia, a counterpart to the claustrophobia evoked elsewhere:

> Every object in it appeared to exist by itself in total separateness from the rest. Each bush, tree, stone and flower lived in the naked light with its own black shadow sharply defined . . . The place existed for itself. Soon silence closed in again. (*NFH*, pp. 2–3)

The dehumanising potential of this 'impenetrable landscape', where a traveller unwisely venturing away from the road and the bus would easily lose his bearings and become a prey to thirst and mirages, is not fully realised by the light-hearted people travelling in couples; but the elderly widow, the young teacher from Yorkshire, the surly engineer perceive, and in a way visibly represent it, when they are described as

> at the same time totally isolated and yet connected, for each threw a sharp, dark shadow on the ground, a shadow linking them with one another and with the nearby stones and bushes – though not in the human way. This was a beautiful and fearful place for human people to stand alone in. (*NFH*, pp. 5–6)

The bus driver is wearily patient. Around him there seems to gather an aura of quasi-religious symbolism. Though he alerts the travellers to the dangers of venturing alone into the wild spaces, he feels a deep pride in this land, in the deeds of its pioneer explorers and colonisers. His pride is scoffed at by the engineer, who opposes his memories of a country rich in civilisation and history, where 'at every step, and check by jowl with skyscrapers, you come across the medieval church, the Norman castle, the Gothic cathedral, the Elizabethan palace' (*NFH*, p. 10) to the harsh forbidding sublimity of the Australian wilderness. But it is no simple question of nostalgia for an ancient culture. As the young woman from Yorkshire surmises, the wilderness he despises mirrors the void and rawness in the man's own life. 'Always in empty space – your own deserts and plains. Nobody gets near. Sooner or later everyone gets the push.' Reacting to her insight, he accuses the incomer of making facile judgements: 'These incomers! . . . absolute beginners in this land! *You* will go back to your small country . . . We'll hate this place and love it for the rest of our lives!' (*NFH*, pp. 14–15).

His hatred, or at least contempt, for the Australian landscape turns out to be compatible, and indeed perhaps inextricably mixed, with love. A similar love-hate relationship seems to bind the engineer to the driver, in whom he senses 'a whole person in the way that he himself was not' (*NFH*, p. 8) The two are contrasted throughout the story as negation versus acceptance, ruthless egocentrism versus readiness to help, guide and project one's neighbour; but at the end, with the driver suddenly dead and the engineer in a drunken sleep, they appear to share the same boon, which the latter had claimed he was after, all the time: silence. The death of the driver – a gratuitous, though plausible enough, occurrence in terms of realistic fiction – carries for Davie a symbolic meaning which is linked to the emphasis she lays on the significance of empty spaces. These wild expanses unreclaimed by history and unredeemed by civilisation, are an ominous image of the final reality, that which is least of all amenable to human reason and will: the 'undiscovered country from whose bourne/No traveller returns'; the realm of silence and death.[6]

Notes

1.   Elspeth Davie (1918–95) was the daughter of an Ayrshire minister who worked with the international peace movement. She studied at Edinburgh University and the Edinburgh School of Art. She married George Davie, the philosopher of the 'democratic intellect', and began writing when they lived in Belfast. She was awarded the Katherine Mansfield Prize in 1978, as well as two Arts Council Awards.

2.   Elspeth Davie, *The Spark and Other Stories* (Calder, London, 1968), p. 76. Further references to S. Her other publications are: *Providings* [P] (Calder, London, 1965); *Creating a Scene* [CS] (Calder & Boyars, London, 1971); *The High Tide Talker, and Other Stories* [HIT] (Hamish Hamilton, London, 1976); *Climbers on a Stair* [CS] (Hamish Hamilton, London, 1978); *The Night of the Funny Hats* [NFH] (Hamish Hamilton, London, 1980); *A Traveller's Room* [TR] (Hamish Hamilton, London, 1985); *Coming to Light* [CL] (Hamish Hamilton, London, 1989); *Death of a Doctor, and Other Stories* [DD] (Sinclair-Stevenson, London, 1992).

3.   Marina Spunta, 'Elspeth Davie', *Dictionary of Literary Biography*, vol. 139, 'British Short-Fiction Writers, 1945–1980' (1994), p. 50.

4.   For further discussion of the use of space and perception in artistic texts see Jurij Lotman, *The Structure of the Artistic Text*, translated G. Lenhoff and R. Hroov (University of Michigan Press, Ann Arbor, 1977).

5.   See Douglas Gifford, 'Scottish Fiction 1978', *Studies in Scottish Literature* 15 (1980), 243–4; 'The Vital Spark: The Vision of Elspeth Davie', *Books in Scotland* 16 (Autumn 1984), 9–10; Isobel Murray, Creating a Scene', *Scottish International* (September 1971), 35; Alan Spence, 'Really Distorted', *New Edinburgh Review* (May 1980), 31.

6.   Further useful material on Davie is to be found in two unpublished theses: M. van Eijck, *The Novels and Stories of Elspeth Davie: An Introduction*, PhD dissertation, Catholic University of Nijmegen, 1984; Marina Spunta, *The Narrative of Elspeth Davie: A Study of her Short Fiction. A Universe of One's Own?*, University of Bologna, 1992.

37

Designer Kailyard

Deirdre Chapman

Of the many characteristics Scots have tried to find in themselves and in their country, little approximating to charm or sweetness is sought, found or regretted. An endemic brusqueness and rationality is widespread and assumed, while the scenery consistently rises above or falls below prettiness. The notion of sentimentality that 'kailyard' evokes is un-bosky, anti-Arcadian: a perverse nostalgia for thin comforts, a rather clodhopping gaiety, a less aspiring society, all this against a background of extreme physical beauty – an awkward and not entirely matching set of ideas, only in the last instance romantic. Yet its very meagreness, its contrariness, its persistence into the present day, carries a powerful appeal to a number of modern writers of romantic and light fiction, and, more to the point, their readers.

Today's Designer Kailyard does not emerge as a coherent and unified literary style but is, rather, a series of consumer-conscious stabs at intuited Scottishness on the part of some very different storytellers for whom Scotland is a deliberate, never a random setting, with bulky connotations that can be used but not ignored. In *Kailyard*, his study of the McLaren/Crockett/Barrie school, Ian Campbell notes, 'The Kailyard looks back to a just vanished comfortable certainty: to read it from the cities, from overseas, is to be aware of something remembered at first hand . . . still fully credible, possibly discoverable in remote parts of Scotland'.[1] The call of a dream certainty: for a romantic writer and her oeuvre this thing is bigger than both of them and, no creature of glade and bower, may turn wrecker if handled carelessly. Nourished by memories, first or second hand, of those who seek assurance above enlightenment, it is unevolved, unmalleable and market-led.

On the reader's part there is a strong comfort factor in recognition. Even a non-native reader may find security in a parochial Scottish setting: neutered by diminutives, walled in by teacups, the cad does not flourish. Metropolitan philanderers are plucked out of their interiors and put down on moors or in manses, and so badly do the bogus, the egotistical and the unprincipled fare in the reader's immediate interpretation of this society that there can be little or no redemption for them until they submit to its values. Another, more native, gritty and inward-looking genre is concerned with social realism, the struggle for survival played out for its own sake – 'a regularly repeated set of themes which are more self-reflexive than reflective' as Beth Dickson says of the work of popular writers of the beginning of the century such as MacDougall Hay and Neil Munro.[2]

While there are some writers whose entire work lies within and draws from this emotional parish, others are merely visiting. Rosamunde Pilcher, Scottish not by birth but by domicile since her marriage after the war, retains an English perspective while making strong use of Scottish professional and landed country society for some of her bestselling novels, in particular *September* (1990), set in fictitious Relkirkshire, a Southern Highland county. The Steyntons at Corriehill are planning a September dance for their daughter Katy. Invitations are going out far and wide: strangers will return, chickens come home to roost. Meanwhile it is May, and Violet Aird in tweed skirt and cardigan is taking her turn in the village store where there is time to 'marvel at the weather; ask after somebody's mother; watch a small boy choose with painful deliberation a packet of Dolly Mixtures'. A poke-of-sweeties ethos in a prepack present. '"Oh, thank you,"' says Violet, '"my milk and my paper. And Edie wants some furniture polish and a roll of paper towel"'.[3] 'Needs' might be the better word, for it is Violet's furniture that Edie is to polish, but Pilcher is not focused on indigenous minor characters. Her concern here is to set a mood quickly and this she does by having the characters voice thoughts too banal to be uttered in a Hampstead drawing room or a Glasgow pub. Platitudes reliably signal emotional sanctuary.

We are here amongst landed, educated but unostentatious people and their humbler neighbours, the familiar Highland democracy of shared inconvenience and the village shop. The Episcopal church, itself a sign of English influence, needs rewriting: 'Archie Balmerino rallied his meagre troops, chaired committees' (p. 71) and at Balnaid, home of Edmund and Virginia Aird, the committee has just planned a jumble sale:

> As soon as the others had gone, Virginia had disappeared into the kitchen to make tea, and brought it to them on a tray, without ceremony. Three mugs, a brown teapot, a jug of milk, and a bowl of sugar. (p. 72)

Stylish American-born Virginia is more of a Spode and Filipino maid person, but the life she is living here is awesomely unpretentious and her tea-making circumvents yards of explanatory prose. Scotland in this novel is more than a setting, more than a catalyst: it is nothing less than a nice people's Utopia. Virginia's urbane, spooky-cool husband Edmund commutes daily to Edinburgh and jets off occasionally to more hedonistic places, and, while that carries more than a hint of decadence, life for these two would be very different, one feels, in the Home Counties; a London head office staffed by more predatory girls, the stockbroker belt more testing of Virginia's virtue than Relkirkshire. The jumble sale, the brown teapot, imply moral rigor as well as lack of opportunity.

Serpents slither around this Eden. Virginia's days are taken up with her adored son Henry whom Edmund now wishes to send away to boarding school, tempting her to seek other comforts. Her step-daughter Alexa, homely-featured heiress and *cordon bleu* cook in London, has met Noel, party-going yuppie who may be a shade too interested in her money. Then there is Pandora, Archie Balmerino's beautiful feckless sister who ran off twenty years earlier when Edmund turned her down, and has since led a dissolute and copiously alimonied life in America and Ibiza and now, though no one knows it, is terminally ill. Noel and Pandora must be brought north to the dance, to be purified, and to decide.

Noel and Pandora represent life elsewhere, which also beckons Virginia and Edmund. But there is more to Relkirkshire than clean air. The 'curious and obviously satisfying air of stasis to the kailyard' noted by Campbell among the comfortable working class of the kailyard has its counterpart here amongst the statically affluent.[4] Further upward-mobility is not on their minds. The very thought may be disquieting. Quality of life is all, and here the enviable world class scenery weighs in on the side of the brown teapot. In the ensuing battle between good and less good but maybe more fun, there is no doubt that the Highland way of life will ultimately prevail. It is, after all, rather a comfortable upper-crust version. Pandora – 'And the sun and the blue sky and the heather linties cheeping away, and the guns going *crack*, and the poor little grouse tumbling out of the sky. And all those clever doggies' (p. 503) – brings a salutary glimpse of the wrecked and unregenerate sybarite who has chosen exile. For her, rural Scotland will be the final sanitorium, a place to be purged as well as cosseted, pardoned as well as loved. In direct contrast to Pandora, Edie, the Aird family treasure, afflicted by the arrival in the solitary household of her mad, never convincingly dangerous cousin Lottie, is loved and sympathised with but never examined. Lottie's madness, too, seems to be more of an obsessive and righteous malice against upper-class goings-on, perfectly understandable in an ageing rural Scot of limited intellect and horizons moving amongst these privileged people. Pilcher, however, is not writing this sort of book. Deft and convincing on the upper-class characters, she leans heavily on unexamined kailyard conventions whenever she steps outside the drawing room.

Violet's long lifestyle monologue to citified Noel is the key passage:

> Not different, Noel. Ordinary. The most ordinary of folk, who have been blessed with the good fortune to be raised and to live in this incomparable country. There are, I admit, titles, lands, huge houses, and a certain feudalism, but scratch the surface of any one of us, go back a generation or two, and you'll find humble crofters, mill-workers, shepherds, small farmers. (pp. 465–6)

Noel thinks of the awful alternative: 'Calling up friends, meeting in bars, eating in restaurants, trying to find the telephone numbers of all those emaciated and beautiful women' (p. 477) and finally, at the September dance, watching Alexa do the Reel of the 51st (Scottish Country Dancing has a powerful symbolic, catalytic and mythic role in this type of fiction, jumps the right way. In fact, of course, he is opting for middle age. The middle-aged, the old and the very young are the pillars of the Designer Kailyard. Elsewhere, like youth, is shallow, fleeting, illusory. Scotland triumphs: Henry is spared boarding school, Virginia steadies, Edmund thaws, and Pandora, all partied out from California and the Med, is happy to drown herself in the loch of her childhood.

Pilcher uses country-estate Scotland in two other novels – to cure one heroine of her weakness for an English cad, and to rescue another from the precarious charm of California beach life.[5] They are healed, soothed, detoxed, largely by contact with dour and unexamined minor characters such as housekeepers and gamekeepers. So morally unambiguous is the type that a walk-on role is sufficient to flesh out the terms of the exchange – history, dignity, maturity in return for the tacky strobe and sunlight of perpetual youth.

Jan Webster, Lanarkshire-born, now living in Cheshire, has written a number of historical romances chronicling events in the West of Scotland from the 1920s to the present day. In *Lowland Reels* (1992) she uses the device of the special event, this time a wedding, much as Pilcher uses the September dance, to bring strangers home and local people together and to stand acquired values against inherited ones. She too is purveying Scotland to non-Scots, though in her case with an authentically robust native accent.

Her 'Eggleham' is located in Central Belt commuter Scotland, much closer in time and place to the industry its prosperity derives from. The characters are comfortably off, not wealthy, there is a new feel to the money, and the effortless good taste of Relkirkshire is not much in evidence.

> The older women wore dainty shoes and fine nylon. Although it was early autumn some already wore well-made winter skirts with pastel-coloured jumpers and either pearls or chains, while others wore sensible sleeved dresses that had cost enough but would see them comfortably through the season ahead. Fashions did not change all that drastically. There was a kind of contempt for it.[6]

This is the bride's mother's best friend Kizzie, a television personality back from the south, in the role of guide and interpreter to her homeland. The Media in this case rather than the South, stands for ambition, fulfilment, the tug of beyond, the wider view, set against a climate of self-satisfaction and not a little self-doubt. The tension in the story – between bride and groom, between the bride's parents, between Kizzie and her possible partners – stems largely from outgrown identity, from too much consumer comfort and too little stimulus. But the wedding party, the huge sentimental occasion, is something they all do well:

> Now the food came hot and fast – big plates of nourishing chicken soup with hot rolls followed by lavish prawn cocktail followed by a choice of roast meats, steak pie or salads, vegetables by the truckload and potatoes in every variety known to man. It was feasting as Metropolitan London had forgotten about or perhaps had never known, generous to excess, prodigious, perhaps only in the way that people can enjoy food whose antecedents have known hard times, failing harvests, thin pickings. (p. 57)

Nothing here, though, that would be unfamiliar in Yorkshire or rural Ireland. Something is needed – historic, genetic, metaphysical, huge – to stress an ambience that is uniquely and unassailably Scots. Tam, an Irish media person, prompts Kizzie ('Don't you feel you are among your own here?'), and she is given licence to explore her feelings about her genetic heritage – Covenanters, coalminers, farmers – now mingling in spirit with 'the modern Scots who had been to the Seychelles and Florida, strolled in the Louvre or danced in the Tivoli Gardens' (p. 57). The scenery, the history, the achievements . . . what are they if one has only been to Benidorm? The true Scottish fear, the fear of provincialism, is hauled out naked and squirming for all to see.

And still it's not enough. We are more than we are, aren't we? Tam, the outsider (for an outsider's endorsement is worth one hundred of the blood) is given another go:

> Remembering what Edwin Muir the poet had written, about the simple, naturalistic vision of life held by the 'Scottish peasantry' . . . and about life as a thing of sin and pleasure, passing . . . but with the intense vividness of a flame, before something eternal, he thought of Melinda [the bride] now as an embodiment of that idea, like the Border ballads he himself loved above all other poetry. (p. 68)

The prawn cocktail belt is yet capable of simple naturalism; Melinda rises not only on the strength of her own ethereal beauty but because of a spiritual inheritance from Fair Ellen.

What does make the whole gathering inescapably Scots of course are the kilts, the music, the dancing. The book is divided into three sections – 'Pas de Basque', 'Set to Your Partner', 'Travelling Steps' – that echo the movement of a reel, and during an Eightsome the groom is whirled off his feet by his bride, to his serious but not his permanent injury, with future ramifications in the plot. The physical scene is affectionately observed: the conscientious re-remembering of steps, the quite extraordinary level of exertion, the keeping going, shoes and jackets thrown off, to the point of exhaustion, 'the women demanding pots of tea after the champagne, the men looking for beer chasers for their malt whiskies' (p. 64) but perhaps more powerful than the deliberate evocation is the underlying squirm of reader recognition: kailyard reflex, the habit of occasion, the Pavlovian straightening of shoulder at the first tug of an accordion. Here is dancing for its own sake, all-inclusive dancing. The habitually graceful are not seen at their best and the normally awkward become fluent. This *is*, perhaps, singularly Scottish, and writers use it time and time again. In *Lowland Reels* there is a strong appeal to association and an affirmation of the common denominator – a sanctionable couthiness – to soften a story of upwardly mobile people which closes aptly with someone saying 'Come into the body of the kirk'.

By no means all of the writers who approach the bank of this stream of association are electing to cast themselves into the current. Ian Campbell notes that 'The danger of using Scottishness to evoke a calculated response, without the conscious intention of the reader or hearer, is one ever present to the entertainer in any medium who aspires to use "Scottish" material'.[7] Magda Sweetland, Edinburgh-born, now living in England, is a writer whose work borrows strong vernacular locations and evocations for much more complex and ambitious purposes with, sometimes, in her first novel, an untoward effect. She is not alone. Campbell finds that kailyard 'features occur in Neil Munro and Neil Gunn, MacDougall Hay and in Grassic Gibbon – Stevenson and Buchan managed to write about their native Scotland in challengingly original ways, yet in their weaker moments could fall into kailyard traps, as any Scottish writer could (and can), so permeated is the Scottish consciousness with these presuppositions'.[8]

Eightsome Reel (1985), is a lengthy, socially and geographically diverse, constantly reflective novel which takes its tension from the coming together of two people, Esme and Alexis, who defy significant taboos – he is the husband of her aunt. From Edinburgh, where Esme's mother has just died, the scene moves to the countryside around Lochearnhead where her mother's sister Mari and her husband Alexis are having an up-market Guy Fawkes party for a hundred guests.

After the post-prandial fireworks Alexis, whom we are told it is easy to imagine 'helmeted with the cuspid horns of the Viking, shaggy and bearded, red-eyed from smoke and blood-hunting' calls for a piper and works up the allure of the dying bonfire into elements of a pagan fire festival: '"Come, ladies, who will partner me? Who'll keep pace with me step for step?"'[9] Around the bonfire there is 'no shortage of offers', but in the room where the reader sits the chill is palpable, the pages atremble with arrested put-down reflex. The florid speech pattern is part of a move to distance Alexis from his petty bourgeois wife; to help him disguise a guilty grief at her sister's death; and to reach out to a wider al fresco Scottishness: 'Over the loch the pibroch sounded as it had in the days of Bruce who hid in the enclosure of the surrounding hills, or of Charles Edward Stuart, a call to arms, a battle cry, a lament for the dead' (p. 19). But in calling upon such powerful Gods so early and at such a non-native and really rather House and Garden event, of which he is, after all, the host, the balance is further disturbed. The narrative further isolates the inhibited, prim Mari who stands watching helplessly as 'They reared and plunged by the light of the fire. It was primitive, heathen' (p. 20). But Alexis has already lost our vote. He is arrogant, flamboyant, bearded, faithless, and dressed in 'a brocade waistcoat which was a masterpiece of flowers and ferns. Rumour put a price on it and fell short' (p. 19). The kailyard in the Scottish reader has been alerted and now sits, tight-lipped, taking sides. Mari is our girl.

This is especially awkward as Alexis is soon to be paired with the bereaved Esme, an isolated, introverted girl whom we first meet picking apples from neglected trees in her huge Edinburgh garden, rattling down ancient sweaters for their wool, and promising in most details to be agreeably and sympathetically wayward. Each is a half-Scot – Alexis had a Swedish mother, Esme a Polish father – which might seem to allow them moral latitude. The difficulty arises when Scottish vernacular tradition is invoked on their side. They cannot take pride in their Scottish ancestors and rejoice in Scottish superiority as they do, frequently, if they will not play by Scottish rules.

Throughout the novel there is a strong didactic element: a dinner party conversation ranges from Mary, Queen of Scots, the marriage customs of Gretna Green, and the management of Highland estates to Young Lochinvar, and even a bar lunch stresses the quality of Highland pub food: 'no ordinary bar room sandwiches these. Soft baps filled with salmon from the local streams or thin shreds of pinky brown venison' (p. 61). These people feel themselves to be hugely Scots. Scottishness feeds their egos and gives them their references. When Alexis and, increasingly, Esme indulge their flamboyance and their sense of separateness, when they behave with arrogance to more obviously Scottish types like Mari and Graham the gamekeeper (Alexis to Graham: 'confine yourself to your natives. I am out of your sphere,' p. 156) and where even their attempts at sensitivity can seem self-regarding, the narrative has become the victim of its own setting: '"Do you think she hates us?"' asks Esme of Alexis when Fiona, a local girl, serves at table. '"She's serving us food she probably hasn't eaten, except in kitchen scraps, salmon, asparagus, and yet it's from this part of the country." Alexis: '"I wouldn't worry about it too much. Fiona doesn't know fresh from tinned salmon. She's just a village girl"' (p. 127).

Here too, the village-hall dance is a major scene. 'They played liltingly, not the great songs of the country which are all of loss and leaving and the heartbreak of exile, but the second strand of airs that were fitting accompaniment to the jig, the reel, the Strathspey', and Esme is popular because 'she appealed to the large, sandy coloured Highlanders' (p. 154). The high Scottishness is written with great love, but undercut by voice changes. The music of the large, sandy coloured Highlanders is one thing, the men themselves, though she dances with them gladly, Esme keeps verbally at arm's length. She does not wince at Alexis's florid sentences but finds them noble. The romance of her heritage which she finds personified in him – 'High living and plain thinking' – haunts her when she leaves for Canada, and at a party in an Air Force Officers' Mess in Quebec province, she find herself missing him and thinking how she would like to hear him 'say, under his breath, "Come, my bonny burde, let's do a Schottishe and show them how to move"' (p. 241).

There is nothing formulaic or reader-led about Sweetland's writing which is full of esoteric references and quotations. In her second book, *The Connoisseur* (1986), she returns to examine more fully the introverted, solitary thread in the Scottish personality, and her study of a middle-aged aesthete is an economic gem of character observation. But, in *Eightsome Reel*, she demonstrates the dangers in a strongly evoked Scottish context of disregarding the natural bias against pretension and towards the guiltless, the diligent and the plain-spoken. Lack of human warmth is as often the result of hurt as the cause of it. By neglecting to understand the character of Mari, self-righteous, over-aware of propriety and position, but a recognisable figure in plain Scottish terms, she isolates Alexis and Esme and loses them our sympathy.

Sweetland's third novel, *The Hermitage* (1988) moves between professional Edinburgh and London with visits to a Highland estate, and ranges over the fields of politics, theatre, and academe through the medium of the actress daughter of an eerily evoked Nationalist mother; through her husband, an academic, who represents the Edinburgh moral majority; and, widening the perspective, through her lover, an Independent MP who is also heir to the estate. The wide canvas allows her to demonstrate effectively the easy interlinking of disparate disciplines and social groups in modern Scotland, with the volatility she was so anxious to show in *Eightsome Reel* more pointed, but the authorial didactic habit, itself so Scottish, still in evidence. At Scottish Question Time in The House of Commons, 'a fragment of every man present was nationalist, not separatist, but indelibly defiant to English mores and English laws. The clansman was anarchic and like the feral species could never be entirely trusted in domestic habitat'.[10] Her concern is one shared with many Scottish writers, to track, swat and dissect every flying or creeping manifestation of national identity: 'this "everyone" was familiar . . . because the name was so frequently invoked. It was a uniquely Scottish personage, an amalgam of neighbour, gossip, telltale, sneak . . . this ubiquitous critic who was Calvinist and unfriendly. It was the inverse of the laissez-faire spirit which prevailed at Oxford' (pp. 201–2). Occasionally, though, the mission is *de trop*. The thing itself has got there first.

A very different writer – two, in fact – is 'Jessica Stirling', the pen-name that Hugh C. Rae and Peggy Coughlan chose for their collaboration in a range of fiction that is anchored in the industrial working class in the closing years of the nineteenth century and which depicts a community tempering good-natured acceptance with resourcefulness in the face of deprivation. After the death of Peggy Coughlan, Hugh Rae, who also writes quite different fiction under his own and other names, continued alone with the Stirling books. A 'gelling of attitude and myth, a freezing of the possibilities of change or redefinition, a tacit acceptance of a narrow range of character and activity within which to present "real" Scotland' which Campbell lists as distinguishing facets of the kailyard are the template for these books, albeit a template whose strictures the authors frequently resist.[11]

The ugliest of settings – a brick-and-grit Lanarkshire pit village for 'The Stalker Trilogy', a tenement area of Glasgow for 'The Nicholson Quartet' – tax the 'romantic novel' tag, but the eventual redemption of the characters by hard work and love is in kind. There are sensory appeals to the present ('*Sit Down Suppers* . . . from whose doorway wafted a delicious effluvium of pan fat')[12] but much of the attraction to a reader must lie in a past safely passed. Whatever the future may have up its sleeve it will not include hand-washing overalls, darning by gaslight or cooking mutton broth on a range. The form – trilogy, quartet – assumes continuity, homogeneity, *tholing* to Olympic standard, and a reigned-in response to the blows of fate which may release itself in present blusher for the ultimate preservation of peace and order. The characters are lively and well differentiated but the style, tailored to its audience, elects to protect itself against surprise.

The seeds of this containment are sown early. In *The Spoiled Earth* (London, 1974), first of 'The Stalker Trilogy', Mirrin Stalker, marked out from the start as the independent, outspoken one of militant miner Alex Stalker's family, has soon had the limits of her development signalled: 'She was only a girl, of course, and a good-looking lass at that:

consequently her opinions were not taken seriously by the district's militants. Even her father and brother treated her political fervour as something of a joke.'[13] The low-key, conversational noting of the prevailing male ethos is a fair warning that it will not be overthrown. Certainly this ethos is acknowledged, lightly disapproved of even, but since it is hinted that the men's judgement may be right, a point that might be the crux of narrative tension in a novel with a more provocative purpose is effectively defused. Strong feelings and serious issues are not lacking in these books, but the language must often be felt as wrapping paper.

The major event, a pit explosion which kills ninety-five, including two of Mirrin's brothers, and later, from his injuries, her father, is caused by fire damp which the miners had reported, but which the management had failed to find. Houston Lamont, the pit owner, is the obvious target of emotion and blame. Living in his tree-screened mansion house beyond the village whose economy depends equally on his benevolence and on his business sense, he shares to some extent the miners' blighted environment. However, when Alex Stalker, Mirrin's respected and politically astute father, is hauled charred but ranting out of the pit fire – '"find him . . . make him pay"' (p. 45) – it is surely unthinkable that shortly after, her father now dead, Mirrin, the political hot-head, will become Lamont's housekeeper and his lover. Yet this is achieved partly by a judicious mellowing of character on both sides: Lamont, as bosses go, is a responsible man with troubles of his own – his wife, his sister, the price of coal. Mainly, though, the unthinkable liaison is achieved by the parcelling up of feeling, a self-regulating climbing down that happens in the head, a 'thinking down' characteristic of the fiction of resignation, that follows extreme statements of attitude or intent. The process inhibits everything that might push the novels out of their genre. They are contained by the needs of their prospective readers as surely as the characters are circumscribed by their environment. In fact the relationship between Mirrin and Lamont is convincing enough, two strong but fairly complex people well matched but brought together by narrative exigency in a bit of a rush – Lamont's wife is made rather a caricature of heartless, self-seeking, snobbery, and Mirrin's acknowledged but untested sensuality allows her to effect an easy liaison. Her self-limiting sexuality was signalled earlier when she boldly entered the village pub, taboo to women: 'The young men eyed her appraisingly. Mirrin let them gaze their fill. She knew how she appeared, with her thick black hair and her good figure' (p. 87). She was never to be a Joan of Arc, then, but a Strong Woman with all the baggage that brings with it. Nonetheless there is a strong ending to the novel when the death of a miner's child in the river allows the community to be seen in less than idealised accord. Stupid and vengeful with hurt, they turn on Lamont's mad sister, and to save her Mirrin renounces Lamont. As she helps to round up another element in the child's death, Loonie Lachie, the scapegoat, who is to be sent off to an asylum, there is an acknowledgement that all that happens in close communities is not loving or fair, and that to live outside the rules brings reprisal.

Another traditional element in the trilogy is the Getting On theme, one that is handled gingerly in the kailyard for the light it casts on local stasis, which climaxes at the end of the final book. Mirrin's brother Drew who, in the first book, got to Edinburgh to study law on the backs of his hard-working sisters and with Lamont's patronage, has become Scotland's most illustrious advocate. The necessary literary price is to lose touch with his family – including Niall, his bastard son, brought up discreetly by another of his sisters and now, in *The Dark Pasture* (1977), charged with murder after a pit riot. Drew gives up an assured seat on the bench to acknowledge and successfully defend his son in a convincing court scene that illustrates how, in parochial fictional Scotland, the seriously bright must go away to remain credible. The comforting (for the reader) convention that intellect, independence and originality leave no mark on speech pattern becomes a trap when the language of winning advocacy has to come from a man who, had he kept up with his mother, would have had to talk like the back shift. Absence is the cure for difference and also allows for the startling volte face. Drew's brother-in-law, wondering somewhat seditiously about the real reason for Drew's change of heart says:

> 'Do you know what he said to us . . . ? He said "Don't think that I'm being noble. You know me better than that." . . . He also said "The working class will always battle to escape what they are, but when they succeed, they will seize on the first opportunity to cast themselves down again."'[14]

The fresh air of the critical world beyond can almost be tasted here on lips of a writer nearing the end of a long haul at the coal face. Drew tells his son, '"You are, you can be, what you choose to be"' (p. 373). To his nephew who asks '"Do you despise us?"' he replies '"I scorn much of what you are, but only with my head . . . At least . . . that is my excuse"' (p. 374).

The Jessica Stirling books return to late nineteenth-century industrial Scotland for 'The Nicholson Quartet' set in a dockside tenement area of Glasgow, which chart the ascent of the young countrified Nicholsons through an interdependent community of prostitutes, criminals, traders, police and their families. The morality of this wider community is more complex and pragmatic, the ostentatiously affluent operating just this side of the law, those who have to struggle being ethically superior. Craig Nicholson, between acts of valour and compassion, is essentially an unimaginative, touchy, stereotypical farm boy, nonetheless capable of development and maturity. Kirsty, his wife, lighter, brighter, shrewder, more manipulative, has the engaging modernity possibly essential to connect these books to their readers.

The contemporary romantic writer who, perhaps, comes closest to sharing the horizons of the original kailyard school, while introducing a raunchiness that is all her own, is the prolific Christine Marion Fraser whose Rhanna stories, so far seven in all, are set on a fictitious island in the Hebrides, and unfold from just before the Second World War to the late 1960s. (Her later King's series begins in the rural Aberdeenshire of the 1880s and concerns itself with a similar type of character to the Jessica Stirling Nicholson quartet.) In the Rhanna books, red-haired Shona MacKenzie is the central character, maturing from wild child to doggedly sensuous matron in the time span. It is her strong love for and adherence to the ways of the island – and she has choices, one is made to feel – that dominate both ambience and plot.

Shona herself is firmly of the people and there is no sense of distance between writer and character. The dialogue is couthy, earthy, reductive: '"Sit you down and I'll get you a cuppy"'. People who will not sit down and have a cuppy are snooty, ignorant of island custom or deeply troubled in a way that will soon present itself.

The characters have little off-the-page life, and those who are given a history are soon to figure more prominently. Physical beauty, which abounds in the scenery and in the female characters where it is often associated with red hair (women who are not attractive are seldom serious contenders) is constantly undercut by an earthiness of utterance that is so naturalistic as to be occasionally shocking. Humour is robust, lavatorial, and mocks refinement and pretension, but also, on occasion, specs, false teeth, spinsterhood. There is little to choose between the direct speech of one character and another (with the exception of a few choice primitives) thus there is a sanctioned communal voice, and fanciful utterances can be dismissed as daft, often by those who make them.

All the elements of sentimental Scottishness are assembled here. In the second book of the series, *Rhanna At War* (1982), there is a striking set-piece based on the Clydebank Blitz where a remarkably generous selection is deployed in a short time span: the essential goodness of simple people, animals, tea; the blind cruelty or fate; the moral degeneracy of foreigners, whose only path to redemption is by humility, simplicity, sentimentality and, ultimately, assimilation.

Niall, Shona's childhood sweetheart, later to be her husband, has been injured at Dunkirk and is now in lodgings in Clydebank. His 'cheery little Glaswegian landlady', Ma Brodie, has, in spite of rationing, served him a 'hearty meal of thick broth followed by an enormous helping of mashed potatoes, fluffy dumplings and mince'.[15] ('"How do you do it, mo ghaol?"' he asks. '"There are wee ways, son, wee ways a body has."') When the siren goes, Niall, having seen the old people and their pets down to the shelter, hurries off to do his stint as air-raid warden. When he returns he finds the lodging house has taken a direct hit:

> He looked at a crumpled ball of orange fur lying on the cracked pavement and realised it was Ginger Moggy stretched in a pool of his own blood . . . Above him, alive by some freakish escape, Joey perched on a crazily-leaning lampost, feebly muttering 'Good-night Mammy, Mammy's pretty boy.' Miss Rennie's broken body was being lifted from the rubble, the jagged spars of Joey's cage embedded in her chest. Light pink bubbles of lung-blood oozed out of the little holes . . . He found Ma Brodie quite suddenly . . . The teapot was still clutched in her hand, and fragments of a teacup were embedded into the flesh of her arm like crazed paving. Her rib cage had been smashed and splinters of bone stuck through the gay, flowery apron Niall had given her at Christmas. (p. 38)

Above, an exultant Luftwaffe pilot flies over once again to gloat. But his bomb aimer, a country boy, cowering in the fuselage, is escaping from the nightmare by dreaming of the smell of his mother's bread baking, and the rear gunner, a musician, is similarly disaffected. The plane, disabled, wanders out over the Atlantic to crash on the mountains of Rhanna where the disagreeable pilot is captured, while the sentimental bomb aimer, badly wounded, is nursed back to health by Shona's friend Babbie, whom he marries later. The rear gunner is reserved for a further book where he marries Rhanna's blind world-class violinist and composer, Rachel.

In *Song of Rhanna* (1985) Rachel, famous, returns to the island in the wake of her haunting composition of that name which the islanders have been hearing on the radio. 'I had a wee greet to myself it was that nice'.[16] By this time the ban on pretension has been lifted sufficiently to allow quite a lot of cultural activity. Beautiful disabled Ruth has become a poet: 'And the child stole a kiss from its mother's lips, only to give back a millionfold the little that she had taken'[17] Shona quotes to her daughter who is about to go off on a boat in which she will rescue a baby otter called Tubby from a chip-pan fire and die from her burns. This is in *Return to Rhanna* (1984) where, also, Barra McLean, an 'artist wifie' who studied art in Glasgow has retired to the island to open a craft shop. The sudden, bizarre and unaesthetic death of the only child of the central character is redeemed by her angelic nature, and her earlier expressed wish, like Peter Pan, never to grow up. Her mother's subsequent descent towards madness is arrested by the new minister, a young good-looking replacement for the boring, loquacious old one.

Mood swings are balanced by passage of time, new distractions, a nice day, the discomfort of being out of step for too long. George Blake found 'a sort of national infantilism' in the way the first kailyarders ignored the industrialised world.[18] Rhanna, a steamer and a train ride away from that world, wallows in wilful innocence. The narrow local mindset so dominates the tone that small unkindnesses are disregarded and presently obliterated in the great outpouring of good-heartedness, and the robust naturalism is deployed so confidently that the mature Shona can say playfully 'you dirty bugger' to her husband Niall and have it logged as an endearment.[19]

In the most naturalistic of this type of fiction the line between reader and writer has become blurred. They are colluding in a mutually experienced idea uncritically sustained. In *Literary History as a Challenge to Literary Theory* H. R. Jauss takes a spirit level and a T square to the whole caboodle of light reading:

> The distance between the horizon of expectations and the work, between the familiarity of previous aesthetic experiences and the 'horizon change' demanded by the response to new works determines the artistic nature of a literary work along the lines of the aesthetics of reception: the smaller this distance, which means that no demands are made upon the receiving consciousness to make a change on the horizon of unknown experience, the closer the work comes to the realm of 'culinary' or light reading.[20]

Designer Kailyard, then, is irrefutably culinary, but not at the dessert end. Light, but as light goes, heavy. The perpetual kailyard, where no palm tree or shopping plaza will ever flourish, brings to its readers their own perceived gravitas, an antidote to candyfloss. The writer, working alongside a strong school of challenging literary fiction, can shake off the charge of neglecting contemporary reality. The reader, closing the book, looks up from something agreeably salutary.

'Kitsch,' says Milan Kundera in *The Art of the Novel*,

> is something other than simply a work in poor taste. There is a kitsch attitude. Kitsch behaviour. The kitsch-man's need for kitsch: it is the need to gaze into the mirror of the beautifying lie and to be moved to tears of gratification at one's own reflection.[21]

In Scottish Kitsch the mirror is tilted to ennoble rather than to beautify. It is the reflection of the restricted life well employed that asks to be seen, a use of time that might be model to others, a lifestyle that, had it not been inherited, might have been freely chosen.

Notes

1. Ian Campbell, *Kailyard* (Ramsay Head, Edinburgh, 1981), p. 15.
2. Beth Dickson, 'Functions of the Modern Scottish Novel', in *The History of Scottish Literature*, ed. Cairns Craig, 4 vols (Aberdeen University Press, Aberdeen, 1987), vol. 4, p. 50.
3. Rosamunde Pilcher, *September* (Hodder & Stoughton, London, 1990), p. 13. All further references are to this edition.
4. Campbell, *Kailyard*, p. 365.
5. Rosamunde Pilcher, *Wild Mountain Thyme* (Hodder & Stoughton, London, 1978); *The End of Summer* (Hodder & Stoughton, London, 1971).
6. Jan Webster, *Lowland Reels* (Hale, London, 1992), p. 20. All future references are to this edition.
7. Campbell, *Kailyard*, p. 124.

8.   Campbell, *Kailyard*, p. 11.
9.   Magda Sweetland, *Eightsome Reel* (Macmillan, London, 1985), p. 19. All further references are to this edition.
10.   Magda Sweetland, *The Hermitage* (Macmillan, London, 1988), p. 277. All further references are to this edition.
11.   Campbell, *Kailyard*, pp. 10–11.
12.   Jessica Stirling, *The Good Provider* (Pan Books, London, 1988), p. 43.
13.   Jessica Stirling, *The Spoiled Earth* (Hodder & Stoughton, London, 1974), p. 20. All further references are to this edition.
14.   Jessica Stirling, *The Dark Pasture* (Hodder & Stoughton, London, 1977), p. 365. All further references are to this edition.
15.   Christine Marion Fraser, *Rhanna At War* (Collins, London, 1982), p. 25. All further references are to this edition.
16.   Christine Marion Fraser, *Song of Rhanna* (Collins, London, 1985), p. 34.
17.   Christine Marion Fraser, *Return to Rhanna* (Collins, London, 1984), p. 162.
18.   George Blake, *Barrie and the Kailyard School* (A. Barker, London, 1951), p. 9.
19.   *Return to Rhanna*, p. 158.
20.   H. R. Jauss, 'Literary History as a Challenge to Literary Theory', *New Literary History* 2 (1970).
21.   Milan Kundera, *The Art of the Novel*, translated by Linda Asher (Faber, London, 1988), p. 135.

38

Twentieth-century Poetry II:
The Last Twenty-five Years

Dorothy McMillan

Scottish women's poetry is probably having a better time now than it has ever had, assisted perhaps by important Scottish women of letters like Tessa Ransford, founder of the Scottish Poetry Library and editor of *Lines Review*, and Joy Hendry, editor of *Chapman*. The main problem facing women writers today may be the curse of acceptance rather than neglect. For readers not unsurprisingly tend to read their work in terms of a challenge to or resentment of past neglect. This tendency to attribute to women writers the same plot means that the writers are now often being tied down by their readers' willingness to sympathise with battles that they are not always fighting and certainly not only fighting. Modern psychoanalytic criticism has the danger built into it of teasing out the same story over and over again, but even historical and contextual criticism is usually too willing to read women's writing as having as its sole aim the speaking back of marginalised or even colonised female voices. I hope to show that while it is often the case that women writers are reclaiming lost ground they frequently move on from this reclamation to the planting of crops far more various and exotic than are covered by the simple formula of women's experience. In other words while it would be merely perverse to claim that contemporary women poets are unmotivated by their gendered experience of time and place, we should not feel that pointing out such motivation is tribute enough. This is true, I think, even when poets admit that their project is giving voice to the hitherto voiceless. Speaking of her own poetry in *Dream State* Elizabeth Burns admits that she is conscious of Scottish poetry as having been a 'mainly male domain'.[1] Her own poetry, she says, reflects an 'interest in women's ways of seeing and writing. "Valda's Poem/ Sleevenotes", for instance, takes the context of the Scottish poetic tradition and wonders how it might appear to a woman looking in from the outside'. The poem was provoked by a sleevenote to Hugh MacDiarmid's record *Whaur Extremes Meet* with the poet enjoying conversation and whisky with MacCaig, 'Valda in swimsuit, working in the garden, or keeping the soft-coated Wheaten and Border Terrier quiet for the recording'. Burns, no doubt conscious that the very sleevenote undermines the claims of the record's title, offers Valda's perception of the afternoon. The woman is in tune with the natural world that she cultivates; as she lets the 'sun's hands . . . finger the frail flesh of my breasts/rub gold into the crease and wrinkle of my stomach' she feels a diffused desire that diminishes the 'two old men', the 'bottle of whisky', the 'two fat volumes of collected poems' that, fat as they are, leave so much out:

> In the afternoon I sit against the apple tree
> feeling the dent of bark on my bare shoulders
> I close my eyes and the murmur of their voices
> blurs with the birdsong that maybe
> when we listen to the finished record
> will have swum inside the poems

Yet to speak of the special qualities of this poem or of the haunting 'Mother and Child in the Botanic Gardens' merely in terms of theme or feminist revisioning is, as Donny O'Rourke explains, to miss the point by insisting on one. O'Rourke speaks rather of a 'dreamy but meticulous reconstruction of a moment and a mood'.[2] That 'dent of bark' on Valda's shoulders or the baby in the Kibble Palace in Glasgow's Botanic Gardens laying her head 'in the creamy pillow/of a lily flower' confirm a poetry not of absence but of full, if mysterious, presence. Elizabeth Burns is also, like so many contemporary Scottish poets, a contextualising poet, exploring the lesser in the greater and vice versa. Scottishness is not an issue in her poetry but it is a constant point of departure for the imagination as well as the body.

Carol Ann Duffy

Ironically the most famous of the women that Donny O'Rourke includes in his anthology is not uncomplicatedly characterisable as a Scottish poet. But Carol Ann Duffy has herself enabled her identification as a poet whose Scottish origins and, through her mother and her Scottish friendships, continuing Scottish connections, permit complex evaluations of place and the languages of place, in the poetic experience. She was born in Glasgow in 1955 and 'lived firstly in the Gorbals and then in Nitshill, a place name which, I remember, embarrassed me then! My family moved to England in the early 1960s and I spent most of my childhood in Stafford, feeling very much an outsider and trying to change my accent to sound like the English kids'.[3] It is not, however, until her third published collection that Carol Ann Duffy makes significant space in her poems for a reading of that early migration.[4] The two earlier volumes, *Standing Female Nude* and *Selling Manhattan*, experiment with a series of contemporary voices, many on the margins of experience, but it is not until *The Other Country* that Duffy contemplates the origin of her own voice, the voice which all the others front. This is not surprising: it is only once a poetic vocation has been established that the need to place it within the history of the self, and the self within larger histories, begins to obtrude itself. *The Other Country* opens with a poem, 'Originally', which in its subtle miscegeration of child and adult viewpoints questions the notion of originality for people and poets:

> We came from our own country in a red room
> which fell through the fields, our mother singing
> our father's name to the turn of the wheels.

The poem continues to chart the processes of loss and acquisition in the light of the speaker's sense that 'All childhood is emigration', that the identification of self and country involve tangles of the inexplicable:

> Do I only think
> I lost a river, culture, speech, sense of first space
> and the right place? Now, *Where do you come from?*
> strangers ask. *Originally* And I hesitate.
>
>   ('Originally', OC, p. 7)

The collection ends with two poems which further explore notions of self, language and place. In 'The Way My Mother Speaks' the mother's Scottish locutions (*'The day and ever'* and *'What like is it?'*) force the poet to think about permanence and the fleeting moment and about the precision that the poet needs to capture them: 'I am homesick, free, in love/with the way my mother speaks'. 'In Your Mind', the final poem, recognises that wherever one is, there is always an 'other country', 'anticipated or half-remembered', the reality of which is guaranteed by the imagination; and the imagination itself is founded on the experience of self and others:

> You know people there. Their faces are photographs
> on the wrong side of your eyes. A beautiful boy
> in the bar on the harbour serves you a drink – What? –
> asks you if men could possibly land on the moon.
> A moon like an orange drawn by a child. No.
> Never. You watch it peel itself into the sea.
>
>   ('In Your Mind', OC, p. 55)

Duffy responds to a question from Jane Stabler about 'home', identified by Robert Crawford as 'one of the great themes of the 1980s':

> Well, the poems most recently written in *The Other Country* and a fair number of those I've written since do seem, however obliquely, to share the idea of 'home' in some way. I perceive this retrospectively – that is, it wasn't a task I set myself. Going back to the childhood bit, I am writing more autobiographically at the moment. Whether I'll feel that the results are of interest to anyone else is another matter. 'Litany' is the most recent example. I'm quite pleased with that.[5]

'Litany' was published in Duffy's last collection, *Mean Time*. The poem testifies to the adult poet's continuing need to rehearse and revaluate her past, and its strategies reveal Duffy's continuing love affair with linguistic potential and ambiguity, with the way in which words function both to obscure and to expose the depths of experience. The poet as a young child pretends to read as she listens to the conversation of her mother and her friends, poring over shopping catalogues as they drink their afternoon tea in 'The Lounge'. The 'litany' in question is the list of desirables prayerfully murmured by the women as yet untouched by the social revolution of the 1960s: *'candlewick/bed spread three piece suite display cabinet'*. But there is much that cannot be spoken: 'language embarrassed them'. Into this atmosphere of whispers and denial, where no one has 'cancer, or sex, or debts', drops the far-from-innocent error of the child:

> *A boy in the playground,* I said, *Told me*
> *to fuck off;* and a thrilled, malicious pause
> salted my tongue like an imminent storm. Then

> uproar. *I'm sorry, Mrs Barr, Mrs Hunt, Mrs Emery,*
> *sorry, Mrs Raine.* Yes, I can summon their names.
> My mother's mute shame. The taste of soap.
>
> ('Litany', *MT*, p. 9)

Both the exploitation of the Proustian moment and the technique of chucking in the unacceptable word or asking the unaskable question to expose evasion and hypocrisy is a characteristic strategy of Duffy's verse from its earliest stages ('Ash Wednesday', *SFN*; 'A Healthy Meal', *SFN*; 'Mouth with Soap', *SM*). In 'Litany' the Proustianism derives its strength from the precision of the poet's acts of memory, capturing the fragile essence of her own past: 'The year a mass grave of wasps bobbed in a jam-jar;/a butterfly stammered itself in my curious hands' ('The Litany', *MT*, p. 9).

In the interview with Jane Stabler, Carol Ann Duffy says that she does not like to be called a woman poet, 'man poet' after all, she claims is not a locution one encounters.[6] Yet Duffy certainly shifted position far enough to allow her to put together for Viking *I Wouldn't Thank You for a Valentine: Anthology of Women's Poetry* (1992).[7] But Duffy may be right to be suspicious of the 'woman poet' label, since it has a way of sticking itself over wider concerns and Duffy is a varied poet: a poet of place and identity, a love poet with a remarkably sure touch ('Meantime', the last poem in the last collection is a little triumph of love and loss: ' . . . unmendable rain/fell to the bleak streets/where I felt my heart gnaw/at all our mistakes.') and also importantly, a public poet, a 'Poet for Our Times'. Invoking this phrase, the ironic title of Duffy's monologue of a *Sun*-type headline writer, Donny O'Rourke says, 'that's precisely what its creator is too. Duffy, for all her sometimes erotic and intimate lyricism, also writes outspoken poems about the condition of the state'.[8] Alan Robinson, in *Instabilities in Contemporary British Poetry*, also treats Duffy as a serious public poet and at the time of writing he had only *Standing Female Nude* as evidence: 'Impressive in its radical protest is the poetry of Carol Ann Duffy, who writes without affectation on the uncomfortable social issues in Britain in the 1980s: racial tension, child neglect, youth anomie and unemployment, moral callousness and drug addiction[9] But while Robinson recognises Duffy's importance he tends to focus his analysis on those poems – 'You Jane', 'A Provincial Party', 'Standing Female Nude', 'Missile', 'Naming Parts' – that allow the identification of a clear feminist perspective even when the speaking voice is male. Robinson has some very useful things to say about male pressures on female experience and the possible repression endemic within our culture of female language. But we may after three further collections by Duffy feel that the pervasiveness of her feminism should by now be regarded, as Kathleen Jamie puts it of her Scottishness, as 'a matter of fact not of worth'.[10]

Accepting this enables a wider view of Duffy's sympathies, for by so thoroughly *understanding* even the hateful speaker of 'You Jane' she enables an extension of the reader's sympathies: it is a peculiar characteristic of Duffy's verse that the anger, even contempt, that sometimes fuels it will not permit facile dismissal of its speaking subjects:

> She says Did you dream, love? I never
> dream. Sleep is black as a good jar.
> I wake half-conscious with a hard-on, shove it in.
> She don't complain. When I feel, I feel here
> where the purple vein in my neck throbs.
>
> ('You Jane', *SFN*, p. 34)

Reviewing *Selling Manhattan* in the *Times Literary Supplement* Lachlan Mackinnon gets to the heart of Duffy's special qualities as a monologist, or perhaps rather a developer of voices. He cites the title poem in which an American Indian speaks his desolation after Manhattan has been sold. The speaker's voice plangently provides an elegy for what America has still to become: 'Man who fears death, how many acres do you need/ to lengthen your shadow under the endless sky?' Mackinnon recognises this as dramatic voice but continues:

> To call this a dramatic monologue slightly misses the point: what the poet is concerned with is not presenting a character or a situation but entering into a different way of seeing or mode of experience.[11]

Duffy presents a 'gallery of psychopaths, mental curiosities, disturbed women and children, but like the American Indian each shows us a rinsed version of the world'.[12]

It is fitting that the *TLS* reviewer of *Mean Time* should be Shena Mackay. Mackay in *Dunedin* tackles the horribleness of the imploding world of urban alienation and disintegration and it is unsurprising that she should recognise the compassionate power in Duffy's rendering of her urban, rainy landscape where the captain of the 1964 *Top of the Form* team deplores his 'stale wife' and 'thick kids', longing for the lost country of his expectant childhood, where the terrible men lurk in the woods awaiting the half fascinated child, where an adulterer pays for it 'in cash, fiction, cab-fares back/to the life which crumbles like a wedding-cake', where a suicide prepares the future suffering of the living, where most commonly the days are 'shortened' and the nights are 'endless'. For Duffy like all the best moralists earns her insights through wit and understanding and supports their bleakness, as does Shena Mackay, by an occasional transfiguring beauty which yields 'moments of grace' as powerful as they are evanescent.

Duffy's use of dramatised voices is the strategy of a kind of passionate non-alignment on the part of the modern poet. The manipulation of other voices is perhaps a characteristic of writing in a plural society or one which is changing too rapidly for most of its members to comprehend it. Thus Duffy as 'state of the nation' poet makes the effort to comprehend the incomprehensible. The use of dramatic forms registers both the desire for a more complete knowledge of social structures, while at the same time it comes out of a certain hopelessness about achieving it. The last poem of *Mean Time* is called 'Prayer' and its authority comes in part from the awareness that it is written by a poet who has earlier written: 'For Christ's sake, do not send your kids to Mass'. The calm reverence of 'Prayer' has not been won without a struggle; it comes, as Hamlet's final peace comes, from being still and listening to the messages in the world around us today and in the quiet hours of our childhood, listening to the shipping forecast with its evocation of a world elsewhere, both exotic and familiar in our homes:

> Some days, although we cannot pray, a prayer
> utters itself. So, a woman will lift
> her head from the sieve of her hands and stare
> at the minims sung by a tree, a sudden gift
>
> . . .
>
> Pray for us now. Grade I piano scales
> console the lodger looking out across
> a Midlands town. Then dusk, and someone calls
> a child's name as though they named their loss.

> Darkness outside, the radio's prayer –
> Rockall. Malin. Dogger. Finisterre.
> ('Prayer', *MT*, p. 52)

Dilys Rose and Marion Lomax

Dilys Rose's characteristic poetic forms are in some ways similar to those of Carol Ann Duffy – she exploits the monologue and the portrait. These methods reach their most sophisticated results in Rose's short stories which are, justly I think, more celebrated than her poetry. But the poems, particularly of *Madame Doubtfire's Dilemma*, offer satisfactions that are often witty and always individual.[13] Dilys Rose's focus is no more wholly feminine than that of Carol Ann Duffy but it is in her revisioning of the plights and adventures of iconic female figures that Dilys Rose finds a distinctive poetic strategy. She gives voice to a Figurehead, to the Sirens, to a Caryatid and to Pandora. She enters the sufferings of the Queen Bee and the Little Mermaid. And in a delightful sequence of poems she takes us inside, literally in the first case, Matryushka, Rag Doll, China Doll, a dressmaker's Dummy, a Maumet, a Fertility Doll, a Performing Doll, a Fetish. And then there is the Artiste and the Succubus and the, happily for the owner, unfeeling Fantasy with fully removable and adjustable parts. The linguistic vitality of Rose's dolls fights against the immobility and impotence of their conditions: 'Faking fragility/Crushed between tons of roof and floor?/Why must I look as if I dance/Beneath my load?' asks the exasperated Caryatid. And the Rag Doll articulates her longing for an impossible transformation:

> All that I am
> Is leftover, scrap
> A confetti of remnants.
> I'm droop-eyed, a flopsy,
> My fluff head nods and lolls.
> Behind my tacked-on grin
> Beneath my bright gladrags
> Can no-one tell I'm in shreds?
> Can no-one feel me burst at the seams
> For the impossible,
> Long to be made new?
> ('Rag Doll', *MDD*, p. 32.)

Carol Ann Duffy and Dilys Rose are in their different ways great exploiters of difference, willing crossers and raiders of borders in the search for appropriate voice and form. *Raiding the Borders* is the title of Marion Lomax's second collection of poems.[14] Like Carol Ann Duffy, Marion Lomax invites appropriation, provided that the complicated meaning of her Scottishness is respected. She was born in Newcastle and grew up in Northumberland; she now spends her time between Aberdeen and London where she is Professor of English at St Mary's University College. Lomax makes raids on historical time lines and on the physical and emotional borders between the countries of the United (perhaps) Kingdom. She gives a voice, both Scots and English, and more significantly a name to Lady Macbeth. Gruoch, the notes explain, was descended from Kenneth III of Scotland (murdered by Malcolm II to secure the throne for his grandson, Duncan). Thus the border-raiding academic revises Scottish history as told by an Englishman:

> Dochter tae a king, faither sin taen,
> mairrit, sin weeda. Aa dinna greet.
> Ma lad, Lulach, maun gang hes ain gait
> an gie's ane bricht chance tae lauch agin.
> > ('Gruoch Considers', *RB*, p. 16)

Questions of history and of national belonging depend on where one is looking from. Yet division may be transcended, borders may be negotiated, raids may not always be bloody. Telling phrases catch the troubled loves and needs that may transcend division:

> On the other side of the border
> they call this *Scozia Irredenta*:
> unredeemed.
> > . . .
> England was never an only child
> but has grown to think so . . .
> > . . .
> > > The bends
> on the border
> > > won't make up their minds.
> Five times
> > > they twist me round, but I still
> head north.
> > > > ('Kith', *RB*, p. 11)

And in 'Raiding the Borders' Lomax uses the past feuds of her own family and the deep personal loss in her mother's death to invoke the 'debateable land' between north and south, past and present, life and death: 'we are', she concludes, 'never free from borders' (*RB*, p. 27).[15]

Kathleen Jamie

Kathleen Jamie has gone even farther out of her way to find something of the meaning of these borders; to investigate her Scottishness and the meaning of her gendered experience of the diverse places she has visited.[16] It is typical of her current assured modesty as a writer that she speaks self-deprecatingly of the products of her travels in Northern Pakistan, Tibet and China. (In her introduction to *The Autonomous Region* she refers to the world events which affected her time in Tibet: 'general strikes, closed borders, and then on 4th June 1989, the Tiananmen Square massacre'. These poems she says are 'my hopelessly inadequate response to those events'.[17]) and that she equally tosses out casually the dedication of her latest volume of poetry: 'This one's for the folks at home'.

The volumes that come out of her travels both divide and connect her collections of poetry, showing how a series of encounters with otherness have assisted her definition of a self and its location; how necessary modifications of social and national voice have worked to generate a poetic voice both individual and generously inclusive. At the same time Kathleen Jamie is wary of labels and pigeonholes and resistant to attempts to pin down the motives of her writing:

> I can't answer the question 'why do you write?' In bursts of enthusiasm I have tried to be a 'woman writer' and a 'Scottish writer' but grow irritated and feel confined. I have no motives, certainly no 'message', but I would like to write some very good poems.[18]

No one reading *Black Spiders*, published by Salamander Press in 1982, could have failed to discern a new fusion of intellectual grip and delicate perception in Scottish writing. Kathleen Jamie was only twenty when this collection of eighteen poems was published and a number of them were written when she was even younger: she had won an Eric Gregory Award in 1981 which enabled the travel which informs some of the poems in this little collection. What still impresses is the way in which such a young writer leaves space in a number of the poems for the imagination of old mysteries, old conflicts, old civilisations while flirting with the desires of new young love. It is true that although Kathleen Jamie shows that she knows what the voices of modern poetry are like, she does not yet quite find a distinctive voice for herself within them. Yet there is consistent promise that the sometimes wilful obscurity will become necessary complexity; that the merely smart has the potential to become emotionally and technically wise.

The title poem of the collection engages with alien place and ancient experience and harnesses these simultaneously to explicate and complicate personal contacts:

> He looked up to the convent
> she'd gone to. She answered no questions
> but he knew by the way she'd turned away
> that morning.
> He felt like swimming to the caves.
>
> *
>
> The nuns have retreated. The eldest still
> peals the bell in glee. although no-one comes
> from the ruins. All their praying was done
> when they first saw the ships and the Turks'
> swords reflecting the sun.
>
> In the convent the cistern is dry,
> the collection boxes empty – cleft skulls
> severed and bleached,
> are kept in a shrine, and stare to the East.
>
> *
>
> She caught sight of him later, below, brushing salt
> from the hair of his nipples. She wanted them to tickle; black spiders on her lips.
>
> ('Black Spiders')[19]

There is perhaps something a little knowing about the deployment of the fashionable technique of teasingly incomplete story-telling and the poem is certainly very determined on its last line. Yet it is a remarkable last line with its faintly threatening sexuality, its gender-mixing sensuality which brings together the sexes so violently and barrenly separated in the centre of the poem. And even at this stage Jamie establishes her self-consciousness about the nature of her art: in 'Permanent Cabaret' Estelle, the highwire artiste, negotiates the claims of life and love made by Coco, her clown lover, and those of her profession:

> Half way across Estelle glitters like frost.
> She has frozen. 'Remain professional.' She
> draws breath through her teeth, wavers
> her hand: 'Let Coco sense something for once!'
> His red boots are edging towards her. He
> coaxes, offers aid – his absurd umbrella.
> The audience wonder: is it part of the show
> this embarrassing wobbling,
> this vain desperation to clutch?[20]

The cunning artistic deployment of the embarrassing wobble and the existential desperation to clutch become part of Jamie's professionalism.

Jamie's next venture was a collaborative one with Andrew Greig. *A Flame in Your Heart* (1986) tells the story of the love affair between a Spitfire pilot and a nurse in 1940, a love tragically although predictably terminated by his death. To Richard Price she says enigmatically, 'If I said I didn't like that book you'd no doubt ask me why, so I won't.' Perhaps the mode of rejection is a clue to the way in which the conception of the book did not quite suit her. In the course of her writing Jamie works through to a distinctive yet plural voice but this is different from the kind of ventriloquism that speaking as a distinct character involves. Possibly the relative fixity that this imposes over the length of a book constrains Jamie's normally provocative openness just as the pressure to tell a predetermined story leaves little scope for the gaps over which her writing teeters like Estelle's act.

Jamie's second collection *The Way We Live*[21] reprints some of the poems from *Black Spiders* and adds characteristic here and there poems which sometimes double as love poems – 'Clearances', 'Poem for a departing mountaineer'; the central section of thirteen poems 'Karakoram Highway' introduces the squalor and the glory, the exoticism and banality of Northern Pakistan, later the subject matter of her travel book, *The Golden Peak*;[22] the concluding section focuses alternately on life's indicative contingencies and on the personal, local, obliquely autobiographical. The controlled miscellaneousness of the whole provides the justification for the final poem, probably still Jamie's most famous:

> Pass the tambourine, let me bash out praises
> to the Lord God of movement, to Absolute
> non-friction, flight, and the scary side:
> death by avalanche, birth by failed contraception.
>   . . .
> Of endless gloaming in the North, of Asiatic swelter,
> to laundrettes, anecdote, passions and exhaustion,
> Final Demands and dead men, the skeletal grip
> of government . . .
> To the way it fits, the way it is, the way it seems
> to be: let me bash out praises – pass the tambourine.
>   ('The Way We Live', *TWWL*, p. 54)

The vitality of the poem needs no underlining but it is important to notice that as the last poem in the collection it is supported by the whole of what has preceded it, which are the poem's credentials, protecting its sentiments from facility.

The Golden Peak and *The Autonomous Region*, in collaboration with the photographer Sean Mayne Smith, were published in 1992 and 1993 respectively. Both books indicate the need to travel to understand 'home' but also the need to come home in order to establish valid senses of both here and there. As a result of her travels Jamie's understanding of Scotland and of the significance of her life within it becomes genuinely philosophical. Her reading of the other regions can never be quite as poised. At some points *The Golden Peak* is a little uncomfortable when in order to convey otherness Jamie gives her Pakistani friends quaint speech modes which seem to make her own stance patronising: Rashida explains. '"We are purdah-observing! The MA is available only at college. This BA I did attain at home. For examinations only I did leave the house."'23 At the same time it is perhaps this very discomfort and Jamie's own sense of her indeterminate position, for she is nothing if not self-examining and her Pakistani friends are nothing if not lovingly critical of the deficiencies of Kathleen's life, that enables her to see the painfulness of the failing 'balancing act' of this society between the local and the foreign, the traditional and the new. *The Autonomous Region* charts a journey across China, a journey which was 'halted at the border of the "Autonomous Region" of Tibet by the events of the time: general strikes, closed borders, and then on 4th June 1989, the Tiananmen Square massacre' (*AR*, p. 6). Jamie's journey is accompanied by two ghosts who repeatedly re-embody themselves in figures of the present – a fourth-century Buddhist monk and Princess Wen Cheng, a seventh-century Eve or Pandora avatar. (Jamie is fond of reincarnating legendary or historical figures, at home Dame Julian of Norwich who is admired for 'banging on at God' about the meaning of evil and disaster and suffering.) Thus the poems of *The Autonomous Region* are located in the space between past struggles for autonomy and contemporary acts of erasure. The rumours of the massacre reach the foreigners each with their own tongues, yet somehow understanding the 'Chinese whispers' that threaten to put an end to all autonomy of life or language. Jamie's answer to the age-old courage of Tibet and its people is to mark it with the old tongue of her own people. The latter day Wen Cheng waits with the terrible story:

> A licht-bulb, hingit fi the ceilin
> by a short cord.
> A slever o gless in the oose
> an a black hair. She tell me
> they've killed 5000 people in Beijing.
>   . . .
> This is a place your friens disappear:
> trust naebody. Luve a.
> The smearit wa's o a concrete room,
> a wumman sweepin.
>   ('For Paola', *AR*, p. 70)

The vernacular tongue is also constantly under erasure unless it is able to reaffirm itself by persistent imaginative acts. As if in preparation for further such acts Jamie concludes *The Autonomous Region* with a look back home: 'A'm waukenet, on a suddenty mindit:/ A'm far frae hame,/I hae crossed China' ('Xiahe', *AR*, p. 78).

In her most recent collection *The Queen of Sheba* 'the travelling poet', as Raymond Friel puts it, 'comes back home'.24 It is the collection in which Jamie most clearly takes on the perplexities of nation and gender. In it Kathleen Jamie finds a voice that is both authoritative and celebratory, yet she does so while still maintaining those secret places of the self within which female experience learns to grow the right to universal comment even while recognising in the modern manner the provisionality of the universal. The voice is a female voice but it is a plural one as far as tongue is concerned. Jamie moves from tongue to tongue with the virtuoso ease of Estelle and again teases the reader with occasional breathtaking hoverings in between. 'A multiple linguistic inheritance', says Bernard O'Donoghue reviewing W. N. Herbert and Kathleen Jamie, 'is a strength, not a gag or humiliation.'[25]

In the title poem of the collection the Queen of Sheba herself has come to Calvin's land in glorious subverting triumph:

> See her lead those great soft camels
> widdershins round the kirk-yaird,
> smiling
> as she eats
> avocados with apostle spoons
> she'll teach us how . . .
> ('The Queen of Sheba', QS, p. 9)

Languages and cultures are stirred in a witch's brew out of which comes new confidence, new sustenance, which enables the expected put-down to be transformed to affirmation:

> Sure enough: from the back of the crowd
> Someone growls:
>
>   *whae do you think y'ur?*
>
> and a thousand laughing girls and she
> draw our hot breath
>   and shout:
>
> THE QUEEN OF SHEBA!
>   (QS, p. 11)

'They', 'she', 'our' – the plural female voice shouts out its refusal of traditional limitations to female power. If these are witches then they are witches like the lawless 'Bairns of Suzie' who are both contemporary children running wild outside the Co-op and, as they career across the braes of the the ancient Fife landscape, incarnations of an ancient, dangerous female potential, a potential which can still perhaps be sniffed out 'among the wifies in headscarfs' ('Bairns of Suzie: A Hex', QS, pp. 25–6). In this way female and national history are brought together: the life of the woman is situated within the life of the country which in turn is placed in wider contexts of place and time. Here in spite of her earlier reservations about being a Scottish poet, Jamie comes closer to the position most clearly laid out by Eavan Boland in her pamphlet, *A Kind of Scar*, and in her interview with Rebecca Wilson.[26] Boland writes as an Irish poet but argues that the issues are not only local and personal but may have wider implications for the woman poet working within a national tradition in which she has more often been a source of poetic subject matter than the author of the poem. She brings the woman and the nation together in ways that Jamie had viewed with suspicion:

> Womanhood and Irishness are metaphors for one another. There are resonances of humilia-
> tion, oppression and silence in both of them and I think you can understand one better by

experiencing the other . . . A 'nation' is a potent, important image. It is a concept that a woman writer must discourse with. I have that discourse and I like to think I have it partially on my terms. But no poet ever discourses with such a powerful image on his or her own terms. There has to be some contact between my perceptions and the national perceptions in Irish literature.[27]

Eavan Boland is a distinguished writer who largely negotiates the potential pitfalls in her own position but it remains problematic. If the woman poet within a national tradition promotes or concedes the metaphorical connection between female oppression and pressure on the nation, then the result may be entrapment within that figuring. The slip into the suffering female figure as emblem of the nation is always possible and always, I think, a concession to male ways of figuring. Jamie's solution is to choose her battleground in the space between the beckoning lures of domesticity and exile. The desire for the clarity of departure to 'there' which cleans away the remnants of life 'here' is brilliantly realised in 'Swallows and Swifts':

> Twitter of swallows and swifts:
> '*tickets and visas, visas and tickets*' –
> winter, and cold rain
> clears the milky-way of birdshit
> where wires cross the lane.
> ('Swallows and Swifts', QS, p. 48)

Yet this departure perhaps achieves clarity at the cost of bleakness. In two deeply personal poems, 'Wee Baby' and 'Wee Wifey', the opposite pull of homeliness is embodied. The former's 'fishy tricks' will surely anchor the traveller for, since her 'kingdom' is within, she is everywhere: 'She blows about the desert in a sand-pram,/O traveller' ('Wee Baby', QS, p. 29); and the latter, however anathematised as a demon, is the ultimate protection against unrootedness:

> It's sad to note
>   that without
>   WEE WIFEY
> I shall live long and lonely as a tossing cork.
>   ('Wee Wifey', QS, p. 30)

But anchorages, rather than safe havens, may be places where the frail vessel rots. Raymond Friel quotes from 'School Reunion' to illuminate this problem:

> Linda   willowy acrobat
> divorce   cartwheels, skirts
> Expecting (again)   cover her face
>
>   a mother's grip
>   *can't you be more*
>   *ladylike,*   women
>   beware
>   gravity.
> ('School Reunion', QS, p. 21)

'Key poems', Friel points out, 'deal with the implications of the gravitational pull in a woman's life – the biological and cultural forces that can be stifling – and explore the possible escapes and compromises.'[28] What lifts the poem above rhythmic grumbling about the female condition is, of course, its nimble linguistic and rhythmic performances. But it is more than this too, for the resonances of Renaissance drama are invoked in disturbing ways. 'Cover her face' surely echoes Ferdinand in Ford's *The Duchess of Malfi* as he looks at the corpse of his sister, the Duchess, dead by his order: 'Cover her face: Mine eyes dazell: she di'd yong' (*The Duchess of Malfi*, IV, 2, 267). The Duchess pays horribly for preferring passionate love to patriarchal codes; in some dwindled sense these once girls, now women, at their Reunion also struggle to maintain passion, to keep alive a youthful flame, 'a coloured twist/within us, like a marble' ('School Reunion', *QS*, p. 24), in a world that strives to obliterate such traces of vitality. In this sense 'women' must 'beware gravity'. But the phrase evokes another Renaissance drama, Middleton's *Women Beware Women*. Kathleen Jamie is too honest to ignore the complicity of women with their oppressions. Just as the little girls who 'pull' their 'soft backsides/through the jagged may's/white blossom' ('Mother-May-I', *QS*, p. 12) are half in love with their own potential degradation by the perverts in the woods, so the big girls of 'School Reunion' may still be their own worst enemies.

But generally this collection is, as the title poem indicates, more celebratory than admonitory. Women are usually seen in a kind of sisterhood of old girls who are capable of finding, even within the tawdry junk of the moment, ancient sources of life-giving power. In 'Fountain' Jamie recovers the ancient meanings that lurk in the debased evidences of contemporary culture. The fountain, far from sacred, is the 'shallow dish' in the city-centre shopping arcade into which we casually toss 5p pieces. What do we mean when we do so?

> So we glide from mezzanine to ground,
> laden with prams, and bags printed
> Athena, Argos, Olympus; thinking: now
> *in Arcadia est* I'll besport myself
> at the water's edge with kids,
> coffee in a polystyrene cup.
>
> . . .
>
> So we flick in coins, show the children how:
> *make a wish!* What for, in the shopping mall?
> A wee stroke of luck? A something else, a nod
> toward a goddess we almost sense
> in the verdant plastic? Who says
> we can't respond; don't still feel,
> as it were, the dowser's twitch
> up through the twin handles of the buggy.
>   ('Fountain', *QS*, p. 17)

Thus the tacky domesticity that still drags women down is transformed into the very source of female power.

As women may defeat the deadening present by tapping ancient sources of strength in a distant past, so the dilemma of here and there, of rootedness and exile is similarly settled by reconciliation. But even as reconciliation is achieved, enough remains that is worrying to prevent its being a facile compromise. A number of poems discover that 'there' is within 'here' and vice versa: it is possible for the Dalai Lama to have a dream on Skye:

> When no one's watching,
> he jumps lightly onto Soay
> and airborne seeds
> of saxifrage, settled
> > on the barren Cuillin
> waken into countless tiny stars.
> ('A Dream of the Dalai Lama on Skye', QS, p. 53)

East and West meet and the barrenness of the mountain is transfigured by an act of loving playfulness.

In 'Another Day in Paradise' the poet on a desert island imagines the intrusion of 'mail' from civilisation brought in on the tide; 'It's a/shoppers-survey come government demand'. She makes the mail into a paper boat and sends it back carrying an *island totem* constructed out of miscellaneous bits and pieces from the island paradise. Thus the traps of the 'here' are transformed into the bearers of messages from the imagined 'there', their threat neutralised by their incorporation into the dream of freedom. The landscape of the desert island is similarly shifting and surprising:

> You gave up gazing at the purple sea
> turned inland. Didn't you know
> whaups flew between palm trees,
> coconuts fell to the banks
> of peaty lochs with a damp thump?
> Didn't you know it could rain here?
> ('Another Day in Paradise', QS, p. 55)

Further reconciliation of the 'here' and 'there', of the imagined and the real, is achieved through language as the poet writes on the sand 'words you thought you'd forgotten;/ *forfauchlet; havers; fowk*' (QS, p. 55). The paradise and 'the shepherd and his daughter' with hard bread, cheese and pipe that are invoked to people it, turn out in the end to be illusions, recognised by the recollecting poet as 'trickery', yet the intensity of the imagining deceives even the poet herself: they were 'so real I could smell them on the bright air'.

The intense yet oddly haphazard efforts of the imagination hold together present and past, here and there, but it is important that the imagination is truthful even if its truths are only equivocally promising. In 'At Point of Ness' at Stromness in Orkney the poet is walking at night across the golf course towards the sea. 'Half-sensed' phenomena take on a half-threatening difference as she approaches the shore:

> I walk on,
> towards the shore, where the night's
> split open, the entire
> archipelago set as sink-weight
> to the sky . . .

She imagines that the surrounding lighthouses beam out a message which is as threatening as it is reassuring:

> *never   ever*
> *harm – this,*
>   *you never could*
> ('At Point of Ness', *QS*, p. 62)

The age of the natural and chastening effect on human insignificance sends her chasing back to her 'own door'. But by day and in sunlight the story is different; the relationship between the natural and the human is perceived in another light:

> Sunshine
> gleams the dry-stane dykes'
> lovely melanoma of lichen. A wren
> flicks on a weathered post
> like a dud lighter, by the track
> that splits the golf course
> from the town's edge to the shore,
> where I walk this afternoon
> for a breath of air.
> ('At Point of Ness', *QS*, p. 63)

The lichen on the dykes is simultaneously lovely and deadly, like melanoma; the wren is perhaps no less lovely for being compared to the used-up products of modern life; and there is a way through, a connection, from the town to the sea, albeit one which traverses the golf course.

Kathleen Jamie has had a wee baby since she published *The Queen of Sheba*. This may not keep her 'here', or not for long. But if it does, we may imagine her continuing to love ruefully even the unacceptable things of Scotland; we may see her in the posture celebrated at the end of the witty poem, 'The Republic of Fife', addressing her fellow Fifers:

> Citizens:
> our spires and doocoots
> institutes and tinkies' benders,
> old Scots kings and dancing fairies
> give strength to my house
>
> on whose roof we can balance,
> carefully stand and see
> clear to the far off mountains,
> cities, rigs and gardens,
>
> Europe, Africa, the Forth and Tay bridges,
> even dare let go, lift our hands
> and wave to the waving citizens
> of all those other countries.
> ('The Republic of Fife', *QS*, pp. 50–1)

Angela McSeveney

Kathleen Jamie has travelled far for her perceptions but the exploration of the meaning of self and place, of roots and uprooting does not need vast distances for its articulation:

> I left home this Summer
> two years after I moved away.
>
> No one heard me say goodbye
> but my roots came up bloodstained.

Angela McSeveney describes the pain not so much of leaving home as of realising that one has done so. The packed little poem registers both the solitariness of separation (since 'goodbye' would still have signalled community), and the problem of transplanting or re-rooting these bloody roots.[29] But it is less the indefiniteness of nation that concerns Angela McSeveney than the problems of community and place within it. In an interview with Carol Gow in *Verse* she admits that she had an early sense that being a Scottish woman writer would be a tough task: 'I began to read articles about women and writing and became aware that if you were Scottish it was going to be tough, you wouldn't be listened to and if you were a woman you wouldn't be listened to. And if you were a Scottish woman you might as well give up!'[30] Yet there is something rather routine about this perception compared to the more clearly personal sense of not belonging which she registers in and out of her poetry. 'I've always been aware of feeling that I don't really come from a particular place.'[31]

> My mother stood her potplants on old saucers,
> all of them survivors from separate sets.
>
> Each item had been packed into a tea-chest at least
>   once
> then laid out on another shelf.
>
> I remember playing among the balled-up newspaper
> on a different kitchen floor.
>
> My mother tended to her red geraniums
> and wondered at the crockery
>   we must have gone through.
>   ('Crockery', *COWI*, p. 19)

Here in a way that characterises much of her verse Angela McSeveney wrests the hidden significances out of common experience. Most of us have experienced at least once the crumpled newspapers from packing chests, and who does not place potplants on old saucers? But here we are made to feel human isolation and fragility through the saucers, still bravely surviving but vulnerable, like their vanished fellows, to the next move. And for the child the 'balled-up newspaper', itself a figure of the temporary, becomes the only stable feature of a series of houses. Angela McSeveney did not come from a really frequently shifting or unstable family but it was a family that did not fit a stereotypical social place and which moved from Highland community to new town to a tied cottage on a Border estate.

At first then it does seem as though the important things to say about Angela McSeveney's poetry do come out of personal and peculiarly gendered experience. And these are largely and quite properly the things that are raised in the *Verse* interview. Here, stress is placed by both parties on the instabilities of Angela McSeveney's life, instabilities that derive not only from uncertainty about her proper place, but also from from her perception of herself as a rather unattractive, unsexy, different woman, self-forced by this perception into at best effacement, at worst pathological withdrawal. Of course, both women make it clear that they do not imagine that poetry is in any simple way autobiographical. What matters in the end, however, is the pressure that this gendered experience places on technique. For the verse itself turns on the twin drives of concealment and violent exposure which the collection's title signals – there would not be so much to come out with had the revelation not been preceded by so much repression. What is repressed again comes out of common experience, rendered uncommon by the oblique perception of how terrible, how threatening is everyday life. There are the lice that must not be spoken of at school ('Lice'); the late period that will certainly come out with it, if its message is true ('Late Period'); the prolific hair concealed by 'long sleeves' and 'dark tights' ('The Hirsute Woman'); the desire that must convert into friendship for a male companion who suddenly announces that he is gay ('Coming Out With It'). More distressing, however, than 'coming out with it' is that revelation does not always bring sympathetic understanding and is, therefore, a prelude not to a new fullness of being but rather to further anguished retreat ('Exposure'). 'At the Shrink' tells the whole story of this process:

> The camp part of me wants a couch
> to lie on but he offers
> only an easy chair.
>
> I try to settle down in it.
>
> I can hear the whisper of his pencil
> against the paper
> as he jots down notes.
>
> The point jerks like a seismograph
> measuring the impact of my answers.
> I blurt out some startling truth
> and watch, baffled,
> when his right hand doesn't move.
>
> ('At the Shrink')

Here the typically witty play on 'camp', 'couch', 'chair' and 'settle' join with the ambivalence of 'lie on' to set a scene of civilised torture and inevitable concealment. The 'whisper' of the pen confirms a secrecy that is violated by the revealing significance of the marks of the pencil on the paper. The 'startling truth' comes out almost unwilled and is met by incomprehension: a self has flashed out and not been recognised. And the true therapy for the reluctant madwoman proves to be not at the 'shrink' but in the expansion of self made possible by compassion for others and in the process of transforming the ordinary from threat to friend. The traumas of the self enable unsentimental pity for others in the present and the past, for the 'victim of violence' ('Victim of Violence'), for Bessie Henderson, scalped when her hair is caught in a loom ('The Pictures'), for Janey, raped at seven and trapped in permanent childhood ('Janey'). That wounded self that in an early poem finds calm in patiently blacking a hearth stone ('Blacking a Hearth Stone') goes on to discover that even in the pathetic 'anaemic and spindly' nightscented stocks that she has sewn there may be a potential garden of 'rosebeds and herbs,/tangles of scarlet runners'.

The paradoxical desire simultaneously to preserve and explode, expose and retreat, also informs Angela McSeveney's linguistic strategies. Like Liz Lochhead and, although to a lesser extent, Carol Ann Duffy, Angela McSeveney manipulates possibilities of cliché, by both affirming its underlying truth and exposing its potential for damaging stereotype. It is not, of course, the case that the use of cliché is particularly gendered – the twentieth-century master of the manipulation of cliché is probably Beckett – yet there does seem to be a sense in which this linguistic feature is particularly serviceable to women writers. Cliché proves attractive, I think, to these women because it is in cliché that the ordinary truths and traps of experience are embedded. And so in cliché it is possible perhaps to find both the sources of female uncertainty and also the possibly enduring beliefs and prejudices on which such uncertainty may be founded.

Angela McSeveney is more explicit than the other poets I have mentioned in her acknowledgement of the cliché as device:

> Once upon a time I uttered words
> as meaningless as myself.
>
> They could only be approximations
> and always of someone else's feelings
>
> but Autumn leaves do look like carpet on the ground
> and hearts can at least come close to breaking.
>   ('Clichés')

Here Angela McSeveney rather sadly admits the chastening near truths embedded in daily linguistic habit. Elsewhere she more often seeks to free experience from the attitudes enshrined in cliché which begin to do their imprisoning work on the growing child. She was 'no beauty', people 'washed their hands' of her ('My Crime'); in adolescence, self-dissatisfied, she 'would like to have opened the door/and shown myself out./But I wasn't going anywhere' ('Retreat'). This use of cliché then enables a more complex investigation of the pressures that social expectation places on the developing self that seeks both to return to the simplicities of these expectations and to flee from their imprisoning restraints. The child within the woman remains as reminder and reproach.

Poetry in Scots: Sheena Blackhall, Ellie McDonald, Alison Kermack

Contemporary poetry written in Scots, of whatever kind, enters into a more or less successful, more or less amicable dialogue with dominant English usage; this is also true of course, of poetry which comes out of the immigrant cultures. In Scottish poetry of the eighteenth and nineteenth centuries the preservers of the vernacular were often women poets, nor was this uniformly a function of conservatism; in the hands of Janet Hamilton, for example, the vernacular has a vigour that nearly does the work of radicalism. In the early part of the twentieth century Jacob and Angus delivered potentially subversive female experience through a deceptively unaggressive use of the vernacular. But after MacDiarmid it is hard not to concede that the vernacular territory has been mapped by men and it was finally in male voices that the use of Scots became a fully rounded political issue. One consequence of the dominance of the male voice in the vernacular poems of the Renaissance and its aftermath (in the writing of Leonard, Crawford, Herbert,

Vettese, O'Neill) is that women poets writing in the vernacular enter willy-nilly into a dialogue not only with English poetry but with Scottish male vernacular poetry and it is a dialogue in which their voices seem less adapted to survival. Sheena Blackhall has unquestionably fashioned a distinctive voice for herself in north-east Scots but in both her poems and short stories she is in a sense self-marginalised, choosing a speech, an angle of vision and a publisher which are firmly located in the north-east. It is a problem of which she is perfectly aware. In conversation with Rebecca Wilson she confesses to preferring painting as a 'universal language' and she concedes that while the 'Scottishness makes for individuality . . . sometimes I swither, because it decreases the size of your reading public. This is not any reflection on the language, it's just a statement of fact'.[32] Blackhall's 'The Tea Pairty' is informed by concerns about linguistic imperialism not dissimilar to those of Tom Leonard's 'Unrelated Incidents', although Blackhall has not quite got a grasp of the wider political and philosophical issues that Leonard handles so effortlessly. But Blackhall's poem is limited too by a north-east Scots much less generally available and, more damagingly, quainter, less hard-edged, than Leonard's urban, if literary, Scots ('scutter', 'mochie', 'hubber').[33]

Ellie McDonald's poems in Dundee Scots are forced, whether she chooses it or not, into dialogue with the intimidatingly intellectual manipulations of the same dialect by W. N. Herbert. Herbert sees his linguistic decisions as career decisions and as theorisable. Herbert explains that most of the poems in *Dundee Doldrums* were initially written in one week in the summer of 1982:

> At that point, I was writing in English and, although I had read MacDiarmid, Garioch etc. with interest, I thought of them as a historically discrete unit, tied up with nationalist dogmas I didn't share.

Herbert remarks the pressures on his poetry of Ginsberg and Kerouac and continues:

> I had just completed my first degree at Oxford. My playground voice seemed very far away. But the poetry I was writing was a curious mixture of English, American(ish), Scots English, and something not quite formed. By the end of the week the English element had been almost wholly overwhelmed. It was like trying to make a career decision. Could I haul the language back towards a standard, or should I let it swerve off along its own route?[34]

Herbert concludes his reminiscence with a discussion of the propriety of using a dictionary to supplement his own remembered Scots; of the problems of the discontinuous history of varieties of urban and rural Scots; of his awareness of the political importance of Tom Leonard coupled with his confession that he cannot share the aggression of his voice. What Herbert understands, however, is that the poet's use of varieties of vernacular is not a simple matter of conscious choice – to some extent the choices seem to force themselves on the poet as the only way to write. Women who write in the vernacular do tend to suggest such uncomplicated positions, as if all that is needed for a fullscale resurrection of Scots is for poets to be sufficiently proud of their tongue to write in it. The politics of language and the need for the language of poetry to achieve authority are nettles never quite gripped by the women writers, although Alison Kermack perhaps comes closest to facing the problems.

It is instructive to compare the Introduction to W. N. Herbert's *Dundee Doldrums* with the Introduction to Ellie McDonald's *The Gangan Fuit*, also published as a collection in 1991.[35] In the first place the author does not write her own Introduction – this is done for her by Anne Stevenson, herself, of course, a well-known poet, but an English-American one despite the time she has spent living in Scotland. The implication that the language of the periphery needs to be validated by the approval of the centre is hard to avoid. Anne Stevenson pays what is clearly sincere tribute to Ellie McDonald's 'Scots tongue' but she does so like a mother who has realised that her child's innocent remarks interrogate the parent's sophistication and this seems still to leave the Scots tongue in the subordinate position. And when McDonald's '"flyting"' and '"smeddum"' are praised with those damaging quotation marks firmly in place, the pass has truly been sold.

Yet Ellie McDonald is herself unabashed and delivers a few telling blows after all to academic writers and to the Scottish male tradition. After all, Herbert and his fellow makars prove not above teasing:

> Nou, the makars scrieve
> translations aneath thir poems
>
> sae that edicatif fowk
> can jalouse thir implications.
> ('Widdershins', p. 25)

Similarly McDonald obliquely asserts the value of her unassertive voice; in 'Flying Lessons' a kind of aggression is latent in her rueful irony. The speaker remarks the herring gulls with their 'littluns' 'soopan and skreichan' round the statue of Burns outside Dundee Central Library. She warns them that in spite of their virtuoso performance:

> Ye'll only need tae hyter aince
> an doun ye'll blatter on the tap o Rabbie's heid.
> But gin ye think life's easier for me
> tak a bit keek owre. That's me, joukan atween thae
> double decker buses, wishan tae hell I had wings.
> (p. 18)

Performance on the ground may eschew the male tradition but it has its own risks: they are risks, however, that seem to have more to do with 'the way we live now' than is figured by Rabbie's statue.

It is tempting simply to agree with Daniel O'Rourke that Alison Kermack 'instead of finding or cultivating a voice of her own has simply (and effectively) taken over Tom Leonard's'.[36] But this both over and under plays her hand. She does not yet seem to me to have turned the trick of vernacular pseudo-orthography into the tool of philosophical and cultural analysis that Leonard has made it but she does gender the orthography in a way that is transformative rather than derivative:

> thi cloak
> oan thi waw
> sezitz timety
>
> get thi bairns reddy
> get thi hoose tidy
> get thi messijis in

get thi tee oan
get inty bed
an gee um hiz conjuggles

thur wizza time when
I

naw thur wizny
('Time and Again')

The 'cloak' on the wall artfully exposes the way time both tyrannises over an ordinary woman's life yet by its very insistence conceals the possibility of an alternative way of living. The defamiliarising orthography of 'messijis' hints at the secret suggestions that lie beneath the deadening habits of daily life. And in 'conjuggles' the implications of 'hiz' confidence trick and 'her' wearily dextrous manipulation of female roles are further deepened by the half comic sense of the woman's secret parts being wielded by her man.

And Alison Kermack is able too to gender her wider political comment while at the same time exploiting, as indeed Tom Leonard does, the visual qualities of the orthography on the page. In 'The Shadow Minister' the speaker explains that a periscope has enabled a glimpse into Number 10, Downing Street:

ah seen thi pee em
sittin inna big arrum chare
in frunty a big coal fyur
hoaldin a mappy scoatlin
oan thi endy a toast foark

funny thing wiz
thoah kidny see it say cleerly
kizzit happind tay faw
oan thi oappisit waw
thi shaddy i thi pee em
wiz dane igzackly thi same thing

It won't do, of course, simply to claim that the cosy domesticity of the act of national incendiarism involves a peculiarly feminine perception; yet the transformation of the map of Scotland into a kind of housewife's local baking speciality – 'yill huv a wee hoat mappy scoatlin wi yer tea?' – does seem oddly gendered. It is in the homes of the great that the oppression of the small quietly proceeds in small-minded ways.

It is hard to predict the future of Scots for poetry by women or men. I have a sense that the way forward is in the non-separatist linguistic projects of Kathleen Jamie and from the other side of the border Carol Ann Duffy. Of course, poets will very properly do what they like and some would no doubt feel that any union with standard English is necessarily a capitulation of the margins to the centre. But perhaps there increasingly is no standard English. Perhaps we should rejoice in the exciting possibility that if the centre cannot hold, it cannot imprison either. The place of the unplaceable today is the special concern of the work of Jackie Kay.

Jackie Kay

Jackie Kay's latest collection is called *Other Lovers*, a title that invites at least a double reading according to where the stress is placed.[37] And it is certainly on both love and otherness that Jackie Kay's special qualities depend. This black woman who lives in London is, when one meets her, in some ways the most Scottish of the young women poets. Both she and her adoptive parents have pleasant clear Scottish voices and the kind of direct, yet thought-out left-wing political firmness that I feel as distinctively Scottish, perhaps even distinctively West of Scotland. But Jackie Kay is also other, also exotic. And her poetry shows her negotiating the meanings of being a black, lesbian poet, daughter, mother, lover in social and political contexts that are not quite used to these conjunctions. Interviewed by Rebecca Wilson for *Sleeping with Monsters*, Jackie Kay speaks of the problems of place and colour which gave rise to the poem 'So You Think I'm a Mule':

> That poem came about because the question, 'Where do you come from?' is one that probably every Black person in this country is asked too many times for comfort. And the question always implies 'You don't belong here.' That's why people ask it. Either they mean 'Go back to where you came from,' or they just have this obsessive curiosity that is all the time trying to deny the fact that you're Scottish.
>
> This irritates me, a lot, that people can't contain both things, being Black and being Scottish, without thinking there is an inherent contradiction there. So that poem 'So You Think I'm a Mule?' is trying to explore that in a humorous way. It was an actual incident. That woman did say, 'You're not pure, are you? You're a mulatto.' All these things in the poem were said exactly like that. So I didn't have to use too much imagination.[38]

The imagination, of course, is in knowing that this conversation is a poem:

> 'Where do you come from?'
> 'I'm from Glasgow.'
> 'Glasgow?'
> 'Uh huh, Glasgow.'
> The white face hesitates
> the eyebrows raise
> the mouth opens
> then snaps shut
> incredulous
> yet too polite to say outright
> liar
> she tries another manoeuvre
> 'And your parents?'
> 'Glasgow and Fife.'
> 'Oh?'
> 'Yes. Oh.'
> Snookered she wonders where she should go
> from here –
> 'Ah, but you're not pure.'
> 'Pure? Pure what.
> Pure white? Ugh. What a plight
> Pure? Sure I'm pure

I'm rare . . . '
('So You Think I'm a Mule?')[39]

Wryly Jackie Kay castrates 'mulatto' to 'mule' and then in the witty routing of her questioner implicitly denies the impotence that attaches to the latter.

Jackie Kay's first collection, *The Adoption Papers*, consists principally of a sequence of poems in which she intuits her history through the voices of her birth mother, her adoptive mother and her younger self. 'The Adoption Papers' is also in a sense a collection of love poetry, achieving its effects by intertwining the roles of daughter and lover, by making the object of love her adoptive mother, Helen, to whom the volume is dedicated. The helpless sadness of the birth mother, excluded from her daughter's development, and the lively vernacular playground perceptions of the child growing into a knowledge of her own difference, are fully imagined. But the poem's triumphs lie chiefly in the recreation of the adoptive mother's anxious loving need. Here she waits for the social worker from the adoption agency:

> I put Marx Engels Lenin (no Trotsky)
> in the airing cupboard – she'll no be
> checking out the towels surely
> All the copies of the *Daily Worker*
> I shoved under the sofa
> the dove of peace I took down from the loo
>
> A poster of Paul Robeson
> saying give him his passport
> I took down from the kitchen
>
> I left a bust of Burns
> my detective stories
> and the Complete Works of Shelley.
> ('The Waiting Lists')[40]

And so the black Scottish baby comes into the home under the deceptive auspices of two revolutionaries, safe because sanctified as literature, and novels that confidently solve puzzles, finger the guilty. 'The Adoption Papers' undermines such simplicities but does affirm the simplicity of love:

> See me and her
> there is no mother and daughter more similar.
> We're on the wavelength so we are.
> Right away I know if she's upset.
> And vice versa. Closer than blood.
> Thicker than water. Me and my daughter.
> ('The Meeting Dream', AP, p. 34)

Fred D'Aguiar, celebrating Jackie Kay of *The Adoption Papers* as 'a new and distinctive voice on the British literary scene', also remarks that 'what is absent from the book are the perspectives of the fathers, both biological and adoptive fathers'.[41] *Other Lovers*, following the pleasant but somewhat didactic book of verse for children, *Two's Company*, provides both new perspectives and new ways of rendering them.[42] The poems of *Other Lovers* are much busier than the earlier poems and, as they do more, they equally force activity on the reader. Communication remains important but the barriers to it are more frequently perceived. On the one hand, language in its various kinds is interrogated about its failures and, on the other, linguistic imperialism is exposed as a peculiarly vicious kind of repression ('Sign'; 'Gastarbeiter'). The ghosts of Jackie Kay's earlier problems of identity and place are now more ruthlessly dealt with:

> walking by the waters
> down where an honest river
> shakes hands with the sea,
> a woman passed round me
> in a slow watchful circle,
> as if I were a superstition;
>
> or the worst dregs of her imagination,
> so when she finally spoke
> her words spliced into bars
> of an old wheel. A segment of air.
> *Where do you come from?*
> 'Here,' I said, 'Here. These parts.'
> ('In My Country', *OL*, p. 24)

In 'Keeping Orchids' (*OL*, p. 28) the speaker explains how she has cared for the orchids that her mother gave her when 'we first met' for twelve days since the meeting. Carrying them 'like a baby in a shawl'. rearranging them when the 'whole glass carafe has crashed/ falling over, unprovoked, soaking my chest of drawers/All the broken waters': the latter figure is, of course, an artful reminder of birth. As the flowers, some recalcitrantly unopened, remind her of the receding encounter with her mother, she catches the draught in her room and reflects: 'Airlocks keep the cold air out./Boiling water makes flowers live longer. So does/cutting the stems with a sharp knife'.

But if *Other Lovers* signals a new confidence in personal identity, it also raises new problems in love and sexualities. Love, lesbian, gay, heterosexual is most often a source of pain, but there is a kind of exhilaration in the unsentimental facing of pain that is oddly bracing. The mother, struck by her adolescent son, has become a 'condemned property' and in her love blames herself for her son's violence:

> I definitely shouldn't have screamed.
> And when he knocked me over,
> I should not have tried to get up.
> Because he wouldn't have had to, then,
> knock me over again. *My lovely boy*.
> ('Condemned Property', *OL*, p. 54)

The terrible tension of the mother's contained hysteria is full felt, as is her unobliterable love.

Other Lovers opens with a sequence of seven poems on the blues singer, Bessie Smith. Bessie Smith's singing awakes memory, bears history: 'a woman's memory paced centuries'

('Even the Trees'). Her voice forces people to recognise themselves: 'On she would come, the Empress, the Voodoo Queen./Blast the blues into them so people remembered who they's been' ('The Right Season'). Kay handles these poems stylishly, slipping in and out of blues rhythms, and finding some lovely, startling phrases: 'the delicate bone-light/that broke hearts' ('Even the Trees'); 'she had a laugh/that could build a raft' ('Blues'); 'her voice was cast-iron' ('Twelve Bar Bessie'). And the experience of Bessie's voice and face enters into Kay's sense of herself through the love that her own loved parents felt for the music:

> Christ, my father says, that's some voice she's got.
> I pick up the record cover. And now. This is slow motion.
> My hand swoops, glides, swoops again.
> I pick up the cover and my fingers are all over her face.
> Her black face. Her magnificent black face.
> That's some voice. His shoes dancing on the floor.
>
> ('The Red Graveyard', *OL*, p. 13)

Looking Backwards and Forwards

The poems of Fleur Adcock, Liz Lochhead, Carol Ann Duffy and Jackie Kay feature in a recent school text of women's poetry.[43] The poets were each born in a different decade of this century from the '30s to the '60s, and it is gratifying to find Scottish writing represented by, let us say, two and a half poets. The penalties of institutionalisation are in evidence too since some of the poems selected privilege accessibility over complexity. More encouraging, however, even than this general visibility is the consistent presence of these poets and of Kathleen Jamie in the pressure groups of poetry, notably the Poetry Book Society. And to find them too as reviewers in the national press and in the journals. In the Winter 1995 Bulletin of the PBS Liz Lochhead writes on the shortlist for the T. S. Eliot Prize chosen by James Fenton, Maura Dooley and herself. The final choice is the result of co-operation among the judges, the poetry-reading public and the academic establishment represented by Gillian Beer. It seems clear then that a number of Scottish writers are well established. Jackie Kay too is beginning to be discussed in critical work on contemporary writing. But there is no cause for complacency or even really congratulation. There are no contemporary Scottish women poets represented in the new Norton Anthology of Poetry. The need for insistence that there are very many good contemporary Scottish women poets remains.

Earlier I made an apology for my selectiveness which was also in a way a celebration of the choices available. I want to conclude by at least signalling my awareness of a few of my omissions. Of the Lochhead generation of writers Valerie Gillies is the most prestigious absence from the story so far. Gillies, born in Canada, brought up in Scotland and educated at the universities of Edinburgh and Mysore, brings these diverse pressures together to forge a distinctive idiom which enables her to scan her native place with an eye attuned to other vistas:

> Tipu had a full view of the line as it passed,
> Seven miles long, looking down on him from the heights:
> Stronghold to stronghold, Seringapatam to Dunfallandy.
> Now Archie's house on its bend of the river
> Faces a continuous conveyor-belt of sound and colour,

> The endless column moving on the dual carriageway.
> As Athol to Karnataka, as Tummel to Cauvery,
> No Tipu, no Archie disrupts the march today.
>   ('Tipu and Archie')[44]

This landscape miscegenetion is matched by Gillies's generic experimentation with the relationships between poetry and music and painting. She collaborated with her daughter's harp (clarsach) teacher, Savourna Stevenson, in *Tweed Journey*, with the artist, Will MacLean, in *The Chanter's Tune*, and with the poet, Harvey Holton, and the artists, Angus McEwan and Douglas Robertson, in a Dundee-based exhibition, *River Spirits*. Gillies's earliest mentor was Norman MacCaig and from time to time in her poetry we find that MacCaig's talent for looking has passed down the line:

> BASS ROCK
> The rock punctuates the sealine.
> Our boat circles the Bass.
> Seals swim beneath us,
> pop fruit-machine heads up
> three at at time, outstare us.
>
> People press towards them,
> lean to starboard all at once.
> We lurch below the cliffs.
> On their dung-yellow rock,
> gannets rest a beak-stab apart.[45]

Among the Anglo-Scots poets distinctive voices can be heard from Elma Mitchell in the older generation and Val Warner in the middle and Alison Fell and Deborah Randall in the younger.[46] Elma Mitchell and Deborah Randall both engage in different ways with Ruskin: the great arbiter of aesthetic and moral taste who discovered to his horror that he had married a woman is a promising quarry for the woman writer. Elma Mitchell points out what lies behind the 'lilies and roses' that Ruskin associates with femininity:

> Their distant husbands lean across mahogany
> And delicately manipulate the market,
> While safe at home, the tender and the gentle
> Are killing tiny mice, dead snap by the neck,
> Asphyxiating flies, evicting spiders
>   . . .
> Spooning in food, encouraging excretion,
> Mopping up vomit, stabbing cloth with needles,
> Contorting wool around their knitting needles,
> Creating snug and comfy on their needles.
>   ('Thoughts After Ruskin')[47]

The artful refusal to be embarrassed by the repetition of 'needles' drives the point home.
    Deborah Randall's tussle with Ruskin takes her into murkier areas. Randall's first collection *The Sin Eater* already showed her willingness to take on areas of the psyche

that she scarcely perhaps herself comprehended and that language was always less than adequate to clarify. Yet at the same time the poems in that collection gave an extraordinary impression of directness, of exuberant sensuality. Sylvia Kantaris in the back-cover blurb finds echoes of Plath and Dylan Thomas and Mackay Brown.[48] Whether she is fixing on local characters ('Danda with a Dead Fish'; 'Gavin'), the lives of broken women – 'And so it came to pass/I had to be taken out to pee/sweetly squatting in the grass/you pull my knickers up and down/just like a mummy' ('Just the Girls to Cope') – or the mysteries of sex and sin, she conveys an overwhelming but not comforting sense that 'the world was saved by victims' ('The Sin Eater') that 'only by acts of uneasiness and imperfection/do we live/like Judas/slinging belief after treachery'. In the light of these perceptions earned from *The Sin Eater* Randall's latest collection focuses on Ruskin and the women with whom he had his more or less disastrous relationships – Effie, his wife, Rose La Touche, Joan Severn. But it is Randall's probing of dark places which she helplessly can neither render nor explain which makes her strain the limits of language and perception in startlingly innovative and thoroughly shocking ways:

> I dream of semen
> Unravelling from the lip and nostril
> Of a phantom horse
> A stallion
> Well-hung
> Who comes for me
> Like a drum
> ('The Demon Horse', WEDA, p. 10)

Alison Fell and Val Warner are from the generation between Mitchell and Randall. Fell reappraises the conventionally feminist concerns that came out of the 1960s in the sourer light of the '80s (Fell worked for the Women's Street Theatre Group and *Spare Rib*):

> Life is short as a shoelace,
> but who knows it?
> '68' I say, 'the politics of desire –
> will we see it again?'
> Liz says she wants everything *now*,
> everything on offer.
> ('Significant Fevers')[49]

Alison Fell's fiction is discussed in some detail by Flora Alexander elsewhere in this volume. Val Warner deserves more attention as a woman of letters than she can be given here. She too is a poet of issues, but is at the same time a sharp observer of the lives of ordinary people and of the natural world. She, like so many of the poets discussed, interrogates the meaning of home and nationality in and out of her poetry ('Going Home', BL, pp. 74–6). To Rebecca Wilson she remarks, 'When I lived in France for a year it seemed much less of a foreign country than Scotland or Wales because nobody is very interested in nationality, but living in Scotland or Wales you're conscious of it all the time. You never forget you're English'.[50]

A recent appearance on the poetry scene has been made by Jenni Daiches (Jenni

Calder), a critic and fiction writer turned poet, reversing the more usual order but following that of Hardy who with MacCaig again might be felt to exert pressure on her verse. Her poetry, she says, 'arises mainly out of everyday experiences of life and work, and is much influenced by place and landscape'. She concludes, in a witty and moving compression of this transfiguration of the commonplace, that 'Life is sensational'.[51]

The Last Word

The last word must go to the young. The *Poetry Book Society Bulletin* for Spring 1996 featured a brief article by Kate Clanchy whose recent first collection *Slattern* won the 1996 Forward Poetry Prize for Best First Collection.[52] Kate Clanchy is, in terms of place, one of these borderline poets that are becoming our new norm: she was brought up largely in Scotland by an academic historian and a girls' school headmistress and now lives and works in London. Many readers on both sides of the border will know her parents and rejoice at Kate Clanchy's generous acknowledgement of her debt to her heritage:

> I couldn't fit my life into the life of the women writers I admired; line up my loving, domestic father who carried me to Nursery School on his shoulders, my remarkable mother, who insisted I should have all the space she had fought for and more, with bullying Barretts or gruesome Plaths. I was offered, instead, and have led, the life that women writers have always dreamed of, I have earned my own money, found my room of my own, controlled my fertility, chosen my friends – I have lived like a man.

Kate Clanchy has some telling things to say too about desire and language:

> So I started, writing about desire just as men always have – for that is all I think the muse is, desire – proclaiming, seducing, reproaching, all of it out loud, all of it in the most accurate language I know, the language that does not seem to me to defer meaning, but to fix it – poetry.[53]

Living like a man, yet loving like a woman allows Clanchy to achieve new freedom and tolerance. Here is the opening poem of *Slattern*:

> MEN
> I like the simple sort, the soft white-collared ones
> smelling of wash that someone else has done,
> of apples, hard new wood. I like the thin-skinned,
> outdoor, crinkled kind, the athletes, big-limbed,
> who stoop to hear, the moneyed men, the unironic
> leisured sort who balk at jokes and have to blink,
> the men with houses, kids in cars, who own
> the earth and love it, know themselves at home
> here, and so don't know they're born, or why
> born is hard, but snatch life smack from the sky,
> a cricket ball caught clean that fills the hand.
> I put them all at sea. They peer at my dark land
> as if through sun on dazzling waves, and laugh.

Notes

1.   Daniel O'Rourke (ed.), *Dream State: The New Scottish Poets* (Polygon, Edinburgh, 1994), p. 40.

2.   *Dream State*, xxxiv.

3.   *Dream State*, p. 2.

4.   Carol Ann Duffy, *Standing Female Nude* [SFN] (Anvil Press Poetry, London, 1985); *Selling Manhattan* [SM] (Anvil Press Poetry, London, 1987); *The Other Country* [OC] (Anvil Press Poetry, London, 1990); *Mean Time* [MT] (Anvil Press Poetry, London, 1993).

5.   'Carol Ann Duffy Interviewed by Jane Stabler', *Verse*, vol. 8, no. 2 (Summer 1991), p. 126.

6.   Stabler interview, p. 127.

7.   Carol Ann Duffy (ed.), *I Wouldn't Thank You for a Valentine: Anthology of Women's Poetry*, illustrations by Trisha Rafferty (Viking, London, 1992; Puffin Books, Harmondsworth, 1995).

8.   *Dream State*, xx.

9.   Alan Robinson, *Instabilities in Contemporary British Poetry* (Macmillan, London, 1988), p. 195.

10.   Kathleen Jamie interviewed by Richard Price, *Verse*, vol. 8, no. 3 and vol. 9 no. 1 (Winter/Spring 1992), 103–6 (p. 106).

11.   Lachlan Mackinnon, review of Carol Ann Duffy, *Selling Manhattan*, *Times Literary Supplement*, 18 March 1988, p. 303c.

12.   Mackinnon, review of *Selling Manhattan*, p. 303c.

13.   Dilys Rose, *Beauty is a Dangerous Thing* (Top Copy, Edinburgh, 1988); *Madame Doubtfire's Dilemma* [MDD] (Chapman, Blackford, Perthshire, 1989); *Our Lady of the Pickpockets* (Secker & Warburg, London, 1989); *Red Tides* (Secker & Warburg, London, 1993).

14.   Marion Lomax, *The Peepshow Girl* (Bloodaxe Books, Newcastle, 1989); *Raiding the Borders* [RB] (Bloodaxe Books, Newcastle upon Tyne, 1996).

15.   Jenny Robertson's first collection of poems which situates itself variously in Scotland and Europe is called *Beyond the Border* (Chapman, Blackford, 1989). With a slightly different nuance Barbara Weightman and Elsie MacRae call their recent anthology of Scottish women's verse *Different Boundaries* (Smeddum Press, Glasgow, 1995). Edwin Morgan's use of the title *Crossing the Border: Essays on Scottish Literature* (Carcanet, Manchester, 1990) signals his desire to see Scotland in a wider context.

16.   It is perhaps worth remarking that voyages of discovery work in the opposite direction too. Gerrie Fellows, a New Zealander who moved to England when she was nine and who has travelled in North and East Africa is in some senses now a Scottish poet: *Technologies* (Polygon, Edinburgh, 1990). But her most recent work is based on a journey back to New Zealand to investigate her origins.

17.   Kathleen Jamie and Sean Mayne Smith, *The Autonomous Region: Poems and Photographs from Tibet* [AR] (Bloodaxe Books, Newcastle, 1993), p. 6.

18.   *Dreamstate*, p. 156.

19.   Kathleen Jamie, *Black Spiders* (The Salamander Press, Edinburgh, 1982), p. 9.

20.   *Black Spiders*, p. 29.

21.   Kathleen Jamie, *The Way We Live* [TWWL] (Bloodaxe Books, Newcastle upon Tyne, 1987).

22.   Kathleen Jamie, *The Golden Peak* (Virago Press, London, 1992).

23.   *The Golden Peak*, p. 21.

24.   Kathleen Jamie, *The Queen of Sheba* [QS] (Bloodaxe Books, Newcastle upon Tyne, 1994). Raymond Friel, 'Women Beware Gravity', *Southfields: Criticism and Celebration*, vol. 1, 29–47.

25.   Bernard O'Donoghue, 'Whae dae ye think ye ur?', *The Times Literary Supplement*, 5 August 1994, p. 19.

26.   Eavan Boland, *A Kind of Scar: The Woman Poet in a National Tradition* (Lip Pamphlet, Attic Press, Dublin, 1989); Gillean Somerville-Arjat and Rebecca E. Wilson (eds), *Sleeping with Monsters: Conversations with Scottish and Irish Women Poets* (Polygon, Edinburgh, 1990) pp. 79–88.

27.   *Sleeping with Monsters*, p. 84.

28.   Friel, 'Women Beware Gravity', p. 31.

29.   Angela McSeveney, 'I left home this Summer', *Coming Out With It* [COWI] (Polygon, Edinburgh, 1992), p. 13. All poems are from this, Angela McSeveney's only published collection.

30.   'Angela McSeveney talking to Carol Gow', *Verse*, vol. 10, no. 1 (Spring 1993), 19–27 (p. 19).

31.   Gow, *Verse*, p. 19.

32.   *Sleeping with Monsters*, p. 187, p. 190.

33.   Sheena Blackhall, 'The Tea Pairty', *The Spik O' the Lan'* (Rainbow Enterprises, Aberdeen, 1986).

34.   W. N. Herbert, *Dundee Doldrums* (Galliard, Edinburgh, 1991), 'Author's Note', p. 3. Most of the poems in *Dundee Doldrums* were originally published by Duncan Glen in *Akros* 51 (1983).

35.   Ellie McDonald, *The Gangan Fuit* (Chapman, Edinburgh, 1991). All poems and comments quoted are from this collection.

36.   *Dream State*, xxxv. Alison Kermack's poems are quoted from this volume.

37.   Jackie Kay, *Other Lovers* [OL] (Bloodaxe Books, Newcastle upon Tyne, 1993).

38.   *Sleeping with Monsters*, p. 121.

39.   Jackie Kay, 'So You Think I'm a Mule?', *A Dangerous Knowing: Four Black Women Poets* (Sheba Feminist Publishers, London, 1988).

40.   Jackie Kay, *The Adoption Papers* [AP] (Bloodaxe Books, Newcastle upon Tyne, 1991), pp. 14–15.

41.   Fred D'Aguiar, 'Have You Been Here Long?: Black Poetry in Britain', in Robert Hampson and Peter Barry (eds), *New British Poetries: The Scope of the Possible* (Manchester University Press, Manchester, 1995), p. 66.

42.   Jackie Kay, *Two's Company*, illustrated by Shirley Tourret (Blackie Children's Books, London, 1992).

43.   *Four Women Poets*, ed. Judith Baxter (Cambridge University Press, Cambridge, 1995).

44.   Valerie Gillies, *The Ringing Rock* (Scottish Cultural Press, Aberdeen, 1995), 'Tipu and Archie', p. 49; Valerie Gillies's earlier collections are: *Each Bright Eye* (Canongate, Edinburgh, 1977); *Bed of Stone* (Canongate, Edinburgh, 1984); *Tweed Journey* (Canongate, Edinburgh, 1990); *The Chanter's Tune* (Canongate, Edinburgh, 1990).

45.   *The Ringing Rock*, p. 23.

46.   Elma Mitchell, *Furnished Rooms* (Peterloo Poets, Calstock, Cornwall, 1983); *People Etcetera* (Peterloo Poets, Calstock, Cornwall, 1987) contains new poems and poems from earlier collections.

  Val Warner, *Before Lunch* [BL] (Carcanet, Manchester, 1986).

  Alison Fell, *Kisses for Mayakovsky* (1984); *The Crystal Owl* (Methuen, London, 1988).

  Deborah Randall, *The Sin Eater* (Bloodaxe Books, Newcastle upon Tyne, 1989); *White Eye, Dark Ages* [WEDA] (Bloodaxe Books, Newcastle upon Tyne, 1993).

47.   *People Etcetera*, p. 10.

48.   *The Sin Eater*, back cover. When *The Sin Eater* was published Randall, born in Hampshire, was living in Kirkwall. She now lives in Ullapool.

49.   *Kisses for Mayakovsky*, p. 43.

50.   *Sleeping with Monsters*, p. 219.

51.   Jenni Daiches, 'Spring', *Mediterranean* (Scottish Cultural Press, Aberdeen, 1995), p. 55.

52.   Kate Clanchy, *Slattern* (Chatto & Windus, London, 1995).

53.   Kate Clanchy, 'Laughter and Some Blood: Kate Clanchy Can't Believe her Luck', *Poetry Book Society Bulletin*, no. 168 (Spring 1996), 8.

39

Contemporary Fiction I:
Tradition and Continuity

Douglas Gifford

This chapter aims to identify some of the most important writers working inside Scotland within the last twenty-five years: it is complemented by Flora Alexander's chapter, 'Contemporary Fiction III: The Anglo-Scots'. Although its period of reference begins around 1970, it aims to set this writing within the overall framework of Scottish women's fiction generally, and within the modern period particularly. Thus reference will be made to writers within the nineteenth and twentieth centuries whose work has significantly contributed to what is happening in the present and especially to writers whose work has not hitherto been discussed either in chapters on particular authors or in period chapters. Where writers like Naomi Mitchison or Muriel Spark have been discussed in previous chapters, the treatment here will of course be more limited and general.

The achievement of contemporary women writers of fiction has arguably been the most substantial of all achievements in Scottish women's writing. It is outstanding in its new confidence in handling a wide range of genres from social realism and satire to recognisably Scottish versions of magic realism, surrealism and historical fantasy, and its willingness to explore the challenges and problems facing women in their personal development, in their relationships with other women, men, families and society generally, and – increasingly – in relation to history and nationality. Given the amount of writers and fiction of the period, and in keeping with the ethos of the volume as a whole, the essay does not seek to follow any particular theoretical approach or single thematic argument; instead, seeking to give wide general information, its organisation falls into three main stages. Firstly, there is consideration or what has probably been the essential preoccupation of the fiction since its first clearly Scottish articulation, in novels like Susan Ferrier's *Marriage* (1818) down through later nineteenth and early twentieth-century fiction to the present, that of personal and sexual identity and the struggle to assert rights of sex and gender within an exceptionally male-dominated society traditionally suspicious of women's voices speaking outside the home. Given this attempt to set the work of the contemporary writers within a very broad Scottish context, the second part of the chapter examines five of the main thematic and formal concerns of the new fiction, together with general discussion of how effectively particular writers exemplify and illustrate these. Briefly described, these concerns are to do with emergence from repression and trauma; with the discovery of a kind of saving interpersonalism, a redemptive interaction with others which greatly helps with problems of self and society; with the rewriting of history and Scotland; with a return to exploitation of magic and mythology; and with a new recognition of gender inclusiveness in which traditional barriers between male and female writing in Scotland are beginning to crumble as increasingly female and male writers avoid specific gender identification in their work, so that a new fiction emerges in which men write women, and women write men. Given the remarkable burgeoning of women's fiction within the period, more detailed consideration of seven of the outstanding contemporary writers, their engagement with the major preoccupations described, and an examination of how they are exploring new ways of presenting their stories, is postponed till the following chapter, 'Contemporary Fiction II: Seven Writers in Scotland'. (In alphabetical order, these are Margaret Elphinstone, Janice Galloway, Sian Hayton, Alison Kennedy, Joan Lingard, Agnes Owens, and Dilys Rose.)

The Historical Context: Novels of Sexual Determination

Jenni Calder has charted the progress of Scottish women's attitudes in fiction of the nineteenth century towards marriage, money and property.[1] Other chapters in this volume focus on a wide range of preoccupations in women's fiction. For the purposes of setting contemporary writers in context, the work of seven novelists over the period 1818 to 1983 may serve as representative of their authors' attitudes towards the major issues of limitation and freedom in debates of sex and gender which confronted women, and representative also as markers of change in social attitudes and values in Scotland and Britain generally. The change is perhaps initially to be seen as taking place in the author's mind and values; but thereafter their novels can be seen to represent sea changes in Scottish society itself; in its broad acceptance of the attitudes expressed in these fictions. These novels powerfully and thoughtfully realise what the author felt at the time of writing to be the desirable extensions and limits to what all these authors feel to be the core complex of women's rights – that of freedom in emotional, sexual, and social choice. The author's choices may ultimately seem to evade or even eliminate sexual activity and partnership; but nevertheless choice is made within such parameters. And the accumulated effect of the fictional choices made by these novelists contributed hugely to the revaluation of women's roles in Scotland and to the release of women from emotional, sexual and social restrictions. It is the essential underpinning of the twentieth-century achievements of writers like Nancy Brysson Morrison, Nan Shepherd and their successors of the 1980s and '90s.

Some of the novels which can be read as milestones in this journey are Susan Ferrier's *Marriage* (1818) and *The Inheritance* (1824), Margaret Oliphant's *Hester* (1883) and *Kirsteen* (1890), Jane and Mary Findlater's *Crossriggs* (1908), Catherine Carswell's *Open the Door!* (1920), Nan Shepherd's *The Quarry Wood* (1928) and *The Weatherhouse* (1930), Willa Muir's *Imagined Corners* (1931), Naomi Mitchison's *The Corn King and the Spring Queen* (1931) and *The Bull Calves* (1947), and, connecting these with the writers of the later twentieth century, Jessie Kesson's *The White Bird Passes* (1958) and *Another Time, Another Place* (1983). There are of course many other revealing perspectives on them; they have been seen, for instance, as speaking with 'the other voice', of caustic detachment from male romanticism, and ironic commentary on male preoccupations with the heroic events of national history, and with their grand symbolic – and often feminine – meanings of landscape.[2] But in terms of a dominating desire for freedom to make one's own emotional and sexual decisions, these novels mark the stages in Scotland of hesitant, stumbling but determined progress towards full independence – or at least an interdependence decided on one's own terms.

All too often the central women of novels by Elizabeth Hamilton, Mary Brunton, Susan Ferrier and Catherine Sinclair – to name the principal figures of early women's fiction in Scotland – are pious, well-bred, sensitive and pale echoes of that recurrent icon in Scottish male fiction, created by the dominant figure in literary culture in the Scottish Enlightenment, Henry Mackenzie. *The Man of Feeling* (1771) had enormous and unfortunate influence, far beyond Scotland, until the age of Scott supplanted its stylised sentimentality and pious pretentiousness with new Scottish and Romantic concerns and values. In virtually all of these women's novels, Harley is transmuted into a long-suffering mature Lady of Feeling who is a pillar of fortitude and beacon of good Christian behaviour to the flightier younger generation; examples include the improving Mrs Mason of Elizabeth Hamilton's *The Cottagers of Glenburnie* (1808), Mrs Mortimer of Mary Brunton's *Discipline* (1814), Mrs Douglas of Susan Ferrier's *Marriage*, and Lady Olivia of Catherine Sinclair's *Modern Accomplishments* (1836). Lady Olivia can represent them all; 'grief had withdrawn her from the world, but she lived in it as a calm, and sometimes even as a cheerful stranger'. Yes, there is often fine social satire around their patient pedagoguery; but their dead hands of didactic propriety reveal to us just how codified and repressively structured Edinburgh and genteel Scottish society was for women – and, sadly, the degree to which women had been conditioned to accept their lot.[3] These women have little to say – as opposed, say, to the fiction of Scott, Hogg and Galt – concerning the important events and changes, social and political, taking place in their Scotland, all too often preferring that the conventions of the English novel of manners should triumph over their lively and entertaining depiction of actual Scottish manners.

That said, these novels have about them a strange dualism; their didacticism runs uneasily alongside some vigorous and hilarious social satire, often far more grotesque and rumbustious than the admittedly subtler ironies of Austen. To the extent that a strong sense of tension is obvious within these writers between their conformist and non-conformist intentions, it can be argued that first steps towards disruption of literary and social convention are taking place. This dualism is the seedbed of more radical departures. Susan Ferrier's *Marriage* places its decision-maker, Mary Douglas, the patient, dutiful stay-in-Scotland daughter of wilful London socialite Lady Juliana, in the predicament of wanting to marry someone of whom her mother disapproves; a situation repeated with the patient, if slightly more vivacious Gertrude of *The Inheritance*, as she falls out over her choice of husband with her guardian, the fustily orthodox Lord Rossville. Neither girl will go against family authority; but, in unusual stirrings of rebellion, neither will accept choices being made for them. Passive resistance in the as yet hardly conscious cause of sexual self-determination has begun, and will develop in the more assertive heroines in the fiction of Margaret Oliphant, such as the unconventional doctor's daughter in *Miss Marjoribanks* (1866), and the protagonists of *Hester* and *Kirsteen* particularly. Oliphant herself, in mid-century, had recorded her exhilaration when she discovered she could publish (with *Margaret Maitland* in 1849) and, contrary to accepted practice for ladies, could act and earn on her own account.[4] In *Hester* she creates a protagonist who rebels restlessly against men who want her as a wife and an inspiration, rather than as wife as fellow doer, sharing intelligently in business as well as bed. Oliphant's ending to the novel mocks conventional conclusion; Hester has what surely all women desire in her two fine suitors for marriage – and yet for her the choice is not real choice at all, since neither offers the possibility of *work*. *Kirsteen* takes this further, in a novel which gently mocks the darker Scottish male novels from Galt's *The Entail* (1823) to Stevenson's frequent representations of domineering patriarchal figures of insensitivity set against hypersensitive sons. Her father recalls Scott's Redgauntlet, although he is a darker and more decadent version, who has made and lost a fortune from the slave trade and now, declining in dreary Argyllshire, tries to use marriage of his daughter Kirsteen to an elderly but rich neighbour to recoup family fortunes. Another daughter has already gone her own way; now Kirsteen, troth already plighted to gallant Highland Ronald, off fighting in the Crimea, runs away over Highland wastes to seek, successfully, her independence as dressmaker in London and Edinburgh. A giant step for Scottish women, perhaps; but there is a sad sting in the tale, and one which sets clear limits around Oliphant's ground-breaking ideology. Ronald is killed in the Crimea; Kirsteen, vivid and attractive, never gives love to another man, preferring to worship at the shrine of the sacred place in her apartments where she has a casket which contains the blood-stained handkerchief found on Ronald's body, and which she had originally given to him. Is there here perhaps a powerful, if unintended symbolism instinctively fusing traditional notions of romantic loyalty with complex and dimly-sensed notions of thwarted sexuality?

Crossriggs, and the work of the Findlaters generally, is discussed at some length in my earlier chapter; but in Alexandra Hope's recognition of the cross-grained and claustrophobic nature of the pressures exerted on her by the claims of her idiosyncratic and practically helpless father, her too-easygoing sister, and her large, fatherless family and her community, together with her own suppressed urges towards recognition of her own sexuality and the altractiveness of the two men who care strongly for her, the next step forward in Scottish women's fiction is taken. It is not a step towards fulfilment; Alex rejects both men, and accepts her family and community lot in a way that anticipates, perhaps, the interpersonalism and community inter-relationships which will emerge as Scottish women's answer to male ideas of the importance of the quest for personal and essential identity, outstandingly in the work of Willa Muir and Nan Shepherd. But Alex recognises, as do so many of the Findlaters' heroines, that there is within herself that powerful yearning for self-realisation in emotional and sexual terms. Is it fear which holds her back from the married man she strongly loves, and from the younger man who so strongly loves her?

It is a situation repeated in Catherine Carswell's *Open the Door!*; only twelve years later Carswell bursts through turn of the century restrictions, encouraging her Joanna Bannerman to have her affair with her married man, and to come back in the end to her younger lover. By mistakes we grow, argues Carswell, in much the same way that sixty-six years later Janice Galloway will take Joy Stone through trauma in *The Trick is to Keep Breathing* to find, at the still point at the heart of crisis, the necessary self-forgiveness and self-entitlement needed to go forward. And Carswell's agenda is followed by Naomi Mitchison, Willa Muir, and Nan Shepherd, in the way that their central characters have to move erratically and hurtfully through mistaken emotional relationships and sexual frustrations, finding out the hard pragmatic way truths about themselves and society, which society doesn't seem to want them to know. *The Corn King and the Spring Queen* sees young Erif Der lose the meaning of her relationship with her husband, the Corn King of Marob, and going on a vast journey through Mediterranean cultures in search of her lost personal magic, in ways which parallel the ancient quest of the Celtic queen with Mitchison's own modern quest for freedom and fulfilment. Fifteen years on, *The Bull*

Calves exploits this kind of historical disguising of authorial quest even more thoroughly, and now with a specifically Scottish application, paralleling Kirstie Haldane's attempts to recreate herself in the aftermath of the Jacobite rebellions with Mitchison's own struggle to remake self and life in Argyllshire during and after the Second World War. Mitchison movingly describes this in *Among you Taking Notes* (1985), that part of her multi-volume autobiography describing her disillusionment with London society and letters, and her move to Scotland to recover from the trauma of the loss of her child, and to rediscover herself.[5] What stands out about Erif Der and Kirstie Haldane, despite the gap of over two thousand years between them, is their refusal to compromise with social expectations, even if this means lonely journeys or clashes with family. But the journeys do have as goal the reintegration of the heterosexually fulfilled self into family and society. For Mitchison, the search for self-fulfilment is accompanied throughout her fiction and prose by the search for the ideal just society, whether in ancient Sparta or Rome, eighteenth-century Scotland, or in science-fiction futures.

Nan Shepherd and Willa Muir share Mitchison's refusal to compromise, although their ideas of what constitutes self-determination can be read as very different. Shepherd's *The Quarry Wood* recognises Martha Ironside's emotional and sexual longing for fellow-student Luke, who is pledged to her friend, and is ironic on his male self-absorption, but argues for eventual fulfilment for Martha in self-containment and service to family and community, with a recognition that romantic and sexual inclinations may be unnecessary delusions and snares. *The Weatherhouse* is even more ironic regarding infatuation and self-deception, yet manages through a deep and humane pity for the endless human capacity for self-deception to assert what Alan Freeman has usefully identified as 'interpersonalism', a term describing a middle way between selfish and ultimately fallacious essentialism and the complete deconstruction of all ideas of self consequent on rigorous psychological analysis.[6] Willa Muir, however, resolves *Imagined Corners*, with its cross-tensions between the self-trapping ideologies of many different characters and types in a small Scottish town, from the confused minister and his family to his parishioners, who include local business men and their wives, as well as bitter shopkeepers and old maids, in slightly different fashion, by suggesting that two women may well be better off together, away from male relations, let alone family and marriage. And the work of Jessie Kesson can be seen as a link between the concerns of these older novelists and the contemporary writers, spanning as it does the period 1958 to 1985, the date of her last novella and stories, *Where the Apple Ripens*. With Kesson and her rural and smalltown Scottish predicaments we recognise the persistence of older Scottish conventions and restrictions, and understand how, even in the late twentieth century, the echoes of the old patriarchal shibboleths continue to resound in the minds of modern women writers. With *The White Bird Passes* and, twenty-five years later, *Another Time, Another Place*, we are left with a strikingly similar image; that of an embattled, lonely and sensitive girl facing, with courage and determination, doorways to an uncertain future in her life. In the first, the orphan with the outcast dead mother challenges the conventions which say that a girl like her shouldn't and probably couldn't write 'literature'; in the second, someone very like the same girl, now married to a dour crofter, in a gossipy community, has violated the conventions which forbade her to sleep with the enemy, the Italian prisoner of war, and is left weeping on a threshold, unsure if Scottish community will re-accept her or not. This is of course not the only tradition in which contemporary Scottish women writers work, but it is one of the strongest, and one of which virtually all would be aware. In the work of writers like Kesson, Lingard, Galloway, and Kennedy, as well as many other of the current fiction-writers, there is a prevailing sense of engagement with and repudiation of traditional Scottish circumscriptions and repressions.

Thematic and Formal Concerns of the New Fiction; Emerging from Repression

If the general argument about the broad aims of Scottish women's fiction from its beginnings is accepted, then modern and contemporary fiction can be examined in its light, to see how it develops and changes nineteenth- and early twentieth-century patterns. It is clear from previous chapters that Scottish women novelists had, and to a lesser extent continue to have, two motives for writing which impel them more strongly than their male counterparts. On one hand they wrote to earn in order to raise families, and on the other, as suggested above, they wrote to alleviate feelings of restriction and boredom, if not downright repression, and to extend their sense of themselves and their freedoms. The second of these two motives is perhaps the stronger by the mid-twentieth century, and very broadly it can be argued that, where serious and ambitious women's fiction in the early part of the century tended to consider, with some negativity and caustic bitterness, the roles and places of women in Scottish society, significant modern and contemporary fiction began to find possibilities of release and hope amidst continuing repressive difficulties. A distinguished group of women – a disproportionate number coming from the north and east of Scotland – created bleak pictures of Scottish history and society, and women's place and influence in it, from just before the First World War until the 1970s. Jacob's portrait in *Flemington* (1911) of a warped and scheming matriarch during the Jacobite Rebellions, and her bittersweet portraits of disappointed country women in her short stories (collected as *The Lum Hat* in 1982), Lorna Moon's long-forgotten novel and stories of tragic unfulfilment in the further north-east in *Dark Star* (1929) and *Doorways to Drumorty* (1926), Nancy Brysson Morrison's poignant, landscape-filled and atmospheric tales of quiet family frustrations and tragedies in novels like *The Gowk Storm* (1933) and *The Winnowing Years* (1949), Hannah Aitken's Edinburgh-set *In a Shaft of Sunlight* (1947), Dorothy Haynes's *Winter's Traces* (1947) and her short stories of real savagery and bitterness as in *Thou Shalt Not Suffer a Witch* (1949) – all these can be added to the work of writers already discussed, as attempting to break clear of family and social restrictions. A few very strong-minded women managed to supply a very few affirmative endings, as in *Open the Door!*, *Imagined Corners* and *The Bull Calves*; but even in these, the women who break through are surrounded by women and men who cannot because they are enmeshed in the strictures of traditional Scottish religion and society, caught up in that intolerant, hypocritical and depersonalising rigidity of behaviour patterning which Willa Muir described in *Mrs Grundy in Scotland* (1936), and which she termed 'McGrundyism'.[7]

That said, it is noticeable that several of these bleak scenarios are qualified with a kind of optimism – often of the slightest, and often presented in the concluding image of women standing on a threshold, between their married or past relationships and a future which they cannot predict, but which cannot be worse than what they have been through. This is especially true of the period after 1945, when the memory, and perhaps, given the role of women during war, the catharsis of wartime tragedy, pity and fear, prompted writers like Mitchison in *The Bull Calves* to exteriorise their complex of pre- and post-war feelings. The sense of standing on a new threshold undoubtedly dominated, so that the memory and pains of past social and familial entanglements would be offset with the possibility of change. Just as *The Bull Calves* ends with Kirstie Haldane's post-Culloden sense of reconciliation and hard-won peace as a historical analogy for Mitchison's sense of having come through a modern valley of death, so Hannah Aitken's poetically elegiac and metaphysically speculative *In a Shaft of Sunlight* (1947) takes her Edinburgh New Town middle-class women through darkness to light, but without ever losing sight of the persistent limitations of family, class, and convention. This is an important and neglected novel, carrying on the intelligent social ironies of the Findlaters, Catherine Carswell and Willa Muir and the poetic sense of landscape and place of Carswell and Morrison. But just as in the male tradition the concerns of the Scottish Renaissance were to peter out in the 1950s, so this immediate post-war moment of epiphany was to give way to more darkly ambiguous statements, like Dorothy Haynes's *Winter's Traces* (1947), a grimly humorous novel which, in its wintry depiction of grimy urban twilight village Magbank, and its sour pictures of trauchled Mrs Boone and disapproving Mrs Lincoln, trapped in loveless marriages, poverty, damp houses, and by squalling children, surely gave a great deal of inspiration to Robin Jenkins as he began his impressive series of Scottish satires in the mid-1950s. It may be that teacher Beattie Mellis will escape to a brighter future in the end; but Haynes observes her selfishness and lack of perception of the plight of the frail, trapped children she abandons with the sardonic eye which most typically characterises the tradition of Scottish women's fiction.

For all this tentative optimism of the immediate post-war period, there is, however, a curious lack of new, exploratory and redefinitive women's writing throughout the '50. Fine work from familiar names like Mitchison, Jane Duncan, March Cost, Elizabeth Kyle continued, as did that staple of Scottish women's writing, historical romance. And although the appearance of fiction from new writers of the '60s like Spark, Lingard and Elizabeth Mavor indicated a resurgence, from the '60s to the '80s it looked as though the older, pre-war agenda had not greatly changed. Even such an ambiguous and enigmatic treatment of Edinburgh character and society as Muriel Spark's *Jean Brodie* (1961) can be read in its last analysis as general condemnation of the stifling inheritance of Calvin which poisons the good intentions of both Jean Brodie, striving at least to bring colour and creativity into her charges' lives, and Sandy Stranger, forced at best by an over-stringent conscience into betrayal and self-destruction.

This cloying background of propriety and coercion can be seen working emphatically in novels like Lingard's *The Prevailing Wind* (1964) and *A Sort of Freedom* (1969), where the prevalent winds are those of Edinburgh's austere conventionality and their eventual triumph over the women who have dared to seek freedom. Their later version in 1979, *The Second Flowering of Emily Mountjoy*, updates that defeat so that a middle-aged woman who dares to take a lover – an actor, too! – is reduced to wise but unfulfilled happiness. The same sense of stagnation can be found in Margaret Thomson Davis's Glasgow *Breadmakers* trilogy (*The Breadmakers*, 1972; *A Baby Might Be Crying*, 1973; *A Sort of Peace*, 1973), which likewise refused to sentimentalise its wartime and working-class Govan bakers, feckless and drink-prone, and their trollopy and feeble wives, allowing Catriona MacNair, the most decent of them all, nothing more than the sad acceptance of failed dreams so typical of Lingard's tired women. Eona Macnicol's Lowland-set stories like *The Halloween Hero* (1969) and *A Carver of Coal* (1979), and Evelyn Cowan's *Portrait of Alice* (1976) set their protagonists in similar repression, Cowan varying previous versions by placing her would-be rebel within the conventions and insistence on privacy of Jewish Glasgow to tragic effect. Even more disturbingly futile and tragic is Elizabeth Sutherland's presentation of a woman trying to make sense of her life as she lies dying, in *Hannah Hereafter*

(1976), with its legitimisation of suicide as a way out of hospitalisation and unbearable memories. In *The Umbrella Maker's Daughter* (1980) Janet Caird presented a traditionally dark picture of an introverted community (based on Dollar in the early nineteenth century) crushing creative talent in her poignant account of would-be poet Mary Tullis; exotic incomers like this are obvious suspects as introducers of cholera, let alone poetry. There's a picture of wasted talent too in Bess Ross's north-east and modern version of a similar theme, in *Those Other Times* (1991), her presentation of the Clark family. Their fisherman father is a decent man, smoking himself to death through unemployment; his shrewish English wife Cis however has little feeling for the ambitions and possibilities of her large family, especially sensitive Marje, whose role is that of a Chris Guthrie from a more squalid background, with far fewer hopes or dignities, and whose fate is to leave her promising school career for service, along with her tough, prospectless sisters and brothers. This, with increased grotesquerie and violence, and an alternation of stories in English with stories in a fierce Lowland Scots, is the substance of Janet Paisley's *Wildfire* (1993), set in a small village in the central belt of Scotland, and fraught with the betrayals and the bitterness of women used to useless and violent husbands. The anger and despair of all these seems distilled in the uniquely claustrophobic nightmares of Bridget Penney's *Honeymoon with Death* (1991).

All these novels by home Scots emphasise the trapped position of sensitive women. And many of the Scots who escaped to wider cultures seem compelled to corroborate this with their obsessive representations of their bleak childhoods or their representations of women, often set in non-Scottish locations, but still cribbed and confined. Flora Alexander describes some Anglo-Scots and their work in her chapter; particularly relevant here, however, are the portraits of neurotic and unhappily limited women in the work of writers like Sheila Macleod (*The Moving Accident*, 1968; *The Snow-White Soliloquies*, 1970; *Letters From the Portuguese*, 1971); Shena MacKay, from *Old Crow* (1967) to *Dunedin* (1992), and Alison Fell's *Every Move You Make* (1984), which graphically reveals the mental baggage carried from her Scottish upbringing in June Guthrie's London rebellion against her background, and her consequent failure to find stable relationships amongst the alternative lifestyles offered by the swinging capital. This reaction against an older Scotland culminates in Elspeth Barker's *O Caledonia!* (1991), with its dark poetry and rich sensual description of northern landscapes working towards the annihilation of its lonely and sensitive adolescent Janet of Achnasaugh; her plight is a quite deliberate – if somewhat distorted and gentrified – representation of dreary big house-and-peasantry Scotland, and its McGrundy imprisonment of genuine spirit.

But if a post-war attitude of sceptical reduction of women's hopes for social and aesthetic freedom persists in women's writing till the present, there emerged a new and different attitude with Jessie Kesson and *The White Bird Passes* in 1958. Once again a voice of real energy and defiance vigorously presented and questioned the situation of women in Scotland, refusing to accept the tired old allocations of roles and duties in its ferociously warm portrait of Janie, the loving daughter of an Elgin prostitute; made an orphan, Janie repudiates all the dreary jobs in shops or service offered to her by the dead hand of traditional charity when she leaves the orphanage, and instead makes that wonderful claim for her rights: 'I don't want to dust and polish . . . and I don't want to work on a farm. I want to write poetry. Great poetry. As great as Shakespeare'.

Kesson was perhaps unaware of how vivid her statement was. At any rate, her next novel, *Glitter of Mica* (1963), resorted to the style of older male writers, in particular that of Ian MacPherson in *Land of Our Fathers* (1933), as though she felt the need to retrench.

The treatment of Helen Riddell in her new novel reverted to that attitude of bleak pessimism regarding possibilities for women which had characterised the work of older writers of the north-east like Jacob and Moon, and now threatened to dominate contemporary women's writing. But *The White Bird* had not passed unnoticed, and twenty-three years later Anne Smith's *The Magic Glass* (1981) refashioned Janie as Stella, the street urchin of the imagined Fife town of Skelf. This portrait, so reminiscent in prose of the paintings of Joan Eardley, vigorously reinforced Kesson's assertion of freedom for young women whose voices had hitherto been ignored in Scotland. Stella raucously and imaginatively survives harsh parents, her school embarrassments, her tough neighbourhood, its dirty old men, her resilience overwhelming all odds. It may be that Smith's version of childhood realism was the encouragement Kesson needed, for she returned, in *Another Time, Another Place*, to her semi-autobiographical account of Janie, now away from the orphanage and married to her decent but conventional crofter, but frustrated by the minimalism of his lovemaking, the insensitivity of neighbours, and the eternity of mundanity which seems to lie ahead. The title indicates her yearning to be somewhere else, exotic and different; it also represents Kesson's insistence on seeing Janie's repression as that of an older era, in another country. For Kesson the past has to be the past, the war marking its boundaries, and life, however painful after the intrusion of the three romantic Italian prisoners of war, can never be the same again.

Another Time, Another Place can be seen as a turning point in Scottish women's writing, both thematically and formally. The image of the young woman standing in the doorway, so recurrent in Scottish fiction, accepting dour Elspeth's 'You'd better come in', implied reconciliation between the older woman's values and the younger woman's shamed yet irreversible breach of community rules. This, taken with Kesson's new-found confidence in presenting her story in an impressionistic mosaic of short, fragmentary episodes, capturing the sense of a break-up of older conventions, literary and social, and with her ability to keep bits of tradition, in song, dance, and storytelling when she wanted, must have suggested to many readers/writers that this new kind of stream of woman's consciousness-in-community could be deployed in interesting contexts, urban and Lowland, as well as in Kesson's northern farm towns.

Kesson repeated the message in the novella *Where the Apple Ripens* (1985), her last major work, but she had been heard. Alison Fell's fiction has developed in ways very different from Kesson's, but it is striking to see how strongly her adolescent Isla Cameron in *The Bad Box* (1987) echoed Kesson's presentation of her determined, imaginative, and often unhappy young women. Fell's presentation of Isla, with her fragments of song, traditional and modern, her private dreams, her swings from poetic idealism to acute realism, and her situation within a family and Highland and Borders communities at once positive and negative, has strong echoes of Kesson – though the triumph of its redemptive magic over Isla's sense of her own negativity, her own 'bad box', places its main thrust beyond Kesson, and within the rediscovery of mythology which is a feature of much contemporary writing, and discussed shortly.

Una Flett's *Revisiting Empty Houses* (1988), took up the theme of persistence through circumscription, so that when her middle-class painter Carla, suffocatingly married to her university tutor, finally confronts Edinburgh, her 'bad dream city', she uses her paintings both as therapy and as a means of gaining emotional and financial independence. And by the time of Lingard's allegory for the importance of women's spiritual unity in *The Women's House* (1989), it was clear that a time of confident experimentation and eclecticism had arrived. Carole Morin made her debut with a stylish punk novel which drew confidently on the fascinatingly repulsive stories of Ian McEwan and the off-beat attractions of Iain Banks's *The Wasp Factory* (1984). The title of *Lampshades* (1991) refers to the alleged uses made of Jewish bodies after death in the concentration camps. Morin's Sophira van Ness, rebellious daughter of a Scottish Big House, sees Hitler as a misunderstood hero; but this apparent sick humour is a cover for rich satire on parental disregard and selfishness not unlike that in Elspeth Barker's *O Caledonia!*, with its comparable, if less extreme misfit Janet. But where Barker's Gothic atmosphere destroys Janet, Sophira and her family house are saved – by black-leathered motor-biking Jack, hero of Hitler movies, and deliberately made incredible, except in *Rocky Horror Show* terms. For all this, the novel carries positive meanings which suggest more than anything else the need for women to think differently, and to exploit extremes of humour and genre.

And by now this new fiction was coming thick and fast. Sharman Macdonald, distinguished as a playwright, showed women taking control of their lives in wayward, confident and hilariously sensual ways in *The Beast* (1986). American Ellen Galford naturalised herself in Edinburgh to the extent that in 1990 she was able to exploit myth in order to mock Scottish and British patriarchy, in her wonderfully zany *Queendom Come* (1990), in which a group of alternative ladies celebrating May Day on Arthur's Seat awaken Gwhyldis, arch-priestess and Merlin-figure to Albanna, the ancient British queen. The re-awakened Gwhyldis has an affair with a gentle lesbian doctor; Albanna goes on to outdo Margaret Thatcher, and Galford has a wonderful time showing the superiority of her alternative lifestyles. The sheer fun of this is important; it illustrates the new ability in Scottish women's writing to laugh at their situation, but always with a view to creating new and liberating perspectives.

A recent collection of stories, Ali Smith's *Free Love* (1995), can be taken as exemplifying many of the changed attitudes of this new writing. The stories are unashamedly personal, giving throughout the collection a sense of linking development. There's a sadness about them which suggests the working out of past pain, as well as an insistence on working out future identity – many of these stories actually say that they're wishing, touching wood, saying 'cold iron', or that they're building, making, growing up. The stories are transitional in respect of gender, too – like Edwin Morgan's love poems, they can almost be read according to preference, as with the title story, in which a girl on holiday in Amsterdam leaves her girlfriend to drift into sex with prostitute Suzi, and finds her first free love, literally, physically and emotionally. Delicately Smith suggests the new horizons opening, through a style which is immediate, slightly breathless, tender, and effective for the subject-matter, itself fleeting, glimpsed, not-to-be-held. Other stories move around familial pain – a dead sister in 'College', a dead mother in 'Cold Iron'. A very modern trait is Smith's presentation of characters with the ability or need to cut off from the past, to simply go quickly away from the ties which bind too constrictingly. The central figure – usually a girl – will go off on impulse to move alone, or quite suddenly get up from father and mother, or lovers and friends, to leave.

Another contemporary qualify of these stories is their fascination with the random and the disconnected – the gulfs in time between people. 'A Story of folding and unfolding' makes curious sensual poetry out of the imagining of a father's strange involvement as an electrician with his unknown wife-to-be's underwear; the summary typically indicating Smith's ability to see from unusual perspectives in imagination and memory. The only way to describe this gift of transforming the conventional worlds of women into new, evocative and dream-like states is as a kind of lyric prose-poetry – and no better example can be given than 'Text for the day', the contemporary parable of Melissa, who suddenly leaves her flat and friends to travel, simply and restlessly moving on, and scattering as she goes the torn out pages of her favourite writers, letting them drift in roadways, graveyards, supermarkets. Atwood, Joyce, Woolf, Hardy, Lawrence, Forster, Gunn, MacDiarmid, Ginsberg, Eliot, Scott . . . Smith's vision of Melissa's beloved pages drifting across desert and sky, bleaching like skulls of small birds, cannot be read as other than a new kind of poetry. There's a kind of unbearable sadness and happiness of a contemporary woman being, changing and dissolving in these sensual, yet wonderfully imaginative stories which mark Smith as an outstanding example of how far Scottish women's writing has come in confidence and range.

Anthologies such as the annual *Scottish Short Stories* volume from Collins, running since 1973, demonstrate the range and quality of fiction from as yet uncollected women writers like Esther Woolfson, Valerie Thornton, Rosalind Brackenbury, Elizabeth Gowans, Elizabeth Burns and many more, as do series like *Original Prints* or shared anthologies such as *Three's Company* (1989), selected by Jessie Kesson from the work of Sheena Blackhall, Rosemary Mackay and Wilma Murray.[8] And of course several of the most important contributors to the development of new ways of defining new women have not yet been discussed. There can be little doubt that Janice Galloway's *The Trick is to Keep Breathing* (1989) and A. L. Kennedy's *Looking for the Possible Dance* (1993) represent the high points of the contemporary novels' questioning of gender roles, of personal, familial, and social obligation. And what of Elphinstone, Hayton, Owens, Rose? These writers, with Joan Lingard, can claim to have done more than most in the redefinition of women in fiction, and are therefore given individual treatment elsewhere.

Thematic and Formal Concerns; Community and Interpersonalism

Alan Freeman has argued that Nan Shepherd was influenced as a student at Aberdeen University by liberal ideas in Scottish philosophy of the early twentieth century, and Willa Muir by the ideas of Bergson concerning the tension between freedom and the imprisoning logic of rational concepts of time.[9] Shepherd, he argues, followed courses in philosophy under James Black Baillie (whose ideas were to be developed by the later Scottish philosophers John Macmurray and John Macquarrie) and shows the influence of such thinking in her insistence on the importance or interdependent relationships within community in her novels.[10] Muir – presumably also aware of similar ideas from her studies at St Andrews University – was fascinated (as *Imagined Corners* reveals) by Bergson's attempts to escape the imprisonment of time (one of Edwin Muir's preoccupations also); and Freeman illustrates her interest in a discussion of her tale, 'Clock-A-Doodle-Doo', in which the Clever Clock's rejection of sun and moon represents a supercilious and introverted rationalism, with its remorseless logic which excludes all emotion and aesthetics but considerations of self, a solipsistic analysis which ends in breakdown. The nameless cleaning lady removes him in the morning.[11]

For both women the ultimate point is the same; that under the withering light of modern rationalism, the essential self dissolves, and with it much of the traditional significance invested in the roles of women. For male writers of their period, that of the 'Scottish Renaissance' led by Hugh MacDiarmid, the answer to such deconstructive rationalism lay in assertions of an essentialism of self located in a mystical core of being, perceived for example by Neil Gunn as 'the atom of delight', and found in relation to ancestral landscape and archetypes evolved from history. Thus epic novels such as Gibbon's *Sunset Song* (1932) and Gunn's *The Silver Darlings* (1941) share an emphasis on moments when Chris Guthrie and Finn MacHamish, their respective protagonists, discover their essential selves in circles of ancient stones, places of *mana* which connect with their timeless essences.

Scottish women have generally remained sceptical concerning such mystic links between places, history and living beings. Willa Muir mocks such pretension in her opening descriptions of her east-coast burgh of Calderwick, constantly undermining any possibility of the numinous. Where for Gibbon and Gunn curlews cry in sympathy with Pictish descendants, Muir sardonically remarks that 'the larks, the crows and the gulls, after all, were not ratepayers. It is doubtful whether they even knew they were domiciled in Scotland', and she sustains throughout an ironic commentary on the validity of interweaving sea, land, and psyche.[12] It is a scepticism which goes back to Susan Ferrier's *Marriage*, with its disenchanted perspectives on bleak castles, rainy moors, muddy cattle. This is not to say that women always devalue the role of setting and landscape in their fiction. The Findlaters, Carswell, and Morrison exploit the possibilities of landscape and weather to the great enhancement of their narratives, and Carswell especially would seem to exploit both the women's and men's traditions to the full. Shepherd and Muir herself will make use of vivid settings – but none of these women allow consideration of intimations of land and immortality to cloud their main issue, which is simply that of the importance of human relations within community. And in this respect, however intriguing Freeman's suggestions concerning the significance of Scottish and European philosophy for women's writing may be (and his intriguing ideas merit extensive further research) these early twentieth-century women writers were surely also re-emphasising older Scottish traditions of community awareness, to be found from David Lindsay's mid-sixteenth century *Ane Satyre of the Thrie Estaitis* through to the work of Ramsay, Fergusson, Burns, Hogg, and Galt, but fading in the nineteenth century in the new Scotland of industry and Empire.

In virtually all the major fiction by women after Carswell, Shepherd and Muir until the Second World War there is this emphasis on the interaction of women seeking fulfilment for themselves with other women, and with their communities. Chapters in this volume on these writers have stressed their ultimate involvement with others rather than with self. Shepherd's protagonists learn such involvement, while Muir's learn to understand the motivations of others in a very different tolerance than, say, that of Gibbon's malicious community gossip throughout *A Scots Quair*. But a change was to take place following that short period of post-war and post-Renaissance hopefulness in novels like *The Bull Calves* and *A Shaft of Sunlight*, which clearly maintain that emphasis on interpersonalism which distinguished earlier fiction. Thereafter, serious women writers were for almost two decades to emphasise the loss of such traditional community. Morrison's *The Winnowing Years* is significantly placed at 1949 as a simultaneous celebration of and lament for four different historical periods of thick-textured rural Scottish community. Subsequently, women took an even darker view. So too did many of the men – from Jenkins, Friel, and Crichton Smith to Kelman and the dark urbanites of the present like Welsh, McLean and Meek, 'Scotland' and its cities are seen as mutually contradictory. On one hand 'Scotland' is perceived as a conglomeration of phoney representations and spurious traditions, with false mythologies of land and community, while on the other its cities are dumb, unrelated, unimagined, as in the famous complaint of Duncan Thaw in Gray's *Lanark* (1981).

In contrast, for all their post-war pessimism, it is striking that women writers refused to throw the ailing baby of community out with the industrial bathwater. Haynes's *Winter's Traces* differs from the novels of Jenkins in that, for all its corrosive view of pathetic people and pathetic hopes and pretensions, there's always a qualifying restraint on condemnation, whereby even balding baker Lincoln who murders his wife to become talk of the town, is given a residual community sympathy and blessing on his execution. In the short stories of *Thou Shalt Not Suffer a Witch* (1949) Haynes is even more savage about lonely people in communities in decline, as in the novels of Jane Duncan with her webs of complex interrelationships, showing the breaking up of traditional community; but their sardonic pictures of decay are shot through with moments of redemptive kindness.

Amongst the more negative of the later novels, it's possible to see that, however malicious or critical community becomes, there's nearly always a saving grace. Even the fiction which depicts grim families in deprived urban and rural settings insists on emphasising social setting, neighbours, gossip, not so much protesting the death of community, as accepting that, however warped, it's a given. For all its gossip, backbiting, and new-fangled radio songs, *Another Time, Another Place* is haunted with echoes of a supportive community, with its fragments of old ballads and the singing of old songs like 'Rowan Tree' which are filled with memories of hearth and home and arrest the novel in mid-gossip so that for a moment community is rediscovered, even with the jarring presence of the condescending laird-farmer and his lady. And isn't Elspeth's open door a sign of possible redefinition of community, given that Elspeth is clearly represented as the backbone of serious inter-relationships? Moira Burgess's *The Day Before Tomorrow* (1971) presents a thickly-textured version of Glasgow's slum Cowcaddens, using the threat to the community of a sexual killer to explore community responses in ways which, while seeing all the bleak features of her subjects, finds redemption in human relations in a finally positive human setting. Apparently less sympathetic to community is her later novel *A Rumour of Strangers* (1987), the gap of sixteen years perhaps accounting for the presentation of her West Highland community of Finaway in more caustic terms, with the gossip of its two-faced locals waspishly circling around the incomers who run a guesthouse, a woman who has lost her child and her near-alcoholic husband. The attitudes towards townsfolk, gypsies, and incomers in this novel can even seem uncertain in their movements from satire to acceptance; and this description is not meant so much as criticism as recognition that many modern writers have genuinely ambivalent attitudes towards Scottish community and its many faces. The short stories of Eona Macnicol, such as her *A Carver of Coal* (1979), a grainy series of pictures of 'any mining village in Scotland', evoke Lowland industrial village community – and its terrible flaws – in ways close to the film representations of rural slums in Bill Douglas's *My Childhood* trilogy (1979).

Thereafter, in the sheer pain and bitterness of their writing, novels like *The Magic Glass, Those Other Times, O Caledonia!,* or *Lampshades,* and the short stories of *Honeymoon with Death* or *Wildfire,* suggest a painful recognition or the extent of the loss. Is there not a terrible yearning implied in Barker's presentation of lonely Janet? And the work of Agnes Owens, taken with the writing of Duncan McLean and Irvine Welsh, demonstrates strongly that for some contemporary writers traditional community has dramatically altered for the worse.

It's now clear, however, that an increasing number of contemporary women have begun to recreate positive representations of Scottish old and new communities. Mitchison's *Early in Orcadia* (1987), her account of the first primitive settlers in Orkney, is very much based on intuited and shared relationships, reminiscent of Golding's communal Neanderthals in *The Inheritors*; Elphinstone's *The Incomer* (1987) announced that one of the main themes of her projected trilogy was to be the search by her protagonist Naomi for something like Mitchison's 'just society'; while Lingard's *The Women's House* (1989), with its recognition of the need for the mutual interdependence of women and of men, is perhaps her answer to the search of all her lonely and disappointed women since *The Prevailing Wind* of twenty-five years before.

This important regenerative movement comes to a head in the work of Lingard and Elphinstone particularly, although both Galloway and Kennedy have deepened their awareness of the importance of community relationships as their work progresses.

Thematic Concerns; Rewriting Scotland and History

There is something of a paradox in the fact that, until comparatively recently, Scottish women writers, while working extensively over the field of Scottish history, and especially in the twentieth century, have in a deeper sense failed to grapple with Scottish historical realities, in the way of Scott, Galt, or Stevenson in the nineteenth century, and Gibbon, Gunn and contemporaries like Crichton Smith and Harry Tait in the twentieth. There are some outstanding exceptions; Violet Jacob's dark presentation of malign oppositions in the time of the Jacobite rebellions, *Flemington* (1911), works magnificently in the tradition of acute and often iconoclastic reinterpretation of Scottish history which runs from *Waverley* through Galt's *Ringan Gilhaize* and Stevenson's *The Master of Ballantrae* down to the great body of work produced by Naomi Mitchison.[13] The writers of robust and satisfying accounts of Mary, Queen of Scots, Montrose, Claverhouse, Prince Charles Edward, and of periods of civil war and Highland Clearance, are to be numbered in dozens; the genre began before Scott's Waverley novels with Jane Porter's rumbustious account of her giant hero William Wallace in *The Scottish Chiefs* (1810), and in the twentieth century some of the most prolific and outstanding practitioners include Margaret Irwin, Jane Lane, Jane Oliver, Jean Plaidy, and more recently, Pamela Hill, Mary Stewart, Nan Webster, Elizabeth Sutherland, Alanna Knight, Agnes Short, Jessica Stirling, and Joan Lingard. In the 1950s, when women's writing seemed to lose its characteristic and effective ironic comment on Scottish society, the women's historical romance flourished, as though escape from drab greyness to an imagined and colourful Scotland was infinitely preferable. It has to be said, however – as Moira Burgess corroborates in her chapter on women's historical writing – that very often the psychological motivation and the sexual relationships of characters in these novels remains that of the twentieth century – or, more exactly, that of the conventions of love interest in the twentieth-century popular novels. Neither did many of these writers attempt to reassess in any very extensive way the position of women within history – for example, a fine novel reworking the life of Walter Scott, Jean Oliver's *The Blue Heaven Bends Over All* (1971), remains well within conventional fictional and patriarchal perspectives in its traditional study of its massive subject.

Nevertheless, some of these writers sometimes transcend these basic limitations in individual novels. Eona Macnicol's two painstakingly researched novels about the life and achievement of sixth-century St Columba of Iona, *Colum of Derry* (1955) and and *Lamp in the Night Wind* (1965) take up Scottish Druid-Christian history where Gunn left off in *Sun Circle* (1933), and go a long way towards successfully recreating the period in history which Gunn always regretted not tackling, that in which took place the symbolic and crucial meeting between Druid King Brude and the new faith of Columba. The short stories of Macnicol and Dorothy Haynes have a true historical sense. The latter's *Thou Shalt Not Suffer a Witch* (1949), set around Lanark, has stories like 'The Head' and the title story which recreate medieval brutalities with a lack of sentimentality which is finely balanced with redemptive tenderness.[14] Following Gunn and Macnicol, and before Naomi Mitchison's *Early in Orcadia* (1987) or the *Hidden Daughters* trilogy (1989–93) of Sian Hayton, Marion Campbell's *The Dark Twin* (1973) vividly recreated the world-picture and the interaction with landscape of Celtic people in Argyll before the coming of Christianity and Vikings. In her narrative of Drost, co-ruler with golden Ailill, King of the Boar People, and his ritual dark twin, there is real imaginative power in the attempt to fathom the utterly alien conceptions and living conditions of the lost folk who left the astonishing mounds and standing stones of Dunadd and Kilmartin. This active recreation of other times and people is continued in Elizabeth Sutherland's *The Seer of Kintail* (1973) and *The Eye of God* (1977), which explore the life of the Brahan Seer and sixteenth-century witch trials as a linked pair of studies of north-east supernatural tradition, and *The Weeping Tree* (1980), an account of Highland Clearance, which, like Joan Lingard's *Greenyards* (1981) tries hard to render from a woman's point of view a realistic account of hardship in removal and emigration.

In the main, however, most women writers were traditionally – and by convention – less interested in the deeper considerations of the metaphysics of race, history and great patterns of social change. Perhaps, just as they were less impressed by soulful conceptions concerning the relationship between history, landscape and psyche, and irritated by the habit of Scott, Gibbon and Gunn of ennobling women, with a touch of condescension alongside a great deal of limitation, into epic protagonists like Jeanie Deans, Chris Guthrie and Dark Mhairi of the Shore, they simply suspected the men of being on one hand woolly in their anthropomorphic thinking and on the other typically manipulative in forcing women into Earth-Mother and national-soul roles which they had never sought. It will be obvious from previous discussion that when Scottish women work at their most ambitious levels of fiction they focus on the more immediate problems of self, family, society.

That does not mean to say, however, that modern women writers do not deal with large issues of Scotland and history. Carswell's *Open the Door!* is as good a picture of Glasgow in its end-of-the-century period as can be found since Sarah Tytler's *St Mungo's City* (1885), with Carswell's analysis of the effects of the 1843 Disruption in the Church of Scotland on second and third generations. Morrison's *The Winnowing Years* effectively juxtaposes three historically discrete periods and ministries in the village of Drumban, thereby comparing social and political mores in the mid-sixteenth century, the period of French and American revolutions, and the two World Wars of the twentieth century. Outstandingly, the work of Naomi Mitchison has explored points of crucial division in Scottish history, and the legacy of Highland and Lowland division, in great depth and perception, from the *The Bull Calves* and *The Big House* (1950), with their very different ways of resolving ancient tensions between the aristocracy and peasantry of Scotland, to investigations of modern social and economic problems in Argyllshire in the lighter-hearted yet still serious *Lobsters on the Agenda* (1952) and *Early in Orcadia*, her later attempt to imagine the earliest settlers and their mindsets as they crossed to unpopulated Orkney. Mitchison is of course prolific in her historical writing, much of which has a Celtic bias, as in *The Corn King and the Spring Queen* or *The Conquered* (1923), which sets Meromic the Gaul and his barbarian inheritance against Roman imperialism and values in much the same way that *The Corn King* sets the primitive earth magic of Marob against sophisticated Grecian culture, and with the same conclusion that the peripheral had, for all its backwardness, fundamental significances denied to centralised and elitist societies. Even in novels with apparently very different themes, such as *Blood of the Martyrs* (1939), Mitchison finds herself arguing consistently for underdogs and outsiders against impersonal systems – in this case, early Christians against authoritarian Rome. Dorothy Dunnett, whose work is looked at with Mitchison's in more depth by Moira Burgess in another chapter, is arguably Mitchison's only rival in the scope of her Scottish epics, from *The Game of Kings* sextet to, outstandingly, her recreation of the character and achievement of Macbeth in *King Hereafter* (1982). With daring speculation, she identifies Macbeth and Earl Thorfinn of Orkney as one and the same, thus greatly extending his power and importance. This is not all; she reinterprets him as a great king and as a visionary who, poised between the dark of prehistory and new Christianity, plans for an immensely distant future. Such use of history, with its meticulous awareness of historical possibilities and compexities, goes beyond her achievement in the wonderfully entertaining *Game of Kings* adventures of Francis Crawford of Lymond which, marvellously researched and richly detailed in settings that range across all Europe, deliberately and effectively create in Crawford a hero whose charismatic character and almost superhuman abilities are those of the modern James Bond.

The outstanding present-day exponents of historical fiction in Scotland are undoubtedly Margaret Elphinstone and Sian Hayton, examined later. But there is, of course, more than one way to grapple with Scottish fundamentals than through historical narrative. In this respect it's striking to see just how many modern writers manage to weave a critique of Scottish attitudes, modern and historical, into their apparently modern stories. The title of Barker's *O Caledonia!*, playing sarcastically on Scott's 'O Caledonia, stern and wild/Meet nurse for a poetic child', Galford's hilarious reversal of patriarchal focus and dominance in *Queendom Come*, even Mackay's *Dunedin* (1992), with its indication of dark Scottish-New Zealand skeletons in cupboards behind its modern London location and satire, and Morin's *Lampshades*, in its repudiation of northern values for their polar opposites in decadence and punk – all these carry a hidden commentary on accumulated Scottish values and conventions, with a mixture of criticism and relish. The work of Lingard, Galloway, Kennedy, Owens and Rose will show that throughout their work there is close engagement, often expressed in surreal and parodic terms, with the matter of Scotland, its history and its values. All these writers, and especially these last, are rewriting traditional Scotland as narratives and interpretations, Scotlands of multi-faceted minorities and communities, some of them unashamedly imagined Scotlands.

Thematic Concerns; The Return to Magic and Mythology

Closely connected to the revaluation of attitudes towards Scottish history and values is the way in which contemporary women writers present a synthesis of old and new, and often sharply conflicting, perspectives on Scotland. Indeed, one of the most striking features of women's writing in the last fifteen years, has been its rapidly growing confidence in joining men's writing in reviewing the pessimistic perspectives of the '50 and '60s, and its deployment of a striking new range of formal amd imaginative approaches in doing so. Amongst these new approaches the exploitation by women of the possibilities of traditional Scottish folk legends and myths, of Scottish fictional traditions of the supernatural, and of modern magic realism, is impressive. Older writers like Lorna Moon in *Dark Star* (1929), with its echoes of ancient family evil, or Morrison in *The Gowk Storm*, with its use of folk-hints, omens and portents as a suggestive and supernatural music of the past, had continued something of the traditional supernatural found in writers like Margaret Oliphant, George Macdonald and Stevenson. A few writers like Dorothy Haynes, Naomi Mitchison, and Marion Campbell (in, for example, *Thou Shalt Not Suffer a Witch*, *Five Men and A Swan* (1958), and *The Dark Twin*, respectively) continued to work in the tradition of the classic Scottish supernatural tale, albeit with very different emphases and tone. The title story of the collection *Five Men and A Swan* is an outstanding story in the Renaissance manner of, say, Linklater's 'The Goose Girl', only here evoking a woman's perspective on the old legends of the bird-woman, and now deploying tradition to make a strong point against Scottish male sexual aggression. Mitchison posited the existence of actual magic in *The Corn King and the Spring Queen*, with many moments suggestive of the working of ancient and genuine earth-magic (amongst many examples of the supernatural, Erif Der's bringing back to life of a dead flower through hand-magic, the significance of oracular prophecy, and the serpent apparitions on the death of Kleomenes stand out). It is significant however that some fifteen years later, and after the war, Mitchison's use of magic changes; in *The Bull Calves*, American Indian magic and Scottish witchcraft are exploited in the light of her reading of Jung's ideas on the reintegration of the broken self, so that Indian ritual and lore is viewed as psychologically healing, while Kirstie's involvement with a coven is readable as simply a result of her distorted mental state. After *The Bull Calves*, there are several important strands of the supernatural in Mitchison's fiction, from *The Big House* (1950) and *Travel Light* (1952) with their wonderfully magic and mythic journey-quests, and *Five Men and a Swan*, to the very different kinds of magie in stories which explore it from the viewpoint of a distinct people and culture in *Images of Africa* (1980), and in *What Do You Think Yourself?* (1982), stories set in Scotland which exploit the supernatural in allegorical and surrealistically suggestive ways which are new for Mitchison. And Muriel Spark has continued to employ supernatural elements in her work from the use of traditional Scottish demonic and black magical subtexts in *The Ballad of Peckham Rye* (1960) and *Jean Brodie* (1961) to her recent *Symposium* (1990), with its echoes of traditional Scottish witchery. But in the last fifteen years the attitude towards Scottish magic and supernatural has fundamentally changed.

In a recent essay I claimed that Scottish fiction is now changing direction. Contrasting the fiction and the cultural values of the Scottish Renaissance with those of the period following the Second World War, I argued that, after the failure of ideologies of National Socialism, and their supportive traditionalism, a mood of social realism and sceptical materialism emerged which was distrustful of Renaissance ideology and mythology, with its respect for the traditional and the supernatural, and its emphasis on the intimate and fundamental relationship between landscape and character. Most of the major poets after the war, like Norman MacCaig and Iain Crichton Smith, for all their obvious connections with Scottish highlands and islands, preferred to leave out Scottish Renaissance subtexts of profound archetypal and mythic meaning, those resonances with the 'collective unconscious' so beloved of MacDiarmid and Muir, Gibbon and Gunn. This reaction culminated in the work of post-1945 writers such as Robin Jenkins, George Friel, and James Kelman, with their sardonic and reductive attitude towards old and new presentations of Scotland as a vital and colourful interaction between Highland and Lowland histories, with a continuation of romantic folk tradition and culture. These authors – perhaps because of the collapse of ideas of National Socialism in Europe, but perhaps even more strongly the grimness of living conditions in the post-war industrial conurbations of the Scottish Lowlands – concentrated on emphasising the spiritual bleakness and hopelessness of modern Scotland, stripping away what they saw as a phoney conglomeration of representations of Scotland past and present, utterly irrelevant to the majority of people living in arid non-communities and employed, if at all, in soul-destroying monotony. This was the dominant tendency in Scottish fiction and literature from the 1950s till the '70s, and it still carries weight in the present-day work of writers like Kelman, Irvine Welsh, and Duncan McLean, and in some women's writing, like that of Agnes Owens, Janet Paisley and even some of Galloway and Kennedy (although it would be fair to say that when the last two work in this vein they do so in a way which embeds it within wider and more therapeutic overall narratives and transformations).

The essay then argued that a major change took place through the 1980s, with writers like Edwin Morgan, Alasdair Gray, and Liz Lochhead, in poetry, fiction and drama, developing a new kind of imaginative relationship with their country and its culture, a relationship which refused to accept a simple realism of generally bleak and economically deprived urban character. Instead, the connection of the urban with the rural, and the idea of the future possibilty of a whole modern Scotland, linking past with present and future, began to be emphasised; and these and many other writers insisted on reintroducing, albeit in different form from Renaissance usage, elements of magic and myth, employed for symbolic and social-political reasons. The changes of these writers in approach and ideology, and of the contemporary writers who follow them, have radically altered the directions of Scottish literature, and fiction especially.[15]

A new grouping of writers is emerging who refuse to accept the old polarities, and who create in their novels an interlocking and interweaving of ideas which refuses to accept the premises of Scottish writing in its previously polarised twentieth-century attitudes. These writers include Iain Banks, Margaret Elphinstone, Janice Galloway, Andrew Greig, Sian Hayton, Alison Kennedy, and Carl MacDougall in fiction, as well as writers like Robert Crawford, Carol Ann Duffy, Douglas Dunn, W. N. Herbert, Jackie Kay, Liz Lochhead and Edwin Morgan in poetry. The range of impressive adaptions in drama of mytho-poetic Scottish fiction, as well as powerful new versions of the ideologies of rural and urban, as in Liz Lochhead's *Mary Queen of Scots Got Her Head Chopped Off* (1987) and her translation into Scots of Molière's *Tartuffe* (1985), Edwin Morgan's translation into Scots of *Cyrano de Bergerac* (1992), Sue Glover's *Bondagers* (1991), or Bill Bryden's *The Ship* (1991), and the recent impressive adaptations of *A Scots Quair* (1993), exhibit these eclectic, reforming and often literally magical new ways of thinking about past and future Scotlands.

What is the significance of all this reorientation? It is surely that Scottish literature of the 1980s is marked by its commitment to radical new ground-breaking; to reassessing its older texts, and to exploring ways of using a recognisably Scottish perspective in viewing the world outside, while simultaneously reasserting the validity of Scottish fictional and literary tradition as source material for contemporary creativity. Not least is its commitment to re-examining the identity and place of women in gender, in relationships, in society. In every aspect of literary productivity, from financing to deciding on topic and theme, the post-war ambience of scepticism and negativism was examined and challenged; and while this challenge was tempered by the post-referendum disappointment of 1979, it can be seen now to have been merely slowed. The underlying forces of insistent Scottish identity-making were moving, and are moving, inexorably in the direction of synthesis, but a synthesis which is permissive of multiple perspectives and a plurality of approaches through different genres. This new spectrum of possibility is based on a new willingness to allow a multi-faceted Scotland, no longer demanding allegiance to a single

MacDiarmid agenda, but recognising other people's right to perceive Scotland differently, and to imagine it differently also. There is simultaneously a desire to retain amidst the plethora of possible Scotlands a unifying sense of a force-field or web of connections which hold together what would otherwise deconstruct into meaningless regional variants, each of them susceptible to further deconstruction, so that as 'authenticity' is lost, so also is any awareness of identity or permanence. This desire to hold together 'Scotlands' in a net of deliberate casting is, of course, not a rational wish, but a willed creation of irrationalities which are perceived as more significant and important than the results of endless logical analysis, a logical deconstruction which must of course, if followed through to its reductive conclusion, reduce national aspirations – and, in the end, the human condition – to pointless temporality.

It is towards countering the pointlessness of placeless temporality that so many of the new Scottish writers, and especially the women writers, direct their imaginative energies. In many ways it is the contemporary writing of women which best exemplifies this move away from reductive social realism towards the new and non-essentialist use of the magical and the mythic as an imaginatively playful way of exploring possibilities and implying reformative agendas.

Following the inspiration of Naomi Mitchison, whose *Inheritors*-like *Early in Orcadia* had appeared in 1987, Margaret Elphinstone and Sian Hayton have developed a fascinating vein of quasi-historical, speculative and magical fiction. Mitchison wasn't the only inspiring writer; outstandingly, the work of George Mackay Brown from the mid-1960s ploughed a comparatively lonely furrow, in celebrating Orkney past and present in a way which continued Renaissance values. It would be true to say that Brown kept the anthropomorphic and mythical alive in fiction when most others had turned from it. Aware of the work of Mitchison and Brown, Elphinstone and Hayton have developed their own way of handling the mythic, the non-rational, the edges of experience. Elphinstone has written two novels concerning the wanderings of singer-poet Naomi, as she moves around Galloway and the Lake District – only a Galloway changed, a region of the future after apocalypse, a world returned to basic communities, isolated and unsure. Elphinstone's visionary Green Light in *The Incomer* (1987) and her dark discovery of poisoned lands in *A Sparrow's Flight* (1989), were new slants on modern issues extrapolated into the future, handled with delicacy and power from a quietly feminist position. Magic and myth played an even more central and poetic part in Elphinstone's short-story collection, *An Apple From a Tree* (1991), with its encounters in Galloway with Pan, its unapologetic supernatural events – used by Elphinstone in a curiously straightforward yet clearly allegorical way. Her most recent novel, *Islanders* (1994), shows a deliberate change of tack, however; she portrays the quiet lives of Fair Isle farmers and peasants without any hints of the magical, yet somehow still manages to embed these lives in a world-view deeply aware of the rhythms of seasons, seas, and the importance of tradition. This is an attempt to winnow the stuff of Renaissance writers like Gunn, Linklater and Mitchison to the grain, to see how plain the telling and presentation can be without becoming the grim view of the urban writers. It is, to my mind, outstandingly successful, and marks the high point of the new synthesis; although the work of Sian Hayton is almost as impressive in her *Hidden Daughters* trilogy; *Cells of Knowledge* (1989), *Hidden Daughters* (1992), *The Last Flight* (1993). These stories tell of the Celtic daughters of the giant Uthebhan, women of superhuman powers and great spiritual strength, but doomed to be distrusted by the new male-dominated Christian era. Set around the end of the first millenium, the stories contrive to lose history in myth; places are named in ways which hint at what they are now, but suggest a very different origin and society. Again, a sense of allegory hangs over all; but quite what the allegory means Hayton doesn't clearly suggest. Is it that the old woman-led Celtic society is measured against male-Christian dominance, and found to be greatly superior? Hayton allows no clear narrative to emerge, but permits hints, echoes, and occasional mentions of previous sisters and situations to loosely hold her trilogy together. She also begins in the Christian world, only gradually revealing her lost and hidden magic; then returns to the Christian, posing unanswered questions as to what will happen to the sisters and their descendants. In all this the past is shown to be protean, as flux; but a flux which hints towards the present, with disturbing implications for our values and gender relations.

It is clear that this new use of the magical in eclectic ways is no passing phase. Ellen Galford's hilarious recreation of ancient Celtic magic in contemporary Edinburgh in *Queendome Come*, discussed above in its ways of showing emergent women's power, uses a blend of traditional lore and modern invention to make its powerful satiric statements, while her *The Dyke and the Dybbuk* (1993) presents a lesbian London taxi-driver having a quarrelsome affair with Kobos, a demon employed by Mephisto PLC to work out ancient curses. This new supernaturalism can be deployed for psychological exploration as well as satirical humour; in the work of A.L. Kennedy, outstandingly in *So I Am Glad* (1995), with its introduction of Cyrano de Bergerac in modern Glasgow, it reaches its apotheosis.

Thematic Concerns; Breaking Down Gender Difference

Since Scott's *The Heart of Midlothian* (1818), male writers of Scottish fiction have frequently represented Scottish women prominently, but in ways which suggest that this foregrounding is something of a back-handed compliment. The compliment lies in the way the figure of a Scottish woman, usually but not necessarily of humble origin, is placed at the centre of the novel as carrier of essential national identity, as tradition bearer, and often as having mythic and regenerative power. Scott's Jeanie Deans, the humble cow-feeder's daughter, is made to speak for the grass roots resilience and fundamentally sound morality of Scotland and the Scottish peasantry. Scott had been unable to locate this healing and archetypal power in his male protagonists, defeated as they were in their heroic enterprises by the plain facts of history.[16] And following Scott, writers such as Stevenson, George Macdonald, Neil Gunn and – outstandingly – Lewis Grassic Gibbon in *A Scots Quair* (1932–4), often stepped outside history to locate a Scottish ideal in their symbolic women (the simple and very common names chosen for them, like Jeanie, Kirstie, and Chris reinforcing the sense of their being very much the product of their race). Women writers used this strategy also; Oliphant's independent protagonist in *Kirsteen*, Carswell's Joanna Bannerman (with a touch of mockery in the notion that at last it was the turn of a bannerwoman?) in *Open the Door!* and Mitchison's Kirstie Haldane in *The Bull Calves* all work with reference to Scott's regenerative ideology.

The back-handed nature of Scott's, and Gibbon's, compliment to women in allowing them such core status lies in its limitation of alternative and more ambitious roles for women, together with a restriction of emotional and social range. Women as guardians of national soul tend to be enduring witnesses rather than agents of significant change – although, to be fair to Scott, his Jeanie Deans was allowed to enact considerable social change in her role as guiding spirit as minister's wife in Scott's 'island' of Roseneath, where both 'island' and Jeanie's influence on its natives were to stand as Scotland and its potential changing character in microcosm. Later writers limited the scope of their archetypal women's actions, so that Gunn's strong women are seen as the knots which hold history together, tough and elemental figures of endurance, and Gibbon's Chris Guthrie becomes in his trilogy increasingly side-lined as witness to Land, Change, and Death, a passive Earth Mother eventually fading back into the land itself while her son Ewan emerges out of that land to become the future, the political and social New Man. This archetyping of Scottish women continued up to the '50s, with Neil Paterson's Thirza Gair, the epic fisherwoman in *Behold Thy Daughter* (1950), and Robin Jenkins's Bell MacShelvie, the urban version of the symbolic figure in *Guests of War* (1956).

This chapter has already noted the way in which several women writers of the first half of the twentieth century reacted against such usage of female figureheads. In particular, Violet Jacob, Willa Muir, and Nan Shepherd all refashion this tradition, in varying ways and degrees, parodying and ironically exposing its limitations in ways which recall Stella Gibbons's effective and hilarious undermining in *Cold Comfort Farm* (1932) of 'the answer lies in the soil' fictional tradition as represented by writers like Mary Webb and D. H. Lawrence.

If, in the contemporary burgeoning of both Scottish women's writing and Scottish writing generally, there are indeed signs of new acceptance and syntheses of rural and mythic concerns rejected in the pessimism of the post-1945 period, then perhaps one of the strongest indications of a new direction for Scottish writing – and, one would hope, for what has for so long been a pretty male-dominated Scottish society – lies in the way that new male writers are trying to empathise with women, and the way that both men and women writers are challenging conventions of gender difference.

Signs that a shift in male fictional perceptions of women was under way can be read in the novels and stories of Alasdair Gray, outstandingly in *1982, Janine* (1984), *Something Leather* (1990) and *Poor Things* (1992). Gray's genuine recognition of repression and maltreatment of women by men, with its awareness of the nuances involved in Scottish variants, struck many readers of *Janine*, but left as many again misunderstanding the motives behind what seemed in the first part of the book to be an indulgence in male erotic fantasy. The second half, in which the suicidal and aggrieved fantasist, Jock McCleish, is forced to come to terms with the way he has victimised (and been victimised by) the women in his life, represents a new openness and honesty, to the point of vulnerability, in Scottish male writing. And Gray's subsequent work has made it clear that for him revaluation of gender stereotypes and sexual relations is of paramount importance. *Something Leather* again plays with predictable reader expectations and reactions, again turning tables on those who naively read the grouping of women in this novel as a portrayal of sexual deviation. For once, unhappy women organise together, and Gray takes comic delight in their new potency, as he does in his grotesque and ferocious recreation of ideas of Mary Shelley and Stevenson in his provocative account of the creation of a sexual and gender-unconditioned *tabula rasa* in the manmade female Frankenstein, Bella Baxter, the girl who becomes the symbolic and potential New Woman of Scotland, 'Bella Caledonia', and whose social and sexual unconventional frankness shocks all who meet her.

Working in a different vein and genre, but with many of the same aims, the fiction of Iain Banks has also sought to revalue and replace the roles of women in fiction, from *The Bridge* (1986) and *Canal Dreams* (1989) to *The Crow Road* (1992) and, in particular, *Whit* (1995). In these novels women are frequently stronger than men, taking dominant roles, but in ways which the author/protagonist accepts, if not as a happy state, at least as natural and unsurprising. *Canal Dreams* deliberately plays with stereotypes in its presentation of an ugly female violin-playing counter-terrorist of matchless ferocity; while *Whit* sees Banks going further than anyone else, with the exception of Gray in *Poor Things*, in his creation of a new kind of female archetype to Scotland, the initially naive heiress to the leadership of a bizarre religious sect, who learns through betrayal and comic-epic journey to take complete initiative away from double-dealing male relatives and male-dominated society. 'Whit', one of her names, refers also to the epiphanetic quality of her new social role.

Other male writers have shown this empathy, alongside an exploration of gender boundaries, perhaps the most important being Ronald Frame, Stuart Hood, and more recently (and in critical work also) Christopher Whyte (in *Gendering the Nation*, 1995). Frame's novels are consistently presented from the perspective of middle-class women, in ways which are deeply sensitive to the particular pains and problems of women coping with the difficulties of class conventions, none the less complex and hurtful for their proximity to wealth and privilege, which so readily disappear for these straitened and mysterious women. Stuart Hood's impressive run of novels, from *A Storm from Paradise* (1985) to *The Book of Judith* (1995), explore many issues from the narrow-mindedness of smalltown Scots to the morality of international terrorism, but always with the new emphasis on treating the dimensions of gender with empathy and argument for women's balanced place. And Christopher Whyte's provocative coat-trailing to draw out cries of outraged conventionality in *Euphemia McFarrigle and the Laughing Virgin* (1995) explicitly seeks to force reassessment of traditional male-female roles, natural and supernatural, as to a lesser extent does Andrew Greig in *Electric Brae* (1992) and *The Return of John McNab* (1996), with their forceful females taking emotional and unconventional initiatives within traditionally male activities like climbing and hunting – with the author giving these pursuits some unusual twists.

But the outstanding example of new male writing working through a female persona has without doubt been Alan Warner's *Morvern Callar* (1994). *Morvern Callar* is the contemporary, rural, and female version of Trocchi's *Young Adam*; it wouldn't be going too far to say that what Trocchi began against the grain of Scottish literature in the 1960s is taken up and developed in Warner's novel. Warner doesn't go for Trocchi's violence; Morvern simply finds her older boyfriend with his throat cut, and doesn't tell anyone about it. But both novelists conceal and withdraw from all 'normal' social obligations, and both speak with a spare yet powerful, apparently controlled voice of the subsequent events, with the major difference that now it is a woman who withdraws from social obligation. Morvern, like Trocchi's Joe and Kelman's chancers, works on the edge – here, as a storehand in the supermarket in a West Highland town (quite deliberately never named, but clearly identified via railways, islands, hotels, and its hilltop folly as Oban). Where Joe's story started with him haunted by the memory of the body of girlfriend Cathie, Morvern wakes up one morning to find her older boyfriend has cut his throat and left a disc from his PC as suicide note. Where Joe goes about his cool business, so does Morvern, telling no one, but working as normal, giving out Christmas presents, partying and having far-out sex and crunching around snowy Oban in the small hours. She's just as, if not more, laconic than Joe; and her environment is handled in the same minimal, yet evocative way. It is one of Warner's singular achievements that he manages to strip his/her West Highland town of tourist and romantic associations, so that its essentially seedy bars, lanes, and railway cuttings are seen through the eyes of locals, disenchanted and not a bit different from locals in city housing estates. That doesn't mean that Oban and hills disappear; but for the reader the effect is of recognising a dissociation between place and people, as though sea and hills are just there. It is a dissociation which parallels the central dissociation of conventional gender patterns. Warner makes Morvern acutely alive to physical detail, textures, weather; a contemporary Chris Guthrie, she can respond to 'nature' as well, as when she goes camping outside Oban, and vividly senses water, fire-smells, smoke in her hair. But in another sense she is a repudiation of the older gender categories expressed in Chris Guthrie and her community. For Morvern, it is the here and now which matter, and the reader isn't all that surprised to realise that one reason for the camping is to take little parcels of her lover's body for burying, camping being the perfect cover.

Slowly the effect takes hold; a realisation of Morvern's suppressed feelings, masked totally; a realisation of her survival capability; an awareness of just how surprising, yet credible she is in her mixture of gallus shrieking laughter, mortal drink-drug sessions, warmth towards friend Lanna, strange qualified loyalty towards her foster-father and his new woman, and apparently heartless treatment – some of it dangerously hilarious – of her lover's body and his loft, filled with model trains. Grotesque surprises and situations arise quite casually, as when she has to abandon her promising driving test because she suddenly sees from the car that men from the council are about to fix the roof of her flat – and will find the body. What this humour conceals, however, is Morvern's depth of character, which is slyly understated; the reader has to tune in to see why Morvern acts as she does, and to read past the extremes of 'bad taste' in which Morvern thoughtlessly indulges to find the new woman Warner represents in her.

The story takes risks halfway through, leaving Oban for the Mediterranean and the world of instant holidays. Morvern has taken her lover's card, which she can use, sent off his novel under her name to a publisher, and skedaddled with Lanna for sunshine. With something of the send-up of Janice Galloway's *Foreign Parts* (1994) Warner shows up the sex-and-drink-drenched falsity of the cheap tours; but he somehow controls the transition to this totally different scene by continuing the strange perspective that is Morvern's concealing account. The reader *knows* that she is concealing, that something slow to articulate itself is building up, and recognises why she has to leave Lanna and – as she did when camping – go back to sensations of weather, sea, night. She's still Morvern; she still goes to raves, but never connecting in real human terms.

For she is completely now a misfit. Her unknown parents, her place as foster-child of society as well as of Red Hanna, her loss of her articulate, yet finally insufficient lover who might have taken her out of limbo – all these are exacerbated by the 'escape' to Europe; so that three years later she will return to the West pregnant by an unknown father, with a child of the rave scene. It's virtually impossible to know how to take Warner's ending, as she heads on down to the port, except that the reader knows that Morvern being Morvern will survive, as quarry worker, as author (for the novel is to be published), as triumph of the new ungendered dispossessed, just as Kelman's Sammy or Galloway's Joy will survive. Morvern is original, fresh, tough, and utterly believable as a girl, and a person. Warner has arguably succeeded, as no other since Lewis Grassic Gibbon introduced us to Chris Guthrie, in presenting a woman so completely that awareness of male authorship disappears. There's one crucial difference, however, which is a measure of change; where Gibbon created Chris in terms of connections with landscape, maternity, relationships with men which were boundaries marking the territories women were supposed to occupy, allocated by men, Warner strips these connections down so that Morvern is a creature, so alive to place and people that she defies gender allocations, taking initiatives which centuries have said she shouldn't, refusing commitments, sure only of a few basic things – her right to decide where she'll go, who she'll have sex with, and her recognition that she's alone. There are many other achievements – the grasp and control of Morvern's voice, with its Oban-yet-not-Oban phrases, strange syntactic turns, the ferocious, unpredictable local and Mediterranean characters, and Warner's strange, dark poetry of place; but it is the creation of Morvern herself which marks a significant reorientation in the gendering of Scottish fiction.

Conclusion

If this last section has dealt with the work of male writers, it is because the change in male perspectives is arguably long overdue and highly significant. Women have been writing men from the beginning, albeit with certain understandable orientations, towards the traditionally feminine interests in marriage and family. But since Willa Muir their acceptance of marriage and family domesticity has been drastically modified, and in this respect the changes in contemporary women's writing have been less dramatic. That said, it is noticeable in the work of Galloway, Kennedy, McWilliam (the title of whose *Debatable Land*, 1994, points to its subject matter of Scottish definitions of gender and inherited gender roles and behaviour as matter worthy of redefinition and catharsis through debate) and Rose particularly, that there is now no discernible bias towards either sex. Instead, there is a willingness, as in the poetry and drama of Liz Lochhead, or the plays of Rona Munro, like *Bold Girls* (1991), to apportion blame in terms of particular cases, and to make a continual implicit plea for a cessation of sexual and gender hostilities, and for the recognition and deconstruction of the assertive and defensive barriers which centuries of British and Scottish patriarchal and religious social conditioning have erected. Never before have male and female writers worked as closely in terms of aims and thematic preoccupations; the fact that consideration of contemporary fiction of men and women becomes increasingly difficult to separate into work by men and work by women is a measure of this change.

In this account of the increasing success of the new women's writing it is only fair that the achievement of women be placed finally in the context of the astonishing burgeoning of contemporary creative writing in Scotland generally. The beneficial effect of the work of writers like Jenkins, Mackay Brown, Crichton Smith, Gray, Kelman, Frame, Banks and many others should not be underestimated; it provided examples of new confidence, of wider range in novels, and the writers gave explicit acknowledgement of the aims of women and encouraged them, in writers' circles and workshops, and in the narratives themselves, to seek these aims. Quite simply, modern Scottish women and men writers are to a great extent working out problems of Scottish history, identity, gender, relation to environment, and future direction, in terms of mutual respect for each other's ideals and values, and with an increasing sense of the possible synthesis of these ideals and values. In the next chapter closer attention is paid to the best work of the most outstanding of the new women writers who have produced fiction which explores and illustrates the major themes and preoccupations discussed above.

Notes

1. Jenni Calder, 'Heroes and Hero-makers: Women in Nineteenth Century Scottish Fiction', in Douglas Gifford (ed.), *The History of Scottish Literature*, vol. 3 (Aberdeen University Press, Aberdeen, 1988), pp. 261–74.
2. See, for example, Moira Burgess, *The Other Voice: An Anthology of Scottish Women's Writing*, and Douglas Gifford, 'Myth, Parody and Dissociation in Scottish Fiction 1814–1914',

in *The History of Scottish Literature*, vol. 3 (Aberdeen University Press, Aberdeen, 1988), pp. 236–9.

3. Willa Muir's *Mrs Grundy in Scotland* (Routledge, London, 1936) is a perceptive and entertaining study by a later Scottish novelist of the increasing and repressive narrowness of social manners in nineteenth-century Scotland.

4. Calder, 'Heroes and Hero-makers', p. 264.

5. Naomi Mitchison, *Among You Taking Notes: The Wartime Diary of Naomi Mitchison 1939–1945*, ed. Dorothy Sheridan (Gollancz, London, 1985).

6. Alan Freeman, *Scotland's Missing Zolas: Fiction By Women 1900–1940*, unpublished doctoral thesis, University of Edinburgh, 1992. I am indebted to Alan Freeman for many ideas from this thesis, and from discussion with him on the Findlaters, Carswell, Muir, and Shepherd especially.

7. Muir, *Mrs Grundy in Scotland*.

8. Twenty-three annual volumes have appeared from Collins since the first, *Scottish Short Stories 1973*, eds Douglas Gifford and Neil Paterson (Collins, London and Glasgow, 1973). The *Original Prints* series is published by Polygon, Edinburgh.

9. Freeman, pp. 161–74.

10. James Black Baillie, *Studies in Human Nature* (Bell and Sons, London, 1921); John Macmurray, *Persons in Relation* (Faber and Faber, London 1970); John Macquarrie, *Existentialism* (Pelican, London, 1972).

11. Freeman, pp. 164–6; Willa Muir, 'Clock-A-Doodle-Doo', in J. H. Whyte (ed.), *Towards a New Scotland: A Selection from The Modern Scot*, McElhose, London, 1935), pp. 184–91.

12. *Imagined Corners* (1931; Canongate, Edinburgh, 1987), p. 2.

13. The work of these two women is discussed in separate chapters.

14. A useful new edition of *Thou Shalt Not Suffer a Witch* has been edited with an excellent introduction by Angela Cran and James Robertson (B&W Publishing, Edinburgh, 1996).

15. Douglas Gifford, 'Imagining Scotlands: the Return to Mythology in Modern Scottish Fiction', in Susan Hagemann (ed.), *Studies in Scottish Fiction: 1945 to the Present* (Peter Lang, Frankfurt am Main, 1996), pp. 17–49.

16. For a fuller version of this argument, see Douglas Gifford, 'Myth, Parody and Dissociation', pp. 217–61.

40

Contemporary Fiction II:
Seven Writers in Scotland

Douglas Gifford

The years 1989 and 1990 saw the publication of Margaret Elphinstone's *A Sparrow's Flight*, Janice Galloway's *The Trick is to Keep Breathing*; Sian Hayton's *Cells of Knowledge*, Alison Kennedy's *Night Geometry and the Garscadden Trains*, Joan Lingard's *The Women's House* and Dilys Rose's short-story collection, *Our Lady of the Pickpockets*. Taken in conjunction with work around this time from writers like Barker, Fell, Ross and Owens there was a clear signal that a significant new development in women's writing in Scotland was taking place, in which there was a heightened consciousness of the need to explore female identity in relation to past, present and future. Hayton's fiction, for example, looked back to Celtic concepts of womanhood, imagining an older integration of male-female co-operation in work and family which the Christian church was to destroy; *The Trick is to Keep Breathing* explored present-day pressures surrounding women in urban society by looking at a woman, struggling to reintegrate her mind and life after the tragic death of her lover; Elphinstone's *The Incomer* and *A Sparrow's Flight* moved into the future, conjecturing as to future roles and identities for women in a post-nuclear holocaust society. And since then several women have produced an impressive body of work which deserves fuller consideration than given in the previous chapter. This chapter introduces the novels and short stories of seven of the home Scottish writers; the next deals with the work of some of the Anglo-Scottish writers.

Margaret Elphinstone

Underpinning Elphinstone's first two novels is the premise that Britain has suffered a great nuclear disaster which has taken it back to dark ages, with isolated communities around the Borders and Galloway struggling to develop. She does not record this, and the reader is left to find this out through hints and clues, the strongest of which emerge in *A Sparrow's Flight* (1989), with its journeys placed in a Cumbria rumoured to have suffered a great poisoning from what would appear to be related to a nuclear disaster at Sellafield. In *The Incomer* (1987) Naomi is a wandering minstrel. She seems recently to have faced a crisis in her life, in which the claims of family in a past community have yielded to the claims of her art. Elphinstone captures the new sense of time of her neo-medieval communities well, and their new-old mindset, with its superstitious fear of ever referring to holocaust. She recreates this community in Clachanpluck, one of the new settlements somewhere in southern Scotland. The village consciously embeds itself in a strange and organic relationship with nature, its members having reverted to a deep reborn respect for earth, plants and trees. Within this relationship with nature lies the village's secret, which Naomi and the reader never quite discover. Elphinstone is of course creating a kind of allegory for quests which modern society has forgotten, and Naomi is her mouthpiece, as she gives music and help to the village – especially to its women. For though Naomi has not lost her desire for men, she is hurt from her past, and the matriarchal village and its strong women attract her. Like Hayton, Elphinstone seems to be suggesting that women seek new kinds of relationships, drawing from older and deeper versions of matriarchy as sources of new identity. Clachanpluck is outraged by the rape of a villager girl, an unheard-of event which in allegorical reading surely stands as the archetypal breach of ideal trust between sexes. Elphinstone makes the rape symbolic of the bad old ways which somehow destroyed the old world, and its fierce expiation an archetypal recommendation. And in Naomi's glimpse of Clachanpluck's vital connection with the Green Light, the spirit of Nature, elusive as Pan in *The Wind in the Willows*, Elphinstone reiterates Grahame's deepest and quasi-religious message.

A *Sparrow's Flight* has different mythic resonances. Naomi is still the wanderer, following her own music, but her journey is now from an Edenic island in the East (Lindisfarne?) over Border mountains, avoiding the poisoned valleys and their inhabitants. Once again she is witness and enabler, this time for Thomas, seeking to relieve the agony of his people in their hidden valley in the Lakes country. The journey echoes *The Pilgrim's Progress*; and exploits Tarot imagery to lend an air of fabulous and predestined significance to its stages. Elphinstone is rightly concerned that her work avoids becoming science fiction, and is thus economical with her occasional glimpses of the Old World of science and its aftermath – there's a shunned place of overgrown ruins, a hatred of one particular coastal place (Sellafield?) and Naomi's discovery of sheet music in Thomas's valley home, and that's almost all. This music is from the past, however, and shows Naomi that something rich can be salvaged from there, which can lead her in the future to a richer music than that which she plays now at weddings and fairs. The novel is in the end about human and sexual relations and their redefinition; Naomi makes a new kind of relationship with Thomas which breaks with gender stereotypes. This is epic work which is comparable in many respects with the similar aims of Sian Hayton, but it also suggests strongly that it represents important quests of Margaret Elphinstone herself.

An *Apple From a Tree* (1991) showed that Elphinstone could create delightful short stories, working with the kind of earth-magic of her first novel, as well as drawing from the magic of traditional Border balladry. The volume could aptly have been titled *The Green Man*, since the first story, with that title, sets the tone. A girl walking across the old railway lines of Galloway comes across the strangest earth-coloured tent, and a man with green hair, eyes, skin. After making love, Lin (Tamlin?) withdraws from her to his own and other landscape, unable to face the despoliation of the land. Echoing Mitchison's *Five Men and a Swan* (1958), and the central ideas of George Mackay Brown, but making unusual play with traditional male-female roles, Elphinstone places women at the centre of the fight for renewal and resistance to earth pollution. Three more stories, including the title story, present otherworld visitors, two of them using Oddny the Earth Mother, guardian of the primal Well, symbol of essential purity. But the preaching is light; Oddny takes time off to advertise in the modern press for an earth girl to take her place, and the accounts of the relative difficulties of the two to adjust to each other's world is hilarious. More seriously, Oddny takes on Sellafield and its spiritual and physical poisoning of the land around; Elphinstone is here unashamedly politically motivated. But her women aren't always guardians; there are stories here that show that they can be malign. But the sense of this world next to another is always present, outstandingly in the title story, in which Alison bites an apple in Edinburgh's Botanic Garden; the earth reels, and she is in an alien land with otherworld Nosila; reverse the situation, and the two girls are frantic in a hostile Waverley Station. The otherworldliness can be comic, like this – or, as in 'A Life of Glory', deeply disturbing; an idyllic love affair in the Grand Canyon is then seen from the embryo's perspective, in its overwhelming desire to escape this earth for the oneness of space. It achieves this leap – but through miscarriage and death. Elphinstone's sense that we walk a crust on this earth which can break and precipitate us into strange landscapes works within the tradition of 'the two moods of Scottish literature', moving from worldly detail to 'the horns of Elfland', described by Gregory Smith in *Scottish Literature: Character and Influence* (1919).

But her most impressive work must surely be *Islanders* (1995), her ambitious and extensively researched recreation of life on Fair Isle (which she renames as Fridarey) in the twelfth century. Her manner of presenting island history is very different from her previous mytho-poetic creations, with their magic and mythic resonances. Here these are almost eliminated (but it is an important qualifying 'almost') and instead replaced by slow turns of season and details of the island life of a few families of farmers, fishermen and Viking raiders over two generations. It is almost as though Elphinstone wishes to explore how far she can reduce her mythic elements and yet somehow keep a residual bedrock of tradition and legend which will carry forward the events of these ordinary lives to become the myths of the future. Neil Gunn had worked in much this way in the trilogy of *Sun Circle, Butcher's Broom* and *The Silver Darlings* (1932–41), by showing how contemporary events translate into legend and ossify into myth; Eric Linklater had recreated saga times and styles in *The Men of Ness* (1932) and clearly the work of Naomi Mitchison in *The Corn King and the Spring Queen* (1931), *The Bull Calves* (1947), and, particularly, *Early in Orcadia* (1987), with its recreation of early island life, has influenced Elphinstone's novel. But there is no sense of imitation of any of these, as Elphinstone's spare, steady narrative has its own rhythms, appropriate to her own aims of suggesting the triumph of the ordinary business of living over Viking adventure. The result lies between Linklater's impersonal saga style and Gunn's recounting of generations, and represents a singular and impressive new way of writing history. Indeed, from the opening pages with their map of the islands which turns north and south upside down to reflect the orientation of the island worldview, the reader's conventional perspectives on peripheral cultures is destabilised, and resettled in a view from a rock perched far in the Atlantic, looking at Europe, Britain, and even Orkney and Shetland from a very different value-centre.

This is no Romance. Events are low-key, if sometimes tragic. Apart from the shipwrecking of the child Astrid on Fridarey at the beginning there are few more melo-dramatic incidents, the main events being to do with their farming calendar, occasional social gatherings of the four or five families on the island. Ships are built, stores laid up, winters endured, rumours of power shifts amid Viking raids heard, and occasionally a man is tempted to join the raiding. But times are changing, and the twelfth century sees the dying of the tradition of piracy, made disreputable by the new trading.

In addition to recreating the men and women of Fridarey in rare depth and individu-ation, Elphinstone successfully recreates that tension of cultures surrounding Fridarey which saw both raiding and trading as legitimate foraying for food and goods, with honour in valour valued alongside profit. These movements in history are encapsulated in the story of Astrid, caught between old and new worlds. Originally from Dublin, chance has thrown her on Fridarey. She learns slowly that life in her peripheral island is better than at the centre, that Fridarey holds in microcosm all that life can offer. She has her chance to leave, but her journey through Shetland with Thorvald, her Fridarey companion, seeking ways of return to Dublin, reveals that even in Shetland the new world is filled with predators. Astrid's life has been a balance of chance (her shipwreck, the men she meets in Fridarey, her dangerous encounters now on Shetland) and the stability of life on Fridarey. In contrast to the new opportunists of Shetland and beyond, the farmers of Byrstada and Shirva are men and women who assume that people have a natural equality, born of sharing tasks and avoiding the controls of church and state, timelessly decent, if sometimes violent or jealous. Elphinstone seems to be arguing that, in a world where chance is more important than myth, such hard gleaned order emerges as more important than religion or myth. That said, she has a sting in the tale; when Astrid and Thorvald return to Fridarey, two seals guide their boat to shore; but this is a residual flicker of magic which serves to highlight just how different Elphinstone's aims have become. This is genuine historical recreation of times and their agents, rather than historical stagesetting for modern psychology and romantic dilemmas. This is a world which can still be related to its very changed present in its early versions of placenames, institutions and its changing economic orientations. But above all it is a world of people whose actions can be understood in their time.

Janice Galloway

Of all the new Scottish fiction, arguably that of Janice Galloway and Alison Kennedy is the most sophisticated and powerful, and Galloway's first novel, *The Trick is to Keep Breathing* (1989), one of the strongest of the new statements of the need to redefine the place of women in society. Galloway works in the context of that astonishing revival of fiction in the West of Scotland which began with Alasdair Gray and James Kelman; indeed, her novel exploits techniques which Kelman used in *The Busconductor Hines* (1984) and Gray in *1982, Janine* (1984). The presentation of Hines's life in a long series of fragmented episodes separated from each other by a heading row of three small circles is adopted here to present Joy Stone's situation; and Gray's account of a disillusioned middle-class drunk coming to terms with traumatic memories through dialogues with his own inner voices is refashioned in young teacher Joy's negotiation with her traumatic memories. Like *Janine* this is a journey towards rehabilitation – or at least a beginning. In each case the protagonist has no illusions as to immediate future happiness, but at least they have learned to make the positive statement 'yes' to their deepest selves. Joy's lover has drowned, and perhaps her mother also; Joy comes close to drowning amidst her turbulent and traumatised life thereafter, but just in time discovers that the trick, as in swimming, is to keep breathing. Like *The Busconductor Hines* this novel makes no concessions to cliché or falsely contrived narrative, taking Kelman's risks in incorporating the mundane alongside the occasionally funny, grotesque or moving event.

Galloway finds her own voice, however, with a more immediate sense of the absurd and a keener eye for banal detail than either Gray or Kelman. She opens her novel in something of the way of *Lanark*, with the reader struggling *in media res*, with the sense of something tragic having occurred. But where Gray uses fantasy in order to convey the breakdown of his central figure, Galloway presents a more immediate sense of horror, as Joy struggles to shut out memory and images of her drowned lover in a way that shockingly conveys unexpected tragedy. Joy allows the reader the barest glimpses of the accident; not till well on in the novel does the reader know all. Sudden sharp images of the pool, of the body, interrupt her teaching, her interviews with the Housing Department (will she get to keep the house she shared with her lover, not being married to him?), her meetings with friends. But two things force themselves through Joy's understandably self-centred grief. Even in her darkest moments she is aware of the ridiculous and condescending aspects of her interviews with social workers, headmasters, officials. This aspect becomes a sustained satire on the insufficiencies of male-dominated systems like education, health, social services, well-meaning but insensitive in their dealings; and on the way ordinary people are exploited through the slick banality and clichés of advertising in a ruthless consumer society, in its endless messages designed to programme and to take away genuine choice. The reader is perhaps less sympathetic to Joy in regard to the other message which forces itself through grief to her; Joy will finally realise that much of the trauma she endures comes from guilt; Michael has left his wife and family for her, and Joy, in failing to extend understanding to herself or to Michael's wife and family, is drowning in the subconscious guilt which she cannot articulate in order to come to terms with it.

Yet for all its darkness, the novel is often hilariously and embarrassingly funny as Galloway recounts the absurd situations Joy gets into. Galloway captures the variety of ways in which she is patronised in her hospital treatment, by social workers, by her headmaster, by her best friend's smothering mother. There are grimmer situations; her unwillingness to face her alcoholic sister, or the memories of her ferocious mother (has her mother committed suicide?). Joy's bouts of loveless sexuality, where she is unable to distinguish between genuine concern or unable to avoid allowing herself to be sexually exploited, are used by Galloway to create a suffocating sense of Joy's loss of will and direction. But just as the very intensity of her confession begins to create a sense of emotional claustrophobia for the reader, Galloway subtly turns the implication of all this around. Forced to follow Joy's interpretation of events, and perhaps becoming intolerant of her monotony of self-interest, the reader begins to realise that Joy is hiding something which lies behind all her tortured diary entries, her anorexia, her binges followed by vomiting, her use of sleazy men as escape, her solitary drinking and her introversion. This is that guilt, partly her own and partly induced and promoted by her society, concerning Paul, the man she lived with and left for Michael, and Michael's wife and family, and all her own buried familial guilt. Galloway doesn't allocate blame. Instead she simply shows Joy's subtle and unsubtle ostracisation, together with the guilt she feels, which must be externalised. The crucial penultimate paragraph, with its reminders of the voice which spoke to Jock McLeish in Alasdair Gray's *Lanark* (1981), prompting self-forgiveness and release, is the first step in Joy's self-rediscovery. Alone, drinking, Joy tells us that

> The voice is still there.
> I forgive you.
> I heard it quite distinctly, my own voice in the empty house.
> I forgive you.

All through the novel, as with the healing voice in *Janine*, this voice has been struggling, a subconscious and self-healing identity, to make its subject listen. Galloway uses some of the typographical experimentations of *Janine*, with thoughts printed in the margin to suggest the marginalisation of our deepest selves amidst the pressures of contemporary society. This voice, finally achieving utterance, surely marks the book's most significant achievement in its insistence that the real concerns and the real voices of contemporary women should genuinely be heard in Scottish society, and not just paid condescending lip service.

The combination of sensitive interpretation of women's pain and a sharp eye for the farcical, the grotesque, and the excesses of modern society are found in Galloway's next book, the collection of short stories, *Blood* (1991). Again, one can see connections with the grotesque strand in the work of James Kelman, for example, in the running 'Scenes from the Life' of which numbers 23, 29, 26 and 27 are given here. Galloway reveals here that she can handle West of Scotland macho humour very effectively, exploiting it in order to parody and show up entrenched male attitudes. Number 23, 'Paternal Advice', is an old West of Scotland urban folk-tale retold here as a mini-drama. Sammy (archetypal West of Scotland punter) is mulling over a tricky problem. He stands up suddenly and calls into the sitting room Wee Sammy. Genially he persuades his son to climb on to the mantelpiece and to jump into his arms – only when the boy does so '*boy crashes lumpily into the tiles of the fire surround. His father sighs and averts his eyes, choking back a sob.* SAMMY: Let that be a lesson to you son. Trust nae cunt.'[2] What Galloway has done is to expand a piece of black Glasgow humour, reinforcing it with Kelman-like detail, and perhaps with a touch of the surreal emphasis of Ivor Cutler. And this strand runs through her collection, as in 'Two Fragments', where a girl retells her mother's old tale of how her father lost his fingers by eating his chips too quickly, or how her mother boiled the tom cat in the washhouse. On the collection's appearance there were some reviews suggesting that these stories were more sick than funny. This is to miss Galloway's satiric point; she is merely working with what's out there in traditional urban-Scottish humour, so that she is simultaneously reflecting and satirising the way in which it mingles the humane and the cruel, the sympathetic and the savagely sceptical. In addition to these sketches, she further exposes hypocritical male attitudes in stories like 'Fair Ellen and the Wanderer Returned', a kind of ballad lampoon in which she pours scorn on men's expectations that women should give unqualified fidelity; or in 'Need for Restraint', which shows a girl witnessing street violence being told so repeatedly by her man that it's nothing to do with her that she finally breaks down and they separate.

Another of Galloway's aims is to find ways of handling the unbearable. If she is angered at social and official indifference and condescension, she also recognises that there is a huge amount of unavoidable human pain. In 'Scenes from the Life 26' an old woman is seen by a health visitor, and after giving the visitor tea in exchange for banalities, kills herself (the reader will remember Galloway's attitude towards the authoritarian do-gooders of *The Trick is to Keep Breathing*). Galloway's detached stage-setting of the visit and the old lady's calm preparations for death emphasise loneliness in a way which which comes out in story after story of individuals who, like Joy Stone, are locked inside themselves. The last and longest story, 'A Week with Uncle Felix', eschews the previous grotesquery and simply tells itself from the point of view of a young girl away for a week with her dead father's brother and his wife. Very little happens, apart from trips, teas, desultory chat, but Galloway captures the girl's isolated unhappiness perfectly along with the sadness of her uncle and his unsuccessful attempts to bridge the gap between them.

If Galloway's opposite extremes are compassion for human pain and sardonic satire, some of the most impressive stories here work with a rich poetic imagery and symbolism which often becomes grotesque and surreal. In a significant new experimentation with traditional supernatural, 'Breaking Through' has a girl visit an old lady in an out of the way house; on one visit she finds Blackie the cat 'framed in flames', burning in the fireplace.

Galloway ends the story with a curious appropriateness when the old lady steps into the fire herself, calm and ready, her time over, the child instinctively lifting the poker to assist in her pyre. In 'It Was', a girl out walking – is she lonely, distraught, perhaps having a breakdown? – finds a tiny human face in the ground; she dusts it down, and it is her dead Uncle George. She goes off happily to have tea with him. And the title story, while never surreal, uses images and ideas of blood in rich variation to capture the changing moods of a schoolgirl during one difficult day, with a power and poetic resonance only to be found in the work of Liz Lochhead.

The sense of Galloway beginning to experiment with very different themes and expressions is borne out in her novel of 1994, *Foreign Parts*, very different in its style and conclusion from any previous work. There is still the wickedly and hilariously accurate analysis of consumer society, this time in her sharp and detailed presentation of the pressures of commercial tourism, the background to the novel's central relationship between two lady friends of around forty on holiday. They have totally different ways of perceiving the holiday and its aims, and these surface as tips of the iceberg of far deeper and older tensions between them. But this is an immensely humane study. Just as *The Trick is to Keep Breathing* moves towards personal forgiveness so here the novel moves towards the beginning of genuine mutual understanding.

The two friends are Cassie and Rona, welfare workers on holiday. The novel opens with them on the ferry to France, following them through Normandy and their visits to war graveyards to cathedral and château towns like Saumur and Chartres. Cassie is impulsive and anxious, the 'artistic' of the two. Rona is practical and calm, her huge handbag filled with something to meet every eventuality. Cassie yearns and theorises, dreams and agonises; Rona drives and tells her to shut up. Galloway's treatment of their holiday relationship is masterly in its perceptions of friends irritating each other in new ways they could not have imagined, Cassie clutching her superior sensitivity to *Madame Bovary* as proof of her superiority to unimaginative Rona. She hates the ferry, the sticky table-tops, the games machines, the macho peasants and most of all the blurbs for tourists; she rages as she reads

> It is easy to love ANGERS. All it takes is the time to know the city and soon its melange of characters, from the Tapestry of the Apocalypse and the Chant du Monde to the giants from the Toussaint Church, live in the mind. Take a leisurely visit and do not let Angers' natural modesty lead you to miss the hidden architectural jewels . . . [3]

'Christ's teeth, Rona', thinks Cassie. Galloway's style here is more leisurely than her previous fictions, mixing Cassie's thoughts with conversation. All through, Cassie (in this sense resembling Joy Stone) is remembering things she doesn't want to remember, such as other holidays, when she always gave in to her selfish longterm lover Chris (who was always reminding her that it's *his* flat) in Greece or Istanbul, where his encounters with Turkish football supporters led him off to happy male occasions, and where her needs were always secondary.

What is important in this novel is Galloway's dissipation of bitterness. The claustrophobic and deliberately unattractive aspects of *The Trick is to Keep Breathing*, arising from Joy's endless caricaturing of health visitors, doctors, teachers, and ministers, many of whom did indeed wish to help her, was accurate and unkind. Here the same perceptive scepticism is tempered with Cassie's slow realisation of affection for experience and people. The cathedral town of Chartres becomes a place of a modest epiphany, with its sheer size, its quality of light, and even its gargoyles; amidst its yellow sunflowers it yields peace in a way which allows Cassie and Rona slowly to harmonise. There is a trace of the old asperity in Cassie's diatribes against men – who needs them? – and these can seem out of tune with the slow pace of movement through France, and through Cassie's exploration of herself. But Galloway places these angers in the context of Cassie's realisation of the waste of human life in the Normandy graveyard, a perception which makes her look at her own life and frustration. Rona too has been heading for this graveyard, carrying her grandfather's last postcard home. The ending is typically, but hopefully, low-key. Cassie has been sounding off about men at supper, and has suggested that she and Rona might live together; Rona, she realises, is snoring gently. What is clear is that Cassie has mellowed – and that Rona has understood *Madame Bovary* much more than Cassie imagined.

The garish cover of *Where You Find It* (1996), Galloway's next collection of short stories, is a parody of an overblown St Valentine's Day card. And the title holds implied questions – what is to be taken where it's found? Love, yes; but of what kind? Whatever is available, even if second-rate? A large group of these stories circle around the endless varieties of contemporary sexual and emotional relationships. They present couples in typical modern premarital live-in and already worn-out situations. The rites of passage of these mismatched couples are well-observed, from their going home to stuffy parents with a new partner and the hypocritical sleeping arrangements to the taboo subjects over Sunday lunch, and the wary circling around old dangers. The point of consciousness is usually the woman's. Galloway captures the way her women endure the continual vagaries of their men – the man's habit of stealing the last piece of meat off the woman's plate, his economy with the truth, casual selfishness and macho behaviour. The stories range from the gentler exposure of so-called male camaraderie, as workers mock their young workmate's Valentine's Day heart-shaped sandwiches, to the harsher presentation of the stay-at-home girl in the ironically titled 'Valentine' who begins to realise why her partner has to wash his hair so often, or, harshest of all, the anxiety and dawning awareness of the girl who finds out that her man hasn't got flu, but Aids. Like Alison Kennedy, Galloway circles around these moments of truth, so that fragmented impressions, fleeting clues, crystallise like the story itself into final order and meaning. The stories are often short, sometimes almost prose-poetry, as in the title story with its sensual exploration of the nuances involved in the superlative kissing powers of Derek, or the atmospheric short account in 'Waiting for Marilyn' of a woman waiting for her favourite hairdresser, revealing that her urgency is sexual, but not to be requited, as Marilyn, standing so close, but so unobtainable, prattles on about her engagement. Like Lochhead, however, Galloway has a sympathy for both parties in male-female relations, a sympathy which is more detached than Lochhead's, which stands well back watching the game, letting the women's voices be heard as often querulous and irritating. In these domestic and apparently mundane stories women can be seen in unattractive lights, as in 'Home', which captures the ineffable mixture of love, boredom and nausea of a man locked in marriage with a sweetly made-up, complacent, magazine-and -chocolate devouring couch potato. 'While He Dreams of Pleasing His Mother' shifts the relationship, so that a son's dreams project the domination of his mother into a film set in Californian desert and a heat haze in which gleaming juggernaut lorries bear down on him, with the dimly-seen figure of his mother behind their windscreens.

This last story also begins to shift into Galloway's surreal mode. Galloway's realism is always tinged with oddity, as though she sees the surreal constantly threatening to take over. In another grouping of stories the boundary is apparently crossed; again, however, the surreal is never too far from the real. 'Tourists from the South Arrive in the Independent State' parodies Tourist Board icons of Scottish Hospitality and post-independence notions of a better Scotland in a hilarious but wicked description of the nice foreigners who expect a Highland welcome and get instead what disturbingly resembles the rainy Sunday treatment offered by many present-day establishments. 'After the Rains' presents a world where rain has fallen for months, then give way to glorious sunlight and gigantic rainbows – while people start turning into flowers and fruits. There's Bradbury horror in this, and the reader might begin to ask where the central theme of the collection is to be found here. Is it perhaps in the variant reading of the title which now suggests that love, human warmth, and happiness are elusive and can transmogrify horrifically? The concluding story of the volume combines realism and surrealism beautifully; in 'Six Horses' the girl's visions of wild horses accompany her journey in search of love, in ways which endlessly suggest rather than define.

The final grouping of stories, bleak, sad, and ferociously horrific, take the meanings of the title beyond the possibility of love, to those areas of darkness in our society where it's just not to be found. 'A Night In' simply shows teenagers huddling together for warmth in an abandoned house; 'Last Thing' empathises with the mind of a girl who is being murdered in a sex attack; 'Someone Had To' is a dramatic monologue in which a high-pitched, increasingly angry voice justifies its punitive abuse of a young girl, shut in a cupboard for staring, burned with cigarette ends for dumb insolence, and scalded to death. The reader understands the traumatised staring, and Galloway has an ability to force empathy with almost unbearable experience which rather shows up much of that fashionable contemporary Scottish fiction which indulges in horrific reality but which lacks Galloway's detached but deep human compassion. Perhaps the most poignant of this group of stories is 'Baby-sitting', which tells of two wee boys ferreting in their father's pockets for money for fish suppers. Their squalid living conditions are seen – or not seen – from their point of view, as is their bewilderment about their father. Neither the brusque outsiders, the lady in the chip shop, nor the boys, know that the father is dead. This is a quality and kind of writing Galloway and Alison Kennedy have made very much their own.

Sian Hayton

If Galloway and Kennedy can be paired in terms of their shared background, topics and modes, then Elphinstone and Hayton can likewise be seen as sharing broad themes and method. Both use the traditional ways of life to shed light on the present; both exploit magic and myth; both have a series of novels which develop large movements of people and history. Their individual ways of creating characters in alien backgrounds are, however, very different. Where Elphinston has realised her creations in ever more solid and deliberate terms, Hayton has moved in the opposite direction, so that her historical novels have moved increasingly into myth and enigma.

From the beginning her aims and meanings have been deliberately placed in Celtic mist, so that large implications are sensed rather than realised – although that description should not disguise the careful and Celtic knotting and interlinking of ambitious overall design throughout her trilogy *Cells of Knowledge* (1989), *Hidden Daughters* (1992), and *The Last Flight* (1993). It is set in a recreated tenth century Scotland, and is a work of distinction and originality (the first volume won the Saltire First Book of the Year award for 1989). The trilogy is, however, best read as such, the individual parts being tightly interlinked by plot, character, theme and narration. In *Hidden Daughters* Barve, one of the daughters of the giant Uthebhan (Yspaddadn in Celtic folklore), tells her travelling gaurd and companion, the monk Hw, that 'the truth is a torc made of many wires, and it is more twisted than you could realise', and her metaphor can apply to the strands and twists of the meticulously plotted trilogy with its interrelationships between characters. Such is the complexity of Hayton's interweavings and hidden connections that attentive reading and re-reading are required to appreciate just how careful and thoughtful the author's planning and plotting have been.

The action of the trilogy concerns the entry of the giant Uthebhan's daughters into the outside world. Two main social, political and cultural groups are used by Hayton to demonstrate the patriarchal nature of this tenth-century Scotland. The daughters interact in various ways with both the Culdee monks and the warrior clans. The relationships between the daughters and these men are used to show male perceptions of the female. Marighal, Barve, Olwen and their sisters, all descendants of the Celtic gods and possessed of strange supernatural powers, are viewed as demonic, unnatural and dangerous. The confrontations between Celtic and Christian, magic and physical strength are delineated as gendered concerns. There is, however, no simplistic male/female schema to the trilogy. Hayton's mixing of genres (historical, fantastic, and Celtic traditional) allows her to confuse and confound any notions of gender being a simple determinant of social and cultural power relationships. In the trilogy the daughters are not human women; Kigva, mother of Culhuch, is human but possesses great supernatural and political power. The giant Uthebhan is simultaneously Celtic god, wood-demon and autocratic father. Grig and his kin are dwarves. Monks and warriors are shown to be almost different races. By populating her Scottish past with such a diversity of fantastic peoples Hayton is recreating history and creating new legend and myth. She deliberately blurs the boundaries between the two, for her overall aim is to create an equality of space for her Celtic female alongside the male, a space which conventional histories would not allow. Working from the basis of the Celtic folk-tale (which often, indeed, gives women credit for brains, initiative and courage), Hayton's aim in *Cells of Knowledge* particularly was to explore what might happen when a Celtic heroine confronted the rapidly expanding tenth-century European Church face to face, at a time when it was eroding the status of women.

By bringing Celtic stories and legends into her historical trilogy Hayton is therefore rewriting history. *Cells of Knowledge* has Marighal the Celtic heroine encountering the Culdee monks of the monastery of Rintsnoc (Portpatrick in Galloway). Selyf, a monk, writes to tell of the events to the Bishop of Alban. The novel is presented in the form of Selyf's letters with Marighal's and his tales as the core text. The wide margins of the page contain the interpolated comments of another monk, whom we later discover to be Hw, Selyf's son and the monk who writes the letters which make up the text of *Hidden Daughters*. This as yet unnamed narrator has to prepare a case providing that there is no heresy amongst his seniors, especially Selyf. The same method of narration continues until the final volume where Josiah, marginal narrator of *Hidden Daughters*, writes his letter to Eugenius Calvus with no marginal gloss. This use of the printed page gives the trilogy an added complexity and sophistication, raising questions of voice and authority which conventional methods of narration could not provide. In a sense the marginalia suggests that in Hayton's re-vision of the past it is the male voice and text which is marginalised, with the female action for once holding centre stage and page. Conventional history written by men about men is shown as narrowmindedly incapable of understanding Marighal and her sisters (although Hw and some other monks do find that, against their orders and desires, they establish relationships of genuine respect and some awe for these more than human daughters of great ones. The removal of the margins in *The Last Flight* may be meant to carry the implication that the daughters have finally broken free from the confines of the strict dogma of ordered Christianity and history; the trilogy as a whole certainly carries an overall message that the traditional, inherited, and latent power of women, as exemplified in Celtic women, is colossal and necessary for any viable human development.

In *Cells of Knowledge* the two voices, central and marginal, counterpoint each other resulting in a fascinating recreation of early Christian and superstitious wonder, ignorance and prejudice against both Celticism and Celtic women, and women at large. Marighal is shown in the first half of the novel to be a resourceful, energetic leader of men as well as women, skilled in metal work and practical affairs. But Christianity rejects her for, as the novel proceeds, she grows in stature both literally and figuratively till she stands revealed, with her giant of a father, as one of the last of the Great Ones of the elder world, magical and superhuman. The shift in genre from relatively naturalistic to grotesque supernaturalism has been criticised as unpredicted and over sudden; but re-reading will show that, from the first fabulous prelude and later hints, the ground has been laid. It is a shift akin to that occurring with grotesque suddenness in traditional Celtic folk-tales and medieval romances such as *Gawayne and the Green Knight*. It is also in direct correspondence with Celtic folk-tale. Much of what happens in the magical parts of *Cells of Knowledge*, where Kynan defeats his foster-father Uthebhan with the aid of Marighal, is a reworking of traditional matter contained in stories such as 'The Battle of the Birds'. Such episodes show Hayton handling her own mixture of Celtic, Arthurian and Irish-Scottish legend with superb delicacy, suggestiveness and control. For, as the trilogy develops, echoes are awakened for the reader – the daughters have legendary names like Olwen, Esseult, and Fand. Hayton thus creates a world which is akin to that mytho-historic recreation developed by Neil Gunn in *Sun Circle* or Naomi Mitchison in *Early in Orcadia*, in which the imagined realisation of alien mindsets and values is perhaps more important than events and social contexts. Hayton is offering her glimpses of the tribal, shadowy, confused happenings which were later mythologised and shaped into destiny stories. A theme begins to emerge of the crucial significance of the conscious, intuitive, and magical knowledge and power of Celtic Women, and the matriarchal sisterhood of benign and more than human Hidden Daughters, born of the elemental forces of earth, air, water and fire, who are in tune with these earth-forces and therefore instinctively good. These women *have* to fall into the world of man, so that – while men are not simplistically seen as evil or superstitious or useless – a new world can evolve from the female-male and Celtic-Christian confrontation.

Hidden Daughters opens with the strange nomad-queen Kigva's story told from her point of view, a retelling of the tale which opened *Cells of Knowledge* as told by the male warrior Kilidh, father of Kynan. Again more questions are raised than are answered: what is Kigva's role in the trilogy? She isn't a 'hidden daughter', so how is her painful story interwoven? She is the mother of Culhuch (Kilhwch in Welsh Saga), half-brother of Kynan. She is in fact enemy to the daughters, a kind of malicious genius with magical powers who hates Uthebhan and his offspring, a Iago-destroyer. *Hidden Daughters* shows her poison at its worst, nearly destroying Culhuch's queen, Olwen, and her friend, the wise Merthun. This is Hayton at her most challenging and difficult, hinting at archetypal divisions amongst women themselves. Readers lacking the awareness of earlier narrative and theme would find it difficult to fathom her meaning and direction here. The reader of the trilogy who follows the deep-woven strands throughout will, however, be increasingly aware of the trilogy's sense of direction and destiny which emerges through the unremitting battles, cruelties and sacrifices, the maimings, martyrdoms, and betrayals. The wisdom of the sisters triumphs. Barve finds her sister; Olwen is reconciled with Culhuch and her mother-in-law; Culhuch dies, witness for the church of these ultimately unknowable events.

The Last Flight lacks a folk-tale, magical introduction; but the church is still witness, with Josiah writing his letters which tell of the events. And the events are even stranger. The reader learns that the giant isn't dead; that the daughters are almost immortal, that they can be reborn, that they can commune with each other over space and time. This is now Esseult's story, told through the Icelander Guaire, descendant of the race of Kynan, and told through Josiah, and by Esseult herself. Marighal's son Drost, half-human, half of the giant's race, will kill his father – if killing Uthebhan can ever be final. Imagination is stretched to its limit here; for the killing has Guaire and Drost fighting the giant in the form of a volcano in Iceland. Is this how legends are born? For in one sense Drost fights natural elemental forces with reason and science; yet simultaneously he accepts he has a supernatural opponent. In this weird world in which reason and dream go hand in hand, Hayton creates her special magic, dimly suggesting that this is one possible version of the beginning of the Fiann cycle of legends (for Drost will go to Ireland in the end to stay with Fand, and in Fiann legend Fand was the lover of Cuchullain). In similar vein Merthun will reappear as prophet by the crystal house in the forest, suggesting the prehistory of the legendary Merlin of Arthurian and pre-Arthurian legend. Hayton is even-handed in her recreations of legend, the male characters are allowed their place alongside their female counterparts.

Hayton's trilogy marks a return to a kind of epic myth-making of a serious nature which recalls Naomi Mitchison in *The Corn King and the Spring Queen* and Henry Treece in *The Green Man* (1966). While her trilogy adds to the rediscovery of myth seen in Scottish writing in recent years, returning to the full-bodied poetic atavism of *Sun Circle*, her original and manipulative exploitation of gender traits isolates her (perhaps with Naomi Mitchison and Margaret Elphinstone nearby) in her revisioning of a Scottish past where women, human or superhuman, have more than their traditional part to play.

Her other and unrelated novel, *The Governors* (1992), set in the present, does indeed use fantasy as its main vehicle – but in very different ways for very different ends. For all its strange worlds, this is a novel which belongs to that category of contemporary writing identified as dealing with emergence from trauma. Here is the familiar theme of a woman coming to terms with her recent and drastic personal disasters, disasters both her own and illustrative of problems of female experience in the twentieth century. This – for this once – links Hayton's work with that of writers such as Janice Galloway and A. L. Kennedy.

Hesione (named after a sea-spirit by her father; also called Hester), is suffering an identity crisis. Pregnant, suffering problems with her in-laws, she is trying to come to terms with the death of her father, a marine biologist killed in a car crash. Everybody around her appears threatening and offensive to her, just as she imagines her lumpen shape appears to them. What makes this novel different from other novels charting loss of self is Hayton's underplot which links it with her other work. Increasingly Hester/Hesione (earth- or sea-spirit?) dreams or wakingly imagines that she is called towards the sea and its selkies, mermen, the talking denizens of the deep. These vivid fantasies take over to such an extent that the dreams are more real than reality, and nightmare echoes of her father's death and her family intrude at the edge of these alternative experiences.

The sea-dreams and often disgusting rites of therapeutic passage mark the beginning of Hester's quest for integrity and wholeness. They represent her necessary subconscious drownings in the past, in her guilts and fears, to cleanse or more appropriately naturalise her. Some of the grotesque and savage scenes with sea-creatures relate strongly to the Celtic trilogy and are effective in Hayton's visionary depiction of female experience of the world. Increasingly, however, the surreal world of Hester's dreams becomes comic, which tends to jar with its serious and mythic significance. Hayton may well be suggesting that through comic abandonment lies redemption, but the reader may find the climactic meeting with Mer Maid, in her Homes and Garden undersea dwelling, and the therapeutic sex with the Bull Ray fish, over-ambitious in its attempt to mingle the real with the surreal, threatening Hayton's former ability to suspend her reader's disbelief in the *Cells of Knowledge* trilogy. The title indicates that by such dream-links with their own sea-origins, and with their deepest biological and tidal rhythms, humans are governed; such profound suggestions sit uneasily with the cartoon comedy of Mer Maid and Bull Ray, comic archetypes which lack so much of the poetic and mythic power and integrity of the great characters of Hayton's trilogy. *The Governors* is nevertheless a disturbing and novel exploration of the unconscious. Hayton's experiment here stands as evidence of that continuing return to magic and myth in Scottish women's writing.

Alison (A. L.) Kennedy

Alison Kennedy's first volume of stories, *Night Geometry and the Garscadden Trains* (1990), was immediately striking in its arresting title and its quality of near-complete unity of vision of its stories. Like Alan Spence's Glasgow stories in *Its Colours They are Fine* (1977), it has a coherence emerging from different perspectives, tones, and narratives, so that the reader has a final sense of the author's whole way of looking. The blurb described the stories as being about 'characters often alone and sometimes lonely, as they ponder the mysteries of sex, death and public transport at the end of the twentieth century', which seems fair till stories like 'Translations' are brought into account. There, a death-fated South American native purges his own and his race's shame, along with the guilt of their Scottish missionary masters, in a story which moves disturbingly between dream and reality. Nor, at the other extreme, can a story like 'Genteel Potatoes' be fitted into a simplistic overall description; a grandmother remembers her rebellion against patronising posh employers in rejecting their left-over middle-class potatoes, and how she got the sack and a thrashing at home for her wilful 'we wouldn't feed these to our pigs!'.

While the stories can be very different, there are many marked by their empathy for modern losers, which Kennedy captures in graphic pictures: teenage Grace, whose sluttish mother has abandoned her to her Aunt Ivy (when her aunt dies Grace is raped by one of her mother's menfriends); the girl who sits in a car for days watching for a glimpse of the father she doesn't really want to see; the couple who can't communicate as they witness the police search for a lost child, since he's been caught by her having sex with her best friend. Or, strikingly, and significantly, given Kennedy's future development, the story 'Cap O' Rushes', which mingles acid comment on real families and real husbands with a hint of fantasy; a woman worn down with her Goblin Family leaves, to learn to be herself, ever on the look out for Goblins around her – they may not look like Goblins, but you never can tell.

The title story is typical of Kennedy's conjoining of realism with disturbing sub-real images. The Garscadden trains are real enough, as is their unreliability; but as images of transience, moving lights at the back of dreary housing schemes, as well as representing too-often failed connections through society, they foreground the volume's running themes of restless shifting, temporariness, breakdown; the way we live and – if we're lucky – work now. A girl comes back home early, her train connection broken. She finds her lover Duncan in bed with his old girlfriend. Somehow it is the ordinariness, the mid-morning low-key drabness, which makes the betrayal so embarrassingly poignant – as well as the fact that Duncan is also her best friend. The total effect is typically obtained firstly by Kennedy's way – comparable to that of Galloway or Rose – of having the teller circle around the deferred central revelation, with hints of unease, insufficiency, betrayal, together with prevailing images of claustrophobia or desired escape. Secondly, there is nearly always a running imagery – in this case the Garscadden trains – which at first seems inconsequential, but which can in the end be seen as a kind of correlative, a summing-up in metaphor of the central issue. The overall result is a powerful yet low-key presentation of West of Scotland social deprivation, boredom, frustration, expressed paradoxically through sensitive and perceptive personae.

The reader should also be open to deeper subtleties. Kennedy will switch modes, looking at this subject matter from very different angles, as in 'The Role of Notable Silences in Scottish History', where she widens her net to include a commentary on broader issues of the State of Scotland from an acid tongue-in-cheek perspective;

> Buses are the transport of the poor, trains being rendered inflexible by their rails, cars improbable by their expense, and taxis impossible by their extravagant fares and their disinclination to make for destinations the poor might choose . . . Those rendered insensible by drink may find in any bus an audience for sentimental ballads, a steadying hand, a patient ear, directions to any location, a corner to sleep in, and a floor on which to deposit their most recent meal.[4]

This commentator researches the author who pelted his wife with boiled potatoes once a month, the legends of the evil McIvers, queues for Housing, Post Office counter service and Dole, *Bonnie Charlie's Glasgow Cookbook*, and *Killing Time: Seven centuries of Scottish slaughter*, with its informative chapter for children on 'Playing Dead'. This story, like 'Translations', may seem to break the volume's coherence; but the perceptive reader will not only see through the diversity to the thematic linking through situations of exploitation, home and abroad, past and present, seriously, ironically, or surrealistically represented, but will begin to see more bizarre linking – in images of potatoes, in ideas of the trains of society going off the rails, and in quirky connections between stories. A fine example of this last connects the first story, 'Tea and Biscuits', the account of the girl who picks up Aids from the older man she loves, too-late tired of 1960s permissiveness, with the next strange dream-story, 'Translations'. The first ends with the girl's recognition of her body clock's winding down, and her speculation about her lover Michael's stories of Indian tribes: 'Those Indians. They thought that we went through life on a river, all facing the stern of the boat and we only ever looked ahead in dreams. That's what I'll have to do now', she thinks (p. 8) – and the next story is about Indians, dreamtime, and assuagement of guilt. In these stories Kennedy works on many different levels.

Looking for the Possible Dance (1993) is a novel which shares the attitudes and moods of new grouping of affirmative Scottish texts, like Carl MacDougall's *The Lights Below* (1993) Iain Banks's *The Crow Road* (1992), and Andrew Greig's *Electric Brae* (1992). Where MacDougall used light as metaphor – the lights being literally those of Glasgow seen from high tenements, but also the hidden lights of decent people and older community values, and deepburied personal hope and resilience Kennedy uses dance. Margaret's earliest memories are of dancing with her father; she clumsily dances/makes love with Colin, but even more significantly, she searches throughout 'for the possible dance, the step, the move to beat them all'. That ambiguous 'beat' sums up much of Margaret's predicament.

We have to work out from a narrative expressed in fragmented experiences, and from short passages of reflection, who and where Margaret is. We piece together that she's around twenty-three, and is wrapped self-protectively in a cocoon of love for her dead father. This love isn't unnatural in any sexual way, but unhealthy in its perpetuation to the exclusion of commitment to Colin. Margaret has been raised since three by her father, her mother having left; she doesn't remember her mother, and when she remembers her father through anxious and tender love, he is a caring, lovable man with an absurd sense of humour, accepting his loneliness as the price for looking after his daughter.

One of the achievements of this novel is its identification of the terrible sadness underlying love, particularly in the case of parental love, with its inevitable recognition of the two final issues of growing apart and death. Kennedy handles these fundamentals with a poise of lightness and gravity. On one hand, Margaret is trapped in Fatherland, unable to cross to Colin. On the other, she is a project leader in peripheral Glasgow, shown as sympathetic and lively in her relations with her charges, in something of the way Kelman presented schoolteacher Patrick Doyle and his classes in *A Disaffection* (1989); these adolescents are nobody's fools, rough in banter but loyal, idealistic and quick to resent betrayal. Ironically, it is one of them, on drugs, who betrays Margaret and her job; otherwise, as in *The Lights Below*, ordinary people are treated with an impressive mixture of ferocity and hilarity. Margaret's most loyal friend is the autodidact Graham, a born survivor, and her colourful children include Toaty Boadie, a three-foot-high seven-year-old who brings tears to glass eyes with her singing.

Kennedy's love of the bizarre goes further; Margaret learns fire-breathing, a Chinese acupuncturist sings Sinatra songs at her ceilidh, and she has a touching and delightful encounter with a dumb spastic on the London train. All of these unusual episodes are related to the main development, that of her complex and evasive relationship with Colin. The tug of her adolescents and her rapport with unusual people all help to pull her out of her sad and frozen love for her father, to the point where she can share her love for him with Colin and a complex, ugly, human world. The ending is significant in its discovery of hope and renewal in non-urban landscape, in a way which is shared by MacDougall, Banks and Greig, as well as many other recent Scottish novels. Colin has been horrifically attacked, leaving him emotionally traumatised as well as physically damaged. Helped by her assorted friends, Margaret takes him to the ancient landscape around Kilmartin, where burial mounds, stones, and relics of the past are the setting for rediscovery of self, love and possibility. Moving in this place of ancient rhythms, Margaret rediscovers the possible dance; dance has been prefigured in the dance motif of the novel, from folk to modern; now it is the dance of life which Margaret and Colin must join.

If this novel seemed part of a new approach which sought a synthesis of urban and rural, together with an admission of traditional references and values which post-war fiction had excluded, then Kennedy's next volume, the short stories of *Now That You're Back* (1994) made its statements about new ideas and topics in Scottish writing in very different ways. Dreich urban realism is rejected in these astonishingly varied stories, which move from first-person confession and self-exposing dramatic monologue to a use of third person which is first person in disguise, to authorially detached storytelling and a bizarre surrealism which can strike from unexpected angles. And in this collection it's this last approach which dominates. 'On Having More Sense' reflects upon the penguin ('no city has ever been besieged by penguins . . . no glistering genocidal design has ever been pursued by penguins . . . Penguins Have More Sense'[5]). A Wise Old Man tries to tell his tribe of these singular Penguin virtues, but his people just wander off. 'The Mouseboks Family Dictionary' uses lowly animals as commentary on humans even more viciously; it lists the main terms and proverbs used by the lying, nasty, doomed Mouseboks family, a tribe who seem disturbingly like the human race writ small, in their pursuit of sex, money and power. There's real Swiftian satire and bite in these entries; for example, '**family:** Spending time within the Mouseboks Family might be likened to drifting in an open boat filled with cannibals precisely at tea-time. Their company is always enlivening and their interest in others very sincere, if not deeply alarming' (p. 112). Or '**future:** A usefully inexhaustible source of *Despair* and *Fear*, terminated only by *Death*' (p. 114); or '**guilt:** . . . a huge source of satisfaction to all Mousebokses, although tremendous guilt prevents them from celebrating it too openly' (p. 114). The dictionary becomes an imaginative and nasty way of describing ourselves.

Most of the stories are touched by surrealism, if less strikingly. A pair of weird parents destroy their son through systematic repression and religious mania, describing the process with unctious concern; a southern gal buries her husband alive out of love for a serial killer, likewise recounting her ghastly deeds with self-approval, this time in a prissy moral southern drawl which talks as though it is the most normal thing in the world for a woman to sigh with annoyance at the dirty feet of the killer who has been burying his most recent victim in the woods. And sometimes Kennedy will vary her surreal approach by using the explicitly and socially realistic supernatural as in 'Christine', where a strange and accident-prone girl can telepathise feelings and comfort across the world. The effect, however, is surreal, as though the tale itself were a parody of Stephen King, an unreal wish-story.

Alongside these clear examples of the strange and bizarre run stories of recognisable human situations in straightforward narrative. Even here, though, there are striking and unusual features. In 'Bracing Up', a Welsh actor can't handle love and sex, believing that his utterly hairless body must only disgust, so he ejects his one-night lover just when she is becoming really interested in him. Instead, when he's not playing the fool in Lear he takes refuge in playing Punch and Judy shows on the beach – in the braced-up box he can feel safely concealed. Kennedy shows another side here, in her psychological understanding of the way the actor's grandfather has scarred him. She also shows this humane understanding in 'Like a City in the Sea', where a dancer is dying in the care of her much younger husband. Kennedy juxtaposes the private tenderness of his love for her with the public face she shows to the world while making a film of her life. Sympathy for damaged and private people invaded by public curiosity is very much a theme of this strand of the collection. The hidden forces behind these damaged lives are implied, often left unstated; the title story never tells of the profound anguish which has in the past separated Tom from his bigger brothers Phil and Billy. Instead, Kennedy lets the present reunion speak for itself, with its touching attempt by the three to rediscover some shreds of family in a caravan holiday by the sea. It's now that they're all back together that's the triumph, not the mysterious and traumatised past.

All Kennedy's strands of fiction come together – sensitive human analysis, surrealism and supernatural satire on Scotland and humanity generally – in her audacious novel of 1995, *So I Am Glad*. It is a love story set in contemporary west-end Glasgow (although

Kennedy's emphasis on the setting is slight; like many present-day Scottish writers she wears her sense of place easily and confidently, avoiding topographical explanation or local dialect). The novel opens like a mundane story of all-too-recognizable stress-related decline – in this case, the decline of Jennifer Wilson, whose profession as a radio announcer and voice-over for adverts may imply that, like the oracle in Gray's *Lanark*, she wilfully prefers disembodiment to reality – 'until reality breaks in'. The 'reality' that breaks in comes in the form of a new lodger in her house whose body gives off a blue glow when he sweats, who has lost all memory, and consequently suffers from acute agoraphobia. He also happens to be Cyrano de Bergerac, somehow translated from seventeenth-century France to become Jennifer's responsibility as he struggles with the nightmare transition.

Once again a new kind of treatment of fantasy and supernatural accepts few or no limitations to its scope, and is no longer contained by traditional folk and Gothic rules. In many ways this novel develops the contemporary rediscovery of magic and myth splendidly, extending the worlds of Gray's *Lanark* and *Poor Things* (1992), Lochhead's *Dreaming Frankenstein* (1985), or Morgan's *Sonnets From Scotland* (1984), until the Scottish and mainly urban present intermingles with anything and anywhere the author cares to imagine. The domestication of the nobly comic French spirit in such an unlikely setting is audaciously effective; to see Savinien Cyrano de Bergerac weeding a scrubby Glasgow garden has its charm; and to witness the growing tenderness between damaged Jennifer and disorientated Cyrano is equally pleasing. And Kennedy keeps the reader guessing for long as to the legitimacy of Cyrano, in the tradition of ambivalence which is the hallmark of the Scottish novel from Hogg and Stevenson to Spark and Gray. Has unhappy Jennifer invented the lover needed to repair the traumas of her deviant love-life? How then do her flatmates, Arthur the bluffly kind, Liz the abrupt, the intermittent Peter, all recognise the new lodger's problems? The reader feels the need to re-read, to check if the flatmates simply humoured Jennifer and her new lover, leaving her alone in her fantasy of love. And yet . . . if that's the case, what happens to Cyrano in the powerful and moving ending which takes them to Paris and his birthplace? This novel deliberately echoes older Scottish fiction of the supernatural, with its doppelgangers and dualisms, always with its insistence that these are echoes, and not rules or conventions to be adhered to.

Thus Kennedy exploits two perspectives; on one hand, a marvellously inventive and ambiguous reworking of the classic Scottish 'either/or' tension between the supernatural and the psychological, and on the other a modern Scottish story of the kind exemplified in work from Trocchi to Gray, Banks to Galloway, Welsh to Warner, in the depiction of a traumatised mind using displacement and fantastic imagination to simultaneously avoid and redeem the damage from which it hides. Cyrano is realised tactfully and sensitively; his oddity never extreme, even his nose underdone. Yet when he finds his feet in this post-Thatcherite world, after the horrific experience of being down-and-out, he is impressive, intellectually as well as physically; his mind is disarmingly honest, his speed of reflex awesome, as his psychopathic Glasgow enemy discovers. But does Jennifer invent him? A psychological reading is attractive; she has been insidiously warped since childhood by the explicit sexuality of her parents – perhaps not physically, but certainly mentally, abused. Her own sexuality has become deviant; with the submissive Steven, she goes to the edge of mental as well as physical tolerance, perhaps over the edge. She has revulsion for herself as woman, for her job as media liar, for the world she lives in; Kennedy constantly juxtaposes Jennifer's personal problems with glimpses through her of a sick society, a world of atrocity and sadistic exploitation which recalls that of *Janine*, with its linking of the personal pain and amorality of Jock McLeish with that of the world. Jennifer needs both to avoid and atone; Cyrano answers both needs. He has lived with violence, yet has a code of honour; is disfigured, yet acceptable; and has sensitivity unavailable to modern males. He can understand distortion and articulate dilemma – and Jennifer desperately needs to understand and articulate. He is the correlative for her yearning to be free of herself. Read thus, the book is about a process of self-healing in a nasty modern world, and about Jennifer's aquisition of a new personality, confidence and tone in her voice which had hitherto been lacking (a nice touch this; this new 'tone' threatens her studied broadcasting neutrality and thus her ability to exploit her voice in advertising and announcement). Cyrano is her means of cure; she must then paradoxically move towards losing him, since he represents her lack and need, which fulfilled, removes him. 'So I am glad', she realises; she recognises the healing and the affirmative meaning behind her experience. Questions remain, of course; what about her flatmates seeing Cyrano? His presence, even as 'Martin', seems real enough. And even if she alone makes him into Cyrano, while the others see merely a love affair with Martin, there remains the puzzle as to the disappearance of 'Martin' in the end. And in the end the answers – or evasions – are the postmodern sleights of *Lanark*. Kennedy teases her readers, anticipating their old-fashioned questions of how and why; but she retains older and community values – kindness, charity, honour – in a way which combines tradition and innovation.

Joan Lingard

Joan Lingard has produced nearly twenty novels since *Liam's Daughter* in 1963. Some of these novels, such as *The Prevailing Wind* (1964) and *The Second Flowering of Emily Mountjoy* (1979) have already been discussed in the previous chapter. Along with writers like Naomi Mitchison, Jessie Kesson and Elspeth Davie she has consistently successfully depicted modern Scottish society, especially in Edinburgh, and especially in regard to the way in which women were hemmed in by conventions of class and gender. This chapter seeks to deal with outstanding contemporary fiction, and so the novels treated here are her major novels of the last ten years, *The Women's House* (1989), *After Colette* (1993) and *Dreams of Love and Modest Glory* (1995).

It would appear that with *The Women's House* Lingard's fiction developed a stronger and more affirmative stance on women's issues. Set in a southern English town, its group of strangely assorted women, an elderly writer, a middle-age mime artiste, and a traumatised slum waif, live in Shangri-la, a vast and decaying mansion. Facing it across the road is its prosperous, well-kept mirror twin, which is maintained by wealthy Italian restaurateurs. This mafioso-style family bought Shangri-la when its owner died, hoping to turn it into a casino. The trio who live there have leases which give perpetuity, but gentle and rough hints are made to them regarding their unwantedness, and when they stay, a series of casual Italian waiters flows through Shangri-la. In Lingard's way of viewing human relations nothing is conventional. Anna, middle lady of Shangri-la, has an affair with Tonelli senior, 'the king'. The rich Tonelli neighbours are at once friends and enemies, and out of the tensions between British femininity and aggressive Italian maleness emerges a strange charity. Shangri-la is burned down by the most aggressive Tonelli, 'prince' Roberto, and with it the elderly writer. Anna's affair must end with Tonelli guilt. The protective haven is finally destroyed; Roberto gets off, and the casino is set to be built. Male power has triumphed, and the novel does not evade truth by suggesting last-minute surprises. But as Anna and young Holly sit alone after the funeral of their friend, the prevailing sense is of rebirth rather than death; they have reordered their lives, are touring New England with Anna's mime shows, and have – with their dead friend's money – bought a house, and purged themselves with the endless labour of turning it into the new, fresh, sweet-smelling women's house. Lingard uses the burning of the old house with suggestions of mythic exorcism, as though these women are closing doors on a past which was too ramshackle, too self-protective and self-deluding. In this sense the novel continues the opening of doors begun by Carswell in 1920.

In another sense, the doors seemed to open for Lingard also; for with her next two novels she worked on a far bigger scale and with more sophisticated techniques than ever before. *After Colette* breaks out from the Scottish and Ulster settings of most of the previous fiction, interweaving lives in France and Scotland. Two women are born at the same time in the Burgundy village of Saint-Sauveur-en-Puisaye in 1873; one is Berthe-Amelie Grenot, the other is Sidonie-Gabrielle Colette. The novel is not about the best-loved and most famous of French women writers, the elegist of the lost country of childhood in the Claudine accounts, but her presence runs like a strong motif through the lives of the women whose interlinked stories over a hundred years are told here. Colette's work powerfully impresses young Berthe; and marks her descendants, Eugenie and Aimee. In several senses, they are all 'after Colette', in time, in ideas, and in pursuit of that elegant, poised life-style which continually eludes them as more earthbound, less talented natures. Poverty, war and chance deal less favourably with them than with cat-like and cat-lucky Colette, with her adoring men, her elegant rooms, her ability to edit messy things like her daughter and family out of her life. Ordinary mortals like Berthe and her children stumble through harsher marriages and lives, in France and Edinburgh, with the banal realities of squalling children and money worries. It's not that Colette is seen as guilty; rather, in the glimpses of her rooms with their blue lamps and delicate paperweights, or in her gracious reception of Berthe's descendants, she's representative of a dream, an ideal which has haunted the generations. The 'I' who opens and closes the story is the unnamed Edinburgh cousin of Aimee/Amy Balfour, trying to trace Aimee, who in her sixties has gathered her poor possessions and disappeared, last seen as a lonely figure in the Gare de L'Est. The dream of following Colette has dominated Aimee's life. Ever since her ritual introduction to her, she has followed her, making a career out of a onewoman show which re-enacts Colette's life, repeating it endlessly, at Edinburgh Festivals and throughout the world till people ask if she is Colette.

The novel is about the sadness of lives in shadow: Berthe's struggles with family and sick husband, yet still reading Colette at night; Eugenie's abiding sense that there's more to life than Edinburgh grimness, and her flight after her French lover; and lost, divided Aimee, yearning for the mother who abandoned her, just as did Colette. Thus Colette mars lives without remotely knowing. Lingard never overtly criticises her – after all, why should she? Colette is invariably kind and interested to the visiting Grenots. Quotations from her books head the novel's chapters. But the inference is clear. There are ideal, remote dream-lives, and there are real lives; and the Grenots, for all their pain, are real. The Edinburgh cousin has a gallus friend, Jessie, not intelligent, a creature of steamies and pubs who chats up men in her seventies and shows her knickers. Nothing could be further from Colette and Paris than Jessie and working-class Edinburgh, or Grannie Balfour, Scottish, disapproving, grimly living in a world where art is meaningless and survival enough. These become the opposite poles to Colette, the realities of life set against the dream. The choice of narrator in the intrigued cousin is clever, since it helps poise the two worlds against each other, asking endless questions which can't be answered.

Yet the ending suggests one more meaning to 'after Colette', beyond those of dependency on suspect values. When Amy goes East, she is perhaps at last rejecting Colette for the earthier world of human intermingling and pain. After a life-time of playing someone else, and the Grenots following irrelevant ideals, Amy may in tragedy at last have become herself. Thus the theme of *The Women's House*, of self-discovery through the painful shedding of self-protective layers, is projected on to a European canvas.

Dreams of Love and Modest Glory widened and deepened the European dimensions. That sense of apparent authorial detachment of the author from generations of pain, spanning space and time in *After Colette* (apparent rather than real, since the 'detached' author is in fact arranging events to create a profound sense of the sadness of the human condition) is maintained here, as witness this time to huge historical events. Lingard follows the Russian Revolution and the Latvian struggle for independence from 1913 to 1993, and from several perspectives. These are those of the Aberdeen twins, Lily and Garnet Mackenzie, and their respective husbands, Thomas Zale of Riga and Count Sergei Brunov of St Petersburg. In a sense the perspectives on European upheaval are also those of Scotland, Latvia, and Russia, since the central protagonists are effectively made to represent essential characteristics of their nationalities – with the pairing of Lily and Garnet cleverly presented as a kind of traditional polarisation of Scottish head and heart, although Lingard is far too sophisticated to simply recreate a conventional dualism of Scottish fiction.

The title is drawn from Pushkin ('Our dreams of love and modest glory/delusive hopes now quickly sped') and the dreams are those of the two couples and their respective countries. From the meeting of the girls with the two foreign architects in Britain, and their hopes for the future, the novel moves to the crumbling of aristocratic Sergei's dreams as Russia under the Czar moves into poverty and revolution, and his self-indulgent family with it, to the tensions in Latvia, caught between exploitation by Germans and by Russians, with Thomas's dreams moving from career and family to concern for his suffering country as the huge nightmare of the First World War begins. Lingard moves on the grand scale of historical fiction here, embedding her convincing characters in richly detailed and controlled settings in several countries. What is all-important in her success is the connection, drawn strongly and persuasively, between history and its effects on individuals – and vice versa. All this is imbued with the essential tragic sense of Pushkin, as Lingard sets his grim Russian God of snowstorms, pot-holed roads, cockroaches, cripples and famine at the heart of early twentieth-century Russia and Europe – with the striking contrasts of the palaces of the Czar and the Burnovas set like jewels amidst trash, a striking metaphor which echoes the Colette/ Grenot opposition of dream and reality in her previous novel.

The novel is held together through the twins; Lily, sensitive and withdrawn, Garnet, bold and decisive. Their strong Aberdeen background, the world Lingard knows so well of Scottish middle-class homeliness, with its gossip, tea-parties, Salvation, Army good works, is here used less to expose narrow convention and repressive intolerance (though these, unsurprisingly, still thrive), than to allow that, set against the darkness of central European chaos, this mundane Scottish community life has compensating virtues of understated kindliness, stability and peace. It is the norm, manifest in the values and attitudes of the twins, against which they measure the differences of their new lives in Latvia and Russia, and against which later horrors are defined. The twins see Europe very differently, but always with their deep-bonded Aberdeen sensibility, and through their eyes Lingard subtly forces the reader to reassess Scottish identity and Britishness, by setting the relationship of Latvia and its traditional sense of community and colourful peasant culture with the inequality and arrogance of Russia against the relationship of Scotland and England. It's always done implicitly, and never obviously or simplistically, but the effect is to reorientate the novel and its Scotland so that – in keeping with so much of contemporary Scottish writing – the reader locates it within a European rather than a British cultural context.

The patterning within the novel echoes the essential dualism of Lily and Garnet. Lily finds her character fits comfortably in Latvia, while Garnet's volatility finds – at first – a home in Russia. Tom, Lily's husband, is modest and dependable, while Garnet's Sergei is a selfish womaniser. But the patterning is qualified. Garnet is to be trapped almost until her death in St Petersburgh, losing the two husbands whose natures reflect another dualism, this time that within the soul and economy of Russia itself. Garnet's hard experience, her eventual hatred of Russian cruelty after Lenin, and her return to reconcile herself with her sister before dying in Aberdeen, is conveyed with great power. And gentle Lily has wronged Garnet; she has succumbed to Sergei at the very start of her marriage, and her twins have different fathers. This old family secret, a fatal flaw at the heart of the lives of the four, once again works within patterns of larger divisions within countries and within Europe – as if Lingard is implying esoteric connections between individual moral actions and the actions of nations. Lily's children, one Russian, the other Latvian, thus enact the larger conflicts within family relations. Lily and Garnet were estranged when Nikolai's paternity emerged, just as war was to break out.

In addition to Lingard's control of her implicated generations and her rich mirror-image patterning, the novel works through consistent and sustained imagery and motifs. And there is yet another layer to the patterning. The events are framed within the view of cousins Katrina Zale and Lydia Burnova, grandchildren of Lily and Garnet, visiting Latvia in 1993 to find out what happened in 1944 between Russian officer Nikolai and Latvian Alex. The movement between modernity and past events creates effects of time and forgiveness which echo the narrative's movement to the tragic event which finally purges the disease of the generations which started in 1913. With its command of place and time, its sureness of control over vast movements of people and power, and its exploration of profound moral issues, this novel takes its place alongside the best of contemporary Scottish fiction of that internationally orientated kind produced by writers like Allan Massie, Stuart Hood and William Boyd.

Agnes Owens

The work of Agnes Owens first appeared in the novel *Gentlemen of the West* in 1984, and in short stories in *Lean Tales* (1985), along with stories by Alasdair Gray and James Kelman. It would be fair to say that their encouragement has helped this self-taught, original writer to develop her deceivingly straightforward and simple stories of hard life at the edges of society to the point where she must be considered as one of the most significant of contemporary women's voices. Her novel appears at first to be a series of rough episodes in the life of the young sometimes bricklayer Mick/Mac. He comes from a small community – if it can be called that – to the north of Glasgow. He and his mates, like the wino Paddy MacDonald, are feckless, reckless and sad cases. Ejections from pubs, fights and stitches, hangovers, and cadging for drink make up their activities. Their local is a tatty bar with a humourless barman. Their tales take the reader back to the world of Patrick MacGill's epic account of exiled Irish and working-class labourers looking for work, drink and fights in Scotland at the turn of the century, in *Children of the Dead End* (1914); local treacheries, dog-thefts, old scores, famous booze-ups, death from drink and hypothermia are their matter, and style and character drawing seems crude, like naive painting. The sheer hardness at first repels, in its portrayal of world without human dignity. But the monotony of topic and violence has its purpose, very much as in the work of Kelman, to show the debilitation of all this, so that Mac's problems in changing his life are seen not just as his own, but as a complex of events around him. In Paddy's death he sees his warning, and there is a moment of feeling communication with his atrophied mother, before he leaves for a crack at a job in the north. The spiral has at least turned upwards, although we cannot predict an outcome.

This is a voice more primitive, yet as truthful and in its own way as effective, as Kelman's. And the stories from Owens in *Lean Tales*, if more contrived than the earlier fiction, have even more pain and hardness. Here a cynical mother, knowing well that her son is at fault, destroys an assertive headmistress; a woman has a strange encounter with a violent teenager in the park – is he her dead son?; a reclusive woman mothers dogs and smothers sanitary inspectors. The vision darkens, although a grotesque comic sense survives, to re-emerge in the continuation of Mac's career in *Like Birds in the Wilderness* (1987). Mac in Aberdeen has tried hard to find work, but it's elusive. When he gets it he can't keep it, with his temper and his hangovers. Shady deals attract him, but so does the nippy but lovely Nancy, who thinks she can redeem him. And while the comedy of Mac's picaresque career is often hilarious, it's also tragi-comedy, in the picture of his gullibility, his weakness for drink, his growing fecklessness. Owens comes close to the surreal in the closing account of Mac and Nancy's quest in the wild Highlands for the mysterious men who promised him work, but in the end it can be seen that the absurd wild goose chase of the birds in the wilderness has really been a graphic picture of Mac, the archetypal, unreliable, drink-orientated Scot, all gab and no delivery. Farce becomes national tragedy.

A Working Mother (1994) is short, a novella which, however, shows Owens developing her style from straightforwardly effective characterisation and narrative into a darker and more devious subtlety. Her wife and mother Betty, who tells her own story, is neither naive or crude in her telling, although her actions are throughout in fine bad taste. She's married to Adam, handsome, balding, boring in his tales of how he's been damaged by the war. Or was he ever in the war? The problem is that the reader can't trust Betty an inch, as she monotonously tells her boss, Mr Robson, a dirty old man whom she leads on, her agent, the fortune teller Mrs Ross, her friend Mai, whom she betrays, anything that will remove her own blame for her drinking, her lust, her cheating, and transfer it to Adam or her lover, the disgusting Brendan.

But Betty has style, in a way which recalls Spark's Dougal Douglas in *The Ballad of Peckham Rye* (1960). There's Gray as well as Spark in this tale, and that is not to demean it in the least, with its nasty humour and black surprises. Betty's wiles earn her a place in a mental hospital – and once again the reader is tempted to see her as representative of more than just herself, as perhaps a commentary on the backbiting female equivalent of Scottish male deficiencies.

In her latest collection of stories, *People Like That* (1996), Owens fuses the blackness of the novella with a narrative style which mangages to imply *Waiting for Godot*-style unreality, as though the repetitive pointlessness and monotony of so many of her characters' situations hypnotises the reader into a kind of slow-motion viewing of sad lives. The title story suggests who these people are; in it an old woman waits in a central Glasgow station, endlessly asking strangers when the Manchester train will arrive, so that she can meet her son Brian. She tries to engage them in chit-chat, but is constantly repelled. Then she thinks that she recognises her husband of twenty years ago in a drunk man – and in politely asking him if this is so ends up being disgustingly raped – remembering almost casually as this happens that Brian died of an overdose two years ago. Fragments of memory – of trips to Ayr, of Brian's dead gerbils – reveal to us that Brian was a bad lot; but the old woman's naivety, innocence, and indomitable stupidity, have a genuine pathos about them which makes us angry with the station clerk who simply dismisses her, when the attendants from her home finally catch up, with 'we have them in here all the time – people like that'.

'People like that', outsiders, down-and-outs, alcoholics and no-hopers, are – in the main – the subject of these stories. 'The Collectors' has an old man and an alcoholic in uneasy partnership, gathering lost golf balls; the off-centre location, and the contrast of the pair with the well-to-do players, effectively emphasises the forlorn pointlessness of disconnected lives. 'The Warehouse' has old Mavis, deserted during a drinking session by her man, dropping into maundering memory, fragments of song, even forlorn little prayers before going up in flames as she falls asleep while smoking. The imagery of a discarded old woman in a discarded old coat burning alive captures the idea of her utter redundancy, as though she is simply rubbish burning on a wasteland.' A Bad Influence' shows how, with effortless ease, a boy goes to the bad, setting bins alight and cutting off from family; and 'Intruders' perfectly captures the essential vision of Agnes Owens in its portrayal of two tinkers with a child in a pram circling endlessly round drinking binges, quarrels, deserted houses. And it is a vision; bleak, nasty, world-weary, detached, devoid of political and moral comment, but making its point in a way that Irvine Welsh works much harder to do. There are stories which don't quite fit; the first, 'The Lighthouse', can't really claim to be about 'people like us' when the protagonists are two small children who wander too far on the beach, one falling horribly and the other getting picked up by a child-molester. This comes close to the manner and content of one of Janice Galloway's stories in its effective horror – but it is disconnected from the main theme. So too are the stories set in France, which seem a bit out of place, and, for all its humour, the final autobiographical piece describing a weird funny-and-macabre search for work in the Highlands called 'Marching Into the Highlands and into the Unknown'. But Owens has a unique voice, not to be undervalued because she refuses to compromise with what she sees as the unfairness of life for her characters, women and men, and which refuses to find redeeming magic or meaning in town or country.

Dilys Rose

Dilys Rose established herself as one of the outstanding new poets in Scotland with *Madame Doubtfire's Dilemma* in 1989, that *annus mirabilis* for new women's writing in Scotland. Her strong use of imagery and her wry, self-mocking feminism translates to her first book of short stories in the same year, *Our Lady of The Pickpockets*, set in New York, Mexico and Scotland. Her focus is on underdogs and misfits, mainly women, and the men with whom they have complicated and uneasy relationships, but sometimes children, old men or victims of racial prejudice. A recurrent protagonist is a girl alone, abroad; afraid yet resilient; the impression which comes over strongly is of Rose using experience and materials from her own extensive travel. Rose has a rare ability to get under the skin of very different nationalities, characters and ages. She is able to convey a sense of vulnerable, yet intense, identity through her characters' voices in short dramatic monologues which compel the reader to empathise with their alien situations. In 'I Can

Sing, Dance, Rollerskate' a tough, lonely and pregnant New York girl who is desperately looking for a job hopes that her condition won't show up in tough downtown interview before she's hired. In 'Maya', the British girl traveller feels guilt at abandoning her travel-friend, a pregnant German girl, for freedom and sex. 'New York' finds a Scottish girl on her first night in that lonely city discovering that her dreams don't work out quite as she envisioned, as she succumbs too quickly to the aggressive pushiness of the man in the bar, and fends off loneliness with casual sex.

She presents women from an astonishing range of angles. Several, like 'Before Oscar', focus on women who reveal themselves trying to come to terms with their post-pregnancy bodies and their bored marriages; 'Drifter' anticipates the atmospheric stories of the later volume *Red Tides* in its vivid juxtaposition of Fiona's Glasgow memories with her slow drifting across America, and casual relationships; the 'hard dark seam' of Scotland, guilt, and perhaps integrity pushes her out of a drunken dance-floor to seek something else. Love is usually qualified or slightly comical; only sometimes 'almost romantic', as in the shabby, guilty affair of the Edinburgh hotel domestics in 'Reading the Sheets'. The closest that women come to fulfilment is in a kind of tired, affectionate truce with their partners, or in the warm female sharing of perception in 'The Original Version'. Men are revealed too; usually from the outside, however, but with sympathy along with the sardonic perception of their weaknesses. 'Little Black Lies' is a bittersweet and economical presentation of Sonny, the homosexual black dancer who makes a marriage of convenience; in this and stories like 'Landa Opportunity' Rose demonstrates a remarkable chameleon ability in her adoption of voices far removed from her Scottish roots. The title story transfers the innocence of the recurrent girl traveller to the 'innocence' of the manipulative Mexican child who latches on to a childless American couple, homing in on the childless woman's yearning for what she can't have. When this fails, the boy tries desperately to interest the couple in group sex – if that's the only way to get to America – and, on failing again, wryly accepts defeat, settling for their watches and going back to the fallen realities of street poverty. Rose's interpretations of the stories of her damaged yet defiant victims are authentic and original.

Amongst these powerful statements of the predicaments of women and innocents abroad are more traditional and conventional stories like 'Child's Play', 'Self-portrait, Laughing', or 'Magnolia'. These sometimes seem to derive more from Rose's reading than her travel experience, recalling respectively the stories of Ray Bradbury, O. Henry, and Elspeth Davie. A child gives an account of the accidental death of a playmate in a game, in which the telling is revealed to be as nasty as the event; a neglected painter contrives a posthumous revenge on his detractors, who include his wife; a magnolia plant exercises a strange fascination on those who see it, the story exploiting that obsessive, almost surreal quality so typical of Elspeth Davie's work. This last is almost a tribute to the older storyteller; perhaps it should overtly say so.

Rose continued to explore possibilities of style and the short-story genre with even greater success in *Red Tides* (1993). This is marked by its sheer assurance in its symbolic and poetic integration of theme. It's rare to find a volume of short stories whose individual tales subserve a whole purpose; but in Rose's skilful circling round her stories' subjects, and in her avoidance of the over-direct statement, there are shared underlying directions, the movements, ebb and flow, of the red tides of the passions; love, jealousy, desire, anger – usually, but not always, defining themselves in terms of what Rose sees as the passions of women. The title story is the last; the red tides are literally the noxious algae, rust- and blood-coloured, clinging like a scarf or bandage to an American beach where Carla,

Lois and storyteller lie out in their time off from waitressing. The story moves slowly, like the sluggish tides; like the girls, it seems to be going nowhere, filled with a world-weary, experienced and tough tone, touched with that kind of worldly sadness which was the hallmark of Scott Fitzgerald. The girls tan, talk sex, simply lie on the beach. Each has a man of the moment, or is in between men – no big deal, sex is tidal, will come and go. They are there for fun, sun and fucking. The story has moved on from the innocents of the earlier volume to more worldly concerns. Now the focus is on Lois's aimless life, on her obsession with her current lover; on Carla's Jimmy, who is going to carve up her ex; on the teller herself, caught up one weekend in a wild spree with Blind Bill the piano-tuner and the pianist Lyall. That's all – nothing disastrous appears to have happened. But with marvellous suggestive power Rose and her uneasily knowledgeable teller have warned us, in this story of sea, and sand and boredom, that the red tides are moving, inexorably, towards storms – or the weathering down of change, age, and death.

Drifting tides and human emptiness are caught in different images and metaphors throughout the tales. 'Wings' has the same sense of windblown and random chance, and again reminds the reader of Davie's story-reflections. A Japanese boy has come to Canada; his business-man father – always in too much of a hurry – once made him a kite, back in Japan. Now the boy, blown by winds of life into this alien culture, sits in a bus station with a stranger reflecting on wind. What is wind? We can die without ever knowing ... and slowly Rose's imagery of delicately made paper-and-wood craftsmanship unfolds, Japanese-style, as a metaphor. This gently paced, yet effective story, is beautifully and symbolically released with the young man's cutting of the cord of the kite; now it can fly free, accepting the winds of life.

But Edinburgh, Scotland and Britain are here too; and for all that Rose usually centres her stories on womens' consciousness, male voices are to be heard as well. In 'Friendly Voices' Rose juxtaposes the streams of consciousness of a well-meaning but cerebral woman doctor and her rough-spoken slum patient (and his alsatian, Raj); as so often in her work, the aim is nothing to do with the potential melodrama of the situation, but to reveal human essences and human distances from each other. And while Rose usually remains at the edge of violence, implying rather than revealing, she can explore violence when it is appropriate; in 'Street of the Three Terraces' a horrific murder is presented with photographic detachment, the inhumanity of the telling voice chillingly echoing its theme. And Rose can show violence from other angles, as in the anger at yobbo abuse of foreigners in Waverley Station in 'Barely an Incident'.

But it would be wrong to separate consideration of these stories into 'home' and 'away' groupings. It is the intermingling of the contrasting and very different voices and the settings of these stories which achieves their impressive overall effect. With typical balancing of themes and tensions, Rose moves easily from local-accented tales of family pressures and frustrations in urban Scotland to tales of London street-life or travellers abroad. A drunken and dying American phones Scotland in the middle of the night and pours out his dammed-up macho vulgarity in a messy tide which swamps his unhappy listener; a tourist gets too close and trusting with a Turkish carpet-seller, and has to run from the flow of emotion and sexuality she has prompted; a woman backing singer with a big voice and a big personality loses both when her young lover withdraws from their relationship.

In the end the overall impression is of human ebbing and flowing, bleeding and enduring. What holds all of them together is a broad yet very personal sympathetic feminism. It's a feminism which can be immensely concerned with men; 'The Worst of It' shows a sensitive understanding of the decent Deep South hippie fisherman who knows of, but doesn't openly articulate to himself, his wife's infidelity. But the essence of the volume is its endless exploration of the tides of female thinking and emotion. From the opening story, 'This is Tomorrow', a sad-funny tale of a mother-writer at last getting some personal space to go on her own to a writers' conference, but in her hotel room sleeping in, from sheer accumulated domestic fatigue, right through the time she should have given her own reading, to the final 'Red Tides', the heart of the matter is the ambivalence that women feel in intimate relations, in their families, amongst the endlessly changing and down-wearing claims of love and sex.

Notes

1.   Janice Galloway, *The Tride is to Keep Breathing* (Polygon, Edinburgh, 1989; Minerva, London, 1991), p. 235. Reference is to the Minerva edition.
2.   Janice Galloway, *Blood* (Secker & Warburg, London, 1991; Minerva, London, 1992), p. 16. Reference is to the Minerva edition.
3.   Janice Galloway, *Foreign Parts* (Jonathan Cape, London, 1994; Vintage, London, 1995), p. 145. Reference is to the Vintage edition.
4.   A. L. Kennedy, *Night Geometry and the Garscadden Trains* (Polygon, Edinburgh, 1990; Phoenix, London, 1993), p. 65. This and further references in the text are to the Phoenix edition.
5.   A. L. Kennedy, *Now That You're Back* (Jonathan Cape, London, 1994), p. 34.

41

Contemporary Fiction III: The Anglo-Scots

Flora Alexander

Some contemporary Scottish women writers of fiction are living in England, and in several cases they have also been educated in England, so that their Scottishness may not be immediately apparent. Nevertheless Emma Tennant, Alison Fell Shena Mackay, Sara Maitland and Candia McWilliam were all born either in Scotland or into a Scottish family, have all spent at least a part of their childhood in Scotland, and their work has, in varying degrees, a Scottish dimension. Scotland provides Tennant, Fell and McWilliam with a significant body of material for their writing, and Mackay and Maitland make occasional use of Scottish material. All of them carry with them some sense of their Scottish origins. Their family backgrounds differ: Tennant, Maitland and McWilliam, all privately educated at English schools, have had access to socially privileged circles, whereas Fell positions herself firmly as a woman with Scottish working-class origins.

Emma Tennant

Emma Tennant, born in 1937, is the daughter of the 2nd Baron Glenconner and Lady Glenconner, but unusually for a woman from such a background she has become a writer of fiction which is radical in its treatment of class and sexual politics. Her output is prolific. Her first novel, which appeared in 1964 under the name Catherine Aydy, was unfavourably received, and after that she published no fiction for nine years, but since *The Time of the Crack* (1973) she has produced more than a dozen novels. She was also influential as the founding editor, from 1975 to 1978, of the innovative literary magazine *Bananas*. She has been general editor since 1985 of Viking's series Lives of Modern Women. She herself classifies her fiction in three categories.[1] There are comic satirical fantasies, such as *The Time of the Crack*, *The Last of the Country House Murders* (1974), and *Hotel de Dream* (1976), which offer a critique of various aspects of modern society. Another group of novels, notably *Wild Nights* (1979) and *Alice Fell* (1980), depend largely on Tennant's poetic evocation of atmosphere, in treatment of subjects such as childhood and adolescence. The third and largest category, not in itself homogeneous, is a body of feminist writing. Because of her interest in women's relationship with power, Tennant's work has affinities with much of the fiction written by English women since the early 1970s, although she avoids the realist approach favoured by writers like Margaret Drabble, preferring to work with postmodern and fantastic modes in a manner closer to that of

Angela Carter. She has made a particular niche for herself in rewriting male-authored fictions, to present a critique of aspects of patriarchal activity. In *Queen of Stones* (1982) for example, a female version of William Golding's *Lord of the Flies* (1954), which is in its turn based on R. M. Ballantyne's *Coral Island* (1857), Tennant places a group of girls and young women in isolation, demonstrating how the various pressures on them lead to savage behaviour. The confident Freudianism of a male psychiatrist who deals with one of the young women (based on Freud's *Fragment of an Analysis of a Case of Hysteria* – the case of Dora) exposes as inappropriate the crude application of male perspectives and terminology to female experience. In *Faustine* (1992), Tennant adapts the Faust legend to explore the way in which for women power is related to a youthful and attractive appearance. Her *Tess* (1993) reworks the materials of Thomas Hardy's *Tess of the D'Urbervilles* (1891) to produce a history of repression of women, and the development of myths of male superiority, and puts forward an argument for matriarchy, for which the narrator claims to find evidence in early Celtic society.

Although most of Tennant's life since childhood has been spent in England, she is emphatic that she comes from the Scottish Borders. She points out that James Hogg wrote stories about the wood outside her bedroom window in Glen House near Peebles, where she spent her wartime childhood. This was for her an important formative experience, and she sees the shock and sadness of leaving the Borders for London after the war as a loss of Eden.[2] She ascribes to this background some of the qualities of her writing, believing that it explains why her imagination is 'so completely unlike a lot of English novelists'.[3] Borders and boundaries are frequent motifs in her writing, and she is consistently interested in differences between Scotland and England, and the ways in which Scottish people have their own ways of thought and expression. She traces to Edwin Morgan and Karl Miller the source of her thinking about the effects that language has on the construction of identity, and of her awareness that the situation of being balanced between Scottish and English cultures may foster a psychological splitting in the individual, and contribute to the strong Scottish interest in the idea of the double.[4] She also reflects on the colonised condition of Scotland, and on the sense in which women's exclusion from power places them in a similarly colonised position.[5] Tennant's home is not now in Scotland, but her fiction conveys an impression that she is more interested in the country because she no longer lives there, so that it becomes for her a country of the mind, and a powerful source of myth.

In two of her novels she reinterprets Scottish dualist texts, exploring the phenomenon of splitting or fragmentation of the self. *The Bad Sister* (1978) is based on James Hogg's *The Private Memoirs and Confessions of a Justified Sinner* (1824), and the later *Two Women of London* (1989) is a rewriting of R. L. Stevenson's *Dr Jekyll and Mr Hyde* (1886). The predominant focus in both of these novels is on the fragmentation of the female individual which results from pressures placed on women by patriarchal culture. Theoretically aware, Tennant discusses the difficulties of the female subject in patriarchy in terms which resemble those used in contemporary French feminist work to explore how women are affected by the Symbolic Order: the woman's tension between powerlessness and rationality is dangerous and destructive. In both of these reworkings of Scottish novels Tennant combines an interest in the general question of women's relationship with male power, and discussion of some specific issues which emerge from contemporary sexual politics, including the destructiveness of some militant forms of radical feminism.

In *The Bad Sister* Hogg's character Robert Wringhim is turned into a fragmented female subject, Jane Wild, haunted by a double, and ensnared by a powerful female figure, Meg

Gilmartin, who is derived from Hogg's diabolic Gilmartin. Jane's first-person narrative reveals her severe psychological disturbance: she feels a need to destroy her 'bad sister', whom she identifies with Miranda, her partner's former girlfriend, and also an urge to seek wholeness or completeness in relationship with Meg Gilmartin. Jane's quest for wholeness is presented in terms that recall, in Kristevan terms, the desire to return to the semiotic state, undivided from the mother, while at the same time an element of destructiveness in their relationship is signalled by a suggestion of vampirism. Tennant preserves Hogg's device of an Editor, and an 'Editor's Narrative', which includes a letter and a spoken testimony by other witnesses. By using this open form she organises multiple perspectives on the confused state of the central character. We can see Jane alternatively as a victim of patriarchal oppression, or, as the Editor suggests, as an easy prey for the influence of Meg's fanatical radical feminism. According to this view, Meg uses the pretext of fighting patriarchy and capitalism, to incite Jane to kill her father and then her half-sister, in the hope of acquiring her father's money.

When Tennant returns to Scottish Gothic materials in *Two Women of London*, she explores women's responses to sexual violence. As in *The Bad Sister*, she avoids a simple feminist position. Her Mrs Hyde murders, or 'executes', a man whom she mistakes for a rapist, so that a misguided feminist revenge replaces the non-specific evil suggested by Stevenson's Mr Hyde. The almost entirely male society of Stevenson's tale is transformed into a closely knit group of female professionals, including the lawyer and doctor of the source text, who observe and discuss the events, and to some extent participate in them. The novel is polyphonically constructed as a collection of edited documents including video- and audio-taped testimonies, so that it displays a spectrum of women's reactions to Mrs Hyde's action in avenging her sisters. These range from the filmmaker who expresses her support by using Mrs Hyde's face for a photomontage depicting women's resistance to oppression, to the measured dissent of the moderate feminist Scots lawyer, Jean Hastie. Jean is so appalled by the hatred of men which she identifies among her former friends, that she formulates a wish to erase the word 'W-O-M-A-N' from her typewriter, and leaves London with a resolution to work henceforth in Edinburgh on eighteenth-century philosophy of the Scottish Enlightenment. Tennant maintains in this novel her interest in Scottish dualism, which is in part fed by her familiarity with Karl Miller's work in *Cockburn's Millennium*, where Miller places *Dr Jekyll and Mr Hyde* in the complex tradition of Scottish thinking about divided lives.[6] Tennant's own use of ideas of Scottishness is not stable. At times she finds in it a congenial source of the extravagant and picturesque, as when she quotes in an interview Scott's words, 'Caledonia, stern and wild,/Fit nurse for a poetic child'.[7] Yet she also finds, as in her comic pastiche of an eighteenth-century memoir, *The Adventures of Robina, By Herself* (1986), that a Scottish background can provide a useful contrast of rigorousness and repression against which the dissolute life of the south can be explored.

Shena Mackay

Shena Mackay was born in Edinburgh in 1944, and brought up in England in a Scottish family. She was educated at grammar and comprehensive schools in Kent and London, left school at the age of sixteen, and thereafter worked in a variety of places including an antique shop, a factory and a library. She made a remarkable literary debut in 1964 with two novellas, published as a single volume, *Dust Falls on Eugene Schlumberger and Toddler on the Run*, both written while she was still in her teens. Since then she has produced six further novels and three collections of short stories. Both novellas are narratives of young love cut short by the death of the man, handled with a minimum of background, and emphasising the emotions and perceptions of the central characters. In *Dust Falls on Eugene Schlumberger*, Mackay relates in twenty-one brief chapters the growth of love between Eugene and the schoolgirl Abigail, the disruption of their relationship when he is imprisoned for stealing a car and dangerous driving, and his death trying to escape from prison. Emotional intensity is created by a combination of terse, elliptic narration with extravagant imagery and an inventive use of language. Images of dark skies, silver stars, frost and snow generate what is up to a point a conventional romantic atmosphere of youthful love. But sentimental pathos, as in the observation of the 'poor worn out sad sand stained paws' of a rabbit killed by the lovers' car, is deployed against a narrative voice made astringent by puns and witty metaphor. The book creates a sense of understated despair. *Toddler on the Run* similarly deals with passionate love, and ends with a young woman alone, choking on the salt of her tears, after the accidental death of her lover, mistaken by the authorities for a toddler because of his short stature. In both texts death is present at the periphery, in apparently incidental bereavements and fatal accidents, as well as at the centre. The love stories are accurately located in the culture of the early 1960s, voicing a youthful challenge to the authority of traditional institutions in education and religion. Mackay has a fresh approach to fictional conventions, combining sharp observation of the contemporary setting with a Gothic evocation of melancholy and a humour which is often black and at times surreal.

Old Crow (1967), still the work of a very young woman, is a disturbing version of the novel of English country life. In the rich, fertile setting of the natural world, and through the traditional institutions of parish council, village school, church, and pub, Mackay focuses on intolerant attitudes to a single mother, persecuted by the community because her cottage spoils the appearance of the village. Intense sensuous beauty is juxtaposed with an unsparing vision of squalid modern life: courtship in the overripe orchard leads to the birth of a winter baby placed in 'cold frilled nylon'. Recurrent references to brutal behaviour, and glimpses of a severed head, introduce an awareness of horror, which leads to the final image of the young woman hanging from a fence like a scarecrow. The author's characteristic puns, both in dialogue and in the voice of the narrator, add a grim humour, as in the snatch of dialogue overheard in the village surgery: "'Sometimes I feel I can't go on, Doctor. . .' 'Go on, Mrs Roe'". In later novels Mackay continues to probe the dark secrets that lie beneath the surface absurdities of English life. In *A Bowl of Cherries* (1984) she creates an outrageous concentration of vices and eccentricities in the lives of one Surrey family and their associates, bringing an improbable narrative to a conclusion in which, although virtue does not triumph, deception and oppression are clearly seen for what they are. Her writing characteristically combines a fondness for bizarre situations with a capacity for exact observation and accurate recall of the details of everyday life.

Throughout her career, Shena Mackay has written short stories. Many of them were originally published in journals such as *New Review* and *Critical Quarterly*, or read on BBC Radio, and they are collected as *Babies in Rhinestones* (1983), *Dreams of Dead Women's Handbags* (1987), and *The Laughing Academy* (1993). Her subjects, as in the novels, are both painful and comic: delicate revelations of bleakness and despair are combined with satirical exposure of complacency and malice, in the lives of families, friends, and lovers. Her condensed mode of writing allows her to pack extensive meaning into the short story: thus in 'Dreams of Dead Women's Handbags', which occupies a few hours in the consciousness of a novelist travelling to perform at a writers' weekend, a complex of images of bags and their contents, associated with shells and other sea objects, unlocks not only the secrets of her literary imagination, but also the repressed crisis of her early life, in which she was the accidental cause of the deaths of her parents. An ironic narrative voice adds further significance to the text by introducing an element of distance in the presentation of the central character.

Although Mackay writes largely about southern English life, her Scottish heritage appears in her work in the form of Scottish characters, turns of phrase, and fragments of traditions, songs, and rhymes. In the title story of *The Laughing Academy*, a study of two people brought together by mutual need and fears for their sanity, the entertainer Vincent McCloud is positioned between different worlds, clinging to an identity as son and Scotsman which is no longer valid. Professionally he is expected to 'wester home via the low road to Marie's wedding and his ain folk', but now he has only a one-night stand at Bexhill-on-Sea to look forward to. Scotland is the source of his recollections of his mother, now dead. It also provides the sentimental language which he applies to his children, and the sweets he buys for them, both inappropriate since the children are now adult. The Soor Plooms come to symbolise his own bitterness, and the Edinburgh Rock is expanded into a network of associations referring to holidays and the family life which he can no longer recover. Scottish material is also important in *Dunedin* (1992), a novel which extends Mackay's range by addressing political as well as personal issues. Dunedin in the novel is both the New Zealand city, named after Edinburgh, and the name of the London house to which Jack Mackenzie, a Scottish minister, retreats with his family after his career in New Zealand is ended by a sexual adventure with a part-Maori woman. The name Dunedin also contains an intimation of the lost Eden which troubles the lives of Mackenzie's descendants. Brief opening and closing sections present the family's colonial experience in 1909 and 1910, and the bulk of the novel traces, through a panoramic view of London life, its consequences in the personal lives of Mackenzie's middle-aged grandchildren Olive and William and on his illegitimate great-grandson, Jay Pascal, the ill-fated relic of the minister's scandalous love-affair. While Emma Tennant speaks of Scotland as colonised, Mackay's interest is in the Scot as coloniser. Just as Jack Mackenzie exhibits a male arrogance towards women, the Scots settlers treat the native people of New Zealand with condescension. Symbols emphasise the critique of imperialism: a sacred shrunken head, taken by Mackenzie from the house of his Maori mistress, is found abandoned in the London house, and a Maori chief's cloak becomes first a child's plaything and finally feather dusters. A central element of the plot, in which Olive, disturbed and unhappy, steals a black woman's child, functions as a modern parody of imperialist behaviour.

Alison Fell

Alison Fell was born in Dumfries in 1944, and spent much of her childhood in rural Scotland. She has written of the importance for her of years spent in Kinloch Rannoch from 1949 to 1953.[8] Highland space gave her freedom and fed her imagination, and when the family left the Highlands so that her parents could live with her maternal grandmother in Lochmaben she experienced a great loss. For her fictional character Isla in *The Bad Box* (1987), a similar move is like 'being torn out of paradise', and the language here is close to the words used by Tennant describing her childhood move from the Borders to London. From Dumfries Academy, Fell went to Edinburgh College of Art where she specialised in sculpture. In the late 1960s, after her marriage, she lived in Leeds, where in

1969 she was a co-founder of the radical theatre group, *Welfare State*. She separated from her husband and moved to London in 1970, at the point when the Women's Movement was beginning to be active in Britain, and was associated with the feminist theatre group Monstrous Regiment, and with feminist and left-wing journalism, especially the magazine *Spare Rib*. She writes fiction and poetry, has edited anthologies of women's work and collections of feminist short stories, and has provided artwork for collectively-authored books. Feminism is central to her view of the world, and she has argued that it needs to be seen not as simply a set of campaigns and political strategies, but as something which 'can and does transform women's consciousness of themselves at a very deep level', and which should 'shock some awareness of life's larger issues back into literature'.[9]

Fell's first novel, *Every Move You Make* (1984), draws heavily on autobiographical materials, presenting in first-person narration the experience of a working-class Scots woman who goes to London and works on a feminist magazine. It is a story of conflict, breakdown, and adjustment, told in realist mode with stilted dialogue and an excess of detail. While showing few signs of the quality of her later fiction, it contains a powerfully concise formulation of the narrator's recollection of Scotland: 'I thought of dry-eyed grim funerals and joyless maudlin weddings'. Other early work provides more indication of Fell's lively intellect and powerful imagination. A novel for children, *The Grey Dancer* (1981), makes use of her background in the Highlands and in the Borders, and exploits traditional Scottish shapeshifting legend, and historical material from the period of the Highland Clearances, in her treatment of twentieth-century Scottish social and political problems.

In *The Bad Box*, Fell continues to draw on personal experience, in a *Bildungsroman* which treats the childhood and adolescence of Isla Cameron, first in a Highland and then in a Lowland village, ending with the accidental death of her childhood sweetheart and her departure for art college in Edinburgh. This novel is written in a more experimental mode than *Every Move You Make*, and is much more successful. Isla's consciousness is presented as complex, and while her point of view records sharply and clearly the detail of Scottish life in the 1950s, her mind is at the same time engaged in multiple story-telling activities, including an extensively developed legend of a dumb girl, the child of a white hind, locked in a difficult relationship with father and lover. The 'bad box', carrying associations of confinement, symbolises Isla's psychological unease. The analysis of family and sexual relationships is interwoven with an account of salient features of Scottish life and culture. Through Isla's perceptions the nature of Scotland as an amalgam of contrasting subcultures is displayed. Removed from a Highland Eden to the South where she is not understood, she is regarded as being either depressed or mad. Highland myths contribute to her formation, and her father's socialism and anti-clericalism are important influences. Vividness of Highland imagination is contrasted with Lowland dullness as is her father's idealistic socialism with the subservient Toryism which Isla first encounters in the south of Scotland.

Fell won the Boardman Tasker Award for Mountain Literature for *Mer de Glace* (1991), a postmodern fiction in which a framework of psychoanalytic dialogue provides a structure for a series of documents. These include letters, a journal, dreams, fantasies, and contradictory narratives written in first and third person by the central figure Kathleen or by her married lover Will, who is younger than her and is also her pupil. Psychoanalysis and storytelling are mixed, so that event and fantasy cannot be reliably distinguished, and 'maybe it doesn't matter what really happened if the trajectory of the love story is irresistible'. Recollections of her unresolved difficulties with the father who wanted a boy and the mother who resented her daughter are connected with aspects of Kathleen's present sexual relationship; in each case there is a triangle, and patterns of behaviour between parent and child are introduced into Kathleen's relationship with Will. Fell's writing here shows the influence of French feminism, and in particular of Luce Irigaray, who is quoted in the text, and whose work is a likely source for the punning resonances Fell creates for 'Mer de Glace'. The phrase suggests in different chapter headings ice mirror, ice mother, and sea of ice. It also connects with allusions to the fairy tale 'The Snow Queen', which contributes to Fell's psychological theme the image of the boy who saw the whole world as ugly because a fragment of the Snow Queen's mirror had lodged in his eye. Alongside the myth-making and the condensed poetic language, Fell introduces direct discussion of left-wing politics, and of contemporary aspects of female-male relationship.

In *The Pillow Boy of the Lady Onogoro* (1994) Fell, while maintaining her interest in women's sexuality and in the theme of storytelling, creates an entirely different fictional world. A medieval Japanese poet is helped to reach orgasm with her lover, the General, by a young blind man who tells her erotic stories from behind a screen. Within the framing narrative, which ends with the death of the General and the beginning of love between Onogoro and the storyteller, Fell provides a series of embedded tales which show women as strong, resourceful, and sexually assertive.

As well as writing novels, Fell pursues her feminist agenda as editor and contributor to three volumes of short stories each organised around a theme: *The Seven Deadly Sins* (1988), *The Seven Cardinal Virtues* (1990), and *Serious Hysterics* (1992). Her Introduction to *Serious Hysterics* clarifies her feminist perspective, as she argues that historically the disorder engendered in women by patriarchal oppression had been categorised as deviance, that psychoanalysis, in spite of its phallocentricity, is a more humane remedy than earlier kinds of exorcism, but that for writers these things which fall outside patriarchal discourse are material with which 'to make poetry and mayhem'.[10]

Sara Maitland

Sara Maitland was born in 1950 into a well-to-do Scottish family, and brought up in Scotland but educated at a Wiltshire boarding school. She studied English at Oxford, and since then has worked as a reviewer, journalist and biographer, as well as writing short stories (her preferred form), novels and theology. Like Alison Fell she became involved in feminist activities at the beginning of the Women's Movement in Britain. What gives Maitland a distinctive position is her conversion, at more or less the same time as she discovered feminism, to Anglo-Catholic Christianity, and her work is marked by strenuous efforts to incorporate into her fiction both her religion and her sexual politics. She explains in 'A Feminist Writer's Progress', that feminism gave her material for fiction, but that at the beginning of her career this came into conflict with her belief that 'great writing' and politics were incompatible.[11] Participation in a Feminist Writers' Group helped her to find a way of writing which avoids crude polemic, and also to try to avoid what she continues to see as the danger of producing work inaccessible to the common female reader. A significant amount of her work has been done collaboratively, and she is a contributor to two of the collections of feminist short stories edited by Alison Fell, *The Seven Deadly Sins* and *The Seven Cardinal Virtues*. She values the principle of collectivity, because in working together writers 'are forced to give up their traditional privileges, of control, of assertion, of dominance'.[12]

In her impulse to write about women, arguing for their rights and celebrating their strengths, and to conduct in her fiction debates about such matters and issues as sexuality and essentialism, she has much in common with other women novelists of the 1970s and 1980s. She occupies a more radical position than, for example, Margaret Drabble, and in her questioning and her talent for outraging conventional pieties her work has more in common with the fiction of Emma Tennant or Angela Carter. Religious conviction is an essential element in her writing. Finding appropriate modes of expression for an approach to Christianity which will include women's experience has been a high priority in her work. She has commented, in a 1988 interview, that when she became interested in religion she found that there was a lack of books that expressed feminist spirituality, and in her early novels, *Daughter of Jerusalem* (1978) and *Virgin Territory* (1984), she herself is attempting to supply that need.[13] Since then, she has found the spiritual dimension that interests her, in work by British writers like Jeanette Winterson and Michelene Wandor, and American writers like Mary Gordon and Annie Dillard,.

In *Arky Types* (1987), an epistolary metafiction written collaboratively with Michelene Wandor, Maitland remarks that she has no enthusiasm for social realism, but that she is 'quite interested in muddling around the categories. . . .I think this is called Magic Realism nowadays'. And in an essay on 'Futures in Feminist Fiction' she notes that the novels of the Women's Movement are not particularly innovative structurally, and looks forward to the development of a type of fiction which will be truthful but which will accommodate some kind of vision.[14] Her own writing is moderately innovative in the way in which she incorporates into it non-realist traditional materials, such as legend and myth and fairytale. She frequently employs a repetitive style which draws attention to the emotional dimensions of her narratives, and emphasises thematic significance. Her collections of short stories, *A Book of Spells* (1987) and *Women Fly When Men Aren't Watching* (1993), emphasise the strength and complexity of women, rewriting conventional notions of the feminine to disclose destructiveness and rebellion, and challenging stereotypes of passivity and mildness. She also displays aspects of male oppression of women which have traditionally been concealed or glossed over, as in the short story 'Triptych', which is the story of Abraham, Sara and Hagar rewritten in a way that exposes the ill-treatment of women hidden in the Biblical version, and introduces the idea of a deity which may have a female aspect. Like Carter and Tennant, she rewrites myths and by this means works towards what Carter has called 'a decolonization of the mind'.[15] Her first novel, *Daughters of Jerusalem*, is at one level a treatment of a woman's experience of attending a fertility clinic, handled with a bold disrespect for traditional kinds of male authority, but the significance of each chapter is extended by a concluding passage which recreates the experience of Biblical women, or pairs of women such as Rachael and Leah, and Elizabeth and Mary. Maitland's interest in aspects of women's lives which are cyclic and timeless picks up a way of theorising femininity which has something in common with recent French feminist work.[16]

In her second novel, *Virgin Territory* (1984), Maitland achieves a fuller integration of the mythic with the naturalistic. It is a narrative of development in which the vocational crisis of a nun, Sr. Anna, and her discovery of lesbian love, are explored through a complex network of symbols. In Maitland's appropriation of the symbolism of family relationships, Anna's father is linked with the oppressive Fathers of the Church, and with patriarchy more generally; mothers are not simply Anna's absent biological mother, but also a series of mothers, like Mother Church and the Mother of God, whom Anna perceives as taking the side of the Fathers by restricting the freedom of women. Anna's resistance to the authority of the Fathers is encoded in a discourse which stretches language to capture something of the essence of the semiotic, and resembles the representation in the novel of the consciousness of a pre-verbal child, a voice which, typography indicates, goes below or beyond words, and confronts chaos.[17] An epigraph to this novel, in a quotation from Sheila Rowbotham, gives notice of an idea pursued in the text: that 'for feminists the existence of universal and ahistoric psychic patterns clearly has to be contested because these inevitably confirm and legitimate male power.' Maitland revises archetypes daringly, crossing traditional boundaries of decorum. She introduces the thought that on the analogy of the virgin forest, the virgin is not barren, but is free from man's control, and she puts into the mouth of a lesbian character the idea that 'The dyke is the positive image of the negative virgin.' Women's strength is indicated through the key image of the Visitation, the meeting of two strong Biblical women, Mary and Elizabeth, and it is suggested that God is mother as much as father.

Maitland's probing of the lives of women continues in *Three Times Table* (1990) and *Home Truths* (1993). *Three Times Table* traces the interaction between women of three generations, mother, daughter, and granddaughter, in a narrative which brings together personal and working lives, science and politics, realism and fantasy. The scope of the novel includes a professional crisis in a scientific career, the discovery of breast cancer, and a young woman's loss of a childhood fantasy life as she enters puberty. The emphasis is on the wide range of women's experience. A shooting lodge in the Scottish Highlands is the setting for *Home Truths*, in which a young woman, in the company of her brothers and sisters, tries to remember and come to terms with an accident on a mountain in Zimbabwe, in which she lost her right hand, and may have caused the death of her lover. This novel shows a further development of Maitland's interest in the interaction between Christianity and homosexuality, and also of her perception that while women are at times oppressed, they may also be capable of hatred and destructive behaviour.

Candia McWilliam

Candia McWilliam, born in Edinburgh in 1955, is the daughter of the architectural historian Colin McWilliam, who was officer-in-charge of the Scottish National Monuments Record, and devoted much of his life to the preservation of Scottish historic buildings. She was educated first in Edinburgh and, from the age of thirteen, at school in England, after which she read English at Cambridge. She has worked in advertising and in journalism. Her first novel, *A Case of Knives* (1988), was joint winner of the Betty Trask Award, which is given for works of traditional fiction by young writers, and she continues to produce fiction of a fairly conventional kind. *A Case of Knives* is a story of corrupt relationships, in which four narrators successively reveal their manipulation of each other in a plot that turns on a marriage arranged for several concealed reasons. Occasionally the same event is related from different perspectives by two characters, but in general each narrator adds a new dimension to the story. Lucas Salik, a successful heart surgeon at the centre of the narrative, has been contriving to provide a bride for his homosexual lover Hal, and although the young woman, Cora, is an object of their manipulation, she herself chooses to take advantage of this opportunity to provide a father for her unborn child. When Lucas is stabbed, at the instigation of animal rights activists who deplore his use of laboratory animals in his work, his assailant turns out to be Hal, and he is jailed. In the novel's conclusion Lucas, previously intensely misogynist, becomes part of a family unit where he and his long-standing friend Anne Cowdenbeath become 'parents' to the 'bride' Cora and make a home for her and her female child. This plot is the basis for a psychological study of obsessive behaviour, and also allows McWilliam to examine fluidity in gender and family roles, highlighting for example Anne Cowdenbeath's androgynous qualities, and the irony by which the misogynist Lucas, who formerly thought of Cora as 'a doll for [Hal] to break', ends in a version of marriage with Anne as wife and Cora and her baby as daughter and granddaughter.

The title, taken from George Herbert's poem 'Affliction (IV)', has ramifications which McWilliam exploits ingeniously. Anne's reflection that 'Language is a case of knives' more or less reproduces the thought in Herbert's poem, but the significance of the basic perception that thoughts can wound the heart opens out into further reflections on several levels. Knives relate to the activity of Lucas, the heart surgeon, the fact that he is himself vivisected, and the vulnerability of the human body in general. In the exploration of gender roles, Cora has a feminine fantasy that she wishes to enter Lucas's body through a hole in his side and become a rib of Adam. McWilliam is linguistically daring. She revels in description, enlarging on food and decoration and paying loving attention to visual and tactile details. She creates varied discourses for her four narrators, of which Cora's is particularly complex and includes word-play, metaphor, allusion, and a deliberate exploitation of cliche. Anne Cowdenbeath, who joins with Lucas to take over the role of parents to Cora, is Scottish, and through Anne Scotland is introduced as a country different from England, presented in recollection through most of the narrative, but also, at the end of the novel, directly, when she and Lucas retire there with the newly constituted 'family'. While the references to Scotland are sometimes no more than a conventional mention of rain or of Calvinism, Anne recognises the idea of crossing the border back into Scotland as vitally important for her, and her awareness of its difference includes freshly observed detail of Scottish habits of speech, architecture, and landscape.

A Little Stranger (1989) makes effective use of first-person narration for an account of how an intelligent young mother blinds herself to the very evident psychological illness of her nanny, and through the two characters McWilliam explores women's experience of two complementary eating disorders: over-eating in the mother and bulimia in the nanny. The voice created for Daisy the narrator, like Cora's in A Case of Knives, is sophisticated, allusive, and witty.

McWilliam's third novel, Debatable Land (1994), moves beyond the limited social worlds of the first two and addresses major issues of identity and nationhood. It is a narrative of a yacht's voyage with a crew of six from Tahiti to New Zealand. McWilliam uses the device of the small, closed group of characters to pursue personal histories and tensions which are resolved at the end of the journey. There is a Conradian allusion in the violent storm which brings the emotional dynamics of the voyage to a resolution. The narrative focuses on interaction between the six people on the boat, and on their individual reflections. Three of them are Scots from different backgrounds, and the debatable land of Scotland forms a subject of their conversations and recollections. Scottish identity is explored through their recollections of their northern country from the South Pacific. Resonances from Robert Louis Stevenson contribute to this perspective on Scotland, and in particular on Edinburgh. McWilliam's Scotland is built up through a complex interaction of visual appearance, weather and atmosphere, and the nuances of Scottish speech and customs. The visual evocations of Scotland in the memory of the artist Alec Dundas are especially exact, as in his childhood view of Edinburgh through the Camera Obscura: 'The colours were true to the tabby, pewter, lilac and soot of the slate and smoke of the city'. The impression of Scottish civilisation is made substantial and vital with history and legend, and fragments of song. Like Alison Fell, McWilliam stresses that Scotland is a hybrid place which encompasses different cultures. Highland and Lowland traditions are recognised. Alec's working-class background is very different from Elspeth Urquhart's privileged upbringing, and they remember two quite different Edinburghs. The nation accommodates Anglo-Scots and American-Scots like Elspeth and Logan. McWilliam's portrayal of Edinburgh also takes note of the importance of Scots-Italian culture. Scotland is a debatable land because there are different Scotlands in the experience of different people, and also because its future is seen as a subject of literal debate. Recurrent metaphors convey something of the qualities of the national consciousness. 'Ardent Spirit', the name of the yacht, stands not only for whisky, but also for a kind of Scottish temperament, the Celtic 'feast-or-famine gene', exemplified in Alec's wife Lorna, who remains at home in Edinburgh. This contrasts with Alec's asceticism, explained when he says 'I saw the bones in things only because I so feared the flesh taking me over'. And yet Alec's is not a simple asceticism, since in the Scottish tradition of doubleness (and here the debt to Stevenson is conspicuous) he admits to a Jekyll and Hyde-like split between repression at home and promiscuous relations with other women. McWilliam's treatment of Scottish identity is wide-ranging and done with acute perception and great sensitivity.[18]

Notes

1. Sue Roe and Emma Tennant, 'Women Talking about Writing', in Moira Monteith (ed.), *Women's Writing: A Callenge to Theory* (Harvester Wheatsheaf, Brighton, 1986), p. 150.
2. John Haffenden, *Novelists in Interview* (Methuen, London, 1985), pp. 282–3.
3. Monteith, *Women's Writing*, p. 124.
4. Haffenden, *Novelists in Interview*, p. 292.
5. Monteith, *Women's Writing*, pp. 124–5 and p. 135.
6. Karl Miller, *Cockburn's Millennium* (Duckworth, London, 1975).
7. Monteith, *Women's Writing*, p. 128.
8. Alison Fell, 'Rebel with a Cause', in Liz Heron (ed.), *Truth, Dare or Promise: Girls Growing up in the Fifties* (London, 1985), p. 16.
9. Alison Fell (ed.), *Hard Feelings: Fiction and Poetry from Spare Rib* (London, 1979), Introduction, p. 6.
10. Alison Fell (ed.), *Serious Hysterics* (London, 1992), Introduction, p. 5.
11. Sara Maitland, 'A Feminist Writer's Progress', in Michelene Wandor (ed.), *On Gender and Writing* (London, 1983), p. 19.
12. Sara Maitland, 'Futures in Feminist Fiction', in Helen Carr (ed.), *From My Guy to Sci-fi: Genre and Women's Writing in the Post-Modern World* (London, 1989), p. 198.
13. *The Sunday Times*, 17 July 1988, p. 4.
14. Maitland in Carr (ed.), *From My Guy*, p. 202.
15. Angela Carter, 'Notes from the Front Line', in Wandor (ed.), *On Gender and Writing*, p. 71.
16. See Julia Kristeva, 'Women's Time', trans. Alice Jardine and Harry Blake, in Toril Moi (ed.), *The Kristeva Reader* (Oxford University Press, Oxford, 1986), pp. 187–213.
17. I use 'semiotic' in the sense in which it is used by Julia Kristeva in 'Revolution in Poetic Language', trans. Margaret Waller in Toril Moi (ed.), *The Kristeva Reader*, pp. 89–136.
18. Further material of interest will be found in: Flora Alexander, *Contemporary Women Novelists* (London, 1989); Carol Anderson, 'Listening to the Women Talk', in Randall Stevenson and Gavin Wallace (eds), *The Scottish Novel since the Seventies: New Visions, Old Dreams* (Edinburgh University Press, Edinburgh, 1993); Sara Maitland, *Very Heaven: Looking Back at the 1960s* (London, 1988).

42

The Mirror and the Vamp:
Liz Lochhead

Anne Varty

Liz Lochhead was born in Motherwell in 1947, she trained at Glasgow School of Art, and when she was twenty-four published *Memo for Spring*, her first and most personally reminiscent collection of poems, which sold nearly 5,000 copies. Since 1972 she has become one of Scotland's most significant and prolific writers, whose work is distinguished by its protean character. Often defying generic classification, it works within and across boundaries of poetry, prose, drama and film. Her style is marked by two political features: it is fundamentally transgressive and it is also popular. Formal transgression, a refusal to sit squarely as 'poetry', 'drama', or even 'rap' – let alone divisions within these categories such as 'ballad', or 'lyric' – is matched by a provocative tone of ironic feminism. This allows Lochhead to move into what has been predominantly male territory, at the same time permitting a negotiation with rank-and-file feminist politics. The popularity of her work is just as complex. Her vocabulary, whether literary or theatrical, contains the demotic, taking particular strength from spoken idiom. Sensitivity to regional varieties of contemporary Scots, English and American goes hand in hand with a subject-matter that draws on topics of current political debate, folk history and pop culture. Capable of sounding an intimate, unpretentious voice, her work is that of one woman speaking to many, and one person speaking for many. Poetry readings, revue work, and more formal performances (Verena in *Quelques Fleurs* for both stage (1991) and radio (1992), and Pernelle in *Tartuffe* (1994) which she also directed at the Edinburgh Festival before transferring to the Glasgow Mayfest in 1995) permit a direct (if 'in personae') relationship with her audience. Participation in cultural activity that is not accorded the status of 'high' art, yet which addresses in variously crafted media matters of personal and political concern for a wide audience, is a significant dimension to her work as a writer.

An early example of the transgressive and popular dimensions of her work is provided by the poem 'Morning After' contained in *Memo for Spring* (1972). The title itself proclaims the popular idiom on which the poem depends. Predictable lament is yoked with lyrical intensity so that where the reader expects cliché she finds sincerity, generated by the verb 'I shiver' and its position in the blank verse. Although gender roles are not assigned by the text, the reader draws assumptions from the stereotypes of popular culture which dictate that the lyrical 'I' is a female voice, addressing herself in the presence of a male partner. The reader, no less than the speaker of the poem, is therefore dependent on stereotype for her position. The monologue takes place over the Sunday papers:

> Me, the Mirror
> reflecting only on your closed profile.
> You, the Observer
> encompassing larger, Other issues.[1]

The two newspapers named are both English; the allusion is therefore to the hierarchy of British politics. Syntactic elision of the verb 'to read' makes a metaphor of the relationship between reader and paper, so that the woman is not just associated with the tabloid, she actually is 'the mirror', a reflective role that is not so far from that of 'observer' as a first glance suggests. Despite the possible collapse of the distinction between 'mirror' and 'observer', conflicts between powerful and powerless, active and passive, man and woman, Scots and English, recurring polarities of Lochhead's work, operate here. And they anticipate her view that 'the English are like men – nonchalant and unquestioning about existing,' while 'Scotland is like a woman; the Scots know they are perceived from the outside'.[2]

Defiantly aware how culture and commerce shape women for the pleasure of the male gaze, Lochhead couples this with a self-conscious analysis of nationhood. Her work reflects upon the distortions and refinements of cultural conditioning, as if to provide a response to the metaphoric deployment of the mirror in the philosophy of the Scottish Enlightenment. Adam Smith, in his *The Theory of Moral Sentiments* (1759) imagines a solitary 'human creature':

> Bring him into society, and he is immediately provided with the mirror which he wanted before. It is placed in the countenance and behaviour of those he lives with . . . ; and it is here that he first views the propriety and impropriety of his own passions, the beauty and deformity of his own mind . . .
> [B]y placing ourselves before a looking-glass, or by some such expedient, [we] endeavour, as much as possible, to view ourselves at the distance and with the eyes of other people.[3]

Comments on the education of the noble savage, and his desire for approbation, contrast with the representation of woman, who is already corrupt and must be chastened:

> A woman who paints, could derive, and should imagine, but little vanity from the compliments that are paid to her complexion. These, we should expect, ought rather to put her in mind of the sentiments which her real complexion would excite, and mortify her the more by the contrast.[4]

But why does she 'paint' in the first place? What has the patriarchal looking-glass taught about her image? The case for a woman's response is strong and Lochhead questions such inherited assumptions about the female and the Scottish identity. Providing her readers and her audiences with 'the eyes of other people', she regularly exposes divisions which have resulted from the moral hypocrisies and double vision governing the formation of 'self' in the face of 'Other'. And her weapon against Smith's censorious 'ought' is playfulness, a voice mischievously on the game, coupled with an exposure of feminine follies, vices, and hurts, more generously corrective:

> The other woman
> lies
> the other side of my very own mirror.
> Sweet, when I smile
> straight out for you, she
> puts a little twist on it, my
> right hand never knows what her left is doing.
> She's sinister.
> She does not mean you well.
>
> ('The Other Woman')[5]

The affirmation of gender stereotyping in 'Morning After', and the means by which it is achieved, demonstrate how the reader is compromised by patriarchy. But if, in 'Morning After', the voice of the lyrical 'I' is disappointed and vulnerable, it is also implicitly critical. It heralds a more vigorous criticism of the social roles assigned to women that is typified by Lochhead's more recent poetry. In 'Almost Miss Scotland' (*Bagpipe Muzak*, 1991) the gender of the voice is unmistakably female, and the conceit of the monologue is to make the speaker herself entertain the (im)possibility of a gender swop in the situation of a beauty contest:

> How would they like their mums to say that their bums
> Had always attracted the Ladies' Glances,
> And nothing wrang wi it, they'd aye gone alang wi it
> And encouraged them to take their chances?
> And they were Good Boys, their Mum's Pride & Joys,
> Saving it for their Future Wives?[6]

The setting for the poem is an event in popular culture. It should not, therefore, be surprising that the language used is demotic Scots. Yet even here Lochhead jolts her reader by using ungroomed diction and syntax in a situation where grooming is at a premium. Linguistic propriety has been breached, and this carries other political unorthodoxies in tow. The confessional aspect of the monologue generates comic effect, again defying expectation since a beauty competitor is rarely also a stand-up-comedian (a form of entertainment where women are a minority amongst performers anyway): 'Yet fur this dubious prize I'd have scratched oot their eyes/And hoped they'd get *plooks*, so I'd win!' ('AMS', *BM*, p. 4). It is the whole context of the competitive environment that the speaker comes to reject in the process of taking part. But instead of instigating a 'bacchanalian Revenge of the Barbie Dolls', 'I/Just stuck on my headsquerr and snuck away oot o therr . . . And I let my oaxters grow back in/Really rid and thick and hairy.' She justifies her withdrawal, and recovered pride in her body on the grounds that 'the theory of feminism's aw very well/But yiv got tae see it fur yirsel' ('AMS', *BM*, pp. 5–6). If Lochhead's politics sometimes appear crude, this is to expose by matching, the implicit yet invisible grotesqueness of the female role, and her voice addresses 'yirsel' directly.

Recalling her school days at Dalziel High (1960–5) in Motherwell, Lochhead notes that the environment was 'completely unsexist', but 'there was nothing that actually allowed you to express your *femaleness*'.[7] Being a 'proxy boy' was no solution to the problem of growing up to inhabit a woman's body. Keen to observe sexual difference, she has written frequently about the transition from girlhood to womanhood. 'Revelation', the opening poem of *Memo for Spring*, for which she won her first public prize (a Radio Scotland Poetry award in 1971) describes a girl's passage from innocence to experience. This involves the recognition of a sexual identity that is different from 'the hot reek of him', the farmyard bull. The poem, Lochhead states, is based on a childhood memory, and the scene is narrated by a mature woman looking back, 'I remember once being shown the black bull' it begins.[8] But the reminiscent voice refrains from doing more than place symbols of the encounter in front of the reader. It is for our experienced eye to interpret the prophecy of the farmyard 'revelation', to know with hindsight what inspires the girl's flight, and what her tokens of eggs and milk (which she fears to shatter and spill) stand for. The girl's sense of her own fragility, and her effort to save the goods for which she was sent, tell with great economy of her own fertility to come, and the social role she will be expected to play even in the face of male threat. With 'The Ariadne Version' in the later *Grimm Sisters* (1981), Lochhead uses cultural memory or legend, typical of that collection as a whole, to describe the adolescent girl whose body now craves experience. This time the 'bull' is internalised, yoking her adult desire and pain:

> It had burst inside her recently
> like a bull in a china shop.
> She was grown up.[9]

The tone is ironic, the tokens anachronistic, the fate inevitable. The story is told from Ariadne's point of view, a perspective only superficially at odds with the way legend renders the teenager's destiny general and impersonal. In contrast to the reaction of the girl in 'Revelation', Ariadne flees into the arms of trouble. But this is just a trick of narrative. Both of them have their path laid out and directed by the social condition of their sex.

With 'Mirror's Song',[10] the last poem in *Dreaming Frankenstein* (the collection that couples with *Blood and Ice* in addressing the monstrous compulsion to write creatively), Lochhead offers a more violent, if open-ended attack on conventional female constriction. As the final line avows, it recounts the difficult and painful labour of 'a woman giving birth to herself'. The farewell here is not to childhood, but to the materialist trappings of womanhood. Patriarchal norms of feminine appearance and behaviour are not just rejected, but destroyed. There is a fundamental ambiguity in the poem about the identity of the speaker, as befits its discussion of the tangled relationship between a woman and her appearance. It begins:

> Smash me looking-glass glass
> coffin, the one
> that keeps your best black self on ice.
> Smash me, she'll smash back –
> without you she can't lift a finger.

'Me', 'you' and 'she' are difficult to distinguish, and the reflecting quality of the mirror is caught by the repetition of 'glass' in the first line. The mirror demands to be broken, recognising both her power over the image she throws back, and its lifelessness. Without a controlling self-image the woman is free to reassemble herself. A vast list of dressing-table equipment is junked. This includes the brand names 'Valium' and 'Thalidomide', drugs designed to ease the symptoms of illness or discomfort commonly associated with women. Illness disguised is not health, any more than 'panstick' guarantees beauty or a 'chafing iron' assures virginity. All these pretences and placebos are disposed of in an abandon of rage marked by breathless enjambement and abrupt caesuras:

> let her
> rip up the appointment cards for the
> terrible clinics,
> the Greenham summonses, that date
> they've handed us. Let her rip.
> She'll crumple all the
> tracts and the adverts, shred
> all the wedding dresses, snap
> all the spike-heel icicles
> in the cave she will claw out of –
> a woman giving birth to herself.

It is not simply commercial aids to enhance appearance that are rejected, but also the political system which determines such products and which turns the conforming woman herself into a commodity. This includes Government control of female solidarity and rebellion represented during the 1970s by demonstrations at the nuclear weapons store at Greenham. The technique of naming brand names together with more general terms is typical of Lochhead's style. It provides precise temporal and social location, asserts the immediately spoken quality of the verse, and at the same time generates a metaphoric gloss about commerce as a means of social control.

The mirror here may have elected for her own destruction, but Lochhead has other tricks for shattering received images of women. 'The Furies', a sequence of three dramatic monlogues, lets the 'Harridan', the 'Spinster' and the 'Bawd' speak for themselves. Placed in the collection *The Grimm Sisters*, these monologues contribute to Lochhead's extensive revision of fairy tale material. The fairy tales with which we are all familiar have their origins in folk narratives told by women to each other, often as they worked. These were collected and anthologised by the Brothers Grimm and became the stuff of childhood in the nineteenth and twentieth centuries. Because of their importance in our cultural lives, often before full consciousness, such fairy tales are open to cynical media exploitation on the one hand and radical feminist revision on the other. Parodic exploitation by one group is matched by urgent critique by the other. Lochhead is typically sensitive to the claims of both camps and her work here is profoundly ironical, taking on the lessons in propriety, cunning, and good fortune afforded by the childhood stories as well as their questionably normative cultural values and their more sinister step-sisters in the commerce of contemporary adult life. Although the three 'furies' do not emerge from any one narrative, they are archetypes which lurk through many stories, and stereotypes which figure in social attitudes today. In each case Lochhead invites the reader behind the scenes, to hear how the woman determines to construct herself according to type. The roles are therefore simultaneously made and unmade, adopted and abandoned, to reveal various kinds of difficulty experienced by the single woman in securing her social place.

The speaker of 'Harridan'[11] begins at some distance from the mask she will adopt, subjecting the figure of 'Mad Meg', from Bosch, Breughel and Magritte, to art-historical consideration: 'took pains . . . to reduce it all to picture planes'. The first stanza ends, 'discussed: Was Meg 'mad' or more the Shakespearian Fool?' The rejoinder in the second stanza takes off from this:

> The fool I was! Mad Meg, Sour-Tongued Margot,
> maddened slut in this mass of misery, a Virago
>   . . .
> Oh that kitchen knife, that helmet, that silent shout,
> I know Meg from the inside out.

Irregular line length is punctuated by the insistently recurring rhyme of the couplets so that chilling senses of order and inevitability shape the expression of anger. Experience intervenes between stanzas and radically changes the perspective of the earnest student. She is hurled into the picture, and becomes herself the creature once viewed with dispassion. The 'shout' which on canvas was necessarily seen and not heard, continues to be 'silent', despite the loud emotion of the speaker, simply because society will not listen. One way in which society conspires to collective deafness is to make the aggrieved woman laughable, and Lochhead points to this with the incongruous collocation of 'kitchen knife' with 'helmet', details lifted directly from Breughel's picture. This locates the battle field in the home, toys swiftly with the tendency to ridicule and at the same time highlights both the pathos and the nightmare of the situation. The submerged narrative of what has befallen the speaker is indicated by the accusations of the final stanza:

> Oh I am wild-eyed, unkempt, hellbent, a harridan.
> My sharp tongue will shrivel any man.
> Should our paths cross
> I'll embarrass you with public tears, accuse you with my
>   loss.

She now revels in the persona of Mad Meg, welcomes the opportunity to express her unreasonable grief. Her 'loss' is not simply that of a loved one, but also of her composure and assured social status. She is separated from her lover, and with that she is outcast from the larger community.

'Spinster',[12] the voice of another kind of outcast, presents from inside the problem of having no obvious function as wife or mother. She must find other ways of constructing a social identity. And the extent to which the speaker has internalised the fact that the community deals with the literal eccentricity of her situation by finding it funny is expressed by her comic rhymes: 'My life's in shards./I will keep fit in leotards', or the final couplet, 'I'll grow a herbaceous border./By hook by crook I'll get my house in order'. While the first example is playful, reflecting a self-mocking desire for routine and discipline, the last example, on which the poem closes, for all its syntactical self-assertion, carries a note of resignation. The allusions suggest that the speaker will be assimilated with the figure of the witch ('herbaceous border' to provide the ingredients for cures and spells), and also that she is destined to be a figure of nursery rhyme fun. 'By hook by crook' alludes to the predatory wolf who will blow down the house of the three little pigs. The spinster is both social aggressor and victim. She wants her house to be allowed to stand. 'Accept' is the imperative that is repeated four times in the three-stanza poem, and this is addressed not just to herself but also to her audience, the community. Yet it seems that her efforts to make the best of a bad job all lead her further into eccentricity and stereotype. 'Bawd'[13] imagines a different way of acting out her fate. This woman decides to be bad, now that 'I've hauled my heart in off my sleeve': 'I'll let my hair down,/go blonde, be a bombshell, be on the make,/I'll gold-dig, I'll be frankly fake.' She confesses pell-mell the tactics she will use to get herself the reputation of 'fatal dame', hiding behind a breathtaking repertoire of clichés. In contrast to 'Spinster', this speaker finds it only too easy to acquire a vocabulary and a style. But the very fact that the bawd speaks such idiomatic English means that the last stanza of the confession is not, technically, a surprise: 'I'll be a bad lot./I've a brass neck. There is mayhem in my smile./No one will guess it's not my style.' The linguistic cast-offs she has picked up, together with too solid a protestation of bad intent already labelling herself as others will, reflect the inauthenticity of the stance and a bitter sense that there is a better life (both in terms of pleasure and ethics) than the one she adopts.

An altogether different strategy for confronting stereotype is afforded by 'What The Pool Said, On Midsummer's Day'.[14] This opening poem of Dreaming Frankenstein, presents by its title the poet in her role as medium. The pool speaks, its sex is female ('The woman was easy./Like to like, I called her, she came.'), and it wants a mate ('But it's you I want, and you know it, man'). Because this is a spirit of nature speaking ('it's only water talking'), the encounter is elementally sexual, licensed to intoxicate beyond social proprieties. Even so, the anima tricks out her identity with a semblance of conventionally erotic underwear, using a description of woman entering her depths as a means of enticing the man: 'slipping on my water-stockings / . . . being cupped and clasped/in my glass green bra.' Designed for the male gaze, the male prey is imagined taken, and underwear turns to undergrowth, things felt, not seen: 'my wet weeds against your thigh, it/could turn nasty'. The man is coaxed out of his safe, socially constructed, expression of sexual desire, and invited to encounter something unknowable. The penultimate stanza rejects the man's attempt to control the sexual encounter through requests to conform with the pattern of familiar erotica. The incongruity of conventional female display with the things of nature at her disposal exposes his desire as absurd and somehow corrupt. 'You'd make a fetish of zazzing dragonflies?/You want I should zip myself up/with the kingfisher's flightpath, be beautiful?' The pool has an answer for every objection. By the final stanza the conventional power balance has been reversed. The man has been turned into an object of her gaze, the pool's notional passivity is a token of her power as he is compelled to act: 'I watch. You clench,/clench and come into me.' This pool is harridan, spinster and bawd all in one. A powerful expression of sexual desire, it justifies male fear, but it also invites to something mutually transforming. The anachronistic technique which grafts contemporary reference, puns, and allusion onto a moment of enchantment that supposedly stands outside the temporal, is a bold recognition of the fact that not even sex escapes the interference of socially learned convention. The conceit of letting 'nature' speak sidesteps residual social unease at articulations of female desire, while the decision to let the 'pool' speak, rather than the mermaid who traditionally tempts men from the water, eschews patriarchal stereotype contained by folklore.

If, in reading poetry, it is important to remember that 'Poets don't bare their souls, they bare their skill' as Lochhead states (however ironically) in 'A Giveaway',[15] then this is even more pertinent when considering performance work which often, in Lochhead's case, involves the physical presence of the writer. Since 1978 in tandem with her publication of poetry, Lochhead had also been contributing regularly to various kinds of revue. Some of what she had written as poetry was of immediate use to her as a performer, even though she describes her dramatic monologues as dramatisations of 'psychic states rather than . . . what someone would say'.[16] 'Spinster' and 'Bawd' became turns for the first Sugar and Spite revue that Lochhead put together with the writer Marcella Evaristi and the musician Esther Allan at the Traverse Theatre in Edinburgh. But Lochhead herself insists that a fundamental distinction is to be made between work that is written to read and work written for performance. 'A play is something that doesn't exist when you have written it. It only exists when it begins to be performed. Whereas a poem . . . even if it's lying under the bed, there it is; it's a thing . . . '.[17] If a play script is an artefact-in-waiting, then the inscribed transitoriness of material written for revue which lacks even the cohesive power of sustained narrative, is so much more conspicuous. Little of what she has written for such occasions survives in published form. What there is has been collected in the 'black book',[18] *True Confessions and New Clichés* (1985). *Sugar and Spite* transferred from the Traverse to the Tron Theatre in Glasgow in 1979, where its ephemeral status seemed to be compounded by the fact that the performance space used was the public bar, although it played to 'full houses' (a seating capacity of sixty-five), and was invited back, rematerialising in 1981 as *True Confessions* now with the actor Siobhan Redmond and the musician Angie Rew.

Narrative is absent, but technique and theme are brought to the fore. Claiming an insider's permissiveness, she states '[t]he subject was Women In Love. Hence *True Confessions*' and the technique was 'taking the (gentle) mickey out of women (i.e. ourselves)'.[19] The tautology of 'true confessions' and the oxymoron of 'new clichés', signal the artfulness with which these raps, songs, monologues and sketches have been constructed. Parody of a wide range of ostensively female experience is lightly turned to a political tool. And the variety of voices, from 'Mae West' and 'Phylis Marlowe' to the more local Mrs Abernethy at the Manse, shows Lochhead appropriating a whole library of women's magazine attitudes for her purposes. But it is not just the situations which women find themselves in that are made fun of. The stylistic cross-dressing in which parodic reference is made to narrative by Hammet, and songs by, for instance, Shirley Bassey ('Phyllis Marlowe: Only Diamonds Are Forever', *TC*, pp. 16–19) and Frank Sinatra ('Gentlemen Prefer Blondes', *TC*, pp. 52–3), deploys forms of popular entertainment from the '50s that would have been familiar turns at the Working Men's Club or the local Free and Easy. (*The Big Picture*, an unpublished play produced at Dundee Repertory Theatre in 1988, reflects extensively on the seductive risks of '50s pop culture.) The new – female – context for these versions still insists on their popularity, but also asserts a woman's right to reply by ironising what balladeer or crooner have to say.

Nor is she afraid to put herself into the picture. 'Liz Lochhead's Lady Writer Talkin' Blues (*Rap*)' satirises the cliché that writers plunder their lives for their art:

> He said Mah Work was a load a' drivel
> I called it detail, he called it trivial
> Tappin' out them poems in mah tacky room
> About mah terrible cramps and mah
> Moon Trawled Womb –
> Women's trouble?
> Self Pity. (*TC*, p. 38)

Stereotypical 'male' judgements about 'women's writing' are mocked, but at the same time they are legitimated since the rap is about precisely the kind of therapeutic indulgence that parades personal problems in poetic form. Yet the stylised language, and the comic posturing, distance the author from the text and the experience represented by it. The use of her own name in the title may invite a confessional relationship with the spectator but the style of the verse steers the critic firmly away from a biographical approach. Under scrutiny here are stock responses to romantic rejection, and stock ways of articulating disappointment. Misunderstanding between partners is presented as misunderstanding the processes of creative writing. The rap is a free-standing and self-referential parody; it may also be viewed as a satirical gloss on the play about female creativity which Lochhead had recently been working on, *Blood and Ice*.[20]

Some targets of 'True Confessions' are more serious than others. 'Page Three Dollies' (*Rap*, *TC*, pp. 40–1) airs one of the most polemical issues in feminist debate, pornography. Here Lochhead is presenting attitudes to the 'soft porn' of the tabloid press. The refrain 'they're laughing all the way to the bank' leaves the spectator in no doubt about what to think about who is the more exploited. The vulgar tongue assaults the ear ('we're more rosy aureole/than perked up clit'), as the ideas assault the imagination ('And if you keep my pic in mind/As you go through the motions'), brandishing in public what is more comfortably kept private. This ability to throw out a disturbing 'turn' is maintained by the collected songs of the pantomime-revue *Same Difference* (1984), where 'Sins of the Fathers' (*TC*, pp. 100–1), about child abuse, introduces a chilling tone. The snippets of nursery rhyme lend the song a superficially light air. They emphasise the abused child's inability to mature, suggest a manner in which the father might approach his child, and tease the listener by withholding rhymes which must be socially and psychologically suppressed.

> Shocking shocking shocking
> A mouse ran up my stocking
> The higher up the mountain
> The greener grows the grass
> The higher up that mousie climbs
> The nearer to my –
> Ask no questions, tell no lies,
> Keep your mouth shut
> Catch no flies.

The veering shift of rhythm in the last three lines quoted suggests the disturbed and enforced shying away from what happens. The consequences are left for the refrain (subtly changed each time) to tell, in dialogue with the subjectivity of the verses.

> And the sins of the fathers
> Will visit the children
> Nightly in their beds
> and there's grown-up mothers
> Who are still little children
> In the darkness of their heads.

Anticipating here the representation of Queen Elizabeth's nightmare in scene 5 of *Mary Queen of Scots Got Her Head Chopped Off*, we are reminded that the sins of the fathers are manifold.[21]

'New Clichés', a short but impressive 'rag bag' (*TC*, p. 111), closes the volume of performance pieces. 'Postcard Us When The Wean Says Bananas' ('The Greeting Card Song', *TC*, pp. 132–3), a rhyming romp through the greetings card rack, laughs at the bizarre collection of 'personal' messages, but more seriously reminds us how commerce generates clichés that rob us of expression while promising to provide it.

> Seasons Greetings, Aw the Best
> Good Luck on Your Driving Test
> Blank for Your Message, Glad to Be Gay
> Have a swell St Swithin's Day, . . .

Its observant social satire picks up a sensitivity to local idiom that has been manifest in Lochhead's work since the first time she looked at a culture from the outside in 'Letter From New England'.[22] The carefully-placed last 'rap' of the book, 'Men Talk' (*TC*, pp. 134–5) toys with the proliferation of terms that denote the ways in which women speak ('rabbit', 'tattle', 'titter', 'prattle' . . .), while men, of course, just 'talk' (and need 'a good listener'). This seals an ironic judgement on the collection as a whole. It is hardly surprising that responses to this collection vary according to gender, and that, as Lochhead notes, '*some* men (not *our* Real Pals)' felt 'a bit got at' by it (*TC*, p. 2). Male discomfiture arises from the fact that far from intruding on an exclusively female domain, men – the Adam Smiths – are made to see their own part in the construction of female roles.[23]

Since 1982 Lochhead has written at least one new script every year, and since 1985 work for performance has claimed most of her energy. *Blood and Ice* (1982), about Mary Shelley and her vexed relationship with the imagination is the first major piece for the stage. Its gothic style and dream reality anticipate the adaptation of *Dracula* (1985), and the screenplay *Latin For A Dark Room* (1994). The rhymed translation into Scots of *Tartuffe*[24] in 1985 initiated accomplished dramatic writing in Scots that was quickly followed by *Mary Queen of Scots Got Her Head Chopped Off* (1987) which offers a remarkable blend of realism and romance. More straightforward realism is afforded by the television play *Sweet Nothings* (1984) and the radio play *Fancy You Minding That* (1986). The two-hander *Quelques Fleurs* with its origins in the 'Verena' revue monologues (published in *True Confessions and New Clichés*, and *Bagpipe Muzak*) enjoys a protean existence as a play both for stage and radio requiring minimal adaptation for either medium.

She has also recast texts from the literary canon for modern audiences: her version of The York Mystery Cycle was staged at the York Theatre Royal in 1992 (again in 1996), and her adaptation of *The Tempest* for children, *The Magic Island*, was produced at London's Unicorn Theatre in 1993 before an extensive Scottish tour by TAG brought the play as far as the real islands Orkney, Islay and Skye in 1995. Her linguistic strategy in adapting both of these pieces is to allow the language of the original to be heard alongside and through domestic and contemporary idiom. Variegated diction couples, in both pieces, with a bold theatrical style inspired by pantomime, to create multi-layered dramas which can be understood differentially by different audience members. In Lochhead's mystery cycle, Mrs Noah, conceived as one of the most defiant female characters to leap from sacred drama to the medieval profane, retains the comedy of stubborn stereotype:

> MRS NOAH CLAPS HER HANDS OVER HER EARS AND BEGINS
> MUTTERING UNDER HER BREATH HOW IF EVER WOMAN HAD HELL TO
> PUT UP WITH HERE ON EARTH MORNING NOON AND NIGHT DAY IN DAY
> OUT . . . AS THE WATER RISES AND NOAH EXPLAINS TO HER DEAF EARS,
> YET AGAIN,
> THE OBVIOUS TRUTH.[25]

Yet her grief, after the flood, is not trivial. In Lochhead's version as in the original, she speaks for a lost community. Her last words are 'Noah where are now all our kin/And t'company we knew before?'. Noah's response: 'Dame, all are drowned! Hush thy din./'T was the wages of their sin full sore'.[26] Is Mrs Noah a justly and comically chastened shrew, or does the male assertion of individual privilege against a more generous female concern represent polarised gender differences in attitude towards unquestionable Authority? With God on one side and natural justice on the other, the rhyming divergence of Mrs Noah's 'kin' with Noah's 'din' succinctly and ironically suggests an evolution of social values after the deluge.

In *The Magic Island* Lochhead alters the narrative frame of Shakespeare's world purged by water to suit her young audience, but keeps the grown-ups happy with teasing comic intertextual references to popular culture. Prospero was the magician at the Empire Theatre before his wicked managerial brother sold him out for shares in cinema. With Empire fortunes swindled, Prospero the Entertainer sails with the Titanic, to find himself and Miranda washed up on the set of Desert Island Discs complete with gramophone, Bible and Shakespeare. Paradoxically it is here that we really meet the ideology of a brave new world. Miranda, speaking directly to the audience about the relationship between her Dad and Caliban, says:

> See, I was only fourteen and to be fair to my dad, he honestly didn't think there was anything wrong with trying to civilise old Caliban.
>
> Ask your Mums and Dads, wasn't there a time when you went to the cinema, and the Indians were the baddies, the cowboys were the goodies, no question.[27]

But if this world is post-colonial, it is also pre-pubescent and Ferdinand emerges as Miranda's best female friend Ferdanelle. While both plot and dialogue make some concessions to the audience of under-twelves and the politics they will inherit, Lochhead refuses to patronise them by glossing some of the most famous lines from *The Tempest*. She therefore retains elements of difficult verse such as Ariel's song and Prospero's late arias ('*We* are such stuff as dreams are made of!' declares the professional performer[28]). Dangerous nostalgia for the world which Shakespeare's Prospero governs is channelled into a celebration of theatre magic, made here infinitely more intoxicating than wicked Antonio's new-fangled cinema. The script calls for skilled physical performers, musicians, acrobats, and real magicians. *The Magic Island* negotiates difficult political territory, while exciting sheer pleasure in performance.

The publication in 1989 of two plays, *Mary Queen Of Scots Got Her Head Chopped Off* and *Dracula*, represents Lochhead's dual interest in womanhood and nationhood. 'To be is to be perceived', but by whom? The history of Mary Stuart has been as manipulated as the Queen herself in the service of other agendas, Schiller's *Maria Stuart* (1800), for example, used the story about two queens on one island to plead for German unification. Lochhead's deployment of the same material was written in and about 'Thatcherland', to present a politically divided Britain and a people that has inherited divisive cultural values. It is a play with history rather than a history play, for its focus is on the present, marked by the gleeful anachronisms of stage properties, and borne out by the distinguishing models of characterisation for the two queens. Elizabeth was inspired by the 'Thatcher monster',[29] the references are contemporary and were picked up by most newspaper reviews. By contrast, the characterisation of Queen Mary is folkloristic, drawing on legends of the mermaid as well as Scottish nostalgias about the young French monarch. References in the stage directions to Mary's long and beautiful hair abound; this, together with the mirror (represented metaphorically by Mary's quest for approval from her male court and her English cousin), comprise the iconography of the mermaid, whose fabled beauty tempts men to their destruction. 'Beware of women, the charms o' their hair – beware for adultery begins wi' the eyes', Knox warns Bothwell. 'Burn the hoor!' the assembly chants, after Mary has slept with Bothwell (*MQ and D*, p. 48, p. 60).

The inclusion of a play-within-the-play, the 'Masque of Salome' during which Riccio is murdered, also blends ancient and modern (*MQ and D*, pp. 52–6). A common device on the Renaissance stage, one of the best remembered is 'Pyramus and Thisbe' from Lochhead's favourite Shakespeare play, *A Midsummer Nights' Dream*. But Lochhead's subject would have been censored by the 1559 legislation against stage representation of religious matter which was invoked in 1892 to ban Wilde's *Salome*. Within Lochhead's play, the masque slurs Mary as a 'fatal dame', while intertextually recalling Shakespeare's supposed reference to her bewitching powers in the *Dream* as 'a mermaid on a dolphin's back'.[30] Technically bold, in narrative as in staging, the story of the power struggle between the two women opens with a parade of circus animals, ringmastered by La Corbie the sardonic choric crow, and it closes with 1950s tenement children playing 'Mary Queen of Scots Got Her Head Chopped Off'. They represent Lochhead's own generation. La Corbie introduces the audience to the action, setting the scene in a 'Scotland' which is 'a peatbog', 'Princes Street or Paddy's Merkit' (*MQ and D*, p. 11), a composite of times and places found only in the imagination. The location referred to by the children within the rhyme of their closing game is '*Glesca* Green' (*MQ and D*, p. 63) again taking the action away from the seat of power in Edinburgh or London and locating it in the popular imagination.

Elizabeth and Mary each contain female types that Lochhead has treated previously. Posturing as queenly versions of 'Harridan', 'Spinster' and 'Bawd', each monarch seems unable to eschew stereotype. Their roles are further fragmented by the multiple identities which each adopts. Elizabeth also plays Bessie, Mary's maid, and Leezie a 'tarty' beggar lass, while Mary plays Marian, Elizabeth's gentlewoman, and Mairn, Leezie's friend. Constantly paired, up and down the social scale, these women complement and complete each other. Masculine and feminine, Protestant and Catholic, repressed and oppressed, adult and child, English and Scottish, virgin and whore, imprisoned and free, the binaries of the argument multiply, swop, and converge. Audience perspective is kaleidoscoped and surprised, although here as in every epic, we know what happens next. And neither side wins. The expectation of the emergence of what Derrida would term a 'violent hierarchy', in which one set of qualities is prized above the other, is frustrated.

Judgement is withheld. It is a play about power, prejudice and bigotry which is not itself partisan or jingoistic. In narrative terms, one important means of achieving this even-handedness is the displaced conclusion in which adult manoeuvres become children's games. Far from diminishing their seriousness, this emphasises the deep-rooted nature of cultural conditioning. The last scene is called 'Jock Thamson's Bairns', pointing the way forward to Lochhead's fiercer satire on the totems of Scottish identity, *Jock Tamson's Bairns*, which she scripted with Communicado to open Glasgow's year as 'Culture Capital of Europe' on Burns' Night in 1990. Another technique by which balance is maintained between the poles of debate is the paradoxical sisterhood that is struck between the fighting cousin queens. Despite themselves, they share the difficulty of maintaining power over men. England, represented by a woman, is therefore unusually self-conscious about appearances: 'I said, Leicester, if I married you and we lay down together as King and Queen, then we should wake as plain Mister and Mistress Dudley. The Nation would not have it' (*MQ and D*, p. 24). Elizabeth engineers her whole political strategy out of this insight (a match for the confusions of Mrs Thatcher's attempts to be perceived as both distinct from and at one with the people, epitomised by her pronouncement 'we are a grandmother'). Mary, or Scotland, learns too late. Elizabeth cunningly selects her cousin's husband and Knox, Mary's Protestant Fury, voices the complaint,

> For by the same act o' takkin' a man tae her bed, she makks a king tae a people.
> We, the people, should choose a husband fur a lassie raither than a silly wee furrin lassie should choose a king for a hale people. (*MQ and D*, p. 34))

Mary's male heir succeeded to the English throne, and England became, in Lochhead's terms, 'nonchalant' about her appearance, while Scotland played increasingly to the view from Westminster. The fragmentation of the queens' experience into a variety of roles ascribed to them by the patriarchies which they ostensibly control links the women so that gender politics metaphorically override those of race or religion. Once the audience has seen their alter egos it is impossible to see either monarch without simultaneously seeing the shadows of her other selves. This is a theatrical technique which guarantees and authenticates for the audience Lochhead's assertion that projected identity is conditioned by the gender and the nationality of the beholder. Further confirmation comes from the reception of the play in England. When Communicado toured south, after winning a 'Fringe First' at the Edinburgh Festival in 1987 (the quatercentenary of Mary's execution), and when the Manchester Contact Theatre mounted a new production in 1991, press complaints were loud that the play was incomprehensible because of the Scots dialogue.

Bram Stoker's *Dracula* (1898) typifies various male *fin-de-siècle* anxieties about sex and the 'new woman'; the pure, innocent, childish Lucy turns into a grotesque vamp and must be staked through the heart for men, women and children to sleep easily once more. The fantasy is designed to titillate male desire, and the narrative upholds a tested but victorious Christian patriarchy. Lochhead's adaptation of the novel revises the vampire legend for our own, more secular, and more knowing, *fin-de-siècle* that nevertheless craves the exotic, the spectacular, and the sensational. The popular dimension of the fable was captured by proliferating press photographs of the playwright shot in the Glasgow Necropolis at the time of the premier. But recognising contemporary gothic taste, the play's commentary upon it teases us with indulgence. Lochhead's use of Stoker's novel as a source of stage directions is particularly manipulative. Stoker's fantasy of Jonathan Harker's visitation by the vampire brides (scene 9) embedded in her own directions, is one example: '*a deliberate voluptuousness which is both thrilling and repulsive . . . she arches her neck . . . licks her lips . . . Lower and lower goes the head . . . ' Quote, unquote . . . '* (*MQ and D*, p. 100). Her citation from the novel at the moment of the Undead Lucy's apparition to Seward clearly signals her revisionary purpose as the tone of her directions, '*lovely and terrifying and etherial*' juxtaposes with the equal but opposite prejudice of Stoker's '*her eyes blaze with unholy light and her face becomes wreathed in a voluptuous smile*' (*MQ and D*, p. 134).

Her most radical revision of the novel is to balance the valorisation of male and female sexual desire. Count Dracula's disruption of patriarchal control is represented as a liberating force for the expression of female sexuality. The men who battle against him do not acquire the heroic status that is bestowed on them by the novel; his female 'victims' are transfigured into sexual maturity, distorted more by the signs of oppression (corsets, wedding dresses) than by the vampire signature at their throats. From the beginning of the play the audience is made aware of how women are trained to perform to the male gaze. Lucy, in her underwear, swings in the garden on Midsummer morning '*her armful of frou-frou petticoats, mirror in her hand, singing*'. Her first words are: 'Who shall I marry?'; her first action: '*she kisses her own lovely reflection in the mirror*', in love with an image that she believes men will find attractive.

> The day they put me in stays and made me wear my hair up I swore blind if I was to be pinched and skewered then I was to have the thinnest thinnest waist and the highest highest hair,

she continues (*MQ and D*, p. 73). The Garden is corrupted at the outset by the invisible but omnipresent sense of the male spectator. Mina, in Lochhead's version Lucy's big sister, whose entrance is described by a pun across semiotic codes as '*Proper English rose, a peach, eating one*' (*MQ and D*, p. 73) is preparing for the arrival of her fiancé Jonathon Harker. 'Behold the bridegroom cometh!' (*MQ and D*, p. 75) Lucy teases, her satirical allusion to the 'Song of Solomon' (one of Lochhead's favourites)[31] confirming the elevated status of men in this society, while her actions ('*a pantomime of tizz . . . parodying* Lady's Home Companion') (*MQ and D*, p. 75) skirmish with the propriety Mina seeks to maintain despite her obvious appetite for forbidden fruit.

The decision to emphasise sisterhood, and to drop the class issue which plays in the novel where Mina is Lucy's unmonied friend, concentrates attention on feminist politics. As the ironically lovely garden fades into scene two, '*lights change and suddenly it's grim nurses with fouled laundry in the asylum*' (*MQ and D*, p. 75), the unbalanced, constrained, and disturbing nature of the girls' microcosm is explicated by juxtaposition. Renfield's madness is expressed verbally by his vatic confusion of nursery rhymes, Shakespeare, and sex. Like the sisters, he is infantilised by a threatened male hegemony. Obsessively he eats flies and is sedated with opiate, providing further comment on the treatment of women, a link made even more explicit by the use of a split stage and composite action in scene 10 where Renfield is straitjacketed as Mina is pinned into her wedding dress. Renfield's fate also parallels Lucy's developing anorexia and her tormented wish to please her master, 'exercise like the lady doctor in the *Lady's Home Companion* recommends. Swedish callisthenics!' (*MQ and D*, p. 105). These neurotic symptoms are timed to Dracula's arrival in England, her menstruation, and Seward's return. She is briefly pacified by the false promise extracted from her fiancé that he will 'sneak back in and kiss' her once she has fallen asleep (*MQ and D*, p. 112). Satisfaction of her desire is fatally deferred, Seward is diminished by his feeble lie, and Dracula is invited in. His shape-changing manifestations, from the bestial to the aristocratic, mercifully destroy the fixtures of *Home Companion* life. Dracula has no image. He is the invisible, omnipresent eye, which can be caught by no 'Kodak' (*MQ and D*, p. 91), and reflected by no mirror (*MQ and D*, p. 98); Lucy is released by her assimilation with this vantage point. Dracula himself figures as an ironic Transcendental Phallus that we shall see again in Lochhead's work, particularly in *Latin for a Dark Room*.

This twenty-three minute screenplay, shown first at the Edinburgh Film Festival in 1994, is a gothic fantasy of *fin-de-siècle* intrigue set in Edinburgh's Camera Obscura. The story is about Mrs Maria McKillop, an optician who has developed her interest in vision into a 'private scientific folly', the Camera Obscura. She falls in love with Mr William Archer, an English engraver who is developing the art of photography.[32] Passion grows, and she decides to murder her husband. But after William has entrusted her with the poison, she discovers that he pays prostitutes to pose for porn shots not unlike a photograph which he had taken of herself. She poisons her lover instead of her husband, but the final scene in which Mr McKillop offers his wife a poke of green grapes leaves us guessing about her fate at his hands. The story is deceptively simple. It is a Bataillesque fantasia, a story of the eye, in which Maria's erotic 'I' acquires definition through a semiotic playfulness, riddled with Freudian gags and Hitchcockian clues. As one optician's chart which hangs in her surgery states

IN PRO
SE BUT
BY MEIN
POE
TRY

the telling of the tale is a form of poetry.

Poetic narration begins with the puns concealed in the title, and as the action unfolds its conceits are teased out. The Latin for 'a dark room' is *camera obscura*, a term which was also used in the nineteenth century to refer to the eye, and later – in shortened form – to denote the instrument by which the film itself is made. The action is set in a variety of *camerae obscurae*, of which the dark room of the imagination, where escapist and erotic fantasy have free play, is most significant. The film starts with the leisurely precision of Maria McKillop's voice explaining over a black screen and the title credits,

> As your eyes become accustomed to the lack of light, as the rods and cones of the retina adjust, you will see from a new angle the architectural marvels of this our capital city, the Athens of the North.

Her face appears on the screen, and we are at a show inside the Camera Obscura in Edinburgh, the dark room of the cinema turns into a dark room in the fiction presented. Plato's cave myth and the Pauline revision of it are inevitably evoked by the 'camera' technique of refracting images, and in this story they are used profanely to signal the altered perception that follows once blinding love is killed by revelation of duplicity. Maria discovers her lover's dealings with prostitutes during an Obscura show when she chances on him paying a whore in a graveyard. Her opening exposition continues, with the provenance of her technology,

> The ancient Greeks and the Romans were known to have employed it. One single pinhole of light in a dark room, and they could throw on to a wall *projectarae* ... moving images of bloody deeds and dramas enacted outside, for them to view obliquely inside.

Her account becomes a self-reflexive allegory about the relationship between this film and the workings of the erotic imagination. Latent within it is reference to the occasional Ancient Greek practice of representing the phallus tipped with an eye, which like the light waves she controls, would go on a dark journey 'passing through the locked treasure room of the pinhole'. She explains, 'artists used it as a drawing aid, although its exquisite exactness far surpassed the utmost skill of any painter to express'. Her optician's pride in precision will be challenged when she finds herself the artist's model, captured on film, and apparently valued as a whore. But the traditionally gendered relationship between artist and model is subverted by the narrative voice of the film itself. The camera overtly represents the tunnels of her lens system as a vagina, an unseen but seeing eye. Or are we taken inside a kind of transcendental phallus, at its tip the panoramic views of the capital and its secrets? This ambiguity renders the camera through which the audience sees like Archer's lens in that it adulterates truth, representing a costume drama extravaganza, but also like Maria's lens, for it never lies.

The poised androgeneity of the medium is confirmed when images of Edinburgh are thrown onto the embracing couple, as their uniting bodies mask the screen of the Camera Obscura. Issues of gender stereotyping, and the Scots/English dichotomy, inform the drama from a comfortable distance. Maria comments that her husband dislikes her profession, while William does not understand her Scots response to his gift of an engraving called 'Camera Obscura' in which togaed figures watch through the lens how a woman castrates a man. 'A penny geggy, a rae ri' sha',' she explains, 'I'll make a spectacle of myself'. Her vision may be clear, but her expression is opaque to her English lover who eventually falls victim to her unfathomable action. William's sight is also good, so that he does not need the spectacles which she makes for him of clear glass, but he fails to read the writing on the wall of her surgery. Another test chart reads 'LORD ASKED/ OUR NAME/TO BE RIT/INN THE/BOOK AS/WAS DUN/BY MR. W.', uncannily predicting not just the pharmacist's request for his signature when he buys the poison. The dream logic of the film trusts only the audience to distinguish between seeing and understanding. The English man is captivated by the power of artifice, he makes graven images and is uncaring of how they may appear to the sensitive viewer; the Scots woman makes glasses, correcting nature's deficiency. She makes eyes for him, but is compromised by making eyes at him, while the ambiguity of his behaviour suggests to the audience that she may be fatally over-sensitive to the image he makes of her. In that photograph she is both madonna and whore, holding the white lilies of annunciation and death, sporting Virgin blue with his top hat at a rakish angle. Recalled here is one of Lochhead's earliest poems, 'Object':

> In whose likeness
> do you reassemble me?
>   . . .
> But you, love,
> set me down in black and white exactly.
> I am at once
> reduced and made more of.[33]

Is William's photograph really so unfaithful to her? The last picture of him is cast by Maria's vengeful imagination, internalising the photographer's dark room. He is posed naked in black and white, layed out in his coffin; coppers hide his eyes and his phallus is blindfolded by the coloured blue top hat. But when Mr McKillop who, like the audience has been an unheeded spectator, intrudes on the final scene, Maria's crunch on his grape, heard against a black screen, is the last word.

This is a film about passion and perception which is generous to the audience, at once empowering and teasing. Its exotically textured semiotics represent a contemporary gothic taste. The full story is wittily elusive, allowing escapades of what Maria McKillop (referring to her Camera Obscura, but echoing our 'Lady Writer') calls 'trivial amusement' in her 'enchanted garden'. These play in the popular imagination also at the level of casting. Lochhead selected one of her favourite actors, Siobhan Redmond, as Maria, while William Archer is played by Neil Pearson. Both are well-known television actors from a high-brow BBC cop soap *Between the Lines* in which they are work partners. The twentieth-century ghosts of their *fin-de-siècle* characters add a further dimension of postmodernity to *Latin for a Dark Room*. Affirmation, albeit disappointingly crude, that the screenplay taps in to contemporary delight in polysemous puns is given by its BBC billing, on 4 January 1995, as one of three 'Tartan Shorts' (instancing precisely the labelling and marginalisation of Scottish identity to which Lochhead objects), while the inadequate review in *The Scotsman* commented that 'many viewers would have been most tickled to find Siobhan Redmond and Neil Pearson from *Between the Lines* actually between the sheets'.[34] Joe Aherne's direction contributes to the complex successes of the film. Familiar actions are made strange by the use of oblique perspectives, and the camera is nosey, even flirtatious, lingering over slowly-paced action. The narrative technique toys with audience perception, matching the thematic focus of the script. Together, script, direction, and performance, conspire to make this most transparent of media into an opaque reflector of the viewer's imagination.

The indeterminacy of action represented here leaves an open end. As long as Lochhead celebrates that 'ink is ink'[35] her own career is likewise open-ended:

> To tell the stories was her work.
>
> . . .
>
> Night in
> she'd have us waiting held
> breath, for the ending we knew by heart.[36]

And *pace* her typically feminine experience of a divided self which led her to suggest that her poems and performance work are 'written by two different people',[37] her explorations of a complex but constant range of images, mental states, and stories in the range of stylistic vocabulary at her command, offer us a diverse corpus of remarkable organic integrity.

Notes

1. Lochhead, 'Morning After', *Dreaming Frankenstein and Collected Poems* (Polygon, Edinburgh, 1984).
2. Liz Lochhead, interviewed by John Cunningham, *The Guardian*, 8 February 1990.
3. Adam Smith, *The Theory of Moral Sentiments*, ed. D. D. Raphael and A. L. Macfie (1759; Clarendon Press, Oxford, 1976), pp. 110, 112.
4. Smith, *Theory*, p. 115.
5. Liz Lochhead, 'The Other Woman', *The Grimm Sisters* (1981); *Collected Poems*, pp. 92–3.
6. Liz Lochhead, 'Almost Miss Scotland', ['AMS'] *Bagpipe Muzak* (Penguin, Harmondsworth, 1991), p. 5
7. 'Liz Lochhead: Speaking in her own Voice', by Alison Smith, in *Liz Lochhead's Voices*, ed. Robert Crawford and Anne Varty (Edinburgh University Press, Edinburgh, 1993), p. 4.
8. Liz Lochhead, 'Revelation', *Collected Poems*, p. 124.
9. Liz Lochhead, 'The Ariadne Version', *The Grimm Sisters*; *Collected Poems*, p. 96.
10. 'Mirror's Song', *Collected Poems*, pp. 67–8.
11. 'Harridan', *Collected Poems*, pp. 74–5.
12. 'Spinster', *Collected Poems*, p. 75.
13. 'Bawd', *Collected Poems*, p. 76.
14. 'What the Pool Said, on Midsummer's Day', *Collected Poems*, pp. 8–9.
15. 'A Giveaway', *Dreaming Frankenstein*, *Collected Poems*, p. 43.
16. Liz Lochhead interview, 'Hearing Voices: Monologues and Revues', by Jackie Clune, in *Liz Lochhead's Voices*, p. 85.

17. Liz Lochhead interviewed by Emily Todd, in *Verse*, 8.3/9.1 (Winter/Spring 1992) 87.
18. Lochhead interview, *Verse*, 86.
19. Liz Lochhead, *True Confessions & New Clichés* (Polygon, Edinburgh, 1985), p. 2. Henceforth *TC*.
20. For discussion of this play see Elaine Aston, *An Introduction To Feminism & Theatre* (Routledge, London, 1995), 143–7; Jan McDonald and Jennifer Harvie, 'Putting New Twists To Old Stories: Feminism and Lochhead's Drama', *Liz Lochhead's Voices*, pp. 124–47; Anne Varty, 'Scripts and Performances', *ibid.*, 148–69.
21. Liz Lochhead, *Mary Queen of Scots Got Her Head Chopped Off and Dracula*, (Penguin, Harmondsworth, 1989). Further references in the text will be given to *MQ and D*.
22. *Collected Poems*, pp. 142–5.
23. The feminist and all-female platform of Lochhead's early revues has given way during the mid-1990s to her collaboration with the Dundee musician Michael Marra in the double bill 'In Flagrant Delicht' (for example, Glasgow Tron Theatre, August 1995; Glasgow Keeble Palace, June 1996). Her performance material is still drawn from *True Confessions*, its irony moderated by the presence of her male colleague.
24. Liz Lochhead, *Tartuffe* (Polygon, Edinburgh, 1985). Further references are to *T*. For discussion of this play see Randall Stevenson, 'Re-enter Houghmagandie: Language as Performance in Liz Lochhead's *Tartuffe*', in *Liz Lochhead's Voices*, pp. 109–23.
25. Lochhead, *York Mystery Cycle*, unpublished typescript, p. 22.
26. *York Cycle*, p. 26.
27. Lochhead, *The Magic Island*, unpublished typescript, p. 21.
28. *Magic Island*, p. 64.
29. Liz Lochhead, *Time Out*, 16–23 September 1987.
30. Oberon speaks these words. Shakespeare, *A Midsummer Night's Dream*, ed. Harold F. Brooks, Arden Edition (Routledge, London, 1979), II. i. 150–4.
31. 'Song of Solomon', *Grimm Sisters*; *Collected Poems*, 86–7.
32. All quotations are taken from the BBC 2 screening of the film on 4 January 1995.
33. 'Object', *Islands* (1978); *Collected Poems*, pp. 155–7.
34. *The Scotsman Magazine*, 5 January 1995.
35. Liz Lochhead interviewed by Peggy Reynolds, BBC Radio 4, Kaleidoscope, 30 May 1992.
36. Liz Lochhead, 'Storyteller', *Grimm Sisters*; *Collected Poems*, p. 70.
37. Liz Lochhead, *Verse*, Interview, 86.

43

Women's Writing in Scottish Gaelic Since 1750

Meg Bateman

Introduction

For writers of a minority language, culture is of greater significance than gender. In the case of Gaelic, 'writer' itself is a misnomer for a great many of its producers of words. 'Writer' brings with it a misleading set of expectations which do not apply to 'oracy' – expectations perhaps of originality in content and form and certainly of distinctiveness in voice. Cultural criticism in general is geared to plotting progress as a series of movements in those fields. But originality has to be thought of differently in an oral culture where the transmission of verbal pieces depends utterly on their acceptance by the group. Nowadays, as it is mostly in printed form that we know this originally orally transmitted work, it is imperative that we recognise its oral origins and its essential difference from work conceived for and transmitted in writing. Almost by definition, oral work is not individualistic. It uses formulae, fugitive passages, runs, stock characters and the like, and the very process of oral transmission subverts our notions of authorship. Possibly it is not a matter of forgetting, but of non-ownership, that accounts for the vast majority of this work being anonymous. The work is generally heavily conventionalised in both form and content; voice remains generically rather than personally determined, and attitudes are group-generated. The undeniable identity of individual pieces is primarily aural, afforded by rhythm (even in prose), rhyme and tune, and the occasional unusual image.

Only in the last few decades have the practice and the consumption of writing produced the sort of individualism in some Gaelic authors that makes reasonable comparison with other written literatures. Writing skills in Gaelic among the ordinary people were connected with the publication of the Bible in Scottish Gaelic, made widely available after 1807. It is significant that the work of Màiri Mhòr (1821–98), though belonging to the latter half of the nineteenth century, was still produced without recourse to writing – her songs in many ways being an extension of the 18,000 lines of traditional poetry she knew by heart. From the formal point of view, she composed new words to old tunes, often using existing rhyme schemes. She maintains however that it was the *personal* matter of her humiliation in court that was the initial impetus to her composing. The poetry itself is a *public* service; she speaks out for her people on such matters as the lost homeland, Clearance and Land Law Reform. Viewed on the page without the tunes, without the social context, without the political urgency, her verse is often said to lack intensity. Surely it is folly to expect the same intensity from a song that was designed to be sung and appreciated in a group, with the mood maintained and indulged over forty-odd quatrains, that might be expected from a shorter lyric, designed to be read several times in private. Similarly it is folly to expect a sustained personal view in this sort of work; a personal view is used only in so far as it is representative of the group as a whole. In Gaelic, idiosyncrasy is a late twentieth-century development among a few women writers (it appears a little earlier among the men) and it continues to be absent in the work of a good many others. Its absence is noteworthy in the autobiographies from the 1980s and 1990s, for an autobiography whose principal focus is not the individual, sounds, in established literary theory, like a contradiction – another indication that a literary culture needs to be judged on its own terms.

The existence of a few licentious poems of female authorship in the courtly love tradition of the sixteenth century, and the frank tone of women's work in the waulking songs of the seventeenth and eighteenth centuries have raised hopes of finding a continuing unsuppressed tradition of women's work in Gaelic. To further this hope, women in the seventeenth and eighteenth centuries composed songs about clan politics, and, in the nineteenth century, it was Màiri Mhòr who was the most voluble of the poets in campaigning for her people. Such sexual and political forthrightness from women was not seen again in published form until the 1980s, doubtless the result of the university system and female consciousness-raising in Europe and America as a whole. The enormous social upheaval in the intervening period can probably be held responsible for the tameness of the intervening writing. Clearance and emigration, the change from a subsistence to a capitalist economy, new lifestyles in the industrialised parts of Scotland and elsewhere were all probably too disorientating to admit mould-breaking creativity.

Many apologists for women's writing point to the lack of models for more than a limited set of accepted female genres; this lack is much more acute in a minority culture where the business of the major institutions (with the exception of the churches) is conducted through another language. The post-1872 education system rendered most Gaelic speakers incapable of writing in their mother-tongue. The literature of this period is mostly nostalgic (to comfort emigrant Gaels with evocations of the lost homeland), or religious (positing an exchange of the uncertainties of this life for the rewards of the next). The same social responsibility is exhibited in women's writing in Gaelic up to the present time – story-books for children, text books, autobiography (with its instructive purpose to record a passing way of life) and even the novels with their high moral tone. In the collections of oral tradition, women have shown a great commitment to the language in being transmitters of tales, Fenian lays, songs, proverbs and charms, but this too was a service to the community rather than to the Muse. The exploration of the individual psyche may well be the subject of most literature in English of the period, but it is a matter of less urgency when the whole of a community is in a state of change, and, perhaps more importantly, when the mores of that close-knit community did not foster individualism. The culture as a whole, accustomed to a corpus of formalised work where the individual's emotions are subsumed by convention, finds something appalling (I think to this day) in the display of individualised angst.

Traditional Song Poetry

The fascination of traditional song poetry lies in the counterpoint between the dignity of expressing the personal in conventional terms and the freshness conveyed by the occasional inclusion of some telling detail. Most exponents of the kind are known for only one or two songs. Rather than poetry being the outpourings of uniquely gifted individuals, it appears that the tradition equipped its participants with the tools to create songs when the occasion demanded, typically at times of bereavement. This point is well illustrated by a song from 1953, made up of traditional elements, in which the author explains she is not a poet but that it is the acuteness of her nostalgia for Cape Breton which has led her to start composing (BAN 73, vv. 3 and 7).[1] The importance of song in Gaelic society explains both its appropriateness as commemoration of the dead and the ease with which apparent novices were able to compose orally, long and metrically complex poems.

Many characteristics of the tradition can be illustrated from the song, 'Ailein Duinn, shiùbhlainn leat' (CC vol. 1, 1), the only song we know of by Anna Chaimbeul of Scalpay, composed in 1768 in response to her lover's drowning on his way to their wedding. The work is conventional in both content and diction; with the exception of the reference to an English-language schooling, it could belong anywhere in the tradition of women's laments over the preceding two centuries. Yet the whole is intensely visualised and the conventional is made personal by the inclusion of specific detail – the names of ports, their meeting at school, his gifts of spotted silk. Events are not related in chronological order; rather the progression is from one emotional climax to another: her anxiety over the storm, the elegance of his slim, black vessel sailing to Man, the tenderness of her memory of him, the outrage of the wetness of his shirt and of his body being rent by sea-monsters, her desire to be with him wherever he has been washed up and to drink his blood in defiance of her people, her anxiety that God should reward him, her wish to be dead beside him. The lack of a chronology differentiates this tradition from the ballad; the juxtaposing of different emotions differentiates it from the lyric.

Typical of traditional diction is the frequent use of negative antithesis and under-statement. Incremental repetition (where tension is built up through parallel structures) becomes all the more intense when the words are sung, as each line is repeated, first as the second line of a couplet, and then as the first line of the next couplet. It is not merry-making that is on her mind, but the force of the storm; her bad news is not the small number of her cattle, or their thinness in Springtime, but the wetness of her lover's shirt (this being the first oblique reference to his having drowned); it is not the red wine of Spain she desires but a drink of his blood. The general tendency to understate (as with the quiet reference to the lovers' private conversations and their being on the hills together) allows maximum effect to startling notions like the blood-drinking.

The subject matter of these songs, depicting the speaker in extremis, as well as their diction, gives a distinct unity to the tradition. There are drownings (of a husband, son and brother-in-law between Coll and Tiree, of two brothers in Cape Breton trying to save their herring-net from the ice), laments for absent menfolk (brothers who have emigrated, a son who has left to fight in Spain) and laments for the dead (a brother fatally wounded falling into the hold of an emigrant ship, a daughter, the fourth casualty of five brothers), and there are complaints about disappointments in courtship.

Again and again, emotional states are depicted by their pressures on the body: the hair has grown white and thinned, the breasts have become like an old woman's, the kidneys are wounded, sight and hearing have failed. The most desperate of these signs, often occurring as the climax of a song, is the threat of imminent dementia, expressed physically by the need for some agent (another man or God) to keep the author and her senses united. States of contentment may likewise be evoked in physical terms, with an unabashed delight in the material (e.g. BT, 236, v. 5). The conventional is suddenly rendered actual by specific detail. Very commonly the day of the week on which bad

news was received is noted. Mrs MacFadyen's otherwise conventional praise for the three
drowned members of her family (BT, pp. 26–7) includes these unconventional and specific
details of her husband:

> Mo cheist am beul mun robh 'n fhaitheam.
> 'S an làmh a dhèanadh rud grinn;
> Ni nach fac thu fo d' chomhair
> Thug do mheomhair e nìos . . .
> (My beloved the mouth that was circumspect,
> and the hand that could make a beautiful object;
> anything that you could not see before you
> your imagination could conjure up . . .)

The speaker's account of the disparity between her own estimation of her son-in-law and
that of the rest of the community is also unconventional. In another poem (BL, p. 167) a
conventional description of a brother's attractiveness – slim red lips, regular teeth, round
blue eyes – includes the detail that his face would not look cold on coming home in
the snow:

> Nuair a rachadh tu 'n clachan
> Is a shileadh an sneachda,
> Bhiodh t' aghaidh bhruich mheachair gun fhuachd oirr'.

Another individualising detail is found when (BT, p. 406) the speaker describes a burial
where she finds herself utterly surrounded by Lowlanders.

Despite the general tendency in this tradition to side-step the author's individuality, her
grief functioning as a measure of the value of the lost one, there are occasional glimpses
of self-reflection. A woman proudly remembers her husband's delight in her which was as
great as if she had provided him with a field full of cattle (BT, 25, v. 2); another is proud
of having maintained composure at her brother's deathbed (BT, 406, v. 3). One woman,
despite the shame of pregnancy, advises other girls to follow their love (BAN, 49, v. 6),
and another blames her sex for her inability to board a ship and visit her sorely-missed
brothers in Nova Scotia (GColl, 335, v. 5). Throughout there is an empathy for the
womenfolk attached to the male casualties. Anna Chaimbeul is grateful that the death
of her dead lover's mother will protect her from knowledge of his death (CC, vol. 1, no.
1); another poet considers the plight of the family trying to survive through the winter
without the man who kept everything in order (GColl 364, v. 5).

All this poetry is structured by emotion and not chronology. The circumstances
surrounding a tragedy typically do not emerge till the middle of a poem, and emotional
tack changes, even within a single verse. In a love poem of only six verses (BAN, 49),
for example, the speaker expresses all of the following: shame, indifference, the wish for
absolution and death, and the defiant recommendation that other girls should do the same
as she. Equally typical of the tradition is the understated way her pregnancy is suggested:

> 'S ann Di-Sathuirn' a ghluais mi,
> Chaidh mi sheòladh mu thuath leat . . .
>
> (It was on Saturday that I left,
> I went sailing north with you . . .)

It is clear that this tradition inherited some of the rhetoric of the learned heroic poetry of the preceding centuries. This is evident in the praise of the beloved for his hunting and sea-faring skills, for his generosity, good looks, his presence at table. That tradition also furnished the women poets with certain powerful metaphors (a tree without apples, a man as a salmon), and the strong sense of the visual, especially in the slow-paced descriptions of burials and the special focus given to the shirt as the physical realisation of a woman's encompassing care for her beloved. In the hands of the professional poets these elements had become stale; it is the genius of the longer-lived women's tradition that they are given fresh impetus. In Anna Chaimbeul's lament for her drowned lover, the fine, embroidered shirt, seen in heroic poetry as a sign of a man being cherished by noble women, becomes, in its soaked version, a shocking mockery of her desire to encompass him with her care.

There are two or three poets of the latter half of the nineteenth century who deserve special attention because a considerable amount of their work has survived, in these cases because of publication rather than acceptance into the oral tradition. The nine songs of Lady D'Oyly published in 1875 are a typical product of the Celtic Twilight. They have a sense of not being inhabited by their author. They seem to be assembled from the *topoi* of older songs, with none of the details or change in tone that made that tradition exciting. Literacy lends these songs a regularity of structure and versification which combines with uniformity of mood to risk boredom. Spurious antiquity sits uncomfortably with fashionable nostalgia. The only cheerful song, ironically enough, is addressed to Bonnie Prince Charlie.

Mary MacKellar (1836–90) shows the same tendency to evoke the past rather than engaging with the present. Her poetry never challenges or seeks out uncomfortable truth: rather it prettily clothes set pieces. She compares a fresh-water spring on the shores of Loch Eribol to a humble woman, content to pour out her sweetness unnoticed, wherever she finds herself. The celebration of the role of a subservient woman is doubtless a comfortable one for a disempowered culture and MacKellar also confines evocations of the heroism of its menfolk to pre-Culloden times. MacKellar is impressive in her complete mastery of Gaelic technique – she is able to echo the great seventeenth- and eighteenth-century poets in her descriptions of the chiefs' drinking halls, of nature and sea voyages (of which she had first-hand experience as the wife of a sea-captain). Her bicultural education is evident in her introduction of various dramatic techniques (lighting, the appearance of ghosts, etc.) and a general nineteenth-century taste for worthiness.

It is in Màiri Mhòr nan Òran (1821–98) that we at last find a poet plucky enough to examine her own times and to analyse, however crudely, how and why the Clearances occurred. Far from being made invisible by her sex, Màiri Mhòr is one of the principal icons of Gaelic poetry. This is probably because of her warm-hearted championing of her fellow Highlanders at the time of Clearance and emigration and because of her practical help in rallying support for the land-raiders and those MPs committed to bettering the crofters' lot. She was very prolific (some 9,000 lines were published) and her songs gained a wide currency in the Gaelic music-hall culture of the Lowlands. The circumstances of her coming to poetry at the age of fifty are well known and often mentioned in her songs: she claims that it was the humiliation of being wrongly found guilty by the Inverness Court of stealing some clothing from her employer that 'brought her poetry to life':

'S e na dh'fhulaing mi de thàmailt
A thug mo bhàrdachd beò.
(MM, 61)

She connects her personal experience of humiliation with the humiliation of Clearance experienced by the Highlands as a whole, and articulates her rage with greater forthrightness than any other nineteenth-century Gaelic poet. In other songs she is passionately enthusiastic about, and optimistic for, her people, and this loyalty combines with the memory of her impressively protective stature (seventeen stones of it) to ensure her a place of special affection.

It may then be with a sense of disappointment that we first read her work. We find it unfocused, unstructured, sentimental and full of now obscure references. It goes over the same ground time and again, and as if each song were not long enough, the material is further padded out with clichés and line-fillers. She can also exhibit a crass jingoism, the noble Gaels contrasted with the English, the sole villains of the Clearances. The rhythms become tedious and have none of the subtleties of the older songs.

It is possible to defend her against all these charges by taking her in the context of the oral tradition and of almighty social upheaval. It is also possible to specify positive qualities. Since the subject matter of her songs is based in the near-contemporary world of political rallies, shinty clubs, and paddle-steamers, it is easy to overlook her utterly traditional method and purpose. The oral tradition goes a long way to explaining the apparent diffuseness of her songs. Repetition of subject matter between songs is common to most oral poets (and present-day politicians) where there is a need, as nothing can be taken 'as read', to present the whole case every time. As a traditional poet, she had a public function in her community. The nostalgic songs she produced for the Gaelic music-hall culture, depicting an idealised view of the lost homeland, were what people needed in their displaced state. The allusions to local characters and recent current events suggest that her concern was primarily to communicate to a particular community rather than to the abstract readership addressed by more conventional poets.

It is when she is read as part of the oral tradition that her strengths become apparent. Poetry had always been the vehicle for exposing injustice (cf. the use of satire and *tàmailt*, or Iain Lom's poetic campaign against the perpetrators of the Keppoch murders). Màiri Mhòr uses that function of poetry too, to insist, without making any defence for herself, on her innocence in the court case. She says how essential her clear conscience was during her time in prison:

'S b'fheumail cogais shaor dhomh 'n uair sin –
Chùm i suas mi 's rinn i m'èideadh.

The wild exuberance of such songs as 'Fàistneachd agus Beannachd do na Gàidheil' (A Prophesy and Blessing for the Gaels) should be seen as serving the pragmatic purpose of 'brosnachadh catha' (battle incitement) when the niceties of fact may well be dispensed with in support of the cause, in this case, the righting of the wrongs of the Clearances.

It may still be argued that worthy aims do not make for worthy poetry, but there are attractive, as well as functional, aspects to her work. Her nostalgic songs for Skye strongly evoke freedom, plentifulness, community: her petticoat is tugged by the heather, barrels overflow with salted meat, trips are made to weddings and waulkings in the winter, with the path lit by a glowing peat.

As well as exposing those who betrayed her in court, she castigates the clergy for neglecting to defend their flocks against the Clearances:

> Tha luchd-teagaisg cho beag cùraim
> Faicinn càramh mo luchd-dùthcha,
> 'S iad cho balbh air anns a' chùbaid
>   'S ged bu bhrùidean bhiodh gan èisdeachd.
>
> (MM, 74)
>
> (Some preachers are quite unconcerned on seeing the condition of my people, and in the pulpit they are as silent on the matter as if their congregation were dumb beasts.)

Satire is often her weapon against the offences of the times. She mocks the legislation that would prevent a crofter from helping himself to an oyster in the middle of the sea (MM, 94), the over-zealous troops battering the skulls of the gentle women of the Braes (MM, 101) and the hypocrisy of the converted who denounce as vanity the songs which uniquely nourish her people (MM, 100).

Màiri Mhòr must be read in the context of her times, with her public and pragmatic aims in mind. Such pragmatism does not conform with our modern notions of Art, but it is a misrepresentation (and a loss to ourselves) to measure her by inappropriate yardsticks.

Traditional Religious Poetry

A single song survives from Anna Nic Ealair (fl. c.1810): it expresses her ecstasy in being loved by Christ. Her joy communicates itself through the resonances and tensions created by her selection of material. She appeals to our erotic susceptibility by using the voluptuous images of wine and apple trees to evoke Christ's abundant grace. It is the *mood* rather than the *basis* of affirmation that is communicated. The reader is uplifted without needing to accede to the doctrine. This is the fifth of eight verses:

> Is mìlse leam do ghaol na'm fìon
>   Seadh am fìon nuair is treis' e
> 'S nuair a thug thu dhomh do ghràdh
>   'S ann a dh'fhàilnich mo phearsa.
>
> (Sweeter to me your love than wine
>   even wine at its strongest,
> and when you gave me your love
>   it made my body falter.)

Its mood derives from the Evangelical awakenings of the late eighteenth and early nineteenth centuries, but the diction comes from the woman's oral tradition, with new material ('The Song of Songs') from the recently published Gaelic Bible.

Bean Torra Dhamh/Mary MacPherson or Mrs Clark (fl. mid-late eighteenth century), unlike Anna Nic Ealair, was literate and produced highly structured and occasionally didactic hymns. Seven, from a supposed thirty, survive. She comments on the abuse of power and wealth and envisages a reformed society where its leaders conduct themselves according to God's law. Here she notes the injustice of the system of heritable jurisdictions (abolished in 1748) by which local barons could profit personally from the penalties they imposed:

> B' uamhasach an cleachdadh tìre,
> Croich is binn air àird gach cnocain,
> Cùirt nan spleagh gun lagh gun fhìrinn,
> 'S tric a dhìt an tì bha neo-chiont'.
>
> ('Beachd Gràis air an t-Saoghal', v. 7)

> (Terrible the custom of the land,
> Gallows and a sentence atop each hillock,
> A court of lies, without law or truth,
> Often was an innocent one condemned.)

The hymn, 'Ard Rìgh na Flathais', expresses relief and celebration at being with Christ, and wonder at His works, exemplified for her by her own growth within the womb (v. 7). Another hymn, 'Truailleachd Nàdair', captures a state of weakness and misgiving with two voices, one doubting whether she has the tenacity in the face of loneliness and poverty to allow herself to be saved, the other, faithful voice, refuting her own argument. A third example, 'Togarrach a bhith maille ri Crìosd', like Anna Nic Ealair's song, represents Christ as her lover who has initiated her conversion.

Catrìona NicDhòmhnaill (Staffin, Skye, twentieth century) is close to Anna NicEalair and Bean Torra Dhamh in her almost exclusively celebratory tone. There is almost nothing of the frightening coercion and threats of eternal damnation nor of the exhaustive accounts of the scheme of Redemption of Dùghall Bochanan or the medieval tradition. The women use the claims of love alone rather than the dual male tactic of reward and goad. For them, the world is an irrelevance rather than an object of loathing, a passage to the next world rather than a trap. In the opening two verses of 'Mo Chalman' she gives Christ a voice:

> Mo chalman tha falach an sgoltadh nan creag,
> 'N ionad dìomhair a' bhruthaich nis cluinneam do ghuth;
> Na fuirich air d'aineol, 's na deòir air do ghruaidh,
> 'S mi sireadh do thàladh le cridhe làn truais.

> Is mise d'fhear-pòsd', 's tha mo ghràdh dhut toirt bàrr
> Air gràdh athar no màthar, piuthair no bràth'r;
> Is àill leam thu thilleadh gu m'ionnsaigh gu saor
> Gus an dèan mi do phasgadh nam ghàirdeanan caomh'.

> (My dove who is hiding in the cleft of the rocks/In a secret place
> in the cliff I now hear your voice;/Don't be a stranger with the
> tears on your cheeks/While I seek to draw you with a pitying heart.

> I am your spouse, and my love of you exceeds/love of father or
> mother, sister or brother;/I desire you to turn to me of your
> free-will/so I may enfold you tenderly in my arms.)

As with secular verse, it is clear in the religious verse that the 'traditional' is not super-seded by the 'modern'. Catrìona's sixty-four hymns published in the 1980s are entirely traditional; the imagery is conventionally religious, her voice is public and she refers to herself only in so far as she is representative of her fellow sinner:

> Tha mo chridh' cho seachranach
> Is uairean tioram cruaidh,
> Ach Crìosda nì E còmhnaidh ann
> 'S thig blàths an àit' an fhuachd;
> Is bruchdaidh as a' chridhe sin
> Ceòl nach buin don t-saogh'l –
> A cùirt nam Flaitheas thàinig e
> 'S cha dèan sìorraidheachd a thrao'dh.

> (My heart is so wayward
> and sometimes hard and dry
> but Christ comes and dwells in it
> and warmth replaces cold;
> and out of that heart there springs
> music that belongs not to the world –
> from the court of the Kingdom it came
> and in all eternity it will not ebb.)

Poetry in the Modern Idiom

The main point of departure for women writers of non-traditional modern Gaelic poetry could only be the male poets of Sorley MacLean's generation, whose work, anthologised in *Nua-Bhàrdachd Ghàidhlig* (1976), was widely used in formal Gaelic education. Like those poets, the women all had access to higher education and absorbed the characteristics of poetry in modern European idioms.

Five of the six poets that I will refer to represent a younger generation than the poets of *Nua-Bhàrdachd Ghàidhlig*, and thematically have not much in common with them. The world has moved on and different issues are to the fore. That place the world derided (to paraphrase Donald MacAulay's description of the Outer Hebrides) now attracts a constant stream of incomers; established religion does not threaten the women as it did the older male poets whose rejection of it (often for 1940s nihilism) had almost become an orthodoxy amongst Gaelic *literati*.

The oldest of this group of poets is Màiri NicDhòmhnaill, who published a collection of sixteen poems (eight with English translation) and some of her drawings and photographs in *Mo Lorgan Fhìn / My Own Footprints* in 1985. The naturalistic props of her poems achieve a symbolic resonance. Màiri writes in the context of looking after an elderly mother, of watching the attenuation of her culture, of love and with an awareness of the individuality underlying her social being.

In 'Teine Beò' she comes to visit an old woman in her thatched house, and is relieved by the sight, in what first seemed a completely dark interior, of the embers which the old woman fans up in welcome. The poem is modest, understated, depending on fire's connotations of life and conviviality to amplify her satisfaction in the old woman's wellbeing, made all the more poignant in the case of a dying culture. The attenuation of that culture means that the poet is in part disenfranchised from expressing herself through it. The Fenians brush past her in 'Tuireadh na Gaoithe' but do not wait for her: their historical distance from mainstream society reflects her own distance from the archetypes of her culture. The overall sense of the poem, 'Mo Lorgan Fhìn', is the poet's regret that her mother did not survive into the summer to return to the islands once more. The practical considerations of getting a crippled old woman onto the sands and the natural cadences of the conversation between mother and daughter effectively contrast with the metaphorical overtones of 'going home'. Likewise the fancifulness of the old woman's chatter about her tracks going back to her youth and forward into the next world contrasts with the finality of her daughter's realisation that from now on summer will be conditioned by this sorrow.

A final example of how Màiri achieves an uncontrived symbolism may be seen in the poem 'Crom-lus Arrais'. She describes herself picking a poppy from the battlefields of Arras and extends the conventional poppy symbolism to include its rootedness in that soil which expresses the irrevocability of the loss and burial there of the particular soldier she has come to remember. Here is the final verse:

> Chùm mi am flùr
> Gu socair, maothail
> An cuachadh mo làimh –
> Buille chràitich mo chridhe
> A' plosgartaich 's a' crith
> Nam bileagan
> Nis a' crìonadh.
> Carson a spìon mi thu?
> A dh' altrum mi thu greis bheag
> 'S do fhreumhan fighte gu bràth
> An duslach Arrais.

> (I held the flower
> gently, tenderly
> cupped in my hand –
> the painful pulse of my heart
> in the throbbing and quivering
> of the petals
> now wilting.
> Why did I pick you?
> So as to nurse you for a moment
> though your roots are woven forever
> in the dust of Arras.)

Catrìona NicGumaraid (b.1947) is the most productive of the six poets and her voice has become stronger over the years. Her first, mostly love, poems, published in 1974, are often too obvious in their collocations or too redolent of Sorley MacLean to communicate their passion afresh. There are three aspects of her later voice I particularly enjoy – a delicate affirmativeness, a taste for irony and satire, and the unusual perspectives from which she views her world. Her poetry is mostly concerned with Gaelic culture, with love, mental anguish and the eventual peace she finds with Christ.

The poems 'Eilidh' and 'An Taigh Beag' locate a joy that can survive her fears for her own Gaelic culture. I quote the first poem in full:

> Bha dùil a'm gum biodh tu agam
> measg chreag is tiùrr' is ghlinn,
> 's gun ionnsaicheadh tu cainnt Dhiarmaid
> gu siùbhlach bhuamsa fhìn –
> chan ann an seo san ear-bhaile,
> far nach tuig mi cleas na cloinn';
> ach a-nochd gur dlùth an dàimh, a chagair,
> 's tu torghan air a' chìch.

> (I thought that I would have you
> midst rock, sea-wrack and glen
> and that you would learn Diarmid's language
> fluently from myself –
> not here in this east coast city
> where I don't understand the children's play
> but tonight the kinship is close
> as you gurgle at the breast.)

With her child at her breast, she can discount the difference of language that will, one day, separate her from her child. In the second poem she spots an old neighbour climbing the hillside where she and her little girl are playing at houses. Things have changed since her own childhood: the girl has plastic utensils for her house, and the whole area has become heavily anglicised. While the hosting of the *cèilidh* with the neighbour in a make-believe house sharpens the poignancy of the erosion of the real community, it cannot detract from the joy in the communication taking place at all. Irrevocable cultural erosion and the glimpsing of some redemptive aspect is the subject of a famous poem by Sorley MacLean, 'Hallaig', but Catrìona's treatment of the subject, utilising the modest topos of child-play, is also uniquely satisfying.

She uses satire and irony very effectively to expose the absurdities and injustices that arise when a once threatened culture has been weakened to the point where it can only ornament the dominant culture. The historical irony is maintained throughout the speech she puts in the mouth of a chief, soliciting funds from the descendants of the very people his forebears evicted ('Gu Dòmhnallaich Aimeireagaidh'). 'Làraich' is more subtle in its observation that though English-speaking gentry may own the Highlands, their presence is far too recent and recreational to endure in toponymy or topography. The subject of incomers raises dangerous temptations. In 'Roag 2000' she sees the icons of her youth – sheep, byres smelling of milk, the Gaelic language – being replaced by those of the incomer – ornamental dogs, craft shops and English.

Catrìona's poems first appeared in *A' Choille Chiar*, 1974, along with seventeen poems by her sister, Mòrag NicGumaraid (b. 1949). In Mòrag's work one finds flames, tides, berry-eating, cockle shells; certain rhythms come and go and suggest sex, child-birth, lost love affairs, a lost homeland. One poem stands out, in which she longs for the household to wake up to give her day shape, and begins to reformulate the world according to her own myths ('Goid Rìoghachd nam Ban Mara' and 'An-raoir a-rithist') as a way of dealing with the worn topos of leaving the homeland. In this connection too she shows herself capable of parodying traditional songs.

Màiri NicGumaraid (b.1955, not a sister to Catrìona and Mòrag) has the most distinctive style of the modern women poets. Her language is uniquely musical, not by means of established metres, but through her own patternings. Repetition of lines provides aural decoration as well as reflecting the meditative, circular nature of her thought. Reading her poetry has been well described by Christopher Whyte as feeling like eavesdropping, and as with eavesdropping, the point is sometimes inaudible. In addition to this quiet tone, two other voices are apparent in her poetry – one, childish, that allows her the innocent forthrightness of the boy in the 'Emperor with No Clothes', the other, cutting and angry, for use in political satire against landlordism and imperialism.

As her style is original, so often is the subject matter. It is the joint singing of songs she commemorates from an early love affair. In her relationship with the Gaelic culture, she refuses to accept easy answers or to offer flattering stereotypes. She cannot claim to be a direct heir to the old crofting way of life; she too has to learn about it in museum and book, knowing only the grief, and not the details, of a dying culture ('An Taigh-tasgaidh 's an Leabhar'). Biculturalism inhibits her from being able to identify herself with the Gaelic renaissance ('An t-Ordugh a-mach') and indeed she suspects such group behaviour robs the participants of their individuality. She admits to feelings she knows herself are not politically correct. She feels embarrassed by her attitude to Gaelic learners who with enormous effort achieve next to nothing, and to English incomers, whom she prefers not to like. It is this sort of paradoxical honesty that I find most intriguing in her poetry.

Meg Bateman (b. 1959)

It is seven years since I wrote much. I dried up with the sense that I had come to parody myself: the poems are mostly tight eight-line structures with some central paradox experienced in love, demonstrated through a single image. The thematic catalyst for me was Sorley MacLean. His comprehension of a hurtful and unbridgeable divide between what love inspired him to be and what he was in reality exactly corresponded to my own youthful experience. The exultation of love was impossible to maintain and I did not have the maturity to accept myself without that drug. Muted passion became an insult to love and life itself. Other women voiced criticism at my constant tone of emotional vulnerability; I would reply that I sought not to recommend a political stance but to reflect an emotional reality (however ill-founded).

Unlike the other writers discussed in this chapter, I am a learner of the language I choose to write in. It was not foresight into the growing fashionability of Gaelic that prompted this decision, nor hope for easy publication; it seemed a natural extension to having had my poetic tastes shaped by taking a degree in Celtic.

Anne Frater

Anne Frater (b. 1967) is the youngest of the six poets. Her work, anthologised in *An Aghaidh na Sìorraidheachd* in 1991, develops from what should probably be regarded as prentice pieces (e.g. 'Grian' or 'Loch an t-Sìthein') to some powerful and original work. Some of her work (e.g. 'Ar Cànan 's ar Clò') seems too derivative of Derick Thomson in its use of an image from the old way of life as a metaphor for its decline. In addition, the interpretation of the metaphor is often schematic and allegorical, without much emotional resonance. Other poems, however, such as 'Aig an Fhaing', '9mh den t-Samhainn 1989' or 'Màiri Iain Mhurch' Chaluim' are superbly observed and paced, allowing a build-up of tension and involvement through a perfectly judged use of stage props as emotional sign-posts. The first poem describes the poet and her neighbours working with the sheep. From standing cold at the edge of the fank, she is gradually drawn into the work, the language she finds herself using with the others being the ultimate sign of her belonging. The second poem watches an old woman being helped through the Brandenburg Gate by a young soldier, her slow approach to where she would have been shot even the night before reflecting the clumsiness and arbitrariness of political solutions. In the third poem, about her grandmother's loss, as a little girl, of her father with the sinking of the *Iolaire*, Anne uses images of the ship's rigging and of the sea to amplify the meaning of memory and forgetting. In these poems and many others there is an attractive rigour. Some of her nationalist poems may not work as poetry, but at their best they are witty and caustic, with well-timed endings. This review comes too soon for coverage of her forthcoming collection *Fon t-Slige/Under the Shell*.

Prose

Prose plays a relatively small part in the tradition. Whereas countless anonymous people participated in the song tradition, Gaelic literary prose is the work of a small number of known writers. Oral narrative, of course, existed, first alongside and subsequently outliving a manuscript tradition of medieval tales and romances. A collection of oral tales was published in 1860 by John Francis Campbell: it tried to record the way the tales were told in a communal setting. As Highland communities broke down and as printing presses became more numerous, oral tales were moulded into literary form. The Gaelic is superbly rich and idiomatic, and though the inversions and rhythms of speech are still to be heard, the overall sense of proportion and the polish of each sentence spring from the opportunity to revise and rewrite. A distinct nineteenth-century sensibility is very clear when such tales are compared with 'unimproved' versions. Lisa Storey published a collection, *Bha Siod Ann Reimhid* in 1975, with the intention of giving children, no longer in a story-telling society, access to that culture. While the later editor took down the stories verbatim, leaving their robust, amoral quality intact, the late nineteenth-century editors adapted and selected tales which gave them scope to exercise current tastes encountered in the first place through English.

The literary tales very often have an improving purpose, either religious, cautionary or educational: the stories self-consciously seek to inform young Gaels about the practices of their forebears. Most marked is the insistence (especially among women writers) on extremes of emotion. Coming after a tradition in which emotion tended to be understated, such detailed evocations of turmoil, with accompanying extremes of weather and light, strike a new note. The writers seem to be fascinated with the affective power of written words read in privacy. Whereas in traditional renditions, thought and feeling are only revealed through action, now every emotion is teased out for maximum effect. The carefully imagined tableaux are very much in line with contemporary painting, where pathos is evoked for its own sake. This Romanticism, formerly foreign to Gaelic culture (though the movement had taken much of its impetus from James Macpherson's handling of Gaelic material), was enthusiastically taken up by literate Gaels to articulate their own sense of lost glory.

Some of these points may be illustrated from the writings of Katherine Whyte Grant, published in 1911 in *Aig Taigh na Beinne*. She takes pains to give her highly polished literary tales atmospheric settings suitable for oral renditions – people waiting by a huge fire on a blustery night for a ferry-crossing; a grandmother seeking to keep the children from disturbing their mother at her needlework. A story, 'Moileag', heard from her grandmother, is significantly divided into chapters in its literary form. The emotional pitch is maintained throughout. It describes how a little girl, the only child and constant companion of her mother, is stolen by tinkers. She escapes and is hidden by an elderly godly woman who takes her in and makes arrangements for her to go into service with a doctor. There, twelve years after her kidnapping, she recognises her father, who comes to the door as a pedlar, a livelihood he took up to allow him to search for his daughter. Father and daughter are united; the mother has died of a broken heart. The story is paced for maximum dramatic effect, focusing on scenes of especial tenderness – the old woman telling the child about God, their deathbed farewell, the unification of father and daughter, the exquisite sadness lingering at the end made bearable in the religious message of a meeting in the next world. The relative morality of, at one end of the scale, the thieving and bestial tinkers who stole the child and ransacked the old woman's house in a menacing attempt to find her, and, at the other, the respectable doctor who has the sensitivity to remove himself discreetly from the scene of reunion, shares the contemporary equation of virtue with wealth. It was this same sort of thinking that was used to justify the Clearances, and its occurrence here is indicative to me of the lack of social engagement in Gaelic writers of the time.

A different approach is taken by the few women writers published by Ruaraidh Erskine of Mar in *Guth na Bliadhna* and *An Sgeulaiche* in the first two decades of this century. In accordance with his editorial directives, these women appear to be writing from a belief in the intrinsic rather than pragmatic worth of literature. Their work, though not substantial in volume or purport, is refreshingly unromantic and not at all moralistic. One story, 'Balaich na Calluinn', describes young boys' jinks at Hogmanay and the rather menacing practical jokes played on them by some older boys. Their talk and their behaviour is naturalistic. Another story seeks to interest children in the Gaelic lore on what various birds and animals say. The information is anecdotal and fragmented; there is no attempt to augment it; nor does the author shy from telling her young readers the benefits of drink in comprehending the animals.

This sort of playful 'realism' is a pointer towards what was to become the major prose genre in Gaelic – the modern short story. A minority culture, too fragmented to sustain a novel requiring a stable and full society, may be ideally portrayed in the short story especially in its modern manifestations where a sense of alienation is often evoked. Yet the extreme and sometimes psychotic states of alienation portrayed by Iain Crichton Smith and John Murray do not seem centrally to interest the main female exponents of the short story – Eilidh Watt (b. 1908, Skye) and Mary MacLean (b. Grimsay, early twentieth century).

Of the two, Mary is the less sophisticated. She uses the idiom of the short story in so far as it allows her to examine a character (usually female) at a critical moment in her life. Often her story only scantily clothes a religious message ('Oidhche na Stoirme'), sometimes a story seems all melodrama with little attempt at human psychology ('Mòr NicFhionnlaigh'). Yet melodrama and psychological insight come together in 'Còrd Tri-fhillte' which deals with a woman who chooses to isolate herself in her grief until, challenged by a minister, she realises that involvement may cure her: she seems on course to marry the minister and adopt the orphan her husband drowned to save.

Eilidh Watt is very prolific and has written some extremely beautiful short stories. Her language, unlike Mary MacLean's, is consistently colloquial. In many stories, in particular those illustrating the second sight, she uses the technique of the storyteller with audience. Nevertheless her stories are in the modern idiom, especially in their faultless achievement of unity of effect. She is endlessly inventive in devising situations which reveal varieties of character. In a single story she may sustain several 'sentient centres' at once and touch on several different themes. Her interest in human relationships derives from her observation of Highlanders but her focus is not exclusive. A sort of warm spirituality (and not piety as with Mary MacLean) pervades her stories which optimistically suggest that the pure, fair response to a situation may produce the greatest happiness for all. Her stories, like those of Iain Crichton Smith, are concerned with the fulfilment of the individual, but where Crichton Smith's characters serve his philosophical ideas and are controlled by his symbolism, Watt *appears* much less interventionist.

Autobiography

I will look at two autobiographies: *Air Mo Chuairt* by Ealasaid Chaimbeul (1982) and *Mo Bhrògan Ura* by Catrìona NicNèill (1992). I have already suggested that a reader who comes to Gaelic autobiographies with preconceptions based on non-Gaelic autobiography will fail to read them on their own terms, for the focus of the Gaelic autobiography is not an individual but a way of life. The Gaelic authors hold themselves up as being entirely representative of their communities. When the sort of personal experience that is the meat of conventional autobiography is encountered, the Gaelic authors hurry over it as being too differentiating or simply too private for elaboration. Of the death of her mother in 1940, Ealasaid Chaimbeul says only 'Thuig mi an uair sin dè bh' ann an lèireadh. Ach feumaidh an saoghal a dhol air aghaidh' (p. 36). (I understood then what pain was. But life has to go on.) She notes her marriage without any former mention of a man: ''S ann a thàinig e nis fainear dhomh pòsadh, oir bha mi air a dhol suas am bliadhnachan' (p. 38). (I thought to marry for I was getting on in years.)

The job in hand then is the depiction of a way of life at a time of rapid change. Very often an educative purpose is transparent in the treatment of such topics as children's games, diet, dairy and wool work and so on. The writers have no real critical perspective: they refer to social injustice and the decay of Gaelic culture without analysis. (The male writer, Aonghas Caimbeul, is exceptional in the independence of judgement of his autobiography.) The reader gains no inside knowledge of the author, but the very absence of such knowledge is itself indicative of the way of life depicted. In their disinclination to voice opinions that could antagonise or differentiate them from the group, they manifest those very qualities that make group-existence possible. The tendency towards stoicism in the face of adversity, an ability to see the humorous side of things, a disinclination to dwell on loss and a total absence of self-aggrandisement are further features of their group responsibility. The mores of the community are made evident then, not through the analysis of an aloof spectator, but through the bearing of the writers themselves.

Such writing has value both for social history and for its linguistic richness. These elderly women were monoglot until school-age and their richly idiomatic language is striking. Few younger people have Gaelic so free of English structures. Ealasaid Chaimbeul moves to the language and rhetoric of poetry to express emotion. This is indicative both of the importance of song within the community and once more of the culture's tendency to shy away from idiosyncratic expression. Catrìona NicNèill's liberal use of proverbs demonstrates her desire to give personal observation an established form of expression. Yet in both books some flashes of specific detail relieve the somewhat schematic approach adopted elsewhere.

The Novel

The chief virtue of Màiri NicGillEain's novel *Gainmheach an Fhàsaich* (1971) is as a repository of language. Yet her vast vocabulary and range of expression often tempt her to overwrite. Her novel treads uneasily between different traditions, a certain pietism attempting to bond the different elements together – fairy story, adventure story and religious odyssey. It is in one sense a religious love story which invites identification with the heroine, perhaps with the aim of awakening or strengthening the faith of the reader. The story concerns a wellbred young woman whose greedy stepmother forces her to leave her home. She seeks out the sweetheart of her youth in Africa, only to find him a ruined opium addict. Inspired by the religious faith of her godmother, she refuses to view him as an enemy, or herself as a victim. She nurses him to a state of mental health in which he can make peace with God and die. She is doubly rewarded for her fortitude by a marriage proposal from an equally God-fearing, handsome and well-to-do Gael. The elements of the traditional story – wicked step-mother, fairy godmother, the equation of wealth and beauty with goodness – sit uncomfortably in what purports to be a modern adventure story. The narrative is also marred by a degree of xenophobia. The characterisation is rather flat and the assumption that a woman's best hope is in marriage seems like a tired joke. The potentially most interesting issues like the change in the relationship between father and daughter on his remarrying are not explored. The narrator's voice is intrusive and didactic in a period when we have come to expect authorial effacement and reader input or at least some sense of ironic distance from cliché and convention.

The attempt to use a romantic tale as a vehicle for a religious message is characteristic of the improving ideals of the more conservative of Gaelic writers. Màiri NicGumaraid, however, sets her novel *Clann Iseabail* (1993) in the bicultural world of contemporary Gaels. She gives a sense of the world inhabited by modern Gaels, equally at home in the Islands and in Glasgow. She portrays the networks of extended families spanning these places, with their mutual obligations, loyalties, irritations and tolerance. The view is unromanticised. Her language and her representation of dialogue is natural and unforced. Some of the characterisation is very good too. There is occasional humour and some finely developed sequences of emotional change (in the narrator's realignment with her original boyfriend, or the reaction to a drowning in the family).

The novel examines the repercussions of various political practices: most telling is the needless death of a young man caused by the entanglement of his fishing nets with submarines on military exercise. The unstructured approach of the novel leaves many loose ends and unexplored questions: this is either courageous or messy. But the presumed allegiance of the reader to the author's Republican viewpoint is probably irritating. NicGumaraid never really tries to argue out her political positions: interesting questions of identity, political effectiveness and the purpose of writing are raised but never resolved. NicGumaraid employs recurrent devices (such as the accusation of being 'inquisitive', the injunction, 'bi fìor', the appearance of the dog, Howler) but their significance never quite pushes beyond the ornamental. The narrative is too diffuse, focusing neither on politics, nor the family network, nor the development of the narrator from romantic to realist. The tone is problematic too, veering from the didactic to the confessional. If the narrator's politics are compromised on the one hand, her feminism, on the other, is perhaps suspect (compare Annag's pathetic attempt to attract her husband with pink nighties with the narrator's confused attempt to attract a man through her writing). The text's feminist positions (that, for example, the personal is the political) pull the narrative into the present day but perhaps NicGumaraid's technical ability has not caught up with her politics.

Conclusion

In Ireland, Nuala Nì Dhomhnaill is producing startling poetry in which she expresses her sexuality through the fantastic and energetic language of traditional Irish tales. Her poetry reformulates the way we see ourselves. In Scotland, the poetry of Sorley MacLean produced something of the same shock in the 1940s when people realised that the Gaelic language which had seemed in thrall to nostalgia could engage with contemporary concerns with dignity and passion. No woman writing at present in Scottish Gaelic has achieved a stature comparable to either writer. But it may be the case that the movement from communal to individualistic writing is a more traumatic one for women who still must struggle with their own as well as the group's charges of aggression and immodesty. It would be surprising, however, if Gaelic women writers, having already come so far, did not push further down the road of linguistic, social and political invention.

Note

1. Compiling a bibliography for traditional Gaelic poets presents singular difficulties, given the occasional and sporadic nature of much of the traditional material. In order to facilitate further reading, this note gives Collections, followed by works by individual authors. Rev. Hector Cameron, *Na Bàird Thirisdeach*, (Stirling, 1932) [henceforth BT in the text]; J. L. Campbell, and F. Collinson, *Hebridean Folksongs*, vol. 1, (Oxford, 1969) [CC]; Duncan Kennedy, *An Laoidheadair Gaelic* (Glasgow 1786 and 1836); Keith Norman MacDonald, *The MacDonald Bards* (Glasgow, 1900); Malcolm C. MacLeod (ed.), *Modern Gaelic Bards* (Glasgow, 1913); Calum Iain M. MacLeòid, *Bàrdachd a Albainn Nuaidh*, (Gairm, Glasgow 1970) [BAN]; Dòmhnall Eachann Meek (ed.), *Màiri Mhòr nan Oran* (Gairm, Glasgow 1977) [MM]; Rev. A. Maclean Sinclair, *The Gaelic Bards 1715–1765* (Charlottetown, Nova Scotia, 1892); *The Glenbard Collection* (Charlottetown, Nova Scotia, 1890) [GColl]; *Na Bàird Leathanach/The MacLean Bards*, vol. 2, (Charlottetown, Nova Scotia, 1900) [BL]; Archibald Sinclair, *An t-Oranaiche* (Glasgow 1876); Christopher Whyte, *An Aghaidh na Sìorraidheachd* (Polygon, Edinburgh 1991).

Poetry (individual authors)
Meg Bateman, *Orain Ghaoil* (Coiscéim, Dublin 1990); Cairistiona Chaimbeul, *Measg Sguaban Bhaois* (Glasgow 1971); Catrìona Dhùghlas, *Sàr-Orain: na h-Orain is an Ceòl gu h-uile le Catrìona Dhùghlas*, ed. Domhnall Budge (Dunbheagain, 1971); Anne Frater, *Fon t-Slige/Under the Shell* (Gairm, 1995); K. W. Grant, *Aig Taigh Na Beinne* (Oban, 1911); Christine MacLeod, *An Sireadh* (1952); *Ceòlraidh Cridhe* (1943); Mary MacPherson/Màiri Mhòr nan Oran (of Skye) see Dòmhnall Eachann Meek, *Màiri Mhòr nan Oran* (Glasgow, 1974, Skye, 1985); Catrìona NicGumaraid (Catrìona Montgomery), *A' Choille Chiar* (Glasgow, 1974; also contains work by Mòrag NicGumaraid); *Rè na h-Oidhche/The Length of the Night* (Canongate, Edinburgh 1994); Màiri NicGumaraid (Mary Montgomery), *Eadar Mi 's a' Bhreug* (Coiscéim, Dublin 1988); Mòrag NicGumaraid (Mòrag Montgomery), *A' Choille Chiar* (Glasgow, 1974).

Prose
Ealasaid Chaimbeul, *Air mo Chuairt* (Acair, Stornoway 1982); Cairistiona Dick, *Raonaid* (Aberfeldy, 1981; teenage novel); *Calum Cille*, co-authored with Iain Bannerman (Glasgow, 1982; history); *Dal Riata*, co-authored with Iain Bannerman (Glasgow, 1987; history); K. W. Grant, *Aig Taigh Na Beinne* (Oban, 1911; prose and poetry); Màiri NicGillEain, *Gainmheach an Fhàsaich* (Inverness, 1971; novel); *Lus-Chrùn à Griomasaigh* (Inverness, 1970; short stories);

Màiri NicGumaraid (Mary Montgomery), *Clann Iseabail*, (Acair, Stornoway, 1993; novel); Catrìona NicNèill, *Mo Bhrògan Ura* (Gairm, Glasgow, 1992; autobiography); Eilidh Watt, *A' Bhratach Dheàlrach* (Inverness, 1972; short-stories); *Gun Fhois* (Loanhead, 1987; short stories); over forty short stories in *Gairm* from no. 68 (1972) onwards.

Drama
Catrìona Ghrannd, *An Sgoil Bheag agus a' Mhaighdean-Mhara* (Glasgow, 1910); Mary MacKinnon, *Ri Guaillibh a Chèile* (Glasgow, 1930).

Children's Books
Many modern Gaelic books by women are aimed at young children. A full list of the titles can be found in the catalogues of the Gaelic Books Council, Glasgow.

Select Bibliographies of Scottish Women Writers

Fiona Black and Kirsten Stirling

The following select bibliographies of writers are divided into pre- and post-twentieth century, although there are obviously some borderline cases. The pre-twentieth-century bibliography has been compiled principally by Kirsten Stirling, who thanks Pat Clark for the assistance of her bibliography of Scottish women's writing which will form the basis of her forthcoming (Tuckwell) directory of Scottish women's writing from 1700 to 1900. The twentieth-century bibliography is based on the descriptive bibliography of Scottish women's writing by Karen Stewart, prepared for the 'Glasgow 1990' celebrations, a copy of which is deposited in Glasgow University Library. It has been revised and augmented by Fiona Black with assistance from Kirsten Stirling. Decisions about inclusion in the bibliographies have tended towards openness in the interpretation of Scottishness.

Pre-Twentieth Century

Some anthologies of poetry containing work by women:

Gaelic

The Book of the Dean of Lismore: Poems from the Book of the Dean of Lismore, ed. E. C. Quiggin, Cambridge University Press, Cambridge, 1937; *Scottish Verses from the Book of the Dean of Lismore*, ed. W. J. Watson, Oliver & Boyd, Edinburgh, 1978

Duncan Kennedy, *An Laoidheadair Gaelic*, Glasgow, 1786 and 1836

D. C. McPherson, *An Duanaire*, 1868

Archibald Sinclair, *An t-Oranaiche*, 1876–9

The Glenbard Collection, Charlottetown, Nova Scotia, 1890

Rev. A. Maclean Sinclair, *The Gaelic Bards 1715–1765*, Charlottetown, Nova Scotia, 1892

Keith Norman MacDonald, *The MacDonald Bards*, Glasgow, 1900

Na Bàird Leathanach/The MacLean Bards, Charlottetown, Nova Scotia, 1900

A. and A. MacDonald, *The MacDonald Collection of Gaelic Poetry*, 1911

Malcolm C. MacLeod, *Modern Gaelic Bards*, Glasgow, 1913

Rev. Hector Cameron, *Na Bàird Thirisdeach*, Stirling, 1932

Alasdair MacAsgaill, *Rosg nan Eilean*, Glasgow, 1966

J. L. Campbell, and F. Collinson, *Hebridean Folksongs*, 3 vols, Oxford, 1969; 1977; 1981

Calum Iain M. MacLeòid, *Bàrdachd a Albainn Nuaidh*, Gairm, Glasgow 1970

For further bibliographical information about Gaelic women poets see the chapters by Frater and Bateman.

Scots and English

Allan Ramsay (ed.), *Scots Songs*, 1718; *The Ever Green*, 1724; *The Tea-Table Miscellany*, 1724

J. Gillies (ed.), *A Collection of Ancient and Modern Gaelic Poems and Songs*, Perth, 1786

J. Johnson (ed.), *Scots Musical Museum*, 6 vols, London, 1787–1803; ed. D. A. Low, Scolar Press, Aldershot, 1991

Walter Scott, *Minstrelsy of the Scottish Border*, 1802–3, 4 vols, ed. T. F. Henderson, Blackwood, London, 1902

James Hogg (ed.), *Jacobite Relics of Scotland*, W. Blackwood, Edinburgh and London, 1819–21

T. G. Stevenson (ed.), *The Ballads and Songs of Ayrshire*, 2 vols, published for the editor, Ayr, 1846–7

William Stenhouse (ed.), *Illustrations of the Lyric Poetry and Music of Scotland*, W. Blackwood, Edinburgh and London, 1853

Charles Rogers (ed.), *The Modern Scottish Minstrel: Or the Songs of Scotland of the Past Century*, 6 vols, A. & C. Black, Edinburgh, 1855–8; *The Sacred Minstrel: A Collection of Spiritual Songs with Biographical Sketches of the Authors*, Hulston & Wright, London, 1859

William Motherwell (ed.), *The Harp of Renfrewshire*, A. Gardner, Paisley, 1872

James Grant Wilson (ed.), *The Poets and Poetry of Scotland*, 2 vols, Blackie, London, 1876–7

Modern Scottish Poets, 16 vols, D. H. Edwards, Brechin, 1880–97

James Beveridge (ed.), *The Poets of Clackmannannshire*, J. S. Wilson, Glasgow, 1885

The Glasgow Ballad Club, Publications from 1885–

Malcolm McLachlan Harper (ed.), *The Bards of Galloway: A Collection of Poems, Songs, Ballads etc by Natives of Galloway*, T. Fraser, Dalbeattie, 1889

Robert Brown (ed.), *Paisley Poets*, 2 vols, J. J. Cook, Paisley, 1889–90

Alexander G. Murdoch, *Recent and Living Scottish Poets*, Porteous Brothers, Glasgow, 1890

Sarah Tytler and J. L. Watson (eds), *The Songstresses of Scotland*, 2 vols, Strahan & Co., 1891

Robert Ford (ed.), *The Harp of Perthshire*, A. Gardner, Paisley, 1893

  Ballads of Bairnhood, A. Gardner, Paisley, 1894

George Eyre-Todd (ed.), *Scottish Poetry of the Eighteenth Century*, Glasgow 1896

  The Glasgow Poets: Their Lives and Poems, W. Hodge & Co., Glasgow and Edinburgh, 1903

John Macintosh (ed.), *The Poets of Ayrshire from the Fourteenth Century to the Present Day*, Thomas Hunter, Dumfries, 1910

W. Macneile Dixon (ed.), *The Edinburgh Book of Scottish Verse, 1300–1900*, Meiklejohn & Holden, London, 1910

Roger Lonsdale (ed.), *Eighteenth Century Women Poets*, Oxford University Press, Oxford, 1989

Germaine Greer, S. Hastings, J. Medoff and M. Sansone (eds), *Kissing the Rod: An Anthology of Seventeenth-Century Women's Verse*, Virago Press Ltd, London, 1988

Tom Leonard (ed.), *Radical Renfrew: Poetry from the French Revolution to the First World War by Poets Born, or Sometime Resident in the County of Renfrewshire*, Polygon, Edinburgh, 1990

Catherine Kerrigan (ed.), *An Anthology of Scottish Women Poets*, Edinburgh University Press, Edinburgh, 1991

Roderick Watson (ed.), *The Poetry of Scotland: Gaelic, Scots and English*, Edinburgh University Press, Edinburgh, 1995

Information about the Ballads and the women who have been involved in their transmission is best sought in the chapters by Brown and Petrie. The bibliographical complexities of early women's writing are discussed in Dunnigan's chapter, and Frater and Bateman deal with Gaelic verse.

Readers looking for further work by women poets are recommended to consult the Scottish Poetry Collection of the Mitchell Library, Glasgow and the Scottish Poetry Library, Edinburgh.

Poets not accorded separate entries in this bibliography include: Margaret Ballantyne, Margaret Bean, Jean Clerk, Emma Dickson, Lydia Falconer Fraser, Janet Graham, Mary Gray, Dorothea Gregory, Agnes Hall, Helen Harper, Elizabeth Hartley, Flora Hastings, Lizzie Hunter, Rebecca Hutcheon, Jeanie Johnstone, Isabella Ledgerwood, Agnes Lyon, Katherine Mann, Agnes Marshall, Lady Elliot Murray, Jeanie G. Paterson, Joanna Picken, Alice Pringle, Margaret Stewart Sandeman, Mary Anne Shaw, M. C. Smith, Helen Stewart, Mary Bruce Strange, Cecile McNeill Thomson, Margaret Wallace Thomson, and many others.

For further information about fiction see:
Moira Burgess, *The Scottish Fiction Reserve: Directory of Authors Included in the Scheme*, 3rd edn, National Library of Scotland, Edinburgh, 1995

Pre-Twentieth Century: Select Bibliography

Adams, Jean (1710–65) 'Miscellaneous Poems, by Mrs Jane Adams, in Crawfordsdyke', James Duncan, Glasgow, 1734; see also Tytler & Watson, 1871

Aird, Marion Paul (1815–88) *The Home of the Heart; and Other Poems Moral and Religious*, James McKie, Kilmarnock, 1846; *Heart Histories: Violets from the Greenwood*, Johnstone & Hunter, London & Edinburgh, 1853; *Sun and Shade*, James McKie, Kilmarnock, 1860

Allhusen, Beatrice May (née Butt) (?1850–1918) *Verses*, S. C. Mayle, Hampstead, 1905; *Fragments*, Longmans, Green & Co., London, 1912

Anderson, Jessie Annie ('Patience') (1861–?) *Across the Snow*, 1894; *Songs in Season*, Milne & Stephen, Aberdeen, 1901, *Songs of Hope and Courage*, 1902; *An Old-world Sorrow; and Other Sonnets*, 1903, *Lyrics of Life and Love*, 1903; *Legends and Ballads of Women*, 1904; *Lyrics of Childhood*, 1905; *A Handful of Heather*, 1906; *The Book of the Wonder Ways*, 1907; *Flower Voices*, 1908 (all Milne & Stephen, Aberdeen); *Dorothy's Dream of the Months*, Horace Cox, London, 1909; *Breaths from the Four Winds*, Milne & Stephen, Aberdeen, 1911; *This is Nonsense: Verses Light and Satirical*, Aberdeen Press & Journal, Aberdeen, 1926; *A Singer's Year*, Aberdeen Press & Journal, Aberdeen, 1928; *Lewis Morrison-Grant, His Life, Letters & Last Poems*, ed. J. A. Anderson, A. Gardner, Paisley, 1894.

Appleton, Elizabeth *Private Education: Or a Plan for the Studies of Young Ladies, with an Address to Parents, Private Governesses and Young Ladies*, Henry Colburn, London, 1813

Baillie, Lady Grisell (1665–1746) *The Household Book of Lady Grisell Baillie 1692–1733*, ed. R. Scott-Moncrieff, Scottish History Society Publications, 2, vol.1, Edinburgh, 1911. See Ramsay, *Tea-Table Miscellany* and Kerrigan, 1991

Baillie, Joanna (1762–1851) *Poems; Wherein it is Attempted to Describe Certain Views of Nature and of Rustic Manners*, Joseph Johnson, London, 1790; *A Series of Plays: In Which It Is Attempted to Delineate the Stronger Passions of the Mind, Each Passion Being the Subject of a Tragedy and a Comedy*, 3 vols, T. Cadell & W. Davies, London, 1798–1812; Epilogue to the theatrical representation at Strawberry-Hill, written by Joanna Baillie, spoken by the Hon. Anne S. Damer, November 1800, London, 1804; *Miscellaneous Plays*, Longman & Co., London, 1804; *De Monfort: A Tragedy*, Longman, Hurst, Rees and Orme, London, 1807; *The Family Legend: A Tragedy*, J. Ballantyne & Co., Edinburgh, 1810; *Metrical Legends of Exalted Characters*, Longman & Co., London, 1821; *The Martyr: A Drama in Three Acts*, Longman & Co., London, 1821; *The Bride: A Drama in Three Acts*, Henry Colburn, London, 1828; *Fugitive Verses*, Edward Moxon, London, 1840; *Ahalya Baee: A Poem*, Spottiswoode & Shaw, London, 1849; *The Dramatical and Poetical Works of Joanna Baillie*, Longman, Brown, Green and Longmans, London, 1851; (ed.), *A Collection of Poems Chiefly Manuscript and from Living Authors*, Longman & Co., 1823

Ballantyne, Jane B. *Poetical Fragments*, Edinburgh, 1876; *A Summer Trip to the Highlands*, Edinburgh, 1880

Bannerman, Anne (fl.1816) *Poems*, Mundell & Son, Edinburgh, 1800; *Tales of Superstition and Chivalry*, Vernor & Hood, London, 1802

Barbour, Margaret Frazer *The Way Home: A Religious Manual for the Young*, Edinburgh, 1856; *The Child of the Kingdom*, J. Nisbet & Co., London, 1862; *The Soul Gatherer*, London, 1864; *The Irish Orphan in a Scottish Home*, Edinburgh and London, 1866; *Three Burdens Laid Down*, Morgan & Scott, London, 1874; *A Memoir of Mrs Stewart Sandeman by her Daughter*, J. Nisbet & Co., London, 1883

Barnard, Lady Anne Lindsay (1750–1825) *The Lays of the Lindsays; Being Poems by the Ladies of the House of Balcarres*, Edinburgh, 1824; *South Africa a Century Ago: Letters Written from the Cape of Good Hope (1797–1801) by Lady Anne Barnard*, ed. with a memoir etc. by W. H. Wilkins, Smith, Elder, & Co., London, 1901; Alexander Crawford Lindsay, *Lives of the Lindsays*, 2 vols, J. Murray, London, 1849; Dorothea Fairbridge, *Lady Anne Barnard at the Cape of Good Hope, 1797–1802*, illustrated by a series of sketches made by Lady Anne Barnard, Clarendon Press, Oxford, 1924; *Auld Robin Gray: A Ballad*, ed. Sir Walter Scott, J. Ballantyne, Edinburgh, 1925

Beaton, Mary (c.1543–c.1597) see Dunnigan chapter

Begbie, Agnes Helen *Edinburgh Vignettes: Verses*, Cummings & Erskine, Edinburgh, 1900; *The Rosebud Wall; and Other Poems*, W. J. Hay, Edinburgh, 1906; *Christmas Songs and Carols*, Elkin Mathews, London, 1908

Bell, Maria (d.1899) *The Country Minister's Love Story*, Hodder & Stoughton, London, 1895; *Songs of Two Homes*, Oliphant, Anderson & Ferrier, Edinburgh & London, 1899

Bernstein, Marion (fl.1876) *Mirren's Musings*, McGeachy, Glasgow, 1876; see also Tom Leonard, *Radical Renfrew*, 1990

Bishop, Isabella Bird (1831–1904) *The Englishwoman in America*, John Murray, London, 1856; *A Revival in America*, by an English Eye-witness, James Nisbet & Co., London, 1858; *The Aspects of Religion in the United States of America*, 1859; *Notes on Old Edinburgh*, 1869; *The Hawaiian Archipelago*, John Murray, London, 1875; *A Lady's Life in the Rocky Mountains*, 1879; *The Golden Chersonese; and the Way Thither*, 1883; *Unbeaten Tracks in Japan*, 1885; *Journeys in Persia and Kurdistan*, 1891 (all John Murray, London); *Heathen Claims and Christian Duty*, Morgan & Scott, London, 1894; *Among the Tibetans*, London, 1894; *Japan and the Faith of Christendom*, J. Townsend, Exeter & London, 1898; *Korea and Her Neighbours*, John Murray, London, 1898; *The Yangtze Valley and Beyond*, John Murray, London 1898; *Chinese Pictures: Notes on Photographs Made in China*, Cassell & Co., London, 1900; *A Traveller's Testimony*, London, 1905

Blamire, Susanna (1747–94) *The Poetical Works of Susanna Blamire*, ed. H. Lonsdale, with Preface, notes and memoir by Patrick Maxwell, John Menzies, Edinburgh, 1842; Woodstock Facsimile Series, ed. Jonathan Wordsworth, 1994; *Songs and Poems*, Routledge, London, 1866

Blaze de Bury, Marie Pauline Rose, Baroness (née Stuart) (1813–94) *Racine and the French Classical Drama*, Knight, London, 1845; *Molière and the French Classical Drama*, Knight, London, 1846; *Germania: Its Courts, Camps and People*, Colborn, London, 1850; *Memoirs of the Princess Palatine, Princess of Bohemia*, Richard Bentley, London, 1853; *All For Greed: A Novel*, Little & Gay, Boston, 1868

Brunton, Mary (1778–1818) *Self-Control: A Novel*, 1811; *Discipline*, 1814; *Emmeline, with Some Other Pieces*, 1819 (all Manners & Miller, London)

Buchanan, Harriet Flora Macdonald *Diary*, 1817

Burgess, Mary Anne (1763–1813), *The Progress of the Pilgrim Good Intent*, 1800

Burton, Ella (1845–?) *The Norman Conquest Illustrated by the Bayeux Tapestry*, Edinburgh Publishing Co., Edinburgh, 1878; see also Kerrigan, 1991

Bury, Lady Charlotte Susan Maria (née Campbell) (1775–1861) *Poems on Several Occasions*, 1797; *Self-Indulgence*, 1812; *Conduct is Fate*, 1822; *Suspirium Sanctorum; Or, Holy Breathings: A Series of Prayers*, 1826; *Flirtation: A Novel*, 1828; *A Marriage in High Life*, 1828; *Journal of the Heart*, Colburn & Bentley, London, 1830; *The Separation: A Novel*, Colburn & Bentley, London, 1830; *The Exclusives*, 1830; *The Disinherited; and The Ensnared*, 1834; *The Devoted*, 1836; *The Divorced*, Henry Colburn, London, 1837; *Love*, 1837; *The Murdered Queen! Or, Caroline of Brunswick*, 1838; *Diary Illustrative of the Times of George IV*, H. Colburn, London, 1839; *The History of a Flirt; Related by Herself*, 1840; *Family Records; Or, The Two Sisters*, Saunders & Otley, London, 1841; *The Manoevering Mother*, 1842; *The Wilfulness of Women*, 1844

Cailéin, Iseabail Nî Mheic (Isabel, Countess of Argyll) (fl.1500) see *The Book of the Dean of Lismore*; see also Kerrigan, 1991

Calderwood, Margaret (of Polton) see J. G. Fyfe (ed.), *Scottish Diaries and Memoirs 1746–1843*, with an Introduction by J. D. Mackie, Eaneas Mackay, Stirling, 1942; *Letters and Journals of Mrs Calderwood of Polton*, D. Douglas, Edinburgh, 1884

Callcott, Lady Maria Graham (née Dundas) (1788–1842) *Letters on India with Etchings and a Map*, Constable & Co., Edinburgh, 1814; *The Captain's Wife: The South American Journals of Maria Graham 1821–23*, compiled and edited by Elizabeth Maver, Weidenfeld & Nicolson, London, 1993; and others

Campbell, Anna (of Scalpay, Harris) (fl.173) see Kerrigan, 1991

Campbell, Elizabeth (1804–?) *Poems*, printed for the Author, Arbroath, 1862; *Songs of My Pilgrimage*, A. Elliot, Edinburgh, 1875

Campbell, Harriette (1817–41) *The Only Daughter: A Novel*, Colburn, London, 1839; *The Cardinal Virtues; or, Morals and Man*, John W. Parker, London, 1841; *Self-devotion; or, The History of Katherine Randolph*, Harper & Row, New York, 1842

Carlyle, Jane Welsh (1801–66) *Letters and Memorials Prepared for Publication by Thomas Carlyle*, 3 vols, ed. James Anthony Froude, Longman & Co., London, 1883; *Early Letters of Jane Welsh Carlyle*, ed. David G. Richie, S. Sonnenschein & Co., London, 1889; *New Letters and*

Memorials of Jane Welsh Carlyle, ed. A. Carlyle, John Lane, London, 1903; *Jane Welsh Carlyle: Letters to Her Family, 1839–63*, ed. L. Huxley, John Murray, London, 1924; *I Too Am Here: Selections from the Letters of Jane Welsh Carlyle*, ed. A. and M. Simpson, Cambridge University Press, Cambridge, 1977; *Jane Welsh Carlyle: A New Selection of Her Letters*, Gollancz, London, 1950; *Collected Letters of Thomas and Jane Welsh Carlyle*, 25 vols, ed. C. R. Sanders, K. J. Fielding, C. de L Ryals, W. Bell, J. Campbell, A. Christianson, J. Clubbe, H. Smith, Duke University Press, Durham, North Carolina, 1970–97

Carnegie, Susan *Dunottar Castle: A Poem*, Aberdeen, ?1796

Carstairs, Christian (fl.1763–86) *The Hubble-Shue: A Farce*, c.1780; with an Introductory Notice by J. Maidment, Andrew Shortrede, Edinburgh, 1834; *Original Poems. By a Lady*, 1786

Cassady, Mary H. ('Vera') *Sweet Vale of Orr: Lays and Lilts of Galloway*, Castle Douglas, 1890

Chalmers, Anne *Letters and Journals of Anne Chalmers*, ed. by her daughter [Matilda Grace Mackie], privately printed, London, 1912

Cleland, Elizabeth *A New and Easy Method of Cookery*, printed for the author, Edinburgh, 1755

Clephane, Elizabeth Cecilia Douglas see David P. Thomson, *Women of the Scottish Church*, no. 2: 'The Sweet Singer of Melrose': the Story of Elizabeth Clephane and her Famous Hymn

Cockburn, Alicia (Alison Rutherford) (1713–94) 'The Flowers of the Forest', *The Blackbird*, Edinburgh, 1765; *Letters and a Memoir of Her Own Life by Mrs Alison Rutherford or Cockburn*, ed. T. Craig-Brown, David Douglas, Edinburgh, 1900

Cockburn, Catharine (née Trotter) (1679–1749) *Agnes de Castro: A Tragedy. . .Written by a Young Lady*, 1696; *Fatal Friendship: A Tragedy*, London, 1698; *Love at a Loss; or, Most Votes Carry It: a comedy*, London, 1701; *The Unhappy Penitent: A Tragedy*, London, 1701; *A Defence of the Essay of Human Understanding*, 1702; *The Revolution of Sweden: A Tragedy*, London, 1706; *A Discourse Concerning a Guide in Controversies*, 2nd edn, 1728; *Remarks upon the Principles and Reasonings of Dr Rutherford's Essay on the Nature and Obligations of Virtue: in vindication of the contrary principles and reasonings, inforced in the writings of the late Dr Samuel Clarke*, published by Warburton, 1714; *The Works of Mrs Catherine Cockburn*, with an Account of the Life of the Author by T. Birch, J. & P. Knapton, London, 1751; *Poems by Eminent Ladies*, ed. M. Barber, 1755

Colquhoun, Lady Janet (1781–1846) *The World's Religion as Contrasted with Genuine Christianity*, 2nd edn, John Johnstone, Edinburgh, 1839

Cook, Eliza (1818–89) *The Poetical Works of Eliza Cook*, Frederick Warne & Co., London, 1899

Corcadail, Aithbhreac Inghean (c.1460) see *The Book of the Dean of Lismore*

Cortis-Stanford, Florence *Westering Winds: Poems*, Gowans & Gray, London and Glasgow, 1922

Cousin, Anne Ross (1824–1906) *The Last Words of Rev. Samuel Rutherford with Some of his Sweet Sayings*, James Taylor, Edinburgh, c.1860; *Immanuel's Land, and Other Pieces*, 1876

Craig, Isa (Knox) (1831–1903) *Poems*, William Blackwood, Edinburgh, 1856; *The Burns Festival: Prize Poem Recited at the Crystal Palace*, Bradbury & Evans, London, 1859; *Duchess Agnes*, Alexander Strachan, London, 1864; *Esther West: A Story*, Cassell, Petter & Galpin, London and New York, 1870; *In Duty Bound*, Harper & bros, New York, 1870; *Songs of Consolation*, 1874; *Hold Fast By your Sundays*, new edn, Home Words, London, 1889

Craik, Helen (1750–1825) *Julia de Saint Pierre*, 1796; *Henry of Northumberland, or The Hermit's Cell*, 1800; *Adelaide de Narbonne, with Memoirs of Charlotte de Cordet*, 1800; *Stella of the North; or The Foundling Ship*, 1802; *The Nun and her Daughter*, 1805

Cross, Mary (1885–1922) *Under Sentence*, Ward & Downey, London, 1890

Crowe, Mrs Catherine [Ann] (née Stevens) (1790–1876) *Aristodemus: A Tragedy*, W. Tait, Edinburgh, 1838; *Susan Hopley; or, The Adventures of a Maidservant*, W. Tait, Edinburgh, 1942; *Men and Women; or, Manorial Rights*, Saunders & Otley, London, 1844; *The Story of Lily Dawson*, Henry Colburn, London, 1847; *The Night-Side of Nature; or, Ghosts and Ghost-Seers*, T. C. Newby, London, 1848; *Light and Darkness, or, Mysteries of Life*, H. Colburn, London, 1850; *The Adventures of a Beauty*, Colburn, London, 1852; *The Cruel Kindness: A Play in Five Acts*, Routledge, London, 1853; *Linny Lockwood: A Novel*, D. Appleton, New York, 1854; *Ghosts and Family Legends*, Newby, London, 1859; *Spiritualism and the Age We Live In*, T. C. Newby, London, 1859; *Pippie's Warning: A Tale for Young People*, J. & J. L. Gihon, Philadelphia, 1860

Dalrymple, Christian *Private Annals of My Own Time by Miss Dalrymple of Hailes 1765–1812*, Edinburgh, 1914

Darling, Isabella F. (1861–1903) *Whispering Hope,* J. Menzies, Edinburgh; Simpkin & Marshall, London, 1893; *Poems and Songs,* H. Nisbett, Glasgow, 1889; *Songs from Silence,* A. Gardner, Paisley, 1904; *A Certain Rich Man,* J. McLeod, Shotts, 1913

Davidson, Harriet Miller (1839–83) *Lines for Little Lips,* H. M. Davidson, London, 1856; *The Two Babies: A Sketch of Every-day Life. By a Mother,* Simpkin & Marshall, London, 1859; *Isobel Jardine's History,* Scottish Temperance League, Glasgow, c.1865; *Christian Osborne's Friends,* c.1865

Davies, Mrs Christi[an]na [Jane] (née Douglas) **(1822–87)** *The Heir of Ardennan: a Story of Domestic Life in Scotland,* Colburn, London, 1852

Davies, Lady Lucy Clementina (née Drummond) **(1795–1879)** *Recollections of Society in France and England,* Hurst & Blackett, London, 1872

Dixie, Lady Florence (1857–1905) *Abel Avenged: A Dramatic Tragedy in Three Acts,* London, 1877; *Across Patagonia,* R. Bentley & Son, London, 1880; *Waifs and Strays; or, The Pilgrimage of a Bohemian Abroad,* Griffith, Farran, Okeden & Welsh, London, 1880; *A Defence of Zululand and its King,* Chatto & Windus, London, 1882; *In the Land of Misfortune,* R. Bentley, London, 1882; *Redeemed in Blood,* Henry & Co., London, 1884; *Aniwee; or, The Warrior Queen: A Novel,* Henry & Co., London, 1890; *Gloriana; or, The Revolution of 1900,* Henry & Co., London, 1890; *The Young Castaways; or, The Child Hunters of Patagonia,* Shaw & Co., London, 1890; *The Horrors of Sport,* Humanitarian League, London, 1891; *Little Cherie; or, The Trainer's Daughter: A Racing and Social Novel,* Treherne & Co., London, 1901; *The Mercilessness of Sport,* Humanitarian League, London, 1901; *Songs of a Child and Other Poems* by Darling, 2 vols, Leadenhall Press, London, 1901 and 1903; *Isola; or, The Disinherited: A Drama in Verse,* Leadenhall Press, London, 1902; *The Story of Ijain; or, The Evolution of a Mind,* Leadenhall Press, London, 1903; *Izra: A Child of Solitude,* John Long, London, 1906

Douglas, Elizabeth (fl. 1587) See Dunnigan chapter

Douglas, George (i.e. Lady Gertrude Georgina Douglas) (1842–93) *Brown as a Berry: A Novel,* Tinsley Bros, London, 1874; *The Red House by the River: A Novel,* Tinsley Bros, London, 1876; *Linked Lives,* London, 1876; *Nature's Nurseling: A Romance from Real Life,* Kegan Paul & Co., London, 1885; *A Wasted Life* and *Marr'd,* Hurst & Blacket, London, 1892

Duncan, Mary Grey Lundie *History of Revivals of Religion in the British Isles, Especially in Scotland,* 1836; *Memoir of Mrs Mary Lundie Duncan,* 1841; *Rhymes for My Children,* 1842 (all W. Oliphant & Son, Edinburgh); *The Children of the Manse,* Carter & Bros, New York, 1851

Eliot, Jean (of Minto) (1727–1805) ('The Flowers of the Forest') see Tytler and Watson, 1871, and Lonsdale, 1989

Ferrier, Susan (1782–1854) *Marriage: A Novel,* William Blackwood, Edinburgh, 1818; *The Inheritance,* William Blackwood, Edinburgh, 1824; *Destiny,* R. Cadell, Edinburgh, 1831; 'Maplehurst Manor' (outline sketches for undeveloped novel) in *Susan Ferrier 1782–1854,* National Library of Scotland Exhibition Catalogue, Edinburgh, 1982; *Memoir and Correspondence of Susan Ferrier, 1782–1854,* ed. John A. Doyle, John Murray, London, 1898

Fleming, Marjory ('Pet Marjory') (1803–11) *The Complete Marjory Fleming, Her Journals, Letters & Verses,* transcibed and edited by Frank Sidgwick, Sidgwick & Jackson, London, 1934

Fletcher, Eliza (née Dawson) **(1770–1858)** *Autobiography of Mrs Fletcher of Edinburgh,* privately printed, Carlisle, 1874

Fraser, Mrs Augusta Zelia ('Alice Spinner'; née Webb) **(?1868–1925)** *A Study in Colour,* T. Fisher Unwin, London, 1891; *Lucilla: An Experiment,* Kegan Paul & Co., London, 1895; *A Reluctant Evangelist and Other Stories,* E. Arnold, London, 1896

Gerard, Dorothea (Mme Longard de Longgarde; 'E. D. Gerard') (1855–1915) *Orthodox,* Longmans & Co., London, 1888; *A Queen of Curds and Creams,* Eden, Remington & Co., London, 1892; *An Arranged Marriage,* Longmans & Co., London, 1895; *The Wrong Man,* Blackwood & Sons, Edinburgh and London, 1895; *A Forgotten Sin,* Blackwood & Sons, Edinburgh and London, 1898; *The Conquest of London,* Methuen & Co., London, 1900; and more than thirty others

Gerard, Emily Jane (Madame de Laszowski) (1855–1915) *The Land Beyond the Forest,* 1888; *Bis: Four Tales,* 1890; *A Secret Mission,* 1891; *A Foreigner,* 1896; *An Electric Shock and Other Stories,* 1897 (all Blackwood, Edinburgh & London); *The Voice of a Flower,* A. D. Innes & Co.,

London, 1893; *The Tragedy of a Nose (A Brief Delirium)*, Digby, Long & Co., London, 1898; *The Extermination of Love*, Blackwood, Edinburgh & London, 1901

Gerard, Dorothea and Emily *A Sensitive Plant*, 3 vols, Kegan Paul & Co., London, 1891; *The Heron's Tower: A Romance*, Methuen, London, 1904; *Honour's Glassy Bubble*, William Blackwood, London, 1906

Glover, Jean (1758–1801) ('O'er the Muir Amang the Heather') see Tytler and Watson, 1871 and Kerrigan, 1991

Godwin, Mrs Catherine Grace (née Garnett) **(1798–1845)** *The Night Before the Bridal, and other poems*, 1824; *Reine Canziani: A Tale of Modern Greece*, 1825; *The Wanderer's Legacy*, 1829; *The Reproving Angel: A Vision*, 1835; *Cousin Kate; or, The Punishment of Pride*, 1836; *Basil Harlow; or, Prodigality is not Generosity*, 1836; *Alicia Grey; or, To Be Useful is to be Happy*, 1837; *Josephine; or, Early Trials*, 1837; *Louisa Seymour; or, Hasty Impressions*, 1837; *Scheming: A Tale*, 1838; *The Poetical Works of Catherine Grace Godwin*, ed. with a sketch of her life by A. Cleveland Wigan 1854 (all published in London)

Gordon-Cumming, Frederica Constance (1837–1924) *At Home in Fiji*, William Blackwood & Sons, Edinburgh and London, 1881; *From the Hebrides to the Himalayas: A Sketch of Eighteen Months, Wanderings in Western Isles and Eastern Highlands*, Sampson Low etc., London, 1876; *A Lady's Cruise in a French Man-of-War*, Blackwood, Edinburgh and London, 1882; *Fire Fountains: The Kingdom of Hawaii*, Blackwood, Edinburgh and London, 1883; *Granite Crags: An Account of Travels in California*, Blackwood, Edinburgh and London, 1884; *In the Himalayas and on the Indian Plains*, Chatto & Windus, London, 1884; *Via Cornwall to Egypt*, Chatto & Windus, London, 1885; *Wanderings in China*, Blackwood, Edinburgh and London, 1886; *The Last Commandment: A Word to Every Christian*, Church of England, Missionary Society, 1889; *Two Happy Years in Ceylon*, Blackwood, Edinburgh and London, 1892; *Memories*, Blackwood, Edinburgh, 1904; and others

Graham, Clementina Stirling (1782–1877) *Mystifications (in prose and verse)*, privately printed, Edinburgh, 1859

Grant, Anne (of Laggan) (née MacVicar) **(1755–1838)** *Poems on Various Subjects*, Longman and Co., Edinburgh and London, 1803; *Letters from the Mountains; being the Real Correspondence of a Lady between the Years 1773 and 1803*, 3 vols, Longman and Co., London, 1806; ed. in 2 vols, with notes and additions by J. P. Grant, Longman, Brown, Green and Longmans, London, 1845; *Memoirs of an American Lady with Sketches of Manners and Scenery in America as They Existed Previous to the Revolution*, 2 vols, Longman and Co., London, 1808; *Essays on the Superstitions of the Highlanders of Scotland, with Translations from the Gaelic*, 2 vols, Longman and Co., London, 1811; *Eighteen Hundred and Thirteen: A Poem*, 1814; *Memoir and Correspondence of Mrs Grant of Laggan*, ed. J. P. Grant, 3 vols, Longman, Brown, Green and Longmans, London, 1844

Grant, Elizabeth Grant (of Carron) (1745–1814) ('Roy's Wife of Aldivalloch') see Eyre-Todd, 1896 and Rogers, 1855–8

Grant, Elizabeth (of Rothiemurchus) (1797–1885) *Memoirs of a Highland Lady*, ed. Lady Strachey, J. Murray, London, 1898; 2 vols, ed. Andrew Tod, Canongate, Edinburgh, 1988; *The Highland Lady in Ireland*, ed. Patricia Pelly and Andrew Tod, Canongate, Edinburgh, 1991; *The Irish Journals of Elizabeth Smith 1840–1850*, ed. Thomson and McGusty, Oxford University Press, London, 1980 *A Highland Lady in France*. ed. Patricia Pelly and Andrew Tod, Tuckwell, East Linton, 1996

Halket, Lady Anne (1623–99) *The Autobiography of Lady Anne Halket*, Edinburgh, 1701; modern edition, ed. J. Loftis, Clarendon Press, Oxford, 1979; *Meditations on the Twentieth and Fifth Psalm*, Edinburgh, 1701; *Meditations and Prayers upon the First Week*, Edinburgh, 1701; *Meditations upon the Seven Gifts of the Holy Spirit*, 1702; *Meditations upon Joshbeshi's Request*, 1702

Hamilton, Elizabeth (1756–1816) *Translation of the Letters of a Hindoo Rajah; Written Previous to, and during the Period of his Residence in England. To Which is Prefixed a Preliminary Dissertation on the History, Religion and Manners of the Hindoos*, for G. G. and J. Robertson, London, 1796; *Memoirs of Modern Philosophers: A Novel*, for R. Crutwell, Bath, 1800; reprinted 1992 with an introduction by Peter Garside. *Letters on the Elementary Principles of Education*, for H. Colbert, Dublin, 1801; *Letters on Education*, for G. G. and J. Robertson, Bath, 1801; *Memoirs of the Life of Agrippina, the Wife of Germanicus*, for G. G. and J. Robertson, Bath, 1804; *Letters Addressed to the Daughter of a Nobleman on the Formation of*

Religious and Moral Principle, for T. Cadell and W. Davies, London, 1806; *The Cottagers of Glenburnie: A Tale for the Farmer's Ingle-nook*, Manners & Miller, Edinburgh, 1808; *Exercises in Religious Knowledge*, Manners & Miller, Edinburgh, 1809; *A Series of Popular Essays Illustrative of Principles Essentially Connected with the Improvement of the Understanding, the Imagination, and the Heart*, Manners & Miller, Edinburgh, 1813; *Examples of Questions Calculated to Excite and Exercise the Infant Mind*, Walker & Greig, Edinburgh, 1815; *Hints Addressed to the Patrons of Schools: Principally Intended to Shew that the Benefits Derived from the New Modes of Teaching May be Increased by a Partial adoption of the Plan of Pestalozzi. To Which are Subjoined Examples of Questions Calculated to Excite and Exercise the Infant Mind*, Longman, Hurst, Rees, Orme & Brown, London, 1815; *Memoirs of the Late Mrs Elizabeth Hamilton with a Selection from Her Correspondence and Other Unpublished Writings* 2 vols, ed. Elizabeth Benger, Longman, Hurst, Rees, Orme, Brown & Green, London, 1818

Hamilton, Janet (1795–1873) *Poems and Essays of a Miscellaneous Character on Subjects of General Interest*, Thomas Murray, Glasgow, 1863; *Poems of Purpose and Sketches in Prose of Scottish Peasant Life and Character in Auld Langsyne*; with a glossary, Thomas Murray and Son, Glasgow, 1865; *Poems and Ballads*, Thomas Murray, Glasgow, 1868; *Poems Essays and Sketches*, James Maclehose, Glasgow, 1870

Hamilton, Mary, Lady (1739–1816), *Munster Village* 1788; new edn, Pandora, London and New York, 1987

Hardy, Robina Forrester (d.1891) *The Pearl Necklace: A Story for the Young*, John S. Marr & Sons, Glasgow, 1880; *Whin-bloom* (new edn) Oliphant, Anderson & Ferrier, Edinburgh, 1883; *Jack Halliday: A Grassmarket Hero; or, Sketches of Life and Character in an Old City Parish* 1883; *Glenairlie; or, The Last of the Graemes*, 1884; *Within a Mile o' Edinburgh Town* (2nd edn) 1886 *Fickle Fortune*, 1886 (all Oliphant, Anderson & Ferrier, Edinburgh); *Frieda's First Lesson*, T. Nelson & Sons, London, 1887; *The Ghost of Greytoun Manor*, T. Nelson & Sons, London, 1887; *Life to Those That are Bound. . .*, new edn,. . .Oliphant, Anderson & Ferrier, 1887; *Diarmid; or, Friends in Kettletoun*, Oliphant, Anderson & Ferrier, 1889; *The Story of a Coral Necklace*, T. Nelson & Sons, London and New York, 1889; *Kilgarvie*, Oliphant, Anderson & Ferrier, Edinburgh, 1889; *Archie: a Story of Changing Fortunes, and Other Stories*, Oliphant, Anderson & Ferrier, 1890; *Tibby's Tryst, or 'I will lift up mine eyes unto the hills'*, Oliphant, Anderson & Ferrier, Edinburgh and London, 1891; *The Launch of the Victory*, T. Nelson & Sons, London and New York, 1891

Hartley, Elizabeth, *The Prairie Flower and Other Poems*, Dumbarton, 1870

Hawker, Mary Elizabeth Morwenna Paulin, 'Lanoe Falconer' 1848–1908) *Cecilia de Noel*, Macmillan & Co., London and New York, 1891; *Mademoiselle Ixe*, 7th edn, Unwin, London, 1891; *The Hotel d'Angleterre, and other stories*, Cassell, New York, 1891; *Shoulder to Shoulder*, Griffith & Farran, London, 1891; *Old Hampshire Vignettes*, Macmillan & Co., London and New York, 1907

Hawkins, Susannah (1787–1868) *The Poems and Songs of Susanna Hawkins*, printed for the author by J. M'Diarmid & son, Dumfries, 1846

Hering, Jeanie (afterwards Acton) (1846–1929) *Garry: A Holiday Story*, Bell & Daldy, London, 1868; *Little Pickles: A Tale for Children*, Cassell, London, 1872; *Golden Days*, London, 1873; *Through the Mist*, Virtue, Spalding & Daldy, London, 1874; *Honour and Glory; or, Hard to Win*, London and New York, 1876; *The Child's Delight*, G. Routledge & Sons, London, 1878; *A Banished Monarch and Other Stories*, Cassell & Co, London, 1880; *The Dog Picture Book*, G. Routledge & Sons, London, 1880; *A Rough Diamond*, 1880; *The Town Mouse*, 1880; *Wee Lammie*, 1880; *Minnie's Dolls*, 1880 (all G. Routledge & Sons, London); *Honour is My Guide*, The Golden Mottoes Series, 1886; *Elf: A Tale*, G. Routledge & Sons, London, 1887; *Put to the Test*, 1889 *Adventures of a Perambulator: True Details of a Family History*, 1894 (both G. Routledge & Sons, London)

Holdsworth, Annie E. (d.1910?) *Spindles and Oars, or Chronicles of Skyrle*, C. H. Kelly, London, 1893; *The Years that the Locust Hath Eaten*, W. Heinemann, London, 1896; *The Gods Arrive*, W. Heinemann, London, 1897; *The Valley of the Great Shadow*, W. Heinemann, London, 1900; *Great Lowlands*, Hodder & Stoughton, London, 1901; *A Garden of Spinsters*, Walter Scott Publishing Co., London and Newcatle upon Tyne, 1904; *A New Paulo and Francesco*, John Lane, New York and London, 1904; *The Iron Gates*, T. Fisher Unwin, London 1906; *Lady Letty Brandon*, John Long, London, 1909; *The Little Company of Ruth*, Methuen & Co.,

London, 1910; *Dame Verona of the Angels: A Study in Temperament*, Methuen & Co., London, 1912; *The Book of Anna*, Hutchison & Co., London, 1913

Hume, Anna (fl.1630–44) translation of Petrarch's *The Triumphs of Love, Chastity and Death*, Evan Tyler, Edinburgh, 1644; reprinted in Bohn, *Petrarch by Various Hands*, 1859

Hunter, Anne (née Home) (1742–1821) *Poems*, T. Payne, London, 1802 *The Sports of the Genii*, London, 1804 *A New Ballad Entitled 'The Times'*, ?1804; *Songs, with Memoir*, see Rogers, vol. 1, 1855

Inglis, Mrs Margaret Maxwell (née Murray) (1774–1843) *Songs, with Memoir*, see Rogers vol. 1, 1855; and *Miscellaneous Collection of Poems, Chiefly Scriptural*, Edinburgh, 1838

Irving, Elizabeth Jane *Fireside Lays*, Robert Anderson, Glasgow, 1872

Jay, Harriet ('Charles Marlowe') (1857–1932) *The Queen of Connaught*, 1875; *The Dark Colleen*, R. Bentley & Son, 1876; *Madge Dunraven*, London, Guildford, 1879; *The Priest's Blessing; or, Poor Patrick's Progress from This World to a Better*, F. V. White & Co., London and Edinburgh, 1881; *Through the Stage Door*, 1881; *Two Men and a Maid*, 1881; *My Connaught Cousins*, 1883; *A Marriage of Convenience*, 1885 (all F. V. White & Co., London and Edinburgh); *The Strange Adventures of Mr Brown*, R. Buchanan, London, 1897; *Robert Buchanan: Some Accounts of his Life, his Life's Work and his Literary Friendships*, T. Fisher Unwin, London, 1903; as Charles Marlowe with Robert Buchanan, *The Strange Adventures of Miss Brown: A Farcical Play in 3 Acts*, French, London, 1921

Jenkin, H(enrietta) C(amilla) (née Jackson) (?1807–85) *Violet Bank and its Inmates*, 1858; *Cousin Stella*, 1859; *Who Breaks – Pays*, 1861; *Skirmishing*, 1862; *Once Again*, 1865; *Two French Marriages*, London, 1868; *A Psyche of Today*, New York, 1868; *Madame de Beaupres*, New York, 1869; *Within an Ace*, London, 1869; *Jupiter's Daughters*, London, 1874

Johnston, Ellen (c. 1835–73) *Autobiography, Poems and Songs of Ellen Johnston, the Factory Girl*, William Love, Glasgow, 1867

Johnston, Grace L. Keith ('Leslie Keith') *What an Old Myth May Teach*, London, 1878; *Master Troublesome*, M. Ward & Co., London, 1879; *Nobody's Laid*, J. F. Shaw & Co., London, 1880; *Surrender: A Novel*, Sampson, Law & Co., London, 1881; *Alasnam's Lady: A Modern Romance*, Bentley & Son, London, 1882; *Venetia's Lovers: An Uneventful Story*, Bentley & Son, London, 1884; *The Chilcotes; or, Two Widows*, Ward & Downey, London, 1886; *St Cecilia: Her Dream and its Fulfillment*, Kent & Co., London, 1887; *Uncle Bob's Niece: A Novel*, Ward & Downey, London, 1888; *A Hurricane in Petticoats*, Bentley & Son, London, 1889; *Ralph Ellison's Opportunity, and East and West*, Religious Tracts Society, London, 1889; *Of all Degrees*, Religious Tracts Society, London, 1890; *The Halletts: A Country Town Chronicle*, R. Bentley & Son, London, 1891; *Our Street*, Religious Tracts Society, London, 1892; *When the Bour-Tree Blooms*, Religious Tracts Society, London, 1894; *A Troublesome Pair*, R. Bentley & Son, London, 1894; *For Love of Prue*, A. D. Innes & Co., London, 1895; *My Bonnie Lady*, Jarrold & Sons, London, 1897; *The Mischief Maker*, R. Bentley & Son, London, 1898; *Penance*, Hodder & Stoughton, London, 1901; *Scots Thistle*, Religious Tracts Society, London, 1902; *The Deceiver*, London, 1905

Johnstone, Christian Isobel ('Meg Dods') (1781–1857) *The Saxon and the Gael: or, The Northern Metropolis: Including a View of the Lowland and Highland Character*, T. Tegg & T. Dick, London, 1814; *Clan-Albin: A National Tale*, Macredie, Skelly and Muckersy, Edinburgh, 1815; *The Wars of the Jews, as Related by Josephus. Adapted to the Capacities of Young Persons*, Harris & Son, London, 1823; *The Cook and Housewife's Manual: Containing the most Approved Modern Receipes etc* (under the pseudonym, 'Mrs Margaret Dods, of the Cleikum Inn, St Ronans'), Edinburgh, for the Author, 1826; *Scenes of Industry Displayed in the Bee-hive and the Ant-hill*, J. Harris, London, 1827; *Elizabeth de Bruce*, William Blackwood, Edinburgh, 1827; *The Students; or, Biography of Grecian Philosophers*, John Harris, London, n.d.; *Diversions of Hollycot; or, The Mother's Art of Thinking*, Oliver & Boyd, Edinburgh, 1828; *Nights of the Round Table; or, Stories of Aunt Jane and her Friends*, Oliver & Boyd, Edinburgh, 1832; *True Tales of the Irish Peasantry, as Related by Themselves. Selected by Mrs Johnstone from the Report of the Poor-law Commissioners*, P. Brown, Edinburgh, 1839; *The Edinburgh Tales* (including some work by others), W. Tait, Edinburgh, 1845–6

Keddie, Henrietta, ('Sarah Tytler') (1827–1914) *Phemie Millar*, 1854; *The Nut Brown Maids*, 1859; *My Heart is in the Highlands*, 1861; *Heroines in Obscurity*, 1871; *A Douce Lass*, 1877; *Kincaid's Widow*, 1895; *Three Generations: The Story of a Middle-Class Scottish Family*, John Murray, London, 1911; and others; as **Sarah Tytler**: *Citoyenne Jacqueline*, London, 1865; *Songstresses* *of Scotland*, with J. L. Watson, Strahan, London, 1871; *St Mungo's City*, Chatto & Windus, London 1884; *Logie Town*, Ward & Downey, 1887; *Miss Nanse*, J Long, London, 1890; and over 100 others

Kennedy, Grace (1782–1824) *The Decision, or, Religion Must be All, or is Nothing*, Edinburgh, 1825; *Dunnallan, or Know What You Judge a Story*, 1825; *Profession is not Principle; or, The Name of Christian is not Christianity*, 4th edn, 1825; *Anna Ross: A Story for Children*, 3rd edn, 1826; *The Word of God; or, The Word of Man Addressed to Irish Catholics*, 1827 *Father Clement: A Roman Catholic Story*, (all W. Oliphant, Edinburgh), 1835

Laird, Margaret Thomson (1810–69) *Anniversary Lines on the Death of My Only Son – Memorial Volume of Poems*, printed for private circulation, Alex Gardner, Paisley, 1893; see also Leonard, 1990

Lawson, Jessie Kerr (1838–1917) *The Epistles o' Hugh Ainslie*, 1888; *The Curse that Came Home*, Oliphant, Anderson & Ferrier, Edinburgh 1891; *A Vain Sacrifice*, Oliphant, Anderson & Ferrier, Edinburgh, 1892; *Dr Bruno's Wife*: A Toronto Society Story, Simpkin & Marshall, London, 1893; *Euphie Lyn; or, The Fishers of Old Inweerie*, Oliphant, Anderson & Ferrier, Edinburgh, 1893; *The Harvest of Moloch: A Story of To-day*, John Poole and Co., Toronto, 1908; *Lays and Lyrics*, William Briggs, Toronto, 1913

Lindsay, Christian (fl.1580s) no surviving texts; see Dunnigan chapter

Little, Janet (1759–1813) *The Poetical Works of Janet Little, The Scotch Milkmaid*, Ayr, 1792

Lundie, Jane Catherine (1821–84) *America as I Found it by the Mother of Mary Lundie Duncan*, R. Carter & Bros, New York, 1852; see also Kerrigan, 1991

Mabon, Agnes Stuart (of Jedburgh) *Homely Rhymes from the Banks of the Jed*, J. & R. Parlane, Paisley, 1887

MacDonald, Cicely/Sìleas Na Ceapaich (?1729–?1660) see C. O. Baoill, *Bàrdachd Shìlis na Ceapaich*, Edinburgh, 1972 see Kerrigan, 1991 and Watson, 1995

Macgregor, Mrs, of Glenstrae (c. 1570) see Watson, 1995

McKellar, Mary (1836–90) *Poems and Songs in Gaelic and English*, 1880

MacKenzie, Hannah Brown *Kitty's Cousin*, Blackie & Son, London, 1885; *Worthy of Trust*, Blackie & Son, London 1885; *After Touch of Wedded Hands*, Oliphant & Co., Edinburgh & London, 1891; *Crowned Victor: A Story of Strife*, Oliphant & Anderson, Edinburgh & London, 1894; *Hector MacRae: A Modern Story of the West Highlands*, Simpkin, Marshall & Co., London, 1898; *A Late Repentance*, S. W. Partridge & Co., London, 1902

MacLeod, Mary/Màiri Nighean Alasdair Ruaidh (?1615–?1706) *Gaelic Songs of Mary MacLeod*, ed. J. C. Watson, Oliver & Boyd for the Scottish Gaelic Texts Society, 1965

MacNaughtan, Sarah (?1864–1916) *Selah Harrison*, R. Bentley & Son, London, 1898; *The Fortune of Christina McNab*, Methuen & Co., London, 1901; *The Gift*, Hodder & Stoughton, London, 1904; *The Expensive Miss Du Cane*, William Heinemann, London, 1907; *Four-Chimneys*, Thomas Nelson & Sons, London, 1907; *Three Miss Graemes*, John Murray, London, 1908; *Us Four*, John Murray, London, 1909; *The Andersons*, John Murray, London, 1910; *Peter and Jane; or The Missing Heir*, Methuen & Co., London, 1911; *Snow upon the Desert*, Hodder & Stoughton, London, 1913; *A Green Englishman and Other Stories of Canada*, Smith Elder & Co., London, 1914; *A Woman's Diary of the War*, T. Nelson, London, 1915; *My War Experiences in Two Continents*, ed. Mrs Lionel Salmon, John Murray, London, 1919

Macpherson, Mary (of Skye)/Màiri Nic a'Phearsain (Màiri Mhòr nan Oran) (1821–1898) *Comhradh nan Cnoc: Torr-a-bheathain agus Creag-phadruig*, Archibald Sinclair, Glasgow, 1887 see also Dòmhnall Eachann Meek, *Màiri Mhòr nan Oran*, Gairm, Glasgow, 1970

MacRae, Flora Maitland *Wonderful Tales of God's Goodness and Love*, J. E. Hawkins, London, 1887; *The Private Note Book Opened; or, A Broken Heart Bound Up*, Drummond's Tract Depot, Stirling, 1888; *Jack Clayton*, Geol Stoneman, London, 1904; *The Book at the Bottom of the Sea*, Chas. J. Thynne, London, 1907; *Under the Burning Sun; or, The Two Ministers*, Elliot Stock, London, 1910; *Hymns of Comfort for the Sick and Sorrowful*, Drummond's Tract Depot, Stirling, 1911

Maitland, Mary (fl. 1586) no surviving texts; see Dunnigan chapter

Marchbank, Agnes *Some Edinburgh Bohemians*, Tovani & Co, Auchterarder, 1891; *An Angel's Visit and A Guid Tocher (2 Tales)*, W. W. Gibbings, London, 1892; *Songs of Labour, Home and Country*, Tovani & Co., Auchterarder, 1892; *The Covenanters of Annandale*, J. & R. Parlane, Paisley, 1895; *Ruth Farmer: A Story*, Jarrold & Sons, London, 1896; *A Swatch o' Hamespun*, R. W. Hunter, Edinburgh, 1896

Mary, Queen of Scots (1542–87) *The Poems of Mary, Queen of Scots*, ed. Julian Sharman, 1873; *The Silver Casket, Being the love Letters and Love Poems attributed to Mary, Queen of Scots*, ed. Clifford Bax, n.d.; *Mary, Queen of Scots, An Anthology of Poetry*, ed. Antonia Fraser, 1981; *Bittersweet within My Heart: The Collected Poems of Mary, Queen of Scots*, ed. and translated by Robin Bell, Pavilion, London, 1992

Maughan, Janet Leith (Mrs Story) (1828–1926) *Charley Nugent; Or, Passages in the Life of a Sub*, 1860; *The St Aubyns of St Aubyn*, 1862; *Richard Langdon; or, Foreshadowed*, 1863; *The Co-Heiress*, 1866; *The Man of Mark*, 1866; *Equal to Either Fortune*, 1869; *Kitty Fisher, the Orange Girl*, Marr & Sons, Glasgow, 1881; *Early Reminiscences*, James Maclehose & Sons, Glasgow, 1911; *Later Reminiscences*, James Maclehose & Sons, Glasgow, 1913

Maxwell, Anna Maria *Letters from the Dead to the Living; and Moral Letters*, new edn, Reid & Hedderson, Paisley, 1820

Mayo, Isabella Edward, Garrett, (née Fyvie) (1843–1914) *Seen and Heard*, Strahan & Co., London, 1872; *Her Object in Life*, The Girls Own Paper Office, London, 1884; *Thoughts and Stories for Girls*, G. Routledge & Sons, London, 1884; *The Mystery of Allan Grale*, R. Bentley & Son, London, 1885; *Ways and Means; or, Voices from the Highways and Hedges*, Religious Tracts Society, London, 1889; *A Daughter of the Kelphts; or, A Girl of Modern Greece*, W. & R. Chambers, London & Edinburgh, 1897; *Other People's Stairs*, Religious Tracts Society, London, 1898; *Recollections of What I saw, What I Lived Through and What I Learned, during More than Fifty Years of Social and Literary Experience*, John Murray, London, 1910

Mclvill, Elizabeth, Lady Colville of Culross (fl.1603) *Ane Godlie Dream Compylit in Scotish Meter by M. M. Gentlewoman in Culros, at the Requeist of her Friendis*, Robert Charteris, Edinburgh and Aberdeen, 1603; see Greer, *Kissing the Rod*, 1988

Montgomery, Florence (1843–1923) *Misunderstood: A Tale*, London, 1867; *A Very Simple Story Being a Chronicle of the Thoughts and Feelings of a Child*, 1867; *Seaforth: A Novel*, London, 1878; *Herbert Manners and Other Tales*, R. Bentley & Son, London, 1880; *The Blue Veil: A New Series of Moral Tales for Children*, R. Bentley & Son, London, 1883; *Transformed; or, Three Weeks in a Lifetime*, R. Bentley & Son, London, 1886; *The Fisherman's Daughter*, Hatchards, London, 1889; *Colonel Norton: A Novel*, R. Bentley & Son, London, 1895; *Tony: A Sketch*, R. Bentley & Son, London, 1898; *An Unshared Secret and Other Stories*, Macmillan & Co., London, 1903; *Behind the Scenes in the Schoolroom. Being the Experiences of a Young Governess*, Macmillan & Co. London, 1913

Mure, Elizabeth (of Caldwell) see J. G. Fyfe (ed.), *Scottish Diaries and Memoirs 1746–1843*, with an Introduction by J. D. Mackie, Eaneas Mackay, Stirling, 1942

Murray of Stanhope, Lady *Memoirs of the Lives and Characters of the Right Honourable George Baillie of Jerviswood and of Lady Grisell Baillie*, Edinburgh, 1822

Napier, Catherine *A Month at Oostcamp*, London & Bruges, 1844; *The City of the World*, privately printed, London, 1845; *The Lay of the Palace*, J. Olliver, London, 1852

Nicholson, Ellen Corbet with James Nicholson: *Poems*, Hamilton, Adams & Co, London, 1880; *Willie Waugh, and other poems*, Menzies & Co., Edinburgh & Glasgow, 1884

Norton, Caroline (1808–77) *The Undying One, and Other Poems*, London, 1830; *The Dream, and Other Poems*, Henry Colburn, London, 1840; *The Child of the Islands: A Poem*, London, 1845; *Stuart of Dunleath: A Story of Modern Times* London, 1851; *Lost and Saved*, Hurst & Blackett, London, 1863; *Old Sir Douglas*, London, 1868; *Selected Writings of Caroline Norton*, Facsimile Reproductions with an introduction and notes by James O. Hoge and Jane Marcus, Scholars Facsimiles and Reprints, New York, 1978

Ogilvy, Dorothea Maria of Clova (1823–95) *Poems*, Aberdeen, 1865; *Willie Wabster's Wooing and Wedding*, Montrose, 1868

Oliphant, Carolina, Baroness Nairne (1766–1845) and Oliphant, Caroline (the Younger) (1807–1831) *The Life and Songs of the Baroness Nairne; with a Memoir and poems of Caroline Oliphant, the Younger* (London, 1869); both: see Ford, *The Harp of Perthshire*, 1893

Oliphant, Margaret (1828–97) *Margaret Maitland*, Colburn, London, 1849; *Caleb Field*, Colburn, London, 1851; *Merkland: A Story of Scottish Life*, Colburn, London, 1851; *Adam Graeme of Mossgray*, Hurst & Blackett,, London, 1852; *Katie Stewart*, Blackwood, Edinburgh & London, 1853; *Harry Muir*, Hurst & Blackett, London, 1853; *The Quiet Heart*, Blackwood, Edinburgh, 1854; *Magdalen Hepburn*, Hurst & Blackett, London, 1854; *Zaidée*, Blackwood,

Edinburgh, 1856; *The Days of My Life*, Hurst & Blackett, London, 1857; *The Laird of Nordlaw*, Hurst & Blackett, London, 1858; *Sundays*, Nisbet, London, 1858; *Lilliesleaf*, Hurst & Blackett, London, 1859; *Lucy Crofton*, 1860; *The House on the Moor*, 1861; *The House of Edward Irving*, 1862 (all Hurst & Blackett, London); *The Doctor's Family, and Other Stories*, Blackwood, London, 1863; ed. Merryn Williams, World's Classics, 1986 *Salem Chapel*, Blackwood, Edinburgh & London, 1863; *The Perpetual Curate*, Blackwood, Edinburgh & London, 1864; *Agnes*, 1865; *Miss Marjoribanks*, Blackwood, Edinburgh & London, 1866; ed. Penelope Fitzgerald, Virago, London, 1987; *A Son of the Soil*, Macmillan, London, 1866; *Francis of Assisi*, Macmillan, London, 1868; *The Minister's Wife*, Hurst & Blackett, London, 1869; *John: A Love Story*, Blackwood, Edinburgh, 1870; *Squire Arden*, Hurst & Blackett, London, 1871; *Ombra*, Chapman & Hall, 1872; *Innocent: A Tale of Modern Life*, Sampson Low, 1873; *A Rose in June*, Hurst & Blackett, London, 1874; *Whiteladies*, Chatto, London, 1875; *The Curate in Charge*, Beccles, 1876; ed. Merryn Williams, Alan Sutton, London, 1987; *Phoebe Junior: A Last Chronicle of Carlingford*, Hurst & Blackett, London, 1876; *Mrs Arthur*, Hurst & Blackett, London, 1877; *A Beleaguered City*, Macmillan, London, 1880; *The Ladies Lindores*, Blackwood, Edinburgh, 1880; *A Little Pilgrim in the Unseen*, Macmillan, London, 1882; *Hester*, Macmillan, London, 1883; ed. Jennifer Uglow, Virago, London, 1984; *Sir Tom*, Macmillan, London, 1884; *A Country Gentleman and His Family*, Macmillan, London, 1886; *A House Divided Against Itself*, Blackwood, Edinburgh, 1886; *The Land of Darkness*, Macmillan, London, 1888; *Lady Car*, Longmans, 1889; *Kirsteen*, Macmillan, London, 1890; ed. Merryn Williams, Everyman Classics, 1984; *The Railway Man and his Children*, Macmillan, London, 1891; *The Cuckoo in the Nest*, Hutchinson, London, 1892; *A Beleaguered City, and Other Stories*, Macmillan, London, 1892; ed. Merryn Williams, World's Classics, 1986; *The Marriage of Elinor*, 1892; *Lady William*, Macmillan, London, 1893; *Who was Lost and is Found*, Blackwood, Edinburgh, 1894; *Sir Robert's Fortune*, Methuen, London, 1895; *Jeanne d'Arc*, Putnam, 1896; *The Sisters Brontë*, Hurst & Blackett, London, 1897; *A Widow's Tale and Other Stories*, Macmillan, London, 1898; *The Autobiography of Margaret Oliphant*, ed. Mrs Harry Coghill, Blackwood, Edinburgh, 1899; ed. Elizabeth Jay, Oxford University Press, Oxford, 1990; and others

Oxlie, Mary (of Morpeth) (fl.1620s) 'Commendatory Verse To William Drummond of Hawthornden' in 1656 edition of his *Poems*; see Greer, *Kissing the Rod*, 1988 and Dunnigan chapter

Pagan, Isobel (1742–1821) *A Collection of Songs and Poems on Several Occasions*, Glasgow, 1803

Pickering, Anna (afterwards Stirling) *The Adventures of Prince Almero: A Tale of the Wind-spirit*, J. Heywood, Manchester, 1890; *Memoirs . . . of Anna Maria Wilhelmina*, ed. by her son S. Pickering, Hodder & Stoughton, London, 1903; *Coke of Norfolk and His Friends*, John Lane, London & New York, 1908

Porter, Anna Maria (1780–1832) *Artless Tales*, printed for the author, 1795; *Original Poems on Various Subjects*, Cadell, London, 1798; *The Hungarian Brothers*, J. B. Williams, Exeter, 1807; *Ballad Romances and Other Poems*, 1811; *The Recluse of Norway*, Routledge, London, 1814; *The Barony*, Longman, Rees, Orme, Brown & Green, 1830; and others

Porter, Jane (1776–1850) *The Two Princes of Persia: Addressed to Youth*, Crosby & Letterman, London, 1801; *Thaddeus of Warsaw*, Longman & Rees, London, 1803; *Aphorisms of Sir Philip Sidney with Remarks*, Longman, Hurst, Rees & Orme, London, 1807; *The Scottish Chiefs: A Romance*, Longman, Hurst, Rees & Orme, London, 1810; *The Pastor's Fireside: A Novel*, Longman, Hurst, Rees, Orme & Brown, London, 1817; *Duke Christian of Luneburg; or, Traditions from the Hartz*, Longman, Hurst, Rees, Orme, Brown & Green, London, 1824; *Tales Round a Winter Hearth* (with **Anna Maria Porter, 1780–1832**) Longman, Rees, Orme, Brown & Green, London, 1826; *Coming Out and The Field of the Forty Footsteps* (with **Anna Maria Porter**) Longman, Rees, Orme, Brown & Green, London, 1828; *Sir Edward Seaward's Narrative of His Shipwreck and Consequent Discovery of Certain Islands in the Caribbean Sea: With a Detail of Many Extraordinary and Highly Interesting Events of His Life from the Year 1733–1749 as Written in His Own Diary*. Edited [i.e. written] by Miss Jane Porter, Longman, Rees, Orme, Brown & Green, London 1831

Pyper, Mary (1795–1870) *Select Pieces (in verse)*, Edinburgh, 1847; *Sacred Poems*, Andrew Elliot, Edinburgh, 1865; *Hebrew Children: Poetical Illustrations of Biblical Character*, 1858

Reid, Marion *A Plea for Woman*, William Tait, Edinburgh, 1843; with introduction by Susanne Ferguson, Polygon, Edinburgh, 1988

Riddell, Maria (1772–1808) *Voyages to the Madeira and Leeward Carribee Islands, with Sketches of*

the Natural History of these Islands, Hill & Cadell, Edinburgh, 1792; *The Metrical Miscellany*, ed. Maria Riddell and containing some of her verses, Cadell & Davies, Edinburgh, 1802

Russell, Jessie (b. 1850) *The Blinkin' o' the Fire and Other Poems*, Cossar, Fotheringham & Co., Glasgow, 1877

Saxby, Jessie (née Edmonston) (1842–1940) *Glamour from Argyllshire (in prose and verse)*, Inveraray, Edinburgh, 1874; *Lichens from the Old Book*, Edinburgh, 1874; *Daala-Mist; or, Stories of Shetland*, J. T. Reid, Edinburgh, 1876; *Geordie Roye; or, A Waif from the Greyfriars Wynd*, J. S. Marr & Sons, Glasgow, 1979; *Snow Dreams*, Johnstone, Hunter & Co., Edinburgh, 1882; *Ben Hunson: A Story of George Watson's College*, Oliphant, Anderson & Co., Edinburgh, 1884; *The Lads of Lunda*, Nisbet & Co., London, 1887; *Oil on the Troubled Waters: A Story of the Shetland Isles*, Religious Tracts Society, London, 1888; *The Yarl's Yacht*, J. Nisbet & Co., London, 1889; *West-Nor'-West*, J. Nisbet & Co., London, 1890; *Wrecked on the Shetlands; or The Little Sea-Kings*, Religious Tracts Society, London, 1890; *Viking-Boys: A Tale)*, J. Nisbet & Co., London, 1892; *Auld Lerwick: A Personal Reminiscence*, Morrison & Gibb, Edinburgh, 1894; *Breakers Ahead; or Uncle Jack's Stories of Great Shipwrecks of Recent Times: 1869 to 1880*, T. Nelson & Sons, London, 1896; *The Saga-book of Lunda*, J. Nisbet & Co., London, 1896; *Shetland Traditional Lore*, Grant & Murray, Edinburgh, 1932; *Threads from a Tangle Skein: Poems and ponderings*, T. & J. Manson, Lerwick, 1934

Schaw, Janet (?1737–?1801) *Journal of a Lady of Quality: Being the Narrative of a Journey from Scotland to the West Indies, North Carolina and Portugal in the Years 1774 to 1776*, ed. Evangeline Walker Andrews and Charles McLean Andrews, Yale University Press, New Haven, 1921; 2nd edn, 1934; 3rd edn, with additional material, 1934

Scott, Lady Caroline Lucy (née Douglas) (1784–1857) *A Marriage in High Life*, London, 1828; *Trevelyan*, London, 1834; *Exposition of Types and Archetypes of the Old and New Testament*, London, 1856; *The Old Grey Church*, R. Bentley, London, 1856; *Incentives to Bible Study*, London, 1860; *Acrostics: Historical, Geographical and Political*, London, 1863

Scott, Lady Harriet Anne (née Shank) (1819–94) *The MP's Wife; and The Lady Geraldine*, 1838; *The Henpecked Husband*, 1847; *Percy; or, The Old Love and the New*, 1848; *Hytton House and Its Inmates*, 1850; *The Pride of Life*, 1854; *The Only Child: A Tale*, 1858; *The Skeleton in the Cupboard*, 1860; *The Dream of a Life*, 1862 (all London)

Scott, Lady John see Spottisuode, Alicia Anne

Sinclair, Catherine (1800–85) *Holiday House*, W. Whyte & Co., Edinburgh, 1839; *Modern Accomplishments*, Edinburgh & London, 1836; *Beatrice; or, The Unknown Relatives*, Ward, Lock & Tyler, London, 1852; *Hill and Valley*, W. Whyte & Co., Edinburgh, 1838; *Scotland and the Scotch*, Simpkin & Marshall, Edinburgh, 1841; *Modern Flirtations; or, A Month at Harrowgate*, W. Whyte & Co., Edinburgh, 1841; *Scotch Courtiers and the Court*, W. Whyte & Co., Edinburgh, 1842; *Charlie Seymour*, Edinburgh, 1844; *Jane Bouverie: or, Prosperity and Adversity*, Edinburgh, 1846; *The Journey of Life*, London, 1847; *Sir Edward Graham*, London, 1849; *Lord and Lady Harcourt*, London, 1850; *Beatrice*, London, 1852; *Popish Legends and Bible Truths*, Longman, Brown, Green & Longmans, 1852; *London Homes*, London, 1853; *Lady Mary Pierrepoint*, London, 1853; *Frank Vansittart; or, the Model Schoolboys*, London, 1853; *The Priest and the Curate*, London, 1853; *The Mysterious Marriage*, London, 1854; *Cross Purposes: A Novel*, London, 1855; *The Cabman's Holiday*, Ipswich, London, 1855; *Torchester Abbey*, 1857; *Anecdotes of the Caesars*, Ipswich, London, 1858; and others

Skein, Lilias (?–1697) *A Warning to the Magistrates and Inhabitants of Aberdeen: An Expostulary Epistle, Directed to Robert Macquare Delivered Some Months since at his House in Rotterdam*, in Robert Barclay the Elder, *Apology for the True Christian Divinity etc*, Benjamin Clerk, London, 1679; see also William Walker, *The Bards of Bon-Accord, 1375–1860*, Edmond & Spark, Aberdeen, 1887

Skene, Felicia (1821–99) *The Isles of Greece*, London, 1843; *Wayfaring Sketches among the Greeks and the Turks, and on the Shores of the Danube*, Chapman & Hall, London, 1847; *Use and Abuse: A Tale*, F. & J. Rivington, 1849; *The Tutor's Ward: A Novel*, Colburn, London, 1851; *St Alban's; or, The Prisoners of Hope*, London, 1853; *Hidden Depths*, Edmonston & Douglas, Edinburgh, 1866; *Awakened*, The Christian World Annual, London, 1874; *A Memoir of Alexander Bishop of Brechin*, J. Masters, 1876; *The Shadow of the Holy Week*, Masters & Co., London, 1883; *Dew Drops*, A. R. Mowbray & Co., Oxford & London, 1888

Somerville, Mary (1780–1872) *The Mechanism of the Heavens*, 1831; *On the Connection of the Physical Sciences*, John Murray, 1834; *Physical Geography*, 2 vols, 1848; *On Molecular and*

Microscopic Science, London, 1869; *Personal Recollections from Early Life to Old Age, with a Selection of Her Correspondence*, by her daughter, Martha Somerville, John Murray, London, 1873; *An Unpublished Letter of Mary Somerville, with a Comment by F. E. Hutchison*, reprinted from the 'Oxford Magazine', Oxonian Press, Oxford, 1929

Spence, Elizabeth Isabella (1768–1832) *Summer Excursions*, 1809; *Sketches of the Present Manners, Customs and Scenery of Scotland*, Longmans, London, 1811; *Letters from the North Highlands, Written during Summer 1816*, London, 1817; *A Traveller's Tale of the Last Century*, 1819; *Old Stories*, London, 1822; *How to be Rid of a Wife*, Longman, Hurst & Co., 1823; and others

Spottiswoode, Alicia Anne (Lady John Scott) (1810–1900) *Poems and Songs*, ed. E. David Douglas, 1904

Steel, Flora Annie (1847–1929) *From the Five Rivers*, W. Heinemann, London, 1893; *The Flower of Forgiveness*, Macmillan & Co., London, 1894; *Tales of the Punjab*, Macmillan & Co., London, 1894; *The Potter's Thumb*, Heinemann, London, 1894; *Red Rowans*, Macmillan & Co., London, 1895; *On the Face of the Waters*, Heinemann, London, 1896; *In the Permanent Way*, Heinemann, London, 1898; *The Hosts of the Lord*, Heinemann, London, 1900; *In the Guardianship of God*, Heinemann, London, 1903; *India*, A. & C. Black, London, 1905; *A Book of Mortals*, Heinemann, London, 1905; *A Prince of Dreamers*, Heinemann, 1908; *The Gift of the Gods*, Heinemann, London, 1911; *King-Errant*, Heinemann, London, 1912; *The Adventures of Akbar*, Heinemann, London, 1913; *Dramatic History of India*, K. & J. Cooper, Bombay, 1917; *Mistress of Men*, Heinemann, London, 1917; *English Fairy Tales*, Retold by F. A. Steel (illustrated by Arthur Rackham), Macmillan & Co., London, 1918; *The Builder*, John Lane, London, 1928; *The Curse of Eve*, John Lane, London, 1929; *The Garden of Fidelity*, Macmillan & Co., London, 1929; and others

Stopes, Charlotte (1841–1929) (née **Carmichael**) *British Freewomen: Their Historical Privilege*, Swann Sonnenschein & Co., London, 1894; *The Constitutional Basis of Woman's Suffrage*, Darien Press, Edinburgh, 1908; *Shakespeare's Stage*, Alexander Moring, London, 1913

Strain, Mrs Euphans H. (née **McNaughton**) **(d. 1934)** *A Man's Foes, Ward, Lock & Bowden*, London, 1896; *School in Fairyland*, T. F. Unwin, London, 1896; *Elmslie's Drag-Net*, Methuen & Co., London, 1900; *Laura's Legacy*, T. F. Unwin, London, 1903; *A Prophet's Reward*, W. Blackwood & Sons, Edinburgh & London, 1908

Stuart, Lady Louisa (1757–1851) *Lady Louisa Stuart: Selections from Her Manuscripts*, ed. J. A. Home, D. Douglas, Edinburgh, 1899; *Letters*, selected and introduced R. Brimley Johnson, John Lane, London, 1926; 'Biographical Anecdotes of Lady Mary Wortley Montagu', in Lady Mary Wortley Montagu, *Essays and Poems*, ed. Robert Halsband and Isobel Grundy, Clarendon Press, Oxford, 1977; *Memoire of Frances, Lady Douglas*, ed. and introduced by Jill Rubenstein, with a preface by J. Steven Watson, Scottish Academic Press, Edinburgh, 1985

Thomson, Lady Margaret *Verses*, Glasgow, 1874; *Poems*, ed. by her children, 1888

Todd, Margaret Georgia ('Graham Travers') (1859–1918) *Mona Maclean: Medical Student*, W. Blackwood & Sons, Edinburgh, 1892; *Fellow Travellers: A Novel*, W. Blackwood & Sons, Edinburgh & London, 1896; *Windyhaugh: A Novel*, W. Blackwood & Sons, Edinburgh & London, 1896; *Growth: A Novel*, Archibald Constable & Co., London, 1906; *The Way of Escape*, John Murray, London, 1908; *The Life of Sophia Jex-Blake*, Macmillan & Co., London, 1918

Tytler, Sarah see Keddie, Henrietta

Veitch, Sophie Frances Fane ('J. A. St. John Blythe') *Wise as a Serpent* (as Blythe), R. Bentley, London, 1869; *Wife or Slave* (as Blythe), R. Bentley & Son, London, 1872; *The Saga of Halfred the Sigskald* (trans), 1886; *James Hepburn, Free Church Minister*, A. Gardner, London, 1887; *The Dean's Daughter*, A. Gardner, Paisley & London, 1888; *Duncan Moray, Farmer*, A. Gardner, Paisley & London, 1890; *Margaret Drummond, Millionaire*, A. & C. Black, London, 1893; *A Modern Crusader: A Novel*, A. & C. Black, London, 1893.

Waldie, Charlotte Ann (1788–1859) *Days of Battle, or Quatre-Bras and Waterloo; by an Englishwoman Resident in Brussels in June 1815*, John Murray, London, 1817; *Continental Adventures: A Novel*, Hurst, Robinson & Co., London, 1826

Waldie, Jane (1791–1826) *Sketches Descriptive of Italy in the Years 1816 and 1817*, London, 1820

Walford, Lucy Bethia (née **Colquhoun**) **(1845–1915)** *The Merchant's Sermon, and other Stories*, Edinburgh, 1870; *Mr Smith*, Edinburgh & London, 1874; *Pauline*, Edinburgh & London, 1877; *Cousins: A Novel*, Blackwood, Edinburgh & London, 1879; *Troublesome Daughters*, 1880; *Dick Netherby*, 1881; *The Baby's Grandmother*, 1884; *Nan, and Other Stories*, 1885;

The History of a Week, 1886 (all Blackwood); *Her Great Idea, and Other Stories*, Sampson Low & Co., London, 1888; *A Sage at Sixteen*, Spencer, Blackett & Hallam, London, 1889; *A Stiff-necked Generation*, Blackwood, Edinburgh & London, 1889; *The Mischief of Monica*, Longmans & Co., London, 1892; *Bertie Bootboy*, Christian Knowledge Society, London, 1892; *The One Good Guest*, Longmans & Co., London, 1892; *A Question of Penmanship*: Stories, Griffith, Farran & Co., London, 1893; *Stay-at-homes*, Longmans & Co., London, 1893; *The Matchmaker*, Longmans & Co., London, 1894; *'Ploughed', and Other Stories*, Longmans & Co., London, 1894; *Merrielands Farm*, Christian Knowledge Society, London, 1895; *Successors to the Title*, Methuen & Co., London, 1896; *Iva Kildare: A Matrimonial Problem*, Longmans & Co., London, 1897; *The Intruders*, Longmans & Co., London, 1898; *Leddy Marget*, Longmans & Co., London, 1898; *The Little Legacy, and Other Stories*, C. A. Pearson, London, 1899; *Sir Patrick: the Puddock*, C. A. London, 1899; *One of Ourselves*, Longmans & Co., London, 1900; *The Black Familiars*, James Clarke & Co., London, 1903; *Charlotte*, Longmans & Co., London, 1902; *Leonore Stubbs*, Longmans & Co., London, 1908; *Memories of Victorian London*, Edward Arnold, London, 1912; *Recollections of a Scottish Novelist*, Williams & Norgate, London, 1910; reissued Waddesdon, Bucks., 1984; *Star*, Thomas Nelson & Sons, London, 1922; and others

Wallace, Lady Eglantine (née Maxwell) (d.1803) *The Ton; or, Follies of Fashion: A Comedy*, London, 1788; *Letter from Lady Wallace to Captain William Wallace, aid de camp to Colonel Maxwell at Bangalore*, Debrett, 1792; *The Conduct of the King of Prussia and General Dumourier Investigated*, London, 1793; *A Sermon Addressed to the People, Pointing out the Only Sure Method to Obtain a Speedy Peace and Reform*, S. & J. Reed, London, 1794; *The Whim: A Comedy in Three Acts*, Margate, 1795

Wardlaw, Lady Elizabeth (1677–1727) *Hardyknute: A Fragment*, 1719

Watt, Christian (1833–1923) *The Christian Watt Papers*, ed. and with an Introduction by David Fraser, Paul Harris, Edinburgh, 1983

Werner, Alice (1859–1935) *A Time and Times: Ballads of East and West*, T. Fisher Unwin, London, 1886; *Tom Winter's Life-Work*, Sunday School Union, London, 1886; *O'Driscoll's Weird and Other Stories*, Cassell & Co., London, 1892; *The Humour of Italy*, 1892; *The Humour of Holland*, 1893; *Chapenga's White Man: A Story of Central Africa*, Chatto & Windus, London, 1901; *The Natives of British Central Africa*, Constable, London, 1906; *African Mythology*, Marshall Jones Co., Boston, 1925; *African Stories*, Watts & Co., London, 1932; *Myths and Legends of the Bantu*, Harrap, 1933

Wright, Frances (afterward D'Arusmont) (1795–1852) *Altorf: A Tragedy*, M. Carey & Sons, Philadelphia, 1819; *Views of Society and Manners in America: in a Series of Letters from that Country to a Friend in England, during the Years 1818, 1819 and 1820*, By an Englishwoman, Longman, Hurst, Rees, Orme & Brown, London, 1821; *A Few Days in Athens, Being the Translation of a Greek Manuscript Discovered in Herculaneum*, Longman & Co., London, 1822; *Course of Popular Lectures, as Delivered by Frances Wright, in New York, Philadelphia and Other Cities of the United States*, Office of the Free Enquirer, New York, 1829; *Introductory Address, Delivered by Frances Wright, at the Opening of the Hall of Science, New York . . .* , George H. Evans, New York, 1829; *Address containing a Review of the Times, as First Delivered in the Hall of Science, New York, May 9, 1830*, New York, 1830; *Fables*, New York, 1832; J. Watson, London, 1842; *Parting Address, as Delivered at the Bowery Theater to the People of New York in June 1830*, New York 1830; *What is the Matter? A Political Address*, published for the author, New York, 1838; *Tracts on Republican Government and National Education Addressed to the Inhabitants of the United States of America*, New York (Robert Dale Owen wrote the tract on Republican Government and Fanny Wright that on National Education); *Biography, Notes and Political Letters of Frances Wright D'Arusmont*, J. Myles, Dundee, 1844; Boston 1848; *England the Civiliser: Her History Developed in its Principles*, London, 1848

1900–Present: Select Bibliography

This bibliography deals with writers whose work mainly appears after 1900. Where possible, dates of birth and death are given, as with publishers of individual books. Works by authors writing for children are not listed, apart from a small number whose influence is generally regarded as unusually significant. Considerations of space preclude listing all authors; the names of other significant writers of popular, historical and romantic fiction are listed at the end of the bibliography.

For information regarding the location of contemporary unpublished plays, see Jan McDonald's chapter, 'Scottish Women Dramatists since 1945'.

Adam, Agnes, *Great Expectations*, 1966; *Batcherlor's Club: A Play About Robert Burns*, 1973; *Birds of Prey: A One-Act Scots Comedy*, 1973; *The Wedding Presents: A One-Act Play for Seven Women*, 1977; *Community Centre: A Three-Act Scots Comedy*, 1978; *Robing of the Minister*, 1980; *Well Connected*, 1937; *The New Hell*, 1938; *Braidlands*, 1940; *5 Brick Lane*, 1940; *William the Conqueror*, 1941; *The Birthday*, 1947; *The Door that Opens*, 1948; *The Lass wi' the Tocher*, 1948; *Sing a New Song: A One Act Scots Play for Eight Women*, 1946; *Spring Song*, 1949; *The World at Your Fingertips*, 1949; *A Bit of Land*, 1949; *With Decorum and Economy*, 1950; *The Whustle*, 1950; *A Great Occasion: A One Act Scots Play*, 1950; *The Bone Setter*, 1951; *China Dogs*, 1952; *The Masterfu' Wife: A One Act Scots Comedy*, 1952; *All on a Summer's Evening*, 1954; *Dow's Doughnuts*, 1954; *Sunshine Voyage*, 1954; *Forbid Them Not*, 1954; *Christmas*, 1954; *Between Two Thieves*, 1955; *Treasure in Heaven*, 1955; *Home Sweet Home*, 1955; *Aunt Janet*, 1956; *The Old Chest*, 1957; *Old Maid*, 1957; *The Paisley Shawl*, 1957; *A Cameo from Cranford*, William Maclellan, Glasgow, 1946; *Caller Merrin*, Galashiels, 1958; *The Letter*, 1959; *A Matter of Diplomacy*, 1959; *High Tea*, 1959; *I Bequeath*, 1960; *The Crack O' Doom*, 1960; *The Cracked Crown*, 1960; *Coronets and Cows*, 1962; *Happy Families*, 1962; *House of Shadows*, 1963; *Sunshine Susie*, 1964; *Paddy Muldoon's Ghost*, 1964; *A Pearl of Great Price*, 1965; *The Strawberry*, 1965; *Miss Primrose's Husband*, 1966; *Still Waters*, 1966 (all published by Brown Son and Ferguson, Glasgow, unless otherwise listed)

Adamson, Margot Robert (1898–) *A Year of War and Other Poems*, 1917; *The Desert and the Sown and Other Poems*, 1921; *Up the Hill of Fairylight*, 1925; *A Northern Holiday*, 1928; *A Treasury of Middle English Verse*, 1930; *The Forester's Wife*, 1931; *One Fine Day I Was Walking Along: A Travel Book for Those Who Stay at Home*, 1933; *Render Unto Caesar*, 1934; *Chapter and Verse*, Edinburgh, 1937; *A Rope of Sand*, 1965 (all published in London unless otherwise listed)

Aird, Catherine *The Religious Body*, Macdonald, London, 1966; *Slight Mourning*, Collins, London, 1975; *Some Die Eloquent*, Collins, London, 1979

Aitken, Hannah Mary (1911–77) *In a Shaft of Sunlight*, 1947; *Whittans*, 1951; *Seven Napier Place*, 1952; *Music for the Journey*, 1957 (all Hodder & Stoughton, London); (ed.) *A Forgotten Heritage: Original Folktales of Lowland Scotland*, Scottish Academic Press, Edinburgh, 1973

Allan, Betty (1930–) *Awa' fae Ballater: Scots Verses*, E. Allan, Skene, 1987

Allan, Dot (1892–1964) *The Syrens*, Heinemann, 1921; *Makeshift*, Andrew Melrose, 1928; *The Deans*, Jarrolds, 1929; *Deepening River*, Jarrolds, 1932; *Hunger March*, Hutchinson, 1934; *Virgin Fire: The Story of Marion Bradfute*, Hutchinson, 1935; *John Mathew, Papermaker*, Hodder & Stoughton, 1948; *Mother of Millions: The Story of Margaret Carnegie Fletcher of Saltoun*, Robert Hale, 1953; *The Passionate Sisters*, Robert Hale, 1955; *Charity Begins at Home*, Robert Hale, 1958 (all titles published in London)

Anderson, Jessie Annie (1861–?) *Songs in Season*, 1901; *Songs of Hope and Courage*, 1902 (both Milne & Stephen, The Caxton Press, Aberdeen); *Lyrics of Life and Love*, 1903; *Old-World Sorrow*, Milne & Stephen, The Caxton Press, Aberdeen, 1903; *Lyrics of Childhood*, Milne & Stephen, The Caxton Press, Aberdeen, 1905. *A Book of the Wonder Ways*, 1907; *Flower Voices*, Milne & Stephen, The Caxton Press, Aberdeen, 1908; *Breaths from Four Winds*, 1911; *This is Nonsense*, Aberdeen Press and Journal Office, Aberdeen, 1926; *A Single Year*, 1928

Andrew, Moira *Light the Blue Touch Paper*, Iron Press, 1986; *Summer Child*, Santone Press, Sancton, 1988

Angus, Marion (1866–1946) *The Lilt and Other Poems*, Wylie, Aberdeen, 1922; *The Tinker's Road and Other Verses*, Gowans & Gray, London and Glasgow, 1924; *Sun and Candlelight*, 1927; *The Singin' Lass*, 1929; *The Turn of the Day*, 1931 (all Porpoise Press, Edinburgh); *Lost Country, and Other Verses*, Gowans & Gray, Glasgow, 1937; *Selected Poems*, ed. Maurice Lindsay, Serif Books, Edinburgh, 1950

Armstrong, Kate *Wild Mushrooms: Writings*, Blind Serpent, Carnoustie, 1993

Bannerman, Chrissie/Criosaidh Dick (1934–) *Roanaid*, Clo Chailleann; *Calum Cille*, Gairm; *Dal Riata*, Gairm; *Na Loidsearan Neonach*, Acair, Stornoway; *An Turas Eiquinneach*, Canongate, Edinburgh

Barker, Elspeth (1940–) *O Caledonia!*, Hamish Hamilton, London, 1991

Bateman, Meg (1959–) *Cuart Filiochta*, Irish Arts Council; *Orain Ghaoil*, Coisceim, Dublin, 1990; *Cat a'Mhinisteir*, with Hamish Whyte, Mercat Press, Edinburgh, 1994

Biggar, Joan (1932–   ) *The Maiden Voyage*, Molendinar Press, Glasgow, 1977; *Edwina Alone*, Pan Books, London, 1980

Black, Laura *Glendraco*, 1977; *Castle Raven*, 1978; *Wild Cat*, 1979 (all Hamish Hamilton, London)

Blackhall, Sheena (1947–   ) *The Cyard's Kist and Other Poems*, 1984; *The Spik o'the Lan'*, 1986; *Hame-drauchtit*, 1987 (all Rainbow Books, Aberdeen); *Curfew for Now*, 1988; *Fite Doo Black Crow*, 1989; *A Nippick o'Nor'East Tales: A Doric Hairst*, 1989 (all Keith Murray, Aberdeen); *The Nor' East Neuk*, Charles Murray Trust, Aberdeen, 1989; *Reets*, Keith Murray, Aberdeen, 1991; *A Toosht o' Whigmaleeries*, Hammerfield, Aberdeen, 1991; *Three's Company: A collection of Stories from Aberdeen by Three Leading Writers: Sheena Blackhall, Rosemary Mackay, Wilma Murray*; selected and introduced by Jessie Kesson, Keith Murray, Aberdeen, 1989; *A Hint o' Granite: 20 Tales in Scots and English*, 1992; *Back o' Bennachie: Poems in Scots and English*, 1993; *Druids, Drauchts, Drochules*, 1994 (all Hammerfield, Aberdeen)

Blair, Anna, (1927–   ) *A Tree in the West*, Collins, London, 1976; *The Rowan on the Ridge*, Molendinar Press, Glasgow, 1980; *Tales of Ayrshire*, Shepheard-Walwyn, London, 1987; *Tea at Miss Cranston's*, Shepheard-Walwyn, London, 1985; *Scottish Tales*, Richard Drew, Glasgow, 1987; *Croft and Creel*, Shepheard-Walwyn, London, 1987; *The Goose Girl of Eriska*, Richard Drew, Glasgow, 1989; *Seed Corn*, Shepheard-Walwyn, London, 1989; *More Tea at Miss Cranston's*, Shepheard-Walwyn, London, 1991

Bone, Lady Gertrude Helena (1876–1953) *Provincial Tales*, 1904; *Women of the Country*, 1913; *The Brow of Courage and Other Tales*, 1916 (all Duckworth & Co., London); *Mr Paul*, Jonathan Cape, London, 1921; *The Furrowed Earth*, Chatto & Windus, 1921; *Oasis*, Jonathan Cape, London, 1924; *This Old Man*, Macmillan, London, 1925; *Of the Western Isles*, T. N. Foulis, London, 1925; *The Hidden Orchis*, The Medici Society, London and Boston, 1928; *The Cope*, The Medici Society, London, 1930; *Days in Old Spain*, Macmillan, London, 1938; *Came to Oxford*, Blackwell, Oxford, 1952

Bone, Kate (1897–   ) *St Kentigern*, Oxford University Press, London, 1948; *Thistle By-blaws*, Castlelaw Press, West Linton, 1972

Bowie, Jeanetta *Penny Buff: A Clydeside School in the 'thirties*, 1975; *Penny Boss: A Clydeside School in the 'fifties*, 1976; *Penny Change: Clydeside Schools in the 'seventies*, 1977 (all Constable, London)

Boyd, Elizabeth *Cross-Country Walks in the West Highlands*, Oliver & Boyd, Edinburgh, 1952

Boyle Mary E. (1881–?) *Pilate in Exile at Vienne*, 1915; *Aftermath*, 1916 (both W. Heffer & Sons, Cambridge); *Daisies and Apple Trees*, E. Mackay, Stirling, 1922; *Herodias Inconsolable*, Chelsea Publishing Co., London, 1923

Brackenbury, Rosalind *Telling Each Other it is Possible*, 1987; *Making for the Secret Places*, 1989; *Going Home the Long Way Round the Mountain*, 1993 (all Taxus Press, Exeter); *Golden Goose Hour: First Shore Poet's Anthology*, ed., with Brian Johnstone, Taranis, Edinburgh, 1994

Bray, Madge Dudgeon *Poems*, Sarah & Blair Spence, Inverness, 1976

Broomfield, Janet *A Fallen Land*, Bodley Head, London, 1990

Brown, Margaret Gillies (1929–   ) *Give Me the Hill-Run Boys*, 1978; *The Voice in the Marches*, 1979; *Hares on the Horizon*, 1981 (all Outpost Publications, Walton-on-Thames); *No Promises*, Akros Publications, Nottingham/Edinburgh, 1984; *Looking Towards Light*, Blind Serpent Press, Dundee, 1988; *Footsteps of the Goddess*, Akros Publications, Nottingham/Edinburgh, 1994

Burgess, Moira (1936–   ) *The Day Before Tomorrow*, Collins, London, 1971; *A Rumour of Strangers*, Collins, London, 1987; *Streets of Stone: An Anthology of Glasgow Short Stories*, ed., with Hamish Whyte, Salamander, Edinburgh, 1985; *Directory of Authors in the Scottish Fiction Reserve*, National Library of Scotland, Edinburgh, 1986; *The Glasgow Novel: A Survey and Bibliography*, Scottish Library Association/Glasgow District Libraries, Motherwell, 1986; (ed.) *The Other Voice: Scottish Women's Writing Since 1808: An Anthology*, Polygon, Edinburgh, 1987; *Streets of Gold: Contemporary Glasgow Stories*, ed., with Hamish Whyte, Mainstream, Edinburgh, 1989

Burns, Elizabeth (1957–   ) *Ophelia and Other Poems*, Polygon, Edinburgh, 1991

Butler, Rhoda *Shaela: Shetland Poems*, Thuleprint Ltd., Sandwick, 1976

Caird, Janet (1913–92) *Murder Reflected*, 1966; *Perturbing Spirit*, 1966; *Murder Scholastic*, 1967; *The Loch*, 1968 (all Bles, London); *Murder Remote*, Doubleday, New York, 1973; *Some Walk a Narrow Path*, Ramsay Head, Edinburgh, 1977; *The Umbrella Man's Daughter*, Macmillan, London, 1980; *A Distant Urn*, 1983; *John Donne, You Were Wrong*, 1988 (both Ramsay Head, Edinburgh)

Calder, Jenni (1941–) *There Must be a Lone Ranger*, Hamish Hamilton, London, 1974; *Women and Marriage in Victorian Fiction*, Thames & Hudson, London, 1976; *The Victorian Home*, Batsford, London, 1977; *Heroes: from Byron to Guevera*, Hamish Hamilton, London, 1977; *The Robert Louis Stevenson Companion*, Paul Harris, Edinburgh, 1980; *Robert Louis Stevenson: A Life Study*, Hamish Hamilton, London, 1980; *The Enterprising Scot: Scottish Adventure and Achievement*, HMSO, Edinburgh, 1986; *The Story of the Scottish Soldier*, HMSO/National Museums of Scotland, Edinburgh, 1987; *Scotland in Trust*, Richard Drew, Glasgow, 1990; *Margaret Oliphant*, Scottish Academic Press, Edinburgh, as Jenni Daiches, *Mediterranean*, Scottish Cultural Press, Aberdeen, 1995

Cameron, Isabel *Gorry*, T. D. Davidson, Elgin, 1925; *A Highland Chapbook*, Eneas Mackay, Stirling, 1928; *Boysie*, T. D. Davidson, Elgin, 1929; *Good Cheer*, Hodder & Stoughton, London, 1932; *Stories of the Doctor*, Religious Tracts, Society, London, 1936; *A Second Highland Chapbook*, Eneas Mackay, Stirling, 1948; *From a Cottage in Penny Cook Lane*, London, 1933; *Gillian Munro, a Highland Preacher*, Religious Tracts Society, London, 1934; *The Adventures of Elizabeth Gray*, Religious Tracts Society, London, 1934; *The Street of the Spinners*, Lutterworth Press, London, 1936; *Red Rowans in Glen Orrin*, Lutterworth Press, London, 1936; *Angus Our Precentor*, Religious Tracts Society, London, 1936; *Folk of the Glen: Tales Told in the Smiddy*, Lutterworth Press, London, 1937; *White Bell Heather*, Lutterworth Press, London, 1938; *The Girl Who Lost Things*, London, 1939; *A Pot of Gold*, Methuen, London, 1939; *The Cockle Ebb*, Methuen, London, 1940; *Cross Gaits*, 1945; *The But and Ben*, 1948; *Green Park Terrace*, 1949; *Tattered Tartan*, 1950; *Heather Mixture*, 1952; *The Kirk of the Corrie*, 1956 (all Lutterworth Press, London); *The Fascinating Hat*, London, 1961

Cameron, Mary *Sarah – Joy in the Morning: Blessings of Bereavement*, Marshall, Morgan & Scott, Basingstoke, 1986; *Methil: History and Trail*, 1986; *Kirkland: Village History and Trail*, 1987 (both Wemyss Environmental Education)

Campbell Marion, (1919–) *The Dark Twin*, Turnstone, London, 1973

Carrothers, Annabel *Kilcaraig*, Heinemann, London, 1982

Carswell, Catherine (Roxburgh) (1879–1946) *Open the Door!*, Melrose, London, 1920; *The Camomile: An Invention*, 1922; *The Life of Robert Burns*, 1930; *The Savage Pilgrimage: A Narrative of D. H. Lawrence*, 1932 (all Chatto & Windus, London); *A National Gallery: Being a Collection of English Character* (with Daniel George Bunting), Martin Secker, London, 1933; *The English in Love: A Museum of Illustrative Verse and Prose Pieces from the 14th to the 20th Century* (with Daniel George Bunting), Martin Secker, London, 1934; *The Fays of the Abbey Theatre: An Autobiographical Record* (with William Fay), Rich & Cowan, London, 1935; *The Scots Week-end and Caledonian Vade-mecum for Host, Guest and Wayfarer*, (ed with Donald Carswell), Routledge, London, 1936; *The Tranquil Heart: Portrait of Giovanni Boccaccio*, Lawrence & Wishart, London, 1937; *Lying Awake: An Unfinished Autobiography, and Other Posthumous Papers*, (ed. John Carswell), Secker & Warburg, London, 1950

Casciani, Elizabeth *Oh How We Danced*, Mercat Press, Edinburgh, 1994

Caudwell, Sarah, *Thus Was Adonis Murdered*, Collins, London, 1981

Christie, Anne *My Secret Gorilla*, Loughton, 1981; *First Act*, London, 1983; *An Honest Woman*, London, 1985; *Growing Wings*, London, 1993 (all published by Piatkus)

Clanchy, Kate (1965–) *Slattern*, Chatto & Windus, London, 1995

Cleland, Mary (Margaret Barbour Wells) *The Silver Whistle*, London, 1920; *The Two Windows*, Hodder & Stoughton, London, 1922; *The Sure Traveller*, Hodder & Stoughton, London, 1923; *The Forsaken Way*, London, 1927

Cook, Margaret Fulton, *Spell Bound*, Itinerant, Gourock, 1989

Cost, March, (Margaret Mackie Morrison) (?–1973) *The Oldest Wish*, Simpkin Marshall, London, 1928; *A Man Named Luke*, 1932, 1948; *The Dark Glass*, 1935; *The Dark Star*, 1939; *Rachel: An Interpretation*, 1947; *The Bespoken Mile*, 1950; *The Hour Awaits*, 1952; *Invitation from Minerva*, 1954; *By the Angel, Islington*, 1955; *Her Grace Presents*, 1957; *A Woman of Letters*, 1959 (all Collins London); *The Interpreter*, 1959; *The Countess*, 1963; *The Year of the Yield*, 1965; *After the Festival*, 1966; *The Veiled Sultan*, 1969; *Two Guests for Swedenborg*, 1971; *A Key to Laurels*, 1972 (all Cassell, London)

Cowan, Evelyn (1926–) *Spring Remembered: A Scottish Jewish Childhood*, Southside, Edinburgh, 1974; *Portrait of Alice*, Canongate, Edinburgh, 1976

Crow, Christine (1940–) *Miss X or the Wolf Woman*, Women's Press, London, 1990

Cros, Janet Tessier du (née **Grierson**) *Divided Loyalties; A Scotswoman in Occupied France*, Canongate, Edinburgh, 1990

Cruickshank, Helen B(urness) (1886–1975) *Up the Noran Water and Other Scots Poems*, Methuen, London, 1934; *Sea Buckthorn*, Macpherson, Dunfermline, 1954; *The Ponnage Pool*, Macdonald, Edinburgh, 1971; *Octobiography*, Standard Press, Montrose, 1976; *More Collected Poems*, Gordon Wright, Edinburgh, 1978

Czerkawska, Catherine Lucy (1950–) *White Boats: Poems with Andrew Greig*, Garret Arts, Edinburgh, 1973; *Fisherfolk of Carrick: A History of the Fishing Industry in South Ayrshire*, Moledinar Press, Glasgow, 1975; *A Book of Men, and Other Poems*, Akros, Preston, 1976; *Shadow of the Stone*, Richard Drew, Glasgow, 1989; *The Golden Apple*, Century, London, 1990

D'Ambrosio, Margaret (1957–) *Meggie's Journeys*, Polygon, Edinburgh, 1987

Davie, Elspeth, (1919–95) *Providings*, John Calder, London, 1965; *The Spark and Other Stories*, Calder & Boyars, London, 1968; *Creating a Scene*, Calder & Boyars, London, 1971; *The High Tide Talker and Other Stories*, 1976; *Climbers on a Stair*, 1978; *The Night of the Funny Hats*, 1980; *A Traveller's Room*, 1985; *Coming to Light*, 1989 (all Hamish Hamilton, London); *Death of a Doctor and Other Stories*, Sinclair-Stevenson, London, 1992

Davis, Margaret Thomson (1926–) *The Breadmakers*, 1972; *A Baby Might Be Crying*, 1973; *A Sort of Peace*, 1973; *The Prisoner*, 1974; *The Prince and the Tobacco Lords*, 1976; *Roots of Bondage*, 1977; *Scorpion in the Fire*, 1977; *The Dark Side of Pleasure*, 1981; *The Making of a Novelist: An Autobiography*, 1982; *A Very Civilised Man*, 1982 (all Allison & Busby, London); *Light and Dark*, 1984; *Rag Woman, Rich Woman*, 1987; *Daughters and Mothers*, 1988; *Wounds of War*, 1989 (all Century Hutchinson, London); *A Woman of Property*, Random Century Group, London, 1991; *A Sense of Belonging*, Arrow, London, 1993; *Hold Me Forever*, Century, London, 1994; *Kiss Me No More*, Century, London, 1995

Derwent, Lavinia (Elizabeth Dodd) (?–1989) *The Fairy Fiddler*, Glasgow, 1938; *Tammy Troot*, London, 1945; *Clashmaclavers: A Mixty-Maxty of Prose and Verse in the Couthy Tradition*, Oliver & Boyd, Edinburgh, 1947; *The Kirk Moose and Other Stories*, W. MacLellan, Glasgow, 1948; *Macpherson*, Burke, London, 1961; *The Boy From Sula*, Gollancz, London, 1973; *Macpherson's Lighthouse Adventure*, Blackie, London, 1977; *Another Breath of Border Air*, 1977; *A Border Bairn*, 1979; *God Bless the Borders!*, 1981; *Lady of the Manse*, 1983 (all Hutchinson, London); *Song of Sula*, Gollancz, London, 1986; *Beyond the Borders*, Century Hutchinson, London, 1988

Douglas, O. (Anna Buchan) (1877–1948) *Olivia in India*, 1913; *The Setons*, 1917; *Penny Plain*, 1920; *Ann and Her Mother*, 1922; *Pink Sugar*, 1924; *The Proper Place*, 1926; *Eliza for Common*, 1928; *The Day of Small Things*, 1930; *Priorsford*, 1932; *Taken By the Hand*, 1935; *Jane's Parlour*, 1937; *People Like Ourselves* (contains: *Priorsford, Penny Plain, Pink Sugar*), 1938; *The House That is Our Own*, 1940; as **Anna Buchan**: *Unforgettable, Unforgotten*, 1945; *Farewell to Priorsford: A Book By and About Anna Buchan (O. Douglas)* 1950 (all published by Hodder and Stoughton, London)

Douglas, Sheila (1932–) *Sing A Song of Scotland*, Thomas Nelson, London, 1982; *The King o' the Black Art and Other Folk Tales*, Aberdeen University Press, Aberdeen, 1987; *The Sang's the Thing*, Polygon, Edinburgh, 1992; *Fair Upon Tay*, Tayside Regional Council, Dundee, 1993

Drummond, Cherry (Cherry Evans) (1928–) *Love From Belinda*, 1961; *Lalage in Love*, 1962; *Creatures Great and Small*, (all Hodder, London) 1968

Duffy, Carol Ann (1955–) *Standing Female Nude*, 1985; *Selling Manhattan*, 1987; *The Other Country*, 1990; *Mean Time*, 1993 (all Anvil Press, London); *Selected Poems*, Penguin/Anvil Press, London, 1994; *Grimm Tales Adapted from the Brothers Grimm*, Faber & Faber, London, 1996

Duffy, Margaret *A Murder of Crows*, 1987; *Brass Eagle*, 1988; *Death of a Raven*, 1988; *Who Killed Cock Robin*, 1990; *Rook-Shoot*, 1991; *Man of Blood*, 1992; *Gallows Bird*, 1993 (all published by Piatkus, London)

Dugdale, Blanche ('Baffy') *The Diaries of Blanche Dugdale 1936–1947*, ed. N. A. Rose; foreword by Meyer Weisgel

Dunbar, Dorothy (1915–) *David Dale's Daughters: A Play in Two Acts*, 1979; *Cutty Sark*, 1981; *The Warlock and the Gipsy*, 1981 (all published by Brown Son & Ferguson, Glasgow)

Duncan, Jane (Elizabeth Jane Cameron) (Janet Sandison) (1910–76) *My Friends the Miss Boyds*, 1959; *My Friend Muriel*, 1959; *My Friend Monica*, 1960; *My Friend Annie*, 1961; *My Friend Sandy*, 1961; *My friend Martha's Aunt*, 1962; *My Friend Flora*, 1962; *My Friend Madame Zora*, 1963; *My Friend Rose*, 1964; *My Friend Cousin Emmie*, 1964; *My Friends the Mrs Millers*, 1965;

My Friends from Cairnton, 1965; *My Friend My Father*, 1966; *My Friends the Macleans*, 1967; *My Friends the Hungry Generation*, 1968; *My Friend the Swallow*, 1970; *My Friend Sashie*, 1972; *My Friends the Misses Kindness*, 1974; *Letter from Reachfar; an Autobiography*, 1975; *My Friends George and Tom*, 1976 (all MacMillan, London)

as **Janet Sandison**: *Jean in the Morning*, 1969; *Jean at Noon*, 1971; *Jean in the Twilight*, 1972; *Jean Towards Another Day*, 1975 (all MacMillan, London)

Dunlop, Eileen (1938–) *Robinsheugh*, 1975; *A Flute in Mayferry Street*, 1976; *The Valley of Deer*, 1989 (all Oxford University Press, London); *Scottish Traditional Rhymes*, with Antony Kamm, Chambers, Edinburgh, 1991

Dunn, Mary Alice (Mary Alice Faid) (1897–?) *Trudy's Uphill Road*, Pickering & Inglis, London, 1951; *Love will venture in*, Hurst & Blackett, London, 1963; *Trudy in Demand*, Pickering & Inglis, London, 1964; *The Walls of Rossa*, Hurst & Blackett, London, 1967

Dunnett, Dorothy (1923–) *The Game of Kings*, 1961; *Queen's Play*, 1964; *The Disorderly Knights*, 1966 (all Cassell, London); *Dolly and the Singing Bird*, Cassell, London, 1968; Houghton, 1968, as *The Photogenic Soprano*; Arrow, 1991, as *The Rum Affair; Pawn in Frankincense*, Cassell, London, 1969; *Dolly and the Cookie Bird*, Cassell, London, 1970; Houghton, 1970, as *Murder in the Round; The Ringed Castle*, Cassell, London, 1971; *Dolly and the Doctor Bird*, Cassell, London, 1971; Houghton, 1971, as *Match for a Murderer; Dolly and the Starry Bird* (as Dorothy Halliday), Cassell, London, 1973; Houghton, 1973, as *Murder in Focus; Checkmate*, Cassell, London, 1975; *Dolly and the Nanny Bird* (as Dorothy Halliday), Michael Joseph, London, 1976; *King Hereafter*, Michael Joseph, London, 1982; *Dolly and the Bird of Paradise*, Michael Joseph, London, 1983; Arrow, 1991, as *Tropical Issue; Niccolo Rising*, Michael Joseph, London, 1986; *The Spring of the Ram*, Michael Joseph, London, 1987; *The Scottish Highlands*, with Alastair Dunnett, photographs by David Pearson, Mainstream, Edinburgh, 1988; *Race of Scorpions*, Michael Joseph, London, 1989; *Moroccan Traffic*, Chatto & Windus, London, 1991; Harcourt, Brace, 1992, as *Take a Fax to the Kasbah; Scales of Gold*, Michael Joseph, London, 1991; *The Niccolo Dossier*, 1992; *The Niccolo Dossier 2*, 1992; *The Unicorn Hunt*, Michael Joseph, London, 1993; *Roman Nights*, Arrow, 1993; *To Lie With Lions*, Michael Joseph, London, 1995

Elphinstone, Margaret (1948–) *The Incomer*, Women's Press, London, 1987; *The Holistic Gardener*, with Julia Langley, Thorsons, London, 1987; reprinted as *The Green Gardener's Handbook*, Thorsons, 1990; *Organic Gardening*, Greenprint, London, 1990; *Outside Eden*, Sundial Press, London, 1990; *A Sparrow's Flight*, Polygon, Edinburgh, 1989; *A Treasury of Garden Verse*, Canongate, Edinburgh, 1990; *An Apple From a Tree*, Women's Press, London, 1991; *Islanders*, Polygon, Edinburgh, 1994

Evaristi, Marcella (1953–) *Mouthpieces*, Crawford Centre for the Arts, St Andrews, 1980; *Commedia*, Salamander Press, Edinburgh, 1983; *The Works in Plays Without Wires*, Sheffield University Press, Sheffield, 1989; *Wedding Belles and Green Grasses*, 1981; *Terrestrial Extras*, 1987

Fell, Alison (1944–) *The Grey Dancer*, Collins, London, 1981; *Kisses for Mayakovsy*, 1984; *Every Move You Make*, 1984; *The Bad Box*, 1987 (all Virago, London); (ed.), *The Seven Deadly Sins*, Serpent's Tail, London, 1988; *The Crystal Owl*, Methuen, London, 1988; (ed.), *The Seven Cardinal Virtues*, Serpent's Tail, London, 1990; *Mer de Glace*, Methuen, London, 1991; *Serious Hysterics*, Serpent's Tail, London, 1992; *Pillow Boy of the Lady Onogoro*, Serpent's Tail, London, 1994

Fellows, Gerrie (1954–) *Technologies*, Polygon, Edinburgh, 1990

Findlater, Jane Helen (1866–1946) *The Green Graves of Balgowrie*, 1896; *A Daughter of Strife*, 1897; *Rachel*, 1899 (all Methuen, London); *The Story of a Mother*, James Nisbet, London, 1902; *Stones From a Glasshouse*, James Nisbet, London 1904; *All that Happened in a Week*, 1905; *The Ladder to the Stars*, Methuen, London, 1906; *Seven Scots Stories*, John Murray, London, 1912; *A Green Grass Widow and Other Stories*, John Murray, London, 1921

Findlater, Mary (1865–1963) *Songs and Sonnets*, 1895; *Over the Hills*, 1897; *Betty Musgrave*, 1899; *A Narrow Way*, 1901; *The Rose of Joy*, 1903 (all Methuen, London); *A Blind Bird's Nest*, 1907; *Tents of a Night*, 1914 (both Smith, Elder and Co., London)

Findlater, Jane and Mary *Tales That are Told*, Methuen, London, 1901; *The Affair at the Inn* (with Kate Douglas Wiggin and Allan McAuley) 1904; *Crossriggs*, 1908; *Robinetta* (with Kate Douglas Wiggin and Allan McAuley), 1911; *Penny Monypenny*, 1911; *Seen and Heard Before and After 1914*, 1916; *Content with Flies*, 1916 (all Smith, Elder and Co., London); *Beneath the Visiting Moon*, Hurst & Blackett, London, 1923

Fine, Anne (1947–) *The Summer-House Loon*, Methuen, London, 1978; *The Granny Project*, Methuen, London, 1983; *The Killjoy*, Bantam, London, 1986; *Madame Doubtfire*, Hamish Hamilton, London, 1987; *Stranger Danger*, Hamish Hamilton, London, 1989; *Taking the Devil's Advice*, Viking, London, 1990

Finlay, Ann *Seed Time and Harvest*, Tragara Press, Edinburgh, 1978

Flett, Una *Falling from Grace: My Early Years in Ballet*, Canongate, Edinburgh, 1981; *Revisiting Empty Houses*, Canongate, Edinburgh, 1988

Forrest-Thomson, Veronica (1947–75) *Identi-Kit*, Outpost Publications, London, 1967; *Twelve Academic Questions*, the author, Cambridge, 1970; *Language-Games*, School of English Press, University of Leeds, Leeds, 1971; *On the Periphery*, Street Editions, Cambridge, 1976; *Poetic Artifice: A Theory of Twentieth-Century Poetry*, Manchester U.P., Manchester, 1978; *Collected Poems and Translations*, Allardyce Barnett, London, 1990

Fraser, Amy Stewart (1892–) *The Hills of Home*, Routledge & Kegan Paul, London, 1973

Fraser, Olive (1909–77) *The Pure Account: Poems 1909–1977*, Aberdeen University Press, Aberdeen, 1981; *The Wrong Music: The Poems of Olive Fraser 1909–1977*, Canongate, Edinburgh, 1989

Galford, Ellen (1947–) *Moll Cutpurse: Her True History*, Stramullion, Edinburgh, 1984; *The Fires of Bride*, Women's Press, London, 1986; *Queendom Come*, Virago, London, 1990; *The Dyke and the Dybbuk*, Virago, London, 1993

Galloway, Janice (1956–) *The Trick is to Keep Breathing*, Polygon, Edinburgh, 1989; *Blood*, Secker & Warburg, London, 1991; *Foreign Parts*, Jonathan Cape, London, 1994; *Where You Find It*, Jonathan Cape, London, 1996

Garry, Flora (1900–) *Bennygoak and Other Poems*, Akros, Preston, 1974; *Collected Poems*, Edinburgh, Gordon Wright, 1995

Gavin, Catherine Irvine (1907–) *Louis Philippe, King of the French*, Methuen, London, 1933; *Clyde Valley*, Barker, London, 1938; *The Hostile Shore*, Methuen, London, 1940; *The Black Milestone*, Methuen, London, 1941; *Britain and France: A Study of Twentieth Century Relations, the 'Entente Cordiale'*, Jonathan Cape, London, 1941; *Edward the Seventh: A Biography*, Jonathan Cape, London, 1941; *The Mountain of Light*, Methuen, London, 1944; *Liberated France*, Jonathan Cape, London, 1955; *Madeline*, Macmillan, London, 1958; *The Cactus and the Crown*, 1962; *The Fortress*, 1964; *The Moon into Blood*, 1966; *The Devil in the Harbour*, 1968; *The House of War*, 1970; *Give Me the Daggers*, 1972; *The Snow Mountain*, 1974; *Traitor's Gate*, 1976; *None Dare Call It Treason*, 1978; *Now Sleep the Brave*, 1980 (all Hodder & Stoughton, London); *The Glory Road*, Grafton, London, 1987; *A Dawn of Splendour*, Grafton, London, 1989; *The French Fortune*, Harper Collins, London, 1991

Gerber, Pat (1934–) *Maiden Voyage*, Kailyards Press, Glasgow, 1992; *The Search For The Stone of Destiny*, Canongate, Edinburgh, 1992

Gibson, Magi (1943–) *Kicking Back*, Taranis Books, 1993/Clydeside Press, Glasgow, 1995

Gillies, Valerie (1948–) *Trio: New Poets from Edinburgh*, with Roderick Watson and Paul Mills, ed. Robin Fulton, New Rivers Press, New York, 1971; *Poetry Introduction 3*, Faber, London, 1975; *Each Bright Eye: Selected Poems 1971–1976*, Canongate, Edinburgh, 1977; *Bed of Stone*, Canongate, Edinburgh, 1984; *Leopardi: A Scottis Quair*, Edinburgh University Press, Edinburgh, 1987; *Tweed Journey*, with Judy Steel, Canongate, Edinburgh, 1989; *The Chanter's Tune*, Canongate, Edinburgh, 1990; *The Ringing Rock*, Scottish Cultural Press, Aberdeen, 1995

Gladstone, Mary (Mary Drew) *Catherine Gladstone by her Daughter*, Nisbet & Co., London, 1919; *Acton Gladstone and Others*, Nisbet & Co., London, 1925; *Mary Gladstone (Mrs Drew) her Diaries and Letters*, ed. Lucy Masterman, Methuen, London, 1930

Glover, Sue (1943–) Major plays performed include: *Bondagers*, 1990; *The Seal Wife*, Edinburgh Festival, 1980; *An Island in Largo*, Byre Theatre, 1981; *The Bubble Boy*, Tron, 1981; *The Straw Chair*, Traverse, 1988; *Bondagers*, Traverse, 1991; *Sacred Hearts*, 1994 (of these, so far only *Bondagers* has been published, in *Made in Scotland: An Anthology of New Scottish Plays*, eds Ian Brown and Mark Fisher, Methuen, London, 1995)

Gordon, Katherine *The Emerald Peacock*, 2 vols, 1978–9; *Peacock in Flight*, 1979; *In the Shadow of the Peacock*, 1980; *The Peacock Ring*, 1981; *Peacock in Jeopardy*, 1982 (All Hodder & Stoughton, London)

Gordon, Janette R. *Left by the Tide: Poems*, Alex P. Reid, Aberdeen, 1977

Grant, Katherine Whyte (1845–?) *Dusgadh na Fienne, Dealbh – Chluich Mir Son na Cloinne*, J. & R. Parlane, Paisley, 1908; *Aig Tigh na Beinne (Tales and Poems, Original and Translated)*, Hugh

Macdonald, Oban, 1911; *Myth, Tradition and Story from Western Argyll*, The Oban Times Press, Oban, 1925

Hamilton, Margaret (1915–72) *Bull's Penny*, MacGibbon & Kee, London, 1950

Hanagan, Eva *Playmates*, Duckworth, London, 1978; *The Upas Tree*, 1979; *Holding On*, 1980; *A Knock at the Door*, 1982 (all Constable, London)

Haynes, Dorothy K(ate) (1918–87) *Winter's Traces*, Methuen, London, 1947; *The Gibsons of Glasgow*, 1947; *Robin Ritchie*, Methuen, London, 1949; *Thou Shalt Not Suffer a Witch and Other Stories*, Methuen, London, 1949; *Haste Ye Back*, Jarrold's, London, 1973; *Peacocks and Pagodas and the Best of Dorothy K. Haynes*, Paul Harris, Edinburgh, 1981; *Lanark in Old Postcards*, European Library in Zaltbommer, Netherlands, 1983; *Thou Shalt Not Suffer a Witch* (new edition), B&W Publishing, Edinburgh, 1996

Hayton, Sian (1933–) *Cells of Knowledge*, Polygon, Edinburgh, 1989; *The Governors*, Balnain Books, Nairn, 1992; *Hidden Daughters*, Polygon, Edinburgh, 1992; *The Last Flight*, Polygon, Edinburgh, 1993

Hedderwick, Mairi (1939–) *An Eye on the Hebrides*, 1989; *Highland Journey*, 1992 (both Canongate, Edinburgh)

Henderson, Meg *Finding Peggy: A Glasgow Childhood*, Corgi, London, 1994

Hendry, Joy (1953–) *Literature and Language: The Way Forward*, SNP Publications, West Lothian, 1981; *The Land for the People*, ed., with Irene Evans, Scottish Socialist Society, Blackford, 1985; *Sorley Maclean: Critical Essays*, ed., with Raymond J. Ross, Scottish Academic Press, Edinburgh, 1986; (ed.) *Norman MacCaig: Critical Essays*, Edinburgh University Press, Edinburgh, 1990; *Neil M. Gunn Centenary Lecture*, Peglet Press, Ampthill, 1992; *Gang Down Wi' a Sang*, Diehard Press, Edinburgh, 1995

Hodgman, Jackie (1953–) *The Fish in White Sauce Incident*, Keith Murray, Aberdeen, 1992

Hunter, Mollie (Maureen McIlwraith) (1922–) *A Love Song for My Lady*, Evans, London, 1961; *Stay for an Answer*, French, London, 1962; *Patrick Kentigern Keenan*, Blackie, London, 1963; *A Pistol in Greenyards*, Evans, London, 1965; *The Ghosts of Glencoe*, Evans, London, 1966; *The Bodach*, Blackie, London, 1970; *The Haunted Mountain*, 1972; *The Stronghold*, 1974; *A Stranger Came Ashore*, 1975 (all Hamish Hamilton, London); *Talent is Not Enough: Mollie Hunter On Writing For Children*, Harper, New York, 1976; *The Kelpie's Pearls*, Puffin, Harmondsworth, 1976; *The Brownie*, Byways Bairns, 1986; *The Enchanted Boy*, Byways Bairns, 1986; *Escape from Loch Leven*, Canongate, Edinburgh, 1987; *Walking Stones*, Mammoth, 1991; *The Stronghold*, Canongate, Edinburgh, 1995

Jacob, Violet (1863–1946) *The Sheep Stealers*, 1902; *The Infant Moralist*, with Lady Helena Carnegie, Grant & Son, Edinburgh, 1903; *The Golden Heart and Other Fairy Stories*, 1904; *The Interloper*, 1904; *Verses*, 1905 (all Heinemann, London); *Irresolute Catherine*, John Murray, London, 1908; *The History of Aythan Waring*, Heinemann, London, 1908; *Stories Told by the Miller*, 1909; *The Fortune Hunters and Other Stories*, 1910; *Flemington*, 1911; *Songs of Angus*, 1915 (all John Murray, London); *More Songs of Angus, and Others*, Country Life, London, and Charles Scribner's Sons, New York, 1918; *Bonnie Joan and Other Poems*, John Murray, London, 1921; *Tales of my Own Country*, John Murray, London, 1922; *Two New Poems*, Porpoise Press, Edinburgh, 1924; *The Good Child's Year Book*, Foulis, London, 1928; *The Northern Lights and Other Poems*, John Murray, London, 1927; *The Lairds of Dun*, John Murray, London, 1931; *The Scottish Poems of Violet Jacob*, Oliver & Boyd, Edinburgh, 1944; *The Lum Hat and Other Stories: Last Tales of Violet Jacob*, ed. Ronald Garden, Aberdeen University Press, Aberdeen, 1982; *Diaries and Letters from India, 1895–1900*, ed. Carol Anderson, Canongate, Edinburgh, 1990 *Flemington* ed. Carol Anderson, Association for Scottish Literary Studies, Aberdeen, 1994

Jamie, Kathleen (1962–) *Black Spiders*, Salamander Press, Edinburgh, 1982; *A Flame in Your Heart*, with Andrew Greig, Bloodaxe, Newcastle, 1986; *The Way We Live*, Bloodaxe, Newcastle, 1987; *The Golden Peak*, Virago, London, 1992; *The Autonomous Region*, with Sean Mayne Smith, Bloodaxe, Newcastle, 1993; *The Queen of Sheba*, Bloodaxe, Newcastle, 1994

Johnson, Alison, (1947–) *A House By the Shore*, 1986; *Scarista Style*, 1987; *Islands in the Sound*, 1989 (all Gollancz, London); *Children of Disobedience*, Andre Deutsch, London, 1989; *The Wicked Generation*, Blackstaff, Belfast 1992

Kay, Jackie (1961–) *The Adoption Papers*, Bloodaxe, Newcastle, 1991; *That Distance Apart*, Turret Books, London, 1991; *Two's Company*, Blackie, London, 1992; *Other Lovers*, Bloodaxe, Newcastle, 1993

Kennedy, A. L. (1965–) *Night Geometry and the Garscadden Trains*, Polygon, Edinburgh, 1990; *Looking for the Possible Dance*, Secker & Warburg, London, 1993; *Now that You're Back*, Cape, London, 1994; *So I Am Glad*, Cape, London, 1995; *Original Bliss*, Cape, London, 1997

Kesson, Jessie, (1916–94) *The White Bird Passes*, Chatto & Windus, London, 1958; Hogarth Press, London, 1987; B & W Publishing, Edinburgh, 1996; *Glitter of Mica*, Chatto & Windus, London, 1963; Hogarth Press, London, 1988; *Another Time, Another Place*, Chatto & Windus, London, 1983; *Where the Apple Ripens and Other Stories*, Chatto & Windus, London, 1985; *The Jessie Kesson Omnibus*, Chatto & Windus, London, 1991

Knight, Alanna *Legend of the Loch*, 1969; *The October Witch*, 1971; *Castle Clodha*, 1972; *This Outward Angel*, 1972; *Lament for Lost Lovers*, 1972; *The White Rose*, 1973; *Fanny Osbourne*, Milton House, Aylesbury, 1974; *A Stranger Came By*, 1974 (all Hurst & Blackett, London); *The Passionate Kindness: The Love Story of Robert Louis Stevenson and A Drink for the Bridge*, Macmillan, London, 1976; *The Wicked Wynsleys*, Nordon Publications, New York, 1977; *Girl on an Empty Swing*, New Playwrights Network, Macclesfield, 1978; *The Black Duchess*, Macdonald Futura, London, 1980; *The Private Life of Robert Louis Stevenson*, Wilfron Books, Paisley, 1983; *Castle of Foxes*, Prior, London, 1981; *Colla's Children*, Macdonald, London, 1982; *The Clan*, Macdonald, London, 1985; (ed.), *RLS in The South Seas*, Mainstream, Edinburgh, 1986; *Estella*, Macdonald, London, 1986; *Enter Second Murderer*, 1988; *Blood Line*, 1989; *Deadly Beloved*, 1989; *Killing Cousins*, 1990 (all Macmillan, London); *The Sweet Cheat Gone*, Severn House, Wallington, 1992; *A Quiet Death*, Macmillan, London, 1992; *Strathblair*, BBC Books, London, 1993; *The Evil That Men Do*, Macmillan, London, 1993; *Inspector Faro and the Edinburgh Mysteries: (Enter Second Murderer; Blood Line; Deadly Beloved)* Pan, London, 1994; *To Kill A Queen*, 1992; *Bull Slayers*, 1995; *The Missing Duchess*, 1994; *The Bull Slayers*, 1995 (all Macmillan, London)

Kyle, Elisabeth (Agnes Mary Robertson Dunlop) (?–1982) *The Begonia Bed*, Constable, London, 1934; *Orangefield*, Constable, London, 1938; *Broken Glass*, 1940; *Visitors from England*, 1941; *The White Lady*, 1941; *But We Are Exiles*, 1942; *Behind the Waterfall*, 1943; *The Pleasure Dome*, 1943; *The Skater's Waltz*, 1944; *The Seven Sapphires*, 1944; *Holly Hotel*, 1947; *Lost Karin*, 1947; *The Mirrors of Castle Doone*, 1947; *West Wind*, 1948; *The House on the Hill*, 1949; *Douce*, 1950; *The Provost's Jewels*, 1950; *The Lintowers*, 1951; *The Tontine Bell*, 1951; *The Captain's House*, 1952 (all Davies, London); *The Reiver's Road*, 1953; *The House of the Pelican*, 1954; *Caroline House*, 1955; *Vanishing Island*, 1956; *Run to Earth*, 1957 (all Nelson, London); *The Money Cat*, Hamilton, London, 1958; *Eagle's Nest*, Nelson, London, 1961; *High Season*, Davies, London, 1968; *The Stilt Walkers*, 1972; *Through The Wall*, 1973; *The Yellow Coach*, 1976 (all Heinemann, London); *All the Nice Girls*, Davies, London, 1976; *The Key of the Castle*, Heinemann, London, 1976; *The Stark Inheritance*, Davies, London, 1978; *A Summer Scandal*, Davies, London, 1979; *The Deed Box*, Robert Hale, London, 1981

Lingard, Joan (1933–) *Liam's Daughter*, 1963; *The Prevailing Wind*, 1964; *The Tide Comes In*, 1966; *The Headmaster*, 1967; *A Sort of Freedom*, 1969; *The Lord on Our Side*, 1970; (all Hodder & Stoughton, London); *Across the Barricades*, 1972; *Into Exile*, 1973; *The Clearance*, 1974; *A Proper Place*, 1975; *The Gooseberry*, 1978 (all Hamish Hamilton, London); *The Second Flowering of Emily Mountjoy*, Paul Harris, Edinburgh, 1979; *Greenyards*, 1981; *The Winter Visitor*, 1983; *Sisters by Rite*, 1984; *Reasonable Doubts*, 1986; *The Guilty Party*, 1987; *Rages and Riches*, 1988; *Tug of War*, 1989; *The Women's House*, 1989; *Glad Rags*, 1990; *Between Two Worlds*, 1991 (all Hamish Hamilton, London); *After Colette*, Sinclair-Stevenson, London, 1993; *Dreams of Love and Modest Glory*, Sinclair-Stevenson, London, 1995

Lochhead, Liz (1947–) *Memo for Spring*, Reprographia, Edinburgh, 1971; *Islands*, Glasgow Print Studio, Glasgow, 1978; *The Grimm Sisters*, Next Editions, London, 1981; *Blood and Ice*, Salamander, Edinburgh, 1982; *Silver Service*, Salamander, Edinburgh, 1984; *Dreaming Frankenstein, and Collected Poems*, Polygon, Edinburgh, 1984; *True Confessions and New Cliches*, Polygon, Edinburgh, 1985; *Tartuffe, a translation into Scots*, Polygon, Edinburgh, 1985; *Mary Queen of Scots Got Her Head Chopped Off, and Dracula*, Penguin, Harmondsworth, 1989; *Bagpipe Muzak*, Penguin, Harmondsworth, 1991. Other unpublished productions include: *The Big Picture*, 1988; *Them Through the Wall* (with Agnes Owens), 1989; *Patter Merchants*, 1989; *Jock Tamson's Bairns*, 1990

Lochhead, Marion (Cleland) (1902–85) *Poems*, Gowans & Gray, Glasgow, 1928; *Painted Things, and Other Poems*, Gowans & Gray, Glasgow, 1929; *Anne Dalrymple*, 1934; *Cloaked in Scarlet*, 1935; *Adrian was a Priest*, 1936; *Island Destiny*, 1936; *Feast of Candlemas, and Other Devotional*

Poems, 1937; *The Dancing Flower*, 1938 (all Moray Press, Edinburgh); *Fiddler's Bidding*, Oliver & Boyd, Edinburgh, 1939; *Highland Scene*, Smiths, Glasgow, 1939; *On Tintock Tap: Being Lowland and Other Tales for Children*, 1946; *Saint Mungo's Bairns: Being the Story of Glasgow Told for Children*, 1948; *A Lamp Was Lit: The Girls' Guildry through Fifty Years*, 1949 (all Moray Press, Edinburgh); *John Gibson Lockhart*, 1954; *Their First Ten Years*, 1956; *Young Victorians*, 1959; *Elizabeth Rigby, Lady Eastlake*, 1961; *The Victorian Household*, 1964 (all John Murray, London); *Portrait of the Scott Country*, Hale, London, 1973; *The Battle of the Birds, And Other Celtic Tales*, James Thin, Edinburgh, 1981; *Magic and Witchcraft of the Borders*, Hale, London, 1984; *The Renaissance of Wonder in Children's Literature*, Canongate, Edinburgh, 1977; *Scottish Tales of Magic and Mystery*, compiled by Marion Lochhead, Johnston & Bacon, 1978, 1990; *Scottish Love Stories*, compiled by Marion Lochhead, Johnston & Bacon, London, 1979;

MacArthur, Bessie Jane Bird (1889–?) *Clans of Lochan*, Urquhart, Edinburgh, 1928; *The Starry Venture*, Elkin Mathews and Marrot, London, 1934; *The Starry Venture*, Elkin Mathews and Marrot, London, 1934; *Last Leave*, Oliver & Boyd, Edinburgh, 1943; *From Daer Water: Poems in Scots and English* H. T. Macpherson, Dunfermline, 1962; *And Time Moves On*, Castlelaw Press, West Linton, 1972; *Sang o' the Lairock*, Biggar Museum Trust, Biggar, 1976

McCabe, Mary (1950–   ) *Everwinding Times*, Argyll Publishing, Glendaruel, 1994; *Streets Schemes and Stages*, with Ewan MacVicar, Strathclyde Regional Council, Glasgow, 1991

McDermid, Val *Report for Murder*, 1988; *Common Murder*, 1989; *Final Edition*, 1991 (all Women's Press, London); *Dead Beat*, Gollancz, London, 1992; *Kick Back*, Gollancz, London, 1993; *Union Jack*, Women's Press, London, 1993; *Crackdown*, 1994; *Clean Break*, 1995; *Mermaids Singing*, 1995; *Suitable Job For A Woman: The World of Female Private Investigators*, 1995 (all Harper Collins, London)

McDonald, Ellie (1937–   ) *The Gangan Fuit*, Chapman, Edinburgh, 1991

MacDonald, Mairi (1821–?) *Dain Agus Orain Ghaidhlig*, Mac-Coinnich, Inverness, 1891; *Orain Luaidh*, A. Matheson, Glasgow, 1949; *Mo Lorgan Fhin (My Own Footprints)*, Crois-Eilein Publications, Inverness, 1985

Macdonald, Sharman (1951–   ) *When I Was a Girl I Used to Scream and Shout*, Faber & Faber, London, 1985; *The Beast*, Collins, London, 1986; *Night Night*, Collins, London, 1988; *When I Was a Girl I Used to Scream and Shout; When We Were Women; The Brave*, 1990; *All Things Nice*, 1991; *Shades*, 1992 (all Faber, London)

Macgregor, Helen *The Collected Poetry*, Regency Press, London, 1976

McGregor, Iona (1929–   ) *The Popinjay*, Faber, London, 1969; *The Burning Hill*, Faber, London, 1970; *Edinburgh Reel*, Canongate, Edinburgh, 1986; *Death Wore a Diadem*, Women's Press, London, 1989; *Alice in Shadowtime*, Polygon, Edinburgh, 1992

MacInnes, Helen (1907–85) *Above Suspicion*, 1941; *Assignment in Brittany*, 1942; *The Unconquerable*, 1944 (all Harrap, London); *While Still We Live*, Little Brown & Co., Boston, 1944; *Horizon*, Harrap, London, 1945; *Friends and Lovers*, Little Brown & Co., Boston, 1947; *Rest and Be Thankful*, Harrap, London, 1949; *Neither Five Nor Three*, 1951; *I and My True Love*, 1953; *Pray for a Brave Heart*, 1955; *North from Rome*, 1958; *Decision at Delphi*, 1961; *Venetian Affair*, 1964; *The Double Image*, 1966; *The Salzburg Connection*, 1969; *Message from Malaga*, 1972; *Agent in Place*, 1976; *Prelude to Terror*, 1978; *Hidden Target*, 1980; *Cloak of Darkness*, 1982 (all Collins, London)

Mackay, Rosemary (1951–   ) *Three's Company: A Collection of Stories from Aberdeen by Three Leading writers: Sheena Blackhall, Rosemary Mackay, Wilma Murray*, selected and introduced by Jessie Kesson, Keith Murray, Aberdeen, 1989

Mackay, Shena (1944–   ) *Dust Falls on Eugene Schlumberger and Toddler on the Run*, Deutsch, London, 1964; *Music Upstairs*, Deutsch, London, 1965; *Old Crow*, Cape, London, 1967; *An Advent Calendar*, Cape, London, 1971; *Babies in Rhinestones and Other Stories*, Heinemann, London, 1983; *A Bowl of Cherries*, Harvester Press, Brighton, 1984; *Redhill Rococco*, 1986; *Dreams of Dead Women's Handbags*, 1987; *Dunedin*, 1992; *The Laughing Academy*, 1993 (all Heinemann, London); *Collected Short Stories*, Penguin, Harmondsworth, 1994; *The Orchard on Fire*, Heinemann, London, 1996

MacKenzie, Agnes (Muriel) Mure (1891–1955) *Spilt Ink: Carmina Togata*, W. W. Lindsay, Aberdeen, 1913; *Without Conditions*, Heinemann, London, 1923; *Robert the Bruce, King of Scots*, Maclehose, Glasgow, 1924; *The Half Loaf: A Comedy of Chance and Error in 3 Acts*, 1925; *The Quiet Lady*, 1926; *Lost Kinellan*, 1927 (all Heinemann, London); *The Playgoers Handbook to the English Renaissance Drama*, Jonathan Cape, London, 1927; *The Process of Literature: An*

Essay Toward Some Reconsiderations, Allen & Unwin, London, 1929; *Keith of Kinellan*, 1930; *Cypress in Moonlight: An Operetta in Prose*, 1931; *Between Sun and Moon*, 1932 (all Constable, London); *An Historical Survey of Scottish Literature to 1714*, Maclehose, Glasgow, 1933; *Single Combat*, Constable, London, 1934; *The Rise of the Stewarts*, 1935; *The Scotland of Queen Mary and the Religious Wars 1513–1638*, 1936; *The Passing of the Stewarts*, 1937 (all Maclehose, Glasgow); *The Foundations of Scotland*, Chambers, Edinburgh, 1938; *I was at Bannockburn*, Moray Press, Edinburgh, 1939; *The Kingdom of Scotland: Short History*, Chambers, Edinburgh, 1940; *Scotland in Modern Times 1720–1939*, Chambers, Edinburgh, 1940; *The Arts and Future of Scotland*, Oliver & Boyd, Edinburgh, 1942; *Scottish Principles of Statecraft and Government*, McLellan, Glasgow, 1942; *Scottish Pageant*, (4 vols), Oliver & Boyd, Edinburgh, 1946–50 *A History of Britain and Europe for Scottish Schools*, 3 vols, Grant Educational, Glasgow, 1949–51; *Apprentice Majesty*, Serif, Edinburgh, 1950; *Scotland on Freedom*, (ed.), Saltire Society, Edinburgh, 1950; *Rival Establishments in Scotland 1560–1690*, SPCK, London, 1952; *David I: A Study in Principles of Administration*, Saltire Society, Edinburgh, 1954; *A Garland of Scottish Prose*, Maclehose, Glasgow, 1956;

Mackenzie, Helen B. *The Sassenach*, Canongate, Edinburgh, 1980; *To Cry Loyal*, Lochar, Moffat, 1989

Mackinnon, Rayne (1937–) *The Spark of Joy and Other Poems*, John Humphries, Thurso, 1970; *The Hitch-hiker and other Poems*, Outpost Publications, Walton-on-Thames, 1976; *The Blasting of Billy P. and other Poems*, Enitharmon, London, 1978; *Northern Elegies*, Netherbow Centre, Edinburgh, 1986

Mackintosh, Elizabeth (pseudonyms Josephine Tey, Gordon Daviot) (1897–1952) *Kif: An Unvarnished History*, Benn, London, 1929; *The Man in the Queue*, Methuen, London, 1929; *The Expensive Halo*, Benn, London, 1931; *Richard of Bordeaux*, 1933; *The Laughing Woman*, 1934; *Queen of Scots*, 1934 (all Gollancz, London); *A Shilling for Candles*, Methuen, London, 1936; *Claverhouse*, Collins, London, 1937; *The Stars Bow Down*, Duckworth, London, 1939; *Leith Sands, and Other Short Plays*, Duckworth, London, 1946; *Miss Pym Disposes*, 1946; *The Franchise Affair*, 1948; *Brat Farrar*, 1949; *To Love and Be Wise*, 1950; *The Daughter of Time*, 1951; *The Privateer*, 1952; *The Singing Sands*, 1952 (all Peter Davies, London); *Plays*, 3 vols, Duckworth, London, 1953–4

Mackintosh, May *Roman Adventure*, Collins, London, 1976

Macleod, Christina (1880–1954) *An Sireadh*, E. Mackay, Glasgow, 1952; *Ceolradh Cridhe* (with Kenneth Macleod), Alex Maclaren & Sons, Glasgow, 1943

MacLeod, Sheila (1939–) *The Snow-White Soliloquies*, Secker & Warburg, London, 1970; *Xanthe and the Robots*, Bodley Head, London, 1977; *Circuit Breaker*, Bodley Head, London, 1978; *The Moving Accident*, Faber, London, 1968; *Letters from the Portuguese*, Secker & Warburg, London, 1971; *Axioma*, Quartet, London, 1984; *The Art of Starvation: An Adolescent Observed*, Virago, London, 1981; *Lawrence's Men and Women*, Heinemann, London, 1985; *Meallada am Malta*, Acair, Stornoway, 1993

McNeill, F(lorence) Marian (1885–1973) *Iona: A History of the Island*, Blackie & Son, London, 1920; *The Scots Kitchen*, Blackie & Son, London, 1929; *The Book of Breakfasts*, 1932; *The Road Home*, 1932; *The Camper's Kitchen*, 1933 (all A. Maclehose, London); *Recipes From Scotland*, Albyn Press, Edinburgh, 1946; *An Iona Anthology*, E. Mackay, Stirling, 1947; *The Scots Cellar*, 1956, Lochar, Moffatt, 1992; *The Silver Bough*, 4 vols, William Maclellan, Glasgow, 1956–68

Macnicol, Eona (1910–) *Colum of Derry*, Sheed & Ward, London, 1955; *Lamp in the Night Wind*, Maclellan, Glasgow, 1965; *The Halloween Hero, and Other Stories*, Blackwood, Edinburgh, 1969; *The Jail Dancing, and Other Stories of an Old Scottish Town*, Ramsay Head, Edinburgh, 1979; *Carver of Coal*, Ramsay Head, Edinburgh, 1979

MacPhail, Catherine *Run, Zan, Run*, Blackie, London, 1994; *Blue Lights and Bandages* (with Jack Kirkland), Seanachaidh, Greenock, 1989

MacPherson, Elizabeth *Letters from a Scottish Village*, Methuen, London, 1936; *Letters From a Highland Township* (with Ian MacPherson), W&R Chambers, London and Edinburgh, 1939

McSeveney, Angela (1964–) *Coming Out With It*, Polygon, Edinburgh, 1992

McWilliam, Candia (1955–) *A Case of Knives*, 1988; *A Little Stranger*, 1989; *Debatable Land*, 1994 (all Bloomsbury, London)

Maitland, Sara (1950–) *Daughter of Jerusalem*, Blond & Briggs, London, 1978; *Telling Tales*, Journeyman, London, 1983; *Virgin Territory*, Michael Joseph, London, 1984; *Vesta Tilley*,

Virago, London, 1986; *A Book of Spells*, Michael Joseph, London, 1987; *Three Times Table*, Chatto & Windus, London, 1990; *Women Fly When Men Aren't Watching*, Virago, London, 1993; *Home Truths*, Chatto & Windus, London, 1993; *Big-Enough God: Artful Theology*, Mowbray, New York, 1994

Malcolm, Fiona (1906–) *A Child's Fancies: Little Poems*, J. N. Mackinlay, Glasgow, 1914

Manners, Alexandra (Anne Rundie) *Sable Hunter*, Collins, London, 1978; *The White Moths*, Collins, London, 1979

Mavor, Elisabeth (1927–) *Summer in the Greenhouse*, New Authors Ltd., London, 1959; *The Temple of Flora*, Hutchinson, London, 1961; *Virgin Mistress: A Study in Survival: The Life of the Duchess of Kingston*, Chatto & Windus, London, 1964; *The Redoubt*, Hutchinson, London, 1967; *The Ladies of Llangollen: A Study in Romantic Friendship*, Penguin, Harmondsworth, 1973; *A Year With the Ladies of Llangollen*, Penguin, Harmondsworth, 1984

May, Naomi (1934–) *The Adventurer*, 1970; *At Home*, 1970; *Troubles*, 1976 (all John Calder, London)

Miller, Christian (1920–) *The Champagne Sandwich*, 1969; *Daisy, Daisy*, 1980; *A Childhood in Scotland*, Murray, London, 1981; Canongate, Edinburgh, 1989

Millington, Rosemary Irene (1935–) *A Nation of Trees*, New Authors, London, 1962; *The Islanders: a Hebridean Experience*, Hutchinson, London, 1966

Milne, Elizabeth *Displaced Persons: a play in one act*, H. F. W. Deane, London, 1951; *Happy Exit: a comedy in one act*, H. F. W. Deane, London, 1952; *The Wee Black Coo: a comedy in one act*, Oliver & Boyd, Edinburgh, 1953; *The Cracket Joug, a one-act Scots comedy*, Brown Son & Ferguson, Glasgow, 1957; *Henrietta*, Hurst & Blackett, London, 1960

Mitchell, Elma (1919–) *The Poor Man in the Flesh*, Peterloo, Stockport, 1976; *The Human Cage*, Peterloo, Liskeard, 1983; *Furnished Rooms*, Peterloo, Liskeard, 1983; *People Etcetera: Poems New and Selected*, Peterloo, Calstock, Cornwall, 1987

Mitchison, Naomi (1897–) *The Conquered*, 1923; *When the Bough Breaks and Other Stories*, 1924; *Cloud Cuckoo Land*, 1925; *The Laburnum Branch*, 1926 (all Cape, London); *Anna Comnena*, Howe, London, 1928 *Black Sparta: Greek Stories*, 1928; *Nix Nought Nothing; Four Plays for Children*, 1928 *Barbarian Stories*, 1929 (all Cape, London); *Comments on Birth Control*, Faber, London, 1930; *The Hostages and Other Stories for Boys and Girls*, Cape, London, 1930; *Boys and Girls and Gods*, Watts, London, 1931; *The Corn King and the Spring Queen*, 1931; *The Price of Freedom: A Play in Three Acts*, with L. E. Gielgud, 1931; *Powers of Light*, 1931; *The Delicate Fire: Short Stories and Poems*, 1933 (all Cape, London); *The Home and A Changing Civilization*, Lane, London, 1934; *Vienna Diary*, Gollancz, London, 1934; *Beyond This Limit*, Cape, London, 1935; *We Have Been Warned*, 1935; *The Fourth Pig: Stories and Verses*, 1936; *An End and a Beginning and Other Plays*, 1937 (all Constable, London); *Socrates*, with Richard H. S. Crossman, Hogarth Press, London, 1937; *The Moral Basis of Politics*, Constable, London, 1938; *As It Was in the Beginning*, with L. E. Gielgud, Cape, London, 1939; *The Alban Goes Out*, Raven Press, Harrow, Middlesex, 1939; *Blood of the Martyrs*, Constable, London, 1939; Canongate, Edinburgh, 1988; *The Kingdom of Heaven*, Heinemann, London, 1939; *The Bull Calves*, Cape, London, 1947; Richard Drew, Glasgow, 1985; *Nix-Nought-Nothing and Elfen Hill: Two Plays for Children*, Cape, London, 1948; *Men and Herring: A Documentary*, Serif, Edinburgh, 1949; *The Big House*, Faber, London, 1950; *Spindrift*, with Denis Macintosh, French, London, 1951; *Lobsters on the Agenda*, Gollancz, London, 1952; *Travel Light*, Faber, London, 1952; Virago, London, 1985; *Graeme and the Dragon*, Faber, London, 1954; *The Swan's Road*, Naldrett Press, London, 1954; *Land the Ravens Found*, Collins, London, 1955; *To the Chapel Perilous*, Allen & Unwin, London, 1955; *Little Boxes*, Faber, London, 1956; *Behold Your King*, Muller, London, 1957; *The Far Harbour*, Collins, London, 1957; *Five Men and a Swan: Short Stories and Poems*, Allen & Unwin, London, 1958; *Other People's Worlds*, Secker & Warburg, London, 1958; *Judy and Lakshmi*, Collins, London, 1959; *A Fishing Village on the Clyde*, Oxford University Press, 1960; *The Rib of the Green Umbrella*, Collins, London, 1960; *The Young Alexander The Great*, Max Parrish, London, 1960; *Karensgaard: The Story Of A Danish Farm*, Collins, London, 1961; *Presenting Other People's Children*, Hamlyn, London, 1961; *Memoirs of a Spacewoman*, Gollancz, London, 1962; Women's Press, London, 1985; *The Fairy who Couldn't Tell a Lie*, Collins, London, 1963; *Alexander the Great*, Longman, London, 1964; *Ketse and the Chief*, Nelson, London, 1965; *When We Become Men*, Collins, London, 1965; *Friends and Enemies*, Collins, London, 1966; *Return to the Fairy Hill*, Heinemann, London, 1966; *Cloud Cuckoo Land*, Hodder & Stoughton, London, 1967; *The Big Surprise*, Kaye and Ward, 1967; *African Heroes*, Bodley

Head, London, 1968; *Sun and Moon*, Bodley Head, London, 1968; *Don't Look Back*, Kaye & Ward, 1969; *Family At Ditlabeng*, Collins, London, 1969; *The Africans: A History*, Blond, London, 1970; *Cleopatra's People*, Heinemann, London, 1972; *Danish Teapot*, Kaye & Ward, 1973; *A Life for Africa: The Story of Bram Fisher*, Merlin Press, 1973; *Small Talk: Memories of an Edwardian Childhood*, Bodley Head, London, 1973; Richard Drew, Glasgow, 1988; *Sunrise Tomorrow: A Story of Botswana*, Collins, London, 1973; *When the Bough Breaks and Other Stories*, Bodley Head, London, 1974; *Oil for the Highlands*, Fabian Society, 1974; *All Change Here: Girlhood and Marriage*, Bodley Head, London, 1975; Richard Drew, Glasgow, 1988; *Sittlichkeit (38th Haldane Memorial Lecture)*, Birkbeck College, 1975; *Solution Three*, Dobson, London, 1975; *Snake!*, Collins, London, 1976; *The Cleansing of the Knife and Other Poems*, Canongate, Edinburgh, 1978; *The Two Magicians*, Dobson, London, 1978; *You May Well Ask: A Memoir 1920–1940*, Gollancz, London, 1979; Scottish Academic Press, Edinburgh, 1986; *Images of Africa*, Canongate, Edinburgh, 1980; *The Vegetable War*, Hamish Hamilton, London, 1980; *Mucking Around; Five Continents Over Fifty Years*, Gollancz, London, 1981; *Margaret Cole 1893–1980*, Fabian Society, London, 1982; *What Do You Think Yourself? Scottish Short Stories*, Paul Harris, Edinburgh, 1982; *Not By Bread Alone*, Marion Boyars, London & Boston, 1983; *Among You Taking Notes: The Wartime Diary Of Naomi Mitchison 1939–1945*, ed. Dorothy Sheridan, Gollancz, London, 1985; *Beyond This Limit: Selected Shorter Fiction of Naomi Mitchison*, ed. Isobel Murray, Scottish Academic Press, Edinburgh, 1986; *Early in Orcadia*, Richard Drew, Glasgow, 1987; *As It Was: Small Talk and All Change Here*, Richard Drew, Glasgow, 1988; *A Girl Must Live*, Richard Drew, Glasgow, 1988; *The Oath Takers*, Balnain Books, Nairn, 1991; *SeaGreen Ribbons*, Balnain Books, Nairn, 1991

Moon, Lorna (Nora Low) (1886–1930) *Doorways In Drumorty*, Cape, London, 1926; Gourdas House, Aberdeen, 1981; *Dark Star*, Gollancz, London, 1929; Gourdas House, Aberdeen, 1980

Morin, Carole (1964–   ) *Lampshades*, Secker & Warburg, London, 1991; *Dead Glamorous*, Gollancz, London 1996

Morrison, Nancy Brysson (1907–86) *Breakers*, John Murray, London, 1930; *Solitaire*, John Murray, London, 1932; *The Gowk Storm*, Collins, London, 1933; Canongate, Edinburgh, 1988; *The Strangers*, Collins, London, 1935; *When the Wind Blows*, Collins, London, 1937; *These Are My Friends*, Geoffrey Bles, London, 1946; *The Winnowing Years*, Hogarth Press, London, 1949; *The Hidden Fairing*, Hogarth Press, London, 1951; *The Keeper of Time*, Church of Scotland, 1933; *The Following Wind*, Hogarth Press, London, 1954; *The Other Traveller*, Hogarth Press, London, 1957; *They Need No Candle: The Men Who Built The Scottish Kirk*, Epworth Press, London, 1957; *Mary Queen Of Scots*, Vista Books, London, 1960; *Thea*, Robert Hale, London, 1963; *The Private Life of Henry VII*, Robert Hale, London, 1964; *Haworth Harvest: The Lives of the Brontës*, 1969; *King's Quiver: The Last Three Tudors*, 1972; *True Minds: The Marriage of Thomas and Jane Carlyle*, 1974 (all Dent, London)

Muir, Marie *Leezie Lindsay*, Macmillan, London, 1955; *The Mermaid Queen*, Constable, London, 1978; *The Cup of Froth*, Constable, London, 1980

Muir, Willa (1890–1970) *Women: An Inquiry*, Hogarth Press, London, 1925; *Five Songs from the Auvergnat Done into Modern Scots*, Samson Press, Warlingham, 1931; *Imagined Corners*, Martin Secker, London, 1931; Canongate, Edinburgh, 1989; *Mrs Ritchie*, Martin Secker, London, 1933; *Mrs Grundy in Scotland*, Routledge, London, 1936; *Living With Ballads*, Hogarth Press, London, 1965; *Belonging*, Hogarth Press, London, 1968; *Laconics, Jingles and Other Verses*, Enitharmon Press, London, 1969; *Imagined Selves (Imagined Corners; Mrs Ritchie; Mrs Grundy in Scotland; Women: an Enquiry)*; 'Women in Scotland', ed. Kirsty Allen (Canongate, Edinburgh, 1996)

Munro, Rona (1959–   ) *Fugue*, Salamander, Edinburgh, 1983; *Piper's Cave, in Plays by Women*, ed. Micheline Wandor and Mary Remnant, Methuen, London, 1985; *Saturday Night at the Commodore, in Scot Free*, ed. Alisdair Cameron, Nick Hern, London, 1990; *Bold Girls*, Samuel French, London, 1991; Hodder & Stoughton, London, 1995; *The Maiden Stone*, Nick Hern, London, 1995; *Your Turn to Clean the Stair/Fugue*, Nick Hern, London, 1995

Murray, Wilma (1939–   ) *Three's Company: A Collection of Stories from Aberdeen by Three Leading writers: Sheena Blackhall, Rosemary Mackay, Wilma Murray*: selected and introduced by Jessie Kesson, Keith Murray, Aberdeen, 1989

Nelson, Gillian (1932–   ) *The Cypress Room*, Bodley Head, London, 1981; *The Spare Room Cupboard*, Hamish Hamilton, London, 1984; *A Secret Life*, Hamish Hamilton, London, 1985

Nicol, Jean *Home is the Hotel*, Michael Joseph, London, 1976

NicGumaraid, Catriona (Catriona Montgomery) (1947–) *A Choille Chiar:* with Morag NicGumaraid, Clo-beag, Glasgow, 1974; *Fionn na Fuamhairean 's daoine beaga*, Acair, Stornoway, 1992; *Re na h-Oidhche-Bardachd/The Length of The Night*, Canongate, Edinburgh, 1994

NicGumaraid, Mairi (Mary Montgomery) (1955–) *Eadar Mi'sa' Bhreug*, Coisceim, Dublin, 1988; *Baile Beag Annasach*, Acair, Stornoway, 1990; *Clann Iseabail*, Acair, Stornoway, 1993

NicGumaraid, Morag (Morag Montgomery) *A Choille Chiar*, with Catriona NicGumaraid, Clo-beag, Glasgow, 1974

Orr, Christine (Grant Millar) (1899–1963) *The Glorious Thing*, 1919; *Kate Curlew: A Romance of the Pentland Country*, 1922; *The House of Joy*, 1926; *Hogmanay*, 1928 (all Hodder & Stoughton, London); *The Loud Speaker and Other Poems*, Porpoise Press, Edinburgh, 1928; *The Marriage of Maida*, Leng, Dundee, 1928; *Artificial Silk*, Hodder & Stoughton, London, 1929; *The Price of Love*, Leng, Dundee, 1929; *The Gulf Between*, Leng, Dundee, 1930; *The Player King: A Romance*, Hodder & Stoughton, London, 1931; *Limericks: A Farcical Comedy*, Brown Son & Ferguson, Glasgow, 1932; *Immortal Memory: The Comedy of a Reputation*, Hodder & Stoughton, London, 1933; *No Hawkers: A Farce*, Brown Son & Ferguson, Glasgow, 1933; *Clothes Do Make a Difference: A Comedy in One Act*, Brown Son & Ferguson, Glasgow, 1934; *Tattered Feathers*, Hodder & Stoughton, London, 1934; *Hope Takes the High Road*, Leng, Dundee, 1935; *The Flying Scotswoman*, Rich & Cowan, London, 1936; *Gentle Eagle: A Stewart Portrait*, International Publishing Company, London, 1937; *Catriona MacLeod*, Leng, Dundee, 1937; *The Happy Woman*, Brown Son & Ferguson, Glasgow, 1947; *You Can't Give Them Presents*, Rich & Cowan, London, 1949; *Other People's Houses*, Rich & Cowan, London, 1951

Owens, Agnes (1926–) *Gentlemen of the West*, Polygon, Edinburgh, 1984; *Lean Tales* (with Alasdair Gray and James Kelman), Jonathan Cape, London, 1985; *Like Birds in the Wilderness*, Fourth Estate, London, 1987; *A Working Mother*, Bloomsbury, London, 1994; *People Like That*, Bloomsbury, London, 1996

Paulin, Dorothy Margaret *Country Gold and other poems*, Moray Press, Edinburgh and London, 1936; *The Wan Water and other poems*, Blackwell, Oxford, 1939; *Solway Tide*, William Hodge, Glasgow, 1950; *Springtime by Loch Ken and other poems*, J. H. Maxwell, Castle Douglas, 1963

Penney, Bridget (1964–) *Honeymoon With Death and other Stories*, Polygon, Edinburgh, 1991

Pitman, Joy (1945–) *Telling Gestures*, Chapman, Edinburgh, 1993

Raine, Kathleen (1908–) *Shore and Flower: Poems 1935–43*, Nicholson & Watson, London, 1945; *The Pythoness and other Poems*, 1949; *The Collected Poems*, 1956; *The Hollow Hill and other Poems*, 1965 (all Hamish Hamilton, London); *Defending Ancient Springs*, Oxford University Press, London, 1967; *Farewell Happy Fields*, 1973; *The Land Unknown*, 1975; *The Lion's Mouth*, 1977 (all Hamish Hamilton, London); *Collected Poems 1935–1980*, Allen & Unwin, London, 1981; *Autobiographies*, Skoob Books, London, 1991

Ramsay, Dorothy Macnab *Honey in the Mead*, 1991; *The Flame Within*, 1993; *The Harps Are Hushed*, 1994 (all Pittenhope, Glenrothes)

Randall, Deborah (1957–) *The Sin-Eater*, Bloodaxe, Newcastle, 1989; *White Eyes, Dark Ages*, Bloodaxe, Newcastle, 1993

Ransford, Tessa (1938–) *Poetry Of Persons*, Quarto, London, 1976; *While it is Yet Day*, Quarto, Feltham, 1977; *Light Of The Mind*, 1980; *Fools and Angels*, 1984; *Shadows From The Greater Hill*, 1987 (all Ramsay Head, Edinburgh); *A Dancing Innocence*, Macdonald, Edinburgh, 1988; *Seven Valleys*, Ramsay Head, Edinburgh, 1991; *Medusa Dozen and other Poems*, Ramsay Head, Edinburgh, 1994

Reid, Netta Blair *The Shepherd Beguiled: A Play in Two Acts*, Brown Son & Ferguson, Glasgow, 1986

Reynolds, Margaret *At the Heart's Edge, Poems*, Tamarind Press, Penicuik, 1976

Robertson, Edith Anne (1883–1973) *Collected Ballads and Poems in the Scots Tongue*, 1967; *Forest Voices*, 1969 (both Aberdeen University Press, Aberdeen)

Robertson, Jenny (1942–) *Easter Story*, 1979; *Dark Journey*, 1987; *The Hidden House*, 1987 (all Scripture Union, London); *Ghetto: Poems of the Warsaw Ghetto*, Lion, Oxford, 1989; *Beyond the Border*, Blackford, Chapman, Edinburgh, 1989; *Bright Dawn*, Scripture Union, London, 1989; *Fear in the Glen*, 1990; *Branded!*, 1991; *Coroskirr*, 1992; *Season in St Petersburg*, 1994 (all Lion, Oxford); *Loss and Language*, Chapman, Edinburgh, 1994

Rose, Dilys (1954–) *Beauty is a Dangerous Thing*, Top Copy Press, Edinburgh, 1988; *Madame Doubtfire's Dilemma*, Chapman, Blackford, 1989; *Our Lady of the Pickpockets*, Secker & Warburg, London, 1989; *Red Tides*, Secker & Warburg, London, 1993

Ross, Bess (1945–) *A Bit of Crack and Car Culture,* 1990; *Those Other Times,* 1991; *Dangerous Gifts,* 1994 (all Balnain Books, Nairn)

Sangster, Maureen (1954–) *Different People, Poems by Maureen Sangster, Kenny Storrie, Colin Kerr,* Straightline, Edinburgh, 1987

Scott-Moncrieff, Ann (1914–43) *Aboard The Bulger,* Methuen, London, 1934; *The White Drake,* 1936; *Auntie Robbo,* Constable, London, 1941

Shepherd, Nan (Anna) (1893–1981) *The Quarry Wood,* Constable, Edinburgh and London, 1928; Canongate, Edinburgh, 1987; *The Weatherhouse,* Constable, Edinburgh and London, 1930; Canongate, Edinburgh, 1988; *A Pass in the Grampians,* Constable, Edinburgh and London, 1933; *In the Cairngorms: Poems,* Moray Press, Edinburgh and London, 1934; *The Living Mountain: A Celebration of the Cairngorm Mountains of Scotland,* Aberdeen University Press, Aberdeen, 1977; *The Grampian Quartet (The Quarry Wood, The Weatherhouse, A Pass in the Grampians, The Living Mountain),* Canongate, Edinburgh, 1996

Shepherd, Stella *Like a Mantle, the Sea,* G. Bell & Sons, London, 1971

Smith, Ali (1962–) *Free Love and other Stories,* Virago, London, 1995

Smith, Anne (1944–) (ed.), *The Art of Emily Brontë,* Vision Press, 1976; (ed.), *Lawrence and Women,* Vision Press, 1978; *The Magic Glass,* London, Michael Joseph, 1981; *Women Remember,* Routledge, 1990; Canongate, Edinburgh, 1992

Somerville-Arjat, Gillean (1947–) *Sleeping with Monsters: conversations with Scottish and Irish Woman Poets,* ed., with Rebecca Wilson, Polygon, Edinburgh, 1990

Spark, Muriel (1918–) *Out of a Book,* Millar & Burden, Leith, 1933; *Tribute To Wordsworth,* ed., with Derek Stanford, Wingate, London and New York, 1950; *Child of Light: A Reassessment of Mary Wollstonecraft Shelley,* Tower Bridge, London, 1951; revised and published as *Mary Shelley,* Constable, London, 1988; *The Fanfarlo and Other Poems,* Hand and Flower Press, Aldington, 1952; (ed.), *A Selection of Poems By Emily Brontë,* Grey Walls Press, London, 1952; *Emily Brontë: Her Life and Work* (with Derek Stanford), Peter Owen, London, 1953; *John Masefield,* Peter Neville, London, 1953; *My Best Mary: The Letters Of Mary Shelley,* ed., with Derek Stanford, Wingate, London, 1953; *The Brontë Letters,* Neville, London, 1954; *The Comforters,* Macmillan, London, 1957; *The Letters of John Henry Newman,* ed., with Derek Stanford, Owen, 1957; *The Go-Away Bird and Other Stories,* 1958; *Robinson,* 1958; *Memento Mori,* 1959; *The Ballad of Peckham Rye,* 1960; *The Bachelors,* 1960; *Voices At Play,* 1961; *The Prime of Miss Jean Brodie,* 1961; *Doctors of Philosophy,* 1963; *The Girls of Slender Means,* 1963; *The Mandlebaum Gate,* 1965; *Collected Poems,* vol. 1, 1967; *Collected Stories,* vol. 1, 1967; *The Public Image,* 1968; *The Very Fine Clock,* 1969; *The Driver's Seat,* 1970; *Not To Disturb,* 1971; *The Hothouse by the East River,* 1973; *The Abbess of Crewe,* 1974; *The Takeover,* 1976; *Territorial Rights,* 1979 (all Macmillan, London); *Loitering with Intent,* Bodley Head, London, 1981; *Bang-Bang You're Dead and Other Stories,* Bodley Head, London, 1981; *Going Up To Sotheby's and Other Poems,* Granada, London, 1982; *The Only Problem,* Bodley Head, London, 1984; *The Stories Of Muriel Spark,* Bodley Head, London, 1987; *A Far Cry From Kensington,* 1988; *Symposium,* 1990; *Curriculum Vitae,* 1992; *Reality and Dreams,* (all Constable, London) 1996

Squair, Olive M. (1902–) *A Tale to Tell,* Club Leabhar Ltd., Inverness, 1970; *Scotland in Europe: a study of race relations,* Graphis Publications, Inverness, 1976

Stevenson Anne (1933–) *Travelling Behind Glass: Selected Poems 1963–73,* Oxford University Press, London, 1974; *Enough of Green,* 1977; *The Fiction-Makers,* 1985; *Selected Poems 1956–86,* 1987; *The Other House,* 1990; *Four and a Half Dancing Men,* 1993 (all Oxford University Press, Oxford)

Stevenson, Dorothy Emily (1892–1973) *Mrs Tim: Leaves from the Diary of an Officer's Wife,* Cape, London, 1932; *Vittoria Cottage,* 1949; *Mrs Tim Filies Home: Leaves from the Diary of a Grass-Widow,* 1952; *Charlotte Fairly,* 1954; *The Tall Stranger,* 1957; *Still Glides the Stream,* 1959; *The House on the Cliff,* 1966; *Crooked Adam,* 1969; *Gerald and Elizabeth,* 1969 (all Collins, London)

Stewart, Agnes Charlotte *Biddy Grant of Craigengill,* Blackie, London, 1979

Stewart, A. J. (Ada F. Kay) (1929–) *Man from Thermopylae,* Scottish Society of Playwrights, Glasgow, 1981; *Died 1513– Born 1929: The Autobiography of A. J. Stewart,* Macmillan, London, 1978; *King's Memory,* W. Maclellan, Glasgow, 1981; *Falcon: The Autobiography of His Grace King James IV, King of Scots,* W. Maclellan, Glasgow, 1982

Stewart, Ena Lamont (1912–) *Starched Aprons* (1945), Scottish Society of Playwrights, Glasgow, 1976; *Business in Edinburgh,* Scottish Society of Playwrights, Glasgow, 1977; *Men Should Weep*

(1947), 7:84 Publications, Edinburgh, 1983; *Walkies Time*, Methuen, London, 1991; *Towards Evening*, Methuen, London, 1991

Stewart, Isobel *The Doctor's Daughters*, 1976; *Girl From Nowhere*, 1976; *Stranger in her Heart*, 1976; *Man From Yesterday*, 1977; *Sing No Sad Songs*, 1977; *Storm Over Yesterday*, 1977; *So Dear the Stream*, 1979; *The Desperate Dawn*, 1979; *The Heather on the Hills*, 1980; *Strangers No More*, 1980; *The Return*, 1988; *Beyond the Far Horizon*, 1990 (all Hale, London)

Stewart, Mary (1916–) *Wildfire At Midnight*, 1956; *Nine Coaches Waiting*, 1958; *The Ivy Tree*, 1961; *This Rough Magic*, 1964; *Thunder On The Right*, 1969; *My Brother Michael*, 1969; *The Crystal Cave*, 1970; *Airs Above The Ground*, 1972; *Little Broomstick*, 1973; *The Hollow Hills*, 1973; *Touch Not The Cat*, 1976; *The Last Enchantment*, 1979; *Walk in Wolf Wood*, 1981; *The Wicked Day*, 1983; *Thornyhold*, 1988; *Frost on the Window*, 1990; *Stormy Petrel*, 1991 (all Hodder & Stoughton, London); *Madam, Will You Talk?*, S. Thornes, 1991; *The Moon-Spinners*, Oxford University Press, Oxford, 1991; *The Prince and the Pilgrim*, Hodder & Stoughton, London, 1995

Strick, Ivy *Scot Free: A Novel*, Canongate, Edinburgh, 1979

Stuart, Alice Vandocken (1899–1981) *The Far Calling*, Poetry Lover's Fellowship, London, 1944; *The Dark Tarn*, George Ronald, Oxford, 1953; *David Gray The Poet Of The Luggie*, Burgh Of Kirkintilloch, Kirkintilloch, 1962; *The Door Between and Other Poems*, H. J. MacPherson, Dunfermline, 1963; *The Unquiet Tide*, Ramsay Head, Edinburgh, 1971; *Voice and Verse: A Jubilee Anthology*, compiled by Alice V. Stuart and Charles Graves, Ramsay Head Press, Edinburgh, 1974

Sulter, Maud (1960–) *As A Black Woman*, Akira, London, 1985; *Zabat: Narratives*, 1989; *Necropolis*, 1990; (ed.), *Passion: Discourses on Black Women's Creativity*, 1990 (all Urban Fox Press, London); *Echo: Works By Women Artists 1850–1940*, Tate Gallery, London, 1991

Sutherland, Elizabeth (Elizabeth Marshall) (1926–) *Lent Term*, 1973; *The Seer of Kintail*, 1974; *Hannah Hereafter*, 1976; *The Eye Of God*, 1977; *The Prophecies Of The Brahan Seer – Coinneach Odhar Fiosaiche, with a foreword, commentary and conclusion by Elizabeth Sutherland*, 1977; *The Weeping Tree*, 1980; *Ravens and Black Rain: The Story of Highland Second Sight, including a new collection of the prophecies of the Brahan seer*, 1985; (ed.), *The Gold Key and the Green Life: Some Fantasies and Celtic Tales by George MacDonald and Fiona MacLeod*, 1986; *In Search of The Picts*, 1994 (all Constable, London); *The Black Isle: Portrait of the Past*, Protheroe Books, Fortrose, 1973

Swan, Annie S. (1859–1943) *Ups and Downs: A Family Chronicle*, Charing Cross, 1878; *The Guinea Stamp: A Tale of Modern Glasgow*, Oliphant, Edinburgh, 1892; *The Bridge Builders*, Hodder & Stoughton, London, 1913; *The Fairweathers: A Story of the Old War and the New*, Hodder & Stoughton, London, 1913; *Closed Door*, J. Leng, London & Dundee, 1926; *The Pendulum*, Hodder & Stoughton, London, 1926; *The Marching Feet*, Hodder & Stoughton, London, 1931; *The Last of the Laidlaws: A Romance of the Borders*, J. Leng, London & Dundee, 1933; *My Life: An Autobiography*, Nicholson & Watson, London, 1934; *The Collected Stories of Annie S. Swan*, Clarke, London, 1941; *The Letters of Annie S. Swan*, ed. Mildred Robertson Nicoll, Hodder & Stoughton, London, 1945. (This is an abbreviated listing for this prolific popular writer.)

Symon, Mary (1863–1938) *Deveron Days*, D. Wyllie, Aberdeen, 1933

Taylor, Rachel Annand (1876–1960) *Poems*, J. Lane, London and New York, 1904; *Rose and Vine*, E. Mathews, London, 1909; *The Hours of Fiametta*, E. Mathews, London, 1910; *The End of Fiametta*, 1923; *Aspects of the Italian Renaissance*, G. Richards, London, 1923; *Leonardo the Florentine*, G. Richards, London, 1927; *Dunbar, the Poet and his period*, Faber & Faber, London, 1931

Tennant, Emma (1937–) *The Colour of Rain*, Weidenfield & Nicolson, London, 1964; *The Time of the Crack*, Cape, London, 1973; *The Last of the Country House Murders*, Cape, London, 1974; *Hotel de Dream*, Gollancz, London, 1976; *The Bad Sister*, Gollancz, London, 1978; *Wild Nights*, Cape, London, 1979; *Alice Fell*, Cape, London, 1980; *The Boggart*, Granada, 1980; *The Search For Treasure Island*, Puffin, New York, 1981; *Queen of Stones*, Cape, London, 1982; *Woman Beware Woman*, Cape, London, 1983; *The Ghost Child*, Heinemann, 1984; *Black Marina*, Faber, London, 1985; *The Adventures of Robina: by Herself*, Faber, London, 1986; *The House of Hospitalities*, Viking, London, 1987; *A Wedding of Cousins*, Viking, London, 1988; *The Magic Drum: an Excursion*, Viking, London, 1989; *Two Women of London: The Strange*

Case of Ms Jekyll and Mrs Hyde, Faber, London, 1989; *Sisters and Strangers*, Grafton, London, 1990; *Faustine*, Faber, London, 1992; *Tess*, Harper Collins, London, 1993; *Pemberley*, Hodder, London, 1993

Thompson, Alice *Killing Time*, Penguin, Harmondsworth, 1991; *Justine*, Canongate, Edinburgh, 1996

Thornton, Valerie (1954–) *Working Words: Scottish Creative Writing*, Hodder & Stoughton, London, 1995

Tytler, Sarah (Henrietta Keddie) (1827–1914) *Women Must Weep*, 1901; *The Machinations of Janet*, 1903; *Hearts are Trumps*, 1904; *The Girls of Inverbarns*, 1906 (all John Long, London. This is an abbreviated list of works by this popular author. See also the Pre-Twentieth Century; bibliography, under Keddie, Henrietta.)

Ure, Joan (Elisabeth Carswell) (1919–78) *Two Plays by Joan Ure*, Scottish Theatre Editions, Inverkeithing, 1970; *Five Short Plays*, Scottish Society of Playwrights, Glasgow, 1979; *The Woman Who Got a Government Grant*, Scottish Society of Playwrights, Glasgow, n.d.

Warner, Val (1946–) *These Yellow Photos*, Carcanet, Chedle, 1971; *Under the Penthouse*, Carcanet, Chedle, 1981; *Tristan Corbiere: The Centenary Corbiere*, translated by Val Warner, Carcanet, Manchester, 1975; (ed.), *The Collected Poems and Prose of Charlotte Mew*, Carcanet/Virago, 1982; *Before Lunch*, Carcanet, Manchester, 1986

Watt, Eilidh (1908–) *A'bhratach Dhealrach*, Club Leabhar, Inverness, 1972; *Latha a Choin Duibh: Agus Ipilidh: Sgeulachdan/(Na Dealbhan Le Seumas Donn)* Club Leabhar, Inverness, 1972; *Gun Fhois*, Macdonald, Loanhead, 1987

Webster, Jan (1924–) *Collier's Row*, 1977; *Saturday City*, 1978; *Beggarman's Country*, 1979; *Due South*, 1982 (all Collins, London); *Muckle Annie*, 1985; *One Little Room*, 1987; *The Rags Of Time*, 1987; *I Only Can Dance With You*, 1990; *Abercrombie's Aunt and Other stories*, 1990 (all Hale, London); *A Different Woman*, Ulverscroft LP, 1991; *Bluebell Blue*, Ulverscroft LP, 1992; *Taillie's War*, Hale, London, 1993; *Lowland Reels*, Ulverscroft LP, 1993; *Makalienskis Bones*, Hale, London, 1995

Wells, Nancy K(atharin) (1875–?) *Diverse Roads: A Novel*, Grant & Murray, Edinburgh, 1932; *Byronic Comments on the Twentieth Century*, Michael Slains, Collieston, 1962; *George Gordon, Lord Byron: A Scottish Genius* (with foreword by Hugh MacDiarmid), Michael Slains, Collieston, 1962; *The Golden Eagle*, Castle Wynd Printers, Edinburgh, 1962

Whyte, Betsy (1919–88) *Yellow On The Broom: The Early Days Of A Traveller Woman*, Chambers, Edinburgh, 1979; *Red Rowans and Wild Honey*, Mainstream, Edinburgh, 1990

Wood, Wendy (1892–1981) *I Like Life*, Moray Press, Edinburgh & London, 1938; *Tales of the Western Isles*, Oliver & Boyd, London, 1952; *Astronauts and Tinklers*, ed. Joy Hendry, Heritage Society of Scotland, Edinburgh 1985

Significant additional writers of Scottish popular historical and romantic fiction, prose and poetry whose work is too extensive to be listed here include (alphabetically):

Sybil Armstrong, Honor Arundel, Tessa Barclay, Lilian Beckwith, Janet Beaton, Janet Broomfield, Marian Chesney, Mercedes Claraso, Mary Cummins, Doris Davidson, Inga Dunbar, Margaret Duffy, Christine Marion Fraser, Julia Hamilton, Pamela Hill, Evelyn Hood, Margaret Irwin, Marion Lamont, Jane Lane, Sheila Lewis, Catherine McArthur, Elspeth McCutcheon, Mairi MacDonald, Mairi McLachlan, Alison McLeay, Elizabeth McNeill, Jean Matheson, Roseleen Milne, Jane Oliver, Judith O'Neill, Francis Paige, Rosamunde Pilcher, Jean Plaidy, Helen Pryde, Rona Randall, Stella Shepherd, Isobel Stewart, Agnes Short, Magda Sweetland, Alison Thirkell, Janet McLeod Trotter, Lady Margaret Sackville West, Flora Wood. (See also Deirdre Chapman's chapter on 'Designer Kailyard'.)

Notes on Contributors

Flora Alexander is Senior Lecturer in English Literature at the University of Aberdeen.

Carol Anderson lectures in the Department of Scottish Literature at the University of Glasgow.

Meg Bateman is a poet who lectures in Gaelic Literature at the University of Aberdeen.

Fiona Black is a postgraduate student at the University of Glasgow.

Valentina Bold is a Research Fellow at the University of Aberdeen and a tutor with the Open University.

Mary Ellen Brown is Professor at The Folklore Institute, and Director of the Women's Studies Programme, at the University of Indiana.

Moira Burgess is a novelist and literary historian.

Catriona Burness lectures in the Department of History of the University of Durham.

Peter Butter is Emeritus Professor of English Literature at the University of Glasgow.

Jenni Calder is a poet, biographer of Naomi Mitchison, and editor who is Head of Publications for The National Museums of Scotland.

Gerard Carruthers is Research Fellow at the Centre for Walter Scott Studies, University of Aberdeen.

Deirdre Chapman is a journalist and short-story writer.

Aileen Christianson lectures in English Literature at the University of Edinburgh.

Robert Crawford is a poet and critic, and Professor of Modern Scottish Literature at the University of St Andrews.

Beth Dickson lectures in Scottish Literature at the University of Glasgow.

Sarah Dunnigan is a postgraduate student at the University of Edinburgh.

Margaret Elphinstone is a novelist, and lectures in Scottish and English Literature at Strathclyde University.

Anne Frater is a poet and works in Gaelic programmes with the BBC.

Douglas Gifford is Professor of Scottish Literature at the University of Glasgow.

Amanda Gilroy lectures in English Literature at the University of Groningen.

Susanne Hagemann is Reader in English at the Faculty of Applied Linguistics and Culture Studies of the University of Mainz.

Francis Hart is Emeritus Professor of English at the University of Massachusetts in Boston.

Lorena Hart is a graduate of Middlebury College and Boston University.

Ralph Jessop lectures in Philosophy and English at the University of Glasgow.

Kirsteen McCue is Director of the Music Information Centre in Glasgow.

Margery Palmer McCulloch lectures in the Department of Scottish Literature at the University of Glasgow.

Jan McDonald is Professor of Theatre Studies and Drama at the University of Glasgow.

Dorothy McMillan lectures in the Department of English Literature at the University of Glasgow.

Isobel Murray is a Senior Lecturer in English at Aberdeen University and biographer of Jessie Kesson.

Glenda Norquay is Reader in English at Liverpool Polytechnic.

Elaine Petrie is Head of the School of Communication and Media at Falkirk College of Further and Continuing Education.

Valentina Poggi is Professor of English at the University of Bologna.

Aileen Riddell is a postgraduate student at the University of Glasgow.

Adrienne Scullion lectures in Theatre Studies and Drama at the University of Glasgow.

Kirsten Stirling is a postgraduate student at the University of Glasgow.

Anne Varty lectures in Theatre and Media Studies, and English at Royal Holloway, University of London.

Elizabeth Waterston is Emeritus Professor of English Literature at the University of Guelph.

Roderick Watson is Professor of Literature and Director of the Institute for International Studies at the University of Stirling.

Christopher Whyte is a poet and novelist who lectures in the Department of Scottish Literature at the University of Glasgow.

Merryn Williams is a poet and critic, and the biographer and editor of Margaret Oliphant.

Index